The Law in Context Series

Editors William Twining (University College London) and
Christopher McCrudden (Lincoln College, Oxford)

Since 1970 the Law in Context series has been in the forefront of the movement to
broaden the study of law. It has been a vehicle for the publication of innovative scholarly
books that treat law and legal phenomena critically in their social, politial and economic
contexts from a variety of perspectives. The series particularly aims to publish scholarly
legal writing that brings fresh perspectives to bear on new and existing areas of law
taught in universities. A contextual approach involves treating legal subjects broadly,
using materials from other social sciences, and from any other discipline that helps to
explain the operation in practice of the subject under discussion. It is hoped that this orientation is at once more stimulating and more realistic than the bare exposition of legal
rules. The series includes original books that have a different emphasis from traditional
legal textbooks, while maintaining the same high standards of scholarship. They are
written primarily for undergraduate and graduate students of law and of other disci-
plines, but most also appeal to a wider readership. In the past, most books in the series
have focused on English law, but recent publications include books on European law,
globalisation, transnational legal processes, and comparative law.

Books in the Series

Anderson, Schum & Twining: *Analysis of Evidence*
Ashworth: *Sentencing and Criminal Justice*
Barton & Douglas: *Law and Parenthood*
Bell: *French Legal Cultures*
Bercusson: *European Labour Law*
Birkinshaw: *European Public Law*
Birkinshaw: *Freedom of Information: The Law, the Practice and the Ideal*
Cane: *Atiyah's Accidents, Compensation and the Law*
Clarke & Kohler: *Property Law: Commentary and Materials*
Collins: *The Law of Contract*
Davies: *Perspectives on Labour Law*
Dembour: *Who Believes in Human Rights?: The European Convention in Question*
de Sousa Santos: *Toward a New Legal Common Sense*
Diduck: *Law's Families*
Elworthy & Holder: *Environmental Protection: Text and Materials*
Fortin: *Children's Rights and the Developing Law*
Glover-Thomas: *Reconstructing Mental Health Law and Policy*
Goldman: *Globalisation and the Western Legal Tradition: Recurring Patterns of Law
and Authority*
Gobert & Punch: *Rethinking Corporate Crime*
Harlow & Rawlings: *Law and Administration: Text and Materials*
Harris: *An Introduction to Law*

Harris, Campbell & Halson: *Remedies in Contract and Tort*
Harvey: *Seeking Asylum in the UK: Problems and Prospects*
Hervey & McHale: *Health Law and the European Union*
Holder & Lee: *Environmental Protection, Law and Policy: Text and Materials*
Lacey & Wells: *Reconstructing Criminal Law*
Lewis: *Choice and the Legal Order: Rising above Politics*
Likosky: *Transnational Legal Processes*
Maughan & Webb: *Lawyering Skills and the Legal Process*
McGlynn: *Families and the European Union: Law, Politics and Pluralism*
Moffat: *Trusts Law: Text and Materials*
Monti: *EC Competition Law*
Morgan & Yeung: *An Introduction to Law and Regulation*
Norrie: *Crime, Reason and History*
O'Dair: *Legal Ethics*
Oliver: *Common Values and the Public–Private Divide*
Oliver & Drewry: *The Law and Parliament*
Picciotto: *International Business Taxation*
Reed: *Internet Law: Text and Materials*
Richardson: *Law, Process and Custody*
Roberts & Palmer: *Dispute Processes: ADR and the Primary Forms of Decision-Making*
Scott & Black: *Cranston's Consumers and the Law*
Seneviratne: *Ombudsmen: Public Services and Administrative Justice*
Stapleton: *Product Liability*
Turpin and Tomkins: *British Government and the Constitution: Text and Materials*
Twining: *Globalisation and Legal Theory*
Twining: *Rethinking Evidence*
Twining & Miers: *How to Do Things with Rules*
Ward: *A Critical Introduction to European Law*
Ward: *Shakespeare and Legal Imagination*
Zander: *Cases and Materials on the English Legal System*
Zander: *The Law-Making Process*

Cases and Materials on the English Legal System

Southampton
SOLENT
University

ander's
bserver
it faces

on, the
appeal
ding of
ored by
bodies,

naterial.
Reform
iminal
Codes
05, the
arrange-
uspect's
vice, the
Review
n paper
QCs, the
Services

chool of
n Royal

Commission on Criminal Justice .... d author
and researcher, he is also a regular journalist, a frequent broadcaster on radio
and television, and is recognised as the leading authority on the workings of the
legal system.

Cases and Materials on the English Legal System

Tenth Edition

MICHAEL ZANDER QC FBA

Emeritus Professor of Law, London School of Economics and Political Science

CAMBRIDGE
UNIVERSITY PRESS

CAMBRIDGE UNIVERSITY PRESS
Cambridge, New York, Melbourne, Madrid, Cape Town, Singapore, São Paulo

Cambridge University Press
The Edinburgh Building, Cambridge CB2 8RU, UK

Published in the United States of America by Cambridge University Press, New York

www.cambridge.org
Information on this title: www.cambridge.org/9780521675406

© Michael Zander 2007

Ninth edition published by Butterworths 2003
Tenth edition published by Cambridge University Press 2007

Printed in the United Kingdom at the University Press, Cambridge

A catalogue record for this publication is available from the British Library

ISBN 978-0-521-67540-6 paperback

Contents

Preface to the tenth edition   page xxiii
Preface to the First edition   xxv
Acknowledgments   xxvi
Command papers, Hansard, House of Commons papers and
    other official publications excerpted   xxvii
Books, pamphlets, memoranda, speeches and articles excerpted   xxviii
Table of statutes   xxix
Tables of cases   xl

CHAPTER 1
The organisation of trial courts   1

1. Introduction   1
2. The work handled by the courts   3
   (1) The civil courts   3
       The High Court   3
       The county court   7
       Magistrates' courts   9
       Family court work   10
       The allocation of cases between higher and lower civil trial
          courts   11
       Toward a unified civil court   13
   (2) The criminal courts   16
       The Crown Court   16
       Magistrates' courts   19
3. Managing the courts   34
       Lord Justice Auld's Review   34
       The Courts Act 2003   37
       Auld's proposal for a middle tier of jurisdiction rejected   39
4. IT for the courts   40
5. The tribunal system   42

CHAPTER 2
Pre-trial civil proceedings   47

1. **Introduction**   47
    The court's duty to manage cases   50
        The three tracks   50
    The Civil Procedure Rules   51
        The Human Rights Act and the CPR   53
        User-friendly language under the CPR   53
        Research on the Woolf reforms   54

2. **Few cases are ever started and fewer reach court**   55
    The myth of the 'compensation culture'   55
    The attrition of claims   56
    The advantages of 'repeat players'   58
    Legal privileges that promote settlement   60
    The pre-action protocols   60
        Are the protocols a success?   62

3. **Legal proceedings**   63
    Who can sue? Representative parties and group litigation   63
        Woolf and multi-party actions   65
    Which court?   67
    What kind of proceedings should be started?   67
    Contents of the claim form   68
    Contents of the particulars of claim   69
    The statement of truth   69
    The drafting of documents – out with old-style pleadings?   69
    The cost of initiating proceedings   71
    Venue   73
    Issue and service of proceedings   74
    Responding to a claim   76
    Acknowledgment of service   76
    A defence   77
    Claimant's right of reply   77
    Allocation to track   78
    Counterclaim   79
    Seeking more information   79
    Making applications for pre-trial court orders   79
    Amendments   80
    Judgment in default   80
    Summary judgment   81
    Part 36 offers to settle and payment into court 82

4. **Getting the documentary evidence**   86
    Disclosure (formerly 'discovery') from one's opponent   86
        Woolf on discovery   87

The new rules (CPR, Part 31)   88
No disclosure if legal professional privilege applies   90
No disclosure if public interest immunity applies   94
Disclosure from someone who is not (or is not yet) a party   95
Medical records   96
Disclosure from a third party to correct wrongdoing
        (the Norwich Pharmacal principle)   97
The 'mere witness' rule   98
Subsequent use of disclosed document   98

5. Getting evidence from witnesses   99
There is no property in a witness   99
Interim remedies   101
Obtaining advance notice of one's opponent's witnesses and of
        their evidence   104
Revolution in the rules for the exchange of evidence   105
Has the exchange of witness statements proved beneficial?   106
Who can inspect the witness statements?   108
The expert witness in the pre-trial process   108

6. Pre-trial case management   114
The Woolf reforms   115
Small claims   115
Fast track   116
Multi-track   116
Case management conferences, pre-trial reviews, listing
        hearings   117
Utility of pre-trial hearing   118
What to do about delay?   119
The systems approach of official committeees   120
The 1995 Practice Directions   124
The Woolf reforms   125
American research on the effects of case management   126
Sanctions and the new rules   128
Assessment of the Woolf reforms   132
Apparent benefits deriving from the Woolf reforms   133
Issues of concern or uncertainty   134
Conclusion   140

7. Alternative dispute resolution (ADR)   141
Woolf and ADR   143
The costs sanction   145
Low take-up   146

CHAPTER 3
Pre-trial criminal proceedings   151

1. Introduction – the overriding objective   151
   Evaluating criminal justice systems   155

2. Questioning of suspects by the police   156
   The importance and quality of police questioning   156
   The danger of false confessions   159
   The Judges' Rules   159
   Whom can the police question?   161
   The citizen is not normally obliged to answer police questions   161
       When the citizen is under a duty to answer   162
       Arrest for failure to give name and address   164
       Obstructing the police   165
   The legal consequences of silence in the face of police
       questioning   165
       The Criminal Law Revision Committee   166
       The Philips Royal Commission   167
       The 'right of silence' debate reopened   168
       The Runciman Royal Commission   169
       The Criminal Justice and Public Order Act 1994   170
       Judicial interpretation of the right to silence provisions   172
   Empirical evidence on the right to silence changes   173

3. Safeguards for the suspect   175
   Access to a lawyer   175
       The Philips Royal Commission   176
       PACE   176
       Getting a lawyer   178
       Statistical data   179
       The adviser in the police station   180
   Informing someone that one has been arrested   182
   Tape-recording of interviews   183
       Exchanges that are not recorded   186
   The regime in the police station – the Codes of Practice and the
       custody officer   187
       Information to the person in custody   188
       Records of interviews   188
       Conditions of detention   189
       Medical treatment   190
       Conduct of interviews   190
       The questioning of juveniles, and mentally disordered and
           otherwise mentally vulnerable persons   190
       Interpreters   191
       Questioning of deaf persons   191
   Rules preventing improper pressure on suspects   191

4. **Stop, arrest, detention**   192
    Stops in the street   192
        The Philips Royal Commission on stop and search   195
        PACE   196
        The Code of Practice powers of stop and search   196
        Power to stop and search randomly   197
        Abolition of 'voluntary' searches   198
        Records of stops and searches   198
        Recording of stops that do not result in a search   199
        Statistics   199
    Can a person be held in the police station if he is not under
        arrest?   199
    Arrest   200
        Arrest under warrant   200
        Arrest without warrant at common law   200
        Arrest without warrant under statute – new PACE s. 24   201
        Detention for thirty minutes by a civilian   203
        Procedure on arrest   203
        Summons or arrest?   205
        Remedies for unlawful arrest   206
    Detention for questioning   207
    The time limits on detention for questioning   208
        The Philips Royal Commission   209
        PACE   209
        Charging   211
        Statistics on length of detention and charges   211
    Terrorism cases   212
        Indefinite detention of terroriat suspects without charges   213
        Indefinite detention without charges replaced by control
            orders   214

5. **Establishing the suspect's identity**   217
    Fingerprints   217
    Footwear impressions   218
    Photographs   218

6. **Getting the evidence**   219
    Identification evidence   219
    Search after an arrest   220
        Searching the arrested person   220
        Searching premises after an arrest   220
        Intimate searches, X-rays and ultrasound scans   222
        Intimate and non-intimate samples   223
        When samples can be retained   224
    Powers to enter premises other than after an arrest   225
        At common law   225

The Philips Royal Commission   227
PACE   228
Excluded material   228
Special procedure material   230
Search warrants   231
Search by consent and executing a search warrant   232
Conduct of searches   233
Telephone tapping, 'bug and burgle' and other surveillance by
   the security agencies and police   234
Seizure of evidence   239
The Philips Royal Commission   239
PACE   239
The power to freeze the suspect's assets   240

7. The prosecution process   241
The police have a wide discretion   241
Class bias in prosecutions   243
Proposals for an independent prosecution process   244
The Philips Royal Commission   245
The Government's response   245
The Crown Prosecution Service (CPS)   246
The Glidewell Report   247
The Government's response to Glidewell   247
The Auld Review   248
The CPS takes on the task of charging   248
The decision to prosecute   250
The Code for Crown Prosecutors   250
Guide to case disposal   253
Reducing discretion by new 'charging standards'   254
Cautioning as an alternative to prosecution   255
Discontinuance by the CPS   258
Judicial control of police discretion in prosecution policy   260
Remedies for the prosecution's failure to prosecute   262
Is the CPS independent of the police?   263
The three stages of the CPS' history   264
Other prosecutors   266
The Law Officers   266
Serious Fraud Office   267
Customs and Excise   267
Prosecution by other public bodies   268
Private prosecutions   268
Duries of prosecuting lawyers   270
The prosecutor and those instructing him   271
The barrister and the judge

8. Bail or remand in custody   273
   Bail on the street   275
   Bail from the police station   275
   Bail decisions by courts   276
      The Bail Act 1976   277
      How many bail applications?   282
      Length of periods of remand   283
      Appeals against a refusal of bail   283
      Appeals against a grant of legal aid   284
   Causes for concern   285
   New developments   286

9. Information supplied to the opponent ('Disclosure')   287
   Evidence the prosecution intend to use   288
   Evidence the prosecution do not intend to use ('unused
      material')   290
      Common law 1946–1981   290
      Attorney General's 1981 Guidelines   290
      Common law 1989–1995   291
      Runciman Royal Commission   292
      Auld on disclosure   293
      The Criminal Justice Act 2003 and further changes   294
      Prosecution disclosure of sensitive material – public interest
       immunity (PII)   297
   Scientific evidence   299
   Other issues of prosecution disclosure   301
   Disclosure by the defence   302
      The common law position   302
      Alibi exception   302
      Philips Royal Commission   302
      Expert evidence exception   302
      Roskill Committee   303
      Runciman Royal Commission   304
      The special case of expert evidence   306
      Auld on defence disclosure   307
      Criminal Justice Act 2003   308
      Defence disclosure in the magistrates' courts   310
   The 2006 Disclosure Protocol   310
   The prospects regarding disclosure   312

10. The allocation of cases between higher and lower criminal trial
    courts   315
   History   315
      The origins of the right to trial by jury   316
   The debate over allocation 1975–2002   316

James Committee (1975)   316
1986 consultation paper   317
1990 Practice Note   318
Runciman Royal Commission (1993)   318
1995 consultation paper   319
Criminal Proceure and Investigations Act 1996, s.49(1)   319
Narey Report   320
Mode of Trial Bill No. 1 (1999)   320
Mode of Trial Bill No. 2 (2000)   320
Auld Report (2001)   321
July 2002, the Government gives up   321

11. The guilty plea   322
Why do defendants plead guilty?   322
The innocent who plead guilty   322
The role of the lawyers   324
Other factors in guilty pleas   325
The sentence discount   326
The judge's involvement in plea discussions   327
Making the discount explicit   329
Use of the sentence discount – or even total immunity –
    for helping the prosecution   334
Taking a plea before mode of trial decision as to venue   337

12. Committal or transfer proceedings   340
The introduction of 'paper committals' (1967)   341
Reform or abolition?   342
The Runciman Royal Commission   343
Apparent abolition – Criminal Justice and Public Order Act
    1994, s. 44   343
Abolition of committal proceedings for indictable-only
    offences   344
Transfer proceedings to replace committal   345

13. The voluntary bill of indictment   346

14. Case management and pre-trial preparation   347
Pre-trial hearings   349
Plea and case management hearings (PCMH)   349
Preparatory hearings under the Criminal Justice Act 1987,
    ss. 7–10 for serious or complex fraud cases   350
Pre-trial rulings   350
Magistrates' courts – early administrative hearings (EAH)   351
Magistrates'courts – pre-trial review (PTR)   351
Empirical evidence about the value of pre-trial hearings   351
Auld on pre-trial hearings   352
Auld on 'pre-trial assessment'   354

Sanctions as a management tool in criminal justice   355
Case Preparation Project   357

15. Preparation of cases by the defence   362

16. Delays in criminal cases   365
Time-limits   366
Overall time limits   366
Custody time limits   366
Extension of custody time limits   367
Stay of prosecution becausee of delay   368

17. Publicity and contempt of court   370
Publicity before criminal proceedings are active   370
Publicity when criminal proceedings are active   371
Proceedings to enforce the law   371
Reporting of committal and transfer proceedings   374
Publicity at the time of the trial prejudicing a retrial   375
Power to order postponement of reports   375
Publishing material not heard by the jury   375
Research as to the (minimal) effect of pre-trial publicity   376
Anonymity for victims (and defendants) in sexual offence cases   376
No reporting of names of vulnerable witnesses – the
Government climbs down   377

CHAPTER 4
The trial process   379

1. The adversary system compared with the inquisitorial   379
The adversary system   380
Judicial intervention   380
Calling witnesses   382
Civil court acting of its own motion   382
Small claims hearings   382
Where the interest of children are concerned   389
Prosecution disclosure   390
Duties of the defence   390
Duties of an expert witness   390
Professional rules of conduct   391
Lord Woolf and the Runciman Royal Commission on the
adversary system   393
The inquisitorial system   395
Tribunals and the adversary system   398

2. Does being represented make a difference?   402
Representation in magistrates' courts   402
Representation in small claims cases   402
Representation in tribunals   404

3. Handicaps of the unrepresented   405
        In the lower courts   405
        In tribunals   407
        Litigants in person   408

4. Establishing the facts: the unreliability of human testimony   411
        Perjury   411
        Human fallibility   413

5. The principle of orality   415

6. The taking of evidence   417

7. Justice should be conducted in public   422
        Physical access to the proceedings   423
            Are small claims hearings in public?   424
            Special measures directions   425
            Access to court documents and the judgment   425
            Physical access to proceedings in chambers   427
        Reporting of judicial proceedings   428
            Televising trials   430
        Protecting the witness   431
            Special measures directions for vulnerable witnesses   431

8. The exclusionary rules of evidence   435
        Evidence excluded because it might be unduly prejudicial   435
            Bad character and prior convictions   435
        Evidence excluded because it is inherently unreliable   442
            Children   442
            Persons of defective intellect   445
            Parties   445
            Spouses of parties   445
            Hearsay evidence   446
            Identification evidence   459
        Evidence excluded because its admissibility would be against the
            public interest   462
            The evidence of spouses in criminal cases   462
            Evidence that might incriminate the witness   463
            The accused is not a compellable witness   463
            Legal professional privilege   466
            Evidence obtained at a 'trial within a trial'   467
            To protect police informers   468
            Cross-examination of rape victims   468
            Phone-tap evidence   469
            Evidence obtained by improper means   470
                Confessions   470
                    Evidence, including confessions, illegally or improperly
                        obtained   477

The ECHR and the fairness of trials   483
Abuse of process   484

CHAPTER 5
The jury   486

1. The origins of the jury system   486

2. Eligibility for jury service   486
    Composition of the jury list   486
    Those ineligible, disqualified or excused   487

3. The process of jury selection   492

4. Challenging of jurors   493
    Peremptory challenge   493
    Challenge for cause   494
        The judge's discretion   496
        Jury selection and pre-trial publicity   497
        Procedure for challenge for cause   497
    Stand by for the Crown   498
    Juries and the problem of race   498
    Jury vetting   500
        The use made of jury vetting   501

5. The size of the jury   502

6. Who serves on juries?   502

7. The extent to which juries are used   503
    Civil cases   503
        Juries for libel and slander cases – the Faulks Committeee   507
        Juries and damages in defamation cases   507
    Criminal cases   509

8. Aids to the jury   510

9. The quality of jury decision-making   513

10. Respective roles of judge and jury   519
    Summing up the law   519
    Summing up on the facts   521
    Directing an acquittal   523
    Directing a conviction   525
    Should the jury be prohibited from returning a perverse verdict?   527
    Asking the jury questions   528
    Is the jury's unreasoned verdict compatible with the European
        Convention on Human Rights?   529

11. Majority jury verdicts   530

12. Retrials on jury disagreement   532

13. Will the courts consider what happened in the jury room?   532

14. Publication of the secrets of the jury room   536

15. Does the jury acquit too many defendants?   537

16. Trial on indictment without a jury   540
  'Diplock courts' in Northern Ireland   541
  Defendant allowed to opt for trial by judge alone   542
  Non-jury courts for fraud and other complex trials   543
   Lord Justice Auld's report   545
   The White Paper   545
   The Criminal Justice Act 2003   546
  Trial by judge alone because of jury tampering   548
  Trial by jury of sample counts only   548
  Young defendants   549

17. The operation of the jury (and trials) in former times   550

CHAPTER 6
Costs and the funding of legal proceedings   556

1. The new rules   556
  Who pays?   557
  Factors to be taken into account in assessing the amount of costs   558
  Assessment (formerly 'taxation')   558
   The different bases of costs   561
   Non-contentious costs   562

2. Controls on costs   562
  'Between party' and 'solicitor and own client' assessment of
   costs   563
  Fixed costs   563
  Scale fees   566
  Pre-emptive cost-capping orders   567
  Remuneration certificates in non-contentious matters   568
  Legal aid work   568
  Wasted costs orders   569

3. Should costs follow the event?   571
  Civil cases   571
   The costs-follow-the-event rule and group actions   573
   The costs liability of non-parties   575
  Criminal cases   576

4. Exceptions to the rule that costs follow the event   577
  No costs in small claims in county courts   577
  Legal aid cases   578
  Some costs of litigants in person   579
  Where the winner is not liable to pay – the indemnity principle   581
  Contemptuous damages   582

Family law ancillary relief applications	585
Public interest cases	583
5. The legal aid system	**585**
Introduction	585
(1) The civil legal aid scheme	587
The nature of provision	588
The funding priorities	589
Exclusions from the scheme	590
Exceptions to the exclusions	590
The merits test	591
The means test and contributions	592
The statutory charge	593
'Legal Help'	593
'Help at Court'	594
Immigration and asylum work	594
The system in operation	596
Quality control	599
Peer review	601
Specialist Support reprieved	602
(2) The criminal legal aid scheme	603
The merits test	604
The means test and contributions	605
Very High Cost cases	610
Duty solicitor schemes in magistrates' courts	610
Duty solicitor schemes in police stations	611
Public defenders	612
Law centres	614
Legal aid for tribunals?	615
The not-for-profit sector in legal services	615
The declining proportion of the population eligible for legal aid	616
Why has the cost of criminal legal aid risen so much?	616
Where now with the funding of legal aid?	618
The Carter Review	620
International comparisons	629
6. Conditional fees and contingency fees	**630**
CFAs – the history	631
CFAs – the start	632
Recoverability of success fees and insurance premiums	633
Claims management companies	635
'Costs wars'	636
CFAs – the balance sheet	640
The courts and contingency arrangements	641

Should contingency fees be permitted?   643
Contingency Legal Aid Fund (CLAF)   646

7. Legal expenses insurance (LEI)   648

8. Pro bono work done by the profession   651

CHAPTER 7
Appeals   654

1. The structure of appeal courts   655
Civil cases   655
Radical reform of civil appeals following Bowman   658
Criminal cases   661
The Judicial Committeee of the Privy Council   662

2. The appeal process   664
A right to appeal?   664
Civil cases   664
Criminal cases   666
Appeals by the prosecution   666
Abolition of the double jeopardy rule   668
Practice and procedure of appeals   671
The procedure for civil appeals   673
The procedure for criminal appeals   673
Appeals by way of case stated   677
Leapfrog appeals   677
General   678
Skeleton arguments   682
Restrictions on oral argument?   683

3. Appeal decisions   685
The grounds of appeal   685
Only one appeal   686
Powers of the Court of Appeal   687
Civil cases   687
Criminal cases   687
The grounds for allowing appeals   687
Court of Appeal Civil Division   687
Court of Appeal Criminal Division   687
Cooper and the 'lurking doubt' test   693
Quashing the jury's verdict on account of error at trial   696
Quashing the jury's verdict on account of pre-trial
malpractice or procedural irregularity   697
Applying the proviso   699
The redrafting of s. 2   700
The power to receive fresh evidence   708
New points taken on appeal   713

The power to order retrials   714
 In fresh evidence cases should the Court of Appeal order
  retrials or decide for itself?   716
Does the criminal appeal system make sense?   718

4. **Dealing with alleged miscarriage of justice cases**   719
 Powers of the Home Secretary   720
  Free pardon   720
  Conditional pardon   721
  Remission   721
  Reference to the Court of Appeal, Criminal Division under
   the Criminal Appeal Act 1907, s.17   721
  Other powers   721
 The principles upon which the Home Secretary exercised his
  powers   721
 The case for an independent body   722
  The Runciman Royal Commission   723
 The Criminal Cases Review Commission (CCRC)   725
 Compensation for wrongful conviction   730

CHAPTER 8
The legal profession   735

1. **The component parts of the profession**   735
 The Bar   735
  Origin   735
  Inns of Court   735
  Entry and training   736
  Numbers at the Bar and recruitment   742
  Chambers   742
  The barrister's clerk   745
  Queen's (or King's) Counsel   748
  Partnerships among barristers   752
  Women at the Bar   754
  Ethnic minorities at the Bar   755
  Circuits   755
  Advertising by barristers   756
  Management of the Bar   757
  Employed and 'non practising' barristers   760
 The solicitors' branch   761
  Origin and history   761
  Entry and training   761
  Number of solicitors   766
  The structure of the solicitors' profession   766
  Legal executives   767

      The distribution of solicitors' offices in the community   768
      Women in the solicitors' profession   768
      Ethnic minorities in the solicitors' profession   769
      Management of the solicitors' branch   770

2. The divided profession   773

3. Law centres   775

4. The use of solicitors, and clients' perceptions   776

5. Reform of the profession – current issues   777
      Rights of audience for lawyers   784
      Rights of audience for non-lawyers   790
      Conducting litigation   794
      Claims assessors   795
      Legal Services Consultative Panel   796
      Right of direct access to the Bar for professional and lay clients 797
      Non-practising employed barristers   800
      Queen's Counsel   801
      BarMark and Quality Mark   806
      Partnerships between lawyers and between lawyers and
          non-lawyers   807
      Partnerships between barristers   807
      Partnerships between barristers and members of other
          professions   809
      MNPs and MDPs for solicitors   809
      Incorporation and limited liability partnerships (LLPs)   814
      Conveyancing   815
      Probate   818
      Cost information and client care   819
      Complaints   820
      EU lawyers – reciprocal rights   821

6. From the Clementi Review to the Legal Services Bill   823
      The regulatory system   824
      Complaints   828
      Alternative Business Structures (ABSs)   829

7. Clementi – what has happened?   834
      The Bar Council and the Law Society separate regulatory from
          representational functions   834
      Prospects for Alternative Business Structures   835
      The Northern Ireland 'Clementi' takes a different view   836
      The Irish Competition Authority follows Clementi   839
      Reform of the regulation of legal services in Scotland   840

    Index   843

Preface to the tenth edition

This book was first published thirty-five years ago. The fact that it is still around and seems to be worth continuing is gratifying.

There have been a few structural changes since the first edition. The chapter on the legal profession was added in the fourth edition. The chapter on enforcement of civil judgments was dropped in the seventh edition. The time has clearly come to add a chapter on the judges. I considered including it in this volume but decided, partly on grounds of the length of the book, that it would be better to introduce it into the next edition of the companion volume, *The Law Making Process*.

Probably the most important change between the first and this tenth edition is the different balance between excerpted material and the author's own text. The preface to the first edition said that the book did not attempt to replace standard descriptive texts – 'rather it attempts to supplement them by focusing through the basic texts on points where the legal system is under stress or is the subject of controversy'. It still is not a textbook but I would say that it could perfectly well serve instead of one. Gradually over the course of the successive editions a higher and higher proportion of the book has consisted of the author's own text.

There have been a great number of developments since the ninth edition – far too many to list here. Some of the main ones include the Constitutional Reform Act 2005, new research on the effect of the Woolf reforms, the White Paper on unifying the civil courts, the Criminal Procedure Rules 2005, significant changes to PACE and revised PACE Codes (January 2006), the Serious Organised Crime and Police Act 2005, the Prevention of Terrorism Act 2005 and the Terrorism Act 2006, new arrangements for the charging of suspects, the Disclosure Protocol 2006, the suspect's right to ask for an indication of sentence, general eligibility for jury service, the introduction of fixed fees for some categories of litigation, Lord Carter's Review of the procurement of legal aid (July 2006) and the 2006 consultation paper *Legal Aid: A Sustainable Future?*, the new system for appointing QCs, the Clementi Review of regulation of legal services (2004) culminating in the Legal Services Bill (2006). There have also been an extraordinary number of official Consultation papers and, of course, many important judicial decisions.

A minor but possibly useful change in this edition is the removal to footnotes of most of the references that were previously in the text. There was too much clutter on the page. There are also more headings to help the reader find his way.

But the essence of the book remains the same as it has been from the start – an exploration of the important issues involved in the operation of the legal system. The book aims to convey not just the current position but enough of the background to make sense of the developing story.

As always, the legal system is a moving target. Even since delivery of the manuscript to the publishers there have been a large number of important changes that had to be noted. The text is up to date to 1 February 2007. (On 27 February, the very last day on which the author dealt with corrections to the text, *The Times* carried the dramatic news that the Government was about to announce the splitting of the functions of the Home Office. Police, serious organised crime, counter-terrorism strategy, MI5, immigration and nationality, passports, drugs and antisocial behaviour would remain in the Home Office, which would be like a continental Ministry of the Interior. Prisons, probation, criminal justice policy, the Office for Criminal Justice, sentencing and victims would go to the Department for Constitutional Affairs which would effectively become a Ministry for Justice.)

I thank Julian Roskams, my excellent copy editor with whom I have worked for many years. I thank also the team at Cambridge University Press – Sinead Moloney, Stephanie Thelwell and above all Wendy Gater – for the efficient and courteous way they handled a difficult manuscript and what must have been for them a tiresome author who kept on coming along with further final amendments.

The first five editions of the book were published by Weidenfeld & Nicolson which launched the Law in Context series. The last four editions were published by Butterworths/LexisNexis which took it over from Weidenfelds. In 2003 Cambridge University Press took over from LexisNexis. This is therefore the first edition of the book to be published by Cambridge.

In 1972, this was the fourth book to be published in the Law in Context series. There are now 52. It seems appropriate to thank Robert Stevens and William Twining who started the whole thing off. I was present at the initial meeting they called to discuss the project. I doubt whether any of us imagined it would develop so impressively. Their vision deserves much commendation from the long list of their authors.

MZ
February 2007, London

Preface to the first edition

This book is concerned with dispute settlement in courts and tribunals in England and Wales. The aim is to make available a selection of materials which reveal the actual workings of the system, its problems and difficulties, and which suggest ways in which it might be improved. The emphasis is contemporary and critical. The materials selected come from a wide variety of sources. Some, of course, are drawn from conventional legal sources – statutes and judicial decisions. But many more are taken from articles, official reports, books and surveys. Wherever possible they draw on empirical work, though there are still far too many areas of concern where no empirical investigation has yet been undertaken. The work is intended mainly as a source-book for those taking courses on the English legal system for a law degree or an equivalent course for a degree in some other subject. My intention is not merely to make a collection of scattered sources conveniently accessible, but also to stimulate constructively critical thought about the subject. I also hope that anyone who wishes to learn about the actual operation of the legal system or who is interested in its reform will find it useful.

The book does not attempt to cover all topics that are sometimes included in legal system courses, such as the sources of law, the legal profession, the machinery of law reform and sentencing. Excellent works on each of these topics are readily available, and it would not have been possible to do justice to these subjects within short compass. Nor does this book attempt to replace standard descriptive texts. Rather it attempts to supplement them by focusing through the basic texts on points where the legal system is under stress or is the subject of controversy. The aim is to give a better understanding of the reality of the law in action.

Michael Zander
July 1972, London

Acknowledgements

All the materials in the book appear here with the permission of those who hold the copyright. I wish to express my sincere gratitude to all the individuals and institutions who have so kindly and generously allowed the material to be reprinted in this form. In particular I wish to thank the Controller of Her Majesty's Stationery Office for permission to include extracts from official publications; the Incorporated Council of Law Reporting for England and Wales for extracts from the *All England Law Reports*. I am indebted to the following publishers and journals for permission to use extracts: Sweet & Maxwell Ltd for extracts from *Civil Justice Quarterly*, the *Criminal Law Review* and the *Criminal Appeal Reports*; to the *Law Quarterly Review*, *Legal Action*, the *Magistrate*, the *Modern Law Review*, the *Solicitor's Journal*, the *Law Guardian*, the *New Law Journal*, the *Law Society's Gazette*, the *International and Comparative Law Quarterly*, *New Society*, *The Times* and *The Guardian*. The Social Administration Research Trust gave permission for use of an extract from Susanne Dell's book *Silent in Court*. The BBC and Sir Robert Mark gave permission for use of an extract from Sir Robert's Dimbleby lecture on BBC television. The *New Statesman* and CR Rolph allowed me to use the extract from Mr Rolph's 1969 article on police discretion.

Command papers, Hansard, House of Commons papers and other official publications excerpted (in chronological order)

Final Report of the Committee on Supreme Court Practice and Procedure, 1953, Cmnd 8878 (Evershed Committee)   **395–96**

Report of the Departmental Committee on Jury Service, 1965, Cmnd 2627 (Morris Committee)   **486–87**

Report of the Committee on Personal Injuries Litigation, 1968, Cmnd 369 (Winn Committee)   **70, 131**

Criminal Law Revision Committee, 'Evidence (General)', 11ᵗʰ Report, 1972, Cmnd 4991   **166**

Report of the Personal Injuries Litigation Procedure Working Party, 1979, Cmnd 7476 (Cantley Committee)   **120**

Report of the Royal Commission on Criminal Procedure, 1981, Cmnd 8092   **176, 340–41**

Report of the Farquharson Committee, 'The Role of Prosecution Counsel', 1986 and 2002   **270, 273**

Crown Prosecution Service, *Code for Prosecutors*   **250–52**

Report of the Royal Commission on Criminal Justice, 1993, Cm 2263   **169, 292, 304, 694–95, 697–98, 714–15, 723**

Lord Woolf's *Interim Report on Access to Justice: the Civil Justice System*, 1995 and Final Report, 1996   **128, 130, 393**

Lord Justice Auld's *Review of the Criminal Courts*, 2001   **35, 40–44, 293, 307, 353, 355, 366**

Sir David Clementi's Review of the Regulatory Framework for Legal Services in England and Wales, December 2004   **835**

Disclosure: A Protocol for the Control and Management of Unused Material – the Crown Courts, February 2006   **311–12**

Legal Services in Northern Ireland: Complaints, Regulation, Competition, November 2006   **837, 838, 839**

Books, pamphlets, memoranda, speeches and articles excerpted

Baldwin, John, *Video-taping Police Interviews with Suspects – an Evaluation,* Home Office, Police Research Series Paper No 1, 1992 **157–58**

Blom-Cooper, Louis, *The A6 Murder* (Harmondsworth, Penguin, 1963) **396–97**

Bridges, Lee, see McConville

Dell, Susanne, *Silent in Court,* Occasional Papers in Social Administration, No 42 (London, Bell and Sons, 1971) **405–06**

'Diogenes', *New Society,* 31 August 1973 **414–15**

Hodgson, Jacqueline, see McConville

Kalven, Harry, Jr, and Hans Ziesel, *The American Jury* (Boston, Little Brown & Co, 1966) *New Society,* 25 August 1966 **514**

Knight, Michael, *Criminal Appeal* (London, Stevens and Sons, 1970) pp. 9–53 **699–700**

Lambert, John, 'The Police Can Choose', *New Society,* 18 September 1969 **242–43**

Law Society, *A Guide to the Professional Conduct of Solicitors,* 2003 **99**

Mark, Sir Robert, 'Minority Verdict', BBC Dimbleby Lecture, 1973 **537–38**

McCabe, Sarah and Robert Purves, *The Shadow Jury at Work* (Oxford, Basil Blackwell, 1974) **515**

McConville, M., Hodgson, J., Bridges, L., and Pavlovic, A., *Standing Accused* (Clarendon Press, 1994) **362–64**

Pavlovic, Anita, see McConville

Purves, Robert, see McCabe, Sarah

Ratliff, John, 'Civil Procedure in Germany', in *2 Civil Justice Quarterly,* 1983, **398**

Rolph, CR, 'Police Discretion', *New Statesman,* 2 February 1969 **242**

Lord Woolf's 'Background Notes' on the Criminal Justice Bill 2002–03 **458**

Table of statutes

Access to Health Records Act 1990 96
Access to Justice Act 1999 ....178, 586,
634, 646
 s 6(1) 589
 s 6(8) 590
 s 11 ....578, 579
 s 23 589
 s 26 676
 s 27 634
 s 28 647
 s 29 634
 s 31 ....581, 634
 s 35(3) 797
 s 36 786
 s 37 786
 s 40 794
 s 42 786
 s 46 759
 s 51 821
 s 54 664
 s 55(1) 659
 s 56 660
 s 57 ....660, 678
 s 59 656
 s 70 660
 s 78 20
 s 87 31
 s 91 31
 Sch 2 para 1(a) 590
 Sch 3 para 5(2) 604
 Sch 5 797
  para 5 786
  para 6 786
Administration of Criminal Justice Act
1855 316

Administration of Justice Act 1960
 s 12(1) 427, 429
Administration of Justice Act 1969
 s 12(3) 677–78
 s 20 120
 s 22 120
Administration of Justice Act 1970 3–4
 s 31 95
 s 32 96
Administration of Justice Act 1977
 s 12 774
Administration of Justice Act
1985 815
Administration of Justice
(Miscellaneous Provisions) 1933
 s 2 346
Anti-Terrorism, Crime and Security
Act 2001 218
 s 21 213
 s 23 213
Appellate Jurisdiction Act 1876 657

Bail Act 1976 277
 s 3(6) 279
 s 4 277
 s 5 281
 s 6ZAA 279
 s 7(3) 280
 s 9 281
 s 9AA (2) 278
 Sch 1 ....277, 282
  para 7 277
  para 9 277
Bail (Amendment) Act 1993 284
 s 1 284

Banking Act 1987
  s 41 163
  s 42 163
Bill of Rights Act 1990 (New Zealand) 483

Champerty Act 1897 (Ontario) 644
Children Act 1989 ....5, 9, 10, 664
  s 97(2) 429
  s 108(5) 429
  Sch 13 para 14 429
Children and Young Persons Act 1933
  s 38 ....443, 445
  s 39 429–30
  s 49 429
Civil Evidence Act 1938 450
Civil Evidence Act 1968 450–51
  s 11 442
Civil Evidence Act 1972 450
Civil Evidence Act 1995 ....416, 451
  s 2 451
  s 3 452
  s 4 452
Civil Evidence (Scotland) Act 1988 451
Civil Justice Reform Act 1990 127
Civil Procedure Act 1997 52
  s 7 103
  s 8 96
Companies Act 1985 164
  s 431 163
  s 432 163
  s 434(5) 707
  s 447 163
Compensation Act 2006 635–36
Competition Act 1998
  s 9 779
  Sch 4 779
Constitutional Reform Act 2005 657–58
  s 1 2
  s 2 3
  s 3 2
  s 40(3) 666
  s 41 663
  s 59(1) 2
  s 106 22
  s 148(4) 658
  s 148(5) 658
  Sch 4 para 326 38

Constitutional Reform Act 2005 (cont.)
  Sch 12 para 2 2
  Sch 13 2
Contempt of Court Act 1981
  s 2(2) 370
  s 3(1) 371
  s 4 428
  s 4(1) 375
  s 4(2) 375
  s 8 ....489, 513, 533, 536
  s 10 97
  s 11 428
  Sch 1 paras 3-5 370
County Courts Act 1959
  s 19 11
  s 20 11
  s 75A 11
  s 75B 11
  s 75C 11
Court Services Act 2000
  s 56 256
Courts Act 1971 ....16, 17
Courts Act 2003 ....1, 11, 37–39
  s 1 37
  s 5(1) 38
  s 6(2)(b) 38
  s 10 ....22, 38
  s 27(2) 38
  s 27(4) 38
  s 29 ....31, 38
  s 93 374
Courts and Legal Services Act 1990 778
  s 4 ....11, 569
  s 6 385
  s 11 793
  s 17(1) 785
  s 17(3) 785
  s 20 796
  s 21(1) 796
  ss 21–26 820
  s 28 794
  s 29 794
  ss 34–52 816–17
  s 54 ....782, 818, 819
  s 55 ....782, 818, 819
  s 58 ....633–34, 638–39
  s 58A 634

Courts and Legal Services Act 1990 (*cont.*)
s 66 ....784, 807, 809
s 89 810
s 111 569
s 112 569
Sch 2 796
Sch 9 818
Sch 14 810

Crime and Disorder Act 1998
s 25 197
s 35 465
s 39 256
s 46 289
s 49 33
s 50 33
s 51 ....345, 367, 374
s 51A...345
s 51B...345
s 52A...374
s 54(1) 280
s 54(2) 279
s 55 280
s 56 278
s 65 256
s 66 256
Sch 3 para 2(4).................................344

Crime and Punishment (Scotland) Act
1997
s 24 726

Crimes Act 1961 (New Zealand)
s 361 542

Criminal Appeal Act 1907
s 4 691–93
s 17 721

Criminal Appeal Act 1966
s 2 691

Criminal Appeal Act 1968...................697
s 1(2)(b)..685
s 2 ....691, 693, 699, 700–01
s 7 714
s 17 728
s 23(2) 709
s 23A...728

Criminal Appeal Act 1995...........719, 725
s 1 666
s 2 ....691, 701–02
s 4(1) 709

Criminal Appeal Act 1995 (*cont.*)
s 5 728
s 13(1) 726
s 13(2) 726
s 14(4) 727
s 14(4A)..727
s 14(4B)..727
s 14(6) 727
s 18 728
s 19 728
s 20 728

Criminal Code (Canada)
s 473 542
s 476 542

Criminal Defence Service Act
2006..605, 608

Criminal Evidence Act 1898
s 1(b)...463

Criminal Evidence Act 1999
s 34 419
s 35 419
s 38 419

Criminal Justice Act 1925
s 13(4)(a) 449

Criminal Justice Act 1967 341–42
s 2 452
s 3 374
s 9 ....416, 452
s 11 302
s 17(3) 531
s 67(1) 285

Criminal Justice Act 1972
s 36 666–67

Criminal Justice Act 1982....................316
s 59 283
s 72 464
Sch 9...283

Criminal Justice Act 1987....................267
s 2 163
s 4 342
s 4(1)(b) 343
s 5 342
s 6 342
s 7(1) 350
s 7(3) 303
s 9(5) 303
s 9(7) 304

Criminal Justice Act 1987 (*cont.*)
s 24(1) 200
Criminal Justice Act 1988.....240, 317, 452
s 23 ....453, 456
s 24 453
s 25 456
s 26 456
s 31 511
s 32 432
s 32(1) 431
s 33A 443
s 34 445
s 36 667
s 43 714
s 55(7) 432
s 119 487
s 133 731
s 133(1) 732
s 133(4A)..732
s 154 282
s 155 283
s 158 377
s 159 428
Sch 2..452
Sch 12 731
Criminal Justice Act 1991....................316
s 52 443
s 54 432
s 55(7) 343
Criminal Justice Act 1993....................163
Criminal Justice Act 2001
s 131 279
Criminal Justice Act 2003........18, 152–53,
205, 210, 294, 308–10,
340, 667–68
s 4(3) 275
s 6(1) 279
s 7 209
s 10 224
s 11 151
s 13(1) 279
s 14 278
s 16 284
s 16(3) 280
s 17 284
s 18 284
s 22 258

Criminal Justice Act 2003 (*cont.*)
s 23 258
s 24 258
s 27 31
s 29 206
s 32 296
s 33(2) 309, 310
s 33(3) 310
s 34 309
s 35 308
s 36 ....308, 310
s 37 296
s 39 ....308, 310
s 40 309
s 43 ....541, 546, 547
s 44 ....541, 548
s 46 ....495, 548
s 75 669
s 76 669
s 77 670
s 78 670
s 79 670
s 82 670
s 84 670
s 85 670
s 86 670
s 99 438
s 100 438
s 101(1) 439
s 101(3) 441, 442
s 103 ....439, 442
s 103(1) 440
s 104(1) 440
s 105 440
s 106 440
s 112 439
s 114 455–56
s 114(1)(d) 457, 458
s 116 ....456, 458
s 117 ....456, 458
s 118 456
s 119 456
s 120 456
s 121 ....457, 458
s 123 457
s 124 457
s 125 457

Criminal Justice Act 2003 (*cont.*)
s 126 457
s 137 434
s 137(1) 457
s 139 457
s 154 30
s 154(1) 321
s 155 321
s 172 332
s 174 422
s 282 321
s 306 212
s 309 350
s 313 728
s 315 727
Sch 2 249
    para 2(2) 211
    para 3 276
Sch 3 367
    para 5 331
    para 6 331
    para 18 345
    para 19 374
    para 23 321
    para 26 345
Sch 3 para 23 ....331, 345
Sch 4 668
Sch 5 669
Sch 33 488
    para 3 490
    para 15 ....488, 489
Sch 36 para 21 296

Criminal Justice and Court Services
    Act 2000
s 57 224

Criminal Justice and Police Act 2001
ss 50-66 240
s 74 183
s 76 186
s 79 222
s 80(1) 223
s 82 224
s 129 281
Sch 1 240
Sch 2 240

Criminal Justice and Public Order Act
    1994 ....166, 170–72

Criminal Justice and Public Order Act
    1994 (*cont.*)
s 25 ....278, 366–67
s 26 278
s 27 276
s 29 276
s 32(1) 461
s 33 461
s 34 ....170, 171, 172
s 34(1) 170
s 34(2) 170
s 35 ....171, 465
s 36 171
s 37 171
s 38(3) 171
s 43 ....376, 518
s 44 343–44
s 48 330
s 60 197
s 81 197
Sch 2 344
Sch 4 343

Criminal Justice (Scotland) Act 1980 ...164
s 2 209

Criminal Law Act 1967 201
s 2 201
s 2(6) 226
s 4 165

Criminal Law Act 1977 317
s 62 ....182, 183

Criminal Procedure and Investigations
    Act 1996 ....287–88, 292
s 3(1) 296
s 3(8) 296
s 4 416
s 5 305
s 5(5) 312
s 5(7) 306
s 6 310
s 6(2) 306
s 6A(1) 309
s 6A(4) 310
s 6B 310
s 6C 309
s 6D 308
s 6E(2) 308, 312
s 6E(4) 310

Criminal Procedure and Investigations
   Act 1996 (*cont.*)
  s 7(2) 296
  s 7A...296
  s 8(2) 297
  s 8(5) 297
  s 11(2)(e) 308
  s 11(2)(f)...308
  s 11(3) 306, 308, 512
  s 11(5) 310
  s 12 296
  s 13(1) 296
  s 13(3) 297
  s 21A...309
  s 29 350
  s 30 350
  s 39(3) 350
  s 40 ....350, 351
  s 44 344
  s 45 ....344, 416
  s 49 ....289, 337
  s 49(1) 319
  s 52(2) 283
  s 54 ....495, 667
  Sch 1 ....344, 416
Criminal Procedure (Scotland) Act
   1995...164–65
  s 13 164
  s 13(1) 194
  s 13(7) 194
  s 194C..727
Crown Prosecution Act 1985 246
  s 23 246

Data Protection Act 1984 96
Data Protection Act 1998
  s 8(2) 96
Domestic Violence, Crime and Victims
   Act 2004 548
  s 17 541
  s 18 ....541, 549
  s 19 541
  s 20 541
Drug Trafficking Offences Act 1986 240
Drugs Act 2005 224
  s 3 222
  s 5 222

Enterprise Act 2002 779
Fair Trading Act 1973
  s 2 778
Family Law Act 1996
  s 8 142
  s 13 142
  s 27 142
  s 29 142
Financial Services Act 1985 ....163, 164
Financial Services and Markets Act
   2000................................143, 818, 829
Firearms Act 1968..................................195

Government of Wales Act 1998
  s 109 663
  Sch 8...663
    para 29 663
    para 32 663
    para 33 663
Greater London Council (General
   Powers) Act 1968...........................226

Human Rights Act 1998 ....33, 53, 162,
   704–05

Insolvency Act 1986...............................164
  s 236 163
  s 237 163
Insurance Companies Act 1982 164
  s 43A...163
Interception of Communications Act
   1985...234

Judicature Act 1873 761
Juries Act 1825.......................................487
Juries Act 1974 ....486, 487
  s 9(1) 490
  Sch 1 ....487, 488, 489, 490
Justice Statute Law Amendment Act
   2002 (Ontario) 646
  s 20.1 646
  s 28.1 646
  s 28.8 646
Justices of the Peace Act 1997 ....31, 38

Legal Aid Act 1949.................................586
Legal Aid Act 1982........................606, 610

Legal Aid Act 1988.................586, 606, 610
  s 15(2) 591
  s 15(3) 591
  s 18 578
  s 21(7) 605
  s 22 604
Legal Profession and Legal Aid
  (Scotland) Bill 2006......................841
Legal Services Bill 2007 784
  cl 1...824
  cl 1(3) 833
  cl 2...824
  cl 3(2) 824
  cl 8...825
  cl 11...833
  cl 12...825
  cl 17..825, 826
  cl 25...826
  cl 27(3) 825
  cl 30...826
  cl 31...826
  cl 31(3)(b)..826
  cl 34...826
  cl 36...826
  cl 38...826
  cl 40...826
  cl 54...826
  cl 56...827
  cl 57...827
  cl 58...827
  cl 58(4) 827
  cl 60(1) 827
  cll 70–108..832
  cl 94...826
  cll 109–157..828
  cl 123...829
  cl 135...828
  cl 158...826
  cl 166...827
  Sch 1..824
    para 1 825
    para 2 825
  Sch 2..825
  Sch 3..825
  Sch 4..825
    para 16 825
    para 17(1)(a) 825

Legal Services Bill 2007 (*cont.*)
    para 19(1) 826
  Sch 6..826
  Sch 7..826
  Sch 8..826
  Schs 10–14 832
  Sch 11
    para 11 833
    para 13 833
  Sch 13
    para 3 833
    para 4 833
    para 6 833
  Sch 15 para 1.......................................829
  Sch 16 para 74......................................832
Limited Liability Partnerships Act
  2000..814
Litigants in Person (Costs and
  Expenses) Act 1975 579–80

Magistrates Court Act 1980 416
  s 1(1) 200
  s 6 416
  s 6(1) 342, 344
  s 6(2) 342, 344
  s 8(4) 374
  s 19 337
  s 19(2)(a) 331
  s 20(3) 331
  s 20(4) 331
  s 20A(3)..331
  s 43(1) 208
  s 43(4) 208
  s 102 ....416, 452
  s 111(1) 677
  s 127 366
Metropolitan Police Act 1839
  s 66 195
Misuse of Drugs Act 1971 195

NHS Redress Act 2006 57–58
Northern Ireland Act 1998
  s 11 663
  s 79 663
  s 82 663
  Sch 10..663
    para 32 663

Official Secrets Act 1911

s 6 162

Police Act 1997

s 91 238
s 91(2) 236
s 92 235
s 93 236
s 93(2) 235
s 94 236
s 95 236
s 96 236
s 97 236
s 103(2) 236

Police and Criminal Evidence Act
    1984...151
s 1 196
s 2 198
s 3 199
s 4 182
s 8 182
s 8(1A)..231
s 8(1C)..231
s 8(1D) 231
s 8(1)(d)..229
s 9 182
s 10 ....229, 466
s 11 ....228, 229
s 12 ....228, 229
s 13 229
s 15 231
s 15(2A)...231
s 16(4) 234
s 16(5) 232
s 16(5)(a) 233
s 16(9) 231
s 16(10) 231
s 17(1) 226
s 17(5) 226
s 17(6) 226
s 18(1) 221
s 19 ....222, 231, 239
s 19(6) 239
s 21(1) 240
s 21(3) 240
s 21(8) 240
s 22(2) 239

Police and Criminal Evidence Act (*cont.*)

s 24 201
s 24(5) 164
s 24A...202
s 25 201
s 25(3) 164
s 27 218
s 28 205
s 29 200
s 30 ....205, 275
s 30B...275
s 32 ....221, 231
s 34 210
s 36 187
s 37 249
s 37(1) 210
s 37(2) 208, 209, 276
s 37(7) 210
s 37(7)(d) 211
s 37D 276
s 38(1) 211
s 38(1)(a) 276
s 39 210
s 39(1) 188
s 39(6) 188
s 41 209
s 42 ....182, 209
s 43 ....182, 209
s 43(4) 210
s 43(4)(b) 210
s 43(12) 210
s 44 ....182, 209, 210
s 46(2) 211
s 51(3) 161
s 51(d) 210
s 55 222
s 55A...222
s 56 ....182, 183, 188
s 56(1) 183
s 56(5) 183
s 56(6) 183
s 56(8) 183
s 58 182
s 58(1) 176
s 58(2) 176
s 58(4) 176
s 58(8) 177, 178

Police and Criminal Evidence Act (*cont.*)
s 60A...186
s 61(1A)..218
s 61(1B)..218
s 61(3) 217
s 61(4) 218
s 61(6) 218
s 61A...218
s 62 223
s 63 224
s 63B...224
s 63C...224
s 64 224
s 64A...218, 219
s 65 223
s 67(1) 151
s 67(8) 152
s 67(10) 152
s 67(11) 152
s 68 ....452, 453
s 69 454
s 76 ....468, 474, 475, 476
s 78 ....178, 441, 479–81, 483,
                                                698–99
s 80 462
s 81 302
s 116 182
Sch 1 ....182, 230, 233
Sch 1A 201
Sch 2
   para 1 452
   para 2 452
Sch 5...182
Police and Magistrates' Courts Act
   1994..31, 152
Police Reform Act 2002 ....203, 240
Sch 4...203
Sch 5...203
Powers of Criminal Courts
   (Sentencing) Act 2000
s 3A...321
s 3C...345
s 5A...345
Sch 9 para 198..................................256
Prevention of Crime Act 1953
s 1 196
s 1(9) 196

Prevention of Terrorism Act
   2005..214–15
s 1(4) 215
s 2(1) 215
s 3(2) 215
s 4(7) 215
Prevention of Terrorism (Temporary
   Provisions) Act 1974
s 11 162–63
Prevention of Terrorism (Temporary
   Provisions) Act 1976
s 11 162–63
Prevention of Terrorism (Temporary
   Provisions) Act 1989 178
s 18 163
Proceeds of Crime Act 1995................240
Proceeds of Crime Act 2002.........240, 335
s 327 91
s 328 91
s 329 91
s 338(4) 91
Prosecution of Offences Act
   1985..151, 245
s 2 366
s 6(2) 269
s 16 577
s 18 576
s 19B...374
s 22 368
s 23 269

Regulation of Investigatory Powers
   Act 2000 237
s 17 469
s 26(2) 237
s 28 238
s 29 238
s 32 238
s 35 238
s 36 238
s 62 238
s 80 238
Road Traffic Act 1972
s 159 193
Road Traffic Act 1988
s 4 226
s 163 ....193, 226

Scotland Act 1998
    s 32 663
    s 33 663
    s 98 663
    s 103 663
    Sch 6 663
        para 32 663
Security Services Act 1989
    s 1(2) 235
    s 1(3) 235
Security Services Act 1996.....................235
Serious Organised Crime and Police
        Act 2005 182
    s 62 164
    s 63 164
    s 64 164
    s 65 164
    s 71(1) 336
    s 73 335
    s 110 ....164, 201, 202
    s 113(4) 231
    s 113(7) 231
    s 114(2) 231
    s 114(8)(a) 231
    s 116 218
    s 117(2) 218
    s 118 218
    s 120 187
    s 121 187
    Sch 7 182
        para 43(3) 221
        para 43(6) 221
        para 43(7) 209
        para 43(8) 210
        para 43(10) 177
        para 43(13) 230
Sex Offences Act 1997 256
Sexual Offences Act 1956 461
Sexual Offences (Amendment) Act
        1976
    s 2 468
Sexual Offences (Amendment) Act
        1992..377
Solicitors Act 1972 (Ontario)..............646
Solicitors Act 1974 ....563, 630, 820
    s 20 794
    s 23 819

Solicitors Act 1974 (*cont.*)
    s 39 809
Special Immigration Appeal
        Commission Act 1997...................214
    s 23 214
Summary Jurisdiction Act 1879...........316
Supreme Court Act 1981..............656, 660
    s 15(3) 671
    s 33 95
    s 34 96
    s 37 102
    s 37(1) 102
    s 37(3) 102
    s 51 ....11, 556
    s 54(2) 656
    s 69(1) 503
    s 69(3) 503
    s 72 104
    Sch 3 para 8................................11

Terrorism Act 2000 ....163, 185
    s 19 163
    s 32 195
    s 33 195
    s 34 195
    s 35 195
    s 36 195
    s 37 228
    s 44 198
    s 89 194
    Sch 5 ....230, 233
        para 6 228
    Sch 8
        para 29 212
        para 36 212
Terrorism Act 2006
    s 23(7) 212
Theft Act 1968
    s 12 284
    s 12A...284
Transport Act 1981
    s 5 225
    s 25 225
    Sch 8 225
Tribunals, Courts and Enforcement
        Bill 2006....................................44–46
    Sch 6 45

Youth Justice and Criminal Evidence Act
    1999
    s 9 164
    s 16 ....433, 434
    s 17 434
    s 21(5) 433
    s 23 432
    s 24 432
    s 25 432
    s 25(3) 425, 432
    s 26 432
    s 27 432
    s 27(2) 433
    s 28 ....431, 432, 434
    s 29 432

Youth Justice and Criminal Evidence Act
    1999 (*cont.*)
    s 41 469
    s 44 378
    s 46 378
    s 53 444
    s 54(5) 444
    s 55 444
    s 55(6) 445
    s 55(8) 445
    s 58 171
    s 59 708
    s 60 454
    Sch 3 ....164, 708

Table of cases

A, Re [2006] EWCA Crim 4, [2006] 2 All ER 1 423
A v Secretary of State for the Home Department [2004] UKHL 56, [2005]
    2 AC 68, [2005] 2 WLR 87 214
A v Secretary of State for the Home Department (No 2) [2005] UKHL 71, [2006]
    1 All ER 575 481
AB v Leeds Teaching Hospital NHS Trust [2003] EWHC 1034, QB 567, 568
Abse v Smith [1986] QB 536...784
Afrika v Cape Plc; X v Schering Healthcare Ltd; Sayers v Merck, SmithKline
    Beecham Plc [2001] EWCA Civ 2017, [2002] 1 WLR 2274 574
A-G for New South Wales v Perpetual Trustee Co Ltd [1955] AC 457.........................260
A-G v Associated Newspapers Ltd [1994] 1 All ER 556 537
A-G v Birmingham Post and Mail Ltd [1998] 4 All ER 49...............................373
A-G v Blake [1998] 1 All ER 133...240
A-G v Leveller Magazines [1979] AC 440, HL 423, 428
A-G v MGN Ltd [1997] 1 All ER 456 373
A-G v New Statesman and Nation Publishing Co Ltd [1980] 1 All ER 644 536
A-G v News Group Newspapers Plc [1998] 2 All ER 906......................................371
A-G v Scotcher [2005] UKHL 36, [2005] 3 All ER 1 534
A-G v Scriven, 4 February 2000, unreported, CA..421
A-G v Sports Newspapers Ltd [1992] 1 All ER 503 371
A-G v Times Newspapers (1983) Times, 12 February.......................................372
Agassi v Robinson [2005] EWCA Civ 1507...581
A-G's Reference (No 1 of 1975) [1975] 3 WLR 11 667
A-G's Reference (No 1 of 1990) [1992] QB 630..368
A-G's Reference (No 3 of 1999), Re [2000] 4 All ER 360 224
A-G's Reference (No 2 of 2001) [2003] UKHL 68. [2004] 1 All ER 1049 369
A-G's Reference (No 1 of 2004) R v Edwards Note [2004] EWCA Crim 1025,
    [2004] 4 All ER 457 350
A-G's Reference (No 5 of 2002) [2004] UKHL 40, [2004] 4 All ER 901 ....237, 238
A-G's Reference (No 14 and 15 of 2006) French and Webster [2006] EWCA Crim
    1335...332
Ahmed v Powell [2003] EWHC 9011 (Costs)...636
Aiden Shipping Co Ltd v Interbulk Ltd, The Vimeira [1986] 2 All ER 409 573
Air Canada v Secretary of State for Trade [1983] 1 All ER 910................................94, 383
Albert v Lavin [1981] 3 All ER 878...165
Alderson v Booth [1969] 2 QB 216 ....203, 204

Alfred Crompton Amusement Machines v Customs and Excise Commissioners
(No 2) [1974] AC 405 ....92, 94
Allen v Sir Alfred McAlpine & Sons Ltd [1968] 2 QB 229 119
Anderton v Clwyd County Council [2002] EWCA Civ 933, [2002] 1 WLR 3174 75
Anton Piller KG v Manufacturing Processes Ltd [1976] 1 All ER 779, CA 103
Arab Monetary Fund v Hashim (No 5) [1992] 2 All ER 911 97
Aratra Potato Co Ltd v Taylor Joynson Garrett [1995] 4 All ER 695, Div Ct...............631
Arbuthnot Latham Bank Ltd v Trafalgar Holdings Ltd [1998] 2 All ER 181 119
Arkin v Borchard Lines Ltd [2005] EWCA Civ 655, [2005] 3 All ER 613 ....575, 576
Arthur HS Hall & Co v Simons[2002] 1 AC 615, [2000] 3 All ER 673.......................571
Ashworth Hospital Authority v MGN Ltd [2002] UKHL 29, [2002] 1 WLR 2033,
[2002] 4 All ER 193 97
Assicurazioni Generali Spa v Arab Insurance Group (BSC) [2002] EWCA Civ
1642, [2003] 1 WLR 577 ....672, 691
Averill v United Kingdom (2001) 31 EHRR 839...171
Awwad v Geraghty & Co [2000] 1 All ER 608 641

Balfour v Foreign and Commonwealth Office [1994] 1 WLR 681, [1994] 2 All ER
588..94
Bankers Trust Co v Shapira [1980] 1 WLR 1274, [1980] 3 All ER 353.........................97
Banks v Cox [2000] CA transcript 1476...53
Bannister v SGB Plc [1997] 4 All ER 129 122
Barclay-Johnson v Yuill [1980] 1 WLR 1259 102
Barclays Bank Plc v Eustice [1995] 4 All ER 511, CA 93
Bayer AG v Winter [1986] 1 All ER 733 104
Beck v Ministry of Defence [2003] EWCA Civ 1043 114
Beckles v United Kingdom (2003) 36 EHRR 13 173
Begum v Klarit [2005] EWCA Civ 210..638
Benmax v Austin Motor Co Ltd [1955] AC 370 689
Bentley v Brudzinski [1982] Crim LR 825 193
Bevan Ashford v Geoff Yeandle (Contractors) Ltd [1998] 3 All ER 238 634
Biguzzi v Rank Leisure Plc [1999] 1 WLR 1926, [1999] 4 All ER 934....................53, 131
Biogen Inc v Medeva Plc [1997] RPC 1...689
Birkett v James [1978] AC 297...119, 123
Blackshaw v Lord [1983] 2 All ER 311 690
Bostock v Bostock [1950] P 154 60
Boston v Bagshaw & Sons [1966] 1 WLR 1135n 532
Bowman v Fels [2005] EWCA Civ 226, [2005] 4 All ER 609 91
Bradford City Metropolitan Council v K and K [1990] Fam 140................................450
Brazil v Chief Constable of Surrey [1983] 3 All ER 537 220
Briscoe v Briscoe [1966] 1 All ER 465, Div Ct 382
British Coal Corpn v Dennis Rye Ltd (No 2) [1988] 1 WLR 1113, [1988] 3 All ER
816..93
British Steel Corpn v Grenada Television Ltd [1981] AC 1096....................................97
Brits-Mat Ltd v Elcombe [1988] 1 WLR 1350 392
Brogan v United Kingdom (1989) 11 EHRR 117 212
Brooks v Metropolitan Police Commissioner [2005] UKHL 24, [2005] 2 All ER
489..262

Brown v Stott (Procurator Fiscal Dunfermline) [2001] 2 All ER 97, PC 162
Buckland v Watts [1970] 1 QB 27, CA 579
Budgen v Andrew Gardner Partnership [2002] EWCA Civ 1125 86
Bullivant v A-G of Victoria [1901] AC 196 93
Burchell v Bullard [2005] EWCA Civ 358 146
Burmah Oil Co Ltd v Bank of England [1980] AC 1090, [1979] 3 All ER 700,
    HL 94

Cable & Wireless Plc v IBM European Union Ltd [2002] EWHC 2059, [2002]
    1 All ER (Comm) 104 145
Calcraft v Guest [1898] 1 QB 759 93
Calderbank v Calderbank [1975] 3 All ER 333 83
Callery v Gray [2001] EWCA Civ 117, [2001] 3 All ER 833, [2001] 1 WLR 2112 636
Callery v Gray [2002] UKHL 28, [2002] 3 All ER 417, [2002] 1 WLR 2000 637
Callery v Gray (No 2) [2001] EWCA Civ 1246, [2001] 4 All ER 1, [2001] 1 WLR
    2142 637
Campbell v MGN (No 2) [2005] UKHL 61, [2005] 4 All ER 793 .... 632, 634
Campbells Cash and Carry Property Ltd v Fostiff Property Ltd [2006] HCA 41 576
Carlson v Townsend [2001] EWCA Civ 511, [2001] 3 All ER 663 111
Castle v Cross [1985] 1 All ER 87 447
Causton v Mann Egerton [1974] 1 All ER 453 382
CC v United Kingdom [1999] Crim LR 228 278
Chappell v United Kingdom [1989] FSR 617 392
Chic Fashions (West Wales) Ltd v Jones [1968] 2 KB 299 239
Chief Constable of Gwent v Dash [1985] Crim LR 674 198
Chief Constable of Hampshire v A Ltd [1984] 2 All ER 385 240
Chief Constable of Kent v V [1982] 3 All ER 36 240
Chief Constable of Leicestershire v M [1988] 3 All ER 1015 240
Chief Constable of Thames Valley Police v Hepburn [2002] EWCA Civ 1841,
    [2002] 147 Sol Jo LB 59 232
Chilton v Saga Holidays Plc [1986] 1 All ER 841 385
Christie v Leachinsky [1947] AC 573 .... 204, 206
CIBC Mellon Trust Co v Stolzenberg (No 3) [2005] EWCA Civ 628 575
Clark (Inspector of Taxes) v Perks [2001] 1 WLR 17 660
Clark v Chief Constable of Cleveland Constabulary (1999) 21 LS Gaz 38 687
Clarke v Chief Constable of North Wales Police (4 April 2000, unreported) 204
Clarke v Malborough Fine Art (London) Ltd (Amendments) [2002] 1 WLR 1731,
    Ch D 69
Clibbery v Allen [2002] 1 All ER 865 .... 423, 427
Closwer v Chaplin, Finnigan v Sandford [1981] Crim LR 643, HL 225
Cockerill v Tambrands Ltd [1998] 3 All ER 97 123
Codent Ltd v Lyson Ltd [2005] EWCA Civ 1835 83
Collier v Hicks (1831) 2 B & Ad 663 408
Collins v Wilcock [1984] 1 WLR 1172 193
Columbia Picture Industries Inc v Robinson [1986] 3 All ER 338 103
Compagnie Financière du Pacifique v Peruvian Guano Co (1882) 11 QBD 55 86
Condron v United Kingdom (No 2) [2001] 31 EHRR 1, [2000] Crim LR 679 ... 173, 529,
    705

Connolly v Dale [1996] QB 120 100
Conway v Hotten [1976] 2 All ER 213 472
Conway v Rimmer [1968] AC 910...94
Cosgrove v Pattison [2001] CP Rep 68, (2001) Times, 13 February 113
Crane v DPP [1921] 2 AC 299 715
Cranfield v Bridegrove Ltd [2003] EWCA Civ 656, [2003] 3 All ER 129 76
Crawford v Washington (2004) 541 US 36 ....458, 459
Crouch v King's Healthcare NHS Trust [2004] EWCA Civ 1332, [2005] 1 All ER 207 85
Cullen v Chief Constable of the Royal Ulster Constabulary [2003] UKHL 29,
    [2003] 1 WLR 1763 177
Culver v Beard [1937] 1 All ER 301..690
Customs and Excise Commissioners v Barclays Bank Plc [2006] UKHL 28.............102
Cutts v Head [1984] Ch 290 83

D v National Society for the Prevention of Cruelty to Children [1978] AC 171 94
Dallison v Caffery [1964] 2 All ER 610 290
Daniel v Morrison [1980] Crim LR 181...195
Daniels v Walker [2000] 1 WLR 1382 ....53, 111, 113
Darmalingum v Mauritius [2000] 1 WLR 2303 369
Davies v Eli Lilly [1987] 3 All ER 94...573
Davis v Lisle [1936] 2 KB 434 225
Dawes v DPP [1995] 1 Cr App Rep 65 ....200, 203
Days Healthcare UK Ltd v Pihsiang Machinery Manufacturing Co Ltd [2006]
    EWHC 1444, QB, [2006] 4 All ER 233..559
Derby & Co Ltd v Weldon (No 2) [1989] 1 All ER 1002, CA.....................................102
Dering v Uris [1964] 2 QB 669 582
Designers Guild Ltd v Russell Williams (Textiles) Ltd [2001] 1 All ER 700...............690
Dial v State of Trinidad and Tobago [2005] 1 WLR 1660..718
Dian AO v Davis Frankel & Mead [2004] EWHC 2662 (Comm), [2005] 1 All ER
    1074..426
Director of Revenue and Customs Prosecutions (R) v Criminal Cases Review
    Commission [2006] EWHC Admin 3064 726
Dixon v Dixon (1983) 133 NLJ 305...710
Donnelly v Jackman [1970] 1 All ER 987...192–93
Dosoruth v Mauritius [2004] UKPC 51, [2005] Crim LR 474 711–12
DPP v Blake [1989] 1 WLR 432...476
DPP v Hawkins [1988] 3 All ER 673 205
DPP v M [1997] 2 All ER 749 444
DPP v Morrison [2003] EWHC Admin 683, (2003) Times, 21 April 195
DPP v Ping Lin [1975] 3 All ER 175..473
DPP v Stonehouse [1978] AC 55..525
DPP v Wilson [2001] EWHC Admin 198, [2002] RTR 37 162
Dubai Bank Ltd v Galadari (No 7) [1992] 1 All ER 658...92
Dunnett v Railtrack Plc [2002] EWCA Civ 303, [2002] 1 WLR 2434, [2002] 2 All
    ER 850...145

E (SA), Re [1984] 1 WLR 156 389
Eagil Trust Co Ltd v Pigott-Brown [1985] 3 All ER 119...690

Edward and Lewis v United Kingdom (2003) 15 BHRC 189....................................298
Edwards v Edwards [1986] 1 FLR 187...450
Electrolux Northern Ltd v Black and Decker [1996] FSR 595 392
Elgindata Ltd, Re [1993] 1 All ER 232..557
Elguzouli-Daf v Metropolitan Police Commissioner [1995] 1 All ER 833, CA 269
Elias v Passmore [1934] 2 KB 164...239
Ellis v Deheer [1922] 2 KB 113 533
EMI Records Ltd v Wallace Ltd [1982] 2 All ER 980 562
Emmanuel v Emmanuel [1982] 12 Fam Law 62..104
English and Scottish Co-op Properties Mortgage and Investment Society Ltd v
    Odhams Press Ltd [1940] 1 KB 440 690
Entick v Carrington (1765) 2 Wils 275 ....233, 239
Esso Petroleum Co Ltd v Southport Corpn [1956] AC 218................................69
Evans v Chief Constable of Surrey [1988] QB 588, [1989] 2 All ER 594 95

F (an infant) v Chief Constable of Kent [1982] Crim LR 682 ....467, 468
Fisher v Oldham Corpn [1930] 2 KB 364, 46 TLR 390......................................260
Fitt v United Kingdom (2000) 30 EHRR 441, [2000] Crim LR 586 298
Flowers v Jamaica [2000] 1 WLR 2396...369
Forbes v Smith [1998] 1 All ER 973 ....425, 427
Ford v GKR Construction Ltd [2000] 1 WLR 1397, [2000] 1 All ER 802 85
Foster v Attard [1986] Crim LR 627..226
Frank Truman Export Ltd v Metropolitan Police Commissioner [1977] 3 All ER
    431..239

G (Chambers Proceedings: McKenzie Friend), Re [1999] 1 WLR 1828.......................409
G (Children) (Care Proceedings: Wasted Costs), Re [2000] 2 WLR 1007, [1999]
    4 All ER 371 570
G v DPP [1997] 2 All ER 755 444
G v G (Minors: Custody Appeals) [1985] 1 WLR 647......................................691
Gaming Board for Great Britain v Rogers [1973] AC 388 94
Garfinkel v Metropolitan Police Commissioner [1972] Crim LR 44 239
Garratt v Saxby [2004] EWCA 341..53
Garrett v Halton Borough Council and Myatt v National Coal Board [2006]
    EWCA Civ 1017..640
General Mediterranean Holdings v Patel [2000] 1 WLR 272, [1999] 3 All ER
    673...91, 383
General of Berne Insurance Co v Jardine Reinsurance Management Ltd [1998]
    2 All ER 301 581
Ghani v Jones [1969] 3 All ER 1700 239
Giambrone v JMC Holdings Ltd [2002] EWHC 2932, QB, [2003] 1 All ER 982 561
Gibbs v Rea [1998] AC 786 232
Giles v Thompson [1993] 3 All ER 321 630
Gleaner Co Ltd v Abrahams (2003) Times, 22 July...509
Goddard v Nationwide Building Society [1987] QB 670 93
Godwin v Swindon Borough Council [2001] EWCA Civ 1478, [2002] 1 WLR
    997...53, 75
Goodwin v United Kingdom (1996) 22 EHRR 123..98

Goswell v Metropolitan Police Commissioner, *Legal Action,* September 1998 207
Grainger v United Kingdom (1990) 12 EHRR 469...608
Grant v Gorman [1980] RTR 119..204
Grant v The State [2006] UKPC 2, [2006] Crim LR 837 458
Greaves v D [1980] Crim LR 435..472
Gregory v Turner [2003] EWCA Civ 183, [2003] 2 All ER 1114.........................563, 664
Gregory v United Kingdom (1988) 25 EHRR 577...535
Greig Middleton & Co Ltd v Denderowicz (No 2) [1997] 4 All ER 181 122
Grobelaar v News Group Newspapers Ltd [2001] EWCA Civ 33, [2001] 2 All ER
    437...689
Grobelaar v News Group Newspapers Ltd [2002] UKHL 40, [2002] 4 All ER 732 689
Guardian Newspapers Ltd, Re [2004] EWHC 3092, Ch 426
Guinness Peat Properties Ltd v Fitzroy Robinson Partnership [1987] 1 WLR 1027,
    [1987] 3 All ER 816 93
Gundry v Sainsbury [1910] 1 KB 645 581

H v H; K v K [1990] Fam 86 450
Haggis v DPP [2003] EWHC 2481, [2004] 2 All ER 382 683
Haiti v Duvalier [1990] 1 QB 202, CA 102
Halford v United Kingdom (1997) 24 EHRR 523 234
Halloran v Delaney [2002] EWCA Civ 1258, [2003] 1 All ER 775, [2003] 1 WLR
    28..637
Halsey v Milton Keynes General NHS Trust [2004] EWCA Civ 576, [2004] 4 All
    ER 920 ....145, 149
Hamilton v Al-Fayed (2001) Times, 16 January, CA...708
Hamilton v Al-Fayed (No 2) [2002] EWCA Civ 932 575
Hanlon v Law Society [1980] 2 All ER 199 593
Harmony Shipping Co SA v Davis [1979] 3 All ER 177...93, 100
Harrington v North London Polytechnic [1984] 3 All ER 666.......................................98
Harris v DPP [1952] AC 694..478
Hart v Aga Khan Foundation (UK) [1984] 1 WLR 994..580
Hart v Chief Constable of Kent [1983] Crim LR 117..225
Hashtroodi v Hancock [2004] EWCA Civ 652 53
Hellewell v Chief Constable of Derbyshire [1996] 1 WLR 804....................................219
Henry v BBC [2005] EWHC 1034, QB 559
Henry v BBC [2005] EWHC 2503, QB, [2006] 1 All ER 154.......................................568
Hertfordshire Investments Ltd v Bubb [2000] 1 WLR 2318...708
Hertsmere Primary Care Trust v Administrators of Balasubranamium's Estate
    [2005] EWHC 328, [2005] 3 All ER 274 392
Hickman v Blake Lapthorn [2006] EWHC 12, QB 145
Hickman v O'Dwyer [1979] Crim LR 309 201
Hill v Chief Constable of West Yorkshire [1989] 1 AC 53, [1988] 2 All ER 238...262, 263
HIV Haemophiliacs Litigation, Re [1990] NLJR 1349 95
Hodges v Harland and Wolff Ltd [1965] 1 All ER 1086, CA...505
Hodgson v Imperial Tobacco Ltd [1998] 2 All ER 673 ....427, 576
Holgate-Mohammed v Duke [1984] AC 437, [1984] 1 All ER 1054 207
Hollington v F Hewthorn & Co Ltd [1943] KB 587 442
Hollins v Russell [2003] EWCA Civ 718, [2003] 4 All ER 590..............638, 639, 640, 642

Holmes v SGB Services Plc [2001] EWCA Civ 354..48, 49
Honeywell Ltd v Alliance Components Ltd, 22 February 1996, unreported 392
Hope v Great Western Rly Co [1937] 2 KB 130...503
Hoskyn v Metropolitan Police Commissioner [1978] 2 All ER 136 462
Howells v Dominion Insurance Co Ltd [2005] EWHC 552, QB.............................63, 66
Hsu v Metropolitan Police Commissioner [1997] 2 All ER 262 207
Huck v Robson [2002] EWCA Civ 398, [2002] 3 All ER 263...86
Hurst v Leeming [2001] EWHC 1051, [2003] 1 Lloyd's Rep 379, Ch 145
Hurwitt v Hurwitt [1979] 3 FLR 194 450

IJL v United Kingdom (2000) 9 BHRC 222 708
Ikarian Reefer [1993] 2 Lloyd's Rep 68...390
Ikarian Reefer [1995] 2 Lloyd's Rep 455..689
Independent Publishing Co Ltd v A-G of Trinidad and Tobago [2004] UKPC 26,
    [2005] 1 All ER 499 373
Independiente Ltd v Music Trading On-Line (HK) Ltd [2003] EWHC 470, Ch...........63
Ingleton v Dibble [1972] 1 All ER 275 165
Interbrew SA v Financial Times [2002] EWCA Civ 274, [2002] 2 Lloyd's Rep
    229...97
Iraqi Ministry of Defence v Arcepey Shipping Co SA [1981] QB 65n 102
IRC v Rossminster Ltd [1980] 1 All ER 80..231

Jackson v Marley Davenport Ltd [2004] EWCA Civ 1225 93
James Cramp v Hastings Borough Council; Rainbow Phillips v London Borough
    of Camden [2005] EWCA Civ 1005, [2005] 4 All ER 1014......................................665
Jasper v United Kingdom (2000) 30 EHRR 1, [2000] Crim LR 586.............................298
Jeffrey v Black [1978] 1 All ER 555 ....239, 478
John v Mirror Group Newspapers Ltd [1996] 2 All ER 35..508
John v Rees [1970] Ch 345..63
Jones v National Coal Board [1957] 2 QB 55, CA 380, 381
Jones v University of Warwick [2001] EWCA Civ 535, [2001] All ER (D) 135
    (Apr) 557
Jones v Whalley [2006] UKHL 41, [2007] Crim LR 74..256

Keegan v Chief Constable of Merseyside Police [2003] EWCA Civ 936.......................232
Keegan v United Kingdom, Application No 28867/03 [2006] All ER (D) 235 232
Kelley v Corston [1997] 4 All ER 466 571
Kenlin v Gardiner [1967] 2 QB 510...192, 193
Khan (Sultan) v United Kingdom (2000) 32 EHRR 1016, [2000] Crim LR 684 483
Khan v Armaguard Ltd [1994] 3 All ER 545..106
Khan v Lord Chancellor [2003] EWHC 12, QB, [2003] 2 All ER 367..........................580
Kinetics Technology International v Cross Seas Shipping Corpn (The Mosconici)
    [2001] 2 Lloyd's Rep 313..86
King v Telegraph Group Ltd [2004] EWCA Civ 613, [2005] 1 WLR 2282...556, 569, 634
King v Telegraph Group Ltd [2005] EWHC 90015 (Costs) 559
KU v Liverpool City Council [2005] EWCA Civ 475 ....637, 638
Kuruma, Son of Kaniu v R [1955] AC 197...477–78

L (a minor), Re [1997] AC 16, [1996] 2 All ER 78, HL 92, 101, 389
Ladd v Marshall [1954] 1 WLR 1489, CA 708, 709, 711
Lambert v Roberts [1981] 2 All ER 15 225
Lawrie v Muir 1950 JC 19 482
Leigh v Michelin Tyres Plc [2003] EWCA Civ 1766 561
Lewis v Chief Constable of South Wales Constabulary [1991] 1 All ER 206 205
Lewis v Daily Telegraph Ltd [1964] AC 234...690
Liliy Icos v Pfiza Ltd (No 2) [2002] EWCA Civ 2, [2002] 1 WLR 2253...........................99
Lilley v Pettit [1946] KB 401 450
Lindley v Rutter [1981] QB 128...220
Linton v Ministry of Defence (1983) 133 NLJ 1103 711
Livesey v Jenkins [1985] AC 424...389
Lloyds Bank Plc v Parker Bullen [2000] Lloyd's Rep PN 51..86
Lodwick v Sanders [1985] 1 All ER 577 194
London Scottish Benefit Society v Chorley (1884) 13 QBD 872 579
Lownds v Home Office [2002] EWCA Civ 365, [2002] 1 WLR 2450 560
Lucas v Barking, Havering and Redbridge Hospital NHS Trust [2003] EWCA Civ
    1102, [2003] 4 All ER 720 93
Ludlow v Burgess [1971] Crim LR 238 192

M v Secretary of State for the Home Department [2004] EWCA Civ 324, [2004]
    2 All ER 863 214
McGlinn v Waltham Contractors [2005] EWHC 1419, [2005] 3 All ER 1126, TCC.......61
McGuinness v Kellogg Co of Great Britain Ltd [1988] 2 All ER 902.............................106
McIntyre Estate v Ontario [2002] 61 OR (3d) 257, CA 630, 644, 645
McKenzie v Mckenzie [1971] P 33, CA 408
McLeod v Metropolitan Police Commissioner [1994] 4 All ER 553 226
McLeod v Metropolitan Police Commissioner [1999] Crim LR 155 226
McLorie v Oxford [1982] QB 1290...220, 239
MConnell v Chief Constable of Greater Manchester Police [1990] 1 WLR 364..........226
McPhilemy v Times Newspapers Ltd [1999] 3 All ER 775...71
McPhilemy v Times Newspapers Ltd (No 2) [2001] EWCA Civ 933, [2001] 4 All
    ER 861, [2002] 1 WLR 934 562
Mainwaring v Goldtech Investments Ltd [1997] 1 All ER 467 579
Makanjuola v Metropolitan Police Commissioner [1992] 3 All ER 617 94
Malkinson v Trim [2002] EWCA Civ 1273, [2003] 2 All ER 356...................................579
Malloch v Aberdeen Corpn (No 2) [1973] 1 All ER 304..579
Malone v United Kingdom (1985) 7 EHRR 14..234, 470
Mareva Cia Naviera SA v International Bulk Carriers SA [1980] 1 All ER 213n,
    [1975] Lloyd's Rep 509, CA 102
Marks v Beyfus (1890) 25 QBD 494...468
Markt and Co Ltd v Knight Steamship Co Ltd [1910] 2 KB 1021....................................63
Maxwell v DPP [1935] AC 309...700
Medcalf v Weatherill [2002] UKHL 27, [2003] 1 AC 120 570
Mole v Mole [1951] P 21...60
Momodou v Liman [2005] EWCA Crim 177, [2005] 2 All ER 571, [2005] Crim
    LR 588 418

Monnell and Morris v United Kingdom (1987) 10 EHRR 205....................................675
Moore v Green [1983] 1 All ER 663 165
Morris v Bank of America National Trust [2000] 1 All ER 954, CA.............................118
Morris v Beardmore [1981] AC 446, HL..225
The Mosconici, Kinetics Technology International v Cross Seas Shipping Corpn
    [2001] 2 Lloyd's Rep 313...86
Mulholland v Mitchell [1971] AC 666 713
Murray (John) v United Kingdom (1996) 22 EHRR 29...171
MV Yorke Motors v Edwards [1982] 1 All ER 1024 682
Myers v DPP [1965] AC 1001 ....447, 452

Neave v Neave (No 2) [2003] EWCA Civ 325..84
Neilson v Laugharne [1981] 1 All ER 829 94
Nembhard v R [1987] 1 All ER 183 449
New Zealand Maori Council v A-G of New Zealand [1994] 1 AC 466 583
Nizami v Butt [2006] EWHC 159, QB 640
Noor Mohamed v R [1949] AC 182 478
Norwich Pharmacal Co v Customs and Excise Commissioners [1973] AC 133............................97

O (Disclosure Order), Re [1991] 1 All ER 330...463
Official Solicitor to the Supreme Court v K [1965] AC 201..................................389, 450
O'Hara v Chief Constable of the Royal Ulster Constabulary [1997] AC 286, [1997]
    1 All ER 129 202
Ohio v Roberts (1981) 448 US 56..459
Osman v United Kingdom (2000) 29 EHRR 245 263
Oxfordshire County Council v M [1994] Fam 151, [1994] 2 All ER 269...............................389

P v BW [2003] EWHC Fam 1541, [2003] 4 All ER 1074..429
P v P (Ancillary Relief Proceeds of Crime) [2003] EWHC Fam 2260, [2003] 4 All
    ER 843..91
Painting v University of Oxford [2005] EWCA Civ 161...86
PCW (Underwriting Agencies) v Dixon [1983] 2 All ER 697..102
Peach v Metropolitan Police Commissioner [1986] 2 All ER 129 93
Pedro v Diss [1981] 2 All ER 59..192, 204
Peet v Mid-Kent Healthcare NHS Trust [2000] EWCA Civ 1703, [2002] 1 WLR
    210, [2002] 3 All ER 688 112
Perotti v Collier-Bristow [2003] EWCA Civ 1521, [2004] 2 All ER 189..............................408
Persaud v Persaud, Case No AC9500972, CA, 6 March 2003, unreported................................570
Petrotrade Inc v Texaco Ltd [2001] 4 All ER 853...85
Petursson v Hutchinson 3G UK Ltd [2004] EWHC 2609, TCC...568
PG and JH v United Kingdom [2002] Crim LR 308 483
Pilbrow v Pearless de Rougemont & Co [1999] 3 All ER 355 820
Pool v Pool [1951] P 470..60
Popek v National Westminster Bank Plc [2002] EWCA Civ 42...113
Price v Messenger (1800) 2 Bos & P 158 239
Prudential Assurance Co Ltd v Newman Industries Ltd [1981] Ch 229.................................63
Prudential Assurance Co Ltd v Prudential Insurance Co of America [2002]
    EWHC 2809, (2003) Times, 2 January..60

R v A (No 2) [2002] AC 45, [2001] 3 All ER 1 469
R v Abdroikov [2005] EWCA Crim 1986, [2005] 4 All ER 869 488
R v Ahluwalia [1992] 4 All ER 889 686
R v Al Khwaja [2005] EWCA Crim 2697 458
R v Alladice (1988) 87 Cr App Rep 380...178
R v Andrews [1987] 1 All ER 513 449
R v Andrews (Tracey) [1999] Crim LR 156 ....373, 497
R v Argent [1997] 2 Cr App Rep 27..173
R v Ashton [2002] EWCA Crim 2782 172
R v Ashton [2006] EWCA Crim 794, [2006] Crim LR 1004...155
R v Askov (1990) 79 CR (3rd) 273, 56 CCC (3rd) 449 (SCC) 366
R v Ataou [1988] 2 All ER 321...90
R v Atkinson [1976] Crim LR 307..226
R v Atkinson [1978] Crim LR 238..329
R v Attfield (1961) 45 Cr App Rep 309...521
R v B (1990) Times, 1 March 443
R v B [2003] 2 Cr App Rep 197...368
R v B [2006] EWCA Crim 417, [2006] Crim LR 745 390
R v Badham [1987] Crim LR 202 ....221, 222
R v Baggott (1927) 20 Cr App Rep 92...420
R v Bansall, Bir, Mahio and Singh [1985] Crim LR 151.......................................498, 499
R v Barry (1991) 95 Cr App Rep 384, CA 477
R v Bass [1953] 1 QB 680..200
R v Beales [1991] Crim LR 118...475
R v Beckles and Montagu [1999] Crim LR 148, CA..173
R v Bedingfield (1879) 14 Cox CC 341 449
R v Benedetto [2003] 1 WLR 1545..461
R v Benjafield [2002] UKHL 2, [2003] 1 AC 1099, [2002] 1 All ER 815 727
R v Bentley [1991] Crim LR 620...460
R v Bentley [2001] 1 Cr App Rep 307, [1999] Crim LR 330 706
R v Berrada (1989) 91 Cr App Rep 131n...521
R v Betts and Hall [2001] EWCA Crim 224, [2001] 2 Cr App Rep 257 ....172, 173
R v Binns [1982] Crim LR 522 ....498, 499
R v Bird [1978] Crim LR 337...329
R v Blake [1989] 1 WLR 432..477
R v Blastland [1986] AC 41 448
R v Boal [1992] 3 All ER 177 686
R v Boodram [2001] UKPC 20, [2002] 1 Cr App Rep 103 686
R v Bow County Court, ex p Pelling [1999] 4 All ER 751 409
R v Bow Street Stipendiary Magistrates, ex p South Coast Shipping Co Ltd [1993]
    1 All ER 219 269
R v Bowden [1999] 2 Cr App Rep 176..172, 173
R v Bowers [1998] Crim LR 817, CA..172
R v Bowles [1992] Crim LR 726 382
R v Brasier (1779) East PC 443 443
R v Brentwood Justices, ex p Nicholls [1990] 3 All ER 516...510
R v Bromley Magistrates, ex p Smith and Wilkins, R v Wells Street Magistrates
    Court, ex p King [1995] 4 All ER 146...291

R v Brophy [1981] 2 All ER 705, HL 467

R v Brown (1987) 87 Cr App Rep 52...468

R v Brown and Brown [1997] 1 Cr App Rep 112..382

R v Brown and Routh [1983] Crim LR 38 463

R v Brown (Davina) [2001] Crim LR 675, CA 524

R v Brown (Winston) [1997] 3 All ER 769, HL...302

R v Bryant and Dickson (1946) 31 Cr App Rep 146.......................................290

R v Butcher [1992] 2 NZLR 257 483

R v Butt [2005] EWCA Crim 805 422

R v Cain [1976] Crim LR 464 ....326, 329

R v Cairns [2000] Crim LR 473 711

R v Caley-Knowles and Jones [2006] EWCA Crim 1611, [2007] Crim LR 61 526

R v Central Criminal Court, ex p Francis & Francis [1989] AC 346 229

R v Central Criminal Court, ex p Guney [1996] 2 All ER 705.........................281

R v Chaaban [2003] EWCA Crim 1012...347

R v Chalkley [1998] 2 Cr App Rep 79, [1998] 2 All ER 155 ....236, 703, 704

R v Chandler (No 2) [1964] 1 All ER 761 494

R v Chesterfield Justices, ex p Bramley [2000] 1 All ER 411 240

R v Chief Constable of Devon and Cornwall, ex p Central Electricity Generating
    Board [1981] 3 All ER 826 261

R v Chief Constable of Kent County Constabulary, ex p L and R v DPP, ex p B
    (a minor) [1993] 1 All ER 756, Div Ct..261

R v Chief Constable of Sussex, ex p International Trader's Ferry [1999] 1 All ER
    129, HL 261

R v Chief Constable of the West Midlands Police, ex p Wiley [1995] 1 AC 274,
    [1994] 3 All ER 420 94

R v Chung (1990) 92 Cr App Rep 314, CA 477

R v Churchill [1989] Crim LR 226 222

R v Civil Service Appeal Board, Ex p Cunningham [1992] ICR 816............................422

R v Cleary (1963) 48 Cr App Rep 116 470

R v Clemo [1973] RTR 173n...525

R v Clewer (1953) 37 Cr App Rep 37 381

R v Clinton [1993] 2 All ER 998 686

R v Coleman [1974] RTR 359...194

R v Collister and Warhust (1955) 39 Cr App Rep 100....................................301

R v Connor and Mirza [2004] UKHL 2, [2004] 1 All ER 925, [2004] Crim LR
    1041 ....533, 534

R v Cook [1987] Crim LR 402 448

R v Cooper [1969] 1 QB 267, CA 693–94

R v Cowan [1996] QB 373 ....173, 466

R v Cox (Andrew Mark) [1995] Crim LR 741 714

R v Coxhead [1986] Crim LR 251, CA...261

R v Crabtree, Foley and McCann [1992] Crim LR 65 685

R v Cranwell [2001] EWCA Crim 1216..705

R v Criminal Cases Review Commission, ex p Pearson [1999] 3 All ER 498...............726

R v Cronin [1940] 1 All ER 618..715

R v Crown Court at Guildford [1989] 3 All ER 7 496

R v Crown Court at Inner London Sessions, ex p Baines & Baines [1987] 3 All ER
    1025..229
R v Crown Court at Ipswich, ex p Reddington [1981] Crim LR 618 281
R v Crown Court at Maidstone, ex p Lever [1995] 2 All ER 35 281
R v Crown Court at Manchester, ex p McDonald (1999) 1 Cr App Rep 409, [1999]
    1 All ER 805 368
R v Crown Court at Reading, ex p Bello [1992] 3 All ER 353....................................280, 281
R v Crown Court at Wood Green, ex p Howe [1992] 3 All ER 366..............................281
R v Crozier [1991] Crim LR 138...391
R v Cumberwell Green Youth Court, ex p D and G [2005] UKHL 4, [2005] 2 Cr
    App Rep 1 433
R v Customs and Excise Commissioners, ex p Popely [1999] STC 1016, Div Ct.........229
R v D [2002] EWCA Crim 990, [2003] QB 90..444
R v D and J [1996] 1 All ER 881, CA...712
R v Danvers [1982] Crim LR 680 498
R v Davis, Johnson and Rowe (1993) 97 Cr App Rep 110, CA 297
R v Davis, Johnson and Rowe [2000] Crim LR 1012..703, 705
R v Davis [1979] Crim LR 167...329
R v Davis and Ellis [2006] EWCA Crim 1155, [2007] 70...431
R v Davison [1988] Crim LR 442 475
R v Day [2003] Crim LR 1060 ....685, 686
R v Delaney (1988) 88 Cr App Rep 338, CA 477, 480
R v Derby Magistrates Court, ex p B [1996] AC 487..90
R v Dervish and Anori [2001] EWCA Crim 2789, [2002] 2 Cr App Rep 105.............172
R v Doolan [1988] Crim LR 747 476
R v Doolan (1991) 12 Cr App Rep(S) 634, CA 477
R v Dorking Magistrates, ex p Harrington [1983] 3 All ER 29 666
R v DPP, ex p C [1995] 1 Cr App Rep 136 262
R v DPP, ex p Lee (1999) 2 Cr App Rep 304, [1999] 2 All ER 737 ....289, 297
R v DPP, ex p Manning [2001] QB 330..262
R v DPP, ex p Manning and Melbourne [2000] 3 WLR 463...263
R v DPP, ex p Threadaway (1997) Times, 31 October...263
R v Du Plooy [2003] SCCR 640...332
R v Dunford [1991] Crim LR 370 178
R v Dunlop [2006] EWCA Crim 1354, [2007] 1 All ER 593...671
R v Edwards (1991) Cr App Rep 48...301
R v Eel [1983] Crim LR 806..220
R v Ensor [1989] 1 WLR 497 685
R v Epping and Harlow Justices, ex p Massaro [1973] QB 433..............................289, 341
R v Everett [1988] Crim LR 826 ....476, 477
R v Evesham Justices, ex p McDonagh [1988] 1 All ER 371 428
R v Farid (1945) 30 Cr App Rep 168 700
R v Fergus (1993) 98 Cr App Rep 313 460
R v Fiak [2000] EWCA Crim 2381 204
R v Flower (1965) 50 Cr App Rep 22..709
R v Ford (1989) 89 Cr App Rep 278, [1989] 3 All ER 445............................496, 498, 499
R v Foster [1984] Crim LR 423..720

R v Frazer [1987] Crim LR 418..498
R v Fulling [1987] QB 426 475
R v Galbraith [1981] 1 WLR 1039, [1981] 2 All ER 1060, CA 341, 523, 524
R v Gautam [1988] Crim LR 109..685
R v Geen [1982] Crim LR 604 195
R v General Council of the Bar, ex p Percival [1990] 3 All ER 137...............................261
R v Gibson (1887) 18 QBD 857...456
R v Gleeson [2003] EWCA Crim 3357, [2004] Crim LR 579...390
R v Glennon (1992) 173 CLR 592 497
R v Goldenberg [1988] Crim LR 678 476
R v Goodyear [2005] EWCA Crim 888, [2005] 3 All ER 117, [2005] Crim LR 659.....333
R v Governor of Canterbury Prison, ex p Craig [1990] 2 All ER 654...........................368
R v Governor of Glen Parva Young Offender Institution, ex p G [1998] 2 All ER
    295...280
R v Governor of Pentonville Prison, ex p Osman [1989] 3 All ER 701 341
R v Governor of Winchester Prison, ex p Roddie, [1991] 2 All ER 931 367
R v Gowan [1982] Crim LR 821 472
R v Grafton [1992] Crim LR 826...382
R v Grant [2005] EWCA Crim 1089, [2005] Crim LR 955 484
R v Graves [1978] Crim LR 216..713
R v Grays Justices, ex p Tetley (1979) 70 Cr App Rep 11......................................289, 341
R v Gunning (1983) 78 Cr App Rep 23 380
R v H and R v C [2004] UKHL 3, [2004] 2 AC 134, [2004] 1 All ER 1269...291, 298, 299
R v Haddy (1944) 29 Cr App Rep 182..700
R v Hamilton [1969] Crim LR 486...381
R v Hanratty (decd) [2002] EWCA Crim 1141, [2002] 3 All ER 534, [2002] Crim
    LR 650 ....707, 713
R v Hanson, Gilmore and Pickstone [2005] EWCA Crim 824, [2005] 1 WLR
    3169..439, 440
R v Haringey Justices, ex p DPP [1996] 1 All ER 828...382
R v Harris [2005] EWCA Crim 1980..390
R v Harrison [2002] EWCA Crim 2309 686
R v Haughton, Case No 589/SI/91, 21 May 1992, unreported................................695–96
R v Hayes [1977] 1 WLR 234..443
R v Hennessey (1978) 68 Cr App Rep 426 290
R v Hester [1973] AC 296 445
R v Hewitson and Bramwich [1999] Crim LR 307...703
R v Highton, Van Nguyen and Carp [2005] EWCA Crim 1985, [2005] 1 WLR
    3472..440, 441
R v Hircock [1969] 1 All ER 47...522
R v Hoare and Pearce [2004] EWCA Crim 784 173
R v Holmes, ex p Sherman [1981] 2 All ER 612 208
R v Hooper [2003] EWCA Crim 2427..368
R v Hopkins-Husson (1949) 34 Cr App Rep 47, CA 692
R v Horseferry Road Magistrates Court, ex p Bennett [1994] AC 42, [1993] 3 All
    ER 138...484
R v Horsham Justices, ex p Farquharson [1982] QB 762 428
R v Houghton and Franciosy (1978) 68 Cr App Rep 197 208 207

R v Howell [1981] Crim LR 697 201
R v Howell [2003] EWCA Crim 1, [2003] Crim LR 405 173
R v Hubbert (1975) 29 CCC (2d) 279 497
R v Hudson (1980) 72 Cr App Rep 163 208
R v Hudson [1981] Crim LR 107 472
R v Hunjan (1978) 68 Cr App Rep 99 460
R v Inwood [1973] 2 All ER 645 ....200, 203, 204
R v IRC, ex p Mead [1993] 1 All ER 772 261
R v Irwin [1987] 2 All ER 1085 686
R v Isleworth Crown Court, ex p Clarke [1988] 1 Cr App Rep 257, DC......................284
R v Jasper, 24 April 1994, unreported 477
R v Jisl [2004] EWCA Crim 696 347
R v Johnson [1988] 1 WLR 1377 468
R v Johnson [2005] EWCA Crim 971, [2006] Crim LR 253 172
R v Jones (Douglas) (1999) Times, 17 February..529
R v Joyce and Joyce [2005] EWCA Crim 785 456
R v K [2005] EWCA Crim 346, [2005] Crim LR 574 534
R v K [2006] EWCA Crim 724, [2006] Crim LR 1012 348
R v Kansal (No 2) [2001] UKHL 62, [2002] AC 69, [2002] 1 All ER 257 727
R v Keane (1994) 99 Cr App Rep 1 ....291, 297
R v Kearly [1992] 2 AC 228, [1992] 2 All ER 345, HL..447
R v Kelleher [2003] EWCA Crim 3525...526
R v Kennedy [1999] 1 Cr App Rep 54 703
R v Khan [1994] 4 All ER 426..236
R v Kidd (Canavan) [1998] 1 WLR 604 549
R v King [1969] 1 AC 304, PC 220
R v King [1983] 1 All ER 929 93
R v Kirifi [1992] 2 NZLR 8 483
R v Kirk [1999] 4 All ER 698..211
R v Kuimba (2005) Times, 17 May..675
R v Kulynycz [1970] 3 All ER 881 ....205, 206
R v Lam Chi Ming [1991] AC 212, [1991] 3 All ER 172, PC..472
R v Lawson (1990) 90 Cr App Rep 107 291
R v Leer [1982] Crim LR 310..525
R v Leicester City Justices, ex p Barrow [1991] 2 All ER 437 ....408, 409
R v Leveller Magazines Ltd [1979] AC 440, HL...423, 428
R v Leyland Justices, ex p Hawthorn [1979] 1 All ER 209..290
R v Liverpool Juvenile Court, ex p R [1988] QB 1, [1987] 2 All ER 668 ....468, 474
R v Llewellyn (1978) 67 Cr App Rep 149 329
R v Loizou [2006] EWCA Crim 1719..173
R v Lord Chancellor, ex p Child Poverty Action Group [1998] 2 All ER 755 583–84
R v Lord Chancellor, ex p Lightfoot [2000] QB 597...73
R v Lord Chancellor, ex p Witham [1997] 2 All ER 779..73
R v Lyons [2002] UKHL 44, [2002] 4 All ER 1028 ....705, 707, 727
R v McCalla [1986] Crim LR 335 498
R v McCarthy (1980) 70 Cr App Rep 270 474
R v McCay [1991] 1 All ER 232 151
R v McGovern (1990) 92 Cr App Rep 228 477

R v McGowan, O'Donnell [2005] SCCR 497...332
R v McGrath [1949] 2 All ER 495...713
R v McGuiness [1999] Crim LR 318, CA 170
R v McKenna [1960] 1 QB 411 715
R v McKenzie (1992) 96 Cr App Rep 98, CA 476
R v McVeigh [1988] Crim LR 127 519
R v Maguire (1989) 90 Cr App Rep 115, CA..477
R v Makanjuola and Euston [1995] 2 Cr App Rep 469, [1995] 3 All ER 730..............461
R v Malvern Justices, ex p Evans [1988] 1 All ER 371, Div Ct 423
R v Manchester Crown Court, ex p Williams and Simpson [1990] Crim LR
   654..346
R v Mansfield (1977) 65 Cr App Rep 276..523
R v Martinez-Tobon [1994] 2 All ER 90, CA..463
R v Marylebone Magistrates Court, ex p Amdrell, trading as 'Get Stuffed,' and
   Robert and Pauline Sclare (1998) 162 JP 719, [1998] NLJR 1230 233
R v Mason [1980] 3 All ER 777..489
R v Maxwell,Transcript of pre-trial ruling, 27 April 1995...497
R v Maynard (1979) 69 Cr App Rep 309 713
R v Metropolitan Police Commissioner, ex p Blackburn [1968] 2 WLR 893, CA 260
R v Metropolitan Police Commissioner, ex p Blackburn (No 3) [1973] 1 All ER
   324..261
R v Middlesex Quarter Sessions Chairman, ex p DPP [1952] 2 QB 758......................666
R v Mills [1995] Crim LR 884..460
R v Mills (No 2), Poole (No 2) [2003] EWCA Crim 1753, (2003) Times,
   26 June 687, 717
R v Mondon (1968) 52 Cr App Rep 695 420
R v Moore (1972) 56 Cr App Rep 373..470
R v Moss (1990) 91 Cr App Rep 371, CA..477
R v Mount (1934) 24 Cr App Rep 135 462
R v Mullen [2000] QB 520, [1999] Crim LR 561...703, 704
R v Murray (Kevin Sean) [1994] 1 WLR 1 ....172, 173
R v Mushtaq [2005] UKHL 25, [2005] 3 All ER 885 475
R v Mussell; R v Dalton [1995] Crim LR 887 460
R v Nangle [2002] Crim LR 506 686
R v Neal [1949] 2 KB 590...715
R v Neaven [2006] EWCA Crim 955, [2006] Crim LR 909..712
R v Newton Rose (1981) Times, 11 November...498
R v Nickolson [1999] Crim LR 61, CA..172
R v Northallerton Magistrates' Court, ex p Dove [1999] Crim LR 760 577
R v Northam (1967) 52 Cr App Rep 97..472
R v Nottingham Justices, ex p Davies [1980] 2 All ER 775 282
R v Nycander (1982) Times, 7 December 208
R v Obellin, Williams and Martin [1997] 1 Cr App Rep 355.......................................489
R v O'Brien, Hall, Sherwood [2000] Crim LR 676, CA..707
R v Oliva [1965] 1 WLR 1028...382
R v Olotu [1997] 1 WLR 328 367
R v Oosthuizen [2005] EWCA Crim 1978 333
R v P [2001] 1 AC 146, HL...483

R v Paraskeva [1983] Crim LR 186..301
R v Paris, Abdullahi and Miller (1992) 97 Cr App Rep 99 475
R v Parris [1989] Crim LR 214 177
R v Pendleton [2001] UKHL 66, [2002] 1 All ER 524, [2002] Crim LR 398 716
R v Perks [1973] Crim LR 388 380
R v Pigg [1983] 1 All ER 56..531
R v Pinfold [1988] 2 All ER 217..686
R v Pitman [1991] 1 All ER 468..329
R v Pitt [1982] Crim LR 513 462
R v Pointer [1997] Crim LR 676, CA 170
R v Ponting [1985] Crim LR 318...526
R v Poole [2003] EWCA Crim 1753, [2003] Crim LR 60.................................726
R v Powell [2006] EWCA Crim 3, [2006] Crim LR 71 444
R v Prager [1972] 1 WLR 260...472
R v Preston [1993] 4 All ER 638 291
R v Ptohopoulos [1968] Crim LR 52...381
R v Puddick (1865) 4 F & F 497..270
R v Rabbitt (1931) 23 Cr App Rep 112...381
R v Rafferty [1998] Crim LR 433..337
R v Rajcoomar [1999] Crim LR 728..703
R v Rampling [1987] Crim LR 823..185
R v Randle and Pottle [1991] 1 WLR 1087 526
R v Rankine [1986] QB 861 468
R v Ras Behari Lal (1933) 50 TLR 1, PC 533
R v Rasheed (1994) 158 JP 941 302
R v Reigate Justices, ex p Argus Newspapers (1983) 5 Cr App Rep (S) 181 423
R v Renda [2005] EWCA Crim 2826, [2006] 2 All ER 553 442
R v Rennie [1982] 1 All ER 385 473
R v Renshaw [1989] Crim LR 811 381
R v Reynolds [1981] 3 All ER 849...531
R v Rezvi [2002] UKHL 1, [2003] 1 AC 1099, [2002] 1 All ER 801....................727
R v Richards [1999] Crim LR 764 425
R v Robinson [2002] EWCA Crim 2489 535
R v Roble [1997] EWCA Crim 449..173
R v Rose [1982] 2 All ER 731, HL...715
R v Rothfield (1937) 26 Cr App Rep 103...346
R v Salt [1996] Crim LR 517...487
R v Samuel [1988] QB 615..177
R v Sang [1980] AC 402, [1979] 2 All ER 1222..478
R v Sargent [2001] UKHL 54, [2003] Crim LR 276 703
R v Sat-Bhambra (1988) 88 Cr App Rep 55 474
R v Saville of Newdigate, ex p A [1999] NLJR 965 431
R v Secretary of State for the Home Department, ex p Bentley [1993] 4 All ER
    442...720
R v Secretary of State for the Home Department, ex p Chubb [1986] Crim LR 809,
    Div Ct..731
R v Secretary of State for the Home Department, ex p Gunn [2001] EWCA Civ 891,
    [2001] 3 All ER 481 579

R v Secretary of State for the Home Department, ex p Harrison [1988] 3 All ER
86 731
R v Secretary of State for the Home Department, ex p Hickey (No 2) [1995] 1 All
ER 490 728
R v Sellick [2005] Crim LR 722 ....456, 458
R v Shaheed [2002] 2 NZLR 377, CA 483
R v Shahzad [1996] 1 All ER 353 484
R v Sharp [1993] 1 All ER 225 381
R v Sheffield Crowm Court, ex p Brownlow [1980] QB 530 492
R v Sheffield Justices, ex p Turner [1991] All ER 1 858 368
R v Silcott, Braithwaite and Raghip (1991) Times, 9 December 476
R v Slinger (1961) 46 Cr App Rep 244 700
R v Smith [1959] 2 QB 35 ....471, 473
R v Smith [1990] Crim LR 354 329
R v Smith [2005] UKHL 12, [2005] 2 All ER 29, [2005] Crim LR 476 ....534, 535
R v Smith (Lance Perceval) [2003] EWCA Crim 283, [2003] Crim LR 633................499
R v Smith (Percy) [1976] Crim LR 511 448
R v Smolinski [2004] 2 Cr App Rep 661 368
R v Soneji [2005] 3 WLR 303 155
R v Southampton Justices, ex p Green [1976] QB 11 280
R v Sparkes [1956] 1 WLR 505 713
R v Spencer [1986] 2 All ER 928 533
R v Stone [2005] EWCA Crim 105, [2005] Crim LR 569 461
R v Stovell [2006] EWCA Crim 27, [2006] Crim LR 760 420
R v Sultan Khan [1997] AC 58 483
R v Sussex Justices, ex p McCarthy [1924] 1 KB 256 422
R v Swabey [1972] 2 All ER 1094 713
R v Symons [2006] EWCA Crim 856, [2006] 2 Cr App Rep 23 368
R v Tahery [2006] EWCA Crim 529 458
R v Taylor and Taylor (1993) 98 Cr App Rep 361 372
R v Thakrar [2001] EWCA Crim 1096 686
R v Thomas (1989) 88 Cr App Rep 370 ....498, 499
R v Thomas [2000] 1 Cr App Rep 447 703
R v Thomas [2002] EWCA Crim 941, [2002] Crim LR 912 687
R v Thompson [1962] 1 All ER 65 532
R v Thompson (1978) Times, 18 January 470
R v Togher [2001] Cr App Rep 457, [2001] 3 All ER 463 ....703, 705
R v Tower Bridge Metropolitan Stipendiary Magistrates, ex p Chaudhry [1994]
1 All ER 44 269
R v Townsend [1987] Crim LR 411 448
R v Turnbull [1977] QB 224 460
R v Turnbull [1984] 80 Cr App Rep 104 450
R v Turner [1970] 2 QB 321 ....326, 328
R v Uxbridge Justice, ex p Heward-Mills [1983] 1 WLR 56 280
R v Walhein (1952) 36 Cr App Rep 167 531
R v Wallace Duncan Smith [2002] EWCA Crim 2007, [2003] 1 Cr App Rep 648 687
R v Wallwork (1958) 42 Cr App Rep 153 443

R v Walsh [1989] Cr App Rep 161 ....178, 480
R v Wang [2005] UKHL 9, [2005] 1 All ER 782 525
R v Ward [1993] 2 All ER 577, (1993) 96 Cr App Rep 1, CA 291, 297, 299
R v Warley Magistrates Court, ex p DPP [1998] Crim LR 684....................................337
R v Waterfield, R v Lynn [1964] 1 QB 164...239
R v Waters [1989] Crim LR 62, CA 477
R v Watson [1988] QB 690 531
R v Wells [1995] 2 Cr App Rep 412..346
R v West [1996] 2 Cr App Rep 374...373
R v Westlake [1979] Crim LR 652 472
R v Whybrow (1951) 35 Cr App Rep 141...700
R v Williams (1992) Times, 6 February 186
R v Wong Kam-Ming [1980] AC 247, PC 467
R v Wood [1982] Crim LR 667 448
R v Wright (1987) 90 Cr App Rep 91 443
R v X Justices, ex p J [2000] 1 All ER 183, Div Ct..185
R v Xhabri [2005] EWCA Crim 3135...458
R v Young [1995] QB 324 533
R v Z [1992] 2 QB 355...443
R v Zaveckas [1970] 1 All ER 413 ....471, 473, 476
R (on the application of Bucher) v DPP [2003] EWHC Admin 580............................193
R (on the application of Campaign for Nuclear Disarmament) v Prime Minister
    [2002] EWCA Admin 2712, Case AC9500930 584
R (Corner House Research) v Secretary of State for Trade and Industry [2005]
    EWCA Civ 192, [2005] 4 All ER 1 584
R (Cowl) v Plymouth City Council [2001] EWCA Civ 1935, [2002] 1 WLR 803 145
R (on the application of CPS) v Chorley [2002] EWHC 2162 Admin, (2002) 166
    JP 764 279
R (on the application of CPS) v Registrar General of Births, Deaths and Marriages
    [2002] EWCA Civ 1661, [2003] 1 All ER 540 462
R (on the application of Daghir) v Secretary of State for the Home Deparment
    [2004] EWHC 243..732
R (on the application of DPP) v Havering Magistrates' Court [2001] 1 WLR 805,
    [2001] Crim LR 902, Div Ct 280
R (on the application of Factortame Ltd) v Secretary of State for Transport, Local
    Government and the Regions (No 8) [2002] EWCA Civ 932, [2003] QB 381,
    [2002] 4 All ER 97 642
R (on the application of Faulkner) v Secretary of State for the Home Department
    [2005] EWHC Admin 2567 204
R (Gazette Media Co Ltd) v Teeside Crown Court [2005] EWCA Crim 1983,
    [2005] Crim LR 157 430
R (on the application of Gibson) v Winchester Crown Court [2004] EWHC 361,
    [2004] Crim LR 839 367
R (Gillan) v Commissioner of the Metropolitan Police [2006] UKHL 12 198
R (on the application of Jarrett) v Legal Services Commission [2001] EWHC
    Admin 389, [2001] All ER (D) 111 (June)..590
R (on the application of Joseph) v DPP [2001] Crim LR 489 263

R (on the application of Laporte) v Chief Constables of Gloucestershire and
    Thame Valley and the Commissioner of the Metropolitan Police [2004] EWHC
    Admin 253, [2004] 2 All ER 874...201
R (on the application of McGowan) v Brent Justices [2001] EWHC Admin 814,
    [2002] Crim LR 412 422
R (Mondelly) v Metropolitan Police Commissioner [2006] EWHC Admin 2370 261
R (Mount Cook Land Ltd and Mount Eden Land Ltd) v Westminster City Council
    [2003] EWCA Civ 1346..585
R (Mullen) v Secretary of State for the Home Department [2002] EWHC Admin
    230, [2002] 1 WLR 1857 731–32
R (Mullen) v Secretary of State for the Home Department [2004] UKHL 18,
    [2004] 3 All ER 65, [2004] Crim LR 837...732
R (on the application of Murphy) v Secretary of State for the Home Department
    [2005] EWHC Admin 140, [2005] 2 All ER 763..731
R (on the application of O) v Harrow Crown Court [2003] EWHC Admin 868........278
R (O) v Harrow Crown Court [2006] UKHL 42, [2006] 3 All ER 1157 278
R (on the application of O'Brien) v Independent Assessor [2003] EWHC Admin
    855, [2003] NLJR 668..733
R (R) v Durham Constabulary [2002] EWHC Admin 2486, [2003] 3 All ER 419......256
R (R) v Durham Constabulary [2005] UKHL 21, [2005] 2 All ER 369 256
R (S) v Chief Constable of South Yorkshire, R (Marper) v Same [2004] UKHL 39,
    [2004] 4 All ER 193 225
R (S) v Waltham Forest Youth Court [2004] EWHC Admin 715, [2004] 2 Cr App
    Rep 355 433
R (Wardle) v Leeds Crown Court [2001] UKHL, [2001] Crim LR 468 367
R (on the application of Wulfsohn) v Legal Services Commission [2002] EWCA
    Civ 250, [2002] All ER (D) 120 (Feb) 580
Ragho Prasad s/o Ram Autar Rao v R [1981] 1 All ER 319.......................................474
Raja (Representative for the Estate of Mohammed Sabir Raja, decd) v Van
    Hoogstraten [2006] EWHC 1315, Ch 77
Rank Film Distributors Ltd v Video Information Centre [1982] AC 380....................103
Rantzen v Mirror Group Newspapers [1993] 4 All ER 975...508
Raphael Partners v Liam [2002] OJ No 3417, 10 September 2002 (Docket No
    C36074) 643
Rastin v British Steel Plc [1994] 1 WLR 232, [1994] 2 All ER 641 ....122, 129
Reid v R [1980] AC 343, PC...715
Rennie v Frame [2005] SCCR 608..332
Reynolds v Metropolitan Police Commissioner [1982] Crim LR 600....................206–07
Reynolds v Metropolitan Police Commissioner [1984] 3 All ER 649..........................231
Rice v Connolly [1966] 2 QB 414, Div Ct 161–2, 165, 167
Richard Saunders & Partners v Eastglen Ltd [1990] 3 All ER 946 106
Ricketts v Cox [1982] Crim LR 184..162
Ridehalgh v Horsefield [2004] Ch 205, [1994] 3 All ER 848.......................................570
Rockwell Machine Tool Co Ltd v EP Barrus (Concessionaires) Ltd [1968] 2 All ER
    98..87
Rogers v Merthyr Tydfil County Borough Council [2006] EWCA Civ 1134 639
Rondel v Worsley [1969] 1 AC 191, HL 571
Rowe and Davis v United Kingdom (2000) 30 EHRR 1, [2000] Crim LR 584 298

Royal Bank of Canada Trust Corpn Ltd v Secretary of State for Defence (2003)
Times, 14 May, Ch D 145
Royal Brompton Hospital NHS Trust v Hammond [2001] EWCA Civ 550, (2001)
Times 11 May 82
Rush & Tompkins Ltd v Greater London Council [1988] 3 All ER 737, HL 60

Saif Ali v Mitchell & Co [1980] AC 198, HL 571
Samonini v London General Transport Services [2005] EWHC 90001 (Costs),
19 January 2005 649
Sander v United Kingdom (2001) 31 EHRR 1003 535
Saric v Denmark, Application no 31913/96, 2 February 1999 529
Sarwar v Alam [2001] EWCA Civ 1401, [2001] 4 All ER 541 ....649, 650
Saunders v United Kingdom (1996) 23 EHRR 313 ....163, 164, 708
Scarth v United Kingdom (1999) 27 EHRLR CD 37 ....425, 428
Scott v Scott [1913] AC 417 423
Scribes West Ltd v Relsa Anstalt [2004] EWCA Civ 965 660
Secretary of State for the Home Department v JJ [2005] EWCA 1141 216
Secretary of State for the Home Department v MB [2006] EWCA 1140 216
Sefkali, Banamira, Ouham [2006] EWHC Admin 894 27 February 2006 194
Sekhon [2003] 1 WLR 1655 155
Sharratt v London Central Bus Co [2003] EWCA Civ 7128, [2003] 1 WLR 2487,
[2003] 4 All ER 590 638
Sharratt v London Central Bus Co (No 2) [2004] EWCA Civ 575, [2004] 3 All ER
325 635
Sherman and Apps, Re (1981) 72 Cr App Rep 266 208
Siporex Trade SA v Comdel Commodities Ltd [1986] 2 Lloyd's Rep 48 102
The Siskina [1979] AC 210 102
Sisu Capital Fund Ltd v Tucker [2005] EWHC 2321, Ch, [2006] 1 All ER 167 579
Smith v DPP [2001] EWHC Admin 55, [2001] Crim LR 735 193
SmithKline Beecham Biologicals SA v Connaught Laboratories Inc [1999] 4 All
ER 498, CA 99
Snook v Mannion [1982] RTR 321 225
Solutia UK Ltd v Griffiths [2001] EWCA Civ 61, [2001] 2 Costs LR 247 567
Sparks v R [1964] 1 All ER 727, PC 446
Spicer v Holt [1977] AC 987, HL 200
Squires v Botwright [1972] RTR 462 ....193, 194
SS Hontestroom (Owners) v SS Sagaporack (Owners) [1927] AC 37, HL 688
Stafford v DPP [1974] AC 878 716
Stanton v Stanton [2006] EWCA Civ 878 429
Starrs v Procurator Fiscal [2000] LRC 718 19
Steel and Morris v United Kingdom (2005) Times, 16 February 590
Steele v Money [2005] EWCA Civ 96, [2005] 2 All ER 256 76
Stevens v Gullis [2000] 1 All ER 527 112
Stevens v Walker [1936] 2 KB 215 690
Stewart v Engel [2000]1 WLR 2268 53
Stirland v DPP [1944] AC 315 ....699, 714
Storer v British Gas Ltd [2000] 1 WLR 1237 428
Subramaniam v Public Prosecutor [1956] 1 WLR 965 448

Sumitomo Corpn v CrÈdit Lyonnais Rouse Ltd [2001] EWCA Civ 1152, [2002]
   4 All ER 68 92
Sunworld Ltd v Hammersmith and Fulham Borough Council [2000] 2 All ER 837,
   Div Ct..677
Swain v Hillman [2001] 1 All ER 91, CA 81
Swales v Cox [1981] 1 All ER 1115 226

Tanfern Ltd v Cameron MacDonald (Practice Note) 1 WLR 131 ....658, 659, 664, 691
Tarling, Re [1979] 1 All ER 981 713
Taylor v Anderton [1995] 1 WLR 447, [1995] 2 All ER 420, CA 94
Taylor v Chief Constable of Cheshire [1987] 1 All ER 225 447
TGA Chapman Ltd v Christopher [1998] 1 WLR 12 575
Theodoropoulas v Theodoropoulas [1964] P 311..60
Third Chandris Shipping Corpn v Unimrine SA[1979] QB 645 102
Thomas v Sawkins [1935] 2 KB 249 226
Thompson v Metropolitan Police Commissioner [1997] 2 All ER 762......................509
Thompson v Thompson [1986] 1 FLR 212n 450
Three Rivers DC v Bank of England (No 3) (Summary Judgment) [2001] UKHL
   16, [2001] 2 All ER 513 49
Three Rivers DC v Bank of England (No 4) [2002] EWCA Civ 1182, [2002] 4 All
   ER 881 96
Three Rivers DC v Bank of England (No 6) [2004] UKHL 48, [2004] 3 WLR
   1274 ....91, 92
Total Spares & Supplies Ltd v Antares SRL [2006] EWHC 1537, Ch 576
Toth v Jarman [2006] EWCA Civ 1028 382
Tri Level Claims Consultants Ltd v Kolionitis (2006) 15 CPC,(6th) 1241 641
Trustor AB v Smallbone [2000] 1 All ER 811..428

Universal Thermosensors Ltd v Hibben [1992] 3 All ER 257 103
Uphill v BRB (Residuary) Ltd [2005] EWCA Civ 60, [2005] 3 All ER 264 ....664, 665

Vapormatic Co Ltd v Sparex Ltd [1976] 1 WLR 939..103
Various Ledward Claimants Meadway HA [2003] EWHC 2551, QB..........................567
Vasiliou v Hajigeorgiou [2005] EWCA Civ 236, [2005] 3 All ER 17 114
Ventouris v Mountain, The Italia Express [1991] 1 WLR 607, [1991] 3 All ER
   472 92
Vernon v Bosley (No 2) [1999] QB 18, [1997] 1 All ER 614....................................89, 392
Verrechia v Metropolitan Police Commissioner [2002] EWCA Civ 605, [2002]
   3 All ER 385 ....86, 557
Vinos v Marks & Spencer Plc [2001] 3 All ER 784, CA 75
Voise v Delavel 1 TR 11, 99 ER 944 532

W v Egdell [1990] 1 All ER 835 391
Wallersteiner v Moir (No 2) [1975] 1 All ER 849 631
Ward v Guinness Mahon & Co [1996] 4 All ER 112 573
Ward v James [1966] 1 QB 273, [1965] 1 All ER 563, CA 504, 505
Waters v Bigmore [1981] Crim LR 408..204
Watson Wyatt v Maxwell Batley (2002) Times, 15 November......................................145

Waugh v British Railways Board [1980] AC 521, [1979] 2 All ER 1169, HL..................93
Webb v Webb [1986] 1 FLR 541 450
Weight v Lang [1986] Crim LR 746..193
Weir v Secretary of State for Transport, 21 April 2005, unreported, QBD 584
Wershof v Metropolitan Police Commissioner [1978] 3 All ER 540 ....201, 206
West Mercia Constabulary v Wagener [1981] 3 All ER 378 240
Whitehouse v Jordan [1981] 1 All ER 267 689
Wilkey v BBC [2002] EWCA CIv 1561, [2003] 1 WLR 1 76
Williams v Home Office [1981] 1 All ER 1151 94–95
Willmott v Atack [1977] QB 498 165
Wouters, Case C-309/99 [2002] ECR I-1577 813

X v Y [1988] 2 All ER 648 98

Yams v Plender [2001] 1 WLR 32 664
Yousif v Salama [1980] 1 WLR 1540 103
Yuill v Yuill [1945] P 15, [1945] 1 All ER 183, 61 TLR 176..380

ZYX Music GmbH v King [1995] 3 All ER 1 107

Chapter 1

The organisation of trial courts

1. Introduction

The English courts system has developed slowly over centuries and still shows many signs of its history but in recent decades there have been several major changes and in the past few years the pace of reform has quickened.

Up to 1979 the courts, other than the magistrates' courts, had been run by the Lord Chancellor's Department (LCD). In that year their administration was transferred to an executive agency called the Court Service. That agency was responsible for the functioning of the Supreme Court of England and Wales (comprising the Court of Appeal, the High Court and the Crown Court), county courts and seven tribunals. The running of the magistrates' courts was not included. They were run by local committees under the general supervision of the Home Office until 1991 and since that date by the LCD.[1]

In 2001, in his *Review of the Criminal Courts System*,[2] Lord Justice Auld recommended a 'single and nationally funded administrative structure, but one providing significant local autonomy and accountability'. This proposal was accepted by Government. The Courts Act 2003 made the necessary statutory changes to allow for the creation of Her Majesty's Courts Service (HMCS) as a new executive agency with some 20,000 staff. (Bringing the magistrates' courts into the national system doubled the complement of staff.) The change took effect in April 2005. HMCS is accountable to the Lord Chancellor/Secretary of State for Constitutional Affairs.[3] HMCS

---

[1] For the successive recent developments in the story of the administration of the magistrates' courts see the 9th edition of the present work, pp. 29–31.

[2] www.criminal-courts-review.org.uk.

[3] On 12 June 2003, the Prime Minister, Mr Tony Blair, announced that the ancient title of Lord Chancellor dating back to the eleventh century would be abolished and replaced by the title Secretary of State for Constitutional Affairs. The Prime Minister's announcement proved to be somewhat hasty. The Lord Chancellor's Department (LCD) was renamed the Department of Constitutional Affairs (DCA) by a stroke of the Prime Ministerial pen, but in the event the office of Lord Chancellor survived. The holder of the office is now both Lord Chancellor and Secretary of State for Constitutional Affairs.

has forty-two areas each with an Area Director and an advisory Courts Board.[4]

The highest court, the House of Lords, is outside this administrative structure. Hitherto it has been run by the LCD, now the DCA. Under the Constitutional Reform Act 2005, the House of Lords in its judicial capacity is to be transformed into the new Supreme Court with its own administrative structure including a chief executive. It will be situated in the Middlesex Guildhall, opposite Parliament. Getting that building ready for its new role is a major project that will take some years.[5] It is not expected to be finished before the end of 2009. Until then, the House of Lords as the final court of appeal will continue in its traditional home in the Palace of Westminster sitting under its traditional title and administered as before by the Government Department.

Calling the final court of appeal the Supreme Court necessitated a re-naming of the existing Supreme Court of England and Wales. This will be known as 'The Senior Court of England and Wales'.[6]

The Constitutional Reform Act 2005 made other major constitutional changes, the most important of which is the transfer of responsibility for the appointment of the judiciary from the Lord Chancellor[7] to a new Judicial Appointments Commission with a lay chairman and a significant number of lay members.[8] The Act for the first time gives explicit recognition to the special responsibility of the Lord Chancellor for the rule of law[9] and for the independence of the judiciary.[10] There is however no longer any guarantee that the Lord

---

[4] The Boards have seven members – a judge, two magistrates, two people to represent the local community and two people with experience of the courts in the area (lawyers, victim support, advice agencies etc.).

[5] The task was costed at £30 million. The cost of moving the old courts into new premises would be another £20 million. (There is every reason to suppose that these would prove to be considerable underestimates.) The costs of running the new Supreme Court would be of the order of £8–10 million a year compared with £3–4 million in the House of Lords. For a drawing of what the new Supreme Court would look like see *Law Society's Gazette*, 14 September 2006, p. 4.   [6] Constitutional Reform Act 2005, s. 59(1).

[7] For a description of the previous system see Sir Thomas Legg, 'Judges for the new Century', *Public Law*, 2001, pp. 62–76. *Legal Studies* in March 2004 devoted the whole of issues 1 and 2 to judicial appointments.

[8] The 2005 Act (Sch.12, para. 2) provides for the Commission to consist of a lay chairman, five judicial members, two practitioners, five lay members, one tribunal member and one lay justice The first chairman is Baroness Usha Prashar. The names of all but one of the other fourteen appointees were announced on 23 January 2006. (See the Lord Chancellor's Ministerial Statement, House of Lords, *Hansard*, 23 January 2006, WS 45.) The Commission was launched on 3 April 2006. The Act (Sch. 13) also provides for a lay Judicial Appointments and Conduct Ombudsman whose duties would also commence on 3 April 2006.

[9] Section 1 states that the Act does not adversely affect '(a) the existing constitutional principle of the rule of law, or (b) the Lord Chancellor's existing constitutional role in relation to that principle'.

[10] Section 3 of the Act states that 'the Lord Chancellor, other Ministers of the Crown and all with responsibility for matters relating to the judiciary or otherwise to the administration of justice must uphold the continued independence of the judiciary'.

Chancellor will necessarily be either a member of the Upper House or a lawyer.[11]

At least of equal importance is the so-called 'Concordat'[12] between the Lord Chancellor and the Lord Chief Justice, a 28-page document setting out in detail their respective roles in relation to a long list of topics.[13]

The chapter starts with a description of the existing trial courts structure. (The appellate system is treated in Ch. 7.)

2. The trial courts – work and organisation

(1) The civil courts

There are three different levels of trial courts for civil cases: the High Court, the county court and the magistrates' court.

The High Court
History[14]

The High Court is divided into three Divisions: the Queen's Bench Division, the Chancery Division and the Family Division. The High Court came into existence in the Judicature Acts of 1873–5, in replacement for the ancient Queen's Bench Court, Court of Common Pleas, Court of Exchequer, Chancery Court, and the Probate, Divorce and Admiralty Court. Under the 1873–5 legislation these five separate courts became the five Divisions of the High Court. In 1888 the three common law courts (Queen's Bench, Common Pleas and Exchequer) were merged into a single Division, the Queen's Bench Division (QBD). The Probate, Divorce and Admiralty Division was broken up by the Administration

---

[11] Section 2 of the Act (headed 'Lord Chancellor to be qualified by experience') provides that the person who holds the office of Lord Chancellor must be someone who appears to the Prime Minister to be qualified by experience as a Minister, a member of either House of Parliament, a practitioner, a university law teacher or 'other experience that the Prime Minister considers relevant'.

[12] The Concordat is on the DCA's Website as a consultation paper entitled *Constitutional Reform: The Lord Chancellor's judiciary-related functions* (since referred to as 'the agreement' and also 'the Concordat'): www.dca.gov.uk/consult/lcoffice/judiciary.htm. The Concordat was negotiated on behalf of the judiciary by the Lord Chief Justice, Lord Woolf. For a lecture in which he explains it see 'The Rule of Law and a Change in the Constitution', 63 *Cambridge Law Journal*, 2004, pp. 317–30.

The topics dealt with in the Concordat include: key statutory responsibilities of the Secretary of State and the Lord Chief Justice, judicial independence, judicial posts held by the Lord Chancellor, leadership of the judiciary in England and Wales, oath-taking, provision of resources, deployment, 'leadership posts', appointments to committees, boards and similar bodies, the making of procedural rules for judicial fora, rule committee appointments, Practice Directions, education and training, judicial complaints and discipline, judicial appointments commission – process and judicial appointments commission – membership.

[13] The remarkable story of the Constitutional Reform Act 2005 is the subject of a two-part article by Lord Windlesham in *Public Law*, 2005, pp. 806–23 and 2006, pp. 35–57.

[14] For an outstanding historical account see B. Abel-Smith and R. Stevens, *Lawyers and the Courts* (Heinemann, 1967).

of Justice Act 1970 which allocated its functions between the QBD, the Chancery Division and the new Family Division.

The High Court today

The jurisdiction of the High Court is to be found in the provisions of the Supreme Court Act 1981.

The Queen's Bench Division (QBD) This consists of the Lord Chief Justice and some seventy High Court judges. It deals primarily with claims for contract and tort. The largest single category of work is for goods sold and delivered, work done, materials supplied or professional work done. The next largest categories typically are claims for breach of contract, personal injuries and the recovery of land or property.

The number of cases dealt with by the QBD has been declining dramatically in recent years. One reason is the transfer of cases from the QBD to the county court (see below pp. 11, 67). In 1990 the number of proceedings started in the QBD was over 350,000. In 1997 it was down to some 121,000. Four years later by 2001 it had slumped to a mere 21,600. In 2005 it was down to 15,317![15]

The QBD additionally has two special types of jurisdiction. One is the Admiralty Court, previously part of the Probate, Divorce and Admiralty Division until it was abolished by the Administration of Justice Act 1970. Admiralty cases typically concern collisions at sea, damage to cargo and personal injuries suffered at sea. (In 2005 there were 102 claims issued in admiralty cases but only three cases were actually tried!) The second category is the Commercial Court, which has judges specially chosen for their experience to try heavy commercial cases. (There are currently twelve Commercial Court judges.) The cases consist of matters relating to ships, aircraft, insurance, banking, carriage of cargo and the construction and performance of mercantile contracts. Many of the cases have a strong international flavour. (In 2005 there were almost a thousand (981) claims started.)

The Divisional Court of the Queen's Bench Division exercises an important first instance jurisdiction by way of review of the acts of Ministers, their civil servants and local councilors and officials. Traditionally this was by way of the ancient prerogative writs (*certiorari, mandamus, prohibition* and *habeas corpus*). Then such cases were dealt with by an application for judicial review under what was Order 53 of the Rules of the Supreme Court (RSC). The part of the QBD that dealt with these applications was known as the Crown Office List. From October 2000 the Crown Office List was renamed the Administrative Court.[16] The applicant now applies for mandatory, quashing and prohibiting orders. Unlike the position for ordinary actions, permission (formerly called 'leave') is

---

[15] The figures are to be found in the annual *Judicial Statistics*.
[16] *Practice Note* [2000] 1 WLR 1654, [2000] 4 All ER 1071. For commentary see 20 *Civil Justice Quarterly*, 2001, pp. 1–5 and *Public Law*, 2001, pp. 4–20.

required to start such proceedings. Applications for permission are heard normally by a single judge. In 2005 there were 4,660 applications to apply for judicial review in civil matters, of which more than half (58 per cent) concerned immigration issues.

The Chancery Division The Chancery Division is the successor to the ancient Chancery Court. It consists of the Vice Chancellor and seventeen High Court judges. It deals with corporate and personal insolvency disputes, business, trade and industry disputes, the enforcement of mortgages, professional negligence, intellectual property matters, copyright and patents, trusts, wills and probate matters. The Chancery Division also includes a specialist Companies Court and Patents Court. In 2005 the total number of proceedings was just over 34,000, of which some 14,000 were Companies Court matters and 13,000 were bankruptcy petitions.

The Family Division The Family Division was created in 1970 when the Probate, Divorce and Admiralty Division was split up. It consists of the President and some seventeen High Court judges. It hears defended divorce cases and ancillary disputes over children and property. It also deals with wardship, guardianship of infants, adoption and legitimacy cases. The Family Division nominally also deals with non-contentious probate work but in practice this work is handled by administrative or bureaucratic rather than by judicial proceedings. (As will be seen, the Children Act 1989 established a concurrent family jurisdiction across the High Court, the county court and family proceedings courts in the magistrates' courts.)

There are two other special jurisdictions:

The Technology and Construction Court (TCC) – formerly the Official Referees Court. The Official Referees Court was renamed the Technology and Construction Court in 1998. Its jurisdiction remained the same, namely difficult or technical issues of fact on reference from the Queen's Bench Division or the Chancery Division after an application made by either party. Usually the cases involve complex building and construction disputes. The judges used to be Circuit judges (lower in the judicial hierarchy than High Court judges), but on the renaming of the court in 1998, a High Court judge was put in charge (on a part-time basis) and the Official Referees were renamed 'judges' to be addressed as 'My Lord' instead of 'Your Honour'. In June 2005 the Lord Chief Justice said that because of the number and importance of the cases heard by the TCC the High Court judge in charge would in future be full-time. No fewer than forty-one Circuit judges were engaged on these cases in London (seven full-time) and eleven other court centres – and twenty-three Recorders (part-time judges) were authorised to hear TCC cases as and when required.[17]

In 2004–05 there were 655 TCC cases started and eighty-nine contested trials – thirty-eight in London and fifty-one in Birmingham, Salford and Leeds.[18]

---

[17] [2005] 3 All ER 289.
[18] *Annual Report of the Technology and Construction Court, 2005.* NB The *Judicial Statistics* are plainly inaccurate in stating in Table 3.16 that there were only three contested TCC trials in 2005.

The Court of Protection This is responsible for the management and administration of the property and affairs of people suffering from mental disorder. Most of the work is done by masters and deputy masters (see below) rather than by judges, but judges of the Chancery Division and the Family Division do exercise some of the powers. There are normally some 30,000 estates under administration.

The hands-on management of the affairs of patients unable to manage for themselves is done by the Public Guardianship Office (PGO) which was established as an executive agency in 2001. Its main function is to promote the interests of its clients by overseeing the activities of Receivers appointed by the Court of Protection.

In December 1997 the Government published a consultation paper, *Who Decides? Making Decisions on Behalf of Mentally Incapacitated Adults*, based on the recommendations of the Law Commission.[19] This proposed that the Court of Protection should cease to exist as an office of the Supreme Court and instead become a superior court of record. By 2006 no decision on this issue had been announced.

Judges in High Court cases

One of the features of the English system is the overlapping jurisdiction of judges. The fact that a case is heard in the High Court does not mean that it will be heard by a High Court judge. Thus in 2005 the High Court case load was shared between High Court judges (56 per cent), Circuit judges (full-time judges) (21 per cent), Deputy High Court judges (retired judges, practitioners or experienced Circuit judges) (18 per cent), District judges (full-time judges) (3 per cent) and Lords Justices of Appeal and Recorders (practitioners sitting as part-time judges) (2 per cent).[20]

Interlocutory work in the High Court

Most trials are handled by judges, but the pre-trial (called 'interlocutory') work is conducted in London by Masters in the Queen's Bench and Chancery Divisions and by District judges (formerly called registrars) in the Family Division. Outside London there are no Masters. High Court interlocutory business outside London is handled in District Registries by District judges who are normally also the District judges for the county court. District Registries are physically located in county courts. There are over a hundred District Registries. All the District Registries deal with Queen's Bench, Chancery and Family Division work. Most, though not all, are authorised to take undefended divorce cases. County courts are now divided into Civil Trial Centres and Feeder Courts. Groups of feeder courts are supervised by designated Circuit judges who sit in the trial centres.

---

[19] *Mental Incapacity* (1995) Law Com. 231.
[20] Source: *Judicial Statistics, 2005, Revised*, calculated from Table 10.2, p. 133.

The county court

The county court was established in 1846 with a jurisdiction limited to £20 for actions in contract and tort. Over the next 150 or so years its jurisdiction rose from £20 to £5,000.[21] In 1990 the ceiling was abolished. As from 1 July 1991 county courts were able to deal with all contract and tort claims and recovery of land actions, regardless of value, plus equity matters where the value of the trust fund or estate does not exceed £30,000. In practice, however, the great majority of high value cases are handled by the High Court.

Most of the business of the county courts is money claims. Actions of this kind are mainly for goods sold and delivered, work done, materials supplied and professional fees. The other largest categories of work done by the county court are undefended divorce[22] and ancillary relief with regard to children and matrimonial property and actions for the recovery of land and premises. The county court also has an admiralty and equity jurisdiction, can hear contested probate actions, and deals with bankruptcy and companies winding up.

There are two tiers of judges in the county courts. The lower tier (District judges) deal with the case management work plus the great bulk of less complicated/lower value hearings and most of the housing possession and family related claims. The upper tier (Circuit judges) deal with the more serious cases, the trials of care cases and the more difficult private law Children Act applications.

Small claims in the county court

A 1970 study of the county court by the Consumer Council (*Justice out of Reach*) showed that individuals hardly ever used the county courts as plaintiffs. This led to changes in county court procedure designed to make them more 'user friendly' to ordinary citizens. The main reform was the introduction in 1973 of what was originally called 'arbitration' but which soon came to be known as the small claims procedure. This had several special features, notably, hearings in private,[23] less formal procedure, and costs rules under which each side basically pays its own costs.[24]

The limit for small claims cases in 1973 was £75 but it has increased hugely and is now £5,000 other than for personal injury and housing disrepair cases where it is £1,000.[25]

---

[21] During the first hundred years the jurisdiction was increased very slowly – to £50 in 1850, £100 in 1903 and £200 in 1938. In 1955 the jurisdiction of the county courts was raised to £400. In 1966 it went up to £500, in 1969 to £750 and in 1974 to £1,000. It next jumped to £2,000 in 1977 and in 1981 it was more than doubled to £5,000 – and in equity matters £30,000.

[22] About three-quarters of the 220 county courts are authorised to deal with undefended divorce work.

[23] As will be seen, this has been changed. To make the procedure compatible with the European Convention on Human Rights a trial now has to be conducted in public. See p. 424 below.

[24] See further below – with regard to small claims less formal trial methods, pp. 384–88, and with regard to costs, pp. 577–78.

[25] The £75 limit was raised to £200 in 1975. In 1979 it went up to £500 and in 1991 to £1,000. Lord Woolf's *Interim Report Access to Justice* in June 1995 proposed that it be increased to

The reason for the difference is to take account of the need for lawyers to assist with such claims. The small claims system does not allow for recovery of lawyers' fees whereas in claims outside the small claims system lawyers' fees can be recovered by the winning party. In personal injury and housing disrepair cases access to the help of lawyers has been considered sufficiently important to justify the lower limit. In May 2004, the Government's Better Regulation Task Force recommended that the Government should undertake research into raising the limit for personal injury cases so that they were brought into line with the rest of civil claims. This it said would 'increase access to justice for many as it will be less expensive, less adversarial and less stressful'.[26] The Association of Personal Injury Lawyers (APIL), unsurprisingly, labelled this proposal, which it said would affect more than half of all personal injury, 'a disaster',[27] but it was not just the personal injury lawyers who were opposed. A report published by the Civil Justice Council agreed with APIL that the starting point for recovery of costs in personal injury claims below £5,000 should remain at £1,000:[28]

> There is no evidence to suggest that the resolution of personal injury claims between £1,000–5,000 is working unsatisfactorily for the consumer. Only a very small number of such claims do not settle and litigation to trial in these cases is a very infrequent last resort . . . [T]here is simply no benefit to be gained by raising the small claims limit in personal injury cases. Rather, any such move that would remove cost recovery in such cases would work contrary to the public interest by removing quality controlled and regulated law firms from their role in resolving such claims which are still important to the injured consumer. The resulting gap in access to justice would be filled either by unrepresented consumers who would be unequal to the task of taking on the complexities of personal injury law, or by non-lawyers whose only means of remuneration would be to deduct a contingency fee from the injured consumer's damages.[29]

APIL's view also received support from a MORI poll published in April 2005.

Footnote 25 (*cont.*)
   £3,000, save for personal injury cases. This was implemented in January 1996. When the 'Woolf reforms' were implemented in April 1999, the general jurisdiction was raised to £5,000.
[26] *Better Regulation Task Force, Better Routes to Redress*, May 2004, p. 27 – www.brc.gov.uk. A report by the House of Commons Constitutional Affairs Committee in December 2005 recommended that the limit for personal injury cases and for housing could be raised to £2,500 without disadvantage to claimants – *The Courts – Small Claims*, HC 519, December 2005. For earlier discussion of the question of raising the limit see J. Baldwin, 'Increasing the small claims limit', 148 *New Law Journal*, 27 February 1998, p. 27; *Monitoring the Rise in the Small Claims Limit*, LCD Research Series 1/97, Lord Chancellor's Department, 1997 and *Lay and Judicial Perspectives on the Expansion of the Small Claims Regime*, LCD, Research Series 8/02, September 2002.
[27] The President of APIL was quoted as saying: 'it cannot be right that someone who is not legally trained is expected to put together a personal injury claim, gather medical reports and work out how much compensation they are entitled to. Thousands of people . . . may find bringing a claim against the person or company which injured them practically impossible', *New Law Journal*, 18 March 2005, p. 397.
[28] *Improved Access to Justice – Funding Options and Proportionate Costs*, September 2005 – www.costsdebate.civiljusticecouncil.gov.uk.   [29] *Ibid*, p. 16, para. 2.

According to the poll, 64 per cent of more than 2,000 respondents said they would be unlikely to pursue their case without a lawyer and 80 per cent believed that without a lawyer to help them they would not receive the right amount of compensation from an insurance company.[30]

As the jurisdiction has expanded, the small claims system has assumed increasing importance. In 1973, when it began, only 8 per cent of trials in the county court were heard under the small claims procedure. A quarter of a century later the proportion had soared ten-fold to over four-fifths.[31] In 2004 and 2005, it was 74 per cent and 73 per cent respectively.[32] This has been an astonishing development. Professor John Baldwin, the leading academic expert on the small claims system, said of this,[33] 'it is no exaggeration to say that the development of the small claims procedure in England and Wales has for many years been slowly bringing about a revolution in civil procedures in the county courts'.[34]

Magistrates' courts

Magistrates' courts have always had a significant jurisdiction in the civil field. Most of it was in the field of domestic relations – especially maintenance for deserted wives and children, custody disputes, adoption, guardianship, and protection of battered wives. A different kind of civil jurisdiction is the collection of various statutory debts such as income tax, national insurance, social security, rates and legal aid contributions.

In the field of domestic relations there was a great deal of overlap between the jurisdiction of the magistrates and that of the county court. The issue of what to do about this jurisdiction culminated in the Children Act 1989 which led to a significant re-casting both of the relevant law and of the responsibilities of the different levels of civil courts. The magistrates' courts functions in this field have been renamed 'family proceedings courts'.

---

[30] *New Law Journal*, 8 April 2005, p. 529.

[31] Between 1997 and 2003 the proportions were 83 per cent, 87 per cent, 87 per cent, 78 per cent, 81 per cent, 80 per cent and 77 per cent.

[32] Calculated from *Judicial Statistics*, the table headed 'Proceedings disposed of by trial or small claims hearing by region' – Table 4.7 or, in 2005, Table 4.8.

[33] J. Baldwin, *Lay and Judicial Perspectives on the Expansion of the Small Claims Regime*, September 2002, LCD Research Series, No. 8/02, p. 7. For an overall description of the system see N. Madge, 'Small Claims in the County Court', 23 *Civil Justice Quarterly*, 2004, pp. 201–11.

[34] In June 2005 the Department for Constitutional Affairs issued a consultation paper (CP 12/05) regarding a proposal from the European Commission for a European Small Claims Procedure. The Commission's suggestion was that the procedure should be available not only for cross-border disputes but also for internal cases. The new system would be an alternative to, not a replacement for, whatever already exists in Member States. The UK Government welcomed the proposed new procedure but wished it to be confined to cross-border cases – a view with which the House of Commons Constitutional Affairs Committee agreed in its report in December 2005 (n. 26 above).

Family court work

In 1974 the Finer Report[35] recommended the setting up of a unified family courts system to combat what it considered to be the chaotic effect of the jurisdictional split between the High Court, county courts and magistrates' courts. The report was not implemented. In 1986 an interdepartmental *Review of Family and Domestic Jurisdiction* consultation paper canvassed various models for the Finer Report's proposed unified family court. Again, however, the unified family courts project was not taken forward.

The Children's Act 1989, implemented in 1991, established not a unified but a concurrent family jurisdiction across all tiers of civil courts. All three courts were given (albeit differing) jurisdiction to act, though the rules provided that certain business had to be started or tried in particular courts:

The High Court The High Court has jurisdiction to hear all cases relating to children and has an exclusive jurisdiction in wardship cases. It also hears appeals from family proceedings courts and cases transferred from the county court or the family proceedings courts.

County courts There are county courts with no family jurisdiction. There are divorce county courts which can issue all private law family law proceedings but contested matters are transferred to family hearing centres for trial. Family hearing centres can issue and hear all private law family law matters whether or not they are contested. There are care centres which have full jurisdiction in both private and public family law matters. There are also Specialised Adoption Centres.

(Public law cases are those usually brought by local authorities or the NSPCC and include care, supervision and emergency protection orders. Private law cases are brought by individuals generally in connection with divorce or separation.)

Family Proceedings Courts (magistrates' courts) Full private and public law jurisdiction except for divorce. Either lay magistrates alone or a District judge sitting with lay magistrates. They have been specially trained.

Public law cases must start in the family proceedings court but can be transferred to the county court to minimise delay or where the matter is grave, complex or important. (In 2005 there were a total 24,600 public law applications, of which 64 per cent were heard in the family proceedings courts, 35 per cent were heard in the county court and 1 per cent were heard in the High Court.[36])

Private law cases can be started at any family proceedings court or county court. (In 1992 private law applications ran at around 50/50 – 52,900 in county courts and 51,500 in family proceedings courts, but since then there has been a dramatic shift. In 2005, 82 per cent of the 104,400 private law cases were heard in the county courts as against 17 per cent in the family proceedings courts and 0.2 per cent in the High Court.[37])

---

[35] *Report of the Committee on One-Parent Families*, 1974, Cmnd. 5629.
[36] *Judicial Statistics 2005 (Revised)*, Table 5.1.   [37] *Ibid.*

The Courts Act 2003 provided for a new unified set of rules in family law matters. The new rules (the Family Procedure Rules or FPR) apply in all courts exercising family jurisdiction.

The allocation of cases between higher and lower civil trial courts

Since 1846, when the county court was established, there has been the question of the proper relationship of the High Court and the county court. The two courts had concurrent jurisdiction up to the limit of the county court's jurisdiction. As has been seen, it was repeatedly raised[38] until 1991 when the ceiling was abolished. There were costs incentives to encourage litigants to have the case dealt with in the cheaper county court. Thus when the county court ceiling was £5,000 and the plaintiff in the High Court recovered less than £3,000 he was penalised by getting his costs on the county court scale. If he recovered less than £600 he got no costs at all.[39] When the ceiling was abolished in 1991, the High Court was given the power to reduce the costs recoverable by the successful party by up to 25 per cent if it thought the case should have been brought in the county court.[40] The courts had the power to transfer cases up or down either at the request of the parties or of its own motion.[41] Despite these incentives, a surprising number of cases within the jurisdiction of the county court were brought in the High Court.

In 1988, the *Civil Justice Review*[42] recommended that:

• The High Court and the county court should remain separate.
• There should be no upper limit for the jurisdiction of the county court.
• There should be a lower limit of £25,000 for cases in the High Court
• All cases below that should be heard in the county court unless they involved public law or specialist problems, or were cases of unusual complexity.
• Cases involving amounts between £25,000 and £50,000 should be heard in either the High Court or the county court.
• All personal injury cases should start in the county court.
• Registrars should be given the title of district judge and have their jurisdiction increased from £1,000 to £5,000.

The Lord Chancellor announced his broad acceptance of these proposals in April 1989 and they were implemented by the Courts and Legal Services Act 1990. The effect of the changes was that cases were allocated for trial according to substance, importance and complexity. Generally, cases involving amounts

---

[38] Always over the strenuous opposition of the Bar fuelled by the fact that barristers enjoyed a monopoly over the right to appear in the High Court whereas in the county court barristers and solicitors had an equal right of audience. For the history see B. Abel-Smith and R. Stevens, *Lawyers and the Courts* (Heinemann, 1963).

[39] County Courts Act 1959, ss. 19, 20.

[40] Courts and Legal Services Act 1990, s. 4 amending s. 51 of the Supreme Court Act 1981.

[41] Supreme Court Act 1981, Sch. 3, para. 8 inserting new s. 75A, Band C into the County Courts Act 1959. See also *Practice Direction* [1991] 3 All ER 349.   [42] Cm. 394.

below £25,000 were to be tried in the county court, those involving amounts above £50,000 in the High Court, and amounts in between, in either court depending on the criteria and judicial availability.[43]

However within those parameters and subject to the court's power to transfer a case, the choice of level of court was left to the parties. This continued until the implementation in 1999 of 'the Woolf reforms' based on two reports, both entitled *Access to Justice*[44] by Lord Woolf.[45]

The origin of the Woolf inquiry on civil justice was the Lord Chancellor's request to Lord Woolf to remove unnecessary differences between the procedural rules of the High Court and the county court. Lord Woolf got the Lord Chancellor's approval for expansion of this original remit to a much wider brief. It turned into a wide-ranging re-examination of the whole of the civil justice process.

In his *Interim Report* in June 1995 Lord Woolf proposed that the rules of the High Court and the county court should basically be the same (and that he would produce a draft of a single code of rules for High Court and county court cases), that an action could be commenced at any court and that the court rather than the parties should have the responsibility for allocating the case to the appropriate track. He suggested that these recommendations 'will mean that the question of whether a case is a High Court or a county court case will be of reduced significance'.[46]

Lord Woolf's proposal, implemented in 1999, was that, in addition to the existing small claims track, there should be two new tracks – the 'fast track' for cases involving amounts between £5,000 and £15,000 unless they were unsuitable for that track because of their complexity or importance and the 'multitrack' for cases involving sums above £15,000 or which were not suitable for the fast track. Lord Woolf envisaged that fast track cases would be handled in the county court but that multi-track cases would 'straddle' the High Court and the county court with procedural judges allocating the cases to the appropriate level of court.[47]

---

[43] *Practice Direction* [1991] 3 All ER 722.

[44] *Access to Justice, Interim Report, 1995; Final Report, 1996.* For a book of essays commenting on the *Interim Report* see *The Reform of Civil Procedure – Essays on Access to Justice* (eds. Zuckerman and Cranston, OUP, 1995). See also the lengthy note in 14 *Civil Justice Quarterly,* 1995, pp. 231–49. The Woolf reforms are enshrined in the Civil Procedure Rules (CPR). They can be accessed on the Website of the Department for Constitutional Affairs – www.dca.gov.uk.
    The writer was one of the few commentators who was basically opposed to the Woolf reform project – on the ground that it would have more adverse than beneficial results . See especially M. Zander, 'The Woolf Report: Forwards or Backwards for the new Lord Chancellor?' 16 *Civil Justice Quarterly,* 1997, pp. 208–27. For consideration of the pros and cons of the issues raised see pp. 132–40 below.

[45] In 1994 when he was first asked to undertake the project Lord Woolf was a Law Lord. In 1996, when he completed his report, he was Master of the Rolls. In 2000 he became Lord Chief Justice. He retired in 2005.   [46] *Interim Report,* p. 73, para. 4.

[47] For the different characteristics of the fast track and the multi-track cases see p. 50 below; for allocation to tracks see p. 78 below.

Toward a unified civil courts system

Lord Woolf rejected the suggestion that the High Court and the county court should be merged or amalgamated. One reason was the constitutional need to preserve the separate status of the High Court bench. This would be more difficult if there were a single civil court, but his reforms would move the system toward a closer alignment of the two levels, in particular through common rules of procedure and common though not identical jurisdictional rules and powers. The proposed new Head of Civil Justice would have responsibility for the management of civil cases throughout the system. Outside London the High Court and the county court shared the same buildings. Their administration was separate but that would be unnecessary when the common rules of procedure were introduced.[48]

In the last edition of this work in 2003 the writer said, 'the question of the possible amalgamation of the High Court and the county court seems to have disappeared as an issue'. This proved to be mistaken. In February 2005 the Department of Constitutional Affairs published a consultation paper entitled *A Single Civil Court?*[49] The paper (CP) outlined what a unified jurisdiction might look like and asked whether the proposed model, which included the Family Proceedings Courts, was feasible and appropriate. The CP said, 'it has been argued that unifying these jurisdictions would represent the next logical step following the fundamental reforms of civil procedure introduced in 1999'.[50] The CP suggested that there were three broad options. One was to do nothing. A second was to simplify and streamline the system further by secondary legislation. The third was to introduce primary legislation which would:

- Abolish the county courts.
- Create a new Civil Court.
- Adjust the powers, procedure and judiciary to ensure that it had all the features of a court covering all that the High Court and the county courts now do.

The title and special status of High Court judges would be preserved and certain powers would be reserved wholly or mainly to them. So, for instance, judicial review could be reserved to High Court judges and Circuit judges or Recorders specifically authorised by the Lord Chief Justice, but generally there would be few statutory restrictions on what cases could be tried by the different tiers of judges. It would be for the judiciary to make the necessary detailed rules about allocation of work between tiers through rules, Practice Directions etc.

The arguments for unifying the High Court and the county courts applied equally to the family law area. The arguments suggested a case for a single Family Court alongside the single Civil Court to handle all the family law business currently undertaken in the High Court, the county court and the Family Proceedings Courts (FPCs). That would have the effect of giving lay magistrates

---

[48] *Interim Report*, pp. 73–5.   [49] CP 06/05.   [50] At p. 6.

greatly increased powers – though rules could restrict their jurisdiction in particular categories of work. (As has been seen, a single family court had been the
chief recommendation of the Finer Committee in 1974.)

Consideration would have to be given to the various specialist courts – the
Patents Court, the Admiralty Court, the Commercial Court (and its county
court equivalent, the Mercantile Court), the Administrative Court, the
Companies Court, the Bankruptcy Court and the Technology and Construction
Court. Of these, only the first three were recognised in statute. With one exception, the CP suggested, there would be no reason to retain any statutory provision for specialist jurisdictions. The judiciary would provide for them through
rules and Practice Directions maintaining all or some of those that now exist
and adding others in future. The exception might be the Commercial Court in
order to preserve its international prestige and status.

The CP also addressed the question whether the divisions of the High Court
(QBD, Chancery and Family) had any remaining role. This topic was considered in the 1987 Civil Justice Review *General Issues* consultation paper which
commented that there was no comprehensive planning or forecasting procedure available for the purpose of reviewing the total workload of the High Court
and its Divisions. Each Division managed its affairs virtually independently of
the others which stood in the way of overall management of civil business.[51]
Professor Ian Scott, one of the country's leading experts on courts' management, wrote: 'it may be argued that the present three-fold Division structure
stands in the way of development of a range of procedures suited to the many
varieties of business arising in the High Court and that what is required nowadays is not three divisions but multiple, "substance-sensitive" procedural and
administrative arrangements reflecting the wide jurisdiction of the Court'.[52]

Lord Woolf in his *Interim Report* in 1995 said that it could be argued that separate practices and a separate culture between the Chancery and the Queen's
Bench Divisions might cause difficulties for outsiders. On the other hand, the
Chancery Division provided a convenient umbrella for a number of specialist
jurisdictions which were serviced by specialist judges and specialist members of
the bar. These jurisdictions, which included companies, bankruptcy and the
administration of estates and trusts, were of a quasi-administrative nature and
required a different approach from other litigation. The sense of team spirit
among the Chancery judges and their special relationship with the Chancery
Bar resulted in a more effective and efficient disposal of work. Moreover, if the
Chancery judges were amalgamated with the judges of the QBD they might
just be absorbed to meet the needs of the QBD. Lord Woolf's conclusion was
that it was not desirable, at least at that stage, to merge the two Divisions.[53]
Implementing his other recommendations would involve other changes of a
very substantial nature and it was preferable not to add to those changes the

---

[51] CP, para. 68.   [52] 8 *Civil Justice Quarterly,* 1989, p. 5.
[53] *Interim Report,* p. 77, para. 23.

upheaval that a merger of the two Divisions would involve. He would, however, follow the suggestion that judges should be nominated to lists according to their expertise, regardless of which Division to which the lists belonged. So a judge could be attached not only to lists in the Chancery Division but also to the Commercial Court in the QBD. If, however, the retention of the Chancery Division proved inimical to the uniform and flexible approach which he considered essential, the question of a merger could be reconsidered.

In his *Final Report*, Lord Woolf confirmed that he accepted that, although the administration of the two divisions should be brought closer together, they should not be merged.[54]

The DCA's 2005 CP did not argue the case. It said there were three broad options. One was to abolish the concept of divisions altogether. The second was to retain the divisions basically as now with a Family Court (if established) and a Civil Court divided into Queen's Bench and Chancery divisions with the divisions then incorporating the various specialist courts/lists. Consideration would be required as to whether to extend the concept of divisions to judges of the Circuit and District benches. The third option would be to change the concept so that divisions no longer applied to the issue and allocation of business but referred rather to groupings of judges.

The responses to the consultation paper were published on 19 October 2005.[55] There had been 131 responses. Some two-fifths of respondents (41 per cent) were said to be broadly in favour of the idea of a unified civil court, just under a third (31 per cent) were broadly against, with the remainder (28 per cent) neutral. Judges and solicitors were more in favour, barristers were more against.

On the same day the Lord Chancellor announced that he had concluded that reform to create single Civil and Family Courts would be feasible and beneficial: 'the idea of unifying the civil and family court jurisdictions has been gathering momentum for many years. We will be reforming the system to create a structure suitable for twenty-first century customer needs – making the courts simpler to understand and to access'.[56] This would be a long-term project. In the meanwhile, further steps would be taken to streamline the system and to improve efficiency.

A consultation paper issued that day (*Focusing judicial resources appropriately*)[57] outlined some of those steps. The CP considered the size, nature and relative position within the justice system of the judges of the High Court. It proposed that more should be done to ensure that High Court judges were reserved for cases that required that level of experience and competence. The exceptional features of cases requiring a High Court judge it suggested were: (1) the unusual complexity of the case either in points of law or points of fact or specialist evidence; (2) public impact, importance and significance (for instance

[54] *Final Report*, p. 261, para. 6.   [55] DCA, CP (R) 06/05.
[56] Press Release, Government News Network, DCA 265/05, 19 October 2005.
[57] DCA, CP 25/05.

'right to life' cases or ones involving high profile litigants or witnesses) and (3) cases raising points of law that would set precedents. If a claim were issued in the High Court it would need to be backed by a certificate explaining the reasons. A procedural judge would monitor the allocation process.

There could be four categories of case:

- Category 1 – Must be heard by a specialist High Court judge – such as most judicial review cases or cases claiming a declaration of incompatibility with the European Convention on Human Rights.
- Category 2 – Must be heard by a High Court judge or a Deputy High Court judge – such as cases involving claims of over £5 million.
- Category 3 – Could be heard by a High Court judge or by a less senior judge (but would normally be heard by Recorders or others sitting as Deputy High Court judges). Examples would be claims involving claims of £1–5 million.
- Category 4 – Not heard by High Court judges.

The DCA published the responses to the consultation paper on 18 September 2006 – www.dca.gov.uk (103 pages).

(2) The criminal courts

There have always been two levels of criminal court. Prior to 1972 the higher level consisted of Assize courts and Quarter Sessions courts. These were replaced by the Crown Court.

The Crown Court

The Crown Court dates from 1 January 1972, the day on which the Courts Act 1971 came into force. The 1971 Act was the result of the *Report of the Royal Commission on Assizes and Quarter Sessions*.[58] The Royal Commission under the chairmanship of Lord Beeching was set up to investigate and propose reforms to a system that had remained substantially unchanged for centuries.

The Royal Commission found that the then existing system was seriously defective. The ancient assize towns were no longer necessarily main centres of population; the fact that the same judge did both civil and criminal work meant that the civil cases always had to wait for the more urgent criminal cases to be finished first; the sittings of the assize courts were fixed long before anyone had any idea as to the likely case load; when the allotted time was up the judge had to go to the next assize town, rather than finish the list; the judges spent too much of their time on the road travelling between assize towns and whilst he and the court staff were all travelling, the entire courts system was inaccessible.

The solutions recommended by the Beeching Commission to the ills it had diagnosed were clear cut:

[58] 1969, Cmnd. 4153.

- The abolition of Assizes and Quarter Sessions and their replacement by a new higher criminal court to be called the Crown Court. This court would sit as and where needed. The siting of Crown Courts would be based on the principle 'that virtually the whole population will be within reasonable daily travelling distance of at least one such site, and that no regard shall be paid to civic boundaries established for other purposes'.
- The division of the criminal from the civil business of the higher courts so that civil litigants would no longer have to wait for the completion of criminal cases.
- Instead of the judges processing from town to town, they should to a much greater extent sit in court centres in permanent or more or less permanent session. In addition, there should be mini-circuits to handle the criminal work that could not be dealt with in the main court centres.
- Cases should be divided into different categories and allocated to judges by reference to their gravity and the level of seniority of judge required.
- The judges should all be able to sit in any Crown Court anywhere in the country.
- County court judges should be restyled Circuit judges, who should sit both in Crown Courts to conduct criminal cases and in county courts to conduct civil business.
- There should be a new title of Recorder for part-time judges eligible to sit in any Crown Court, who could be solicitors as well as barristers.
- The country should be divided into six, as compared with the previous seven, circuits. Each circuit should be run by two Presiding judges and a Circuit administrator.

The Royal Commission was set up by a Labour Government. Its report was implemented by the incoming Conservative Government. It accepted every one of the recommendations listed above. The Courts Act 1971 provided for the establishment of the Crown Court, whose business was to be handled by High Court judges, Circuit judges and Recorders. (The Crown Court for the City of London was, however, allowed to keep its hallowed name 'The Central Criminal Court', otherwise known as the Old Bailey.)

The Crown Court sits at some 90 locations throughout the country. The court centres are of three kinds. First-tier centres are those visited by High Court judges, Circuit judges and Recorders for the full range of Crown Court work – as well as by High Court judges of the Queen's Bench Division and Family Division for civil work. Second-tier centres are those at which Crown Court work (but not civil business) is dealt with by High Court judges, Circuit judges and Recorders. Third-tier centres are those visited only by Circuit judges, Recorders or Deputy Circuit judges.

At the start of the 1990s the number of cases committed for trial in the Crown Court was around 100,000 per year. In 1993 the figure dropped to 86,800 and since then it has fluctuated between a high of 91,100 (in 1997) and a low of 71,000 (in 2000). In 2005 it was 80,000.

The distribution of business in the Crown Court is governed by directions given by the Lord Chief Justice with the concurrence of the Lord Chancellor.[59] These divide offences, for the purposes of trial, into three (formerly four)[60] classes.

The most serious (Class 1) are generally to be tried by a High Court judge. They include treason, murder and espionage, but murders can be released by or on the authority of the Presiding judge for trial by a Deputy High Court judge, a Circuit judge or a Deputy Circuit judge who has been approved ('ticketed') for the purpose.

Offences in Class 2 must be tried by a High Court judge unless released by, or on the authority of, a Presiding judge for trial by a Circuit judge or Recorder. The offences include manslaughter, rape and abortion. Rapes and other serious sex offences can only be released to judges who have been ticketed for such trials.

Cases in Class 3 can be heard by any judge eligible to sit in the Crown Court though they are normally heard by a Circuit judge or Recorder. They include grievous bodily harm with intent, robbery and conspiracy and all 'either-way' offences.

Committals for sentence only

Crown Courts have also had a jurisdiction in sentencing defendants who were committed for sentence only by magistrates once the case had been concluded in the magistrates' courts. (In 2005 the Crown Court dealt with 32,300 such committals.) This jurisdiction in the Crown Court was exercised by a judge sitting with two lay magistrates. In his *Review of the Criminal Courts, 2001*, Lord Justice Auld recommended that this jurisdiction be abolished – a recommendation that the Government moved to implement in the Criminal Justice Act 2003.[61]

Appeals heard by the Crown Court

The Crown Court also has a jurisdiction in hearing appeals in respect of conviction and/or sentence in criminal cases decided by magistrates. (In 2005, there were 12,800 such appeals.) These are heard by a judge sitting with two, or sometimes one, lay magistrate. The judge should be the resident judge or a specifically designated judge or an approved experienced Recorder but failing that, another judge can be selected.

Crown Court judicial manpower

It is instructive to consider what has happened with regard to the requirements of judicial manpower since the Beeching Report in 1969 not yet forty years ago.

---

[59] The Consolidated Criminal Practice Direction III.21.1–2 and IV 33. [2002] 3 All ER 904 at 914, 923 as amended on 26 May 2005.

[60] The four classes became three in June 2005.

[61] See p. 321 below. As will be seen, most of the proposed change was included in the Act but implementation was postponed.

The Beeching Report estimated that there would be a need for some 150 full-time Circuit judges and 120 part-time Recorders – totalling 270.

In fact, as at September 2006, there were 637 Circuit judges and 1,363 Recorders – a total of exactly 2,000, almost a ten-fold increase.

In 2005, Crown Court work was divided between the different levels of judges as to 4 per cent by High Court judges, as to three-quarters (74 per cent) by Circuit judges and as to two-fifths (20 per cent) by Recorders.[62] The remaining 2 per cent was handled by Deputy High Court and Deputy Circuit judges.[63]

'Ticketing' of judges

The system of 'ticketing' judges as suitable for particular types of cases was criticised by Lord Justice Auld in his *Review of the Criminal Courts.* There were, for instance, some 50 Circuit judges approved to try murder cases and another 25 who were approved to try attempted murder. There were about 340 Circuit judges approved to try rape or other serious sexual offences. This system of selection involved the Lord Chief Justice, the Senior Presiding judge, the Presiding judges, the Resident judge of each court centre and his listing officer. The system, Lord Justice Auld said, was 'unduly bureaucratic and rigid'.[64] It was a rough-and-ready means of marking suitability. It also made for invidious distinctions between judges. The system, he suggested, should be changed by giving Resident judges responsibility for allocating cases at their court centres – subject to regular and systematic appraisal to determine the experience and interests of judges and a precondition of appropriate training by the Judicial Studies Board before taking particular types of cases.

Magistrates' courts

Magistrates' courts, which are manned mainly by lay justices, handle over 96 per cent of all criminal cases. In 2005 there were 1.9 million cases tried in magistrates' courts. Of these, nearly half (45 per cent) were minor motoring charges, just under one-third (30 per cent) were other summary cases that could only be tried in the magistrates' courts, and the remaining one-fifth (22 per cent) were cases that could have been tried in the Crown Court but the defendant chose instead to have the case dealt with summarily before the magistrates.[65]

---

[62] Until 2000 part-time judges started as Assistant Recorders. This rank of judge was abolished in light of the Scottish decision in *Starrs v. Procurator Fiscal* [2000] LRC 718 in which the High Court of Justiciary held that temporary sheriffs were insufficiently independent of the executive for the purposes of Article 6 of the European Convention on Human Rights because they had insufficient security of tenure. This was felt to apply equally to Assistant Recorders in England and Wales. In April 2000 the LCD announced that in future part-time judicial appointments would be for five years with a right of automatic renewal save in cases of misconduct or incapacity. For the various decisions taken by the Lord Chancellor after a review of the implications of the decision see *Judicial Appointments Annual Report 1999–2000*, paras. 2.14–2.18.

[63] Calculated from Table 10.2 in *Judicial Statistics 2005*, p. 134. (The total of Crown Court days sat in the published text is stated as 86,010. It should be 93,526.)   [64] Auld, para. 22, p. 236.

[65] *Criminal Statistics*, Home Office, RDS, 19/06, Fig. 2.1, p. 12.

(On this last category, called 'either-way' offences, see further pp. 316–17 below.)

There are some 450 magistrates' courts, some of which sit every day, some of which sit only occasionally. They are manned by just under 29,000 lay – and unpaid – magistrates and by some 135 professional, full-time and paid magistrates formerly called 'stipendiaries' and from 1999 called District Judges (Magistrates' Courts).[66] The lay justices typically sit once a week or once every two weeks.[67] The jurisdiction of the District Judges (Magistrates' Courts) is the same as that of the lay justices except that the District Judge normally sits on his or her own,[68] whereas the lay justices sit with one or, more usually, two others. Whatever its composition, the magistrates' court is supposed to have a court clerk who is supposed to be appropriately qualified to advise the bench on law and procedure.[69]

Considering the vast amount of attention given by commentators to trial by jury, trial in the magistrates' court gets very short shrift. The point was made forcefully by Dr Penny Darbyshire, a court clerk turned academic, with a formidable array of evidence. She pointed to the fact that by far the majority of criminal cases are heard in the magistrates' courts and that numerically there were far more contested trials in the magistrates' courts than in the Crown Court. ('The decisions which matter are those of the police and prosecutors as to charge, the defendant's decision as to plea and the magistrates' decisions as to verdict and sentence, aided by their clerks; yet the making, teaching and analysis of criminal law and evidence often proceeds as if things were as in Blackstone's day'.[70]) Juries heard only 1 per cent of all criminal cases that come before the courts; magistrates sentenced about 95 per cent of all defendants who come before the criminal courts.

There had been an enormous growth in the jurisdiction of the magistrates during this century with indictable-only offences downgraded to either-way and either-way offences to summary-only.[71] ('The list of offences triable by magistrates includes: causing death by aggravated vehicle taking, wounding or inflicting grievous bodily harm, cruelty to and abduction of children, indecent assault and many other sex offences, most burglaries, thefts, frauds and forgeries, arson not endangering life, manufacturing, supplying and misusing all illegal drugs, some perjury, all betting and gaming offences and most firearms offences'.[72])

---

[66] The change of title was made in the Access to Justice Act 1999, s. 78. For the history of the office see P. Seago, C. Walker and D. Wall, 'The Development of the Professional Magistracy in England and Wales', *Criminal Law Review*, 2000, pp. 631–51.

[67] The basic rule is a minimum of twenty-six half-day sessions per year but in practice they often sit much more.

[68] However a District Judge sits with lay justices in Family Proceedings Courts and in Youth Courts.   [69] On the issue of the qualification of court clerks see pp. 31–32 below.

[70] P. Darbyshire, 'An Essay on the Importance and Neglect of the Magistracy', *Criminal Law Review*, 1997, pp. 627–43 at 643.

[71] See pp. 00–00 below for explanation of the distinction between these categories.

[72] *Criminal Law Review*, 1997, 627 at 630.

Magistrates also dealt with almost all young offenders. ('The importance of the youth court is impossible to exaggerate . . . [but] it is a jurisdiction almost entirely forgotten in traditional law books and by the public, probably because it goes on behind closed doors, unreported'.[73]) The Attorney General had the power to appeal an unduly lenient sentence given by the Crown Court (p. 667 below). There was no equivalent for unduly lenient sentences given by magistrates. The decisions of the Divisional Court on appeal from the magistrates' court got far less notice in the law reports than decisions of the Court of Appeal. ('When the Court of Appeal or House of Lords develop criminal law and evidence they speak in the language of trial on indictment and pay no regard to how their reasoning will apply to summary trial. Stipendiaries and justices' clerks are left to agonise on how to translate these *rationes* into their world, in articles sounding exasperated, in *The Justice of the Peace* and *Local Government Law*'.[74])

The same blindness, she suggested, affected many academics.[75] Again, the Runciman Royal Commission on Criminal Justice had focused almost exclusively on trials on indictment. The legislation that followed the Runciman Report had been flawed in its application to magistrates' courts.[76] Part of the problem lay in the weakness of justices' clerks, court clerks and magistrates as a lobbying force. Even the Law Commission was capable of producing reform proposals that completely ignored summary proceedings.

In a subsequent article,[77] Dr Darbyshire critically examined the rhetoric about magistrates. The magistrates on the whole had a poor reputation. ('Praise of the magistracy is as rare as pro-jury rhetoric is common'.[78]) Almost no one extolled the virtues of the magistracy who was not either a magistrate or the Lord Chancellor of the day addressing magistrates. Blackstone – 'for whom the jury was the most admirably constituted fact-finding body in the world' – had deplored the mischiefs that resulted from demoting cases from jury trial to trial before justices. In modern times Mr Michael Mansfield QC dismissed magistrates in his book *Presumed Guilty* (1993) with only a page of discussion. Lord Gifford QC in his book *Where's the Justice?* (1984) described lay justices as 'white, middle class, middle-aged people sitting in judgment over young, working class and often black defendants'. Mr Geoffrey Robertson QC condemned lay justices as 'ladies and gentlemen bountiful', politically imbalanced, unrepresentative of ethnic minority groups, and women, who 'slow down the system and cost a fortune'. We should replace them, he told the House of

---

[73] *Ibid* at 633.   [74] *Ibid* at 635.

[75] The writer was one of those criticised for the disparate treatment in this book of trial by jury and trial by magistrates (*ibid*, p. 637). I am indebted to Dr Darbyshire for prompting the addition of this section.

[76] Dr Darbyshire instanced the botched attempt at abolition of committal proceedings, the new rules on disclosure and on preparatory hearings (*ibid*, p. 638).

[77] 'For the New Lord Chancellor – Some Causes for Concern about Magistrates', *Criminal Law Review*, 1997, pp. 861–74.   [78] *Criminal Law Review*, 1997, p. 861.

Commons Home Affairs Committee, with juries or 'sensible stipendiary magistrates'.[79] According to Bar lore the burden of proof was reversed in magistrates' courts where police evidence was too readily believed. The James Committee had cited defendants' negative view of 'magistrates, who inevitably become "case-hardened" and may be too ready to accept the prosecution case'.[80] Later surveys repeated this view.[81]

The text that follows draws heavily on Dr Darbyshire's writings. It draws also on a report commissioned jointly by the Lord Chancellor's Department and the Home Office by Rod Morgan and Neil Russell[82] and on Lord Justice Auld's *Review of the Criminal Courts, 2001.*[83]

Selection process Magistrates have always been appointed by the Lord Chancellor and that remains the position under the new arrangements for the appointment of judges,[84] though the new Judicial Appointments Commission has the power to advise on the matter.[85] The LCD/DCA has had to rely on local Advisory Committees to nominate suitable appointees and that too will continue to be the case[86] though it does not follow that the existing Advisory Committees will necessarily continue in being. What follows describes the system as it has existed up to now.

Not much is known about those processes. In 1995, the Magistrates' Association, in evidence to the House of Commons Home Affairs Select Committee said: 'the present method of recruitment is shrouded in mystery but, as far as we can see from the outside, the system is a self-perpetuating oligarchy'.[87] That even the Magistrates' Association should describe the selection process in such terms speaks for itself. There were some one hundred local Advisory Committees which nominated potential candidates to the Lord Chancellor. The

---

[79] House of Commons, 52-II, Home Affairs Committee, Third Report, *Judicial Appointments Procedures*, 1995–96, vol. II, para. 611 (the report is referred to here as the *Home Affairs Report*).

[80] *The Distribution of Criminal Business between the Crown Court and Magistrates' Courts*, Cmnd. 6323, 1975, p. 18, para. 36.

[81] Darbyshire cited A.E. Bottoms and J. McLean, *Defendants in the Criminal Process*, 1976, p. 89; D. Riley and J. Vennard, *Triable-either-way-cases: Crown Court or Magistrates' Court?*, 1988, Home Office Research Study No. 98; C. Hedderman and D. Moxon, *Magistrates' Court or Crown Court? Mode of Trial Decisions and Sentencing*, 1992, Home Office Research Study No. 125; J. Vennard in *Contested Trials in Magistrates' Courts*, 1982, Home Office Research Study No. 71, pp. 2–3.

[82] Morgan and Russell, *The judiciary in the magistrates' courts*, 2000. Accessible at www.homeoffice.gov.uk/rds/pdfs/occ-judiciary-pdf.

[83] See also A. Sanders, *Community Justice: Modernising the Magistracy in England and Wales*, 2001, IPPR.   [84] Courts Act 2003, s. 10.

[85] The Ministerial Statement made by the Lord Chancellor on 23 January 2006 said that the Judicial Appointments Commission would not assume responsibility for advising on the appointment of magistrates 'until it indicates that it is ready to do so'. Until such time the existing system would continue.

[86] The Constitutional Reform Act 2005, s. 106 provides that the Lord Chancellor must ensure that arrangements for the appointment of lay justices 'include arrangements for consulting persons appearing to him to have special knowledge of matters relevant to the exercise of those functions'.   [87] *Home Affairs Report*, n. 79 above at para. 241.

names of the Secretary to the Advisory Committees were available – they are even given on the Department's Website – but the names of committee members were not easily available. (Two-thirds of the members are magistrates.)

The chairmen of Advisory Committees and of sub-committees are appointed by the Lord Chancellor – usually on the advice of the outgoing chairmen![88] (The chairman of the local bench is not permitted to sit as a member of the local Advisory Committee.) Local Advisory Committees are left to determine their own ways of recruiting new magistrates. Both the Advisory Committee and the bench they are responsible for selecting are supposed broadly to reflect the local community in terms of gender, ethnic origin, geographical spread, occupation and, until now, political affiliation, but the Committee is left to obtain its own information in that regard. In his report Lord Justice Auld commented that without reliable information the Committees are not equipped to fulfil this responsibility.[89]

Serving magistrates are recruited in different ways – nomination by local organisations, advertisements, being invited by existing committee members and in recent years by a variety of other outreach efforts. Darbyshire noted: 'many magistrates are councillors and many have multiple membership of other local organisations such as health authorities or trusts or school governing bodies'.[90] In some areas the Freemasons seemed to have disproportionate numbers.

Darbyshire urged that advertising be undertaken by the Department on a national basis emphasising that anyone can apply. This suggestion was adopted.[91] Auld said that many local Advisory Committees 'largely rely on the network, and overlapping membership of local bodies, with the result that there is an undue draw towards the local "great and good" '.[92] He contrasted the money devoted to attract members of the public to become magistrates (£35,000) to that devoted to attract them to serve in the Territorial Army (£4.7 million).[93] He said he was concerned at the low level of financial assistance given to local Advisory Committees. He endorsed criticism of the LCD made by Morgan and Russell as to its failure to maintain a proper database as to the composition of the magistracy using the same classification as the national census.[94] The Department acted on this suggestion.[95]

---

[88] Statement of Lord Mackay of Clashfern in evidence to the Home Affairs Committee, *Home Affairs Report*, n. 79 above, para. 504.   [89] Auld, p. 122, para. 68.

[90] *Criminal Law Review*, 1997 at p. 867.

[91] In 2004 the DCA started a major national recruitment campaign to attract more magistrates of diverse backgrounds. The aim was over three years to increase the number of new appointments from 1,500 per year to 2,500. Advertisements were placed in many quarters. They even appeared on the side of buses. It will be of interest to discover what difference such a campaign makes to either the number or the type of candidates.   [92] Auld, p. 121, para. 66.

[93] Auld, p. 122, para. 67. The national advertising campaign referred to in n. 91 above had a budget of £3.3 million.   [94] Auld, p. 122, para. 69.

[95] See the *National Strategy for the Recruitment of Lay Magistrates* issued by the DCA in October 2003 – www.dca.gov.uk – Magistrates – Appointment Procedures. For a sceptical assessment see G. Robson, 'Diversifying the Magistracy: Plain Sailing or Rocks Ahead?', 167 *Justice of the Peace*, 2003, pp. 906–9.

Also, as from 1999, an explanation of how to become a magistrate, the duties of magistrates and other relevant information, including the application form and notes for guidance, have been on the Department's Website.

The Department now issues a lengthy (150 or so pages) document (accessible on the DCA's Website) advising Advisory Committees on the processes of selection. It covers functions, organisation and composition, appointments, sources of candidates, interviewing, ancillary matters and conduct.

Composition of the bench

On composition of the bench, Darbyshire wrote: 'lay magistrates are too white, middle class, Conservative and, I would add, old'.[96]

Gender There are almost exactly equal numbers of male and female lay magistrates.[97]

Age A magistrate can be appointed at any age from eighteen[98] to sixty-five. The retirement age is seventy. Darbyshire reported that her observations suggested that sitting magistrates were skewed towards the retired. DCA figures published in 2003 showed that just over a third (35 per cent) were between sixty and seventy, 45 per cent were between fifty and sixty, 16 per cent were between forty and forty-nine and 4 per cent were under forty.[99] The DCA has recently made considerable efforts to attract more young people.[100]

Ethnic minority representation Morgan and Russell wrote, 'the composition of the lay magistracy is now approaching ethnic representativeness, that is 2 per cent black, 2 per cent of Indian sub-continent or Asian origin and 1 per cent other' – as against a national picture of 94 per cent white, 2 per cent black, 3 per cent Indian sub-continent or Asian origin and 1 per cent other.[101] Strong efforts are being made by the DCA to increase representation of the ethnic minorities on the magistrates' bench.

Social class mix It has been accepted for decades that there are insufficient numbers of 'working class' magistrates, despite strenuous efforts by successive Lord Chancellors to increase the proportion. One factor may be that magistrates are not paid, though they can claim travel expenses (including a per mile bicycle allowance!), a subsistence allowance and a modest financial loss allowance, on proof of actual loss. Another factor no doubt is the attitude of employers – and

---

[96] Darbyshire, *Criminal Law Review*, 1997, p. 863.

[97] As at April 2005, 14,519 were men and 14,346 were women, *Judicial Statistics, 2005*, p. 138.

[98] The minimum age was reduced in 2004 from 27 to 18.

[99] *Home Affairs Report*, n. 79 above, Appendix D.

[100] In September 2005 there was considerable publicity on the appointment to the North Sussex bench of Anand Limbachia, described as a 19-year-old Asian civil servant. In September 2006 similar publicity attended the appointment of 19-year-old law student Lucy Tate to the bench in Pontefract. *The Guardian* (11 September) reported that one of her fellow JPs in Pontefract described the appointment as 'an absolute folly'.

[101] Morgan and Russell, p. 14. This assumed that the 11 per cent of magistrates whose ethnic identity is recorded as unknown are all white.

fellow employees.[102] Another may be the somewhat demanding requirements of the job. Thus for instance the 'understanding and communication' requirement is described as follows: 'ability to understand documents, identify and comprehend relevant facts, and follow evidence and arguments – ability to concentrate – ability to communicate effectively'. One factor is likely to be that most working class people probably do not relate to the idea of being a magistrate. An important factor may be the 'old boy network' of the selection process.

There have been a number of studies of the social class composition of the magistracy.[103] One by Dignan and Wynne is especially useful as they compared their data with those of previous surveys.[104] The proportion of wage earners had risen from 15 per cent of male magistrates in 1947 to 26 per cent in 1989–90. Although an increase, this did 'nothing to dispel the overall picture of a magistracy that is still drawn from the middle classes'.[105] The rateable value of their houses showed equally 'that magistrates in Whitechurch tend to be drawn from the more affluent sectors of the communities they reside in, irrespective of the overall prosperity of those communities'.[106]

Morgan and Russell sent questionnaires to 1,916 lay magistrates in the ten courts selected for their study. Just under three-fifths (58 per cent) replied. Of these, 69 per cent gave as their current or former occupation a professional or managerial position, 12 per cent said they had a clerical or other non-manual jobs, 3 per cent were skilled manual workers and 5 per cent said they were unemployed. As many as two-fifths (40 per cent) said they were retired.[107] Possibly also relevant was the fact that 86 per cent of those responding said they did not claim loss of earnings and almost a quarter (23 per cent) said they seldom or never claimed expenses.

Political balance Politics is supposed to play no part in the appointment of judges but for many years it has been official policy that attention be given to the political balance on the magistrates' bench. The policy developed from the report of two Royal Commissions (1909–10 and 1946–48) both of which suggested that the Conservative Party was over-represented on the bench and that it was important to have a broader mix. The directions to Advisory Committees stated that the bench should reflect the political balance of the local electorate as judged from the result of the last two general elections. Nominees were asked to state their political affiliation, though not all did so. Nominating committees were asked to state the current balance of the parties on the bench and in the local electorate.

---

[102] Lord Falconer, the Lord Chancellor, said in 2004 that the Government planned to introduce legislation to encourage employers to give employees time off to serve on the bench similar to s. 47 of the Employment Act 2002 which deals with variations in employment contracts to provide flexible working hours for parents of children under six or who have disabilities.

[103] See, for instance, J. Baldwin, 'The Social Composition of the Magistracy', 16 *British Journal of Criminology*, 1976, p. 171.

[104] J. Dignan and A. Wynne, 'A Microcosm of the Local Community', 37 *British Journal of Criminology*, 1997, pp. 170–93. Though published in 1997 it was based on 1989–90 data.

[105] *Ibid at* p. 188.   [106] *Ibid at* p. 189.   [107] Morgan and Russell at p. 16.

It is likely however that in many, if not most, cases the actual distribution of political allegiances was not 'balanced' as recommended in the directions. In the study by Dignan and Wynne (above), for instance, 'there was a marked contrast between the declared voting intentions of the Whitechurch bench and the pattern of voting in local council elections at the time'.[108]

In October 1998 the LCD issued a consultation paper (*Political Balance in the Lay Magistracy*) raising the question whether the attempt to achieve a political balance on the bench should be scrapped in favour of a new system that would attempt to achieve a balanced bench on the basis of a broader range of socio-economic factors. The responses were inconclusive with about half in favour of the existing system and half in favour of a broader approach. Lord Justice Auld said that the outcome of this consultation exercise was that the Lord Chancellor concluded 'though reluctantly, that for the time being the requirement for polit-ical balance should remain, but that work should continue on searching for a more appropriate measure of social balance, possibly using occupational group-ings, either alone or with social groupings based on National Statistics classifi-cation'.[109] In Auld's view that was the right approach. The only basis for the political balance to be used was that it was regarded 'as a crude proxy for occu-pational and/or social groupings'.[110] Political views, he said, 'balanced or other-wise, are hardly relevant to the fairness or ability of a tribunal'.[111]

This view was given effect in 2003 when it was announced that the political affiliation test would be taken out of the application form.[112]

Auld said there were various options for making the magistracy more repre-sentative.[113] One was to make the role and terms of service more manageable for a wider range of persons; another would be short term conscription like jury service; a third was co-option of citizens on a rotating basis – serving a speci-fied number of times per year; a fourth was election. He thought that only the first was worthy of serious consideration. The only concrete suggestion he made in that regard was reviewing the sitting arrangements. ('There may be scope for magistrates to sit more or less often, for longer or shorter periods at a time and more flexibly, according to their individual circumstances. This might increase the pool of candidates for appointment'.[114]). One has to say that it is difficult to believe that changes in sitting arrangements of that kind would have much impact.

In October 2003, the DCA launched a National Recruitment Strategy aimed at achieving a more diverse magistracy. One of the initiatives was a shadowing

---

[108] Dignan and Wynne, n. 104 above. While the area returned a large majority of Labour councillors only just over a quarter of magistrates said they intended to vote Labour. Conversely, while almost half the magistrates identified with the Conservatives, the party had only 16 per cent of local council seats at the time (p. 191). No fewer than twenty-seven of the seventy wards in the division had no magistrates living in them, while five wards had thirty-three magistrates – almost a third of the total number (p. 192).

[109] Auld, p. 128, para. 85.   [110] *Ibid.*   [111] *Ibid.*

[112] DCA Press Release, 6 November 2003.   [113] Auld, p. 123, para. 72.

[114] Auld, p. 124, para. 73.

scheme whereby people from black neighbourhoods are given the opportunity of seeing what magistrates do, but the evaluation report on the first phase of this scheme said: 'shadowers were in the main already engaged in community activities and were well respected and trusted members of their communities'. In other words, it seemed that they were the kind of people who were already likely to come forward as potential magistrates.[115]

Training The LCD told the House of Commons Home Affairs Committee that until 1989 'training was negligible. It was really a matter of learning by experience'.[116] There was a brief induction course, followed by some basic training in the first year and further basic training in the second and third year. The training consisted of courses following a syllabus. There was no evaluation or assessment process.

In 1998 a new system of training was started based on competences – a combination of skills, knowledge and attributes. It considers not just knowledge of law and procedure but such topics as reaching impartial decisions (e.g. 'one's own conditioning and personal prejudices, labelling and stereotyping, language and cultural differences and body language') and effective participation on the bench (e.g. ensuring equality of treatment to all court users, ensuring that witnesses are not bullied, note-taking, observing people/conduct, contributing to a structured decision-making process, challenging discriminatory views, helping to identify the issues etc.). New magistrates are assigned experienced magistrates as mentors. Competences are assessed through appraisal. The appraisal system applies not only for new magistrates. Existing magistrates are also appraised, in principle, every three years – though benches are allowed up to five years for the first appraisal. There is now also training and appraisal for chairmen of benches. The required competences depend on the work that each magistrate is actually doing.

Reviewing the new training system, Auld[117] said that it had been much criticised for its complexity – 'for example there are 104 "competences" even for those who sit only as "a winger" '.[118] Two years after the introduction of the scheme no national standards had been set with regard to competences. The Judicial Studies Board had issued an evaluation of the new system[119] in which it concluded that although the basic concepts were sound there was too great a variation in the manner of its implementation. It recommended the introduction of national performance standards, the weighting of consequences and simplification of documents. Auld added that the lack of consistency as between areas applied to all the training of magistrates. This was a matter of legitimate concern 'particularly in its contribution to wide variations in the effectiveness

---

[115] G. Robson, 'Diversifying the Magistracy: Plain Sailing or Rocks Ahead?' 167 *Justice of the Peace*, 29 November 2003, pp. 906–9.   [116] The *Home Affairs Report*, n. 79 above at p. 151.

[117] Auld, pp. 131–32, para. 92.

[118] The bench normally consists of the chairman and two 'wingers'.

[119] *Magistrates New Training Initiative: Evaluation of Implementation, Final Report* (December 2000).

of case management and in sentencing patterns'.[120] In his view there was 'an urgent need for clearer and simpler national standards in the training of magistrates and for more consistency in and monitoring of its provisions'.[121] The Judicial Studies Board, he said, should be made responsible for devising and securing the content and manner of training of magistrates.

In June 2004 the Judicial Studies Board published proposals regarding the training of magistrates.[122] In November 2004 the DCA published its proposals for new rules for the training of magistrates.[123] The new rules[124] were introduced as from 1 April 2005. They provide, *inter alia*, that a magistrate may not sit either as chairman or member of the adult court, the family proceedings court or the youth court until he has completed the relevant approved training.[125]

However whilst more training for lay justices increases their professionalisim there is a view that it may not be wholly desirable. This view was expressed by Mark Davies of Sussex Law School in his article 'A new training initiative for the lay magistracy in England and Wales – a further step towards professionalisation'.[126] His point was that part of the value of the lay magistracy is that it is 'lay' which was threatened by greater training. There was a dilemma:

> On the one hand, an increasingly skilled and knowledgeable magistracy is better able to meet the demands of a complex judicial system. On the other hand, the very attributes which are celebrated strengths of the magistracy, for example, impartiality (including an impartial attitude to the legal system); the ability to approach cases free of the ingrained presumptions which come with the professional socialisation of lawyers; and generally, the freedom and variety of thought which comes with a judicial body drawn from a far wider cross section of the community than salaried judges drawn only from the ranks of lawyers . . . [The] idea that the role of magistrates is an embodiment of society in the legal process – a direct democratisation of that process – requires magistrates to be amateurs who lack training and expertise. This very lack of expertise is essential if the community is to be protected from the dominance and abuse of power by experts such as lawyers. The essential role of the magistrate, therefore, is to bring common sense and knowledge of the locality and the local community to the criminal justice process . . . It is therefore open to question whether developments in the training and appraisal of lay magistrates, and the development of other characteristics which fit models of professionalism, are desirable. This is the "paradox of training" a lay body. This in turn leads to the distinction between "legal justice" – the application of pre-determined rules by trained professionals – and "community

---

[120] Auld, p. 132, para. 96.   [121] *Ibid.*

[122] *Proposals for the Organisation and Management of Magisterial Training in the Unified Courts Administration,* 28 June 2004.

[123] *Proposals for New Rules for Training, Development and Appraisal,* 17 November 2004.

[124] Justice of the Peace (Training and Appraisal) Rules 2005, SI 2005/564.

[125] For a description and discussion of the new system see G. Robson, 'Changing the Culture of the Lower Courts', 169 *Justice of the Peace,* 22 January 2005, pp. 53–6.

[126] 12 *International Journal of the Legal Profession,* March 2005, pp. 93–119.

justice" – justice which reflects the values of the community it serves. The English and Welsh criminal justice system is a hybrid of the two types. The strong presence of lay participants reflects a long commitment to community justice, albeit recognising that this operates within a legal framework. The increased training, and therefore professionalisation of the lay magistracy, risks removing this community element from the majority of criminal cases.[127]

The balance between lay and professional magistrates

In 1998, the LCD issued a consultation paper (*Unification of the Stipendiary Bench*) as to whether there should be a single national judicial corps of stipendiary magistrates. The professional magistrates get through cases at a considerably greater rate than lay justices. (The CP suggested that, according to research, a single stipendiary did the work of about thirty lay justices in the provinces and of twenty-three in London.[128])

Morgan and Russell's report was a comparison between lay and stipendiary magistrates. It confirmed that stipendiaries dealt with their work more quickly. They knew the law and therefore did not need to consult their legal adviser. They sat alone and therefore did not need to consult colleagues. They therefore withdrew less often and for shorter periods, but they also asked more questions than lay magistrates. They granted fewer adjournments. They were less likely than lay justices to grant bail over police objections (19 per cent compared to 37 per cent) and more likely to give defendants immediate custodial sentences (25 per cent compared to 12 per cent).[129] The finding that stipendiaries are more severe in sentencing confirmed earlier research:[130]

- If only direct costs were considered, Morgan and Russell said, lay justices were much cheaper as they were not paid and many did not claim loss of earnings or even travel expenses (£3.59 per appearance against £20.96). However, when the cost of buildings and court administration were included the gap obviously narrowed (£52.10 against £61.78).
- The study found that in London, where there are a large number of stipendiaries, they did the full range of magistrates' courts work. Outside London their caseload was more slanted toward 'heavy business'.[131]
- A nationally representative sample of 1,753 members of the public was interviewed as to their views on and knowledge of the magistracy.[132] Most had heard of magistrates and magistrates' courts but only a minority had heard of lay as opposed to stipendiary magistrates. When the difference between them was explained, almost three-quarters (73 per cent) said they were not aware of the difference. When comparing single magistrates with

---

[127] *Ibid*, pp. 112–13.   [128] At para. 33.   [129] Note 82 above at pp. 26–7.
[130] See S.S. Diamond, 'Revising Images of Public Punitiveness: Sentencing by Lay and Professional English Magistrates', 15 *Law and Social Inquiry*, 1990, pp. 191–221 and 'The Assessment of Sentencing Choice through Triangulation: A Reply to Walker', 17 *Law and Social Inquiry*, 1990, pp. 115–22.   [131] Note 82 above at pp. 26–7.   [132] *Ibid*, Ch. 5.

panels, a large majority thought that the more serious decisions of guilty/ not guilty (74 per cent) and imprisonment (76 per cent) should be taken by panels.

The establishment in 1999 of Lord Justice Auld's *Review of the Criminal Courts* raised expectations in some quarters that he would recommend a change in the overall balance between lay and professional magistrates – and possibly even abolition of the lay bench – but he did not do so. ('Nor can I see any basis for recommending any significant change in their respective numbers'.[133])

Lord Justice Auld also rejected the suggestion that lay and professional magistrates sit together in a hybrid magistrates' court. ('The overwhelming evidence in the Review is that they each do a good job in their separate ways. And neither magistrates nor District Judges would welcome such a general transformation and diminution of their respective roles'.[134]) However, somewhat inconsistently, he did recommend that a new intermediate criminal court (District Division) be set up consisting of a professional judge and two lay magistrates (on which see pp. 39–40 below).

In June 2005, the House of Commons Public Accounts Committee recommended that the DCA should consider whether the use of stipendiary magistrates led to better management of the trial process,[135] obviously unaware of the fact that stipendiary magistrates no longer existed having several years earlier become District Judges (Magistrates' Courts).

There is no sign that the DCA plans any significant change in the balance between the lay and the professional bench.[136]

Extent of summary jurisdiction

Auld also rejected suggestions for either a general increase or decrease in summary jurisdiction. ('I can discern no wide or well-based support for a change in the general limit of six months' custody or £5,000 fine now applicable to District Judges and magistrates alike'.[137]) He acknowledged that their sentencing powers were greater than those given to lay tribunals in other countries but, in his view, 'they are increasingly well trained for their task and have their legal advisers to assist them, where necessary, on points of law or procedure'(*ibid*). There were remarkably few appeals from their decisions.

As will be seen (p. 321 below), the Government disagreed. Hoping to reduce the proportion of cases committed for sentence to the Crown Court it included a provision in the Criminal Justice Act 2003 to extend magistrates' sentencing power from six months' to twelve months' imprisonment (s. 154). This power was supposed to be implemented in October 2006 – but this did not happen and it was not clear when (if at all) it would be implemented.

---

[133] Auld, p. 111, para. 2.   [134] Auld, p. 109, para. 40.
[135] Recommendation 5 of the 22nd Report of the Committee, Session 2004–05, 16 June 2005.
[136] See G. Robson, 'Never Off the Agenda: The Issue of the Lay Magistracy', 169 *Justice of the Peace*, 6 August 2005, pp. 611–14.   [137] Auld, p. 101, para. 20.

Justices' chief executives, justices' clerks and court clerks

The justices' clerk used to be the person responsible both for the administration of the magistrates' court and for advising the bench. Their duties included keeping the accounts, handling the collection of fines and other enforcement procedures, running the licensing sessions, training the justices and listing of cases. In large court complexes the justices' clerk was so busy with administrative duties that he rarely sat in court. Some justices' clerks would have one or two benches; some had a large number.[138]

In 1994 the Police and Magistrates' Courts Act established the post of justices' chief executive to act as the single head of service for each Magistrates' Courts Committee (MCC). Each MCC was required to appoint a chief executive to manage the courts in its area. As a result there was a drastic reduction in the number of posts. In 1989 there were 275 full-time justices' clerks. By 2006, there were only seventy.

Justices' clerks continued to be responsible for many administrative matters. The Justices of the Peace Act 1997 separated the legal and administrative functions of the job. The Access to Justice Act 1999, s. 87 took this process further in providing that the chief executive need not be someone qualified to be a justices' clerk. The policy was that justices' clerks should concentrate on their legal and judicial functions which were rapidly expanding.[139]

The Courts Act 2003 was an even more radical step. Instead of the justices' clerks being appointed as before locally by MCCs they are now appointed by the Lord Chancellor (s. 27). MCCs were abolished and the new system was centralised as recommended by Lord Justice Auld. The 2003 Act (s. 29) guarantees the independence of justices' clerks with regard to judicial and quasi-judicial functions. (When the Bill was going through Parliament fears were expressed that making justices' clerk appointees of the executive could put them under improper pressure.[140])

A consultation paper issued by the DCA in May 2006 (*A Model for the Provision of Justices' Clerks in England and Wales*)[141] made it clear that the local connection between the magistrates' courts and their justices' clerk was likely to become increasingly tenuous as the range of their territorial responsibility was enlarged.[142]

The court clerk – qualifications Each magistrates' court when sitting is supposed to be served by a court clerk. Ideally the court clerk should be a qualified lawyer but many are not. A consultation paper issued by the LCD in 1998 (*The Professionalisation of Court Clerks*) said that some 40 per cent of the 1,500

---

[138] Darbyshire stated that when in 1997 the Kent Magistrates' Courts Committee amalgamated the whole county under one clerkship the clerk would be serving fourteen benches with 800 justices (*Criminal Law Review*, n. 77 above at p. 873).

[139] The Access to Justice Act 1999, s. 91 for instance transferred responsibility for fines and fees accounts to the justices' chief executive.

[140] N. Hanson, 'Clerks seek justice', *Law Society's Gazette*, 17 June 2004, pp.18–20.

[141] CP (L) 08/06, 10 May 2006 – www.dca.gov.uk – Publications – Consultation papers.

[142] For critical commentary on the thrust of the consultation paper see G. Robson, 'A Long Farewell', 170 *Justice of the Peace*, 22 July 2006, pp. 548–51.

or so court clerks in magistrates' courts were not so qualified. Since 1980, all courts clerks should have at least a Diploma in Magisterial Law, though not all in fact satisfy that test. Darbyshire wrote: 'diploma students and part-time distance learners may be authorised to be a clerk on completion of just one year of the course'.[143] The LCD's 1998 consultation paper invited views on a proposal that all court clerks should be professionally qualified as barristers or solicitors. It presented two broad options. One was that from a given date only persons qualified as barristers or solicitors would be eligible to take courts. The second was that this would only apply to new entrants as from that date.

The Government initially decided that court clerks appointed after January 1999 would have to be fully qualified and that existing clerks would have to become so qualified within ten years. Subsequently, the Government retreated slightly in the face of criticism and announced that this new rule would not apply to serving clerks aged forty or over.[144]

Auld said that in March 2001 there were some 1,800 legal advisers, two-thirds of whom were qualified. He warmly approved of the increasing professionalism of the court clerks but he recommended that District judges, being themselves professionally qualified, should normally sit without a legal adviser.[145]

The clerk and the bench The function of the court clerk vis-à-vis the bench has undergone important changes. Basically the function is to guide the justices on matters of law and procedure.

In the 1950s it was laid down that the clerk must be, and be seen to be, subservient to the bench and that although the clerk could, for instance, retire with the bench when they went to consider their decision, he should do so only on invitation and should emerge before the justices.[146] In recent years the crucial role played by the clerk has increasingly been recognised and the courts have now changed their emphasis when dealing with the delicate balance of power between the clerk and the bench.

The next Practice Direction was issued in July 1981.[147] It said that '*if it appears to him to be necessary*' (emphasis supplied) or 'he is so requested by the justices', the clerk had the responsibility to 'refresh the justices' memory as to any matter of evidence and to draw attention to any issues involved in the matters before the court' as well as advising on the penalties available and giving guidance as to the choice of penalties. The clerk could advise the justices in their retiring room, though if they wished to consult him about the evidence they should normally do so in open court.

---

[143] Darbyshire, *Criminal Law Review,* 1997, p. 872. Under the Justices Clerks (Qualification of Assistants) Rules 1979 a person can serve as a court clerk if he has passed a preliminary professional examination and has served for two years or, in the case of clerks who had served for five years before 1980, if he has a 'certificate of competence' from the magistrates' court committee.

[144] Press statement by Mr Geoff Hoon, MP, Minister of State LCD, 12 November 1998.

[145] Auld, p. 117, para. 53. On recruitment difficulties in getting court clerks see 153 *New Law Journal,* 5 September 2003, p. 1297.   [146] *Practice Direction* [1953] 2 All ER 1306.

[147] [1981] 2 All ER 831.

It was argued that advice on law from the clerk should always be given in open court.[148] This view was implemented in the Practice Direction issued on 2 October 2000, the day the Human Rights Act came into force:[149]

> 8. At any time, justices are entitled to receive advice to assist them in discharging their responsibilities. If they are in any doubt as to the evidence which has been given, they should seek the aid of their legal adviser, referring to his/her notes as appropriate. This should ordinarily be done in open court. Where the justices request their adviser to join them in the retiring room, this request should be made in the presence of the parties in court. Any legal advice given to the justices other than in open court should be clearly stated to be provisional and the adviser should subsequently repeat the substance of the advice in open court and give the parties an opportunity to make any representations they wish on that provisional advice. The legal adviser should then state in open court whether the provisional advice is confirmed or, if it is varied, the nature of the variation.

In recent years the trend has been to give more and more responsibility to the clerk and especially the clerk to the justices. The first step in that direction was taken in the Justices' Clerks Rules of 1970, which allowed clerks to hear applications for summonses and warrants, to grant adjournments, renew bail, issue witness orders, take pleas, order a means inquiry and vary the payment of a fine.

It has been suggested that court clerks should be allowed to rule formally on the admissibility of evidence and to sum up points for the justices. They would then be acting very much like the judge with a jury. One strong argument for such a development is that it would make the administration of justice more open. The parties would be able to see on what basis the case was being approached and what law was being applied.

In February 1997, the Narey Report[150] proposed that justices' clerks should take over from magistrates many of the functions of court management such as handling pre-trial reviews or early administrative hearings, extending bail, varying conditions of bail, ordering defendants to produce their driving licences etc. The decision as to bail or custody would, however, remain one for the bench. In its response to the Narey Report the Government said it accepted in principle that there was a role for clerks to the justices in assisting in case management. Under rules made by virtue of the Crime and Disorder Act 1998, ss. 49 and 50, justices' clerks have the power to perform a variety of tasks recommended for transfer by Narey.[151] (As originally drafted the Crime and Disorder Bill would have given clerks even wider judicial powers – including varying of bail conditions without consent, remanding an accused in custody

---

[148] A. Heaton-Armstrong, 'The Verdict of the Court and its Clerk? Can Justice be Seen to be Done Behind Closed Doors?', *Justice of the Peace*, 31 May 1995, p. 340 and 7 June 1995, p. 357.

[149] *Practice Direction* [2000] 1 WLR 1886, [2000] 4 All ER 895. This is now para. V 55.7 of the Practice Directions given under the Criminal Procedure Rules 2005.

[150] *Review of Delay in the Criminal Justice System*, 1997. Mr Martin Narey was a senior Home Office official who shortly thereafter became Director-General of the Prison Service.

[151] Justices' Clerks Rules 1999, SI 1999/2784.

for a medical report, making an order for joint or separate trials, determining mode of trial on an additional charge and prohibiting press publicity, but after opposition from, *inter alia*, the Lord Chief Justice and the Magistrates' Association, s. 49(3) was added expressly to prevent those functions being delegated to clerks.[152])

Lord Justice Auld said that the majority of justices' clerks were frustrated by the limitations of their newly-acquired jurisdiction and wanted enhanced powers. He did not support them. ('I recommend that there should be no extension of justices' clerks case management jurisdiction'.[153]) The Government, so far at least, seems to have accepted that view.

See further on magistrates' courts: Sir Thomas Skyrme, *The Changing Image of the Magistracy*, (Macmillan, 1979) and *History of the Justices of the Peace* (1994); P. Carlen, *Magistrates' Justice* (Martin Robertson, 1976); Elizabeth Burney, *Magistrate, Court and Community* (Hutchinson, 1979); P. Darbyshire, *The Magistrates' Clerk* (Barry Rose, 1984); S. Brown, *Magistrates at Work*, 1991.

3. Managing the courts

Lord Justice Auld's review

The criminal justice system currently operates on a budget of some £12 billion and consists of three Government Departments – the Department of Constitutional Affairs, replacing the Lord Chancellor's Department, the Home Office and the Attorney General – and a number of separate agencies. Describing management for the system, Lord Justice Auld said:

> The whole edifice is structurally inefficient, ineffective and wasteful . . . The basic problem lies in the shared, but also divided, responsibilities of the three Government Departments for the system. Each, necessarily, must guard its constitutional independence and, in respect of some of its responsibilities, its functions from the others and have regard to its separate financial accountability to the Treasury and to Parliament. The Public Accounts Committee, in its 2000 Report, observed: 'the most common constraints to effective local inter-agency liaison include conflicting objectives and priorities, which can prevent agreement . . . Current performance in progressing criminal cases is not satisfactory and needs to be improved through more concerted joint monitoring and management of performance across the criminal justice system'.[154]

Auld continued:

> It does not have to be this way. It is axiomatic that overall political accountability for investigation, prosecution and adjudication should remain separate, but beneath that level there needs to be a mechanism for securing some central direction and joint management of the achievement of shared objectives.[155]

---

[152] See, generally, P. Darbyshire, 'A Comment on the Powers of Magistrates' Clerks', *Criminal Law Review*, 1999, pp. 377–86.   [153] Auld, p. 119, para. 58.
[154] Auld, Ch. 8, para. 14, pp. 319–20.   [155] *Ibid*, para. 15, p. 420.

He recommended that a Criminal Justice Board should replace all the existing national planning and operational bodies, including the Strategic Planning Group[156] and the Trial Issues Group (TIG).[157] It should be responsible for planning and setting criminal justice objectives, budgeting and the allocation of funds, securing the national and local achievement of its objectives, the development of an integrated IT system and research and development. The Board should be the means by which the Government Departments and agencies dealing with criminal justice provided overall direction of the criminal justice system. It should have an independent chairman and should include senior civil servants from the three main departments and chief executives of the main criminal justice agencies plus a small number of non-executive members.[158]

The Government's White Paper *Justice for All* (July 2002, para. 9.5) stated that a new National Criminal Justice Board would be established to replace the Strategic Board. It would be chaired by the Permanent Secretary at the Home Office and would include the Permanent Secretary at the Lord Chancellor's Department, the DPP, the chief executives of the criminal justice agencies, the president of the Association of Chief Police Officers and a senior judge. The Board would report to the Cabinet Committee, chaired by the Home Secretary and including the Lord Chancellor and the Attorney General whose function was to co-ordinate broad policy on criminal justice. The existing tripartite Criminal Justice Joint Planning Unit would be answerable to the Board and would establish co-ordinated business plans and priorities. The White Paper did not mention Auld's recommendation as to the Board's functions but it was clear that the Government did not accept that the Board would allocate budgets.

Auld recommended that local Criminal Justice Boards, replacing Area Strategy Committees and local TIGs, should be responsible for giving effect at the local level to the national Board's directions and for management of the system at their level.[159]

The 2002 White Paper (para. 9.11) said that the Government would set up forty-two local Criminal Justice Boards to oversee the new joint working agreements between local agencies in each area. Local Chief Officers from the police, CPS and Probation Service as well as senior representatives of the courts would provide the core membership. Each local Board would be required to establish

---

[156] This consisted of the Criminal Policy Directors and senior Finance Officers of the three departments, other senior officials including a representative of the Treasury and a member of the Prime Minister's Policy Unit. It met every six weeks. It made recommendations to the Ministerial Group chaired by the Home Secretary which included the Lord Chancellor and the Attorney General. However, according to a recent study by Professor Sue Richards cited by Auld, the Strategic Planning Group 'is not strategic and it does not plan' (Auld, Ch. 8, paras. 22, 25, pp. 322, 323).

[157] Established in 1995. It consisted of senior civil servants and officials drawn from all the main criminal justice agencies and organisations. Monthly meetings. A creature of the three departments. Operated as their planning and co-ordinating agent through sub-groups, pilot studies, instructions and guidance. Supported by six specialist sub-groups and local TIGs based on the forty-two criminal justice areas (Auld, Ch. 8, paras. 26–27, pp. 324–25).

[158] Auld, Ch. 8, paras. 43–72, pp. 330–43.   [159] Auld, Ch. 8, paras. 73–77, pp. 343–44.

advisory and consultative machinery involving input from the judiciary, magistrates, voluntary groups and members of the community including victims (para. 9.12). The local Boards would agree annual local delivery contracts with the National Board and would be responsible and accountable for local delivery of criminal justice system objectives, improvements in the delivery of justice, the service provided to victims and witnesses and in securing public confidence.

Auld said that the existing Criminal Justice Consultative Committee was 'ill-equipped to undertake the wide-ranging and comprehensive consultative and advisory role that the Government needs'.[160] It should be replaced by a strengthened Criminal Justice Council chaired by the Lord Chief Justice and with a proper secretariat and research staff to keep the whole system under review and to advise the Government.[161]

The White Paper (para. 9.7) stated that the Criminal Justice Consultative Council would be replaced by a new Criminal Justice Council with membership from the Commission for Racial Equality, the Law Society, victim and witness organisations and academics, as well as the core membership of the judiciary, the Bar and the magistracy. There was no mention of the secretariat or research capacity.

Auld recommended that the Crown Court and the magistrates' courts should be replaced by a unified Criminal Court.[162] The Government rejected this recommendation. The White Paper (para. 4.6) said that the benefits Auld saw flowing from unification could be realised through 'a closer alignment of the magistrates' courts and the Crown Court, without a complete re-ordering of the court system and without adversely affecting the civil and family jurisdictions'. The Government would legislate to bring the two courts closer together. They would be known as 'the criminal courts'.

With regard to the forty-two MCCs and the Greater London Magistrates' Courts Authority, the White Paper (para. 9.16) said that Lord Justice Auld had found their 'differences in practices, procedures, management and culture to be confusing, divisive and inefficient'. Organisational boundaries between the different court services in each area formed an institutional barrier to the effective management of the courts. There were wide variations in their performance. The Government accepted Auld's recommendation of a new agency to replace the Courts Service. ('The aim of the new agency will be to enable management decisions to be taken locally by community focused local management boards, but within a strong national framework of standards and strategy direction . . . In an integrated system, local managers will have much greater freedom to balance workloads across the civil, criminal and family jurisdictions . . . Unification will also make it simpler to transfer cases from magistrates' courts to the Crown Court and easier for the courts to engage directly with other criminal justice agencies'.[163])

---

[160] *Ibid*, para. 79, p. 347.   [161] *Ibid*, paras. 78–88, pp. 346–51.
[162] Auld, Ch. 7, paras. 2–15, pp. 270–73.   [163] White Paper, *Justice for All*, paras. 9.17, 9.20.

At the same time the White Paper said that management of the courts needed to reflect local considerations. ('The new structure will need to ensure sufficient local flexibility and devolved decision-making about management issues of importance to the local area'.[164])

There also needed to be greater accountability to the local community. MCCs largely consisted of magistrates appointed by magistrates. ('There is no requirement for court users, the local community or local authorities to be consulted about key management decisions'.[165]) The Government said that it would expect managers of courts to be accountable to new local management boards which would include representatives drawn for example from the judiciary, the magistracy, local court user groups, victim support groups, local authorities and the local community.[166]

However local flexibility could not be used to excuse wide variations in performance. ('Local services will need to satisfy clear national standards in performance, financial reporting and meeting national policy aims'.[167]) The chief executive of the new agency would be accountable to Ministers and Parliament for national functions including setting and monitoring standards across the courts, stepping in to take action when an area was under-performing and managing major programmes and projects like IT.[168]

As noted above, the new unified courts system run by HM Courts Service (HMCS) was established as from 3 April 2005.

Auld recommended that a Joint Inspection Unit should be established under the collective control of the six Criminal Justice Chief Inspectors: of the Crown Prosecution Service, of the Constabulary, of Prisons, of Probation, of the Magistrates' Court Service and of Social Services. The Magistrates' Courts Inspectorate should be superseded by an Inspectorate for the unified Criminal Court.[169]

The Government accepted both these recommendations. On joint inspections, it said, 'the more the CJS comes to be managed as one overall system, with consistent measures of performance, the more important it will be that future inspections are conducted and delivered in a cohesive and consistent manner' (para. 9.43). But, as will be seen, this did not come to pass.

On inspecting the courts, the White Paper said (para. 9.46): 'We will set up a new independent inspectorate to look at improving administrative performance of the magistrates' courts, the Children and Family Court Advisory Service and, for the first time, of the Crown Court and county courts'.

The Courts Act 2003
The Courts Act 2003 gave effect to some of these proposals:

• Part I (Maintaining the Court System) – section 1 places a duty on the Lord Chancellor to provide an efficient and effective system to support the carrying

[164] *Ibid*, para. 9.22. [165] *Ibid*, para. 9.23. [166] *Ibid*, para. 9.24. [167] *Ibid*, para. 9.25.
[168] *Ibid*, para. 9.26. [169] Auld, pp. 351–52.

on of the business of all the main courts in England and Wales, namely the Court of Appeal, the High Court, the Crown Court, the county courts and the magistrates' courts. The Act did not set out a blueprint for the new agency. However the Explanatory Notes accompanying the Act stated: 'this responsibility will be discharged, in practice, by a new executive agency, as part of the Lord Chancellor's Department, replacing the Courts Service and the forty-two Magistrates' Courts Committees (MCCs).[170] This agency will have local community links through Court Boards'. The function of the Boards is 'to scrutinise, review and make recommendations about the way in which the Lord Chancellor is discharging his general duty in relation to the courts with which the Board is concerned' (s. 5(1)).[171]

The scheme based on forty-two Local Justice Areas which was the basis of the Courts Act 2003 did not last long. In the consultation paper issued in May 2006 the DCA said:

> HMCS [Her Majesty's Court Service] is a national organisation and so former geographical boundaries should not be a constraint. Further, the advent of police boundary reform and the impact that this will have on the potential shape of HMCS means that the forty-two boundaries are of little if any relevance or constraint on the future provision of justices' clerk posts.[172]

The paper said that the Government envisaged that there would be twenty-two HMCS areas.
- The office of justices' chief executive was abolished.[173]
- Part 2 (Justices of the Peace) – largely re-enacted Part II of the Justices of the Peace Act 1997. The main change was to give lay magistrates a national jurisdiction, though they would be assigned to a local justice area (s. 10).
- As already noted, justices' clerks are now appointed by the Lord Chancellor. They have to have a five-year magistrates' courts qualification, or be a barrister or solicitor or have previously been a justices' clerk (s. 27(2)). The Lord Chancellor is obliged to consult the chairman of the lay justices before assigning a justices' clerk to a different area (s. 27(4)). (The Constitutional Reform Act 2005, Sch. 4, para. 326, added the requirement of consultation also with the Lord Chief Justice.[174]) A section in the Courts Act headed 'Independence' states that when exercising their legal functions justices' clerks are not subject to the direction of the Lord Chancellor or any other person and that assistants are not subject to the direction of anyone other than the justices' clerk (s. 29).

[170] The House of Lords debates on the Bill focused particularly on the issue of centralisation of powers and the resulting loss of local input regarding the running of magistrates' courts. (For an article about the Bill by the Minister, published after the completion of the House of Lords stage, see Baroness Scotland, 'Courts Bill', 167 *Justice of the Peace*, 24 May 2003, p. 384. The purpose of the article was plainly to persuade magistrates who had expressed considerable disquiet about the Bill that the Government's amendments sufficiently met their concerns.)
[171] For a sceptical appraisal of the Courts Boards see G. Robson, 'What Next for Local Justice?', 168 *Justice of the Peace*, 3 April 2004, p. 246.   [172] Note 141 above, section 7, para. 3.
[173] Section 6(2)(b).   [174] Schedule 4, para. 326.

- Part 5 (Inspectors of Court Administration) – provides for the establishment of a new inspectorate to be known as Her Majesty's Inspectorate of Courts Administration to replace the existing Courts Service Inspectorate. It had the power to inspect all magistrates' courts, county courts and the Crown Court. However this was rapidly overtaken by events. In March 2005 the Government announced that the public sector inspectorates would be reduced from eleven to four. In the same month, the DCA, the Home Office and the Attorney General issued a consultation document[175] proposing the amalgamation of the five existing criminal justice inspectorates[176] into one. In November 2005 they issued a Policy Statement under the same title that the plan would be implemented by legislation. The Police and Justice Bill 2005–06, Part 4 provided for a single inspectorate for Justice, Community Safety and Custody. Its remit would include the courts system and the criminal justice system (defined to include the police, criminal proceedings, the Crown Prosecution Service, protection of witnesses, support of victims, prisons and probation). This reform was fiercely and ultimately successfully opposed by a wide spectrum of informed opinion on the ground that the establishment of a single inspectorate would inevitably mean the loss of focus and expertise of the previous separate bodies. On 11 October 2006 the proposed amalgamation of the inspectorates was overwhelmingly defeated in the House of Lords, by 211 to 98, and, facing the inevitable, the Government abandoned the project.
- Part 7 (Procedure Rules and Practice Directions) – provides for the amalgamation into a single new Criminal Procedure Rule Committee of the two existing separate Rule Committees for the Crown Court and magistrates' courts. (This has already led to important developments in the form of the promulgation of the Criminal Procedure Rules – see pp. 153–55 below.)

Auld's proposal for a middle tier of jurisdiction rejected

Lord Justice Auld proposed that there be a new court – to be called the District Division – between the magistrates' court and the Crown Court:[177]

> There should be a third tier for the middle-range of cases that do not warrant the cumbersome and expensive fact-finding exercise of trial by judge and jury, but which are sufficiently serious or difficult, or their outcome is of such consequence to the public or defendant to merit a combination of professional and lay judges, but working together in a simpler way.[178]

Such cases, Auld suggested, 'could be those where, in the opinion of the court, the defendant could face a sentence of imprisonment of up to, say, two years or a substantial financial or other punishment of an amount or severity to be determined'.

[175] *Inspection Reform: Establishing an Inspectorate for Justice and Community Safety*, March 2005.
[176] The Police, the Crown Prosecution Service, court administration, prisons and the National Probation Service.   [177] Auld, pp. 275–81.   [178] *Ibid*, p. 277, para. 26.

The proposal attracted a great deal of criticism, especially for its likely effect in reducing cases tried by juries and it was rejected. The Government's July 2002 White Paper stated: 'we are not convinced that there is a strong enough case to justify introducing a new "intermediate tier" court, as was recommended by Sir Robin Auld'.[179]

4. IT for the courts

The story of IT for the courts has, at least until very recently, been one of dismal failure. The main problem is failure to integrate a system that operates in all the relevant agencies. It has been the subject of sharp criticism by one official committee after another. In 1995 a Government study (the Masefield Report) said progress had been 'very slow' and 'a step change' was now needed. ('There is a pressing need for agencies to share goals, to work more proactively together to improve systems and to be far more outward-facing in their strategies. The systemic nature of criminal justice must be more effectively recognised and managed if major inefficiencies and seriously under-optimal investment is to be avoided'.) In 1998 the Glidewell Report on the Crown Prosecution Service, having quoted the above words from Masefield, said: 'what is sad is that this statement of the obvious can be repeated with equal relevance three years later' (*ibid*). Only now there was even greater urgency because of the major commitments that already existed or were about to be made by the various agencies. Contracts with providers would be for seven to twelve years and would be difficult and/or costly to alter:

> The fact that within the criminal justice system a number of largely uncoordinated projects are about to be contracted seems to us, at best, to be a sure recipe for sub-optimisation and at worst, to signal the possibility of near disaster.[180]

In 1999 the same problem was described in the National Audit Office's Report, *Criminal Justice: Working Together*.[181]

> Each organisation in the criminal justice system is independently responsible for developing its own business processes and information flows, and for identifying, developing and procuring information technology to support them. As a result, information systems have historically been developed in isolation. Moves toward the automated exchange of information have been slow and constrained by the different systems in use and the fact that they were not designed to communicate with each other.

In October 2001 Lord Justice Auld again repeated this analysis:

> Each of the main criminal justice agencies has introduced, or is about to introduce, a system designed for its own needs, and with varying or no ability to

---

[179] White Paper, p. 72, para. 4.19.   [180] Glidewell, p. 186.
[181] HC 29, Session 1999–2000, at p. 117, para. 6.6.

communicate directly its electronically stored information to other agencies that need it.[182]

Auld described as 'a public disgrace' the fact that manual systems still played an important part in the operation of the criminal justice system.[183] The inefficiency of the development of IT for the criminal justice system was even more of a public disgrace.[184] He made a series of recommendations, the most important of which was that the project of linking the six main IT systems in the criminal justice system be scrapped in favour of a single integrated system for all the agencies.[185]

Since then there has been some progress – more in the criminal than in the civil courts. The extent of the progress with regard to the criminal justice system can be traced on www.cjit.gov.uk which gives details of the various projects and of the state of play with regard to each.[186] (It states that the Government had invested 'an unparalleled £1.95 billion into the Criminal Justice Information Technology programme'.[187]) In March 2006 it was reported that a national case progression system (PROGRESS) connecting defence lawyers, the CPS, Crown Courts and magistrates' courts had been given a funding go-ahead with a view to introduction in phases from 2007.[188]

The judge with the main responsibility for taking the issue forward initially was Lord Justice Brooke. In a lecture in 2004[189] he said that his main concern was with regard to the civil justice system:

> In January 2001 the Court Service published a consultation paper on *Modernising the Civil Courts*. This paper described the very serious difficulties very frankly. Six months later a judges' working group, led by Mr Justice Cresswell, published its own report. They started with a description of the problems which nearly every judge in the country faces every day. The list began: 'insufficient staff – high staff turnover leading to the use of inexperienced staff – missing or chaotic files – court orders take too long to be drawn and are often drawn incorrectly – lack of proper administrative support for the judiciary'.

---

[182] Auld, Ch. 8, p. 353, para. 92, n. 73.   [183] Auld, Ch. 8, p. 394, para. 94.

[184] 'At best the system is inefficient and wasteful' (Auld, p. 355, para. 99).

[185] Auld, pp. 308 and 365–66.

[186] CPS – COMPASS case management system fully implemented; Police – NSPIS custody system live in seventeen out of forty-two areas; NSPIS case preparation system live in twenty-one areas; magistrates' courts – LIBRA live in two areas; LINK project (national roll out of information and communication technology infrastructure across the Court Service) – completed by spring 2006; Probation and Prison Service – Offender Risk Assessment System (OASys) giving updated offender information to both organisations by linking the two separate OASys systems – supposedly completed March 2006; XHIBIT – providing case progress to Crown Courts and approved members of the criminal justice community (police, CPS, prisons, probation, Youth Offending Teams etc.) – live in all forty-two areas; CJS exchange XHIBIT portal – permitting approved criminal justice agencies access to Crown Court hearing information via XHIBIT will benefit the police, witnesses, victim support etc. – live in all areas; secure e-mail for criminal justice agencies– live in all areas.

[187] www.cjit.gov.uk.   [188] *Law Society's Gazette*, 2 March 2006, p. 11.

[189] 'Court modernisation and the crisis facing our civil courts' a lecture to the Society of Advanced Legal Studies, London, given by Lord Justice Brooke on 24 November 2004 (www.dca.gov.uk– Judges – Speeches).

Later on they said that very few members of court staff had real IT expertise, and that there was a chronic lack of funds even for basic equipment . . .

These were the problems. Part of the solution was to install an IT infrastructure into all the main civil and family court centres, and to provide judges and court staff with the specialist software they needed so as to introduce order out of chaos. There were also plans for new business centres, so that undefended business could be dealt with somewhere else, and the court centres could concentrate on defended business.

But the plans had gone awry.

In July 2002 the Treasury pulled the plug on all this. We had been allocated £30 million for the start of the programme in 2003–4, and this sum seemed to be carried forward each year until April 2006. In other words, it looked as if £100 million in all would be available, but without further funding we could not possibly complete the job and commission the specialist software we needed. The project team working on that part of the programme had to be disbanded immediately. In the event the limited funding was cut by a quarter . . .

Two and a half years ago I really thought we were on the way to creating new arrangements for civil and family justice of which this country could be proud. Now I see no light on the horizon at all. I do not even see any evidence that the scale of the problem is being properly addressed because there are so many other initiatives currently being pursued, which are distracting the attention of our policy-makers. And so long as the Treasury insists on its full cost recovery regime, things can only get worse. Much worse.

Lord Justice Brooke was clearly in despair about the miserable state of progress in IT for the civil system. But the fact that the criminal justice system was getting so much more in funding did not seem to translate into operational success.

By the end of 2006, Libra, the magistrates' court system, was 'over-budget and behind schedule'. It was only 'live' in nine courts. COMPASS, the CPS system, was up and running connecting the 2,800 CPS lawyers, police charging centres, and courts.[190] However, a report in October 2006 by the House of Commons Public Accounts Committee said that, having procured COMPASS at a cost of £300m over ten years, 'the Crown Prosecution Service has yet to make full use of the system's capabilities'. Staff failed to update the information on file in the system, correspondence was misfiled or sent to the wrong address. COMPASS and LIBRA would not be integrated for at least another year.[191]

5. The tribunal system

The work of the courts is supplemented by the large number of administrative tribunals. Tribunals sit for more days than the High Court and the county courts

---

[190] 'Taking the CPS into the 21st century', *Law Society's Gazette*, 21 September 2006, p. 15.
[191] House of Commons Public Accounts Committee, *Crown Prosecution Service: Effective Use of Magistrates' Courts Hearings*, July 2006, HC 982, p. 10.

put together and hear many more contested cases than the ordinary courts. The Leggatt inquiry into tribunals published in March 2001[192] stated that there were some seventy tribunals and that between them they dealt with nearly one million cases a year – though only twenty of the seventy tribunals dealt with more than 500 cases a year and many were defunct. Their quality varied from excellent to inadequate. The so-called tribunal system was not a system at all:

> What we have found . . . is that the present collection of tribunals has grown up in an almost entirely haphazard way. Individual tribunals were set up, and usually administered by departments, as they developed new statutory schemes and procedures. The result is a collection of tribunals, mostly administered by departments, with wide variations of practice and approach, and almost no coherence. The current arrangements seem to us to have been developed to meet the needs and conveniences of the departments and other bodies which run tribunals, rather than the needs of the users.[193]

Leggatt said that the lack of coherence had brought with it many difficulties and weaknesses in the performance of tribunals. The report outlined what would be a new 'single, overarching structure'. There would be nine subject divisions dealing with immigration, social security and pensions, land and valuation, financial including taxation, transport, health and social services, education, regulatory and employment. Appeals would go to a single appellate division which would sit in panels related to the nine divisions. There would be a new Tribunals Service operating parallel to the Courts Service and under the Lord Chancellor – so that administration of tribunals would be taken away from their parent Government Departments.

In August 2001 the Government published a consultation paper (*Tribunals for Users*) inviting views. Unsurprisingly, there was resistance in Whitehall to the suggestion that departments should lose stewardship of their respective tribunals.[194] Nevertheless, in March 2003, Lord Irvine, in one of his last acts as Lord Chancellor, announced that the main Leggatt recommendation of the establishment of a new unified Tribunals Service was to be implemented.[195]

The unified Tribunals Service would have as its core the top ten non-devolved tribunals which currently existed: the Appeals Service, the Immigration Appellate Authority, the Employment Tribunals Service, the Criminal Injuries Compensation Appeals Panel, the Mental Health Review Tribunal, the Office for Social Security and Child Support Commissioners, Tax Tribunals, Special Education Needs and Disability Tribunals, the Pensions Appeal Tribunal and the Lands Tribunal. They would be included in the new unified service between 2006 and 2008. Any new tribunal would be brought into the unified system.

---

[192] *Tribunals for Users: One System, One Service* (www.tribunals-review.org.uk).
[193] Leggatt, p. 15.
[194] Lord Justice Brooke wrote: 'departments of state could not see why they had to surrender part of their fiefdom to Lord Irvine's growing empire' (*Counsel*, November 2004, p.11). Sir Henry Brooke was the Lord Chief Justice's nominee to help prepare the reform. He was subsequently replaced by Lord Justice Carnwath.   [195] LCD Press Notice 106/03, 11 March 2003.

In July 2004, developing its plans, the Government published a wide-ranging White Paper (*Transforming Public Services: Complaints, Redress and Tribunals*). It covered not just dispute resolution in the context of tribunals but a wider range of administrative justice including ombudsmen and the courts. It emphasised the desirability of proportionate dispute resolution, with the maximum number of disputes being resolved without recourse to hearings. Ombudsman services were especially commended: 'Ombudsman services have shown that perfectly sound decisions can be made which fully respect the rights of parties without formal hearings'.[196] (The Financial Services Ombudsman Service (FOS) in particular was praised for its tiers of intervention – ranging from initial advice through to conciliation and adjudication, with a final decision by the ombudsman only if necessary.[197]) The proposed new Tribunals Service, the White Paper said, should be a 'new type of organisation which will not only provide formal hearings and authoritative rulings where these are needed but will have as well a mission to resolve disputes fairly and finally either by itself or in partnership with the decision-making department, other institutions and the advice sector'.[198] The White Paper envisaged that tribunal staff would have the power to innovate in finding new ways of resolving disputes.

The Tribunal Service (website www.tribunalsservice.gov.uk), the new executive agency to run the tribunals system, was launched in April 2006. It has responsibility for 21 tribunals.

The Tribunals, Courts and Enforcement Bill to give legislative effect to the new system was finally published and introduced in the Lords on 16 November 2006. The Explanatory Notes attached to the Bill described its main features:

> 13. The Government's response to Sir Andrew Leggatt's recommended single tribunal system was to create two new, generic tribunals, the First-tier Tribunal and the Upper Tribunal, into which existing tribunal jurisdictions can be transferred. The Upper Tribunal will be primarily, but not exclusively, an appellate tribunal from the First-tier Tribunal.
>
> 14. The Bill also provides for the establishment of 'chambers' within the two tribunals so that the many jurisdictions that will be transferred into the tribunals can be grouped together appropriately. Each chamber will be headed by a Chamber President and the tribunals' judiciary will be headed by a Senior President of Tribunals . . . [199]

---

[196] White Paper, para.6.20.

[197] For a description of the FOS see R. James and P. Morris, 'The Financial Ombudsman Service: a brave new world in "Ombudsmanry?"', *Public Law*, 2002, pp. 640–49. The FOS (website www.financial-ombudsman.org.uk) was established in 2000 taking over the functions of five existing ombudsman schemes: the Banking Ombudsman, Building Societies Ombudsman, Insurance Ombudsman, Investment Ombudsman and Personal Investment Authority Ombudsman. In 2004–05 it received over 110,000 new complaints. Over half (55 per cent) of the complaints handled in the year were dealt with informally by 'guided mediation'; 38 per cent were handled more formally, generally involving adjudication; only 7 per cent were resolved by decisions of an ombudsman. The complainant is charged nothing. The unit cost (total costs divided by completed cases) was £496 per case (Annual Report, 2004–05).

[198] White Paper, para. 4. 21.   [199] The first President appointed was Lord Justice Carnwath.

17. The Bill creates new offices for the First-tier and Upper Tribunal. It creates new titles (giving the legal members the title of judges) and a new system of deployment. Judges of the First-tier Tribunal or Upper Tribunal will be assigned to one or more of the chambers of that tribunal, having regard to their knowledge and experience. The fact that a member may be allocated to more than one chamber allows members to be deployed across the jurisdictions within the tribunal. It is expected that members of existing tribunals will become members of the new tribunals.

Reviews and appeals and the judicial review jurisdiction of the tribunals

18. Currently there is no single mechanism for appealing against a tribunal decision. Appeal rights differ from tribunal to tribunal. In some cases there is a right of appeal to another tribunal. In other cases there is a right of appeal to the High Court. In some cases there is no right of appeal at all. The Bill provides a unified appeal structure. Under the Bill, in most cases, a decision of the First-tier Tribunal may be appealed to the Upper Tribunal and a decision of the Upper Tribunal may be appealed to a court. The grounds of appeal must relate to a point of law. The rights to appeal may only be exercised with permission from the tribunal being appealed from or the tribunal or court, as the case may, being appealed to.

19. It will also be possible for the Upper Tribunal to deal with some judicial review cases which would otherwise have to be dealt with by the High Court or Court of Session. The Upper Tribunal has this jurisdiction only where a case falls within a class specified in a direction given by the Lord Chief Justice or in certain other cases transferred by the High Court or Court of Session, but it will not generally be possible for cases to be transferred to the Upper Tribunal if they involve immigration or nationality matters.

20. Instead of tribunal rules being made by the Lord Chancellor and other government Ministers under a multiplicity of different rule-making powers, a new Tribunal Procedure Committee will be responsible for tribunal rules. This committee has been modelled on existing rule committees which make rules of court.

Transfer of tribunal functions

21. It is intended that the new tribunals will exercise the jurisdictions currently exercised by the tribunals listed in Parts 1 to 4 of Schedule 6, which constitute most of the tribunal jurisdictions administered by central government. The Government's policy is that in the future, when a new tribunal jurisdiction is required to deal with a right of review or appeal, that right of appeal or review will be to these new tribunals.

22. Some tribunals have been excluded from the new structures because of their specialist nature. Tribunals run by local government have for now been excluded, as their funding and sponsorship arrangements are sufficiently different to merit a separate review.

The role of the new Tribunal Service is wider than merely running an efficient executive operation. Its task includes taking the initiative across Whitehall to ensure that more decisions are right first time and that disputes are resolved, so far as possible, without recourse to hearings before tribunals at all.

Under the Bill, the Council on Tribunals,[200] which oversees tribunals, will be renamed the Administrative Justice and Tribunals Council (AJTC). Following the recommendations of the Leggatt report, its remit will include important new functions: keeping under review the performance of the administrative justice system as a whole; reviewing the relationship between the components of the system (in particular ombudsmen, tribunals and the courts) to ensure that these are clear, complementary and flexible; identifying priorities for research; and providing advice and making recommendations to ministers.

See generally Professor M. Adler, 'Tribunal Reform: Proportionate Dispute Resolution and the Pursuit of Administrative Justice' (2006) 69 *Modern Law Review* pp. 958–85, and Genevra Richardson and Hazel Genn, 'Tribunals in Transition: Resolution or Adjudication?' *Public Law*, 2007, pp. 116–41. See also S. Prince, 'Mandatory Mediation: The Ontario Experience', 26 *Civil Justice Quarterly*, 2007, pp. 79–95.

---

[200] The Council (website www.council-on-tribunals.gov.uk) was set up by the Tribunals and Inquiries Act 1957 as a watchdog on the working of tribunals. It publishes an annual report.

Chapter 2

Pre-trial civil proceedings

1. Introduction

This chapter deals with the problems of the pre-trial stages of a civil action which set the stage for the trial – if there is one. There are two main reasons why the pre-trial stage of litigation is vital. One is that in the great majority of cases the proceedings never reach trial. Secondly, in the rare cases that go to trial, the outcome is usually determined by what has been achieved by way of collection and preparation of evidence in the pre-trial stage.

Pre-trial civil process has repeatedly been the subject of reports and inquiries – more than sixty over the past hundred years! (These are issues and problems that seem not to go away.) Since 1968 there has been the report of the Winn Committee,[1] the Report of the Cantley Committee,[2] the massive Civil Justice Review 1985–88[3] and the Heilbron-Hodge Working Party set up jointly by the Bar and the Law Society.[4] The recommendations of these bodies were dealt with extensively in earlier editions of this work. For reasons of economy of space, they are treated here lightly, since the new system which took effect in April 1999 was based essentially on the recommendations made by Lord Woolf in his June 1995 *Interim Report*[5] and his July 1996 *Final Report* both entitled *Access to Justice*. Virtually every topic dealt with in this chapter is affected by the Woolf Report.

The gestation period from the *Final Report* of *Access to Justice* to implementation in April 1999 was just under three years. Given the radical nature of the changes made and their immense scope, this was a remarkable achievement.

The Woolf reforms, like those of previous attempts at reform of civil justice, were mainly aimed at the three problems of cost, delay and complexity. As will

---

[1] *Report of the Committee on Personal Injuries Litigation*, 1968, Cmnd. 369.
[2] *Report of the Personal Injuries Litigation Procedure Working Party*, 1979, Cmnd. 7476.
[3] For a full account of its recommendations, see the 30-page note in the *Civil Justice Quarterly*, 1988, pp. 281–312. See also the reflections of a member of the Civil Justice Review formerly with the National Consumer Council: Richard Thomas, 'Civil Justice Review – Treating Litigants as Consumers', 6 *Civil Justice Quarterly*, 1990, p. 51.
[4] *Civil Justice on Trial – the Case for Change*, 1992.
[5] For an extended account of its recommendations, see the 30-page note in 11 *Civil Justice Quarterly*, 1995, pp. 231–49.

be seen, the main thrust of the project was to transfer the chief responsibility for progressing cases from the parties and their lawyers to the court.

The overriding objective At the heart of the new system is the 'overriding objective' which is set out in Part I, r. 1.1 of the new Civil Procedure Rules (CPR). The opening words of the new rules state: 'these Rules are a new procedural code with the overriding objective of enabling the court to deal with cases justly'. Rule 1.1(2) then articulates what is meant by dealing with a case justly. 'Dealing with a case justly includes, so far as is practicable: (a) ensuring that the parties are on an equal footing;[6] (b) saving expense; (c) dealing with the case in ways which are proportionate (i) to the amount of money involved; (ii) to the importance of the case; (iii) to the complexity of the issues; (iv) to the financial position of each party; (d) ensuring that it is dealt with expeditiously and fairly; and (e) allotting to it an appropriate share of the court's resources, while taking into account the need to allot resources to other cases'.

These propositions are intended to have an impact at all times. CPR 1.2 states that these factors must be taken into account whenever the court exercises any power given to it by the rules or interprets any rule. Moreover, the duty to comply with the overriding objective applies not only to the courts but also to the parties. Rule 1.3 states: 'the parties are required to help the court to further the overriding objective'. This applies to all stages of a dispute. So, for instance, the Practice Direction on Pre-action Protocols (p. 60 below) states that the court will expect the parties, 'in accordance with the overriding objective', to act reasonably in exchanging information and documents and generally in trying to avoid the necessity for the start of proceedings (para. 4).

Lord Woolf's *Final Report* said that the overriding objective 'provides a compass to guide courts and litigants and legal advisers as to their general course' and this has become a reality.

It will be noted that the listed considerations which make up the overriding objective are very broad and not necessarily consistent. In truth, they will justify any decision the court is minded to make. As the practitioner's bible, the *White Book* said: 'it is probably true to say that, in almost any circumstances in which the court exercises a power given to it by the CPR, it would be possible to justify (at least in part) the particular manner in which the power is exercised in the light of one or other of the aspects of the overriding objective'.[7]

In *Holmes v. SGB Services Plc*[8] the judge granted an application to vacate the trial date, to amend particulars of claim and to re-instruct the expert. He said there was a tension between rules emphasising the maintaining of trial dates and the interests of justice in achieving a fair trial. Dismissing the other side's appeal, the Court of Appeal doubted whether any such tension existed. Lord

---

[6] It has been held that this concept of a 'level playing field' does not mean that it is wrong for one side to instruct a QC where the other has only a junior barrister (*Maltez v. Lewis* (1999) 21 Gaz 39, (1999) Times, 4 May).   [7] *Civil Procedure*, 2002, vol. 1, p. 9.

[8] [2001] EWCA Civ 354.

Justice Buxton said that in making the case management decision, the court has to balance all the criteria in CPR 1.1 without giving any of them undue weight. Striking a balance was a matter for the judge and it would be wrong for the Court of Appeal to give, or for judges to seek, any direction suggesting that one or other of the criteria was more or less important.

It is unrealistic to say that the tension does not exist. Clearly it does. If, as in *Holmes,* two or more of the criteria point in different directions, the judge, having weighed them, must decide which he favours. So in each such case one or more of the criteria will be held to be 'more important' than others.

The crux of the matter is whether the court should give primary weight to the determination of cases justly in the sense of substantive justice on the facts of the case or whether substantive justice on the facts of the case is only one of the factors to be taken into account. The point was made strongly by Professor A. Zuckerman, editor of the *Civil Justice Quarterly*:

> The CPR are founded on three imperatives: reaching substantively correct outcomes, by means of proportionate resources, and in a reasonable time. The overriding objective consists in 'enabling the courts to deal with cases justly' (CPR, r. 1.1(1)). Doing justice is the goal of any enlightened system of civil litigation. However the notion of doing justice is capable of a variety of interpretations. Under the previous system doing justice was thought to require merely arriving at a judgment that was correct as a matter of fact and law. That is to say, doing justice consisted of reaching a correct decision no matter how long it took and how much it cost the litigants and the court. The CPR broke with this tradition by establishing that doing justice on the merits is not the sole overarching principle. Rather, justice on the merits has to be achieved within a reasonable time and by using no more than proportionate resources.[9]

The context was the grotesque saga of the case brought against the Bank of England by the liquidators of the Bank of Credit and Commerce International AS (BCCI).[10] What had gone wrong there, Zuckerman argued, turned on the decision of the majority of the House of Lords in which the Law Lords had reverted to the pre-CPR philosophy.[11] The result of such an approach, he warned, would be fatal to the CPR reforms: 'unless all levels

---

[9] 25 *Civil Justice Quarterly*, 2006, pp. 287–311 at 307.

[10] The claim was estimated to involve potential damages of over £500 million. It dragged on for twelve years. The case came to an end in November 2005 on day 256 of the trial when the claimants abandoned the action. Ten years earlier, in November 1995, Justice Clarke had ruled that the bank was entitled to summary judgment on the ground that the claimant's case had no prospect of success. The Court of Appeal upheld the decision 2–1. The House of Lords, allowing the claimant's appeal by 3–2, held that it was not a case for summary judgment – the evidence should be heard. The decision of the majority (Lords Steyn, Hobhouse and Millett) resulted in ten more years of fruitless litigation with astronomical costs. (The Bank of England's costs were agreed at £75 million.)

[11] *Three Rivers DC v. Bank of England (No 3) (Summary Judgment)* [2001] UKHL 16, [2001] 2 All ER 513.

of judiciary can be persuaded to embrace the overriding objective that incorporates the requirements of proportionality and expedition, as well as the need to do justice on the merits, the entire CPR system may become a colossal wreck'.[12]

The court's duty to manage cases

Traditionally civil litigation in the pre-trial stage was run by the parties, with the courts playing only a supporting or facilitating role, intervening basically only when requested. The new rules impose a positive duty on the courts to manage cases. CPR 1.4(1) states that the court must further the overriding objective by actively managing cases. It continues:

> 1.4(2) Active case management includes: (a) encouraging the parties to co-operate with each other in the conduct of the proceedings; (b) identifying the issues at an early stage; (c) deciding promptly which issues need full investigation and trial and accordingly disposing summarily of the others; (d) deciding the order in which issues are to be resolved; (e) encouraging the parties to use an alternative dispute resolution procedure if the court considers that appropriate and facilitating the use of such procedure; (f) helping the parties to settle the whole or part of the case; (g) fixing timetables or otherwise controlling the progress of the case; (h) considering whether the likely benefits of taking a particular step justify the cost of taking it; (i) dealing with as many aspects of the case as it can on the same occasion; (j) dealing with the case without the parties needing to attend at court; (k) making use of technology; and (l) giving directions to ensure that the trial of a case proceeds quickly and efficiently.

The court is given power (unless a rule or other enactment prevents it) to exercise its powers on its own initiative. It may give a person likely to be affected an opportunity to make representations but it need not do so. A party affected by such an order has the right to seek to have it set aside, varied or stayed.

For a positive assessment of whether judicial detachment and impartiality is compatible with the new duty of active trial management see Lightman J., 'The case for judicial intervention'.[13] For a positive assessment of court control with regard to fact finding see A.J. Cannon, 'Effective Fact-finding,' 25 *Civil Justice Quarterly*, 2006, pp. 327–48.

The three tracks

Under the CPR, cases must be assigned to one of three tracks: small claims, fast track or multi-track. Each track has its separate regime.

---

[12] Note 9 above at p. 311. For the same critique arising from a decision of the Court of Appeal, see J. Sorabji, 'B v. B: Forwards or Backwards for the Overriding Objective', 24 *Civil Justice Quarterly*, 2005, pp. 414–23.

[13] 149 *New Law Journal*, 3 December 1999, p. 1819 and www.lcd.gov.uk/judicial/speeches/speechfr.htm.

Small claims

As has been seen, the limit for small claims cases is £5,000 except for personal injury and housing cases where it is £1,000. Under the Woolf reforms, small claims involve mainly very limited pre-trial court management, few, if any, pre-trial hearings and a trial where the judge runs the proceedings in whatever way seems right to him.

Before April 1999, a case involving sums within the jurisdiction would go to small claims unless it raised a difficult question of law or fact or was of exceptional complexity or the parties agreed that the case should be tried in court or that it would be unreasonable.[14] Under the Woolf regime, the court allocates the case to its appropriate track. The Practice Direction on small claims says: 'the small claims track is intended to provide a proportionate procedure by which most straightforward claims with a financial value of not more than £5,000 can be decided, without the need for substantial pre-hearing preparation and the formalities of a traditional trial, and without incurring large legal costs'.[15] 'Cases generally suitable for the small claims track will include consumer disputes, accident claims, disputes about the ownership of goods and most disputes between a landlord and a tenant other than those for possession'.[16]

Fast track

The fast track is for cases involving amounts between £5,000 and £15,000 unless they are unsuitable for this track. The original concept was a set timetable of no more than thirty weeks to trial, limited pre-trial procedure, a trial confined to no more than three hours, no oral evidence from experts and standard fixed costs recoverable from the other side. This, broadly, was the scheme that was implemented, though the proposed three-hour limit on the hearing was extended to five hours and fixed costs applied originally only to the costs of the actual hearing.

Multi-track

The multi-track is for cases involving amounts in excess of the fast track limit or for cases involving lesser amounts which are too complex or too important to be dealt with as small claims or fast track cases. They are given a more intensive form of court management probably including pre-trial hearings.

In the first five years of the CPR, over half of cases (50–60 per cent) were allocated to the small claims system, between a fifth and a third (21–33 per cent) were fast track and slightly fewer (15–20 per cent) were allocated to the multi-track.[17]

The Civil Procedure Rules

One of the important parts of the Woolf reform project was the unification of the rules of the High Court in the *White Book* (formerly the *Annual Practice,*

---

[14] CCR Order 19, r. 1(5).   [15] 26 PD 8.1(1)(a).   [16] 26 PD 8.1(1)(c).
[17] DCA Statistical Branch annual figures for 1999–2003 quoted by Peysner and Seneviratne, DCA Research Report 9/2005, Table Two, p. 18.

now *Civil Procedure*) with those for the county court in the *Green Book* (*County Court Rules*). Under the Civil Procedure Act 1997, a new Rule Committee was established, replacing the two committees previously responsible respectively for the Rules of the Supreme Court (RSC) and the County Court Rules (CCR). The new committee was charged with the task of preparing a new single procedural code, to be known as the Civil Procedure Rules (CPR).

Previously the rules were divided into Orders. In the CPR they are divided into Parts. Most Parts are accompanied by Practice Directions that amplify or clarify the rules. These have a major role (J. Jacob has rightly said: 'the development of procedure is now by Practice Direction as much as by precedent or change of rule'),[18] but whereas the Rules are made by the Rule Committee, the Practice Directions are made by Heads of the different divisions.[19]

The Civil Procedure Rules – as amended from time to time – are accessible on the Department's Website – www.dca.gov.uk. The fact that the Website is up-to-date is of considerable value given the number of amendments and additions. From April 1999 to January 2006 there were no fewer than forty supplements.

The significance of calling the CPR a 'new procedural code? The *White Book* comments editorially that in many cases the judges have stressed the statement in r. 1.1 that the CPR are 'a new procedural code'. It suggests that they do so to ensure that the innovative provisions in the CPR are given their full intended effect 'and are not limited by practices and attitudes that attached to the former rules of court' and also to make it clear that provisions that are plainly based on former rules will not necessarily be interpreted and applied in accordance with the old case law, but it warns that the assertion 'should not be relied upon as an excuse for dealing with important procedural issues as matters of first impression rather than as matters requiring rigorous legal analysis (in their historical context, if necessary)'.[20]

J. Jacob has described the effect on precedent:

> The CPR are a step toward 'Teflon precedents'. Old decisions, even those after April 1999, will not stick. Of course, cases will continue to be reported, read by lawyers and to judges. What has changed is that a continued primacy is given to the Rules and even more importantly the spirit that underlies them (the Overriding Objective, CPR, Part 1.2(b)). To this extent, the doctrine of precedent is being modified. Previous authority, even apparently binding authority, will become guidance. The judge, in managing cases, will have prime regard to the rules themselves not what some other judges have said about them.[21]

---

[18] *Civil litigation practice and procedure in a shifting culture*, 2001, Emis, pp. 21–2.
[19] For the QBD by the Lord Chief Justice, for the Chancery Division by the Vice Chancellor, for the Court of Appeal Civil Division by the Master of the Rolls and for the county courts by the Lord Chancellor. (See the note on Practice Directions first published in the HMSO version of the CPR, 23rd Supplement, May 2001 and see also J.A. Jolowicz, 'Practice Directions and Civil Procedure Rules', *Cambridge Law Journal*, 2000, pp. 53–61.)
[20] *Civil Procedure*, 2006, vol. 1, 1.3.9, p. 23.
[21] Note 18 above at p. 13.

The trouble is that there is no way of knowing in advance whether the court will find the precedent helpful and therefore to be followed, or not helpful and therefore not to be followed.[22]

The Human Rights Act and the CPR

There are many provisions in the CPR that arguably might provoke challenges under the Human Rights Act 1998 but the courts have made it clear that it is most unlikely that such challenges will be successful. The reason is that in the view of the senior judiciary the rules to be found in the CPR are consistent with the European Convention on Human Rights. Lord Woolf expressed this in *Walker v. Daniels*[23] in which he said the matter was more than adequately covered by the requirement in the CPR that the court deal with cases *justly*. There was therefore no need to pray in aid the ECHR:

> It would be unfortunate if case management decisions in this jurisdiction involved the need to refer to the learning of the European Court of Human Rights in order for them to be resolved. In my judgment, cases such as this do not require any consideration of human rights issues, certainly not issues under Article 6. It would be highly undesirable if the consideration of case management issues was made more complex by the injection into them of Article 6 style arguments. I hope that judges will be robust in resisting any attempt to introduce those arguments.[24]

On the impact of the Human Rights Act and the ECHR on the CPR see Joseph Jacob's valuable book, *Civil Justice in the Age of Human Rights* (forthcoming 2007, Ashgate).

User-friendly language

One of the features of the new Woolf era was the scrapping of old-fashioned legal terms and, in particular, the banishment of time-honoured Latin phrases used by lawyers. Thus new terms for practitioners and judges to master included: 'claimant' instead of 'plaintiff', 'disclosure' instead of 'discovery', 'statement of case' instead of 'pleading', 'application' instead of 'motion', 'litigator's friend' instead of 'next friend' and 'guardian *ad litem*', 'without notice' instead of '*ex parte*', 'witness summons' instead of '*subpoena duces tecum*', 'with permission' instead of 'with leave', 'service by an alternative method' instead of 'substituted service', 'between parties' instead of '*inter partes*', 'search order' instead of 'Anton Piller order', 'freezing order' instead of 'Mareva injunction' etc. For lawyers such changes are minor irritants. Opinions differ as to whether

---

[22] In *Hashtroodi v. Hancock* [2004] EWCA Civ 652 the court said that earlier authorities were generally not relevant. It cited to similar effect *Biguzzi v. Rank Leisure Plc* [1999] 1 WLR 1926 at 1934 and *Godwin v. Swindon BC* [2001] EWCA Civ 1478 at [42], but it acknowledged that there were cases 'where this court has derived assistance from cases decided under the former rules'. It cited *Banks v. Cox* [2000] CA Transcript 1476 at [41]; *Stewart v. Engel* [2000] 1 WLR 2268 at 2276 and *Garratt v. Saxby* [2004] EWCA 341 at [18].

[23] [2000] 1 WLR 1382.   [24] At 1387.

it actually benefits lay people involved in litigation or whether it is mainly a manifestation of political correctness.

Research on the Woolf reforms

Pre-Woolf reforms For an assessment of the research situation in March 1997 plus recommendations see a report commissioned by the LCD – T. Goriely, *Evaluating the Woolf Reforms – Obtaining Baseline Data on the Cost and Length of Civil Litigation.*[25] In 2002 the DCA published a snapshot of non-family civil justice at the county court and High Court in Sheffield.[26] Although it was published after the Woolf reforms had been introduced, it related only to a period before they were introduced.

Post-Woolf There have so far been only two proper research studies of the impact of the Woolf reforms. The first, on the effect of the reforms on pre-action behaviour, was carried out for the Civil Justice Council (CJC) and the Law Society ('Goriely et al').[27] The study was based on interviews with fifty-four lawyers, insurers and claims managers, of whom thirty specialised in personal injury (PI) work, twelve specialised in clinical negligence and twelve specialised in housing disrepair. In the case of PI work it also included comparison of 150 claimant solicitor files concluded before April 1999 ('pre-Woolf') and 150 opened and closed post-Woolf files.

The second, on the case management aspects of the reforms, was conducted for the DCA by Professors Peysner and Seneviratne.[28] The study, carried out in 2003–04, focused on eight county courts with a varied diet of town and country. In each court in-depth interviews were conducted with judges, and relevant court staff, notably listing officers and diary managers. Focus groups were conducted with solicitors practising in the area. The authors reported: 'what was surprising about our findings was the almost uniform views we encountered in very different environments, about the impact and level of success of the reforms' (para. 3). The study did not generate any new quantitative data.

---

[25] The 34-page report was published by Social Legal Research, 227a Richmond Road, Twickenham TW1 2NJ.

[26] J. Shapland, A. Sorsby and J. Hibbert, *A Civil Justice Audit*, DCA Research Report 2/2002. The study drew together data about the use of the courts, the progress of cases through the stages of civil justice, the costs etc. For the Executive Summary, see www.dca.gov.uk – Publications – Research. For an article based on the study by one of its authors, see J. Shapland, 'The Need for Case Management? Profiles of Liquidated and Unliquidated Cases', 22 *Civil Justice Quarterly*, 2003, pp. 324–48.

A second study conducted for the DCA of defended, litigated cases in six county courts by Professor H. Genn, *The Pre-Woolf Litigation Landscape in the County Courts* was not published as the Department decided it wanted to compare the data with post-Woolf data. At the time of writing the DCA study in question had not been completed.

[27] T. Goriely, R. Moorhead and P. Abrams, *More Civil Justice? The impact of the Woolf reforms on pre-action behaviour* (Law Society, 2002) Research Study No. 43, 420 pp. A 33-page summary is accessible on www.research.lawsociety.org.uk (Publications).

[28] J. Peysner and M. Seneviratne, *The Management of Civil Cases: the Courts and the Post-Woolf Landscape*, DCA Research Report 9/2005. The research was summarised by the authors in 'The Management of Civil Cases – a Snapshot', 25 *Civil Justice Quarterly*, 2006, pp. 312–26.

The LCD's publications on evaluation of the Woolf reforms – *Emerging Findings* (March 2001)[29] and *Further Findings* (August 2002)[30] – drew on a combination of sources: reports of the Law Society's Woolf Network based on responses by some 130 solicitors knowledgeable in the field who agreed to answer periodic questionnaires on how in their view the reforms were working in practice[31] and surveys by the Expert Witness Institute, and Court Service User Satisfaction Surveys in March and November 2001 and June 2002. There have also been reports made by individual law firms. There are quite a number of articles written by a variety of authors of the 'Woolf reforms one/two/three years on' variety based on a mixture of opinion and impression – and plenty of anecdotal evidence.

For the writer's assessment of how the Woolf reforms have worked out see pp. 132–40 below.

2. Few cases are ever started and fewer reach court

The myth of the 'compensation culture'

There has in recent years been increasing alarm about a growing 'compensation culture' leading to a 'litigation crisis'. (Entering the phrase 'compensation culture' into a UK-only Google search in December 2004 and confining the search to the previous twelve months generated no fewer than 25,500 web pages.[32]) The concern is fuelled by a sense that people resort too readily to law when things go wrong and that the courts are too ready to give compensation. The evidence, if anything, points to a different conclusion. The Government's Better Regulation Task Force in a report in 2004 compared national expenditure on tort claims, at 0.6 per cent of GDP in this country as lower than that of ten other industrialised countries including Canada, Australia, Germany and the US. Only Denmark spent less.[33] Its report, which the Government said it accepted,[34] denied that Britain was in the grip of a compensation culture. It based this view partly on the opinion of 'almost everyone' who gave evidence to

---

[29] www.dca.gov.uk/civil/emerge/emerge.htm. For a summary of the findings, see 'Effects of the Civil Justice Reforms', 20 *Civil Justice Quarterly*, 2001, pp. 301–2.

[30] www.dca.gov.uk/civil/reform/ffreform.htm.

[31] They were published roughly twice yearly: No. 1 in September 1999, the last, No. 7, in July 2004. The last four are accessible on www.lawsociety.org – Civil Litigation.

[32] K. Williams, 'State of Fear: Britain's "Compensation Culture" Reviewed', 25 *Legal Studies*, 2005, pp. 499–514 at 499. Williams' article is a helpful review of the evidence. See also R. Lewis, A. Morris and K. Oliphent, 'Is there a Compensation Culture in the UK?, *Journal of Personal Injury Law*, 2006, pp. 87–103 and the report of the House of Commons Constitutional Affairs Committee, *Compensation Culture*, 3rd Report, 2005–06, HC 754, March 2006.

[33] Better Regulation Task Force, *Better Routes to Redress*, May 2004, p. 15. See www.brc.gov.uk; 154 *New Law Journal*, 11 June 2004, p. 873.

[34] *Tackling the 'Compensation Culture'*, Government response to the Better Regulation Task Force Report, *Better Routes to Redress*, November 2004.

the inquiry and partly on the declining number of personal injury claims regis-tered in recent years.[35] The real problem it suggested was perceptual. Too many of us have been persuaded by media stories and by the advertising campaigns of claims management companies that large sums of money are easily accessible.[36] According to the Task Force, there is no objectively sound basis for such beliefs or for asserting that Britain is suffering from a 'have a go culture'.[37]

However, in November 2005, the Government introduced the Compensation Bill. Its main purpose was to establish a regulatory system for claims manage-ment companies but s. 1 directly addressed the perception of a 'compensation culture' issue. It provides: 'a court considering a claim in negligence or breach of statutory duty may, in determining whether the defendant should have taken particular steps to meet a standard of care (whether by taking precautions against a risk or otherwise), have regard to whether a requirement to take those steps might (1) prevent a desirable activity from being undertaken at all, to a particular extent or in a particular way or (2) discourage persons from under-taking functions in connection with a desirable activity'.

The general consensus seems to be that s. 1 adds nothing to the existing law which it simply restates. The Constitutional Affairs Committee in its March 2006 report *Compensation Culture* said that the clause was unnecessary and that it should not be in the Bill.[38] The Government, however, did not follow this advice. The Bill, still including s. 1, received Royal Assent in July 2006.

The attrition of claims

If legal problems are seen in the form of an iceberg, the ones that reach a court are those at the very tip. The great majority never even get to a lawyer. Of those that get to a lawyer, the great majority get sorted out without any form of court hearing, sometimes before legal proceedings are started, often between the ini-tiation of legal proceedings and the hearing.

The first solid empirical evidence regarding the progress of claims came from a large study of personal injury cases conducted in the 1980s by the Oxford Socio-Legal Centre.[39] The study was based on a national household survey which produced a random sample of 1,711 accident victims all of whom had suffered some impairment for at least two weeks. Of these, only 26 per cent

---

[35] K. Williams reached the same conclusion: 'there is virtually no reliable evidence about the number of bogus or exaggerated claims or whether they constitute a grave (or increasing) problem' (www.dca.gov.uk/civil/reform/ffreform.htm, note 32 above at p. 513).

[36] The Government's response to the Better Regulation Task Force Report, n. 32 above, said: 'there is no place for advertising of whatever kind, whether by claims management companies or lawyers, that either raises false expectations of large compensation pay outs for minor injuries, or indirectly promotes the bringing of frivolous claims' (p. 8). For commentary, see A. Morris, 'Claims Advertising: Access or Excess?', *New Law Journal*, 11 March 2005, p. 345.

[37] *Better Routes to Redress*, n. 33 above at p. 11.

[38] 3rd Report of Session 2005–06, HC 754, para. 67.

[39] D. Harris et al, *Compensation and Support for Illness and Injury* (Clarendon Press, 1984).

had even considered claiming damages, 14 per cent had actually consulted a solicitor, most of whom (12 per cent) actually got damages,[40] suggesting that the great majority were valid cases. In the cases in which damages were obtained, a writ had been issued in under half (40 per cent).[41] There were only five cases which ended with a court hearing! This represented 2.7 per cent of the 182 cases in which damages were obtained, but only 0.2 per cent of the 1,711 accident cases in the sample.

In Professor Hazel Genn's study *Paths to Justice*[42] 4,125 randomly selected adults were surveyed to find out how they had experienced and dealt with a variety of problems for which there might be a legal solution. About 40 per cent of the sample had experienced one or more of fourteen types of justiciable problems during the previous five years. Overall, about 5 per cent had done nothing at all to try and solve the problem, about one third tried to resolve the problem without help and about 60 per cent tried to resolve the problem with advice. (The most common first adviser was a solicitor, followed by a Citizens' Advice Bureau.) About one third of the problems were eventually resolved by agreement (in some 3 per cent after the commencement of legal proceedings). Very limited use had been made of formal legal proceedings. In eight out of ten cases no legal proceedings were started, no ombudsman was contacted and no alternative dispute resolution (ADR) process was used. The matter ended with a court, tribunal or ombudsman's decision in 14 per cent of all cases but the majority of these cases were ones in which the respondent to the survey was being pursued rather than him or herself initiating action. Among respondents having action taken against them, over half (56 per cent) said their case had been decided by a court, tribunal or ombudsman, compared with only 9 per cent of those who initiated action.[43]

According to Genn's study, most people therefore do not even use the informal and 'user-friendly' small claims system – see p. 389 below.[44]

A recent study in the NHS suggests that claim frequency is close to one claim per hundred patients damaged by negligence.[45] (The Government's NHS Redress Act 2006 aimed at providing a fast track scheme to enable the settlement without the need to commence legal proceedings of clinical negligence claims

---

[40] *Ibid*, Figure 2.1, p. 26.   [41] *Ibid*, p. 112.   [42] Oxford, 1999.

[43] At p. 151. The Cantley Committee in their report in 1979 stated: 'in round figures, for every 9,000 personal injury writs issued in London there are no more than about 300 judgments. Outside the personal injuries field, for every 100,000 writs issued in London there are fewer than 300 judgments after trial. The figures for District Registries are not dissimilar' (*Report of the Personal Injuries Litigation Procedure Working Party*, 1979, Cmnd. 7476, para. 9).

[44] See also the 2001 and 2004 surveys carried out for the Legal Services Commission by the Legal Services Research Centre – P. Pleasence et al, *Causes of Action: Civil Law and Social Justice* (2nd edn, 2006). Both surveys had over 5,000 respondents. See also P. Pleasence et al, 'Causes of Action: First Findings of the LSRC Periodic Survey', 30 *Journal of Law and Society*, 2003, 11–30.

[45] P. Pleasence et al, 'The experience of clinical negligence within the general population', 9 *Clinical Risk*, 2003, p. 211.

up to a limited amount – initially £20,000.[46] It was anticipated that this would result in an increase in the number of claims.)

For a comparative study of the literature on the use of lawyers see T. Goriely with A. Paterson, *Access to Legal Services: A European Comparison* (Law Society, 2000). The first part of the work considered the evidence as to how and why people use legal services. The second part looked at the actual use of legal services in England, Wales and Scotland. The third part dealt with the use of legal services in six European countries (Sweden, Norway, Holland, Germany, France and Ireland) with regard to personal injury, dismissal and consumer claims.

Who uses the small claims system? Although the main purpose of establishing the small claims system was to provide more user-friendly access to justice to individuals, in fact, like the county court itself, the small claims system is used to a significant extent by business concerns. In 2005, two-fifths of all claimants were businesses.[47]

It is also striking that, according to Professor Baldwin, in the main, individual litigants using the small claims system are middle class. ('Most litigants contacted in this study, especially those who appeared as plaintiffs, were relatively well-heeled and articulate individuals. Over two-thirds of those in paid employment were in professional or managerial occupations . . . Very few litigants were from ethnic minority groups. The genuinely poor make few appearances at small claims hearings, and when they do, it is typically as defendants to face landlords or money-lenders'.[48])

The advantages of 'repeat players'

It is not surprising that the ordinary citizen is apprehensive about starting litigation. He will be nervous about the likely costs, both in terms of time and money. He will worry whether he may have to appear in court – unaware of the fact that most cases settle out of court. He will be unfamiliar with the procedures of the legal system and will not know how to 'use the system'. He will not be in regular contact with lawyers who can take up his case. He will not know how to calculate the pros and cons of taking up the cudgels in terms of the likely outcome as against the costs of the case.

---

[46] The Act was based on the recommendations of Sir Liam Donaldson, the Chief Medical Officer, in *Making Amends*, consultation paper, June 2003 – www.dh.gov.uk/assetRoot/04/0609/45/ 04060945.pdf. Entitlement to compensation would be assessed initially by the NHS Litigation Authority. An offer of compensation would be made 'without prejudice' and could not therefore be used in subsequent litigation. The claimant would retain his right to sue up to acceptance of the amount offered under the scheme. See M. Rowles, 'Does the Redress Bill make Amends?', 155 *New Law Journal*, 16 December 2005, p. 1919. One issue to be resolved was finding an acceptably economical way of giving claimants an independent medical assessment of the claim and an independent legal assessment of the appropriate compensation. The Government indicated that both would be provided at fixed fees without charge to the claimant.

[47] *Judicial Statistics, 2005*, Table 4.10, p. 51 – based on a three months' sample from selected county courts.

[48] J. Baldwin, *Small Claims in County Courts in England and Wales* (Clarendon Press, 1997) p. 166.

None of these factors inhibits the large institution or, at least, not nearly to the same extent. Professor M. Galanter, a noted American scholar in the field of the sociology of law, in a famous study analysed the differences between parties who have only occasional recourse to the law ('one-shotters') as against those who take part in litigation repeatedly ('repeat players').[49]

The repeat players' advantages included the following:

- Having done it before, they can structure the next transaction and thus gain over the one-shotter. It is the repeat player who writes the standard form contract and who can adjust it if a particular clause has been interpreted unhelpfully in a previous case.
- Repeat players develop expertise, can employ specialists, enjoy economies of scale and have low start-up costs for any new case.
- Repeat players have developed informal relations with those who work the legal system, such as lawyers and court officials.
- Repeat players can play the odds. Because they have large numbers of cases they can afford to take risks with particular cases providing they come out ahead overall. The one-shotter by comparison cannot afford to lose his one case and therefore cannot take the risks involved in going for the maximum result.
- Repeat players can play to alter the rules through test case litigation or even by lobbying for legislative or administrative changes. Repeat players can select from among their cases the most favourable ones to fight into the courts and up the appellate levels in order to achieve the best results. This gives them advantages in the area of law-making through litigation.

Once a case begins there are immense pressures to settle. This was always so, but it is even more the case following the Woolf reforms which place such emphasis on the value of early settlement. The CPR actually lays on the court a positive duty of 'helping the parties to settle the whole or a part of the case' (CPR 1.4(2)(e)).

On the process of negotiating a settlement, see further J. Phillips and K. Hawkins, 'Some Economic Aspects of the Settlement Process: A Study of Personal Injury Claims', *Modern Law Review,* 1976, p. 497 and H. Genn, *Hard Bargaining: A Study of the Process of Out of Court Settlement In Personal Injury Actions 1987* (OUP, 1988). For a picture of the strategies of defence lawyers, see R. Dingwall, T. Durkin, P. Pleasence, W.L.F. Felstiner and R. Bowles, 'Firm Handling; the Litigation Strategies of Defence Lawyers in Personal Injury Cases', 20 *Legal Studies,* 2000, p. 1.

For a powerful argument that settlement is not necessarily a good thing, see O. Fiss, 'Against Settlement', *Yale Law Journal,* 1984, p. 1073.

For an assessment of the role of settlement in light of the Woolf reforms, see S. Roberts, 'Settlement as Civil Justice', 63 *Modern Law Review,* 2000, p. 739.

---

[49] M. Galanter, 'Why the "Haves" Come out Ahead', 9 *Law and Society Review,* 1974, p. 95 and 'Explaining Litigation', *ibid,* p. 347.

Legal privileges that promote settlement

Negotiations designed to explore the possibility of settlement are assisted by legal privileges. One such is for negotiations conducted 'without prejudice'. This is the rule that if in the course of written exchanges headed with the magic words 'without prejudice' a party makes an offer or concession it cannot be used as evidence against him if the negotiations break down and the case comes to court.[50] The current trend is for the scope of the 'without prejudice rule' to be narrowed.[51]

Another example of rules to promote settlement is the privilege accorded to mediators or conciliators such as marriage guidance counsellors, clergymen, doctors or even family friends who are working with a couple in a matrimonial dispute. Unless they have the consent of both spouses, they may not reveal the content of any communication from either spouse. In effect such communications are treated as having been made 'without prejudice'.[52]

The pre-action protocols

One of the important innovations of the Woolf reforms is that the conduct of the parties in the pre-litigation stage will be taken into account by the court both during the case and at the end when it comes to allocation of costs. One of the chief means to this end is the pre-action protocols. This was an idea pioneered by Lord Woolf. They were developed by working parties of experts representing the different interest groups in litigation. By the time the new rules came into force in April 1999, pre-action protocols had been promulgated for personal injury litigation and the resolution of clinical disputes. By 2003 they also existed for construction and engineering, defamation, professional negligence and judicial review, all of which are supplemented by a Pre-Action Protocol Practice Direction.

This represents a major new development in civil litigation. The Practice Direction accompanying the protocols says their objective is to encourage the exchange of early and full information about the prospective claim, to enable parties to avoid litigation by settlement and, where litigation cannot be avoided,

---

[50] For an illustration of the rule, see *Rush & Tompkins Ltd v. Greater London Council* [1988] 3 All ER 737, HL. See C. Mulcahy, 'Lifting the Veil on Without Prejudice Negotiations', 144 *Solicitors' Journal*, 12 May 2000, p. 444; J. Ross, 'The Without Prejudice Rule', 152 *New Law Journal*, 4 October 2002, p. 1488 and S. Akhtar, 'Listen Without Prejudice', 153 *New Law Journal*, 11 April 2003, p. 538.

[51] See, for instance, *Prudential Assurance Co Ltd v. Prudential Insurance Co of America* [2002] EWHC 2809, (2003) Times, 2 January, Ch where the Vice Chancellor emphasised the importance of Article 10 of the ECHR. The 'without prejudice' rule, he said, should be applied with restraint and only in cases in which the public interest underlying the rule was plainly applicable. See K. Awadella, 'The Privileged Few', 147 *Solicitors' Journal*, 17 January 2003, p. 43.

[52] See *Mole v. Mole* [1951] P 21; *Pool v. Pool* [1951] P 470 and cf *Bostock v. Bostock* [1950] P 154. The principle extends to cover direct negotiations between the spouses themselves where no third party intervenes: *Theodoropoulas v. Theodoropoulas* [1964] P 311.

to support the efficient management of the litigation. The introduction to the personal injury protocol (PIP) says that its aims are more pre-action contact between the parties, better and earlier exchange of information, better pre-action investigation by both sides and to enable proceedings to run to the court's timetable and efficiently. ('The court will be able to treat the standards set in protocols as the normal reasonable approach to pre-action conduct' (para. 1.4).)

The PIP says that it is designed especially for road traffic, tripping and slipping and accident at work cases in the fast track range, but the 'cards on the table' approach advocated in the PIP was 'equally appropriate to some higher value claims' (PIP, para. 2.4):

> The spirit, if not the letter of the protocol should still be followed for multi-track type claims. In accordance with the sense of the civil justice reforms, the court will expect to see the spirit of reasonable pre-action behaviour applied in all cases, regardless of the existence of a specific protocol' [para. 2.4].

The PIP suggests that the claimant may wish at a very early stage to notify the defendant and his insurer that a claim is likely to be made. It includes a specimen letter of claim. This is completely different from the traditional uninformative letter before action. It should 'contain a clear summary of the facts on which the claim is based with an indication of the nature of any injuries received . . . Sufficient information should be given in order to enable the defendant's insurer/solicitor to commence investigations and at least put a broad valuation on the risk' (paras. 3.1 and 3.5). It states that the defendant has a maximum of three months to investigate a claim and to respond stating whether liability is admitted, and if not, giving reasons (para. 3.7). In the hope of getting agreement on a single expert, before either party instructs a medical expert, he should try to agree the name of an expert with the other side.

The pre-action protocol on medical negligence disputes is similar. It was based on extensive consultation with the major vested interests in the medico-legal system.

The Practice Direction accompanying all the pre-action protocols says (para. 2.3) that if, in the opinion of the court, non-compliance with the protocols has led to the commencement of proceedings which might otherwise not have needed to be commenced, or has led to unnecessary costs being incurred, it can impose a financial penalty on the party at fault.

It also says (para. 4.1) that in cases not covered by a specific protocol, 'the court will expect the parties, in accordance with the overriding objective and the matters referred to in CPR 1.1(2)(a), (b) and (c), to act reasonably in exchanging information and documents relevant to the claim and generally in trying to avoid the necessity for the start of proceedings'.

When a claimant abandons a claim (either wholly or in part) during the pre-action protocol stage he is not normally liable to pay the costs incurred in respect of that work as costs 'incidental to' any subsequent proceedings. The point arose in *McGlinn v. Waltham Contractors Ltd.*[53] The court held that costs incurred at the pre-action protocol stage could be recoverable but that it would be contrary to the whole purpose of the protocols, which were such an integral part of the CPR, if claimants were routinely penalised if they decided not to pursue claims in court which they had originally included in their protocol claim letters. The whole purpose of the protocols was to narrow issues and to enable a prospective defendant to demonstrate that a particular claim was doomed to fail. Unless the claimant had behaved unreasonably, those costs were not recoverable from him.

In October 2001, the LCD issued a consultation paper on whether there was a need for a general pre-action protocol. The responses were generally not favourable with many respondents stating that there would be difficulty in successfully producing a protocol capable of applying to all disputes, and that it would add to costs and lead to delays. However, amendments to para. 4 of the Practice Direction that came into force in April 2003 achieve much the same effect.[54]

Are the protocols a success?

Research commissioned by the Law Society and the Civil Justice Council[55] showed that those involved in personal injury and clinical negligence work felt positive about the protocols. ('By establishing clear ground rules on how claims should be formulated and responded to, protocols were thought to focus minds on the key issues at an early stage and encourage greater openness. This smoothed the way to settlement'.[56]) In fact housing practitioners reported similar changes even though there was no protocol covering their work.

Research by Professors J. Peysner and M. Senviratne of Nottingham Law School, Nottingham Trent University found that the protocols generated better preparation of cases, a more co-operative attitude between parties (including in fields where there was no protocol), more voluntary disclosure and more widespread employment of single joint experts.[57]

---

[53] [2005] EWHC 1419, [2005] 3 All ER 1126, TCC. The defendants sought an interim payment of £20,000 expended they said in costs thrown away in dealing with the abandoned issues. For a discussion of the implications of the decision, see S. Cavender, 'Pre-action Protocol Costs: Settle or Fight?', 155 *New Law Journal*, 2 September 2005, p. 1275.

[54] For details see D. de Ferrars, 'Entry via the Back Door?', 153 *New Law Journal*, 4 April 2003, pp. 519–20.

[55] T. Goriely, R. Moorhead and P. Abrams, *More Civil Justice? The impact of the Woolf reforms on pre-action behaviour* (Law Society, 2002) Research Study No. 43, 420 pp. A 33-page summary is accessible on www.research.lawsociety.org.uk – Publications. As noted above, the research was based on interviews with fifty-four lawyers, insurers and claims managers, of whom thirty specialised in personal injury (PI) work, twelve specialised in clinical negligence and twelve specialised in housing disrepair. In the case of PI work it also included a comparison of 150 claimant solicitor files concluded before April 1999 ('pre-Woolf') and 150 opened and closed post-Woolf files.   [56] Goriely et al, summary of Research Study No 43, p. v.

[57] *The Management of Civil Cases: the courts and the post-Woolf landscape*, 2005, DCA Research Report 9/2005.

On the other hand, it is generally agreed that one of the effects of the protocols has been 'front-loading' of costs not only for cases that are ultimately contested but equally for those that settle – including cases that would previously have settled at lower cost.

See also S. Burns, 'Pre-action protocols under the CPR', *Legal Action*, October 2001, pp. 6–9.

In October 2006 the Law Society proposed a new scheme (dubbed 'Fast and Fair') for handling personal injury cases worth less than £10,000. The claimant solicitor would complete a standard early notification form to be sent within seven days of receipt of the client's instructions, providing enough information to enable the insurance company to consider the claim. No further work would be done by the solicitor for 21 days to give the insurance company time to offer an apology, or admit liability and make an early offer of compensation. After 21 days the claimant's solicitor would send a simple claim form, plus medical report, any other evidence and an offer of settlement.[58]

3. Legal proceedings

Who can sue? Representative parties and group litigation

Traditionally, the system was based on the concept that legal proceedings were brought by individuals, but there was provision in the rules for persons to be represented in proceedings by other persons. They were known as 'representative proceedings'. (The old rules were in RSC Order 15, r. 12; the new rules are in CPR 19.6.[59])

The old rule required that those who were represented 'have the same interest' in the proceedings and this requirement is also in CPR 19.6. The requirement used to be interpreted very narrowly. The classic case was *Markt & Co Ltd v. Knight Steamship Co Ltd*,[60] but gradually the courts have adopted a broader approach.[61]

In public law anyone with a 'sufficient interest' may apply for judicial review and the courts have given a generous interpretation to 'sufficient interest'. Organisations like Greenpeace and the Consumers' Association have been held to have a sufficient interest to bring proceedings in private law cases. Claimants must show that they themselves have a legal right which they are seeking to enforce. In February 2001 the LCD issued a consultation paper *(Representative*

---

[58] *Law Society's Gazette*, 19 October 2006, p 3; and www.lawsociety.org.uk.
[59] Inserted by the Civil Procedure (Amendment) Rules 2000, SI 2000/221.
[60] [1910] 2 KB 1021.
[61] See, for instance, *John v. Rees* [1970] Ch 345 permitting representation of members of the local divisional Labour Party even though there was some division of opinion between the plaintiff and those he claimed to represent; *Prudential Assurance Co Ltd v. Newman Industries Ltd* [1981] Ch 229 permitting representation by minority shareholders of all other shareholders; and, more recently, *Independiente Ltd v. Music Trading On-Line (HK) Ltd* [2003] EWHC 470, Ch and *Howells v. Dominion Insurance Co Ltd* [2005] EWHC 552, QB.

claims: proposed new procedures) which proposed that this distinction between public law and private law cases be removed and that it should be possible for a representative claim in private law to be brought by an appropriate body or person with a sufficient interest – such as consumer groups, environmental organisations and trade associations.[62] But in April 2002 the LCD issued a statement to the effect that a new general provision for claims of this nature would not meet the needs of the diverse situations where representative claims would be beneficial. Instead the Government would bring forward legislation dealing with specific topics.[63] (This has not yet happened.)

In recent years there has been considerable development of group or multiparty litigation. In the United States class actions are used on a significant scale. Rule 23 of the Federal Rules of Civil Procedures allow such actions where (1) the class is so numerous that joinder of all members is impracticable; (2) there are questions of law or fact common to the class; (3) the claims or defences of the representative are typical of the claims or defences of the class; and (4) the representative parties will fairly and adequately protect the interests of the class.

The first massive group action for damages along American lines in the English courts was the claim of some 1,500 plaintiffs against Eli Lilly, the manufacturers of the drug Opren. The actions were co-ordinated by a consortium of a small number of solicitors' firms. Instead of separate statements of claim, plaintiffs were using two-page schedules which referred to a master statement of the claim running to over a hundred pages. In July 1986 Justice Hirst ruled that a number of 'lead cases' should be chosen to be litigated on the different issues of liability. The remaining actions would then be stayed pending the result in these cases.

Technically, the position is different from that in an American class action. Under the American procedure, the result binds all members of the class. In the English system this is not so. Any Opren litigant could in theory have continued to fight his own case after the conclusion of the 'test cases', but this is pure theory. In reality, the members of the class in the English situation are just as much bound by the result. Those on legal aid would not be allowed to continue the case and those not on legal aid would not be able to afford to do so.

It had been thought that the procedural problems posed by the English rules for representative actions could be circumvented by the 'lead case' device where one strong case was selected as a test case. Typically, a plaintiff on legal aid poor enough to be on a nil contribution would be selected. The other plaintiffs would issue their proceedings but their claims would be stayed until the test case was determined. It was thought that the costs of the litigation could be thrown on to the state through this use of the legal aid fund. However in the Opren case the Court of Appeal held that if the action failed, the costs would have to be met

---

[62] On the consultation paper, see P. Bowden and M. Bramley, 'Representative claims', 145 *Solicitors' Journal*, 6 July 2001, p. 629 and a note by Professor Ian Scott in 20 *Civil Justice Quarterly*, 2001, p. 205.   [63] LCD Press Notice 141/02, 26 April 2002.

by all the plaintiffs, other than those on legal aid. This in effect meant that, absent support from the legal aid fund, such actions were impossible to fund.

For the role of the legal aid fund in supporting multi-party litigation in a series of major disaster case – the Zeebrugge ferry disaster, the King's Cross fire, the Clapham and Purley rail crashes, the Lockerbie air crash, the Hillsborough football stadium tragedy and lawsuits against the makers of the Dalkon Shield contraceptive device and Benzodiazepene-based tranquillisers – see the article by the Director of Legal Practice at the Law Society, A. Lockley, 'Regulating Group Actions', *New Law Journal*, 9 June 1989, p. 798.[64]

Woolf and multi-party actions

Lord Woolf devoted 25 pages of his *Final Report* to multi-party actions and ended with eighteen separate recommendations for procedural reform.[65] The new procedures should provide access to justice both where large numbers of individuals had a claim that was too small to make individual action uneconomic and when individual damages were large enough to make an action viable but the number of claimants made the case unmanageable. There should be full-scale case management throughout. Where proceedings will or might require collective treatment, either the parties or the Legal Aid Board should make an application to the court for a declaration that the action meets the criteria for a multi-party situation (MPS). The court itself should equally have the power to initiate such an application. The criteria suggested by the Law Society were: ten or more persons with claims in respect of the same or similar circumstances, a substantial number of which give rise to common questions of fact or law and the interests of justice would be served by treating the case as an MPS. Lord Woolf agreed subject to two modifications. The number ten should be a guide not a rule. In some instances five might be sufficient. Secondly, the common issues need not necessarily predominate over issues affecting only individuals. The MPS format should be sufficiently flexible to handle all the different types of multi-party actions – local housing and environmental actions, consumer cases, single 'one off' disasters and large-scale complex environmental actions and product liability cases, including pharmaceutical and medical cases.

The subsequent procedure would broadly follow the scheme proposed by the Law Society. The case should be certified as an MPS. A managing judge should be appointed to control all the cases. He would make decisions about notification of the action, lead lawyers, arrangements for representing the interests of the group, as to how to balance the generic issues and the individual cases, and

---

[64] The Legal Aid Board played a major role in the development of this form of action. See its reports *Issues Arising for the Legal Aid Board and the Lord Chancellor's Department from Multi-Party Actions*, May 1994 and *When the Price is High*, 1997. This policy was continued by the Legal Services Commission (LSC). Its annual reports give information about multi-party actions funded by the LSC. Such cases are handled by the Special Cases Unit as part of its remit with very high cost cases.   [65] *Final Report*, pp. 223–48.

as to how costs were to be dealt with. Individuals would participate by entering their names on a register. The judge would probably need the assistance of a Master – who might be a Deputy Master or Deputy District judge drawn from practitioners with experience of such cases.

Lord Woolf accepted that there was nothing wrong with lawyers 'taking the initiative in multi-party actions'.[66] The typical claimant in such cases was 'often poorly informed or ignorant of the particular facts, and it will only be the lawyer who recognises the potential for claiming', but the interests of the lawyers and their clients could conflict. Both the legal aid authorities and the court should supervise and control the way the case was handled by the lawyers. Clients might be represented by a 'trustee' appointed and paid for out of public funds who would maintain a watching brief on the public interest elements of the case. There was a strong case for requiring court approval of any settlement in such cases.

In 1997 the LCD issued a consultation paper, *Access to Justice – Multi-party Situations: Proposed New Procedures.*

The CPR deals with the matter in Part 19, rr. 19.10–15 – headed Group Litigation. The rules provide a framework for the case management of 'claims which give rise to common or related issues of fact or law' (CPR 19.10). The court has power to make a group litigation order (GLO) enabling the court to manage the claims in a co-ordinated way. The GLO will contain directions about the establishment of a group register listing the claims and specifying the management court. Judgment orders and directions of the court will be binding on all claims within the GLO (CPR 19.12(1)). The court can select particular claims as test claims and appoint individual solicitors to be the 'lead' solicitor for the claimant or defendants (CPR 19.13(b),(c) and 19.15). The Practice Direction allows costs to be apportioned in advance.

For the position regarding the vital matter of costs in relation to these cases see pp. 573–74 below.

For a discouraging assessment of the future for group litigation orders see J. Robins, 'Another One Bites the Dust', *The Lawyer*, 2 June 2003, p. 18 – www.thelawyer.com/lawyernews. See generally J. Seymour, 'Representative Procedures and the Future of Multi-party Actions', 62 *Modern Law Review*, 1999, pp. 564–84.

See also R. Mulheron's two-part article 'Some Difficulties with Group Litigation Orders – and Why a Class Action is Superior', 24 *Civil Justice Quarterly*, 2005, pp. 40–68 and 'From Representative Rule to Class Action: Steps Rather than Leaps', *ibid*, pp. 424–49. Mulheron argues that although the courts have moved the representative action some way toward a fully fledged class action system, important differences remain and that the way forward now should be reform through legislation.[67]

---

[66] *Final Report*, p. 242, para. 70.
[67] Reform through legislation is the preference equally of J. Seymour in her discussion of the decision in *Howells v. Dominion Insurance Co.Ltd*, 24 *Civil Justice Quarterly*, 2005, pp. 309–15.

Which court?

As has been seen, until 1990 the High Court and the county court had concurrent jurisdiction up to the limit of the county court's jurisdiction (at that time, £5,000). In disputes within the jurisdiction of the county court, the plaintiff therefore had a choice as to whether to start the action in the higher or the lower level court. Reforms in 1990–91 following the report of the Civil Justice Review aimed to shift a significant volume of High Court cases to the cheaper county court. Lord Mackay said that the reason was 'too many cases of relatively low importance, substance and complexity were being handled and tried at an inappropriately high level. This was wasteful of High Court resources, inflated the costs of smaller cases and clogged up the courts, exacerbating delay'.[68] It was provided that personal injury cases had to commence in the county court unless the amount in dispute was over £50,000, but for other cases there remained some degree of choice as between the two levels of court. As from April 1999, however, the rule is that no proceedings can be started in the High Court unless the amount claimed is over £15,000 or in personal injury cases, £50,000.[69] The choice as to where to issue proceedings now applies only to cases involving sums of over £15,000 or in the case of personal injury claims, over £50,000.

There are various reasons why lawyers may prefer the High Court to the county court. They may feel they will get higher damages, the enforcement process is thought to be more efficient, the quality of the judges is likely to be better, the level of costs may be higher. But the court has the power to transfer a case from one level to the other (CPR Part 30). The Practice Direction on Case Management in the High Court states that, if started in the High Court, cases involving sums of under £50,000 will generally be transferred to a county court (CPR 29PD, 2.2).

When, as now seems possible, the High Court and the county courts are amalgamated into a single Civil Court, this problem would disappear. The DCA's 2005 consultation paper *A Single Civil Court?* stated: 'it should in principle be possible to commence any proceedings at any court office' (para. 27). Subject to some exceptions the litigant would issue his case at the court business office most convenient for him. Post-commencement, the system would direct cases to the appropriate venue as part of case management.

What kind of proceedings should be started?

Until 1999, there were a variety of ways of starting legal proceedings: in the High Court, writ of summons, originating summons, originating motion and petition; in the county court, summons (also known as plaint). Lord Woolf's *Interim Report* stated that his new code of procedure would provide for a single method of starting all types of claim.[70] Under the CPR, for most cases

---

[68] Lord Mackay, 'Litigation in the 1990s', 54 *Modern Law Review*, 1991, p. 171.
[69] Practice Direction to CPR, Part 7.   [70] At p. 209, para. 11.

there is now only one claim form regardless of whether it is a case in the High Court or the county court. (However, if there is no substantial issue of fact, a claim in the form of what was previously an originating summons is retained – CPR, Part 8. This is used extensively, notably in proceedings where the only issue is costs.)

As noted above, with regard to small claims, in March 2005 the European Commission proposed the establishment of a European Small Claims Procedure which would apply to claims of up to 2,000 euros and which would apply to internal as well as to cross-border cases. The claimant would choose whether to use his own internal system or the new European system. The DCA's consultation paper asking for views said the Government took the view that there was no legal basis for applying the provision to internal cases and that the proposal was likely to be administratively complex, costly and confusing for litigants.[71] At the time of writing it was not known whether and, if so, when this initiative might bear fruit.

Contents of the claim form

Part 16 of the CPR and its supporting Practice Direction set out the matters that must be included in the particulars of claim (unless the originating summons procedure is used). A claim form must contain a concise statement of the nature of the claim, specify the remedy claimed, including any claim for interest on the judgment and the grounds for claiming any aggravated or exemplary damages, and contain a statement of value of the claim. The particulars of the claim can either be stated on or with the claim form or they can be sent subsequently, in which case the claim form must state that they will follow.

Previously, the court could only grant a remedy that had been asked for and practitioners would end the request for remedies with general words to the effect of 'and such further or other relief as the court thinks appropriate'. The rules now give the court the power to award any remedy to which the claimant is entitled, even if this is not specified in the claim form.

The claim form asks for a statement of value in order to enable the court to allocate the case to the appropriate track. The claim form must state whether the claimant expects to recover more than £5,000, between £5,000 and £15,000 or more than £15,000, or that the claimant cannot say what the claim is worth. If the statement of value is omitted, the district judge will need more information in order to allocate the case to its proper track.

The law distinguishes between 'special damages' where the amount is based on specific amounts that can be precisely quantified – the cost of clothes damaged in the accident, taxi fares to and from the hospital, cost of rented car

---

[71] The covering letter inviting view – CP(L)12/05 – www.dca.gov.uk – Publications – consultation papers – 2005. The Regulatory Impact Statement (para. 10) said that the Government's view was shared by 'most Member States'.

etc. – and 'general damages' where there is no precise way of quantifying the amount claimed – such as damages for pain and suffering resulting from the injuries suffered in the accident. Claims for general damages in the past did not have to be quantified. Under the CPR, if a figure is given on a claim for general damages, this is treated by the court as the statement of value for the purposes of allocation to the right track. Moreover, if no defence is entered, the claimant is entitled to ask for judgment in the amount claimed (though the defendant can apply to have the judgment set aside).

Contents of the particulars of claim

The particulars of claim must include a concise statement of the facts on which the claimant relies. In a personal injuries case the particulars must include brief details of the claimant's injuries and a schedule of past and future losses. If medical evidence is relied on, a medical report must be served with the particulars.

It is optional whether the particulars include points of law relied on and the names of witnesses to be called.

The statement of truth

In order to improve the quality of the documents exchanged between the parties, either the claim form or the separate particulars of claim must contain a statement by the claimant or the claimant's solicitor: 'I believe that the facts stated in these particulars are true'. Particulars that do not contain this statement are liable to be struck out. The same rule applies to defendants and to the statements of all witnesses (see CPR, Part 22). The purpose of the statement of truth is to eliminate claims in which a party has no honest belief and to discourage the pleading of cases unsupported by evidence which are put forward in the hope that something may turn up either pre-trial or at the trial.[72]

The drafting of documents – out with old-style pleadings?

The pleadings are the formal documents exchanged between the parties which define the issues in the case so as to enable each party to prepare its evidence for the trial. Strictly, parties are limited at the trial to matters which have been pleaded – though the court has a discretion to admit by amendment issues that were not pleaded.[73]

Under the old rules the pleadings were supposed to contain a statement of the facts on which the party relied in his claim or defence – not the evidence by which the facts were to be proved (RSC, Order 18, r. 7(1)), but although pleadings were intended to reveal to each side what the other's case would be,

---

[72] *Clarke v. Marlborough Fine Art (London) Ltd (Amendments)* [2002] 1 WLR 1731, Ch D, per Justice Patten.

[73] For a case in which the pleadings determined the outcome of the case with disastrous results for the plaintiff, see *Esso Petroleum Co Ltd v. Southport Corpn* [1956] AC 218.

practitioners were adept at seeing that they did not have this effect. They drafted the pleadings in such a way as to conceal rather than reveal.

The Winn Committee made some acid comments on the state of pleadings.[74] 'A perusal of the RSC Order 18 . . . constitutes a fascinating experience, for a practitioner, in the nature of a trip through territory unknown to him and in a climate which he has not experienced in his daily life. No set of rules could have been more carefully devised, no judicial comment could be more cogently expressed; practice all too regrettably often reveals little relationship to the Rules; the judicial comments pass unregarded':

> 252 . . . It is all-important to make clear in the pleading the causal connection between the facts alleged and the breach of duty which is alleged to flow from them. Thus it happens that a statement of claim pleads that the plaintiff sustained a fall at work (without saying how or why) and adds that this was 'caused' by the negligence and/or breach of statutory duty of the defendants. There follows an assortment of complaints, such as failing to fence a stock-bar, failing to maintain the floor, failing to provide protective clothing, etc. This may conceal a perfectly coherent case, e.g. that the plaintiff tripped in a cavity in the floor, caught his sleeve in an unfenced stock-bar, and was whirled across the room, falling and breaking his ankle, which would not have occurred had he been provided with boots instead of plimsolls. Yet the pleading discloses nothing . . .
>
> 254. In road traffic cases, the statement of claim seldom requires any great intellectual effort and, perhaps for this reason, tends to be a shoddy product. Far too many such pleadings follow a stock form of which the dominant characteristic is that no cause of collision known to practitioners is omitted. In this type of litigation superfluity and irrelevance are rampant vices . . .
>
> 266. We have no hesitation in saying it is in defence that the current practice of pleading calls for the harshest criticism. One of the most experienced Queen's Bench Masters told us that at present 'the defence is a blot on our procedure' and he regrets that trial judges seem to be unwilling to penalise unsuccessful formal denials by an order for costs.

The position in the 1990s when Lord Woolf reported was much the same as that described in 1968 by the Winn Report.

Woolf on pleadings Lord Woolf's report referred to 'incomplete, obscure, evasive or long-winded pleadings' and to 'slapdash pleading and deliberate misuse'. He said that while he accepted that compliance with existing rules would improve the position, 'the fact that they are so often ignored only accentuates the need for a completely new approach and a change of culture'.[75] The answer, he said, lay in a switch to a 'managed system of litigation' which must extend to the way in which parties set out their claims and defences. Mere exhortation would achieve little. It was time to return to the basic functions of pleadings – to state the facts of the case. He therefore proposed that:

---

[74] *Report of the (Winn) Committee on Personal Injuries Litigation*, 1968, Cmnd. 369, p. 237.

[75] *Interim Report*, p. 154, para. 6.

- The claimant and defendant should each set out 'all the material matters on which they rely'.
- The claim and defence would be considered by the procedural judge after the defence is filed.
- The procedural judge gives directions which could include directions to clarify points in the claim or defence. If the factual allegations are so unclear that the matters in dispute cannot be identified, he would hold a case management conference. If the case was on the 'fast track', the conference would normally be on the telephone.[76]

A major aim of the case management conference would be to produce an agreed statement of the issues in dispute. This would take over from the pleadings. As a consequence, the need for further exchanges between the parties (requests for further and better particulars, notices to admit and interrogatories) should largely be eliminated.

The new rules of procedure for both the High Court and county court, Lord Woolf said, should simplify the rules regarding pleadings. One aim would be to avoid technicality. There should be non-prescribed forms of claim for common types of proceedings – possibly in questionnaire format. Statement of claim and defence might face each other in the same document. Eventually this could be computerised. Parties should be required to identify the principal documents on which they relied and would be permitted though not required to attach them to the pleading.

In order to signal a change of culture the word 'pleading' which was synonymous with obfuscation should be replaced by 'statement of case'.[77]

There is nothing in the CPR equivalent to RSC Order 18 dealing with the general principles of pleading. They have to be gathered by looking at what is required in particulars of claim and defences. Lord Woolf's hope, apparently, was that the judges would achieve the miracle of improving standards of drafting by a combination of exhortation based on scrutiny and criticism together with the application of sanctions.

In a decision given shortly after the new rules came into force, Lord Woolf said that although pleadings could now be simpler than before, they were still necessary 'to mark out the parameters of the case that was being advanced by each party', but contests over the precise terms of a pleading were to be discouraged and should take place, if at all, at a hearing where all relevant issues could be resolved. No more than a concise statement of the facts was required.[78]

The cost of initiating proceedings

In recent years the cost of taking civil proceedings has risen very considerably. In 1988–89 the then Conservative Government adopted a policy that the civil

---

[76] *Interim Report*, p. 155, para. 9.   [77] At p. 162, para. 33.
[78] *McPhilemy v. Times Newspapers Ltd* [1999] 3 All ER 775 at 792–93.

justice system should be self-financing. It did so without any public discussion or consultation with the judiciary. Initially the costs of the system that had to be financed by court fees excluded judicial salaries, but in 1991 the Government decided that judicial salaries should also be included. There were swingeing increases in court fees. This policy was fiercely criticised as unconstitutional by Sir Richard Scott, the then first holder of the office of Head of Civil Justice:

> The policy that the civil justice system should be self-financing is, I suggest, indefensible from a constitutional point of view. It treats civil justice as a market place commodity to be paid for by the customer who wants it . . . The system of civil justice is one of the three pillars on which the structure of justice in a civilised community must stand. The other two are the criminal justice system and the police. No-one could seriously suggest that the criminal justice system or the police should be made self-financing. Why should the suggestion be made of the civil justice system? . . . A policy which treats the civil justice system merely as a service to be offered at cost in the market place, and to be paid for by those who choose to use it, profoundly and dangerously mistakes the nature of the system and its constitutional function.[79]

Sir Richard (later Lord Scott) hoped that the Government would 'consign the self-financing of the courts policy to the dustbin'. His call has been echoed repeatedly. In November 2002, the Civil Justice Council, in published advice to the Lord Chancellor, urged that full cost recovery was impossible without inappropriate cross-subsidy, that it arbitrarily limited the nature and quality of the services provided by the civil justice system, limited access to the courts and was wrong in principle.[80] The following month, Lord Woolf, the Lord Chief Justice, added his voice to the chorus of condemnation in a powerful intervention on the Second Reading of the Courts Bill.[81] Indeed his leadership resulted in a defeat of the Government on the issue. An amendment to the Courts Bill, carried by 90–87 on 27 March 2003, required that when setting court fees, the Lord Chancellor must have regard to access to justice.

However there was no sign that the Government would abandon its Treasury-driven policy. On the contrary. There was a further significant rise in January 2005 and in September 2005 the DCA issued a consultation paper (*Civil and Family Court Fees Increase*)[82] proposing yet another major increase. The consultation paper said the Government estimated that the increases would raise an extra £50 million a year and that the aim was to raise 100 per cent of the costs of the county court, the High Court and the Court of Appeal, and two-thirds of the costs of the family courts.

---

[79] Transcript of a speech to the County Court Advisers Group, 16 May 1997.

[80] 'Full Costs Recovery' accessible on www.civiljusticecouncil.org.uk – Publications.

[81] House of Lords, *Hansard*, 9 December 2002, col. 27. For the Legal Action Group's powerfully expressed view, see N. Ardill, 'Courting Trouble', *Legal Action*, February 2003, p. 6. See also A. Jack, 'Court Fee: the New Stealth Tax', 154 *New Law Journal*, 18 June 2004, p. 909.

[82] CP(L) 24/05.

In January 2006 the Government announced that all but two of the proposed increases had been implemented. It also announced that it was undertaking two major reviews. One was to reconsider the system of exemptions from court fees. The second would review the points at which fees are charged with the objective of achieving a closer match of income and 'cost drivers' – in particular through the introduction of trial fees.[83] (The suggestion put forward by the DCA was that fees of £200 per hour might be charged for trials.)

Court fees are not payable by those in receipt of certain benefits: income support, family credit, disability working allowance and income-based job-seeker's allowance. In 1996, Lord Mackay, the Lord Chancellor, abolished this traditional waiver of fees for indigent litigants, but his action was challenged successfully by way of judicial review.[84] The judges found that the Lord Chancellor had infringed a basic constitutional right of access to the courts which Justice Laws described 'as near to an absolute right as any I can imagine'. The Lord Chancellor had the grace (or political sense) not to appeal the decision.[85] In 2003 it was estimated that some five million people were eligible for the automatic exemption from court fees.[86] Another gesture in the same area was the decision announced in 2002 that the fee payable on allocation would no longer be required for claims of under £1,000.

Venue

Pre-Woolf, High Court cases could be started in the Royal Courts of Justice in the Strand or in any District Registry, as the plaintiff chose, subject to provision for transfer to another District Registry or the Royal Courts. Divorce proceedings could be started in any divorce county court. In the county court, by contrast, the rule was that the proceedings should be in the defendant's local court or the court with which the case was most closely connected.

Lord Woolf's *Interim Report* proposed that, irrespective of the nature of the proceedings, the plaintiff should be able to apply to *any* court and it would be for the court to allocate the case to the appropriate track and the appropriate court.[87] This recommendation was adopted in the CPR. The claim can be issued from any court, but if the defendant is an individual and the claim is for a specified amount of money the case will normally be transferred to the defendant's home court, if and when a defence is entered (CPR 26.2).

---

[83] Baroness Scotland, Written Ministerial Statement, House of Lords, *Hansard*, 10 January 2006, WS 5.

[84] *R v. Lord Chancellor, ex p Witham* [1997] 2 All ER 779. See to the same effect the same judge's decision in *R v. Lord Chancellor, ex p Lightfoot* [2000] QB 597 relating to bankruptcy fees.

[85] See R. English, 'Wrongfooting the Lord Chancellor: Access to Justice in the High Court', 61 *Modern Law Review*, 1998, pp. 245–54.

[86] Statement of the Minister during the House of Commons Committee Stage of the Courts Bill, Standing Committee 'D', 8 July 2003, col. 169.   [87] *Interim Report*, p. 36, para. 14.

Issue and service of proceedings

The claim must be 'issued' and it must be 'served' on the other side. Originally proceedings had to be served personally. In the High Court this was done until 1999 by the plaintiff or a professional process server on his behalf. In the county court it was formerly done by the bailiff on behalf of the court until this was stopped in 1983 as an economy measure, since when it was usually sent by the court through the post.

Under the 1999 reforms, service can still be personal but it can also be by first class post, document exchange, fax 'or other means of electronic communication in accordance with the relevant Practice Direction' (CPR 6.2). Service will normally be by the court and the court can choose whichever method of service it prefers (CPR 6.3(2)). (Exceptionally, the Administrative Court will not serve documents, leaving it to the parties to do so.) There are special rules as to how service should be effected on businesses and companies, children, patients and members of the armed services. The 'deemed' date of service is the second day after it was posted rather than, as previously, seven days later.

If ordinary service is not possible because the defendant's whereabouts are not known, the court can be asked for permission to allow service by an alternative method (formerly 'substituted service'), for example by putting an advertisement in a local newspaper. Where a property owner is trying to get back possession of premises occupied by squatters, service on those on the premises (whose names would normally not be known) is allowed to be made by posting up a notice of the proceedings on the door or some other appropriate place.

There is often a considerable delay between issue and service of a writ. The rules used to allow twelve months from issue of the writ for its service. Under CPR 7.5 the general rule is that service of the claim form must take place within four months from the date of issue (or six months if service is outside the jurisdiction). If the particulars are not served with the claim, they must be served within fourteen days thereafter and, in any event, within the overall four or six-month period (r. 7.4).

The Computerised Summons Production Centre In 1990, a computerised Summons Production Centre (SPC) was set up to process summons requests from major 'repeat players' – plaintiffs who issued more than 1,000 summonses a year. Issue and dispatch of summonses is guaranteed within twenty-four to forty-eight hours. Its main customers are banks, mail order companies and utilities – gas, electricity and water companies. It issues roughly half of all summonses. There is a separate Practice Direction for the issue of proceedings by the computerised Summons Production Centre available to bulk issuers. A pilot scheme for issuing the process online – Money Claim OnLine (MCOL) – was launched in December 2001 for claims under £100,000. In the first year of its operation, over 16,000 claims were issued making it the fourth highest issuing source for money claims.[88]

---

[88] 153 *New Law Journal*, 7 February 2003, p. 163.

Case law The case law on this dry procedural topic is an object lesson in how the courts have been struggling to find the right approach to failures to comply with the new rules.

In *Vinos v. Marks & Spencer Plc*[89] V had suffered injuries at work. After lengthy negotiations failed to produce a settlement, his solicitors issued proceedings a week before the expiry of the limitation period but due to an oversight they did not serve the claim form until nine days after the expiry of the four-month period prescribed by the CPR. V applied for an extension of time. Under CPR 7.6 the court can extend the time 'only if (a) the court has been unable to serve the claim form; or (b) the claimant has taken all reasonable steps to serve the claim form but has been unable to do so; and (c) in either case, the claimant has acted promptly in making the application'. These provisions did not cover what happened. The court had not been asked to serve the claim form and V by his solicitor had not been unable to serve the form after taking all reasonable steps to do so. Obviously a procedural slip had occurred, but the Court of Appeal refused to apply the 'slip rule' in CPR 3.10 which provides: 'where there has been an error of procedure such as a failure to comply with a rule or Practice Direction (a) the error does not invalidate any step taken in the proceedings unless the court so orders; and (b) the court may make an order to remedy the error'. The court said: 'the general words of CPR 3.10 cannot extend to enable the court to do what CPR 7.6(3) specifically forbids . . . Interpretation to achieve the overriding objective does not enable the court to say that provisions which are quite plain mean what they do not mean, nor that the plain meaning should be ignored' (para. [20]).

The harsh approach of *Vinos* was applied in *Godwin v. Swindon Borough Council*.[90] In that case the claim form actually arrived in time but by virtue of the 'deeming' provision in CPR 6.7(1) it was deemed to have arrived three days late. In judgments that take twenty-four pages in the law reports, the Court of Appeal held that the deemed day of service was not rebuttable by evidence showing that service had actually been effected in time! Nor could the situation be rescued by application of CPR 6.1(b) (the rules apply except where the court orders otherwise) or CPR 6.9 (the court has the power to dispense with service altogether) because that would be to condone failure to comply with the express terms of the rule about service.

The court's approach was slightly softened in *Anderton v. Clwyd County Council*[91] involving five separate appeals basically on the same issue. The Court of Appeal agreed that the deemed day of service could not be rebutted by evidence of earlier receipt. The aim of CPR 6.7 was to achieve procedural certainty in the interests of all concerned. Justice and proportionality required that there were firm procedural rules which should be observed. General rules should not be construed to create exceptions and excuses whenever those who

---

[89] [2001] 3 All ER 784, CA.   [90] [2001 EWCA Civ 1478, [2002] 1 WLR 997.
[91] [2002] EWCA Civ 933, [2002] 1 WLR 3174.

could easily have complied with the rules had slipped up. However, the power in CPR 6.9 to dispense with service altogether could be applied in exceptional circumstances at least where there had been an ineffective attempt to serve in time (as opposed to a case where the claimant had not even attempted to effect service).[92]

In *Steele v. Mooney*[93] the Court of Appeal had to decide whether the application was to rectify a drafting error in an application for an extension of time or whether it was to ask for an extension of time. Asking for an extension of time was barred by CPR 7.6(3) and therefore could not be achieved by application of the slip rule, CPR 3.10, but here there had been a drafting error in the application for an extension of time and that could be cured by CPR 3.10.

Responding to a claim

A defendant served with a claim has a number of options. He can admit the claim by serving an admission under CPR Part 14, or he can serve a defence under Part 19, or he can admit part of the claim and serve a defence for the part he does not admit, or he can file an acknowledgment of service under Part 10.

Acknowledgment of service

Acknowledgment of service was previously a procedure known only to the High Court. It is now available in all cases. It is appropriate when the defendant is unable to file a defence within fourteen days of service of the particulars of claim. Filing the acknowledgment gives the defendant an extra fourteen days. It is also used when the defendant wishes to dispute the court's jurisdiction. If the defendant can file the defence within fourteen days, the stage of acknowledgment of service can be omitted. (Where a claim has been issued online, acknowledgment of service – as well as defence, part admission and counterclaim – can now also be made online.)

If the defendant fails to file an acknowledgment of service or a defence or an admission within fourteen days, the claimant can move directly to ask for judgment (see default judgments below).

---

[92] In *Wilkey v. BBC* [2002] EWCA Civ 1561, [2003] 1 WLR 1 the Court of Appeal held that the decision in *Anderton* created a presumption that CPR 6.9 would be applied to cases prior to that decision unless the other party could show that he would suffer prejudice or some other good reason why it should not be applied. Avoidable delay would not be a good reason, but the dispensing power should ordinarily not be exercised where service had occurred after the decision in *Anderton*. In such cases a strict approach should generally be adopted. The deemed service rule and the highly desirable certainty which it provided would therefore continue to apply in all but the most exceptional circumstances after the *Anderton* decision. In *Cranfield v. Bridgegrove Ltd* [2003] EWCA Civ 656, [2003] 3 All ER 129 the court said that it could exercise its discretion where there had been some comparatively minor departure from the permitted method of service.   [93] [2005] EWCA Civ 96, [2005] 2 All ER 256.

A defence

As has been seen (p. 70 above), Lord Woolf severely criticised the drafting of defences, especially for failing to reveal the nature of the defence case. Under the CPR, the defence has to be explicit. CPR 16.5 requires a defence to state, *inter alia*, which of the allegations are denied, which are admitted and which are neither admitted nor denied. Where the defendant denies an allegation he must state his reasons for doing so. If he intends to put forward a different version of the facts, the defendant must state his own version. A failure to deal with an allegation is taken as an admission with regard to that allegation (CPR 16.5). Previously, the defendant could put in a simple, totally uninformative denial and the plaintiff tried to get further information by requests for further and better particulars. The position under the new rules is wholly different. The defendant has no choice. With regard to each allegation he must admit it, or deny and explain why, or state that he cannot either admit or deny it.

CPR 3.4(2) gives the court the power to strike out a statement of claim, *inter alia*, if there has been a failure to comply with a rule or Practice Direction. The Practice Direction on striking out a statement of case states that a defence may fall within the rule where it consists of a bare denial or otherwise sets out no coherent statement of facts or if the facts it sets out would not, even if true, amount to a defence. The court can of its own motion strike out the defence or order the defendant to give additional information and, in default, order that the defence be then struck out.[94]

Claimant's right of reply

In his *Interim Report*, Lord Woolf said that the plaintiff need not be given a right to reply, but his *Final Report* allowed that, at least in some circumstances, a reply should be permitted. CPR 16.7 states that a claimant who does not file a reply is taken to admit the matters stated in the defence and that a claimant who fails to deal with something raised in the defence is taken to require that matter to be proved.

[94] For a remarkable example of the use of the strike out power, see *Raja (Representative for the Estate of Mohammed Sabir Raja, decd) v. Van Hoogstraten* [2006] EWHC 1315, Ch. Mr Raja (R) had been the tenant and former business associate of the notorious millionaire Nicholas van Hoogstraten (H). R sued H for an account but before the action came to trial he was murdered by two thugs. H and the two thugs were convicted of the murder. H's conviction was later overturned by the Court of Appeal and on a retrial he was acquitted, but Raja's widow continued the civil action against H. Lightman J., struck out H's defence and counterclaim on the ground that it was established on a balance of probabilities – 'and indeed if it were necessary beyond reasonable doubt' – that H had hired the two thugs to murder Raja to stop his legal action. As the judge put it, there could be no greater reason for striking out a defendant's statement of case than the murder of his opponent with the expectation of his being unable to substantiate his claim. (See L. Flannery and P. Woodfield, 'Deadly Encounter', 156 *New Law Journal*, 29 September 2006, pp. 1468–9.)

Allocation to track

Allocation of the case to its proper track is based on answers given by both sides to a booklet called the allocation questionnaire (Form N150). The court sends the questionnaire to both sides after a defence is filed. It must be completed within the specified time, usually fourteen days. The allocation decision is generally taken by a District judge or a Master (see CPR 26.6). The main consideration is the amount claimed but there are various additional relevant matters including the nature of the remedy sought, the complexity of the facts, law and evidence, the number of parties, the amount of oral evidence, the importance of the claim to persons who are not parties and the views of the parties (see CPR 26.8). If the amount in dispute is under £5,000, the normal track is small claims, but a personal injury claim where the claim for 'general'[95] (as opposed to 'special' damages) is over £1,000 is excluded, so is a residential tenant's claim for damages of more than £1,000 for repairs or if it is a claim for unlawful eviction or harassment. If the claim is for between £5,000 and £15,000 it will normally be allocated to the fast track but again there will be exceptions. To be fit for the fast track the procedural judge must consider that the trial can be completed within five hours and that oral expert evidence will be limited to one expert per party in no more than two fields. All cases that are not allocated to the small claims or fast track are allocated to the multi-track.

The allocation questionnaire asks, *inter alia*, whether the parties wish there to be a one-month stay to attempt to settle the case. (A stay can be ordered without the parties' consent.) It asks whether they have complied with any pre-action protocol, what witnesses of fact it is intended to call and which facts they are witnesses to. There are several questions about expert witnesses, with the emphasis placed on the desirability of single experts jointly instructed. (The questions ask whether expert reports have been copied to the other side, the names of the proposed experts and their fields of expertise, whether the parties will be using the same expert(s) and, if not, why not and whether there is a wish that the expert(s) give oral evidence at the trial.) The parties require consent to use expert evidence at all. There are questions about trial location, legal representation and time estimates. The parties are asked to give an estimate of costs to date and likely overall costs. The final section invites agreed directions (see CPR Practice Direction to Parts 26–29).

By fourteen days after the defence is entered, both parties are therefore required to know a great deal about the case with regard to the facts, the likely evidence and the costs. The Practice Direction makes it clear that the parties are expected to consult one another and to co-operate in completing the allocation questionnaire.

If the solicitors do not give sufficient replies, they are asked to attend an allocation hearing. The person attending the allocation hearing is required to be

---

[95] Damages for pain, suffering and loss of amenity.

someone with personal knowledge of the case and with authority to deal with any issues likely to come up (CPR Practice Direction, Part 26, 6.5).

There are costs sanctions for causing an allocation hearing by failure to return the allocation questionnaire. The party in default will be required to pay – forthwith – the other side's costs of the hearing on the higher 'indemnity' basis (see p. 562 below). If those costs are not paid within the stated time, the court can order that the statement of claim be struck out (CPR, Part 26, 6.6(2)).

Counterclaim

A counterclaim by the defendant is treated like a claim and the claimant can then file a defence to the counterclaim (see CPR, Parts 20.3 and 20.4).

Seeking more information

CPR, Part 18 gives the court the power to order a party to clarify any matter that is in dispute or to give additional information in relation to any such matter 'whether or not the matter is contained or referred to in a statement of case'. A party replying to a request must include a statement of truth (p. 69 above). The accompanying Practice Direction states that a request 'should be concise and strictly confined to matters which are reasonably necessary and proportionate to enable the first party [the requesting party] to prepare his own case or to understand the case he has to meet' (para. 1.2).

If the person to whom the request is addressed (the second party) considers that complying with the request would involve disproportionate expense, he can say so in his reply, with his reasons (CPR Practice Direction, Part 18, 4.1, 4.2). If the second party objects to a request or cannot reply within the stated time, he does not have to make an application to the court. He must simply write to the first party giving his reasons or saying when the reply will be ready.

If the second party fails to respond to the original application, the court will order that the request be replied to without a hearing. The court can make an order as to costs at the end of any such hearing. If it does not do so, the costs cannot be recovered later.

Making applications for pre-trial court orders

Applications (previously called 'motions') have to be in writing. They must be served on the other side as soon as practicable and, save in cases of urgency, at least three days before the application is to be heard. The application can be made by a telephone hearing or a video conference. Where the parties agree on the terms of the order or agree that no hearing is needed, the court has power to deal with an application without a hearing. The court also has the power to make an order without a hearing if it does not consider that a hearing is appropriate. Telephone conferences have now become an accepted part of the system.

Peysner and Seneviratne's research report commented on 'the startlingly wide-spread take-up of case management conferences being conducted by telephone conferencing'. This, they said, 'appeared to be rapidly becoming the norm and during the period of the research most courts reported that a half or more cases were dealt without personal attendances'.[96]

The arrival of the hearing conducted by telephone has now been officially recognised. An amendment to the CPR in April 2006 provided that in the county court *all* allocation hearings, listing hearings, interim applications, case management conferences or pre-trial reviews of no more than an hour in length – or any other application with the consent of the parties and the judge – will be conducted by telephone unless the court orders otherwise. Practice Direction 23B excludes from this new rule applications where all the parties are unrepresented, where more than four parties wish to make representations or where the hearing could result in the final determination of the whole or any part of the proceedings.

This new system was rolled out in stages. London, the last stage of implementation, was due to go live as from 2 October 2006, though in fact at that date only six of the London courts were operating the system.[97]

Amendments

Once served, any amendment to an official document requires either the consent of the other party or of the court.

Judgment in default

If the defendant fails to file an acknowledgment of service or fails to file a defence – provided that in either case the time for doing so has expired – the claimant can normally ask the court to enter what is (and also was previously) called a default judgment. There are some types of case where default judgment cannot be obtained and others where a default judgment requires the consent of the court. (Consent is required, for instance, where the claim is against a child or a patient, or is against the Crown, or is a claim in tort by one spouse against another.) If the claim is for an unspecified sum of money, the default judgment is for an amount to be decided by the court plus costs.

A default judgment can in some circumstances be set aside. It must be set aside if it was entered prematurely or in breach of any of the technical rules (CPR 13.2). If the default judgment is technically correct, the court may set aside or vary it if the defendant can show that he has a real prospect of successfully

---

[96] J. Peysner and M. Seneviratne, *The Management of Civil Cases: the Courts and the Post-Woolf Landscape*, DCA Research Report 9/2005, para. 3.7, pp. 26–7. They found that, if anything, telephone conferences were better rather than worse prepared as 'it was more difficult for a lawyer to operate "off the cuff" on the telephone than in person' (p. 27).

[97] www.courts-service.gov.uk/infoabout/tel_conf/courts_lon.htm.

defending the claim or it appears to the court that there is some other good reason why it should be set aside or varied or the defendant should be allowed to defend the claim (CPR 13.3). In considering whether to exercise this discretion the court must have regard to whether the application to be set aside or vary was made promptly.

Summary judgment

Part 24 of the new rules gives the court extensive power to deal with hopeless cases by way of summary judgment. This power is an extension of the power that previously existed under RSC, Order 14, but whereas the power under Order 14 could only be exercised on application of a party, the power under Part 24 can be exercised by the court of its own motion.

The court can give summary judgment if it considers that the claimant or defendant has no real prospect of success and there is no other compelling reason why the case should be disposed of at trial (CPR 24(2)).[98]

An application for summary judgment can be made in respect of the whole claim or a part of a claim. It can be based either on a point of law or on the evidence or both. At least fourteen days' notice of the hearing must be given. If the application is based on a point of law, the notice must identify the point of law. If it is based on the evidence, the evidence supporting the application must be filed. If the respondent wishes to oppose the application, he must file his evidence at least seven days before the hearing. The applicant must file any reply at least three days before the hearing. Under the new rules an application can be made in a small claims case as well as in fast track or multi-track cases.

The court's approach is treated in the Practice Direction (Part 24, para. 4.1). The old test under Order 14 was no triable issue. The new test is no reasonable prospect of success. Exceptionally, the court can permit the case to go forward on grounds of public interest even though the case appears hopeless.

For sharply critical comment on the new, more restrictive approach to summary judgment see D. O'Brien, 'The New Summary Judgment: Raising the Threshhold of Admission', 18 *Civil Justice Quarterly*, 1999, pp. 132–48. O'Brien suggested that making the test at the summary hearing more demanding had a cost in terms both 'of the substantive accuracy of the adjudication and, more importantly, in terms of procedural fairness' (p. 147). Moreover under the attenuated fast track procedures the parties were already 'being denied access to the full panoply of procedural weapons currently available' (*ibid*). Why then curtail even further their right to adjudication on the merits by insisting that their case have a realistic chance of success? Also, to the extent that funding would increasingly be by way of conditional fee agreements (see pp. 630–41 below), there should be even less need to screen unmeritorious claims since that function would already have been performed by the claimant's solicitor in

---

[98] On this test see *Swain v. Hillman* [2001] 1 All ER 91, CA.

deciding whether to take the case. O'Brien said that the dramatic extension of the court's summary powers might turn out to be the most radical of Lord Woolf's reforms and one beset with difficulties. It would be a fertile field for satellite litigation 'with parties investing a great deal of their resources and energy to fighting and, if unsuccessful, then appealing applications for summary judgment' (p. 148). The 'knock-on effects might be to undermine the very objectives the new rule was intended to achieve, namely speedy and cost effective resolution of disputes'.

However, in 2006 Lord Woolf himself criticised the courts for allowing weak cases to drag on and not using the power of summary judgment enough. Without naming names, he had in mind especially huge cases in the Commercial Court.[99]

There are other provisions in the CPR that could have a similar effect to summary judgment:

- CPR 1.4(1) states that the court must further the overriding objective by 'actively managing' cases. CPR 1.4(2) states that active case management includes, *inter alia*, identifying the issues at an early stage (CPR 1.4(2)(b)) and deciding promptly which issues need full investigation and trial and accordingly 'disposing summarily' of the others (CPR 1.4(2)(c)).
- The court's 'general powers of management' include the power to exclude an issue from consideration (CPR 3.1(2)(k)). (The Court of Appeal has held however that a claim arguable on the pleadings needs to be decided and should not be excluded by exercise of the court's powers under CPR 3.1(2)(k).[100])
- CPR 3.4(2) states that the court may strike out a statement of case on the ground that (1) it discloses no reasonable grounds for bringing or defending the claim; (2) it is an abuse of the court's process or is otherwise likely to obstruct the just disposal of the proceedings; or (3) that there has been a failure to comply with a rule, Practice Direction or court order.

Part 36 offers to settle and payment into court

'Payment into court' has for a long time been a device to promote settlement. The defendant paid a sum of money into a court account as an offer of settlement. If the claimant accepted the money, the case was ended and he got his costs as well. If the claimant refused the offer, the defendant could increase his payment-in. If the claimant still refused and the case went to trial, the matter was determined by the outcome. If the claimant recovered more than the

---

[99] A lecture reported in *The Lawyer*, 13 March 2006, p. 32. Two cases in point were the £500 million claim brought by the liquidators of BCCI against the Bank of England abandoned on the 256th day of the trial and the £2.6 billion negligence claim brought by Equitable Life against Ernst & Young thrown out by the trial judge.

[100] See *Royal Brompton Hospital NHS Trust v. Hammond* [2001] EWCA Civ 550, (2001) Times, 11 May.

amount paid in, he got his damages plus the costs in the normal way. If, however, he did not recover more than the amount paid in, the court ordered that he pay the costs of both sides from the date of payment-in.

Pre-CPR the rule was applied inflexibly. The consequence of 'getting it wrong' was extremely serious as failing to beat the sum paid in could result in the plaintiff losing the greater part or even the whole of his damages.

The trial court would not be informed of the fact or the amount of any payment-in, lest its assessment of damages be influenced – though on appeal sometimes the Court of Appeal might become aware of it. Payment into court did not apply to small claims.

Technically the system applied only where the case concerned a damages or other money claim, but the same principle was adapted for use in other cases. So, if the defendant made an offer of settlement 'without prejudice save as to costs', this was treated by the courts in virtually the same way as if it were a payment into court. (The technique is known as a Calderbank letter after the case of *Calderbank v. Calderbank*.[101]) The Court of Appeal held in *Cutts v. Head*[102] that the court could look at a letter marked 'without prejudice' but expressly reserving the issue of costs. In a case where a payment into court was not practicable, this would suffice. Where payment-in was practicable, however, it would still be required to achieve the effect.

For an analysis of payment into court and other economic aspects of the settlement process, see J. Phillips and K. Hawkins, 'Some Economic Aspects of the Settlement Process: A Study of Personal Injury Claims', 39 *Modern Law Review*, 1976, p. 497.

Woolf on payment into court Lord Woolf, in his *Interim Report* in June 1995, made a number of proposals regarding payment into court:[103]

- That the actual payment-in of money should stop and that instead a Calderbank letter would suffice in all cases. [This was not adopted.]
- An offer should be capable of being made either in respect of the whole case or of specific issues. [This was adopted.]
- The plaintiff too should be able to make an offer to settle – as was already permitted in a number of Australian and Canadian jurisdictions. [This was adopted.]
- If the plaintiff's offer was refused and he then was awarded as much or more, he should be entitled to 'additional costs' in the form of costs on the 'indemnity' basis (see p. 562 below) plus interest at an enhanced rate. The scope of this recommendation was qualified by the caveat that it should only apply to 'multi-track cases' and therefore not to the much larger number of 'fast track cases' because 'it would detract from the predetermined costs regime which is

---

[101] [1975] 3 All ER 333. For a recent exploration of the topic, see the Court of Appeal's decision in *Codent Ltd v. Lyson Ltd* [2005] EWCA Civ 1835 – discussed in E. Gold, 'The Calderbank Effect', 156 *New Law Journal*, 21 July 2006, p. 1156.
[102] [1984] Ch 290.   [103] At pp. 194–8.

an integral feature of that track'. [Adopted as to payment of costs on the indemnity basis and as to interest at an enhanced rate, unless unjust to do so – limited to 10 per cent over base rate (CPR 36.21). Not adopted as to the proposed limitation to multi-track cases.]

• If the plaintiff beats the defendant's offer but not his own, Lord Woolf proposed that he should only be entitled to normal costs. [Adopted unless 'unjust to do so'.]

• An offer by either side should be capable of dealing either with the whole case or with one or more issues and should be capable of being made even before the start of proceedings. [This was adopted.]

• Courts should have (and should exercise) a discretion to modify the normal cost rule in the light of the way in which offers are made – to take account, for instance, of sham offers or last minute offers or withdrawals of offers.

The new rules on payment into court (CPR, Part 36) There are several significant differences in the post-1999 rules. First, the court can mitigate the harshness of the traditional rule under which the claimant would automatically be ordered to pay the costs of both sides if he failed to get a penny more than the amount paid in by the defendant.

When a claimant fails to get more than the amount paid in, the claimant will normally still be ordered to pay the defendant's costs from the latest day for acceptance of the payment in. (As a rule, twenty-one days from the date the offer is made.) In *Neave v. Neave (No 2)*[104] the Court of Appeal said that the effectiveness of the Part 36 regime would be undermined if the ordinary consequences of the payment into court rule did not follow. The offeror was not to be deprived of his costs after having beaten the payment-in without good reason.

However, if the court considers that that is 'unjust', it can decide otherwise. In considering this question, the factors the court can take into account include the terms of any offer, the stage in the process reached, the information available at the time the offer was made and the conduct of the parties with regard to giving information (CPR 36.21(5)).

Secondly, the new rules provide for a claimant's offer – stating what he would accept by way of settlement. If in the event he obtains more, the court can assess costs on the higher indemnity basis and can allow interest at a rate that is no more than 10 per cent above bank rate. The rules provide for Part 36 offers before commencement of proceedings. Such an offer would be taken into account by the court when deciding on costs at the end of the case. If the offer is by the defendant, it must be followed by a Part 36 payment of an equal or greater amount within fourteen days of service of the claim form.

Part 36 payment applies to money claims. Where the claim is not for money the defendant can make a Part 36 offer (as opposed to a Part 36 payment) with

---

[104] [2003] EWCA Civ 325.

the same basic rules. This is the equivalent of the 'Calderbank letter'. The courts have now accepted, however, that in some circumstances discretion (under CPR 44.3) can be exercised to accept a Part 36 offer as if it were a Part 36 payment.[105] In *Crouch v. King's Healthcare NHS Trust*[106] this discretion was exercised in favour of an NHS trust. The offer was made in order to conserve NHS moneys. If this discretion is extended to other reputable defendants, including insurance companies, it would amount to implementation by the back door of Lord Woolf's recommendation in his *Interim Report* that actual payment be no longer required.

Curiously, Part 36 only applies 'where at trial' the claimant fails to beat a Part 36 payment. It therefore does not apply to cases ending with summary judgment. However, in such cases, where appropriate, the court can order indemnity costs and enhanced interest (up to 10 per cent).[107]

Allowing the claimant to make an offer of settlement under the CPR has proved to be a welcome reform. What has proved to be a serious problem significantly undermining the value of payment-in is the uncertainty created by the court's discretion not to apply the ordinary costs rule when justice so requires. Commenting on this, Professor A. Zuckerman, in an editorial note in the *Civil Justice Quarterly*, wrote:

> The result is that one can never be absolutely confident of the consequences of an offer under CPR 36 until after the event . . . The plain fact is that once we move away from the principle that costs follow the event and from the stipulated CPR 36 consequences, the costs outcome becomes wide open and virtually impossible to predict in advance . . . In these conditions litigants find it difficult to assess the consequences of offers to settle with any certainty and are exposed not only to an unknowable risk of costs but also to the risk of further and expensive proceedings about costs. On their part the courts have to devote time and energy to disputes about costs with no certainty that such disputes can be finally put to rest without one appeal or more. The question therefore arises whether the CPR 36 procedure continues to serve a useful purpose.[108]

Cases that illustrate the uncertainty created by the new rule include:

- *Ford v. GKR Construction Ltd*[109] – Court of Appeal refused to interfere with judge's decision to award the claimant all her costs although she had failed to

---

[105] In an article reviewing the cases in *Law Society's Gazette*, 2 December 2004, p. 35 a cartoonist illustrated the point with the caption: 'that's quite plain! If you offer to settle and offer to pay into court, you may be treated as having paid in, but costs might be ordered as if you had not – or the court might make a different order!'

[106] [2004] EWCA Civ 1332, [2005] 1 All ER 207.

[107] *Petrotrade Inc v. Texaco Ltd* [2001] 4 All ER 853. Lord Woolf, giving judgment, speculated that Part 36 did not apply probably because the Rule Committee took the view that it should not apply to ordinary debt collecting. ('By making a Part 36 offer, a claimant could put himself in a position where indemnity costs and enhanced interest orders could be made when it was not appropriate' (para. 61).)

[108] 'CPR 36 offers', 24 *Civil Justice Quarterly*, 2005, p. 167 at 182 and 183.

[109] [2000] 1 WLR 1397, [2000] 1 All ER 802.

beat the sum paid in (£85,000 as against £95,000). She had been reasonable and the defendants had disclosed their damaging video regarding the claimant's mobility very late.

- *Lloyds Bank Plc v. Parker Bullen*[110] – £100,000 paid in, judgment given for £400,000 but only 80 per cent of costs awarded due to exaggeration of claim.
- *Kinetics Technology International v. Cross Seas Shipping Corpn (The Mosconici)*[111] – Judgment beat payment-in but after conduct was considered the successful claimant was ordered to pay two-thirds of the defendant's costs from the date of payment-in.
- *Budgen v. Andrew Gardner Partnership*[112] – Judgment for £330,000 beat payment-in by £44,000 but the claimant only got 75 per cent of his costs from date of payment-in because he lost on a point that took a substantial proportion of the seven-day trial.
- *Verrechia v. Metropolitan Police Commissioner*[113] – Claimant originally sought £141,500. Later made Part 36 offer of settlement of £98,600. Payment-in of £5,500. Judgment for £53,225. Without giving reasons the judge made no order of costs on the basis that the case had been 'an effective draw'. The Court of Appeal declined to interfere.
- *Huck v. Robson*[114] – Defendant offered 50–50 on liability; claimant made Part 36 offer of 95–5. Judge gave claimant 100 per cent but did not give indemnity costs or interest because the 95–5 split was 'derisory'. Court of Appeal allowed the appeal.[115]
- *Painting v. University of Oxford*[116] – Claimant's personal injury claim originally was for over £400,000. Defendants paid in £184,442 but on the basis of video evidence of the claimant's injury they got permission to withdrew all but £10,000. The trial judge awarded the claimant £23,331 but gave her costs because she had beaten the payment-in. The Court of Appeal allowed an appeal on the ground that the claimant had greatly exaggerated her claim. She had to pay all the defendant's costs from the date of payment-in.

4. Getting the documentary evidence

Disclosure (formerly 'discovery') from one's opponent

Under the old rules (RSC Order 24 and CCR Order 14) the parties had to 'make discovery' after close of pleadings. Making discovery consisted basically of making available to each other all documents that the party had or had had in his possession, custody or power which related to any matter in issue.[117] The

---

[110] [2000] Lloyd's Rep PN 51.   [111] [2001] 2 Lloyd's Rep 313.   [112] [2002] EWCA Civ 1125.
[113] [2002] EWCA Civ 605, [2002] 3 All ER 385.
[114] [2002] EWCA Civ 398, [2002] 3 All ER 263.
[115] For comment see G. Exall, *Solicitors' Journal*, 29 March 2002, pp. 288–9.
[116] [2005] EWCA Civ 161.
[117] See *Compagnie Financiere du Pacifique v. Peruvian Guano Co* (1882) 11 QBD 55 at 63.

effect of the Woolf reforms was to retain the concept but considerably to narrow its scope. ('Discovery' is now called 'disclosure'.)

There were two stages – first, making a list of the documents, which had to be done within fourteen days of the close of pleadings and, secondly, physical production of the documents or giving an opportunity for their inspection or copying. The list of documents was in two categories – those that would be produced without objection and those discovery of which was opposed by virtue of a claim of legal professional privilege or public interest immunity (on which see pp. 90–95 below). Discovery took place automatically, but if the opponent defaulted on this obligation, an application could be made to the court for enforcement or appropriate penalty.

The duty to make disclosure as required by the rules lay on both parties and their lawyers. In *Rockwell Machine Tool Co Ltd v. EP Barrus (Concessionaires) Ltd*[118] Justice Megarry pointed out that litigants often had little appreciation of the scope of discovery and the duty of making full disclosure: 'accordingly it seems to me necessary for solicitors to take positive steps to ensure that the client appreciates at an early stage of the litigation, promptly after writ issued, not only the duty of discovery and its width but also the duty of not destroying documents which have to be disclosed'.

Woolf on discovery

In his *Interim Report* Lord Woolf stated that he had received many submissions that in a minority of complex cases discovery created a significant problem in terms of a burden of resources and cost. (There was then and is now no empirical evidence as to the extent of the problem.) Lord Woolf's view was that discovery should be retained but curbed. He differentiated four categories of documents: (1) the documents relied on by the parties; (2) adverse documents which could help the other side; (3) other relevant documents; and (4) documents which could lead to a train of inquiry that might produce relevant documents. The category that generated most of the problem, he suggested, was the third.

Lord Woolf categorised (1) and (2) as suitable for 'standard discovery' and (3) and (4) as 'extra discovery'.

With regard to the fast track case, he proposed only standard discovery should normally be permitted. Additional discovery could be ordered if a case could be made out. In fast track cases this would be very rare. The parties would have to certify that they had disclosed all documents required under standard discovery.

In multi-track cases, Lord Woolf suggested that the approach would have to be adjusted to the needs of the case. The procedural judge would decide on the scope and extent of discovery at the case management conference (p. 117 below). Discovery might be ordered on the basis of a rolling programme.

[118] [1968] 2 All ER 98.

The core of the problem was how to avoid lawyers having to trawl through all category (3) documents in order to eliminate the possibility of overlooking category (2) documents. The Bar suggested that initial disclosure should be confined to documents which are 'capable of being located without undue difficulty and expense'. Lord Woolf said that he supported this approach but he formulated the test slightly differently: 'initial disclosure should apply to documents of which a party is aware at the time when the obligation to disclose arises'.[119] It was for consideration whether this formula should be enlarged to include potentially adverse documents of which a party would have been aware if he had not deliberately closed his mind to their existence.

The new rules (CPR, Part 31)

Adopting the Woolf proposals, the CPR create a much more restrictive disclosure regime. Disclosure on the fast track and the multi-track are subject to the principles of necessity and proportionality under the 'overriding objective' (p. 48 above). There is no longer an automatic duty to disclose. Instead, disclosure is ordered by the court. Whether the court orders it and, if so, to what extent, depends on the court's view of what is appropriate having regard to the amount of money involved, the importance of the case, the complexity of the issues and the financial position of the parties. It is usually much more restrictive in fast track cases than in multi-track cases. The court can dispense with disclosure altogether. Also the parties can agree to dispense with disclosure – typically where disclosure has already occurred in pre-action exchanges.

The normal order is for 'standard disclosure'. This requires the party to disclose documents on which the party relies, or which adversely affect the party's case or another party's case, or which support another party's case, or which the party is required to disclose by a relevant Practice Direction. By way of example, the personal injury pre-action protocol suggests that in a tripping on the highway case the highway authority should disclose (for the previous twelve months) the records of inspection, the maintenance records, minutes of meetings where the maintenance or repair policy had been discussed, records of complaints about the state of the highway and records of other accidents on that stretch of the road.

The definition of 'standard disclosure' represented something of a retreat from Lord Woolf's *Interim Report* which proposed that it should only cover documents that 'to a material extent' adversely affected a party's case or supported the case of another. The dropping of the words 'to a material extent' represented an enlargement of what must be disclosed. On the other hand, the new requirement of disclosure is much narrower than the old rule. Highly material documents that previously would have been disclosed now need not

---

[119] *Interim Report*, p. 171, para. 34.

be disclosed. (The practitioner's bible *Hollander on Disclosure* stated in 2003 that the profession was acting much as before 'as though the change is too radical for lawyers to believe it has really taken place and thus they are assuming it never did occur'.[120]) The critical difference is that whereas previously one had to disclose anything which had the potential of leading to something that could assist the other side, now disclosure is only required if the document itself supports or adversely affects the case, but, as Hollander says, very few documents have the characteristic of the 'smoking gun'. The category (3) 'background' documents which now need not to be disclosed are often crucial. ('Usually, these documents do not in themselves support or adversely affect the case of either party; they are simply the central or core documents, those which are directly relevant to the issues in the case. Those are the "background" documents. They can be vital'.[121])

As has been seen, the original suggestion was that disclosure was only required with regard to documents of which a party was 'aware', but the new rules introduced a duty to search. A party has to conduct 'a reasonable search' for documents which are or have been in the party's control. In determining the extent of a reasonable search, account is to be taken of the number of documents involved, the nature and complexity of the proceedings, the ease and expense of retrieval of any document and the significance of any document likely to be located during the search. The Practice Direction accompanying Part 31 of the CPR says it may be reasonable to decide not to search for documents coming into existence before a certain date or to limit a search to particular categories of documents (Part 31, Practice Direction, para. 2).

The duty to disclose is a continuing one. If a party finds out about a new disclosable document there is a duty to inform the other party immediately.[122]

Disclosure has to be accompanied by a 'disclosure statement' which is supposed to be signed not by the solicitor but by the party personally, saying:

> I state that I have carried out a reasonable and proportionate search to locate all the documents which I am required to disclose under the order made by the court on . . . I did not search for documents: (1) predating . . .; (2) located elsewhere than . . .; (3) in categories other than . . . I certify that I understand the duty of disclosure and to the best of my knowledge I have carried out that duty. I certify that the list . . . is a complete list of all documents which are or have been in my control and which I am obliged under the order to disclose.[123]

Where the party making the statement is a firm or a company, the disclosure statement has to be made by someone who holds an office or position which entitles him to make it – which does not include the firm's solicitor.

In practice the requirements that the disclosure statement be signed by the client rather than by the solicitor and that it gives details of the extent of the searches that were and were not carried out are widely ignored, but the courts

---

[120] C. Hollander QC, *Documentary Evidence* (8th edn, 2003) para. 9–12.   [121] *Ibid*, para. 9–16.
[122] *Vernon v. Bosley (No 2)* [1999] QB 18, [1997] 1 All ER 614.   [123] Annex to PD 31.

sometimes insist that the rules, though tiresome and even unreasonable, be followed.[124]

If a party thinks that the other side's disclosure is inadequate, the court can be asked to order specific disclosure or specific inspection or even a specific search (CPR 31.12). In deciding whether to make such an order the court will take into account all the circumstances, and in particular, the overriding objective, that the means should be proportionate. By the same token, refusal to permit inspection can be based not only as before on the grounds of legal professional privilege (see pp. 90–94 below) or public interest immunity (see pp. 94–95 below), but also on the ground that to permit inspection would be disproportionate. An unsuccessful application will result in an order to pay costs, summarily assessed and payable immediately.

As pre-Woolf, disclosure does not apply in small claims cases. The standard directions on that track merely require each party to supply the court and the other parties with copies of all documents, including experts' reports, to be relied on, not less than fourteen days before the hearing and to bring the original documents to the hearing itself.

The main sanction for failing to comply with the disclosure rules is that the party will not be able to rely on the document without permission of the court (CPR 31.21).

In their study of the Woolf reforms Professors Peysner and Seneviratne said: 'Our interviewees reported that the disclosure regime was working well and specific disclosure applications were much reduced from the position before the introduction of the CPR'. The exception was pre-issue disclosure applications made when the prospective defendant failed to make available material required to be produced by the pre-action protocols. Such applications permitted the claimant to see whether he had a case.[125]

No disclosure if legal professional privilege applies

It is important that clients should be able to communicate fully with their legal advisers without fear that these communications will become known to the other side. Legal professional privilege is therefore an exception to the principle of disclosure. It applies equally in criminal proceedings. Where it exists, legal professional privilege is absolute and is therefore not subject to the weighing of competing public interests – *R v. Derby Magistrates' Court, ex p B*.[126] In *Ataou* the Court of Appeal had held that the court must undertake a balancing exercise in deciding whether privilege applied where the issue was someone's innocence being established. The House of Lords unanimously held that even in that situation the privilege was absolute. The

---

[124] J.M. Collins, 'Disclosure Pitfalls . . . and How to Avoid them', 154 *New Law Journal*, 23 September 2004, p. 1385. Collins suggests that the rule is misconceived since the client does not know what documents are relevant or irrelevant and has no idea whether the list drawn up by the solicitor complies with the rules.   [125] Note 96 above at para. 3.5.

[126] [1996] AC 487 overruling *Ataou* [1988] 2 All ER 321.

principle cannot be derogated from, for instance, by provisions in the CPR.[127] As a corollary, lawyers are generally under a duty to keep the client's affairs confidential.

As will be seen (p. 229 below) legal professional privilege does not apply to communications that take place with the intention *by anyone* to further a criminal purpose. There are also circumstances where the duty to keep the client's affairs confidential is overridden by the lawyer's statutory duty to report – notably with regard to drug trafficking and money laundering. The Proceeds of Crime Act 2002 (PCA) appeared to go much further by laying on the lawyer a duty to report suspicions about the client's possible criminal conduct generally.[128] The interpretation given to the PCA by Dame Butler-Sloss in *P v. P*[129] had extraordinary ramifications. (In a letter to *The Times* a member of the Law Society's Family Law Committee stated: 'if a client seeking a divorce tells her solicitor that her husband insisted on paying a tradesman in cash "to save VAT", their entire assets, as they include assets deriving from evasion of VAT, are regarded as the proceeds of crime'. The offence would be not only that of the spouses but of their solicitors. The only way for the lawyers to avoid committing the offence would be to make 'an authorised disclosure' to one of the specified authorities.) It is arguable that these provisions, as well as being unduly burdensome, may be incompatible with the European Convention on Human Rights.[130] However, in *Bowman v. Fels*[131] the Court of Appeal held that, in the absence of express words to the contrary, the legislature could not have intended to override legal professional privilege. The duty to report created by s. 328 of the PCA did not apply to the ordinary conduct of litigation or any step taken by lawyers in furtherance of litigation. Lord Justice Brooke cited with approval the opinion of Lord Scott that 'communications between clients and lawyers . . . should be secure against the possibility of any scrutiny from others, whether the police, the executive, business competitors, inquisitive busy-bodies or anyone else'.[132]

Legal professional privilege applies to confidential communications between lawyers and their clients for the purposes of getting or giving legal advice whether or not in the context of litigation ('advice privilege') and to confidential

---

[127] See *General Mediterranean Holdings v. Patel* [2000] 1 WLR 272 where the Divisional Court held that CPR 48.7(3) giving the court power to order the disclosure of a privileged document for the purposes of a wasted costs order was *ultra vires*.

[128] If the lawyer knows that the transaction will constitute an offence under ss. 327–329 of the Proceeds of Crime Act 2002 he may disclose communications about the transaction to his Money Laundering Reporting Officer (MLRO) and probably must do so to avoid committing an offence himself. He should equally report to the MLRO where he merely suspects that the transaction may constitute a money laundering offence. In making such a report the lawyer would be protected by the PCA 2002, s. 338(4).

[129] *P v. P Ancillary Relief Proceeds of Crime* [2003] EWHC Fam 2260, [2003] 4 All ER 843. ('An illegally obtained sum of £10 is no less susceptible to the definition of "criminal property" than a sum of £1 million' [56].)   [130] *Family Law*, December 2003, p. 909.

[131] [2005] EWCA Civ 226, [2005] 4 All ER 609.

[132] *Three Rivers DC v. Bank of England (No 6)* [2004] UKHL 48, [2004] 3 WLR 1274 at [34].

communications between lawyers, clients and third parties, with a view to litigation ('litigation privilege'). It covers instructions and briefs to counsel and counsel's opinions. It applies not only to consultations between a lawyer and his clients regarding the client's legal rights and obligations, but also legal advice and assistance to a client who is participating in an official inquiry.[133]

Privilege does not apply to documents obtained by solicitors for the purposes of preparing for litigation if the documents did not come into existence for the purposes of the litigation.[134]

Privilege also does not attach to a communication passing between a party and his non-professional agent or a third party, unless the communication was made after a decision which would lead to solicitors being instructed to start or defend legal proceedings.[135]

In *Re L (a minor)*[136] the House of Lords held by three to two that although legal professional privilege was absolute and could not be overridden even in wardship and care proceedings involving children, it did not cover a report by a pathologist prepared in the course of care proceedings at the request of the child's mother which the judge held could be disclosed to the police. There was a clear distinction between the privilege attaching to communications between solicitor and client and that attaching to reports by third parties prepared on the instructions of a client for the purposes of litigation. Litigation privilege had no place in care proceedings which were non-adversarial.[137]

Normally, if an original document does not have privilege, a photocopy likewise does not have privilege even if the photocopy came into existence for the purpose of seeking legal advice,[138] but if a solicitor has exercised skill

---

[133] *Three Rivers DC v. Bank of England (No 6)* [2004] UKHL 48, [2004] 3 WLR 1274. The House of Lords reversed the Court of Appeal's decision which had confined 'advice privilege' to communications regarding legal rights and obligations and that privilege did not apply where the advice concerned an official inquiry. However, the House of Lords did not express a view about the Court of Appeal's decision that the client on the facts of that case was a small unit in the Bank of England so that advice privilege did not attach to other employees of the bank even though they were engaged in gathering material relevant to the inquiry. For a commentary on the decision, see N. Andrews, 'Legal Advice Privilege's Broad Protection – the House of Lords in Three Rivers (No 6)', 24 *Civil Justice Quarterly*, 2005, pp. 185–93.

[134] *Ventouris v. Mountain, The Italia Express* [1991] 1 WLR 607, [1991] 3 All ER 472.

[135] *Alfred Crompton Amusement Machines Ltd v. Customs and Excise Comrs (No 2)* [1974] AC 405.

[136] [1997] AC 16, [1996] 2 All ER 78.

[137] For criticism of the distinction drawn by the majority in *Re L (a minor)* between litigation privilege and advice privilege, see C. Passmore, 'The Future of Legal Professional Privilege', *International Journal of Evidence and Proof*, 1999, vol. 3, no. 2, pp. 71–86. Passmore argued that this is not an isolated exception to the general principle. He gave a series of other recent examples in case law and elsewhere, including money laundering legislation and CPR, r. 35(10) (an expert's report 'must state the substance of all material instructions, whether written or oral on the basis of which the report was written' and the instructions 'shall not be privileged'). He suggested that the time was ripe for debate as to the extent to which the rules on privilege need refinement to meet new policy objectives based on the principle of 'cards on the table'. See also D. A. Ipp, 'Lawyers Duties to the Court', 114 *Law Quarterly Review*, 1998, 63 at 68–76.

[138] *Sumitomo Corpn v. Credit Lyonnais Rouse Ltd* [2001] EWCA Civ 1152, [2002] 4 All ER 68 overruling *Dubai Bank Ltd v. Galadari (No 7)* [1992] 1 All ER 658.

and judgment in selecting the document for consideration it may attract privilege.[139]

Where a document is prepared for a dual purpose, the test of whether it is privileged is what was the dominant purpose. In *Waugh v. British Railways Board*[140] privilege was denied to a British Railways internal inquiry as to the circumstances of a fatal accident. The report had two purposes – the prevention of accidents for the future and assistance in dealing with the particular claim. The House of Lords held that its dominant purpose was the prevention of accidents and it therefore was not privileged.[141]

The privilege is that of the client and only the client can waive it. It is not lost because the client has died.[142] If, however, a copy of the document has somehow (even through improper means) come into the possession of the other side, evidence of its contents can be given unless the court can be persuaded to grant an injunction against such use on the ground that it would involve breach of confidence.[143]

Material supplied by the instructing party to an expert as the basis on which he is asked to advise is to be treated as part of the instructions.[144] CPR 35.10(4) states that although it is it is technically not privileged, the court will only order disclosure if satisfied that there are reasonable grounds for considering that the expert's statement as to the substance of the instructions he has received are inaccurate or incomplete.[145]

In the case of expert witnesses, legal professional privilege attaches to confidential communications between the solicitor and the expert, but it does not attach to the chattels or documents on which the expert based his opinion, or to the independent opinion of the expert himself.[146] This rule applies to criminal as well as to civil cases. In a criminal trial the Crown can therefore sub poena as a witness a handwriting expert whom the defence has consulted but does not wish to call as a witness, and is also entitled to the production of documents sent to the expert for examination and on which he based his opinion provided they are not covered by legal professional privilege. In *R v. King*[147] Lord Justice Dunn said: 'it would be strange if a forger could hide behind a claim of legal professional privilege by the simple device of sending all the incriminating documents in his possession to his solicitors to be examined by an expert'.

---

[139] *Barclays Bank Plc v. Eustice* [1995] 4 All ER 511, CA.
[140] [1980] AC 521, [1979] 2 All ER 1169, HL.
[141] See similarly *Peach v. Metropolitan Police Comr* [1986] 2 All ER 129.
[142] *Bullivant v. A-G of Victoria* [1901] AC 196.
[143] *Calcraft v. Guest* [1898] 1 QB 759; *Goddard v. Nationwide Building Society* [1987] QB 670, [1986] 3 All ER 264; *Guinness Peat Properties Ltd v. Fitzroy Robinson Partnership* [1987] 1 WLR 1027, [1987] 2 All ER 716; and *British Coal Corpn v. Dennis Rye Ltd (No 2)* [1988] 1 WLR 1113, [1988] 3 All ER 816.
[144] *Lucas v. Barking, Havering and Redbridge Hospitals NHS Trust* [2003] EWCA Civ 1102, [2003] 4 All ER 720.   [145] *Jackson v. Marley Davenport Ltd* [2004] EWCA Civ 1225.
[146] *Harmony Shipping Co SA v. Davis* [1979] 3 All ER 177 at 181.   [147] [1983] 1 All ER 929.

See generally I.H. Dennis, *The Law of Evidence* (3rd edn, Sweet and Maxwell, 2006) Ch. 10; A. Zuckerman, *Civil Procedure* (Lexis Nexis, 2006) Ch. 14.

No disclosure if public interest immunity applies

The second main ground of immunity from disclosure is where it is contrary to the public interest. Such immunity may arise because of the contents of the document or because the document belongs to a class or category which has immunity regardless of its contents.

It is for the courts, not the executive, to determine whether a document has immunity. This crucial issue was settled in 1968 by the House of Lords in *Conway v. Rimmer*.[148]

Before deciding on a claim for public interest immunity the court can call for the actual documents in question and can look at them without showing them to the party applying for access to them, but in *Air Canada v. Secretary of State for Trade (No 2)* the House of Lords held that the court should only do this if the party applying for discovery had shown that the information in the documents was likely to assist his case, in the sense that there was a reasonable probability that it would – not merely a speculative belief that it would do so.[149] See also *Balfour v. Foreign and Commonwealth Office*[150] where the Court of Appeal held that once there was an actual or potential risk to national security demonstrated by an appropriate certificate by a minister the court should not exercise its right to inspect the documents.[151]

There have been many examples over the years of public interest immunity. In *Alfred Crompton Amusement Machines v. Customs and Excise Comrs (No 2)*[152] the House of Lords gave protection to information obtained confidentially by the Crown for the purposes of valuing goods for tax purposes; in *Gaming Board for Great Britain v. Rogers*[153] the House of Lords protected confidential inquiries by the Gaming Board from the police as to applicants; in *D v. National Society for the Prevention of Cruelty to Children*[154] the House of Lords upheld a claim to avoid disclosure by NSPCC of the name of an informant about child cruelty where the mother wanted to sue the informant or the NSPCC;[155] in *Williams v.*

---

[148] [1968] AC 910.   [149] [1983] 1 All ER 910.   [150] [1994] 1 WLR 681, [1994] 2 All ER 588.

[151] See generally N. Zaltsman, 'Public Interest Immunity in Civil Proceedings: Protecting the Supply of Information to the Public Authority', *Public Law*, 1984, p. 423.

[152] [1974] AC 405.   [153] [1973] AC 388.   [154] [1978] AC 171.

[155] See also *Burmah Oil Co Ltd v. Bank of England* [1980] AC 1090, [1979] 3 All ER 700, HL in which immunity was granted in relation to documents exchanged between Government ministers and the Bank of England regarding the price to be paid by the Treasury for the purchase of Burmah Oil shares. In *Neilson v. Laugharne* [1981] 1 All ER 829 and *Makanjuola v. Metropolitan Police Comr* [1992] 3 All ER 617 immunity was allowed for statements given to the police in connection with an inquiry into a complaint against the police, but these decisions were overturned by the House of Lords in *R v. Chief Constable of the West Midlands Police, ex p Wiley* [1995] 1 AC 274, [1994] 3 All ER 420. The House of Lords held that a class claim to immunity in such cases was unjustified since it tended to defeat the object it was designed to achieve. By contrast, see *Taylor v. Anderton* [1995] 1 WLR 447, [1995] 2 All ER 420, CA.

Home Office[156] immunity was refused to hundreds of pages of internal Home Office documents relating to the establishment of 'control units' in prisons; in *Evans v. Chief Constable of Surrey*[157] the Divisional Court said there could be no disclosure of reports from the police to the DPP about a murder in which the applicant was implicated; in *Re HIV Haemophiliacs, Litigation*[158] the Department of Health was ordered by the Court of Appeal to hand over documents for which public interest immunity had been claimed regarding the plaintiffs' infection with AIDS. The 900 or so plaintiffs had shown a *prima facie* case against the department in negligence and the claim to immunity was overridden by the public interest in the full and fair trial of the plaintiffs' claim. (This decision led to an out-of-court aggregate settlement of £42 million for the plaintiffs.)

The doctrine applies also to criminal cases. A spectacular illustration was the so-called Matrix Churchill case in which the trial judge, Judge Smedley, quashed public interest immunity certificates served by the prosecution, designed to suppress evidence about intelligence sources, information held by the Security Service (MI5) and the Secret Intelligence Service (MI6) and high level inter-departmental and ministerial contact over a licence application to export material for a super-gun to Iraq. The judge's decision led to the collapse of the prosecution against the executives in the machine tool company who had been charged with deception in obtaining export licences.[159] It led also to the establishment of the 'arms for Iraq' inquiry by Lord Justice Scott.

Disclosure from someone who is not (or is not yet) a party

Discovery was traditionally only available against the person who was the object of the proceedings. Information or documents in the possession of third parties could normally only be obtained by issuing a subpoena *duces tecum* requiring them to come to the trial with the documents.

The objection that discovery only applied if proceedings had actually started and only applied to parties was considered by the Winn Committee in 1968. It recommended that discovery by order of the court should be available where a claim in respect of personal injuries or in respect of someone's death was 'likely to be made'. The Administration of Justice Act 1970, s. 31 implemented this recommendation, which only applied, however, to actions arising out of personal injuries or death. The power was to be found in s. 33 of the Supreme Court Act 1981.

The Winn Committee proposed a second exception to the general rule with regard to claims for damages arising out of personal injuries or death. This was

---

[156] [1981] 1 All ER 1151.   [157] [1988] QB 588, [1989] 2 All ER 594.
[158] [1990] NLJR 1349.
[159] See A. Tomkins, 'Public Interest Immunity after Matrix Churchill', *Public Law*, 1993, pp. 650–68. For a detailed account of the case, see D. Leigh, *Betrayed: The Real Story of the Matrix Churchill Trial* (Bloomsbury, 1993).

to allow a party to seek an order for discovery against a third party who was holding relevant documents. This recommendation was implemented in s. 32 of the Administration of Justice Act 1970 and was to be found in s. 34 of the Supreme Court Act 1981 and RSC Order 24, r. 7A.

Lord Woolf proposed that pre-action disclosure both from likely parties and from non-parties should be extended to all cases and the Civil Procedure Act 1997, s. 8[160] gave effect to this recommendation (see CPR, rr. 31.16 and 17).

It is not necessary to establish on a balance of probabilities that the evidence will support the applicant's case or undermine the opponent's case – only that it may well do so.[161] Such applications are now common, especially in personal injury cases, and the costs of a successful application are normally recoverable by the claimant.[162]

Medical records

The Access to Health Records Act 1990 established a right for a patient, or someone authorised to apply on his behalf, to get medical records created after November 1990. Note also the Data Protection Act 1984 which gave a person a right of access to information about him which is held in computerised form, but the right to get data on computer is qualified by secondary legislation which states that there is no right to inspect a health record if access would be likely to cause serious harm to the physical or mental health of the applicant or would be likely to disclose another person's identity.[163]

The pre-action protocols on personal injury claims and medical negligence claims (p. 61 above) had a wider provision for access to medical records. ('It is Department of Health policy that patients be permitted to see what has been written about them, and that healthcare providers should make arrangements to allow patients to see all their records, not only those covered by the Access to Health Records Act 1990'.) Use of the forms was said to be entirely voluntary and did not prejudice any statutory rights. The aim was 'to save time and costs for all concerned for the benefit of the patient and the hospital and in the interests of justice. Use of the forms should make it unnecessary in most cases for there to be an exchange of letters or other enquiries' (Practice Direction, Annex B).

The Data Protection Act 1998, which came into force in 1999, replaced the Access to Health Records Act 1990. It broadly made similar access provisions – though s. 8(2)(a) provides a new exemption where supply of the information would involve 'disproportionate effort'.

---

[160] Also the Civil Procedure (Modification of Enactments) Order 1998, SI 1998/2940.
[161] *Three Rivers District Council v. Bank of England (No 4)* [2002] EWCA Civ 1182, [2002] 4 All ER 881.
[162] J. Surti and R. Strong, 'Defensive Pre-action', 155 *New Law Journal*, 21 October 2005, p. 1569.
[163] Data Protection (Subject Access Modification) (Health) Order 1987, SI 1987/1903.

Disclosure from a third party to correct wrongdoing (the Norwich Pharmacal principle)

The courts have developed a further exception to the general rule, under which discovery could be ordered against a third party who has information which is needed to deal with wrongdoing. Thus in *Norwich Pharmacal Co v. Customs and Excise Commissioners*[164] the House of Lords held that the Customs authorities had to disclose the names of persons importing materials allegedly in breach of the plaintiff's patent because dishonest traders did not deserve protection. Lord Reid said that 'if through no fault of his own a person gets mixed up in the tortious acts of others so as to facilitate their wrongdoing he may incur no personal liability but he comes under a duty to assist the person who has been wronged by giving him full information and disclosing the identity of the wrongdoer'. The same principle was applied by the House of Lords in *British Steel Corpn v. Granada Television Ltd*[165] to order Granada to hand over to British Steel the name of the 'mole' who had passed it confidential documents relating to the company's handling of the steel strike. Granada, like the Customs in *Norwich Pharmacal*, was an innocent third party, but the courts ordered discovery in order to permit the plaintiff to get a remedy with regard to wrongdoing.

The same doctrine was applied in *Bankers Trust Co v. Shapira*[166] when the court ordered a bank to reveal the details of a customer's account in order to give effect to a defrauded plaintiff's equitable right to trace his money. By contrast, see *Arab Monetary Fund v. Hashim (No 5)*[167] – disclosure by a non-party was not ordered because the potential benefit was outweighed by the detriment.

Where the power to order such disclosure concerns the press it raises the issue of freedom of expression protected by s. 10 of the Contempt of Court Act 1981 and Article 10 of the European Convention on Human Rights. In *Ashworth Hospital Authority v. MGN Ltd*[168] the House of Lords upheld the Court of Appeal's decision ordering the *Daily Mail* to reveal to the hospital the name of the person who supplied a journalist with information about the notorious 'Moors murderer' Ian Brady. The Law Lords concluded that it did not matter if the wrongdoing was tortious or in breach of contract. In the Court of Appeal Lord Woolf went further in suggesting, *obiter* (at [53]), that it may extend to criminal wrongdoing – but this conflicts with the Court of Appeal's ruling in *Interbrew SA v. Financial Times*[169] in which five media organisations were ordered to hand over to the company a leaked document about a contemplated take-over. In *Interbrew* the Court of Appeal said that if the purpose of the leak was to bring wrongdoing to public notice it would deserve a high degree of protection, but if the purpose was to wreck legitimate commercial activity it would be less deserving of protection. These two cases also establish that a *Norwich*

[164] [1974] AC 133.   [165] [1981] AC 1096.   [166] [1980] 1 WLR 1274, [1980] 3 All ER 353.
[167] [1992] 2 All ER 911.   [168] [2002] UKHL 29, [2002] 1 WLR 2033, [2002] 4 All ER 193.
[169] [2002] EWCA Civ 274, [2002] 2 Lloyd's Rep 229.

Pharmacal order can be made even where the applicant does not intend to pursue court action against the wrongdoer.[170]

In *X v. Y*[171] the court refused to order a reporter to disclose the source of his story. A fine for contempt of court on the paper and a permanent injunction stopping the paper publishing the information was sufficient. In *Goodwin* both the Court of Appeal and the House of Lords had held that a journalist had to pay a fine of £5,000 for contempt of court for refusing to disclose the source of an article, but the European Court of Human Rights held that this constituted a violation of Article 10 of the Convention. The interests of a democratic country in having a free press outweighed the company's interest in tracking down the source of the leak to the journalist.[172]

The 'mere witness' rule

The person against whom the order is made must somehow be involved. It would not be possible under the *Norwich Pharmacal* doctrine, for instance, to order a passer-by who saw a road accident to reveal the name prior to the hearing of the action. He would be a 'mere witness'. This rule was prayed in aid in *Harrington v. North London Polytechnic*[173] by lecturers at the polytechnic who had been ordered by the court to disclose the names of picketing students. The action was brought by Patrick Harrington, a member of the National Front, after he had been prevented from pursuing his studies by other students who objected to his presence. He obtained an injunction against the polytechnic, but when the injunction was ignored by picketing students, Harrington asked for a further order requiring certain teachers to identify persons in photographs taken of the picketing. The lecturers claimed they were not parties to the action and that they should be protected from the order by the 'mere witness' rule. They also said that an order against them would be contrary to public policy since it would damage the special relationship between staff and students. The Court of Appeal held that they were not 'mere witnesses'. In fact they were not witnesses at all since they had not been present at the time of the picketing. They could be made subject to such an order as employees of the polytechnic, but since they had not been given a chance to put their argument, the case was sent back to the High Court for proper argument on the public policy aspects.

Subsequent use of disclosed document

The rule used to be that disclosure was made subject to an undertaking that the document disclosed would not be used for any 'improper, collateral or ulterior purpose' (RSC Order 24, r. 14A). This has now been replaced by CPR 31.22 which states that a document that has been disclosed may only be used for the

---

[170] See M. Amos, 'A Storm Brewing', 152 *New Law Journal*, 9 August 2002, p. 1230.
[171] [1988] 2 All ER 648.   [172] *Goodwin v. United Kingdom* (1996) 22 EHRR 123.
[173] [1984] 3 All ER 666.

purpose of the proceedings in which it is disclosed except where '(a) the document has been read to or by the court, or referred to, at a hearing which has been held in public; (b) the court gives permission; or (c) the party who disclosed the document and the person to whom the document belongs agree'. Even where a document has been read by or to the court or referred to at a public hearing, the court can make an order restricting or prohibiting its use (CPR 31.22(2)). Documents read by the judge out of court before the hearing on which he based his decision were held to be documents referred to at a hearing held in public.[174]

5. Getting evidence from witnesses

There is no property in a witness

The formal position is that since 'there is no property in a witness' one can approach anyone and ask for a statement about the matter in issue – including someone who is likely to give evidence for one's opponent, but the person approached is not under an obligation to co-operate. If he is from the opponent's camp, he will almost certainly decline and, in the improbable event that he might be willing to give a statement, the opponent's lawyers would advise him not to do so. Even the neutral witness may decline, whether because he has already given a statement to the other side, or because he simply does not feel like it or for any other reason. There is no procedure that can compel the potential witness to give a statement. He can of course be compelled to give evidence at the trial by serving him with a subpoena, but no sensible lawyer would call a witness at the trial unless he had previously found out what the witness was going to say, so that is not a practical option.

The rule that there is no property in a witness is set out in the Law Society's *Guide to the Professional Conduct of Solicitors*:[175]

21.10 Interviewing Witnesses Principle

It is permissible for a solicitor acting for any party to interview and take statements from any witness or prospective witness at any stage in the proceedings, whether or not that witness has been interviewed or called as a witness by another party.

1. Principle 21.10 stems from the fact that there is no property in a witness and applies both before and after the witness has given evidence at the hearing.

2. A solicitor must not, of course, tamper with the evidence of a witness or attempt to suborn the witness into changing evidence. Once a witness has given

---

[174] See *SmithKline Beecham Biologicals SA v. Connaught Laboratories Inc* [1999] 4 All ER 498, CA, a decision under former RSC Order 24, r. 14A. For considerations material to an order maintaining confidentiality after the trial has finished, see *Lily Icos v. Pfiza Ltd (No 2)* [2002] EWCA Civ 2, [2002] 1 WLR 2253. See also S.M.C. Gibbons, 'Protecting Documents Disclosed under Pre-action Protocols against Subsequent Use', 21 *Civil Justice Quarterly*, 2002, pp. 254–70.   [175] Online version February 2006 – www.lawsociety.org.uk.

evidence, the case must be very unusual in which a solicitor acting for the other side needs to interview that witness without seeking to persuade the witness to change evidence . . .

3. A solicitor should be aware that in seeking to exercise the right to interview a witness who has already been called by the other side or who to the solicitor's knowledge is likely to be called by them, the solicitor may well be exposed to the suggestion that he or she has improperly tampered with the evidence. This may be so particularly where the witness subsequently changes his or her evidence.

4. In order to avoid allegations of tampering with evidence it is wise in these circumstances for such solicitor to offer to interview the witness in the presence of a representative of the other side. If this is not possible, a solicitor may record the interview, ask the witness to bring a representative, and ask the witness to sign an additional statement to the effect that the witness has freely attended the interview and has not been coerced into giving the statement or changing his or her evidence.

In practice, in civil cases solicitors are very chary about even approaching a witness associated with the other side for fear of running foul of the prohibition on tampering with the evidence. By contrast, in criminal cases both the prosecution and the defence may find it necessary to interview the same witnesses. It was held to have been contempt of court for the police deliberately to impede inquiries by a private investigator working for the defence who was trying to find potential alibi witnesses in a murder case. The accused's alibi was that he stayed overnight at a hostel with three 'travellers' known to him only by their first names. The police had asked the hostel management to ensure that the hostel staff not talk to the investigator.[176]

The rule that there is no property in a witness applies also to expert witnesses. This was established by the Court of Appeal in *Harmony Shipping Co SA v. Davis*.[177] The plaintiffs approached a handwriting expert to advise on the authenticity of a document the genuineness of which was crucial to their case. The expert advised that the document was not genuine. Subsequently he was approached for advice by the other side. Not realising that he had already advised the plaintiffs in the same case, he advised the defendants that the document was not genuine. Later he realised what had happened and told the defendants that he could not accept any further instructions in the matter from them. The defendants, who wanted him to testify as to the genuineness of the document, issued a subpoena requiring him to attend to give evidence. The plaintiffs tried to have the subpoena set aside on the ground that there was an express or implied contract that the expert would not advise both sides and that the defendants were therefore not able to call him. The Court of Appeal unanimously rejected this contention. The court held that the rule that there was no property in a witness applied to experts as much as to witnesses of fact. The only difference was that an expert could not be required to give evidence about matters that were covered by legal professional privilege. Insofar as he had been

---

[176] *Connolly v. Dale* [1996] QB 120.   [177] [1979] 3 All ER 177.

told things in confidence by the solicitors, such information was privileged and could not be made the subject of testimony, but anything not covered by legal professional privilege was available to the defendants as much as to the plaintiffs.[178]

In the United States, there is a procedure to permit a party to take a pre-trial statement from a potential witness. The rule that there is no property in a witness therefore has much more meaning there. Each party can require not only the other party but also anyone with knowledge of relevant facts to answer questions in an oral examination called 'taking a deposition' with regard to those facts and to produce all relevant documents. Any party may take the testimony of such a person either by way of oral examination or written interrogatories. Under the Federal Rules of Civil Procedure a witness, including a party, must give names, addresses and other details of all witnesses known to him. If the pre-trial examination of a witness is oral, his testimony can be used to impeach the witness (for example, to challenge the evidence that he gives at trial). For a graphic illustration of the American system in action, see R. Rashke, *The Killing of Karen Silkwood*.[179] The book, which was the basis of a film starring Meryl Streep, describes the case brought by Miss Silkwood's estate against her employers, alleging that her death was due to its negligence with regard to contamination by plutonium. Most of the inquiries made by the lawyers were pursued through the means of pre-trial depositions. In the end there were over 6,000 pages of such depositions. The case ended with a verdict awarding damages of $10 million. It is difficult to imagine that the case could have had a successful outcome in England, where there is no equivalent procedure permitting a party to require a potential witness of fact to answer questions pre-trial.

Interim remedies

The Civil Procedure Rules, like the old rules, provide for a variety of interim remedies that can be obtained before the hearing of the case. CPR 25(1) lists nineteen different kinds of interim remedies, of which perhaps the best known is the interim injunction. They include interim declarations, orders for the inspection or preservation of relevant property or for information to be provided. The procedure for obtaining an interim remedy is dealt with in CPR, Part 25. (It provides for application by telephone in urgent cases – though this facility is not available to litigants in person, only to lawyers! (Practice Direction 25, para. 4.5(5)).)

Special rules apply to two particularly formidable interim remedies – for freezing assets and for searching premises. (They have been described as the 'two nuclear weapons of the law'.) Because of their fearsome character they can only be granted by High Court judges or 'any other judge duly authorised' (Practice Direction 25, para. 1.1).

[178] See also *Re L* [1996] 2 All ER 78, HL.   [179] Sphere Books, 1983.

A *'freezing order'* *(formerly called a Mareva injunction)* prevents the other party from transferring his assets abroad or disposing of them so as to defeat the plaintiff's hope of satisfying any judgment he may ultimately win. The power derives from a 1975 case, *Mareva Cia Naviera SA v. International Bulkcarriers SA*.[180] The Court of Appeal held that an injunction to prevent assets from being removed could be granted in any case in which the court thought it to be just or convenient.[181] The new jurisdiction was recognised in the Supreme Court Act 1981, s. 37, which made it clear that such orders can be made regardless of whether the subject of the order is domiciled, resident or even merely present within the jurisdiction.

Section 37(1) of the 1981 Act empowered the High Court to grant an injunction in all cases in which it appears to the court to be just and convenient to do so. Section 37(3) extended that power to restraining a party to any proceedings from 'dealing with' assets within the jurisdiction. 'Dealing with' includes disposing of, selling, pledging or charging an asset. The order in effect freezes the assets pending the outcome of the proceedings. It has been held that such an order can apply to assets worldwide: *Derby & Co Ltd v. Weldon (No 2)*,[182] but that such worldwide orders should be granted only in exceptional circumstances: *Republic of Haiti v. Duvalier*.[183]

In 2006 the House of Lords held that a bank which authorised payments from a customer's account in breach of a validly served freezing order did not owe a duty of care to a claimant who was unable to enforce its judgment because of that breach. The bank's failure could be punished by the court as a contempt but that only arose if it knowingly took steps to frustrate the order.[184]

Usually the order only relates to the amount of the claim – leaving the defendant free to use the rest of his assets. The defendant must be left enough to meet his reasonable living expenses and to meet certain debts (*PCW (Underwriting Agencies) Ltd v. Dixon*).[185] The defendant must also normally be allowed to make payments in the ordinary course of business conducted in good faith (*Iraqi Ministry of Defence v. Arcepey Shipping Co SA*).[186]

Mareva injunctions became very popular. (In a case in 1986, Justice Bingham said that such applications had become 'commonplace, hundreds being made each year and relatively few refused'.[187])

The procedure is dealt with in the Practice Direction for CPR Part 25.

A *'search order'* *(formerly called an Anton Piller order)* The other draconian order originally developed by the courts in the 1970s was the Anton Piller

---

[180] [1980] 1 All ER 213n, [1975] 2 Lloyd's Rep 509, CA.
[181] See especially *Third Chandris Shipping Corpn v. Unimarine SA* [1979] QB 645 at 668–69; *The Siskina* [1979] AC 210 at 261; *Barclay-Johnson v. Yuill* [1980] 1 WLR 1259.
[182] [1989] 1 All ER 1002, CA.   [183] [1990] 1 QB 202, CA.
[184] *Customs and Excise Comrs v. Barclays Bank Plc* [2006] UKHL 28. See A. Craig, 'Meltdown for Freezing Orders?', 156 *New Law Journal*, 29 September 2006, p. 1470.
[185] [1983] 2 All ER 697.   [186] [1981] QB 65n.
[187] *Siporex Trade SA v. Comdel Commodities Ltd* [1986] 2 Lloyd's Rep 428 at 539.

order,[188] which permits the plaintiff to enter the defendant's premises to search for evidence. (The court's jurisdiction to make the order was put on a statutory basis by the Civil Procedure Act 1997, s. 7.)

The application is made without notice (previously *ex parte*) to the defendant and is generally heard *in camera* so as not to alert the other side to the application and thus risk that the material may be destroyed.

Search orders are governed by CPR 25.1(1)(h) and the Practice Direction accompanying Part 25. The plaintiff must satisfy the court that he has a very strong *prima facie* case on the merits, that he is likely to suffer very serious actual or potential damage from the defendant's actions, and that there is clear evidence that the defendant has incriminating material on his premises which he would be likely to destroy if no order were made. If the court is satisfied that the effect of such an order would not be excessive or out of proportion, it may order the defendant to permit the plaintiff to enter his premises, to search for goods or documents which are relevant to his claim and to remove, inspect, photograph or make copies of such material.

The plaintiff has to give an undertaking that he will pay the defendant damages if a judge should later hold that damages ought to be paid because of the way the order was executed. The order must be precise. It should be enforced with circumspection and the claimant's solicitor being an officer of the court should be present. The defendant must be allowed to contact his solicitor and, unlike the police with a search warrant, if the defendant refuses entry, the claimant is not entitled to use force, but the defendant may find himself liable to proceedings, including committal to prison, for contempt of court.[189] The procedural requirements set out in *Universal Thermosensors* are now included in the Practice Direction to CPR, Part 25 of which deals at length with search orders. In particular, it requires that there always be a solicitor to supervise the actual entry.[190]

---

[188] The name derived from the decision which initiated this development – *Anton Piller KG v. Manufacturing Processes Ltd* [1976] 1 All ER 779, CA. The plaintiffs wanted to restrain a breach of copyright by a rival firm. They feared that if the defendants knew, they would destroy the documents showing their guilt. They therefore applied for an *ex parte* order, which was granted. The Court of Appeal held that such an order should, however, only be made in an extreme case where there was grave danger of property being smuggled away or vital evidence destroyed.

[189] For pre-CPR cases, see especially *Rank Film Distributors Ltd v. Video Information Centre* [1982] AC 380; *Vapormatic Co Ltd v. Sparex Ltd* [1976] 1 WLR 939; *Yousif v. Salama* [1980] 1 WLR 1540. In *Columbia Picture Industries Inc v. Robinson* [1986] 3 All ER 338 it was held that the order had been carried out in an oppressive manner by the plaintiff's solicitors. The court ordered them to pay the defendant damages of £7,500 plus £2,500 for his company. For discussion and comment, see *Civil Justice Quarterly*, January 1987, p. 10. See generally A. Staines, 'The Protection of Intellectual Property Rights: Anton Piller Orders', 46 *Modern Law Review*, 1983, p. 274 and M. Dockray and H. Laddie, 'Piller Problems' 106 *Law Quarterly Review*, 1990, p. 601. See also the strong decision of the Vice Chancellor in *Universal Thermosensors Ltd v. Hibben* [1992] 3 All ER 257.

[190] For a detailed appreciation of the importance of this institution by someone who had performed the role twenty to thirty times, see T. Willoughby, 'The Role of the Supervising Solicitor', 18 *Civil Justice Quarterly*, April 1999, pp. 103–12.

A variety of other safeguards are covered in the Practice Direction: (1) execution should be on working days during office hours so that the defendant can get legal advice if he wishes to have it; (2) where the supervising solicitor is a man and the respondent is likely to be an unaccompanied woman, he must be accompanied by a woman and (3) unless it is impracticable, a detailed list of what is taken away must be prepared on the premises and the defendant must be given an opportunity to check the list before anything is removed.

The Supreme Court Act 1981, s. 72 cancelled the privilege against self-incrimination in the context of proceedings for infringement of intellectual property (patents, trade marks, copyright etc.) but provided that answers given or documents handed over cannot be used in subsequent criminal proceedings. A search order in such cases is therefore not covered by the privilege. A consultation paper issued by the LCD in 1992 (*The Privilege against Self-incrimination in Civil Proceedings*) recommended that the privilege should no longer apply in civil proceedings generally but this recommendation was not acted upon.

The 'search' (Anton Piller) order and the 'freezing order' (Mareva injunction) were developed primarily in intellectual property, passing off and other commercial matters. Anton Piller orders were often sought by employers against ex-employees to prevent them using confidential information such as customers' lists, price lists etc. They can be used equally in matrimonial proceedings. Thus in *Emanuel v. Emanuel*[191]an Anton Piller order was granted to enable a wife to search at her former husband's home for documents which he had unreasonably refused to produce with regard to his income.

Stopping the defendant leaving the country In *Bayer AG v. Winter*[192] the Court of Appeal held that in support of a Mareva injunction and Anton Piller order the court could also give further relief in the form of a requirement that the defendant hand in his passport and an order that he not leave the country.

Obtaining advance notice of one's opponent's witnesses and of their evidence

Traditionally there was no procedure to enable one party to obtain the names of his opponent's witnesses, let alone their statements, and there was equally no procedure for oral examination of the other side's witnesses in advance of the trial, but in this area there have been some dramatic changes which completely transformed English pre-trial procedure.

The Winn Committee in 1968 considered but rejected the proposal for compulsory exchange of witness statements (called 'proofs') and for pre-trial examination of the other side's witnesses. With regard to the suggestion that proofs of witnesses should be exchanged, the Committee said simply: 'we do not think the time has yet come, if it ever will, when this fundamental change should be

---

[191] (1982) 12 Fam Law 62.   [192] [1986] 1 All ER 733.

recommended'.[193] There was no further treatment of the subject nor any discussion of what made the suggestion inappropriate.

With regard to the suggestion that names of witnesses should be exchanged together with their addresses, the Committee said: 'we equally think that this should not take place. Foreign jurisdictions seem to be equally divided in relation to the exchanging of names of witnesses. Except in some American states the strong tendency of countries operating in a common law atmosphere is against exchange' (para. 370). Again there was no further discussion. In relation to the suggestion that the other side's witnesses should be examinable by some form of pre-trial examination, the Committee said this would so complicate, delay and increase the cost of litigation that it should be rejected (para. 355).

However, although the Winn Committee in 1968 was against a general principle of exchange of witness statements it did favour *some* exchange. It described the traditional approach to litigation as one of 'trial by ambush': 'our present procedures . . . adopt the adversary system as "trial by ambush". The courtroom resembles an arena. It is regarded as good tactics to keep the other side in the dark so far as it is possible, and if one party can spring a surprise upon the other, then an advantage has been obtained by which such party may profit' (para. 131).

Revolution in the rules for the exchange of evidence

The Winn Committee recommended that medical evidence be subject to a rule of exchange and that where such exchange had been ordered, no medical evidence should be admitted at the trial unless its substance had been exchanged in advance. This recommendation became the basis of the rapid change in English procedure which resulted in new rules requiring each side in civil cases, save in exceptional circumstances, to give to the other pre-trial the statements of *any* witness they intend to call. Failure to comply normally results in not being permitted to call that witness at the trial.[194]

By the time that Lord Woolf started his inquiry, pre-trial disclosure of statements of both expert witnesses (RSC Order 38, rr. 36 and 37) and non-expert witnesses (RSC Order 38, r. 2A) had been mandatory in the High Court for several years. Indeed, the matter had gone further still in that the witness statement was normally used not merely pre-trial, but stood as the witness' evidence at the trial itself. That rule was promulgated in January 1995 by the Lord Chief Justice and the Vice Chancellor in a Practice Note[195] stating: 'unless otherwise ordered, every witness statement shall stand as the evidence-in-chief of the witness concerned'. This was equally stated to be the position in the Civil Procedure Rules – CPR 32.4(2) and 5(2).

---

[193] *Report of the Committee on Personal Injuries Litigation*, 1968, Cmnd. 369, para. 368.
[194] For a detailed account of the successive stages of this reform process, see a note in 12 *Civil Justice Quarterly*, 1993, pp. 5–8 and the note in 14 *Civil Justice Quarterly*, 1995, pp. 228–30.
[195] [1995] 1 All ER 385.

In a matter of ten years or so therefore the English system had gone from the position where witness statements were never available before trial to a position where they are virtually always available – and indeed normally constitute that party's evidence-in-chief at trial.

There are however exceptional situations where exchange will not be ordered. In *Richard Saunders & Partners v. Eastglen Ltd*[196] it was held that an order would not be made under Order 38, r. 2A where fraud was alleged and it might be necessary to preserve an element of surprise, or where exchange would be oppressive because there would be great difficulty or expense in obtaining a statement, or where the application is made too late and the preparation of witness statements at that stage would add to rather than save costs. In *McGuinness v. Kellogg Co of Great Britain Ltd*[197] the Court of Appeal approved a decision to allow the defendants to show a video of the plaintiff made by the insurance company's inquiry agent in a personal injuries case – without first disclosing it pre-trial to the plaintiff or his advisers. But the Court of Appeal took the opposite view in a later similar case *Khan v. Armaguard Ltd*[198] on the ground that it was precisely in cases where video evidence exposed the plaintiff's fraud that pre-trial disclosure was appropriate.

Has the exchange of witness statements proved beneficial?

The exchange of witness statements was introduced as a way of improving the process of civil litigation but to some critics it has made matters worse. A county court judge, Judge Nicholas Brandt, published a letter to Lord Woolf in March 1995 in which he said:

> Exchange of witness statements was thought to promote settlements, and, in default, to speed up trials, thereby reducing expense. Experience has demonstrated the futility of these aspirations. The overwhelming majority of cases (about 97 per cent) settle anyway and there is no evidence that this device has increased the percentage. There is overwhelming evidence that the preparation of these statements has turned into a cottage industry. I have talked to members of the Bar who cheerfully confess to spending hours drafting these documents. *Cui bono?* – not the litigant. Incidentally, some are badly drafted, containing much irrelevance and hearsay, leading to applications to strike out and more expense.[199]

---

[196] [1990] 3 All ER 946.   [197] [1988] 2 All ER 902.   [198] [1994] 3 All ER 545.
[199] 'Some Serious Thoughts from Essex on Civil Justice', 145 *New Law Journal*, 10 March 1995, p. 350. For a wide-ranging critique of the cost and delays inherent in the modern insistence on 'cards on the table' – discovery, witness statements, interrogatories, pleadings etc. – see A. Jack, 'Radical Surgery for Civil Procedure', 142 *New Law Journal*, 18 June 1993, p. 891. For similar views see A. Speaight, 'A Bonfire of the Paper Mountain', *Counsel*, November/December 1994, p. 4. Speaight suggested that witness statements gave a significant advantage to the wealthier litigant. If they stand as the witness' evidence-in-chief, the ascertainment of the truth becomes more difficult because the judge no longer has the opportunity of seeing the witness telling his story in his own words. The cost of trials had been considerably increased.

Lord Woolf, in his *Interim Report*, said that his inquiry had received 'a considerable volume of information indicating that the exchange of statements is not proving as beneficial as had been intended'.[200] 'At a meeting of the Commercial Court Users' Committee on 1 February 1995, there was general agreement that it was having a devastating effect on costs. This was because statements were being treated by the parties as documents which had to be as precise as pleadings and which went through many drafts'. A Commercial judge said that 'an enormous amount of time is now spent by lawyers ironing and massaging witness statements; that is extremely expensive for clients, and the statements can bear very little relation to what a witness of fact would say'. A leading QC said that in a case of his, £100,000 had been expended in preparing witness statements.

Lord Woolf concluded: 'there is justification for the concerns which are being expressed about the results of requiring witness statements to be exchanged. The problem is primarily in relation to the heavier litigation. Nonetheless, it does spread to more modest litigation and it needs to be addressed'. He nevertheless firmly endorsed the practice of requiring the exchange of witness statements as a way of ensuring that the parties are aware before the trial of the strengths and weaknesses of the case they have to meet. 'The sooner a party is aware of this, the more likely it is that the outcome of the dispute will be a just one, whether it is settled or tried'.[201]

However the excesses should be eliminated. The new industry devoted to the creation of witness statements would be more likely to wither, Lord Woolf suggested, if the courts adopted a more relaxed attitude to the statements: 'if it is generally understood that a witness will be allowed to develop points already referred to in a witness statement, most of the benefits which are to be derived from the exchange of witness statements should still be achieved, but without the need for exhaustive drafting intended to achieve pedantic accuracy'.[202] (To that end, the new rules state that a witness giving oral evidence may with the permission of the court 'amplify his witness statement' and also 'give evidence in relation to new matters that have arisen since the witness statement was served on the other parties' (CPR 32.5(3)).) Lord Woolf concluded this section with a hope repeated several times in his *Interim Report*: 'in the case of witness statements . . . the solution to the present problem will depend on practitioners behaving in a sensible and co-operative way. If the court is prepared to adopt

In the same issue of *Counsel*, F. Bawdon said that witness statements had taken on a significance undreamed of hitherto: 'witness statements are getting longer and longer, and lawyers are spending hours and hours working on them with their clients. In many cases they became not so much witness statements as lawyers' statements'. She quoted a leading commercial QC: 'the lawyer knows what has to be proved. It is lawyers' language which is used. As a result of statements being so finely crafted, the potential for injustice increased. You are effectively manufacturing evidence'. On abuse of witness statements, see also *ZYX Music GmbH v. King* [1995] 3 All ER 1 per Lightman J. and the note on the case in 14 *Civil Justice Quarterly*, October 1995, p. 228.   [200] *Interim Report* at p. 176, para. 6.
[201] *Interim Report* at pp. 176 and 177, paras. 9 and 10.   [202] *Ibid* at p. 178, para. 13.

a more flexible attitude, the parties and their advisers will need to respond by adopting a more sensible approach to the preparation of witness statements. If they do not, the court must make it clear that they will bear the cost'.[203]

A remarkable further proposal in Lord Woolf's *Interim Report* was that cross-examination on the contents of witness statements should only be allowed with the leave of the judge. 'Such leave should not be given for cross-examination in detail. Nor should it usually be necessary even when a more significant feature is relied upon. The advocate's comment will be all that the judge will usually require'![204] This proved too radical. In the new rules the proposal that cross-examination should require the permission of the court was adopted for hearings other than a trial but was not adopted for the trial itself (CPR 32.7).

Who can inspect the witness statements?

CPR 32.13(1) provides that a witness statement that stands as evidence-in-chief is open to inspection 'during the course of the trial' unless the court otherwise orders.

Anyone can ask for a direction that a witness statement is not open to inspection (CPR 32.13(2)), but the court will not give such a direction unless it thinks it should because of the interests of justice, the public interest, the nature of expert medical evidence, the nature of any confidential information in the statement, or the need to protect the interests of a child or patient (CPR 32.13(3)).

Under the former rules[205] the presumption was that witness statements were not open to inspection but anyone, such as a media representative, could ask for a direction permitting inspection. If granted, such inspection could take place both during the trial and beyond the end of the trial. The presumption is now reversed but the time for inspection appears to be restricted to the trial. The *White Book* suggests that presumably an interested person could apply for a direction that inspection be permitted after the end of the trial.[206]

The expert witness in the pre-trial process

As has been seen, the pre-Woolf rules required the parties to exchange the reports and statements of the experts on whom they intend to rely at the trial. In his *Interim Report* Lord Woolf said that the subject of expert evidence had caused his inquiry much concern. Concern had been expressed in particular that the need to engage experts was 'a source of excessive expense, delay and in some cases, increased complexity through the excessive or inappropriate use of experts'.[207] Concern had also been expressed regarding a lack of independence of experts.

Most of the problems with expert evidence arose because the expert was initially recruited as part of the team and then had to change roles and seek to

---

[203] *Ibid* at p. 179, para. 21.   [204] *Ibid* at p. 179, para. 18.
[205] RSC Order 38, r. 2A(12)–(16) and CCR Order 20, r. 12A(12)–(16).
[206] *Civil Procedure*, 2006, p. 830.   [207] *Interim Report* at p. 181, para. 1.

provide the independent expert evidence which the court was entitled to expect. The judges often exercised their power to ask the experts to meet to try to agree, but this did not seem to deal with the problem of the partisan approach of the respective experts. Before such meetings, the experts were quite often instructed by their respective parties not to agree to anything. Alternatively they were told that anything agreed between the experts had to be referred back to the lawyers for ratification.

Lord Woolf cited an editorial in the Bar's journal *Counsel* in November/ December 1994 which said that expert witnesses were 'hired guns'. There was, the editorial suggested, a 'new breed of litigation hangers-on, whose main expertise is to craft reports which will conceal anything that might be to the dis- advantage of their clients'. The disclosure of expert reports 'which originally seemed eminently sensible, has degenerated into a costly second tier of written advocacy'. This 'deplorable development' had been unwittingly encouraged by a generation of judges who wanted to read experts' reports before coming into court and by Practice Directions stipulating that the reports be lodged in court to enable them to do so.

Waiting for experts' reports, Lord Woolf said, was also a cause of much delay. It was not uncommon for six to nine months to elapse between a request for a report and its delivery.[208]

This unhappy situation had become institutionalised. Lawyers repeatedly instructed a limited class of consultants for reports. There was a serious short- age of suitable experts. The best doctors tended also to be the busiest.

Lord Woolf proposed changes that would address these issues:

- In multi-track cases the judge at the initial case management conference would distil the issues from the parties' statements of case and, if necessary, would decide what expert evidence was needed on each issue. The key issues should then be narrowed through exchange of experts' reports and through meetings of experts, so that only areas of disagreement would have to be decided by the court.[209]
- In some cases the court should appoint an independent expert. There was already power to do so under RSC Order 40 on application by either party – a power that was hardly ever used. Parties did not like it because the cost was in addition to their own experts and they did not trust the court expert. Lord Woolf said these were real concerns, but 'as long as they are borne in mind, there will be cases where it will be the best course to appoint an independent expert'.[210] If the parties could not agree on the appropriate independent expert, the relevant professional body could be asked to make the appointment.
- Rules of court should permit the court to appoint an independent expert of its own motion and to limit the parties' power to call any expert save under

[208] *Interim Report* at p. 184, para. 12.   [209] *Ibid* at p. 185, para. 18.
[210] *Ibid* at p. 186, para. 22.

the direction of the court.[211] This would not however prevent the parties from having their own expert to guide them, especially with regard to cross-examination of any other expert who gave evidence. The additional cost of the neutral expert would usually be justified 'by helping to achieve a settlement, or in the assistance he will provide to the judge'.[212] There should be a wide power for the court of its own motion to refer issues to experts either for determination or report.

- All experts should address their reports to the court. Any instructions they received from the party employing them should be disclosed in the report. The report should end by a declaration that it included everything the expert regarded as relevant.[213]

- If experts met at the direction of the court it should be understood that they were under a duty if possible to reach any agreement that was appropriate. If they could not do so they should specify the reasons. It should be unprofessional conduct for an expert to accept instructions not to reach agreement at such a meeting. Once an expert had been instructed to prepare a report for use of the court, any communications between the expert and the client or his advisers should no longer be privileged.[214]

- No subpoena for attendance of a medical expert should be issued without leave of the procedural judge.[215]

- In fast track cases, because the timetable was very tight and trial would be limited to three hours, it would be necessary for the court to be able to resolve expert issues without oral evidence. In order to achieve that the court should choose from among the following options: (1) the joint appointment of an expert at the outset, chosen, if possible by the parties, if not by the court; failing that no more than one expert per side; (2) separate reports from the experts with the court deciding the issue on the basis of the reports plus argument by counsel; or (3) the reference of the issue to an expert to determine or report when the expert would communicate with experts appointed by the parties before coming to his conclusion.[216]

In his *Final Report* Lord Woolf devoted fifteen pages to the problem of expert evidence. He said that there had been widespread agreement with his criticisms of the way in which expert evidence was used, but his specific proposals had 'provoked more opposition than any of [his] other recommendations'.[217] Most respondents favoured the retention of the full-scale adversarial use of expert evidence and resisted proposals for wider use of single experts ('the idea is anathema to many members of the legal profession') and for disclosure of communications between experts and their instructing lawyers.

The basic premise of his approach, he said, was that the expert's function was to assist the court. He did not recommend a court-appointed expert or a single

---

[211] *Ibid* at p. 187, para. 23.   [212] *Ibid.*   [213] *Ibid* at p. 188, para. 27.
[214] *Ibid* at p. 188, para. 28.   [215] *Ibid* at p. 189, para. 29.   [216] *Ibid* at pp. 189–90, para. 32.
[217] *Final Report* at p. 137, para. 5.

expert for every case. The court should have a range of options. The appointment of a single expert 'would not necessarily deprive the parties of the right to cross-examine, or even to call their own experts in addition to the neutral expert if that were justified by the scale of the case'.[218]

Lord Woolf admitted that, given the strength of opposition to his proposals, 'it would not be realistic to expect a significant shift towards single experts in the short term',[219] but it was possible to initiate a shift in that direction. The rules should specify that as a general principle single experts should be used where the issue concerned an established area of knowledge and where it was not necessary to sample a range of opinions. Where two experts were appointed they should if possible write a joint report. Expert reports should contain the contents of all written and oral instructions.

The CPR regime In the CPR, expert evidence is treated in Part 35. Rule 35.3 states that 'it is the duty of an expert to help the court' and 'this duty overrides any obligation' to those instructing him.[220] No expert may be called and no expert evidence may be put in evidence without the court's permission (CPR 35.4). The court will consider whether an expert's report is necessary. (The *White Book* says: 'it can be very difficult for the parties and their lawyers to anticipate in advance when the court will decide that expert evidence is necessary'.[221]) The accompanying Practice Direction starts with the statement: 'Part 35 is intended to limit the use of oral expert evidence to that which is reasonably required. In addition, where possible, matters requiring expert evidence should be dealt with by a single expert'. In fast track cases an expert will only be directed to attend a hearing if it is necessary in the interests of justice (CPR 35.5). That would not prevent either side from asking the expert to attend but that might have to be at their expense.

A procedural innovation was that each side can put written questions to the other side's expert. If the expert fails to answer such questions, the court can direct that the expert's evidence not be admitted or that his fees not be recoverable from the other side (CPR 35.6). The court can direct that the evidence on an issue be given by one expert only (CPR 35.7). If the parties cannot agree on selecting the single expert, the court can select him from a list prepared by the parties (CPR 35.7). The fact that the defendant does not object to the expert proposed and then used by the claimant does not mean that he should be regarded as an expert who has been jointly instructed whose report is available to both sides. The claimant retains his privilege regarding the expert's report.[222]

---

[218] *Final Report* at p. 141, para. 17. In *Daniels v. Walker* [2000] 1 WLR 1382 the Court of Appeal (including Lord Woolf) held that the fact that a joint expert had been instructed did not preclude a party who was dissatisfied with the joint expert's report being allowed to instruct and call his own expert.   [219] *Final Report* at p. 141, para. 20.

[220] For cases illustrating the point, see J. Hughes, 'Expert Evidence: Three Key Lessons from Recent Case Law', 153 *New Law Journal*, 28 February 2003, p. 291.

[221] *Civil Procedure*, 2006, 35.4.1.

[222] *Carlson v. Townsend* [2001] EWCA Civ 511, [2001] 3 All ER 663.

Both sides can instruct the single expert provided they send a copy of the instructions to the other party (CPR 35.8). However neither can meet with the expert in the absence of the other.[223] The court can limit the amount that can be paid to the expert (CPR 35.8).[224] The expert's report must state the substance of all material instructions, whether written or oral, on the basis of which the report was written (CPR 35.10).[225] The expert's report must state that 'the opinions I have expressed represent my true and complete professional opinion'. Where there is more than one expert, the court can direct them to meet to try to reach agreement, failing which to report as to the nature of their disagreement (CPR 35.12).

In December 2001 the official *Code of Guidance on Expert Evidence* was published after a long gestation period. The Code was not annexed to the CPR – though it is included in the *White Book* at the end of Part 35. In July 2005 the Civil Justice Council launched the *Protocol for the Instruction of Experts to give Evidence in the Civil Courts*.[226] The Protocol replaced the *Code of Guidance.* (It can be accessed on the Website of the Expert Witness Institute – www.ewi.org.uk – the law and you.[227])

There have been cases where the courts have exerted a new strong disciplinarian role vis-à-vis experts. In *Stevens v. Gullis*,[228] for instance, the Court of Appeal dismissed an appeal after the trial judge had refused to allow an expert witness to be called after he had failed to comply with the requirements of PD35 (which only came into force a month later). Lord Woolf said of the expert that 'he demonstrated by his conduct that he had no conception of the requirements placed upon an expert under the CPR'.

The LCD's August 2002 report on the Woolf reforms[229] compared a sample of 1997 pre-CPR cases with a sample of 2000–01 post-CPR cases. In the 1997 sample, in 8 per cent of the cases an expert had been appointed by one party only. In the post-CPR sample the proportion (9 per cent) was about the same. In the 1997 sample, in 12 per cent of cases both parties had appointed experts.

[223] *Peet v. Mid-Kent Healthcare NHS Trust* [2000] EWCA Civ 1703, [2002] 1 WLR 210, [2002] 3 All ER 688.

[224] In February 1999 District judge Frenkel wrote: 'under the present regime, the total cost of calling two orthopaedic experts can be £2,000' (149 *New Law Journal*, 19 February 1999, p. 254).

[225] For a discussion of the problem of the loss of legal privilege in the context of this rule, see C. Phipps, 'Being Frank with Experts', 144 *Solicitors' Journal*, 4 February 2000, p. 90.

[226] K. Elsmore and C. Langford, 'A New, Single Protocol – with Teeth', 155 *New Law Journal*, 29 July 2005, p. 1155.

[227] The Protocol (para. 7.6) states that expert witnesses may not work on the basis of a fee contingent on the outcome of the case. The logic behind this has been queried. 'So, what then, is the difference between lawyers for whom conditional fees are ethical and expert witnesses for whom they are not?' (J. Jacob, *Civil Litigation Practice and Procedure in a Shifting Culture*, 2001, p. 104).

The launch of the Protocol coincided with the release of the Code of Practice for Experts (covering Europe) agreed jointly by the Academy of Experts and the Expert Witnesses Institute.   [228] [2000] 1 All ER 527.

[229] *Further Findings: A Continuing Evaluation of the Civil Justice Reforms.*

In the post-CPR sample the proportion (9 per cent) had gone down. In the 1997 sample there had been no cases of single joint experts. In the post-CPR sample there was a joint expert in 15 per cent of cases.[230]

What is striking in these figures is that although single joint experts have clearly become an established feature of the system, especially in fast track cases, parties are still being allowed to employ their own experts where the case justifies it. As Sir Louis Blom-Cooper QC, Chairman of the Expert Witness Institute, put it:

> The underlying fear within the legal profession that the single joint expert would be the thin edge of the wedge, inexorably adopting the exclusivity of court-appointed experts in the European fashion, has distinctly not been realised . . . Expert witnesses are still called by the respective parties; as such the expert's overriding duty to the court, cannot of itself erase the image of partisanship so redolent of the English mode of civil trial. Thus the reforms in Part 35 do not substantially detract from, or even seriously impinge upon, the English way of conducting civil litigation.[231]

When there is a single joint expert it is usually someone agreed between the parties. Typically, the claimant's solicitor puts forward two or three names and the defendants agree to one. The process of having to get the other side's consent to a name obviously promotes the use of experts who have a reputation for being neutral and fair-minded as opposed to those known to be fiercely partisan. In the research by Goriely et al[232] respondents concerned with personal injury litigation were reported as welcoming the fact that experts were now less partisan and that they were instructed in a more neutral way. The research by Professors Peysner and Seneviratne came to the same conclusion: 'the overall effect of [the Woolf reforms] is that the days of the "hired gun", the expert generally instructed by one side only and perceived to be "pro-claimant" or "pro-defendant", are largely over and neither practitioners nor judges expressed any nostalgia'.[233]

However, the single joint expert does not mean that the parties do not also have their own experts. Preparing effective instructions and written questions to a single joint expert requires skill in the relevant field, so the use of 'shadow' experts to advise rather than to write reports has increased.[234]

Sometimes the court, having first directed that there be a single joint expert, has agreed to allow a party dissatisfied with the joint expert's report to instruct a different expert.[235]

---

[230] Figure 9, p. 15.

[231] 'Experts and Assessors: Past Present and Future', 21 *Civil Justice Quarterly*, 2002, p. 341 at 350.

[232] *More Civil Justice? The impact of the Woolf reforms on pre-action behaviour*, 2002.

[233] *The Management of Civil Cases: the Courts and the Post-Woolf Landscape*, DCA Research Report 9/2005, para. 3.6.

[234] D. Hall, 'Under Scrutiny', 145 *Solicitors' Journal*, 14 December 2001, Supplement, pp. 18–19.

[235] *Daniels v. Walker* [2000] 1 WLR 1382, CA; *Cosgrove v. Pattison* [2001] CP Rep 68, (2001) Times, 13 February; cf *Popek v. National Westminster Bank Plc* [2002] EWCA Civ 42 where the Court of Appeal upheld the judge's decision not to allow a claimant's late application to be allowed to adduce additional expert evidence to that of the single joint expert.

Where one party is given permission to call an expert and for any reason then wishes to call a different expert the court must be asked for permission. In order to discourage 'expert shopping', such permission is likely to be subject to a condition that the first expert's report be disclosed to the other side.[236] The court requires that legal professional privilege in respect of the first report be waived as a condition of obtaining a second expert opinion. However, this only operates if the order giving the party permission to call an expert names him. If, without naming him, it merely states that he may call an expert in a particular field of expertise, the party does not require the court's permission to instruct a second expert and therefore no condition can be imposed.[237]

6. Pre-trial case management

At the heart of the Woolf reforms was pre-trial case management. Not that the concept was new. Pre-trial case management was previously achieved by directions given by the court without a hearing or by some form of pre-trial hearing. The purpose of pre-trial directions and pre-trial hearings was to prepare the case for trial in order to reduce cost and delay. A side effect was the promotion of pre-trial settlement.

In the past there were various kinds of pre-trial hearings in the High Court and the county court. One was the so-called summons for directions. The Evershed Committee which reported in 1953 on how to simplify civil procedure, after deliberating for six years, said that the best hope for reducing delays and costs was a' robust summons for directions',[238] but this hope was not realised. The normal summons for directions was a perfunctory affair lasting only a few minutes conducted by clerks in front of the Master.[239] In a paper prepared for a Workshop on Civil Procedure in London in 1970, Sir Jack Jacob wrote: 'in most personal injury actions the Summons for Directions is a very mild affair and cannot possibly be called robust, since the only order that is made is the limitation of medical and perhaps other experts, plans and photographs, and place and mode of trial, and setting down'.

In 1968, the Winn Committee recommended that because the summons for directions had become a formality, it should be recognised by making the process automatic.[240] Provision should be made for automatic directions without a summons and without an order. At the time this proposal was not implemented. In 1979, the Cantley Working Party, taking the same approach, said: 'in practice competent solicitors know what they want and agree it in advance or in chambers and a two minute hearing suffices in nearly all personal

[236] *Beck v. Ministry of Defence* [2003] EWCA 1043.
[237] *Vasiliou v. Hajigeorgiou* [2005] EWCA Civ 236, [2005] 3 All ER 17. For a critical commentary, see the editorial note in *Civil Justice Quarterly*, 2005, pp. 293–7.
[238] *Final Report of the Committee on Supreme Court Practice and Procedure*, 1953, Cmnd. 8878.
[239] Master Diamond, 'The Summons for Directions', 75 *Law Quarterly Review*, 1959, p. 43.
[240] Paragraph 352.

injury cases . . . In fact the two minute hearing to obtain the Master's order on an agreed summons is in most cases quite unnecessary'.[241]

The proposal that there should be automatic directions unless the parties asked for something different was implemented for High Court cases in 1980 in RSC Order 25, r. 8, with regard to personal injury actions. A similar change was made in Chancery cases in 1982.

The Civil Justice Review Body in its *Final Report* in 1988 recommended that standard directions should be devised for all cases where such directions were appropriate. The parties should be free to apply to the court for additional or different directions or for a general stock-taking. The court should be entitled to initiate a general stock-taking on any hearing whether or not it was applied for by either of the parties.[242]

In cases where there were no automatic directions it should continue to be possible to have a summons for directions or, in the county courts, a pre-trial hearing.

The Woolf reforms

Lord Woolf's *Interim Report* and the January 1996 consultation paper for fast track cases envisaged a 'directions hearings'. The January 1996 consultation paper stated that there would be 'suitably tailored standard directions' linked to the timetable for the case. District judges would thus see all defences when filed, decide venue, allocate cases to the appropriate track, give the necessary directions, set a timetable and allocate a hearing week.[243] Other options at the directions hearing would be an application for summary disposal, striking out of the claim if it had no realistic chance of success, or because no valid defence was shown (previously Orders 13 and 14).

The Woolf 'directions hearing' sounded remarkably like the 'robust summons for directions' envisaged in 1953 by the Evershed Committee!

The 1999 rules provide for directions to be given by the court as part of its case management functions – in small claims and fast track cases usually without any actual hearing, on the basis of the allocation questionnaire.

Small claims

In small claims cases, after allocation, the court gives 'standard directions' or 'special directions' and fixes a date for the final hearing (CPR 27.4). 'Standard directions' are defined to mean a direction that each party shall at least fourteen days before the date fixed for the hearing, file and serve on the other party copies of all documents (including any expert report) on which he intends to rely at the hearing (CPR 27.4). In road accident cases these may include witness statements, invoices and estimates for repairs, documents relating to loss of earnings, sketch

---

[241] *Report of the Personal Injuries Litigation Procedure Working Party*, 1979, Cmnd. 7476, para. 33.
[242] Paragraph 254.   [243] At p. 14, para. 59.

plans and photographs. Before the hearing the parties should try to agree the cost of repairs and other losses. The accompanying Practice Direction gives similar indications with regard to building disputes, landlords' claims for repairs, holiday and wedding claims. 'Special directions' are directions in addition to standard directions.[244]

Fast track

Directions in fast track cases are given at two stages. One is at allocation. The other is on the filing of the listing questionnaire. A directions hearing is held 'if necessary and desirable' (PD 28, para. 2.3). The directions fix a trial date not more than thirty weeks later or fix a period, not exceeding three weeks, within which the trial is to take place (CPR 28.2). An appendix to Part 28 sets out forms of directions regarding requests for further information, disclosure of documents, witness statements, expert evidence, filing of documents with the listing questionnaire, the date for the filing of the listing questionnaire and the documents that must be filed at that time. The Practice Direction states that a typical timetable from allocation might be: disclosure (four weeks), exchange of witness statement (ten weeks), exchange of experts' reports (fourteen weeks), sending of listing questionnaire by the court (twenty weeks), filing of listing questionnaire (twenty-two weeks) and hearing (thirty weeks). On listing, the court confirms the trial date, specifies the place of trial and gives a time estimate. So far as possible, the court's further directions should be based on prior agreement between the parties.

The style of case management envisaged for the fast track was outlined by Lord Woolf in his *Interim Report*:

> The procedure I have outlined above envisages a pro-active role for the District judge in communicating with the parties or, more often, their legal advisers by telephone,[245] letter or fax . . . Where appropriate this should include tripartite discussions between the judge and the parties by means of a telephone conference facility . . . The fast track procedure is designed to dispense with any procedures which create uncertainty or unnecessary preparation or generate additional cost. Although there will be no case management conference or pretrial review, the District judge will be able to ensure that the case is reasonably fit for the hearing by monitoring the checklist and the documentation. To enable District judges to fulfil this role effectively, it is essential that they are provided with appropriate information technology.[246]

Multi-track

Directions for multi-track cases can be given at allocation, at a case management conference, at a pre-trial review or at listing. On the allocation of a claim to the multi-track the court considers whether it is necessary or desirable to hold a case management conference straight away or whether it is appropriate

---

[244] For examples, see CPR, PD, Form F.
[245] As was seen above (pp. 79–80) research indicates that telephone conferences are now normal (ed.)   [246] At p. 44, paras 14–15.

instead to give directions on its own initiative. The directions should, so far as is appropriate, be based on agreement between the parties. To obtain the court's approval, agreed directions must set out a timetable by reference to calendar dates for the taking of steps for the preparation of the case. The court will not approve the timetable if it proposes a date for a case management conference that is later than is reasonably necessary. Agreed directions should also deal with such matters as filing of any reply or amended statement of case, dates for the requests for further information, the disclosure of evidence, the use of a single joint expert or the exchange of expert reports. If the court gives directions on its own initiative, its general approach will be based on standard disclosure, disclosure of witness statements by simultaneous exchange and a single joint expert ('unless there is good reason not to do so'). If directions are not agreed and the court cannot give them on its own initiative, it will direct a case management conference to be listed (PD 29).[247]

Case management conferences, pre-trial reviews, listing hearings

Lord Woolf's report envisaged an early case management conference sometimes for fast track cases and usually for multi-track cases. Pre-trial reviews nearer the time of the hearing, he suggested, would be usual in multi-track cases. These recommendations are reflected in the rules. Where one party has filed a listing questionnaire but the other has not, there will also be a listing hearing (PD 29, para. 8.3(2)). The court will fix the trial date or the period in which the trial is to take place as soon as practicable (CPR 29.2(2)). Postponement of the trial will not occur unless it is unavoidable ('Litigants and lawyers must be in no doubt that the court will regard the postponement of a trial as an order of the last resort' (PD 29, para. 7.4(6).) The legal representative attending such a hearing must be personally familiar with the case and have authority to deal with issues that arise. Failure to comply will be punished by a wasted costs order (PD 29, para. 5.2(3)). The lay party may also be required to attend (r. 29.3). (In practice, this very rarely occurs.)

The Practice Direction on the multi-track covers a great variety of issues. The topics to be considered at a case management conference will include whether the case is clear, what disclosure of documents is necessary, what factual or expert evidence should be disclosed, what arrangements should be made for the

---

[247] For an early approving assessment of case management, see Mr Justice Lightman, 'The Case for Judicial Intervention', 149 *New Law Journal*, 3 December 1999, p. 1819. For an appraisal of the significance of the reforms, see N. Andrews, 'A New Civil Procedural Code for England – Party Control "Going, Going, Gone"', 19 *Civil Justice Quarterly*, 2000, pp. 19–38. For a report on the range of judicial views regarding case management, see J. Plotnikoff and R. Woolfson, *Judges' Case Management Perspectives: the View of Opinion Formers and Case Managers*, LCD 3/2002 – www.dca.gov.uk/ researchintrofr.

For an assessment of case management based on interviews with judges, court officials and practitioners in 2003 and 2004, see M. Peysner and M. Seneviratne, *The Management of Civil Cases: the Courts and the Post-Woolf Landscape*, DCA Research Report 9/2005.

putting of questions to experts, whether there should be a split trial or a trial of preliminary issues. The court will set a timetable for the steps to be taken. Case management is to be tailored flexibly to the needs of the case. It is generally conducted by a Master, District judge or Circuit judge. In complex cases it is conducted by the trial judge.[248]

In small claims cases there is normally no pre-trial hearings, but the court can hold a preliminary hearing where it considers that special directions are needed to ensure a fair hearing and it is necessary to get a party to court to ensure that he understands what he must do to comply with the special directions or to enable the court to dispose of the claim on the basis that one party has no real prospect of success (PD 27, para. 27.6). If all parties agree, the preliminary hearing can be treated as the final hearing.

Utility of pre-trial hearing

It is common sense to suppose that a pre-trial hearing will reduce cost and delay – but there is empirical evidence suggesting that this is not necessarily the case. The procedure for small claims cases introduced in 1973 originally included a pre-trial review but this was dropped after it was found that it was more of a nuisance than a help. The preliminary hearing concept also had a somewhat unsuccessful test in the Family Division. In 1979 it was announced that the 'pre-trial review' concept would in future be applied to contested matrimonial causes in the Family Division.[249] The Practice Direction stated that 'the prime objective behind the pre-trial review procedure is to enable the registrar to ascertain the true state of the case and to give such directions as are necessary for its just, expeditious and economic disposal'. In practice, where it had been tried experimentally it had been found that 'under the registrar's guidance the parties are often able to compose their differences, or to drop insubstantial charges and defences, and to concentrate on the main issues in dispute'. This scheme did not, however, prove successful. It ran as an experiment for fourteen months before being cancelled by a further Practice Direction in June 1981.[250] Research revealed that the reason for the failure of the scheme was that it did not sufficiently achieve the objectives of securing more settlements or even of clarifying issues for the trial.

A study of matched samples in 3,000 personal injury cases in New Jersey found that while pre-trial conferences improved preparation, they did not shorten trials. The researchers concluded that they therefore lowered rather than raised the efficiency of the system by absorbing a great deal of court time without any compensating savings.[251]

---

[248] See *Morris v. Bank of America National Trust* [2000] 1 All ER 954, CA.

[249] *Practice Direction* [1979] 1 All ER 112.   [250] See *New Law Journal,* 1981, p. 623.

[251] M. Rosenberg, *The Pre-trial Conference and Effective Justice* (Columbia University Press, 1964) p. 68.

    See also the study of serious fraud cases done by Professor M. Levi for the Runciman Royal Commission on Criminal Justice. With regard to pre-trial reviews, Levi said: 'none of the

There are no empirical data showing the impact of pre-trial case management since the introduction of the Woolf reforms.

What to do about delay

The problem of what to do about delay in civil litigation is common to all legal systems.

The common law approach The traditional approach of the English courts was relatively relaxed. In *Allen v. Sir Alfred McAlpine & Sons Ltd*[252] the Court of Appeal held that the power to dismiss for lack of prosecution of the case should only be exercised where the court was satisfied either (1) that the default had been intentional and contumacious, or conduct amounting to an abuse of the court or (2) that there had been inordinate and inexcusable delay by the plaintiff or his lawyers and that such delay would give rise to a substantial risk that it was not possible to have a fair trial of the issues in the action or it had caused or was likely to cause serious prejudice to the defendant. These principles were approved by the House of Lords in *Birkett v. James*.[253] Moreover, the Law Lords said there that delay before issuing the writ within the limitation period was irrelevant. The delay under consideration must have occurred since the writ was issued, though it did accept that if he had delayed at first, it was incumbent on the plaintiff to move with all due speed after the writ was issued, but at that time the applicant had to be able to establish that the delay caused him serious prejudice. An adverse effect on the system as a whole was not sufficient.

Twenty years later in *Arbuthnot Latham Bank Ltd v. Trafalgar Holdings Ltd*,[254] decided in the countdown to implementation of the CPR, the attitude was very different. The Master of the Rolls, Lord Woolf, giving the Court of Appeal's decision, said that in *Birkett v. James* the broader consequences of inordinate delay was not a consideration which was in issue, but in the new era of managed litigation it was going to be a consideration of increasing significance.

Litigants and their legal advisers must therefore recognise that any delay which occurs from now on will be assessed not only from the point of view of the prejudice caused to the particular litigants whose case it is, but also in relation to the effect it can have on other litigants who are wishing to have their cases

---

defence lawyers I interviewed argued that pre-trial reviews had any significant effect on the development of the case' (*The Investigation, Prosecution and Trial of Serious Fraud*, Royal Commission on Criminal Justice, Research Study No. 14, 1993, p. 105).

See, to the same general effect, the *Crown Court Study*. Judges in Crown Court cases were asked whether they thought the pre-trial review had saved much time and money at trial. Two-thirds (66 per cent) said no, a quarter (24 per cent) said a little and 8 per cent said a fair amount of time had been saved. Only 1 per cent said a great deal of time had been saved (M. Zander and P. Henderson, *Crown Court Study*, Royal Commission on Criminal Justice, Research Study No. 19, 1993, section 2.8.9).   [252] [1968] 2 QB 229.
[253] [1978] AC 297.   [254] [1998] 2 All ER 181.

heard and the prejudice which is caused to the due administration of civil justice.[255]

The systems approach of official committees

Since the Second World War the problem of delay was considered by no fewer than six committees: the Evershed Committee (1953), the Winn Committee (1968), the Cantley Committee (1979), the Civil Justice Review (1986–89), the Heilbron-Hodge Committee (1993) and Lord Woolf (1995–96).

The Evershed Committee[256] as has been seen, placed its faith in 'the robust summons for directions', but this totally failed. The summons for directions never became robust.

The Winn Committee[257] thought that delay was 'a very great reproach'. It proposed various remedies. One was interest on damages – to encourage insurance companies to pay up quicker. This was implemented in the Administration of Justice Act 1969, s. 22. Another was the power to order interim payment of part of the damages in a case where it was reasonably clear that damages would ultimately be awarded. This was implemented in the Administration of Justice Act 1969, s. 20. Thirdly, the Committee thought delays should be reduced by keeping the procedure on tighter reins so far as time limits were concerned. The need, it thought, was to increase the penalties for delay.

The Cantley Committee[258] did not think that the problem of delay was so serious. Generally the system worked tolerably well:

> 8. The basic principle of litigation as at present conducted in our courts is that the litigation is the litigation of the parties: the court is there to assist the parties and finally to resolve the dispute between the parties if asked to do so, but the court does not intervene unless asked to do so by the parties. Some of the weaknesses of our system derive from this fact but so do many of its strengths and given a competent legal profession, which, with some exceptions, we have, one should not lightly interfere with this method of conducting litigation and encourage an undue degree of court intervention if to do so would lose the advantages of economy and flexibility which our system brings.

Most accidents which led to claims, it said, did not lead to writs and most writs did not lead to trial and judgment. These cases were settled 'and settlement is an essential ingredient in our system of disposing of actions' (para. 9). Moreover, a delay which enabled and encouraged the parties to settle their dispute on reasonable terms was not an undue delay and 'any solution which brought cases to the point of trial more quickly but which brought more cases to trial than at present would have the double disadvantage of being more costly

---

[255] For a discussion of the case, see I.R. Scott, 'Disregard of Procedural Time Limits as Abuse of Process', 17 *Civil Justice Quarterly*, 1998, pp. 83–7.

[256] *Final Report on Supreme Court Practice*, 1953, Cmnd. 8878.

[257] *Committee on Personal Injuries Litigation*, 1968, Cmnd. 369.

[258] *Report of the Personal Injuries Litigation Procedure Working Party*, 1979, Cmnd. 7476.

for those cases which might otherwise have settled and, by bringing more cases to the point of trial, delay the trial itself' (para. 9).

However, Cantley agreed that there were some cases of egregious delay. Having canvassed various solutions to this issue, the one it most favoured was that if within eighteen months after the issue of a writ in a personal injury case the action had not been set down for trial, the plaintiff's solicitor should be required to report to the court as to what stage the proceedings had reached. If appropriate, the court could then issue a summons for the purpose of giving directions, but this sensible proposal foundered because at that date – and for many years after – the court system had no way of identifying the cases in which a case had not been set down eighteen months after the issue of the writ.

The approach to the problem of delay of the Civil Justice Review[259] was very different from that of the Cantley Committee. Where Cantley emphasised that civil litigation was essentially a private matter between the parties, the Civil Justice Review thought of it rather as a matter of public concern:

- It caused personal stress, anxiety and financial hardship to plaintiffs and their families.
- These pressures sapped the morale and determination of plaintiffs, often resulting in acceptance of low settlement offers.
- It reduced the availability of evidence and eroded the reliability of the evidence which was available.
- It led to inefficient business dealing with files opened and reopened over months and years.
- Compensation was delayed until long after it was most needed.
- It lowered public estimation for the legal system.[260]

The Civil Justice Review proposed a variety of remedies for delay. They included:

- Reducing the time limit for bringing a personal injuries action from three years to one year. [Not adopted.]
- Requiring solicitors handling personal injury cases to have a specialist qualification. [Not adopted.]
- Obliging a solicitor to start proceedings within a fixed period of his first meeting with his client. [Not adopted.]
- A system of paper adjudication for cases involving amounts of under £5,000. [Not adopted.]
- Laying down and enforcing a strict timetable for larger cases. [Adopted ten years later for Lord Woolf's fast track.]
- Requiring litigants personally to sign applications for adjournments. [Not adopted.]

---

[259] The Review produced five consultation papers on *Personal Injuries* (1986), *Small Claims* (1986), *Commercial Court* (1986), *Enforcement of Debt* (1987) and *Housing Cases* (1987). Its final report, *Report of the Review Body on Civil Justice*, Cm. 394, was published in 1988.

[260] Civil Justice Review, *The Personal Injuries Consultation Paper*, 1986, para. 86.

- Giving court administrators targets for trials. [Adopted in Lord Woolf's fast track.]
- The court should control the time taken in litigation. [Adopted by Lord Woolf.]
- Implementing the proposal made by Cantley that where a case had not been set down for trial within a stated time from the issue of the writ the lawyers should be asked to report the reasons. There should be different periods for different kinds of cases. [Not adopted.]
- Better court management information.

The net impact of the Civil Justice Reform project in terms of reducing delay was therefore negligible.

In October 1990 a new rule was introduced in the county court without prior consultation or even warning – County Court Rules Order 17, r. 11 – providing for *automatic striking out* of an action if a request for a hearing had not been made within the time limit. The time limit was six months from the close of pleadings. The pleadings were deemed to be closed fourteen days after delivery of a defence or twenty-eight days after the delivery of a counterclaim. Unless the court had already fixed a hearing, the action was automatically struck out if no request to fix a hearing was made within fifteen months of the close of pleadings. The rule applied to any default or fixed date action, i.e. one begun by plaint. This meant most actions.

The Civil Justice Review envisaged that the court would send out a warning notice but this did not happen – not least because the court lacked the technology to discover which cases were at risk of being struck out. Practitioners therefore had to watch the diary to make sure that they did not fall foul of the rule.

The court had a discretion to extend time limits retrospectively but in *Rastin v. British Steel Plc*[261] the Court of Appeal held that the discretion should be exercised sparingly. The plaintiff had to be able to show that he had prosecuted the case with reasonable diligence.

The automatic strike out rule resulted in thousands of cases being struck out.[262] It generated a flood of satellite litigation which in the end required drastic action by the Court of Appeal. In April and May 1997 three of its members (Lord Justices Saville, Brooke and Waller) in a seven-week period decided more than a hundred appeals and applications arising out of Order 17, r. 11.[263] This stopped the flood of cases to the Court of Appeal. A year later, in May 1998, Lord Justice Brooke said that there was only one case involving Order

---

[261] [1994] 2 All ER 641.

[262] According to Judge Greenslade there had been no fewer than 34,000 cases where the automatic striking out rule had been applied – *Reform of Civil Procedure – Essays on Access to Justice* (ed. A.A.S. Zuckerman and R. Cranston, Clarendon Press, 1995) p. 122.

[263] The decisions, which take seventy pages in the law reports, were reported in *Bannister v. SGB Plc* [1997] 4 All ER 129 and *Greig Middleton & Co Ltd v. Denderowitz, Olaleye-Oruene v. London Guildhall University* [1997] 4 All ER 181.

17, r. 11 awaiting decision.[264] However, the automatic strike out rule had been a catastrophic failure.

The Heilbron-Hodge Report[265] was produced by a committee established by the Bar and the Law Society. Surprisingly, given that it was a committee of practitioners, one of the main villains with regard to delay, it thought, were lawyers: 'progress of actions lies with the parties and their lawyers rather than the courts. This is often a recipe for unacceptable and otherwise avoidable delay as well as unnecessary cost'.[266] Heilbron-Hodge called for 'a radical reappraisal of the approach to civil litigation from all its participants'. 'It is time for many of the deeply ingrained traditions to be swept away and for their replacement by pragmatic and modern attitudes and ideas. In essence what is needed is a change in culture'.[267]

This allegedly much needed new ethos in the civil courts was embodied in ten basic principles of reform enunciated by Heilbron-Hodge. One was 'litigants and their lawyers need to have imposed upon them, within sensible procedural time frames, an obligation to prosecute and defend their proceedings with efficiency and despatch. Therefore, once the process of the court is invoked, the court should have a more active and responsible role over the progress and conduct of cases'.[268] Judges should adopt a more interventionist role 'to ensure that issues are limited, delays are reduced and court time is not wasted'.[269]

Under the heading of 'Court Control of Litigation' the committee recommended that the issue of all originating processes should be computerised. Each stage in an action should be computer monitored, triggering 'prompts' where the time prescribed by the procedural rules had expired without any extension of time being ordered or mutually agreed. The court should ensure that extensions of time agreed between the parties should only rarely be allowed beyond set limits.[270]

The automatic striking out rule introduced by Order 17, r. 11 should be applied to the High Court. (Heilbron-Hodge seemed unconcerned about the grave problems that the automatic strike out rule had caused.)

The proposed system of court control of litigation, the committee said, should incorporate powers to dismiss claims which were not expeditiously prosecuted. The existing rules on dismissal for want of prosecution would then become redundant.[271]

Pending the introduction of such a system the decision in *Birkett v. James*[272] should be reversed. (As has been seen, in that decision the House of Lords held that delay before issuing a writ did not count. Even if the claim had previously been dismissed for want of prosecution, if the plaintiff could issue a writ within the time limit, the action should not be dismissed save in exceptional circumstances.)

---

[264] *Cockerill v. Tambrands Ltd* [1998] 3 All ER 97 at 99.
[265] *Civil Justice on Trial – the Case for Change*, 1992.   [266] At p. 5, para. 1.7(iv).
[267] At p. 6, para. 1.8.   [268] At p. 6, para. 1.8(ii).   [269] At p. 6, para. 1.8(iv).
[270] At p. 34, para. 4.11.   [271] At p. 39, para. 4.30(i)   [272] [1978] AC 297.

Within a short period of setting down an action a 'pre-trial review' should be fixed. This should be heard by a High Court judge and in some long and complex cases by the trial judge. The matters to be dealt with would include identification of all witnesses and the extent of documentation to be presented at the trial, estimates of the length of trial, the agreement of non-contentious facts and the fixing of an approximate trial date.[273]

It is obvious that Heilbron-Hodge paved the way for the Woolf Report.[274]

In January 1994, the firm KPMG Peat Marwick published the results of a study into the causes of delay in the High Court and county courts. The study was commissioned by the Lord Chancellor's Department in July 1993. The research was based on court records of a small sample of personal injury cases and interviews with persons involved in the cases. The conclusion was that there were many causes of delay. They included: (1) the anatomy of the case itself; (2) delay caused by the parties for some of which they could be blamed and some of which was not their fault; (3) delay caused by the lawyers, especially solicitors, again, partly their fault, partly not; (4) external factors such as the difficulty of getting reports from medical and other experts; (5) the attitudes of the judiciary; (6) court procedures; and (7) court administration and especially problems created by listing.

The report stated that the two factors that gave rise to the most significant delay were inexperience or inefficiency in the handling of cases by the parties' solicitors and time taken to obtain medical or other expert reports.

The 1995 Practice Direction

In 1995, while Lord Woolf was preparing his *Interim Report*, the Lord Chief Justice, Lord Taylor, unexpectedly entered the fray with a strongly worded Practice Direction. It was headed 'Civil Litigation – Case Management' and it took effect in the Queen's Bench Division and the Chancery Division:

> ***Practice Note (Civil Litigation – Case Management)* [1995] 1 All ER 385**
> The paramount importance of reducing the cost and delay of civil litigation makes it necessary for judges sitting at first instance to assert greater control over the preparation for and conduct of hearings than has hitherto been customary. Failure by practitioners to conduct cases economically will be visited by appropriate orders for costs, including wasted costs orders.

It then set out a series of new rules. The court would exercise its powers to limit discovery, the length of oral submissions, the time allowed for the examination and cross-examination of witnesses, the issues to be addressed and reading aloud from authorities. Unless otherwise ordered, witness statements would stand as the evidence-in-chief of the witness. The rules on pleadings would be

---

[273] At pp. 40–1, para. 4.33(iii).
[274] For a descriptive note about the Heilbron-Hodge report, see 14 *Civil Justice Quarterly*, January 1994, pp. 11–14.

strictly enforced. Parties should use their best endeavours to identify and limit the issues. Rules about court bundles would be strictly enforced. In cases lasting more than ten days, a pre-trial review would be normal. Opening speeches should be succinct. The rule requiring skeleton arguments summarising submissions to be sent to the other side and to the court must be adhered to. The pre-trial checklist required the lawyers to state whether alternative dispute resolution (ADR) had been considered.[275]

From this history it is clear that when Lord Woolf was working on his Report in 1994–95 the conceptual basis for his eventual recommendations had already been laid in the reports of the Civil Justice Review, the Heilbron-Hodge Committee and the 1995 Practice Directions. Lord Woolf's analysis of the problem was unique, however, in that in his *Interim Report* he laid all the blame for the ills of the system on one cause – the uncontrolled nature of the litigation process.[276] 'In particular there is no clear judicial responsibility for managing individual cases or for the overall administration of the civil courts'.[277]

The reason suggested was that without effective judicial control the adversarial process was 'likely to encourage an adversarial culture and to degenerate into an environment in which the litigation process is too often seen as a battlefield where no rules apply'. The consequence was that expense was often excessive, disproportionate and unpredictable and delay was unreasonable. This was because the conduct, pace and extent of litigation were left almost completely to the parties. There was no effective control of their worst excesses.[278]

The Woolf reforms

As has been seen, the remedy prescribed by Lord Woolf was court control. Thus the first of the 124 recommendations in his *Interim Report* was: 'there should be a fundamental transfer in the responsibility for the management of civil litigation from litigants and their legal advisers to the courts'.[279] Apart from case management, the other chief remedy for delay in the Woolf reforms was the strict timetabling of fast track cases with a trial date fixed at a relatively early stage. (In practice the court generally fixes a 'trial window' of one, two or three weeks rather than give an actual date.) The *White Book* states: 'early fixing of the trial date or "trial window" – and insisting upon it – is of the essence of the fast track'.[280]

CPR 28.2 states that when the court allocates a case to the fast track, the court will give directions for the management of the case and set a timetable. 'The standard period between the giving of directions and the trial will be not more than thirty weeks' (CPR 28.2(4)).

The LCD's August 2000 report on the Woolf reforms had several pages of figures and graphs showing the time from issue to hearing in the years 1994 to

---

[275] Six days later a similar Practice Direction was issued by the President of the Family Division – [1995] 1 All ER 586.
[276] There was no reference in his report to the more nuanced view of delay in the report by KPMG Peat Marwick.   [277] *Interim Report* at p. 7, para. 1.   [278] *Ibid* at p. 7, para. 5.
[279] *Ibid* at p. 223.   [280] *Civil Procedure*, 2006, para. 28.2.3.

late 2001 based on data collected by the Court Service.[281] The figures provided some evidence that delay in multi-track and fast track cases had decreased: 'average time from issue to trial was lower post-CPR; 498 days in 2000–01 following a rise pre-CPR from 546 days in March 1994 to 639 days in September 1997 . . . The decline in average time from issue to trial between 1997 and 2000–01 was spread across cases regardless of type or value'.[282]

The report by Goriely, Moorhead and Abrams for the Law Society and the Civil Justice Council[283] also had information on the length of time from issue to settlement, but since their figures were based on comparison of the solicitors' files for pre-CPR and post-CPR personal injury cases, the researchers were also able to take into account pre-issue work. This is critical for any proper evaluation of the effect of the Woolf reforms. The research was conducted between twenty and twenty-eight months after the introduction of the Woolf reforms. It therefore only included small simple cases normally concluded within two years. The research measured the total time taken from the solicitor first receiving instructions to the conclusion of the matter.

This showed that the overall time had remained much the same. Both before and after the reforms, the average standard fast track case took thirteen months to conclude. This was true whether one took the mean or the median figure.[284]

The early stages of a case had become slower. It now took longer to write the first letter of claim. (The median number of days pre-Woolf was thirteen and post-Woolf was thirty-six.[285]) Equally it took longer to instruct a medical expert, no doubt because the two sides had to try to agree on a name. (The median number of days from first instruction to medical instruction had risen from sixty-seven days pre-Woolf to 113 days post-Woolf.[286]) There had been a slight increase in the delay before receipt of the medical report. (From a median of sixty-four days to eighty-three days.[287])

By contrast, the later stages had become quicker. Once a medical report had been received, settlements were arrived at more quickly.[288]

However, overall the delays were unchanged. The speeding up of one part was cancelled by the slowing down of the other.

There are no further empirical data regarding delay as a result of the Woolf reforms.

American research on the effects of case management

A few months after Lord Woolf published his *Final Report*, the Institute of Civil Justice at the Rand Corporation in California published a massive study of the effect of judicial case management in the United States. The study was based on

---

[281] *Emerging Findings*, pp. 20–3.
[282] Paragraph 6.4. The figures for small claims showed fluctuations – see Figure 12, p. 22.
[283] *More Civil Justice? The Impact of the Woolf Reforms on Pre-action Behaviour*, 2002.
[284] *Ibid* at p. 171.   [285] *Ibid* at p. 70.   [286] *Ibid* at p. 131.   [287] *Ibid* at p. 132.
[288] *Ibid* at p. 171.

a five-year survey of 10,000 cases in twenty federal courts drawn from sixteen states. The object was to investigate the impact of procedural reforms introduced under the Civil Justice Reform Act 1990. They included differential case management for different tracks, early judicial management, monitoring and control of complex cases.

The results, to say the least, were discouraging. The package of reforms as implemented, it was found, 'had little effect on time disposition, litigation costs, and attorney satisfaction and views of the fairness of case management'.[289] The reason was that whereas some of the changes introduced had a beneficial effect, these were cancelled by others that had an adverse effect. In particular, 'early case management is associated with significantly increased costs to litigants, as measured by attorney work hours'.[290] The Rand Report explained that case management tends to increase rather than reduce costs because it generates more work by lawyers: 'lawyer work may increase as a result of early management because lawyers need to respond to a court's management – for example, talking to the litigant and to the other lawyers in advance of a conference with the judge, travelling and spending time at the courthouse, meeting with the judge, and updating the file after conference'.

In addition, once judicial case management has begun, a discovery cut-off date has usually been established and attorneys may feel an obligation to begin discovery.[291] Doing so, the report said, 'could shorten time to disposition, but it may also increase lawyer work hours on cases that were about to settle when the judges began early management'.[292] Experiments were conducted to see whether it made any difference if early case management was applied somewhat earlier or later. It did not. Reflecting on this, the report said: 'this finding suggests that the *fact* (sic) of management adds to the lawyer work hours, not the "earliness" of the management' (p. 14). But of course the earlier the case management starts, the more cases are brought within its scope: 'starting earlier means that more cases would be managed because more cases are still open, so more cases would incur the predicted increase in lawyer work hours. Early management involves a trade-off between shortened time to disposition and increased lawyer work hours'.[293] (There was no sign in Lord Woolf's two reports that this basic point had been absorbed.)

With regard to delay, the Rand study found that 'what judges do to manage cases matters'. 'Early judicial case management, setting the trial schedule early, shortened time to discovery cut-off, and having litigants at or available for settlement conferences are associated with a significantly reduced time to disposition' (p. 1). Setting an early trial date was said to be 'the most important component of early management' (p. 14). No other aspect of early judicial

---

[289] At p. 1. The quotations here are from the executive summary of the study, J.S. Kakalik et al, *Just, Speedy and Inexpensive? An Evaluation of Judicial Case Management under the Civil Justice Reform Act, 1996.* The results of the study were the subject of an article by the writer – *New Law Journal*, 7 March 1997, p. 353. See also the writer's postscript – 147 *New Law Journal*, 11 April 1997, p. 539.   [290] At pp. 1–2.   [291] At p. 14.   [292] At p. 14.   [293] *Ibid.*

management had a consistently significant effect on time to disposition, costs or attorney's satisfaction or views of fairness.

On the US approach to case management and delay see J. Plotnikoff, 'Judges as Case Managers', 4 *Civil Justice Quarterly*, 1985, pp. 102–11 and 'Case Control as Social Policy: Civil Case Management Legislation in the United States', 11 *Civil Justice Quarterly*, 1991, pp. 230–45. For an overall view by an American expert on the problem of delay see G. Hazard, 'Court Delay: Toward New Premises', 5 *Civil Justice Quarterly*, 1986, p. 236; see also P. A. Sallman, 'Observations on Judicial Participation in Caseflow Management', 8 *Civil Justice Quarterly*, 1989, pp. 129–51.

For comments by American scholars on the 'managerial judging' proposals in Lord Woolf's report see R. Marcus, 'Déja Vu All Over Again' in *Reform of Civil Procedure – Essays on Access to Justice* (eds. A.A.S. Zuckerman and R. Cranston, Clarendon, 1995) pp. 219–43 and S. Issachoroff, 'Too Much Lawyering, Too Little Law', *ibid*, pp. 245–51.

For a description of the Australian approach to case management see P. McManus, 'Case Management in the Family Court of Australia', 10 *Civil Justice Quarterly*, July 1990, pp. 280–99 and B.C. Cairns, 'Managing Civil Litigation: An Australian Adaptation of American Experience', 14 *Civil Justice Quarterly*, January 1994, p. 67.

Sanctions and the new rules

In his *Final Report* Lord Woolf devoted a whole chapter to sanctions. It started:

> When considering the problems facing civil justice today I argued in chapter 3 of my *Interim Report* that the existing rules of court were being flouted on a vast scale. Timetables are not adhered to and other orders are not complied with if it does not suit the parties to do so. Orders for costs which do not apply immediately have proved to be an ineffective sanction and do nothing to deter parties from ignoring the court's directions. There was overwhelming support from all sides for effective, appropriate and fair sanctions.[294]

Lord Woolf said he would stress four important principles:

> (a) The primary aim of sanctions is prevention, not punishment. (b) It should be for the rules themselves in the first instance to provide an effective debarring order where there has been a breach, for example that a party may not use evidence which he has not disclosed. (c) All directions orders should in any event include an automatic sanction for non-compliance unless an extension of time has been obtained prospectively. (d) The onus should be on the defaulter to apply for relief, not on the other party to seek a penalty.[295]

Striking out a claim or defence was a draconian sanction. 'Nonetheless, where parties do fail without reasonable excuse to comply with the court's directions,

---

[294] *Final Report* at p. 72, paras. 1 and 2.   [295] *Ibid* at p. 72, para. 4.

particularly where they do so more than once, the court must be willing to exercise appropriate discipline over them'.[296] Costs orders – to be paid immediately – also had 'an important part to play',[297] but parties might think a costs order 'a price worth paying for the delay and inconvenience which their action causes the other party'.[298] It was essential that 'case management itself, and other sanctions, should play their part in suppressing misbehaviour'.[299]

Lord Woolf conceded that there should be a limited right to apply for relief from a sanction but the onus should be on the defaulter to apply, not on the other party to enforce the sanction.[300] Relief should be given on the basis of the test in *Rastin v. British Steel Plc*[301] where the court was satisfied that the breach was not intentional, that there had been substantial compliance with other directions and that there was a good explanation.

Lord Woolf said that to a large extent the effectiveness of sanctions would revolve around judicial attitudes. ('There is no doubt that some judges at first instance, especially Masters and District judges, will need to develop a more robust approach to the task of managing cases and ensuring that their orders are not flouted'.[302]) They must, in particular, be resistant to applications to extend a set timetable, save in exceptional circumstances and they would need to be supported by courts hearing appeals. ('Procedural decisions must not be overturned lightly . . . This is not simply a matter of limiting appeals. It goes to a change of culture in which judges can make orders confident that parties will not feel that they can ignore orders or that they can escape unscathed by appealing'.[303])

The new rules provide for seven different kinds of sanctions: striking out a statement of case; excluding argument or evidence;[304] orders for security for the sum in issue and for present and future costs; orders for payment (or non-payment) of costs, in some cases on the indemnity principle and for the immediate assessment and payment of costs; orders for payment of interest at penal rates; proceedings for contempt; and wasted costs orders. The court can impose a sanction on its own initiative with or without holding a hearing and with or without an opportunity for the party affected to make representations (CPR 3.3). However, a party whose case is struck out can apply to have it reinstated.

Thus, the court has the power to strike out a statement of claim if 'there has been a failure to comply with a rule, Practice Direction or court order' (CPR 3.4) or if the claimant does not pay the fee payable when an allocation questionnaire or listing questionnaire is served (CPR 3.7). Where a party has failed to comply with a rule, Practice Direction or court sanction, any sanction for such failure takes effect unless the party in default applies for and gets relief from the court (CPR 3.8). CPR 3.9 sets out nine considerations that the court should take into account. They include the interests of the administration of

---

[296] *Ibid* at p. 75, para. 11.   [297] *Ibid* at p. 75, para. 12.   [298] *Ibid* at p. 72, para. 13.
[299] *Ibid* at p. 75, para. 13.   [300] *Ibid* at p. 75, para. 14.   [301] [1994] 1 WLR 732.
[302] *Final Report* at p. 76, para. 15.   [303] *Ibid*.
[304] For instance, CPR 3.1(2)(k) where a claimant fails to provide further information or a schedule of damage or r. 32.10 if a witness or summary is not provided within the time limit.

justice, if the application for relief was made promptly, whether there is a good explanation for the failure and the effect that granting relief would have on each party. As has been seen, there is also a general 'slip rule' giving the court power to cure any error in procedure such as a failure to comply with a rule or Practice Direction (CPR 3.10).

There is one new rule that somewhat eases the pressure created by time limits. CPR 2.11 says that, unless the rules or a Practice Direction provide otherwise, the parties can give each other permission to extend time limits by written agreement. The rule then cites the cases where this is not possible. One is where a rule, Practice Direction or court order requires something to be done within a specified time and also specifies the consequences of failure to comply (CPR 3.8(3)). Another is an extension of time that would cause an alteration of the fast track case management timetable in respect of the return of the listing questionnaire or the date of the trial (or trial period) (CPR 28.4). A third is an extension of time that would cause an alteration of the multi-track timetable in respect of the case management conference, a pre-trial review, the return of the listing questionnaire or the trial (or trial period) (CPR 29.5). In these instances, an extension of time requires the consent of the court.

There is no Practice Direction on how the courts should approach the application of sanctions and no specific reference, save in the overriding objective, to the doctrine of proportionality.

In his report, Lord Woolf made clear that adherence to the new rules had to be strictly enforced, especially with regard to time limits. With regard, for instance, to the fast track:

> I regard adherence to the overall timetable, with strict observance of the set trial date, as an essential component of the fast track. For this reason, the directions order will be framed as a series of requirements which must be completed by specified dates and will include an automatic sanction for non-compliance, unless an extension order has been obtained prospectively. Parties will be in breach of the order unless they comply with the directions by the date specified.[305]

Mr Justice Lightman, lecturing at the Judicial Studies Board shortly before the Woolf reforms were due to take effect, gave full support to this dramatically different approach. At common law, he said, time was of the essence. Equity modified this rule. In equity, time was not of the essence. In 1873, with the merger of common law and equity, the rules of equity prevailed and that was the prevalent attitude in respect of rules in the pre-Woolf era. The traditional attitude of the courts had been that every default in respect of the rules was venal and so remediable. Save in exceptional circumstances every litigant should be allowed his day in court. That approach was no longer maintainable and was out of accord with the new rules. With regard to time limits, he said: 'time is now of the essence, but in cases where a sufficient cause exists, an application may be

---

[305] *Final Report* at p. 35, para. 15.

made for relief from the draconian sanctions for non-compliance and relief may be granted if to do so accords with the overriding objective'. There was therefore no scope for a presumption that apparently draconian provisions should be interpreted narrowly. 'The judges at the coal face must be robust'.[306]

For a very different philosophy see Sir Jack Jacob, doyen of civil proceduralists, in his dissent to the report of the Winn Committee in 1968:

> The admonition by Lord Justice Bowen that 'courts do not exist for the sake of discipline' should be reflected in the principle that rules of court should not be framed on the basis of imposing penalties or producing automatic consequences for non-compliance with the rules or orders of the court. The function of rules of court is to provide guidelines not trip wires and they fulfil their function most where they intrude least in the course of litigation.[307]

The first important post-CPR decision given by Lord Woolf in *Biguzzi v. Rank Leisure Plc*[308] sounded a distinctly more emollient note than his earlier rhetoric might have suggested. The claimant was injured in 1993. His action got bogged down through default on both sides. Shortly before the CPR came into force, the District judge struck out the action even though the delay had not caused serious prejudice to the defendants or to the chances of a fair trial – on the ground that there had been a wholesale disregard of the rules amounting to an abuse of process. After the CPR came into force an appeal was allowed mainly on the ground that there was nothing unfair in allowing the case to go forward largely because the defendant as well as the claimant had been guilty of serious default. The Court of Appeal upheld that decision. Lord Woolf said that the draconian step of striking-out, whilst available to a procedural judge in his wide-ranging discretion, was one which did not achieve justice in this particular case. Such an order simply led to hard fought appeals and satellite litigation with disproportionate costs. The advantage of the CPR over the previous rules, he said, was that the courts' powers were much broader than they had been. 'In many cases there will be alternatives which enable a case to be dealt with justly without taking the draconian step of striking the case out' (p. 940). There were a range of alternative sanctions such as requiring the claimant to make a payment into court by way of security for costs or ordering the defendant to pay costs on the higher indemnity basis. The courts had to apply the overriding objective of dealing with cases justly which included a need to show that non-compliance with time limits would not be tolerated.

This leaves the matter largely in the hands of judges at first instance:

> Judges have to be trusted to exercise the wide discretions which they have fairly and justly in all the circumstances, while recognising their responsibility to litigants in general not to allow the same defaults to occur in the future as have occurred in the past. When judges seek to do that, it is important that this court

---

[306] Mr Justice Lightman, 'Sanctions under the New Rules', *New Law Journal*, 5 March 1999, p. 336.
[307] *Report of the Committee on Personal Injury Litigation*, 1968, Cmnd. 369, pp. 151–2.
[308] [1999] 4 All ER 934.

should not interfere unless judges can be shown to have exercised their powers in some way which contravenes the relevant principles (p. 941).

When considering whether to grant relief from a failure to comply with a rule under r. 3.9 the court will weigh the matters that are specifically listed and any others that seem relevant in the particular circumstances. The relevance of case law is debatable. Counsel try to persuade the court that they have precedents that are significant. The courts often indicate that each case must be judged in light of its particular facts and that precedents are therefore not useful.

In 2004, in her regular updating column on the Civil Procedure Rules, Suzanne Burns wrote: 'the thrust of most recent cases continues to be that justice takes precedence over procedural fault, unless the latter is very serious or the conduct is repeated'.[309]

For a review of the case law by Professor A. Zuckerman see his 'Enforcing Compliance with Deadlines', 23 *Civil Justice Quarterly*, 2004, pp. 231–43. As has been noted, Zuckerman favours the disciplinarian approach to failure to comply with the rules. He regretfully concluded that 'the court seems willing to countenance further extensions of time even where there have been repeated failures to comply with time limits culminating in breach on an unless order'. Equally worrying, he thought, was 'the growing list of cases interpreting, explaining and refining the meaning and significance of the factors mentioned in the checklist of CPR, r. 3.9 which must be studied when dealing with an application to relief from sanctions'.[310] On the other hand, he welcomed the increasing tendency of the court to require defaulting litigants to pay money into court as a condition for receiving an extension of time for fulfilling procedural requirements. This was a powerful and effective tool for promoting compliance, though it could lead to further disputes and give rise to further court hearings.

See also a recent important contribution to this debate by D.S. Pigott, 'Relief from Sanctions and the Overriding Objective', 24 *Civil Justice Quarterly*, 2005, pp. 103–29.

Assessment of the Woolf reforms

The writer was from the start and consistently a critic of the Woolf reform project on the ground that on balance they would make things worse rather than better.[311] This, however, was very much the minority view. Both branches of the legal profession, the judiciary and both the lay and the legal press strongly

---

[309] *Legal Action*, March 2004, p. 13.   [310] At pp. 231–2.

[311] See M. Zander, 'Are There Any Clothes for the Emperor to Wear?', 145 *New Law Journal*, 3 February 1995, p. 154; 'Why Lord Woolf's Proposed Reforms of Civil Litigation Should be Rejected' in *Reform of Civil Procedure – Essays on Access to Justice* (eds. A.A.S. Zuckerman and R. Cranston, Clarendon, 1995, pp. 79–95); and the Chancery Bar Association Lecture, 'The Woolf Report: Forwards or Backwards for the New Lord Chancellor?', 16 *Civil Justice Quarterly*, July 1997, pp. 208–27. Lord Woolf used the occasion of the Gee Lecture at the Royal College of Physicians to reply, 'Medics, Lawyers and the Courts', 16 *Civil Justice Quarterly*, October 1997, pp. 302–17, also on www.lcd.gov.uk/judicial/speeches/speechfr.htm.

supported the Woolf reforms.[312] The only serious issue raised by those who supported the reforms was whether the Government would put in the necessary resources to make them work, notably with regard to IT. (As was seen above, fears about IT resources for the civil courts proved to be well founded.)

Writing in 2006, seven years having elapsed since the reforms went live in April 1999, what can be said about how they have worked out?

Apparent benefits deriving from the Woolf reforms

The majority of those concerned with the civil litigation business believe that the Woolf reforms are working quite well. Even those who have concerns are mainly, on balance, positive.

The indications from a variety of sources seem to justify the following propositions as to the benefits flowing from the implementation of the Woolf reforms:

- A less adversarial culture between the parties is developing – confounding the views of pessimists such as the writer who considered such a development improbable. Peysner and Seneviratne (2005) reported: 'the overall view was that the culture had changed for the better. The general feeling, shared by judges, court staff and practitioners, was that the reforms had achieved the objective in this respect and that this was an improvement on the previous system'. The parties are more co-operative toward each other – partly at least because of the consequences under the CPR of not being co-operative.
- Pre-action protocols appear to be working to promote *earlier* settlement and probably *more* settlement.
- Settlements are also promoted by the fact that under the CPR the question of costs can be treated separately.
- Since pre-action protocols result in more work being done earlier, cases that would have settled anyway are likely to settle on the basis of more relevant information.
- Part 36 payments or offers of payment – and especially the possibility of Part 36 offers by claimants – seem to be helping to achieve earlier and perhaps more settlements.
- The use of single joint experts is working better than critics feared. (However, in some cases, parties hire their own experts to shadow the joint expert.[313])
- The fact that under the CPR parties can be ordered to pay the costs of interlocutory applications right away has resulted in fewer interlocutory applications.

For the writer's riposte see 'Woolf on Zander', 147 *New Law Journal*, 23 May 1997, p. 768. For a broader view of the issues see the writer's Lionel Cohen Lecture given at the Hebrew University in Jerusalem, 'What can be done about Cost and Delay in Civil Litigation?', 31 *Israel Law Review*, 1997, pp. 703–23.

[312] For a very positive early assessment of progress by the civil servant in charge of implementation, see D. Gladwell, 'Modern Litigation Culture: The First Six Months of the Civil Justice Reforms in England and Wales', 19 *Civil Justice Quarterly*, 2000, pp. 9–18.

[313] J. Peysner, 'Controlling Costs', 153 *New Law Journal*, 25 July 2003, pp. 1147 and 1148.

- Considerable efforts have been made to promote consistent approaches to case management throughout the country. Courses are run by the Judicial Studies Board which have to be attended by all new judges.

However, there are important issues that give rise to concern and others where there is uncertainty.

Issues of concern or uncertainty
The fall in the number of cases issued

It was one of Lord Woolf's aims that more cases would settle without the need for legal proceedings.

At around the time of the introduction of the Woolf reforms, for whatever reason, there was a significant drop in the number of claims issued. In 1999, the year the Woolf reforms were introduced, the total number of county court proceedings issued was 2 million. In 2000 it had fallen to 1.87 million and in the years 2001–04 it was 1.71 million, 1.63 million, 1.57 million and 1.6 million. In 2005 it rose again to 1.87 million.[314] Commenting (before the possibly significant rise in 2005), Professors Peysner and Seneviratne said: 'the number of cases seem to have declined rapidly as soon as the CPR was introduced. This may have been a function of legal conservatism with litigators having issued as many cases as possible under the pre-CPR arrangements and waiting for others to make mistakes in the new system. However, this would cause a temporary dip and could not be responsible for the long term substantive drop in numbers'.[315]

The long term substantive drop in numbers of cases issued is not however just a phenomenon of the post-Woolf reforms era. It started well before the Woolf reforms were introduced.

In the twenty years from 1958–78 the figure for proceedings issued in the county court was stable at 1.3–1.5 million. In the next ten years to 1988 it rose to 2.3 million. By 1990 it had again hugely increased to 3.3 million and it rose to a peak of 3.5 million in 1992.

Since 1992, year by year, there was a steady drop: 1993, 2.98 million, 1994, 2.65 million, 1995, 2.44 million and 1996, 2.34 million. Since there was a considerable fall year by year from 1992 onwards, the further fall since 1999 cannot be attributed exclusively or even mainly to the Woolf reforms. The effect the reforms have had in this regard is unknown and probably unknowable.

The drop over recent years in the number of cases being handled by the civil courts has also occurred in other countries.[316]

---

[314] *Judicial Statistics, 2005*, Table 4.1, p. 46.
[315] *The Management of Civil Cases: the Courts and the Post-Woolf Landscape*, DCA, 9/2005.
[316] The *American Journal of Empirical Legal Studies* devoted the whole of its vol.1, no. 3, 2004 (nearly 1,000 pages!) to the phenomenon of the 'vanishing trial'. See especially the long first article by M. Galanter, 'The Vanishing Trial: An Examination of Trials and Related Matters in Federal and State Courts', pp. 459–565 and H.M. Kritzer's, 'Disappearing Trials? A Comparative Perspective', pp. 735–54 in which he deals with England and Ontario.

One unfortunate side-effect of the drop in the number of civil cases is a corresponding fall in the income derived from court fees. While the DCA, no doubt driven by the Treasury, continues to insist on the full recovery of the costs of the civil court system from litigants, this will have the inevitable result of forcing the level of court fees even higher, which could in turn further reduce the number of cases.

Costs

A central aim of the Woolf reforms was that the cost of litigation would be more affordable, more predictable and more proportionate to the value and complexity of individual cases.

The research evidence so far derives from the research by Goriely, Moorhead and Abrams,[317] from the study conducted for the Civil Justice Council by P. Fenn and N. Rickman[318] and from the report by Professors Peysner and Seneviratne.[319]

The study by Goriely, Moorhead and Abrams looked at the effect of the Woolf reform on costs both through interviews with the players and by examining pre-Woolf and post-Woolf files of concluded cases.

Claimant solicitors said that different changes had had different effects. The fact that fewer claims were issued was thought to lead to obvious cost reductions. It was also suggested that cases 'were now more focused with fewer unnecessary disputes over side issues'.[320] The courts were also felt to put more emphasis on proportionality, with a consequent downward pressure on costs.[321] On the other hand, costs had been increased by 'front-loading' with more work needed at an earlier stage. More work was necessary before issue 'as the fast track timetable left little time to obtain expert evidence or witness statements once litigation had begun'.[322] By and large, claimant solicitors thought front-loading was right (in that it was work that should be done) but they suggested that, inevitably, it had a cost impact. Claimant solicitors disagreed as to whether costs, overall, had gone up, down or had stayed about the same.

By contrast, insurers 'were united in their views. They all said that, since April 1999, the average cost of a personal injury claim had increased markedly. They felt this to be the reforms' "major weakness" '.[323]

After considering various sets of figures the researchers concluded: 'the evidence produced by the insurance industry is strong *prima facie* evidence that the cost of personal injury claims has increased',[324] but the figures only related

---

[317] *More Civil Justice? The Impact of the Woolf Reforms on Pre-action Behaviour*, 2002 – www.civiljusticecouncil.gov.uk and www.lawsociety.org.uk.

[318] *Cost of Low Value RTA Claims 1997–2002*, January 2003, www.civiljusticecouncil.org.uk. The study was of settled claims. It used various large databases including 27,378 from one insurance company, 11,420 from a second, 150,000 cases handled by claims negotiators for twenty different insurance companies and 5,852 cases handled by a claimant solicitor's firm.

[319] *The Management of Civil Cases: the Courts and the Post-Woolf Landscape*, DCA Research Report 9/2005.   [320] *Ibid* at p. 172.   [321] *Ibid.*   [322] *Ibid.*   [323] *Ibid* at p. 174.

[324] *Ibid* at p. 175.

to claims settled in-house, before proceedings had been issued. 'One cannot be sure of the overall impact of the reforms, until one is able to take into account the costs of litigated claims. These may take another few years to work their way through the system'.[325]

The authors also reported on the figures in the study of files of actual cases. These were all small cases that had settled quickly with little substantive dispute. The median amount paid by opponents in post-Woolf cases was £1,576, compared with £1,393 for pre-Woolf cases – a difference that was just statistically significant. (The mean rose from £1,580 to £1,761, a rise of 11 per cent which was lower than in the figures produced by the insurance industry but higher than inflation (8 per cent).[326])

The study by Fenn and Rickman In their conclusions they reported that for low value (<£15,000) road traffic accident cases at the end of July 2001, mean base costs (excluding disbursements) were approximately £2,000 and mean disbursements were approximately £500. This represented a rise of approximately 25 per cent in base costs over the previous eighteen months (i.e. from mid 2000 to end 2001) and of approximately 10 per cent in disbursements.[327]

The increases in base costs and disbursements were greatest in the cases in which legal proceedings had not been issued – 50 per cent and 25 per cent respectively. ('To the extent that these agreed costs reflect legal inputs, it appears that much more work is being done at the pre-issue stage in cases settling from 2000 onwards. This is consistent with Woolf-driven cost increases – though more work would be required to confirm this with statistical confidence' (p. 11).)

The increases were not different as between conditional fee (CFA) cases and non-CFA cases.

Costs rose proportionately to damages and to the complexity of the case.

The authors ended their list of findings:

> The trends in costs we have reported *appear consistent* with the effect of Lord Woolf's reforms on the 'front-loading' of casework. This is particularly the case given that the changes are concentrated on non-CFA, pre-issue cases, at a time when 'Woolf cases' were beginning to be settled in significant numbers.

However, again the authors emphasised that more work was needed to establish with statistical confidence whether the apparent causal relation suggested by logic and timing between the Woolf reforms and the rise in costs was real.

The Peysner–Seneviratne study of case management was not designed to generate hard data on costs but almost a third of their report was devoted to this issue. In his introduction to his *Interim Report* Lord Woolf stated that the problem of costs was the most serious problem besetting the litigation system. Costs were central to the changes he wished to bring about and he noted that

[325] *Ibid.*   [326] *Ibid.* The rise was not due to recoverable success fees (p. 176).
[327] *American Journal of Empirical Legal Studies*, n. 314 above, at p. 17.

virtually all his recommendations were designed at least in part to tackle the problem of costs.

The Peysner–Seneviratne report said there was no doubt that the reforms had had the effect of front-loading costs: 'the major finding we made, unequivocally confirming the findings at the development stage, and agreed unanimously by all interviewees is that costs are front-loaded'.[328] This, it said, was the inevitable result of the Woolf objective that court proceedings should be a last resort and only launched when cases were in order. Unless procedures in the pre-action protocols were reduced in scope, or costs were fixed and reduced in the pre-litigation and early litigation phases, case management had no impact on this forward-loading effect.

With regard to proportionality of costs the report said: 'we consistently found among the judiciary a feeling that costs, particularly in the fast track, were disproportionate and that the CPR had not cured this problem'. The report quoted a Circuit judge: 'in the sort of small fast track claims, which may only be for £1,000 if it is personal injuries, you find that the solicitors have run up a bill of £10,000 or £11,000. It is very concerning that a case has been brought, a very simple whiplash for £1,500 or something, and £10,000 has been expended on it'.[329]

As to whether costs overall had risen, the report cited the impressions of different players. The judges had no doubt that costs had risen. ('Certainly the judiciary, who see those costs claimed in formal bills and make assessments, offered a consistent view: costs were high before the CPR and they became higher after the introduction of the CPR'.[330]) In one sense this was a surprising finding insofar one might have thought that by the time the case came for assessment of costs, the front-loading effect of the reforms would have worn off. 'Yet the judiciary's view is that, case-by-case, costs have increased not merely been front-loaded . . .'[331] One reason was that assessing judges had abandoned the old broad brush approach to costs and were looking for evidence of work done to support claims for costs. This in turn had resulted in practitioners producing highly detailed bills, often professionally drawn, that captured more time spent on the case. 'Thus, the so-called "cost industry" meets the demand that no costs should be paid unless they are evidenced, by ensuring that no activity is lost, and the result is cost inflation'.

Practitioners were not quite so ready to accept that overall bills were higher but none said they had gone down. They argued that the system required a level of detailed activity that produced high costs.[332]

In their conclusion on the issue of costs, Peysner and Seneviratne said: 'in effect we draw the same conclusion as Rand, that case management (which in this context includes pre-action protocols, the fast track and individual case control) is effective in cutting delay but it is ineffective in cutting costs, or indeed

---

[328] *More Civil Justice?*, n. 317 above, para. 6.6, p. 62.   [329] *Ibid*, para. 6.6, p. 63.
[330] *Ibid*, para. 6.6, p. 65.   [331] *Ibid*, para. 6.6, p. 66.   [332] *Ibid*, para. 6.6, p. 67.

may increase costs. Lord Woolf's aspiration that case management would achieve his aims in relation to costs has not been achieved'.[333]

In other words, all the indications are that the direct effect of the Woolf reforms is that costs have not gone down as promised, they have gone up. What is not widely known is that at a very late stage, when the reform process was already well on the way, Lord Woolf himself admitted that this would happen. In the Gee lecture given in May 1997, he said: 'while I favour the greater case management which is now possible I recognise that case management does involve the parties in more expense'.[334]

As to predictability, the erratic decisions of the courts with regard to Part 36 offers and payment into court (above) and equally as regards the rule that costs follow the event (below) have introduced a major new degree of uncertainty into the litigation process.

On the other hand, as will be seen there have been important post-Woolf developments with regard to fixed costs (p. 564 below).

Delay

The annual *Judicial Statistics* tell us that the average waiting time[335] from issue of claim to trial in the county court, which in 1990 was eighty-one weeks and in 1998 was eighty-five weeks, has since decreased considerably. In 2005 it had gone down to fifty-two weeks.[336] The average time from issue to allocation is around half a year.[337] The average time from allocation to trial hovers around the thirty weeks allowed in fast track cases.[338]

In the High Court, there has also been improvement. The average waiting time between issue and trial in the Queen's Bench Division in the years 1998–2001 fluctuated between 178 and 164 weeks. In 2002 it dropped to 149. The following year it rose somewhat to 164 weeks but in 2004 it dropped to 97 weeks.[339] The average time from issue to setting down for trial, which fluctuated from 1996–2003 between a high of 143 weeks and a low of 103 weeks, had dropped to forty-three weeks in 2004 – a remarkable reduction. The average time from setting down to trial has gone rather the other way. In the two years 1999 and 2000 it was an average of thirty-three and thirty-one weeks respectively but since then it has climbed rather than fallen – in the four years from

---

[333] *Ibid*, para. 6.6, p. 71.
[334] 16 *Civil Justice Quarterly*, 1997, p. 302 at 314 and also www.dca.gov.uk/judicial/speeches/speechfr.htm.   [335] Based on a sample size of 862.
[336] Table 4.17. In 1999, it was seventy-nine weeks, in 2000, it was seventy-four weeks, in 2001, it was seventy-three weeks, in 2002, it was fifty-eight weeks, in 2003, it was fifty-nine weeks and in 2004, it was fifty-three weeks.
[337] Table 4.17. In 2002, it was twenty-eight weeks, in 2003, it was also twenty-six weeks, in 2004, it was twenty-five weeks and in 2005, it was twenty-four weeks.
[338] Table 4.17. In 2002, it was thirty-one weeks, in 2003, it was thirty-two weeks, in 2004, it was down to twenty-eight weeks and in 2005, it was also twenty-eight weeks.
[339] Table 3.9. The *Judicial Statistics, 2005*, for reasons that are not explained, did not carry this table.

2001–04 it was an average of thirty-eight, forty-seven, fifty-five and fifty-four weeks.[340]

The annual statistics appear encouraging but, as was seen above, they do not establish that the Woolf reforms have brought down delay. The reason is that the statistics measure the length of the case from the issue of proceedings to the trial. If instead one measures the length of the case from the time the lawyer was first instructed to trial, the study conducted for the Civil Justice Council by Goriely et al (p. 126 above) shows that there has not been any reduction. This is because the lawyers spend more time than before in the pre-issue stage in order to investigate and prepare the case according to the pre-action protocols.

There are no later data that throws further light on this important question. Delay is generally presented as wholly bad. Certainly this was how the Woolf reports presented it, but this not necessarily so. A study by the Rand Corporation found that litigants seem more concerned about the fairness of the process than about delays, or even whether they won or lost.[341]

Inconsistent decisions

One effect of the Woolf reforms is undeniably to increase judicial discretion in the decision-making of pre-trial judges – District judges, Masters, Circuit judges and High Court judges. Appeals in interlocutory matters are not encouraged. The result is a great increase in inconsistent but unappealable decisions. The Law Society's practitioners' Woolf Network's responses to the periodic questions posed about the state of the reforms repeatedly highlighted this issue of inconsistency with regard to the assessment of costs, sanctions generally, timetable targets, the use and numbers of experts, case management decisions, pre-action disclosure and security for costs. Peysner and Seneviratne's report (2005) said some practitioners thought that the overriding objective gave too much discretion to the court. 'The system was now inconsistent and unpredictable, even "airy fairy" '. There was a view that the previous system resulted in more certainty about outcomes, and that this resulted in cost saving. Many solicitors also said that this uncertainty meant that they might not make applications where they would have done so in the past.

In the writer's view the problem of inconsistency of decision-making is a serious issue and it is one that cannot be significantly improved whether by

---

[340] Table 3.9.

[341] See M. Zander, 'What Litigants Think of the Tort System', 139 *New Law Journal*, 20 October 1989, p. 1422. See also R. Dingwall, T. Durkin and W.L.F. Felstiner, 'Delay in Tort Cases: Critical Reflections on the Civil Justice Review', 9 *Civil Justice Quarterly*, October 1990, pp. 353–65 which showed that, for expert litigators, delay was simply a resource to be managed in the best interests of the clients; and Dingwall and Dinkin, 'Time Management and Procedural Reform: Some Questions for Lord Woolf' in *Reform of Civil Procedure – Essays on Access to Justice* (eds. A.A.S. Zuckerman and R. Cranston, Clarendon Press, 1995), pp. 371–392.

judicial training or supervision or guidance from appellate level courts or anywhere else. It is part of the price that has to be paid for the benefits of the reforms.

Unjust application of sanctions

When disproportionate sanctions are imposed – *pour encourager les autres* – the result is, by definition, unjust in the particular case. Lord Woolf insisted that the courts would need to enforce the rules and it is clear that to an extent they are doing so. The Court of Appeal decisions described above (pp. 75–76) on failures with regard to service of claims, illustrate the point. As those cases show, the Court of Appeal believes that enforcing procedural rules is even more important than achieving justice in the particular case.

Again, inconsistency aggravates the problem. Judges differ as to how rigorous they are prepared to be in applying the rules and sanctions for breach. Even individual judges who on one day are strict, may on the next day in similar circumstances be more lenient. The result is unpredictability.

Conclusion

Contrary to the view of most, the writer remains of the view that on balance the disadvantages of the reforms outweigh the advantages.[342] He believes that if Lord Woolf had presented his package of reforms with an admission that, in addition to the great upheaval involved, they would end by costing most litigants more, that their effect on delay was uncertain and that they would hugely increase uncontrollable judicial discretion, it is doubtful whether they would have been implemented. Benefits of various kinds are resulting from the reforms but in the writer's view they are not sufficient to compensate for the detriments.

If that is right, it is legitimate to ask why judges and lawyers seem on the whole to think the reforms to have been well worthwhile. In the case of the judges, could it be because they generally approve of the increased powers given by the reforms to the courts? In the case of the practitioners, could it at least partly be because legal costs have risen rather than fallen?

FURTHER READING

For basic pre-Woolf reading on the topic of this chapter see especially the 1986 Hamlyn Lectures given by Sir Jack Jacob QC published under the title *The Fabric of English Civil Justice* (Sweet & Maxwell, 1987).

For reference see the major commentaries issued annually – the *White Book, Civil Procedure* (Thompson–Sweet & Maxwell), *Civil Practice* (Blackstone) and *Civil Court Practice* (Lexis Nexis).

---

[342] For a generally downbeat overall assessment, see also S. Burns, 'The Woolf Reforms in Retrospect', *Legal Action*, July 2003, pp. 8–11.

For major texts see N. Andrews, *English Civil Procedure* (OUP, 2003) and A. Zuckerman, *Civil Procedure* (2nd ed, Sweet & Maxwell, 2006)

For an excellent assessment of the significance of the CPR see Joseph Jacob, *Civil Litigation practice and procedure in a shifting culture* (2001, Emis Professional Publishing, £15).

For an examination of the impact of the ECHR and the Human Rights Act on English civil procedure see Joseph Jacob, *Civil Justice in the Age of Human Rights* (Ashgate, forthcoming 2007).

For a valuable series of occasional articles commenting on the frequent amendments and other CPR related developments see S. Gold in *New Law Journal* and S. Burns in *Legal Action*.[343]

7. Alternative dispute resolution

In the last few years there has been a dramatic upsurge in new schemes and systems of alternative dispute settlement (ADR) which now has a large literature of its own and much support. ADR has not yet become directly part of the court system, as has happened in the United States, but it has increasingly been brought into connection with the ordinary legal system – a development that was given great further emphasis through the CPR.

In December 1993, a Practice Direction in the Commercial Court introduced questions about ADR into the pre-trial checklist to be answered by the parties. Legal advisers were urged to ensure that parties were fully informed of the most cost effective means of resolving disputes.[344] In January 1995, the Lord Chief Justice's Practice Direction (p. 124 above) gave strong backing to the importance of ADR. The Practice Direction gave the text of the pre-trial checklist to be lodged with the court. This specifically asked solicitors to state whether some form of ADR might 'assist to resolve or narrow the issues in this case' and whether there has been exploration with the client or the other side of the possibility of resolving the dispute (or particular issues) by ADR.

In 1996, the judges of the Commercial Court announced that in appropriate cases they would invite the parties to take positive steps to set in motion ADR procedures. The judge might adjourn the proceedings for a specified period of time to encourage and enable the parties to take such steps. If, after discussion with both sides, it appeared that an early neutral evaluation was likely to assist in the resolution of the matters in dispute, the judge might offer to provide that evaluation or to arrange for another judge to do so. The judge who provided the early neutral evaluation would, unless the parties agreed otherwise, take no further part in the case.[345]

---

[343] See also S. Burns, 'The Human Rights Act and Civil Procedure', *Legal Action*, September 2001, p. 33.

[344] [1994] 1 All ER 34.

[345] See on this development *Law Society's Gazette*, 19 June 1996, pp. 36 and 39; *Solicitors' Journal*, 16 October 1999, p. 936; and more generally on ADR for heavy commercial cases, *Law Society's Gazette*, 5 November 1997, pp. 22–7.

Another field in which ADR, in the form of mediation, appeared to be making some progress was that of matrimonial disputes and divorce. Mediation is a method of resolving disputes by having a neutral third party guide the parties to their own solution. Lord Woolf's report called it a form of 'facilitated negotiation'. In 1995, the Government announced that it intended that mediation should have a formal role in a new form of no-fault divorce.[346] Mediation, it said, would reduce bitterness, would improve communication between couples and would help them reach agreement. Also, it should be more cost effective. The White Paper said that the Government was satisfied that even when mediators were paid more than had been the case in the pilot studies, 'family mediation will still prove to be more cost effective than negotiating at arm's length through two separate lawyers and even more so than litigating through the courts'.[347]

Though mediation was not to be compulsory it was to be strongly promoted. Part II of the Family Law Act 1996 which provided for no-fault divorce, also included a requirement (s. 8) to attend an information meeting at which the parties would get information about marriage counselling and on conflict resolution and mediation. Intending divorcees would be told that mediation might be a better alternative to litigation and confrontation in the courts. Part II also had a power for the court to direct that the parties attend a meeting to explain mediation (s. 13). Part III provided that legal aid could be given for mediation in family matters (s. 27). Before the Legal Aid Board could consider an application for legal aid, clients were supposed to attend an appointment with a mediation provider to see whether mediation would be suitable. Only if it was deemed to be unsuitable could the client get legal aid for representation for legal proceedings.

The Legal Aid Board initiated a number of pilot studies to test this system, but the pilot studies proved disappointing. Many tried to avoid the intake interview. Fewer were deemed suitable for mediation than had been hoped. The Advisory Board under the Act said in its *Second Annual Report* in May 1999: 'while the implementation of s. 29 has clearly already had some impact, the proportion of cases in the pilot franchises electing to use mediation remains as yet very small' (para. 2.25). The result of low usage was that the average cost per case amongst mediation providers was high, as their fixed costs were spread over a small number of cases. Interim findings from research into the pilots conducted by Newcastle University suggested that only 7 per cent of people who attended the s. 8 information meetings went on to mediation. Four out of ten people reported that after attending these meetings they were more likely in future to go to a solicitor.[348]

An announcement about implementation of Part II of the 1996 Act was expected in summer 1999 but in June 1999, in a written parliamentary answer,

[346] White Paper, *Looking to the Future: Mediation and the Grounds for Divorce*, Cm. 2799, 1995.

[347] White Paper at p. 42, para. 5.19.

[348] For the implications, see D. Hodson, 'Family Law Act 1996; Where Now?' *Solicitors' Journal*, 2 July 1999, p. 632 and *Law Society's Gazette*, 21 July 1999, p. 22 at 31. For the background see S. Roberts, 'Decision-Making for Life Apart', 58 *Modern Law Review*, 1995, pp. 714–22. For

the Lord Chancellor, Lord Irvine, announced that implementation of Part II of the Act would be postponed until 2000 when the full results of the pilot studies would be available.[349] Experts predicted that in reality this spelled the end of the provisions – or at least that the Lord Chancellor had decided that they would not be implemented in the then current Parliament. They were proved to be right. It has not been implemented.

There was speculation as to the reasons. Had the Lord Chancellor been persuaded that mediation would not after all be cheaper? Was he worried about political rows over no-fault divorce? Did he see the compulsory information sessions to 'push' mediation instead of court proceedings as an infringement of civil liberties? Whatever the reason, the abandonment of the project was plainly a setback for the mediation bandwagon.

Another technique of ADR is the ombudsmen who deal with complaints in a variety of contexts in both the public and the private sector. The public sector ombudsmen include the Parliamentary Commissioner, the Local Government Commissioner and the Legal Services Ombudsman.[350] Private sector ombudsmen exist in a number of industries such as insurance, building societies, pensions, banking and estate agencies. (The Financial Services and Markets Act 1999 amalgamated several of these schemes in the person of one 'overlord' Financial Services Ombudsman.)

Woolf and ADR

Lord Woolf's *Interim Report* devoted a chapter to ADR. He did not propose that ADR should be imposed compulsorily on parties to civil litigation but he greatly welcomed the development and the strengthening of ADR. He suggested that in multi-track cases at the case management conference and pre-trial review the parties should be required to state whether the question of ADR had been discussed and, if not, why not. The Lord Chancellor and the Court Service should treat it as one of their responsibilities to make the public aware of the possibility offered by ADR.

In his *Final Report*, Lord Woolf urged that people should be encouraged to use the growing number of grievance procedures, ombudsmen[351] or other available

---

a discussion of the problem and possible solutions see G. Bevan et al, 'Piloting a Quasi-Market for Family Mediation among Clients Eligible for Legal Aid', 18 *Civil Justice Quarterly*, 1999, pp. 239–48. See also A. Baker and P. Townsend, 'Is our Faith in Mediation Misplaced?', 163 *Justice of the Peace*, 20 March 1999, p. 224.

[349] House of Lords, *Hansard*, 17 June 1999, vol. 602, WA col. 39.

[350] See on this subject, for instance, R. Nobles, 'Access to Justice through Ombudsmen: the Courts' Response to the Pensions Ombudsman', 21 *Civil Justice Quarterly*, 2002, pp. 94–117.

[351] In his *Interim Report* Lord Woolf expressed the hope that the private ombudsmen system 'which has an impressive track record in relation to the service industries' should be extended to cover consumer complaints in the retail sector. They had many advantages including the fact that they are free and that complainants do not need the assistance of lawyers. Using the ombudsman did not prevent the complainant from taking legal proceedings if in the event the ombudsman was not able to provide a satisfactory outcome. Also there should be a closer relationship between ombudsmen and the courts. Ombudsmen should have the right to apply

ADR method before taking judicial review proceedings.[352] He repeated his *Interim Report* recommendations on ADR and added a new one – that when considering what order to make as to costs, the court should be able to take into account a party's unreasonable refusal to attempt ADR or lack of co-operation in ADR.

ADR features prominently in the rules. CPR 1.4(1) states that 'the court must further the overriding objective by actively managing cases'. CPR 1.4(2) goes on by elaborating twelve different examples of what active case management means. The fifth of these is 'encouraging the parties to use an alternative dispute resolution procedure if the court considers that appropriate and facilitating the use of such procedure'. The duty is therefore that of the court, but under CPR 1.3 the parties have the obligation of helping the court to further the overriding objective. When filing the allocation questionnaire a party may make a written request for the proceedings to be stayed 'while the parties try to settle the case by alternative dispute resolution or other means' (CPR 26.4). Also the court can order a stay of its own initiative (CPR 26.4(2)(b)). The court can also, of its own initiative, order the parties to consider ADR (CPR PD 29). If a party considers that ADR is not suitable, it must file a witness statement setting out the reasons why.

The Practice Direction on Pre-Action Protocols was amended as from April 2006 to strengthen the ADR provision. Paragraph 4.7 now reads:

> 4.7 The parties should consider whether some form of alternative dispute resolution procedure would be more suitable than litigation, and if so, endeavour to agree which form to adopt. Both the Claimant and Defendant may be required by the Court to provide evidence that alternative means of resolving their dispute were considered. The Courts take the view that litigation should be a last resort, and that claims should not be issued prematurely when a settlement is still actively being explored. Parties are warned that if the protocol is not followed (including this paragraph) then the Court must have regard to such conduct when determining costs.

The paragraph then refers to three ADR options for consideration: discussion and negotiation, early neutral evaluation by an independent third party and mediation. It refers to a booklet on ADR published by the Legal Services Commission.[353]

Footnote 351 (*cont.*)

    to a court for a ruling on a point of law without requiring the complainant to commence legal proceedings. It would be an advantage if the courts were able to refer issues to an ombudsman, subject to the parties' consent and that of the ombudsman in question. In any subsequent proceedings, the ombudsman's findings of fact would be accepted as being correct in the absence of evidence to the contrary. This would involve changes to the statutory position of public ombudsmen. The same concept should be applied to private sector ombudsmen if they thought it acceptable (*Interim Report* at pp. 139–140).

[352] At p. 251, para. 7.

[353] 'Alternatives to Court', CLS Direct Information Leaflet 23 – www.cls.org.uk/legalhelp/leaflet23.jsp.

The paragraph ends: 'it is expressly recognised that no party can or should be forced to mediate or enter into any form of ADR'.

The DCA five-year strategy for 2004–09 stated that the Department aimed to achieve 'earlier and more proportionate resolution of legal problems and disputes'. The target was by March 2008 to reduce the proportion of court cases going to a hearing by 5 per cent. A key element in that strategy was to encourage more use of ADR.

The costs sanction

Sabotaging the effort at ADR can be penalised in costs if the case comes back to the courts. This happened in *Dunnett v. Railtrack Plc*[354] where the Court of Appeal refused to give the successful defendants their costs because they had refused to consider ADR which the trial judge had urged should be attempted when he granted leave to appeal from his decision.[355]

However, a litigant's refusal to engage in ADR is not always treated as unreasonable. In *Watson Wyatt v. Maxwell Batley*,[356] Mr Justice Colman refused the claimant's application to block part of the defendant solicitors firm's costs because their refusal to mediate had not been unreasonable. The judge held that three separate invitations to mediate were not genuine but had been employed as an aggressive tactic. In *Hurst v. Leeming*,[357] Mr Justice Lightman held that a barrister involved in professional negligence proceedings was entitled to his full costs even though he had refused to mediate. His refusal was not unreasonable because the personality of the opponent made it improbable that mediation would succeed.[358]

The leading case is *Halsey v. Milton Keynes General NHS Trust*.[359] The claimant in a clinical negligence case failed in her action but then sought to have the defendant health authority penalised in costs because it had repeatedly refused to mediate. The Court of Appeal rejected her contention, holding that the health authority had been justified in refusing to mediate because it reasonably believed that it would win the case. Some cases were not suitable for

---

[354] [2002] EWCA Civ 303, [2002] 1 WLR 2434, [2002] 2 All ER 850. For commentary see I. Grainger, 'The Costs Consequences of a Failure to Mediate', 23 *Civil Justice Quarterly*, 2004, pp. 244–7.

[355] See to similar effect *Cable & Wireless Plc v. IBM United Kingdom Ltd* [2002] EWHC 2059, [2002] 2 All ER (Comm) 1041 and *R (Cowl) v. Plymouth City Council* [2001] EWCA Civ 1935, [2002] 1 WLR 803. See also *Royal Bank of Canada Trust Corpn Ltd v. Secretary of State for Defence* (2003) Times, 14 May, Ch D in which the judge refused to award any costs to the Department of Defence even though it had won on the substantive issue because of its 'surprising' rejection of an offer of mediation by the claimants. The judge said he was influenced in particular by the Government's 2001 pledge that 'ADR will be considered and used in all suitable cases wherever the other party accepts it'.

[356] (2002) Times, 15 November, *Solicitors' Journal*, 29 November 2002, p. 1072.

[357] [2001] EWHC 1051, [2003] 1 Lloyd's Rep 379, Ch.

[358] See similarly *Hickman v. Blake Lapthorn* [2006] EWHC 12, QB where the judge said the test was whether counsel's refusal to consider mediation was unreasonable – which on the facts of the case it was not. For commentary see S. Prince, 'Negotiating Mediation', 156 *New Law Journal*, 17 February 2006, p. 262 and 'Costs Cutting', 156 *New Law Journal*, 5 May 2006, p. 737.   [359] [2004] EWCA Civ 576, [2004] 4 All ER 920.

mediation – for instance where fraud was alleged, where what was wanted was to establish a precedent by a judicial decision or where an injunction was sought. Article 6 of the European Convention on Human Rights guaranteed the right to have a dispute determined by an impartial tribunal. Parties could not be compelled to mediate. Even when the court ordered mediation therefore, this was no more than very strong encouragement to mediate. Forcing an unwilling party to mediate, Lord Justice Dyson said, 'would impose an unacceptable obstruction on their right of access to the court'.

Whether the winning party would be penalised in costs for a refusal to mediate would depend on the case. It was for the losing party to persuade the court that the winning party's refusal had been unreasonable. The Court of Appeal rehearsed factors that could be relevant: the nature of the dispute, the merits of the case, the extent to which other settlement methods had been attempted, whether the costs of mediation would be disproportionately high, whether delay in establishing mediation would be prejudicial and whether the mediation had a reasonable prospect of success.[360]

What is not clear is whether coercing ADR through use of the threat of the costs sanction is compatible with the ECHR's requirement in Article 6 for a fair and public trial.

Low take-up

While the 'mood music' of the courts is certainly therefore in favour of ADR, it is making slow headway on the ground as a means of resolving civil disputes.

The abandonment of mediation under the Family Law Act was an obvious example. Another was the modest success of the scheme to promote ADR set up in January 1996 at the Central London county court. All defendants facing non-family civil disputes of over £3,000 were offered mediation at the nominal rate of £25. Research on the project by Professor H. Genn of University College, London found that, despite the negligible cost, only 5 per cent of litigants approached took up the offer. Those who did use the service achieved a settlement in 62 per cent of cases and generally were satisfied. The process promoted and speeded up settlement and reduced conflicts, but it was unclear to what extent the mediation saved costs and, where the mediation was unsuccessful, it had the effect of increasing costs. Also the level of damages was distinctly lower than that of the courts – a possible explanation why most practitioners seem less than enthusiastic.[361]

[360] See also *Burchell v. Bullard* [2005] EWCA Civ 358.

[361] H. Genn, *The Central London County Court Pilot Mediation Scheme*, LCD Research Series 5/98. For a substantial report on the state of ADR in the UK construction industry see N. Gould and M. Cohen, 'ADR: Appropriate Dispute Resolution in the UK Construction Industry', 17 *Civil Justice Quarterly*, 1998, pp. 103–27. The conclusion was that although formalised mediation was only rarely invoked it was a technique that was available for appropriate cases.

[362] For evaluations of three of these schemes see L. Webley, P. Abrams and S. Bacquet, *Evaluation of the Birmingham Court-Based Civil (Non-Family) Mediation Scheme*, November 2005, DCA

However, the scheme has continued and indeed developed. By 2003 there were comparable schemes at four other county courts – Birmingham, Leeds, Exeter and Guildford.[362]

In 2002 the LCD published another study by Professor Genn – *Court-based ADR initiatives for non-family civil disputes: the Commercial Court and the Court of Appeal.*[363] The Commercial Court judge may make an order directing the parties to attempt ADR to resolve the dispute. The study covered the four-year period from July 1996 to June 2000. The number of orders had grown considerably since the introduction of the CPR. Where pre-CPR the average rate was about thirty annually, in the last six months there had been sixty-eight such orders. During the whole period there were 233 cases in which an ADR order had been made. Information was available regarding 184. Of these, 103 (56 per cent) tried mediation.

Summarising her research on ADR orders in the Commercial Court, the Court of Appeal ADR scheme and the earlier Central London county court mediation scheme, Professor Genn drew the following conclusions:[364]

- Voluntary take up of invitations to enter ADR schemes remained at a modest level, even when the mediator's services were provided free or at a nominal cost.
- Outside of commercial practice, the profession remained very cautious about the use of ADR. Positive experience of ADR did not appear to be producing armies of converts. Explanations might lie in the amount of work involved in preparing for mediation, the incentives and economics of mediation in low-value cases and the impact of the Woolf reforms. More pre-issue settlements and swifter post-issue settlements might diminish the perceived need for ADR in run-of-the-mill cases.
- An individualised approach to the direction of cases toward ADR was likely to be more effective than general invitations at an early stage in the litigation process.
- Subjective perceptions of the profession supported the view that successful ADR saved the likely costs of proceedings to trial and might save expenditure by promoting earlier settlement than might otherwise have occurred. However, unsuccessful ADR could increase the costs for parties.
- ADR generally resulted in a high level of customer satisfaction.

The research carried out in 2003–04 in eight county courts by Professors Peysner and Seneviratne confirmed this basically pessimistic appraisal.[365] After reviewing the evidence on ADR they concluded:

> It seems that ADR has not become incorporated into the court process. Cases are settling, but this is not because they are being mediated. The judges are reluctant

---

Research Series and S. Prince and S. Belcher, *An Evaluation of the Effectiveness of Court-Based Mediation Processes in Non-Family Civil Proceedings at Exeter and Guildford County Courts*, May 2005, DCA Research Series.   [363] LCD Research Series 1/2002.

[364] See the executive summary at www.dca.gov.uk – Research.

[365] *The Management of Civil Cases: the Courts and the Post-Woolf Landscape*, DCA Research Report 9/2005, section 4.5.

> to order mediation because of the lack of facilities and resources ...
> Practitioners said that mediation was inappropriate at the beginning of the lit-
> igation process because there was insufficient information to know the strength
> of the case. Towards the end, all the costs had been incurred, so there was little
> point in not going ahead with the trial.[366]

It seems that, despite the hype and its success when used, ADR is only used in a
tiny proportion of cases.

Reasons for the low take up of ADR by litigants have been suggested by the
Centre for Effective Dispute Resolution (CEDR):

- The process is unfamiliar to clients and practitioners. The latter in particular
  and not unnaturally they prefer to stick to what they know and how they normally operate unless there are incentives to do otherwise.
- Classic positional negotiation behaviour in conflict makes it awkward for a
  party to suggest talks or even talks about talks.
- People resist going to third parties (including advisers and the courts) unless they
  either (1) are familiar with the process; (2) see it as the only real option and (3)
  accept it as a 'socially credible' (i.e. a known and acceptable) option.[367]

Frustration at the slow development of ADR has led the DCA to experiment
with some form of quasi-compulsion. The basic philosophy of mediation is that
it is a voluntary, consensual process,[368] but an experiment in Ontario appeared
to justify the view that mediation could be successful and could give satisfaction
even when the parties were forced to mediate against their will.[369]

In March 2004 the DCA announced the establishment of a scheme in the
Central London county court for the automatic referral of selected cases to
mediation (ARM).[370] The ARM scheme involved random allocation of 100
cases per month to mediation at the point at which a defence was entered.
Trained mediators from one of four mediation organisations were to be allocated on a rotation basis. The mediation would last up to three hours and would
cost £100 per party.

The referral was therefore automatic but the parties were able to object to the
referral. Where one or both parties objected, the matter would be heard by a

---

[366] At pp. 45–6.
[367] *CEDR Response to LCD Discussion Paper on Alternative Dispute Resolution*, February 2000.
[368] See M. Roberts, 'Voluntary Participation in Family Mediation', 36 *Family Law*, January 2006,
   pp. 57–61. (The article ends with the words: 'with compulsion, mediation will cease to be the
   kind of process we now commonly understand it to be'.)
[369] www.attorneygeneral.jus.gov.on.ca/english/manmed/exec_summary_recommend.pdf. The
   Ontario Mandatory Mediation Programme which started in 1999 applied to non-family
   cases in Ontario and Toronto. The evaluation was based on data collected from over 3,000
   mediations. The results showed significant reductions in the time taken to dispose of cases,
   lower costs, earlier settlement and considerable satisfaction of both litigants and lawyers. (See
   S. Prince, 'Mandatory Mediation: The Ontario Experience', 26 *Civil Justice Quarterly*, 2007,
   pp. 79–95.)
[370] The Press Release of 24 March 2004 said that the pilot was based on the Ontario scheme and
   that it would run for twelve months from April.

District judge. The press notice stated that if the judge decided that the case should nevertheless go for mediation and one of the parties still declined to accept the ruling, 'they risk being liable to costs under existing case law and CPR 44.5'.

The DCA commissioned an evaluation of the scheme which it was hoped after a year would be based on around a thousand cases, but in May 2004, only weeks after the scheme began, the Court of Appeal gave its decision in *Halsey v. Milton Keynes NHS Trust* (above) holding that the courts had no power to order cases to go to mediation. The decision in *Halsey* effectively wrecked any chance that the scheme had of testing the question of compulsion or quasi-compulsion to mediate. In the event, as many as 80 per cent of those referred to the scheme opted out, with the result that the number of cases in the evaluation was only a quarter of what had been expected.

At the time of writing, the evaluation report by Professor Genn (*Mediating Civil Disputes: Evaluating Court Referral and Voluntary Mediation*) was in manuscript.[371] The draft report showed an overall settlement rate of 42 per cent. (It was 55 per cent for the cases where there had been no objection to mediation and 33 per cent for the cases where both parties had objected but had been persuaded to undertake mediation. Where mediation occurred after one party had objected, the settlement rate was 50 per cent.)

The settlement rate in the voluntary schemes in Birmingham, Exeter and Guildford was 64 per cent, 40 per cent and 56 per cent respectively.

Whether the DCA (and the Treasury) considers that these 'success' or 'failure' rates of mediation are such as to warrant greater efforts to push litigants toward mediation remains to be seen.

In June 2006 the Technology and Construction Court (TCC) started a controversial pilot scheme under which the *judges* would mediate in construction cases. The very idea of the scheme provoked criticism not only from lawyers but also from mediators.[372]

---

[371] It dealt with both the ARM scheme and with the voluntary mediation programme that had been running at the Central London county court (now the Central London Civil Justice Centre) since 1996 and that had previously been evaluated by Professor Genn in 1998.

[372] *The Lawyer*, 5 June 2006, reported the start of the pilot on p. 1 under the heading 'uproar as TCC hands judges mediation role'. Solicitors, arbitrators and mediators were reported as describing it as 'a terrible idea'. The Technology and Construction Solicitors' Association (TECSA) were said to be against it because judges were not good at mediation. The judges were to have special training in mediation but it has to be said that the mediating role is significantly different from that of a judge. *The Lawyer*, commenting editorially, quoted Australia's leading mediator, former Chief Justice, Sir Laurence Street: 'the involvement of a custodian of power as mediator imports the real risk of a party feeling a sense of coercion and hence disenchantment with the mediated outcome that can reflect back adversely on the court', but the scheme had the support of the Chief Justice. The mediations could be handled either by the trial judge or by another judge. TECSA's chairman was quoted as saying that his group were in favour of the scheme. ('The system's only going to be used by consenting adults. It will be interesting to see if it's taken up'.)

FURTHER READING

M. Palmer and S. Roberts, *Dispute Processes – ADR and the Primary Forms of Decision Making* (Cambridge University Press, 2005); S. Roberts 'Institutionalised Settlements in England: A Contemporary Panorama', 10 *Williamette Journal of International Law and Dispute Resolution*, 2002, p. 17; P. Brooker and A. Lavers, 'Issues in the Development of ADR for Commercial and Construction Disputes', 19 *Civil Justice Quarterly*, 2000, pp. 353–70; P. Brooker, 'Commercial and Construction ADR: Lawyers' Attitudes and Experience', 20 *Civil Justice Quarterly*, 2001, pp. 327–47; S. Shipman, 'Court Approaches to ADR in the Civil Justice System', 25 *Civil Justice Quarterly*, 2006, pp. 181–218; B. Tronson, 'Mediation Orders: Do the Arguments Against Them Make Sense?', 25 *Civil Justice Quarterly*, 2006, pp. 412–18.

See also R.L. Abel, *The Politics of Informal Justice* (Academic Press, 1982); J. Auerbach, *Justice without Law* (Oxford, 1983) and 56 *Modern Law Review*, 1993, the whole issue entitled 'Dispute Resolution: Civil Justice and its Alternatives'.

Chapter 3

Pre-trial criminal proceedings

1. Introduction – the overriding objective

This chapter deals with one of the most important aspects of any legal system – how suspects are dealt with pre-trial – and police powers. It offers a great deal of scope for discussion of matters of both principle and practice. It is also an area where a considerable volume of empirical work has been done.

The topic is dominated by the central piece of legislation in the field of police powers, the Police and Criminal Evidence Act 1984 (known as 'PACE').[1] This Act was the result of the Philips Royal Commission on Criminal Procedure ('Philips').[2] The Philips Commission's Report also resulted in the Prosecution of Offences Act 1985 which established the Crown Prosecution Service ('CPS').

PACE is accompanied by Codes of Practice. Originally there were four. Now there are seven: Code A on Stop and Search, Code B on Search of Premises, Code C on Detention, Questioning and Treatment of Persons in Custody, Code D on Identification, Code E on Tape Recording of Interviews, Code F on Visual Recording with Sound of Interviews and Code G on Arrest. In July 2006 a new Code H was added setting out the rules (equivalent to those in Code C) for the detention, treatment and questioning of terrorist suspects.

PACE has been the subject of countless legislative amendments. The Codes too have been amended from time to time. The latest major revision came into force on 1 January 2006.

The Codes are the result of extensive consultation by the Home Office with interested bodies and persons. New codes and major amendments to the Codes have to be approved by Parliament.[3] (The latest version of the Codes are accessible on www.police.homeoffice.gov.uk/operational-policing/powers-pace-codes/pace-codes.html.)

Technically, the Codes are not law,[4] nor can a breach of the Codes be made the subject of an action for damages or a criminal prosecution against a police

---

[1] On PACE, see M. Zander, *The Police and Criminal Evidence Act 1984* (5th edn, Sweet & Maxwell, 2005 and First Supplement, 2006).   [2] 1981, Cmnd. 8092.
[3] PACE, s. 67(1) as amended by the Criminal Justice Act 2003, s. 11.
[4] In *McCay* [1991] 1 All ER 232 the Court of Appeal said that the Codes had the full authority of Parliament behind them and that therefore there was statutory authority (sic) for a breach

officer (PACE, s. 67(10)). Originally PACE (s. 67(8)) provided that a breach of the Codes was automatically an offence against the police disciplinary code, but this section was repealed by the Police and Magistrates' Courts Act 1994. (Hardly any disciplinary proceedings for breaches of PACE had in fact been brought.[5])

The main formal sanction behind the Codes is that a judge may exclude evidence obtained in breach of the rules or, if the judge fails to do so, the appeal court may quash a conviction (s. 67(11)). As will be seen below (p. 480), this has happened often.

Reference is made in this chapter to the famous (or infamous) Eleventh Report of the Criminal Law Revision Committee (CLRC), published in June 1972.[6] This report made a number of fundamental and highly controversial recommendations for changes in the rules of evidence and procedure in criminal cases. The CLRC's report was received with such a volume of criticism, notably on the problem of the right of silence, that its recommendations (including some that were not controversial) were not implemented at the time.[7] However, many of its recommendations, including, above all, those on the right to silence, were implemented years later.

This chapter also deals extensively with the Report of the Runciman Royal Commission on Criminal Justice ('Runciman'). The Runciman Commission (of which the writer was a member) was announced in 1990 on the day that the Birmingham Six had their convictions quashed. It reported in 1993.[8] The writer was also responsible for the *Crown Court Study* which was the Royal Commission's main piece of research.[9]

The latest major report in this area was Lord Justice Auld's *Review of the Criminal Courts of England and Wales* published in October 2001 ('Auld').[10] The Government gave its response to the Auld Review in the White Paper *Justice for All*.[11] The Criminal Justice Act 2003 gave effect to many of its proposals. The

---

Footnote 4 (*cont.*)

     of the normal hearsay rule! This was a case of Homer nodding. The Codes have no statutory authority.

[5] See Report of the Runciman Royal Commission on Criminal Justice, 1993, p. 48, para. 102.

[6] *Evidence, General*, Cmnd. 4991.

[7] See M. Zander, 'The CLRC Evidence Report – a Survey of Reactions', *Law Society's Gazette*, 7 October 1974.

[8] Cm. 2263. For a critical assessment of the Runciman Commission's Report see for instance *Criminal Justice in Crisis* (eds. M. McConville and L. Bridges, Edward Elgar, 1994).

[9] M. Zander and P. Henderson, *Crown Court Study* (Royal Commission on Criminal Justice, Research Study No. 19, 1993). The study was based on questionnaires addressed to the participants in every completed case in a two-week period in every Crown Court in the country. Questionnaires were completed by the judge, the prosecution and defence barristers, the CPS, the defence solicitor, the police, the court clerk, the jurors and the defendant. There were some 3,000 cases in the sample.

[10] The 686 page report is accessible on www.dca.gov.uk – Major Reports. For appraisal of the Auld Report see, for instance, the April 2002 issue of the *Criminal Law Review*. See also the writer's seventy-five page response accessible on www.dca.gov.uk – Major Reports/Auld Report/Comments received.   [11] Cm. 5563, July 2002.

Criminal Justice Act 2003 also implemented changes to PACE recommended by the *Joint Review of PACE and the Codes of Practice* by the Home Office and the Cabinet Office published in November 2002.[12]

In August 2004 the Home Office published a consultation paper entitled *Policing: Modernising Police Powers to Meet Community Needs.*[13] Many of its proposals were included in the Serious Organised Crime and Police Act 2005.

One of the recommendations of the Auld Report was that there should be a Criminal Procedure Code: 'what is needed is . . . a concise and simply expressed statement of the current statutory and common law procedural rules and the product of the present overlay of Practice Directions, codes of guidance and the like. It should be in a single instrument and laid out in such a form that it, the Code, can be readily amended without constant recourse to primary legislation and without changing the "geography" or the familiar paragraph and section numbers governing each topic'.[14]

This recommendation was taken up. The Criminal Procedure Rules came into force on 4 April 2005.[15] They are arranged in ten main subject divisions, starting with 'General matters' and then proceeding chronologically from 'Preliminary proceedings' to 'Appeals' and 'Costs'.

The new rules are more than a consolidation. They introduced a new 'overriding objective' equivalent to the 'overriding objective' in the CPR (p. 48 above):

The overriding objective

(1) The overriding objective of this new code is that criminal cases be dealt with justly.

(2) Dealing with a criminal case justly includes –
  (a) acquitting the innocent and convicting the guilty;
  (b) dealing with the prosecution and the defence fairly;
  (c) recognising the rights of a defendant, particularly those under Article 6 of the European Convention on Human Rights;
  (d) respecting the interests of witnesses, victims and jurors and keeping them informed of the progress of the case;
  (e) dealing with the case efficiently and expeditiously;
  (f) ensuring that appropriate information is available to the court when bail and sentence are considered; and
  (g) dealing with the case in ways that take into account –

---

[12] For the text of the Joint Report see www.cabinetoffice.gov.uk/regulation/publications/archive.asp. For critical commentary see M. Zander, 'The Joint Review of PACE: a Deplorable Report', 153 *New Law Journal*, 14 February 2002, p. 204.   [13] www.homeoffice.gov.uk.

[14] Auld, para. 274, p. 509.

[15] SI 2005/384. They are available online both on the HMSO and on the DCA's Websites: www.hmso.gov.uk and www.dca.gov.uk respectively. For commentary see P. Plowden, 'Make Do and Mend, or a Cultural Evolution?' 155 *New Law Journal*, 2005, p. 328 and 'Case Management and the Criminal Procedure Rules', *ibid*, p. 416; A. Keogh, 'A Criminal Revolution', *Law Society's Gazette*, 16 June 2005, p. 36. They were the subject of an editorial in the *Criminal Law Review*, 2004, pp. 397–400.

(i)   the gravity of the offence alleged,
(ii) the complexity of what is in issue,
(iii) the severity of the consequences for the defendant and others affected, and
(iv) the needs of other cases.

1.2 The duty of the participants in a criminal case

(1) Each participant, in the conduct of each case, must –
  (a) prepare and conduct the case in accordance with the overriding objective;
  (b) comply with these Rules, Practice Directions and directions made by the court; and
  (c) at once inform the court and all parties of any significant failure (whether or not that participant is responsible for that failure) to take any procedural step required by these Rules, any Practice Direction or any direction of the court. A failure is significant if it might hinder the court in furthering the overriding objective.
(2) Anyone involved in any way with a criminal case is a participant in its conduct for the purposes of this rule.

1.3 The application by the court of the overriding objective

The court must further the overriding objective in particular when –
(a) exercising any power given to it by legislation (including these Rules);
(b) applying any Practice Direction; or
(c) interpreting any rule or Practice Direction.

Rule 1.1(a) equates convicting the guilty with acquitting the innocent. This seems at variance with the traditional view that it is even more important that an innocent person be acquitted than that a guilty person be convicted – expressed most clearly in the requirement that proof of guilt must be beyond a reasonable doubt.

Again, rule 1.1(b) in requiring fairness to both prosecution and defence obscures the fact that the two sides are hardly on an equal footing, do not have equal resources and do not have an equal interest in the outcome of the case.

Rule 1.1(c) does specifically recognise the rights of the defendant.

Rule 1.1(g) introduces a notion of proportionality into the criminal justice process by requiring that the case must be dealt with in a way that takes account of the gravity, complexity and seriousness of the case as well as the 'needs of other cases'. It has been suggested that this could be interpreted to permit 'justice on the cheap' for matters where the penalty is low or where courts have to deal with many other cases without taking into account the fundamental principle that the trial must be fair.[16]

Rule 1.3 regarding the duty of the court to advance the overriding objective is neither surprising nor controversial. The same cannot be said of rule 1.2. This

---

[16] See P. Plowden, n. 15 above at p. 329.

not only requires each participant in criminal cases to prepare and conduct the case in accordance with the overriding objective, but in rule 1.2(c) lays on participants a novel duty to inform the court of 'any significant failure' whether of their own or of any other participant which might hinder the court in furthering the overriding objective.

The courts have made it clear that where there is a failure to comply with procedural rules the court must consider whether Parliament intended the underlying act to be invalid. Generally this would not be the case. In that situation the only issue is whether there is prejudice to the defence. If not, the procedural failing is not to be allowed to thwart the overriding objective of the rules to convict the guilty and acquit the innocent.[17]

Evaluating criminal justice systems

The terms of reference of the Philips Royal Commission were: 'having regard both to the interests of the community in bringing offenders to justice and to the rights and liberties of persons suspected or accused of crime and taking into account also the need for the efficient and economical use of resources', to consider whether changes were needed in the system. The Philips Commission referred frequently to the need to strike a fundamental balance between the interests of the suspect and of the prosecution.

The terms of reference of the Runciman Royal Commission required it to 'examine the effectiveness of the criminal justice system in England and Wales in securing the conviction of those guilty of criminal offences and the acquittal of those who are innocent, having regard to the efficient use of resources'.

The terms of reference of Lord Justice Auld's inquiry, somewhat narrower than those of Philips and Runciman, were to inquire into 'the practices and procedures of, and the rules of evidence applied by, the criminal courts at every level, with a view to ensuring that they deliver justice fairly, by streamlining all their processes, increasing their efficiency and strengthening the effectiveness of their relationships with others across the whole of the criminal justice system, and having regard to the interests of all parties including victims and witnesses, thereby promoting public confidence in the rule of law'.

Superficially, the different terms of reference of the three inquiries might suggest that each had a different agenda, but the essence of each was the same. Sensible assessment of the criminal justice system unavoidably has to take account of the proper concerns of all the relevant interests. The most obvious are those of the prosecution and of the defence and the need to achieve due

---

[17] *Ashton* [2006] EWCA Crim 794, [2006] Crim LR 1004. The cases considered included *Soneji* [2005] 3 WLR 303; and *Sekhon* [2003] 1 WLR 1655. The commentary in the *Criminal Law Review* described the decision in *Ashton* as 'one of the most striking examples of the sea-change in judicial attitude in recent years to the correct approach to remedying procedural flaws in the criminal process.' The new approach was 'far less likely to yield to a defence submission for a case to be discharged or stayed as an abuse of process' (pp. 1006–7).

economy and efficiency. Auld's terms of reference added the interests of the victim and witnesses. Both of these interests have come to the fore even more strongly since the publication of the Auld Report.

On some topics primary weight is given to the interests of the prosecution (sometimes called the 'crime control' perspective); on others to the interests of the suspect (sometimes called the 'due process' perspective); on others again to the need for economy and efficiency. The civil libertarian will strike the balance differently from the police officer. The task of an external inquiry such as that of a Royal Commission is to consider all the evidence and then to reach a considered view as to the pros and cons of all the arguments.[18]

For the contrasting view that principle rather than a search for a proper balance should guide reform of criminal justice systems, see A. Ashworth and M. Redmayne, *The Criminal Process* (3rd edn, OUP, 2003) Ch. 3. See also Professor Ashworth's Hamlyn lectures, *Human Rights, Serious Crime and Criminal Procedure* (Sweet & Maxwell, 2002).

The first substantive topic dealt with here is the questioning of suspects.

2. Questioning of suspects by the police

The importance and quality of police questioning

The questioning of suspects plays a central part in the police handling of the functions of prosecution.[19] A Home Office study of 12,500 custody record forms and observation over a total of 4,000 hours in twenty-five police stations showed that six out of ten detainees were interviewed in custody.[20] The overwhelming majority (96 per cent) were interviewed only once. Even in serious cases only one in five was interviewed more than once.

It was not always so. The 1929 Royal Commission on Police Powers and Procedure said that the law then was that where an arrest was necessary the constable should make it clear that the person was under arrest on a specific charge

---

[18] The fifteen person Philips Royal Commission and the eleven person Runciman Royal Commission both consisted of a mixture of people knowledgeable about the system (judges, lawyers, police officers, academics etc.) and lay people with no prior experience of the criminal justice system. In both cases the chairman was a layman. Despite their mixed membership, both Royal Commissions were unanimous in the overwhelming majority of their recommendations. By contrast, although Lord Justice Auld had an advisory group, he basically conducted his inquiry on his own. (As to the desirability of that see M. Zander, 'Reforming the Criminal Justice System: Too Difficult to be Left to One Individual?' 151 *New Law Journal*, 30 November 2001, p. 1774.) Both Philips and Runciman commissioned substantial empirical research reports. Auld generated virtually no new research.

[19] See for instance M. McConville and J. Baldwin, *Courts, Prosecution and Conviction* (Clarendon Press, 1981) Ch. 7; B. Mitchell, 'Confessions and Police Interrogation of Suspects', *Criminal Law Review*, 1983, p. 596; M. McConville, A. Sanders and R. Leng, *The Case for the Prosecution* (Routledge, 1991) Ch. 4.

[20] T. Bucke and D. Brown, *In police custody: police powers and suspects' rights under the revised PACE codes of practice*, 1997, Home Office Research Series No. 174 ('Bucke and Brown 1997').

and 'thereafter he should not question the prisoner . . . although he should make a note of anything he says and should bring him straight to the police station for formal charging' (para. 137). Whether this is what actually happened is a different question but that was the formal position. It was only recently that the courts directly recognised that the police could hold a suspect for questioning (see p. 207 below).

Various studies have found that over half of suspects in detention confess when questioned. In Bucke and Brown 1997[21] confessions were made by 58 per cent. White suspects confessed more often than Afro-Caribbean and Asian suspects – 60 per cent compared with 48 per cent and 51 per cent respectively. Having legal advice is associated with fewer confessions. Two-thirds (66 per cent) of those who had not had legal advice confessed compared with 47 per cent of those who had had legal advice.[22]

Until quite recently the police received little or no training in questioning. Research conducted for the Home Office by Professor John Baldwin of Birmingham University showed that the results were not unduly impressive. The research was to inquire into video taping of interviews but a side product was the first independent assessment of the quality of police interviews.[23]

Overall, Baldwin found that 64 per cent of interviews were conducted 'competently', 25 per cent were 'not very well conducted' and 11 per cent were conducted 'poorly'.[24]

The main weaknesses identified were: 'a lack of preparation, a general ineptitude, poor technique, an assumption of guilt, unduly repetitive, persistent or laboured questioning, a failure to establish relevant facts and the exertion of too much pressure' (*ibid*):

> The image of police interviewers as professional, skilled and forceful interrogators scarcely matched the reality. Officers sometimes emerged as nervous, ill at ease and lacking in confidence. Even in the simplest cases, they were unfamiliar with the available evidence, and the video cameras often showed them with their eyes glued to a written statement, clearly unacquainted with its contents . . . Many officers enter the interview room with their minds made up. They treat the suspect's explanation, if they bother to listen to it at all, with extreme scepticism from the outset. They are not predisposed, either from training or temperament, to think that they might be wrong. The questions asked (often leading questions starting as they do, from an assumption of guilt) merely seek to persuade suspects to agree to a series of propositions. If this is unsuccessful, discussion tends to be unhelpfully polarised, with claims and counterclaims, allegations and denials following a familiar circular path, descending often into a highly repetitive series of questions . . . Some officers adopted an unduly harrying or aggressive

---

[21] *Ibid.*   [22] *Ibid* at pp. 33–4.

[23] The study was based on 400 video recordings and 200 audio recordings of interviews conducted by the police in the West Midlands, West Mercia and London – J. Baldwin, *Video Taping Police Interviews with Suspects – an Evaluation* (Home Office, Police Research Series, Paper No. 1, 1992).   [24] Baldwin, Table 3, p. 14.

approach in interviewing, and though this arose in a relatively small number of cases, these were the ones in which the present writer felt greatest unease about the outcome, particularly where they involved juveniles and young persons.

Another part of the mythology is that the great majority of interviews are with suspects who are awkward or aggressive. There are of course some interviews which are of this nature, but the great majority are not. Most involve relatively simple and straightforward matters with reasonably compliant suspects. Because officers assume the opposite to be the case (as do most training manuals), training often fails to deal with the commonplace and the humdrum . . . In only twenty-seven cases (4.5 per cent of the whole sample) did the officer's manner seem unduly harsh or aggressive. In almost two-thirds of all cases, the style of interviewing could not even be described as confrontational, since no serious challenge was made to what a suspect was saying . . . Fewer than one in eight suspects sought to exercise their right to remain silent in any significant way, and taking interviews as a whole, it emerged that four out of every five were with such co-operative or compliant individuals that they should have presented no serious difficulties to a moderately competent interviewer.[25]

Professor Baldwin suggested that 'the importance of this simple finding can scarcely be overstated'.[26]

Partly in response to this research and partly because of the concerns about police misconduct in questioning of suspects leading to miscarriages of justice, the police service commissioned outside experts to help it design a new interviewing training package. In its report in 1993 the Runciman Royal Commission referred with approval to this development. The new approach had been signalled in a Home Office circular[27] which stated, *inter alia*: 'the role of investigative interviewing is to obtain accurate and reliable information from suspects, witnesses or victims in order to discover the truth about matters under police investigation . . . Investigative interviewing should be approached with an open mind . . . When questioning anyone a police officer must act fairly in the circumstances of each individual case'.[28]

A new training package based on these principles, involving a full week of training, was introduced in 1993. All police officers were supposed to be exposed to the course.[29] The essence of the interviewing method, one might say, was less talking and more listening!

---

[25] At pp. 14–18.

[26] At p. 18. For other writings by Professor Baldwin on this research see 141 *New Law Journal*, 8 November 1991; 'Police Interview Techniques: Establishing Truth or Proof?', *British Journal of Criminology*, 1993, pp. 325–52. For an account of research comparing the strikingly different tenor of police interviews as reflected in police summaries (pre-PACE) and tape recordings (post-PACE) see I. Bryan, 'Shifting Images: Police–Suspect Encounters during Custodial Interrogations', 17 *Legal Studies*, 1997, pp. 215–33.

[27] 22/1992, dated 20 February 1992.   [28] Runciman, p. 13, para. 21.

[29] For an article on investigative interviewing by one of those most responsible for its introduction see Chief Superintendant T. Williamson, 'Policing', Winter 1992, pp. 286–99. See also the series of articles by Detective Sergeant G. Shaw in nine consecutive issues of *Police Review* starting 5 January 1996.

The danger of false confessions

The phenomenon of false confessions is now widely recognised and accepted. One of the world's leading authorities on the subject identified four different types of false confessions:

- False confessions borne of a desire to attract publicity or notoriety, or to relieve guilt about real or imagined misdeeds, or from an inability to distinguish between reality and fantasy.
- False confessions to protect others.
- False confessions to gain a short-term advantage such as respite from questioning or bail.
- False confessions which the suspect is persuaded by the interrogator are true.

See further G.H. Gudjonsson, *The Psychology of Interrogations, Confessions and Testimony* (Wiley, 1992) and 'The Psychology of False Confessions', 142 *New Law Journal*, 18 September 1992, p. 1277. The same author later published *The Psychology of Interrogations and Confessions: A Handbook* (Wiley, 2003) described in a review as 'seminal, comprehensive, dispassionate, sound, scholarly and most crucially, authoritative'.[30]

For a useful review of the problem of false confessions and of the measures taken to counter the problem in the UK and the US (plus relevant literature) see J. Lowenstein, 'The Psychological and Procedural Issues in the Occurrence of False Confessions by Vulnerable Individuals', 170 *Justice of the Peace*, 25 March 2006, pp. 207–11.

The Judges' Rules

For most of the last century the process of questioning suspects was governed principally by the Judges' Rules – rules formulated by the judges of the Queen's Bench Division in the form of a brief code. They were not law, and breaches of the Judges' Rules did not necessarily give rise to any adverse consequence for the police. Evidence obtained in breach of the Judges' Rules could in theory be held to be inadmissible, but this hardly ever occurred unless the defendant's statement was held by the court to be 'involuntary' (see pp. 471–72). There was also the theoretical possibility that a breach of the Rules (especially one revealed in court) could be made the occasion for police disciplinary proceedings against the officer concerned. That too, however, was very rare.

The Judges' Rules had three parts. There was, first, the preamble which set out five principles that were said to apply generally: (1) that citizens had a duty to help the police discover and apprehend offenders; (2) that no one could be compelled to come to the police station otherwise than by arrest; (3) that anyone in

---

[30] *Criminal Law Review*, 2005, p. 672.

a police station could communicate with and consult privately with a solicitor at any stage provided that it did not cause unreasonable delay or hindrance to the processes of investigation or the administration of justice; (4) that when the officer had enough evidence to charge the suspect he had to cause that to be done without delay; and (5) that a precondition for the admissibility of any confession was that 'it shall have been voluntary in the sense that it has not been obtained from him by fear of prejudice or hope of advantage, exercised or held out by a person in authority, or by oppression'.

There then followed the actual rules dealing with the stages of questioning. Rule I stated that the police could question anyone. Rule II required the police to caution the person being questioned as soon as the police officer had enough evidence to afford reasonable grounds for suspecting that he had committed an offence. The caution warned him that he was not obliged to say anything. Rule III required a second caution when he came to be charged and stated that thereafter questions should only be put in exceptional cases. ('Such questions may be put where they are necessary for the purpose of preventing or minimising harm or loss to some other person or to the public or for clearing up an ambiguity in a previous answer or statement'.) However, a third caution had to be given before such further questions were asked. Rule IV regulated the taking of a statement and required the officer to allow the suspect to put it in his own words.

In addition to the Judges' Rules there were Administrative Directions accompanying the rules, drafted not by the judges but by the Home Office. These dealt with a variety of matters concerning the handling of suspects in the police station.[31]

The Judges' Rules and the Administrative Directions were criticised on various counts. One was that there were many aspects of the process of detention and questioning which they did not cover at all. Another was that they were badly drafted and that in many important respects they were vague. A third ground of objection was that they did not have the status of law. It seemed to be widely accepted that they were frequently flouted by the police and that breaches were usually ignored by the courts.

The Philips Royal Commission on Criminal Procedure concluded that it was desirable 'to replace the vagueness of the Judges' Rules with a set of instructions which provide strengthened safeguards to the suspect and clear and workable guidelines for the police'.[32] The Code of Practice on Detention, Treatment and Questioning of Persons by Police Officers (Code C of PACE) laid down a mass of detailed rules regulating most aspects of the process of questioning. (In the 2006 HMSO version of the Codes, Code C runs to no fewer than eighty-five pages. The Judges' Rules by contrast were two pages long with another two pages for the attached Administrative Directions.[33])

---

[31] For the full text of the Judges' Rules and the Administrative Directions, see [1964] 1 WLR 152.
[32] Paragraph 4.109.　　[33] Note 31 above.

Whom can the police question?

The police can ask questions of anyone both before and after arrest. There is no such thing as immunity from questioning by virtue of one's rank or occupation. This right continues after arrest, though, as will be seen, according to the principles of the English system, questioning is normally supposed to cease after the suspect has been charged. From that moment he is notionally under the control of the court and the police are basically supposed to regard themselves as having completed their function.

The citizen is not normally obliged to answer police questions

The fact that the police are entitled to ask questions does not mean that the citizen must answer them. The rule of English law on this critical point is that there is normally no such duty. This is the citizen's so-called 'right of silence'. Thus a person who is silent in the face of questioning cannot be charged with obstructing the police in the exercise of their duties.

    This fundamental rule was stated authoritatively by the Divisional Court in 1966:

> ### *Rice v. Connolly* [1966] 2 QB 414, Divisional Court
> [The appellant was seen by officers in the early hours of the morning behaving suspiciously in an area where on the same night breaking offences had taken place. On being questioned he refused to say where he was going or where he had come from. He refused to give his full name and address, though he did give a name and the name of a road, which were not untrue. He refused to accompany the police to a police box for identification purposes, saying, 'if you want me, you will have to arrest me'. He was arrested and charged with wilfully obstructing the policy contrary to the Police Act 1964, s. 51(3).]

The court's decision was given by the Lord Chief Justice:

> Lord Parker CJ:. . . the sole question here is whether the defendant had a lawful excuse for refusing to answer the questions put to him. In my judgment he had. It seems to me quite clear that though every citizen has a moral duty or, if you like, a social duty to assist the police, there is no legal duty to that effect, and indeed the whole basis of the common law is the right of the individual to refuse to answer questions put to him by persons in authority, and to refuse to accompany those in authority to any particular place; short, of course, of arrest.
>
>   Mr Skinner has pointed out that it is undoubtedly an obstruction, and has been so held, for a person questioned by the police to tell a 'cock-and-bull' story to put the police off by giving them false information, and I think he would say: well, what is the real distinction? It is a very little way from giving false information to giving no information at all. If that does in fact make it more difficult for the police to carry out their duties, then there is a wilful obstruction.
>
>   In my judgment there is all the difference in the world between deliberately telling a false story – something which in no view a citizen has a right to do –

and preserving silence or refusing to answer – something which he has every right to do. Accordingly, in my judgment, looked upon in that perfectly general way, it was not shown that the refusal of the defendant to answer the questions or to accompany the police officer in the first instance to the police box was an obstruction without lawful excuse.

Marshall and James JJ concurred, though James J said he would not go so far as to say that silence combined with conduct could not amount to obstruction. Whether it did amount to obstruction would depend on the facts of the actual case.

However, see *Ricketts v. Cox* [1982] Crim LR 184, Divisional Court. See also K. Lidstone, 'Minding the Law's Own Business', *New Law Journal*, 14 October 1982, p. 953. Silence, together with awkward, abusive behaviour, may constitute the offence of obstruction.

When the citizen is under a duty to answer

The general principle of the common law is therefore that it is not a criminal offence not to answer questions – and especially questions the answer to which would be incriminating, but there are some statutory exceptions to this fundamental common law rule.

Motorists In certain situations the police have a right to arrest someone who refuses to give his name and address. The most common example is where the police officer has reasonable grounds for thinking that a vehicle has been involved in an accident or traffic offence. It is an offence not to give up one's driving licence and to state one's name and date of birth if one is driving a car and one is asked to do so by a police officer. The duty to provide information about the driver of a car applies not only to the driver himself but also to 'any other person'. The Judicial Committee of the Privy Council held that it is not a breach of the Human Rights Act 1998 to require the motorist to give these details.[34]

Official Secrets There is a provision in the Official Secrets Act 1911, s. 6 (as amended in 1939) that if a chief constable is satisfied that there is reasonable ground for suspecting that an offence under the Official Secrets Act has been committed and for believing that someone is able to furnish information about the offence, he can ask the Home Secretary for consent to use powers of coercive questioning. If such permission is granted, an officer not below the rank of inspector can require the person concerned to attend at a stated time and place and to answer questions. Failure to comply is a criminal offence.

Terrorism A power to require answers on pain and penalties for refusal has also existed under the special legislation concerning terrorism. The earliest form of it was in s. 11 of the Prevention of Terrorism (Temporary Provisions)

---

[34] *Brown v. Stott (Procurator Fiscal Dunfermline)* [2001] 2 All ER 97, PC – a simple question or two was not a disproportionate response to the problem of road accidents. See also *DPP v. Wilson* [2001] EWHC Admin 198, [2002] RTR 37.

Acts 1974 and 1976 which made it an offence for a person who had information that he knew or believed might be of material assistance in preventing an act of terrorism or to secure the arrest, prosecution or conviction of anyone involved in terrorism offences, to 'fail without reasonable excuse to disclose that information as soon as reasonably practicable'.

In his 1978 report on the operation of the Act, Lord Shackleton recommended that this provision be allowed to lapse on the ground that 'it has an unpleasant ring about it in terms of civil liberties'.[35] However, the 1983 inquiry into the operation of the Act reached the opposite conclusion.[36] A total of only fourteen people had been charged under s. 11, of whom nine were convicted. Despite the small numbers of persons charged under s.11, Lord Jellicoe thought retention of the section was warranted and it was retained as s. 18 of the Prevention of Terrorism (Temporary Provisions) Act 1989. The offence carried a maximum penalty of five years' imprisonment.

However, in 1996 Lord Lloyd of Berwick's *Inquiry into legislation against terrorism*[37] also recommended that it be dropped and the Government followed the recommendation in the Terrorism Act 2000.

The Criminal Justice Act 1993 made it a criminal offence to fail to disclose to the police as soon as practicable knowledge or suspicion acquired in the course of one's trade, profession, business or employment that someone is providing financial assistance for terrorism. This is now s. 19 of the Terrorism Act 2000.

Companies Act, bankruptcy, insolvency, liquidations, banking etc. There are many statutes and statutory instruments that require persons to answer questions or to produce documents or information where such answers, documents or information may incriminate them. Refusal can lead to penalties.[38] How do such powers stand in relation to the privilege against self-incrimination?

In the case of Ernest Saunders, the European Court of Human Rights (ECHR) ruled that statements taken compulsorily (in that case by the Serious Fraud Office) cannot be used in evidence in subsequent criminal proceedings as they infringe the right not to incriminate oneself guaranteed by Article 6 of the Convention.[39] This decision affected many statutory provisions. In February 1997, the Attorney General advised prosecutors that statements taken

---

[35] *Review of the Operation of the Prevention of Terrorism Acts*, 1978, Cmnd. 7324, para. 133.

[36] *Review of the Operation of the Prevention of Terrorism (Temporary Provisions) Act 1976*, Cmnd. 8803, 1983, Ch. 9.   [37] Cm. 3420, 1996.

[38] The Companies Act 1985 requires officers and agents of companies to assist inspectors appointed to investigate the affairs of the company under ss. 431, 432 and 447. Refusal to answer questions can be dealt with under ss. 431 and 432 as contempt of court and under s. 447 as a criminal offence. Similar powers exist in a variety of other regulatory contexts – e.g. under the Financial Services Act 1986, for administrators, receivers and liquidators of insolvent companies under the Insolvency Act 1986, ss. 236 and 237, under the Insurance Act 1982, s. 43A and under the Banking Act 1987, ss. 41 and 42. The Serious Fraud Office has the same power under the Criminal Justice Act 1987, s. 2 – though in that case the statements taken can only be used in evidence in criminal proceedings to challenge an inconsistent statement (s. 2(8)).   [39] *Saunders v. United Kingdom* (1996) 23 EHRR 313.

compulsorily under statutory powers should not be used in future in evidence either as part of the prosecution case or in cross-examination.[40]

To bring the law into compliance with the Strasbourg ruling in *Saunders*, the Youth Justice and Criminal Evidence Act 1999, s. 9 and Sch. 3 prohibited the use of evidence obtained by the prosecution under a number of statutory powers, mostly concerning financial investigations, e.g. the Insurance Companies Act 1982, Companies Act 1985, Insolvency Act 1986 and Financial Services Act 1986.

The Serious Organised Crime and Police Act 2005 (SOCPA), Part 2 gave the CPS and the Revenue and Customs Prosecution Service the power to authorise a police officer, a member of the staff of the Serious Organised Crime Agency (SOCA) or an officer of Revenue and Customs the power to issue a 'disclosure notice' to anyone they believe has information relating to a matter under investigation in relation to specified offences. The disclosure notice is a notice to (1) answer questions with respect to any matter relevant to the investigation; (2) provide information and (3) produce such documents as are specified in the notice. Failure to do so is an offence. A statement made by someone in response to a disclosure notice cannot be used in evidence against him in any criminal proceedings (other than for perjury or for failure to comply with the notice).[41]

Arrest for failure to give name and address

PACE did not alter the law regarding the duty to answer questions. However, as will be seen, it did give the police a power to arrest someone for a non-arrestable offence where the officer cannot find out the name of the suspect or his address for the purpose of serving a summons on him.[42] This comes close to creating for suspects a duty to reveal one's name and address.

A similar but even stronger power exists in Scotland, originally under the Criminal Justice (Scotland) Act 1980 and now under the Criminal Procedure (Scotland) Act 1995, s. 13:

> Where a constable has reasonable grounds for suspecting that a person has committed or is committing an offence at any place, he may require (a) that person . . . to give his name and address and may ask him for an explanation of the circumstances which have given rise to the constable's suspicion; (b) any other person whom the constable finds at that place . . . who the constable believes has information relating to the offence, to give his name and address.

---

[40] 148 *New Law Journal*, 13 February 1998, p. 208. See P. Davies, 'Self-Incrimination, Fair Trials, and the Pursuit of Corporate and Financial Wrongdoing' in B. Markesinis (ed.), *The Impact of the Human Rights Bill* (OUP, 1998) pp. 31–61. See also N. Hood, 'Compulsory Questions', 153 *New Law Journal*, 25 July 2003, p. 1140.

[41] SOCPA, ss. 62–5. For critical comment see D. Corker, 'Time to Get Serious', 156 *New Law Journal*, 26 May 2006, p. 874.

[42] This was PACE, s. 25(3)(a), (b) and (c). As will be seen (p. 201 below), the distinction between arrestable and non-arrestable offences was abolished by SOCPA which made all offences arrestable. The power is now in the revised s. 24(5)(a) of PACE introduced by SOCPA, s. 110.

Under the 1995 Act the officer can require such a person to remain with him for such time as may be necessary to note the name, address and explanation given and to verify the name and address, but he may only require the person to remain with him for this purpose briefly. The requirement ceases if there is unreasonable delay in obtaining verification of the name and address. Reasonable force may be used to ensure that the person does remain with the officer, and failing to give a name and address or failing to remain with the officer are both offences, but failing to proffer an explanation is not made an offence and to that extent the right of silence is preserved in Scotland.

Obstructing the police

As already noted, the right of silence must be distinguished from the question of actively misleading or hindering the police. This can constitute an offence. In *Ingleton v. Dibble*,[43] for instance, it was held to be obstruction of the police in the execution of their duty for a motorist to take a swig of whisky to defeat a breathalyser test. In *Moore v. Green*[44] it was held to be obstruction for a probationer police officer to warn the landlord of a public house that his premises were under police surveillance and that a raid to enforce the licensing laws was to be made that evening. By contrast, in *Willmott v. Atack*[45] it was held not to be obstruction for a person to intervene between a police officer and a motorist who was resisting arrest when the purpose of the intervention was to help the police officer by persuading the motorist to desist. The motorist did in fact obstruct the officer, but the Divisional Court held that it had to be shown that he intended to impede the officer.

The Criminal Law Act 1967, s. 4 made it an offence to do anything intended to impede the apprehension or prosecution of someone known or believed to have committed an arrestable offence.[46] Section 5 of the same Act also made it an offence to accept money or other consideration for not disclosing information that would lead to the prosecution of an arrestable offence. In *Albert v. Lavin*[47] the House of Lords held that it was not merely the right but also the duty of a citizen in whose presence a breach of the peace is being, or appears about to be, committed, to attempt to stop it, if necessary by detaining the person responsible.

The legal consequences of silence in the face of police questioning

The citizen's right of silence in the face of police questioning was supported by three main rules. One was that already shown in *Rice v. Connolly* (p. 161 above) – that silence cannot be made the subject of a charge of obstructing the police in the execution of their duties or, with a few exceptional instances, any

---

[43] [1972] 1 All ER 275.   [44] [1983] 1 All ER 663.   [45] [1977] QB 498.
[46] See G. Williams, 'Evading Justice', *Criminal Law Review*, 1975, pp. 430, 477 and 608.
[47] [1981] 3 All ER 878.

other criminal offence. The second was the rule that the prosecution could not comment on the fact of silence and that the judge could not suggest to the jury that silence was evidence of guilt. (As will be seen below, this rule was abolished by the Criminal Justice and Public Order Act 1994.) The third was that a person being questioned by the police had to be cautioned that he was not under an obligation to say anything.

The Criminal Law Revision Committee

The start of the campaign to get the law changed was the 1972 Eleventh Report of the Criminal Law Revision Committee (CLRC) (*Evidence (General)*),[48] in which the CLRC recommended that the failure during police questioning to mention a fact on which the defendant sought subsequently to rely at his trial could be made the subject of adverse comment by the prosecution and the court, and that adverse inferences could be drawn against the accused from such silence or failure. The accused would still have the right to silence, but he would exercise it at the risk that adverse inferences might be drawn against him if the jury or magistrates thought that it would have been reasonable to expect him to have mentioned the facts in question while being questioned. This would apply not only to facts raised in his own evidence but equally to facts referred to in the evidence of any of his witnesses:

> To forbid it seems to us to be contrary to common sense and, without helping the innocent, to give an unnecessary advantage to the guilty. Hardened criminals often take advantage of the present rule to refuse to answer any questions at all, and this may greatly hamper the police and even bring their investigations to a halt. Therefore the abolition of the restriction would help justice . . . [para. 30].

The Committee said that if this proposal regarding silence under interrogation were accepted, it would mean a change in the caution required by the Judges' Rules. The Committee said that the caution was of no help to an innocent person, 'indeed it might deter him from saying something which might serve to exculpate him'. On the other hand the caution 'often assists the guilty by providing an excuse for keeping back a false story until it becomes difficult to expose its falsity'. The caution, it said, stemmed from the ancient fallacy that fairness in criminal trials required that a guilty person should not be allowed to convict himself too easily. It was illogical for the police to have to start an interrogation by saying that the suspect need not say anything (para. 43).

The Committee's proposals on the right of silence and the caution provoked furious controversy. Most of the comment was hostile[49] and it was this above all that led at the time to the rejection of the CLRC's entire report. It was argued by the critics that to allow adverse comment on silence would amount almost to a reversal of the burden of proof. It would put a premium on a suspect's articulateness when most suspects were notoriously inarticulate as well as confused

---

[48] Cmnd. 4991.   [49] See n. 152 above.

and frightened. The critics also denied that silence necessarily indicated guilt. There were many possible innocent reasons for silence, including a desire to protect someone else, fear, contempt for the accusation or failure to understand the accusation.

The matter was next considered by the Philips Royal Commission on Criminal Procedure.

The Philips Royal Commission

The Philips Royal Commission felt that basically the law should *not* be changed. In relation to the situation before an arrest, it regarded the decision in *Rice v. Connolly* (p. 161 above) as correct. ('We adhere to the decision in *Rice v. Connolly* that the duty to assist the police is a social one and not legally enforceable' (para. 4.47).) Once a suspect was arrested the situation was different since he then had to submit to being questioned, but if adverse inferences could be drawn from the fact of silence it might 'put strong (and additional) psychological pressure upon some suspects to answer questions without knowing precisely what was the substance of and evidence for the accusations against them' (para. 4.50). This, in the Commission's view, 'might well increase the risk of innocent people, particularly those under suspicion for the first time, making damaging statements'. On the other hand, a guilty person who at present remained silent would still tend to remain silent since it would be more prudent to hope that the case against him would not be proved in spite of any adverse inferences.

Moreover, the Commission said: 'to use a suspect's silence as evidence against him seems to run counter to a central element in the accusatorial system at trial' (para. 4.51). There was an inconsistency of principle 'in requiring the onus of proof at trial to be upon the prosecution and to be discharged without any assistance from the accused, and yet in enabling the prosecution to use the accused's silence in the face of police questioning under caution as any part of the case against him at trial'.

A minority of the Commission agreed with the police view that the right of silence should be abolished, but the majority concluded 'that the right of silence in the face of police questioning after caution should not be altered' (para. 4.53). The Conservative Government accepted this recommendation.

The caution The Philips Commission proposed that the first caution should be administered not when the police had enough admissible evidence to justify suspicion but when they had enough evidence to justify an arrest (para. 4.56). This was accepted by the Government. Code of Practice C (para. 10.1) states that 'a person whom there are grounds to suspect' must be cautioned 'before any questions about it . . . are put to him'.

Under the Code of Practice the suspect had to be cautioned again before he was interviewed at a police station. The text of the caution was formerly: 'You do not have to say anything unless you wish to do so, but what you say may be given in evidence'.

The text of the caution has now changed to take account of the 'abolition of
the right to silence' (pp. 170–72 below) but the suspect still has to be cautioned
and the rules as to when cautions are required have not changed. Whether the
suspect is given the 'old' caution' or the 'new' caution now depends on whether
he has or has not been given an opportunity to get legal advice.

If questioning is interrupted, the suspect must be made aware that he is still
under caution when it is resumed (Code C, para. 10.8). After he is charged he
must again be cautioned (Code C, para. 16.2).

From that point he should be questioned only where questions are necessary
'to prevent or minimise harm or loss to some other person or the public, to clear
up an ambiguity in a previous answer or statement' or 'in the interests of justice
for the detainee to have put to them, information concerning the offence which
has come to light since they were charged. Before such questions are put he
should be cautioned again' (Code C, para. 16.5).

The 'right of silence' debate reopened
The issue seemed to be settled but in July 1987, the then Home Secretary, Mr
Douglas Hurd, unexpectedly re-opened the debate by a speech in which he
asked whether it was really in the public interest for experienced criminals to be
able to refuse to answer questions 'secure in the knowledge that a jury will never
hear of it'. In 1988 he announced the setting up of a Working Party to consider
not whether the CLRC's 1972 proposal should be adopted, but 'the precise form
of the change in law which would best achieve our purposes'.

In October 1988 the Secretary of State for Northern Ireland laid before
Parliament the draft Police and Criminal Evidence (Northern Ireland) Order
1988 which was first approved and then made on 14 November and came into
force one month later.[50]

The Northern Ireland Order permitted the court to draw adverse inferences
from the accused's failure before being charged or on being charged to
mention any fact relied on in his defence at trial. As recommended by the
CLRC in 1972, the Order stated that such silence could also be corroboration
of other evidence.

The Northern Ireland Order also provided that adverse inferences could be
drawn where someone who had been arrested and cautioned about the matter
failed to explain 'any object, substance or mark' that the officer reasonably
believed suspicious (Article 5). Similarly, adverse inferences could be drawn
from failure to explain one's presence at the scene of the crime. In Northern
Ireland it can also be corroboration of other evidence (Article 6).

Report of the Home Office Working Group
The *Report of the Home Office Working Group on the Right of Silence* was published in July 1989. It recommended changes that were similar but not identical

[50] SI 1989/1341.

to those already introduced for Northern Ireland. The Government, however, did not implement the recommendations of the Working Group, possibly out of a sense that it would be inappropriate in a climate dominated at the time by concern about miscarriages of justice generated in particular by the trio of IRA cases: the Guildford Four, the Maguires and the Birmingham Six.

The Runciman Royal Commission

The Runciman Royal Commission (1991–3), like the Philips Royal Commission, recommended by a majority that the traditional protection for the right to silence be retained. Nine of the eleven members considered that to allow the prosecution and the judge to suggest that silence was evidence of guilt could produce false confessions and therefore more miscarriages of justice:

> The majority of us, however, believe that the possibility of an increase in the convictions of the guilty is outweighed by the risk that the extra pressure on suspects to talk in the police station and the adverse inferences invited if they do not may result in more convictions of the innocent. They recommend retaining the present caution and trial direction unamended. In taking this view, the majority acknowledge the frustration which many police officers feel when confronted with suspects who refuse to offer any explanation whatever of strong *prima facie* evidence that they have committed an offence, but they doubt whether the possibility of adverse comment at trial would make the difference which the police suppose. The experienced professional criminals who wish to remain silent are likely to continue to do so and will justify their silence by stating at trial that their solicitors have advised them to say nothing at least until the allegations against them have been fully disclosed. It may be that some more defendants would be convicted whose refusal to answer police questions had been the subject of adverse comment, but the majority believe that their number would not be as great as is popularly imagined.
>
> It is the less experienced and more vulnerable suspects against whom the threat of adverse comment would be likely to be more damaging. There are too many cases of improper pressures being brought to bear on suspects in police custody, even when the safeguards of PACE and the codes of practice have been supposedly in force, for the majority to regard this with equanimity.[51]

The Report then cited with approval the view of the Philips majority (cited above) to the effect that if adverse inferences could be drawn from silence it might put strong additional pressure on some suspects and might result in more false confessions:

> The minority of two of the Runciman Commission however favoured the view that both the prosecution and the judge should be permitted to invite the jury to draw adverse inferences from silence. In the view of many police officers 'a significant number of suspects, by refusing to answer questions, seriously impede the efforts of investigators to fulfil their function of establishing the facts of the case'.

[51] Runciman, pp. 54–5, paras. 22 and 23.

The minority recommended that silence in response to questions 'asked in a room with audio or visual recording, preferably with a legal representative present, but at least after the suspect has been offered the opportunity of taking legal advice, would qualify for later comment at trial'.[52]

The Criminal Justice and Public Order Act 1994

The Home Secretary, Mr Michael Howard, made his position clear shortly after the Royal Commission reported. Speaking at the Conservative Party Conference that October he said:

> As I talk to people up and down the country, there is one part of our law in particular that makes their blood boil . . . It's the so-called right of silence. This is of course a complete misnomer, what is at stake is not the right to refuse to answer questions, but if a suspect does remain silent should the prosecution and the judge or magistrates be allowed to comment on it? Should they have the right to take it into account in deciding guilt or innocence? The so-called right to silence is ruthlessly exploited by terrorists. What fools they must think we are. It's time to call a halt to this charade. The so-called right to silence will be abolished.

Mr Howard made good his promise in the provisions of the Criminal Justice and Public Order Act 1994 (CJPOA). There are five sections that are especially relevant.

CJPOA 1994, s. 34 gave the court the power to invite the jury (or in the case of the magistrates, themselves) to draw an adverse inference from silence. The right arises only if the suspect has been cautioned and if he is being questioned by a constable 'trying to discover whether or by whom the offence had been committed'.[53] The inference can be drawn if he 'failed to mention any fact relied on in his defence' or failed to mention any such fact on being charged, being a fact 'which in the circumstances existing at the time the accused could reasonably have been expected to mention when so questioned' or charged (s. 34(1)). The inferences to be drawn can be 'such inferences from the failure as appear proper' (s. 34(2)).

The new caution to take account of the change in the law in CJPOA 1994, s. 34 is more complex than the old caution: 'You do not have to say anything, but it may harm your defence if you do not mention when questioned something which you later rely on in court. Anything you do say may be given in evidence' (Code C, para. 10.5). (The old much simpler caution was misunderstood by many suspects. The new more complex caution poses even more difficulties.[54] A team of psychologists read the new caution to 109 ordinary people. On average about half thought it made sense but only one in four actually understood the

---

[52] *Ibid*, p. 51, para. 10.

[53] So if the police know that they are going to charge before the interview starts no inference can be drawn – *Pointer* [1997] Crim LR 676, CA, but if they still have an open mind pending the results of the interview, inferences can be drawn – *McGuiness* [1999] Crim LR 318, CA.

[54] See I. Clare and G. Gudjunsson, *Devising and Piloting an Experimental Version of the 'Notice to Detained Persons'* (Royal Commission on Criminal Justice, Research Study No. 7, 1992).

first part which tells the individual of his right to remain silent, one in eight understood the second element which warns that exercise of the right may harm one's defence later and one in three understood the third part which says that anything said may be used in evidence. They concluded that the length and complexity of the new formula 'ensures that it is beyond the ability of most people in the street to absorb, let alone comprehend'.[55])

A further complication has now been added by legislation preventing a court from drawing adverse inferences until the suspect being interviewed at the police station has had the opportunity to get legal advice.[56] This applies even to terrorism suspects. So someone who is interviewed before he has 'been allowed an opportunity to consult a solicitor' must be cautioned in terms of the old formula. If he is then interviewed after he has had an opportunity to get legal advice he must be cautioned again in terms of the new formula! (PACE Code C, paras. 10.4–10.10).

CJPOA 1994, s. 35 provides that adverse inferences may be drawn from the accused's failure to give evidence at his trial: see pp. 463–66 below.

CJPOA 1994, s. 36, like the Northern Ireland rule, permits the court to invite adverse inferences from the accused's failure or refusal to account for suspicious objects, substances or marks. Section 37, again like the Northern Ireland rule, permits adverse inferences from the accused's failure or refusal to account for his presence at the scene of the crime at the time it was committed. In both cases the suspect must first have been cautioned by the constable. Under ss. 36 and 37 adverse inferences can be drawn from the mere failure to respond to the question. It is not necessary, as under s. 34, to show that the defendant relied on a fact in his defence that he failed to disclose when being questioned, but he must have been cautioned by the appropriate 'special warning'. Under s. 36 he must have been advised that the objects, marks or substances found on his person, or his clothing or footwear seem suspicious and must be asked for an explanation. Where the suspect is arrested at the scene of the crime at the time it is committed, the s. 37 caution must inform him what offence is being investigated, what fact he is being asked to account for, that the officer believes that fact may be due to his having taken part in the offence and that failure to account for the fact could lead to adverse inferences being drawn at the trial. (Home Office research has shown that when such special warnings are given they rarely result in any satisfactory account being given.[57])

CJPOA 1994, s. 38(3) states that silence on its own can never be enough. There must always be a *prima facie* case before any adverse inference can be drawn.

---

[55] *Counsel*, September–October 1995, p. 4.
[56] Youth Justice and Criminal Evidence Act 1999, s. 58; Criminal Evidence (Northern Ireland) Order 1999, SI 1999/2789, r. 36. These statutory provisions resulted from decisions of the European Court of Human Rights in Strasbourg – *Murray (John) v. United Kingdom* (1996) 22 EHRR 29, para. 66; *Averill v. United Kingdom* (2001) 31 EHRR 839.
[57] T. Bucke and D. Brown, *In Police Custody: Police Powers and Suspects' Rights under the Revised PACE Codes of Practice*, 1997, Home Office Research Series No. 174, p. 38.

The provisions can result in the defence solicitor being called as a witness with regard to the advice he gave his client in the police station.[58]

For an evaluation of the practical effect of the reform see T. Bucke, R. Street and D. Brown, *The right of silence: the impact of the Criminal Justice and Public Order Act 1994* (Home Office Research Study, 2000). For an assessment of the Northern Ireland experience see J. Jackson, M. Wolfe and K. Quinn, *Legislating Against Silence: The Northern Ireland Experience* (Northern Ireland Office, 2000).

For caustic, overall assessments of the new law by two leading scholars see D. Birch, 'Suffering in Silence: A Cost–Benefit Analysis of Section 34 of the Criminal Justice and Public Order Act 1994', *Criminal Law Review*, 1999, pp. 769–88 and I. Dennis, 'Silence in the Police Station: the Marginalisation of Section 34', *Criminal Law Review*, 2002, pp. 25–38.

See also R. Pattenden, 'Silence: Lord Taylor's Legacy', 5 *International Journal of Evidence and Proof*, 1998, p. 141 and D. Wolchover, *Silence and Guilt* (2001).

There is a bibliography on the right to silence in M. Zander, *The Police and Criminal Evidence Act 1984* (5th edn, 2005), pp. 501–2.

Judicial interpretation of the right to silence provisions

The House of Lords deciding *Murray (Kevin Sean)*[59] on the Northern Ireland provisions held that adverse inferences may be drawn if they are suggested by the application of common sense.[60] The case law has become voluminous but the theme of common sense has continued to be dominant.[61]

Among the propositions that have been established by the cases, the more important include the following:

Strict interpretation Because the provisions restrict important rights they must be construed strictly.[62]

Reliance on facts need not be in defendant's evidence It can occur through evidence of others, or cross-examination,[63] but mere hypothesising is not reliance.[64] Nor is a bare admission of facts in the prosecution's case.[65]

The failure to mention a fact can be at any stage up to the time of being charged.[66] It could consist of lying in the interview and asserting 'the truth' at trial.[67]

Adverse inferences can only be drawn from silence in the face of questioning If the suspect refuses to come out of his cell to be questioned, the statutory provisions do not apply and no adverse inferences can be drawn.[68] (To deal with this situation, Code C provides that if the suspect declines to leave his cell to be

---

[58] See on this D. Wright, 'The Solicitor in the Witness Box', *Criminal Law Review*, 1998, pp. 44–7.

[59] [1994] 1 WLR 1.

[60] Referred to in *Report of the Working Group on the Right of Silence*, Home Office, 1989, App. C.

[61] On the case law see, for instance, M. Zander, *The Police and Criminal Evidence Act 1984* (5th edn, 2005) pp. 480–98.   [62] *Bowden* [1999] 2 Cr App Rep 176 at 181.

[63] *Bowers* [1998] Crim LR 817, CA.   [64] *Nickolson* [1999] Crim LR 61, CA.

[65] *Betts and Hall* [2001] EWCA Crim 224, [2001] 2 Cr App Rep 257.

[66] *Dervish and Anori* [2001] EWCA Crim 2789, [2002] 2 Cr App Rep 105.

[67] *Ashton* [2002] EWCA Crim 2782.

[68] *Johnson* [2005] EWCA Crim 971, [2006] Crim LR 253.

questioned he can be cautioned and told that his failure to agree to be questioned can be given in evidence.[69])

'The accused' means the actual accused 'When reference is made to the "accused" attention is drawn not to some hypothetical, reasonable accused of ordinary phlegm and fortitude but to the actual accused with such qualities, apprehensions, knowledge and advice as he is shown to have had'.[70]

The fact that the defendant was advised to be silent by his lawyer must be given appropriate weight[71] ('If it is a plausible explanation that the reason for not mentioning facts is that the particular appellant acted on the advice of his solicitor and not because he had no or no satisfactory answer to give then no inferences can be drawn'.[72]) *Howell*[73] decided that whether legal advice to be silent will prevent adverse inferences being drawn depends on whether the jury considers it to be plausible that that was the reason he was silent, rather than that he had no or no satisfactory answer to give. ('There is a public interest in reasonable disclosure by an accused when confronted with incriminating facts. This would be thwarted if silence based on legal advice allowed the systematic evasion of the drawing of adverse inferences'.[74]) In *Hoare and Pierce*[75] the Court of Appeal refined this further by stating that the jury must also believe that it was reasonable for the defendant to have relied on the legal advice to be silent.[76]

Valid reasons for advising silence include: little or no disclosure by the police so the solicitor cannot advise the suspect (*Roble*),[77] the suspect's condition – ill-health, confusion, intoxication or shock, or genuine inability to recollect events without reference to documents or other persons (*Howell*).

Explaining the reasons for legal advice to be silent will probably amount to a waiver of privilege: Bowden[78] and *Loizou.*[79]

The jury may draw whatever inferences they think proper: Cowan[80] and *Beckles and Montagu.*[81] The test is common sense – *Murray (Kevin)*[82] and *Argent.*[83]

Empirical evidence on the right to silence changes

Pre-CJPOA 1994 empirical evidence showed that relatively few suspects actually relied on their right of silence. David Brown of the Home Office conducted an

---

[69] At para. 12.5.   [70] *Argent* [1997] 2 Cr App Rep 27 at 33.

[71] *Condron v. United Kingdom (No 2)* (2001) 31 EHRR 1, [2000] Crim LR 679.

[72] *Betts and Hall* [2001] EWCA Crim 224, [2001] 2 Cr App Rep 257.

[73] [2003] EWCA Crim 1, [2003] Crim LR 405.

[74] For comment see C. Jowett, 'Inferences from Silence', 153 *New Law Journal*, 7 March 2003, p. 344 and A.L.-T. Choo and A.F. Jennings, 'Silence on Legal Advice Revisited: *R v. Howell*', 7 *International Journal of Evidence and Proof*, 2003, pp. 185–190. See also E. Cape, 'Rebalancing the Criminal Justice Process: Ethical Challenges for Criminal Defence Lawyers', *Legal Ethics*, vol. 9, Pt 1, 2006, p. 56.   [75] [2004] EWCA Crim 784.

[76] See also the decision of the ECHR in *Beckles v. United Kingdom* (2003) 36 EHRR 13. For commentary on *Hoare and Pierce* and *Beckles* see *Criminal Law Review*, 2005, pp. 562 and 568 and B. Malik, 'Silence on Legal Advice: Clarity but not Justice? *R v. Beckles*', 9 *International Journal of Evidence and Proof*, 2005, pp. 211–16.   [77] [1997] Crim LR 449.

[78] [1999] 2 Cr App Rep 176.   [79] [2006] EWCA Crim 1719.   [80] [1996] QB 373 at 381–2, CA.

[81] [1999] Crim LR 148, CA.   [82] [1994] 1 WLR 1 at 12, HL.   [83] [1997] 2 Cr App Rep 27 at 33.

analysis of studies on the right of silence for the Runciman Royal Commission on Criminal Justice. His conclusion was that 'outside the Metropolitan Police district, between 6 per cent and 10 per cent of suspects exercise their right to silence to some extent, while within the Metropolitan Police district the equivalent percentage is between 14 per cent and 16 per cent. The number of those who refuse to answer any questions at all is estimated at 5 per cent at most in provincial police force areas and 9 per cent at most in the Metropolitan Police district'.[84] A different Home Office study pre-CJPOA based on a sample of 4,250 suspects detained between September 1993 and March 1994 found 10 per cent refused to answer all questions and another 13 per cent refused to answer some questions.[85]

The first Home Office research on the impact of the changes made by the CJPOA showed a reduction in suspects using the right of silence.[86] Where in the pre-CJPOA 1994 study 10 per cent gave 'no comment' interviews by refusing all questions from officers, in the post-CJPOA 1994 study this had fallen to 6 per cent. Where 13 per cent had answered some questions in the 'pre' study, in the 'post' study this had fallen to 10 per cent. The downward trend was observed across all police stations. Even more significant was that reductions in the use of silence were greatest among those receiving legal advice, presumably because lawyers advised of the dangers of remaining silent under the new provisions.

The same data was used again in another Home Office study published in 2000.[87] Also in 2000 the Northern Ireland Office published a similar study.[88]

The results of the two studies and of the position generally were assessed by Professor John Jackson.[89] The Home Office study established that the silence provisions had had a marked effect on both pre-trial and trial practices but that it was much less clear that they had increased the likelihood of defendants being charged and convicted. It was more common for investigating officers to disclose the main features of the evidence against the accused, thus enabling legal advisers to give suspects better advice as to whether and, if so, how to respond to police questions. This in turn meant that stories could be checked out earlier, weak cases could be stopped and in cases that went to court, the prosecution's hand could be strengthened. More defendants were testifying but, on the other hand, the silence provisions made trials more complex. Judges had to exercise extreme care in directing juries on the right to silence issue. Jackson suggested that the overall

---

[84] Runciman, p. 53, para. 15.

[85] C. Phillips and D. Brown, *Entry into the Criminal Justice System: a Survey of Police Arrests and their Outcomes* (Home Office Research Study No. 185, 1998) p. 75.   [86] *Ibid.*

[87] T. Ucke, R. Street and D. Brown, *The Right of Silence: the Impact of the Criminal Justice and Public Order Act 1994* (Home Office Research Study No. 199, 2000).

[88] J. Jackson, M. Wolfe and K. Quinn, *Legislating against Silence: the Northern Ireland Experience*, 2000. For a summary see M. Zander, 'Silence in Northern Ireland', 151 *New Law Journal*, 2 February 2001, p. 138. The study was based on an examination of all trials in Belfast Crown Court for 1990–5, more detailed examination of thirty terrorism trials in 1995, comparison with all trials in the same court in 1987 and 1991, statistics on legal advice in 1997 and interviews with judges, lawyers and police officers.

[89] 'Silence and Proof: Extending the Boundaries of Criminal Proceedings in the United Kingdom', 5 *International Journal of Evidence and Proof*, 2001, pp. 145–73.

effect had been to make the police interview a formal part of the proceedings against the accused without certain basic procedural safeguards. The suspect had no right to disclosure of the police case at that stage and legal advice as to whether or not to say anything was problematic since the courts had left to the jury the question whether it was reasonable for the suspect to accept this advice.[90]

3. Safeguards for the suspect

The suspect in the police station is in a very vulnerable position. The question arises as to how he can be protected from police abuse of power. A variety of approaches have been developed in recent years, of which the most important are treated below: access to a lawyer, informing the outside world of the fact of arrest, tape recording of the interview and rules to regulate the regime in the police station and to prevent oppressive questioning.

Access to a lawyer

The presence of a lawyer during questioning provides the accused with much-needed advice and at the same time helps to minimise the risk of oppressive interrogation.[91]

Until 1986 when PACE came into operation, access to a solicitor in the police station was governed by the Judges' Rules and some judicial dicta. The Preamble to the Judges' Rules stated that the Rules did not affect the principle 'that every person at any stage of an investigation should be able to communicate and to consult privately with a solicitor. This is so even if he is in custody, provided that in such a case no unreasonable delay or hindrance is caused to the processes of investigation or the administration of justice by his doing so'. This appeared to give a qualified right of access to a solicitor in the police station. The Administrative Directions supplementing the Rules stated that provided no hindrance was reasonably likely to be caused to the processes of investigation or the administration of justice, 'he should be allowed to speak on the telephone to his solicitor or to his friends'. They added that not only should persons in custody be informed of their right orally, but notices describing this right should be displayed at convenient and conspicuous places and the attention of persons in custody should be drawn to them.[92]

In practice, however, the police were reluctant to allow a suspect to summon a solicitor. The studies that were done before PACE all agreed that the proportion of suspects who actually saw a solicitor was tiny.[93]

---

[90] At p. 173.

[91] However, in two of the most celebrated cases in which oppressive questioning led to confessions in murder cases being held to be inadmissible the suspect had had a legal adviser present throughout: see p. 476 below.   [92] Paragraph 7(a) and (b).

[93] P. Softley, *Police Interrogation: An Observational Study in Four Police Stations*, 1980, p. 68; J. Baldwin and M. McConville, 'Police Interrogation and the Right to see a Solicitor',

The Philips Royal Commission

The Philips Royal Commission thought the availability of legal advice for suspects was a matter of considerable importance. In the Commission's view a suspect should be informed of his right to have a lawyer. It rejected the view that there should be an absolute right to have a solicitor. There were situations in which the police should be entitled to refuse access to a lawyer:

> 4.91. Accordingly our general view is that the power to refuse access should be exercised only in exceptional cases. In the first place it should be limited to cases where the person in custody is suspected of a grave offence. Further, even in the case of such offences, the right should be withheld only where there are reasonable grounds to believe that the time taken to arrange for legal advice to be available will involve a risk of harm to persons or serious damage to property; or that giving access to a legal adviser may lead to one or more of the following: (a) evidence of the offence or offences under investigation will be interfered with; (b) witnesses to those offences will be harmed or threatened; (c) other persons suspected of committing those offences will be alerted; or (d) the recovery of the proceeds of those offences will be impeded.

The Commission estimated that if all the 720,000 suspects interviewed at police stations in connection with indictable offences were to take up their right to see a solicitor the cost would be some £30 million but the likely take-up, it thought, would be of the order of one-fifth which would mean an annual cost of some £6 million. (In 2005–6 the cost of legal advice in police stations was £172 million!)

PACE

PACE s. 58(1) provides that 'a person arrested and held in custody in a police station or other premises shall be entitled, if he so requests, to consult a solicitor privately at any time'. The right is both to have legal advice before being interviewed and to have the lawyer present during the interview. Even a suspect arrested under the Terrorism Act has those rights – though in some circumstances a senior officer can instruct that an interview with a terrorism suspect can be conducted in the sight and hearing of an inspector.

The provision of the lawyer is free regardless of the suspect's means. A suspect who comes to the police station under arrest or is arrested there must be informed of the right to have free legal advice both orally and in writing (Code C, paras. 3.1, 3.2 and 6.1).

If a person makes such a request it must be recorded in the custody record and, subject to the exceptions that are mentioned, he must be allowed to have access to a solicitor 'as soon as is practicable' (PACE s. 58(2) and (4)). Delay in

Footnote 93 (*cont.*)
> *Criminal Law Review*, 1979, pp. 145–52; M. Zander, 'Access to a Solicitor in the Police Station', *Criminal Law Review*, 1972, p. 342 and 'The Investigation of Crime', *Criminal Law Review*, 1979, p. 215; B. Mitchell, 'Confessions and Police Interrogation', *Criminal Law Review*, 1983, pp. 597 and 599–600.

compliance with such a request is only permitted where (1) the detainee is being held in connection with an indictable offence (formerly it was a serious arrestable offence)[94] and (2) an officer of the rank of, at least, superintendent authorises delay.

Delay The circumstances in which such authorisation may be given are defined in s. 58(8):

> . . . an officer may only authorise delay where he has reasonable grounds for believing that the exercise of the right [of asking for a solicitor]
>
> (a) will lead to interference with or harm to evidence connected with an indictable offence or interference with or physical injury to other persons; or
> (b) will lead to the alerting of other persons suspected of having committed such an offence but not yet arrested for it; or
> (c) will hinder the recovery of any property obtained as a result of such an offence.

If such a delay is authorised, the detainee must be told the reasons for it, the reasons must be recorded on the custody record (see below) and, once the reasons cease to exist, he must be allowed to see a solicitor.[95]

The maximum period of delay in allowing access to a solicitor is thirty-six hours, or, in the case of terrorism suspects held under the Terrorism Act 2000, forty-eight hours.[96]

There has been a considerable amount of case law on the interpretation of PACE s. 58(8). Most of the cases have involved defence assertions that the police wrongly delayed access to a solicitor and that subsequent confessions or admissions should not be (or should not have been) admitted. The leading case is *Samuel*.[97] The suspect's request for a solicitor was refused on the ground that the offences were serious and that there was a risk of accomplices being inadvertently alerted. Subsequently he confessed. The trial judge admitted the interview in which he confessed. The Court of Appeal quashed the conviction. The right of access to a solicitor, it held, was a 'fundamental right of a citizen' and if a police officer sought to justify refusal of the right, he had to do so by reference to the specific circumstances of the case. It was not enough to believe that giving access to a solicitor *might* lead to the alerting of accomplices. He had to believe that it probably would.[98]

A Note for Guidance in Code C says that an officer's decision to delay access to a specific solicitor 'is likely to be a rare occurrence' and is permissible only if

---

[94] Substituted for serious arrestable offences by the Serious Organised Crime and Police Act 2005 (SOCPA), Sch. 7, Part 3, para. 43(10). Serious arrestable offences were abolished by SOCPA.

[95] The House of Lords has held by a majority that breach of the statutory duty to give reasons for authorising delay of an arrested person's right of access to a solicitor did not give the arrested person a private law remedy in damages, though it could be the subject of judicial review – *Cullen v. Chief Constable of the Royal Ulster Constabulary* [2003] UKHL 39, [2003] 1 WLR 1763.   [96] Code C, Annex B, para. 6; Code H, Annex B, para. 6.

[97] [1988] QB 615.   [98] See to like effect *Parris* [1989] Crim LR 214.

he has reasonable grounds to believe that the suspect is 'capable of misleading that particular solicitor and there is more than a substantial risk that the suspect will succeed in causing information to be conveyed which will lead to one or more of the specified consequences' – alerting accomplices etc. (Code C, Annex B, Note B3).

Research shows that the police now hardly ever claim to be entitled to delay access to a solicitor. In a massive study carried out by David Brown of the Home Office Research Unit involving two samples of 5,000 each taken in 1991, there was only one case of legal advice delayed.[99] In the post-CJPOA Home Office study of 12,500 cases by Bucke and Brown there was not a single one in which the power to delay legal advice had been used.[100]

Unsurprisingly, in terrorism cases, delay is more frequent. A study of this problem by Brown showed that delay of access to a solicitor was authorised in 26 per cent of cases.[101]

The fact that there has been a breach of s. 58(8) does not mean that the court will automatically exclude the resulting statement. It will depend on the court's evaluation of all the circumstances. In *Dunford*[102] the Court of Appeal took into account the fact that the suspect had a record and was therefore familiar with the police station. He answered several questions with 'no comment' and before reaching the police station he declined to answer any questions. The court held that the judge had been entitled to allow the confession. In *Walsh*[103] the Court of Appeal said that to admit evidence obtained following a 'significant and substantial' breach of s. 58 would inevitably have an adverse effect on the fairness of the proceedings within the meaning of s. 78 (see pp. 479–81 below), but that did not mean it had necessarily to be excluded. The task of the court was not only to consider whether there would have been an adverse effect on the fairness of the proceedings but such an adverse effect that justice required the evidence to be excluded. Where the suspect knows his way around in the police station situation it is less likely that a breach of s. 58 will result in exclusion of the evidence.[104]

Getting a lawyer

PACE originally required the Law Society to establish Duty Solicitor schemes for police stations. They are now the responsibility of the Legal Services Commission (LSC) established by the Access to Justice Act 1999 and are run by its Criminal Defence Service (CDS). Every police station in the country is covered by the system, using solicitors in private practice. The duty solicitor is contacted through a telephone service run by FirstAssist, part of the Royal and

---

[99] Brown et al, *Changing the Code: Police Detention under the Revised PACE Codes of Practice* (Home Office Research Study, 1992) p. 68.   [100] Note 20, p. 156 above, at p. 23.

[101] D. Brown, *Detention Under the Prevention of Terrorism Provisions Act 1989: Legal Advice and Outside Contact* (Home Office Research and Planning Unit, Paper No. 75, 1993) p. 16).

[102] [1991] Crim LR 370.   [103] (1989) 91 Cr App Rep 161.

[104] *Alladice* (1988) 87 Cr App Rep 380.

Sun Alliance Group of companies. The police call the service on the suspect's behalf; the service calls the solicitor. The solicitors are private practitioners operating either on a rota or on a panel. In rota schemes a named solicitor is on duty; in panel schemes the service calls the solicitors on the panel in the order in which they appear on the list.

In October 2005 the LSC began a pilot of a new system under which requests for a duty solicitor go instead to CDS Direct. The essence of the approach being tested was that initial advice would be given over the telephone by solicitors employed by CDS. Unless the case concerns an indictable-only offence (i.e. one triable only at the Crown Court) or the police already know the time at which the suspect is to be interviewed, the CDS lawyer, having given initial advice, would decide whether attendance in the police station by a solicitor is required. Where the service is restricted to telephone-only advice[105] all duty solicitor services throughout the country are handled by CDS Direct.[106]

If the detainee does not know of a solicitor, he must be told of the availability of a Duty Solicitor and be shown a list of solicitors who have indicated they are available for this purpose. In about two-thirds of all cases the suspect asks to speak to his own solicitor, rather than the Duty Solicitor, but the state pays the cost regardless of means in any event.

For the recommendations of the Carter Review (2006) regarding police station legal advice see p. 621 below.

Statistical data

In Brown's first 1991 sample of 5,000 taken before April 1991, 24 per cent asked for legal advice. The 1991 revision of the Code required that the suspect be specifically told legal advice was free and that posters advertising the fact be put up in police stations. The 1997 study by Bucke and Brown showed that the take-up had risen to 40 per cent.[107]

Afro-Caribbean and Asians were much more likely to request legal advice (46 per cent and 44 per cent) than white suspects (36 per cent).[108] Afro-Caribbeans were more likely to have been arrested for violence against the person, robbery, fraud and forgery than whites, all of which are offences for which there is a relatively high request rate.

A factor in take-up could be the way the police communicate the right to consult a solicitor. Sanders and Bridges identified a long list of 'ploys' used by the police to discourage suspects from asking for solicitors. These included speaking too quickly or saying that the charge was not very serious, that getting a solicitor

---

[105] From Spring 2004 the LSC introduced cost-saving rules to reduce attendance at police stations. Thus, attendance, for instance, has to be for the purpose of giving advice that could not have been given over the phone, but if the suspect is a juvenile or for any other reason is eligible for assistance from an 'appropriate adult' (see p. 190 below) or he requires an interpreter or he complains of serious maltreatment by the police, attendance is permitted.

[106] *Legal Action*, April 2005, p. 16, October 2005, p. 12; *Independent Lawyer*, May 2004, p. 4.

[107] Note 20, p. 156 above, at p. 19.   [108] *Ibid*, p. 20.

would involve considerable delays, that the solicitor probably would not come anyway, or that one was unnecessary.[109] The Code (Code C, para. 6.5) requires the custody officer to ask the suspect who declines legal advice for his reasons, but Bucke and Brown found that this rule is often honoured in the breach. Less than half of those refusing legal advice were asked for their reasons.[110]

Since 1991, the Code has specifically stated that no attempt may be made to dissuade a suspect from obtaining legal advice (Code C, para. 6.4). Brown's research conducted both before and after the 1991 change did not find much evidence of 'ploys' if that word is taken to connote conscious attempts to dissuade or discourage the suspect from seeking legal advice. (In the great majority of cases 'details of rights were given in exemplary fashion, both slowly and clearly' – though in some cases it was given too quickly or incompletely or the language used was not readily comprehensible.)

The fact that one asks for legal advice and that the police allow one to have it does not always mean that such advice is actually obtained. Earlier research showed a non-contact rate as high as a quarter, but this seems to have gone down. Bucke and Brown found no contact was made with an adviser in only 11 per cent of cases.[111]

Sometimes the reason for 'non-contact' is that the suspect changes his mind, or he is released from custody before the adviser arrives or he decides to see the lawyer at court instead. Overall, a third of suspects (34 per cent) actually had legal advice.[112]

However, even if the solicitor advises in person it does not mean that he will necessarily stay while the suspect is interviewed. In Bucke and Brown 1997, of 2,181 suspects interviewed in custody, just over half (52 per cent) had no legal advice, just over a third (37 per cent) had their legal adviser present at all interviews, just under a tenth (9 per cent) received advice only pre-interview and the remaining 2 per cent had the adviser present at some but not all interviews (p. 32). This showed a considerable rise from previous studies in the proportion of cases of the adviser being present during interviews.

The adviser in the police station

The police are not allowed to refuse someone access to a solicitor because he might advise the suspect to be silent or because he has been asked to act by someone else – providing the suspect does actually want to see the solicitor (Code C, Annex B, A, 4).

Note 6J to Code C states that a person consulting a solicitor in the police station 'must be allowed to do so in private' and that 'this right to consult or communicate in private is fundamental'. It specifies that the right will be compromised if the advice is listened to, overheard or read.

---

[109] A. Sanders and L. Bridges, *Advice and Assistance at Police Stations and the 24 Hour Duty Solicitor Scheme* (LCD, 1989).   [110] Note 20, p. 156 above, at p. 21.   [111] *Ibid*, p. 23.
[112] *Ibid*, p. 24.

If a person has asked for legal advice he may not be interviewed or continue to be interviewed until he has received such advice unless an officer of the rank of superintendent reasonably thinks that one of the specified grounds for allowing legal advice to be delayed applies (Code C, para. 6.6).

If a person who wanted legal advice changes his mind, an interview may take place if that person agrees in writing or on tape and an officer of the rank of inspector or above, having asked the suspect for his reasons, agrees (Code C, para. 6.6(d)).

The right to get legal advice under s. 58 contemplates that the adviser will be a solicitor but in practice this often is not the case. Bridges and Hodgson (1995) said: 'it appears from the available research evidence that a significant proportion, probably between two-fifths and one-half, of all attendances at police stations by legal advisers are carried out by persons other than fully qualified solicitors'.[113] Often the adviser is a former police officer! The use of non-solicitors as police station advisers is particularly common when the firm used is the client's own solicitor (as opposed to the Duty Solicitor).[114]

The quality of legal advice in police stations was the subject of criticism in several research studies.[115] Thus McConville and Hodgson in a study done for the Runciman Royal Commission found that in 86 per cent of cases, the adviser made no inquiries about the case of the custody officer. In half the cases the adviser spent under ten minutes in private conversation with the client and many such consultations appeared cursory in nature.[116] Dixon et al reported that 'legal advisers are largely passive and non-interventionist in police interrogations'. The role of many was 'to act purely as witness to the proceedings'.[117] Baldwin, in a study of 182 audio or video tapes of police interrogations where a legal adviser was present, found that in two-thirds of these cases the adviser said nothing at all in the interview.[118]

Concern about the quality of the work done in police stations led the Law Society to produce an elaborate new training scheme for police station advisers. It led also to the Legal Aid Board insisting that it would only pay for advice done by persons who had qualified themselves under the new 'accreditation scheme'. As from February 1995, legal aid only paid for police station work done by 'own solicitor' representatives if they were on the accreditation list and

---

[113] L. Bridges and J. Hodgson, 'Improving Custodial Legal Advice', *Criminal Law Review*, 1995, p. 104.

[114] In Bucke and Brown 1997, n. 20, p. 156 above, when the advice at the police station was given through the duty solicitor scheme, the adviser was a qualified solicitor in 92 per cent of instances. When the advice was given by the suspect's chosen firm, the adviser was a solicitor in 75 per cent of cases (p. 27).

[115] For a review of this evidence see Bridges and Hodgson, n. 113 above.

[116] M. McConville and J. Hodgson, *Custodial Legal Advice and the Right to Silence* (Royal Commission on Criminal Justice, Research Study No. 16, 1993).

[117] D. Dixon et al, 'Safeguarding the Rights of Suspects in Police Custody', 1 *Policing and Society*, 1990, p. 124.

[118] J. Baldwin, *The Role of the Legal Representatives at Police Stations* (Royal Commission on Criminal Justice, Research Study No. 3, 1992) p. 49.

non-solicitor representatives and trainee solicitors were also brought into the accreditation scheme.[119] This policy was continued by the Legal Services Commission.[120]

Bucke and Brown noted the length of consultations. Nearly half took less than fifteen minutes. Only 2 per cent lasted over an hour.[121]

For a discussion of the effect of poor legal advice on cases especially with regard to exclusion of evidence see E. Cape and J. Hickman, 'Bad Lawyer, Good Defence', 152 *New Law Journal*, 2 August 2002, p. 1194.

Note – 'serious arrestable offences' abolished

'Serious arrestable offences' (SAOs) were defined in Sch. 5 of the Act to mean any of certain specified offences such as murder, manslaughter, rape, using explosives to endanger life or property, and possession of firearms with intent to injure or with criminal intent. Apart from the identified offences, under s. 116 an offence was an SAO if it either had led or was likely to lead to serious harm to the security of the state, serious interference with the administration of justice or the investigation of offences, or death, serious injury or substantial financial gain or loss to anyone.

Research showed that, according to the police, only about 2 per cent of suspects were identified as being involved in serious arrestable offences.[122]

Where an offence was an SAO the police had special powers under PACE – in respect of road checks (s. 4), search warrants (s. 8), special procedure applications (s. 9 and Sch. 1), length of detention (ss. 42, 43 and 44), delay in notifying police of the fact of detention (s. 56) and delay in permitting access to legal advice (s. 58).

SAOs were abolished by the Serious Organised Crime and Police Act 2005 (SOCPA) which substituted indictable offence for serious arrestable offence.[123] An indictable offence is one triable either in the Crown Court or the magistrates' court. That greatly increased the number of instances in which the additional powers could be utilised.

Informing someone that one has been arrested

Almost a decade before PACE, in the Criminal Law Act 1977, s. 62, a suspect was given the right to have the fact of his arrest and his whereabouts communicated to someone reasonably named by him – without delay or, where some delay is necessary in the interests of the investigation or prevention of crime or the apprehension of offenders, with no more delay than is so necessary.

---

[119] For a detailed assessment see L. Bridges and J. Hodgson, 'Improving Custodial Legal Advice', *Criminal Law Review*, 1995, pp. 106–13.

[120] For details of the accreditation schemes see www.legalservices.gov.uk and www.lawsociety. org.uk.   [121] Note 20, p. 156 above, p. 27.

[122] D. Brown, *Detention at the Police Station under the PACE Act 1984* (Home Office, 1989) pp. 48–9.   [123] SOCPA, Sch. 7, Part 3.

Section 62 was recreated with minor modification in s. 56 of PACE. The person to be informed is now 'one friend or relative or other person who is known to him or who is likely to take an interest in his welfare' (s. 56(1)).

Delay is only permitted where the offence in question is an indictable offence (formerly a serious arrestable one) and is authorised by an officer of at least the rank of inspector.[124] The only permitted ground is that informing someone of the fact of the suspect's arrest 'will lead to interference with or harm to evidence connected with an indictable offence or interference with or physical injury to other persons, or will lead to alerting of other persons suspected of having committed such an offence but not yet arrested for it, or will hinder the recovery of any property obtained as a result of such an offence' (s. 56(5)). If delay is authorised, the person must be told the grounds and they must be recorded on his custody sheet (s. 56(6)). The right to have someone informed of his whereabouts applies anew every time that the suspect is brought to a new police station (s. 56(8)).

The Code of Practice (Code C, s. 5) adds further details. Thus the suspect has the right to have someone informed of his whereabouts at public expense. If one person cannot be reached he has the right to nominate someone else. The police right to delay informing someone does not apply in the case of a juvenile or someone who is mentally disordered or vulnerable.[125] Efforts must be made to notify his parent or guardian, or, where he is subject to a supervision order, his supervisor and the appropriate adult (see pp. 190–91 below).

The Code of Practice also provides for a foreign national or Commonwealth citizen to be allowed to communicate with his embassy, high commission or consulate at any time, and this right may not be suspended or delayed (para. 7.1 and note 7A).

It seems that under one-fifth of suspects seek to avail themselves of this right.[126] Delays are hardly ever imposed by the police.[127]

Tape recording of interviews

It would be a very unusual suspect who could take a note (let alone a coherent note) of the questioning he undergoes in the police station. The police on the other hand are well placed to make a record of the process. For many years there was a serious issue as to the accuracy of this record. It happened not infrequently that the suspect claimed that he had (in the jargon) been 'verballed', meaning that an alleged admission or confession had been invented by the police.

---

[124] It was altered from superintendent by the Criminal Justice and Police Act 2001, s. 74.

[125] Code C, Annex B, note B3.

[126] D. Brown, *Detention at the Police Station under PACE* (Home Office Research Study No. 104, 1989) p. 34.

[127] Brown et al (1992, note 99, p. 178 above) p. 68 found that delays were imposed in 0.1 per cent of cases.

The best way to safeguard the accused from police malpractice of this kind is obviously to have the entire transaction on tape. The tape also protects the police from false accusations of improper questioning or fabrication of evidence. Since 1992 tape recording has been compulsory for all interviews in connection with all offences other than summary-only offences.

However, it took a considerable period to reach that position. In 1972, a majority of the CLRC thought the time was not yet ripe to make tape recordings compulsory. It suggested merely that the Home Office mount an experiment. The Philips Royal Commission in its report in 1981 considered various options. It recommended the most modest – that only the final stage of police questioning be tape recorded, namely the formal 'statement stage' when the police assist the suspect to put his previous, usually rambling, account of the matter into a coherent statement. Taping of the whole interview, the Royal Commission thought, would prove too costly.

To its credit, the Conservative Government ignored the advice and went ahead with an experiment into taping the whole interview. The police were initially extremely hostile but the results soon convinced them and they became as enthusiastic about tape recording as any civil libertarians. The reason was that the presence of tape recording seems to increase the proportion of guilty pleas and to reduce challenges to prosecution evidence. Understandable police fears that tape recording would diminish the flow of confessions or information about offences committed by suspects were not realised. Rather surprisingly, suspects seemed just as ready to 'help the police with their inquiries' on tape as before.[128]

Tape recording is done under the procedure laid down in PACE Code E which deals with all the details. It provides that tape recording must be done openly. The master tape is sealed in the presence of the suspect. The second tape is the working copy. There should be a time coding to ensure that the tape is not changed by the police. (There have been no allegations of such abuse.) The fact of breaks, with timings, is supposed to be recorded.

If the suspect objects to the interview being tape recorded, the officer can, but need not, turn the recorder off.

The police also have to make a record of the interview. A 1991 Home Office Circular to the police on tape recorded interviews[129] said that the summary was supposed to be a 'balanced, accurate and reliable summary of what has been said which contains sufficient information to enable the Crown Prosecution Service to decide whether or not a criminal prosecution is appropriate and whether the charges are appropriate'. The summary was supposed to include a verbatim written record of all questions and answers containing admissions by the suspect.[130]

Research funded by the Home Office showed that summaries prepared by

---

[128] For an account of the sea-change in the attitude of the police see J. Baldwin, 'The Police and Tape Recorders', *Criminal Law Review*, 1985, p. 659.   [129] 39/1991.

[130] See, however, J. Baldwin and J. Bedward, 'Summarising Tape Recordings of Police Interviews', *Criminal Law Review*, 1991, p. 671 and J. Baldwin, 'Getting the Record Straight', *Law Society's Gazette*, 3 February 1993, p. 28 to the effect that summaries are often inaccurate.

civilian employees were generally of higher quality than those prepared by police officers. They were more consistently free from bias either toward prosecution or defence and they were better in terms of coverage, accuracy, relevance and literacy. Also they were cheaper.[131] Based on this research, all forces were advised by an efficiency scrutiny in July 1995 to implement a programme to employ civilians to prepare records of taped interviews.[132]

The defence has full access to the tape recording unless there is a valid claim of public interest immunity.[133]

However, in fact it is relatively rare for either the prosecution or the defence lawyers to listen to the actual tapes. They tend instead to work from the summary of the tape. The Law Society has laid down guidelines as to when solicitors should listen to the tape.[134]

Tape recording originally did not apply to interviews with terrorism suspects. There was a fear that giving the defence access to the tapes might result in the identification of the officers involved in questioning such suspects, with possible risk to their lives, but in March 1990 the Home Secretary announced a two-year experiment in London and Merseyside in which the police would tape record summaries of interviews with terrorism suspects. The experiment lasted until 1995 and taping continued after that on a voluntary basis. No report was ever published on the experiment. In 2001 a new system came into force for the mandatory audio recording of terrorism interviews under the Terrorism Act 2000 in England, Wales, Scotland and Northern Ireland. In Northern Ireland in addition there has been video taping of terrorism interviews as from February 2001.

On guidance to the courts on the handling of tape recordings see *Rampling* [1987] Crim LR 823 and *Practice Direction (Crime: Tape Recording of Police Interviews)* [1989] 1 WLR 631.

For a comparison of pre-PACE with post-PACE cases with regard, *inter alia*, to the effect of tape recording see I. Bryan, 'Shifting Images: Police–Suspect Encounters during Custodial Interrogations', 17 *Legal Studies*, 1997, p. 215.

[131] A. Hooke and J. Knox, 'Preparing Records of Taped Interviews', Home Office Research and Statistics Department, Research Findings No. 22, November 1995.

[132] The efficiency scrutiny led in 1995 to further major changes, the main purpose of which was to cut down significantly on police paperwork. In straightforward cases where the defendant is likely to plead guilty in the magistrates' court, the police are now supposed to send to the CPS an abbreviated file with short descriptive notes (SDNs) of taped interviews instead of a record of the taped interview. The SDN should be brief, should refer to relevant tape counter times and should use reported speech. The abbreviated file would have a statement of the victim and key witnesses. The full file has typed copies of all witnesses. For an account of this story and an assessment of the then latest changes see A. Mackie, J. Burrows and R. Tarling, 'Preparing the Prosecution Case', *Criminal Law Review*, 1999, pp. 460–9. For subsequent developments see a report in May 2003 by the Cabinet Office Regulatory Impact Unit entitled 'Making a Difference: Reducing Bureaucracy and Red Tape in the Criminal Justice System' – www.cabinet-office.gov.uk/regulation/PublicSector/reports.htm section 2.2.

[133] In *R v. X Justices, ex p J* [2000] 1 All ER 183, Div Ct, the prosecution successfully argued that the tapes should not be released to the defence as to do so would put an undercover agent with a distinctive voice at risk, but copies of the transcripts were released.

[134] *Law Society's Gazette*, 20 April 1994, p. 29.

A possible future development would be the tape recording of interviews with significant witnesses. For a two-part article by two barristers urging this see D. Wolchover and A. Heaton-Armstrong, 'Tape Recording Witness Statements', 147 *New Law Journal*, 6 June 1997, p. 855 and 13 June, p. 894.

Video taping of interviews A Home Office sponsored pilot experiment with the video taping of interviews with ordinary suspects began in April 2002.[135] It took place in six police force areas under the provisions of new PACE Code F. Code F was extended to all forces on a discretionary basis as from August 2004.

The rules for the handling of video recording are very similar to those for audio recording. Like audio tapes, the master tape has to be sealed in the presence of the suspect. In terrorism cases and other cases where an officer believes that recording or disclosing his identity would put him in danger he is permitted to use his identification number instead of his name and he can have his back to the camera. Receipt of the video tape by the defence is subject to an undertaking by the lawyer that it will not be given to the defendant for fear that it will be used improperly to identify the police officers involved.

Exchanges that are not recorded

It is clear that exchanges take place between suspects and police officers that are not recorded – in the street, in private homes or other premises, in the police car and at the police station. Research done for the Runciman Commission showed that the arresting officers reported having interviewed suspects before arrival at the police station in 8 per cent of cases.[136] The Royal Commission called for more research on the pros and cons of attempting to tape record such exchanges outside the police station,[137] but nothing further seems to have occurred in that regard.

It is to be noted in this context that Code C, para. 11.1 states that, save for exceptional circumstances, 'following a decision to arrest a suspect he must not be interviewed about the relevant offence except at a police station'. No doubt this is because it is only when he gets to the police station that the suspect is advised of his full rights and, in particular, it is only then that he is told about and enabled to get legal advice. Now that silence after caution can 'count' for the prosecution it is at least possible that the courts will be faced with more situations where the police question (and therefore 'interview' – see below) suspects outside the police station.[138]

---

[135] The Criminal Justice and Police Act 2001, s. 76 inserted a new s. 60A into PACE authorising video recording of interviews.

[136] S. Moston and G. Stephenson, *The Questioning and Interviewing of Suspects outside the Police Station* (Royal Commission on Criminal Justice, Research Study No. 22, 1993).

[137] Runciman, pp. 27–8.

[138] In *Williams* (1992) Times, 6 February W claimed that he had been persuaded to confess during an hour-long post-charge 'social visit' in his cell by investigating officers. The Court of

The Runciman Royal Commission recommended that the public parts of police stations should be under constant twenty-four hour a day surveillance through both audio and video recording. That would include the area around the custody officer's desk (the 'custody suite') and the corridors leading to the cells. It would not include the cells themselves. The purpose would be to reduce the danger of unauthorised and improper exchanges, as well as to monitor the nature of any physical interaction between suspects and police officers.[139] The Government's Interim Response to the Royal Commission's Report in February 1994 indicated that this recommendation was accepted and it is now common to have CCTV monitoring of the public space in police stations and custody suites.

The regime in the police station – the Codes of Practice and the custody officer

The Administrative Directions accompanying the Judges' Rules made some provision for the way the suspect was to be looked after in the police station. These dealt with such matters as the way the statement was to be taken and recorded, the record of the questioning, reasonable comfort and refreshment of suspects, special rules for questioning children, young persons and mentally handicapped persons, rules regarding the questioning of foreigners and access to writing materials.

The PACE Codes of Practice very significantly added to these rules and laid on the police a large number of detailed new requirements with regard to the way that suspects must be handled.

Code C starts with the statement that 'all persons shall be dealt with expeditiously and released as soon as the need for detention has ceased to apply' (para. 1.1).

Most of the Code deals with the situation in the police station. It deals with the duties in particular of the custody officer – the person in each police station designated to be responsible for the well-being of suspects. PACE, s. 36 stated that there has to be a custody officer on duty in each 'designated' police station and that normally he should be of the rank of sergeant or above.

However, the requirement that the custody officer be a sergeant was significantly modified by the Serious Organised Crime and Police Act 2005 which permits chief constables to appoint civilian custody officers. This would be a radical departure.[140]

Appeal rejected his appeal that the confession given at a later formal interview should have been excluded by the trial judge.

[139] Report, pp. 33–4.

[140] SOCPA, ss. 120 and 121. Runciman (pp. 30–1) expressly advised against this. It was fiercely opposed by the Police Federation and the Superintendents Association. As at September 2006 no chief constable had yet utilised the new power. However, the Thames Valley force had published a business case with a view to introducing it experimentally in 2007.

It is the custody officer's duty to ensure 'that all persons in police detention at that station are treated in accordance with this Act and any Code of Practice issued under it . . . and that all matters relating to such persons which are required by this Act or by such Codes of Practice to be recorded are recorded in the custody records relating to such persons' (s. 39(1)). Where the suspect is taken to a police station that is not a 'designated' police station, the person acting as custody officer must, if possible, be someone other than the arresting or investigating officers. Where the arresting officer is higher in rank than the custody officer and there is some disagreement between them regarding the handling of the suspect, the custody officer has to refer the matter to an officer of the rank of superintendent or above responsible for that police station (s. 39(6)).

The Code requires the custody officer in each police station to maintain a custody record containing the details of all the relevant events of the detention. A person is entitled to a copy of any part of the custody record and he must be told of his right to have a copy.

Information to the person in custody

One of the most important provisions in the Code relates to the information that must be given to the suspect. The custody officer, before any questioning of the suspect, must tell him the ground of his detention and tell him both orally and in writing of his right to have someone informed about his arrest, to have free legal advice and of his right under s. 5 of the Code to send a message as to his whereabouts to someone outside the police station.

PACE, s. 56 (the right not to be held incommunicado) permits the suspect at his own expense to send letters, or telegrams or make telephone calls, providing Annex B does not apply. (As has been seen, Annex B states that the implementation of certain rights may be delayed if an officer of the rank of inspector (formerly it was superintendent) or above has reasonable grounds to believe that it would lead to 'interference with or harm to evidence connected with an indictable offence', or to the alerting of other persons suspected of having committed such an offence, or will hinder the recovery of property obtained in the course of such an offence.) If letters are sent from the police station, the police are permitted to monitor their contents – other than in the case of letters to a solicitor (Code C, para. 5.7).

The custody record must show that the suspect has been told about his rights, either by his signed acknowledgment or a note that he refused to sign. If he wishes to waive the right to legal advice, this too must be signed (Code C, para. 3.2).

The police must warn the suspect that anything he says in a letter, phone call or message may be used in evidence (Code C, para. 5.7).

Records of interviews

The provisions in Code C regarding the process of keeping proper records of any interview with the suspect require records to be kept of the place of interviews, the time they begin and end and the time of any breaks. The person interviewed must be given the chance to read the record and to sign it as correct or to indicate what he thinks is not accurate. Persons making statements must be allowed to make them in their own words. If the officer writes the statement he should use the words actually spoken by the suspect (Code C, paras. 2.6, 11.7–11.14 and Annex D).

One important addition to the old rules is that records of interviews should so far as practicable be made contemporaneously, or failing this as soon as possible after the interview (para. 11.7(c)). This has caused the police much concern. Also, even if the interview is tape recorded, a written record of the interview must be made and the suspect must be given a chance to read it and to sign it as correct. Where a third person is present at an interview, he has to be given the opportunity to read the written record of the interview and to sign as correct or to indicate the aspects in which he thinks it is inaccurate. If he refuses to do so, this fact should be recorded (Code C, paras. 11.12 and 11.14).

For definition of an interview see Code C, para. 11.1A, but the definition is less important since a record must now be made of relevant comments even if they are made outside the context of an interview (para. 11.13).

For an evaluation of the value of the recording rules see H. Fenwick, 'Confessions, Recording Rules and Miscarriages of Justice: a Mistaken Emphasis', *Criminal Law Review*, 1993, p. 174.

Conditions of detention

The Judges' Rules and Administrative Directions made some, but only rather general, reference to the conditions of detention. The Code puts detailed flesh and blood on the existing skeleton (Code C, ss. 8 and 9).

So far as practicable there should be no more than one person per cell. Cells and bedding should be aired and cleaned daily. There should be reasonable access to toilet and washing facilities. Replacement clothing should be of reasonable standard and no questioning must take place unless the suspect has been offered clothing. There should be at least two light and one main meal per twenty-four hours and any dietary requirements should be met so far as possible. Brief outdoor exercise should be permitted daily, if possible.

A child or young person should not be placed in police cells unless he is so unruly as to be a danger to person or property or there is no other secure accommodation available. Only an inspector or above can authorise such detention.

No more than reasonable force may be used by a police officer to secure compliance with reasonable instructions, to prevent the suspect's escape or to restrain him from causing injury to persons or damage to property or evidence.

If any ill-treatment or unlawful force has been used, any officer who has notice of it should draw it to the attention of the custody officer who in turn must inform an officer of at least the rank of inspector not connected with the investigation. He in turn must summon a police surgeon or other health care professional to examine the suspect. A complaint from the suspect to this effect must be reported to an inspector or above.

Medical treatment

The Code requires that appropriate action be taken by the custody officer to deal with any medical condition – whether or not the person in custody asks for it. This applies not only to obvious medical conditions but where the person is unable to appreciate the nature of the proceedings, or he is incoherent or som-nolent and the custody officer is in any doubt as to the circumstances of his con-dition. The Code specifically warns that a person who appears to be drunk may in fact be suffering from the effects of drugs or some injury. If in doubt the police should call the appropriate health care professional (Code C, Note 9C).

The advice of an appropriate health professional should equally be obtained if the suspect says he needs medication for a serious condition such as heart disease, diabetes or epilepsy (Code C, para. 9.9).

Conduct of interviews

In any period of twenty-four hours the suspect is supposed to be given eight continuous hours for rest, free from questioning, travel or other interruption and, if possible, at night. If he goes to the police station voluntarily, the period is calculated from arrest.

Before a detainee is interviewed, the custody officer, in consultation with the officer in charge of the case and appropriate health care professionals as neces-sary, must assess whether the detainee is fit to be interviewed (Code C, para. 12.3 and Annex G).

Interview rooms are supposed to be adequately heated, lit and ventilated. The suspect should not be required to stand. The interviewing officer should iden-tify his name and rank (or in terrorism cases or if in other cases, revealing his identity would put him at risk, his number). In addition to meal breaks there should also be short breaks for refreshment approximately every two hours unless this would prejudice the investigation.

The questioning of juveniles and mentally disordered or otherwise mentally vulnerable persons

There are detailed provisions in the Code regulating the questioning of persons who are mentally disordered, mentally vulnerable or youthful (Code C, s. 3(b) and Annex E). Broadly, they require that normally questioning should only take place in the presence of an 'appropriate adult' who is either a parent or guardian or a person in whose care he is. If the adult thinks that legal advice should be taken, the interview should not commence until such advice has been taken. However, an interview may take place in the absence of the responsible adult or lawyer if an officer of the rank of superintendent or above reasonably believes that the delay in waiting would involve the risk of immediate harm to persons or serious loss of or damage to property (Code C, para. 11.18).

The Runciman Royal Commission recommended that an expert working party be appointed to consider the role of the appropriate adult.[141] The Home Office set up a Review Group which reported in June 1995. It recommended, *inter alia*, that local panels of appropriate adults should be set up and that guidance as to the role should be available in the form of leaflets. Panels of lay people who volunteer to be on call as appropriate adults now exist in some parts of the country.

Juveniles make up around one-fifth of suspects in police stations. Home Office research has shown that 91 per cent of juvenile suspects had an appropriate adult present for all or some of their time in custody. In three-fifths of cases (59 per cent) it was a parent, in another 8 per cent it was another relative and in almost a quarter of cases (23 per cent) it was a social worker.[142]

Mentally disordered or mentally vulnerable detainees are a smaller group. In the same Home Office study, 2 per cent of detainees were treated as being in those categories – though other research has suggested that the actual proportion is considerably higher. Appropriate adults, usually a social worker, attended police stations in two-thirds of such cases (66 per cent).[143]

For a discussion of the various problems raised by the appropriate adult see J. Hodgson, 'Vulnerable Suspects and the Appropriate Adult', *Criminal Law Review*, 1997, pp. 785–95.

Interpreters

The Administrative Directions accompanying the Judges' Rules referred to statements made by those who could not speak English being translated by an interpreter, but they did not positively require the interpreter to be called. The Code remedies this deficiency and states categorically that a person who has difficulty in understanding English shall not be interviewed save in the presence of someone who can act as interpreter (para. 13.2).

Questioning of deaf persons

The Code (para. 13.5) also provides that where there is a doubt as to a person's hearing, arrangements should be made to have a competent interpreter. If he wishes, no interview should take place without the interpreter. On the other hand, if he does not insist on having an interpreter, the person should sign a waiver to that effect.

Rules preventing improper pressure on suspects

It goes without saying that police officers may not use physical violence or the threat of violence against suspects. Any such action would of course constitute

---

[141] Runciman, p. 44, para. 86.

[142] T. Bucke and D. Brown, *In Police Custody: Police Powers and Suspects' Rights under the Revised PACE Codes of Practice* (Home Office Research Series No. 174, 1997) p. 6.

[143] *Ibid*, pp. 7–8.

the criminal offence of assault (or worse). It would also be actionable in civil proceedings for damages, but civil and criminal proceedings are usually difficult to launch because of the problem of proving the allegations. The use or threat of physical violence could also be the basis of a formal complaint against the officers concerned.

Apart from the inhibiting effect of these possibilities there is also the long-established principle that statements to be admissible in evidence must be voluntary. The requirement that all confessions or admissions be voluntary is considered in Ch. 4. It will be seen there that the Philips Royal Commission proposed that the common law rules be modified and that PACE partly adopted the Commission's proposals. Under the scheme of the Act, confessions obtained as a result of oppression, violence, the threat of violence, or inhuman or degrading treatment are wholly inadmissible. Likewise inadmissible are statements obtained in circumstances that make it likely that any confession obtained in those circumstances would be unreliable. Moreover, if the matter is put in issue, it is for the prosecution to prove beyond reasonable doubt that the statement was not obtained as a result of such conduct, but if these conditions are met, the confession can be admissible even though it was obtained as a result of inducements (see further pp. 476–77).

4. Stop, arrest and detention

Stops in the street

The police can ask anyone any questions – but can they lawfully stop a citizen who does not wish to be stopped without arresting him? This question has arisen in a variety of contexts. In 1967 the Divisional Court gave a clear response in *Kenlin v. Gardiner*.[144] Two schoolboys were going from house to house to remind members of their rugby team about a game. Two plainclothes police officers became suspicious and, producing a warrant card, asked what they were doing. The boys did not believe they were police officers. One boy made as if to run away. The police officer took hold of his arm. The boy struggled violently, punching and kicking the officer. The other boy got involved and struck the other officer. Both were charged with assaulting a police constable in the execution of his duty. Giving the judgment of the court, Lord Justice Winn held that although the boys had assaulted the officers they were acting in justifiable self-defence. The officer had not been legally entitled to take hold of the first boy by the arm to detain him in order to ask questions.[145]

A case that seems to be in conflict with *Kenlin v. Gardiner* is *Donnelly v. Jackman*.[146] A uniformed police officer came up to D in the street to inquire

---

[144] [1967] 2 QB 510.
[145] See to the same effect *Ludlow v. Burgess* [1971] Crim LR 238 and *Pedro v. Diss* [1981] 2 All ER 59.   [146] [1970] 1 All ER 987.

about an offence which he had cause to believe D might have committed. He asked D if he could have a word with him. D ignored the request and continued to walk along the pavement away from the officer. The officer followed and repeatedly asked him to stop and speak to him. At one stage the officer tapped the appellant on the shoulder, upon which D turned round and tapped the officer on the chest saying 'now we are even, copper'. The officer then touched D on the shoulder with a view to stopping him to ask him some questions at which point D turned round and hit the officer with some force. He was arrested and charged with assaulting an officer in the execution of his duty. The magistrates convicted D. On appeal, the Divisional Court upheld the conviction. The court distinguished *Kenlin v. Gardiner* on the ground that in that case each officer had taken hold of a boy and had detained them. Asking the question whether the officers had been acting in the course of their duty, Talbot J for the court said 'it is not every trivial interference with a citizen's liberty that amounts to a course of conduct sufficient to take the officer out of the course of his duties'.

In *Bentley v. Brudzinski*[147] on facts virtually identical with those of *Donnelly v. Jackman*, the Divisional Court went the other way. The respondent and his brother were stopped and questioned by a police officer at 3.30am. They answered his questions truthfully and identified themselves. After waiting some ten minutes while the officer unsuccessfully tried to verify their identities by radio, they walked away. Another officer who came up at that point stopped the respondent by putting his hand on his shoulder and was punched in the face. The Divisional Court held that this was more than a trivial interference with the respondent's liberty and amounted to an unlawful attempt to stop and detain him. Accordingly the respondent was not guilty of assaulting an officer in the execution of his duty. Lord Justice Donaldson added, however, that the respondent would have had no defence to a charge of common assault if one had been laid.[148]

One exception to the general rule is under the Road Traffic Acts. RTA 1988, s. 163 (formerly RTA 1972, s. 159) gives the police the power to stop a vehicle on any ground whatever. It is an offence to fail to stop. This power of stopping the vehicle does not, however, give the police any right to search it unless the driver agrees. As has been seen, the officer can, however, demand to have the name and address of the driver or the owner. The Divisional Court held in 1972 that the power to demand that a motorist gives his name and address includes the power to block his passage for the purpose.[149]

---

[147] [1982] Crim LR 825.

[148] For comment see *Criminal Law Review*, 1982, pp. 481 and 826. See also the contrasting cases of *Collins v. Wilcock* [1984] 1 WLR 1172; *Weight v. Long* [1986] Crim LR 746; *Smith v. DPP* [2001] EWHC Admin 55, [2001] Crim LR 735; and *R (on the application of Bucher) v. DPP* [2003] EWHC Admin 580. For discussion of the last case see N. Parpworth and K. Thompson, 'Physical Contact and a Police Officer's Execution of Duty', 167 *Justice of the Peace*, 7 June 2000, p. 426.   [149] *Squires v. Botwright* [1972] RTR 462.

The courts have held that the police have the right to detain motorists for a short period while they administer the breathalyser.[150]

If the police stop someone to ask him questions and he runs away, this can amount to the offence of wilfully obstructing the police in the execution of their duty. In *Sefkali, Banamira, Ouham*,[151] acting on information about an alleged offence of shoplifting, plain clothes officers approached the three appellants in the street and showed them their warrant cards. The appellants looked at the cards and then ran away. They were chased and caught. The Divisional Court upheld their conviction for obstruction. The police wanted to ask them questions and to see whether they matched the descriptions given to the police by the staff at the shop. The court said the appellants would have been entitled to refuse to answer the police questions. Having refused to answer questions they would have been entitled to say that they were going on their way. But the police were entitled to investigate a suspected offence by questioning and to impede that questioning by running away was obstruction.

As has been seen, in Scotland since 1980 (now under the Criminal Procedure (Scotland) Act 1995), where a constable has reasonable grounds for suspecting that a person has committed an offence he can ask him for his name and address and 'an explanation of the circumstances which have given rise to the constable's suspicion' (s. 13(1)). He can also ask anyone whom he thinks has information relating to that offence to give his name and address. Secondly, the officer can require anyone whose name and address he has asked for to remain with him while he verifies the name and address – provided it can be done quickly. It is an offence not to comply (s. 13(7)).

The Philips Royal Commission did not recommend that the police should have any power short of arrest to detain persons as suspects. It also specifically rejected the idea that witnesses should be liable to arrest if they refused to give their name and address (para. 3.90). Citizens should be left to make up their own minds as to whether to co-operate with the police. Only in one situation should the rule be otherwise. This was where there had been some grave incident (such as a murder on a train of football supporters). The police should then have the right to detain potential witnesses 'while names and addresses are obtained or a suspect identified or the matter is otherwise resolved' (para. 3.93).

This proposal was not implemented.

Under the Terrorism Act 2000, s. 89 an officer may stop a person 'for so long as is necessary to question him to ascertain (a) his identity and movements; (b)

---

[150] *Coleman* [1974] RTR 359 and *Squires v. Botwright* above. See also *Lodwick v. Sanders* [1985] 1 All ER 577. The police stopped a lorry driver who had no excise licence, index plate or brake lights. Becoming suspicious as to whether the lorry was stolen, the officer took the ignition keys to prevent the driver leaving. There was a minor fracas. The driver was charged with assault on the police, but was acquitted on the ground that the officer had not been acting within his duty. Held, on appeal, that this was incorrect. He was entitled to stop the lorry in the first place and, being suspicious, to detain it for a reasonable period while checking out whether it was stolen. He had therefore been acting in the execution of his duty.

[151] [2006] EWHC 894 (Admin) 27 February 2006.

what he knows about a recent explosion or another recent incident endangering life; (c) what he knows about a person killed or injured in a recent explosion or incident'.

The Terrorism Act 2000, ss. 32–6 also give the police the right to cordon off an area for the purposes of a terrorist investigation. In *DPP v. Morrison*[152] the Divisional Court held that the police had a common law power to set up a cordon in a shopping mall as a crime scene because they were entitled to assume that the owner of private land over which there was a public right of way would have consented to the cordon. Hooper J went further in adding *obiter* that he doubted whether consent in such a situation could lawfully be withheld.[153]

The power to stop and search persons arises solely under statute.[154] There are a number of statutes which give the police this power. Pre-PACE the best known of these was the power under s. 66 of the Metropolitan Police Act 1839 to stop and search anyone in the metropolitan area reasonably suspected of carrying stolen goods. This power also existed by virtue of bye-laws in a few other cities. A similar power exists nationally in relation to drugs under the Misuse of Drugs Act 1971 and firearms under the Firearms Act 1968. There are also a variety of archaic powers to stop and search persons suspected, e.g. under the Badgers Act, the Pedlars Act, the Poaching Prevention Act and the Protection of Birds Act.[155]

In *Daniel v. Morrison*[156] the Divisional Court held that the power under s. 66 of the Metropolitan Police Act 1839 to stop, search and detain anyone suspected of having stolen goods included the power to question them as well, if only briefly. Similarly, in *Geen*[157] the court held that the power to search someone suspected of carrying prohibited drugs under the Misuse of Drugs Act 1971 included a power to question him briefly.

The Philips Royal Commission on stop and search

The Philips Royal Commission proposed that the Metropolitan Police power to stop and search for stolen goods should apply throughout the country. It also proposed a new power to stop and search for something possession of which was prohibited in a public place – such as offensive weapons (para. 3.20).

The majority of the Royal Commission thought that the danger of abuse of power could be avoided by the incorporation of proper safeguards, together with the fact that search would only be possible where there were reasonable grounds for suspicion. ('If parliament has made it an offence to be in possession of a

---

[152] [2003] EWHC Admin 683, (2003) Times, 21 April.
[153] See further on the case N. Parpworth and K. Thompson, 'The Lawfulness of a Police Cordon', 167 *Justice of the Peace*, 5 July 2003, pp. 507–10.
[154] The Supreme Court of Canada in *Mann* [2004] SCC 52 recognised a *common law* power of investigative detention short of arrest and with it an incidental power of questioning and of search. See P. Healy, 'Investigative Detention in Canada', *Criminal Law Review*, 2005, pp. 98–107.
[155] For a four-page list see *Report of the Royal Commission on Criminal Procedure: Law and Procedure*, 1981, Cmnd. 8092–1, pp. 75–9.   [156] [1980] Crim LR 181.
[157] [1982] Crim LR 604.

particular article in a public place, the police should be able to stop and search persons suspected on reasonable grounds of committing that offence' (para. 3.21).) The safeguards proposed were: the officer should have to record every search and the reason for it; supervising officers should have a duty to collect and scrutinise figures of searches and their results for evidence that they were being carried out randomly, arbitrarily or in a discriminatory way; the person stopped should have a right to get a copy of the record; and numbers of stops and searches should be given to chief constables' annual reports (para. 3.26). The Commission also thought that searches on the street should be limited to fairly superficial examination of a person's clothing and baggage.

For pre-PACE research on stop and search see D. Smith, *Police and People in London: I.A. Survey of Londoners*, 1983; D. Smith and J. Gray, *Police and People in London: IV. The Police in Action*, 1983; C. Willis, *The Use, Effectiveness and Impact of Police Stop and Search Powers* (Home Office Research and Planning Unit, Paper 15, 1983).

PACE

The Government did not wholly accept the Royal Commission's proposals on stop and search powers. It rejected the argument that there should be a new general power to stop and search anyone reasonably suspected of carrying something possession of which in a public place was forbidden. The police therefore have to continue to manage under the various specific statutes which give them stop and search powers.

PACE, s.1 gives the police the power to search any person or vehicle for stolen goods or prohibited articles.[158]

The Code of Practice for stop and search

The Code of Practice on stop and search is Code A. Paragraph 1.1 states: 'powers to stop and search must be used fairly, responsibly, with respect for people being searched and without unlawful discrimination'. The person stopped can be questioned prior to a search and, if such preliminary exchanges indicate that the suspicion is ill-founded, no search need take place, but a person cannot be stopped in order for grounds for a search to be found. Normally, there has to be prior reasonable suspicion that the person was carrying something possession of which justifies exercise of the power.

Reasonable suspicion requires an objective basis 'based on facts, information, and/or intelligence' (para. 2.2). 'A person's race, age, appearance, or the fact that the person is known to have a previous conviction cannot be used alone or in

---

[158] Prohibited articles include an offensive weapon or an article made or adapted for use in connection with various listed offences such as burglary, theft, taking a motor vehicle or criminal damage. An offensive weapon is defined in the same way as under the Prevention of Crime Act 1953, s. 1 as 'any article made or adapted for use for causing injury to the person, or intended by the person having it with him for such use by him or by some other person' (s. 1(9)).

combination with each other as the reason for searching that person' (para. 2.2). Nor can a search be based on 'generalisations or stereotypical images' (para. 2.2).

These provisions are clearly aimed at the problem of the discriminatory use of the power of stop and search. Having excellent provisions in Code A does not, however, necessarily translate into compliance on the street. This has for years been an issue that provokes controversy. The statistics year-on-year show that people from ethnic minority communities – especially if they are black – are proportionately more likely to be stopped and searched than white people,[159] but this is a notoriously difficult issue to pin down. One of the key questions is the 'availability' of different age groups and different ethnic minorities to be stopped and searched according to time spent on the street and in other public places.[160] Unfortunately, with regard to this highly sensitive question of discrimination in the use of the power of stop and search it seems to be increasingly clear that for a variety of reasons it is not statistically valid to compare the ethnic data in the search figures with local population statistics, but no alternative basis from which to draw valid inferences regarding discrimination has yet been devised.

Power to stop and search randomly

A number of statutes permit stop and search without a requirement that there be reasonable grounds to suspect the particular person. The Criminal Justice and Public Order Act 1994 (CJPOA) provided for this in s. 60 (powers to stop and search in anticipation of serious violence) and in s. 81 (to prevent acts of terrorism). Both sections require a senior officer (under s. 60, an inspector[161] and under s. 81, an assistant chief constable or equivalent) to designate the area in which such powers can be exercised for a limited period (twenty-four hours under s. 60 and twenty-eight days under s. 81).[162] Section 81 only applied to vehicles and their drivers and passengers. The Prevention of Terrorism (Additional Powers)

---

[159] Comparing numbers of stops and searches with the resident population of an area permits the calculation of the number of stops and searches per capita. In one set of figures for England and Wales in 2001–2 the rate for white people was thirteen stops per thousand, compared with 106 for black people and thirty-five for Asians (*Handbook of Policing*, ed. T Newburn, 2003, p. 536. For discussion of this issue see pp. 536–8.

[160] For two recent studies see P.A.J. Waddington, K. Stenson and D. Don, 'In Proportion: Race and Police Stop and Search', 44 *British Journal of Criminology*, 2004, pp. 889–914 (a critique of extant work using research evidence drawn from a study attempting to assess the available population in the Thames Valley); and M. Shiner, *National Implementation of the Recording of Police Stops* (Home Office, 2006) (an assessment of police practice since the new guidelines for recording were introduced).

[161] Under s. 81 of the CJPOA it had to be a superintendent but the Knives Act 1997, s. 8 replaced this by an inspector.

[162] The Crime and Disorder Act 1998, s. 25 permits an officer acting under CJPOA 1994, s. 60 to require the person to remove any item such as a face mask that is being worn wholly or mainly to conceal his identity. (Code A, Note 4 advises that 'where there may be religious sensitivities about ordering the removal of such an item, the officer should permit the item to be removed out of public view'.)

Act 1996 filled the gap by permitting stop and search of pedestrians. The power is now to be found in the Terrorism Act 2000, s. 44 where the officer authorising the power 'considers it expedient for the prevention of acts of terrorism'.[163]

In *Chief Constable of Gwent v. Dash*[164] the Divisional Court held that random stopping of motorists to see whether they were driving with excess alcohol was not unlawful – though randomly requiring motorists to give a specimen of breath would be unlawful. The court said that, provided there was 'no mal-practice, caprice, or opprobrious behaviour', there was no legal restriction on the stopping of motorists by a police officer in the execution of his duty.

Abolition of 'voluntary' searches

Originally the rules on stop and search did not apply where the search was voluntary. Obviously, if this concept is given a wide interpretation there is a danger that a 'coach and four horses' will be driven through the procedural safeguards of PACE. The Home Office Circular on PACE issued to police said: 'voluntary search must not be used as a way of avoiding the main thrust of the safeguards'. However, not all forces and all personnel concerned took this message to heart. In too many situations the concept of the consensual or voluntary search was used as a way of avoiding the main thrust of the safeguards.[165]

The 2003 revision of the Code introduced a new, unambiguous provision:

> An officer must not search a person, even with his or her consent, where no power to search is applicable. Even where a person is prepared to submit to a search voluntarily, the person must not be searched unless the necessary legal power exists, and the search must be in accordance with the relevant power and the provisions of this Code [para. 1.5].

This means that the concept of voluntary search is now effectively banned. A search can only be done if there is the legal power, including reasonable suspicion, and if the Code of Practice is complied with. The only exception, where an officer does not require a specific power to search, is a search of persons entering sports grounds or other premises 'carried out with their consent given as condition of entry' (*ibid*).

Records of stops and searches

✓ Under PACE, s. 2 the police officer who proposes to carry out a stop and search must state his name and police station and the purpose of the search. A plain

---

[163] In *R (Gillan) v. Commissioner of the Metropolitan Police* [2006] UKHL 12 the Law Lords held that this power did not breach the ECHR. (For a critical commentary see *Criminal Law Review*, 2006, pp. 753–7.) The absence of a requirement of reasonable suspicion does not however mean that the police have *carte blanche*. They must not act arbitrarily. They must not stop and search persons who are 'obviously not terrorist suspects' (Lord Bingham at [35]). Intuitive stops were permitted but there had to be a connection to reasons connected with the terrorist threat.   [164] [1985] Crim LR 674.

[165] See D. Dixon, C. Coleman and K. Bottomley, 'Consent and Legal Regulation of Policing', 17 *Journal of Law and Society*, 1990, p. 345.

clothes officer must in addition produce documentary evidence that he is a policeman. The officer must give the grounds for the search. A search in the street must be limited to the outer clothing. The police officer is required to make a record of the search immediately or, if this is not practicable, as soon as possible (s. 3). The record is supposed to state the name of the officer, the name of the person stopped, if known, the object of the search, the ground of the search and its result (s. 3).

Recording of stops that do not result in a search

The Macpherson Report on the murder of Stephen Lawrence (1999) recommended that the police should be required to make records of *all stops* including voluntary stops (recommendation 61). The recommendation was highly controversial. Critics argued that it would significantly increase the burden on the police and to little purpose since there would be no way of determining whether a stop was reasonable, but after piloting the concept, the Government accepted the recommendation and all police forces were required to start implementation by April 2005. A record must be made 'when an officer requests a person in a public place to account for themselves, i.e. their actions, behaviour, presence in an area or possession of anything' (Code A, para. 4.12). The record need not show the name of the person stopped nor the reason for the stop, but it must show the identity of the officer, the date, time and place, the registration number of the person's vehicle, if any, the person's ethnic background and the outcome of the encounter.

Statistics

The annual Home Office statistics on stop and search[166] show that the two most common categories are drugs and stolen property. (In 2004–5 they accounted respectively for 40 per cent and 28 per cent of all recorded stops and searches.) Offensive weapons account for a very small proportion. (In 2004–5 only 9 per cent.)

The 'hit rate' in the sense of arrests following a stop and search, which was 17 per cent in both 1986 and 1987, was 13 per cent in each of the years 1999–2004 and dropped to 11 per cent in 2004–5 (para. 23).

The proportion of *all* arrests for notifiable offences resulting from stop and search is currently around 7 per cent, but in the Metropolitan Police district the proportion is more or less double that. (In 2004–5 it was 13 per cent (para. 15).)

Can a person be held in the police station if he is not under arrest?

It is common to read in the newspapers that a man is 'helping the police with their inquiries'. When asked, the police commonly assert that he is not under arrest.

---

[166] *Arrests for Notifiable Offences and the Operation of Certain Police Powers under PACE.* The latest available was that for 2004–5.

The legal position of such a person is clearly stated in s. 29 of PACE which provides that where a person attends a police station voluntarily 'for the purpose of assisting with an investigation', he is entitled to leave at will unless placed under arrest (s. 29(a)). Secondly, he must be informed 'at once that he is under arrest if a decision is taken by a constable to prevent him from leaving at will' (s. 29(b)). The only gap in the system is that there is no duty on the police to advise the person in question that he need not accompany the officer to the police station unless he wishes to do so. This would be the equivalent of the duty to caution him about his right of silence, but it does not exist and neither the Philips Royal Commission nor PACE made any reference to the issue.

However, if someone who is voluntarily helping the police with their inquiries, whether at a police station or elsewhere, is cautioned he must be informed that he is *not* under arrest, if that is the case (Code C, paras. 3.21 and 10.2).

Arrest

There are two forms of arrest, lawful and unlawful. In *Spicer v. Holt*[167] Lord Dilhorne said: 'whether or not a person has been arrested depends not on the legality of the arrest, but on whether he has been deprived of his liberty to go where he pleases'.[168] So, if a person is being detained by the police against his will, he is under arrest, but whether the arrest is lawful will depend on whether the conditions for a lawful arrest have been fulfilled.[169] If the arrest is not lawful there is a right to use reasonable force to avoid it, but this is clearly not a right to be lightly exercised since the legality of the arrest is best tested after the event when the dust has settled.

A lawful arrest is one authorised by law. There are three basic types of lawful arrest.

Arrest under warrant

The Magistrates' Courts Act 1980, s. 1(1) gives a magistrate power to issue a warrant upon written information being laid before him on oath 'that any person has, or is suspected of having, committed an offence'. Under the Criminal Justice Act 1967, s. 24(1) it is provided that a warrant for the arrest of someone should not be issued unless the offence in question is indictable or is punishable with imprisonment. This reflects the policy that minor offences should be dealt with by summons rather than arrest.

Arrest without warrant at common law

Until 1967 the law of arrest at common law revolved around the distinction between felonies and misdemeanours. Felonies and misdemeanours were

---

[167] [1977] AC 987, HL.
[168] At 1000. See to same effect, *R v. Inwood* [1973] 2 All ER 645 and *R v. Bass* [1953] 1 QB 680.
[169] *Dawes v. DPP* [1995] 1 Cr App Rep 65.

abolished by the Criminal Law Act 1967 which substituted the concepts of arrestable and non-arrestable offences.

There is now only one remaining common law power to arrest – where a breach of the peace has been committed and there are reasonable grounds for believing that it will be continued or renewed, or where a breach of the peace is reasonably apprehended.[170]

Arrest without a warrant under statute – new PACE s. 24

The general power of arrest which formerly was set out in the Criminal Law Act 1967, s. 2, was then to be found in ss. 24, 25 and Sch. 1A of PACE. Section 24 set out the powers of arrest in respect of arrestable offences and in respect of certain non-arrestable offence listed in Sch. 1A. Section 25 gave police officers a power of arrest for non-arrestable offences. (An arrestable offence basically was one carrying a prison sentence of five or more years' imprisonment.)

Under s. 110 of the Serious Organised Crime and Police Act 2005 (SOCPA), ss. 24, 25 and Sch. 1A of PACE were repealed and replaced by new ss. 24 and 25. SOCPA, s. 110 also provided for a new PACE Code of Practice – which is Code G. The new provisions became effective as from 1 January 2006.

Under the new provisions the distinction between arrestable offences and non-arrestable offences has gone. All offences are arrestable.

Arrest by a police officer

Section 24 gives a police officer the power to arrest:

- Anyone who is about to commit or who is in the act of committing an offence, or whom he has reasonable grounds for suspecting to be about to commit or to be committing an offence (subsection (1)).
- Anyone he has reasonable grounds for suspecting has committed an offence (subsection (2)).
- Where an offence has been committed, anyone guilty or reasonably suspected of being guilty (subsection (3)).

However, the power of arrest is only exercisable if the constable has reasonable grounds for believing that for any of the reasons mentioned in subsection (5) it is necessary to arrest the person. The test of 'necessity' is new. Whether it has any effect remains to be seen. The reasons listed in subsection (5) are:

---

[170] See *Wershof v. Metropolitan Police Commissioner* [1978] 3 All ER 540; *Hickman v. O'Dwyer* [1979] Crim LR 309; *Howell* [1981] Crim LR 697. The police were within their power to thwart an apprehended breach of the peace when they stopped three buses heading for a demonstration against the Iraq war five miles from the RAF base where it was due to take place, but they exceeded their powers when they escorted the coach passengers back to London. Their detention for the purposes of taking them back to London was a breach of Article 5(1) of the ECHR entitling the applicant to damages – *R (on the application of Laporte) v. Chief Constables of Gloucestershire and Thames Valley and the Commissioner of the Metropolitan Police* [2004] EWHC 253 (Admin), [2004] 2 All ER 874.

(a) to enable the person's name to be ascertained;

(b) to enable the person's address to be ascertained;

(c) to prevent the person –

(i)   causing physical injury to himself or anyone else;

(ii)   suffering physical injury;

(iii) causing loss of or damage to property;

(iv)   committing an offence against public decency;

(v)   causing an unlawful obstruction of the highway;

(d) to protect a child or other vulnerable person from the person in question;

(e) to allow prompt and effective investigation of the offence or of the conduct of the person in question;

(f) to prevent any prosecution for the offence from being hindered by the disappearance of the person.

Reasons (a)–(d) were previously in s. 25. Reasons (e) and (f) are new.

Citizen's arrest

The power of persons other than police officers to make an arrest are now to be found in s. 24A of PACE also inserted by s. 110 of SOCPA. Previously the power of a citizen's arrest applied to arrestable offences. It now only applies to indictable offences – where the person is committing or is reasonably suspected of committing such an offence (subsection (1)) or, where such an offence has been committed, where the person is guilty or is reasonably suspected of being guilty of it (subsection (2)).

However, the arrest is only lawful if one of the reasons in s. 24A(4) applies and 'it appears to the person making the arrest that it is not reasonably practicable for a constable to make it instead' (subsection (3)). The reasons in subsection (4) are not quite the same as those under s. 24(5) that apply to arrests by police officers. Only four reasons are listed – to prevent the person causing physical injury to himself or someone else, or suffering physical injury, or causing loss of or damage to property, or making off before a police officer can assume responsibility for him.

Reasonable ground to suspect Most statutes granting a power of arrest require that the arresting person has reasonable grounds to suspect. The House of Lords considered this well-worn phrase in deciding *O'Hara v. Chief Constable of the Royal Ulster Constabulary.*[171] O had been arrested for murder committed in the course of a terrorist act in Northern Ireland. The arresting officer had attended a briefing given by a superior officer at which he was told to arrest O because he had been involved in the murder. The officer's suspicion was based solely on that briefing. The trial judge and the Court of Appeal of Northern Ireland held that enough information had been given to the officer to enable him to form the required state of mind. On appeal to the House of Lords it was argued that reasonable grounds had to exist in fact, that the test was objective and therefore required proof of more than what was in the officer's mind. Dismissing the

---

[171] [1997] AC 286, [1997] 1 All ER 129.

appeal, the House of Lords unanimously rejected this argument. The court need look no further than what was in the officer's mind. The officer's suspicion could be based on what he had been told – even by an anonymous informant. It did not have to be established that the facts were true, but in each case it had to be considered whether the officer had enough information to form reasonable grounds for suspicion. Being ordered to make an arrest by a superior officer was not in itself enough. Here, although the information disclosed to the arresting officer at the briefing had been scanty, it was sufficient.

Detention for thirty minutes by a civilian

The Police Reform Act 2002 gives unprecedented powers to civilians acting in support of the police. The Act creates various categories of support with different powers – 'community support officers', 'detention officers', 'escort officers', 'investigating officers' and 'accredited persons' under community safety accreditation schemes.[172] When the Bill was first introduced in the House of Lords it included a power for community support officers to detain people in the street for up to thirty minutes pending the arrival of a police officer. The Government was defeated over these powers. When the Bill went to the Commons the Government successfully moved an amendment to restore the power for community support officers. It did not attempt to restore the power for 'accredited persons'. However, anticipating further defeat in the Lords, it announced on the Third Reading[173] that the power to detain would not be implemented nationally until, first, it had been piloted in up to six force areas over a two-year period and, secondly, there had been a report on the pilot by the Chief Inspector of Constabulary. The pilot and evaluation were positive and the power was activated as from December 2004.

The powers of the community support officer relate to minor misconduct such as issuing fixed penalty notices for being drunk in a public place, cycling on a pavement, littering etc. A community support officer can detain someone reasonably believed to have committed such an offence if he refuses to give his name and address or gives what appears to be a false one. Government ministers repeatedly insisted that detention for up to thirty minutes backed by use of reasonable force did not amount to arrest, merely 'a power of enforcement'[174] – whatever that may be.

Procedure on arrest

The law does not lay down any particular procedure to effect a lawful arrest. In *Alderson v. Booth*[175] Lord Chief Justice Parker said:

---

[172] The powers are set out in Part 4 and Schs. 4 and 5 of the 2002 Act on which see M. Zander, *The Police and Criminal Evidence Act 1984* (5th edn, 2005 and First Supplement 2006) Ch. 12; L. Jason-Lloyd, *Quasi-Policing* (Cavendish, 2003).

[173] House of Commons, *Hansard*, 10 July 2002, cols. 980–1.

[174] House of Commons, Official Report, Standing Committee B (Police Reform Bill), 20 June 2002, col. 266.

[175] [1969] 2 QB 216. See *R v. Inwood* [1973] 2 All ER 645 and *Dawes v. DPP* [1995] 1 Cr App Rep 65. See also G. Williams, 'When is an Arrest not an Arrest', 54 *Modern Law Review*, 1991, p. 408.

Whereas there was a time when it was held that there could be no lawful arrest unless there was an actual seizing or touching, it is quite clear that that is no longer the law. There may be an arrest by mere words, by saying 'I arrest you' without any touching. . . Equally it is clear . . . that an arrest is constituted when any form of words is used which in the circumstances of the case were calculated to bring to the defendant's notice and did bring to the defendant's notice that he was under compulsion.

Giving judgment in a case in 2000, Lord Justice Sedley said:

Although no constable ever admits to saying 'you're nicked for handling this gear' or 'I'm having you for nicking this motor', either will do and, I have no doubt, frequently does.[176]

What is required is words (or actions) that make it clear to the person that he is under arrest.[177]

The other requisite of a valid arrest at common law was that the officer must ensure that the suspect knows immediately, failing which, as soon as practicable, that he is under arrest[178] and the ground of arrest.[179]

In the famous case of *Christie v. Leachinsky*, Viscount Simon in a classic statement said:

(1) If a policeman arrests without warrant upon reasonable suspicion of felony, or of other crime of a sort which does not require a warrant, he must in ordinary circumstances inform the person arrested of the true ground of arrest. He is not entitled to keep the reason to himself or to give a reason which is not the true reason. In other words a citizen is entitled to know on what charge or on suspicion of what crime he is seized. (2) If the citizen is not so informed but is nevertheless seized, the policeman, apart from certain exceptions, is liable for false imprisonment . . . If a policeman who entertained a reasonable suspicion that X has committed a felony were at liberty to arrest him and march him off to a police station without giving any explanation of why he was doing this, the *prima facie* right of personal liberty would be gravely infringed. No one, I think, would approve a situation in which when the person arrested asked for the reason, the policeman replied 'that has nothing to do with you; come along with me . . .'[180]

---

[176] *Clarke v. Chief Constable of North Wales Police* (5 April 2000, unreported) at [36].

[177] In *Alderson v. Booth*, above, after a positive breathalyser test, the officer said: 'I shall have to ask you to come to the police station for further tests'. The magistrates accepted the defendant's somewhat surprising assertion that he thought he was going voluntarily and acquitted him because there had therefore been no lawful arrest from which it followed that the blood sample taken at the station had not been validly taken. The Divisional Court dismissed the police appeal. See also *Fiak* [2005] EWCA Crim 2381 and *R (on the application of Faulkner) v. Secretary of State for the Home Department* [2005] EWHC 2567 Admin, both discussed in N. Parpworth, 'Arrest and Detention: The Necessary Information', 170 *Justice of the Peace*, 7 and 14 January 2006, pp. 7–9.

[178] *R v. Inwood* [1973] 1 WLR 647 and *Pedro v. Diss* [1981] 2 All ER 59.

[179] *Christie v. Leachinsky* [1947] AC 573, HL; *Grant v. Gorman* [1980] RTR 119; *Waters v. Bigmore* [1981] Crim LR 408; *Pedro v. Diss* [1981] 2 All ER 59.   [180] [1947] AC 573 at 589.

The common law is reflected in PACE, s. 28 which states that an arrest is not lawful unless, at the time of or as soon as practicable after the arrest, the person arrested is informed that he is under arrest and of the ground of the arrest. Moreover it is specifically stated that this applies even where the fact of the arrest or its ground is obvious.

The legal consequences of failing to give grounds of arrest were considered by the Divisional Court in *DPP v. Hawkins*[181] and by the Court of Appeal in *Lewis v. Chief Constable of South Wales Constabulary*.[182] In *Hawkins*, the court held that failure to state the reasons for an arrest at the moment when it became practicable to do so had the effect of rendering the initially lawful arrest unlawful as from that moment and not as from the outset. The court therefore refused to allow the lawful arrest to be invalidated retrospectively. In *Lewis*, the officers had told the plaintiffs of the fact of arrest but delayed telling them the grounds for ten minutes in one case and twenty-three minutes in the other. The Court of Appeal (without referring to the *Hawkins* case) said that arrest was not a legal concept but was a matter of fact arising out of the deprivation of a person's liberty. It was also a continuing act and therefore what had been an unlawful arrest could become a lawful arrest. The remedy for the plaintiffs was merely the damages they had been awarded by the jury for the ten minutes and twenty-three minutes of illegality – £200 each.[183]

Under s. 30 of PACE, a person who has been arrested must be taken to a police station 'as soon as practicable', unless his presence elsewhere is reasonably necessary for the investigation. (But see p. 275 below for the new concept of 'street bail' given by a police officer under the Criminal Justice Act 2003.)

Summons or arrest?

Accused persons will either have been charged after an arrest or they will have been summonsed by post.

The proportion arrested for categories of offences varies dramatically. In 2005, of those dealt with for indictable offences, no fewer than 91 per cent were arrested, compared with 35 per cent of those dealt with for summary offences other than motoring charges, and 19 per cent of those dealt with for motoring offences.[184]

However, there are great variations in the policies of different police forces. A study done for the Philips Royal Commission showed that in Cambridgeshire, Cleveland and the Metropolitan Police district only 1 per cent of adults accused of indictable offences were summonsed, compared with over 40 per cent in places such as Thames Valley, West Yorkshire, Wiltshire and North Wales.[185]

---

[181] [1988] 3 All ER 673.   [182] [1991] 1 All ER 206.

[183] For critical comment see J. Marston, 'The Reasons for an Arrest', *Justice of the Peace*, 2 March 1991, p. 131. See also *Kulynycz* [1970] 3 All ER 881.

[184] *Criminal Statistics*, Home Office, RDS, 19/06, Table 4.2, p. 76.

[185] See R. Gemmill and R.F. Morgan-Giles, 'Arrest, Charge and Summons', *Philips Royal Commission*, Research Study No. 9, 1981, App. A, p. 42.

The Philips Royal Commission urged that the less intrusive procedure of summons be used wherever possible (para. 3.77). For whatever reason, the trend is moving instead in the opposite direction. In 1984 and 1986 the proportion of suspects summonsed for indictable offences was 22 per cent, but since then it declined and has been below 10 per cent in each year since 1996. (In 2005 it was 9 per cent.)[186]

Lord Justice Auld in his report recommended that the procedure for issuing a summons on an information laid before magistrates should be abolished and provisions to implement the recommendation were included in the Criminal Justice Act 2003. Section 29 of the 2003 Act (in force as from 6 November 2006) provides for a new system under which a written charge is sent out by the police, together with a requirement ('a requisition') for the defendant to appear before a magistrates' court to answer to the charge.

Remedies for unlawful arrest

A victim of an unlawful arrest has three possible remedies. First, in order to challenge unlawful detention which is still continuing, one can seek to issue a writ for *habeas corpus*. The writ can be applied for by the person unlawfully detained or by someone else on his behalf. There is always a duty judge available at or through the Royal Courts of Justice to hear applications. In emergencies the initial application to the judge can even be by telephone, but many lawyers are not familiar with this procedure and legal aid may not be available. Moreover, the Divisional Court, to whom application must be made, is not easily persuaded to grant the writ.

On the rare occasions when *habeas corpus* proceedings are brought on behalf of someone who is allegedly detained by the police without charges, the normal response from the police is to charge him before the case comes to be heard. Since PACE was enacted with its rigid time limit provisions for detention without charge (see below), *habeas corpus* applications in respect of persons held by the police are virtually unknown.

The second remedy is to use the illegality as the basis of an argument that the subsequent proceedings should be declared null and void. This is unlikely to succeed because of the rule of English law (see pp. 477–78 below) that evidence illegally obtained can nevertheless be admissible. Also, as *R v. Kulynycz* (n. 183 above) shows, the courts may be ready to cure an initial illegality if it was subsequently corrected.

The third remedy is to bring an action for damages for false imprisonment. In cases like *Christie v. Leachinsky* or *R v. Kulynycz* this is of little use since the amount of damages awarded would be purely nominal, but sometimes damages are quite significant. In *Wershof v. Metropolitan Police Commissioner*[187] the plaintiff, a young solicitor, got £1,000 for being arrested and detained for about an hour before being released on bail. In *Reynolds v. Metropolitan Police*

[186] Op. cit. n. 184 above.   [187] [1978] 3 All ER 540.

Commissioner[188]the Court of Appeal rejected an appeal against a jury's award of £12,000 damages for false imprisonment. The plaintiff was arrested in the early hours of the morning in connection with charges of arson for gain. The journey to the police station took two and a half hours. She was detained until 8pm the same day, when she was told there was no evidence against her. She got home by around 11pm. The trial judge in her action for damages against the police ruled that they had had no reasonable grounds for suspecting her of involvement in the crimes.

In *Hsu v. Metropolitan Police Commissioner*[189] the plaintiff was physically assaulted and racially abused when he refused to allow three police officers to enter his house. He was arrested and detained for about seventy-five minutes during which time his house was entered. He suffered post traumatic stress disorder. The jury awarded compensatory damages of £20,000 and exemplary damages of £200,000. The Court of Appeal reduced the total to £35,000. It held that £50,000 was the maximum that should be awarded for exemplary damages. Similarly, in *Goswell v. Metropolitan Police Commissioner*[190] the Court of Appeal reduced exemplary damages of £170,000 awarded by a jury for false imprisonment and assault to £15,000.

Detention for questioning

An arrest has to be based on reasonable suspicion that the person arrested has committed, is committing or is about to commit the offence in question. This is, however, not the same as the degree of suspicion necessary to base a charge. Can the police lawfully hold an arrested person for questioning in order to decide whether there is enough evidence to charge him? The question was only properly settled at common law in the same year that PACE was enacted.

In 1984, in *Holgate-Mohammed v. Duke*[191] the House of Lords held that the police were entitled to hold a suspect for questioning without charges. The plaintiff had been arrested after the theft of jewellery from premises where she was a lodger. She was detained for six hours but was not charged. She brought an action for damages against the police and at first instance won damages of £1,000. The judge held that detention had not been too long and she had been allowed to see a solicitor. Also there had been no improper pressure, but the purpose of detention had been to put her under greater pressure through having her in custody under arrest than would have existed if she had been interviewed without being arrested. The House of Lords confirmed the Court of Appeal's decision allowing the appeal and said that it was legitimate for the police to hold someone for questioning in order to dispel or confirm the officer's reasonable suspicion which led to the arrest.

---

[188] [1982] Crim LR 600.   [189] [1997] 2 All ER 762.   [190] *Legal Action*, September 1998, p. 21.
[191] [1984] AC 437, [1984] 1 All ER 1054.

The first reference to the concept of detention for questioning in any English statute was in PACE. Section 37(2) states that before an arrested person is charged the only ground for detaining him is that there are 'reasonable grounds for believing that his detention without being charged is necessary to secure or preserve evidence relating to an offence for which he is under arrest *or to obtain such evidence by questioning him*' (emphasis supplied).

The time limits on detention for questioning

Before PACE the law on time limits for detention without charges was in a state of muddle.[192] There was a widespread belief that the police were required to bring a suspect before the courts within twenty-four hours of arrest.[193] This was based on a misunderstanding. The only relevant provision that mentioned a time limit was the Magistrates' Courts Act 1980, s. 43(1) which stated, in effect, that a person charged with an offence that was not serious who could not be brought before a magistrates' court within twenty-four hours had to be bailed from the police station to appear before the court. There was no requirement in the section that he be brought before the court within twenty-four hours – only that if he was not, he should be bailed unless the offence was a serious one. (There was no definition of the concept of 'serious offence', which was therefore left to the police to define.)

Prior to 1984, the only other statutory time reference regarding police detention was the provision in s. 43(4) of the Magistrates' Court Act 1980 that 'where a person is taken into custody for an offence without a warrant and is retained in custody he shall be brought before a magistrates' court as soon as practicable'. There was no indication as to what was intended by the words 'as soon as practicable' but it was clear from police practice that this was interpreted by them to mean as soon as practicable after he had been charged and not as soon as practicable after being taken into custody. In his evidence to the Philips Royal Commission, the Commissioner of the Metropolitan Police suggested that the words 'as soon as practicable' were intended to recognise the need to keep some people in custody while inquiries were pursued in order to see whether there was enough evidence for a charge. A person aggrieved by the delay could apply to the Divisional Court for *habeas corpus*.

---

[192] For common law decisions on time limits for detention see *Houghton and Franciosy* (1978) 68 Cr App Rep 197; *Hudson* (1980) 72 Cr App Rep 163; *Re Sherman and Apps* (1981) 72 Cr App Rep 266, sub nom *Holmes, ex p Sherman* [1981] 2 All ER 612; *Nycander* (1982) Times, 9 December.

[193] Research conducted for the Philips Royal Commission established that most suspects spend a relatively short time in police custody. About three-quarters of all suspects were dealt with in six hours or less and about 95 per cent within twenty-four hours. Virtually none was held for more than forty-eight hours. A study based on nearly 50,000 detainees in the Metropolitan Police district showed that the proportion held for more than seventy-two hours was 0.4 per cent. (Philips, para. 3.96, p. 52.)

The Criminal Justice (Scotland) Act 1980, s. 2 authorised detention for questioning for up to six hours.

The Philips Royal Commission

In the Royal Commission's view the proper length of police detention before a suspect had to be brought before a court was a maximum of twenty-four hours. It proposed a scheme under which after six hours the custody officer in the police station would review the need for further detention. Within twenty-four hours the suspect would either have to be charged or released or an application would have to be made to a magistrates' court for permission to hold him for another twenty-four hours. The suspect would have a right to be present at any such hearing and he would equally be permitted legal representation on legal aid. Thereafter, the police would be entitled to go back to the magistrates for further extensions of twenty-four hours at a time. After forty-eight hours' detention, there would be a right of appeal to a judge against continued detention. The Royal Commission did not propose any upper limit of time for such extensions. In theory the magistrates would be free to grant any number of twenty-four hour extensions.

PACE

The Government did not wholly accept the Royal Commission's scheme. Under PACE, when an arrested person is being held under s. 37(2) for questioning he can be held in the first instance for up to twenty-four hours. At that point the necessity of further detention must be considered by a superintendent. He may give authority for further detention until the thirty-six hour point (s. 42).

This authority to extend detention beyond twenty-four hours only applied however to 'serious arrestable offences'. This was changed by the Criminal Justice Act 2003 which applied it to all arrestable offences[194] and, shortly thereafter, by the Serious Organised Crime and Police Act 2005, which restricted the power to indictable offences.[195]

The twenty-four hour period is measured from arrival at the police station. If the suspect is arrested by another force, it starts from the moment he arrives in the police station in the area where he is wanted. If he comes from outside England and Wales, the twenty-four hour period has to start within twenty-four hours of his first arrest (s. 41).

After thirty-six hours, there has to be a hearing in the magistrates' court with the suspect present and, if he wishes, legally represented (s. 43). The magistrates can grant a warrant of further detention for up to a further sixty hours – making a total of 96 hours (ss. 43 and 44), but the maximum period of time allowable by magistrates is thirty-six hours at a time. It follows that if the police want to

---

[194] Section 7 – based on a recommendation by the Home Office/Cabinet Office Joint Review of PACE, 2002.   [195] Schedule 7, para. 43(7).

ask for the full ninety-six hours they have to return to the magistrates for a second hearing (ss. 43(12) and 44).

The magistrates can only authorise further detention if the offence in question is an indictable offence,[196] that is being investigated diligently and expeditiously, and if further detention is necessary to secure or preserve evidence relating to an offence for which the suspect is under arrest or to obtain such evidence by questioning him (s. 43(4)).

PACE, s. 51(d) specifically preserved *habeas corpus*, but any such applications will presumably fail if detention has been properly authorised by the magistrates and the conditions for further detention still apply. However, if they no longer apply, further detention will be unlawful and *habeas corpus* is available.

The time for which a suspect can be held under PACE is affected by the following provisions:

- The custody officer is under a duty to order the immediate release of an arrested person if the grounds for holding him cease to apply and there are no other valid grounds for holding him (s. 34).
- When the suspect first comes to the police station, the custody officer has to decide whether there is at that stage enough evidence to charge him and, if so, he should be charged forthwith (s. 37(1) and (7)). Research has shown that this duty is not performed. Custody officers generally rubber stamp the arresting officer's decision to bring the suspect in for questioning.[197] As will be seen, the Criminal Justice Act 2003 introduced a new system under which responsibility for charging is taken over by the Crown Prosecution Service (CPS). If under this new system a case is referred to the CPS for a decision as to charges there will inevitably be a time delay, but no alteration was made to the provisions in PACE as to the length of detention to allow for this.
- The necessity of further detention must be reviewed regularly throughout the period of detention by an officer of the rank of inspector – initially after the first six hours and thereafter every nine hours. The suspect and/or his legal adviser must be given an opportunity to make representations (s. 39).
- After being charged the arrested person must be released, with or without bail, unless:
  - it is necessary to hold him so that his name or address can be ascertained; or
  - the custody officer reasonably thinks that it is necessary to hold him for his own protection or to prevent him from causing physical injury to anyone or from causing loss of or damage to property; or

---

[196] PACE, s. 43(4)(b) as amended by SOCPA, Sch. 7, para. 43(8).

[197] See I. McKenzie, R. Morgan and R. Reiner, 'Helping the Police with their Inquiries: The Necessity Principle and Voluntary Attendance at the Police Station', *Criminal Law Review*, 1990, pp. 23–4 and M. McConville, A. Sanders and R. Leng, *The Case for the Prosecution* (Routledge, 1991) pp. 42–4 and 119. See also E. Cape, 'Detention Without Charge: What Does "Sufficient Evidence to Charge" Mean?', *Criminal Law Review*, 1999, pp. 875–85.

- the custody officer reasonably thinks that he needs to be held because he would otherwise fail to answer to bail or to prevent him from interfering with witnesses or otherwise obstructing the course of justice; or
- if he is a juvenile, he needs to be held 'in his own interests' (s. 38(1)).

• Once he has been charged, if he is not released, he must be brought before a magistrates' court as soon as practicable and not later than the first sitting after being charged (s. 46(2)). If no court is sitting on the same day as he is charged or the next day (other than a Sunday), the custody officer is under a duty to inform the clerk to the justices so that a court sitting can be arranged (s. 46(3)).

Charging

When the investigating police officer reasonably believes there is a realistic prospect of conviction he must without delay inform the custody officer who is responsible for deciding whether the detainee should be charged.[198] This rule is now subject to the new system under which the CPS advise as to what charges should be brought (for the new system see p. 248 below), but under the new system the actual charging is still done by the police.

Where the detainee is someone the police believe should not be released on bail but the CPS have not yet advised as to what charge(s) to bring and the PACE time limits create a problem, the police can lay a 'holding' charge.[199]

Where someone is detained in respect of more than one offence it is permissible to delay informing the custody officer until the realistic prospect of conviction test is satisfied in respect of all the offences (Code C, para. 16.1).

However, if the other charges are more serious the suspect must be made aware of the fact at an early stage, so that he can consider whether he wants legal advice and how to respond to questions.[200]

Statistics on length of detention and charges

The annual Home Office statistics on length of detention give no figures as to average periods of time. They do however show the total number of cases in which the police apply to the magistrates for a warrant of further detention authorising detention beyond thirty-six hours. In the decade from 1994–2004 the annual number of applications to magistrates for warrants of further detention beyond thirty-six hours ran from a low of 220 to a high of 343. In 2004–5 it jumped to 423.[201]

Evidence of post-PACE average periods of detention prior to charge was given in two Home Office studies by Brown in 1989 and 1992[202] and in a study by Phillips and Brown in 1998. The 1989 report showed that only 1 per cent of

---

[198] Code C, para. 16.1.

[199] PACE, s. 37(7)(d) inserted by the Criminal Justice Act 2003, Sch. 2, para. 2(2).

[200] See *Kirk* [1999] 4 All ER 698 – convictions for manslaughter and robbery quashed.

[201] Home Office Statistical Bulletin, *Arrests for Notifiable Offences and the Operation of Certain Police Powers under PACE*, December 2005, Table PF, p. 15.

[202] *Detention at the Police Station under the Police and Criminal Evidence Act 1984* (HMSO, 1989) and Brown et al, *Changing the Code: Police Detention under the Revised PACE Codes of Practice* (HMSO, 1992).

all suspects in the sample of some 5,500 were held for more than twenty-four hours. As many as 32 per cent were out of the police station within two hours, 59 per cent in four hours and 76 per cent in six hours. Eleven per cent were held more than twelve hours. The mean length of detention was five hours and ten minutes with a median of three hours and nineteen minutes. The 1992 study showed that the position had basically not changed. In the 1998 study the mean time that suspects were held without charge was six hours and forty minutes. In very serious cases (murder or rape) it was just under twenty-two hours. For moderately serious offences it was just over seven hours. For less serious offences the average was just under four hours.[203]

Terrorism cases

The time limits for detention without charges in terrorism cases are different. Under successive Prevention of Terrorism (Temporary Provisions) Acts 1974–1989 a terrorist suspect could be detained for forty-eight hours in the first instance on the authority of the police and thereafter, with the written permission of the Home Secretary, for a further five days.

In 1989 the Strasbourg Court held that detention for four days and six hours under this legislation was a breach of Article 5(3) of the ECHR.[204] The UK Government then entered a derogation from the Convention on the ground of the security situation in Northern Ireland.

The Criminal Justice Act 2003, s. 306 extended the seven-day limit to fourteen days.

Another change was that authority for detention of terrorist suspects beyond forty-eight hours is no longer obtained from the Home Secretary. The Terrorism Act 2000 substituted for the Home Secretary a 'judicial authority' – defined in the Act to mean either the Senior District Judge (Chief Magistrate) or another District Judge (Magistrates' Court) designated for the purpose by the Lord Chancellor.[205]

The Terrorism Bill 2005–6 originally had a provision extending the maximum period of detention of terrorist suspects without charges to ninety days. However, this was a step too far. On 9 November 2005, Tony Blair suffered his first Commons defeat since he became Prime Minister in 1997. MPs rejected the proposal by 322 to 291. The Commons substituted a new maximum of twenty-eight days and the Government decided not to try to restore the ninety-day proposal.[206] Under the Act any extension of detention beyond fourteen days requires an application to a High Court judge and no such extension can be for more than seven days at a time. After fourteen days the suspect is supposed to be transferred to a prison.[207] In the 'aircraft liquid bomb plot' case in 2006, the first case in which the power was used,

---

[203] Note 85, p. 174 above at p. 109. The study was based on a sample of just over 4,000 people detained at ten police stations in 1993–4.

[204] *Brogan v. United Kingdom* (1989) 11 EHRR 117.   [205] Schedule 8, para. 29.

[206] Terrorism Act 2006, s. 23(7) amending the Terrorism Act 2000, Sch. 8, para. 36.

[207] PACE Code H, para. 14.

twenty-four suspects were arrested, of whom seventeen were eventually charged. Eleven were charged between seven and fourteen days after arrest, four between fourteen and twenty-one days, and two between twenty-one and twenty-eight days. Three of the seven released without charges had been held for more than twenty-one days.[208]

The only figures for the length of detention in terrorism cases are derived from a study when the maximum period of detention was seven days. A study of 253 persons detained under the Prevention of Terrorism Act 1989, again by David Brown, found an average period of detention of nearly twenty-nine hours with a median of sixteen hours and twenty-four minutes, but just under 40 per cent of the terrorist detainees had been released within twelve hours and nearly two-thirds within twenty-four hours.[209]

Indefinite detention of terrorist suspects without charges

In the aftermath of the 11 September attack on the Twin Towers in New York the Government rushed through the Anti-Terrorism, Crime and Security Act 2001 (ATCSA) which gave the Home Secretary exceptional powers to detain some terrorist suspects indefinitely without charge. The Act provided that if the Home Secretary reasonably believed a person to be a suspected international terrorist whose presence in the UK was a risk to national security he could issue a certificate under ATCSA, s. 21. The definition of terrorist under the Act includes being a member of, belonging to, or having links with an international terrorist group.[210] (Having links with includes supporting or assisting.[211]) An international terrorist group is defined as one that is subject to the control or influence of persons outside the UK which the Home Secretary suspects of being concerned in the commission, preparation or instigation of acts of international terrorism.[212]

A person who had been certified under s. 21 could be detained indefinitely without charges.[213] Ministers explained that this draconian power was aimed at a small number of persons who could not be prosecuted for insufficiency of admissible evidence nor deported because they would face death or torture in the countries in question. However, if they could find a country prepared to take them, they had a right to go.[214]

During the passage of the Bill most of the controversy centred on the detained suspect's means of challenging certification by the Home Secretary. The Bill provided that appeal would lie to the Special Immigration Appeal

---

[208] Ali Naseem Bajwa and Bernie Duke, 'Pre-charge Detention in Terrorism Cases', 156 *New Law Journal*, 20 October 2006, pp 1578–79. The authors represented one of the suspects.

[209] D. Brown, *Detention under the Prevention of Terrorism Act 1989: Legal Advice and Outside Contact* (HMSO, 1993) p. 50. At that time the maximum period of detention in terrorism cases was seven days.   [210] ATCSA 2001, s. 21(2).   [211] *Ibid*, s. 21(4).

[212] *Ibid*, s. 21(3)(b).   [213] *Ibid*, s. 23.

[214] For commentary on the Act see H. Fenwick, 'The Anti-Terrorism, Crime and Security Act 2001: A Proportionate Response to 11 September?', 65 *Modern Law Review*, 2002, pp. 724–62. On the power of indefinite detention see J. Sawyer, 'Detention Appeals', 152 *New Law Journal*, p. 1357; M. Darwyne, 'The Crumbling Pillars of Justice', *Counsel*, April 2003, p. 27.

Commission (SIAC) established by the 1997 Act of that name, which sits with a High Court judge, an immigration judge and a security expert. The hearings are in camera and the Commission can hear evidence that is not shown to the detainee or his lawyer, though a security vetted lawyer ('special advocate') appointed to represent him would be shown such evidence. An appeal from the Commission lies to the Court of Appeal and House of Lords on a point of law.

The Bill provided that no court or tribunal other than the SIAC could entertain proceedings for questioning the Home Secretary's certificate. During the debates the Government amended the Bill by raising the status of the SIAC to that of a superior court of record, one of the results of which is that it is not subject to judicial review, but the Attorney General pointed out that the SIAC was in some respects more powerful than a court in that it could review the Home Secretary's certificate on its merits.[215]

It was reported in March 2003 that a special self-contained unit would be set up at Woodhill jail in Milton Keynes to house persons held under the ATCSA. Thirteen suspects were being held at different prisons. They would have a choice as to whether to move to the unit or stay where they were. The self-contained unit had been recommended by Lord Carlile of Berriew QC in his review of the operation of the Act. He reported that detainees under the Act complained of being held together with convicted criminals.[216] The authorities had issued no names, no charges had been brought and no explanations for detention had been given.[217]

A challenge to the validity of this system was launched by nine foreign nationals detained under the Act. On 16 December 2004 the House of Lords held by eight to one that the legislation breached Article 14 of the European Convention on Human Rights in that it discriminated against foreign nationals.[218] Section 23 did not rationally address the threat posed by Al-Qa'eda terrorists and their supporters because it did not apply to UK nationals.[219] The House of Lords decision declared that s. 23 was incompatible with the ECHR.

Indefinite detention without charges replaced by control orders

The Government accepted this defeat and quickly introduced new legislation to deal with the problem. The Prevention of Terrorism Bill, introduced on 23 February 2005, received Royal Assent only just over two weeks later on 11 March. The new Act gave the Home Secretary the power to make 'control orders' if he:

---

[215] For a decision by the SIAC cancelling the Home Secretary's certificate under s. 21 of ACSA, which was upheld by the Court of Appeal, see *M v. Secretary of State for the Home Department* [2004] EWCA Civ 324, [2004] 2 All ER 863.

[216] 'Jail within jail to hold terrorist suspects', *The Times*, 7 March 2003.

[217] R. Ford and D. McGrory, '15 foreign suspects held without trial in top-security jail', *The Times*, 17 January 2003.

[218] *A v. Secretary of State for the Home Department* [2004] UKHL 56, [2005] 2 AC 68, [2005] 2 WLR 87.

[219] A few months later, the terrorist threat from UK nationals was made manifest in the London bombings of 7 July 2005.

(a) has reasonable grounds for suspecting that the individual is or has been involved in terrorism-related activity; and

(b) considers that it is necessary, for purposes connected with protecting members of the public from a risk of terrorism, to make a control order imposing obligations on that individual' (s. 2(1)).

There are two kinds of control orders – 'derogating' and 'non-derogating'. To date all the control orders made under the Act have been non-derogating.

A non-derogating order is one the provisions of which are compatible with the Convention. It can be made by the Secretary of State but only if he has applied to the High Court and received permission to make such an order. In an emergency situation the Home Secretary can issue a provisional control order but it must be reviewed by a court within seven days. The court can refuse permission only if it finds that it was 'obviously flawed' (s. 3(2)). If it gives permission, it must give directions for a hearing as soon as practicable, at which point the individual concerned has the right to try to persuade the court that the control order or any of its provisions are 'obviously flawed'.

A derogating order is one the provisions of which are incompatible with Article 5 of the European Convention on Human Rights (the right to liberty) and can only be made if there has been a derogation to the ECHR approved by both Houses of Parliament. A derogating order is made by the High Court on an application by the Home Secretary. The test for the court is the same as that for the Home Secretary (above), except that it must also be satisfied that the risk of terrorism in question arises out of or is associated with the public emergency which resulted in the derogation (s. 4(7)).

Derogating control orders are limited to six months' duration; non-derogating control orders are limited to twelve months' duration. Both can be renewed subject to a right of appeal.

Breach of any condition without a reasonable excuse is a criminal offence punishable on indictment by imprisonment of up to five years or an unlimited fine.

Control orders are extremely far-reaching. They can impose controls on possession of specified articles or substances, on use of specified services or facilities, on carrying on of specified activities, on work or business, on association or communication with others, on place of residence and the persons to whom access is given to the place of residence and on movement. It can require the individual to agree that specified persons can have access to his place of residence and can search it and take away anything found there for testing. He can be required to agree to electronic tagging and to report to specified persons at specified times and places. He may even be required 'to comply with a demand made in the specified manner to provide information to a specified person in accordance with the demand' (s.1(4)).

Lord Carlile of Berriew, the independent reviewer, in his first report on the new Act in February 2006, said the restrictions generally imposed included an eighteen-hour curfew, limitation of visitors and meetings to persons approved by the Home

Office, no cellular communications or internet and a restriction on travel. ('They fall not very far short of house arrest' (para. 43).)[220] Between the coming into force of the legislation in March 2005 and the end of that year, eighteen control orders were made. Having looked at all the material the Home Secretary had available to him, Lord Carlile said: 'I would have reached the same decision as the Secretary of State in each case in which a control order was made' (para. 38).

On 14 February 2006 the Parliamentary Joint Human Rights Committee published a highly critical, 101-page report on control orders in the context of the Government's decision to lay before Parliament a draft order authorising the extension of the control order regime for another year.[221] It expressed concern that the non-derogating control orders that had been made were so restrictive of liberty as to amount to a deprivation of liberty contrary to Article 5(1) of the ECHR. It concluded that they also infringed Article 6(1) rights to a fair trial and the equality of arms, the right of access to a court to contest the lawfulness of their detention in Article 5(4), the right to examine witnesses in Article 6(3) and the most basic principles of a fair hearing and due process long recognised as fundamental by English law.

On 12 April 2006, in the first legal challenge to the new control order system, Sullivan J held that the procedure for legal challenge against the making of a non-derogating control order was incompatible with the right to a fair hearing guaranteed by Article 6(1) of the ECHR.[222] On 1 August 2006, this ruling was overturned by the Court of Appeal composed of the Lord Chief Justice, the Master of the Rolls and the President of the Queen's Bench Division.[223]

On 28 June 2006, Sullivan J quashed control orders imposing an eighteen-hour curfew on six persons on the ground that they deprived them of their liberty in breach of Article 5(1) of the Convention on the ground that they were equivalent to house arrest.[224] On 1 August 2006, the same Court of Appeal dismissed the Home Secretary's appeal.[225] The Home Secretary said he would seek

---

[220] An example of a control order was given in Lord Carlile's first report at Annex 2 – www.security.homeoffice.gov.uk.

[221] Joint Human Rights Committee, *Counter-Terrorism Policy and Human Rights: Draft Prevention of Terrorism Act 2005 (Continuance in Force of Sections 1–9) Order 2006*, 12th Report of Session 2005–6, HL 122, HC 915. The Government's response was published in the form of a letter to the Committee from the Home Secretary which the Committee published as Appendix 1 to its report *Counter-Terrorism Policy and Human Rights: Prosecution and Pre-Charge Detention*, 24th Report of Session 2005–6, 24 July 2006, HL 240, HC 1576.

[222] National press, 13 April 2006.

[223] *Secretary of State for the Home Department v. MB* [2006] EWCA 1140.

[224] [2006] EWHC 1623 Admin; national press, 29 June 2006. They were each required to remain in their one-bedroom flats except for six hours per day (10am to 4pm). During those six hours their freedom of movement was restricted to specified urban areas. Visitors had to be approved by the Home Office. They were not permitted to meet anyone by pre-arrangement who had not had Home Office clearance.

[225] *Secretary of State for the Home Department v. JJ* [2006] EWCA 1141; national press, 2 August 2006.

leave to appeal to the House of Lords. At the time of writing the outcome was not known.[226]

Coincidentally, also on 1 August 2006, the Joint Human Rights Committee made further proposals on dealing with terrorism cases including:[227]

- Suspects should be charged with criminal offences and prosecuted.
- Introducing the system of special advocates into criminal trials would be incompatible with Articles 5(4) and 6(1) of the ECHR.[228]
- There was nothing in the continental investigative approach that should be grafted onto our system.
- The ban on the use of intercept evidence in court should be removed.[229]
- There was scope for more proactive case management of terrorism trials without judges becoming either investigators or prosecutors.
- PACE, Code C should be amended to permit post-charge questioning of suspects and adverse inferences to be drawn from refusal to answer questions.
- There should be an enforceable right to compensation for those held in pre-charge detention who were not charged.
- It should not be necessary to extend the maximum period of pre-charge detention in terrorism cases beyond twenty-eight days.

5. Establishing the suspect's identity

The police have a variety of methods to assist them to establish the identity of, or to track down, suspects.

Fingerprints

Fingerprints may be taken from a person without consent in the following circumstances:

- From someone detained at a police station after being arrested for a recordable offence (PACE, 61(3)).

---

[226] For discussion and comment on the two decisions see L. Dubinsky, 156 *New Law Journal*, 1 September 2006, pp. 1320–1.

[227] *Counter-Terrorism Policy and Human Rights: Prosecution and Pre-Charge Detention*, 24th Report of Session 2005–6, 1 August 2006, HL 240, HC 1576. The Committee did not deal with control orders as they were then the subject of pending judicial proceedings.

[228] The system for special advocates in terrorism cases was described as 'critically flawed' by the Constitutional Affairs Committee in *The Operation of the Special Immigration Appeals Tribunal and the use of Special Advocates*, 7th Report of Session 2004–5, HC 323, April 2005. The Committee highlighted the fact that once the special advocate had seen the classified material he could not communicate with the appellant and his legal advisers as to whether the charges or the evidence could be challenged.

[229] This is equally supported, *inter alia*, by the Attorney General, Lord Goldsmith, the Director of Public Prosecutions, Ken Macdonald, the Association of Chief Police Officers and Liberty – see *The Guardian*, 21 and 22 September 2006. For a review of the competing arguments and issues see G. Langdon-Down, 'Court in the Act', *Law Society's Gazette*, 12 October 2006, pp. 19–20.

- From someone detained at a police station who has been charged with a recordable offence (s. 61(4)).
- From someone who answers to bail at a court or police station where there is doubt as to his identity (s. 61(4)).
- From someone convicted, cautioned, warned or reprimanded for a recordable offence (s. 61(6)) – the person can be required to attend a police station for the purpose (s. 27).
- From someone outside a police station who is reasonably suspected of committing or having committed an offence and the identity of the person is not known (s. 61(6A) and (6B).[230]

See Code D, section 4.

Footwear impressions

The Serious Organised Crime and Police Act 2005 (SOCPA), s. 118 inserted a new s. 61A into PACE to give the police the power to take footwear impressions without consent from a person detained at a police station who has been arrested for, or charged with, a recordable offence. Footwear impressions are recovered from around 20–30 per cent of crime scenes.

Photographs

At common law it was unclear whether the taking of photographs of suspects without consent was lawful. The Philips Royal Commission recommended that photographing should be on the same basis as fingerprinting. Originally there was nothing in PACE on the subject though there were some provisions in Code D on Identification. The first statutory provisions were in the Anti-Terrorism, Crime and Security Act 2001 which inserted a new s. 64A into PACE authorising photographing of detainees. SOCPA, s. 116 extended this power to photographs taken elsewhere than at a police station providing the person has been arrested or has been made subject to a requirement to wait with a civilian community service officer or has been issued with a fixed penalty notice.

Footnote 229 (*cont.*)

    However, Sir Swinton Thomas, the Interception of Communications Commissioner, opposes the move. Interviewed on Radio 4's *File on 4* programme on 21 November 2006, Sir Swinton said that MI5, MI6 and GCHQ had carried out extensive trials to check if intercept material would be valuable in prosecutions. 'Those inquiries have shown very clearly that the number of cases where intercept material would make a substantial difference are very few indeed or possibly even non-existent.' In his view changing the law would harm law enforcement and the security services. ('I deeply believe that if there is a change in the law, huge advantages which the security services and law enforcement agencies have at present would be lost.')

[230] Inserted by SOCPA, s. 117(2). The Explanatory Notes to the Bill stated that approximately 60 per cent of disqualified drivers provide false identities when stopped by the police.

Photographs and images of suspects detained at police stations can be retained provided they are only used or disclosed for purposes related to the prevention or detection of crime (s. 64A). Where the photographs or images were taken elsewhere than at a police station they must be destroyed once they have been used unless the person is charged or he gives informed consent to them being kept (PACE, Code D, para. 3.31).

It has been held that where the police make reasonable use of photographs for the purpose of the prevention or detection of crime they have a public interest defence to an action brought against them by the person whose photograph has been circulated.[231] This would cover the distribution to the media of photographs of suspects wanted by the police.

6. Getting the evidence

Identification evidence

The traditional method of holding an identification parade at which the witness is asked to try to identify the culprit in a line-up is no longer the preferred option. (Code D has detailed rules for the carrying out of identification procedures. In the 2006 revision of the Codes of Practice, Code D runs to no fewer than fifty-four pages.[232])

Video identification (Code D, Annex A) The police can show a witness a video film made after the offence including the suspect and at least eight other people who so far as possible resemble him, if possible, filmed in the same position.[233] This is now the preferred option as being quicker, cheaper and better than ID parades.

Identification parade (Code D, Annex B) Formerly, Code D required that an identification parade had to be held if the suspect asked for one. Since the 2003 revision, Code D (para. 3.12) says that whenever a suspect disputes being the person the witness claims to have seen, an identification *procedure* (not as before, 'identification parade') shall be held unless it is not practicable or it would serve no useful purpose. The suspect 'shall initially be offered a video identification' unless it is not practicable or an ID parade is both practicable and more suitable or group identification applies.

Group identification (Code D, Annex C) A group identification is where the witness sees the suspect in an informal group of people, usually in the police station. It can take place either with the suspect's consent or, if he has refused to co-operate with other methods, covertly.

---

[231] *Hellewell v. Chief Constable of Derbyshire* [1995] 1 WLR 804.
[232] For a detailed overview see M. Zander, *The Police and Criminal Evidence Act 1984* (5th edn, Sweet and Maxwell, 2005) pp. 317–33.
[233] The suspect is photographed. The photograph is then transferred into the computer system which holds a vast digital database. The suspect and his legal advisers are shown a range of photos similar to the suspect and are asked to agree on eight or nine to be used in the video film.

Confrontation (Code D, Annex D) The witness sees just the suspect either directly or behind a one-way mirror. Only used if it is not possible to use one of the other methods.

Search after an arrest

Searching the arrested person

Pre-PACE the common law position was by no means fully supportive of the police wish to search arrested persons. In *Lindley v. Rutter*[234] the Divisional Court held that the police had not been justified in forcibly removing a female suspect's bra. The officers had been acting in accordance with their chief officer's standing order as to searching of prisoners but the court said the order could not be justified since it was not adapted to the circumstances of particular cases. In *Eet*[235] the court held that officers had not been entitled to use force to search a driver suspected of having stolen a car to establish his identity. In *Brazil v. Chief Constable of Surrey*[236] the court held that the police were not acting in the execution of their duty when they searched a female suspect without informing her of the reason for the search. In *King*[237] it was held that where police are searching premises under a search warrant, they are not permitted to search persons there unless the warrant specifically so states.

Searching premises after an arrest

It was for a long time common police practice after arresting someone to go to his home and to search there. The Royal Commission on the Police in 1929 said it was unlawful and should either be permitted by statute or stopped, but no statute was passed to deal with the matter and the practice continued.

In 1982, in *McLorie v. Oxford*[238] the Divisional Court took a very restrictive view of police powers to search premises after an arrest. The police went to M's home looking for a car which they thought had been used by M's brother in an attempt to murder someone. The brother was arrested later that evening at the house where he lived with his father and brother. Subsequently the police saw the car in the backyard of the house and asked M's father for permission to remove it for forensic examination. After the father refused to give permission, the police returned in strength and removed the car forcibly. M, who had resisted the seizure, was charged with, and convicted of, assaulting the police. Quashing the conviction, the Divisional Court held that the police had not been acting lawfully. They would have been entitled to follow a motorist onto his own property in 'hot pursuit' and that would have entitled them to remove the car for forensic examination, but this was not a case of hot pursuit:

> Such is the importance attached by the common law to the relative inviolability of a dwelling house that we cannot believe that there is a common law right

---

[234] [1981] QB 128.   [235] [1983] Crim LR 806.   [236] [1983] 3 All ER 537.
[237] [1969] 1 AC 304, PC.   [238] [1982] QB 1290.

without warrant to enter one either in order to search for instruments of crime, even of serious crime, or in order to seize such an instrument which is known to be there. Certainly if there were, we would expect it to be reflected in the books and it is not.

The Philips Royal Commission on search of the person after arrest and of premises

The Philips Royal Commission thought that the police should not routinely make full searches of all suspects and that the question of how far a search should go should be considered by the station officer. A superficial search should always be permissible. Strip searches, on the other hand, should be rare. If they required a search of intimate parts of the body they should be permitted only in grave offences and only on the authority of a senior officer and should always be conducted by a doctor.

Search of the arrested person's premises and vehicle should be allowed subject to safeguards. The chief safeguard should be that there must be reasonable suspicion that evidence material to the offence may be found on those premises. Search of any other premises should have to require a warrant. The reasons for any search should be recorded by the station officer before the search in order to minimise the risk of 'fishing expeditions' (para. 3.121). Evidence of other offences found in the course of such a search should be admissible if a warrant could have been obtained to look for it, even though no such warrant had been obtained. Searches should be conducted in a manner appropriate to what was being searched for (para. 3.122).

PACE

PACE broadly enacted these recommendations. Section 18 empowered a constable to enter premises occupied or controlled by a person arrested for an arrestable offence to search for evidence relating to that or connected offences. As noted above, 'arrestable offences' was changed by the Serious Organised Crime and Police Act 2005 (SOCPA) to 'indictable offences'.[239] He must have reasonable grounds for believing that there is evidence on the premises that relates to the offence in question or to some offence 'which is connected with or similar to that offence' (s. 18(1)). Authorisation must normally be given in advance by an officer who is at least an inspector.[240] The officer who authorises such a search in advance (or approves one after the event) must make a written record of the grounds for the search and of the nature of the evidence sought.

PACE, s. 32 authorises search of an arrested person and of any premises (including a vehicle) he was in when arrested or immediately before being arrested. Again, SOCPA has added the requirement that the offence for which he was arrested was indictable.[241] The section cannot be used to justify a search

---

[239] SOCPA, Sch. 7, para. 43(3).   [240] *Badham* [1987] Crim LR 202.
[241] SOCPA, Sch. 7, para. 43(6).

several hours after the arrest.[242] A search under s. 32 can be for anything that can be used to assist an escape or for evidence relating to *any* offence (s. 32(2)).

PACE, s. 19 authorises an officer who is lawfully searching any premises (whether after an arrest or not) to seize any article (other than one covered by legal professional privilege) if he reasonably believes that it is evidence relating to the offence which he is investigating 'or any other offence' and that 'it is necessary to seize it in order to prevent its being concealed, lost, damaged, altered or destroyed'.

Intimate searches, x-rays and ultrasound scans

Section 55 of PACE permits a search of bodily orifices (called an 'intimate search'). An intimate search can only be for a weapon or other article that might be used to cause injury or for Class 'A' drugs (i.e. not for 'evidence') and it has to be conducted by a doctor or nurse or, in the case of a weapons search only, a police officer of the same sex provided that an inspector[243] or above reasonably considers that it is not practicable for the search to be conducted by a doctor. In practice virtually all such searches are carried out by doctors.

The Drugs Act 2005, s. 3 added a requirement that a drugs offence intimate search requires written consent. Adverse inferences can be drawn at trial from a refusal of consent.

The Drugs Act 2005, s. 5 inserted a new s. 55A into PACE to permit x-rays or ultrasound scans to be conducted if an inspector has reasonable grounds for believing that a suspect in police detention may have swallowed a Class A drug of which he was in possession with intent to supply. Again, this requires written consent and again, refusal of consent can be the subject of adverse inferences at trial.

A full record has to be kept of such searches – and now also of x-rays and ultrasound scans. Intimate searches are very rare. In David Brown's 1989 Home Office study such searches were found in only seven cases of 5,519 (0.1 per cent).[244] The Home Office annual statistics show that the number of such searches annually ranges from a few dozen to a couple of hundred or so.[245] (In the four years to 2004–5 the number of such searches was 102, 172, eighty-one and ninety-three.) Each year the overwhelming majority are for Class A drugs. (In 2004–5, 87 per cent of all intimate searches were for Class A drugs.) Usually the search produces no evidence. (In 2004–5 that was so again in 87 per cent of cases.[246])

The Joint Parliamentary Committee on Human Rights has suggested that intimate searches under PACE may contravene Article 3 of the European Convention on Human Rights which prohibits 'inhuman or degrading

---

[242] *Badham* n. 240 above. See also *Churchill* [1989] Crim LR 226.
[243] Changed from superintendent by the Criminal Justice and Police Act 2001, s. 79.
[244] Note 202, p. 211 above.
[245] *Arrests for Notifiable Offences and the Operation of Certain Police Powers under PACE.*
[246] Table PG.

treatment'.[247] Article 3 is absolute and permits no justification. The Government told the Committee that it did not agree that the rules contravened the Convention.

For provisions designed to ensure that intimate searches are only undertaken in exceptional circumstances see Code C, Annex A.

Intimate and non-intimate samples

PACE also made provision for the taking of bodily samples from the suspect as part of the process of criminal investigation. With the development of DNA analysis this power has assumed major importance.[248]

The Act distinguishes between two kinds of sample – 'intimate' samples (s. 62) and 'non-intimate' samples (s. 63). The main practical difference is that intimate samples, other than urine, may only be taken with the suspect's written consent, and only by a doctor. Provided an inspector's authority is given, non-intimate samples may be taken, without consent and by a police officer.

Intimate samples are defined as samples of blood, semen, other tissue fluid, urine, pubic hair or a swab taken from a body orifice. Originally, intimate samples could only be taken if the investigation concerned a serious arrestable offence but the CJPOA 1994 provided that it need only be a recordable offence which means an offence carrying a penalty of imprisonment. It requires the consent of an inspector[249] and the written consent of the suspect.

Non-intimate samples are defined (s. 65) as a sample of hair, other than pubic hair, a sample taken from a nail or under a nail, a swab taken from any part of the body including the mouth, other than a body orifice, saliva and a footprint or similar impression of part of a body. A non-intimate sample can be taken without the written consent of the person concerned if an officer of the rank of inspector[250] or above has authorised compulsory taking of the sample.

---

[247] First Report, Criminal Justice and Police Bill, Session 2000–1, HL Paper 69 (2001, HL) para. 75. The Committee's reports are available on www.parliament.uk/parliamentary_committees/joint_committee_on_rights.cfm.

[248] It seems that some DNA evidence is usually left at the crime scene. Home Office research in three police force areas (the Metropolitan Police area, Northumbria and South West Wales) showed that across the three forces more than 85 per cent of cases produced DNA evidence at the crime scene and that, of those, more than two-fifths (42 per cent) matched someone already on the database. The database can even be used to identify suspects who are not on the database by reason of their familial genetic traits.

With 3.6 million profiles the database is the largest in the world. In addition to its use in current cases, it is used increasingly to re-investigate old unsolved serious crimes. In July 2005 the Home Office's Police Standards Unit launched a study of unsolved rapes from 1994–9. By late 2006 the unit had examined nearly 9,000 such cases and selected 1,369 cases for further investigation. 28 per cent of the re-analysed cases resulted in a suspect being identified (*Police Review*, 10 November 2006, pp. 19–21 – www.policereview.com).

[249] The requirement that it be a superintendent was altered by the Criminal Justice and Police Act 2001, s. 80(1) despite concerns expressed by the Parliamentary Joint Committee on Human Rights, First Report, Session 2000–1, HL, Paper 69 (2001), HC 427, para. 81.

[250] The requirement that it be a superintendent was altered by the Criminal Justice and Police Act 2001, s. 80(1).

Section 63 permitted the taking of a non-intimate sample without consent in three situations: (1) following charge for a recordable offence; (2) where the person is in police detention (or is being held in custody by the police on the authority of a court) on the authority of an inspector which can only be given if he reasonably believes that the sample will tend to confirm or disprove his involvement in the offence and (3) following conviction for a recordable offence.

The Criminal Justice Act 2003, s. 10 extended the power to take a non-intimate sample without consent to anyone who has merely been arrested for a recordable offence regardless of whether it might confirm his involvement in the offence. This is mainly to help build up the national DNA database.

A further recent development is the taking of non-intimate samples for drug testing. This began in 2001 under new ss. 63B and 63C, PACE.[251] It arises if a person has been charged with any on a list of 'trigger offences' or if drug misuse is reasonably suspected. It permits the taking of a urine sample or a saliva swab. The Drugs Act 2005 extended these provisions. In the case of adults they now apply where a person has only been arrested. For those between fourteen and eighteen they must have been charged. If, as a result of drug testing the presence of a Class A drug is found, the detainee can be required to attend first, an initial assessment by a suitably qualified person to assess whether he would benefit for treatment and thereafter, a further assessment to draw up a care plan. (Section 17 of Code C – seven pages long – deals with drug testing.)

When samples can be retained

The police place great value on the DNA database which is the largest in the world and already holds some three million entries. The person from whom a sample, fingerprints or footwear impression is taken must be informed that it can be made the subject of a search (called 'a speculative search') against other records with a view to see whether he is wanted in connection with other offences.

However, can the sample be retained on the database if the person from whom it was taken is acquitted? Originally, PACE, s. 64 required samples and fingerprints taken from a suspect to be destroyed if the person from whom they were taken was acquitted, but after two decisions applying this rule provoked public uproar,[252] legislation was passed to change the rule[253] and the amending provision was made retrospective. This has already proved to be of great value in terms of tracking down offenders.[254](A challenge to the amending legislation

---

[251] Inserted into PACE by the Criminal Justice and Court Services Act 2000, s. 57.

[252] Both decisions were given by the same court on the same day. One was a murder case, the other a rape case. The rape case went to the House of Lords. *Re A-G's Reference (No 3 of 1999)* [2000] 4 All ER 360.   [253] Criminal Justice and Police Act 2001, s. 82.

[254] It was reported in January 2006 that retention of samples that previously would have had to be destroyed had led to some 7,500 matches with crime scenes involving 10,700 offences, including eighty-eight murders and 116 rapes. (G. Langdon-Down, 'Coded Warning', *Law Society's Gazette*, 26 January 2006, p. 21.)

brought under the Human Rights Act failed.[255]) Footwear impressions equally can be retained.

Sometimes the police test numbers of persons (sometimes very large numbers) in the hope of discovering a match for a DNA print or other evidence left at the scene of the crime. Ahead of being tested no one is a suspect. In that case fingerprints, footwear impressions and samples must be destroyed 'as soon as they have fulfilled the purpose for which they were taken' (Code D, Annex F, para.1).

Powers to enter premises other than after an arrest

At common law

There is no general common law power to enter private premises in order to investigate criminal acts. In *Davis v. Lisle*[256] a police officer, believing that D's employees had created an obstruction in the highway with a lorry, followed D to his garage. The officer neither had permission to be on the private property nor a warrant. He was first asked and then told to leave, but did not do so. D then struck the officer. He was convicted of assaulting a police officer in the execution of his duty. On appeal the Divisional Court held that the officer was not acting in the execution of his employment. In remaining, despite having been asked to leave, he was a trespasser. See, to like effect, *Lambert v. Roberts*,[257] in which the Divisional Court held that a police officer was not entitled to administer a breathalyser test on a motorist he had followed home when the motorist asked him to leave. But in *Snook v. Mannion*,[258] on virtually identical facts, the decision went the other way. The officers followed the motorist home after observing his erratic driving. They asked him to take a breathalyser test, which he refused, and he told them to 'fuck off'. The magistrates held that this was mere abuse, not a revocation of their implied licence to be on his drive. He was therefore convicted of driving with an excess of alcohol in his blood and the Divisional Court upheld the decision.[259]

The problem in relation to motoring law was altered by the provisions of the Transport Act 1981. (TA 1981, s. 25 stated: 'for the purposes of arresting a person under the power conferred by s. 5 [driving or being in charge of a car while unfit] a constable may enter (if need be by force) any place where that person is or where the constable, with reasonable cause, suspects him to be'.) This power may not, however, cover the situation where the officer wishes to administer a breathalyser test. TA 1981 also gave the police a power of entry where an accident has taken place: see Sch. 8, but these statutory provisions confirm that at common law there is no such power.

---

[255] *R (S) v. Chief Constable of South Yorkshire* and *R (Marper) v. Same* [2004] UKHL 39, [2004] 4 All ER 193. For critical comment see S. Forster, 'Retention of DNA/Fingerprint Samples: A Justified and Lawful Policy', 168 *Justice of the Peace*, 14 August 2004, pp. 628–32.

[256] [1936] 2 KB 434.   [257] [1981] 2 All ER 15.   [258] [1982] RTR 321.

[259] See also *Morris v. Beardmore* [1981] AC 446, HL; *Clowser v. Chaplin, Finnigan v. Sandiford* [1981] Crim LR 643, HL; *Hart v. Chief Constable of Kent* [1983] Crim LR 117.

On the force that can be used by the police in effecting entry, see *Swales v. Cox.*[260]

Lawful entry

A police officer who enters premises without lawful excuse commits a trespass. Prior to PACE, there were three forms of lawful excuse:

- *Under the authority of a search warrant* There are many statutory provisions that permit the police to ask magistrates for a search warrant. The search warrant must specify the correct premises. If it says Flat 45, the police cannot lawfully search Flat 30 even though that was what they actually intended when they asked for a search of Flat 45.[261]
- *To execute an arrest without warrant* This power, which formerly arose under the Criminal Law Act 1967, s. 2(6), now arises under PACE, s. 17(1). The power applies to effect an arrest for an indictable offence and for various summary offences including the offences of driving under the influence of drink or drugs and failing to stop contrary to ss. 4 and 163 of the Road Traffic Act 1988.
- *To deal with emergency situations* There was a common law power to enter premises to deal with, or prevent, a breach of the peace: see *Thomas v. Sawkins.*[262] The power also extended to saving life or limb. It is sometimes used by the police to deal with matrimonial or domestic disputes.[263] The power was preserved by PACE, s. 17(5) and (6), but care has to be exercised in its use. As Lord Justice Purchas said in one case: 'clearly a purely domestic dispute will rarely amount to a breach of the peace, but in exceptional circumstances it might do so'.[264]

It was held by the Divisional Court in 1985 that once the police were on premises lawfully for one purpose, they were there lawfully for any purpose. They could therefore search persons for drugs (which was their real object in being there) even though they had not got a warrant under the Misuse of Drugs Act because they were lawfully on the premises to check out the premises under the Greater London Council (General Powers) Act 1968: *Foster v. Attard.*[265]

According to survey evidence given by the police to the Philips Royal Commission, most searches of premises were under warrant. The survey

---

[260] [1981] 1 All ER 1115.   [261] *Atkinson* [1976] Crim LR 307.   [262] [1935] 2 KB 249.

[263] In *McLeod v. Metropolitan Police Commissioner* [1994] 4 All ER 553 the Court of Appeal held that on the facts the police believed that there was a real and imminent risk of a breach of the peace sufficient to justify an entry while items were removed from the house by the divorced husband in the absence of the wife. (The European Court of Human Rights subsequently took a different view: [1999] Crim LR 155.)

[264] *McConnell v. Chief Constable of Greater Manchester Police* [1990] 1 WLR 364 at 372. For discussion of the cases see N. Parpworth, 'The Lawfulness of a Police Officer's Entry under s. 17(1)(3) of PACE', 169 *Justice of the Peace*, 2 July 2005, pp. 508–11.

[265] [1986] Crim LR 627.

showed that 61 per cent of such searches in London (compared with only 24 per cent in the provinces) were backed by a warrant.[266]

By far the fullest study of the operation of the search warrant power pre-PACE was published in August 1984.[267] The survey showed that search warrants for stolen or prohibited goods represented a mere 8 per cent of all the search warrants issued in that period. (As many as 86 per cent were issued to the Gas and Electricity Boards.)

The researchers observed thirty-two warrant applications. They were not impressed by the way these proceedings were conducted. The magistrate asked questions of the police officer in only four cases – and in only two were the questions directed to the grounds for the application. (Surprisingly, full-time stipendiary magistrates were no more likely to ask questions than part-time lay magistrates.) The information supplied to magistrates was usually minimal – limited to the name of the police officer, the name of the occupier, the address and the nature of the case. The grounds for the application were rarely stated. (Usually it was variations on 'as a result of information received, there is reason to believe . . .') Only occasionally was there any indication that the police had verified the information or had supporting evidence. (The official guidance to magistrates is that police officers should not be required to identify an informant but that it is legitimate to ask whether he is known to the officer and whether it has been possible to make other inquiries.)

The comment from the author was that:

> The reality is then that the judicial hurdle of the warrant application is no more than a stepping stone. Magistrates see the 'information from a reliable source' formula as an impenetrable barrier beyond which they cannot or will not go. This, together with an almost unquestioning trust in the police, the clerk, or both, allied to a lack of knowledge of how the police actually operate and an over-glamourised view of specialist squads, combine to impair the proper exercise of the independent judicial function.[268]

There is no later study from which one could tell whether things have changed since 1984.

The Philips Royal Commission

The Royal Commission on Criminal Procedure recommended that existing powers to get a search warrant to look for prohibited goods such as stolen goods, drugs, firearms, explosives, etc. should be confirmed (para. 3.39). In addition, however, it recommended that there should be a new power to search for evidence whether from guilty persons or from persons totally unconnected with the offence. This power, it thought, should be used very sparingly and subject

---

[266] *The Investigation and Prosecution of Criminal Offences in England and Wales: The Law and Procedure*, Cmnd. 8092–1, 1981, pp. 126–9.

[267] K.W. Lidstone, 'Magistrates, Police and Search Warrants', *Criminal Law Review*, 1984, p. 449.

[268] *Ibid*, pp. 452–3.

to strict controls. It should be granted only in exceptional circumstances and in respect only of grave offences. The seriousness of the intrusion could also be marked by making the issuing authority a Circuit judge. There would be two stages. The court would first order the person holding the material to make it available to the applicant. Non-compliance could result in a search warrant being issued. If there was a danger that the evidence could disappear, the court would issue a search warrant at the first stage.

PACE

When the Police and Criminal Evidence Bill was first published it provided for two different procedures. The normal method for getting permission to search for evidence on private premises was to be by getting a search warrant from the magistrates to look for evidence of a serious arrestable offence. The Government said that the magistrates already granted search warrants in so many different situations that there was normally no need to require a judge's permission. But where the material sought was held in confidence an order from a Circuit judge would be required and would normally be made *ex parte*, i.e. in the absence of the other side.

These proposals provoked an outcry – notably from doctors, priests, journalists and Citizens' Advice Bureaux – claiming that the police would be given the right to search through confidential files and records. As a result, the Government made a number of major changes. First, it was provided that any hearing before a judge (a 'special procedure' application) would be *inter partes* so that the person from whom the material was sought would be entitled to be present unless the police had reason to suspect that he was implicated in the crimes in question. Secondly, various categories of 'excluded material' were defined which would be exempt from any kind of search by the police. (Though if the material could pre-PACE have been the subject of a search warrant it could be made the subject of a special procedure application[269] (see below).)

Excluded material

- *Personal records* held in confidence and acquired in the course of any 'trade, business, profession or other occupation'. 'Personal records' for this purpose means documents or records concerning individuals relating to their physical or mental health, spiritual counselling, social work or similar work involving counselling or assistance and other activities relating to a client's personal welfare or counselling and assistance given by voluntary organisations (ss. 11 and 12). Thus the files and records of doctors, priests, social workers and Citizens' Advice Bureaux are normally exempt from any kind of police search

---

[269] Under the terrorism legislation even excluded material can be the subject of an access order by a court. Only material covered by legal professional privilege is protected from such an order. See now the Terrorism Act 2000, s. 37 and Sch. 5, para. 6.

under PACE. Excluded material also covers human tissue or tissue fluid taken for the purpose of treatment or diagnosis, but if a doctor has the gun used in the crime or the patient's bloodstained clothing, the police would be able to ask a judge for an order requiring it to be produced. They would not be excluded material because they are not 'records' (s. 12).

- *Journalistic material* in the form of documents or records held in confidence. 'Journalistic material' for this purpose means material acquired or created for the purposes of journalism. It is not required that the material be for publication in a national newspaper or that the person holding it be a member of one of the journalists' unions. The material is only 'journalistic material', however, if it is held in confidence and is in the possession of someone who acquired or created it for the purposes of journalism (ss. 11 and 13).[270]

  PACE also provided that items held subject to legal professional privilege cannot not be made the subject of a search warrant application to magistrates (s. 8(1)(d)). Nor can such material be made the subject of a special procedure application or even seizure under s. 19 if actually found during a lawful search.

- *Items covered by legal professional privilege* consist of material exchanged between the client and his lawyer or anyone else acting for the client regarding legal advice, material exchanged between the client and the lawyer or anyone else acting for the client or between the client and such other person in connection with legal proceedings and items enclosed with or referred to in such communications.

However, items held with the intention of furthering a criminal purpose are not subject to legal privilege (s. 10). On this issue see the House of Lords decision in *R v. Central Criminal Court, ex p Francis & Francis*[271] which established that the criminal intent need not be that of the client or the solicitor. It can be that of a third party. In *R v. Crown Court at Inner London Sessions, ex p Baines & Baines*[272] in which it was held that material consisting simply of records of the financing and purchase of a house was not covered by privilege because it was not concerned with the giving of legal advice.[273] See also *R v. Customs and Excise Commissioners, ex p Popely*[274] where it was held that a search warrant cannot authorise seizure of items covered by legal professional privilege but if in the course of a lawful search of a solicitors' office, especially if the solicitor is himself suspected of involvement, the officer inadvertently seizes material which includes items subject to legal privilege, the execution of the warrant is not thereby rendered unlawful.

---

[270] For criticism of the way the courts deal with the seizure of journalistic material see R. Costigan, 'Fleet Street Blues: Police Seizure of Journalists' Material', *Criminal Law Review*, 1996, pp. 231–9.   [271] [1989] AC 346.   [272] [1987] 3 All ER 1025.
[273] See L. Alt, 'Raids: Against the Law', *Solicitors' Journal*, 15 November 1991, p. 1248.
[274] [1999] STC 1016 ,Div Ct.

Special procedure material

If the police seek evidence that is held in confidence but which is not excluded material, they must go to a Circuit judge for permission to seek 'special procedure material'. The procedure is set out in Sch. 1 of PACE. This requires that the judge be satisfied: (1) that there are reasonable grounds for thinking that an indictable offence (formerly a serious arrestable offence)[275] has been committed; (2) that there is 'special procedure material' on premises specified in the police application; (3) that it is likely to be of substantial value to the investigation and that it is likely to be relevant evidence; (4) that other methods of obtaining the material either have been tried or have not been tried because they would be bound to fail and (5) that it is in the public interest that the material should be produced having regard, on the one hand, to the benefit likely to accrue to the investigation and, on the other, to the circumstances in which it is held. Those are called 'the first set of access conditions'. Alternatively, the application can sometimes be made under the 'second set of access conditions'. These apply where pre-PACE the police had a statutory power to get a search warrant to search for the material in question. The applicant must then merely satisfy the court that the issue of a search warrant would have been appropriate. Most applications are made under the first set of access conditions.

If satisfied, the judge orders the person who appears to be in possession of the material to produce it to the police or to give them access to it within seven days from the date of the order. The person against whom the order is sought must normally be given due notice of the application so that he can appear to contest the application. Once a person is served with an order to produce the material, he must not conceal or destroy it. If he disobeys the order he can be dealt with by proceedings for contempt but not normally by the issue of a search warrant.

Special procedure applications are frequently made, especially against banks and other financial institutions.[276] Usually they are uncontested.

In certain circumstances the police can ask the judge for a search warrant instead of an order to produce and in that case the hearing is *ex parte* not *inter partes*. One is where service of notice of the proceedings would seriously prejudice the investigation.

Terrorism cases The terrorism legislation (now the Terrorism Act 2000, Sch. 5, paras. 4–17) gives the police far wider powers to acquire protected information. The judge must be satisfied that a terrorist investigation is underway, that the material would be of substantial value to the investigation and that disclosure would be in the public interest. The person thought to be in possession of the material can be required to state where to the best of his knowledge and belief it is. A production order under the legislation takes effect notwithstanding any restriction on disclosure or obligation of secrecy – an obvious threat to

---

[275] Changed by SOCPA, Sch. 7, para. 43(13).
[276] K. Lidstone reported over 2,000 such applications in the three years between 1986 and 1989: 'Entry, Search and Seizure', 40 *Northern Ireland Legal Quarterly*, 1989, p. 333 at 342.

journalists who might have to disclose material and thereby endanger an infor-mant, but material covered by legal professional privilege is protected.

Search warrants

PACE adopted recommendations made by the Philips Royal Commission on Criminal Procedure regarding the procedure for getting a search warrant (paras. 3.46–7). Section 15 provides that an application for a warrant must state the grounds for making the application, the statutory authority covering the claim and, in as much detail as possible,[277] the object of the warrant and the premises concerned. The Serious Organised Crime and Police Act 2005 (SOCPA) introduced a new concept of an 'all premises warrant' – whereby the warrant can be issued in respect of 'any premises occupied or controlled by a person specified in the application'.[278] The application must be supported by information in writing.[279] The constable must answer any questions put by the justice of the peace on oath. Hitherto each warrant could authorise only one entry but under SOCPA the warrant can now authorise an unlimited number of entries.[280] The warrant must specify the name of the person applying for it, the date of issue, the statutory power under which it is issued and, so far as pos-sible, the articles sought and when the search is to take place. The Act also requires a report to be made by the police to the issuing judicial authority (s. 16(9)). If it is executed, it must be endorsed with a statement showing whether the articles specified or any other articles were seized.

This must be made forthwith after the search. If the warrant is not executed within three months (formerly one month)[281] it must be returned at that point (s. 16(10)).

The rules relating to the issue of search warrants must be seen in light of the study by Ken Lidstone (p. 227 above) showing, at least in that study, the lax way magistrates seem to exercise this power. Lidstone also argued that the police were more likely to use their powers under PACE, ss. 32 (search after an arrest) or 19 (general power of seizure of evidence found incidental to a lawful search) than the power to get a search warrant. Since the police could normally get access to and the right to search premises without having to get a search warrant, they would presumably prefer that.

---

[277] In *IRC v. Rossminster Ltd* [1980] 1 All ER 80 the Inland Revenue obtained a search warrant to look for evidence of suspected tax fraud from the homes of two directors of Rossminster Ltd and its offices. Piles of documents were taken away for inspection. The House of Lords, reversing the Court of Appeal, held that the warrant was sufficiently detailed since it stated that the search was for evidence of tax fraud. It was not necessary, and might be impossible, to be more specific before the documents had been examined. See also *Reynolds v. Metropolitan Police Commissioner* [1984] 3 All ER 649.

[278] SOCPA, s. 113(4) inserting new PACE, s. 8(1A) and s. 113(7) inserting new PACE, s. 15(2A).

[279] This will continue under the new proceedure introduced by the Criminal Justice Act 2003, s. 29 for issuing a requisition as recommended by Lord Justice Auld – see p. 206 above.

[280] SOCPA, s. 114(2) inserting new PACE, s. 8(1C) and (1D).

[281] Changed by SOCPA, s. 114(8)(a).

Until 2006, it was English law that mere incompetence or negligence in applying for a search warrant did not give grounds for an action for damages.[282] Improper motive was necessary.[283] But in *Keegan v. UK*[284] the European Court of Human Rights held that it was a breach of Article 13 of the ECHR for courts to require proof of malice in such cases. The police obtained a search warrant in connection with armed robberies. The suspect had lived at that address previously but the existing tenants were completely unconnected and when they moved in the premises had been unoccupied for over six months. In the Court of Appeal, Lord Justice Kennedy said that if proper inquires had been made there could have been no probable cause to link the suspected robber with the premises. The Court of Appeal rejected the claim because there was no proof of malice. The Strasbourg Court said that Article 8 was geared to 'protecting against abuse of power, however motivated or caused'. Where basic steps to verify the factual basis of the warrant were not carried out, the resulting search could not be proportionate.[285]

See also S. Sharpe, 'Search Warrants: Due Process Protection or Process Validation?', 3 *International Journal of Evidence and Proof*, 1999, pp. 101–34. See generally R. Stone, *Entry, Search and Seizure* (4th edn, Oxford, 2005).

Search by consent and executing a search warrant

The search of premises is regulated by Code B (22 pages).

Search by consent Traditionally the police often somehow managed to get the owner of the place to be searched to consent to a search – though the reality of the consent must frequently have been questionable. This is now much more difficult since Code B requires that, where it is proposed to search by consent without a warrant or arrest, the police must, if it is practicable, get the occupier's consent *in writing* before the search (para. 5.1) and they must tell him that he is not obliged to give such consent (para. 5.2).

Unless it is impracticable to do so, the police must also give the occupier a Notice of Powers and Rights stating whether the search is under warrant or with consent, explaining the rights of the occupier and the powers of the police (para. 6.7). If the person is not suspected of an offence he should be told so (para. 5.2).

Search under warrant Where the occupier of the premises to be searched is present, PACE requires that the constable identifies himself, produces a copy of the warrant and gives him a copy (s. 16(5)). If he is not in uniform, the officer must

---

[282] *Keegan v. Chief Constable of Merseyside Police* [2003] EWCA Civ 936.

[283] *Gibbs v. Rea* [1998] AC 786.   [284] *Application No 28867/03* [2006] All ER (D) 235.

[285] For commentary see P. Ferguson QC, 'Malicious Intent', 156 *New Law Journal*, 29 September 2006, p. 1464 and S. Simblet, *Legal Action*, December 2006, pp. 28–30.

[286] *Chief Constable of Thames Valley Police v. Hepburn* [2002] EWCA Civ 1841, (2002) 147 Sol Jo LB 59. The Court of Appeal increased damages of £600 awarded to H to £4,000 for arrest and

produce documentary evidence that he is a constable (s. 16(5)(a)). A warrant for the search of premises does not legitimise a search of persons on the premises.[286]

An officer executing a warrant may use such force as is reasonable but no more than the minimum degree of force is to be used (Code B, para. 6.6). Searches must be conducted 'with due consideration for the property and privacy of the occupier and with no more disturbance than necessary' (para. 6.10). To have the media in attendance during the execution of a search warrant, even if they do not enter the premises, could be a breach of this provision. In *R v. Marylebone Magistrates' Court, ex p Amdrell Ltd, trading as 'Get Stuffed', and Robert and Pauline Sclare*[287] the applicants sought judicial review of the magistrates' decision to issue search warrants, *inter alia*, on the ground that the police had invited unauthorised persons, namely the press, to attend. The application failed but Lord Justice Rose for the Divisional Court said that save in exceptional circumstances 'it does not seem to me to be in the public interest that legitimate investigative procedures by the police, such as the execution of search warrants, or, for that matter, the interviewing of suspects, which may involve the innocent and may not lead to prosecution and trial should be accompanied by representatives of the media encouraged immediately to publish what they have seen'. Such publication might lead to new witnesses coming forward but it was far more likely 'to impede proper investigation and cause unjustifiable distress or harassment to those being investigated'.

The occupier must be allowed to have a friend, neighbour or other person to witness the search unless the officer reasonably believes that the presence of the person asked for would seriously hinder the investigation or endanger officers or others (para. 6.11).

If the search is for special procedure material under Sch. 1 of the Act or the Terrorism Act 2000, Sch. 5, the officer should ask the occupier to produce the material. He may also ask to see any index to files and to inspect files which according to the index appear to contain any of the material sought, but a more extensive search of the premises can only be made if access to the material is refused, or it appears that the index is inaccurate or incomplete, or if 'for any other reason the officer in charge of the search has reasonable grounds for believing that such a search is necessary in order to find the material sought' (para. 6.15).

Conduct of searches

It has been a fundamental rule for centuries that the police may not ransack a person's home looking generally for evidence against him. The common law rule against 'general warrants' was laid down in 1765 in the great case of *Entick v. Carrington*.[288]

Any lawful entry upon premises for the purposes of a search must always be for a specified reason and the search must be consistent with that reason.

---

detention in a drugs bust of a pub. Drugs were found in the room in which he was held but there had been no reasonable grounds to suspect him at the time of his arrest. He had not been charged with any offence arising from the event.
[287] (1998)162 JP 719, [1998] NLJR 1230.   [288] (1765) 2 Wils 275.

PACE provides that 'a search under warrant may only be a search to the extent required for the purpose for which the warrant was issued' (s. 16(8)). This would obviously make unlawful a search under the floor boards for stolen refrigerators, but if the search was for drugs, such a search would presumably be permitted. The same section also states that entry and search must be at a reasonable time of day 'unless it appears to the constable executing it that there are grounds for suspecting that the purpose of a search may be frustrated on an entry at a reasonable hour' (s. 16(4)). Code B adds that a search under warrant may not continue once the things specified in the warrant have been found or the officer in charge is satisfied that they are not there (paras. 6.9A and 6.9B).

Telephone tapping, 'bug and burgle' and other surveillance by the security agencies and police

Covert surveillance by the security service and the police is not new, but in recent years it has come more to public attention as a result of two quite different developments. One is the growth of technical means available for surveillance. The other is the pressure to regularise such activities in light of the privacy provisions of the European Convention on Human Rights. The traditional ways of handling the problem – informal systems, unpublished non-statutory guidelines and official nods and winks condoning plain illegality[289] – no longer pass muster. Nowadays, such activities have to be 'in accordance with the law' if they are not to run foul of Article 8 of the ECHR which guarantees everyone the right to respect for 'his private life and family life, his home and correspondence'. The UK's record before the European Court of Human Rights on this issue has not been a happy one.[290]

There have been five major recent pieces of legislation in this area: the Interception of Communications Act 1985, the Security Service Act 1989 as amended by a second Act of the same name passed in 1996, the Police Act 1997 and the Regulation of Investigatory Powers Act 2000.

The Interception of Communications Act 1985 This Act was passed to regularise the position after the Strasbourg Court held the UK to be in breach of the Convention because the tapping of Mr Malone's telephone had no statutory basis and was therefore not in 'accordance with the law' as required by Article 8. The Act made it an offence to intercept a communication in the course of its transmission by post or by means of a public telecommunication system unless the Secretary of State had authorised such interception. Detailed provisions were made to govern the issue, form, contents, duration and effect of warrants and to provide for access to a tribunal in case of complaints.

---

[289] As described for instance in *Spycatcher* (1987), the celebrated international bestseller by former MI5 officer Peter Wright.

[290] See *Malone v. UK* (1985) 7 EHRR14; *Halford v. UK* (1997) 24 EHRR 523.

The Security Service Acts 1989 and 1996[291] MI5's traditional role as defined in the Security Service Act 1989 (SSA) was to protect national security, especially against threats from espionage, terrorism and sabotage from the activities of agents of foreign powers 'and from actions intended to overthrow or undermine parliamentary democracy' (s. 1(2)) and also 'to safeguard the economic well-being of the United Kingdom against threats posed by the actions or intentions of persons outside the British Islands' (s. 1(3)).

The SSA 1989 gave the Home Secretary the power to issue warrants for 'the taking of such action as is specified in the warrant in respect of any property so specified' – namely entry of premises for the purpose of bugging.

As a result of the end of the Cold War, MI5 was looking for a new role – and employment for its staff of about 2,000. In 1996, to this end, the Government introduced a new Security Service Bill to amend the Security Service Act 1989 by extending MI5's functions to 'act in support of the prevention and detection of serious crime'. In response to fears expressed by civil libertarians that this would give MI5 a roving brief to act on its own, the Government amended the Bill by clarifying that such actions could not be free-standing but had to be 'in support of the activities of police forces and other law enforcement agencies'.

The SSA 1996 also defined the offences in relation to which the Home Secretary could issue such warrants. The definition was broad – conduct that 'involves the use of violence, results in substantial financial gain or is conduct by a large number of persons in pursuit of a common purpose' or alternatively, the offence is one for which someone over twenty-one with no previous convictions could expect to get a term of three or more years' imprisonment.[292] The minister assured the House of Commons that the SSA would only be used against what the ordinary citizen would understand to be organised and serious crime.[293]

The minister also stated that the Government intended to introduce legislation to regulate the position regarding police surveillance and bugging operations. He acknowledged that it was not satisfactory that the Security Service should be subject to the requirement of getting a warrant for a bugging operation from the Home Secretary while the police could authorise it themselves.[294]

The Police Act 1997 (PA 1997) The Act provides that 'no entry on or interference with property or with wireless telegraphy shall be unlawful if it is authorised by an authorisation' under the Act (s. 92). Authorisation can only be given if the authorising officer believes that 'it is likely to be of substantial value in the prevention or detection of serious crime' and that the objective cannot reasonably be achieved by other means (s. 93(2)). The definition of serious crime is the same as that quoted above from the SSA.

---

[291] See on the Act P. Duffy and M. Hunt, 'Goodbye *Entick v. Carrington*: The Security Service Act 1996', 2 *European Human Rights Law Review*, 1997, p. 11.

[292] This definition was taken from the Interception of Communications Act 1985.

[293] House of Commons, Standing Committee A, 1 February 1996, col. 44.   [294] *Ibid*, col. 78.

Until the PA 1997, entry on premises by the ordinary police for the purpose of bugging had been governed by unpublished guidelines issued by the Home Secretary in 1984. Under the guidelines a chief constable or assistant chief constable could authorise 'encroachment on privacy' through the use of surveillance devices. Though not formally published, the guidelines were extensively quoted by the Lord Chief Justice, Lord Taylor, giving the judgment of the Court of Appeal in *R v. Khan*,[295] a case that arose from the placing of a bug on the exterior wall of a house which enabled the police to tape record a conversation inside the house about drug smuggling.[296]

In the debates on the Bill a great deal of attention was focused on the question of who would be entitled to authorise a bugging operation by the police and in particular, whether and, if so, when the police would have to get approval from someone external to the police service. The Act provides that authorisation must normally be obtained from the chief constable or, in an urgent case, where this is not reasonably practicable, from an officer of assistant chief constable rank (ss. 93 and 94). It must be in writing, though in a case of urgency it can be given orally but it lapses after seventy-two hours unless renewed in writing (s. 95). Any authorisation must be notified as soon as practicable to the Chief Commissioner appointed under the Act (s. 96). The authorisation requires renewal after three months.

In certain circumstances the chief constable's authorisation does not take effect until it also has the written approval of one of the Commissioners appointed under the Act (s. 97(1)). The circumstances are where the property to be bugged is used wholly or mainly as a private dwelling or as a bedroom in a hotel or consists of office premises or the bugging is likely to involve (1) matters subject to legal professional privilege[297] (i.e. bugging of lawyers' offices); or (2) confidential personal information;[298] or (3) confidential journalistic material[299] (s. 97(2)), but this requirement of prior approval from a Commissioner does not apply when the chief constable believes the case is one of urgency. The Commissioner must then be notified with reasons for the urgency as soon as practicable and has the power to quash or cancel it (ss. 97(3) and 103(2)).

Commissioners under the Act must be persons who hold or have held high judicial office (s. 91(2)).

The Act is accompanied by a Code of Practice on Intrusive Surveillance setting out the detailed procedures to be followed. The Code requires the authorising officer to 'satisfy him/herself that the degree of intrusion into the privacy of those affected by the surveillance is commensurate with the seriousness of the offence' (para. 2.3). It says that this is 'the case where the subjects of the surveillance might reasonably assume a high degree of privacy, for instance in their homes, or where there are special sensitivities, such as where the intrusion might affect communications between a minister of any religion or faith and an

---

[295] [1994] 4 All ER 426 at 430–1.   [296] See also *R v. Chalkley* [1998] 2 All ER 155 at 161.
[297] See s. 98.   [298] See s. 99.   [299] See s. 100.

individual relating to that individual's spiritual welfare or where medical or journalistic confidentiality or legal privilege could be affected' or where confidential social security records are involved.

The Home Office press release issued when the Code of Practice was laid before Parliament stated that it was estimated that in 1996 there were some 2,550 chief officer authorisations by the police and customs throughout the United Kingdom. The majority related to the use of tracking devices on vehicles.

Part III of the Act only covers equipment whose placement may cause an act of trespass, criminal damage or interference with wireless telegraphy – for example, bugging devices in a home, a covert video camera in a hotel room and an electronic tracking device attached to a vehicle. It does not cover long-distance microphones or equipment based on laser beam or microwave technology whose use does not involve interference with property. It also does not apply where the police are acting with the consent 'of a person able to give permission in respect of relevant property' (Code, para. 2.1). This could raise difficult questions, for instance, in a landlord–tenant case as to who can give such consent, but presumably an employer could agree to an employee being bugged. The bugging of police cells would always have the approval of the police and would not require the approval of a Commissioner.

The 1984 Home Office guidelines continue to apply to any surveillance operations not covered by the PA 1997.

See further M. Colvin, 'Part III Police Act 1997', 149 *New Law Journal*, 26 February 1999, p. 311 and S. Uglow, 'Covert Surveillance and the European Convention on Human Rights', *Criminal Law Review*, 1999, pp. 287 and 296.

The Regulation of Investigatory Powers Act 2000 (RIPA 2000)[300] Prior to the 2000 Act, the UK had no system of statutory or judicial controls on undercover investigations.[301] In so far as there was any regulation it was in the form, again, of semi-published guidelines (first issued in 1969[302] and reissued by the Association of Chief Police Officers (ACPO) in 1999).[303]

RIPA 2000 puts onto a statutory basis, *inter alia*, 'directed surveillance',[304] 'covert human intelligence' i.e. the use of informers and 'intrusive surveillance' in residential premises or private vehicles including '(a) monitoring, observing or listening to persons, their movement, their conversations or their other activities or communications; (b) recording anything monitored, observed or

---

[300] For the background to the Act see the Government's consultation paper *Interception of Communications in the United Kingdom*, Cm. 4368, 1999.

[301] For the history leading to the 2000 Act see Lord Bingham's speech in *Attorney General's Reference(No 5 of 2002)* [2004] UKHL 40, [2004] 4 All ER 901 at 905–11.

[302] Home Office Circular 97/1969 set out in *New Law Journal*, 1969, p. 513.

[303] They were on the National Criminal Intelligence Service (NCIS) Website – www.ncis.co.uk but are now subsumed in the Code under the RIPA 2000.

[304] Defined as surveillance 'undertaken (a) for the purpose of a specific investigation; and (b) in order to obtain information about or to determine who is involved in the matter under investigation' (s. 26(2)).

listened to in the course of surveillance; and (c) surveillance by or with the assistance of a surveillance device'.

However, the 'bug and burgle' provisions of the PA 1997 (above) remain in being. The provisions of RIPA 2000, ss. 32–40 apply with regard to the surveillance of private property that does not require the physical placing of a device in or on the property. If the activity involves physical trespass on the property, the PA 1997 governs. The 2000 Act applies to private, but not to public, telephone or telecommunication systems.[305]

The authorising officer, designated in the legislation, has to be satisfied the authorised surveillance is proportionate and necessary. Authorisation of 'directed surveillance' and of 'covert human intelligence sources' requires only internal oversight which could be from the organisations carrying out the surveillance (ss. 28 and 29). For the police it is normally at superintendent level.

Authorisation of 'intrusive surveillance' is more narrowly restricted, requiring the decision of the Home Secretary or of one 'of the senior authorising officers'. Senior authorising officers for the police are chief constables (s. 32). (In cases that are urgent authorisation can be obtained from an Assistant Chief Constable.) However, even when such authority has been obtained, the further step is required of notifying the Surveillance Commissioner[306] who must decide whether to approve the authorisation based on a consideration of the relevant grounds and the issue of proportionality (s. 35). The authorisation only takes effect when approved in writing by the Surveillance Commissioner (s. 36).

It should be noted that RIPA 2000 does not impose a duty to obtain authorisation nor does it make unauthorised activity unlawful. If the activity was lawful before the passage of the Act it remains lawful even if it is not authorised under RIPA 2000 (s. 80). What it does do is to make lawful activities that have been authorised which would otherwise be unlawful.

It should also be noted that the fact that evidence has been obtained by means that are unlawful does not mean that it will necessarily be held to be inadmissible (as to which see pp. 477–78 below).

See further Y. Akdeniz, N. Taylor and C. Walker, 'Regulation of Investigatory Powers Act 2000 : Bigbrother.gov.uk: State Surveillance in the Age of Information and Rights', *Criminal Law Review*, 2001, pp. 73–90; E. Cape, 'The Right to Privacy – RIP', *Legal Action*, January 2001, pp. 21–3; D. Ormerod and S. McKay, 'Telephone Intercepts and their Admissibility', *Criminal Law Review*, 2004, pp. 15–38.

---

[305] *Attorney General's Reference (No 5 of 2002)* – n. 294 above. The case related to a private system installed in a police station. See discussion in the commentary on the case in *Criminal Law Review*, 2005, pp. 222–4.

[306] The Chief Surveillance Commissioner is the same Commissioner appointed under s. 91 of the Police Act 1997. RIPA 2000, s. 62 states that his duties cover intrusive surveillance under both Acts.

Seizure of evidence

The law of seizure is closely related to, but separate from, the law of search. Traditionally, the common law required that search be by warrant and that the warrant be particular and faithfully followed. Thus, as already seen, in *Entick v. Carrington*[307] it was held that the police could not ransack a man's house on a general warrant looking for evidence of a crime. In *Price v. Messenger*[308] it was said that a constable who finds goods while searching under a warrant, which are not covered by the warrant, commits a trespass by seizing them.

However, in the late 1960s and the 1970s the common law on this crucial topic considerably modified the strict rule. Since the topic is now governed by PACE and the common law is therefore no longer of practical importance it is no longer covered in this work.[309]

The Philips Royal Commission

The Philips Royal Commission dealt with the problem posed by seizure of evidence not covered by the search warrant. It did not think it realistic to restrict lawful seizure to prohibited articles or evidence specified in the warrant. ('It defies common sense to expect the police not to seize such items incidentally found during the course of a search' (para. 3.48).) It proposed that the police should be permitted to seize evidence of a grave offence which they find incidentally in the course of a lawful search (para. 3.49).

PACE

The Government went somewhat beyond this recommendation. Section 19 of PACE gives the police power to seize articles where a search is carried out lawfully either with the consent of the occupier or under any statutory power. The article may be seized if the officer reasonably believes that it is evidence in relation to an offence which he is investigating *or any other offence* or that it has been obtained in consequence of the commission of an offence and that it is necessary to seize it in order to prevent its concealment, loss or destruction. The only articles exempted are those covered by legal professional privilege (s. 19(6)) and even they may be seized under the new power to 'seize and sift' (below). It is immaterial whether an arrest has or has not taken place and equally whether the occupier is suspected of any involvement in criminal activity.

An article may be held for use as evidence at the trial, for forensic examination or, where it appears to be stolen, for restoration to its lawful owner (s. 22(2)). If requested by the occupier or the person having possession of the

---

[307] (1765) 2 Wils 275.   [308] (1800) 2 Bos & P 158.

[309] For the relevant common law decisions see *Elias v. Pasmore* [1934] 2 KB 164; *Chic Fashions (West Wales) Ltd v. Jones* [1968] 2 QB 299; *Ghani v. Jones* [1969] 3 All ER 1700; *Garfinkel v. Metropolitan Police Commissioner* [1972] Crim LR 44; *Frank Truman Export Ltd v. Metropolitan Police Commissioner* [1977] 3 All ER 431. See also *R v. Waterfield, R v. Lynn* [1964] 1 QB 164; *Jeffrey v. Black* [1978] 1 All ER 555 and *McLorie v. Oxford* [1982] QB 1290.

article, the police must give that person a record of what was seized (s. 21(1)) or a photocopy or photographs of items seized (s. 21(3)). Alternatively, the officer should be prepared to grant access, under supervision, to the items in question (s. 21(3)), but neither photographs, nor photocopies nor access need be granted if 'the officer in charge of the investigation has reasonable grounds for believing that to do so would prejudice the investigation' (s. 21(8)).

Power to 'seize and sift' In *R v. Chesterfield Justices, ex p Bramley*[310] the Divisional Court held that the police could not lawfully take away material that included items covered by legal professional privilege in order to sift and sort them at leisure at police premises. If such material was taken it had to be returned immediately and damages might have to be paid. The Government moved swiftly to change this. The Criminal Justice and Police Act 2001[311] gives the police a power to remove material for the purpose of sifting it elsewhere where it is not practicable to examine it on the spot. The power applies not only to seizure under PACE but to other legislation covering law enforcement agencies. The Police Reform Act 2002 extended the power to civilian investigating officers.

Having sifted the material, they can retain only what they are permitted to seize under the previous seizure powers – though they can hold on to 'inextricably linked material' that cannot be separated. Anyone with a sufficient interest in the material being held can apply to a High Court judge for its return. (For the Code B provisions, see s. 7(b).)

The power to freeze the suspect's assets

A new development in the law in recent years has been the power to freeze assets of a defendant prior to a trial. It is similar to developments in civil procedure, especially of 'freezing orders' (formerly Mareva injunctions) (p. 102 above).

The first step was taken in *West Mercia Constabulary v. Wagener*[312] where the police used civil process to seize and preserve property of a suspect. The High Court judge granted the police an injunction to restrain the alleged proceeds of fraud from being withdrawn from a bank account. The court said that since magistrates could not issue a search warrant to deal with proceeds of an alleged crime held in a bank account, the High Court would fill the gap. The new power was applied by the Court of Appeal in *Chief Constable of Kent v. V*[313] even though the alleged proceeds of crime had been mingled with the defendant's own moneys.[314]

---

[310] [2000] 1 All ER 411.
[311] CJPA 2001, ss. 50–66 and Schs. 1 and 2. See also Code B, paras. 7.7–7.12.
[312] [1981] 3 All ER 378.   [313] [1982] 3 All ER 36.
[314] Cf *Chief Constable of Hampshire v. A Ltd* [1984] 2 All ER 385 where the mingling of the alleged proceeds of crime with other moneys proved fatal to the police request for the same injunction. See similarly *Chief Constable of Leicestershire v. M* [1988] 3 All ER 1015 per Hoffmann J holding that the *proceeds* of crime could not be the subject of an interlocutory injunction. In *A-G v. Blake* [1998] 1 All ER 833 the Court of Appeal granted the Crown an

The common law power to freeze the defendant's assets was supplemented by the Drug Trafficking Offences Act 1986 (DTOA). The basic scheme of the DTOA was to give the court powers to freeze property or assets, whether in the hands of a defendant or a third party, which might subsequently be needed to satisfy the confiscation order for which the Act made provision. (Under the DTOA the court was required to make a confiscation order on every person convicted of a drug trafficking offence who had received any payment or reward in connection with drug trafficking at any time. The requirement was mandatory. The confiscation order was in addition to any sentence including a fine. The amount was the amount assessed by the court to be the full value of the offender's drug trafficking activities. For this purpose the court could assume that, unless the contrary was shown, all the offender's assets, plus any assets he had had in the previous six years, represented the proceeds of drug trafficking.) Similar powers under Part VI of the Criminal Justice Act 1988, by contrast, applied only to offences where the court was satisfied that the proceeds of the crime were more than £10,000.

The power to confiscate the proceeds of crime was greatly expanded by the Proceeds of Crime Act 1995. The relevant powers are now to be found in the Proceeds of Crime Act 2002. They are not restricted to cases where the proceeds are more than £10,000.

The Proceeds of Crime Act provides extraordinary ancillary civil powers which permit the High Court to make a restraint order preventing any dealing with the defendant's assets. Such an order is similar to a 'freezing order' and the prosecutor is given priority over unsecured creditors. The High Court can make disclosure orders requiring disclosure by affidavit of the nature and extent of assets. It can also make receivership orders to manage assets or realise them to enforce payment of a confiscation order made by the Crown Court.[315]

7. The prosecution process

The police have a wide discretion

The police have a major field of discretion in deciding whether and how to respond to criminal conduct. A former police officer turned journalist described once how he had walked from Waterloo Station to Holborn in order to see how many criminal offences he could identify:

injunction to stop the notorious spy, George Blake, from receiving royalties from his autobiography. It was held to be part of the court's support for the criminal law to enforce public policy by restraining receipt by the criminal of further benefit from his crime.

[315] On the 1995 Act see K. Talbot, 'The Proceeds of Crime Act 1995', *New Law Journal*, 15 December 1995, p. 1857 and K. Rees, 'Confiscating the Proceeds of Crime', *New Law Journal*, 6 September 1996, p. 1270.

C.R. Rolph, 'Police Discretion', *New Statesman*, 2 February 1969
I got the following bag:

- A girl feeding the pigeons inside Waterloo Station.
- Two cars with expired Excise Licences.
- Three cars with none at all.
- Twenty-three cars parked wholly or partly on the footway.
- One lorry with its lowered tailboard hiding the rear number plate while in motion.
- A furniture van with its rear number chalked on the back.
- One flag-day girl shaking a collecting box in people's faces.
- One boy throwing a half-eaten egg sandwich into the roadway.
- Three shop awnings that you had to duck under.
- A cycling window cleaner carrying a ladder on his shoulders.
- And a painter on a window sill wearing no means of preventing a fall.

I would say it was a typical lot and among the things too numerous to count were cars bearing advertising 'stickers', vehicles waiting on double yellow lines, and disembarking bus passengers throwing their tickets away.

I've known policemen who would have hated to let any of these escape. They would all have been seen as personal affronts, but even a policeman like that couldn't have coped with more than one of them. If he chose the cycling man with the ladder, who was actually the most dangerous, all the rest would have got away. So perhaps he would have chosen the three shop blinds, on the ground that they might have knocked his helmet off (they ought to be 8ft 6in from the ground).

But it has to be faced that the great majority of policemen would have chosen none of them. Which in itself would have been a choice and the chief constable's 'discretion' is merely the same choice writ large, with the difference that chief constables, who have no time to go around looking for car licences, number plates, flag-day offences, litter bugs and men on window sills, don't exercise their choice until an offence is actually reported and the papers come before them.

A more systematic exploration of the discretionary element in policing was part of a study of policing conducted in the late 1960s by John Lambert. What he wrote then is as relevant today:

J. Lambert, 'The Police Can Choose', *New Society*, 18 September 1969
The policeman is not, and never has been, simply a 'law enforcement officer'. He has *discretion*, in almost all circumstances except catching a murderer actually on the job, about whom he will arrest, investigate or harass, and whom he won't. In this sense, the problem is that of 'normal' policing, because in this exercise of discretion, which is central to all his work, the policeman's own private view of the world comes into play: his opinion, as a citizen, of other citizens; his reaction, as a member of one class or race, towards other classes or races.

The part that discretion plays, necessarily, in British police work is seldom acknowledged publicly. The legal philosophy of a democratic society sees police activities as potentially threatening to individual liberty. So the police, in enforcing the law, are themselves bound by numerous regulations. The theory is that laws apply to all men and the police must enforce the law always, everywhere equally.

Yet *full* enforcement is not possible. Law-breaking is so common that to investigate every infringement, to prosecute every known offender, would require police forces of a size, and involve expenditures on a scale, that would be impracticable and intolerable. So small police forces with small budgets have to enforce laws selectively. Both as an organisation and as individuals, the police have considerable choice about how to organise, which crimes and criminals to prosecute, how to allocate what number of men to different law enforcement tasks, and so on. It's almost a question of artistry, and certainly it's craftsmanship . . .

Crime occurs unevenly in different neighbourhoods of towns and cities. This puts more policemen in some areas than others, with different opportunities to discover offences and to find offenders to process as clients. Opportunities abound for legalistic policemen to cram police cells with the drunk and disorderly and police offices with papers relating to motoring offences. In practice, many are seen but few are processed. How the drunk or the motorist reacts to the policeman's intervention determines the outcome.

What matters is whether the client shows deference or respect to the policeman and which of these is shown depends very much on a two-way perception of status, rank, position and power between policeman and client. Thus law enforcement depends quite precisely on relations between police and public. The legal role of the police is defined by the perceptions of policemen and their ability to manage relationships.

Class bias in prosecutions

Research conducted by Professor Andrew Sanders, then of Birmingham University, explored the question of how far prosecution policy was influenced by class bias. He took 1,200 (non-motoring) cases from six police divisions (two from a large metropolitan county force, two from a small rural force and two from a force that policed both rural areas and a city). He compared police decisions with those of non-police agencies and especially the Factory Inspectorate (HMFI). (See A. Sanders, 'Class Bias in Prosecutions', *The Hansard Journal*, vol. 24, 1985, p. 176.)

He found:

- That the police cautioned very little – in about 4 per cent of cases, whereas the HMFI used cautions as the norm – in the period 1978–1982 cautions were used in 65–73 per cent of cases.
- The overwhelming majority of HMFI prosecutions are directed at the middle class, that is companies and managers, whereas most police prosecutions are of working class or unemployed (previously working class) persons. Despite considerable demographic differences, the police divisions produced very similar class patterns with around only 5 per cent from the middle or upper class. (Also a statistically significant difference emerged in the ability of middle class persons suspected of crime to avoid prosecution by the police.)

- In the police, the decision to prosecute is taken at a relatively junior level (inspector), while the decision not to prosecute is made at a relatively high level (superintendent or above). In the HMFI it is the other way round. The junior (inspector) can caution but it requires a more senior officer to institute a prosecution. Prosecutions are only started by the HMFI for what are regarded as the most serious of the serious cases, whereas the police often prosecute trivial cases.
- The police do not take poverty into account when deciding whether to prosecute. By contrast, if a factory owner or trader says he broke the law because he could not afford to comply, it would be taken into account and would be regarded as a valid reason for not prosecuting.
- Whereas in the police there was an institutional bias in favour of prosecution (reflected in the phrase 'let the court decide'), the HMFI regarded prosecutions as a last resort. The role of HMFI officials was one more of advice and persuasion, getting firms to comply with the law. The police saw their role in prosecutions as such.

In Sanders' view the different decisions of the agencies were the result not of the people concerned but rather of the perspective of the agencies. The police in some circumstances behaved in a similar way – e.g. in fraud cases where it was widely agreed that prosecution was thought of as a last resort for the real rogues. In tax evasion, too, very few are prosecuted. In 1980 there were 22,000 serious cases of tax evasion. One in 122 was prosecuted. By contrast there were 107,000 social security frauds, of which one in four were prosecuted. The total value of social security fraud was estimated at some £108 million in 1979 compared to £3–3.5 billion in tax evasion in the same year. Tax evasion therefore resulted in thirty times more loss to the public purse and yet there were far more prosecutions of social security fraud. On when the Crown Prosecution Service can prosecute, although the Inland Revenue has accepted a pecuniary settlement, see S. Elwes and R. Clutterbuck, 'Tax and Criminal Prosecutions', *Criminal Law Review*, 1999, pp. 139–43.

On class bias see also the research sample reported by McConville, Sanders and Leng in *The Case for the Prosecution* (Routledge, 1991) p. 123.

For evidence of remarkable regional differences in prosecution policies see research by Dr G. Slapper referred to at p. 268 below.

Proposals for an independent prosecution process

In most countries the decision whether to initiate a criminal prosecution is taken not by the police but by the prosecutor (in the USA, the district attorney, in Scotland, the procurator fiscal and in France, the *procureur* or *parquet*). Until 1986, England was one of the few countries in the world where the decision was taken by the police. The power of the police went so far that in the magistrates' courts the police themselves often actually conducted the prosecution. Where they did not conduct the prosecution they instructed either solicitors or solicitors and barristers. In the Crown Court where neither they nor solicitors had the right to appear as advocates, they had to instruct both solicitors and barristers.

This was changed by the Prosecution of Offences Act 1985 which set up the Crown Prosecution Service (CPS). The police still initiated the charge but the question whether the case was continued and, if so, on what charges was transferred to the CPS and it was the CPS which carried the prosecution forward. The change represented a revolution in both the principles and the actual practice of prosecutions. The Criminal Justice Act 2003 took the matter further by introducing the new principle that the CPS rather than the police formulate the initial charge. The police power to lay the charge now only applies in routine minor cases and in serious cases where an early holding charge is required to justify detention.

The origin of the CPS was the 1970 JUSTICE report *The Prosecution Process in England and Wales*, the main thrust of which was that even the honest, conscientious police officer may become psychologically committed to successful prosecution. 'He wants to prosecute and he wants to win'. He is therefore more likely to continue with a prosecution where the evidence may be weak. Also, the police were not well suited to evaluate the public policy aspects of the discretion not to prosecute. The police should not both collect the evidence and conduct the proceedings. The Committee recommended the introduction of the Scottish system where the decision to prosecute in all but very minor cases is taken by the procurators fiscal, under the Lord Advocate, wholly independent of the police. The police report all cases to the procurators fiscal, who decide whether a prosecution is warranted.

The Philips Royal Commission's report

The Philips Royal Commission agreed that a new system was needed but it did not go so far as JUSTICE in recommending the Scottish model. It thought that the initial decision to charge a suspect should continue to be taken by the police but that thereafter all decisions, including any decision to alter or drop the charges, would be taken by a prosecution agency. Each area would have a prosecuting solicitors' department presided over by a Crown Prosecutor of equal status to the chief constable and answerable to the same authority. Each police authority area should have a new committee to be known as the Police and Prosecution Authority, to which the Crown Prosecutor and the chief constable would both be accountable. The minister responsible for the prosecution system should be either the Home Secretary or the Attorney General.

The Government's response

The Government rejected the Royal Commission's view that the new prosecution system would be based on local committees but otherwise it accepted the thrust of the Royal Commission's recommendation.[316] Its White Paper stated

---

[316] For the history of the proposals see the 6th edition of this work, p. 220.

that there should be a single national prosecution service, controlled and directed by the Director of Public Prosecutions. The investigation of criminal offences would remain with the police and they would continue to lay the initial charges but thereafter the responsibility for all prosecution decisions (including the dropping or alteration of charges) would be that of the prosecution service.[317]

The Crown Prosecution Service (CPS)

The Crown Prosecution Act 1985 (CPA 1985) established the Crown Prosecution Service as a national prosecution service for the whole of England and Wales under the general direction of the Director of Public Prosecutions (DPP).

The country was originally divided into areas – twenty-nine in England and two in Wales – with each area headed by a chief Crown Prosecutor, responsible to the DPP for the operation of his area. In 1993 this structure was altered. The thirty-one areas were amalgamated into thirteen larger areas, including one for the whole of London.

The function of the CPS is to conduct all criminal cases against both adults and juveniles (apart from minor motoring offences which have been excluded from the system) that are instituted by or on behalf of the police.

It was also given a power in CPA 1985, s. 23 to discontinue proceedings which is used very often (see further below). This is in addition to the power not to start proceedings where charges have been laid. In summary cases before the court has heard any evidence, and in proceedings in the Crown Court before it or the magistrates' court has heard any evidence, the proceedings can be stopped by notice to the court with reasons. They can also be stopped where someone has been arrested without a warrant before the court has been informed of the charge by notice to the suspect.

The CPS does not, however, have its own investigation machinery or facilities. It relies for that role on the police, but unlike the procurator fiscal in Scotland, the CPS cannot direct the police to carry out an investigation or further investigations. It can only request. The Runciman Royal Commission considered whether the CPS should be given such a power but by a majority of ten to one decided against it. Any dispute between the CPS and the police as to such a question should, it thought, be resolvable between the two agencies, if necessary with the help of the Chief Inspector of Constabulary.[318]

A rocky start The CPS started operation in 1986. For many years the CPS had a poor press. In the early years there were many media stories of muddle and confusion, of lost files, delays and cases bungled. It is generally agreed that the operational efficiency of the service has greatly improved. Such stories are now much rarer, but the CPS continues to be the butt of criticism, often coming

---

[317] *An Independent Prosecution Service for England and Wales,* Cmnd. 9074, 1983.
[318] Runciman, p. 74, para. 26.

from the police because of decisions to discontinue cases. There was also a problem of staff morale – due partly to issues of management.[319]

In April 1997, a month before the General Election, the Labour Party published a document in which it promised that the CPS would be re-organised yet again – this time into forty-two areas each with the same boundaries as the forty-two police areas. It also announced that there would be a review of the working of the CPS by a three-man team headed by Sir Iain Glidewell, a former Lord Justice of Appeal.

The Glidewell Report

The Glidewell Report was published in June 1998.[320] It proved to be a hard-hitting, wide-ranging document highly critical of the CPS. The 216-page report made seventy-five recommendations for changes. The basic themes were:

- A need for improved staff morale.
- Greater devolution of decision-making from the centre – approval for the Government's decision to move from thirteen areas to forty-two.
- Senior lawyers to spend less time on administration and more on casework and prosecuting.
- Headquarters should be 'slimmer, tougher and more directly in control of matters with which it is properly concerned' (p. 165).
- The chief executive should be a lay person.
- Better working arrangements for the interface with the police.
- The police to retain responsibility for investigation and charging but there should be new Criminal Justice Units (CJUs) with a CPS lawyer in charge, civilian employees of the police and senior police officers attached as liaison to direct further investigations. CJUs would deal with 'fast track' cases, magistrates' court cases generally and would instruct counsel for Crown Court cases.
- Better support for prosecuting barristers in the Crown Court.

The Government's response to Glidewell

The Government's reaction to the report was basically positive.[321] It said it saw the future in collaboration and partnership between the police and the CPS.

---

[319] A survey in November 1993 by the First Division Association, the union which represents three-quarters of CPS lawyers, found that their morale was at an all-time low and that the majority had no confidence in the senior management. A poll of the entire membership of the union in November 1995 found the lowest morale and highest dissatisfaction was in the CPS section. Members complained that management was poor and that Government-imposed efficiency and economy drives had put intolerable pressures on them. Disaffection was especially pronounced among senior staff. See D. Bindman, 'Crown Jewels', *Law Society's Gazette*, 7 February 1996, p. 22.

[320] *Review of the Crown Prosecution Service*, 1998, Cm. 3960 ('Glidewell'). For a summary and editorial comment see *Criminal Law Review*, 1998, pp. 517–20.

[321] See statement of the Attorney General on publication, House of Commons, *Hansard*, 1 June 1998, vol. 313, col. 42 and Written Answers, 30 November 1998, col. 67.

The Attorney General told the House of Commons: 'co-location, common administration and integrated working' would 'streamline casework and file handling processes, remove duplication and unnecessary burdens and reduce delay'. The police would retain their responsibility for file preparation and witness warning. The Government had decided 'that it would not be practical or a proper reflection of the respective constitutional priorities of the CPS and the police to require a transfer of responsibilities'.[322]

The Auld Review

Lord Justice Auld in his Review said that most of the Glidewell recommendations had been adopted after local pilots. CPS staff were increasingly located in or close to police stations working in liaison with the police in CJUs and were receiving papers for review shortly after charge. Early signs were that the new system was producing some improvements in efficiency and some savings though not, in the main, in the accuracy of charging.[323]

Disagreeing with both Runciman and Glidewell, Auld recommended that charging of suspects should to a large extent be taken over by the CPS. The chief reason was overcharging by the police. ('A significant contributor to delays in the entering of pleas of guilty and in identifying issues for trial and, in consequence, the prolonged and disjointed nature of many criminal proceedings, is "overcharging" by the police and failure by the CPS to remedy it at an early stage'.[324]) Overcharging, Auld said, led the defence to maintain tactical pleas of not guilty until the last minute. It could also give rise to 'hasty, ill-considered and inappropriate' acceptances by the prosecution of guilty pleas which bewildered and distressed victims.[325]

Auld thought that 'consideration should be given to a move towards earlier and more influential involvement of the CPS in the process to the point where, in all but minor, routine cases, or where there is a need for a holding charge, it should determine the charge and initiate the prosecution'. This became the basis for the new system established by the Criminal Justice Act 2003.

The CPS takes on the task of charging

In response to the Auld proposal, the Home Secretary and the Attorney General decided to start a pilot scheme within the then current legal framework. This took place on nine sites in five areas from February to August 2002. Reports on the pilot were commissioned from independent researchers, PA Consulting Group.[326]

[322] Attorney General, House of Commons, *Hansard*, 19 April 1999, WA col. 398.
[323] *An Early Assessment of Co-located Criminal Justice Units* – available on the CPS Website www.cps.gov.uk.   [324] Auld, Ch. 10, p. 408, para. 35.   [325] *Ibid.*
[326] See *Crown Prosecution Service Charging Suspects: Early Involvement by CPS. A Pilot Final Evaluation*, April 2003.

The pilot involved 3,324 cases in which the CPS gave the police oral advice as to charge and 2,875 cases in which the advice was written. The reported results were very positive:

- Conviction rates improved in six of the nine pilot areas.
- Discontinuance rates were lower than the pre-pilot sample in all areas.
- The proportion of defendants who pleaded guilty increased and the pleas came at an earlier stage.
- There was a consistent fall in all areas in the number of cases where charges were changed or dropped. The early intervention of the CPS, it seemed, made it more likely that the charge was right from the start.
- The proportion of last-minute changes of plea ('cracked trials') decreased.
- The time from arrest to charge increased by an average of twenty-four days but the time from charge to completion reduced by ten days.
- There was some evidence that the quality of files had improved – and not just the files in the pilot.

The Executive Summary of the Report said that all areas were 'fully supportive of early charging advice' and were continuing with the scheme even though the formal pilot had ended. It added: 'we must also highlight the qualitative benefits which have been seen in all areas including enhanced joint working, better quality, skills transfer, and improved confidence, trust and mutual respect' (p. vii). However, not all reactions were equally positive.[327]

In the meantime, the Government's White Paper *Justice for All* had indicated that Auld's recommendation would be adopted and provisions to give it effect were included in Part 4 and Sch. 2 of the Criminal Justice Act 2003.[328]

Under these provisions, s. 37 of PACE is amended to require that the custody officer has regard to guidance from the DPP[329] when determining whether the suspect should be released without charge on bail, or without charge and without bail or charged. Where the case is referred to the CPS to determine whether proceedings should be instituted and, if so, on what charges, the defendant can be released on police bail with or without conditions. In routine minor cases the

---

[327] An earlier assessment of the proposed placement of prosecutors in police stations to offer pre-charge advice to police investigators had been sceptical about its likely benefits – see J. Baldwin and A. Hunt, 'Prosecutors Advising in Police Stations', *Criminal Law Review*, 1998, pp. 521–36. After the scheme was implemented, the *Law Society's Gazette*, 4 August 2004, p. 3, reported: 'concerns are growing among criminal practitioners that the "charging project" is damaging their health, scuppering the legal aid fund, and seeing offenders roam the streets owing to lack of staff'. The article said that both prosecution and defence lawyers were concerned about the 'plight of exhausted lawyers who were doing back-to-back shifts in the police station and courts'. The Director of the Criminal Law Solicitors Association was quoted as saying that CPS staff shortages had left defence solicitors sitting in the police station for hours with their clients waiting for a charging decision – which was likely to increase the burden on the legal aid fund. The police also suffered from the temptation to bail defendants rather than have them sit and wait.   [328] Cm. 5563, July 2002, para. 3.31.

[329] The Director's Guidance document runs to sixteen pages. (See www.cps.gov.uk – Publications – Prosecution Policy and Guidance.)

police continue to charge. In cases where bail would be inappropriate and where the CPS have not yet informed the police what charges to lay, the police are permitted under the DPP's guidance to lay holding charges. In deciding whether to charge, the police and the CPS have to follow the same basic principles.

The new charging system was brought in gradually but by April 2006 it had been activated in all forty-two areas.

For an excellent description of the system see I.D. Brownlee, 'The Statutory Charging Scheme in England and Wales: Towards a Unified Prosecution System', *Criminal Law Review*, 2004, pp. 896–907.

See also R.M. White, 'Investigators and Prosecutors or Desperately Seeking Scotland: Re-formulation of the "Philips Principle"', 69 *Modern Law Review*, 2006, pp. 143–82. White considers the respective roles of investigation and prosecution in the CPS model as compared with that in Scotland and Northern Ireland and that used in the Serious Fraud Office, for prosecutions by the Revenue and Customs and by the new Serious and Organised Crime Agency.

The decision to prosecute

The Code for Crown Prosecutors

The CPS decision as to whether to prosecute is based on the Code for Crown Prosecutors. The current (2004) version is on the CPS Website (www.cps.gov. uk) and is also published at the back of its annual report.[330]

The following text gives key passages as regards the tests that have to be applied in the new charging system. Under that system, unless the new 'Threshold Test' applies, a prosecution can only go ahead if the case has passed both parts of the 'Full Code Test'.

Paragraph 2.2 sets out the basic principle of prosecution:

> **Code for Prosecutors, 2004**
> 2.2 Crown Prosecutors must be fair, independent and objective. They must not let any personal views about the ethnic or national origin, disability, sex, religious beliefs, political views or the sexual orientation of the suspect, victim or witness influence their decisions. They must not be affected by improper or undue pressure from any source . . .

The Full Code Test is set out in section 5. It has two stages.

> **5 The Full Code Test**
> 5.1 . . . The first stage is consideration of the evidence. If the case does not pass the evidential test, it must not go ahead, no matter how important or serious it may be. If the case does pass the evidential test, Crown Prosecutors must proceed to the second stage and decide if a prosecution is needed in the public interest . . .

---

[330] For an explanatory article by the DPP see K. Macdonald QC, 'The New Code for Crown Prosecutors', 155 *New Law Journal*, 7 January 2005, p. 12.

The Evidential Stage

5.2 Crown Prosecutors must be satisfied that there is enough evidence to provide a 'realistic prospect of conviction' against each defendant on each charge. They must consider what the defence case may be, and how that is likely to affect the prosecution case.

5.3 A realistic prospect of conviction is an objective test. It means that a jury or bench of magistrates or judge hearing a case alone, properly directed in accordance with the law, is more likely than not to convict the defendant of the charge alleged . . .

5.4 When deciding whether there is enough evidence to prosecute, Crown Prosecutors must consider whether the evidence can be used and is reliable. There will be many cases in which the evidence does not give cause for concern, but there will also be cases in which the evidence may not be as strong as it first appears . . .

The Code refers to the question whether the evidence might be excluded because of the way it was gathered and whether the evidence is sufficiently reliable.

The Public Interest Stage

5.6 In 1951, Lord Shawcross, who was Attorney General, made the classic statement on public interest, which has been supported by Attorneys General ever since: 'It has never been the rule in this country, I hope it never will be, that suspected criminal offences must automatically be the subject of prosecution'. (*House of Commons Debates*, vol. 483, col. 681, 29 January 1951.)

5.7 The public interest must be considered in each case where there is enough evidence to provide a realistic prospect of conviction. Although there may be public interest factors against prosecution in a particular case, often the prosecution should go ahead and those factors should be put to the court for consideration when sentence is being passed. A prosecution will usually take place unless there are public interest factors tending against prosecution which clearly outweigh those tending in favour, or it appears more appropriate in all the circumstances of the case to divert the person from prosecution.

Factors stated to militate *in favour* of prosecution (para. 5.9) include: (1) the likelihood of a significant sentence; (2) a weapon was used or violence was threatened; (3) the offence was committed against someone who serves the public such as a police or prison officer or a nurse; (4) the accused was in a position of authority or trust; (5) the accused was the ringleader or an organiser; (6) the offence was premeditated; (7) that it was carried out by a group; (8) the victim was vulnerable or was put in fear or suffered personal attack, damage or disturbance; (9) the offence involved discrimination on grounds of ethnic or national origin, sex, religion, political belief or sexual orientation; (10) a marked difference between the actual or mental ages of the accused and the victim, or if there is an element of corruption; (11) the relevance of the accused's record; (12) whether the accused was subject to a court order; (13) the likelihood of repetition and (14) the offence, though not serious in itself, is widespread in that area.

Factors stated to militate *against* prosecution (para. 5.10) include: (1) the likely penalty would be very small or nominal; (2) the offence was committed as a result of a mistake or misunderstanding; (3) the loss or harm is minor; (4) long delay between the offence and the trial, unless the offence is serious or it has only just come to light; (5) prosecution will have a very bad effect on the accused's physical or mental health, always bearing in mind the seriousness of the offence; (6) the accused is old, suffering from significant mental or physical ill-health, unless the offence is serious or there is a real possibility of it being repeated; (7) the accused has already made reparation or paid compensation ('but defendants must not avoid prosecution or diversion solely because they pay compensation') and (8) details may emerge at the trial which could harm sources, international relations or national security.

The CPS prosecutes on behalf of the public at large and not in the interests of any individual. 'However, when considering the public interest, Crown Prosecutors should always take into account the consequences for the victim of the decisions whether or not to prosecute, and any views expressed by the victim or the victim's family' (para. 5.12). It was important that a victim is told about a decision which 'makes a significant difference to the case' (para. 5.13).

The Threshold Test

The Threshhold Test was introduced in 2004. It is applied to cases in which it is not appropriate for the suspect on bail but the evidence to apply the Full Code Test is not yet available and the PACE detention time limit requires that he either be charged or released from custody.

> 6.1 The Threshold Test requires Crown Prosecutors to decide whether there is at least a reasonable suspicion that the suspect has committed an offence, and if there is, whether it is in the public interest to charge that suspect.
>
> 6.4 The evidential decision in each case will require consideration of a number of factors including:
>> the evidence available at the time;
>> the likelihood and nature of further evidence being obtained;
>> the reasonableness for believing that evidence will become available;
>> the time it will take to gather that evidence and the steps being taken to do so;
>> the impact the expected evidence will have on the case;
>> the charges that the evidence will support.
>
> 6.5 The Public Interest Test means the same as under the Full Code Test, but will be based on the information available at the time of charge which will often be limited.

When the police charge a suspect they are supposed to apply the same Evidential Test, Threshold Test and Public Interest Test as the CPS.[331]

[331] For analysis of the 'public interest element' under the previous version of the Code see A. Ashworth, 'The "Public Interest" Element in Prosecutions', *Criminal Law Review*, 1987, p. 595. See also A. Ashworth and J. Fionda, 'Prosecution, Accountability and the Public Interest', *Criminal Law Review*, 1994, p. 894 and R. Daw, 'A Response', *ibid*, p. 904; A. Hoyano et al, 'A Study of the Impact of the Revised Code for Crown Prosecutors', *Criminal Law Review*, 1997, pp. 556–64.

For a strongly argued view that the evidential requirement in the Code is misconceived, see G. Williams, 'Letting off the Guilty and Prosecuting the Innocent', *Criminal Law Review*, 1985, p. 115. Professor Williams' contention was that if the test for proceeding is whether a conviction was likely to succeed (the '51 per cent or realistic prospect of conviction rule') many prosecutions that ought to be brought would not be. The test rather should be whether the prosecutor is satisfied on the evidence that the suspect is guilty, subject to the public interest questions as to whether a prosecution is desirable. Certainly there had to be at the least a reasonable possibility of a conviction, but the effect of the rule that there must be a reasonable probability of a conviction meant, for instance, that corrupt police officers might not be prosecuted because it was notoriously difficult to get a jury to convict a police officer. Where the prosecutor did not believe that the accused was guilty, he should drop the case. An exception to this principle might be where failure to charge someone may bring about a loss of public confidence in the integrity of the prosecution service.

It is not only the Code for Crown Prosecutors that influences the decision whether or not to start and continue a prosecution. Another consideration is the CPS staff member's concern to maintain his employer's approval by not having too many cases that go wrong – i.e. end in acquittal. In an era when performance targets dominate thinking, that will tend to militate in the direction of dropping cases when there is a doubt as to the prospects of a conviction. In former times the prosecution might have left the issue to be resolved by the jury. The same tendency is promoted by the current concern to reduce costs which powerfully affects the members of all public agencies.

In addition to the published Code, CPS staff also work under the influence of the unpublished *Policy Manual* which is for internal use only.

Guide to case disposal

A step in the direction of reducing both discretion and prosecutions came in 1995 with the issue to the police of a new *Case Disposal Manual*. This ranked every offence, motoring, criminal and alcohol-related, on a scale of points from one to five.

Five-point offences, such as murder, would always be prosecuted.

Four-point offences have what the *Manual* terms 'a high probability of prosecution'. This category included GBH, forgery, arson, perjury, burglary and perverting the course of justice.

Three-point offences included indecent assault, theft, handling stolen goods, buggery, prostitution offences, resisting arrest, criminal damage and ABH. In three-point offences the decision whether to charge was to be made by listing the 'aggravating' and the 'mitigating' factors. The *Manual* listed general factors, for instance, the impact on the victim, the accused's prior criminal record, the likelihood of penalty and whether the crime is a prevalent offence causing local concern. The *Manual* also indicated factors specific to particular offences. So possession of drugs (even Class A substances such as cocaine, crack and heroin) would usually be cautioned if only 'small amounts, for personal use' are involved. The possessor of an offensive weapon would not be prosecuted under the *Manual's* guidelines if there was 'no risk, weapon not on display, mistaken belief that there would be no offence if carried for protection only'. Deception offences would not be prosecuted if they were 'committed over a short period, low value' or 'driven by poverty/personal need'. ABH would not be prosecuted if it was a single blow causing only superficial injury.

Two-point offences were those where there was a high probability of a caution and the decision-maker needed to be able to justify the decision not to caution. This category includes begging, kerb-crawling and being drunk and incapable in a public place. A charge for this offence would only be laid if the offender was arrested four times for the same offence within a four-week period.

One-point offences were minor offences for which a formal warning was appropriate or where there was a decision not to proceed with a prosecution. They included such things as throwing litter in the street or sending someone to buy liquor for an underage person.

D. Rose, Home Affairs Correspondent of *The Observer*, commented on this remarkable development in his book *In the Name of the Law: The Collapse of Criminal Justice* (Jonathan Cape, 1996) pp. 163–4:

> The *Case Disposal Manual*, introduced at first in London and several counties, with others rapidly following suit, enlarges police discretion on an unprecedented scale. It requires that officers of junior rank take fundamental decisions with massive implications for the lives of those they arrest, without reference to any court or outside authority. The judgments it demands are even more subjective than some of those required by the Code for Crown Prosecutors. How, for example, do you measure whether a sexual assault is 'trivial'? It is inescapable that many of those judgments will be shaped by factors which have nothing to do with the true merits of the case: the officer's workload; his opinion of the suspect; and the possibility that he may, in return for non-prosecution, become a useful informant in future . . . The *Manual*, drawn up after consultation between the Metropolitan Police, the Association of Chief Police Officers and the CPS, alters institutionalised police practice significantly, but its introduction took place without any trace of public or parliamentary debate.

Reducing discretion by new 'charging standards'

In August 1994 the police and the CPS introduced a new piece of machinery, 'charging standards'. The first such standards were for assault.[332] They were later extended to public order offences, driving offences, dishonesty offences and drugs.

[332] *Justice of the Peace*, 20 August 1994, pp. 554–5. The standards defined the degree of injury that would justify charges respectively of common assault, assault occasioning actual bodily harm ('ABH'), unlawful wounding/inflicting grievous bodily harm ('GBH') and wounding/causing GBH with intent.

The motive for this innovation was stated to be to increase consistency of decision-making throughout the country. It may be that there were also other reasons behind the decision. One such could have been to minimise the occasions when the CPS incurred the annoyance of the police by reducing charges. Another was to reduce costs. The concern expressed in some quarters was that the overall effect would be to downgrade offences.[333]

The Glidewell Report (1998, p. 247 above) said: 'We are very much in favour of charging standards as a useful guide to both members of the police and the CPS' (p. 83). On the question of downgrading of offences, Glidewell said that although it suspected that charges were sometimes downgraded when they should not be, it had no evidence on the question. It noted that charges were only rarely upgraded. Downgrading was usually where the defendant was pleading guilty (pp. 84–5).

Cautioning as an alternative to prosecution

One way to avoid prosecuting the suspect is to administer a caution. This has been a part of the system for decades and has been used especially for young offenders. From 1978 cautioning of young offenders was guided by Home Office circulars which established three conditions for a caution: there had to be sufficient evidence to justify a prosecution, the offender had to admit the offence and the parent or guardian had to consent to the giving of a caution. A caution was not a conviction but on any subsequent court appearance it could be cited.[334]

The Home Office guidelines on cautioning were changed in 1990, largely because of the research showing wide variations in cautioning rates between forces. They were also partly the result of a drop in cautions of persons over seventeen. The presumption in favour of not prosecuting juveniles and the elderly was also to be extended 'to other groups – young adults and adults alike – where the criteria for caution are met'.

Mr Michael Howard, who became Conservative Home Secretary in 1993, took a significantly less positive view of cautioning at least for more serious offences. His tougher approach was reflected in a new Circular (18/1994) issued in March 1994. Its purpose was to provide guidance on cautioning and in particular 'to discourage the use of cautions in inappropriate cases,[335] for example for offences which are triable on indictment only; to seek greater consistency between police forces; and to promote the better recording of cautions' (para. 1).

---

[333] See for instance F.G. Davies, 'CPS Charging Standards: A Cynic's View', *Justice of the Peace*, 1 April 1995, p. 203.

[334] See Judge Richard May, 'The Legal Effect of a Police Caution', *Criminal Law Review*, 1997, pp. 491–3 and R. Evans, 'Challenging a Police Caution using Judicial Review', *Criminal Law Review*, 1996, pp. 104–8. For a warning about the unreliability of cautions and therefore the danger of treating them like previous convictions by citing them in subsequent proceedings see *Criminal Law Review*, 1996, p. 453.

[335] The circular said that, despite earlier discouragement of cautions for the most serious offences, cautions had been administered for offences as serious as attempted murder and rape which 'undermines the credibility of the disposal' (para. 5).

Cautions for juveniles replaced by reprimands and warnings The Crime and Disorder Act 1998 (CDA 1998), ss. 65 and 66[336] provided for the replacement of cautions for juveniles by 'reprimands and warnings'. (The term 'caution' is retained for adult offenders.) A reprimand is a first caution. Normally there is only one reprimand because s. 65(3) provides that if the offender has previously been reprimanded he cannot be reprimanded a second time unless the offence was committed two years after the last warning – and no one can be warned more than twice.

The 'warning' ('final warning') is similar to what has come to be called 'caution plus' schemes which provide some kind of counselling, mentoring or other community support for the young person. The offender is referred to a Youth Offending Team (YOT)[337] which determines whether a rehabilitation programme is appropriate. This may involve some form of mediation. The Home Office has indicated support for the restorative-cautioning initiative pioneered in the Thames Valley area.

Like the old caution, a reprimand or warning is not a conviction[338] and does not constitute a criminal record but the fact of the reprimand or warning and any report on failure to participate in a rehabilitation programme can be cited in court in the same way as a conviction.[339] A person reprimanded or warned for certain sex offences is required to register with the police under the Sex Offences Act 1997.[340] Fingerprints are taken.[341] Reprimands and warnings are entered on the Police National Computer (PNC).[342]

However, unlike the old caution, a reprimand or warning does not require the consent of the young offender or of his parent or guardian. In *R (R) v. Durham Constabulary*[343] the Divisional Court held that despite the decision not to prosecute the final warning process was incompatible with the person's ECHR Article 6 right to a fair and public hearing in the determination of a criminal charge. (Entry on the PNC and the sex offender's register amounted to a public pronouncement of guilt.) The House of Lords[344] unanimously reversed the decision on the ground that neither a reprimand nor a warning were the determination of a criminal charge. Nor was their recording on the PNC and the sex offender's register as access to them was controlled and limited to a small number of authorised persons.

A first offence by a young offender can therefore be met with a reprimand, a final warning or criminal charges depending on its seriousness. After a

---

[336] As amended by the Criminal Justice and Court Services Act 2000, s. 56 and the Powers of Criminal Courts (Sentencing) Act 2000, Sch. 9, para. 198.

[337] Under CDA 1998, s. 39.

[338] However, the assurance given to the person that the caution is instead of prosecution precludes the bringing of a private prosecution by the victim – *Jones v. Whalley* [2006] UKHL 41, [2007] Crim LR 74.

[339] Home Office, *Final Warning Scheme – Guidance for Police*, April 2000.   [340] *Ibid*, para. 77.

[341] *Ibid*, para. 80.   [342] *Ibid*, paras. 82–3.

[343] [2002] EWHC 2486 Admin, [2003] 3 All ER 419.

[344] [2005] UKHL 21, [2005] 2 All ER 369. For comment see *Criminal Law Review*, 2006, p. 88.

reprimand, a further offence leads either to a warning or charge. Normally it would be prosecution.

The CPS Code states:

> Reprimands and final warnings are intended to prevent re-offending and the fact that a further offence has occurred indicates that attempts to divert the youth from the court system have not been effective. So the public interest will usually require a prosecution in such cases, unless there are clear public interest factors against prosecution (para. 8.9).

For an early and highly critical assessment see R. Evans and K. Puech, 'Reprimands and Warnings: Populist Punitiveness or Restorative Justice?' *Criminal Law Review*, 2001, pp. 794–805. Their conclusion was that rather than providing an opportunity for new style restorative justice, 'the legislation is punitive and controlling in principle and in practice' (p. 804). Many of the young people and YOT workers saw the warning scheme as 'arbitrary, unfair, and disproportionate especially as it may involve compulsory participation in a rehabilitation (change) programme' (*ibid*). It suggested that that there was a considerable gap between the rhetoric of the Home Office and the Youth Justice Board and what was actually happening on the ground.

Simple cautions for adults The Home Office updated its guidance on 'simple' cautions in Circular 30/2005 (*Cautioning of adult offenders*). The police can issue a simple caution in all cases except indictable only offences which must be referred to the CPS.

The precondition for a simple caution is that there is enough evidence to satisfy the Threshold Test (above),[345] that the suspect has admitted the offence and that, given the seriousness of the offence, it is in the public interest to use a simple caution to dispose of the case.

As for juveniles, where previously a caution required the consent of the person, this requirement has been dropped.

In April 2006 it was reported that the Home Office had sent the police a document, the Gravity Factor Matrix, as part of a strategy to widen use of cautions. Providing there were no aggravating factors, first-time offenders could receive a caution for nearly one-third of the 180 crimes listed in the document. The crimes were in four categories from the least serious (Level 1) to the most serious (Level 4). The sanction in Level 2 covering some sixty offences was 'normally a simple caution for a first offence'. Level 2 included criminal damage up to £500, theft up to £200 and sex with thirteen- to fifteen-year-olds.[346]

In July 2006 the Lord Chancellor, the Home Secretary and the Attorney General jointly issued a forty-two page policy document entitled *Delivering*

---

[345] The evidentiary test previously required the higher standard of a realistic prospect of conviction.   [346] *Sunday Times*, 2 April 2006.

Simple, Speedy, Summary Justice. It stated that a key component of a simple, speedy, summary criminal justice system was the ability to deal rapidly and effectively with cases where formal court proceedings were disproportionate and remedies such as fixed penalty notices, warnings or cautions were more appropriate.[347]

Conditional cautions The Criminal Justice Act 2003 introduced a new concept of conditional cautions for adults – a caution with conditions attached – which in effect is a form of diversion from the criminal justice system. The conditions must have one or more of the objectives of reparation for the offence or reha-bilitation of the offender, or his punishment (s. 22 as amended by the Police and Justice Act 2006). The 2006 Act (s. 17) added as possible conditions the payment of a penalty of up to £250 or up to twenty hours of community work. The requirements are that the CPS consider that there is sufficient evidence to charge the individual and that the individual signs a document in which it is stated that he admits that he committed the offence, that he consents to the cau-tions and the conditions imposed (s. 23). Failure without reasonable excuse to comply with the conditions makes the person liable to prosecution for the offence (s. 24). The 2006 Act, s. 18 gives the police a right of arrest for breach of the conditions.[348]

The *Delivering Simple, Speedy, Summary Justice* policy paper of July 2006 (above) said that the aspiration was to implement conditional cautioning across the whole of England and Wales by April 2008.[349]

The Government's Fraud Review thought that in exceptional circumstances conditional cautions might be appropriate even in fraud cases – for instance if the condition was to compensate victims of the fraud.[350]

Discontinuance by the CPS

One of the stated objectives for setting up the CPS was better and earlier iden-tification of cases that for any reason should not go forward to prosecution. The 1983 White Paper *An Independent Prosecution Service for England and Wales* said the objectives of the CPS included the promotion of greater consis-tency of policy and uniformly high standards of case preparation and decision-making across the country. The effect, it was said, 'should be that cases which are unlikely to succeed should be weeded out at an early stage' (Cmnd. 9074, p. 14), but the CPS' power to drop a prosecution has given rise to much controversy.

---

[347] Paragraph 7.6, p. 40.
[348] See I. Brownlee, 'Conditional Cautions and Fair Trial Rights in England and Wales: Form versus Substance in the Diversionary Agenda?', *Criminal Law Review*, 2007, pp.129–40.
[349] Paragraph 7.12, p. 41.
[350] Fraud Review, pp. 272–3, para. 11.72.

The Code for Prosecutors (paras. 4.1–4.3) states:

> 4.1 Each case the Crown Prosecution Service receives from the police is reviewed to make sure that it is right to proceed with a prosecution . . .
>
> 4.2 Review is a continuing process and Crown Prosecutors must take account of any change in circumstances. Wherever possible, they should talk to the police first if they are thinking about changing the charges or stopping the case. Crown Prosecutors should also tell the police if they believe that some additional evidence may strengthen the case. This gives the police the chance to provide more information that may affect the decision.
>
> 4.3 The Crown Prosecution Service and the police work closely together, but the final responsibility for the decision whether or not a charge or a case should go ahead rests with the Crown Prosecution Service.

The CPS discontinue around 12–13 per cent of the cases it starts. It is difficult to form a view as to whether this is too high, too low or about right. The police often complain that the CPS drop too many cases, but there is also evidence that it drops too few. (The *Crown Court Study* done for the Runciman Royal Commission showed that in the view of both prosecuting and defence barristers and of judges, the prosecution was weak in about one-fifth of contested cases and that over 80 per cent of these cases ended in acquittal.[351])

Another possible indication comes from acquittal statistics. There are three kinds of acquittals – ordered acquittals, directed acquittals and jury acquittals. 'Ordered acquittals' are where the prosecution offers no evidence at all. The case is dropped at court because the prosecution decide at the last moment not to pursue it, perhaps because a crucial witness fails to turn up or refuses to give evidence. (The rules do not permit the CPS to discontinue a case between committal for trial by the magistrates and trial at the Crown Court. They must therefore go through the process of formally offering no evidence even in cases which their process of review has identified as too weak to continue.) 'Directed acquittals' are where the judge stops the case, usually half way, after a submission by the defence that the prosecution's case is not strong enough even to require a response. Jury acquittals are where the jury has deliberated and found the defendant not guilty. At first blush, ordered and directed acquittals seem to be in the category of weak cases that arguably could and should have been aborted earlier.

In the six years leading to the establishment of the CPS the proportion of acquittals that were either ordered or directed acquittals ranged from a low of 43 per cent in 1982 to a high of 48 per cent in 1985. It might have been expected that with the establishment of the CPS and its presumably better screening methods, the proportion of ordered and directed acquittals would go down. In fact, however, it went up. It is now some two-thirds of all acquittals. (In the five years from 2001–5 it fluctuated between 62 per cent and 69 per cent.) (See the annual *Judicial Statistics*, Table 6.10).)

---

[351] M. Zander and P. Henderson, *Crown Court Study* (Royal Commission on Criminal Justice, Research Study No. 19, 1993) Tables 6.20 and 6.21.

There have been a number of studies as to the reasons why cases are terminated by the CPS or by the court[352] and various initiatives have been tried, but it is not clear that much impact has yet been made on the issue.

Judicial control of police discretion in prosecution policy

The problem of controlling police discretion with regard to prosecuting has only rarely come before the courts. The first modern examples of importance were the cases brought by a private citizen, former Member of Parliament Mr Raymond Blackburn, to compel the police to enforce the gambling and then the obscenity laws.

R v. Metropolitan Police Commissioner, ex p Blackburn [1968] 2 WLR 893, Court of Appeal

[In April 1966, a confidential instruction was issued to senior officers of the Metropolitan Police. Underlying this instruction was a policy decision not to take proceedings against clubs for breach of the gaming laws unless there were complaints of cheating or they had become the haunts of criminals. The applicant, being concerned at gaming in London clubs, brought proceedings for *mandamus* to get the Commissioner to withdraw the confidential instruction.]

Lord Denning MR: the result of the police decision of 22 April 1966, was that thenceforward, in this great metropolis, the big gaming clubs were allowed to carry on without any interference by the police . . .

The duty of the Commissioner of Police of the Metropolis

I hold it to be the duty of the Commissioner of Police of the Metropolis, as it is of every chief constable, to enforce the law of the land. He must take steps so to post his men that crimes may be detected; and that honest citizens may go about their affairs in peace. He must decide whether or not suspected persons are to be prosecuted; and, if need be, bring the prosecution or see that it is brought, but in all these things he is not the servant of anyone, save the law itself. No minister of the Crown can tell him that he must, or must not, prosecute this man or that one. Nor can any police authority tell him so. The responsibility for law enforcement lies on him. He is answerable to the law and to the law alone. That appears sufficiently from *Fisher v. Oldham Corpn*,[353] and *A-G for New South Wales v. Perpetual Trustee Co Ltd*.[354]

Although the chief officers of police are answerable to the law, there are many fields in which they have a discretion with which the law will not interfere. For instance, it is for the Commissioner of Police of the Metropolis, or the chief constable, as the case may be, to decide in any particular case whether inquiries

---

[352] See D. Crisp and D. Moxon, *Case Screening by the Crown Prosecution Service: How and Why Cases are Terminated* (Home Office Research Study No. 137, 1994); B. Block, C. Corbett and J. Peay, *Ordered and Directed Acquittals in the Crown Court* (Royal Commission on Criminal Justice Research Study No. 15, 1993); the study reported in the CPS Annual Report, 1994–5, pp. 7–8 and figures cited in the Glidewell Report, 1999 at p. 90.
[353] [1930] 2 KB 364, 46 TLR 390.   [354] [1955] AC 457.

should be pursued, or whether an arrest should be made or a prosecution brought. It must be for him to decide on the disposition of his force and the concentration of his resources on any particular crime or area. No court can or should give him directions on such a matter. He can also make policy decisions and give effect to them, as, for instance, was often done when prosecutions were not brought for attempted suicide, but there are some policy decisions with which, I think, the courts in a case can, if necessary, interfere. Suppose a chief constable were to issue a directive to his men that no person should be prosecuted for stealing any goods less than £100 in value. I should have thought that the court could countermand it. He would be failing in his duty to enforce the law.

. . . On 30 December 1967, the Commissioner issued a statement in which he said: 'it is the intention of the Metropolitan Police to enforce the law as it has been interpreted'. That implicitly revoked the policy decision of 22 April 1966; and the Commissioner by his counsel gave an undertaking to the court that the policy decision would be officially revoked. We were also told that immediate steps are being taken to consider the 'goings-on' in the big London clubs with a view to prosecution if there is anything unlawful. That is all that Mr Blackburn or anyone else can reasonably expect.

See also *R v Metropolitan Police Commissioner, ex p Blackburn (No 3)*[355] and *R v Chief Constable of Devon and Cornwall, ex p Central Electricity Generating Board.*[356]

But there are limits to police and prosecutorial discretion. In *R (Mondelly) v Metroplitan Police Commissioner*[357] the Divisional Court considered the implications of the downgrading by legislation of cannabis from Class B to Class C and consequential national guidance from the police and the Home Office that a person found in simple possession of cannabis should not be arrested unless there were aggravating factors. The applicant sought judicial review to quash the decision to caution him for simple possession after the police had, by mistake, gone to his premises and were invited in, at which point they noticed a smell of cannabis. He was arrested for allowing his premises to be used for the smoking of cannabis but this charge was not pursued. Instead he was cautioned for simple possession. He argued that in view of the national guidance this was unlawful. The court, in a 2–1 decision (Moses LJ and Ouseley J) refused the application. M's argument was based on the proposition that the national guidance issued to

---

[355] [1973] 1 All ER 324. *Mandamus* to enforce the pornography laws refused on the court being persuaded that the police were doing their best. (Subsequent prosecutions of members of the Obscene Publications Squad for corruption suggested that this was not quite the case.)

[356] [1981] 3 All ER 826. *Mandamus* refused to require the police to help the Electricity Board to remove squatters blocking the building of a nuclear power station. It was for the police on the spot and not the Court to decide when and how to exercise their power.
See further *Coxhead* [1986] Crim LR 251, CA; *R v General Council of the Bar, ex p Percival* [1990] 3 All ER 137, 149–52, Div Ct: In *R v Chief Constable of Kent County Constabulary, ex p L and R v DPP, ex p B (a minor)* [1993] 1 All ER 756 Div Ct; *R v IRC, ex p Mead* [1993] 1 All ER 772; *R v Chief Constable of Sussex, ex p International Trader's Ferry* [1999] 1 All ER 129, HL.   [357] [2006] EWHC 2370 (Admin).

the police had changed the law. That could not be so. If there was a police or CPS policy that an arrest or prosecution for the offence required aggravating factors it would be unlawful. Executive discretion could not change the law. The police retained their discretion as to whether to arrest and to caution.[358]

Remedies for the prosecution's failure to prosecute

In *R v. DPP, ex p C*[359] the Divisional Court, most unusually, allowed an application for judicial review of the decision of the CPS not to prosecute for buggery of a wife by a husband on the ground that the prosecutor had not had in mind certain relevant considerations. Several of the cases have involved ethnic minority complaints about the failure of the CPS to prosecute police officers involved in deaths in police custody of family members.[360]

For the argument that the courts should be prepared to review prosecutorial decisions see generally Y. Dotan, 'Should Prosecutorial Discretion Enjoy Special Treatment in Judicial Review? A Comparative Analysis of the Law in England and Israel', *Public Law*, 1997, pp. 513–31.

In 1988, the House of Lords ruled that the police could not be held liable in negligence for failing to prevent crimes. There was no duty of care to individual members of the public to identify and apprehend an unknown criminal, even though it was reasonably foreseeable that harm was likely to be caused to a member of the public if the criminal was not detected and apprehended. Even if such a duty did exist, it would be against the public interest to hold the police liable.[361] In 2005, the House of Lords applied much the same reasoning in rejecting the negligence claim brought against the police by Duwayne Brooks who survived an attack by a gang of white thugs on him and Stephen Lawrence. Brooks claimed that the psychiatric injury suffered in the attack had been exacerbated by the failings of the police investigation as identified in the report of the inquiry into the Stephen Lawrence case chaired by Sir William Macpherson. The House of Lords held that to impose such a duty of care on the police would cause a diversion of resources from crime investigation to defending claims, would inhibit officers' fearless discharge of their duties as they would tend to act in a detrimentally defensive frame of mind and would involve the courts in making policy judgments better suited to the police.[362]

Where the police are on notice that an attack on a named individual is foreseeable there may be a duty on the police to provide appropriate protection – a duty that could be the basis of an action for damages. This follows from the

---

[358] The dissenting judge, Walker J, considered that there was no sufficient reason for the police to have departed from their policy as explained in the guidance and that it was right for the court to intervene to stop an abuse of process.   [359] [1995] 1 Cr App Rep 136.

[360] See *R v. DPP, ex p Manning* [2001] QB 330 in which the Divisional Court quashed the decision not to prosecute after a death in custody and M. Burton, 'Reviewing Crown Prosecution Service decisions not to prosecute', *Criminal Law Review*, 2001, pp. 374–84.

[361] *Hill v. Chief Constable of West Yorkshire* [1989] 1 AC 53, [1988] 2 All ER 238, a case brought by relatives of one of the victims of Peter Sutcliffe, the 'Yorkshire Ripper'.

[362] *Brooks v. Metropolitan Police Commissioner* [2005] UKHL 24, [2005] 2 All ER 489.

decision of the European Court of Human Rights in *Osman v. United Kingdom*.[363] A teacher had formed an attachment to a fifteen-year-old pupil. He changed his name to that of the boy, broke windows at the family home and slashed car tyres. The school met the police to discuss the matter. Eventually the teacher shot and killed the boy's father and seriously injured the boy. The Court of Appeal rejected an action for negligence against the police in light of the decision in *Hill*. The ECHR held unanimously that there had been a breach of Article 6 of the Convention which guarantees a right to have one's civil rights and obligations determined by a court or tribunal. The ECHR accepted that in *Hill* there were sufficient public policy reasons for excluding liability, but in *Osman* the proximity test seemed to be satisfied as the police appeared to have assumed some responsibility for the Osmans' safety. A blanket immunity for the police established by the House of Lords decision in *Hill* was therefore a disproportionate restriction on the applicant's right of access to a court.

Normally no duty to give reasons for not prosecuting

Normally the police cannot be required to give reasons for not prosecuting,[364] but very occasionally the circumstances might be such as to require reasons to be given. In *R v. DPP, ex p Manning and Melbourne*[365] Lord Chief Justice Bingham held that where there had been a death in custody, the inquest resulted in a verdict of unlawful killing and the identity of the person responsible and his whereabouts were known, it was to be expected that a prosecution would follow. If none did follow, it was appropriate to require the DPP to give his reasons.

Is the CPS independent of the police?

A central part of the case for the establishment of the CPS was that it should be more independent of the police. In one sense the CPS certainly is independent of the police in that the CPS has always taken the decision whether to *proceed* with the case and under the new statutory charging arrangements established by the Criminal Justice Act 2003 the CPS generally now determines the charge from the very outset, but the police still play a crucial role which to an extent constrains the CPS.

The entire investigation of the offence is in the hands of the police. The CPS gets the file prepared by the police and nothing much else.[366]

---

[363] (2000) 29 EHRR 245.   [364] *R v. DPP, ex p Treadaway* (1997) Times, 31 October.

[365] [2000] 3 WLR 463.

[366] In *R (on the application of Joseph) v. DPP* [2001] Crim LR 489 the Divisional Court held that the CPS had been entitled to rely on summaries of video evidence given by the police which led it to discontinue the case despite the fact that in interview one of the alleged culprits admitted carrying a weapon which undermined the self-defence argument on which the CPS decision was based. The commentator in the *Criminal Law Review* wrote: 'this is simply another example of the dependence of the CPS on the accuracy and *bona fides* of the police in preparing and disclosing material' (p. 490).

The Philips Royal Commission envisaged that the CPS would supervise and check the work of the police but in practice this does not happen. The Runciman Royal Commission did not recommend any change in that regard. One reason is simply the lack of manpower resources. Another is that it would generate tensions between the two agencies. Thirdly, since the CPS has no investigatory powers under the Act, it lacks the standing to do so. The CPS basically work with what is provided to them by the police – and in cases where the police decide to take no further action the CPS will not be involved at all.

In Scotland where the prosecutors *do* have investigatory powers, they tend not to use them. Research in the early 1980s showed that normally they acted on the basis of information supplied by the police. They used the power to ask for further information in only 6 per cent of cases. In most cases the decision-making was largely routine. (In 63 per cent of cases the decision was taken on the same day that the procurator fiscal received the papers.) The real discretion of the fiscal at that date came in the 'trial avoidance arrangements' – bargaining over a guilty plea to lesser charges in return for other more serious charges being dropped.[367] A decade later the same researchers found a dramatic increase in the rate of cases not prosecuted from 8–47 per cent resulting from a wider range of formal alternatives to prosecution, notably fiscal penalties and fiscal fines.[368]

At the time when the CPS was established it was regarded as vital that the new organisation be moved physically into its own buildings away from the police, but, as has been seen, the trend is now in the opposite direction toward co-location. Glidewell welcomed closer co-operation and did not think it threatened the independence of the prosecutor. ('When they are working in close proximity to a police station and in association with one or more police officers, they will, we are confident, continue to maintain that professional independence' (p. 132).)

The three stages of the CPS's history

In January 2003, Lord Goldsmith QC, the Attorney General, summed up what he described as the first two stages of the CPS's history:[369]

> *1986–1999* In this first stage the professional culture of the Crown Prosecution Service was established. It is marked, rightly, by a great emphasis on establishing the independence of the CPS from the police. It was essential to move from what had essentially been a solicitor/client relationship with the police to establish instead a culture of independence, and to bring home that a new organisation had come into being.
>
>   These were difficult times. The idea was good in concept, but the execution was poor. The CPS was undoubtedly under-resourced. The organisation itself

---

[367] See S. Moody and J. Tombs, *Prosecution in the Public Interest* (Scottish Academic Press, 1982).

[368] J. Tombs and S. Moody, 'Alternatives to Prosecution: The Public Interest Redefined', *Criminal Law Review*, 1993, pp. 357–67.

[369] Speech to the Crown Prosecution Service Senior Management Conference.

struggled to find the right balance between local autonomy and central direction. It probably became over-bureaucratic. There was a long period of inadequate work, loss of public confidence, and a lack of self-worth, but despite all these pressures, a strong professional culture did develop . . .

1999–2003 The second phase began in early 1999 after the present Government in its first term set about reform. It commissioned the Glidewell Report, and put its recommendations into effect. The CPS was restructured into forty-two areas which matched police force boundaries . . .

The process was started of creating Glidewell co-located units where much police and CPS work could be done under one roof, increasing efficiency and reducing bureaucracy.

In this phase too, this Government addressed the historic under-funding of the CPS. This chronic under-funding, which meant far too few Crown Prosecution staff having to do far too much work, has now been remedied by this Government. In 2001, the CPS received a net increase in funds of 23 per cent. This year it received a further 6 per cent increase in real terms and the figure for the forthcoming financial year is 9 per cent in real terms. These are substantial figures. A nearly 40 per cent increase in resources is a substantial uplift. It takes time for extra resources to translate into additional staff recruited, trained and in post, especially in organisations where a very high degree of professional expertise is required. So we are only now starting to see the benefits of these extra resources in terms of additional, qualified staff on the ground, delivering results.

The next period heralded the third stage for the CPS:

I see the third stage of the CPS especially as one in which the CPS is more outward facing and outcome focused. It is one in which the CPS has an enhanced role at every stage of the criminal process working in co-operation with our criminal justice partners while retaining that independence of prosecution decision-making which is the hallmark of the CPS, but it also means increasing the efficiency and the accountability which were also part of its reason for being.

Some of it would involve a change of culture. Lord Goldsmith listed the features of the new era:

Getting the cases right from the start: This is the most important part of what happens later. The CPS will have an increased role through a new relationship of co-operation between the police and the CPS. The Criminal Justice Act will give the CPS the responsibility for determining the charge in all but routine cases.

Building on the Glidewell co-location and so improving the administration of cases; reducing bureaucracy; getting operational officers in touch with operational lawyers.

Improving the review of cases: The focus of review will be not only to keep careful track of changes which are taking place to see whether cases should be continued but seeing what should be done to strengthen weak cases. This is a very important element and part of the culture change needed.

Taking charge of witnesses: Far too many cases fail because witnesses do not turn up to give evidence. Changing this is a key part of improving performance. The West Midlands pilot will show the potentials for one agency to be in the lead in handling witnesses and that this agency should be the CPS . . .

The new powers will give a role to the prosecutors even at the outset: The new power for prosecutors' cautions in the Criminal Justice Act [see p. 258 above (ed.)] and greater emphasis on getting cases in the right court as changes to magistrates' sentencing powers take place mean prosecutors will have from the start to be concerned with what the eventual disposal ought to be.

The role of the CPS is gradually expanding. A speech by the new DPP, Ken Macdonald, in May 2005 saw the CPS taking a central role in the criminal justice system – controlling the progress of cases from start to finish, dealing directly with victims and prosecution witnesses and appearing as advocates in many more cases.[370]

For an exploration of the ethical dimensions of these developments see J. Jackson, 'The Ethical Implications of the Enhanced Role of the Public Prosecutor', 9 *Legal Ethics*, 2006, pp. 35–55.

For a critical assessment of the CPS's lack of efficiency see the report of the House of Commons Public Accounts Committee in October 2006: *Crown Prosecution Service: Effective Use of Magistrates' Courts Hearings.* The report said the CPS, as effectively the largest law firm in the country, needed to learn how to run its business from the most successful private practices.

Other prosecutors

The Law Officers

The Attorney General has the power to enter a *nolle prosequi* in cases tried on indictment, which has the effect of stopping the proceedings. Equally, he can give or refuse his permission (known as *fiat*) in the considerable number of cases where by statute his consent is required for a prosecution. In 1998 the Law Commission recommended that the consent requirement should be abolished save where it was required in the public interest.[371] No action followed. In 2007 however reform seemed increasingly likely as a result of two high-profile cases. One was Lord Goldsmith's involvement in the controversial dropping of a major corruption inquiry by the Serious Fraud Office into defence sales by BAE Systems to Saudi Arabia. The other was his insistence that as Attorney General he would be the person who ultimately would decide whether the Prime Minister and others close to him should be prosecuted in connection with the 'cash for honours' affair.[372]

---

[370] Adam Cowell memorial lecture, Law Society, 17 May 2005. He called, *inter alia*, for the scrapping of the rule banning the prosecution from conducting pre-trial interviews with witnesses. Allowing the prosecution to interview witnesses to test for themselves the strength of their evidence would allow them to reach better informed prosecution decisions (29 *Independent Lawyer*, June 2005, p. 1).

[371] *Consents to Prosecution*, Law Com. No. 255, 1998.

[372] For the argument that the AG's power should be transferred to the DPP see J. Jackson, 'Let the Director Direct', 157 *New Law Journal*, 5 January 2007, p. 23.

Serious Fraud Office

The Serious Fraud Office (SFO) was set up by the Criminal Justice Act 1987 following the recommendation of the Roskill Committee on Fraud Trials (1986). There is a Director, separate from the DPP, but also under the supervision of the Attorney General. The Director may, in conjunction with the police or any other person, investigate any offence which appears to him to involve 'serious or complex fraud' and may institute and have conduct of any criminal proceedings relating to such fraud investigated. So in the case of the SFO the functions of investigation and prosecution are joined in one organisation.

Customs and Excise

HM Customs and Excise (HMCE) was a large agency enforcing revenue and regulatory law with a wide range of criminal, civil and administrative enforcement options including prosecution, compounding, seizure, forfeiture and civil penalties. It conducted large and complex investigations involving surveillance and undercover investigations. Investigations were carried out by the National Investigations Service. Prosecutions were the task of the Solicitor's Office containing a Prosecutions Group. The Solicitor's Office was solicitor to HMCE generally. The position was therefore like pre-CPS police prosecuting departments with the relationship being that of solicitor and client, but while the investigators decided what to investigate and the solicitors decided if there was sufficient evidence, the decision whether to prosecute was taken by administrators. This led to a series of spectacular failures resulting in a number of severely critical reports.[373] The London City Bond warehouse case, for instance, involved thirteen prosecutions involving 109 accused persons. There were no convictions. The legal aid bill was estimated at £20 million. The Butterfield Report on this case[374] recommended that all prosecution functions should be transferred to a separate prosecuting authority. This was accepted. HMCE and the Inland Revenue were merged into HM Revenue and Customs. As from April 2005, prosecutions are handled by the Revenue and Customs Prosecution Office (RCPO) headed by a Director appointed by and under the supervision of the Attorney General.[375] RCPO will also handle prosecutions resulting from the work of the Serious Organised Crime Agency established in 2006 under the provisions of the Serious Organised Crime and Police Act 2005.

Prosecution by other public bodies

Many prosecutions are conducted by Government departments, nationalised industries, local authorities and other statutory bodies. A study done for the

---

[373] See R.M. White, 'Investigators and Prosecutors or Desperately Seeking Scotland: Reformulation of the "Philips Principle"' at p. 161, n. 120.

[374] *Review of the Criminal Investigations and Prosecutions Conducted by HM Customs and Excise by Mr Justice Butterfield*, 2003.

[375] Commissioners for Revenue and Customs Act 2005. See 'Introducing RCPO', 170 *Justice of the Peace*, 11 February 2006, pp. 91–4.

Philips Royal Commission on Criminal Procedure showed that they amounted to something like one-quarter of all prosecutions. Prosecutions were conducted, in order of frequency, by the Post Office (mainly for television licence offences), the British Transport Police (e.g. for non-payment of fares), the Department of the Environment (in relation to vehicle excise licences), the Department of Social Security (for social security frauds), HM Customs and Excise and Regional Traffic Commissioners (for offences connected with the use of heavy lorries).

Other public bodies with some prosecution functions included the Health and Safety at Work Inspectorate, Water Authorities, the Inland Revenue, Department of Trade and Ministry of Agriculture.[376]

Research has shown that there are extraordinary regional variations in such prosecutions. Analysis of all 9,689 prosecutions brought by organisations other than the CPS at three magistrates' courts in London, Milton Keynes and Newcastle showed that of the 2,320 cases prosecuted by the Department of Transport and DVLA, 80 per cent were in Milton Keynes and only 1 per cent was in the London court. Of the ninety-seven cases brought by the Environment Agency, 89 per cent were in the Newcastle court.[377]

For a study of prosecutions by the Health and Safety Executive see K. Hawkins, *Law as Last Resort: Prosecution Decision-Making in a Regulatory Agency* (OUP, 2002).[378]

Private prosecutions

A private person can bring a prosecution even though he has no direct interest in the matter. (So private bodies such as the NSPCC or NSPCA can bring prosecutions.) The private prosecutor must persuade a magistrate to issue a summons which will be refused if it appears to be a vexatious or improper proceeding. He would also normally have to bear his own costs and if the prosecution fails he might in addition have to pay something in respect of the costs of the defence. The DPP has the right to take over a private prosecution and the Attorney General has the power to stop one by entering a *nolle prosequi.*

A study done for the Philips Royal Commission showed that at that time private prosecutions were 2 per cent of all prosecutions.[379] The great majority were for common assault. In some areas the police had a policy of not prosecuting in shoplifting cases and all prosecutions for this offence were brought by retail stores.

---

[376] See K.W. Lidstone, R. Hogg and F. Sutcliffe, *Prosecutions by Private Individuals and Non-Police Agencies* (Royal Commission on Criminal Procedure, Research Study No. 10, 1980) Table 2.3, p. 15.   [377] G. Slapper, *Organisational Prosecutions* (Ashgate, 2001).

[378] A critical review in *Modern Law Review*, July 2004, pp. 704–9 ended: '. . . notwithstanding its flaws it is an important source of material for students of health and safety in particular, and more generally for those concerned to know and explore the nature and limits of regulatory enforcement in a capitalist democracy'.   [379] Note 376 above, Table 2.13, p. 23.

When the CPS refuses to prosecute or refuses to bring appropriate charges, sometimes the victim (or in cases of death, a relative) wants to bring a private prosecution. In *R v. Tower Bridge Metropolitan Stipendiary Magistrate, ex p Chaudhry*[380] the mother of the deceased victim of a driving accident tried to get a summons for causing death by reckless driving. The driver had been charged with summary-only traffic offences. The Divisional Court held that the decision whether to allow a private prosecution to go forward should be based on consideration of various matters. One was whether the case had already been investigated by a responsible prosecuting authority which was pursuing what it considered to be appropriate charges. Regard should be had to the provision in the Code for Crown Prosecutors – whether the charges reflect the seriousness of the offence and give the court sufficient sentencing powers and whether the charges can be presented in a clear and simple manner. A second consideration would be whether the issue of a summons for a more serious offence would override the discretion of the CPS in a way that would be oppressive to the defendant. Thirdly, the court should bear in mind that the DPP could always intervene to discontinue the proceedings under s. 6(2) of the Prosecution of Offences Act 1985 or to reduce the charges under s. 23. Lord Justice Kennedy suggested that there would have to be special circumstances 'such as apparent bad faith on the part of the public prosecutor' (at p. 51). The court refused the application for judicial review.

In 1995, the family of eighteen-year-old Stephen Lawrence succeeded in launching a private prosecution for murder after the CPS dropped charges against two teenagers who had been charged with the killing. It was believed to be the first time that a private prosecution had been brought in this country in a murder case. Stephen Lawrence, who was black, was killed by a white gang in a racially motivated murder. The case aroused much public attention and a fund was established to pay for the private prosecution. However, in the event, the trial of the three defendants collapsed after the judge ruled that crucial eye witness evidence for the prosecution was too unreliable to be put before the jury.[381]

See also *Elguzouli-Daf v. Metropolitan Police Commissoner*[382] holding that the CPS owes no duty of care toward defendants such that they could sue for failure to dismiss charges earlier after the forensic evidence against them had been discredited.

---

[380] [1994] 1 All ER 44. See also *R v. Bow Street Stipendiary Magistrate, ex p South Coast Shipping Co Ltd* [1993] 1 All ER 219.

[381] See the national press, 26 April 1996. For a discussion of the legal issues see E. Saunders, 'Private Prosecutions by the Victims of Violent Crime', 144 *New Law Journal*, 29 September 1994, p. 1423. For sharp criticism of the Lawrence family's lawyers for having launched a private prosecution that was bound to fail see M. Mears, 'Mansfield, Kamlish and Khan – the Three Wise Men', 149 *New Law Journal*, 26 March 1999, p. 463. See further J. Kodwo Bentil, 'The Unenviable Task of Seeking to Institute a Private Prosecution', 154 *Justice of the Peace*, 26 May 1990, p. 324.   [382] [1995] 1 All ER 833, CA.

Lord Justice Auld in his Review said that although a strong case had been advanced for abolition of the right of private prosecution he was not inclined to recommend it. It was not much used but 'its strength might lie in its availability when needed rather than in the extent of its use',[383] but in his view there was the need for an effective system for alerting the DPP to the initiation of such prosecutions so that he could consider his power to intervene. He recommended that any court which authorised the initiation of a private prosecution should be required to notify the DPP of it in writing.[384]

Duties of prosecuting lawyers

The classic statement on the role and approach of prosecuting counsel was expressed by a judge as long ago as 1865 – they 'are to regard themselves as ministers of justice, and not to struggle for a conviction'.[385]

At the time of the establishment of the Crown Prosecution Service, the Bar set up a committee on the duties and obligations of counsel when conducting a prosecution. The committee produced what have come to be called the Farquharson Guidelines.[386] The introductory passage of the 1986 Guidelines is a classic statement regarding the special position of prosecution counsel:

> There is no doubt that the obligations of prosecution counsel are different from those of counsel instructed for the defence in a criminal case or of counsel instructed in civil matters. His duties are wider both to the court and to the public at large. Furthermore, having regard to his duty to present the case for the prosecution fairly to the jury he has a greater independence of those instructing him than that enjoyed by other counsel. It is well known to every practitioner that counsel for the prosecution must conduct his case moderately, albeit firmly. He must not strive unfairly to obtain a conviction; he must not press his case beyond the limits which the evidence permits; he must not invite the jury to convict on evidence which in his own judgment no longer sustains the charge laid in the indictment. If the evidence of a witness is undermined or severely blemished in the course of cross-examination, prosecution counsel must not present him to the jury as worthy of a credibility he no longer enjoys. Many of the important decisions counsel for the prosecution has to make arise during the trial itself, and then because he has the conduct of the prosecution case, he is the person best fitted to make them. Information will be available to him and not, for example, to the judge of the reliability and background of the witnesses he is proposing to call. It is for these reasons that great responsibility is placed upon prosecution counsel and although his description as a 'minister of justice' may sound pompous to modern ears it accurately describes the way in which he should discharge his function.

---

[383] Auld, Ch. 10, para. 48, p. 414.   [384] Auld, Ch. 10, para. 48, p. 415.
[385] *Puddick* (1865) 4 F & F 497 per Crompton J.
[386] For the name of the chairman Farquharson J. The original Guidelines were published in the *Law Society's Gazette*, 26 November 1986, p. 3599.

The Farquharson Guidelines were reissued in a revised version in 2002.[387] Strangely, the new version did not include anything about the fundamental issues regarding prosecuting counsel's role explained in the original text, but there can be no doubt that the fundamental principle remains unchanged.[388]

At the core of the principle is that prosecution counsel is independent. This is a vital part of the role of the barrister in private practice and most of all for prosecution counsel. In his introduction to the revised version of the Guidelines, the Lord Chief Justice said that the prosecution advocate 'plays an important public role and as such may be considered a cornerstone of an open and fair criminal justice system'. He cannot be that cornerstone unless he is independent, but what does independence of prosecution counsel mean in practice?

The prosecutor and those instructing him

Where the prosecution is handled by a barrister in private practice at the Bar, as is normally still the case in Crown Court cases, the question of independence means counsel's relationship with those instructing him – the CPS and, through the CPS, the police. To what extent is counsel free to take what he considers to be the right decisions with regard to the case he is prosecuting?

That this is a problem area became clear in the *Crown Court Study* conducted for the Runciman Royal Commission.[389] The back page of the questionnaires used in the study was blank. Respondents were asked to use the page to express any particular concerns about the system which they wanted to draw to the Royal Commission's attention. One issue raised over and over again by the barristers was that of unwelcome and inappropriate pressure exerted on them by the CPS.

The 1986 Guidelines said on this issue that in case of disagreement between counsel and those instructing him, counsel's view should prevail subject to the right of the CPS to take a second opinion or to withdraw the instructions and brief another barrister. From a certain point of time, however, it would no longer be practicable to withdraw instructions.

The 2002 revised Guidelines dealt with the issue in more detail:[390]

The Role and Responsibilities of the Prosecution Advocate

3. (c) *Presentation and conduct* While he remains instructed it is for Counsel to take all necessary decisions in the presentation and general conduct of the prosecution . . .

---

[387] Published on the CPS Website at www.cps.gov.uk and the Criminal Bar's Website at www.criminalbar.com.

[388] See also R. Young and A. Sanders, 'The Ethics of Prosecution Lawyers', 7 *Legal Ethics*, 2004, pp. 190–209.

[389] M. Zander and P. Henderson, *Crown Court Study* (Royal Commission on Criminal Justice, Research Study No. 19, 1993).

[390] For reasons of economy of space, the extract that follows only states each main proposition without the explanatory paragraphs.

4. (d) *Policy decisions* Where matters of policy fall to be decided after the point indicated in (b) above (including offering no evidence on the indictment or on a particular count, or on the acceptance of pleas to lesser counts), it is the duty of Counsel to consult his Instructing Solicitor/Crown Prosecutor whose views at this stage are of crucial importance . . .

(e) In the rare case where Counsel and his Instructing Solicitor are unable to agree on a matter of policy, it is subject to (g) below, for Prosecution Counsel to make the necessary decisions . . .

(f) *Attorney General* Where Counsel has taken a decision on a matter of policy with which his Instructing Solicitor has not agreed, then it would be appropriate for the Attorney General to require Counsel to submit to him a written report of all the circumstances, including his reasons for disagreeing with those who instruct him . . .

5. (g) *Change of advice* When Counsel has had the opportunity to prepare his brief and to confer with those instructing him, but at the last moment before trial unexpectedly advises that the case should not proceed or that pleas to lesser offences should be accepted, and his Instructing Solicitor does not accept such advice, Counsel should apply for an adjournment if instructed to do so [to permit other counsel to be instructed] . . .

6. (h) *Prosecution advocate's role in decision making at trial* Subject to the above, it is for Prosecution Counsel to decide whether to offer no evidence on a particular count or on the indictment as a whole and whether to accept pleas to a lesser count or counts . . .

Whether those more detailed propositions have made a difference is not known. Barrister David Jeremy, while welcoming the new Guidelines, expressed anxiety as to whether they would operate as intended. Writing in the *Criminal Bar Association Newsletter*[391] he claimed that the independence of the prosecuting barrister had been ignored by both the Bar Council and the CPS:

> When it comes to the important policy questions such as acceptance of plea, or continuing with a prosecution, a whole generation of barristers has grown up with the idea that they are no more than a conduit between the CPS and the defendant. The pantomime of experienced counsel explaining a serious case over the telephone to a CPS lawyer, who may be totally unfettered by knowledge of the case, and then awaiting the latter's 'instructions', sometimes without even being asked to give his own opinion, has brought the prosecution process into disrepute. It fails to make use of the expertise of the Bar and it renders the CPS vulnerable to defensive decision-making, that is decision making that is motivated by a desire to conceal errors or omissions, that gives too much weight to the views of others such as the police, or that simply seeks the easiest option . . .
>
> The reason why we have been reduced to this situation is presumably because the Crown Prosecution Service perceives a need to appear to be in sole control of decision-making, and the Bar in turn has paid excessive regard to the fact that the CPS is a provider of work. By being too fearful of where the next brief is coming from, we have contributed to the abandonment of any valid claim to be independent prosecutors.

[391] June 2002, pp. 3 and 4.

The problem of the prosecutor's independence also occurs when the prosecution is being presented by the CPS themselves. Independence in that context means freedom to conduct the case as it requires unaffected by extraneous considerations such as the bureaucratic concerns of a large organisation. Worries about this fuelled much of the opposition at the time to proposals to extend rights of audience in the higher courts to CPS advocates.[392]

The barrister and the judge

The Farquharson Guidelines also deal with the relationship between prosecuting counsel and the judge, especially as to whether counsel is right to accept a plea to a lesser charge. The revised Guidelines in 2002 restated the position set out in the original version in 1986:

> 7.(i) If Prosecution Counsel invites the Judge to approve the course he is proposing to take, then he must abide by the judge's decision . . .
>
> (j) If Prosecution Counsel does not invite the Judge's approval of his decision, it is open to the Judge to express his dissent with the course proposed and invite Counsel to reconsider the matter with those instructing him, but having done so, the final decision remains with Counsel . . .
>
> (k) In an extreme case where the Judge is of the opinion that the course proposed by Counsel would lead to serious injustice, he may decline to proceed with the case until Counsel has consulted with the Director [of Public Prosecutions[393]] . . .

For a valuable review of many of the ethical problems of criminal practice see M. Blake and A. Ashworth 'Some Ethical Issues in Prosecuting and Defending Criminal Cases', *Criminal Law Review*, 1998, pp. 16–34. The authors consider a variety of issues: defending a person believed to be guilty; believing that perjury has been committed; the lawyer knows that an error of law or fact has been made which favours the other side; the defence lawyer thinks the client would be better advised to plead guilty but the client wishes to plead not guilty; the client and his lawyer disagree as to how to conduct the defence; the prosecutor realises that evidence has been obtained unfairly; and the prosecutor negotiates for a guilty plea even though he suspects that the prosecution case would fail.

8. Bail or remand in custody[394]

There are many reasons for concern as to whether accused persons should be held in custody while their cases are still pending.[395] Remand in custody for

---

[392] The writer was with the Bar and many of the judges in voicing such fears – M. Zander, 'Will the Reforms Serve the Public Interest?', 148 *New Law Journal*, 3 July 1998, p. 969. On the rights of audience battle see p. 220 below.   [393] Commonly referred to simply as 'the Director'.

[394] See generally on this subject N. Corre and D. Wolchover, *Bail in Criminal Proceedings* (3rd edn, Oxford, 2004).

[395] For a great deal of information on this subject see: www.prisonreformtrust.org.uk and www.innocentuntilprovenguilty.

someone who has not yet been convicted is despite the fact that he is formally presumed to be innocent. To be remanded in custody is a serious matter for the person concerned.

Remand prisoners are disadvantaged in preparing their cases for trial. The remand prisoner will be hindered in getting access to lawyers to prepare his defence, in looking for witnesses and collecting evidence or preparing evidence in mitigation of sentence. If the prison where he is held is remote, he may find that lawyers are not willing to come there at all. Even when it is relatively close to main centres of population he will find it difficult to have the kind of access to advisers that would be possible if he were at liberty.

There is evidence that, *other things being equal,* those who are held in custody are more likely to plead guilty, to be found guilty and to be given a custodial sentence than those who are on bail. In other words, the mere fact of being imprisoned seems to have an effect on one's prospects in the criminal justice system.[396] Also, the defendant in custody is unable to continue with his normal life, may lose his job, may fall behind in paying rent and both he and his family may suffer other financial and other practical difficulties, as well as obvious emotional upset or even trauma. The National Association for the Care and Resettlement of Offenders carried out a study based on interviews with 3,449 prisoners in eight male and two female prisons. Nearly one-third of the sample (31 per cent) were unconvicted prisoners on remand. Two-fifths of the remand prisoners had lost their homes as a result of being in prison and over one-third (35 per cent) of the remand prisoners had lost jobs through being imprisoned.[397]

The suicide rate of remand prisoners is significantly higher than the rate for prisoners who are not on remand.[398] It is generally assumed that the reason is the anxiety and uncertainty of the situation of awaiting trial or sentence, the higher proportion of mental disturbance among remand prisoners and the depressing effect of the poor conditions and restricted regimes in which remand prisoners are held.

Remand prisoners are also a serious issue from the point of view of prison overcrowding. Remand prisoners who have not yet been convicted or are awaiting sentence make up around one-fifth of the prison population. (Of these, roughly, two-thirds are unconvicted, the remaining third are awaiting sentence.) Because of the rapid turn-over of remand prisoners, they are, of course, an even higher proportion of all *receptions* into prison. There have been times when lack of space in prisons has meant that remand prisoners have had to be held in police cells.

Conditions in prisons for remand prisoners are theoretically better than for convicted prisoners. They are allowed more visits, they can send more letters,

---

[396] A.K. Bottomley, *Decisions in the Penal Process* (Martin Robertson, 1973) pp. 88–93.
[397] 'Bail – Some Current Issues', Penal Affairs Consortium, October 1995, p. 2 – referred to here as the 'Penal Affairs Consortium Paper, 1995'.
[398] Remand prisoners were between a fifth and a quarter of the prison population but they accounted for half the suicides (Penal Affairs Consortium Paper, 1995, p. 3).

they can wear their own clothes and be attended by a doctor of their own choice (provided they meet the cost), they can work if they wish like convicted prisoners but cannot be required to do so, they cannot be required to have their hair cut, they can have more cigarettes and may use private cash for purchases from the prison shop. But in practice the regime for remand prisoners is in most ways worse than for those who have been convicted. A paper presented in 1992 to the Criminal Justice Consultative Committee prepared by the Director General of the Prison Service stated: 'Taken as a whole, however, the regime for unconvicted prisoners is in practice far from satisfactory, and is often worse than for the convicted. A variety of factors contribute to this, including antiquated accommodation, a transient and sometimes volatile population, and the pressures placed on establishments by the demands of courts and other work' (para. 4.3). In many prisons they are locked in their cells as much as twenty-three hours a day.

The question of bail arises in three situations: the street, the police station and the court.

Bail on the street

The Criminal Justice Act 2003 introduced the radically new concept of bail granted by a police officer in the street. The Explanatory Notes accompanying the Act said this 'provides the police with additional flexibility following arrest and the scope to remain on patrol where there is no immediate need to deal with the person concerned at the [police] station' (para. 107). It was intended to allow the police 'to plan their work more effectively by giving them new discretion to decide exactly when and where an arrested person should attend at a police station for interview' (ibid).

Section 4 of the Act amends s. 30 of the Police and Criminal Evidence Act 1984 which requires the police to take an arrested person to a police station. The arrested person must be given a written notice stating the offence for which he was arrested and the ground.[399] If he is not told at that time where and when he must attend at a police station, he must be so informed later. No condition other than attendance at a police station may be imposed. Failure to attend at the specified time makes the person liable to arrest.

There is no solid information as to how much this new power is being used. (The writer's impression is that so far at least it is little used.)

Bail from the police station

If a person is arrested on a warrant, the warrant will state whether he is to be held by the police in custody or released on bail, but if, as is much more common, he is arrested without a warrant, the police must decide whether or

---

[399] New s. 30B of PACE inserted by s. 4(7) of the 2003 Act.

not to release the suspect after charge or whilst charges are being considered by the CPS. Before a suspect has been charged, he can only be detained in the police station if the custody officer reasonably thinks that such detention is 'necessary to secure or preserve evidence relating to an offence for which he is under arrest or to obtain such evidence by questioning him' (PACE, s. 37(2)). No distinction is made between serious and other offences.

After a person has been charged, he has to be released from the police station unless his name and address are not known or the custody officer reasonably thinks his detention is necessary for his own protection or to prevent him causing injury to a person or damage to property or because he might 'skip' or interfere with the course of justice (s. 38(1)(a)). A juvenile can be held in custody, in addition, 'in his own interests' (s. 38(1)(b)).

The Criminal Justice and Public Order Act 1994 (CJPOA) gave the police the power to grant bail subject to conditions, similar to the power to grant bail subject to conditions traditionally enjoyed by the court. (On the courts' power to set conditions for bail see p. 279 below.) The power, established by CJPOA 1994, s. 27, followed a recommendation of the Runciman Royal Commission[400] based on the belief that it would result in release of far more persons from police custody.

Under CJPOA 1994, this police power to impose conditions only applied to persons who had been charged. The Criminal Justice Act 2003 extended conditional bail from the police station to persons released pending a decision about charge.[401]

Conditions should only be imposed if it appears to the custody officer that they are necessary to secure that the defendant (1) surrenders to custody; (2) does not commit further offences while on bail and (3) does not interfere with witnesses or otherwise obstruct the course of justice (CJPOA, s. 27(3)). The police, unlike the court, cannot order reports to be prepared nor can the police order the defendant to live in a bail hostel.

The conditions of bail can be made more onerous or less onerous by the original or another custody officer (*ibid*).

The CJPOA, s. 29 gave the police a power to arrest someone who did not answer to police bail.

The great majority of those arrested are bailed by the police. This applies even to arrests for indictable offences. In 2005, four-fifths (80 per cent) of those who were arrested for indictable offences, were bailed from the police station.[402]

Bail decisions by courts

When a court adjourns a case – whether overnight or for a week or a month – it has to decide whether the defendant should be remanded on bail or in

---

[400] Runciman, p. 73, para. 22.   [401] See new s. 37D(3) inserted by Sch. 2, para. 3.
[402] *Criminal Statistics 2005*, Home Office, RDS, 19/06, Table 4.2, p. 76.

custody. Until the Bail Act 1976 the system of bail was to permit the release of the defendant, usually on his own recognisance (his promise to pay a stated sum of money if he absconded and was caught) and often also the promise by sureties that they too would pay a stated sum of money in the same event. (In the English system no money has to be provided by a surety unless the defendant actually 'skips'.) Bail could be granted either with or without conditions. Police objections to bail could be based on a variety of grounds – for example, the likelihood that the defendant would abscond, would interfere with witnesses or would commit further offences.

The Bail Act 1976

Statutory presumption of bail The Bail Act 1976 created a statutory presumption of bail for remand cases (including remands after conviction for reports to be made). This means that the court *must* grant bail unless one of the statutory exceptions applies – even if the defendant does not apply for bail (s. 4).[403]

The main exceptions are set out in the Bail Act. They provide that a court need not grant bail to a person charged with an offence punishable with imprisonment if the court is satisfied that there are substantial grounds for believing that, if released on bail, the defendant would (1) fail to appear; (2) commit an offence while on bail or (3) obstruct the course of justice. Bail also need not be granted if the court thinks he ought to stay in custody for his own protection (or, in the case of a juvenile, for his own welfare), or if there has been insufficient time to obtain enough information about the defendant for the court to reach a decision, or he has previously failed to answer to bail.[404]

In determining whether it is likely that the defendant would skip or commit an offence or obstruct justice, the court should have regard to (1) the nature and seriousness of the offence (and the probable way the court will deal with the defendant); (2) the character, antecedents, associations and community ties of the defendant; (3) his record with regard to any previous grant of bail; and (4) except where the remand is for reports, the strength of the evidence against him.[405]

Exceptions to the statutory presumption In the case of someone charged with an offence punishable with imprisonment who is remanded for reports, bail need not be granted if it appears to the court impracticable to complete the inquiries or make the report without keeping the defendant in custody.[406]

Where the defendant is charged with an offence not punishable with imprisonment, the permissible grounds for refusing bail are narrower. He can be

---

[403] The importance of the presumption was shown by the results of a study carried out over six months in Cardiff. There were almost 500 cases (496). In 395 the police did not object to bail, nothing was said about bail on behalf of the defendant and bail was simply granted. M.J. Doherty and R. East, 'Bail Decisions in Magistrates' Courts', 25 *British Journal of Criminology*, 1985, Table 2, p. 256.   [404] Bail Act 1976, Sch. 1, Part I, paras. 2–6.

[405] Schedule 1, Part I, para. 9. For criticism of the structure of the Bail Act provisions see *Criminal Law Review*, 1987, pp. 438–9 and 1993, p. 1.   [406] Schedule 1, Part I, para. 7.

refused bail if he has previously failed to answer to bail and if the court believes, in view of that failure, that he will again fail to surrender to custody if released on bail.[407]

The CJPOA, s. 25 provided that anyone on a charge of murder, attempted murder, manslaughter, rape or attempted rape who had previously been convicted for one of those offences, in such cases bail was not permitted at all, but this absolute prohibition only lasted four years before it was removed by the Crime and Disorder Act 1998, s. 56. This allows bail in such cases if the court finds it is justified by 'exceptional circumstances'.[408] The CJPOA, s. 25 was contrary to the European Convention on Human Rights.[409] Despite doubts raised in some quarters,[410] the Law Commission concluded that the revised s. 25 could be interpreted compatibly with the Convention on the basis that where the defendant would not pose a real risk of committing a serious offence on bail that would constitute 'an exceptional circumstance'.[411]

Of greater practical significance was s. 26 of the CJPOA which removed the statutory presumption of bail with regard to anyone charged with an offence which is not a purely summary offence where the alleged offence occurred while the defendant was on bail. This was to deal with the alleged scandal of so-called 'bail bandits' – on which see p. 286 below. The court was not bound to refuse bail in such cases; it simply was not subject to the statutory presumption in favour of bail. The Law Commission recommended that this provision might conflict with the ECHR and that it should be amended to make it clear that offending on bail was only one of the considerations to be taken into account rather than being in itself an independent ground for refusing bail.[412] This recommendation was accepted by the Government and the necessary amendment was made in the Criminal Justice Act 2003, s. 14 which provides that the court should give that matter 'particular weight'.[413]

The same Act however created a new restriction on the grant of bail to drug users. The Explanatory Notes accompanying the Act said (para. 148) there was a concern that such offenders if granted bail would merely reoffend in order to fund their drug use. Accordingly the Act states that an alleged offender aged eighteen or over who has been charged with an imprisonable offence will not be granted bail where three conditions exist unless he demonstrates that there is no significant risk of his committing an offence while on bail. The three conditions

---

[407] Chapter 1, Part II, para. 2.

[408] For a decision that bail does not have to be granted to such a defendant even though the custody time limit had expired and had not been extended because of the prosecution's failure to act with due diligence see *R (O) v. Harrow Crown Court* [2006] UKHL 42, [2006] 3 All ER 1157.   [409] *CC v. United Kingdom* [1999] Crim LR 228.

[410] See, for instance, P. Leach, 'Automatic Denial of Bail and the European Convention', *Criminal Law Review*, 1999, pp. 300–5.

[411] *Bail and the Human Rights Act 1998*, Law Com. No. 269, 2001, para. 8.45. This view was upheld by the Divisional Court in *R (on the application of O) v. Harrow Crown Court* [2003] EWHC 868 Admin.   [412] Law Com. No. 269, 2001, para. 4.12.

[413] Inserting new para. 9AA(2) into the Bail Act 1976, Sch. 1, Part I.

are that there is drug test evidence that he has a Class A drug in his body, the court is satisfied that there are substantial grounds for believing that misuse of a Class A drug caused or contributed to the alleged offence and he refuses to undergo an assessment as to his drug dependency.

Bail on condition If bail is granted, it can be conditional or unconditional. Unconditional bail means that the defendant must simply surrender to the court on the appointed date. Failure to do so without reasonable cause is an offence (s. 6(1)) punishable in the magistrates' court with three months' imprisonment and/or a fine, or in the Crown Court with twelve months' imprisonment or a fine.

Conditions can be attached where the court thinks it is necessary to ensure the defendant's presence at court, or so that he does not commit further offences or interferes with witnesses or obstruct the course of justice, or to ensure that he makes himself available for reports or for an interview with lawyers.[414] The Criminal Justice Act 2003 added a further ground – the protection of the defendant.[415]

The most common conditions relate to such matters as reporting to the police daily or weekly, handing in one's passport, living in particular premises or with particular persons, or *not* associating with particular persons or not going to particular places. In 2001, electronic tagging was added as a possible condition for juvenile defendants.[416] In *R (on the application of Crown Prosecution Service) v. Chorley Justices* the Divisional Court upheld the lawfulness of a 'door stepping' condition, under which the defendant was subject to a curfew backed by a condition that he had to show himself at the door if asked to do so by the police.[417]

It seems that conditions are imposed on about two-thirds of grants of bail.[418]

There was previously no right of appeal as such against conditions imposed on the grant of bail. Lord Justice Auld in his Review said this was sensible 'otherwise the appellate process could be corrupted by endless wrangling over conditions',[419] but he recommended that the defendant should be given a right of appeal against conditional grants of bail in respect of conditions to live away from home and to provide sureties or to give security (on which see below).[420] This recommendation was accepted by the Government and a provision to give

---

[414] Section 3(6). The last category was added by the Crime and Disorder Act 1998, s. 54(2).

[415] Section 13(1), following the recommendation of the Law Commission Report, n. 411 above, para. 9A.27.

[416] Criminal Justice and Police Act 2001, s. 131 adding new s. 6ZAA to the Bail Act 1976.

[417] [2002] EWHC 2162 Admin, (2002) 166 JP 764. For a discussion suggesting that the condition is useless see P. Tain, 'Shut that Door', 146 *Solicitors' Journal*, 20 December 2002, p. 1155.

[418] R. Morgan and N. Russell, *The Judiciary in the Magistrates' Court* (Home Office, RDS Occasional Paper No. 66, 2000) p. 49. See generally B.P. Block, 'Bail Conditions: Neither Logical nor Lawful', 154 *Justice of the Peace*, 1990, p. 83; J.N. Spencer, 'Bail Conditions: Logical or Illogical?', 154 *Justice of the Peace*, 24 March 1990, p. 180; J.W. Raine and M.J. Willson, 'The Imposition and Effectiveness of Conditions in Bail Decisions', 159 *Justice of the Peace*, 3 June 1995, pp. 364–7.   [419] Auld, Ch. 10, para. 88, p. 424.   [420] *Ibid.*

it effect was included in the Criminal Justice Act 2003 (s. 16(3)) which also extended the right of appeal to conditions of curfew and electronic tagging.

The Bail Act 1976 did not create an offence of breaking conditions imposed by the court, but s. 7(3) gives the police a power to arrest a defendant on conditional bail where they reasonably suspect that he is likely to break the conditions or that he has already done so. Anyone arrested under this subsection must be brought before a justice of the peace within twenty-four hours. The justice of the peace may then reconsider the question of bail. If he is not brought before the magistrates within twenty-four hours, they cannot remand him in custody since they have no jurisdiction over him.[421]

It has been held that a hearing to deal with alleged breach of bail conditions is not a hearing of a criminal offence so as to give the accused rights under Article 6 (right to a fair trial) of the ECHR and that although Article 5 (right to liberty and security) is applicable, it does not impose any new procedural requirements, but the court must take proper account of the quality of the material available to it.[422]

Sureties The Bail Act 1976 abolished personal recognisances whereby the defendant agreed to pay a sum of money if he failed to appear on the appointed day. The only exception was where the court thought there was a danger the defendant might go abroad, in which case he could be asked to give monetary security. But the Crime and Disorder Act 1998, s. 54(1) restored the general power to order the defendant to give a personal recognisance. Giving a personal recognisance does not require the production of the actual money or even a bond – only providing sufficient evidence to satisfy the court that one has it.

The Bail Act preserved the ancient right of the court to ask for sureties as a condition of bail. The sureties promise to pay in the event that the defendant does not turn up. The court then has a discretion as to whether to order that the amount put up by the sureties be forfeited ('estreated'). The Crime and Disorder Act 1998, s. 55 changed the position by making the surety's recognisance forfeit automatically if the defendant fails to appear, but the court then fixes a hearing to enable the surety to show cause why he should not be ordered to pay the sum in which he was bound.[423]

Standing surety for someone can have catastrophic consequences. In a case in December 1982, for instance, Bow Street magistrates' court demanded payment of £120,000 from a travel agent who promised that amount as surety for two men he hardly knew charged with VAT frauds of over £20 million. For a more lenient attitude see *R v. Crown Court at Reading, ex p Bello*.[424] The

---

[421] *R v. Governor of Glen Parva Young Offender Institution, ex p G* [1998] 2 All ER 295.

[422] *R (on the application of the DPP) v. Havering Magistrates' Court* [2001] 1 WLR 805, [2001] Crim LR 902, Div Ct.

[423] For the principles applied by the courts see *R v. Uxbridge Justices, ex p Heward-Mills* [1983] 1 WLR 56; *R v. Southampton Justices, ex p Green* [1976] QB 11 and A. Eccles, 'New Developments in the Law of Forfeiture of Recognisance', 146 *Justices of the Peace*, 1982, p. 146.

[424] [1992] 3 All ER 353.

Divisional Court upheld the judge's order that the surety lose £5,000, which was half the sum he had agreed to stand for, even though he was entirely blameless. The Court of Appeal disagreed. The court should always consider the question of fault. ('If it was satisfied the surety was blameless throughout it would then be proper to remit the whole of the amount of the recognisance'.) However, in *R v. Crown Court at Maidstone, ex p Lever* [425] the Court of Appeal held that the absence of culpability on the part of the surety was not by itself a reason to reduce or remit entirely the forfeiture of a recognisance if the defendant absconded. It upheld forfeiture even though the surety had been in no way at fault.

In *ex p Bello* (above) the Court of Appeal held that the surety had to be informed of the date when the defendant was required to attend at court. Since he had not been so informed that was in itself sufficient ground to allow the appeal. See also *R v. Crown Court at Wood Green, ex p Howe*[426] holding that courts should consider the surety's ability to pay when deciding how much of the sum promised should be forfeited.

The surety's responsibilities cease when the trial starts. In 1990, the financier Asil Nadir fled Britain for Cyprus after he had been arraigned at the start of his trial for fraud offences. The judge, Tucker J, required a Mr Guney who had stood as surety for £1 million to forfeit £650,000. The Court of Appeal held that since from the moment that the defendant was arraigned at the start of the trial the surety was no longer at risk, the decision to forfeit the surety's money had been wrong.[427]

It is a criminal offence to agree to indemnify a surety – for example, where the defendant or his associates agree to reimburse the surety if he is asked by the court to pay the money he has promised to pay (Bail Act 1976, s. 9). Such an agreement is treated as a conspiracy to pervert the course of justice.

The Bail Act provides that a surety can be relieved of his obligations if he notifies the police that the bailed person is unlikely to surrender. The police can then make an arrest without a warrant.[428]

Procedural formalities The Act requires that the bail decision be recorded and that reasons must be given to the defendant if it is refused or if conditions are attached to the grant of bail. Reasons must also be given if bail is granted over the objections of the prosecution.[429] If the defendant is unrepresented and is refused bail, he must be told of his right to apply to a higher court for bail (s. 5).

What determines the decision on bail? Both the theory and law of bail is that the decision as to whether the defendant is remanded in custody or on bail is made by the court, but in practice the decision is likely actually to be determined

---

[425] [1995] 2 All ER 35.   [426] [1992] 3 All ER 366.
[427] *R v. Central Criminal Court, ex p Guney* [1996] 2 All ER 705.
[428] However, see *R v. Crown Court at Ipswich, ex p Reddington* [1981] Crim LR 618 establishing that the surety is not automatically relieved simply by going to the police.
[429] Criminal Justice and Police Act 2001, s. 129.

by other actors in the criminal justice system. In a study by the Home Office Research Unit it was found that the factor which was most highly correlated with the bail rate in courts was whether the police had given the defendant bail from the police station.[430] In another study, based on 1,524 remand hearings and court records for 2,069 cases, only 9 per cent of the remand hearings were contested. In 85 per cent of cases the CPS did not oppose a remand on bail. When the CPS did oppose bail, the defence did not contest the matter in 42 per cent of those cases. In that author's view, in most cases the effective decision-makers were the police, the CPS and the defence lawyers. Usually the remand decision was made informally before the defendant appeared in court. Even when there was a contested bail application, the magistrates generally agreed with the CPS assessment of bail risk.[431]

How many bail applications?

Originally, an unconvicted person could not be remanded in custody for more than eight days. This ensured that his case would be reconsidered every week and repeated applications could be made to have him released by the magistrates.

In 1980, in *R v. Nottingham Justices, ex p Davies*[432] the Divisional Court held that no fresh application for bail could be made to magistrates unless the circumstances had in some way changed since the last application.

One effect of the decision in the *Nottingham Justices* case was that even competent defence counsel delayed making an application for bail lest the client was prejudiced by the rule. As a result, a client might be remanded in custody longer than would otherwise have been the case. See B. Brink and C. Stone, 'Defendants Who Do Not Ask For Bail', *Criminal Law Review*, 1987, p. 152. This article led to the Criminal Justice Act 1988, s. 154, which requires the courts to consider bail at *each* hearing.[433] Moreover, under s. 154, at the first hearing after the defendant has been remanded in custody his lawyers can deploy any arguments they please, whether or not they have been advanced previously, but at any subsequent hearing the court need not hear arguments heard previously. This helped to defuse part of the problem created by the *Nottingham Justices* case, but there is a doubt as to whether if the defence do not advance any argument regarding bail at the first hearing they are restricted to two hearings or whether the first 'unargued' hearing should be disregarded and not count. It seems that many courts adopt a strict approach and in effect hold that the defendant who does not utilise his first opportunity of arguing for bail has wasted it.

---

[430] F. Simon and M. Weatheritt, *The Use of Bail and Custody by London Magistrates' Courts Before and After the Criminal Justice Act* (HMSO, 1984) p. 15.

[431] A. Hucklesby, 'Remand Decision Makers', *Criminal Law Review*, 1997, pp. 269–81. See also her 'Bail or Jail? The Practical Operation of the Bail Act 1976', 23 *Journal of Law and Society*, 1996, pp. 213–33.   [432] [1980] 2 All ER 775.

[433] The section added a new Part IIA to Sch. 1 of the Bail Act 1976.

Length of periods of remand

As noted, remands traditionally were for a maximum of one week. The Criminal Justice Act 1982, s. 59 and Sch. 9 provided for the longer remand in custody of defendants over seventeen who are legally represented even though they are not physically before the court. The defendant could be remanded in custody for three one-week periods providing this was explained to him when he was first remanded in custody and he gave his consent. This meant that he had to be produced at least every four weeks, but if he wished to change his mind during that period, he could. His lawyer would not normally appear for him in his absence either.

At first this was introduced as an experiment (Criminal Justice Act 1988, s. 155), but in 1991 all courts were given the power to remand a defendant for up to twenty-eight days at a time providing he has been remanded in custody for the offence at least once before. In other words, this power cannot be used on the first occasion. The purpose was to reduce court hearings, to reduce time taking prisoners to and from courts and prisons and to save legal aid money.[434] In 1997, the power to remand the accused in custody for twenty-eight days on the second remand was extended to defendants under seventeen.[435]

Remand hearings are nowadays often heard via video link with the prison where the defendant is being held.

Appeals against a refusal of bail

There were three alternative methods of appealing against a refusal of bail – other than applying again to another bench of magistrates, which was considerably restricted by the *Nottingham Justices* decision.

The first was to apply to the judge in chambers through a barrister or a solicitor. The basic procedure for such applications is set out in CPR SC79.

The alternative was to apply for assistance to the Official Solicitor. The prisoner filled out a form in prison which requested the Official Solicitor to forward an application to the judge in chambers. There was no oral argument. The papers were simply presented to the judge by an official. There was no charge for the service.

Unsurprisingly, the chances of success were much greater through an oral argument presented by lawyers than in appeals by the Official Solicitor.[436]

The third method of seeking to obtain bail after it had been refused by magistrates was through the Crown Court.

---

[434] Magistrates' Courts (Remand in Custody) Order 1991, SI 1991/2667.

[435] Criminal Procedure and Investigations Act 1996, s. 52(2).

[436] According to a parliamentary answer, the success rate for Official Solicitor applications in 1980 was 9 per cent compared with 69 per cent for those privately represented (House of Commons, *Hansard*, 23 November 1981, Written Answers, cols. 274–5). See to like effect N. Bases and M. Smith, 'A Study of Bail Applications Through the Official Solicitor to the Judge in Chambers', *Criminal Law Review*, 1976, p. 541.

Auld recommended that the appeal system be reformed by removal of the right of application to a High Court judge after determination of the matter by either magistrates or the Crown Court. Reopening of the bail issue should be restricted to an appeal on a point of law only.[437] This recommendation was accepted and implemented in the Criminal Justice Act 2003, s. 17, but s. 16 of the Act created a right of appeal to the Crown Court against the imposition by magistrates of certain listed conditions of bail – such as requirements relating to residency, provision of a surety or giving a security, curfew or electronic monitoring.

Appeals against a grant of bail

The Bail (Amendment) Act 1993 gave the prosecution a right of appeal where a magistrates' court granted bail to a person who was charged with or convicted of an offence carrying a sentence of five or more years' imprisonment, or an offence of taking a conveyance without the owner's consent (contrary to the Theft Act 1968, s. 12), or aggravated vehicle taking (contrary to the Theft Act 1968, s. 12A). The Criminal Justice Act 2003, s. 18 applied the right to any imprisonable offence. The right of appeal is against the grant of bail only and therefore cannot be used to challenge conditions imposed.

In order to exercise the right the prosecution must strictly follow the set procedure. First, the prosecution must have objected to bail during the bail hearing (s. 1(3)). At the conclusion of the bail hearing the prosecution must immediately[438] state in open court that it proposes to exercise its right of appeal (s. 1(4)). The clerk of the court announces the time at which this oral notice was given and issues a warrant of detention authorising the detention of the defendant for the time being. This is also recorded in the court register.

If the defendant is unrepresented, the court clerk has to tell him that he has the right to ask the Official Solicitor to represent him at the appeal.

The prosecution must serve written notice on the court and the defendant (not his legal representative). If this is not done within two hours, the appeal is deemed to have been dropped (s. 1(7)).

The appeal hearing must start within forty-eight hours of the day on which oral notice of intention to appeal was given, not counting weekends and public holidays (s. 1(8)). The hearing is before a single judge in chambers in the Crown Court (s. 1(9)). The defendant has no right to be present.[439]

---

[437] Auld, Ch. 10, paras. 84–7.

[438] However, five minutes' delay was held to be acceptable – *R v. Isleworth Crown Court, ex p Clarke* [1998] 1 Cr App Rep 257, DC.

[439] For a review of this system five years on by an experienced prosecutor see D. Tucker, 'The Prosecutor on the Starting Block: the Mechanics of the Bail (Amendment) Act 1993', *Criminal Law Review*, 1998, pp. 728–31. He suggested that the way for the CPS to avoid an unseemly rush after an adverse decision was to decide beforehand whether an appeal would be taken.

Note

1. Time spent in custody pre-trial or pre-sentence can generally be deducted from the ultimate sentence. This is by virtue of s. 67(1) of the Criminal Justice Act 1967.[440]

2. No compensation is paid to persons who have been remanded in custody and then are found not guilty. By contrast, in Germany, France, Holland and Sweden, persons who are detained and then acquitted can sometimes be compensated.

Causes for concern

Bail/remand in custody is a subject that perennially attracts critical comment from all quarters.

The civil libertarians are concerned especially that:

- 'As many as something under half of those at some stage remanded in custody pre-trial by the magistrates' court or the Crown Court are either acquitted, given non-custodial sentences or the case is not proceeded with.[441])
- There are considerable variations in the policy of different courts in remanding defendants on bail or in custody.
- Bail decisions are too hasty. Research has showed 62 per cent of bail hearings lasted less than two minutes and 96 per cent less than ten minutes. Even when bail was refused, 38 per cent were heard in under two minutes and 87 per cent in less than ten minutes.[442]
- Remand prisoners tend to be held in highly unsatisfactory conditions in prisons or in police cells.
- Some remand prisoners spend very long periods of time in custody. (In 2004, some 1,500 prisoners spent more than six months on remand of whom some 400 spent over a year in prison.[443])
- Many of those held on remand have significant problems – drug misuse, poor educational attainment, mental illness and unstable accommodation are particularly prevalent among remand prisoners.[444]

At the same time, discontents are expressed by the police and the media:

[440] However, this is not always the case – N. Yell, 'Credit for Time Spent Remanded in Custody', 146 *Justice of the Peace*, 1982, p. 275; *Criminal Law Review*, 1986, p. 270; 131 *New Law Journal*, 3 October 1980, p. 937.

[441] The 2005 figures show 19 per cent acquitted or not proceeded with, 26 per cent given non-custodial sentences (discharge, fine, community sentence or suspended sentence) and 55 per cent given immediate custodial sentences. (*Criminal Statistics 2005*, Home Office, RDS, November 2006, Table 4.5, p. 79 – percentages based on 75,700 in the 'Acquitted' and 'Convicted' categories. Persons 'Otherwise dealt with' or 'Failed to appear' are not included.)

[442] M.J. Doherty and R. East, 25 *British Journal of Criminology*, 1985, Table 2, p. 256.

[443] NOMS 2005 Caseload Statistics, Supplementary Tables, Table 8.18 – www.homeoffice.gov.uk/rds/pdfs05/hosb1750section8.xis.

[444] *Reducing re-offending amongst ex-prisoners*, Social Exclusion Unit, 2002 – www.socialexclusionunit.gov.uk.

- Too many commit offences while on bail – the problem of what the media call 'bail bandits'.[445]
- Too many people 'skip'. (In 2005, 13 per cent of defendants who had been bailed by magistrates' courts failed to appear at court.[446]) (The Criminal Justice Act 2003, s. 15 provided that someone who previously did not without reasonable excuse surrender to custody while on bail may not be granted bail unless the court is satisfied that there is no significant risk of his jumping bail again.)

The prison authorities are concerned about the cost of remand prisoners, the burdens they create for the prison system including the burden of escorts for prisoners going to court, the rapid turnover in receptions and discharges, and in terms of the problem of prison overcrowding and providing a tolerable regime while they are in custody.

New developments

One helpful development is the Bail Information Scheme now operating in many magistrates' courts. (They began in the mid-1980s as a result of the initiative of the Vera Institute of Justice of New York.[447]) Under these schemes probation officers provide the CPS and the court with verified information about the defendant – his employment status, where he lives, his family situation and other community roots and the like. Research suggests that the provision of bail information has a significant effect.[448]

However, in practice courts often lack the information they need. The Auld Review said: 'as to information, despite the introduction in 1998 of bail information schemes, it is often incomplete and for that and other reasons inaccurate'.[449] A 1998 study commented on the lack of ready availability to the police,

---

[445] For the facts see for instance *Offending While on Bail: a Survey of Recent Studies* (Home Office Research and Planning Unit, Paper No. 65, 1992). This concluded that the percentage of offenders who were convicted of offences committed while on bail had varied little over the previous decade. The studies consistently showed that 10–12 per cent of persons granted bail were convicted of offences committed while on bail. Six years later another Home Office study found that the proportion was 12 per cent for those bailed by the police and 15 per cent for those bailed by the court. (D. Brown, *Offending on bail and police use of conditional bail*, Home Office Research Findings No. 72, 1998.)

[446] *Criminal Statistics 2005*, Home Office, RDS, 19/06, Table 4.8, p. 82.

[447] The concept, based on pioneering work by the Vera Institute in New York, was first proposed in this country by the writer in the late 1960s – see M. Zander, 'Bail: A Reappraisal', *Criminal Law Review*, March 1967.

[448] *Bail Information Schemes: Practice and Effect* (Home Office Research and Planning Unit, Paper No. 69, 1992), but see M.K. Dhami, 'Do Bail Information Schemes Really Affect Bail Decisions?', 41 *Howard Journal of Criminal Justice*, 2002, pp. 242–62. This study was based on hypothetical cases presented to magistrates. The results showed no difference in bail decisions but the information gave magistrates more confidence in their decisions.

[449] Auld, Ch. 10, para. 78, p. 428.

prosecutors and courts of the defendant's criminal record and other relevant information.[450]

Since September 1999 all remand prisons have been required and funded to provide bail information schemes,[451] but the Prison Inspectorate's thematic report in 2000 on the treatment and conditions of remand prisoners recorded a wide variation in performance by establishments throughout the country and poor overall performance.[452]

Another helpful development has been the establishment of bail hostels and other facilities where defendants can be sent by courts. There are also a growing number of bail support schemes usually run by probation involving arrangements to help defendants on bail – through contact with bail support workers, residence requirements, volunteer befriending schemes, debt counselling and the like.

These more hopeful developments must be seen against a background of a continuing huge remand population in prison, held for the most part in their cells for twenty-three out of twenty-four hours a day.

Auld recommended that the courts take more time over bail, that better information be provided to them and that they should always record their bail decisions.[453]

9. Information supplied to the opponent ('disclosure')

The question of advance disclosure of information by prosecution to defence and by defence to the prosecution is one of the most important and most troublesome that confronts the criminal justice system. It is important since it goes to the question whether there has been a fair trial. Many notorious miscarriages of justice have occurred because of a failure by the prosecution to disclose crucial material at the time of the trial. It is troublesome since it is notoriously difficult (probably impossible) to get the actors to comply with the rules.

Disclosure by the prosecution has two aspects – first, the evidence it intends to use and, secondly, material in its possession that it does not intend to use that might in some way assist the defence (called 'unused material'). Disclosure by the defence deals with the material that the defence is required to reveal about its case before the trial.

Disclosure by the prosecution of its own case works tolerably well. The many problems associated with disclosure relate to disclosure of unused material by the prosecution and to defence disclosure.

The subject is covered today principally by the provisions of the Criminal Procedure and Investigations Act 1996 (CPIA) as amended by the Criminal

---

[450] R. Morgan and P. Henderson, *Remand Decisions and Offending on Bail: Evaluation of the Bail Process Project* (Home Office Research Study No. 184, 1998).

[451] Auld, Ch. 10, para. 71, p. 425.

[452] *Unjust Deserts*, 2000, paras. 4.09–4.17 – www.homeoffice.gov.uk/justice/prisons/inspprisons.

[453] *Ibid.*

Justice Act 2003 (CJA 2003), the Code of Practice under the CPIA,[454] the Criminal Procedure Rules 2005, Parts 25–8, the Attorney General's Guidelines on Disclosure (AG's Guidelines),[455] the CPS *Disclosure Manual* (CPS *Manual*)[456] and decisions of the courts. In 2006, there was added a new protocol issued by the judges (*Disclosure: A Protocol for the Control and Management of Unused Material in the Crown Court*).[457]

In February 2006, the Attorney General, announcing the outcome of his review of 'shaken baby syndrome' cases, published a booklet entitled *Disclosure: Expert's Evidence and Unused Material – Guidance Booklet for Experts.*

Evidence the prosecution intend to use

Lord Justice Auld said in his 2001 Review: 'the law is somewhat muddled in its provision for advance notification of the prosecution case and/or evidence, but reasonably satisfactory in its operation'.[458]

The position is different for the two levels of court and for different categories of case.

Cases tried in the magistrates' court The statutory duty on the prosecution in either-way cases to supply its evidence to the defence in advance of the trial only arises if the defence requests it. In that event the prosecution has a choice whether to supply copies of witness statements or a summary of their statements.[459] Because of the ease of photocopying, normally the statements themselves are supplied. For summary-only offences there is no equivalent rule. The defence was expected to manage somehow on the day without any advance notice.

The position for both types of cases changed as a result of the AG's Guidelines on Disclosure issued in November 2000.[460] Technically, the Guidelines do not have the force of law but it is clear that the Attorney General expects them to be followed.

The Guidelines include the following bald statement (para. 57):

> The prosecutor should . . . provide to the defence all evidence upon which the Crown proposes to rely in a summary trial. Such provision should allow the accused or their legal advisers sufficient time properly to consider the evidence before it is called.[461]

---

[454] *Criminal Procedure and Investigations Act 1996 (Code of Practice)* 1997 and 2005.

[455] First issued in 1981, revised in 2000 and re-issued in revised form in April 2005. For the current text see www.lslo.gov.uk.

[456] See www.cps.gov.uk – Legal Guidance and Covert Law Enforcement.

[457] www.hmcourts-service.gov.uk. Sir Igor Judge, President of the QBD, said the protocol would overcome the problems of over-complication and delay caused by the current arrangements for disclosure (156 *New Law Journal*, 24 February 2006, p. 294).

[458] Auld, Ch. 10, para. 117, p. 445.

[459] Magistrates' Courts (Advance Information) Rules 1985, SI 1985/601, r. 4.

[460] *Disclosure of Information to Criminal Proceedings*, 2000.

[461] The 2000 Guidelines went on: 'exceptionally, statements may be withheld for the protection of witnesses or to avoid interference with the course of justice'. This sentence does not appear in the 2005 revision.

This statement covers both summary-only and either-way cases tried in the magistrates' courts.[462]

Cases going to the Crown Court The rule for cases going to the Crown Court was that prior to the committal proceedings in the magistrates' courts the prosecution had to provide the defence with copies of enough of the prosecution evidence to constitute a *prima facie* case.[463] Before the trial took place, or at the latest before the end of the prosecution's case, any other evidence the prosecution intended to call also had to be handed over.

As will be seen below, when the relevant provisions of the Criminal Justice Act 2003 are brought into force, committal proceedings will be abolished. The new system is that cases are sent directly by the magistrates' courts to the Crown Court. In cases sent directly to the Crown Court the rule is that copies of the prosecution's evidence must be provided to the defence forty-two days after the first preliminary hearing there.[464]

Also, the Divisional Court has recognised a residual common law duty on prosecutors to serve proposed evidence earlier, where it is in the interests of justice to do so – for instance, to assist a bail application or an application to stay the proceedings as an abuse of process.[465]

The need for the defence to have early advance disclosure of the prosecution's case is now the greater because of changes that have been made in order to process cases, and especially guilty plea cases, more quickly.[466] These include asking the defendant to indicate his plea before the magistrates decide whether he should be tried at the higher or lower level ('plea before venue')[467] and the rule that when someone is granted bail by the police the return date when he is required to appear at court should, if possible, be the next sitting of the court.[468]

Lord Justice Auld said time between charge and service of the prosecution's evidence was 'dead time' in the life of the case. The Philips Royal Commission had recommended the introduction of a formal and comprehensive framework of rules for advance prosecution disclosure of proposed evidence in all courts, but no rules were made.[469] Auld said he supported that recommendation. The precise time scale should be prescribed by rules.[470] For cases sent to the Crown Court, regulations made in 2005 allow the prosecution seventy days from the

[462] In his covering Foreword to the 2000 Guidelines the Attorney General highlighted this development as one of the new Guidelines' 'highly significant changes addressing areas not covered by legislation'.

[463] *R v. Epping and Harlow Justices, ex p Massaro* [1973] QB 433; *R v. Grays Justices, ex p Tetley* (1979) 70 Cr App Rep 11.

[464] Magistrates' Court Act 1980, s. 5B(2)(c); Crime and Disorder Act 1998 (Service of Prosecution Evidence) Regulations 2000, SI 2000/3305, r. 2.

[465] *R v. DPP, ex p Lee* [1999] 2 All ER 737.

[466] See D. Sunman, 'Advancing Disclosure: Can the Rules for Advance Information in the Magistrates' Courts be Improved?', *Criminal Law Review*, 1998, pp. 799–801.

[467] CPIA, s. 49, pp. 337–38 below.   [468] Crime and Disorder Act 1998, s. 46.

[469] Auld, Ch. 10, paras. 119–20, p. 446.   [470] *Ibid.*

day the case is sent to serve its evidence on the defence and the court. (Where the defendant is in custody, it is fifty days.[471])

Scotland In Scotland until very recently there was no equivalent provision for advance disclosure of its case by the prosecution. Instead, in a feature of the Scottish system that is unknown in England and most other countries, the prosecution handed the defence a list of proposed prosecution witnesses. The defence could then arrange for them to be interviewed ('precognosed') and statements taken. (A study of the effect of the introduction of fixed fees for defence lawyers showed a marked decline in precognition and in pre-trial preparation generally![472])

Evidence the prosecution do not intend to use ('unused material')

The rules regarding disclosure to the defence of material the prosecution do not intend to use ('unused material') were formerly a mixture of common law and guidelines laid down by the Attorney General.

Common law 1946–1981

The first judicial pronouncement on the subject merely required the prosecution to supply the defence with the name and address of any witness they knew could give material evidence but whom they did not intend to call as a witness.[473] There was judicial disagreement as to whether this duty extended to the witness statements themselves.[474]

Attorney General's 1981 Guidelines

In December 1981, the Attorney General issued Guidelines for trials on indictment. These stated that all 'unused material' should normally be made available to the defence solicitor 'if it has some bearing on the offence(s) charged and the surrounding circumstances of the case'.

'Unused material' for this purpose was defined to mean (1) all witness statements and documents not included in the committal bundles served on the defence and (2) where edited statements are included in the committal bundle, the unedited version of such statements or documents. There were stated exceptions: when disclosure might lead to improper pressure on the witness, where it was untrue and where it was against the public interest on account of being 'sensitive', for instance, because it dealt with national security, the identity of an informer or the source of surveillance.

---

[471] Crime and Disorder Act 1998 (Service of Prosecution Evidence) Regulations 2005.

[472] C. Tata and F. Stephen, '"Swings and Roundabouts": Do Changes to the Structure of Legal Aid Remuneration Make a Real Difference to Criminal Case Management and Case Outcomes?', *Criminal Law Review*, 2006, pp. 722–41 at 725 and 728–9.

[473] *R v. Bryant and Dickson* (1946) 31 Cr App Rep 146; *R v. Leyland Justices, ex p Hawthorn* [1979] 1 All ER 209.

[474] *Dallison v. Caffery* [1964] 2 All ER 610 at 618 and 622. See also *R v. Hennessey* (1978) 68 Cr App R 419 at 426.

In the case of any doubt, the material ought to be submitted to counsel for advice. A balance should then be struck between the competing values. If, for instance, the material established the accused's innocence or even if it only tended to show him to be innocent, it should either be disclosed in full or at least with any sensitive passages excised. Any doubt should be resolved in favour of disclosure. If the material was too sensitive to show to counsel, it must be sent to the DPP.

Technically, the Guidelines were not law but the courts could treat failure to comply with them as the basis for quashing convictions.[475]

Strictly, the Guidelines only applied to trials on indictment, but in 1987 the Attorney General told the House of Commons that in summary trials the prosecution were under a general duty of being fair, which required them, *inter alia*, to supply to the defence any materially inconsistent statement, written or oral, of any prosecution witness of which the prosecutor became aware at any stage.[476]

Whether the Attorney General's Guidelines were being followed was another matter. A JUSTICE Committee in December 1987 said that it was the experience of the Committee that the spirit of the Attorney General's Guidelines on prosecution disclosure to the defence was frequently ignored and also that the practice of disclosure varied considerably from area to area.[477]

Common law 1989–1995

The law relating to prosecution disclosure of unused material developed rapidly in the years after 1989 with the result that the Attorney General's Guidelines were to a significant extent displaced as being too narrowly defined.

The courts held that unused material that had to be disclosed to the defence included:

- All preparatory notes and memoranda which led to the making of witness statements.[478]
- Police officers' notebooks, observation logs, crime reports, photofits, artists' impressions from all witnesses, notes of oral descriptions and car registration numbers.[479]
- Any material that was relevant even if it was not admissible.[480]

These decisions required the disclosure of whole categories of material leaving it for the defence to see whether there was anything that was both relevant and helpful to its case.

(The issue of sensitive material is dealt with separately below – see p. 297.)

---

[475] See, for instance, *R v. Lawson* (1989) 90 Cr App Rep 107.

[476] House of Commons, *Hansard*, 5 November 1987, col. 713. The Divisional Court held that this view was correct in *R v. Bromley Magistrates' Court, ex p Smith and Wilkins, R v. Wells Street Magistrates' Court, ex p King* [1995] 4 All ER 146.

[477] JUSTICE, *A Public Defender*, 1987, para. 25.

[478] Ruling of Mr Justice Henry in *Saunders* ('Guiness 1'), August 1998.

[479] *Ward* [1993] 2 All ER 577.

[480] *Preston* [1993] 4 All ER 638 at 664. See also *Keane* (1994) 99 Cr App Rep 1.

Runciman Royal Commission

The Runciman Royal Commission was persuaded by evidence, mainly from the police, that the disclosure regime created by the courts resulted in some cases in excessive burdens on the prosecution:

> The defence can require the police and prosecution to comb through large masses of material in the hope either of causing delay or of chancing upon something that will induce the prosecution to drop the case rather than to have to disclose the material concerned . . .
>
> . . . We strongly support the aim of the recent decisions to compel the prosecution to disclose everything that may be relevant to the defence's case, but we accept the evidence that we have received that the decisions have created burdens for the prosecution that go beyond what is reasonable. At present the prosecution can be required to disclose the existence of matters whose potential relevance is speculative in the extreme. Moreover, the sheer bulk of the material involved in many cases makes it wholly impracticable for every one of what may be hundreds of thousands of individual transactions to be disclosed.[481]

The Runciman Royal Commission proposed a new approach consisting of two stages: 'primary disclosure' which basically would be automatic and 'secondary disclosure' if the defence could persuade the court of its relevance. The Commission's view of the scope of primary disclosure was however not narrow. It would cover 'all material relevant to the offence or to the offender or to the surrounding circumstances of the case'.[482]

The Criminal Procedure and Investigations Act 1996 and the Code of Practice

The recommendations of the Runciman Royal Commission were implemented (with some modification) in the Criminal Procedure and Investigations Act 1996 (CPIA). These provisions, together with regulations[483] and the Code of Practice, came into force in April 1997.

There is general agreement that the system did not work well.[484]

---

[481] Runciman, Ch. 6, paras. 42, 43 and 49, p. 95.

[482] Runciman, Ch. 6, para. 51, p. 95.

[483] Crown Court (Criminal Procedure and Investigations Act 1996) (Disclosure) Rules 1997; Magistrates Court (Criminal Procedure and Investigations Act 1996) (Disclosure) Rules 1997; Criminal Procedure and Investigations Act 1996 (Defence Disclosure Time Limits) Regulations 1997.

[484] See in particular J. Plotnikoff and R. Woolfson, *A Fair Balance?: Evaluation of the Operation of Disclosure Law* (Home Office, RDS Occasional Paper No. 76, 2001); Crown Prosecution Service Inspectorate, *The Inspectorate's Report on the Thematic Review of the Disclosure of Unused Material* and H. Quirk, 'The Significance of Culture in Criminal Procedure Reform: Why the Revised Disclosure Scheme Cannot Work', 10 *Evidence and Proof*, 2006, pp. 42–59. The writer's commentary on Lord Justice Auld's Review of the Criminal Courts has a lengthy section dealing with the issue of disclosure and its problems – www.dca.gov.uk/criminal/auldcom/ar/arindex.html. See also M. Redmayne, 'Disclosure and its Discontents', *Criminal Law Review*, 2004, pp. 441–62 and D. Ormerod, 'Improving the Disclosure Regime', 7 *Evidence and Proof*, 2003, pp. 102–29.

Auld on disclosure

Lord Justice Auld in his report in 2001 cited the report of the CPS Inspectorate in its *Thematic Review of the Disclosure of Unused Material* which found 'that the 1996 Act was not working as Parliament intended and that its operation did not command the confidence of criminal practitioners'.[485] It highlighted the failure of police disclosure officers to prepare full and reliable schedules of unused material, undue reliance by the prosecutors on disclosure officers' schedules and assessment of what should be disclosed and the 'awkward split of responsibilities between the police and the CPS in the task of determining what should be disclosed'.[486]

Joyce Plotnikoff and Richard Woolfson in their research study[487] had reached the same conclusions. ('Our findings confirmed the conclusion of the CPS Inspectorate's *Thematic Review* that poor practice in relation to disclosure was widespread'.[488]) They had found that Government objectives for improvement in efficiency had not been achieved, that in the Crown Court the average length of trial had not fallen as hoped and that the scheme was expensive. ('It had been expected that it would be "cost-neutral" for the criminal justice system, but in fact it was so resource intensive that it cost the CPS as much or more than it saved the police and produced no identifiable, significant savings for the courts'.[489]) Auld concluded with this damning assessment of the system:

> To summarise: the main concerns about the disclosure provisions of the 1996 Act are: a lack of common understanding within the CPS and among police forces of the extent of disclosure required, particularly at the primary stage; the conflict between the need for a disclosure officer sufficiently familiar with the case to make a proper evaluation of what is or may be disclosable and one sufficiently independent of the investigation to make objective judgment about it; the consignment of the responsibility to relatively junior officers who are poorly trained for the task; general lack of staffing and training for the task in the police or the CPS for what is an increasingly onerous and sophisticated exercise; in consequence, frequent inadequate and late provision by the prosecution of primary disclosure; failure by defendants and their legal representatives to comply with the Act's requirements for giving the court and the prosecutor adequate and/or timely defence statements and lack of effective means of enforcement of those requirements; seemingly and confusingly different tests for primary and secondary prosecution disclosure; and the whole scheme, whether operated efficiently or otherwise is time-consuming and otherwise expensive for all involved. The outcome for the criminal justice process is frequent failure to exchange adequate disclosure at an early stage to enable both parties to prepare for trial efficiently and in a timely way.[490]

In Auld's view the best way forward was first to require automatic disclosure at the primary stage of some forms of documents (crime reports, incident report

---

[485] Auld, Ch. 10, para. 163, p. 463.   [486] *Ibid.*   [487] Note 484 above.
[488] Auld, Ch. 6, para. 164, p. 463.   [489] *Ibid.*   [490] Auld, Ch. 6, para. 167, p. 464.

books, police officers' notebooks, custody records, draft versions of witness statements where the draft differs from the final version and experts' reports). It could also include certain types of material by reference to their subject matter as distinct from the category of document.

Beyond that he favoured building on and improving the present system of two-stage prosecution disclosure coupled with greater defence disclosure:

- The test for primary and secondary prosecution disclosure should be made the same.
- The duty of recording unused material should remain with the police but with improved training, rigorous 'spot audits' by HM inspectors and non-compliance being treated as a police disciplinary offence.
- Prosecutors should carefully check police schedules against witness statements and unused material.
- Transferring from the police to prosecutors responsibility for identifying disclosable material.[491]

The Criminal Justice Act 2003 and further changes

Further changes were made by the Criminal Justice Act 2003 (CJA 2003), by the 2005 revision of both the Code of Practice and the Attorney General's Guidelines.[492]

The provisions of prosecution and defence disclosure are closely linked though they cover different types of material. The duty of prosecution material to be disclosed under the rules relates to unused material, i.e. the material the prosecution does not intend to use. The duty of the defence to disclose material relates to its case. (For the treatment of the defence disclosure provisions see below at p. 302.) The prosecution's duty to disclose its own evidence in the case was unchanged by the legislation.

Disclosure officer The Code of Practice provides for a disclosure officer, defined as the person responsible for examining material retained by the police during the investigation, for revealing material to the prosecutor and certifying that he has done so and for disclosing material to the defence (para. 2.1).

Police duty to record information The police are under a duty to record and retain information and material generated in the course of an investigation. The Code of Practice deals with the length of time for which material has to be

---

[491] Plotnikoff and Woolfson, n. 484 above at p. 134, recommended to the contrary that primary responsibility remain with the police – a view shared by the writer.
[492] The Attorney General's Guidelines had been reissued in 2000. Their main focus was to tighten up existing procedures and to clarify the responsibilities of police investigators and disclosure officers, prosecutors and defence practitioners. For the most part they restated and emphasised what was already the position. New provisions included the statement (as seen above) that prosecutors must disclose all their evidence in summary cases, that open access must be given to the defence in respect of material seized but not examined by the prosecution and a list of items that would normally be disclosed as a matter of course if relevant to the defence.

retained. (Thus, where a person has been convicted and given a custodial sentence, all relevant material must be retained at least until he has been released from custody (para. 5.9).)

Two schedules Material which may be relevant to an investigation and which the disclosure officer believes will not form part of the prosecution case must be listed on a schedule (para. 6.2). If any of the material is 'sensitive' – defined now as disclosure of which the officer believes 'would give rise to a real risk of serious prejudice to an important public interest' (para. 6.12)[493] – it must be listed on a separate schedule (para. 6.4). Exceptionally, where disclosing the material on the list would be likely to lead to loss of life or directly threaten national security, the existence of the material must be revealed to the prosecutor separately (para. 6.13).

Schedules have to be prepared in respect of all cases triable only on indictment and of cases triable either way that are likely to be tried on indictment and of summary-only cases if the defendant is likely to plead not guilty. If the defendant changes his mind and pleads not guilty at the last moment, the disclosure schedule has to be prepared as soon as is reasonably practicable (para. 6.6).

Both schedules must be given by the disclosure officer to the prosecution lawyers (para. 7.1). The lawyers must also be given copies of material with information given by an accused person explaining the offence, any material casting doubt on the reliability of a confession or the reliability of a prosecution witness and any material which the investigator believes may fall within the test for prosecution disclosure (para. 7.3).

The trouble with the schedules, as research has shown, is that they are frequently incomplete or insufficiently detailed to be useful. In Plotnikoff and Woolfson's study,[494] lawyer prosecutors judged the information on the principal schedule to be poor in the majority of cases and good in only 3 per cent. Moreover, prosecutors generally do not have either the time or the inclination to pursue the matter further by going back to the police for further information. In the result, frequently they are not in a position to make informed decisions about what should and should not be disclosed.

That is so in ordinary cases. The problem is obviously compounded in cases where the material is unusually heavy. The Government's Fraud Review published in July 2006 highlighted the fact that vast masses of material were now held in digital form on computers, mobile phones, Blackberries and personal digital assistants.[495] The Computer Forensic Unit at the Serious Fraud Office

---

[493] In the previous version of the Code sensitive material was defined simply as 'any material which [the disclosure officer] believes it is not in the public interest to disclose'. The new definition is clearly intended to narrow the concept of sensitive material. A dozen examples are given in para. 6.12 – material that would compromise national security, the identity of informants, methods of covert surveillance etc.   [494] Note 484 above at p. 29.

[495] In a ninety-four day fraud trial, 6,000 man hours (250 complete days) had been spent dealing with disclosure and the defence had spent 2,643 hours just reading the disclosed material. (Fraud Review, p. 213, para. 9.45.)

had calculated that the average case it dealt with now had between 5.3 and 6.7 terabytes of digital material to be analysed. (Five terabytes is roughly the equivalent of a pile of paper sixty-two miles high or twelve Mount Everests.[496])

Prosecution disclosure The CPIA, s. 3(1) required the prosecutor to give 'primary disclosure' of any prosecution material 'which in the prosecutor's opinion might undermine' the case for the prosecution against the accused, or alternatively to give the accused a written statement that there was no material of that description. After defence disclosure (see below) had been made, the CPIA required 'secondary disclosure' of any prosecution material not already disclosed which 'might be reasonably expected to assist the accused's defence as disclosed by the defence statement' or give the accused a written statement that there was no such material.[497]

The CJA 2003, s. 32 changed the definition of what has to be disclosed from the subjective test in the CPIA to an objective test – material that 'might reasonably be considered capable of undermining' the prosecution's case or 'of assisting the accused'.

The CJA 2003 also abolished 'primary' and 'secondary' disclosure. Primary disclosure became 'initial disclosure'[498] and secondary disclosure became a 'continuing duty of disclosure' under which the prosecutor must at all times (and especially after the delivery of defence disclosure) keep under review whether there is prosecution material that ought to be disclosed.[499] In 2004 in *R v. H* and *R v. C*[500] the House of Lords said the golden rule was full disclosure of any material held by the prosecution which weakened its case or strengthened that of the defendant.[501]

The timing of disclosure The duty to give initial disclosure arises with a period measured from 'the relevant day'. For cases dealt with in the magistrates' court, the relevant day is the day the defendant pleads not guilty and for cases dealt with at the Crown Court, it is the day the proceedings are sent to the Crown Court.[502] Although a time limit was envisaged by the 1996 Act, none is fixed for

---

[496] Fraud Review, p. 214, para. 9.49.   [497] Section 7(2).   [498] CJA 2003, Sch. 36, para. 21.

[499] CJA 2003, s. 37 inserting a new s. 7A into the CPIA.

[500] [2004] UKHL 3, [2004] 2 AC 134, [2004] 1 All ER 1269. A single judgment was delivered by Lord Bingham.

[501] The House of Lords laid down a checklist for the court to consider in PII applications: (1) what in detail is the material sought? (2) is the material such as may weaken the prosecution case or strengthen that of the defence? If no, disclosure should not be ordered. If yes, full disclosure should be ordered unless (3), (4) or (5) applied; (3) would full disclosure create a real risk of serious prejudice to an important public interest? If no, full disclosure should be ordered; (4) if the answer to (2) and (3) is yes, can the defendant's interests be protected without disclosure or by some other means such as partial disclosure? (5) the order should be the minimum derogation from the golden rule of full disclosure; (6) if limited disclosure under (4) or (5) would make the trial unfair, fuller disclosure must be ordered even if that would mean that the prosecution drops the case; and (7) the matter must be kept under review throughout the case. For commentary see C. Taylor, 'The Courts and Applications for Public Interest Immunity: *R v. H and C*', 8 *Evidence and Proof*, 2004, pp. 179–85; M. Redmayne, 'Disclosure and its Discontents', *Criminal Law Review*, 2004, p. 441 at 454–9.

[502] CPIA 1996, ss. 3(8), 12 and 13(1).

prosecution disclosure other than 'as soon as practicable', but in *R v. DPP, ex p Lee*[503] the Divisional Court laid down the important principle that the prosecutor must always be alive to the need to make advance disclosure of material of which he is aware (either from his knowledge or because his attention has been drawn to it by the defence) and which he as a responsible prosecutor recognises should be disclosed at an early stage.

Under the disclosure rules the defence do not have the advantage of initial prosecution disclosure before deciding whether to plead guilty in the magistrates' court.

Failure to comply If the accused thinks the prosecution have not complied with their obligation to disclose, he can apply to the court for an order requiring such disclosure (s. 8(2)). The court need not make such an order if it does not think such disclosure to be in the public interest (s. 8(5)). This decision must however be kept under continuing review by the court (s. 15(3)).

Prosecution disclosure of sensitive material – public interest immunity (PII)

The doctrine of public interest immunity (PII) enables the prosecution to withhold disclosure of material where, in the courts' view, the public's interest in non-disclosure outweighs the defendant's interest in having access to the material. In a series of decisions it was held that the court, not the prosecution, is the arbiter of what could be withheld from disclosure.[504] The court must carry out a balancing exercise, though where non-disclosure may lead to a miscarriage of justice the court should *always* order disclosure.[505] The prosecution then has a choice between complying or dropping the case.

In 1993, in *Davis, Johnson and Rowe*[506] the Court of Appeal set out three different procedures for dealing with PII claims. In Type 1, the defence is informed of the application and of the type of material involved and can address the court on the matter. In Type 2, the application is heard *ex parte* but the defendant is informed that the application is to be made without notice as to the type of material in issue. In Type 3, the defence is not even notified of the fact of the application.[507] The CPIA in effect codified the common law.[508]

The Runciman Royal Commision said it believed 'that the procedure laid down in *Davis, Johnson and Rowe* for the disclosure of material that may attract public interest immunity strikes a satisfactory balance between the public interest in protecting such material and the legitimate need of the defence in some cases to see it or to be aware of its existence'.[509]

---

[503] (1999) 2 Cr App Rep 304, [1999] 2 All ER 737.

[504] *Ward* (1993) 96 Cr App Rep 1, CA; *Davis, Johnson and Rowe* (1993) 97 Cr App Rep 110, CA; *Keane* (1994) 99 Cr App Rep 1, CA.   [505] *Keane* (1994) 99 Cr App Rep 1, CA.

[506] [1993] 2 All ER 643.

[507] Type 3 applications are very rare – some twenty a year. (Inspectorate's *Thematic Review*, n. 484 above at para. 6.43.)

[508] See the Crown Court (Criminal Procedure and Investigations Act 1996) (Disclosure) Rules 1997, SI 1997/698, reproducing the procedure laid down in *Davis, Rowe and Johnson*.

[509] Runciman, Ch. 6, para. 47, p. 95.

The Strasbourg Court in *Rowe and Davis v. United Kingdom*[510] agreed that in exceptional circumstances evidence could be withheld from the defence but found that on the facts there had been a breach of the ECHR. The general rule that the prosecution should reveal all its evidence to the defence might in some circumstances have to give way to other competing considerations such as national security, protection of witnesses and preserving secrecy of police investigations (para. 61). However, Article 6(1) of the Convention only permitted exceptions that were strictly necessary. The procedure followed at the applicants' trial in a Type 2 PII application whereby the prosecuting authorities decided to withhold material evidence without informing the trial judge did not meet this standard and the Court of Appeal, which had itself considered the material, was not able to remedy the position as it had not seen the witnesses give their evidence and had to rely on transcripts.

By contrast, in *Jasper v. United Kingdom*[511] given by the same court on the same day, the Strasbourg Court held there was no breach of the ECHR as the PII application had been made in proper form to the trial judge. The defence had had an opportunity of making submissions to the court even though it was not informed as to the category of material being sought.[512]

Lord Justice Auld's Report said that there was 'widespread concern in the legal professions about lack of representation of the defendant's interest [in such hearings] and anecdotal and reported instances of resultant unfairness to the defence'.[513] He proposed the introduction of a scheme for instruction in such cases by the court of special independent counsel to represent the interests of the defendant both at trial and on appeal. Special advocates for this situation are now part of the system. He is made privy to the confidential material and can argue on behalf of the defendant though he is not allowed to reveal the content either to the defendant or to his lawyers. The system was approved by the Strasbourg Court in *Edwards and Lewis v. UK* in July 2003[514] and in February 2004 by the House of Lords in *R v. H and C* (above). The concept had been used for the Special Immigration Appeals Tribunal and in terrorism cases and both the Strasbourg Court and the House of Lords said there were exceptional PII cases in which, despite its problematic nature, it could be helpful. (The Court of Appeal in *R v. H and C* said that in Type 3 hearings a special independent counsel should always be appointed.[515])

In July 2003, Sir David Calvert-Smith QC, the then Director of Public Prosecutions, announced new Joint Operational Instructions on prosecution

---

[510] (2000) 30 EHRR 1, [2000] Crim LR 584 and commentary at 585.

[511] (2000) 30 EHRR 1, [2000] Crim LR 586.

[512] See also to the same effect *Fitt v. United Kingdom* (2000) 30 EHRR 1 and 441, [2000] Crim LR 586.   [513] Auld, Ch. 10, para. 193, p. 477.

[514] (2003) 15 BHRC 189. Endorsed without argument by the Grand Chamber on 27 October 2004.

[515] For discussion of the position of the lawyer acting as special advocate see A. Boon and S. Nash, 'Special Advocacy: Political Expediency and Legal Roles in Modern Judicial Systems', *Legal Ethics*, vol. 9, Pt 1, 2006, p. 101.

disclosure including new rules on public interest immunity applications. A PII application should only be made if disclosure would cause real harm to a genuine public interest.[516] The Joint Operational Instructions were replaced by the CPS' *Disclosure Manual*.[517] (See also the Criminal Procedure Rules 2005, Part 25.) The *Manual* states that if the disclosure rule is applied in the robust manner endorsed by the House of Lords in *R v. H and C* (above), applications to the court for PII certificates should be rare. There should only be derogations from the golden rule in exceptional circumstances.[518]

Scientific evidence

The Runciman Royal Commission emphasised the crucial importance of prosecution disclosure to the defence where exhibits are sent to a laboratory for scientific analysis. Sir John May's inquiry into the case of the Maguires[519] and the Court of Appeal's judgment in the *Judith Ward* case[520] had demonstrated the serious risk of a miscarriage of justice if there were not full disclosure of scientific evidence to the defence. 'Forensic scientists are therefore under a categorical obligation to disclose to the police, and the police to pass on to the CPS, all the scientific evidence that may be relevant to the case'.[521] This duty of disclosure, it said, extended to anything that might help the defence:

> Following disclosure, the defence are entitled to access to notebooks and test results and to information about similar evidence discovered in other or related cases, especially where this tends to undermine the identification of the defendant as the offender. We interpret the Court of Appeal judgment in *Ward* as meaning that, if expert witnesses are aware of experiments or tests, even if they have not carried them out personally, which tend to disprove or cast doubt upon the opinions that they are expressing, they are under an obligation to bring the records of them to the attention of the police and prosecution.

The Royal Commission said that it had 'no hesitation in endorsing the main thrust of the Court of Appeal's judgment in *Ward* as regards the disclosure of scientific evidence' and it was pleased to be able to say 'that this is also accepted by the public sector laboratories concerned'.[522] If the defence thought there might be material at the laboratory which threw doubt on the prosecution's test results, 'they should in our view be entitled to have access to the original notes of the experiment in order to test that belief'. It continued: 'we believe that this is in fact the position, since we have been told by defence experts that they now have full access to everyone and everything relevant to the case in question'.[523]

---

[516] 'Getting it Right – Prosecution Disclosure of Unused Material', 153 *New Law Journal*, 4 July 2003, p. 1020.

[517] www.cps.gov.uk – Legal Guidance – Disclosure and Covert Law Enforcement.

[518] CPS, *Disclosure Manual*, Ch. 13, para. 2.

[519] *Interim Report on the Guildford and Woolwich Pub Bombing*, 1990 (HC 556) and *Second Report on the Maguire Case*, 1992 (HC 296).   [520] [1993] 2 All ER 577.

[521] Runciman, p. 154, para. 45.   [522] *Ibid.*, p. 154, para. 47.   [523] *Ibid*, para. 48.

The Royal Commission recommended that when exhibits were taken for analysis by the prosecution, regard should be had to the potential desire of the defence in due course to carry out their own tests on the material. Where practicable, sufficient material should be collected for the purpose and, so far as practicable, the scene of the crime should remain undisturbed. After a suspect had been charged the defence should have an enforceable right to observe any further scientific tests carried out or the right to remove some of the material for their own analysis.[524]

Defence access to scientific or forensic testing

In 1987, a JUSTICE Committee said that although the police theoretically made their forensic science laboratory facilities available to the defence, 'in practice little or no use can be made of them'. The police would not permit re-examination of an exhibit already examined by one of their own scientists. They would allow their own scientists to conduct tests for the defence or a defence scientist to use their laboratories, but they insisted that their own scientists had to be present, which meant that the prosecution were fully apprised of the experiments and the results. This was 'wholly unacceptable' and 'an erosion of the principle that it is for the prosecution to establish their case'.[525]

Generally the defence did not take advantage of the possibility of using police facilities. Indeed if they did, and if evidence favourable to the prosecution emerged, it would be a gross breach of duty by the defence solicitor to the client.

In April 1991, the Forensic Science Service became an Executive Agency of the Home Office as part of the Conservative Government's policy for making public bodies somewhat independent and financially accountable. It started to charge the police and others using its services. (Previously even the defence experts had the use of the facilities free of charge.) The Framework Document provided that the Agency was free to take on work for the defence, but it seems that was developing slowly.[526]

The problem of provision of adequate scientific facilities for the defence was specifically included in the terms of reference of the Runciman Royal Commission. The Commission said that the public sector forensic science laboratories were prepared to work for the defence for its normal charges – provided the same laboratory was not already working on the case for the prosecution. The exception was the Metropolitan Police Forensic Science Laboratory, and it intended to change this policy, but it was rare that the defence were dissatisfied with tests carried out for the prosecution. It was more likely to be a matter of interpretation of the results. Defence scientists were allowed to use the public sector facilities.[527]

---

[524] Runciman, p. 155, para. 52.   [525] JUSTICE, *A Public Defender*, 1987, para. 30.
[526] See R. Stockdale, 'Running with the Hounds', *New Law Journal*, 7 June 1991, p. 772 raising the question of how to provide adequate forensic scientific services to the defence.
[527] Runciman, p. 146, para. 11.

The Royal Commission proposed that 'all the public sector laboratories should look upon themselves as equally available to the defence and the prosecution and we would expect to see considerable development of the provision of services to the defence as time goes by'.[528]

The Royal Commission thought that the defence should have complete freedom to choose between public sector and private sector forensic scientists.[529] It did not think that public funds should be devoted to establishing separate facilities for the defence.

Other issues of prosecution disclosure

Where a prosecution witness is of known bad character, the prosecution is under a duty to inform the defence of the fact.[530] In *Paraskeva*[531] the Court of Appeal quashed a conviction because the prosecution had failed to comply with this duty. The complainant in a charge of robbery and assault had had a conviction for theft. The Appeal Court said that the defence should have been told, since either the prosecution or the defence were lying and the jury should have had this information in making up their minds which it was. Details of the previous convictions of the accused himself must be supplied by the prosecution to the defence.[532]

See also *Edwards*[533] where the Court of Appeal quashed convictions because disciplinary findings against police witnesses had not been made known to the defence or the court. The court held that the defence were entitled to cross-examine police officers not only about disciplinary findings but also about any earlier trial in which their evidence had been rejected by the jury in circumstances suggesting that they were not believed. The Runciman Royal Commission thought this went too far. It recommended that the prosecution should only be required to disclose disciplinary findings against police witnesses in so far as those records were relevant to an allegation by the defence about the conduct of the witness in the present case. The Commission thought that the prosecution should also not be required to disclose cases in which there has been an acquittal following evidence given by an officer where it would seem that his evidence must have been disbelieved by the jury. Since research in the jury room was not permitted there was no way of knowing why the jury had rejected particular evidence.[534]

The prosecution must disclose to the defence copies of any statement or report made by any prison doctor as to the mental capacity of the defendant. Also, the results of any examination carried out by the Home Office Forensic Science Laboratory should be handed over to the defence, but generally the

---

[528] Runciman, p. 149, para. 24.   [529] Runciman, p. 156, para. 55.
[530] *R v. Collister and Warhurst* (1955) 39 Cr App Rep 100.   [531] [1983] Crim LR 186.
[532] *Practice Direction* [1966] 1 WLR 1184.   [533] (1991) 93 Cr App Rep 48.
[534] Runciman, p. 97, para. 56.

prosecution are not under an obligation to disclose material that goes solely to the credibility of defence witnesses.[535]

Disclosure by the defence

The common law position

Traditionally it was a fundamental principle of the common law that the defendant had a right of silence in the police station and that this extended also to the preparatory stages before the trial and to the trial itself. Subject to a small number of recognised exceptions, the defence was not under any obligation to give advance notice of its case, but this has now changed.

Alibi exception

The first exception was created in 1967 by the Criminal Justice Act of that year, s. 11 of which laid down that an alibi defence must be notified to the police in advance of the trial, so that it could be checked.

Philips Royal Commission

The Philips Royal Commission on Criminal Procedure considered whether the alibi exception should be extended to other forms of evidence. It did not think that the defence should generally be required to disclose its case. It thought there was an 'objection of principle' to any formal requirement of general disclosure by the defence because the burden of proof was upon the prosecution (para. 8.20). It considered that it would be impossible to devise effective sanctions against a defendant who failed to comply with the requirement, since it seemed unlikely that in practice courts would be prepared to prevent a defendant from introducing evidence that demonstrated his innocence. (The experience with the alibi defence rule is that courts are normally lax about insisting on compliance by the defence. The sanction is the comment permitted to prosecution and judge on failure to comply.)

The Commission cited research evidence that even police officers thought that new facts introduced at the trial resulted in unjustified acquittals only in about 1 per cent of cases (para. 8.21), but it thought that special defences should be notified to the prosecution in advance. The obvious examples, it suggested, were defences depending on medical or forensic evidence on which the prosecution would wish to consider calling expert testimony.

Expert evidence exception

Section 81 of PACE granted power to make Crown Court rules to require any party to proceedings before the Crown Court to disclose to the other party any expert evidence which he proposes to adduce in the case. In 1987, the new rules

---

[535]   *R v. Brown (Winston)* [1997] 3 All ER 769, HL. For a report of the case, comparison with *R v. Rasheed* (1994) 158 JP 941 and comment see also *New Law Journal*, 8 July 1994, p. 939.

provided for the disclosure, as soon as practicable after committal, of a statement in writing of any finding or opinion of an expert upon which a party intended to rely.[536] The requirement to give advance notice of expert evidence to the prosecution was extended to magistrates' courts in 1997.[537]

Failure can be penalised by the court refusing permission to adduce the expert evidence, but, like alibi notices, it has not been strictly enforced by the courts.

Roskill Committee

The problem of disclosure by the defence was also considered by the Roskill Committee in its report on Fraud Trials (1986).

Unlike Philips, it concluded, subject to one dissent, that the defence should be required to outline its case in writing at the preparatory stage. Failure to do so should be capable of attracting adverse comment from the prosecution and the judge and the jury could be invited to draw adverse inferences (para. 6.82).

It considered, but ultimately rejected, the case for advance disclosure by the defence of the names of its witnesses and for advance notification to the prosecution as to whether the defendant himself intended to give evidence (paras. 6.83–4).

Roskill implemented The Government accepted the majority's recommendation. The Criminal Justice Act 1987 provided that in serious fraud cases notices could be given under s. 2 requiring persons to give information and to produce documents. This power has been used extensively.

The judge can order the prosecution to 'prepare and serve any documents that appear to him to be relevant' and having made such an order and the prosecution having complied with it, the judge can then make an equivalent order for the defence to provide relevant documents (s. 7(3)). Under this provision, the defence can be required to give the court and the prosecution: (1) a statement in writing setting out in general terms the nature of his defence and indicating the principal matters on which he takes issue with the prosecution; (2) notice of any objections he has to the prosecution's case statement; (3) notice of any points of law he intends to take, including any on the admissibility of evidence and (4) notice of the extent to which he agrees with the prosecution as regards documents and other matters and the reason for any disagreements (s. 9(5)).

Section 10 provides that, in the event of any departure from the case disclosed at the preparatory hearing or any failure to comply with the obligation to make advance disclosure, the judge and, with the judge's leave, the other party may make such comment as he thinks appropriate. (In deciding whether to give such leave the judge is required to have regard to the extent of any departure and whether there was any justification for it.) When making an order to the defence

---

[536] Crown Court (Advance Notice of Expert Evidence) Rules 1987, SI 1987/716.
[537] Magistrates' Courts (Advance Notice of Expert Evidence) Rules 1987, SI 1987/705.

to make advance disclosure, the judge must warn the defence of the possibility of such comment (s. 9(7)).[538]

Runciman Royal Commission

The Runciman Royal Commission on Criminal Justice (1993), by a majority of ten to one, recommended that after the prosecution had produced its case, the defendant should be asked to indicate in outline the nature of his defence:

> 59. With one dissentient, we believe that there are powerful reasons for extending the obligations on the defence to provide advance disclosure. If all the parties had in advance an indication of what the defence would be, this would not only encourage earlier and better preparation of cases but might well result in the prosecution being dropped in the light of the defence disclosure, an earlier resolution through a plea of guilty, or the fixing of an earlier trial date. The length of the trial could also be more readily estimated, leading to a better use of the time both of the court and of those involved in the trial; and there would be kept to a minimum those cases where the defendant withholds his or her defence until the last possible moment in the hope of confusing the jury or evading investigation of a fabricated defence.[539]

The majority thought this would not infringe the right of defendants not to incriminate themselves – anymore than this right was infringed by the duty to advance one's defence at trial. Moreover defendants would still be entitled to remain silent throughout.[540] It was true that 'ambush defences' were relatively rare but the existing system encouraged late preparation of cases which was undesirable:

> 68. In most cases disclosure of the defence should be a matter capable of being handled by the defendant's solicitor (in the same way that alibi notices are usually dealt with at present). Standard forms could be drawn up to cover the most common offences, with the solicitor having only to tick one or more of a list of possibilities, such as 'accident', 'self-defence', 'consent', 'no dishonest intent', 'no appropriation', 'abandoned goods', 'claim of right', 'mistaken identification' and so on. There will be complex cases which may require the assistance of counsel in formulating the defence. Where counsel are involved, they should if practicable stay with the case until the end of the trial; where this is impracticable, the barrister who has been involved with the pre-trial work should pass on his or her preparation to the barrister who is to present the case at trial.[541]

The sole dissentient was the writer:

> 1. The most important objection to defence disclosure is that it is contrary to principle for the defendant to be made to respond to the prosecution's case until it has been presented at the trial. The defendant should be required to respond

---

[538] For a report on how the powers under the CJA 1987 were utilised see M. Levi, *The Investigation, Prosecution and Trial of Serious Fraud* (Royal Commission on Criminal Justice, Research Report No. 14, 1993).   [539] Runciman, p. 97, para. 59.

[540] *Ibid*, para. 60, pp. 97–8.   [541] *Ibid*, para. 68, p. 99.

to the case the prosecution makes, not to the case it says it is going to make. They are often significantly different.

2. The fundamental issue at stake is that the burden of proof lies throughout on the prosecution. Defence disclosure is designed to be helpful to the prosecution and, more generally, to the system, but it is not the job of the defendant to be helpful either to the prosecution or to the system. His task, if he chooses to put the prosecution to the proof, is simply to defend himself. Rules requiring advance disclosure of alibis and expert evidence are reasonable exceptions to this general principle, but, in my view, it is wrong to require the defendant to be helpful by giving advance notice of his defence and to penalise him by adverse comment if he fails to do so . . .

There were also practical grounds of objection:

9. Moreover, a general requirement of defence disclosure would involve significant extra delays, costs and inefficiencies. The lay client would have to be seen to take his instructions. Getting the lay client to come into the solicitor's office or going to see him in prison is often troublesome. Counsel would quite frequently be involved both to advise and often actually to settle the defence disclosure. It could hardly be expected that defence lawyers would go out of their way to be helpful to the prosecution. The prosecution would therefore often find it right to ask for 'further and better particulars', with resulting further delays and costs. These extra costs would apply not only to cases that ended as trials but also to those that ended as last minute guilty pleas ('cracked trials').

10. The present much criticised lack of continuity in counsel's involvement in the case would pose even greater problems than in relation to ordinary pre-trial matters. From the defendant's point of view, the last minute appearance of a barrister he has never seen before would be even more upsetting in a regime where pre-trial defence disclosure was a requirement. It is bad enough that the client should so often be faced on the day of the trial with a new barrister. It would be worse if he knew that the new barrister's ability to represent him was restricted by decisions regarding defence disclosure made by another barrister at an earlier stage whether on paper or at a pre-trial hearing . . .

12. In summary, I am against defence disclosure because it is wrong in principle, and because it would cause extra delay, cost and general inefficiency in the system, to little, if any, purpose.[542]

Runciman implemented The Government accepted the majority view. The Criminal Procedure and Investigations Act 1996 (CPIA) provided for a new regime of compulsory disclosure by the accused in response to primary disclosure by the prosecution. Section 5 said that the accused must give a defence statement to the prosecutor:

(6) For the purposes of this section a defence statement[543] is a written statement –
   (a) setting out in general terms the nature of the accused's defence,

---

[542] Runciman Dissent at pp. 221–3.
[543] On the question what use, if any, the prosecution can make of the defence statement see
      J. Sprack, 'Will Defence Disclosure Snap the Golden Thread?', *International Journal of Evidence*

    (b)   indicating the matters on which he takes issue with the prosecution, and

    (c)   setting out, in the case of each such matter, the reason why he takes issue with the prosecution.

In the case of an alibi, the particulars to be provided included the name and address of any such witness, failing which, information as to how to find him (s. 5(7)).

The regulations impose a tight time limit for defence disclosure. The defence statement must be served within fourteen days of the prosecution's service of prosecution material or statement that there is none. The defence can apply for an extension of time.

If the defendant fails to comply with the obligation to give a defence statement or does so late, or sets out inconsistent defences, or at his trial puts forward a defence inconsistent with what appeared in the defence statement, or advances an alibi of which he has not given advance notice, the judge and, with leave of the court, the prosecution 'may make such comment as appears appropriate' (s. 11(3)(a)). Also 'the court or jury may draw such inferences as appear proper in deciding whether the accused is guilty' (s. 11(3)(b)).

The requirement to produce a defence statement only applies to cases in the Crown Court. In cases being tried summarily, the defence have the option of giving a defence statement but need not do so (CPIA, s. 6(2)).[544]

The special case of expert evidence

The Runciman Royal Commission unanimously recommended that if the defence proposed to contest the prosecution's scientific or other expert evidence they should give advance notice of the grounds on which they disputed that evidence – whether or not they intended to call expert testimony of their own.[545] The *Crown Court Study* done for the Royal Commission showed that the defence called an expert in only one-third of the cases in which they contested the prosecution's scientific evidence. In two-thirds of cases, the challenge was purely in the form of cross-examination,[546] but it is very common in that situation for the defence to be advised by an expert even though he is not called at the trial. The rules only require advance disclosure of evidence one intends to adduce at the trial. The defendant does not have to give notice of tests done which support the prosecution theory of the case.

Footnote 543 (*cont.*)

    and Proof, 1998, vol. 2, no. 4, pp. 224–31; S. Thompson, 'Defence Statements – Weighting the Scales or Tipping the Balance on a Submission of No Case?', *Criminal Law Review*, 1998, pp. 802–7; C. Parry and M.I. Tregilgas-Davey, 'Prosecution Use of Defence Statements', *Solicitors' Journal*, 28 May 1999, p. 520.

[544] For the argument that this is an anomaly that should be remedied see V. Smith, 'Defence by Ambush', 168 *Justice of the Peace*, 17 January 2004, pp. 24–31.

[545] Runciman, p. 157, para. 60.

[546] M. Zander and P. Henderson, *Crown Court Study* (Royal Commission on Criminal Justice, Research Study No. 19, 1993) section 3.2.6.

Auld on defence disclosure

In Lord Justice Auld's view, defence disclosure was not working as intended:

> Many defence statements do not comply with the requirements of the 1996 Act. They do not set out in general terms the nature of the defence or the matters on which issue is taken with the prosecution case and why. Often defence statements amount to little more than a denial, accompanying a list of material that the defence wish to see and without explanation for its potential relevance to any issues in the trial. Most judges, Crown Prosecution Service representatives or practitioners who have commented on the matter in the Review and to the Plotnikoff and Woolfson Study[547] have said that the statements, in the form in which they are generally furnished, do little to narrow the issues at, or otherwise assist, preparation for trial.[548]

The fourteen-day time limit for filing the defence statement was tight and sometimes insufficient. Prosecution primary disclosure might be defective or late, defendants for all sorts of reasons might not give their solicitors instructions or do so in time, the solicitors might misunderstand the instructions, or neither might focus sufficiently on the issues. Judges were likely to be very cautious in permitting the jury to draw adverse inferences from a failure to comply with the requirements.[549]

Auld said that he had considered whether to recommend that the defence be under an obligation to identify defence witnesses and the content of their expected evidence but had concluded against it. Many would find it objectionable as going beyond definition of the issues and requiring the defendant to set out an affirmative case.[550] There were too many instances when the prosecution amended the charges late in the day or failed to provide adequate or timely primary disclosure. There could be no question of punishing a defendant by barring an unannounced defence and only rarely of allowing adverse inferences. Often it would be difficult to establish whether the fault for non-compliance lay with the lawyer or the defendant. Financial penalties, whether on the lawyer or the defendant, were equally unworkable.[551]

Although Auld did not recommend changes in the requirements for defence statements, he did propose a variety of ways for making them more effective:[552] to have full and timely prosecution disclosure, to pay defence lawyers a proper and discrete fee for preparatory work, to make defendants in custody more accessible to their lawyers (including provision of video conferencing facilities) and for prosecution lawyers to request particulars of inadequate defence statements, seeking court directions if necessary.

---

[547] J. Plotnikoff and R. Woolfson, *A Fair Balance? Evaluation of the Operation of Disclosure Law* (Home Office, 2002) p. 13. For further details of the research findings see the writer's response to Lord Justice Auld's report – www.dca.gov.uk – Publications – Reports and Reviews – Comments received – Academics – at pp. 50–1.

[548] Auld, Ch. 10, para. 158, p. 461.   [549] *Ibid*, para. 159, p. 461.

[550] *Ibid*, para. 180, p. 470.   [551] *Ibid*, paras. 180–3.

[552] *Ibid*, para. 183. pp. 471–2.

Auld also recommended that there should be professional conduct rules, training, guidance and in the rare cases where it was appropriate, discipline 'to inculcate in criminal defence practitioners and through them their clients, the principle that a defendant's right of silence is not a right to conceal in advance of trial the issues he is going to take. Its purpose is to protect the innocent from wrongly incriminating themselves, not to enable the guilty, by fouling up the criminal process, to make it as procedurally difficult as possible for the prosecution to prove their guilt regardless of cost and disruption to others involved'.[553]

Criminal Justice Act 2003

In 2002, the Government in its White Paper *Justice for All*[554] indicated its intention to make important changes with regard to defence disclosure – most of which were implemented in the Criminal Justice Act 2003 (CJA 2003):

- Widening the matters on which an adverse inference could be drawn to include significant omissions that the defendant could reasonably have been expected to have mentioned in the defence statement. This was included in the CJA 2003.[555]
- Removing the requirement for permission from the judge before commenting on discrepancies between the defence statement and the defence at trial. This was included in the CJA 2003.[556]
- Incentives and strengthened sanctions aimed at getting prosecution counsel to play a more active role in advising on and challenging the adequacy of defence statements.
- Giving the prosecution a right to apply for an early judicial hearing to enable the prosecution to challenge unreasonable defence requests for prosecution documents.
- Enhancing the requirements of the defence statement. This was included in the CJA 2003 (see below).
- Requiring the judge to alert the defence to inadequacies in the defence statement from which adverse inferences may be drawn. This was included in the CJA 2003 and extended to other failings of defence disclosure.[557]
- Requiring the defence to provide details of any unused expert witness reports. This was not implemented as to the actual reports, but the CJA 2003 does requires the defence to give the name and address of any expert consulted whether or not it is intended to call him.[558]

---

[553] *Ibid*, para. 183, p. 472.   [554] Cm. 5563, July 2002.

[555] New CPIA, s. 11(2)(e) and (f) inserted by s. 39 of the CJA 2003.

[556] Under the CPIA 1996, s. 11(3) adverse comment on 'faults in disclosure by the accused' could be made only with the leave of the court. By contrast, the equivalent provision replacing s. 11 inserted by the CPIA, s. 39 requires the leave of the court only where the 'fault' was not giving advance notice of a point of law raised at the trial, giving a witness notice late or calling a witness who was not named in the witness notice.

[557] New CPIA, s. 6E(2) inserted by s. 36 of the CJA 2003.

[558] New CPIA, s. 6D inserted by s. 35 of the CJA 2003.

In the debate on the measure in the Commons, the Home Office Minister said that the purpose was to 'enable the prosecution to approach and consult expert witnesses with a view to obtaining evidence to support the prosecution case'.[559] Could the prosecution call a defence expert as a prosecution witness? The minister said: 'it would be open to them to do so . . . Of course the legal professional privilege rule would prevent the expert from being questioned about any work done for the defence'.[560] The House of Commons Home Affairs Committee in its report on the Bill said that while it accepted the need for the provision it was not convinced that it would work. The Home Secretary, giving evidence to the Committee, had admitted, 'there would be little or no sanction in practice . . . In terms of the actual trial, if [defence solicitors] had deliberately or negligently failed to identify the names of all experts and the trial has taken place then there is not much that can be done about that'.[561]

• Requiring details of defence witnesses. Implemented by a provision in the CJA 2003 that the defence serve on the court and the prosecutor a notice giving the name, address and date of birth of any proposed defence witness together with any information known to the accused which 'might be of material assistance in identifying or finding' the witness. Any changes or further information must be notified by an amended notice.[562] The House of Commons Home Affairs Committee recommended that the Bill be amended so that when the prosecution wish to interview a defence witness, they should be required to notify the defence and offer to interview the witness in the presence of the defence. Also that the interview should be tape recorded.[563] The Government accepted this and dealt with it in a Code of Practice.[564] The Act provides that the code must include, in particular, guidance as to: the information that must be provided to both the interviewee and the accused regarding such an interview, the attendance of the interviewee's solicitor and the accused's solicitor at the interview and the attendance of any other appropriate person having regard to the age and any disability of the interviewee.

The CJA 2003 made other changes regarding defence disclosure by inserting new provisions in the 1996 Act:

• The accused is required to provide a more detailed defence statement. Thus where previously the Act required disclosure 'in general terms' of the nature of the defence, there is now an obligation to set out 'the nature of the accused's defence, including any particular defences on which he intends to rely' and details of any point of law he wishes to take.[565]

---

[559] HC Official Report Standing Committee B (Criminal Justice Bill) 9 January 2003, cols. 254–5.
[560] *Ibid*, col. 255.   [561] HC 83, 2nd Report 2002–3, paras. 77–8.
[562] New CPIA, s. 6C inserted by s. 34 of the CJA 2003.   [563] HC 83, 2002–3, para. 71.
[564] New CPIA, s. 21A inserted by s. 40 of the CJA 2003.
[565] New CPIA, s. 6A(1) inserted by s. 33(2) of the CJA 2003.

- The Home Secretary is given the power to prescribe in regulations further details that have to be contained in defence statements.[566] In the Committee stage in the Commons, the Government accepted an amendment to require that any such change would require the approval of an affirmative resolution passed by both Houses of Parliament.
- The defence must update the defence statement, as required by regulations.[567]
- Either on his own motion or on the application of any party, the judge may direct that the jury be given a copy of the defence statement (edited to remove any inadmissible evidence) if that would help the jury 'to understand the case or to resolve any issue in the case'.[568]
- Failure to comply with any of the rules regarding defence disclosure can lead to comment by the court or 'any other party' and adverse inferences being drawn.[569]

For consideration of the position of defence lawyers with regard to disclosure see E. Cape, 'Rebalancing the Criminal Justice Process: Ethical Challenges for Criminal Defence Lawyers', 9 *Legal Ethics*, 2006, pp. 56–79.

Defence disclosure in the magistrates' courts

As noted above, in the magistrates' court, the giving of a defence statement is not required. It is optional (CPIA, s. 6).[570] However, in the absence of a defence statement, the defence cannot make a request for specific disclosure under CPIA, s. 8 nor can the court make an order for disclosure of prosecution unused material.

The 2006 Disclosure Protocol

In February 2006, a remarkably ambitious Crown Court *Disclosure Protocol*[571] was issued by HM Courts Service[572] with a covering notice stating that it came from the judiciary.[573] Its aim was nothing less than a total transformation of the culture with regard to disclosure of unused material.[574] The Protocol was

---

[566] New CPIA, s. 6A(4) inserted by s. 33(2) of the CJA 2003.

[567] New CPIA, s. 6B inserted by s. 33(3) of the CJA 2003.

[568] New CPIA, s. 6E(4) and (5) inserted by s. 36 of the CJA 2003.

[569] New CPIA, s. 11(5) inserted by s. 39 of the CJA 2003.

[570] For an analysis of the problem of trial by ambush in the magistrates' court and a plea that this rule be changed see V. Smith, 'Defence by Ambush', 168 *Justice of the Peace*, 17 January 2004, pp. 24–31.

[571] Three months later, an equivalent Protocol was issued for magistrates' courts: *Protocol for the Provision of Advance Information, Prosecution Evidence and Disclosure of Unused Material in the Magistrates' Court*, May 2006 (www.judiciary.gov.uk/docs/judgments-guidance/protocols/mags_courts_ per cent20disclosure.pdf).

[572] *Disclosure: A Protocol for the Control and Management of Unused Material in the Crown Court* (www.hmcourts-service.gov.uk – news).

[573] The Protocol appears on the Courts Service Website under the Court of Appeal's logo. It seems that the prime mover was Lord Justice Judge, President of the Queen's Bench Division.

[574] In an 'Outline Note' issued at the same time it was stated that the Protocol had been drafted by a team, led by two High Court judges, which included representatives from the Crown

drafted in strong, uncompromising language. Its tone was severe. The message, bluntly stated, was that everyone concerned with the problem of disclosure of unused material must do a great deal better – and that the judges would henceforth enforce the rules.[575]

> There needs to be a sea-change in the approach of both judges and the parties to all aspects of the handling of the material which the prosecution do not intend to use in support of their case. For too long, a wide range of serious misunderstandings has existed, both as to the exact ambit of the unused material to which the defence is entitled and the role to be played by the judge in ensuring that the law is properly applied. All too frequently applications by the parties and decisions by the judges in this area have been made based either on misconceptions as to the true nature of the law or a general laxity of approach (however well-intentioned). This failure properly to apply the binding provisions as regards disclosure has proved extremely and unnecessarily costly and has obstructed justice. It is, therefore, essential that disclosure obligations are properly discharged – by both the prosecution and the defence – in all criminal proceedings and the court's careful oversight of this process is an important safeguard against the possibility of miscarriages of justice (para. 1).
>
> For the statutory scheme to work properly, investigators and disclosure officers responsible for the gathering, inspection, retention and recording of relevant unused prosecution material must perform their tasks thoroughly, scrupulously and fairly (para. 13).
>
> It is crucial that the police (and indeed all investigative bodies) implement appropriate training regimes and appoint competent disclosure officers, who have sufficient knowledge of the issues in the case. Each item listed on the schedule should contain sufficient detail to enable the prosecutor to decide whether or not the material falls to be disclosed (para. 14).
>
> The scheduling of the relevant material must be completed expeditiously (para. 15).
>
> Investigators, disclosure officers and prosecutors must promptly and properly discharge their responsibilities under the Act and statutory Code, in order to ensure that justice is not delayed, denied or frustrated (para. 16).
>
> Extensions of time should not be given lightly or as a matter of course. If extensions are sought, then an appropriately detailed explanation must be given. For the avoidance of doubt, it is not sufficient merely for the CPS (or other prosecutor) to say that the papers have been delivered late by the police (or other investigator); the court will need to know why they have been delivered late. Likewise, where the accused has been dilatory in serving a defence statement (where the

---

Prosecution Service, the Serious Fraud Office and the Revenue and Customs Prosecutions Office. (There was no mention of representatives of the legal profession.) The Protocol took effect on 20 February 2006, the date of its issue.

[575] The magistrates' court Protocol had the same message. It concluded: 'the public rightly expects that the delays and failures that have been present in the past where there has been scant adherence to sound disclosure principles will be eradicated . . . It is now the duty of judges and magistrates actively to manage disclosure issues in every case'.

prosecution has complied with the duty to make primary or initial disclosure of unused material or has purported to do so), it is not sufficient for the defence to say that insufficient instructions have been taken for service of this within the fourteen day time limit; the court will need to know why sufficient instructions have not been taken and what arrangements have been made for the taking of such instructions (para. 28).

Judges should not allow the prosecution to abdicate their statutory responsibility for reviewing the unused material by the expedient of allowing the defence to inspect (or providing the defence with copies of) everything on the schedules of non-sensitive unused prosecution material, irrespective of whether that material, or all of that material, satisfies the relevant test for disclosure. Handing the defence the 'keys to the warehouse' has been the cause of many gross abuses in the past, resulting in huge sums being run up by the defence without any proportionate benefit to the course of justice. These abuses must end (paras. 30 and 31).

In the past, the prosecution and the court have too often been faced with a defence case statement that is little more than an assertion that the defendant is not guilty. Defence statements must comply with the requisite formalities. There must be a complete change in the culture. The defence must serve the defence case statement by the due date. Judges should then examine the defence case statement with care to ensure that it complies with the formalities required by the CPIA. If no defence case statement – or no sufficient case statement – has been served by the plea and case management hearing (PCMH), the judge should make a full investigation of the reasons for this failure to comply with the mandatory obligation of the accused under s. 5(5) of the CPIA (paras. 34, 37 and 38).

If there is no – or no sufficient – defence statement by the date of the PCMH or any pre-trial hearing where the matter falls to be considered, the judge must consider whether the defence should be warned, pursuant to s. 6E(2) of the CPIA,[576] that an adverse inference may be drawn at the trial. In the usual case where s. 6E(2) applies and there is no justification for the deficiency, such a warning should be given.

Where there are failings by either the defence or the prosecution, judges should, in exercising appropriate oversight of disclosure, pose searching questions to the parties and, having done this and explored the reasons for default, give clear directions to ensure that such failings are addressed and remedied well in advance of the trial date (para. 41).

The prospects regarding disclosure

There is no doubting the energy behind this Protocol but, in the writer's view, the prospects for its success must be counted as very poor.[577]

---

[576] Failure to provide a defence statement, an updated defence statement and details of intended witnesses.

[577] This section draws heavily on research on disclosure by H. Quirk of the School of Law, Manchester University, published as 'The Significance of Culture in Criminal Procedure

The problem goes beyond a lack of resources, though resources are clearly part of the problem since neither the police nor prosecutors have – or are ever likely to have – the personnel necessary to do what is required of them. To identify the material that needs to be considered for disclosure requires time and effort. It requires training and it requires judgment. The Protocol states that 'investigators and disclosure officers responsible for the gathering, inspection, retention and recording of relevant unused prosecution material must perform their tasks thoroughly, scrupulously and fairly' and that each item on the schedules drawn up 'should contain sufficient detail to enable the prosecutor to decide whether or not the material falls to be disclosed' (para. 14). On the basis of her research, Hannah Quirk (n. 577) says that the pivotal role played by the police in the disclosure regime is one for which police officers are ill-equipped by purpose, training and occupational culture. The responsibility 'is onerous, time-consuming and unpopular'. Every case requires the completion of at least five forms which requires judgments about the legal significance of material, the consideration of multiple possible defences and potentially complex legal argument. 'Police officers are neither qualified nor trained for such a role'. The police officers she interviewed appeared to have little understanding of what was required of them. It is also relevant that the officer in charge of the case is usually a quite junior person. (In the *Crown Court Study*, in 81 per cent of over a thousand cases, the officer in charge of the case was a constable.[578])

Unused material is by definition not relevant to the prosecution's case. Some officers were prepared to acknowledge to Quirk that they were reluctant to give the defence potentially exculpatory evidence. 'Such attitudes militate against the police being able or willing to perform the challenging duty imposed by the CPIA of not merely reviewing evidence objectively, but of considering it from the perspective of the defence'. The *Thematic Review of the Disclosure of Unused Material* by the CPS Inspectorate (2000) found that over one-third (38.5 per cent) of non-sensitive schedules and one-fifth (21.5 per cent) of sensitive schedules were defective. A quarter of the barristers and solicitors Quirk interviewed and one-third of the Crown Prosecutors expressed concern that important material was omitted from the schedules.

In doing their job with regard to disclosure, prosecutors are dependent on what they get from the police. Quirk says: 'it is rare for prosecutors to examine material that the disclosure officer has not identified as potentially undermining' the prosecution case. 'In most cases, prosecutors said they would examine

Reform: Why the Revised Disclosure Scheme cannot Work', *Evidence and Proof*, 2006, pp. 42–59. The research was based on interviews in 1998–9 with twenty-six legal representatives, twenty-six Crown prosecutors, seventeen police officers, sixteen barristers, six justices' clerks, five lay magistrates, two stipendiary magistrates and two judges. In addition 100 questionnaires were completed by police officers. (Quirk, p. 44, n. 2.)

578 M. Zander and P. Henderson, *Crown Court Study* (Royal Commission on Criminal Justice, Research Study No. 19, 1993) section 7.5.1.

the schedules rather than the actual documents listed, unless something alerts them to a potential problem'. Some would make basic checks. 'Others prefer not to create work for themselves . . . as to do so would make their workload unmanageable'. Much of the work in the prosecutors' offices is now done by civilian workers, but even CPS lawyers do not generally have defence or Crown Court experience to draw on.

Prosecuting counsel tended to be more ready to make disclosure to the defence than CPS lawyers but their effectiveness was dependent on the often limited amount of time they had to consider the brief. They were rarely asked to advise formally on the disclosure of unused material. Moreover, the graduated fees scheme which covers most cases does not provide remuneration for prosecuting or defence barristers' time reading unused material.

So far as concerns defence disclosure, the hope that the more detailed defence statements required under the CJA 2003 would be returned completed as required (and within a strict fourteen-day time limit) seems equally unrealistic. It is true that under the CJA 2003 both the prosecution and co-defendants now have the right to comment on any inadaquacies without leave of the court, but it is difficult to imagine that such adverse comment – described in the Protocol as 'the ultimate sanction' – will have much impact on juries. Defence advocates should have little difficulty in finding plausible explanations for failure to comply with the disclosure rules – laying the blame on the lawyers or others rather than the defendant. The threat of adverse inferences is therefore unlikely to make a noticeable dent on the problem of defence laggardness with regard to disclosure rules.

In short, there can be little expectation that the Protocol will change the behaviour with regard to disclosure of police officers, prosecutors, prosecuting and defence barristers or defendants.

There must even be serious doubts as to whether the judges will be prepared to take it on. In the past they have shown little inclination to do so. Where there are failings by either the defence or the prosecution, the Protocol says that judges should 'pose searching questions to the parties, and having done this and explored the reasons for default, give clear directions to ensure that such failings are addressed and remedied well in advance of the trial date'.

However, 'clear directions' from judges that disclosure failings should be addressed does not mean that they will be addressed. The Government's Fraud Review published in July 2006 concluded that 'judges have few effective sanctions available for them to tackle non-compliance with the spirit of the new effective trial management culture'.[579] It thought that this was an area 'that could usefully be looked at further'. It is not obvious, however, what could be achieved by 'looking further'.

The Fraud Review thought that one possible reform would be a requirement of even fuller defence disclosure:

---

[579] Fraud Review, p. 222, para. 9.76.

> The time may now be right to move towards a full 'civil' degree of mutual disclosure between prosecution and defence in fraud and other complex criminal trials. The prosecution are now bound to provide pleadings in the form of a case outline, lists of admissions and issues and they must select relevant unused material to disclose. For the court, the picture can only be complete when the defence is also obliged to provide more than an 'outline' of its case.[580]

It also canvassed the idea that in high volume cases such as serious fraud the prosecution's duty to provide *initial* disclosure of unused material might be postponed until it had received the defence statement. Alternatively, the prosecution could be allowed to seek a judicial ruling that some unused material did not have to be looked at unless the defence could persuade the judge otherwise.[581]

The Fraud Review proposed that in 2008 a working group consisting of judges, practitioners and officials should be set up to consider what, if any, changes were needed with regard to disclosure.[582]

10. The allocation of cases between higher and lower criminal trial courts

History

For hundreds of years there were three criminal courts: assize courts, quarter sessions courts and magistrates' courts. The judges began to go out on assize to hear criminal cases from the early part of the twelfth century. In 1361 a statute provided that justices of the peace were required to keep the peace and to arrest and punish offenders. The following year a further statute required them to meet four times a year – from which the origin of quarter sessions courts is derived. In times of crisis such as the Wars of the Roses in the fifteenth century and the Civil War in the seventeenth century, when it was not possible to assemble the justices at quarter sessions, they started to sit to hear cases out of sessions without a jury. At first this was done without authority, but by the end of the sixteenth century powers of summary jurisdiction were conferred on these meetings, which came to be called petty sessions.

Until the middle of the nineteenth century there were only two categories of offence: those triable on indictment at either assizes or quarter sessions and those triable only summarily by magistrates. From 1847 onwards, however, the legislature also gradually gave magistrates power to deal with various categories of indictable offence.

In 1847 magistrates' powers of sentence were three months' imprisonment or a fine of £3. The modern maximum became six months' imprisonment or a fine

---

[580] Fraud Review at pp. 209–10.   [581] *Ibid.* at p. 220, paras. 9.67–8.
[582] *Ibid.* at p. 321, recommendation 56.

of £5,000. The Criminal Justice Act 1982, Part III, established a system of grading of penalties which had five scale levels. Under the Criminal Justice Act 1991, the actual figures were altered: Level 5 up to £5,000, Level 4 to £2,500, Level 3 to £1,000, Level 2 to £500 and Level 1 to £200.

Origins of the *right* to trial by jury

The commonly held belief that the right of a defendant to choose jury trial goes back to Magna Carta is mistaken. Until the middle of the nineteenth century the normal mode of trial in criminal cases was trial on indictment by judge and jury. Only a small number of offences could be dealt with in the magistrates' court. The development of the magistrates' courts as the court where most criminal cases are handled only started in the mid-nineteenth century. The first statute to give the defendant the right to choose the mode of trial was the Administration of Criminal Justice Act 1855 which gave magistrates jurisdiction to try simple larceny cases involving sums of under five shillings, but only if the defendant consented.[583] In the Summary Jurisdiction Act 1879 the defendant was given the right to claim trial by jury for all offences carrying a maximum sentence of more than three months.

Today, the right to have jury trial exists in relation to all 'either-way' offences. They make up the majority of all cases sent to trial in Crown Courts.

The debate over allocation 1975–2002

The allocation of cases between the higher and the lower criminal court has been actively on the political agenda for over a quarter of a century. From the perspective of Government it has been fuelled mainly by a wish to reduce the cost of criminal proceedings by having more cases handled by the less expensive proceedings in the magistrates' courts.[584]

James Committee (1975)

In 1975 the James Committee[585] recommended the transfer of substantial categories of work to the lower court. It proposed that there should be three categories of case – those so serious that they should be triable only on indictment, those that were not sufficiently serious to justify the elaborate procedures and expense of trial on indictment and an intermediate category

---

[583] In 1847 an Act provided for summary trial for larceny if the defendant was under fourteen, the justices thought this appropriate and the child's parents consented.

[584] In 1993 the Runciman Royal Commission on Criminal Justice stated that the Home Office estimated that the average cost of a contested case in the Crown Court was some £13,500 as against £1,500 in the magistrates' court and the cost of a guilty plea case was £2,500 as against £500 in the magistrates' court – Runciman, p. 5, para. 18.

[585] *The Distribution of Criminal Business between the Crown Court and Magistrates' Courts*, 1975, Cmnd. 6323.

of offences triable either way. The defendant's right to elect for trial by jury should be retained. It was only used in about a tenth of the cases in which it could be exercised, but it was widely regarded as important both by defendants and by those who represented them. If the defendant opted for trial summarily, the magistrates should, however, have the right to send the case for trial at the higher level – having first heard representations from the prosecution. Those proposals were implemented in the Criminal Law Act 1977.

The Committee proposed, further, that certain offences previously triable either summarily or on indictment should become summary-only offences. This should apply, for instance, to all drink-driving offences and to theft of amounts under £20 or criminal damage where the value of the damage did not exceed £100. The Government accepted these recommendations and they were included in the Bill. The Committee's recommendations for making motoring and other offences triable only summarily were implemented in the 1977 Act but, in a foretaste of many battles to come, the proposals to make small theft and small criminal damage cases triable only summarily provoked massive opposition and the Government eventually dropped the proposal from the Bill.

In 1980 criminal damage cases involving amounts under £200 became triable only summarily. The process of transferring cases to the summary-only category continued. In the Criminal Justice Act 1988, criminal damage cases became summary-only if they involved sums of under £2,000 and driving while disqualified, taking a motor vehicle without authority and common assault and battery were all reduced to this category. The £2,000 limit for summary-only criminal damage cases was raised to £5,000 by the Criminal Justice and Public Order Act 1994.

1986 consultation paper

In 1986 a Home Office consultation paper again raised for consideration the controversial question of whether small theft cases should be transferred to the summary-only category.[586] The proposal canvassed in the consultation paper was that there should be a statutory presumption that indictable offences should be tried summarily but trial on indictment would be available 'where special circumstances made the offence one of exceptional gravity'.[587] It would be for the magistrates to decide this question. There might also be a case for allowing a person with no prior conviction for dishonesty to elect for trial on indictment for an offence of that character. The proposal again ran into considerable opposition and in the end the Government decided not to pursue it.[588]

---

[586] *The Distribution of Business between the Crown Court and Magistrates' Courts*, Home Office, 1986, para. 21.   [587] *Ibid*, para. 27.
[588] See House of Lords, *Hansard*, 19 November 1987, col. 309.

1990 Practice Note

In 1990 Lord Taylor, the Lord Chief Justice, issued a Practice Note (offences triable either way: mode of trial)[589] to assist magistrates in making the mode of trial decision. The court, it said, should never make its decision on grounds of convenience or expedition. Also, the accused's prior record was irrelevant. 'In general, except where otherwise stated, either-way offences should be tried summarily unless the court considers that the particular case has one of the features set out in the following pages [relating to named offences] and that its sentencing powers are insufficient'. This was intended to increase the proportion of cases dealt with summarily, but it did not have much effect.

Runciman Royal Commission (1993)

The Runciman Royal Commission recommended a radical change by proposing that the defendant's right to demand trial by jury in either-way offences be abolished. Instead, he should have a right only to ask for Crown Court trial. If the prosecution agreed, that would be sufficient. If the prosecution disagreed, the matter would be decided by the magistrates after hearing representations from both sides. The magistrates' decision should be guided by statutory indications as to what factors should be taken into account. These should include the gravity of the offence, the defendant's prior record, if any, the complexity of the case and the effect of conviction and the likely sentence on the defendant.[590]

The Commission gave various reasons:

- With regard to indictable-only and summary-only offences the decision as to where the case should be tried was made by the legislature. With regard to either-way offences it would be more rational that the decision be made by the court than by the defendant.
- Many defendants chose Crown Court trial because the acquittal rate was higher than in the magistrates' courts. The defendant should no more have the right to choose the court that gave him a better chance of an acquittal than to choose a lenient judge.
- The great majority of those who asked for Crown Court trial in either-way offences in fact eventually pleaded guilty.[591]
- Last minute guilty pleas in the Crown Court (known as 'cracked trials') clogged up the system, caused extra costs in the preparation of cases that then

[589] [1990] 3 All ER 979.   [590] Runciman, pp. 85–9.

[591] In one study, of the convicted defendants who elected for Crown Court trial, 70 per cent pleaded guilty to all charges and another 14 per cent pleaded guilty to some charges. (C. Hedderman and D. Moxon, *Magistrates' Court or Crown Court? Mode of Trial Decisions* (Home Office Research Study No. 125, 1992).) In another study, 74 per cent of those who elected pleaded guilty to all charges. (D. Riley and J. Vennard, *Triable-either-way Cases: Crown Court or Magistrates' Court?* (Home Office Research Study No. 98, 1988).)

were wasted, resulted in witnesses being brought needlessly to court and added to the numbers in prison.

- According to Home Office research:[592]
  - half of those who elected for trial by Crown Court did so in the mistaken belief that if convicted the sentence would be lighter. In fact, judges were three times as likely to impose immediate custody and in like cases Crown Court sentences were on average two and a half times as long;
  - one-third of the defendants who elected Crown Court trial said they would have preferred to have been dealt with at a magistrates' court;
  - in over 60 per cent of cases in which the magistrates declined jurisdiction, the Crown Court imposed a sentence that would have been within the power of the magistrates' to impose.
- The objection that justice in the magistrates' courts was inferior to that in the Crown Court was not a reason to preserve the defendant's right to insist on jury trial. Magistrates handled over 90 per cent of all criminal cases and 'should be trusted to handle cases fairly'.

This was the most controversial of the 352 recommendations made by the Runciman Royal Commission. Critics of the proposal included the Bar, the Law Society and the greatly respected Lord Chief Justice, Lord Taylor.[593]

1995 consultation paper

In July 1995 the Government published a consultation paper *Mode of Trial* which canvassed three options. One was the recommendation made by the Runciman Royal Commission. The second was statutory reclassification of either-way offences to summary-only. (Thus, for instance, reclassification to summary-only status of thefts of under £100 could divert an estimated 9,000 cases from the Crown Court each year.) The third option was a new procedural device of requiring defendants to enter a plea before the mode of trial decision. Home Office research had found that about two-thirds of defendants committed by magistrates reported that they were ready to plead guilty at the first opportunity available to them. This suggested that, if the defendant in such cases could enter a plea at the magistrates' court, some 25,000 defendants dealt with at the Crown Court might have been willing to plead guilty at the magistrates' courts and be sentenced there or have their case transferred to the Crown Court for sentence only.

Criminal Procedure and Investigations Act 1996, s. 49(1)

The CPIA adopted a modified version of the plea before venue option, but rather than the defendant being required to enter a plea before the mode

---

[592] Hedderman and Moxon, n. 591 above.

[593] His objection was principally that the Commission's recommendation would lead to 'two-tier' justice, i.e. jury trial for those with no record and the most reputation to lose, but magistrates' trial for recidivists.

of trial decision, he is invited to indicate his plea. (On this see pp. 337–40 below.)

Narey Report (1997)

Martin Narey, a senior Home Office official, was asked to make proposals to reduce delays.[594] Narey, like Runciman, thought the defendant's right to demand jury trial should be abolished – but in his view the question should always be decided by the court and not be open to agreement between prosecution and defence.

Mode of Trial Bill No. 1 (1999)

In November 1999 the Government introduced the Criminal Justice (Mode of Trial) Bill providing that the magistrates should determine mode of trial after hearing representations from both sides and in light of a number of considerations: the nature and seriousness of the case, their powers of punishment, the effect of conviction and sentence on the defendant's livelihood and reputation and any other relevant circumstances. Whether the defendant had previous convictions could be mentioned as a factor concerning the effect of a conviction on reputation. The Bill adopted Narey's view that the mode of trial issue should always be determined by the court with no power for the parties to determine the matter by agreement.

The Bill ran into great opposition – especially the mention of a defendant's livelihood and reputation as relevant factors which it was argued could create 'two-tier justice' with magistrates discriminating against the poor or unemployed, in favour of defendants with higher economic or social status. The Bill which started in the Lords reached the Committee stage there but, after a series of defeats, it was withdrawn.[595]

Mode of Trial Bill No. 2 (2000)

In 2000 the Government tried again with its Criminal Justice (Mode of Trial) (No. 2) Bill – this time in the House of Commons, but when it reached the Lords it was again defeated and was again withdrawn.[596]

The crucial change between the No. 1 Bill and the No. 2 Bill was the removal of all but one of the factors the court was permitted to take into account when making the allocation decision. These were now reduced to 'the nature of the case' and 'the circumstances of the offence (but not of the accused)'. It no longer referred to appreciation of the relevant circumstances – such as previous convictions and reputation – mentioned in the first Bill.[597]

---

[594] *Review of Delay in the Criminal Justice System*, 1997.
[595] The Committee stage on 20 January 2000 resulted in a defeat for the Government by 222 to 126 on the right of election.
[596] It did not get beyond its Second Reading in the Lords on 28 September 2000.
[597] For an explanation of the reasoning behind the Bill by the Home Secretary see Jack Straw's article in 150 *New Law Journal*, 12 May 2000, p. 670. For the writer's critique of the change

Auld Report (2001)

Lord Justice Auld agreed with Runciman and Narey that the decision as to mode of trial in either-way cases should be made by the court.[598]

July 2002, the Government gives up

No doubt wishing to avoid further political difficulties and defeats in the House of Lords, the Government announced in its White Paper *Justice for All* that it had decided to abandon the whole idea of removing the defendant's right to elect jury trial.

Instead, it proposed two measures to address the problem of too many cases going to the Crown Court. However, at the time of writing, the prospects for these two initiatives were uncertain. Both had been due to be introduced in November 2006, but in both cases implementation was postponed with no indication as to when, or indeed whether, they would be activated.[599] The first was to increase the sentencing power of magistrates from six months to twelve months[600] in order to encourage magistrates to retain more cases. (In 2003–4, almost three-quarters of the either-way cases that went to the Crown Court did so because the magistrates declined jurisdiction.) The second was drastically to reduce the numbers of defendants being sent to the Crown Court for sentence only by abolishing the power unless the defendant is in the category of dangerous offenders.[601]

If and when these new provisions are activated, it is likely that they would result in a significant increase in the prison population. Figures in the Auld Report showed that 55 per cent of the 43,000 persons convicted of either-way offences after being committed for trial and nearly 60 per cent of the 20,000 committed for sentence, received sentences in the Crown Court that were within the powers of magistrates.[602] If the magistrates had the power to give terms of imprisonment of up to twelve months, many of these would presumably receive longer sentences than they got in the Crown Court.

For details of an empirical study indicating that magistrates do not want to take more serious cases see S. Cammiss, '"I Will in a Moment Give You the Full History": Mode of Trial, Prosecutorial Control and Partial Accounts', *Criminal Law Review*, 2006, pp. 38–51.

---

made in the No. 2 Bill see M. Zander, 'Why Jack Straw's Jury Reform has Lost the Plot', 150 *New Law Journal*, 10 March 2000, p. 366.   [598] Auld, p. 200.

[599] The postponement also affected the provisions in Sch. 3 of the Criminal Justice Act 2003 for allocation of cases (40 pages long). For the advice of the Sentencing Advisory Panel to the Sentencing Guidelines Council regarding these provisions see www.sentencing-guidelines. gov.uk – Advice – Allocation (February 2006).

[600] Criminal Justice Act 2003, ss. 154(1), 155 and 282.

[601] Powers of Criminal Courts (Sentencing) Act 2000, s. 3A inserted by the Criminal Justice Act 2003, Sch. 3, para. 23. The power to commit for sentence dangerous young offenders was activated by SI 2006/1835.   [602] Auld, Appendix IV, the second table on p. 678.

11. The guilty plea

The guilty plea plays a critical role in the criminal process since the great majority of defendants do plead guilty. In the Crown Court the proportion is currently around 60 per cent.[603] In the magistrates' courts the proportion is higher.[604] Even in categories of more serious offences, most plead guilty. (In 1983 in a sample of 3,000 magistrates' court cases in five offence categories – shoplifting, assaulting a police officer, possession of cannabis, criminal damage and social security fraud – as many as 83 per cent of the defendants pleaded guilty.[605])

Why do defendants plead guilty?

It seems likely that the main reason why accused persons plead guilty is that they *are* guilty, they know they are guilty, they believe that the police know it and can prove it. Frequently they have made tape recorded admissions or have actually signed a statement admitting the facts alleged against them in the police station.[606] They cannot see any advantage in pleading not guilty whereas there are distinct advantages in pleading guilty – these include getting the whole thing over more quickly, sparing friends or relatives the ordeal of giving evidence and getting a lesser sentence (p. 000 below).

The innocent who plead guilty

Unfortunately even innocent persons sometimes plead guilty.[607] As was noted above (p. 159), it is now recognised that people make false confessions out of some form of psychological condition, but there are innocent people who

---

[603] In both 2003 and 2004 it was 58 per cent. In 2005 it was 60 per cent – see *Judicial Statistics*, Table 6.8. The rate varies from region to region. In 2005 the variance was from a high of 68 per cent in the North East to a low of 49 per cent in London.

[604] The National Audit Office in February 2006 broke down the figures as follows: 61 per cent pleaded guilty, 15 per cent were found guilty in their absence and 5 per cent were found guilty after a trial. In 13 per cent the CPS discontinued the case. Only 2 per cent were acquitted and in 1 per cent of cases due to be committed to the Crown Court the magistrates discharged the cases for lack of evidence. In 4 per cent the case could not be completed because the defendant absconded. (Crown Prosecution Service, *Effective use of magistrates' courts hearings*, National Audit Office, February 2006, HC 798, Session 2005–6, p. 10.)

[605] *Report of a Survey of the Grant of Legal Aid in Magistrates' Courts* (Lord Chancellor's Department, 1983) p. 5.

[606] A study of a large sample of cases tried in the Crown Court in Birmingham and London before tape recording in the police station showed that 88 per cent of those who made statements confessing to the charges pleaded guilty in Birmingham and two-thirds in London. (J. Baldwin and M. McConville, *Confessions in Crown Court Trials*, Royal Commission on Criminal Procedure, Research Study No. 5, 1980, p. 14.)

[607] For consideration of the ethical problems for lawyers in representing clients who claim to be innocent but propose to plead guilty see L. Bridges, 'The Ethics of Representation on Guilty Pleas', *Legal Ethics*, vol. 9, Pt 1, 2006, p. 80. For how the Bar Code of Conduct addresses the problem see Bar Council, *Written Standards for the Conduct of Professional Work*, paras. 11.5.1–11.5.3 – www.barcouncil.org.uk – Code of Conduct.

plead guilty for a variety of other reasons. Clive Davies, a barrister, conducted interviews with 418 men charged with burglary. Of these, eight said that although they were not guilty they intended to plead guilty to the charges. A further twenty-one either said that they were not guilty or said they intended to plead not guilty, but subsequently pleaded guilty.[608] Davies concentrated his focus on the eight who said they would plead guilty from the outset. In one case, after four hours in the police station, the defendant said he agreed to plead guilty to breaking into a shop with intent to steal after being falsely accused by police officers. His reasons – no one would believe him and a guilty plea would entail loss of earnings for only two days compared with many days over weeks or months for a not guilty plea. Another said he agreed to plead guilty to being on enclosed premises with intent to steal a motorcycle even though he did not know how to ride one. He had gone there merely to urinate. His reasons – advice to plead guilty from his solicitor, no one would believe him and to get it over with. (Davies persuaded him to plead not guilty and he was acquitted.) On the basis of his study Davies calculated that some thousands of persons each year plead guilty to charges of which they are innocent.

In a study based on interviews with women in Holloway prison it was found that a significant number pleaded guilty to offences they claimed not to have committed. Of 527 women who had been tried at magistrates' courts, there were fifty-six such cases. The reasons they gave were similar to those mentioned by Davies – police advice or pressure, to save time and avoid remands, fear that pleading not guilty would lead to harsher penalties or the feeling that there was no point when the police evidence would inevitably be preferred.[609]

In a later study by Baldwin and McConville of last-minute change of plea cases tried at the Birmingham Crown Court, 'over half of the sample made some claim to be innocent, and often very vehemently, either of the whole of the indictment to which they pleaded guilty or of individual counts within it'.[610] No fewer than seventy of the 121 defendants interviewed (58 per cent) claimed to be innocent. Some of these claims according to the researchers were somewhat limp, others were scarcely believable and seemed far-fetched to the interviewer. Others were based on a misunderstanding of the law, but there were some whose stories could not be so lightly dismissed. The reasons given for pleading guilty were variations on a few themes: 'the feeling of hopelessness at attempting to rebut the evidence of police officers and the severity of sentence they anticipated if they failed to do so; the weariness caused by the case dragging on for months on end and the consequent anxiety and social disruption caused by frequent remands (especially if in custody); the attractiveness of the bargain held out to them or perhaps merely the negative pressure exerted by counsel' (p. 65).

---

[608] C. Davies, 'The Innocent who Plead Guilty', *Law Guardian*, March 1970, pp. 9 and 11.
[609] S. Dell, *Silent in Court*, Occasional Papers in Social Administration No. 42 (Bell, 1971) p. 30.
[610] *Negotiated Justice* (Martin Robertson, 1977) p. 61.

The role of the lawyers

A factor in the decision to plead guilty in some cases in Baldwin and McConville's sample was the advice of counsel. Some defendants said that their barristers had made it clear that they had no real prospect of an acquittal (p. 70). The independent assessors who examined the cases concluded that in 79 per cent of these cases the likelihood was that the defendant would be convicted, but in 21 per cent they thought there was some chance of an acquittal and in some instances that the chances of an acquittal were good (p. 74).[611]

One of the main contentions of this Baldwin and McConville study was that some guilty pleas are induced by *improper pressure* by the barrister. This suggestion produced a furious denial from the Bar, but a later piece of analysis of the same data by the same two authors revealed the significant fact that the proportion of guilty pleas varied dramatically from one barrister to another.[612] Some apparently like a fight more than others and some may be more inclined to exert pressure on the client to plead guilty. No doubt the barrister honestly believes this to be in the best interests of his client but, because of his psychological 'set', he may take insufficient notice of the client's protestations of innocence.

The converse situation is where counsel may have to consider whether to withdraw from a case rather than to continue to represent a client who is pleading guilty. For an exploration of that situation see L. Bridges, 'The Ethics of Representation on Guilty Pleas', 9 *Legal Ethics*, 2006, pp. 80–100.

Guilty plea rates vary as between different circuits. Solicitor Ole Hansen reported on an informal inquiry into the reasons behind these variations. The circuit administrator in Leeds said that the abnormally high guilty plea rate in his (North Eastern) circuit reflected the robustness of the bench and the legal profession 'and a good dollop of northern common sense',[613] but, Hansen suggested, what seemed like robustness to a circuit administrator might look rather different from the defendant's perspective. A Leeds solicitor told him that 'the local bar was not prepared to fight enough cases'. One of the reasons that he used London counsel a lot was that they were more ready to fight – and they usually won their cases. (The London not guilty plea rate is consistently the highest in the country. The North Eastern circuit consistently has the

---

[611] The *Crown Court Study* conducted for the Runciman Royal Commission on Criminal Justice appeared at first to be a fourth study with evidence of innocent persons pleading guilty. In a pre-publication lecture about the early results of the study, the writer suggested that the study included fifty-three such cases. (M. Zander, 'The Royal Commission's Crown Court Study', 142 *New Law Journal*, 11 December 1992.) Further analysis of the cases showed, however, that very few, if any, were examples of this phenomenon. (M. Zander, 'The "Innocent" who Plead Guilty', 143 *New Law Journal*, 22 January 1993, p. 85 and the Royal Commission's Report, p. 11, para. 43.)

[612] 127 *New Law Journal*, 27 October 1977, p. 1040. See also M. McConville et al, *Standing Accused*, 1994, pp. 257–60.   [613] 136 *New Law Journal*, 27 June 1986, p. 601.

highest guilty plea rate in the country.) Moreover the problem was not confined to the Bar. 'Many solicitors had a similar attitude. They did not believe their client's defences were valid and therefore did not investigate cases fully – preferring instead to maximise their fee income from magistrates' court advocacy. The end result was a client under pressure to plead guilty in the Crown Court'.[614]

Another explanation for the high guilty plea rate, Hansen suggested, was that the judge, the defending and the prosecuting barristers all frequently came from the same chambers, which made defence counsel 'anxious not to appear to "waste" the courts' time'.

Other factors in guilty pleas

Also, Hansen suggested, in the provinces, if a barrister had a number of guilty plea cases in a session he could get a higher level of remuneration than if he only had the one not guilty plea case. A study published in 2006 showed that the introduction of fixed fees had statistically affected the rate of guilty pleas. Lawyers interviewed for the study denied that they themselves had allowed economic considerations to affect their pleading practices but they thought that *other* lawyers had been affected.[615]

Some guilty pleas result from skilful handling of the suspect by the police.[616]

Sometimes a guilty plea occurs despite the fact that the prosecution do not have enough evidence to prove the case.[617] In the *Crown Court Study* prosecution barristers in guilty plea cases were asked: 'if the defendant had pleaded not guilty but the prosecution had gone forward, do you think he/she would have stood a fair chance of an acquittal?' In 9 per cent the response was 'yes, the defendant would have had a fair chance of an acquittal'.[618]

The case for barristers to advise the client to plead not guilty was strongly argued by P. Tague in his article 'Tactical Reasons for Recommending Trials Rather than Guilty Pleas in Crown Court'.[619] A trial was not as risky

---

[614] For confirmation see the disturbing account of the attitude of defence solicitors toward their clients in M. McConville et al, *Standing Accused* – p. 362 below.

[615] C. Tata and F. Stephen, '"Swings and Roundabouts": Do Changes to the Structure of Legal Aid Remuneration Make a Real Difference to Criminal Case Management and Case Outcomes?', *Criminal Law Review*, 2006, pp. 722–41 at 735. See equally the uncomfortable research results in P.W. Tague, 'Barristers' Selfish Incentives in Counselling Defendants over the Choice of Plea', *Criminal Law Review*, 2007, pp. 3–23.

[616] See B. Smythe, 'Police Investigation and the Rules of Evidence', 117 *Solicitors' Journal*, 5 October 1973, p. 718 written by a former police officer. See further M. McConville, A. Sanders and R. Leng, *The Case for the Prosecution* (Routledge, 1991) pp. 60–5.

[617] See J. Baldwin and M. McConville, *Negotiated Justice* (Martin Robertson, 1977) p. 74; S. Moody and J. Tombs, *Prosecution in the Public Interest* (Scottish Academic Press, 1982) p. 307; M. McConville, A. Sanders and R. Leng, *The Case for the Prosecution* (Routledge, 1991) p. 159.

[618] M. Zander and P. Henderson, *Crown Court Study* (Royal Commission on Criminal Justice, Research Study No. 19, 1993) section 6.5.5.

[619] *Criminal Law Review*, 2006, pp. 23–37. Peter Tague, Professor of Law at Georgetown Unversity, has written over many years about criminal justice issues in the US and the UK.

nor a guilty plea as advantageous, as was often believed. The main advantages he suggests are the statistical likelihood of an acquittal, the fact that the sentence after a guilty plea may not in fact be significantly less and that after a not guilty plea there is the possibility of a successful appeal. (The article should be compulsory reading for barristers and solicitors who defend in criminal cases.)

The sentence discount

A very powerful incentive to plead guilty is the fact that a person who pleads guilty is entitled to expect a significantly lower sentence than if he is convicted after pleading not guilty. It is not known when this was first established but it has been part of the English system for decades. Originally the sentence discount for a guilty plea was recognised in statements made by the Court of Appeal,[620] but, as will be seen, it is now proclaimed both in legislation and in official guidelines issued to the courts.

In the early judicial statements the discount was said to be a response to the defendant's remorse. This was a fiction since there was no inquiry as to whether the defendant was in fact remorseful. (The discount for a guilty plea is now treated as separate from the question whether the defendant deserves extra credit for remorse or other mitigating factors (see p. 332 below).) In reality the discount is, and always was, given in recognition of the fact that a guilty plea saves the expense and the trouble of a trial as well as saving witnesses the ordeal of testifying.[621] The benefit to the prosecution is that there is a conviction. The benefit for the defendant is the lower sentence. Whether the victim of the crime believes that the sentence discount gives him or her a benefit must be regarded as doubtful.

The idea of the sentence discount has very widespread support.[622] However, the support is not universal. Professor Andrew Ashworth in particular argues that the sentence discount is against the spirit of four fundamental rights and

---

[620] In *Turner* [1970] 2 QB 321, Lord Chief Justice Parker said that counsel for the defence was entitled to advise his client ('if need be in strong terms') that a guilty plea 'showing an element of remorse is a mitigating factor which may well enable the court to give a lesser sentence than would otherwise be the case'. In *Cain* [1976] Crim LR 464 the Court of Appeal stressed that defendants should appreciate that, in general, a plea of guilty attracts a lesser sentence and that this was 'a glimpse of the obvious'. Lord Widgery said: 'Everybody knows that it is so and there is no doubt about it. Any accused person who does not know about it should know about it. The sooner he knows the better'.

[621] The *Guideline on Reduction in Sentence for Guilty Plea*, issued by the Sentencing Guidelines Council in December 2004 – see p. 000 below – states: 'A reduction in sentence is appropriate because a guilty plea avoids the need for a trial (thus enabling other cases to be disposed of more expeditiously), shortens the gap between charge and sentence, saves considerable cost, and in the case of an early plea, saves victims and witnesses from the concern about having to give evidence' (para. 2.1).

[622] The writer, for instance, does not recall any submission amongst the hundreds made to the Runciman Royal Commission on Criminal Justice that was critical of the sentence discount.

freedoms recognised by the ECHR – the presumption of innocence, the privilege against self-incrimination, the right to be treated fairly and without discrimination, and the right to a fair and public hearing.[623]

Although almost all the literature and case law on the sentence discount relates to the Crown Court, the concept also applies in the magistrates' court.[624] The first mention of it in the Magistrates' Association's Sentencing Guidelines appeared in 1989. A study published in 1990 found that magistrates did not regard a guilty plea as a significant matter in mitigation of sentence,[625] but the 1993 official Guidelines stated unequivocally: 'the guideline sentences represent a broad consensus of view and are based on a first-time offender pleading *not guilty*. A timely *guilty* plea may be regarded as a mitigating factor for which a sentence discount of approximately one-third might be given'.[626]

The judge's involvement in plea discussions

The courts have tried over the years to arrive at an acceptable approach to the problem of communication regarding the plea between the defendant and his lawyers, on the one hand, and the prosecution lawyers and the judge, on the other. It is common for there to be discussion between prosecution and defence to see whether there is a basis for the defendant to plead guilty. These discussions are generally referred to as plea (or charge) bargaining.

Plea bargaining in the United States is different as the prosecutor there is permitted to suggest an actual sentence to the court. This, so far at least, is not permitted in England. It follows that the prosecution cannot do a 'deal' by promising to ask for a particular sentence in return for a guilty plea. (See p. 335 below, however, for the recommendation of the Fraud Review.)

Normally the judge accepts what emerges from the discussions between the two sides, but it is open to the judge to reject any 'deal' struck between the lawyers. In the 'Yorkshire Ripper' case in 1981 the prosecution and defence agreed that Peter Sutcliffe would plead guilty to manslaughter on the grounds of diminished responsibility. The judge refused to accept the plea. There was a long trial, at the end of which the jury found the accused guilty of murder and rejected the diminished responsibility defence.

---

[623] See for instance A. Ashworth and M. Redmayne, *The Criminal Process* (3rd edn, OUP, 2005) pp. 285–96. See also M. McConville, 'Plea Bargaining: Ethics and Politics', 25 *Journal of Law and Society*, 1998, pp. 562–87 and P. Darbyshire, 'The Mischief of Plea Bargaining and Sentencing Rewards', *Criminal Law Review*, 2000, pp. 895–910. (As well as arguing the case, Darbyshire cites the recent literature). For the ethical dilemmas of the defence lawyer see M. Blake and A. Ashworth, 'Ethics and Criminal Defence Lawyer', 7 *Legal Ethics*, 2004, pp. 168–89.

[624] For an empirical study of the operation of the sentence discount in magistrates' courts see R. Henham, 'Reconciling Process and Policy: Sentence Discounts in the Magistrates' Courts', *Criminal Law Review*, 2000, pp. 436–51. The study confirmed that the discount was in regular (if erratic) use.

[625] R.J. Henham, *Sentencing Principles and Magistrates' Sentencing Behaviour* (Avebury, 1990).

[626] Emphasis in the original.

Sometimes the judge becomes directly involved in the discussions. This has dangers. The *locus classicus* of advice to counsel on the practice of discussing these issues with the judge was the Court of Appeal's 1970 judgment in *R v. Turner*.[627] The defendant there changed his plea to guilty after advice from his counsel following a conversation between counsel and the judge. Counsel advised that in his opinion a non-custodial sentence would be imposed if the defendant changed his plea, whereas if he persisted with the plea of not guilty, there was a real possibility of a sentence of imprisonment being passed. Repeated statements were made to him that the ultimate choice of plea was his. Although he did not receive a custodial sentence he nevertheless appealed against his own plea.

The Court of Appeal reluctantly allowed the appeal and quashed the conviction not on the ground that counsel had done anything wrong but because the defendant might have gained the impression that counsel's advice was based on what the judge had said. The court took the opportunity of making some general observations:

> Counsel can advise his client, if need be in strong terms, that a plea of guilty, showing an element of remorse, is a mitigating factor which may well enable the court to give a lesser sentence than would otherwise be the case. Counsel should always emphasise that the client should not plead guilty unless he has committed the act charged.
>
> Any discussion between counsel and the judge must be in the presence of counsel for both prosecution and defence.
>
> Counsel may wish to discuss with the judge whether it would be proper for the prosecution to accept a plea to a lesser offence.
>
> Subject to one exception, the judge should never indicate the sentence which he is minded to impose. A statement that on a plea of guilty he would impose one sentence but that on a conviction following a plea of not guilty he would impose a severer sentence is one which should never be made. This could be taken to be undue pressure on the accused, thus depriving him of that complete freedom of choice which is essential.
>
> What on occasion does appear to happen however is that a judge will tell counsel that, having read the depositions and the antecedents, he can safely say that on a plea of guilty he will, for instance, make a probation order, something which may be helpful to counsel in advising the accused. The judge in such a case is no doubt careful not to mention what he would do if the accused were convicted following a plea of not guilty. Even so, the accused may well get the impression that the judge is intimating that in that event a severer sentence, maybe a custodial sentence, would result, so that again he may feel under pressure. This accordingly must also not be done.
>
> The only exception to the rule is that it is permissible for a judge to say that whether the accused pleads guilty or not guilty, the sentence will or will not take a particular form, e.g. a probation order or a fine, or a custodial sentence.

---

[627] [1970] 2 QB 321, CA.

There were many further decisions regarding the issue.[628] The chief principle that could be distilled from these cases was that the judge should not engage in over-precise indications, let alone bargaining, as to what he intended with regard to sentence.

The fundamental problem with this case law was that the Court of Appeal wanted to have it both ways. On the one hand, it wanted defendants to appreciate that if they pleaded guilty they would get a lesser sentence. On the other hand, it did not want judges to provide defendants with concrete information as to how great the discount would be.

The courts gave two reasons for refusing to provide a defendant with this information. One was that it would create undue pressure to plead guilty. This is unconvincing. The pressure is created by the mere fact of the sentence discount itself. Quantifying the discount can hardly increase the pressure. Indeed, it might reduce the pressure by making it clear that the defendant's fears about the penalty for pleading not guilty are exaggerated. The second reason given was that it was unseemly for the court to be in any sense bargaining or haggling with the defendant. As was said in *Cain*: 'what was being condemned was a more precise offer because the judge was then inviting the defendant to bargain with him'.

Making the discount explicit

Is it better for the judge to give a general indication of the kind of sentence he has in mind which is conveyed to the accused without too detailed an account or should the accused be told more precisely what his options are?

Both practitioners and judges overwhelmingly favour explicit indications. In the *Crown Court Study* the judges and barristers in the sample cases were asked: 'Do you think that *Turner* should be reformed to permit full and realistic discussion between counsel and the judge about plea and especially sentence?' 86 per cent of prosecution barristers, 88 per cent of defence barristers and 67 per cent of judges answered this question 'yes'.[629]

As will be seen, this view has now prevailed. *Turner* has been set aside.

The origin of this major shift of approach was a submission in 1992 to the Runciman Royal Commision from a committee of the Bar Council chaired by Robert Seabrook QC recommending that unofficial plea bargaining should be replaced with a formal system with graduated sentence discounts depending on the stage at which the guilty plea was entered. (A guilty plea at the committal stage should receive a minimum of 30 per cent discount, while those who waited longer would get less – a minimum of 10 per cent was suggested for a plea made between the first Crown Court listing and arraignment.)

---

[628] See for instance *Cain* [1976] Crim LR 464; *Llewellyn* (1978) 67 Cr App Rep 149; *Bird* [1978] Crim LR 237; *Atkinson* [1978] Crim LR 238; *Davis* [1979] Crim LR 167; *Smith* [1990] Crim LR 354; *Pitman* [1991] 1 All ER 468.

[629] M. Zander and P. Henderson, *Crown Court Study* (Royal Commission on Criminal Justice, Research Study No. 19, 1993) section 4.13.1.

The Runciman Royal Commission adopted the recommendation of the Seabrook Committee. Its report said of the sentence discount: 'provided that the defendant is in fact guilty and has received competent legal advice about his or her position, there can be no serious objection to a system of inducements designed to encourage him or her so to plead'.[630] It thought that the system of sentence discounts should remain but that it should be made more effective, in particular by promotion of earlier guilty pleas so as to reduce the very high proportion of last minute guilty pleas (known as 'cracked trials').

The Commission recommended a system of formalised plea bargaining which it called 'sentence canvass'. It could only be initiated by the defence asking the judge at a hearing in chambers what sentence he would impose on a guilty plea. Prosecution and defence would present the case to the judge who, if he felt able and willing, would give an indication as to sentence. If the defendant accepted that sentence, the case would be adjourned into open court and the parties would go through it all again in public. If the defendant did not accept it, he would be free to contest the case in the normal way. The sentencer at a trial would not be bound by the indication given at the sentence canvass.[631]

The proposal was not well received. In particular, the highly influential figure of the Lord Chief Justice, Lord Taylor, made it clear that he strongly opposed it. At the time it seemed unlikely that any version of this recommendation would be implemented.

The Commission also recommended that the earlier the plea, the greater the discount. This was implemented in the Criminal Justice and Public Order Act 1994. This was the first statutory recognition of the sentence discount. Section 48(1) provided that when determining what sentence to pass on an offender who has pleaded guilty the court shall take into account (1) the stage in the proceedings for the offence at which the offender indicated his intention to plead guilty; and (2) the circumstances in which this indication was given. Section 48(2) stated that if the court had used subsection (1) it should state the fact.[632]

In 2000, the Fraud Advisory Panel made proposals to the Lord Chancellor which included a sentence canvass for fraud cases very similar to that proposed

---

[630] Runciman, p. 110, para. 42.   [631] *Ibid.*, pp. 113–14, paras. 50–5.

[632] A study of the impact of s. 48 based on 310 guilty plea cases in six Crown Court centres showed that it was working very imperfectly. In almost half the cases in the sample the judge did not comply with the requirement of saying that he had given a discount for the guilty plea. Of those who did say it, only a third went on to give any explanation of the basis on which they had reached their decision. Under 10 per cent of the whole sample gave a full explanation. Surprisingly, a third of the sentencers told the researchers they regarded a guilty plea 'not particularly important' or 'not important at all' and half said they attached no importance (35 per cent) or no particular importance (15 per cent) to the stage when the guilty plea was entered. There were considerable differences in the way the section was treated in different courts as well as differences in the discounts given for offences. (R. Henham, 'Bargain Justice or Justice Denied? Sentence Discounts and the Criminal Process', 62 *Modern Law Review*, 1999, pp. 515–38. The article also covers the case law and recent literature on the subject.)

by the Runciman Commission.[633] In 2001, Lord Justice Auld in his report on the criminal justice system made a similar proposal, save that he would go further still in allowing the judge to state not only the maximum sentence he would give on a guilty plea, but also the sentence he would give if the defendant was convicted after a not guilty plea.[634]

In July 2002, the Government's White Paper *Justice for All*[635]stated that the Government accepted the basic idea of the sentence canvass. ('We therefore intend to introduce a clearer tariff of sentence discount, backed up by arrangements whereby defendants could seek advance indication of the sentence they would get if they pleaded guilty' (para. 4.42).) The procedure would have to be initiated formally by the defendant in court sitting in private in the presence of the prosecution. The proceedings would be recorded, but, agreeing with Runciman rather than Auld, the court's indication of sentence would not include what it might be after a trial (para. 4.43). The system would not apply to summary-only proceedings but it would apply to either-way cases. The law would be changed to provide that when making their decision magistrates would be informed about the defendant's prior convictions. A trial conducted by magistrates after an advance indication would be handled by a different bench (para. 4.44).

The Criminal Justice Act 2003, Sch. 3 dealt with this issue as it affected magistrates' courts. It included a provision that the magistrates should be informed of the defendant's prior convictions when deciding whether an either-way case is suitable for summary trial.[636] If they reach that view, the defendant 'may then request an indication ("an indication of sentence") of whether a custodial sentence or non-custodial sentence would be more likely to be imposed if he were to be tried summarily for the offence and to plead guilty'.[637] So the indication of sentence would only go to the question of custody or not. The court may, but it need not, give such an indication.[638] If the defendant opts for trial in the Crown Court, the judge there would not have his hands tied by the indication of sentence given by the magistrates.[639] It was expected that this provision allowing the defendant to ask for an indication of sentence would be implemented in November 2006. However, during the summer the Government indicated that implementation would be delayed. There was no information as to whether this would be a short or long delay.

There was nothing in the Act regarding a 'clearer tariff of sentence discount' but that came forward in guidance published by the Sentencing Guidelines

---

[633] 150 *New Law Journal*, 17 March 2000, pp. 398 and 399.   [634] Auld, p. 443.

[635] Cm. 5563.   [636] New MCA 1980, s. 19(2)(a) inserted by Sch. 3, para. 5 of the 2003 Act.

[637] New MCA 1980, s. 20(3) inserted by Sch. 3, para. 6 of the 2003 Act. For consideration of the 'indication of sentence' see the Sentencing Advisory Panel's advice to the Sentencing Guidelines Council, February 2006, paras. 33–47 and recommendation 18.

[638] New MCA 1980, s. 20(4) inserted by Sch. 3, para. 6 of the 2003 Act.

[639] New MCA 1980, s. 20A(3) inserted by Sch. 3, para. 6 of the 2003 Act.

Council[640] in December 2004 on the 'Reduction in Sentence for a Guilty Plea'.[641] It introduced a sliding scale for the discount of one-third reducing to 10 per cent.[642]

A full discount of one-third was only to be given where the guilty plea was entered at the first reasonable opportunity. A defendant who delayed his plea until he was committed for trial might only get a discount of 30 per cent because he could have given the indication at plea before venue in the magistrates' court. The discount was to be reduced to a maximum of one-quarter where a trial date had been set and to a maximum of one-tenth for a guilty plea entered at the door of the court or after the trial had started.

Whether the courts will pay much attention to this sliding scale is questionable. Research[643] suggests they may not. Quite apart from anything else, a judge has a good deal of leeway in arriving at what he thinks is the appropriate sentence by pitching the starting point higher or lower before applying the Guideline discount.

The Guidelines (para 2.3) state that the issue of remorse – or any other mitigating factor, such as admissions to the police in interview – should be treated as a separate matter before calculating the reduction for the guilty plea.

A special section of the Guidelines deals with its application to sentences for murder. Where a full life tariff is imposed, there is no room for any discount. In other cases, the discount is half[644] of that applied to other offences with a maximum discount of five years.

Section 172 of the Criminal Justice Act 2003 states that in sentencing an offender the court 'must … have regard to any guidelines which are relevant to the offender's case'.

In May 2006 the Sentencing Advisory Panel, at the request of the Sentencing Guidelines Council, issued a consultation paper inviting views as to whether the existing Guidelines on the sentence discount should be revised.[645] The consultation exercise was the result of public uproar over the case of Alan Webster, a paedophile convicted of the horrifying rape of a three-year old girl. In calculating the minimum time that he would serve, the judge said that although the evidence against him was overwhelming, he was entitled to the full one-third discount for an early guilty plea. The Attorney General appealed unsuccessfully. The Court of Appeal held that in light of the existing Guidelines the judge had been correct.[646]

In light of the consultation and the Advice received from the Advisory Panel, the Sentencing Guidelines Council issued new draft Guidelines in January 2007.

---

[640] The Council, chaired by the Lord Chief Justice, was established by the Criminal Justice Act 2003, s. 167. The Council is advised by the Sentencing Advisory Panel.

[641] See www.sentencing-guidelines.gov.uk.

[642] Until recently there was no equivalent in Scotland but that has changed – *Du Plooy* [2003] SCCR 640; *McGowan, O'Donnell* [2005] SCCR 497 and *Rennie v. Frame* [2005] SCCR 608.

[643] See n. 658, p 337 below.

[644] This is because in murder cases the judge sets the minimum term and the question of parole does not arise until that term has been served, whereas with determinate sentences the offender can be released on licence half way through his sentence.

[645] For discussion see Firth, n. 647 below.

[646] *A-G's Reference (No 14 and 15 of 2006) French and Webster* [2006] EWCA Crim 1335.

The questions posed in the consultation and the answers given by the Sentencing Council were:

- Does a maximum reduction of one-third properly balance the interests of justice and the encouragement of guilty pleas? [Yes]
- Should there be an upper limit on the amount of the reduction? [Yes]
- Is a 10 per cent discount for pleas at the door of the court sufficient in all cases? [Yes]
- Does the phrase 'first reasonable opportunity' for entering a guilty plea require clarification? In particular does it mean at the police interview or when the case first comes before a court? [It will depend on the facts of the case]
- To what extent, if any, should the fact that the prosecution case is overwhelming influence the level of reduction?

In regard to the last question, the Sentencing Guidelines Council had originally considered adopting the approach taken in previous cases by the Court of Appeal[647] – namely, that the maximum discount should not be given where the evidence was overwhelming so that the defendant had no real alternative but to plead guilty.[648] But it changed its mind.[649] The issued Guideline (para. 5.2), under the heading 'Where an offender is caught red-handed', said there was no reason why credit should be withheld or reduced on these grounds alone.[650]

However the draft Guideline issued in January 2007 in light of the consultation exercise said:'Whilst there is a presumption in favour of the full reduction being given where a plea has been indicated at the first reasonable opportunity, the fact that the prosecution case is overwhelming without relying on admissions from the defendant may be a reason justifying departure from the guideline' – reducing the discount to 20 per cent. (paras 5.3, 5.4)).

R v. Goodyear

As noted, the 2003 Act confined advance sentence indication to magistrates' courts. The Government took the view that the new system could be applied in the Crown Court without legislation. That duly happened in April 2005 when the Court of Appeal gave judgment in *Goodyear*[651] which effectively overruled its 1970 decision in *Turner*. To mark its importance there were five instead of the usual three judges. The decision was given by the Lord Chief Justice.

The court said: 'In essence we accept the recommendation of the report of the [Runciman] Royal Commission' (at [54]). It ruled that it would now be

---

[647] See for instance *Greenland* [2002] EWCA Crim 1748.

[648] The draft Guideline had said that the credit was 'likely to be less for someone caught red-handed'.

[649] Probably in light of the view expressed by the House of Commons Home Affairs Committee that a variable discount 'might be a disincentive to pleading guilty' – see P. Firth, 'Special Offer – One Third Off', 156 *New Law Journal*, 11 August 2006, p. 1279.

[650] Applied in *Oosthuizen* [2005] EWCA Crim 1978.

[651] [2005] EWCA Crim 888, [2005] 3 All ER 117, [2005] Crim LR 659.

permissible for the defendant to give his counsel instructions (which should be in writing) to ask the judge for a prior indication of the maximum sentence he would give on a guilty plea. Provided the question was initiated by the defendant, knowledge of the sentence would not amount to improper pressure. It simply substituted the defendant's reliance on his counsel's assessment of the likely sentence with the more accurate indication provided by the judge himself. It was to be distinguished from an unsolicited indication directed at him by the judge and conveyed to him by his counsel. The judge should not give an advance indication of sentence unless asked to do so by the defendant – though the judge was not prohibited from reminding counsel in open court in the presence of the defendant of his right to seek an advance indication of sentence. In giving such an indication, he should not go further and indicate what the sentence might be after a trial as the comparison would create the risk of improper pressure to plead guilty. Nor should the judge get involved in a plea bargain by indicating what the different sentence would be if the defendant pleaded guilty to different charges. ('Thus for example he should refuse to give an indication based on the possibility that the defendant might plead guilty to s. 18, alternatively s. 20, alternatively s. 47' (at [68]).) *Turner* remained good law only in permitting the judge to indicate that the sentence would be the same whatever the plea – though that would be unusual given the guidance as to the credit to be given for a guilty plea.

The court said that the defence advocate was responsible for ensuring that the defendant appreciated that he should not plead guilty unless he was guilty. An indication should not be sought unless prosecution and defence are agreed on an acceptable plea and on the factual basis to the plea. The agreed basis should be reduced into writing before an indication is sought. The court said it anticipated that a sentence indication would be sought at the plea and case management hearing (as to which see p. 349 below). This was usually the first opportunity for the defendant to plead guilty and the moment when the maximum discount for a guilty plea was available to the defendant, but it could be requested at a later stage – even at the trial itself. In complex cases seven days' notice should be given.

The judge was not obliged to give an indication and he could state that he could not give one at that stage. Any indication given was binding not only on that judge but on any other judge who dealt with the case after the guilty plea. It obviously does not bind the judge after a trial.

The hearing should normally take place in open court with a full recording made, both sides represented and in the presence of the defendant. Reporting restrictions should normally be imposed, to be lifted if and when the defendant pleads or is found guilty.

Use of the sentence discount – or even total immunity – for helping the prosecution

The sentence discount can also be used to persuade defendants to assist the prosecution by giving statements and, if needed, evidence regarding the guilt of others. Utilisation of the sentence discount for this purpose was explicitly recognised in the Serious Organised Crime and Police Act 2005. Section 73 (headed 'Assistance by defendant: reduction in sentence') provides that where a person pleads guilty and has made a written agreement with a prosecutor to give assistance to the prosecution, the court may take into account the extent and nature of that assistance when passing sentence. Unless the court considers it not to be in the public interest to do so, it should state in open court both that it has passed a lesser sentence than it otherwise would have been and what the greater sentence would have been.

The Government's Fraud Review published in July 2006 took this concept even further. It suggested that the time was ripe for a rethink of the traditional English opposition to a formal plea bargaining system as it existed in the United States, i.e. a bargain agreed between prosecution and defence that could be presented as a recommendation to the court.[652]

Commenting sceptically, Peter Kiernan, a partner of Eversheds, said that the average sentence for Serious Fraud Office cases was currently three and a half years. With that relatively low level of sentence there might not be sufficient leeway to persuade a suspect to plead guilty. From the prosecution's point of view, plea bargaining would best take place at a relatively early stage so saving maximum costs, but at that stage the defendant would not necessarily be able to judge whether the prosecution could prove his guilt. ('To motivate someone to admit guilt at an early stage when the evidence is not strong requires a very powerful incentive'.) Also, once guilt was admitted, confiscation of assets would follow under the Proceeds of Crime Act 2002. How would this be dealt with? ('Unless prosecutors will compromise on confiscation, why rush to admit guilt when in consequence you lose all your assets? Then again, imagine the headlines if a major criminal walked away from a case with a substantial portion of their ill-gotten gains intact as part of a deal'.[653])

There are instances where an accused is given *total immunity* from prosecution in return for evidence for, or other assistance to, the prosecution. In 1975 the Court of Appeal said that such an offer of total immunity might have to be made in the public interest but that it should be done only by the Director of Public Prosecutions, never by the police.[654] The practice in England then seemed to have lapsed. It was used extensively for some years more in Northern Ireland but it ceased there too in the mid-1980s after a number of high profile cases went spectacularly wrong for the prosecution.[655]

---

[652] Fraud Review, 2006, pp. 271–2, paras. 11.66 and 11.68.

[653] 'Is Plea Bargaining a Realistic Option for UK Justice', *The Lawyer*, 18 September 2006.

[654] The occasion was the case of Bertie Smalls who was arraigned at the Old Bailey on charges of major robberies and acquitted when the prosecution offered no evidence. In return for a promise of immunity from prosecution he had given the authorities information which had led to the arrest and conviction of twenty-six others in robberies to the value of over £1 million (*The Times*, 25 March 1975, p. 18).

[655] In 1985 the DPP decided not to proceed with a case against Terry Davis, a supergrass who had implicated forty to fifty other people in serious burglaries. Many had been picked up but in

The concept has unexpectedly been revived, however, by a provision in the Serious Organised Crime and Police Act 2005 (SOCPA). Section 71(1) of SOCPA states: 'if a specified prosecutor[656] thinks that for the purposes of the investigation or prosecution of any offence it is appropriate to offer any person immunity from prosecution he may give the person a written notice under this section (an "immunity notice")'. If such a notice is given, no proceedings can be brought save in circumstances specified in the notice. The section applies to both England and Northern Ireland.[657]

Note – TICs

A different form of 'confession' is the admission by someone who either pleads guilty or is found guilty that he committed *other* offences. If this happens before the court case, they are mentioned in court and 'taken into consideration' for the purpose of sentencing. (Hence they are called TICs.) The advantage for the accused is that they cannot later be brought up against him. The advantage for the police is that they can 'clear the books' – the success rate of cleared up crime in that force area improves.

In recent years the police on some forces have taken this one step further by visiting defendants in prison after they have been sentenced to see whether they can get them to admit to other offences.

Unsurprisingly, not all such admissions are true. In August 1986, detectives from Scotland Yard made a series of surprise raids on thirteen police stations in Kent investigating allegations that police officers had been falsifying crime statistics with bogus confessions. It was the sort of police operation usually directed against leading criminals, complete with a 6am briefing at Scotland

Footnote 655 (*cont.*)

the end they were released without charges being brought. In 1986 the convictions of eighteen defendants on the evidence of supergrass Christopher Black were quashed by the Northern Ireland Criminal Appeal Court. Black had been given immunity for a murder charge in exchange for evidence against thirty-eight people charged with 184 terrorist offences. The case against twenty defendants accused on the evidence of William Allen collapsed when the trial judge described his evidence as 'unworthy of belief'. The fourteen men convicted on the evidence of Joseph Bennett all had their convictions quashed on appeal. In October 1986 the DPP decided not to offer any evidence against nineteen defendants accused of terrorist offences on information given by Northern Ireland's first woman supergrass.

See generally A. Jennings, 'Supergrasses and the Northern Ireland Legal System', 133 *New Law Journal*, 1983, p. 1043; T. Gifford, *Supergrasses* (Cobden Trust, 1984); E. Grant, 'The Use of "Supergrass" Evidence in Northern Ireland 1982–1985', 135 *New Law Journal*, 8 November 1985, p. 1125; S.C. Greer, 'The Rise and Fall of the Northern Ireland Supergrass System', *Criminal Law Review*, 1987, p. 663; D. Bonner, *Modern Law Review* 1988, p. 23; S. Greer, 'Supergrasses and the Legal System in Britain and Northern Ireland', 102 *Law Quarterly Review*, 1986, p. 19.

[656] A 'specified prosecutor' in England means the DPP, the Director of Revenue and Customs Prosecutions or the Director of the Serious Fraud Office and in Northern Ireland means the DPP for Northern Ireland.

[657] This new power was referred to favourably by the Government's Fraud Review (July 2006) para. 11.70. For sceptical comment over its re-emergence see M. Lane, 'The Supergrass System – a Metamorphosis', 156 *New Law Journal*, 2 June 2006, pp. 908–9.

Yard and a simultaneous swoop on target police stations. Teams of officers from the Serious Crime Branch were investigating allegations made by a serving Kent officer, PC Ron Walker, that detectives in the area had been 'cooking the books'. He had alleged that the fake confessions were boosting the clear up rate in some areas by as much as 50 per cent. He also claimed that in return for making false confessions, some criminals were given a licence to commit further crimes on release from prison!

Taking a plea before mode of trial decision as to venue

As noted above, the Criminal Procedure and Investigations Act 1996 (CPIA), s. 49 introduced the new procedure of giving the defendant the right to indicate how he would plead before the mode of trial decision. If the defendant declines to indicate how he would plead, the bench decides whether the case should be tried summarily or at the Crown Court in the ordinary way, but if he later decides to plead guilty, he is only entitled to a lower sentence discount.[658]

If he indicates that he would plead guilty, the court then proceeds as if it had been a summary trial – either to sentence him or to commit him to the Crown Court for sentence only. The guilty plea is taken into account by magistrates together with the matters that they would previously have taken into account (set out in s. 19 of the Magistrates' Courts Act 1980) in considering whether their powers of sentencing were sufficient.

If the case is sent to the Crown Court, the defendant remains free to change his plea to one of not guilty at the risk of that raising his sentence if he is convicted.[659]

An assessment in 1999 of the effect of s. 49 by Professor Lee Bridges showed that although the number of cases in which the magistrates sent cases for trial in the Crown Court had declined, it had not had the desired effect of reducing the number of cases going to the Crown Court. The reason was that the number of cases being committed for sentence had risen by far more:

> Between 1996/97 and 1998/99, the number of either-way cases ordered by magistrates to the Crown Court for trial decreased by 4,700 while the number of committals for sentence increased by 15,600, over three times as much. Plea before venue has therefore not led to a reduction in cases being sent to the Crown Court but rather to a change in the status of those cases. Whereas before magistrates

---

[658] *Rafferty* [1998] Crim LR 433. However, this proposition has to be treated with some reserve since research suggests that sentencers pay little or no attention to the decision in *Rafferty*: '. . . defence solicitors in all three sample courts indicated that full credit was almost always given for a guilty plea at the plea and directions hearings in the Crown Court despite the guidance given by the Court of Appeal in *Rafferty* that the maximum sentence discount is reserved for those who indicate a guilty plea at the plea before venue hearing in the magistrates' court' (A. Herbert, 'Mode of Trial and Magistrates' Sentencing Powers: Will Increased Powers Inevitably Lead to a Reduction in the Committal Rate?', *Criminal Law* Review, 2003, p. 314 at 319, n. 28).

[659] For the problems created by the CPIA 1996, s. 49 see *R v. Warley Magistrates' Court, ex p DPP* [1998] Crim LR 684 and commentary pp. 687–90.

would have declined jurisdiction and sent either-way defendants to the Crown Court for trial, where many of them would then have entered guilty pleas, now such defendants will indicate their guilty pleas in the magistrates' court and be sent, as convicted defendants, to the Crown Court for sentence. This change does bring some administrative savings, but the vastly increased use by magistrates of their power to commit defendants to the Crown Court for sentence still involves a considerable waste of resources and any promise that plea before venue held out for defendants of having their cases retained for sentencing in magistrates' courts, because of their early guilty pleas, has proved to be illusory.[660]

Professor Bridges pursued this matter in evidence to the Commons Home Affairs Committee considering the Criminal Justice Bill 2003. He suggested that 'plea before venue' introduced by CPIA 1996 was doomed in light of the provisions in the 2003 Bill for advance 'indication of sentence' (which are not yet in force). Under the CPIA procedure the defendant was asked to indicate a plea before magistrates decided whether the case was suited for summary trial. Under the provisions of the Criminal Justice Bill magistrates would decide on venue before the defendant was asked to indicate his plea. If they decided that it was suitable for summary trial, they would then be able to give an 'indication of sentence' to help the defendant make up his mind as to how to plead.

The effect of taking the decision as to venue before knowing the defendant's plea, Bridges suggested, could be to increase the number of cases going to the Crown Court, thereby reversing the effect of 'plea before venue'. Further, the result of 'indication of sentence' was that much greater information on the circumstances of offences and defendants would need to be routinely available to magistrates at an early stage of the proceedings, with likely resulting delays and costs. The Government, he thought, had failed to think through the implications of its plans for sentence indications. (This could be one reason for the postponement of implementation.)

The Home Affairs Committee made no mention of these concerns in its report on the Bill.

A further spanner in the works emerged from new research into plea before venue and the reasons for magistrates' decisions declining jurisdiction and sending cases to the Crown Court.[661] The research was conducted in three magistrates' courts in the Midlands and Home Counties during 1999 and 2000.[662] Herbert reached the important conclusion that the idea that magistrates are the chief decision-makers regarding mode of trial is mistaken:

> There was . . . considerable evidence in this study to suggest that most mode of trial decisions were effectively not taken by magistrates, but were the result of

---

[660] L. Bridges, 'False Starts and Unrealistic Expectations', *Legal Action*, October 1999, pp. 6–7.

[661] A. Herbert, 'Mode of Trial and Magistrates' Sentencing Powers: Will Increased Powers Inevitably Lead to a Reduction in the Committal Rate?', *Criminal Law Review*, 2003, p. 314.

[662] The data collection consisted of observation of court cases, analysis of court registers regarding more than a thousand cases over a three-month period and interviews with thirty-eight court participants – lay and stipendiary magistrates, legal advisers and defence solicitors.

prior negotiation between lawyers. Defence solicitors only challenged the rec-ommendation of the Crown in 11 per cent of cases and in many of these [about half] adopted various recognised techniques to ensure that the magistrates realised that a contested application was only being made in order to comply with their client's instructions. Lay magistrates reached a decision contrary to the agreed or unchallenged recommendation of the Crown Prosecution Service in only one case out of an observation sample of 123 [p. 318].

Herbert said that the plea before venue provisions had had two prime motiva-tions:

> The first was the crime control objective of encouraging defendants to admit guilt by providing them with the opportunity, at least theoretically, to obtain the maximum sentence discount. The second was to facilitate the completion of more cases by magistrates by giving them the opportunity to consider all offence and offender information and apply the discount before determining whether or not their sentencing powers were sufficient [p. 319].

The responses of defendants and magistrates provided two major explanations for the limited effect of plea before venue.

With regard to the first objective, fewer defendants were prepared to plead guilty at that stage than had been anticipated. Only about half the defendants (51 per cent) indicated a plea at the plea before venue hearing. One reason was what was felt to be inadequate pre-trial prosecution disclosure. Another was the understandable reluctance to plead guilty at the plea before venue in light of the charges as they stood at that stage:

> There was a consensus of opinion among all interviewed court participants, that the majority of mode of trial decisions, possibly as many as 75 per cent, were obvious. They were, however, only obvious on the basis of the charge or charges faced at the mode of trial hearing. As an example, magistrates in the largest sample court unsurprisingly declined jurisdiction in eleven cases of violent dis-order. Yet not one of these defendants was ultimately convicted of that offence, and all those who admitted lesser offences of violence in the Crown Court received community orders. Increased sentencing powers will not influence this predicament . . . There would appear to be little incentive for solicitors to address this perceived problem given their apparent belief that cases which ini-tially present as being serious are better suited to be resolved in the Crown Court [p. 321].

As regards the second main reason behind plea before venue, Herbert's research showed that magistrates were very reluctant to consider taking cases that they felt might be outside their sentencing powers. This was demonstrated by their atti-tude to ordering pre-sentence reports. According to the philosophy behind plea before venue, the appropriate course of action in a case that appears on the facts to warrant a sentence of nine months was to order a pre-sentence report and post-pone any decision until all the information was available, but the research sug-gested that magistrates had not adopted – and do not agree with – this approach.

They appeared to view the decision to order reports as equivalent to a decision to accept jurisdiction. The result was that they were unwilling, or at least reluctant, to order reports in cases that might be outside their sentencing powers, preferring instead to commit the defendant to the Crown Court at the plea before venue. Only 5 per cent of 315 defendants for whom reports were ordered were committed for sentence after consideration of the report. The magistrates interpreted this statistic with approval as an indication that their colleagues had made the right decision at plea before venue. The theory behind plea before venue is that magistrates would make their decision as to venue after considering all the relevant facts, but almost half (45 per cent) of those committed had received a sentence that could have been given by the magistrates and four-fifths of them had been committed without a pre-sentence report (p. 320).

12. Committal or transfer proceedings

If the charge is one on which there is a choice between the magistrates' court and the Crown Court, the defendant must be told of his right to ask for trial at the higher level. Most then opt for summary trial. If the defendant asks for trial at the higher level, his preference prevails. If, however, he asks for summary trial and the prosecutor prefers to have the case tried at the Crown Court, the court will decide. The court can also override the defendant's choice of summary trial if it thinks the case too serious for trial in a magistrates' court.

Hitherto, if the case was to be tried in the Crown Court, the defendant had to be committed for trial by the magistrates' court. Under the Criminal Justice Act 2003, when implemented, committal proceedings are to be abolished. Instead, once the decision is made that the case is not to be dealt with by the magistrates' court, it is sent to the Crown Court.

The history of committal proceedings was conveniently set out by the Philips Royal Commission on Criminal Procedure:[663]

a. Historical background

184. Before the establishment of regular police forces it was the duty of magistrates to pursue and arrest offenders and it was the magistrates who could be referred to as 'detectives and prosecutors'. They had responsibility for the taking of depositions as long ago as the sixteenth century. These were equivalent to the statements taken from witnesses by the police today. The examination of the witnesses took place in private and the accused had no right to be present. In the early part of the nineteenth century the responsibility for enquiring into offences began to pass to the police. In 1848 changes were made in the procedure. The Administration of Justice (No. 1) Act of that year set out to consolidate the law relating to the duties of magistrates in relation to the functions of investigating and inquiring into offences, with such changes as were deemed necessary. The

[663] *The Investigation and Prosecution of Criminal Offences in England and Wales: The Law and Procedure*, 1981, Cmnd. 8092–1, pp. 67–8.

most important change was a provision whereby the accused was entitled, for the first time, to be present at the examination of the witnesses against him, but the inquiry was not required to be in open court, that is in public. The nature of the inquiry by the magistrates was changing before 1848 and continued to do so after that year. During this transitional period, the position of the police as investigators and prosecutors was becoming more clearly established. During the same period, the magistrates' inquiry became a judicial instead of an investigative function. Indeed, by 1848, or soon after, the magistrates' examination (that is committal proceedings) usually took place in open court. As a result of these changes there became grafted onto the system a preliminary judicial hearing.

b. Committal proceedings in the modern era

185. This preliminary judicial hearing continues today, with modifications, as committal proceedings. The link with the magistrates' former investigative functions is evidenced by the statutory reference to committal proceedings as an inquiry into an offence by examining justices, and by the procedure which envisages that the charge will not be formulated until after the 'examining justices' have heard the evidence of the prosecution and that it is the magistrates who will decide upon what charge the accused will be committed for trial . . .

c. Purpose of committal proceedings

187. The purpose of committal proceedings now is to ensure that no person shall stand trial at the Crown Court unless there is a *prima facie* case against him. It is not a purpose of committal proceedings that the defence may hear all the prosecution witnesses, or any particular witness or witnesses, give their evidence in chief or that such witnesses shall be made available for cross-examination. The prosecution are not required to call all their witnesses at committal proceedings; if they can make out a *prima facie* case without calling any particular witness or witnesses, even an important witness, they are entitled to do so and neither the defence nor the court can require any witness to be called.[664] It follows that committal proceedings are not necessarily a means whereby the defence may obtain full disclosure of the prosecution case before trial. In most cases, however, the prosecution do present all their evidence at the committal proceedings, and if they do not, they should give notice before the trial of any additional evidence they propose to call.

The introduction of 'paper committals' (1967)

Before the Criminal Justice Act 1967, committal proceedings were lengthy affairs in which all the evidence had to be taken laboriously, translated into depositions and then signed. In the overwhelming proportion of cases the defendant was committed for trial. The Criminal Justice Act 1967 introduced changes designed to abbreviate this procedure and thus save the time of the courts, lawyers, police

---

[664] *R v. Epping and Harlow Justices, ex p Massaro* [1973] QB 433; *R v. Grays Justices, ex p Tetley* (1979) 70 Cr App Rep 11. See also *R v. Governor of Pentonville Prison, ex p Osman* [1989] 3 All ER 701 and *Galbraith* [1981] 2 All ER 1060, CA.

and witnesses. Instead of the witnesses having to come to the magistrates' courts to have their statements taken down, the statements were now sent to the defence. If the defendant was legally represented, he could agree to be committed for trial on the basis of the prosecution statements. The procedure in that event lasted only a few minutes. If, however, he wanted all or some of the prosecution witnesses to be called for examination and cross-examination, this was open to him. (The procedure was to be found in the Magistrates' Courts Act 1980, s. 6(1) – paper committals – and s. 6(2) – old style full committals.)

In a large Home Office study in 1985 it was found that there was no evidence that full committals resulted in the weeding out of a higher proportion of weak cases than paper committals. The rate of acquittals directed by the judge was considerably higher in the full committal cases.[665] Also, full committals resulted in considerably greater delays.

Reform or abolition?

The Philips Royal Commission on Criminal Procedure thought that committal proceedings were an inadequate filter against weak cases. It proposed the abolition of full committal proceedings and the institution of a new procedure ('application for discharge') whereby the defence could ask for a hearing before the magistrates at which to make a submission of no case to answer. The Royal Commission also proposed the abolition of paper committals on the ground that sifting of weak cases would be done by the proposed new independent prosecution service (the CPS) (paras. 8.24–31).

The Roskill Committee on Fraud Trials in its report in January 1986 also recommended that something drastic should be done about committal proceedings. With regard to full committals, they were time-consuming. Sometimes in complicated cases they lasted for weeks and occasionally even months. The defence desire to use the committal stage as a dress-rehearsal for the trial could be an abuse. Sometimes, for instance, the defence would cross-examine prosecution witnesses simply in the hope of turning up something that would assist the defence.

The Committee recommended a new procedure whereby fraud cases could be sent for trial direct to the Crown Court by the new prosecution authorities recommended by the report. They would issue a 'transfer certificate' subject to the right of the accused to apply to a judge for a discharge on the ground that the prosecution's evidence failed to disclose a *prima facie* case (paras. 4.31–40).

This recommendation was implemented in the Criminal Justice Act 1987, ss. 4–6. A transfer certificate can be issued under s. 4 by the DPP (and therefore anyone in the CPS), the Director of the Serious Fraud Office or the Home Secretary. The basis of a transfer certificate is (1) that in the opinion of one of

---

[665]   P. Jones et al, 'The Effectiveness of Committal Proceedings as a Filter in the Criminal Justice System', *Criminal Law Review*, 1985, pp. 355 and 360.

the above the evidence of the offence would be sufficient for the person charged to be committed for trial and (2) that it reveals a case of fraud 'of such seriousness and complexity that it is appropriate that the management of the case should without delay be taken over by the Crown Court' (s. 4(1)(b)).

Further erosion of the value of committal proceedings occurred in the Criminal Justice Act 1991, s. 55(7), which removed the right of the accused personally to cross-examine a child victim in sex and assault cases at the committal stage.

The debate as to what to do about committals continued. (For the history between 1986 and 1992 see the 6th edn of this work, pp. 304–6.)

In 1992 a study of some 3,000 either-way cases in five Crown Court areas and interviews with magistrates and justices' clerks showed that they thought that full committals rarely achieved any useful purpose.[666] Occasionally they were useful but the resources they absorbed were quite out of proportion to any benefits. Equally there was a strong view that 'paper committals' served no judicial purpose and that there was no point in retaining them in their existing form.

The Runciman Royal Commission

The Runciman Royal Commission, like the Philips Commission and the Roskill Committee, recommended that committal proceedings be abolished on the grounds that paper committals were a waste of time and that there were better ways of achieving the objective of weeding out weak cases than by old style full committals. It commented on the cumbersome procedure of full committals. The Commission said that it did think, however, that there ought to be a way for the defendant to argue that the case against him was so weak that it should not be allowed to proceed. The defendant ought therefore to have the right to submit that there was no case to answer. Such a submission should be considered on the papers, without calling any evidence. The parties should, however, be permitted to present oral argument. In indictable-only cases, the submission of no case to answer should be made to the Crown Court; in either-way cases, it should be made to the magistrates' court but they should be heard by stipendiary magistrates rather than lay justices.[667]

Apparent abolition – Criminal Justice and Public Order Act 1994, s. 44

The Government accepted the recommendation. Committal proceedings were seemingly abolished by s. 44 of the Criminal Justice and Public Order Act 1994. Cases were to be transferred to the Crown Court under provisions set out in Sch. 4 of the 1994 Act. But major snags in the drafting of Sch. 4 were discovered

---

[666] C. Hedderman and D. Moxon, *Magistrates' Court or Crown Court? Mode of Trial Decisions and Sentencing* (Home Office Research and Planning Unit, Paper No. 125, 1992).

[667] Runciman, pp. 90–1, paras. 25–32.

by the Law Society which caused successive postponements, first to July 1995, then to September 1995, then to a date in 1996 and then to a later date in 1996. Finally, to the Government's embarrassment, the difficulties raised by the Law Society and others proved insurmountable. On 25 April 1996 the Home Office wrote to the relevant interested parties that it had decided to move amendments to the Criminal Procedure and Investigations Bill totally abandoning the whole idea of transfer proceedings.

Instead, uncontested 'paper committals' under s. 6(2) of the Magistrates' Courts Act 1980 were retained without change. Contested 'old style committals' under s. 6(1) were reformed by the removal of the right to call witnesses to give oral evidence.

Contested committal proceedings therefore proceeded simply on the basis of witness statements and other documentary material presented by the prosecution and oral argument by both prosecution and defence as to whether there was a case for committal.[668]

NB Schedule 2 of the Act made dramatic changes in the rules for the giving of evidence at the Crown Court. Any statement which formed part of a committal bundle was to be read at trial as evidence of its truth unless the defence asked for the attendance of the witness for cross-examination. Even if the defence did require the attendance of the witness for cross-examination, the judge at the Crown Court had the power to overrule the request and to rule that the evidence should be read.

Abolition of committal proceedings for indictable-only offences

The Labour Government made a further intervention in this area in the Crime and Disorder Act 1998 in the provision for indictable-only cases to be sent direct to the Crown Court without any committal proceedings. Section 51 was headed, 'No committal proceedings for indictable-only offences'. Subject to the power to adjourn, the court was required at the first hearing to send the accused direct to the Crown Court for trial. The transfer applied also to any related either-way offences and any connected summary-only offences carrying imprisonment or disqualification. The defendant could have an early hearing to ask the Crown Court judge to dismiss the charge on the ground that there was not sufficient evidence for a properly directed jury to convict.[669] If a charge was dismissed, no further charges could be brought on the dismissed charge except by way of a voluntary bill of indictment (see below). The defence can raise issues of admissibility, unlike the new procedure on committal. The judge can hear live evidence if it is in the interests of justice to do so (Sch. 3, para. 2(4)).

---

[668] See the Criminal Procedure and Investigations Act, ss. 44, 45 and Sch. 1. For further explanation see A. Edwards, *Criminal Law Review*, 1997, pp. 322–5.

[669] An experienced defence solicitor suggested that this test could be more demanding than the test in the magistrates' courts. See A. Edwards, 'Improving Criminal Procedure?', *Criminal Law Review*, 1999, p. 33.

Transfer proceedings to replace committal

After a successful pilot the new procedure for indictable-only cases was implemented nationally in January 2001.[670]

The magistrates are supposed to send the case to the Crown Court on the first hearing, though they have the power to adjourn. The reasons for an adjournment might be to enable the prosecution to decide whether it is indeed an indictable-only case, for the defendant to get a surety for a bail application or because co-defendants are involved. The first hearing in the Crown Court has to take place within eight days of the magistrates' court hearing in custody cases and within twenty-eight days in bail cases.[671] Most magistrates' courts make 'through legal aid orders' to cover proceedings for the whole case to trial. In the Crown Court, most first hearings are presented by a CPS lawyer, not by counsel, but the defendant is usually represented by counsel. At the first hearing the court asks the defendant to indicate his plea and in contested cases would set the timetable for the case.

An application by the defendant to have the case dismissed can be made not later than fourteen days after service of the papers by the prosecution.[672]

The Auld Report recommended that committal proceedings be abolished and that all either-way cases going to the Crown Court should be 'sent' in the same way as indictable-only cases under s. 51 of the Crime and Disorder Act 1998 (CDA).[673]

The Government accepted the recommendation which was effected in Sch. 3 of the Criminal Justice Act 2003 by applying the s. 51 procedure to either-way cases allocated for trial on indictment,[674] to cases where the defendant is under eighteen[675] and to cases of serious fraud cases previously dealt with under the Criminal Justice Act 1987.[676]

Schedule 3 was due to be activated in November 2006, but in July it was announced that implementation of most of its provisions would be postponed. At the time of writing it was only in force for cases involving juvenile defendants where an indefinite or extended sentence for public protection is a possibility.[677]

---

[670] The pilots found that the average time taken from charge to completion in bail cases was reduced from 228 days to 194 days and in custody cases from 172 days to 141 days. The average number of magistrates' court hearings was reduced from 4.6 hearings per case to 1.4 hearings. That was accompanied by only one additional Crown Court hearing. On a national basis this represented savings of an estimated £16 million.

[671] The time limit runs from receipt of the notice in the Crown Court with the magistrates having four days to send the notice.

[672] Crime and Disorder Act 1998 (Dismissal of Charges Sent) Rules 1998. See generally S. O'Doherty, 'Indictable-Only Offences – the New Approach', *New Law Journal*, 22 December 2000, p. 1891.   [673] Auld Report, pp. 479–81.

[674] New CDA 1998, s. 51 inserted by para. 18 of Sch. 3 of the Act.

[675] New CDA 1998, s. 51A inserted by para. 18 of Sch. 3 of the Act.

[676] New CDA 1998, s. 51B inserted by para. 18 of Sch. 3 of the Act.

[677] New ss. 3C and 5A of the Powers of Criminal Courts (Sentencing) Act 2000 inserted by paras. 23 and 26 of Sch. 3.

13. The voluntary bill of indictment

There was one procedural device to avoid committal proceedings – the voluntary bill of indictment. This was an application to commit a defendant direct to the Crown Court without going via the magistrates' court. The application was made to a High Court judge.[678] Normally it was made when a further defendant emerged after the committal proceedings were already completed. Instead of starting the committal proceedings again, the defendant was belatedly sent for trial on the basis of the evidence already available. The applicant supplied the judge with the committal papers, including proofs of all witnesses, depositions and witness statements. Under the procedure, which obtained until August 1999, prosecutors could, and often did, refuse to give the defence copies of the documents presented to the judge in support of the voluntary bill. The defendant was normally not even given leave to oppose the application which was usually dealt with without a hearing, simply on the papers.

Once the High Court judge had authorised a voluntary bill, the Court of Appeal would not inquire into the exercise of the judge's discretion.[679] Nor was judicial review available,[680] but a Crown Court judge had an inherent jurisdiction to prevent injustice or abuse of process.[681]

The 1990 Practice Direction stated that the judge could invite representations from the proposed defendant but this was not normally done. The procedure was therefore outside the normal rules of fairness and natural justice and, arguably, was contrary to Article 6 of the European Convention on Human Rights.[682] It seems that this point was taken because in July 1999 a new Practice Direction (Crimes: Voluntary Bills) was issued.[683] Prosecutors were required to give the prospective defendant notice of the application and to serve on him a copy of all the documents delivered to the judge. He had to be informed that he could make written submissions to the judge within nine working days. If this procedure was not followed, the judge had to be so informed. The judge was entitled to hold an oral hearing before deciding.

There are no statistics as to the extent of the use of the procedure. The Roskill Committee on Fraud Trials (1986) said that it had been told that it was used at the Central Criminal Court in about six to twelve cases each year.[684]

Lord Justice Auld in his report suggested that once committal proceedings were abolished there would be little point in preserving the voluntary bill

---

[678] The procedure goes back to 1859. It is now regulated by the Administration of Justice (Miscellaneous Provisions) Act 1933, s. 2, Indictment (Procedure) Rules 1971, SI 1971/2084 and the *Practice Direction (Crime: Voluntary Bills)* [1990] 1 WLR 1633.

[679] *Rothfield* (1937) 26 Cr App Rep 103.

[680] *R v. Manchester Crown Court, ex p Williams and Simpson* [1990] Crim LR 654.

[681] *Wells* [1995] 2 Cr App Rep 417.

[682] See S. Farrell and D. Friedman, 'Voluntary Bills of Indictment: the Administration of Justice or a Rubber Stamp?', *Criminal Law Review*, 1998, pp. 617–26.   [683] [1999] 4 All ER 63.

[684] Roskill Report, p. 53, n. 24.

procedure.[685] However, neither the 2002 White Paper nor the Criminal Justice Act 2003 mentioned the voluntary bill.

14. Case management and pre-trial preparation

The Criminal Procedure Rules 2005, Part 3, entitled 'Case Management', applies to the management of all cases in magistrates' and Crown Courts. Rule 3.2(1) states: 'the court must further the overriding objective[686]by actively managing the case'.

Active case management is now a central feature of the criminal justice system. The need for it was emphasised by Lord Justice Judge in *Jisl*:

> Justice must be done. The defendant is entitled to a fair trial and, which is sometimes overlooked, the prosecution is equally entitled to a reasonable opportunity to present evidence against the defendant. It is not, however, a concomitant of the entitlement to a fair trial that either or both sides are further entitled to take as much time as they like or, for that matter, as long as counsel and solicitors or the defendants themselves think appropriate. Resources are limited. The funding for courts and judges, for prosecuting and the vast majority of defence lawyers is dependent on public money for which there are many competing demands. Time itself is a resource. Every day unnecessarily used, while the trial meanders sluggishly to its eventual conclusion, represents another day's stressful waiting for the remaining witnesses and the jurors in that particular trial, and, no less important, continuing and increasing tension and worry for another defendant or defendants, some of whom are remanded in custody, and the witnesses in trials which are waiting their turn to be listed. It follows that the sensible use of time requires judicial management and control.[687]

Improving the efficiency of the system is hardly a new theme. It has been rehearsed over and over again for decades. Active case management is the latest in a long line of initiatives that have been tried. Its immediate origin was the report by Lord Justice Auld which was itself a direct offshoot of the 'Woolf reforms' in the civil justice system.[688] (It was a happy coincidence that the person who launched the Criminal Procedure Rules in April 2005 was Lord Woolf himself, in the role of Lord Chief Justice.)

Active case management is defined in the Criminal Procedure Rules 3.2.2 as 'including':

---

[685] Auld, Ch. 10, para. 58, pp. 418–19.   [686] As to which see p. 153 above.

[687] [2004] EWCA Crim 696 at [114]. For an earlier statement to similar effect see *Chaaban* [2003] EWCA Crim 1012 where the Court of Appeal (Lord Justice Judge presiding) dismissed an appeal brought on the ground that the trial judge had wrongly refused an adjournment to allow the defence to obtain expert evidence. Unnecessary delay was to be avoided. An adjournment culture was a thing of the past. On the culture of adjournments see F. Leverick and P. Duff, 'Court Culture and Adjournments in Criminal Cases: A Tale of Four Courts', *Criminal Law Review*, 2002, pp. 39–52.

[688] The Press Notice announcing the establishment of the Auld Review said: 'this Review is a complement to the highly successful review that Lord Woolf undertook of the civil courts'.

(a) the early identification of the real issues; (b) the early identification of the needs of witnesses; (c) achieving certainty as to what must be done, by whom, and when, in particular by the early setting of a timetable for the progress of the case; (d) monitoring the progress of the case and compliance with directions; (e) ensuring that evidence, whether disputed or not, is presented in the shortest[689] and clearest way; (f) discouraging delay, dealing with as many aspects of the case as possible on the same occasion, and avoiding unnecessary hearings; (g) encouraging the participants to co-operate in the progression of the case; and (h) making use of technology.[690]

The parties and the court must appoint a Case Progression Officer (CPO) who is responsible for progressing the case. The CPO for the parties must keep the court informed of anything that will affect progress and must be available to be contacted during business hours.

The court may give directions on its own initiative as well as on application by a party. It may receive applications by letter, telephone or by any other means of electronic communication and may conduct hearings by such means (r. 3.5).[691]

The parties can agree to vary a time limit fixed by a direction but only if the variation does not affect the date of any hearing that has been fixed or significantly affects the progress of the case in any other way (r. 3.7).

The court's extensive case management powers (set out in r. 3.5) include the power to 'specify the consequences of failing to comply with a direction' (r. 3.5(2)(i)). It is not easy to see, however, what meaningful penalties can be imposed by the courts on either the prosecution or the defence.

Case management of heavy cases poses special problems. In March 2005, the Lord Chief Justice, Lord Woolf, handed down an eleven page 'protocol for the control and management of heavy fraud and other complex criminal cases' directed at cases likely to last longer than eight weeks. [692]

In August 2006, the DCA issued a consultation paper regarding case management in very high cost cases[693] which notoriously absorb a wholly disproportionate share of Crown Court expenditure.[694] The consultation paper proposed that the trial judge should have a new – and unprecedented – power to order the termination of a barrister's or solicitor's involvement in the case where they were in breach of their professional rules of conduct, including

---

[689] In *K* [2006] EWCA Crim 724, [2006] Crim LR, 1012 the Court of Appeal said that the judge's case management powers at the pre-trial stage included the right to restrict argument to written submissions. He was not bound to allow oral submissions and he certainly could put a time-limit on them.

[690] For critical commentary see P. Plowden, ' Case Management and the Criminal Procedure Rules', 155 *New Law Journal*, 18 March 2005, p. 416.

[691] For an account of virtual plea and directions hearings conducted online see *Counsel*, June 2004, p. 20.   [692] [2005] 2 All ER 429.

[693] DCA, *Proposals to Create Judicial Powers to Manage Conflict of Interest and Capacity Issues in Very High Cost Cases*, consultation paper 17/06.

[694] 1 per cent of Crown Court cases absorb 50 per cent of Crown Court legal aid expenditure.

where there is a conflict of interest or where the lawyer 'lacks sufficient capacity adequately to represent their client, such that the efficient progress of the case would be impeded' (para. 5). The defendant would then have up to three weeks in which to apply for a new representation order.

Pre-trial hearings

Lord Justice Auld's report gave strong support to the notion of case management with emphasis on the value of early judicial involvement: 'the sooner the court takes hold of the case at an early preliminary stage, the better'.[695] The rationale was that the parties did not prepare the case for trial as speedily or efficiently as they should and that they needed the goad of the court to make them do their job properly. The vehicle for the application of the goad, Auld said, was a pre-trial hearing of some sort. Pre-trial hearings take various forms:

Plea and case management hearings (PCMH)

Every Crown Court case, other than serious fraud and other complex or long cases for which statutory preparatory hearings (see below) are appropriate, now has a PCMH, formerly known as a plea and directions hearing (PDH). The PDH system was put in place by a Practice Direction in 1995.[696] The PCMH replaced it by a Practice Direction in 2005.[697] The main purpose of the PCMH/PDH is to try to identify the cases that can be dealt with either immediately or very quickly, especially those in which the defendant intends to plead guilty. Where a not guilty plea is confirmed, there is a lengthy questionnaire to be completed by the lawyers[698] which is designed to identify the issues and to enable the judge to give directions that will assist preparation for trial. The Practice Direction states: 'Active case management at the PCMH should reduce the number of ineffective and cracked trials and delays during the trial to resolve legal issues'.[699] It adds that the effectiveness of a PCMH depended in large measure upon preparation by all concerned and upon the presence of the trial

---

[695] Chapter 10, para. 204, p. 481.

[696] *Crown Court: Plea and Directions Hearings* [2002] 3 All ER 904 Practice Direction – consolidation – Part 41 at p. 930. It had been recommended by the Government's Working Group on Pre-Trial Issues in a report issued, but not published, in November 1990. The Runciman Royal Commission, by ten to one, recommended a much more elaborate pre-trial regime – see the Report, Ch. 7, paras. 1–36, pp. 101–9. The writer, dissenting, urged that the Commission's proposed pre-trial regime would make the system less rather than more efficient and urged the introduction of PDHs – Report, pp. 223–33. The Government decided to introduce PDHs.

[697] Amendment to the *Consolidated Criminal Practice Direction (Crime: Case Management)* [2005] 3 All ER 91. It took effect on 4 April 2005, the day the Criminal Procedure Rules came into force.

[698] For the text for PDHs see Annex D of the *Practice Direction* [2002] 3 All ER at 957–60. For the text for PCMHs see Annex E9 and the Guidance Note Annex E10 – www.courtservice.gov.uk. There was a great deal of criticism of the first version of the form and in the summer of 2006 a new version was drafted by the Rules Committee.   [699] Paragraph IV.41.8.

advocate or an advocate who was able to make decisions. (This is frequently a problem.[700])

When the PCMH was first introduced in 2005 the Criminal Bar was greatly exercised by the fact that it involved more work than the PDH with no increase in remuneration. There was even briefly a strike. As will be seen (pp. 620–21 below), Lord Carter's review of legal aid remuneration (July 2006) recommended significant changes aimed at providing more money for the work done at the pre-trial stage – to be implemented in April 2007. (At the time of writing the Government had not yet announced whether it accepted the recommendation.)

Preparatory hearings under the Criminal Justice Act 1987, ss. 7–10 for serious or complex fraud cases

The 1987 Act provided that a preparatory hearing could be ordered by the judge for the purpose of identifying the issues likely to be material to the verdict of the jury, assisting their comprehension, expediting the proceedings or assisting the judge's management of the trial (s. 7(1)). The judge has extensive powers under the 1987 Act to order both sides to prepare and serve any documents that appear to him to be relevant.

Preparatory hearings under the Criminal Procedure and Investigations Act 1996 (CPIA)

CPIA, s. 29 enables a judge, on application or otherwise, to order a preparatory hearing in a case of such complexity, seriousness[701] or length that he thinks substantial benefits will accrue from such a hearing. The purpose of such a hearing is to identify material issues, to assist the jury's comprehension of the issues, to expedite the trial or to assist the management of the trial (s. 29(2)). The preparatory hearing is treated as the start of the trial (s. 30). The judge at such a hearing can make binding rulings. There is an appeal from a judge's ruling on the admissibility of evidence or any question of law.[702]

Pre-trial rulings

CPIA, s. 40 provides that the court may make a ruling as to the admissibility of evidence or any other question of law at a pre-trial hearing, whether on application or on its own motion. A pre-trial hearing is one that takes place before the start of the trial which is defined to mean when the jury is sworn in (s. 39(3)). The significance of this is that it avoids having to swear-in a jury and then send

---

[700] For an upbeat statement of the aims of the Effective Trial Management and the Criminal Case Management Framework from its manager see 57 *Criminal practitioners newsletter*, Law Society, July 2004, p. 3. The pilot studies, it stated, had shown that ineffective trial rates had been reduced, courtroom time had been freed and witnesses had been saved from having to come to court needlessly.

[701] The word 'seriousness' was added by the Criminal Justice Act 2003, s. 309.

[702] As to when it is appropriate to hold different types of preparatory hearings see *Attorney General's Reference (No 1 of 2004) R v. Edwards Note* [2004] EWCA Crim 1025, [2004] 4 All ER 457.

them away for hours or days while lawyers argue legal points. CPIA, s. 40 enables a judge who makes a ruling under the section to order that the ruling is binding, but then goes on to say that such a ruling can be varied by the trial judge 'if it appears to him that it is in the interests of justice to do so' (subsection (4)). However, neither party can seek to obtain a variation in a binding pre-trial ruling unless there has been some material change in circumstances (s. 40(5)).

Magistrates' courts – early administrative hearing (EAH)

The EAH is intended for defendants who intend to contest their guilt. The court typically takes a plea before venue (p. 337 above), determines mode of trial and sets pre-trial review and trial dates as necessary. The Crime and Disorder Act 1998, s. 50 gave single magistrates and court clerks the power to run EAHs.[703]

Magistrates' courts – pre-trial review (PTR)

Many magistrates' courts developed their own local forms of PTR as a way of dealing with pre-trial matters such as which witnesses need to attend, refinement of charges, assessment of the time needed for the hearing and similar aspects of case management.

Empirical evidence about the value of pre-trial hearings

It should not be assumed that pre-trial hearings perform their desired function. Contrary to what common sense would suggest, the existing empirical evidence about pre-trial hearings suggests that, instead of simplifying trials and saving costs, such hearings may do the opposite – increase costs and lengthen trials:

- In the *Crown Court Study*, judges were asked whether they thought the pre-trial review had saved much time and money. As many as two-thirds (66 per cent) said no. A quarter (24 per cent) said that a little time and money had been saved. In 8 per cent a fair amount of time and money had been saved. A 'great deal' had been saved in only 1 per cent.[704]
- Professor Michael Levi's study for the Runciman Royal Commission of serious fraud cases stated with regard to ordinary pre-trial reviews:[705] 'none of the defence lawyers I interviewed argued that pre-trial reviews had any significant effect on the development of the case . . . The problem is that the judge in the pre-trial reviews is seldom the trial judge, has seldom read the papers, and therefore understandably does not wish to become embroiled in complex matters'.[706]

---

[703] For an assessment of the pilot studies of EAHs see P. Tain, 'Reducing Delay: Case Management', *Solicitors' Journal*, 15 October 1999, p. 959.

[704] M. Zander and P. Henderson, *Crown Court Study* (Royal Commission on Criminal Justice, Research Study No. 19, 1993) section 2.8.9.

[705] Pre-trial reviews are not the special preparatory hearings envisaged for serious fraud cases by the Roskill Committee which were established by the Criminal Justice Act 1987.

[706] Royal Commission Research Study No. 14, 1993, p. 105.

- The fate of the more formal preparatory hearings under the serious fraud regime is equally discouraging. The Roskill Committee said that a full day should be set aside for preparatory hearings.[707] In fact, however, in many of the cases brought by the Serious Fraud Office, preparatory hearings take weeks or even months. (In *Guiness 1*, the preparatory hearing took three months!)
- The only proper study of the impact of pre-trial conferences, using *matched* samples, conducted in 3,000 personal injury (i.e. civil) cases in New Jersey,[708] concluded that although they improved preparation, they did not shorten trials. The researchers concluded that they therefore lowered rather than raised the efficiency of the system by absorbing a great deal of court and judge time without any compensating saving in the time required for trials.[709]

Auld on pre-trial hearings

Lord Justice Auld was less convinced of the value of pre-trial hearings in criminal cases than Lord Woolf was for civil cases. PDHs in the Crown Court he suggested were mainly perfunctory: 'taking the form of a report on progress, good or bad, and the fixing of a trial date or the judge chivvying the parties into getting on with basic matters of preparation and to resolving the issues that they may or may not have discussed before then'.[710] The lawyers were not paid adequately for pre-trial work which as a result tended to be done by more junior lawyers than those who would appear at the trial. The courts had no effective sanctions to make the parties prepare cases properly. There were also problems in tailoring the timetabling of pre-trial hearings to the parties' progress or lack of it in preparing for trial. The time limits for holding PDHs were no doubt 'a reassuring target for the Court Service with its own targets and key performance indicators in mind and for the Government with its commendable aim of speeding the criminal justice process',[711] but for cases not needing such a hearing it was 'an unnecessary and expensive intrusion in getting the case to trial', while for cases needing a PDH 'the timing is often too tight'. Often disclosure had not been completed so that by the time of the PDH the parties were 'nowhere near identification of the issues or assessment of the evidential and other requirements for trial, far less a realistic joint estimate of the likely length of the case to enable the court to fix a firm date for listing'. So further costly PDHs might be needed. Or the parties might commit themselves to a trial date for which they were not ready.

---

[707] *Fraud Trials Committee Report*, HMSO, 1986, para. 6.52.

[708] M. Rosenberg, *The Pre-Trial Conference and Effective Justice* (Columbia University Press, 1964) p. 68.

[709] Civil cases are of course not the same as criminal, but if pre-trial conferences do not achieve their intended results in civil cases, it is arguable that they are even less likely to work in criminal cases where the adversarial nature of the proceedings is greater and the defendant is understandably therefore even less inclined to be co-operative or helpful.

[710] Auld, Ch. 10, para. 209, p. 483.   [711] *Ibid*, para. 212, p. 484.

In magistrates' courts, Auld suggested, the PTR 'should perform the same function as plea and directions hearings in the Crown Court, but usually fails to do so . . . because of lack of targets, lack of enforceable sanctions for failure to achieve them, lack of clarity about the aims of the hearing and local variations in practice'.[712] Auld said that in the view of some judges and practitioners pre-trial hearings were a useful means of getting the parties together to focus on the matter of the plea and, in the event of a contest, the issues and the likely evidence required. There was also the convenience to defence practitioners of having defendants in custody brought from prison to court for a conference:

> Frequently the last factor is the most important in the exercise. [For various reasons] defence lawyers are often unable – and sometimes unwilling – to visit and take instructions from clients in custody. In my view this is a major blot on our system of criminal justice. It should be a fundamental entitlement of every defendant, whether in custody or on bail, to meet at least one of his defence lawyers in order to give him instructions and to receive advice at an early stage of the preparation of his case for trial, and certainly before a pre-trial hearing.[713]

The problem to which Auld alluded is serious. According to defence barristers in the *Crown Court Study* (section 2.6.1) there was no pre-trial conference with counsel in 58–9 per cent of cases. This was more common when the defendant ended by pleading guilty but, according to the defence barristers, there was no pre-trial conference in 37 per cent of *contested* cases and according to defence solicitors in 46 per cent. Whichever figure was correct, the proportion was considerable.

Auld suggested the problem could be addressed by promoting video links both to enable remand prisoners to confer with their lawyers and for the holding of court pre-trial remand hearings.[714] The Government's policy paper *Criminal Justice: The Way Ahead* announced that every prison handling remand prisoners would have a video link to a magistrates' court by March 2002.[715] However, this commitment extended only to magistrates' courts. Auld urged that they should be not only available for court hearings. 'They should also be available to enable representatives to speak to their clients and take instructions during the course of the preparation of the case'.

Auld's overall view was that:

> Oral pre-trial hearings should become the exception rather than the rule. They should take place only in cases which, because of their complexity or particular difficulty, require them. In the majority of cases they are unnecessary, expensive, time-consuming and often, because of their timing and the failure of trial

---

[712] *Ibid*, para. 206, p. 482.   [713] *Ibid*, para. 214, p. 485.

[714] See, in particular, p. 502, para. 259 where Auld described experiments that had been conducted and the encouraging results of evaluation. J. Plotnikoff and R. Woolfson, *Video Link Pilot Evaluation* (Home Office, 1999) and *Evaluation of Information Video Link Pilot Project at Manchester Crown Court* (Court Service and HM Prison Service, 2000).

[715] Cm. 5074, 2001, p. 107.

advocates to attend, ineffective. Paradoxically . . . they also often serve to delay rather than speed disposal of cases.[716]

Save for an initial preliminary hearing, pre-trial resort to the court, in Auld's view, should be 'a last recourse' used only when the case requires it.[717] Auld's thesis was that:

> In courts at all levels the main players – the police, prosecutors and defence lawyers – should take the primary responsibility for moving the case on. They should concentrate on improving the quality of the preparation for trial rather than trying to compensate for its poor quality by indulging in a cumbrous and expensive system of often unnecessary and counterproductive court hearings.[718]

The way to do that, he said, was 'by adequate organising and resourcing of the police, prosecutors, defence practitioners and the courts, including the provision of a common information system of information technology for all of them and the Prison and Probation Services' (*ibid*).

Whether these hopes are realistic is a different question.

Auld on 'pre-trial assessment'

Auld suggested that in all Crown Court cases and as appropriate in the magistrates' courts, 'the court and the parties should set a provisional timetable by reference to a suitably adapted standard checklist or case management questionnaire, including a date before which trial should start' and that thereafter 'the parties should liaise with each other, informally communicating progress or lack of it, on key tasks to the court and any others involved'.[719] Courts now had case progression officers whose function it was to remind the parties of imminent deadlines. Such officers could assume a wider role, not only chasing progress, but also involving themselves in arrangements for listing and where appropriate obtaining and transmitting written directions of the judge.[720] In the event of a failure of such liaison the case could be listed for a pre-trial hearing.

The process, Auld said, should culminate in a 'pre-trial assessment' by the parties and the court, with the parties 'signifying in writing to each other and the court their readiness or otherwise for trial and the court responding in writing as appropriate'.[721] Where outstanding matters could not be resolved by written directions, there would be an oral pre-trial hearing. Wherever possible the defendant in custody should be asked to consent to participating by video link. The judge at such hearings should be able to make binding rulings on law, evidence or procedure subject to variation at trial as justice might require. It was

---

[716] Auld, Ch. 10, para. 218, p. 487.
[717] *Ibid*, para. 219, p. 487. For the contrary view that, on balance, the PDH is worth preserving for all Crown Court cases see the writer's response to the Auld Report accessible on www.lcd.gov.uk – Major Reports, Comments at pp. 55–63.
[718] Auld, Ch. 10, para. 220, p. 487.   [719] *Ibid*, para. 221, p. 488.
[720] *Ibid*, para. 210, p. 484, para. 221, p. 488.   [721] *Ibid*, para. 224, p. 489.

vital that trial advocates should attend any pre-trial hearing. All court orders should be recorded (which was not the case at present) and immediately or rapidly issued to the parties in writing. Ideally, it should be done electronically – though, Auld admitted, unfortunately the CREST computer system used in the Crown Court did not have this basic facility.[722]

Auld's 'pre-trial assessment' sounds much like what existed before which did not work. The Runciman Commission said that in 1982 a working party under the chairmanship of Lord Justice Watkins recommended a system of pre-trial discussion between the parties based on the exchange of forms giving information about the likely length of the case, the witnesses to be called, pleas and so on, but an experiment set up to try out the scheme had produced disappointing results. The use of the forms was patchy. Similarly, in the *Crown Court Study*, court clerks said that just under half (47 per cent) of the listing information forms that were supposed to be sent in by the lawyers had not been received and of those that were sent in, many were returned late.[723]

Sanctions as a management tool in criminal justice

Lord Justice Auld in his Review accepted that sanctions are mainly useless or inappropriate in promoting good standards in pre-trial work in criminal cases:

> Throughout the Review I have anxiously searched here and abroad for just and efficient sanctions and incentives to encourage better preparation for trial. A study of a number of recent and current reviews in other Commonwealth countries and in the USA shows that we are not alone in this search and that, as to sanctions at any rate it is largely in vain. In a recent report, the Standing Committee of Attorneys General in Australia commented: '. . . the primary aim is to encourage co-operation with pre-trial procedures. There are inherent practical and philosophical difficulties associated with sanctions for non-co-operation'.[724]

This conclusion stands in marked contrast to the views expressed in the Court Service's consultation paper *Transforming the Crown Court* issued under the imprimatur of the Lord Chancellor in September 1999 and in the Report of the National Audit Office, *Criminal Justice: Working Together* published in December 1999. The Court Service's consultation paper repeatedly stated that compliance with protocols and other case management performance standards must be enforced by sanctions. These it suggested should include on-the-spot fines or fixed financial penalties imposed by judges or by court staff under judicial direction. Financial penalties would apply to the police and other agencies. Consistent failure to comply could lead to agencies' budgets being capped. The National Audit Office Report equally urged that sanctions should play a central

---

[722] *Ibid*, paras. 225–7, pp. 489–90.

[723] M. Zander and P. Henderson, *Crown Court Study* (Royal Commission on Criminal Justice, Research Study No. 19, 1993) section 2.2.8.   [724] Auld, Ch. 10, para. 231, pp. 491–2.

part in court management. It recommended that: 'In taking forward its proposals to change Crown Court procedures, the Court Service should ensure that
appropriate forms of sanctions are introduced to help manage robustly'
(p. 110). It identified the sanctions available to the courts as costs orders against
the lawyers, reprimand in open court, reprimand in the judge's chambers, a
report to the head of chambers or, as the case may be, to the senior partner of
the firm of solicitors, and reference to the practitioner's professional body. The
same view was taken by the writer's fellow Commissioners on the Runciman
Royal Commission. Sanctions, they thought, should include docking fees,
wasted costs orders, or a report to the head of chambers or to the leader of the
circuit.

There is, in other words, a powerful disposition to imagine that sanctions are
an answer to the fact that pre-trial process does not function according to the
rules. (The same philosophy informed Lord Woolf's Report on *Access to Justice*.)
Not that that they are frequently used. The National Audit Office, which was so
enthusiastic about their use, said:

> For sanctions to be effective they need to be workable and appropriate. Magis-
> trates and court staff we spoke to criticised costs orders, which they considered
> to be overly cumbersome since a lawyer's right to make representations against
> an order can prove time consuming and expensive. They are also felt to be inap-
> propriately severe, since a single costs order can damage the reputation of an
> advocate, leading to hostility rather than co-operation between local defence
> solicitors and Crown Prosecution Service staff. Additional hearings may entail
> expenditure greater than the award itself.[725]

In a paper entitled 'What on Earth is Lord Justice Auld Supposed to Do?', the
writer urged Sir Robin to reject this fashionable current philosophy. ('It is time
that the belief in the value of sanctions in securing compliance with performance targets in the context of the justice system is challenged. People on the
whole do their work as best they can according to their abilities, so far as circumstances permit. If in the mass of cases the system is not working as it is supposed to do it is probably not the fault of those doing the work. Sometimes the
fault lies in the design of the system, but often there is no fault'.[726]) I expressed
the hope that, if Sir Robin were persuaded of this, 'it would be very helpful if he
said so in plain terms'. He did precisely that and he set out the reasons.[727] These
may be summarised as follows:

• An order for costs against the defendant is usually not an option because of his
  lack of means and because he cannot be blamed for the faults of his lawyers.
• The fairness of the trial is threatened if the defendant is under threat of sanctions if he or his lawyers misjudge the extent of their obligations to co-operate
  with pre-trial procedures.

---

[725] NAO, 1999 Report, p. 90, para. 4.67.   [726] *Criminal Law Review*, 2000, p. 419 at 429.
[727] Auld, para. 230, p. 491.

- Judges are reluctant to make costs orders against the prosecution involving a transfer of funds from one public body to another.
- In attempting to make wasted costs orders it is difficult to identify who was at fault – on the prosecution side, counsel, those instructing him or the police; on the defence side, counsel, his solicitor or the defendant. (There are of course many other possible culprits – quite apart from the possibility that no one was at fault (ed.).) Wasted costs proceedings are an impracticable and expensive way of achieving efficient preparation for trial.
- There are considerations of public interest, including the fairness of the trial, in extending the court's power to draw adverse inferences against a defaulting party or in seeking to import from civil process the notion of 'strike out', for example by depriving the defendant from advancing part of his case or by too ready a use of the court's power to stay a prosecution for abuse of process.

Despite his conclusion that 'there is little scope for improving on existing sanctions against the parties or their representatives for failure to prepare efficiently for trial',[728] Auld suggested two exceptions. With regard to his proposal that the parties shoulder primary responsibility for the task, having recourse to a pre-trial hearing only when there are matters they cannot reasonably resolve between them, he suggested that they should be penalised if they unnecessarily asked for a pre-trial hearing. The penalty would be loss of the fee for the unnecessary hearing. That would be open to all the same objections that Sir Robin levelled against wasted costs orders. The penalty would be used very rarely – and when used, would result in lengthy and costly debate and successful appeals. It would also be likely to have the effect of discouraging lawyers from asking for a pre-trial hearing in cases where one was actually needed.

Secondly, he suggested, the Bar Council and the Law Society should 'incorporate more stringent and detailed rules in their codes of conduct about preparation for trial' and should issue clear guidance 'as to the seriousness with which the court will view professional failures in this respect'.[729] The danger is that, if implemented, this could be not only useless but counter-productive. The more stringent and detailed the rules, the more they will not be complied with and to say that the courts will regard failure to comply with the stringent and detailed rules with 'seriousness' – having just acknowledged that there are no workable sanctions – is to invite cynicism.

Case Preparation Project

On 30 June 2003, Lord Falconer, newly installed as Secretary of State for Constitutional Affairs and Lord Chancellor, spoke at the national launch of the Case Preparation Project (CPP). The theme was 'Delivering justice – effective trial management'. CPP involves all the key players in the criminal justice

---

[728] Auld, para. 232, p. 492.   [729] Auld, para. 234, p. 492.

system – the police, CPS, judges and magistrates, court staff and the defence. There were six core proposals that would be tested by pilot studies in seven areas:

- *Clearer definition of roles and responsibilities* The responsibilities of the defence, the prosecution and the police in preparing cases at each stage of the case management process from the point of charge to disposal in the courts to be laid down in national protocols with accompanying quality standards. Responsibilities for the courts and the judiciary in supervising the process to be clearly defined.
- *A new case progression function* In each criminal justice area, each agency – the CPS, defence, police, magistrates and Crown Courts – to nominate a person or persons (case progression officers) for progressing cases through the system to the specified protocols and standards. This role to be adequately resourced. The case progression officers (including whoever has been nominated by the defence) to work together as a 'virtual team' to ensure that cases are managed effectively. Primary responsibility to be on the parties to ensure timely and adequate case preparation. The case progression function in the defence, CPS and police to ensure witness availability information is accurate and up-to-date and fed to the courts for listing. The court-based case progression officers to support the judiciary, identifying cases that require intervention and working closely with the listing office to ensure that cases are listed appropriately for trial based on accurate information. Judges and magistrates to have an explicit responsibility for supervising case progression. They would question the parties as to their conduct of the case and would intervene where issues in dispute needed to be resolved, where cases were not making appropriate progress and/or where the parties were not meeting the required standards and responsibilities for case preparation. In the magistrates' courts, specially trained legal advisers would have an enhanced role in supporting the lay magistracy in managing cases consistently – for instance by conducting case progression hearings.
- Process changes in the courts.
- *Magistrates' courts* Make the first hearing more effective. Magistrates, with the legal adviser, to conduct a robust review of the case, deal with allocation decisions, take pleas, identify case needs, make directions and fix a realistic timetable. Legal advisers to carry out pre-trial readiness checks/assessments outside the courtroom. Case progression officers to oversee progress and compliance with directions and orders given by the court.
- *Crown Courts* The new more robust first hearing in the magistrates' court would mean that fewer cases sent to the Crown Court would require a preliminary hearing in the Crown Court. There would be a flexible approach to PDHs – the judiciary, assisted by the court case progression officer and the parties, would decide whether an oral PDH was needed or whether an electronic or paper PDH was more efficient. The judiciary actively to inquire

whether the parties had identified the issues, were preparing adequately for trial and were complying with directions and the agreed timetable. Where appropriate sanctions might be used to penalise poor performance. For certain cases the parties to be required to prepare a case and issues summary to clarify the issues to be decided by the jury. (Not part of the pilots as it probably required legislation.) The parties responsible to certify the court that they were ready for trial in advance of the trial date.

- *Listing* To provide greater certainty, reduce the number of ineffective trials, increase confidence and value for money. More fixed dates. Revised listing practices to be built into a national framework.
- *Interventions to support better case management* The agencies would be given consistent targets and performance measures – for instance with regard to ineffective trials and witness measures. Examples of interventions being considered included, for the agencies, warnings at the local level, warnings at the national level, external inspections or audits; for the defence, audit by the Legal Services Commission or formal inspection.

   Local criminal justice boards to monitor and manage performance against the new targets and to consider what interventions were needed to keep everyone up to the mark. The Criminal Justice Joint Planning Unit to work on CPP as part of its drive to improve delivery nationwide.

- *Actions to 'incentivise' defendant behaviour* The judiciary to apply appropriate sanctions for hindering and obstructing the process – for instance by deliberately failing to attend hearings or keep appointments with lawyers. Requirements of the defendant to be linked to conditions of bail. Sanctions that could be applied could include financial penalties, a period in custody or community service. Defence representatives to be responsible for informing the court if the defendant persistently failed to attend meetings to take instructions or if there was a likelihood that the trial might be jeopardised.
- *Actions to 'incentivise' lawyers to case progression* The solicitor's and barrister's responsibilities for case preparation, case progression and their duty to the court to be articulated in protocols and standards. Fee structures to be adjusted to ensure that these responsibilities were appropriately and explicitly remunerated. This might include front-loading of fees and efficiency payments where cases were brought and concluded expeditiously.
- Persistent failures by an individual practitioner or professional practice (prosecution or defence) to fulfil the case preparation protocols and to meet the agreed standard subject to a range of possible interventions. For the prosecution this could include individual warnings, warnings at national level, inspections or audits. For the defence this could include warnings from the Legal Services Commission (LSC), mandatory audits by the LSC, withholding of fees, peer review and ultimately withdrawal of LSC contracts.

This was an ambitious and far-reaching project to which the Government was committing serious resources. The headquarters unit alone had some fifty persons. The pilots in seven areas were scheduled to take from summer 2003 to summer 2004 with an evaluation over nine to twelve months.

Commenting on the launch the writer expressed reservations about the project:

M. Zander, 'Can the Criminal Justice System be Licked into Shape?' *New Law Journal*, 11 July 2003, p. 1049

Lord Falconer made clear that this programme of criminal justice reform was 'an absolute priority of the Government'.

The overall plans involve all the relevant agencies and, remarkably, at least at this stage, they seem to be on board. (Ken Macdonald QC, the new chair of the Criminal Bar Association, for instance, pledged the full support of the CBA for the reforms.) The project will be well resourced. There will be pilot studies and external evaluation. The plans at this stage are fluid and will be adjusted in light of experience.

Given all this constructive effort aimed at laudable objectives it seems churlish to raise serious doubts about the project. The doubts fall into four distinct categories.

Even though the concerted reform effort is greater than ever before, many of the problems addressed may be too deep-seated to be solved. Experience with one attempt at reform after another suggests that any system that requires the parties to take responsibility for the proper and timely preparation of criminal cases, for monitoring each other, for notifying the court of problems as necessary, for completing forms, will fail in too a large proportion of cases to make successful enforcement action a practical proposition. Frustration at failure will tend to generate either resignation or more and more punitive sanctions – with little practical effect.

Although significant resources are being put into the project, they will be insufficient to test whether the new ideas are practicable. To take only the most obvious example, it will be years before the court IT system is adequate to the task. In the meanwhile the cost of providing sufficient human resources to give the system a chance of working as proposed will be prohibitive.

Worse, some of the proposed solutions to the problems will be counter-productive. Wasted cost orders, for instance, as Lord Justice Auld recognised, tend to generate cumbrous satellite proceedings. Paying lawyers more for pre-trial work will put more money in their pockets, thus pushing up costs to the taxpayer, but will probably not generate either savings or other benefits elsewhere.

More fundamentally, to the extent that the reforms do work, the effort and expense required could be out of proportion to the attainable gains. Ironically, in the very week of the CPP conference, both the Prime Minister and the Trade and Industry Secretary, Patricia Hewitt, acknowledged that maybe the Government had been wrong to devote so much energy to 'delivery' and performance targets. As the Audit Commission recently said, targets and indicators may 'encourage counter-productive activity (for example allocating disproportionate resources to certain activities because they are being measured)'.[730]

---

[730] *Route to Justice*, 2002.

> Lord Falconer said at the conference that his priority was to produce a criminal justice system 'which people trust and above all respect'. The extent of people's trust and respect for the system is based on a complex and shifting bundle of factors. It seems improbable that it could be affected much, if at all, by the outcome of this initiative. The project will be worthwhile if evaluation shows that it has achieved useful results proportionate to the costs and effort expended – regardless of whether the general public knows or cares.

The CPP was carried forward in a variety of ways:

- In June 2004 the new Criminal Procedure Rules Committee met for the first time. The Criminal Procedure Rules were promulgated in April 2005. As was seen above (pp. 153–54), the Rules make it explicit that the judiciary are responsible for case management – notably at the PCMH which replaced the PDH.
- The CPP became the Effective Trial Management programme established by the DCA, the Attorney General and Home Office.
- In July 2004 the Lord Chief Justice, the Attorney General, the Lord Chancellor and Home Office Minister Baroness Scotland issued the Criminal Cases Management Framework (CCMF). A second edition was issued in July 2005 (www.cjs.online.gov.uk/framework). The CCMF (194 pages) provides operational practitioners with guidance on how cases could be managed more efficiently from start to finish. It describes case management procedures and the roles and responsibilities of administrative staff operating these procedures and of the defence. It also sets out the expectations of the judiciary. It includes references to new practices for charging (p. 248 below) and witness management ('No Witness, No Justice')[731] being delivered through the Criminal Case Management Programme.

The CCMF is an impressive document. If everyone acted in accordance with its prescriptions the system would be functioning beautifully.

One measure of efficient management of the system is the proportion of trials that are 'ineffective' in the sense that they cannot go ahead because one or other side is not ready. In 2003 the percentage of ineffective trials in magistrates' courts was 29.4 per cent, in 2004 it was 26 per cent and in 2005 it was 21.7 per cent.[732] This trend is encouraging.

Another set of figures relates to trials that 'crack' i.e. do not go ahead either because the defendant pleads guilty or because the prosecution drops the case. In each of the years 2003, 2004 and 2005 the proportion of trials that cracked because of late pleas was 23 per cent. In the same years the proportion that cracked because the prosecution dropped the case was 14.6 per cent, 14.2 per cent and 13.5 per cent.[733] The figures for cracked trials therefore show little improvement.

---

[731] This project brings together the police and the CPS to meet the needs of victims and witnesses.   [732] *Judicial Statistics 2005 (Revised)*, Table 7.1.   [733] *Ibid*, Table 7.2.

Another set of figures show the average length of hearings in the Crown Court. In the years 2003, 2004 and 2005 the average length of not guilty plea cases was 9.6, 9.5 and 9.8 hours. The average length of guilty plea hearings was 1.2, 1.2 and 1.3 hours. The average length of cases for sentence only was 0.6 hours in all three years.[734] There was therefore no improvement in that respect.

15. Preparation of cases by the defence

A depressing picture of the way cases are (or at least were) prepared by defence lawyers emerged from research conducted by Professor M. McConville and colleagues J. Hodgson, L. Bridges and A. Pavlovic, published as *Standing Accused* (Clarendon Press, 1994). The study was the first to try to explain what defence lawyers actually do. It was based on an examination of files, attending police stations, sitting in on legal advice sessions in police stations, attending questioning of suspects by police officers, interviews with clients, attending interviews with clients in the solicitor's office and at court and conferences with counsel. Interviews were also conducted with the lawyers and their staff.

The main research was conducted over a three-year period starting in October 1988. In that period the researchers observed the practices of twenty-two firms of solicitors in cities and towns in the South West, East Anglia, the South, Central and North Midlands, the North West and the North East of England. 'The firms were chosen for the most part because of their status as mass deliverers of legal services in criminal cases in their localities' (p. 15). In some cases the researcher spent several months with the firm. For most the observation period lasted between four and eight researcher weeks. Shorter periods were spent with firms with smaller practices. The average time spent with each firm was six and a half researcher weeks. In addition to this main sample, another twenty-six firms and three independent agencies were targeted by police station advice and interrogation observation. The average period spent observing this sample of firms was about two weeks. In total therefore there were forty-eight firms in the study and the research covered 198 researcher weeks of observation.

The research came to the following conclusions:

• Almost all those interviewed in the firms 'came to see criminal defence practices as geared, in co-operation with the other elements of the system, toward the routine production of guilty pleas' (p. 71). ('In the process, any notions they have carried with them into practice of criminal defence work being based in an adversarial process and involving careful investigation and construction of the individual's case are disabused' (*ibid*).)
• Many suspects in the police station do not appreciate the significance of the right to free legal advice, some are dissuaded by the police and some are

---

[734] *Ibid*, Table 6.21.

confronted by solicitors who do not want to attend the police station. Many of those who do police station work are former police officers. Non-solicitor clerks generally cannot offer legal advice. 'Advisers of all grades fall in with police routines and are responsive to police expectations that the private interview with the client will be over in a matter of minutes. Consultations are hurried and produce only an outline of the client's account sufficient to enable the adviser to slot the case into one of the "typical case" categories with which advisers are familiar' (p. 100).

Defence advisers present during interviews conducted by the police make few if any objections to the way the interview is conducted:

> Looked at as a whole, advisers who attend police stations accept uncritically the propriety and legitimacy of police action, even where what they witness them-selves, what they hear from clients, and what they suspect goes on, leaves them convinced that the police break the rules and in other ways are beyond the law. The reason for this is that many advisers, like the police, instinctively believe, without requiring substantiation through evidence, that there is a case to answer, and that it is the client who must give the answer. This in turn springs from a working assumption that the client is probably factually guilty [pp. 126–7].
>
> Defence advisers, most of whom are non-qualified staff, are less concerned with establishing the circumstances relating to the alleged offence than with securing from the client a promise to plead guilty. Their dealings with the clients, based on personal relationships, operate on the principle that the client has done something and should plead. Clerks do not assiduously test for the existence of defences or satisfy themselves that all legal requirements of guilt are met, nor do they have the skills to undertake such an inquiry . . . Many solici-tors are court-based, keep a distance from clients and delegate all tasks short of advocacy to non-qualified staff on an ungraded and unsupervised basis [p. 159].

Legally aided clients are not generally encouraged to tell their stories. In so far as their version emerges they are taught that it is not worth recording, that it will not persuade any court and should be abandoned in the face of police evi-dence. Statements of clients are routinely disregarded. The adviser persuades the client that his case is not worth pursuing. Those that survive to trial do so despite, not because of, the process. 'Conviction is achieved in the office of their own adviser through a process whose methodologies most nearly resemble those of the police themselves' (p. 160).

Plea settlement and pleas in mitigation are dealt with in a routine manner. Magistrates' courts are seen by solicitors as places where clients can be processed through guilty pleas. Defence solicitors fail to see their own central role in the production of guilty pleas:

> In magistrates' courts, the principal strength of prosecution cases lies in their heavy reliance upon evidence from the police. Such evidence assumes legitimacy because it is practiced, assertive and depersonalised. Supported by notebook entries and the testimony of fellow officers, the self-legitimating and mutually supporting character of police evidence commends itself to magistrates . . .

> Against this there is often no separate, competing case for the defence. The general lack of investigation and preparation by solicitors and their staff, throws the burden of the defence onto the defendant [p. 237].
>
> So far as conviction or acquittal is concerned, any success defence solicitors have at trials themselves tends to be a product of what they can achieve 'on their feet' in court and whatever 'turns up' on the day [p. 238].

For Crown Court cases a few firms were exceptional in employing competent and experienced staff:

> Here the case was prepared well in advance and a real effort made to engage in proactive defence work. Witnesses were sought and pursued until contacted; enquiry agents were sent to draw up plans of the scene of the crime; and forensic experts were employed in response to the client's assertion of inaccurate or fabricated evidence. However, these individuals were quite exceptional, even within the firms in which they were employed. In the majority of practices much preparatory work is undertaken by non-qualified staff, and solicitors themselves have little contact with routine Crown Court cases . . . In an unacceptably high number of cases, evidence is still being gathered long after the time when it was first available, sometimes during the trial itself . . . The role definition applied to staff leads solicitors to employ junior, casual or part-time individuals who are not otherwise involved in the case at all. The fact that the rates of remuneration are so low shows that it is not just solicitors who undervalue these tasks but the state itself . . . With occasional outstanding exceptions, the average solicitor has little involvement in preparing these cases, and what work is done is often too little and too late [pp. 267–8].

A few barristers were strongly committed to cases and were careful to test the underlying basis of a guilty plea, but most barristers were not:

> Strikingly on the hearing day at court, but also in conferences in chambers, barristers evince little interest in scrutinising the evidence or in attempting to convince the defendant of its weight and probative value. Rather, conferences are treated as 'disclosure interviews', the purpose of which is to extract a plea of guilty from the client. In this process, what the prosecution alleges, what witnesses may say, and what the client wishes to say, are not discussed . . . In place of evidence, a whole gamut of persuasive tactics is deployed against clients enabling barristers to take control of cases and to prevent most clients from becoming, in any real sense, defendants [pp. 268–9].

For a different picture given by the actual participants in the process see the *Crown Court Study*.[735] This confirmed that a high proportion of briefs are received by the barrister in the case at the last minute – 40 per cent of prosecution barristers and 25 per cent of defence barristers got the brief in contested cases after 4pm of the day before the trial (p. 30). 59 per cent of prosecution barristers and 44 per cent of defence barristers said it was a returned brief

---

[735] M. Zander and P. Henderson, *Crown Court Study* (Royal Commission on Criminal Justice, Research Study No. 19, 1993).

(p. 32). A quarter of all barristers said the brief was not adequate (p. 33), but despite this almost all the barristers thought they had enough time to prepare the case (pp. 30–1) and 71 per cent of prosecution barristers and 83 per cent of defence barristers said they had been able to rectify inadequacies in the brief (p. 33).

The judges were asked whether counsel was well-prepared. Nearly half the judges (47 per cent) thought the prosecution counsel was 'very well prepared' and the same proportion thought counsel was 'adequately prepared'. Only 6 per cent thought counsel was 'not well prepared' (p. 47). The judicial assessment of defence counsel was precisely the same (pp. 59–60).

16. Delays in criminal cases

Another measure of efficiency in the system is the extent of delays. Delay is affected by whether the defendant pleads guilty or not guilty and whether he is on bail or in custody.

In the years 2003, 2004 and 2005 the average waiting time from committal for defendants pleading not guilty in the Crown Court was 20.3, 20.9 and 21.3 weeks. In the same years the average waiting time for those pleading guilty was 12.0, 12.4 and 12.0 weeks.[736]

In the same years the average waiting time for defendants on bail was 15.7, 16.2 and 15.9 weeks and for defendants in custody was 13.5, 14.0 and 14.0 weeks.[737]

In the magistrates' courts the delays are of course less. In the years 2003, 2004 and 2005 the average time from first court listing to completion in all criminal cases was thirty-two, thirty-three and thirty-one days.[738]

In either-way cases dealt with in the magistrates' courts the average time from first listing to completion in those years was fifty-six, fifty-five and fifty-four days.[739]

The picture is mixed but overall there cannot be celebration about any strong trend in the direction of improvements.[740]

For a perceptive analysis of the reasons for delays in the criminal justice system see I. Kelcey, 'Delays, the Truth, the Whole Truth and Nothing but the Truth', 152 *New Law Journal,* 15 November 2002, p. 1726.

---

[736] *Judicial Statistics,* Table 6.18.   [737] *Ibid.*   [738] *Ibid,* Table 7.4.   [739] *Ibid,* Table 7.3.

[740] Tables 6.16 and 6.17 of the annual *Judicial Statistics* show the percentage of Crown Court cases dealt with in under eight weeks and under sixteen weeks from committal according to plea and according to bail/custody status. Again the picture is mixed but there is no indication of marked improvement. Indeed compared with the figures for 2001 and 2002 the picture is clearly worse. Thus the proportion of defendants in custody dealt with in under eight weeks in the years 2001–5 was 49.5 per cent, 41.9 per cent, 38.6 per cent, 36.6 per cent and 37.1 per cent. The proportion dealt with in under sixteen weeks in those five years was 78.4 per cent, 72.0 per cent, 69.4 per cent, 67.6 per cent and 69.0 per cent. In both sets of figures there is a consistent year on year deterioration from 2001–4 and the 2005 figures are significantly worse than for 2001.

Time limits

Overall time limits

In Scotland there is a rule that a jury trial must commence within 110 days of committal if the accused is in custody (subject to the court's power to grant an extension) and within one year if he is on bail. If either deadline is passed the prosecution is stayed. The only equivalent in the English system is the rule that summary offences in the magistrates' courts must be started within six months of the alleged offence.[741]

Lord Justice Auld in his report addressed himself to the question whether the English system should adopt the Scottish approach. He was clear that it should not. The Scottish experience was not encouraging:

> The availability of these time limits does not, in general, contribute to the aim of efficient and speedy preparation for trial. To comply with them procurators fiscal[742] frequently have to list cases for trial even when they are not, or may not be, ready and then seek repeated adjournments while the parties continue to prepare for trial. Not only does such necessity defeat the purpose of the time limits, but it also causes much waste of time and other inconvenience to defendants, witnesses, victims and all others involved in the process. In Canada a decision of the Supreme Court[743] interpreting the constitutional right of defendants charged with serious offences to trial within a reasonable time, led to so many motions to stay, that the prosecution dropped thousands of cases awaiting trial. The resultant public outcry contributed eventually to the legislature reclassifying a broad range of offences so as to take them outside that relatively loose time bar.
>
> Similar experiences in other jurisdictions suggest that the Secretary of State has been well advised in not introducing overall time limits here. Compliance with arbitrary and rigid time limits is likely to give only an illusion of speedy preparation for trial, hiding the reality of injustice in substantive and procedural compromises that they may impose on the criminal justice process. At their worst, they may prevent conviction of the guilty while doing little to speed the trial of both guilty and innocent. Neither is conducive to public confidence in the system.[744]

Custody time limits

Custody time limits have been part of the English system since the mid-1980s.[745] When a time limit is exceeded the result is not, as in Scotland, that the case is stayed but rather that the defendant has to be released on bail – subject to the limitations on the right to bail imposed by s. 25 of the Criminal Justice and

---

[741] Magistrates' Courts Act 1980, s. 127.   [742] The Scottish equivalent of the CPS.

[743] *R v. Askov* (1990) 79 CR (3rd) 273, 56 CCC (3rd) 449 (SCC).

[744] Auld, Ch. 10, paras. 263–4, p. 504.

[745] The Prosecution of Offenders Act 1985, s. 2 empowered the Secretary of State to set time limits for the preliminary stages of criminal proceedings by regulations. The time limits are specified in the Prosecution of Offences (Custody Time Limits) Regulations 1987 and the (Amendment) Regulations 1999.

Public Order Act 1994 (p. 278 above). The expiry of a custody time limit could amount to 'exceptional circumstances' within the meaning of s. 25 so as to justify a grant of bail.

In summary-only or either-way cases, the maximum custody period from first appearance to summary trial is fifty-six days. For either-way cases, the limit to trial or committal is seventy days. For indictable-only offences, the limit is seventy days before committal and 112 days from committal. If the case is 'sent' under s. 51 of the Crime and Disorder Act 1998 or now under Sch. 3 of the Criminal Justice Act 2003, the limit is 112 days including time spent in custody at the instance of the magistrates' court or 112 days whichever is the longer.

Each charge has its own time limit. In *R (Wardle) v. Leeds Crown Court*[746] W was charged with murder. On the day the time limit expired the prosecution offered no evidence on that charge but laid a new charge of manslaughter. The House of Lords held that a new seventy-day time limit began on that day, but the prosecution had to show that the new charge had not been brought solely (Lord Hope and Lord Clyde) or primarily (Lord Slynn) to obtain a fresh custody time limit.[747]

Extension of custody time limits[748]

A court may extend the custody time limit if it is satisfied that the need for it is due to 'some . . . good and sufficient cause' and 'that the prosecution has acted with all due diligence and expedition'.[749] The concepts are separate and have separate meanings. They have generated a great deal of case law.[750]

In *R v. Governor of Winchester Prison, ex p Roddie*[751] the prosecution asked for an extension of time because of delays in getting the papers ready due to the police being drastically understaffed. The Divisional Court held that neither the seriousness of the offence, nor the fact that the extension was for a short period, nor that the police were understaffed constituted good and sufficient grounds for an extension of time. Once the time limit had expired there was no discretion to extend it. The accused was held unlawfully for six weeks until the date of his committal. (A person being held unlawfully because of a breach of the custody time limits rules can apply for release on bail or by way of *habeas corpus*, but he cannot obtain damages as the time limit rules do not create a right of action.[752])

However, in *R (on the application of Gibson) v. Winchester Crown Court*[753] the Divisional Court held that an extension could be granted even though the

---

[746] [2001] UKHL 12, [2001] Crim LR 468 and commentary at 469.

[747] Note the powerful dissents by Lords Scott and Nicholls – who said respectively that the majority view was 'absurd' and 'simply nonsense'.

[748] See N. Corrie and D. Wolchover, *Bail in Criminal Proceedings* (2004, Oxford) pp. 476–87.

[749] Prosecution of Offences Act 1985, s. 22(3) as amended. Prior to the amendments introduced by the Crime and Disorder Act 1998, s. 43 the requirement was only 'all due expedition'.

[750] For a helpful brief overview see A. Samuels, 'Application for an Extension of the Custody Time Limit', 168 *Justice of the Peace*, 26 June 2004, pp. 494–6.   [751] [1991] 2 All ER 931.

[752] *Olotu* [1997] 1 WLR 328, [1997] 1 All ER 385.

[753] [2004] EWHC 361, QBD, [2004] Crim LR 839 and commentary at 840.

prosecution had not acted with all due diligence where that was not the cause of delay. The cause there was lack of available courtrooms.

In November 1998, the Lord Chief Justice, giving judgment in five appeals in the Divisional Court, said that the exercise of the discretion to grant an extension was for the judge, taking into account all the relevant factors. It was neither possible nor desirable to try to define what may or may not amount to good and sufficient cause for granting an extension. The Divisional Court would be reluctant to interfere with the judge's decision,[754] but the court said that custody periods should be as short as possible and that the prosecution must prepare cases with all due diligence and expedition. The parties were not permitted to enter consent orders. Great caution should be exercised over a request for an extension by the prosecution based on a shortage of judges or courtrooms. If a case was not remarkable it could be tried by any judge of the appropriate status. Difficulties in listing cases would normally not be a ground for granting an extension of time.

An application for an extension has to be made *before the time limit expires* after two days' notice has been given.[755] This has given rise to considerable difficulties. In *R v. Sheffield Justices, ex p Turner*[756] the accused was charged with murder. Both the CPS and the defendant's solicitor miscalculated the time limit and thought it ended on 23 August when in fact it ended the previous day. The application for an extension of the time limit which was granted on 23 August was therefore technically too late. The Divisional Court ruled that the accused was held unlawfully from 23 August until his committal on 20 September, but that from 20 September he was again held lawfully because on that date he had been committed for trial. The fact that the time limit had expired on 22 August did not invalidate the committal on 20 September.

Auld recommended amendment of s. 22 of the Prosecution of Offenders Act 1985 to enable a court to consider and grant an extension of the custody time limit after it has expired – providing that it is narrowly drawn, including a provision that the court must be satisfied that there is a compelling public interest. Also he recommended that there should be a right of appeal against a refusal of an extension.[757]

Stay of prosecution because of delay

If delay in bringing the prosecution is excessive the case may be stopped ('stayed') as an abuse of the process of the court, but the courts are extremely reluctant to entertain such an application.[758] In *Symons* [759] in March 2006 the

---

[754] *R v. Crown Court at Manchester, ex p McDonald* (1999) 1 Cr App Rep 409, [1999] 1 All ER 805.
[755] In *R v. Governor of Canterbury Prison, ex p Craig* [1990] 2 All ER 654 the Divisional Court held that the notice requirements are directory not mandatory and the court can give an extension if satisfied that there is a good and sufficient reason to do so.
[756] [1991] 1 All ER 858.   [757] Auld, Ch. 10, paras. 267–70, pp. 505–7.
[758] See *A-G's Reference (No 1 of 1990)* [1992] QB 630 at 644; *Hooper* [2003] EWCA Crim 2427 at [76]; *B* [2003] 2 Cr App R 197 at [15]–[18]; *Smolinski* [2004] 2 Cr App R 661 at [7].
[759] [2006] EWCA Crim 756; [2006] 2 Cr. App. Rep. 23.

Divisional Court stated the principles that should be followed: a permanent stay should be exceptional even where delay was unjustifiable, a stay would very rarely be granted where there was no fault on the part of the complainant or the prosecution, no stay should be granted unless the defence was so seriously prejudiced that a fair trial would not be possible and in considering the question of prejudice the court should have regard to its power to regulate the admissibility of evidence. If a fair trial was possible, a stay should not be granted. (In that case S was sentenced to seven years' imprisonment for the rape and indecent assault of his own sisters in the 1970s. The trial judge had allowed the case to go forward. The Court of Appeal held the conviction was not unsafe.)

In *Darmalingum v. Mauritius*[760] the Judicial Committee of the Privy Council allowed an appeal on the ground of undue delay where M's conviction for forgery had been dismissed twelve and a half years after his arrest. The Constitution of Mauritius guaranteed the right to a fair hearing within a reasonable time. Lord Steyn said: 'Even if his guilt is manifest, this factor cannot justify or excuse a breach of the guarantee of disposal within a reasonable time'. The reasonable time requirement was a separate guarantee. It was not necessary to establish that the appellant's case had been prejudiced by the delay.

However, within four months, in *Flowers v. Jamaica*[761] a differently constituted Judicial Committee interpreting an identical provision in the Constitution of Jamaica, came to a different conclusion – the right to trial within a reasonable time was not a separate guarantee but rather part of an overall provision. In order to succeed the appellant had to establish, *inter alia*, prejudice arising from the delay.

The question was considered again in light of Article 6(1) of the ECHR by nine law lords in *Attorney General's Reference No 2 of 2001*.[762] The Court of Appeal had taken the same approach as that of the Judicial Committee in *Flowers*.[763] The House of Lords, by seven to two,[764] upheld the Court of Appeal's decision. Criminal proceedings could be stayed on the ground of delay only if a fair hearing was no longer possible or it was for any other compelling reason unfair to try the defendant. Article 6(1) guaranteed a hearing with certain characteristics. It would be anomalous if breach of the reasonable time requirement had a more far-reaching effect than a breach of other Article 6(1) rights. There were various possible remedies for the breach. If it was established before the trial, action could be taken to expedite the trial. The defendant might be

---

[760] [2000] 1 WLR 2303.   [761] [2000] 1 WLR 2396.

[762] *A-G's Reference (No 2 of 2001)* [2003] UKHL 68, [2004] 1 All ER 1049.

[763] [2001] 1 WLR 1869. For sharp criticism of the decision see A. Webster QC, 'Delay and Article 6(1)', *Criminal Law Review*, 2001, pp. 786–93.

[764] A critical review of the decision commented: 'it is not perhaps surprising that the two dissenting judges came from Scotland where a strict view has long been taken toward the prevention of delay through the imposition of time limits' – J. Jackson and J. Johnstone, 'The Reasonable Time Requirement: an Independent and Meaningful Right?', *Criminal Law Review*, 2005, pp. 3–23 at 4. Lord Hope in his judgment at [62] said that the Scottish 110-day rule had existed for more than three centuries.

released on bail. If it was established after the hearing, there could be an apology, a reduction in sentence or the payment of compensation. It would only be right to quash the conviction if the hearing had been unfair or it had been unfair to try the defendant at all.[765]

17. Publicity and contempt of court

It is a principle of fundamental importance both at common law and under the European Convention on Human Rights that the trial of an accused person should not be prejudiced by inappropriate pre-trial publicity or by publication of prejudicial material during the trial itself. Traditionally, English law controlling the media with regard to publication of pre-trial material has been strict; in practice in recent years it has become far less so.

There are two main different kinds of approach to the problem – to prohibit certain kinds of publication and to penalise breaches by proceedings for contempt of court or, alternatively, to grant a stay or to quash proceedings in the case which is the subject of the publicity. Until very recently almost all English law has been of the former kind, but in recent years there has emerged also the question whether proceedings should be stayed in advance or be annulled retrospectively because of excessive media publicity.[766]

Under the Contempt of Court Act 1981 it is unlawful to publish anything which 'creates a substantial risk that the course of justice in the proceedings will be seriously impeded or prejudiced' (s. 2(2)). The rule takes effect from the moment when proceedings are 'active', which in criminal cases is from the moment of arrest without a warrant or from the issue of a warrant or from the charging of a suspect.[767]

Publicity before criminal proceedings are active

Publication of prejudicial material at a point in time where there is as yet no suspect would therefore not fall foul of the statutory rule, though it could be the common law contempt of intending to prejudice potential criminal proceedings. This was held to apply to *The Sun* newspaper in 1988 when it delayed laying information before magistrates for a private prosecution it was funding until after it had published its story about a doctor allegedly raping an eight-year-old girl. The *sub judice* period did not begin until the information was laid so that the 1981 Act had not been breached, but after the doctor had been

---

[765] For analysis and criticism of the decision see Jackson and Johnstone, n. 764 above. See also J. Jackson, J. Johnstone and J. Shapland, 'Delay, Human Rights and the Need for Statutory Time Limits in Youth Cases', *Criminal Law Review*, 2003, pp. 510–13.

[766] For a general review of developments up to the mid-1990s see D. Corker and M. Levi, 'Pre-trial Publicity and its Treatment in the English Courts', *Criminal Law Review*, 1996, pp. 622–32. For research evidence that pre-trial publicity seems to have little or no impact on jurors see pp. 376–77 below.   [767] Contempt of Court Act 1981, Sch. 1, paras. 3–5.

acquitted, the paper was held to have committed a common law contempt by proclaiming the doctor's guilt. A fine of £75,000 was imposed.[768] By contrast, *The Daily Sport* published the previous convictions of a man the police suspected of kidnapping a girl after the police asked the media not to publish the information. No warrant had yet been issued for the arrest of the man. The editor said that he got the message about the police request not to publish the information too late. The court held that there would not be liability for common law contempt unless there was overwhelming evidence of intent to prejudice the proceedings. The court criticised the paper but did not find such intent.[769] The decision was somewhat surprising as the paper knew that the man was likely to be arrested and obviously appreciated that publication of his previous convictions would be highly prejudicial.

Publicity when criminal proceedings are active

Once criminal proceedings are 'active' the media publish prejudicial material at their peril. They are liable for contempt even though it cannot be proved that they intended to prejudice a fair trial. There is an exception, however, if they can show that they did not know and had no reason to know that criminal proceedings were active (s. 3(1)). It is also a defence if it can be established that publication was part of a discussion of public affairs or matters of public interest if the risk of prejudice to the proceedings is incidental to the discussion (s. 5).

Proceedings to enforce the law

In recent years the standard of compliance with the spirit of the law of contempt in criminal cases has slipped considerably. The media now frequently publish material in the early stages of a case which in former times would have resulted in severe penalties on editors. In the sensational case of the 'Yorkshire Ripper' most of the press published quotes from the police on the day of the arrest of the suspect, Peter Sutcliffe, indicating that the police were jubilant at having caught the man they were hunting. It was clear that the search for the Ripper was over. One or two papers even published photographs of him in spite of the fact that there might well have been issues of identification evidence. The Attorney General happened to be out of the country at the time. The Solicitor General merely issued a letter to editors reminding them of the law of contempt, but no proceedings followed.

Another huge wave of media publicity followed the arrest of Michael Fagan in 1982 after he had been found in the Queen's bedroom at Buckingham Palace. This time proceedings *were* brought against several newspapers for publishing material about Fagan that showed him to be feckless, that he had been a 'junkie'

---

[768] *A-G v. News Group Newspapers Plc* [1988] 2 All ER 906.
[769] *A-G v. Sport Newspapers Ltd* [1992] 1 All ER 503.

and had marriage problems and that other criminal proceedings were pending against him. As *The Times* said (12 February 1983): 'It was fortissimo and it was as lurid as the pettiness of the material permitted. Any idea that while a man has a criminal charge outstanding against him his character is in baulk[770] was thrown to the wind', but, to general surprise, the Divisional Court, with the Lord Chief Justice presiding, rejected all but one of the charges against the papers. It therefore set a lower standard of conduct for the press than would have been thought right before.[771]

In 1994, the Court of Appeal quashed the conviction for murder of two sisters, Michelle and Lisa Taylor, because of prejudicial pre-trial publicity and material irregularities at the trial.[772] The Court of Appeal referred the case to the Attorney General and asked him to consider bringing proceedings for contempt against the newspapers concerned, but the Solicitor General declined to do so. The two sisters were given leave to bring proceedings for judicial review against the Attorney General's failure to take proceedings against the newspapers, but the Divisional Court dismissed the proceedings on the ground that, even though some of the newspaper reports crossed the acceptable limits of fair and accurate reporting, the Attorney General's discretion not to act could not be reviewed by the courts.[773]

In 1995, the trial judge refused to stay the proceedings against the Maxwell brothers, Kevin and Ian (sons of Robert Maxwell), who had been the subject of a great deal of adverse pre-trial publicity before their trial for fraud. In the event, the jury acquitted the defendants. Mr Justice Phillips (now Lord Chief Justice) spoke of the way in which, especially in a long case, all the participants in the case are dominated by the experience:

> It is something that it is impossible to exaggerate. As the weeks go by the trial becomes not merely part of life, but the dominant feature of it so that the stage is reached when one can hardly see behind or beyond it, and I am quite sure that this is true of all who are involved in the trial. The responsibility of reaching verdicts is a heavy one in any case, but in a case such as this it is one of which the jury will be particularly aware. I do not believe that their verdicts will be influenced by anything they may have read about individual defendants before the trial begins.

In October 1995, a trial judge did stop the trial of Geoff Knights, partner of *EastEnders* star Gillian Taylforth, because of what the judge called 'unlawful reporting and scandalous reporting'. (Knights was charged on 17 April 1995. On the following day the *Daily Mail* and *Today* published interviews with witnesses, the *Daily Star* said he 'had gone berserk with an iron bar after catching Miss Taylforth with another man' and a few days later the *Daily Mail* published

---

[770] For the uninitiated, a billiards term meaning 'out of play' (ed.).
[771] *A-G v. Times Newspapers* (1983) Times, 12 February.
[772] *R v. Taylor and Taylor* (1993) 98 Cr App Rep 361.
[773] For comment see B. Naylor, 'Fair Trial and Free Press: Legal Responses to Media Reports of Criminal Trials', 53 *Cambridge Law Journal*, 1994, pp. 492–501.

a lengthy interview with a potential witness along with an account of Knights' previous convictions.[774]) The case was said to be the first where the trial was abandoned before it started, simply because of pre-trial publicity.[775]

The Attorney General brought proceedings against various newspapers for contempt of court arising out of the case of Geoff Knights. He did not succeed. The Divisional Court held that the saturation media coverage given over previous years to the relationship between Geoff Knights and Gillian Taylforth, including his violent behaviour on previous occasions and his previous convictions, had continued until a month before the incident in 1995 which led to the abortive proceedings. It could not be said that any of the publications in April/May 1995 had created a greater risk of prejudice than that which had already been created.[776]

In 1996, the Court of Appeal upheld the conviction of Rosemary West who with her husband Fred West had been charged with multiple horrific murders. After his suicide, she was eventually convicted of ten murders. There had been massive pre-trial press coverage. The question, the Court of Appeal said, was whether it was possible to have a fair trial after such intensive, unfavourable publicity. Lord Chief Justice Taylor said: 'To hold otherwise would mean that if allegations are sufficiently horrendous so as inevitably to shock the nation, the accused cannot be tried. That would be absurd'. The jury had been adequately directed that they must act only on the evidence given in court.[777]

In *A-G v. Birmingham Post and Mail Ltd*[778] the Attorney General did succeed in contempt of court proceedings in respect of an article suggesting that a murder which was then the subject of a trial had been carried out by members of a notorious gang. The article had not identified any of the defendants but the judge had stopped the trial and it started again with a different jury in a different town and ended with convictions. A fine of £20,000 was imposed on the newspaper.[779]

In April 2001, the trial judge stopped the trial on charges of affray of two famous Leeds United footballers, Lee Bowyer and Jonathan Woodgate, after he found that an article in the *Sunday Mirror* had been 'seriously prejudicial'. The article, which framed the case as racially motivated, was published shortly before the end of a long trial. The wasted costs were estimated to be in the region of £8 million. A ten-week retrial ended that December with the acquittal of Bowyer and the conviction of Woodgate on a minor charge.[780] The newspaper

---

[774] See national newspapers on 5 October 1995 and E. Crowther, 'Publish and Then be Damned', *Justice of the Peace*, 13 January 1996, p. 26.

[775] In October 1995, the Attorney General said that at least five trials, including that of Knights, had been halted in the previous three years because the trial judge decided that media coverage would make a fair trial impossible (House of Commons, *Hansard*, 26 October 1995, vol. 264, cols. 797–807).   [776] *A-G v. MGN Ltd* [1997] 1 All ER 456.

[777] *West* [1996] 2 Cr App Rep 374.   [778] [1998] 4 All ER 49.

[779] See also *Andrews (Tracey)* [1999] Crim LR 156.

[780] The publicity over the case was the subject of research published in T.M. Honess, S. Barker, E.A. Charman and M. Levi, 'Empirical and Legal Perspectives on the Impact of Pre-trial Publicity', *Criminal Law Review*, 2002, pp. 719–27.

was fined £75,000 for contempt. It was this case that prompted the Government to include in the Courts Act 2003 a provision permitting a court to make 'a third party costs order' where 'there has been serious misconduct (whether or not constituting a contempt of court) and the court considers it appropriate, having regard to that misconduct' to make such an order.[781]

Reporting of committal and transfer proceedings

Until 1967, committal proceedings provided much lurid material for the press which was lawful since it amounted to reporting of court proceedings, but it was often said that such reporting prejudiced the prospects of a fair trial since the jury might remember what they had read and be affected by it. This was the more so since the normal practice was for the prosecution to present its case at the committal stage but for the defendant to refrain from revealing his defence. The press accounts of the case would therefore inevitably be very one-sided.

The matter came to a head after the trial of Dr Bodkin Adams in 1957 for the murder of one of his elderly patients. The prosecution at the committal proceedings led evidence of the circumstances in which two other patients had died but this was not introduced at the trial. The massive newspaper coverage of the case from the arrest of the doctor to his ultimate acquittal gave the impression that he had been guilty of several murders. As a result of the case, in June 1957, a departmental committee under the chairmanship of Lord Tucker was appointed to consider whether there should be restrictions on reports of committal proceedings.

The report of the committee[782] recommended that restrictions should be imposed and these recommendations were eventually enacted in the Criminal Justice Act 1967, s. 3 (and later s. 8 of the Magistrates' Court Act 1980), which made press reporting of the evidence at committal proceedings unlawful save where asked for by the defence. The press could only publish the formal basic facts and not the evidence (s. 8(4)): the identity of the court, the names, addresses and occupations of the parties and witnesses and the ages of the accused and witnesses, the offence or offences, or a summary of them, with which the accused was charged, any decision of the court to commit the accused for trial and the charges.

The restrictions regarding reporting of committal proceedings were applied to proceedings in the magistrates' court for transferring or sending cases to the Crown Court first, under the Criminal Justice Act 1987 for the transfer of fraud cases, then under s. 51 of the Crime and Disorder Act 1998 in respect of the sending of indictable-only cases and most recently under the Criminal Justice Act 2003 for the sending of either-way cases.[783]

---

[781] Section 93 inserting a new s. 19B into the Prosecution of Offences Act 1985.
[782] *Proceedings Before Examining Magistrates*, 1958, Cmnd. 479.
[783] See Sch. 3, para. 19 inserting a new s. 52A into the 1998 Act.

Publicity at the time of the trial prejudicing a retrial

In October 1998, Michael Stone was convicted of the savage killing of Lin Russell and her daughter Megan and of the attempted murder of her other daughter Josie. The case received a vast amount of media coverage. In February 2001, his conviction was quashed by the Court of Appeal on the ground of the unreliability of fellow prisoner prosecution witnesses. The court ordered a retrial. The defence argued that because of the publicity it would be impossible to have a fair retrial. The Court of Appeal rejected the argument. The court was not satisfied on the balance of probabilities that the publicity, three years on, was such as to make a retrial oppressive or unfair or make a verdict in a retrial unsafe.[784] (At the retrial, Stone was reconvicted.)

Power to order postponement of reports

The Contempt of Court Act 1981, s. 4(1) states that a person is not guilty of contempt of court under the strict liability rule in respect of a 'fair and accurate report of legal proceedings held in public, published contemporaneously and in good faith'. Section 4(2) gives the court the power to order that publication of a report of the proceedings of any court be postponed for such period as the court thinks 'where it appears to be necessary for avoiding a substantial risk of prejudice'. There was no power at common law to make such an order.[785] In the past the power was very rarely used by magistrates but was used quite often by Crown Courts.[786] More recently it has been used increasingly by magistrates' courts.[787]

Publishing material not heard by the jury

The media are not permitted to publish evidence held to be inadmissible. This would normally preclude publication of what takes place in the absence of the jury even though it is fair and accurate and contemporaneous and relates to what occurred in open court. It would not be published 'in good faith' since it would normally be obvious that it was not intended to be seen by jurors and if published might prejudice a fair trial. The contrast with the comparable rule in the USA emerged clearly in the televised trial of O.J. Simpson during which viewers around the world frequently heard evidence not heard by the jury. In the United States the jury in a criminal case is quite often kept together

---

[784] *Criminal Law Review*, 2001, p. 465 and lengthy commentary.

[785] *Independent Publishing Co Ltd v. A-G of Trinidad and Tobago* [2004] UKPC 26, [2005] 1 All ER 499. The Judicial Committee said that without such legislation the court could warn the press of the danger of contempt but that such an order had no validity.

[786] See C. Walker et al, 'The Reporting of Crown Court Proceedings and the Contempt of Court Act 1981', *Modern Law Review*, September 1992, p. 647.

[787] See M. Dodd, 'Lifting the Veil of Secrecy: Reporting Restriction Orders', 165 *Justice of the Peace*, 2001, pp. 498 and 522.

(sequestered) throughout the trial – in a hotel or other suitable facility. In England this only happens after the jury starts to deliberate and under the Criminal Justice and Public Order Act 1994, s. 43 the judge has a discretion to allow them to go home overnight even then.

Research evidence as to the (minimal) effect of pre-trial publicity

A study conducted for the Law Commission of New Zealand explored the effect of pre-trial publicity on jurors. The researchers took a sample of forty-eight high profile jury trials conducted in different parts of the country in 1998. Questionnaires were given to all potential jurors on their arrival at court at the start of the week in which a sample case was starting. These asked whether they knew anything about two or three of the cases starting that week and, if so, from what source. Jurors in the sample cases who agreed were interviewed after the trial. From a potential sample of 575 jurors, 312 were interviewed – an average of 6.5 per jury.[788]

Given that all the sample cases were high profile, a surprising finding was that so few of the jurors were even aware of the pre-trial publicity. In over half the cases (twenty-five out of forty-eight) no juror recalled seeing any pre-trial publicity. In all, only fifty-eight of the 312 jurors (19 per cent) recollected seeing any and only sixteen jurors admitted to knowledge of any details of the alleged offence or the accused's involvement (paras. 7.48 and 7.52). When jurors who had seen the pre-trial publicity were asked whether it had any impact on their thinking about the case, only two acknowledged that it had:

> In summary, therefore, jurors were only rarely aware of sufficient details of pre-trial publicity to enable them to form any bias or prejudgment. When they were, for the most part they reported that they consciously made an effort to put that aside and focus upon the evidence alone; and when they did not, other jurors in the process of collective deliberations generally overrode any individual bias or predetermination [para. 7.57].

As to publicity during the trial:

> While some other jurors were more affected by media coverage during the trial, there is similarly no evidence that any of the collective deliberations of the juries in the sample were ultimately driven or even influenced by this [*ibid*].

Anonymity for victims (and defendants) in sexual offence cases

Since 1976, the victim of rape has been given a measure of anonymity. The Sexual Offences (Amendment) Act 1976 provided anonymity for the victim after someone had been accused of rape, but not earlier. Also the judge could

---

[788] W. Young, N. Cameron and Y. Tinsley, *Juries in Criminal Trials Part Two: A summary of the research findings*, New Zealand Law Commission, November 1999 – www.lawcom.govt.nz.

lift the protection pre-trial if he thought that would cause witnesses to come forward or if the accused's defence would otherwise be prejudiced. At the trial he could lift the protection if satisfied that it was an unreasonable restriction on reporting and that it was in the public interest. The 1976 Act also gave the defendant the same protection.

The Criminal Justice Act 1988, s. 158 extended the protection of anonymity to the victim from the moment of the allegation but withdrew the protection of anonymity from the defendant.

The 1976 and 1988 Acts dealt with rape, attempted rape, incitement to rape and accomplices to such offences. They did not deal with conspiracy to rape or burglary with intent to rape. The Sexual Offences (Amendment) Act 1992 extended the statutory anonymity of rape victims to other sexual offences. Under the 1992 Act the accused can ask for the prohibition to be lifted if he can satisfy the judge that it is necessary to induce witnesses to come forward because the conduct of the defence would otherwise be substantially prejudiced. At the trial, the prohibition can be lifted if the judge considers that the effect of the prohibition is to impose a substantial and unreasonable restriction on reporting and that it is in the public interest to remove it.

Anonymity for defendants In December 2002, the House of Commons Home Affairs Committee in its report on the Criminal Justice Bill 2002–3 said there was a case for extending the anonymity for victims of sex crimes to those accused of such crimes. There was a basis for distinguishing this category of offence in that, first, there was a risk of mistaken prosecutions and, secondly, the stain on a person's reputation was serious and permanent. It urged the Home Secretary to consider amending the Bill to provide for this.[789]

The Home Secretary declined the invitation. At the report stage of the Sexual Offences Bill 2003, Lord Ackner successfully moved an amendment to restore the defendant's right to anonymity in rape cases that he had between 1976 and 1988. The Government was defeated on the issue in the House of Lords by 109–105,[790] but the amendment did not survive. It was reversed in the Commons and when the matter returned to the Lords, the Government won the vote by eighty-six to twenty-six.[791]

No reporting of names of vulnerable witnesses – the Government climbs down

The Youth Justice and Criminal Evidence Bill 1998–9, as originally drafted, would have made it a criminal offence to identify a person under eighteen who might be a victim, a witness or a perpetrator of crimes under investigation unless one of the exceptions applied. Not surprisingly, this extraordinarily

---

[789] HC 83, December 2002, para. 145.
[790] House of Lords, *Hansard*, 2 June 2003, cols. 1084–95.
[791] House of Lords, *Hansard*, 13 November 2003, col. 1622.

far-reaching proposal met with intense opposition, especially from the press and eventually the Government dropped – or at least suspended – the proposal in so far as it affected victims and witnesses. The Bill was amended to require that the provision affecting witnesses and victims be activated by a specific Order in Council and the indications were that this was not likely to happen. The Youth Justice and Criminal Evidence Act 1999, s. 44 maintained the previous rule that a child cannot be identified as the alleged perpetrator of the offence unless the court gives permission on grounds of public interest. It also provided for a new right of appeal against court decisions to lift or not to lift reporting restrictions in the interests of justice and for a right of appeal to the Crown Court against such decisions made in the magistrates' courts.

The Youth Justice and Criminal Evidence Act 1999, s. 46 also gave the court the power to prohibit the reporting of information that would lead to an adult witness being identified in any criminal case if the court considers that coverage will lead to him being intimidated or that his co-operation or his evidence would be adversely affected by fear or distress. The Explanatory Notes to the Act stated: 'neither "fear" nor "distress" was intended to cover a disinclination to give evidence on account of simple embarrassment'. Nevertheless this provision is obviously very far-reaching. The court can lift the restrictions on grounds of the interests of justice.

Chapter 4

The trial process

This chapter deals with the trial itself. The first section considers the particular characteristics of the English adversary method of trial as compared with the so-called inquisitorial method followed on the Continent and, in particular, examines the role of the judge. The second and third sections concern the advantages of representation and the difficulties faced by the unrepresented person in an English trial. The following sections look at the orality of procedure and the evidence of social psychologists that evidence on questions of fact is more apt to be unreliable than the participants appear to realise. The sixth section deals with the most important problems of the rules of evidence.

1. The adversary system compared with the inquisitorial

The common law method of trial has often been described as 'adversary' or 'accusatorial' – as distinct from the continental 'inquisitorial' method. The essence of the distinction is that, whereas in the inquisitorial system the dominant role is played by the court, in the adversary system it is played by the parties. In the adversary system the judge is supposed to remain a mainly passive and silent umpire listening to the evidence produced by the two parties. The parties prepare their respective cases, they decide what witnesses to call and in what order and they examine and cross-examine the witnesses. If both sides decide not to call a witness who has potentially relevant evidence, normally the court will do nothing about it. The burden of preparing the case and of presenting it falls on the parties themselves, which means that a party without a lawyer is at a distinct disadvantage. By contrast, in the inquisitorial system the judge calls the witnesses and examines them, while the parties or their lawyers play a supporting or subsidiary role.

To be sure, as already seen and as will be noted further, the 'pure' adversary system as it has been conducted in England in modern times has been affected as regards civil trials by the implementation of the Woolf reforms with their emphasis on the active judge. Active case management is also now supposed to be a feature of criminal trials and the new Criminal Procedure Rules require the defence to be more helpful to the prosecution than was previously the case. So change is afoot, but despite such developments, the role of the

English judge is still very different from that of his continental opposite number.

The adversary system

Judicial intervention

A classic statement of the pure adversary system was given by Lord Denning deciding that the trial judge, Mr Justice Hallett, had intervened too often:

> ### Jones v. National Coal Board [1957] 2 QB 55, CA
> We are quite clear that the interventions, taken together, were far more than they should have been. In the system of trial which we have evolved in this country, the judge sits to hear and determine the issues raised by the parties, not to conduct an investigation or examination on behalf of society at large, as happens, we believe, in some foreign countries. Even in England, however, a judge is not a mere umpire to answer the question 'how's that?' His object, above all, is to find out the truth, and to do justice according to law; and in the daily pursuit of it the advocate plays an honourable and necessary role. Was it not Lord Eldon LC who said in a notable passage that 'truth is best discovered by powerful statements on both sides of the question'? See *ex p Lloyd*[1] and Lord Greene MR who explained that justice is best done by a judge who holds the balance between the contending parties without himself taking part in their disputations. If a judge, said Lord Greene, should himself conduct the examination of witnesses, 'he, so to speak, descends into the arena and is liable to have his vision clouded by the dust of conflict': see *Yuill v. Yuill*.[2]
>
> Let the advocates one after the other put the weights into the scales – the 'nicely calculated less or more' – but the judge at the end decides which way the balance tilts, be it ever so slightly . . . The judge's part in all this is to hearken to the evidence, only himself asking questions of witnesses when it is necessary to clear up any point that has been overlooked or left obscure; to see that the advocates behave themselves seemly and keep to the rules laid down by law; to exclude irrelevancies and discourage repetition; to make sure by wise intervention that he follows the points that the advocates are making and can assess their worth; and at the end to make up his mind where the truth lies. If he goes beyond this, he drops the mantle of a judge and assumes the robe of an advocate; and the change does not become him well. Lord Chancellor Bacon spoke right when he said that:[3] 'patience and gravity of hearing is an essential part of justice; and an overspeaking judge is no well-tuned cymbal'.

For a comparable criminal case see *R v. Perks*.[4] In *Gunning*[5] the conviction was quashed where the judge asked 165 questions compared with 172 from counsel. In *Matthews*[6] by contrast the Court of Appeal declined to quash a conviction where the judge put 524 questions to counsel's 538. On any view, the court said,

---

[1] (1822) Mont 70 at 72n.   [2] [1945] P 15 at 20, [1945] 1 All ER 183, 61 TLR 176.
[3] 'Of Judicature', *Essays or Counsels Civil and Moral*.   [4] [1973] Crim LR 388.
[5] [1980] Crim LR 592.   [6] (1983) 78 Cr App Rep 23.

the number of judicial interventions and questions was excessive but they did not quite go so far as to divert counsel from his own line of questioning. The court said that a large number of interruptions put the appeal court on notice of the possibility of a denial of justice but the critical issue was not the number but the quality of the interventions 'as they relate to the attitude of the judge as might be observed by the jury and the effect that the interventions have either upon the orderly, proper and lucid deployment of the case for the defendant by his advocate or upon the efficacy of the attack to be made on the defendant's behalf upon vital prosecution witnesses by cross-examination'.[7] Nor will the court interfere merely on the ground that the judge has been guilty of discourtesy, even gross discourtesy, to counsel: *R v. Ptohopoulos*.[8]

In *Hamilton*[9] Lord Chief Justice Parker said the Court of Appeal would overturn a conviction on account of excessive intervention (1) where the interventions invited the jury to disbelieve the defence evidence in such strong terms that they could not be cured by the usual formula that the facts are for the jury; (2) where they prevented defence counsel from carrying out his duty to present the case for the defence; and (3) where the defendant himself was prevented from telling his own story.[10]

For the role of the judge in influencing or directing the jury to convict or acquit, see pp. 523–26 below.

In recent years the traditional English concept of the judge as a passive umpire, as in a tennis match, simply 'hearkening to the evidence' has with regard to civil cases become greatly altered. One reason is that whereas in former times it was normal for the judge to come into court with little knowledge of the case, today far more material is supplied to the court and pre-reading is normal, which means that the judge will form provisional views on the basis of which he can ask questions on matters of evidence as well as questions of law. The Woolf reforms were largely built on the concept of a more active, interventionist judge. No doubt, the primary focus of the reforms was on making the court more active in the pre-trial stage but the reforms have had their impact on the trial stage too. Pre-Woolf, the idea of the judge who played an active role at trial was well established in small claims trials. Post-Woolf, it has become a feature of other civil trials too.

It is important also to appreciate that the nature of the role of the judge described in Lord Denning's judgment in *Jones v. National Coal Board* only applied to the evidence. It had no application to legal argument. Legal argument in a common law case has always involved the judge very actively. Counsel makes his points and submissions but the judge feels free to engage him in discussion by asking questions, raising objections and putting contrary

---

[7] At pp. 32–3.   [8] [1968] Crim LR 52.
[9] [1969] Crim LR 486 (quoted more fully in (1973) 58 Cr App Rep 378 at 382).
[10] See, for instance, *Rabbitt* (1931) 23 Cr App Rep 112; *Clewer* (1953) 37 Cr App Rep 37; *Renshaw* [1989] Crim LR 811; *Sharp* [1993] 3 All ER 225 and generally S. Doran, 'Descent to Avernus', 139 *New Law Journal*, 1 September 1989, p. 1147.

points. The process sometimes almost resembles a seminar. The same is even more true on appeal. As Dr[11] Kate Malleson wrote of the Court of Criminal Appeal: 'The role of the judges in the Court of Appeal is not that of neutral referees but active participators in the proceedings. They ask questions of counsel, make comments, discuss problems, suggest answers, express their opinions and raise new matters in a way which more closely resemble an inquisitorial hearing'.[12]

The higher in the system, the more extensive the exchanges between counsel and the court. (In *The Law Lords* Professor Alan Paterson reports that in *Cassell v. Broome* there were ninety-nine judicial interventions on the first day of argument alone, sixty-one of which came from the presiding judge.[13])

Even on points of law, however, the adversary system works on the basis that the court is not supposed to undertake its own research and is not supposed to go beyond the arguments presented by the parties.[14]

Calling witnesses

The basic common law rule was and remains that it is for the parties, not the court, to call and to examine the witnesses. The parties decide what witnesses to call, in what order and what questions to ask them. In civil cases the court *cannot* call a witness unless the parties agree.[15] In criminal cases the judge technically has the right to call a witness but rarely does so,[16] though it can happen when the purpose is to assist the defence.[17] In *Grafton*[18] doing so led to the conviction being quashed. The Court of Appeal said that the judge's role was to hold the ring impartially and to direct the jury on the law. By acting as he had done, he had in effect taken over the prosecution.

The basic rule is that each party is bound by the evidence of his own witness. One cannot impeach the evidence of one's own witness by cross-examination to show that he is in error, unless the court is persuaded to allow cross-examination on the ground that the witness is 'hostile'.[19] As a result, each side may suppress a witness for fear of what he may say.

The possibility that the parties may suppress evidence that they do not intend to call was illustrated in *Causton v. Mann Egerton*.[20] The plaintiff was considering suing his employers for injuries to his eye suffered through their alleged

---

[11] Now Professor.
[12] 'Decision-making in the Court of Appeal: The Burden of Proof in an Inquisitorial Process', 1 *International Journal of Evidence and Proof*, 1997, p. 175 at 178.
[13] Macmillan, 1982, p. 70; *Toth v Jarman* [2006] EWCA Civ 1028 discussed by J. Levy, in 'Will They Ever Learn?', 156 *New Law Journal*, 3 November 2006, pp. 1671–3.
[14] For consideration of the weaknesses of this rule see N.H. Andrews, 'The Passive Court and Legal Argument', 7 *Civil Justice Quarterly*, 1988, p. 125.
[15] See for instance *Briscoe v. Briscoe* [1966] 1 All ER 465, Div Ct.
[16] For an example that was upheld by the Court of Appeal see *Bowles* [1992] Crim LR 726.
[17] *R v. Haringey Justices, ex p DPP* [1996] 1 All ER 828. See also *Oliva* [1965] 1 WLR 1028 and *Brown and Brown* [1997] 1 Cr App R 112.   [18] [1992] Crim LR 826.
[19] See M. Newark, 'The Hostile Witness and the Adversary System', *Criminal Law Review*, 1986, p. 441.   [20] [1974] 1 All ER 453.

negligence. He agreed to be examined by the insurers' doctors. They were pessimistic about the prospects of his regaining his sight. He was also examined by doctors on his own behalf. On request from the defendants' solicitors, the reports of his doctors were disclosed to them, but when the plaintiff's solicitors asked for reciprocal disclosure of the reports prepared by the insurers' doctors, this was refused.

The Court of Appeal by a majority held that the refusal was legitimate. Disclosure could be compelled if a party was intending to rely on the evidence but neither the opposite party nor the court could require a party to produce privileged testimony which it did not intend to call. Lord Justice Roskill said that to decide otherwise would be to ride roughshod over the clear rule that, in the absence of the parties' consent, the court could not order the production of privileged documents. ('So long as we have an adversary system a party is entitled not to produce documents which are properly protected by privilege if it is not to his advantage to produce them and even though their production might assist his adversary if he or his solicitor were aware of their contents or might lead the court to a different conclusion from that to which the court would come in ignorance of their existence'.[21])

Lord Denning, dissenting, said that the insurers' doctors apparently took a more serious view of the plaintiff's injuries than did his own doctors. The defendants accordingly wished to keep their own reports away from the court and the plaintiff. This would be unfair:

> Counsel for the defendants sought to excuse their conduct by saying that litigation in this country is based on the adversary procedure. By that he means, I suppose, that it is permissible for an insurance company to refuse to co-operate in the doing of justice. It can play with a poker face with the cards hidden from view. I cannot subscribe to that view. Although litigation is based on the adversary procedure, we require the adversaries to play it fairly and openly. The defendants have made the plaintiff put his cards on the table. They should put theirs too.[22]

In the *Crown Court Study* judges were asked: 'Were you aware of any important witness(es) who were not called by either side?' In nearly a fifth (19 per cent) of 743 cases the judge answered yes.[23] The Royal Commission recommended that judges be prepared in suitable cases, where they become aware of a witness who may have something to contribute, to ask counsel in the absence of the jury why the witness has not been called and, if they think appropriate, urge them to rectify the situation. In the last resort judges should be prepared to exercise their power to call the witness themselves.[24] (There is no sign that judges have adopted either recommendation.)

---

[21] At p. 460. See also *Air Canada v. Secretary of State for Trade (No 2)* [1983] 1 All ER 910 and *General Mediterranean Holdings SA v. Patel* [1999] 3 All ER 673.   [22] At p. 458.

[23] M. Zander and P. Henderson, *The Crown Court Study* (Royal Commission on Criminal Justice, Research Study No 19, 1993) section 4.3.12.   [24] Runciman, Ch. 8, para. 18, p. 123.

Lord Justice Auld in his report said that judges were right to use the power to call witnesses only in exceptional cases. The parties might have good reasons, which they could not divulge, consistent with justice and the interests of a fair trial, for not calling a witness. Also, if the witness helped the prosecution, the judge might be thought to be playing the role of auxiliary prosecutor.[25]

There are, however, some situations where the normal principles of the adversary system – that the court is basically passive and it is for the parties to make the best case they can – do not apply.

Modifications or exceptions to the adversary system

Civil court acting of its own motion

The pre-1999 rules had some provisions permitting the court to act of its own motion,[26] but there were few of these. The new rules have many such powers.[27]

Small claims hearings

In small claims cases in the county court the judge is given complete control of what rules of evidence and procedure to adopt. For the first years many of the judges followed the traditional approach of leaving it to the parties to make their case, but gradually and increasingly they took a more active role in getting the parties to make their case. By 2002, Professor John Baldwin reported[28] that 'almost all' the district judges who were interviewed in his study were 'thoroughly enthusiastic about playing a pro-active, interventionist role at hearings'.[29]

The small claims court now handles roughly four out of five contested cases in the county court. (In 2005, 47,521 cases (or 73 per cent) were disposed of as small claims, compared with 17,318 (27 per cent) as ordinary contested hearings.[30])

Nature of hearing From the outset, one of the most important features of the small claims system has been its informality. The Civil Procedure Rules[31] continue this approach:

> The court may adopt any method of proceeding at a hearing that it considers to be fair.
>
> . . .

---

[25] Auld, Ch. 11, para. 36, p. 528.

[26] For example the power to transfer a case from High Court to county court or vice versa.

[27] The court may for example extend or shorten the time for compliance with any rule, Practice Direction or court order, adjourn or bring forward a hearing, require a party or a party's legal representative to attend the court and stay the whole or any part of a case (CPR 3.1(2)).

[28] *Lay and Judicial Perspectives on the Expansion of the Small Claims Regime* (September 2002, LCD Research Series No. 8/02) p. 89.

[29] See generally J. Baldwin, *Small Claims in the County Court in England and Wales: The Bargain Basement of Civil Justice* (Clarendon, 1997) and 'Litigants' Experiences of Adjudication in the County Courts', 18 *Civil Justice Quarterly*, January 1999, pp. 12–40.

[30] *Judicial Statistics, 2005*, Revised Table 4.8.   [31] CPR 27.8(1).

(2) Hearings will be informal.

(3) The strict rules of evidence do not apply.

(4) The court need not take evidence on oath.

(5) The court may limit cross-examination.

(6) The court must give reasons for its decisions.

The judge therefore has complete discretion as to the conduct of the case.

It is true that in *Chilton v. Saga Holidays Plc*[32] the Court of Appeal held that the special rules for small claims did not mean that the basic principles of the adversary system could be set aside. The registrar who heard the case had refused to allow solicitors for the defendants to cross-examine the plaintiff and his wife. ('In cases where one side is unrepresented, I do not allow cross-examination. All questions to the other side will be put through me'.) The county court judge upheld the registrar's decision, but the Court of Appeal held that their view was wrong. The Master of the Rolls said that, although the procedure was designed to be informal, it was fundamental to the adversary system 'that each party shall be entitled to ask questions designed to probe the accuracy or otherwise, or the completeness or otherwise, of the evidence which has been given'.

The Courts and Legal Services Act 1990, s. 6, provided that county court rules may prescribe the procedure and rules for small claims cases and that such rules 'may, in particular, make provision with respect to the manner of taking and questioning evidence'. The Explanatory Notes specifically related this provision to the problem created by the Court of Appeal's decision in *Chilton v. Saga Holidays Plc*. The right to cross-examine lay on the border between procedural rules and the law of substantive evidence, and an enabling power was therefore needed to permit a rule to be made which gave the court the right to dispense with the right, but although CPR r. 32.1(3) states that the court may 'limit' cross-examination it does not say that it may prevent it altogether.

Professor Baldwin was full of praise for district judges:

> . . . district judges have made enormous strides in the past twenty years in providing a pleasant and relaxed setting in which litigants can present their cases at small claims hearings, with or without legal representation . . . It would not be much of an exaggeration to say that what district judges in England and Wales have achieved in providing a congenial arena in which litigants in person can function effectively at hearings has not been equalled at other levels of the judiciary. Moreover, the writer's knowledge of what happens at small claims hearings in other jurisdictions leads him to believe that the judiciary of no other country has achieved a comparable measure of success in this regard.[33]

---

[32] [1986] 1 All ER 841.

[33] *Lay and Judicial Perspectives on the Expansion of the Small Claims Regime* (September 2002, LCD Research Series No. 8/02) pp. 88 and 89 – www.lcd.gov.uk. For a less satisfactory verdict see P. Lewis, 'Litigants in Person and their Difficulties in Adducing Evidence: a Study of Small Claims in an English County Court', 11 *International Journal of Evidence and Proof*, 2007, pp. 24–48.

The judge is expected to be interventionist Despite the decision in *Chilton*, judges in small claims cases are encouraged to take an active role. The 1999 Practice Direction stated, for instance, that the judge may 'ask questions of any witness himself before allowing any other person to do so'.[34] This would be regarded as completely unacceptable in ordinary cases.

Unsurprisingly, the judges vary in their willingness to take on this kind of activist role. Professor Baldwin, writing about this, said:

> The interventionist role is not, however, always easy to play, particularly for judges who (as in this country) have been used to practising within an adversarial setting. It is in fact a role that bears remarkable similarities to the inquisitorial judge. Yet unless adjudicators play this role – and what is more, play it competently and enthusiastically – small claims procedures simply will not work.[35]

Any observer, he said, 'is likely to be struck by the enormous variations between district judges in their interpretation of what it means to be interventionist'.[36] It was rare for the judge to read the papers beforehand. Most did not explain the purpose of the hearing or the nature of the procedure they intended to adopt, whereas some took great pains over the introduction,[37] but most of the judges showed evident relish in playing an interventionist role.

It can, indeed, be said that the judicial shift from the traditional adversarial approach to active interventionism has been achieved in small claims and, however reluctant they may have been in the past, few district judges now show much hesitation about intervening at hearings or express misgivings about doing so.[38]

Baldwin identified four main approaches to being interventionist. One was 'going for the jugular' – identifying the central issues and insisting that the parties stick to them. A second was to allow the parties to say what they want to say. A third was to sit passively and then just ask a few questions. A fourth was to try to achieve a compromise solution like a mediator.

The different styles could affect the outcome of cases. Thus, for instance, judges vary in their approach to the frequent failure of litigants in person to bring all the evidence they need. Preliminary hearings are rare and are discouraged by the rules. It is rare for parties to come with witnesses. (In one of his many studies, in ninety-one out of 109 hearings observed by Baldwin, there were no witnesses.[39]) To avoid an adjournment, a robust judicial approach tended to be adopted, but judges differed widely in their ability and their inclination to ask the pertinent question and to fill in the gaps in the evidence. They

---

[34] PD 27, 4.3(1).

[35] J. Baldwin, 'Small Claims Hearings: The "Interventionist" Role Played by District Judges', 17 *Civil Justice Quarterly*, January 1998, pp. 20 and 21.

[36] *Ibid*, p. 22. The same had been the finding in an earlier study of the small claims system in thirty courts – George Appleby, *Small Claims in England and Wales* (Birmingham Institute of Judicial Administration, 1978) pp. 30–3.

[37] Baldwin, 17 *Civil Justice Quarterly*, January 1998, p. 23.   [38] *Ibid*, p. 24.   [39] *Ibid*, p. 28.

varied also in whether they felt bound to apply the law. A minority thought they should: 'A majority said they were entitled to disregard the law in making decisions if in their view strictly applying it would produce injustice'.[40] In his *Interim Report* Lord Woolf said (p. 109): 'it is questionable whether such differences are acceptable even in a jurisdiction limited to £1,000' and that any inclination to follow common sense rather than the principle of law should be resisted in the interests of consistency. Baldwin agreed with Lord Woolf:

> While there is little doubt that the district judges who compromise the application of law in the broader interests of 'doing justice' act out of laudable motives, it can be dangerous to apply common sense notions even in small claims. Decision-making can easily become inconsistent, capricious, uncertain, even biased, and in the process, the substantive legal rights of individuals may be undermined. Moreover, while flexibility is doubtless desirable in dealing with small claims, it can create great uncertainty for lay litigants and their advisers.[41]

For Baldwin, the variable approaches adopted by district judges 'inevitably weakens one's enthusiasm for the small claims procedure'.[42] Lord Woolf had argued for more guidance and training for district judges in playing the interventionist role to achieve greater consistency.[43] Baldwin suggested that:

> With the trebling[44] in the small claims limit, it is surely no longer acceptable simply to allow the parties to prepare their cases in whatever way they think appropriate and then ask the district judges to make the best of it at hearings. If endless adjournments are to be avoided, then careful attention needs to be paid at an early stage in proceedings to ensure that cases are adequately prepared and, where they are not, that proper directions are given to rectify deficiencies. This tends at present to be done in only a superficial way in many courts, yet it can have a critical bearing upon the fairness of the court procedure.[45]

However, in a further study carried out only a few years later, Baldwin was much reassured at the way the courts had adapted to the increase in jurisdiction and he no longer considered that the way the court handled the case was much, if at all, influenced by the amount involved.[46]

Research on small claims hearings in Canada found, just as Professor Baldwin found, that judges varied greatly in their approach, from the strict legalists to those who seek rather to do justice.[47]

---

[40] *Ibid*, p. 29.   [41] *Ibid*, p. 31.   [42] *Ibid*, p. 33.

[43] *Access to Justice*, Interim Report, pp. 108–10; Final Report, p. 98.

[44] As has been seen, the limit has since been further increased to five times what it was in 1995.

[45] Baldwin, n. 35 above, p. 34.

[46] Baldwin, *Lay and Judicial Perspectives on the Expansion of the Small Claims Regime* (September 2002, LCD Research Series No. 8/02) p. 64.

[47] R.A. Macdonald, 'Judicial Scripts in the Dramaturgy of the Small Claims Court', 11 *Canadian Journal of Law and Society*, 1996, p. 63. The study was described and discussed by the writer: M. Zander, 'Consistency in the Exercise of Discretionary Powers', 146 *New Law Journal*, 1 November 1996, p. 1590.

Litigants' perspective Research has confirmed that the small claims system is popular amongst those who use the civil courts. Professor Baldwin interviewed 352 county court litigants who had used either ordinary or the small claims procedure. The interviews took place in 1996 and 1997. The respondents were a cross-section of plaintiffs and defendants, business and lay, regulars and first timers, winners and losers. The main purpose of the study was to examine the two kinds of county court procedures through the eyes of the litigants.

Most of the litigants in both samples (whether they were private individuals, the representatives of businesses or court 'regulars') said they very much favoured informality of procedures in resolving their disputes. The great majority of small claims litigants accepted without much question the relatively simple and crude methods adopted by district judges and welcomed the opportunity to participate directly in the resolution of their disputes. There were few complaints from the small claims litigants, but these high levels of satisfaction, Baldwin said, 'were certainly not paralleled in the interviews with litigants who had experienced "open court" trial. Almost every interview with litigants in the latter category produced complaints of varying degrees of seriousness. Some produced a veritable catalogue'.[48] Individual litigants complained about the formality and the wigs and gowns. Many were greatly affected by the costs and especially the threat of having to pay the other side's costs if they lost. ('Even though the sums in dispute were in all cases in the sample under £3,000, the costs incurred by some individuals ran into thousands of pounds'.[49]) They were more likely than the small claims litigants to complain about their lawyers and the legal advice they had received. (Whereas 87 per cent of small claims litigants were satisfied with their lawyers, only 45 per cent of 'open court' litigants were.[50]) In short, 'no matter what criterion of litigant satisfaction was adopted, the small claims regime came out ahead – and by a wide margin'.[51]

Baldwin's positive view was confirmed by his further study published in 2002 which ended: 'Although there may be continuing problems and dilemmas in small claims that are yet to be satisfactorily tackled, the small claims procedure is widely acknowledged to be the great success story of civil justice in England and Wales'.[52] He thought it would be worth considering transferring at least a proportion of personal injury claims from the fast track – 'even if such moves would require modification of existing arrangements and would in any event be resisted by sections of the legal profession'.

Had the increase in jurisdiction made any difference? Baldwin suggests that although the threefold increase in the small claims jurisdiction from £1,000 to £3,000 had produced some changes – in the kind of litigant using the system, increases in the level of claim and changes in legal representation – 'one is

---

[48] J. Baldwin, 'Litigants' Experience of Adjudication in the County Courts', 18 *Civil Justice Quarterly*, January 1999, pp. 12–40 at 20.   [49] *Ibid*, p. 28.   [50] *Ibid*, p. 24.
[51] *Ibid*, p. 39.   [52] Note 000 above at p. 91.

nevertheless struck . . . by how little things are changing, not by how much'.[53]
It was especially disappointing that there had been no real increase in the overall
number of litigants using the county court. The main consequence of increasing the jurisdiction seemed to be to shift a certain proportion of ordinary
county court cases to the small claims system.

He reached much the same conclusion in the study published in 2002 which
focused on the increase in jurisdiction from £3,000 to £5,000: 'What has been
striking about recent developments is, therefore, how little difference they have
made, not how much. The effects of the dramatic increases in the small claims
limit, insofar as they have been noticed at all, have been absorbed without
serious disruption'.[54]

Most people won't use the courts – even the small claims court Professor Baldwin
asked why all the changes in court procedure to make the small claims system
more 'user-friendly' had had such little success in attracting would-be litigants.
The answer, in his view, lay in the nature and the image of the courts themselves:

> Although there is a hard-core of regular court users – for the most part busi-
> ness people for whom an occasional county court appearance is an inevitable,
> if somewhat disagreeable, part of commercial life – for most of the rest of the
> population, the courts are regarded as institutions that are to be avoided at all
> costs. It is, it seems, only idealists . . . who see the county courts as providing a
> mechanism through which legal wrongs can be remedied. For most people, it is
> more accurate to say that a situation has to become desperate before legal action
> in the county courts would ever be contemplated.[55]

Where the interests of children are concerned

The courts have held that the ordinary principles of the adversary system do not
necessarily apply in wardship or care proceedings where the primary concern is
the welfare of children. The policy was reflected in a *dictum* of Lord Scarman in
Re E (SA)[56] in which he pointed out that in wardship proceedings the court was
not exercising an adversarial jurisdiction:

> Its duty is not limited to the dispute between the parties: on the contrary, its duty
> is to act in the way best suited in its judgment to serve the true interest and
> welfare of the ward. In exercising wardship jurisdiction, the court is a true family
> court. Its paramount concern is the welfare of its ward. It will, therefore, some-
> times be the duty of the court to look beyond the submissions of the parties in
> its endeavour to do what it judges to be necessary.[57]

[53] J. Baldwin, *Monitoring the Rise in the Small Claims Limit* (1997, LCD Research Series No.
1/97) p. 116.   [54] Note 46 above at pp. 85–6.   [55] *Ibid.* at p. 88.
[56] [1984] 1 WLR 156 at 158–59.
[57] See to the same effect *Oxfordshire County Council v. M* [1994] Fam 151, [1994] 2 All ER 269
per Sir Stephen Brown; and *Re L (a minor)* [1996] 2 All ER 78. Both cases raised the question
whether legal professional privilege applied to reports of experts prepared for the purpose of
litigation. The court in both cases ordered the disclosure of the reports. For other cases see
Livesey v. Jenkins [1985] AC 424 at 437, HL; and *Official Solicitor to the Supreme Court v. K*
[1965] AC 201 at 240, HL.

Prosecution disclosure

As has been seen, the prosecution must reveal to the defence material that tends to undermine the prosecution's case (see p. 296 above).

Duties of the defence

In addition to the duties of defence disclosure, the defence has increasingly been placed under pressure to be forthcoming in ways that are unfamiliar in the adversary system.[58] Traditionally, for instance, if the defence spotted a fatal flaw in the prosecution's case it could wait to take the point on appeal and hope that it would result in the conviction being quashed. In recent years the courts have indicated that this is no longer acceptable[59] and the Bar's Code of Conduct now reflects that view.[60]

Duties of an expert witness

Traditionally the expert witness in the adversary system played his role as a hired gun. In civil cases, as has been seen, this has changed. CPR r. 35.3 provides that an expert witness in a civil case has a duty 'to help the court' which overrides any obligation to those instructing him.[61] This also operates in a criminal case. In the 1993 case of *The Ikarian Reefer*[62] Mr Justice Cresswell listed the requirements for expert witnesses as including independence, objectivity and being non-partisan. An expert's evidence should show the limits of his expertise and make it clear when his report was provisional. These remain the basic principles.[63]

The Criminal Procedure Rules 2005, Part 33[64] states that an expert must help the court to achieve the overriding objective 'by giving objective, unbiased opinion on matters within his expertise' and that this duty overrides any

[58] For discussion see E. Cape, 'Rebalancing the Criminal Justice Process: Ethical Challenges for Criminal Defence Lawyers', *Legal Ethics*, vol. 9, Pt. 1 2006, pp. 56–79.

[59] See for instance *Gleeson* [2003] EWCA Crim 3357, [2004] Crim LR 579. ('For defence advocates to seek to take advantage of such errors by deliberately delaying identification of an issue of fact or law in the case until the last possible moment is, in our view, no longer acceptable given the legislative and procedural changes to our criminal justice process in recent years. Indeed we consider it to be contrary to the requirement on an accused in s. 5(6) of the Criminal Procedure and Investigations Act 1996, in particular para. (b), to indicate "the matters on which he takes issue with the prosecution", and to their professional duty to the court – and not in the legitimate interests of the defendant', per Lord Justice Auld.) For critical commentary see [2004] Crim LR 579 at 581.

[60] A barrister 'must bring any procedural irregularity to the attention of the court during the hearing and not reserve such matters to be raised on appeal' (*Code of Conduct of the Bar of England and Wales*, 8th edn, 2004, para. 708(d)).

[61] For an Australian development that takes the concept even further see G.L. Davies, 'Court Appointed Experts', 23 *Civil Justice Quarterly*, 2004, pp. 37–78 – proposed Queensland rules providing for the appointment of independent court appointed experts prior to litigation.

[62] [1993] 2 Lloyd's Reports 68.

[63] See *Harris* [2005] EWCA Crim 1980 at [271]–[273]; *B* [2006] EWCA Crim 417, [2006] Crim LR 745.

[64] Part 33 was added to the Rules by the Criminal Procedure (Amendment No 2) Rules, SI 2006/2636, Sch. 1, which became operative as from 6 November 2006.

obligation to the person from whom he receives instruction or by whom he is paid.[65] Where more than one party wants to introduce expert evidence, the court may direct the experts to discuss the expert issues in the case and to prepare a statement for the court of the matters on which they agree and disagree, giving their reasons.[66] If the experts refuse to cooperate, their evidence is not admissible without the leave of the court.

An extreme case illustrating the expert's duty is *Crozier*[67] in which the Court of Appeal held that a psychiatrist instructed by the defence in a criminal trial might in exceptional circumstances be justified in showing his report to the prosecution – even though that would be contrary to the wishes of the defence. The circumstances must be such that the public interest in the disclosure of his views to the prosecution was stronger than his duty of confidentiality to his patient. The defendant had pleaded guilty to the attempted murder of his sister. The psychiatrist thought that the defendant was a serious danger to his family and should be detained in Broadmoor. When he came into the courtroom, he found to his consternation that the judge was in the process of imposing a nine-year prison sentence. He told prosecution counsel of his report and as a result the prosecution applied for the sentence to be altered. The judge quashed the sentence of imprisonment and substituted a hospital order with an unlimited restriction of time on release. The Court of Appeal held that the public interest in having the information divulged was greater than in the confidential relationship between doctor and patient.[68]

Professional rules of conduct

Lawyers arguing a point of law in court have always been subject to the rule that they must put before the court all relevant authorities regardless of whether they help or hinder the advocate's case.

Another exception to the adversary principle is the rule of professional conduct that places limits on the extent to which a lawyer can knowingly lend himself to deception of the court. In one instance, sentence of suspension from practice was confirmed on a prominent Queen's Counsel for misleading the court in an action for damages against the police. The QC had put his witness, a police officer, on the stand and examined him as Mr G without alluding to the fact that he had been demoted for misconduct.[69]

If his client confesses his guilt to his own barrister, the barrister is not required to report the fact to the authorities nor need he give up the case, but he may not 'assert as true that which he knows to be false'. He may take points by way of objection to the jurisdiction of the court, to the admissibility of evidence or to the form of the proceedings, but he may not call evidence which he knows to be false. He is entitled to test the prosecution's case by cross-examination and

---

[65] Rule 33.2.   [66] Rule 33.5.   [67] [1991] Crim LR 138.

[68] See to like effect *W v. Egdell* [1990] 1 All ER 835.

[69] *The Times*, 24 November 1961 and 12 January 1962. The original sentence of three-year suspension from practice was later reduced to one year.

he may argue that the prosecution have failed to produce enough evidence to establish their case. Further than that he should not go.[70]

In *Vernon v. Bosley (No 2)*[71] just before the judge gave judgment, defendant's counsel received information anonymously that showed that his opponents had knowingly presented a false picture as to their client's medical/psychiatric state, a material matter in the litigation. The Court of Appeal allowed an appeal based on the new material. Lord Justice Stuart said that it was the duty of counsel to advise his client to make the appropriate disclosure, failing which he should withdraw from the case. Lord Justice Thorpe went further and said that in such circumstances counsel should himself disclose the material to his opponent.[72]

A more robust approach still was adopted by Jacob J in a patent case *Honeywell Ltd v. Alliance Components Ltd.*[73] Jacob J said that where parties relied on experiments they should notify the opponent of any experiments they had conducted which did not support their argument or which undermined it. But in *Electrolux Northern Ltd v. Black and Decker*[74] his colleague in the Patent Court, Justice Laddie, disagreed. If *Honeywell* was right, other potentially fruitful avenues would have to be disclosed and costs and delay would be increased.[75]

Another example of the duty to disclose is where an application is made in the absence of the other side ('without notice' – formerly *ex parte*). In that situation, by definition, the adversary system is not operating and it is therefore the lawyer's duty to make full disclosure to the court so that the decision is made on a fully informed basis.[76] The same is true where an application is made for a 'freezing' (formerly Anton Piller) order (p. 101 above). The lawyer making such an application is under an especially high duty to take care to see that his lay client realises the need for candour and full disclosure.[77]

However, the duty of confidentiality to the client (legal professional privilege) overrides the duty of disclosure. (See p. 90 above.)

As has been seen, under CPR 1.3 the parties are required to help the court to further the overriding objective by co-operating with each other. In *Hertsmere Primary Care Trust v. Administrators of Balasubramanium's Estate*[78] Lightman J held that the defendants had been under an obligation to assist the opponent by informing them in what respect they had not complied with CPR Part 36.

See generally D.A. Ipp, 'Lawyers Duties to the Court', 114 *Law Quarterly Review*, 1998, pp. 63–107, especially pp. 67–76.

---

[70] *Code of Conduct of the Bar of England and Wales* (8th edn, 2004), Written Standards for the Conduct of Professional Work, para. 12.   [71] [1999] QB 18, [1997] 1 All ER 614.

[72] For analysis and comment see A. Speaight QC, 'A Change of Expert Opinion', 147 *New Law Journal*, 7 February 1997, pp. 163–6. See also J. Goodliffe, 'Fair Play Between Lawyers', 147 *New Law Journal*, 5 September 1997, p. 1268.   [73] 22 February 1996, unreported.

[74] [1996] FSR 595.

[75] See B. McConnell, 'Opposing Views', 147 *New Law Journal*, 28 November 1997, p. 1754.

[76] *Brinks-Mat Ltd v. Elcombe* [1988] 1 WLR 1350.

[77] *Chappell v. United Kingdom* [1989] FSR 617.

[78] [2005] EWHC 320 Ch, [2005] 3 All ER 274.

Lord Woolf and the Runciman Royal Commission on the adversary system

As has been seen, Lord Woolf's Interim Report *Access to Justice* published in June 1995 blamed the excesses of the adversary system for much of the cost, delay and complexity of the civil justice system:

> 3. By tradition the conduct of civil litigation in England and Wales, as in other common law jurisdictions, is adversarial. Within a framework of substantive and procedural law established by the state for the resolution of civil disputes, the main responsibility for the initiation and conduct of proceedings rests with the parties to each individual case, and it is normally the plaintiff who sets the pace. The role of the judge is to adjudicate on issues selected by the parties when they choose to present them to the court.
>
> 4. Without effective judicial control, however, the adversarial process is likely to encourage an adversarial culture and to degenerate into an environment in which the litigation process is too often seen as a battlefield where no rules apply. In this environment, questions of expense, delay, compromise and fairness may have only low priority. The consequence is that expense is often excessive, disproportionate and unpredictable; and delay is frequently unreasonable.
>
> 5. This situation arises precisely because the conduct, pace and extent of litigation are left almost completely to the parties. There is no effective control of their worst excesses. Indeed, the complexity of the present rules facilitates the use of adversarial tactics and is considered by many to require it. As Lord Williams, a former Chairman of the Bar Council, said in responding to the announcement of this inquiry, the process of law has moved from being 'servant to master, due to cost, length and uncertainty'.

At various points in the Report, Lord Woolf called for the parties to behave in a more co-operative and less combative or adversarial manner. He stated that one of the objectives of judicial case management would be 'the encouragement of a spirit of co-operation between the parties and the avoidance of unnecessary combativeness which is productive of unnecessary additional expense and delay' (p. 30, para. 17(c)).

The famous proceduralist Sir Jack Jacob wrote: 'The passive role of the English court greatly enhances the standing, the influence and the authority of the judiciary at all levels and may well account for the high respect and esteem in which they are held'.[79] Lord Woolf, by contrast, proposed that the judge should exercise control both before and during trial not only to marshall the case but to control the quantity and quality of evidence received by the court.[80] This policy was enshrined in the CPR. Part 32.1 starts: '(1) The court may control the evidence by giving directions as to – (a) the issues on which it requires evidence; (b) the nature of the evidence which it requires to decide those issues; and (c) the way in which the evidence is to be placed before the court'. Part 32 continues: '(2) The court may use its power under this rule to exclude evidence that would otherwise be admissible. (3) The court may limit

---

[79] *The Fabric of English Civil Justice*, 1987, p. 12.   [80] Page 178, paras. 14 and 15.

cross-examination'. Thus, the judge, if he chooses to exercise it, now has great power to decide which witnesses of fact are called and how they are to give their evidence. Similarly he has some power over the evidence of the expert witnesses. In particular, no expert can be called without the court's permission.

In the view of some this imperils both the search for the truth and the court's appearance of impartiality – see for instance the severe criticisms of C. Dehn, QC, 'The Woolf Report: Against the Public Interest?' in *Reform of Civil Procedure – Essays on Access to Justice* (A. Zuckerman and R. Cranston, eds., Clarendon, 1995) p. 162; and of N. Andrews, 'The Adversarial Principle: Fairness and Efficiency Reflections on the Recommendations of the Woolf Report', *ibid*, pp. 171–183. See also J.A. Jolowicz, 'The Woolf Report and the Adversary System', 15 *Civil Justice Quarterly*, 1996, pp. 198–210. Professor Jolowicz showed how the French civil justice system which, contrary to popular belief, traditionally was mainly adversary, had in recent years become more and more inquisitorial. He suggested that the Woolf reforms would push the English system in the same direction.

For a powerful piece supporting Professor Jolowicz's view, see Lightman J, 'The Case for Judicial Intervention'[81] published a few months after the Woolf reforms had gone live. In the 'old days', he said, the parties did not have to give advance disclosure of their case. The only information the other side had was what little was revealed by the pleadings, the judge did no pre-reading because, apart from the pleadings, there was nothing to pre-read. In those circumstances it was natural and right for the trial judge to be basically silent and passive. Now there was full advance disclosure of the evidence and a requirement of skeleton arguments in which each side set out their submissions and authorities. The judge usually found time to read these before the trial. In Lightman's view it was not merely acceptable but positively desirable that the judge should ask questions based on his reading of the skeleton arguments. This showed the advocate the issues on which the court needed to hear argument. Having read the witness statements in advance the judge was also in a position to ask questions of the witnesses. ('He does not need to wait to see if the question is asked and then what answer is given, and he need not accept the sufficiency of an answer just because the advocate does'.[82]) However, the judge needed to tread very carefully. ('His questioning out of turn may frustrate a planned cross-examination, and if he asks (as he is entitled to) leading questions (questions suggesting their own answer), the witness may psychologically find it difficult to resist the perceived judicial pressure to give that answer'.[83])

However, it is noteworthy that the CPR do not include a new power for the judge to *call* witnesses nor did Mr Justice Lightman urge such a power.

The position with regard to criminal cases remains much more in the traditional mould. By contrast with Lord Woolf's view, the Runciman Royal

---

[81] 149 *New Law Journal*, 3 December 1999, p. 1819. For his later assessment of the adversary system in light of recent developments see Lightman J, 'The Civil Justice System and Legal Profession – the Challenges Ahead', 22 *Civil Justice Quarterly*, 2003, pp. 235–47.

[82] 149 *New Law Journal*, 3 December 1999, at p. 1835.   [83] *Ibid.*

Commission on Criminal Justice did not call for any move towards a less adversary procedure – though it did make some relatively minor proposals for alterations in the way that expert evidence is prepared. It rejected the idea of the court calling its own expert.[84] It equally rejected the concept of judicial supervision of the pre-trial stage of a criminal investigation. Partly its reason was cultural, but partly it was substantive:

> Every system is the product of a distinctive history and culture, and the more different the history and culture from our own the greater must be the danger that an attempted transfer will fail. Hardly any of those who gave evidence to the Commission suggested that the system in another jurisdiction should be adopted in England and Wales; and of those who did, none argued for it in any depth or with any supporting detail.[85]
>
> Our reason for not recommending a change to an inquisitorial system as such is not simply fear of the consequences of an unsuccessful cultural transplant. It is also that we doubt whether the fusion of the functions of investigation and prosecution, and the direct involvement of judges in both are more likely to serve the interests of justice than a system in which the roles of police, prosecutors, and judges are as far as possible kept separate and the judge who is responsible for the conduct of the trial is the arbiter of law but not of fact. We believe that a system in which the critical roles are kept separate offers a better protection against the risk of unnecessarily prolonged detention prior to trial.[86]

For the research evidence on the inquisitorial system done for the Royal Commission, see p. 397 below.

As has been seen, Lord Justice Auld equally accepted that a judge should call a witness in a criminal case only in exceptional circumstances.

The inquisitorial system

In the continental inquisitorial system the main burden of presenting the case at court falls on the court itself. The court calls the witnesses and there is, therefore, not the same danger as exists in the common law systems of the evidence of a particular witness being suppressed because neither side wishes to call him. The witnesses are questioned ('examined') by the presiding judge. The role of the lawyers is supplementary. They can suggest the names of further witnesses that the court should call. They can ask questions of witnesses after the court has finished asking its questions, but the lawyers play a subsidiary role.

The essential differences between the two systems with regard to the taking of evidence was captured fifty years ago by the Evershed Committee:[87]

> 250. (a) There is no doubt that the difference between the English and the continental systems with regard to evidence, i.e. with regard to the rules of evidence

---

[84] Runciman, p. 160, para. 74.   [85] *Ibid.*, p. 4, para. 13.   [86] *Ibid*, para. 14.
[87] *Final Report on Supreme Court Practice*, 1953, Cmnd. 8878.

and the way in which evidence is taken, is very marked; and equally there is no doubt that the difference is one of the main reasons for the fact that litigation in England is substantially more costly than (for example) in France or Germany.

(b) In both France and Germany all (oral) witnesses are the court's witnesses, though generally speaking they are tendered by the parties. In both countries the system is (as has been said), unlike the English system, 'inquisitorial'. There is substantially no cross-examination and for practical purposes none at all by the parties or their legal representatives. The witness in effect makes a deposition before the examining judge who decides what witnesses shall be summoned. The process of taking evidence is almost invariably at an early stage of the proceedings, long before the 'trial' proper.

(c) The witness makes his statement in his own words – there being no 'hearsay' rule. It is for the court to decide the value of what has been said. It is, however, to be noted that the parties themselves are, generally, not competent witnesses in Germany; and in France parents, relatives and servants of the parties and certain other categories of persons are not competent.

(d) In both France and Germany, oral testimony is regarded as of far less significance than in England.

One of the points frequently made in comparisons between the English and the civil law systems of trial is their different approach to the 'search for the truth'. This was the theme of a leading practitioner who is also a scholar, in a book about a famous murder case:

Louis Blom-Cooper, *The A6 Murder*, 1963, pp. 72 and 80–2
In the Continental trial system the starting point of the trial is the accused man. The first thing the court learns about is his medical and criminal antecedents; the court then feels more able to adjudge the man's conduct in relation to the crime, both for testing his culpability in arriving at a verdict and his responsibility for the crime in assessing the treatment he should receive.

The English form of trial is more professional, more aseptic, than the Continental system, a kind of surgical operation, a great deal less painful to the public who are immune from the range of a Continental system of inquiry. The English trial is precise and coldly analytical within the narrow confines marked out by the accusatorial system. Every piece of the puzzle is fitted into a framework which is delineated by the nature of the trial, an accusation on a specific charge against a specific person with all else ruthlessly excluded. The rapier of the prosecution is thrust out; the defence's task is merely to parry it, with no concern other than that the rapier thrust should not strike home. A successful parry means an acquittal and that is that. This precision is claimed to be the English virtue, and certainly the construction of the English trial system does mean that the rules of the game are well defined, and that an accused can prepare himself for it. A more roving inquiry means that the accused may find himself outflanked and may mean also that other suspects may find, in the course of the judicial process, that the pointer of guilt as it swings away from the major suspect shifts towards them.

The Continental system of law, called by contrast the inquisitorial system, believes that a human being is on trial and that the acts of a human being, judged to be criminal, are highly complex. To affix criminal responsibility on an accused, it is not enough to inquire: did this man do the specific act alleged against him? The Continental lawyer wishes to probe deeper in order to determine the full criminal responsibility and the certainty, so far as certainty can be achieved, that the crime is laid at the door of the right perpetrator. It is in essence a search for the truth about the crime.

If your system searches for the truth of the crime, what better start can be made than that the chief suspect 'the accused' should be examined by the court? He must, if any one does, know most about the crime. And so immediately at the outset the scope of the trial is altogether wider. The stage of the trial is taken a step further by the defence and prosecution being allowed to show the real, extended context of the act with which the accused is charged. This intense search for the truth is wholly commendable, since the public, through the agency of the judicial system, is entitled to know not only the criminal but the nature of the crime. For to find out the crime is to make absolute at one fell swoop the nature of responsibility without qualification, and to hamstring the power of the court when determining the sentence. In English law the two functions are kept quite distinct. The mitigating features of the accused's acts are kept away from the eyes and ears of the court – except when . . . the defence chooses to put in a record of the accused's character . . .

The Continental system is therefore fairer to the public, in whose name the trial is being conducted, than it is to those who are the personalities engaged in the trial.

The Runciman Royal Commission on Criminal Justice looked at the question whether it should recommend a move toward the inquisitorial system as proposed by some of those who submitted evidence. It invited Professor Leonard Leigh and Dr (now Professor) Lucia Zedner, both at the time of the London School of Economics, to advise it upon the suitability of the French or German models of procedure for adoption or adaptation in England and Wales. In their report[88] Leigh and Zedner rejected the notion that the inquisitorial model was 'better' or that it should be adopted: 'We do not believe that adoption, certainly in the crude form which is sometimes suggested in respect of the examining magistrates, is either feasible or desirable' (p. 67). In some respect the protections afforded to the suspect in England and Wales were already more extensive than those in France and Germany. 'To reproduce the best features of a foreign system in this country would require much more than the introduction of an office found in the foreign jurisdiction. It would be expensive and time-consuming and would not in our submission, produce better results than could be achieved by an intelligent adaptation of the existing English system' (*ibid*).

Most writing in English contrasting the adversary/inquisitorial features of the common law and continental systems focuses on criminal cases. The extract that follows describes the operation of the civil justice system in Germany from

---

[88] *A Report on the Administration of Criminal Justice in the Pre-trial Phase in France and Germany* (Royal Commission Research Study No. 1, 1992).

which it appears that some of the basic inquisitorial features already observed above seem to operate in civil cases there as well. The procedure has been described by an English lawyer writing about the German system:

John Ratliff, 'Civil Procedure in Germany', 2 *Civil Justice Quarterly*, July 1983, p. 257

The absence of a 'day in court'

There is no single, continuous, oral hearing in German law. Instead proceedings take the form of a series of meetings interwoven with the taking of evidence. German law adheres to the principle that officials should direct the case. This means that the court itself, or an office thereof, is responsible for the initial service of the writ and subsequent exchange of pleadings. Pleadings are sent to the court, which keeps one copy for the official file and sends on two copies to the opposing side, one for the party and one for his lawyer. There is an initial meeting at which the court, after discussion with the parties and on the basis of the written pleadings, decides on what points it will take evidence. The court is not bound to take evidence in any particular order and often hears what it considers to be the decisive evidence first. The actual examination of witnesses takes place in a separate hearing. After the taking of evidence there will be a discussion on what the evidence proves and further appointments for the taking of evidence may be made. This process of taking evidence in instalments succeeded by discussion continues until the court considers the case adequately clarified. One judge is delegated the task of 'reporting' the case, compiling a factual summary of the evidence. At the final hearing the court asks the parties' lawyers if they wish to make any concluding remarks, however, usually a lawyer makes only a 'ritualised reference' to his pleadings. A short discussion on one or two points may follow. The court then retires to come to judgment. The principle of collegiality renders judgment 'off the cuff' impossible. Judgment is later given in court and sent to the parties or their lawyers by registered post or placed in the 'postboxes' which many lawyers' firms have at the courts for receipt of official communications.

In recent years it has increasingly been appreciated in Germany that there may be value at least in some cases in having a trial more in the English sense instead of a series of meetings and written communications between the parties, their lawyers and the court. A new method of handling civil cases (called 'the Stuttgart procedure') was therefore developed. Its essence is to prepare the case so thoroughly beforehand that it can be determined conclusively in one hearing – possibly with the support of a single preliminary meeting. Under the Code of Civil Procedure the judge can if he wishes adopt this mode of proceeding.

See also C.N. Ngwasiri, 'The Role of the Judge in French Court Proceedings', 9 *Civil Justice Quarterly*, 1990, p. 167.

Tribunals

For an evaluation of the tribunal system as to its 'adversary' and 'inquisitorial' features see G. Ganz, *Administrative Procedures* (Sweet & Maxwell, 1974) pp. 29–35. For a very critical view of the decision-making process in industrial tribunals see

A. Leonard, *Judging Inequality* (Cobden Trust, 1987). Leonard studied 300 industrial tribunal cases relating to sex discrimination and equal pay over a three-year period. Her conclusions were disturbing. She found considerable ignorance and misunderstanding about the relevant legislation in the decisions. Many tribunals applied the wrong legal standard. Tribunals were found to be superficial in their analysis of the evidence, too ready to accept vague and generalised statements even when these were inconsistent with other evidence or based on irrelevant considerations. There was a great lack of uniformity in the quality of decision-making as between different tribunals. Some were much more expert than others. The lack of uniformity applied also to the expertise of those assisting applicants. Most claims failed because of the failure by the complainant and his representative to present relevant evidence. The usual pattern was for the parties to present only oral evidence with no more than one or two pre-existing documents. They failed to call supporting witnesses, failed to cross-examine witnesses effectively and made little or no use of statistical or comparative evidence. Complainants who had representatives who were more experienced and knowledgeable about the legislation had much better success rates.

Leonard adopted the view of a previous study[89] that the tribunal should perform an inquisitorial rather than an adversarial function, but in addition to an expert tribunal there would be a need for some form of expert to help the tribunal by organising the presentation of the cases, 'an individual expert in the legislation who in each case reviews the available information, determines what evidence and witnesses would be appropriate and ensures that they are produced by the parties' (p. 147).

FURTHER READING

For further reading about the English system of trial see: Glanville Williams' classic work, *The Proof of Guilt* (3rd edn, Stevens, 1963); S. Bedford, *The Faces of Justice* (Collins, 1961) and *The Best We Can Do* (Collins, 1963; Penguin, 1961); see also R. du Cann, *The Art of the Advocate* (revised edition, Penguin, 1993); P. Devlin, *The Judge* (OUP, 1979) pp. 54–85; and Sir J. Jacob, *The Fabric of English Civil Justice* (Sweet and Maxwell, 1987) pp. 5–19.

For the history see S. Landsman, 'The Decline of the Adversary System', 29 *Buffalo Law Review*, 1980, p. 487 and 'A Brief Survey of the Development of the Adversary System', 44 *Ohio State Law Journal*, 1983, p. 713; J. Langbein, *The Origins of Adversary Criminal Trial* (OUP, 2003) and 'The Prosecutorial Origins of Defence Counsel in the Eighteenth Century: The Appearance of Solicitors', 58 *Cambridge Law Journal*, 1999, pp. 314–65; T.P. Gallanis, 'The Mystery of Old Bailey Counsel', 65 *Cambridge Law Journal*, 2006, pp. 159–73.

On the inquisitorial system see S. Bedford, *The Faces of Justice* (Collins, 1961); B. Kaplan et al, 'Phases of German Civil Procedure', 71 *Harvard Law Review*, 1957–8, pp. 1193

---

[89] J. Corcoran and E. Donnelly, *Report of a Comparative Analysis of the Provisions for Legal Redress in Member States of the EEC in respect of Article 119 of the Treaty of Rome and the Equal Pay, Equal Treatment and Social Security Directive*, 1984.

and 1443 and 'Civil Procedure – Reflections on the Comparison of Systems', 9 *Buffalo Law Review*, 1959–60, p. 409; M. Damaska, 'Evidential Barriers to Conviction and Two Models of Criminal Procedure: A Comparative Study', 121 *University of Pennsylvania Law Review*, 1973, p. 506 and 'Structures of Authority and Comparative Criminal Procedure', 84 *Yale Law Journal*, 1975, p. 480; and J. Langbein, 'The German Advantage in Criminal Procedure', 52 *University of Chicago Law Review*, 1985, p. 230. Langbein's article provoked S.R. Gross, 'The American Advantage: The Value of Inefficient Litigation', 85 *Michigan Law Review*, 1987, p. 734; and R.J. Allan et al, 'The German Advantage in Civil Procedure: A Plea for More Details and Fewer Generalities in Comparative Scholarship', 82 *Northwestern Law Review*, 1988, p. 705 and his reply 'Trashing the German Advantage', 82 *Northwestern Law Review*, 1988, p. 763.

For the position of the defence lawyer in the inquisitorial system see J. Hodgson, 'The Role of the Criminal Defence Lawyer in an Inquisitorial Procedure: Legal and Ethical Constraints', 9 *Legal Ethics*, 2006, pp. 125–44.

For the position of the lawyer in the English civil system see D. Webb, 'Civil Advocacy and the Dogma of Adversarialism', 7 *Legal Ethics*, 2004, pp. 210–30.

For an American view that the two systems are not in fact as different as is often thought because the *juge d'instruction* is only rarely involved and, even when he is, there is still much scope for independent police action see A. Goldstein and M. Marcus, 'The Myth of Judicial Supervision in Three Inquisitorial Systems: France, Italy, and Germany', *Yale Law Journal*, 1977, pp. 240–83. For a comment on this article and a reply to the comment see *Yale Law Journal*, 1978, pp. 1549 and 1570. See also A. Goldstein, 'Reflections on Two Models: Inquisitorial Themes in American Criminal Procedure', 26 *Stanford Law Review*, 1974, pp. 1009 and 1016–25.

See also H. Kötz, 'The Role of the Judge in the Court Room: The Common Law and Civil Law Compared', *Journal of South African Law*, 1987–91, p. 35; C. Menkel-Meadow, 'Is the Adversary System Really Dead? Dilemmas of Legal Ethics as Legal Institutions and Roles Evolve', *Current Legal Problems*, 2004, pp. 85–116.

On the advantages of court control of fact-finding in the context of the systems of South Australia and Germany see A.J. Cannon, 'Effective fact-finding', 25 *Civil Justice Quarterly*, 2006, pp. 327–48.

On the French system see J.R. Spencer, 'French and English Criminal Procedure: A Brief Comparison' in *The Gradual Convergence* (ed. B.S. Markesinis, Clarendon, 1994) pp. 33–45 and M. Delmas-Marty, 'The *Juge d'instruction*: Do the English Really Need Him?', *ibid*, pp. 46–58.

On the French system since the reforms of 2000[90] see Jacqueline Hodgson, *French Criminal Justice: A Comparative Account of the Investigation and Prosecution of Crime in France* (2005, Hart).[91]

---

[90] Loi no 2000-516 du 15 juin 2000, Renforcant la protection de la présomption d'innocence et les droits des victimes.

[91] Dr Hodgson previously published a series of articles based on her research into the French system: 'The Police, the Prosecutor and the Juge d'Instruction', 41 *British Journal of Criminology*, 2001, pp. 342–61; 'Reforming French criminal justice', *Legal Action*, November 2001, pp. 6–8; 'Suspects, Defendants and Victims in the French Criminal Process: The Context of recent reforms', 51 *International and Comparative Law Quarterly*, 2002, pp 781–816; 'Heirarchy, Bureaucracy, and Ideology in French Criminal Justice: Some Empirical Observations', 29 *Journal of Law and Society*, 2002, pp. 227–57; 'Constructing the pre-trial

For a comprehensive review and comparison of the criminal procedure of England, France and Germany originally prepared in the context of the Runciman Royal Commission's inquiries see *Comparative Criminal Procedure* (eds. J. Hatchard, B. Huber and R. Vogler, British Institute of International and Comparative Law, 1996).

For a comparison of the English and Dutch systems see N. Jorg, S. Field and C. Brants, 'Are Inquisitorial and Adversarial Systems Converging?' in *Criminal Justice in Europe: A Comparative Study* (eds. P. Fennell, C. Harding, N. Jorg and B. Swart, Clarendon, 1995) pp. 41–56.

On convergence see B.S. Markesins (ed.), *The Gradual Convergence* (Clarendon Press, 1994).

For a description (by two of its chief authors) of radical reform of the Italian system in 1988 see E. Amodio and E. Selvaggi, 'An Accusatorial System in a Civil Law Country: The 1988 Italian Code of Criminal Procedure', 62 *Temple Law Review*, 1989, p. 1211. The article was the subject of M. Zander, 'From Inquisitorial to Adversarial – The Italian Experiment',141 *New Law Journal*, 17 May 1991, p. 678. See also E. Amodio, 'The Accusatorial System Lost and Regained: Reforming Criminal Justice in Italy', *American Journal of Comparative Law*, 2004, pp. 489–510.

For a lengthy consideration of the adversary/inquisitorial spectrum and where on the spectrum Diplock non-jury trials in Northern Ireland (p. 541 below) should be placed see J. Jackson and S. Doran, *Judge Without Jury: Diplock Trials in the Adversary System* (Clarendon, 1995) especially Chs. 3 and 10. The conclusion of the study was that judges in Diplock courts did not act in a more inquisitorial manner than when sitting with a jury. They varied somewhat in the extent to which they were interventionist but the differences arose from individual characteristics and not from the method of trial.

The Trial on Trial (vol. 1, Oxford, 2004)[92] has two chapters bearing on this topic: P. Duff, 'Changing Conceptions of the Scottish Criminal Trial: The Duty to Agree Uncontroversial Evidence', pp. 51–70; and J. McEwan, 'Ritual, Fairness and Truth: The Adversarial and Inquisitorial Models of Criminal Trial', pp. 71–84. In the same

role of the defence in French criminal procedure: an adversarial outsider in an inquisitorial process?, 6 *International Journal of Evidence and Proof*, 2002, pp. 1–16.

Hodgson's findings regarding the French system included: (1) Interviews with juveniles must be video-recorded but apart from that there is no requirement of tape or video recording; (2) the defence lawyer has the right to 30 minutes with the suspect at the start of detention and again after 20 hours and 36 hours – previously it was 30 minutes after 20 hours; (3) the police must inform the suspect, at the start, of the date and nature of the offence being inquired into; (4) in cases being supervised by the *juge d'instruction* the suspect and his lawyer have the right of full access to the *dossier* – however this affects only some 7 per cent of all cases; (5) in all other cases supervision of the police inquiry is by the prosecutor (*procureur*) – normally conducted over the telephone and by fax; (6) the Ministry of Justice circular says that the suspect should not be told his right to silence at the start of the questioning (neither desirable nor legally required and to do so would encourage the suspect to be silent which would be against his own interest); (7) there is no requirement of an appropriate adult; (8) duty solicitors (*avocat commis d'office*) are mainly young and inexperienced doing it as part of their training; (9) the maximum period of pre-trial detention (*détention provisoire*) is two years or four years depending on the gravity of the offence.

[92] Edited by A. Duff, L. Farmer, S. Marshall and V. Tadros. The essays were the outcome of two workshops under the title of 'Truth and Due Process' and 'Judgment and Calling to Account'. The four editors were due to publish their own book as a final volume.

volume see also J. Jackson, 'Managing Uncertainty and Finality: The Function of the Criminal Trial in Legal Inquiry', pp. 120–45 especially at 134–9; and H. Jung, 'Nothing but the Truth? Some Facts, Impressions and Confessions about Truth in Criminal Procedure', pp. 147–56 especially at 151–4.

For consideration of the effect of the European Convention on Human Rights see J.D. Jackson, 'The Effect of Human Rights on Criminal Evidentiary Processes: Towards Convergence, Divergence or Realignment?' 68 *Modern Law Review*, 2005, pp. 737–64.

For a wide-ranging international comparative study see R. Vogler, *A World View of Criminal Justice* (Aldgate, 2005).

2. Does being represented make a difference?

It would appear obvious that in an adversary system the party who is unrepresented is likely to be at a disadvantage.[93] There is however remarkably little UK statistical evidence on this important question based on court cases. Most of the studies that have statistics on the matter have been of tribunal cases where generally the full adversarial model of trial procedure does not operate.

In 2006 the Association of British Insurers said that a study they had done of 100,000 claims showed that personal injury claimants received more compensation and their claims were settled more quickly when they did *not* have lawyers. Needless to say, the study was dismissed as self-serving nonsense by the lawyers.[94]

Representation in magistrates' courts

In a 1983 study by the Lord Chancellor's Department in some sixty magistrates' courts there were 566 criminal cases in which the defendant pleaded not guilty. The proportion acquitted of those who had legal aid was 42 per cent, for those who were refused legal aid but who were represented privately was 52 per cent and for those who were not represented was virtually the same, 51 per cent. This suggested that representation was not necessarily so significant.[95]

Representation in small claims cases

In its original 1973 pamphlet which first proposed a small claims court, the Consumer Council recommended that legal representation not be permitted in the small claims court, but this recommendation was not adopted. Representation by a lawyer was permitted from the start in 1973 and representation by a non-lawyer has been permitted since 1992.[96] (Representation by

---

[93] For the surprising suggestion by the Master of the Rolls that lawyers might 'be taken out of the loop' in lower-value, less complex litigation where defendants are insured see J. Robins, 'Say it with Flowers', *Law Society's Gazette*, 27 January 2005, p. 22 at 23.

[94] R. Rothwell, 'Solicitors hurt PI claims, say insurers', *Law Society's Gazette*, 13 July 2006, p. 1.

[95] *Report of a Survey of the Grant of Legal Aid in Magistrates' Courts*, LCD, 1983, Table 17.

non-lawyers seems to be very rare. Professor Baldwin reported that in 109 hearings he observed in one of his studies there were only five that featured a lay representative.[97])

Baldwin compared legal representation in the 1996 sample of over 2,500 cases with his 1993 sample of just under 2,000 cases. There were some striking differences with regard to the frequency of representation. In 1993, in 82 per cent of the cases neither side was legally represented; in 1996, that figure had dropped to 55 per cent. In both 1993 and 1996, only the plaintiff was legally represented in 12 per cent of cases. In 1993, only the defendant was legally represented in 4 per cent of cases. The 1996 figure of 5 per cent was virtually the same, but whereas in 1993 both sides had been legally represented in only 2 per cent of cases, in 1996 that figure had risen to 27 per cent.[98] This was an astonishing change over so short a period.

In a previous study for the LCD, Baldwin had established that increases in legal representation were not occurring across the board but were confined to road accident cases. 80 per cent of litigants involved in such cases were legally represented compared with only 14 per cent in other categories of cases.[99] The increase in legal representation seemed therefore to be the result of the fact that many more road accident cases were being handled in the small claims system.

According to the 1996 sample, plaintiffs were significantly more likely to be legally represented than defendants. When the plaintiff was a company or a firm they were legally represented in, respectively, 51 per cent and 41 per cent of cases whereas individuals as plaintiff were legally represented in a third of cases. This difference was less marked in the case of defendants. (27 per cent of companies, 30 per cent of firms and 33 per cent of individual defendants were legally represented.[100]) It is worth noting that even firms and companies are not legally represented in the majority of cases in which they are involved – though they may, of course, be represented by a staff member who is familiar with court procedures.

Baldwin's 1996 figures suggest that legal representation improved a litigant's chances of success by about 10 per cent. He had reached the same conclusion in his earlier study.[101] A more important question is whether legal representation makes a difference when the other side is unrepresented. The 1996 figures showed that in small claims cases it made little difference.[102] Baldwin reflected

---

[96] The Lay Representation (Rights of Audience) Order 1992 giving effect to s. 11 of the Courts and Legal Services Act 1990.

[97] 17 *Civil Justice Quarterly*, January 1998, pp. 20 and 31, n. 31.

[98] J. Baldwin, 'Increasing the Small Claims Limit', 148 *New Law Journal*, 27 February 1998, p. 275.

[99] J. Baldwin, *Monitoring the Rise in the Small Claims Limit* (1997, LCD Research Series No. 1/97).   [100] Baldwin, n. 98 above, p. 275.   [101] *Ibid*, p. 276.

[102] In 87 per cent of the 2,563 cases the plaintiff got an award. When both sides were legally represented the figure was 90 per cent. When neither side was legally represented it was 86 per cent. When the plaintiff alone was legally represented it was 87 per cent. When the defendant alone was legally represented it was 86 per cent (*ibid*).

that this confirmed his earlier research which had indicated how problematic the legal representative's role is likely to be in the small claims context where the court is encouraged to be interventionist. (He had found that the lawyers in small claims cases tended to take a back seat and were sidelined by district judges who preferred to talk directly to the parties.[103])

Representation in tribunals

Another set of statistics regarding the benefit of representation relates to proceedings before national insurance tribunals and supplementary benefit appeals tribunals. In a now somewhat dated study by Professor Kathleen Bell and colleagues conducted in Scotland and the northern region of England in the 1970s, it was found that out of 4,456 cases in national insurance tribunals, the appellant was represented in just over 20 per cent. Representation in three-quarters of the cases was by a trade union representative, in 19 per cent by a relative or friend and in only 3 per cent by lawyers. Overall, the success rate of appeals was 21 per cent, but the success rate was distinctly higher for those who had been represented, regardless of who was the representative.[104]

The Benson Royal Commission on Legal Services in 1979 cited evidence to similar effect with regard to the success rate in over 50,000 supplementary benefit appeal tribunal cases in 1976.[105]

Hazel and Yvette Genn's, *The Effectiveness of Representation at Tribunals* (DCA, July 1989) showed that the presence of a representative 'significantly increases' the probability that cases will be won. In social security appeals the presence of a representative increased the probability of success from 30 per cent to 48 per cent. In hearings before Immigration Adjudicators it went up from 20 per cent to 38 per cent. In Mental Health Review Tribunals it increased the success rate from 20 per cent to 35 per cent. In Industrial Tribunals the impact depended on whether the respondent was represented. When he was not, the presence of a representative for the applicant pushed the success rate up from 30 per cent to 48 per cent. Where the respondent was represented and the applicant was not, the success rate went down to 10 per cent.

What was as striking as the statistical difference in success rate between those who were represented and those who were not was that, again, the nature of the representation made little difference. Thus in immigration appeals, solicitors, barristers and the United Kingdom Immigrants' Advisory Service, which used mainly non-legally qualified advocates, succeeded with virtually identical rates.[106]

Professor Hazel Genn returned with colleagues to the issue in a rich subsequent study, *Tribunals for Diverse Users*, based on three tribunals – the Appeals

---

[103] J. Baldwin, *Small Claims in the County Court in England and Wales: The Bargain Basement of Civil Justice* (Clarendon, 1997) pp. 116–20.

[104] K. Bell, 'National Insurance Local Tribunals', 4 *Journal of Social Policy*, 1975, p. 16. See to like effect House of Commons, *Hansard*, 1 May 1973, vol. 885, cols. 264–5.

[105] Cmnd. 7648, 1979, para. 15.9, p. 169.   [106] *Ibid*, p. 84.

Service (TAS), Criminal Injuries Compensation Appeals Panel (CICAP) and Special Educational Needs and Disability Tribunal (SENDIST).[107] Taking all cases together those who were represented were more successful than those who were unrepresented (73 per cent against 61 per cent). However regression analysis showed that once case type was controlled for, whereas in TAS cases representation (and ethnicity) influenced the outcome of hearings, in CICAP and SENDIST cases representation did not greatly affect outcome.

3. Handicaps of the unrepresented

The formality of English proceedings is often referred to by commentators. Where both parties are legally represented, as they normally are in the High Court or the higher criminal courts, this may not be quite so important, but where they are not legally represented it may be of great significance. There are no figures as to the proportion of defendants in the magistrates' courts who are unrepresented but it is certainly several hundred thousand each year. The essence of the situation was captured by Susanne Dell's study based on interviews with a random sample of 565 prisoners at Holloway prison. The study was conducted many years ago but it would be surprising if the situation of an unrepresented defendant today is very different.

In the lower courts
Susanne Dell, *Silent in Court*, 1971, pp. 17–19
Many of the women who were unrepresented were seriously handicapped by the lack of legal help. An inexperienced defendant is at a disadvantage in court even if well educated and articulate,[108] but for those who have little education, who are scared, nervous and unable to express themselves in the kind of language they believe is expected in court, the handicap can be crippling, particularly if they wish to deny the offence or to plead mitigating circumstances.

. . . When the unrepresented defendant first appears in court, she is in several ways at a disadvantage. The proceedings may be bewildering and unintelligible to her to an extent the court can hardly appreciate. One remanded girl, when asked by the interviewer whether she had asked for bail in court, replied 'What is bail? Is it the same as legal aid?' Many others, even by the time they were inter-

---

[107] H. Genn, B. Lever and L. Gray with N. Balmer (DCA Research Series 1/2006) Ch. 7. Footnote 70 cites other previous studies in which the value of advice and representation were discussed: J. Baldwin et al, *Judging Social Security* (Clarendon, 1992); L. Dickens, *Dismissed* (Oxford, 1985); J. Gregory, *Trial by Ordeal* (Stationery Office, 1989); R. Sainsbury, *Medical Appeal Tribunals* (Department of Social Security, 1992); R. Berthoud and A. Bryson, 'Social Security Appeals: What Do Claimants Want?', 4(1) *Journal of Social Security Law*, 1997, pp. 17–41.

[108] Not many women in the sample fell into that category, but an example was a professional woman who was arrested with others at a political demonstration. She appeared in court with the others, unrepresented, and was remanded in custody untried. When asked by the interviewer why bail had not been allowed, she said she did not know. She knew the police had opposed it, but said that all she heard was a policeman saying that the reason was 'the same as before'. It had not occurred to her to ask in court what bail meant.

viewed, were confused about the correct meaning of terms like 'remand' and 'bail'. This kind of ignorance was not restricted to first offenders, although for them the position is particularly difficult; they do not know what to expect, how to behave, when to speak, and when to be silent. As one girl put it, 'I kept being told to get up and sit down'. It is not easy in such circumstances to do justice to one's own defence.

Frequently, the women said that they had not been able to catch what was being said: a typical comment was 'the Judge mumbles away, and you don't know whether or not he's supposed to be speaking to you'. Many remanded women said they had left the court room without realising what the magistrate had decided: and it was then the police who had had to explain to them that they could not go home, as they had been remanded to Holloway. One first offender who caught the words 'two weeks' thought she was being put on probation for that period, until the police disabused her in the cells . . . The impossibility of expressing themselves in court weighed heavily on many women; not infrequently those who had given the interviewer full accounts of the background to their offences, said that the court had not known of the mitigating circumstances, as they had found themselves tongue-tied and silent at the appropriate moment . . . A few women complained that they never had a chance to explain themselves in court; this, no doubt, reflected their failure to understand the procedure, since they had probably been interrupted when trying to speak at the wrong moment, but the most common situation among the unrepresented was that when invited to do so, they failed to give the court any explanation of their behaviour. When asked 'what have you to say?' they seemed to think that the response expected was a short stereotype like 'I'm sorry' and they felt it impossible and inappropriate in the formality of the atmosphere to talk about the background to their offence. One woman described her feelings when she was invited to speak in court and failed to respond, much as she wished to: 'I was too over-awed and frightened – I didn't want to make a fool of myself – I would only have cried'.

A similar impression of the situation of the defendant in the magistrates' court was given in a book based on observation in magistrates' courts – P. Carlen, *Magistrates' Justice* (1976). See especially pp. 83–5.

A study of litigants in person in the High Court and the county court published by the DCA in 2005[109] said that unrepresented litigants were almost always victims of an imbalance of expertise. A significant minority of unrepresented litigants in family cases had specific indications of some vulnerability

---

[109] R. Moorhead and M. Sefton, *Litigants in person: unrepresented litigants in first instance proceedings* (DCA Research Series 2/2005) available at –
www.dca.gov.uk/research/2005/2_2005.pdf. Moorhead wrote about the study in 'Litigants in Person: Ghosts in the Machine', *Legal Action*, November 2005, pp. 8–9 from which the quotes above are taken. The study considered litigants in person in civil and family cases in the High Court and the county court excluding small claims cases. It was based on 2,432 case records, 748 case files where there were unrepresented litigants and interviews with litigants, lawyers and judges. See also his article 'A Challenge for Judgecraft', 156 *New Law Journal*, 5 May 2006, p. 742.

such as being victims of violence, or having depression, or a problem with alcohol/drug use, or having a mental illness or being extremely young parents. When the unrepresented party was active, they were less likely to defend than represented defendants. ('Activity on cases was often led by the represented party, not the unrepresented party, who participated sporadically and made more errors'.) Another important finding was that the bulk of unrepresented party participation took place via the court office rather than the courtroom.

Unrepresented litigants were far from keen on their day in court and much more likely to deal with court staff than judges. Complexity, jargon and lack of time all rendered courts (and court offices) places unsympathetic to litigants in person. Courts were not confident at guiding unrepresented litigants to alternative sources of help. Staff were uncertain about what services were provided in the locality and tended to rely on very general referral to an unnamed Citizens' Advice Bureau or a haphazardly suggested solicitor.

In tribunals

The 1957 Franks Committee on Administrative Tribunals said (p. 9) that tribunals had certain characteristics which distinguished them from courts – cheapness, accessibility, freedom from technicality and expert knowledge of the tribunal members. It identified three main objectives for the system: namely, openness, fairness and impartiality, but as Genn and Genn pointed out, the Franks Committee did not acknowledge that, to an extent, there is a conflict between the two sets of objectives.[110] Cheapness and informality may be in conflict with fairness and impartiality.

They found that tribunals were decidedly 'more informal and procedurally more flexible than courts' (p. 112), but the price was paid in quality of decision-making, since much of the law dealt with in tribunals is difficult and to present a coherent case on fact and law is not easy. The notion that tribunal cases were straightforward and that therefore there was no great need for a representative was unrealistic (*ibid*, Ch. 4):

> The experience of unrepresented appellants and applicants is overwhelmingly of feeling ill-equipped to present their case effectively at their hearing. They are intimidated, confused by the language and often surprised at the formality of the proceedings. Those who are subjected to cross-examination find the experience stressful, and feel unable to conduct cross-examination themselves. It is difficult to convey the degree of incomprehension common among appellants and applicants who appear unrepresented at tribunals, or the extent of the difficulties experienced by ordinary people trying to present their case in a legal forum.
>
> Representatives perform a number of functions. They prepare the case, act as a mouthpiece, and protect and support appellants and applicants. They act as a physical buffer between the appellant and the tribunal, and between the appellant and the opposing side. Most importantly, representation reduces the sense

---

[110] *The Effectiveness of Representation at Tribunals*, LCD, 1989, p. 111.

of being at a disadvantage experienced by unrepresented appellants. It increases the likelihood that those who appear before tribunals will perceive the process as fair (p. 241).

Litigants in person

A litigant always has the right to represent himself in any court. If he is not legally represented but would like to be, he can ask the court to indicate to the Legal Services Commission (LSC) that legal representation was necessary to ensure a fair hearing. This would be to give expression to Article 6(1) of the ECHR, but the court has no power to do more. It cannot grant legal aid nor can it direct the LSC to grant legal aid – though an indication that it was necessary would probably result in a grant provided the applicant qualified on the means test.[111]

However, if he is not legally represented, can he come with some other kind of person to assist him? In *McKenzie v. McKenzie*[112] the Court of Appeal held that the judge in a defended divorce case had been wrong to exclude an Australian barrister who attended to assist the husband petitioner appearing in person. He had been sitting beside the petitioner prompting and advising him. The court cited the words of Chief Justice Tenterden in *Collier v. Hicks*:[113]

> Any person, whether he be a professional man or not, may attend as a friend of either party, may take notes, may quietly make suggestions, and give advice; but no one can demand to take part in the proceedings as an advocate, contrary to the regulations of the court as settled by the discretion of the justices.
>
> . . . Mr Payne submitted, in my opinion rightly, that the judge ought not to have excluded Mr Hanger from the court, or, rather, ought not to have prevented Mr Hanger from assisting the husband in the way that he proposed to do. And, goes the submission, justice was not seen to be done in those circumstances . . .

This decision led to the start of a new form of assistance in courts known as the 'McKenzie man'. The 'McKenzie man' concept has gone through different phases and has been the subject of conflicting judicial decisions.[114]

In the 1990s it came up in the context of hearings for non-payment of community charge (poll tax). In *R v. Leicester City Justices, ex p Barrow*[115] the Divisional Court held that a party to court proceedings had no *right* to the assistance of a 'McKenzie friend'. It was a matter for the judge or justices to decide whether or not such assistance should be permitted as an exercise of discretion. On appeal the Court of Appeal disagreed.[116] It held that in civil proceedings to which the public had a right of access, the court, as part of its duty to administer justice fairly and openly, was under a duty to permit a litigant in person to have all reasonable

---

[111] *Perotti v. Collyer-Bristow* [2003] EWCA Civ 1521, [2004] 2 All ER 189.
[112] [1971] P 33, CA.   [113] (1831) 2 B & Ad 663 at 669.
[114] For a review and critique of the decisions see R. Moorhead, 'Access or Aggravation? Litigants in Person, McKenzie Friends and Lay Representation', 22 *Civil Justice Quarterly*, 2003, pp. 133–55.   [115] [1991] 2 All ER 437.   [116] [1991] 3 All ER 935.

facilities for exercising his right to be heard in his own defence. This included quiet and unobtrusive advice from another member of the public accompanying him as an assistant or adviser. A litigant did not need leave from the court for this, but in the exercise of its inherent jurisdiction the court could restrict the assistance of an adviser or even require him to leave the court if it became apparent that his assistance was unreasonable or not *bona fide* and was harmful to the proper and efficient administration of justice. There was no evidence that either the applicants or the person who was helping them had any intention of disrupting the court proceedings and the court should have allowed such assistance.[117]

In 1999 the Court of Appeal decided *R v. Bow County Court, ex p Pelling*.[118] Dr Pelling was an experienced McKenzie friend who charged for his services. He had been refused permission to attend to assist G in an application before the senior civil judge. No explanation was given. Dr Pelling brought judicial review proceedings challenging his exclusion. He failed, first, because he had no standing to bring such proceedings. The right to have a McKenzie friend was that of the litigant not of the McKenzie friend. Ultimately, Lord Woolf said, the decision was a matter of discretion for the court, with stronger or weaker presumptions one way or the other depending on whether the hearing was in private. (A hearing in chambers is sometimes in private and sometimes in public.)

Richard Moorhead (n. 109 above) summarised the effect of the decision in *Pelling*:

> (1) If the proceedings are in public whether in court or in chambers, a litigant in person should be allowed to have the assistance of a McKenzie friend unless the judge is satisfied that the interests of justice do not require it.
>
> (2) If the hearing is in private, the nature of the proceedings may make it undesirable in the interests of justice for the litigant to have a McKenzie friend.[119]
>
> (3) The judge should always give reasons for excluding the McKenzie friend.

Moorhead argued persuasively that the more open approach of the Court of Appeal in *Barrow* was to be preferred to that of Lord Woolf in *Pelling*. ('There should be a strong presumption in all cases (whether taking place in chambers and whether private or public) that a court should permit a litigant in person to have the assistance of a McKenzie friend'.[120]) That applied especially to lay assistance short of advocacy. Advocacy, especially when it was provided for payment, was more problematic. Competition for the legal profession from lay representatives who charged fees but did not have formal qualifications, or insurance, or rules of conduct did pose issues, but Moorhead suggests that the question for the courts should be providing help for needy litigants rather than protecting the interests of the legal profession.[121]

---

[117] For an account of this litigation see P.A. Thomas, 'From McKenzie Friend to Leicester Assistant: the Impact of the Poll Tax', *Public Law*, 1992, pp. 208–20.   [118] [1999] 4 All ER 751.

[119] In *Re G (Chambers Proceedings: McKenzie Friend)* [1999] 1 WLR 1828, the McKenzie friend, a solicitor, was refused permission to attend a chambers wardship hearing in private unless he was the solicitor on the record. The Court of Appeal declined to intervene.   [120] At p. 153.

[121] 151 *New Law Journal*, 5 October 2001, p. 216.

In June 2005 the Court of Appeal struck a very positive note regarding the McKenzie friend – at least when he was unpaid. The court allowed three appeals from fathers each of whom had been refused permission to use a McKenzie friend in private proceedings regarding their children. Lord Justice Wall, giving the judgment of the court, said that the President of the Family Division had seen and approved a draft of the judgment.

The three cases, he said, demonstrated the advantages of the presence of a McKenzie friend. The purpose of allowing a person the assistance of a McKenzie friend was to further the interests of justice by achieving a level playing field and ensuring a fair hearing. The presumption in favour of allowing a person such assistance was very strong and such a request should be refused only for compelling reasons. Furthermore, a judge should identify such reasons, he should explain them carefully and fully to both the litigant in person and the would-be McKenzie friend. Where the litigant in person wanted the McKenzie friend in private family law proceedings related to children, the sooner that wish was made known to the court the better and the sooner the court's agreement was obtained the better. In the same way that judicial continuity was important, the McKenzie friend would be most useful to the litigant in person if he could advise the litigant throughout. It was not good practice to exclude the proposed McKenzie friend from the courtroom or the chambers while the application by the litigant was being made since the litigant would require his assistance in making the application.

It was also desirable that any concerns about the McKenzie friend were aired in his presence so that the judge could satisfy himself that the McKenzie friend fully understood his role.

It was understandable that a partner would be wary about allowing a stranger who was not legally qualified to assist his or her estranged partner in a private hearing involving intimate matters and confidential court documents, but, the court said, there were several powerful factors which properly outweighed reliance on such reluctance. The first was Article 6 of the ECHR. In each of the three cases the other side was represented by solicitors and counsel. Even if the litigant in person was unrepresented by choice, the Article 6 argument was powerful.

Proceedings remained confidential. The court should require an assurance from both the litigant in person and from the McKenzie friend that the court documents would only be used for the purpose of the proceedings. The McKenzie friend would need to understand that improper disclosure of court documents would be contempt of court.

The Otton Working Party on litigants in person in the Royal Courts

In June 1995 a committee under the chairmanship of Lord Justice Otton established by the Judges' Council reported on the problem of litigants in person in the Royal Courts of Justice. It said there had been a significant increase in the number of such litigants in the Royal Courts of Justice. The largest number and proportion were in the civil division of the Court of Appeal. In 1993–4, litigants in person were one in three of applicants for leave to appeal though only 10 per cent of actual appellants. The litigant in person was ultimately successful in only 4 per cent of cases – a much lower rate than litigants who had representation. One reason was that some simply had no case at law. Others were prejudiced by the complexity of the proceedings, their lack of knowledge of procedure and the non-availability of low cost or free legal advice and assistance. Court staff gave as much assistance as they could but they could not become legal advisers without prejudicing the independence of the court.

The Working Party referred to the excellent work done for litigants in person by the Citizens' Advice Bureau in the Royal Courts of Justice – as to which see www.bushywood.com/citizens_advice_bureau.htm. The Bureau handles some 18,000 queries a year. It has the voluntary assistance of lawyers from some sixty firms of solicitors.

Moorhead and Sefton report

The report on litigants in person by Moorhead and Sefton[122] drew attention to the fact that not only was non-representation common, it was frequently associated with total non-participation. Litigants in person were what they called 'the ghosts in the machine'. This was especially so in county court cases, including housing possession cases, where over half of all individual defendants did not participate in their cases. Even in High Court cases, over one in five individual defendants did not participate in any way apparent from the court file. More than one in six business defendants in the High Court and over one in four in the county courts did not appear to participate in their cases. Even in family cases, there was a significant minority of unrepresented litigants who did not participate in any way apparent from the court file.

The unrepresented were less likely to defend, less likely to file formal documents or make applications and less likely to attend hearings. Unsurprisingly, they were also more likely to make mistakes.

4. Establishing the facts: the unreliability of human testimony

The majority of both civil and criminal trials involve issues of fact rather than problems of law. One of the difficulties faced by the courts is the danger of perjury by those giving evidence.

Perjury

This is an area where little is known – though most of those connected with the justice business are probably aware that perjury is quite common. The number of prosecutions is tiny – usually 200–300 cases a year.[123] These

---

[122] Note 109 above.

[123] A spectacular example of a perjury prosecution was the case brought against former Tory Cabinet Minister Jonathan Aitken arising out of his failed libel proceedings against *The Guardian* and Granada's *World in Action* programme. Aitken pleaded guilty and was

obviously represent only the tip of the iceberg. An attempt to get some kind of line on the problem was reported by a practising barrister in 1986.[124] David Wolchover had been at the Bar for fifteen years. His aim was to discover how much perjury was committed by police officers. His method was to inquire of his fellow barristers. He accepted that it was far from ideal as a basis for an assessment, but said he thought that there was none better and that it might not be wildly wrong.

He considered that having practised for many years he 'had sufficient experience and acumen to be capable of making a reasonably confident judgment from the details of facts and circumstances in a given case whether police officers were committing perjury'. It had become apparent to him that 'police perjury occurs with great frequency in London' where he practised. His belief that this was so 'was reinforced by hearing, in chambers, in the robing room and Bar mess, the casual and matter of fact way in which the Bar tends to refer to police perjury. It was regarded as commonplace'. Over a two-year period he conducted an informal and statistically haphazard poll of fellow barristers to ask how many shared that view. In the large majority it was shared. For most, it had been between five and twenty years since being called to the Bar and they took part in prosecution and defence work in about equal proportions.

In Mr Wolchover's estimation, perjury took place in as many as three out of every ten criminal trials both summary and on indictment. Forty-one of the fifty-five barristers (75 per cent) he asked thought that this was 'a reasonable estimate with which they could readily concur'. Eight thought it occurred in only one or two out of ten. Four thought its frequency was less than one in ten. Two thought it happened in as many as 50 per cent of their cases (one of these did more prosecution than defence work). Averaged out roughly, this would mean that police perjury was thought to occur in a little over a quarter of all trials.

Mr Wolchover observed that this figure related only to perceptible lying under oath. There would be many other cases where the police officers lied in ways that were not perceptible to the barristers in the case or where the issue of police perjury never became relevant because the defendant pleaded guilty. There would almost certainly be cases where innocent defendants pleaded guilty to trumped-up charges (see p. 322 above) or where some of the prosecution evidence was invented – the gilding of the lily.

For an examination of the sentences given for perjury see S.S.M. Edwards, 'Perjury and Perverting the Course of Justice Considered', *Criminal Law Review*, 2003, pp. 525–40. For a study of offenders convicted of perjury see K. Soothill and B. Francis, 'Perjury and False Statements: A Criminal Profile of Persons Convicted 1979–2001', *Criminal Law Review*, 2004, pp. 926–35.

Footnote 123 (*cont.*)
  sentenced in June 1999 to eighteen months' imprisonment. (For an absorbing account of the story see L. Harding, D. Leigh and D. Palliser, *The Liar: The Fall of Jonathan Aitken* (Penguin, 1997).) [124] 136 *New Law Journal*, 28 February 1986, p. 181.

Human fallibility

However, the problem of perjury in the courts is probably minor by comparison with the problem created by the fallibility of honest witnesses. There is now a mass of evidence based on experiments conducted by psychologists and others showing how distressingly inaccurate human beings are in their powers of observation, recall and reporting.[125]

In the first study listed below in n. 125, the author wrote:

> On the whole, it seems, psychological theory in the field of perception is fairly well advanced. It is now generally recognised that there is an important distinction between 'actual' and 'perceived' characteristics of the environment. In other words, 'we all live in a world of our own psychological reality, a world of personal experience separated from the real world (whatever we choose to mean by that) and from the psychological world of others by a complex neuro-physiological process . . . This process selects, organises and transforms objective information according to conditions existing in the observer at the time'. In short, what a witness recognises perceptually is not necessarily an exact reproduction of the data presented and for legal purposes at any rate the most important finding in this area is that there can be a very considerable discrepancy between the two.
>
> Many of the causes of this discrepancy are already well known, e.g. the adverse effect on accuracy of testimony of poor lighting, long distance, short duration of exposure, etc. Less well-known factors influencing perception include emotion, interest, bias, prejudice, or expectancy, on the part of the perceiver. Take, for instance, the effect of 'expectancy' or 'set'. It is a well-documented fact that we frequently perceive what we expect to perceive. If we expect to see an individual performing a particular action we are more likely than not to interpret a stimulus which is in fact ambiguous as evidence that the person is performing the expected action.
>
> One example of this is provided by a Canadian case where a hunter was mistaken for a deer and shot by his companions. The hunters, who were eagerly scanning the landscape for deer, perceived the moving object (the victim) as a deer. Before the trial, the police recreated the scene under the same conditions, using another man in the place of the deceased. They reported at the trial that the object was clearly visible as a man, but the important psychological difference between the first and second 'shooting' was that the hunters, expecting to see a deer, 'saw' a deer; the police expected to see a man and therefore 'saw' a man.
>
> More recently, a psychologist was called in by the defence in an English case where two men were charged with having committed an act of gross indecency in a public convenience. Complaints had been made to the police that the convenience

---

[125] See in particular D.S. Greer, 'Anything But the Truth? – The Reliability of Testimony in Criminal Trials', 11 *British Journal of Criminology*, 1971, p. 13; Dr E. Slater, 'The Judicial Process and the Ascertainment of Truth', 24 *Modern Law Review*, 1961, p. 721; Dr L.R.C. Haward, 'Some Psychological Aspects of Oral Evidence', 3 *British Journal of Criminology*, 1962–3, p. 342; Dr L.R.C. Haward, 'A Psychologist's Contribution to Legal Procedure', 27 *Modern Law Review*, 1964, p. 656; D. Farrington, K. Hawkins and S. Lloyd-Bostock, *Psychology, Law and Legal Processes* (Macmillan, 1979) especially Part IV; and D. Yamey, *The Psychology of Eye-Witness Testimony* (Free Press, 1979).

was being used for indecent purposes and the accused were apprehended by two policemen who were keeping the convenience under secret observation. The defendants denied that any criminal acts had taken place. The psychologist reproduced the defence version of the facts (i.e. no criminal act) in a series of photographs and he showed these to twelve adults under different conditions of light, for varying lengths of time, and with reference to three different questions: in A they were merely asked to say what they saw in the pictures; in B they were asked if they could see any crime being committed in any of the pictures; in C they were told that some of the pictures actually portrayed criminal acts being committed and they were asked to identify the pictures concerned.

The result was that the number of errors increased considerably from A to B to C. In other words, the witnesses most frequently erred in asserting that a crime was being committed when they were led to expect to see this criminal behaviour. The police, therefore, expecting to see an indecent act being committed might well have put an erroneous interpretation on innocent facts. In the event, the accused were acquitted.

A cautionary tale about being a witness was written in 1973 by *New Society*'s then legal correspondent (later a distinguished Queen's Counsel and Master of an Oxford College):

'Diogenes', *New Society,* **31 August 1973**
Just over two years ago, I witnessed a minor accident. It happened in this way. I was riding in a bus which had new automatic doors at its exit. On reaching the bus stop where I wanted to get off, I found myself behind an old lady who was stepping onto the pavement with some caution. The bus driver evidently had his view of the exit in the mirror blocked because, before she had completed her manoeuvre, he started the bus up. Her arm was caught in the closing doors. Fortunately, my shouts caused the bus driver to stop and the old lady was saved from nothing worse than slight shock, bruises to her arm, and a cut on her shin.

At the time, with a barrister's instinct for a possible civil claim by the old lady against the city bus company, I gave her my name (as a witness, not an advocate), and on my return to my parents' house, some ten minutes later, I wrote out a statement of what I had seen. I was, in other words, the perfect witness. I was on the spot. I had appreciated at once the need for an accurate account of what had happened. I was trained to understand what was and what was not relevant to a claim for negligent driving. And I made a statement within minutes.

Yet, even within that short space of time I found myself forgetting certain details. Had I been directly behind the old lady, or were there other passengers between us? Where had her arm been when it was trapped? How fast was the bus going before it stopped? I argued several points with my wife, who had been with me, and, later that evening, when I furnished another statement to the police, I found myself making minor modifications to my account.

A magistrates' court hearing followed a few months later. I gave my evidence as well as I could; but, by that time, I could not honestly say that I remembered more than the bare outlines of the event, and would have been lost without an ability to refer to my contemporary record – something admissible in evidence like the policeman's notebook. The driver was, however, convicted, in my view quite properly. I felt sorry for the defence solicitor.

I have not been summoned to give evidence in civil proceedings. Nowadays, once a driver has a conviction in respect of an accident, the fact of which can be adduced in evidence, his chances of defending a civil claim are slim indeed. And, I assume, the claim has been settled by the city bus company's insurers.

But, in the ordinary run of things, a trial of a personal injury claim two years after the event would be nothing unusual; slow for a county court, but average for the High Court. And, if I am called on as a witness at this length of time, what do I really retain except a memory of the kind of accident that it was and a feeling that it was the driver's fault?

The point of this reminiscence? Only that every day witnesses purport to give truthful accounts, in the box, of accidents that occurred in split-second circumstances, and in which they were often themselves involved; and that thousands of pounds, indeed an individual's future, may depend on the outcome of the case.

Research has been done on both sides of the Atlantic to discover whether different groups of people are aware of the factors that influence the accuracy of eye witness evidence. To an alarming extent they do not. Even police officers have little appreciation of the relevant factors – and length of service, rank or nature of employment (in uniform or CID) seem not to affect the matter one way or the other.[126]

For the instructive (and entertaining) reflections of an experienced judge on the problems of finding the facts in civil cases, see T. Bingham (later to become, in turn, Master of the Rolls, Lord Chief Justice and senior Law Lord), 'The Judge as Juror', *Current Legal Problems*, 1985, p. 1.

5. The principle of orality

One of the fundamental features of an English trial is the oral examination of witnesses in court. The principle of orality has always been at the heart of the English trial, partly because of the dominant role played for centuries by the jury, though, as will be seen, its importance is gradually being somewhat eroded, especially in civil cases.

One such exception is evidence given on affidavit, a procedure that is common, for instance, in the Chancery Division. The evidence in interlocutory injunction cases is normally taken on affidavit, e.g. in trade union disputes. So too is the evidence on the basis of which the Administrative Court decides applications for judicial review of administrative action, formerly under RSC Order 53, now under CPR Part 54. In theory, the person whose evidence is being read to the court (the deponent) can be asked to come to court to be cross-examined but that rarely happens. The procedure is therefore not well adapted to dealing with disputes as to the facts.

---

[126] P. Bennett and F. Gibling, 'Can We Trust Our Eyes?' 5 *Policing*, Winter 1989, pp. 313 and 320.

A major development in the use of written evidence came in the Practice Directions issued in 1995 for the Queen's Bench Division, the Chancery Division and the Family Division which stated that 'unless otherwise ordered, every witness statement or affidavit shall stand as the evidence-in-chief of the witness concerned'.[127] The CPR restated this principle: 'where a witness is called to give oral evidence under para. (1), his witness statement shall stand as his evidence-in-chief unless the court otherwise orders'.[128]

Another inroad into orality is the rule for fast track cases that expert evidence must normally be given in writing. 'The court will not make a direction giving permission for an expert to give oral evidence unless it believes it is necessary in the interests of justice to do so' (CPR, PD 28, 7.2(4)(b)).

Another exception is when hearsay evidence is given in the form of a witness statement when the witness is not called at all. Under the Civil Evidence Act 1995 the evidence can be given in this form provided notice has been given to the other side and no request has been made for the witness to be brought to court.[129]

Nearly all divorces are obtained through the 'special procedure', which is virtually divorce by post. The court simply looks at the petition and the supporting affidavits and, if they are in order, pronounces the divorce. Normally there is no one present from either side.

Another exception to the general principle that evidence must be given orally in open court is in relation to criminal cases. The Magistrates' Courts Act 1980, ss. 6 and 102 provided for the committal stage to be drastically shortened by the acceptance as evidence of written statements of witnesses, providing that they were signed, that they had been sent in advance to the other side and that the other side did not object. Even if the other side did object, the court retained an overriding discretion to call a witness whose statement had been produced as evidence, but in practice this was rarely exercised. As has been seen, the Criminal Procedure and Investigations Act 1996, ss. 4, 45 and Sch. 1 took this development further by eliminating oral evidence in committal proceedings altogether – before committal proceedings themselves are abolished.

Section 9 of the Criminal Justice Act 1967 had an even wider provision since it related to any criminal case, whether tried summarily or on indictment. It permitted the admission as evidence of a written statement subject to the same conditions as applied to committal proceedings under the Magistrates' Courts Act 1980.

See generally C. Glasser, 'Civil Procedure and the Lawyers – the Adversary System and the Decline of the Orality Principle', 56 *Modern Law Review*, 1993, pp. 307–24. For the argument that commitment to the orality principle seriously weakens the special measures available to protect vulnerable witnesses under the Youth Justice and Criminal Evidence Act 1999 (pp. 431–33 below) see

---

[127] [1995] 1 All ER 385, para. 3, [1995] 1 All ER 586, para. 3.   [128] CPR, r. 32.5(2).
[129] CPR, r. 33.2.

L. Ellison, *The Adversarial Process and the Vulnerable Witness* (OUP, 2001).[130] The book is a critique of the traditional model of oral, adversary trial and its partial reform by the 1999 Act.

6. The taking of evidence

Opening speech In a civil case the case starts with an opening speech for the claimant (formerly 'plaintiff'). In a criminal case tried in the Crown Court the case opens with a speech from the prosecution. (In the magistrates' court the prosecution will not necessarily make an opening speech beyond a statement as to the nature of their case.) The purpose of the opening speech is to set out that side's case and what the witnesses will establish. In Scotland, by contrast, the case starts right away with the first witness – no opening speech is permitted. The danger of the English system is that when there is a jury, it will be prejudiced against the accused by counsel's address and the more so because the prosecution may not actually succeed in proving what counsel's opening speech foreshadowed.

The Runciman Royal Commission on Criminal Justice proposed that unless the judge gave leave, the prosecutor's opening speech should not be longer than fifteen minutes and that opening speeches should be limited to an explanation of the issues at trial.[131] They should refer to the evidence to be called only if that was essential to the jury's understanding of the case. The prosecution should not seek to suggest that particular matters would be proved by the prosecution.[132]

The Royal Commission also proposed that the defence should have the option of making its opening speech immediately after the prosecution's opening.[133] This is occasionally done.

Examination-in-chief The next stage is 'examination-in-chief' when the claimant (formerly 'plaintiff') or prosecutor calls and examines his witnesses. In civil cases, as has already been seen, this stage is nowadays normally skipped as the witness' statement is treated as his evidence-in-chief unless the court otherwise orders. The CPR state that a party may amplify his witness statement or testify in relation to anything new that has happened since the witness statement was served (CPR, r. 32.5(3)).

In a criminal case, however, the witnesses are still normally examined in chief by each side. The prosecution goes first. Examination-in-chief consists of taking

---

[130] See also M. Burton, R. Evans and A. Sanders, 'Vulnerable and Intimidated Witnesses and the Adversarial Process in England and Wales', 11 *International Journal of Evidence and Proof*, 2007, pp. 1–23.

[131] The longest opening speech in British legal history is believed to be 119 days – by counsel for the Bank of England defending an £850 million claim by creditors of the collapsed bank BCCI. The previous record was eighty days by his opponent in the case appearing for the BCCI liquidators (*The Guardian*, 25 May 2005).   [132] Runciman, p. 120, paras. 8 and 9.

[133] Runciman, p. 121, para. 10.

the witness through his story stage by stage. The advocate will base his examination of the witness on the information supplied by his instructing solicitors based on their meetings with the witness, which they have reduced to his statement (or 'proof').

In order to minimise the danger of 'coaching of the witness', the rule in England has been that prosecutors were not permitted to speak about the evidence to their own witnesses prior to the trial. The only general exceptions were the client and an expert witness.[134] In civil cases there is no longer a rule that prohibits a barrister from seeing witnesses but the Code of Conduct states that a barrister should not appear as advocate in a case if he has 'taken' a witness statement – as distinguished from 'settling' a witness statement taken by someone else.[135]

However, the Damilola Taylor case[136] in 2002 led to a reconsideration of this important rule for criminal cases. On 1 May 2003, the CPS issued a consultation paper inviting views as to whether the prosecutor should in future be permitted to interview key witnesses in order to assess their credibility.[137] In 2004 the consultation led to a change in the rules. A prosecutor may now interview his witnesses where it is necessary to confirm the reliability of the witness' evidence or to clarify the evidence which the witness can give.[138]

What is not allowed is any form of 'coaching'. This traditional rule was restated in the clearest terms by the Court of Appeal in *Momodou and Liman*.[139] To familiarise the witness ahead of time with the process, with the layout of the court and even to expose him to a mock cross-examination is permitted, but preparation must not be in the context of the actual case in which the witness is to give evidence. Where an outside agency is employed to conduct witness familiarisation, the CPS should be asked to comment in advance on the proposed format. In the case of the defence, counsel should be asked to advise. The process should normally be supervised by a practitioner.

Examination-in-chief should not generally include 'leading questions'. A leading question is one that suggests the answer ('Did you see the accused at that point raise his arm in a threatening way?' as opposed to 'What did you see then?'). Leading questions are, however, permitted for a matter that is wholly uncontroversial ('Is your name John Smith and do you live at . . . ?'). They are also allowed when the purpose is to elicit a denial from the witness ('Did you kill the deceased?').

---

[134] See the *Code of Conduct of the Bar of England and Wales* (8th edn, 2004), Written Standards for the Conduct of Professional Work, paras. 6.1.3, 6.1.4 and 6.3.1 – www.barcouncil.org.uk. Someone must interview witnesses, since there is obviously no equivalent rule for solicitors – see the Law Society's *Guide to Professional Conduct*, para. 21.10.

[135] *Code of Conduct of the Bar of England and Wales*, n. 132 above, para. 6.2.6.

[136] In April 2002 the trial of four boys for the murder of ten-year-old Damilola ended in a blaze of publicity with all four being acquitted after the fourteen-year-old chief prosecution witness had been shown to be a completely unreliable witness. On 9 August 2006 two other boys were convicted of the killing.

[137] See *Pre-trial Interviews by Prosecutors* – www.cps.gov.uk. The consultation paper included an appendix showing the position in other countries.

[138] Attorney General, *Pre-trial Witness Interviews by Prosecutors Report*, 2004.

[139] [2005] EWCA Crim 177, [2005] 2 All ER 571, [2005] Crim LR 588.

Cross-examination At the end of the examination-in-chief, the witness is offered to the other side for cross-examination. Cross-examination is the attempt to show that the witness was lying or mistaken, or that he is not a person who can be relied on to tell the truth. It may also be used to establish evidence favourable to the cross-examiner's side. Leading questions are permitted. The witness can be cross-examined about his previous convictions, his bias and his reputation for untruthfulness, but the Bar's *Code of Conduct* says that a barrister must not suggest that a witness or other person is guilty of crime, fraud or misconduct or attribute the crime to someone else unless such allegations go to a matter in issue (including the credibility of the witness) which is material to the lay client's case 'and which appear to him to be supported by reasonable grounds'.[140] Also a barrister must not make statements or ask questions which 'are merely scandalous or intended or calculated only to vilify, insult or annoy either a witness or some other person'.[141]

As will be seen (see p. 468 below) in rape cases the defendant's representative is restricted as to the questions that can properly be put to the complainant regarding her sexual experience with other persons.

New rules introduced in the Youth Justice and Criminal Evidence Act 1999, ss. 34 and 35 also state that someone charged with a sexual offence if acting in person (i.e. without legal representation) may not cross-examine either the victim ('the complainant') or a child witness or any other witness if the court so orders. In such a case the court must invite the defendant to arrange for a legal representative to act for him for the purpose of cross-examination, failing which it may appoint a representative for the purpose (s. 38). The rules were introduced because of public outrage at a small number of cases in which a defendant accused of rape subjected the victim to the ordeal of lengthy and humiliating direct cross-examination.[142]

In May 1998 the Lord Chief Justice issued new guidelines to judges to take a more interventionist approach in such cases and either halt questioning, if it sought to humiliate, or order the installation of a screen so that at least the victim did not have to see and be seen by the defendant.[143] The Lord Chief Justice thought that the judges were capable of dealing with the problem without legislation, but the Government decided that legislation would be better.

The general rule is that evidence is not admissible to contradict answers given in answering questions put in cross-examination. The reason is to confine the scope of the case within reasonable limits, but if the witness has made a prior

---

[140] *Code of Conduct of the Bar of England and Wales*, n. 134 above, para. 5.10(h).
[141] *Ibid*, para. 5.10(e).
[142] In 1997, Ralston Edwards, wearing the same clothes as he wore during his sixteen-hour attack on her at her home, spent *six days* cross-examining his victim in his rape trial at the Old Bailey. In another case, in November 1997, the defendant, Brown, sacked his defence team and subjected his victim to merciless cross-examination. (Both men were convicted by the jury.)   [143] *The Times*, 7 May 1998.

statement which is inconsistent with his evidence he can be cross-examined about it.

Occasionally, effective cross-examination can be based simply on what the witness has said by pointing out inconsistencies or improbabilities; usually, however, it requires other material based on work done by those responsible for preparation of the case. Cross-examination is a difficult art and it is not very often that it significantly dents the witness's evidence.

One of the duties of the cross-examiner is to 'put his client's case'. This is because of the technical rule that one cannot call evidence to contradict the opponent's case unless one has challenged the disputed evidence in cross-examination. That is why one so frequently hears counsel say to the witness: 'I put it to you that . . .' – to which the usual reply is some variation on 'no, that is not so'. Nothing much is achieved by such exchanges other than fulfilment of the requirement that the case be 'put' to the witness.[144]

Re-examination At the close of cross-examination, the witness is offered back to the opponent for re-examination. The purpose of re-examination is not to go over the same ground again, but to clarify or to explain evidence that has emerged during cross-examination. Thus, if in cross-examination reference has been made to part of a conversation favourable to the cross-examiner, questions could be put to draw out other parts of the conversation which put a different and less attractive gloss on the matter.

This process of examination-in-chief, cross-examination and re-examination is repeated for each witness in turn. When that process is complete, each party makes a closing speech save that in a criminal case, if the defendant is unrepresented, the prosecution does not make a closing speech.[145] If both sides make a closing speech, the defence in a criminal case has the last word. In a civil case it is the claimant/plaintiff who goes last.

Victim personal statement Since October 2001 the rules have permitted the victim to make a personal written statement.[146] The victim personal statement and any evidence in support 'should be considered and taken into account by the court prior to passing sentence',[147] but the sentencer may not make assumptions unsupported by evidence as to the effect of an offence on the victim. The court should pay no attention to any opinions expressed by the victim.

The statement must be in proper form and must be served prior to sentence on the defendant's solicitor or, if he is not represented, on the defendant.[148]

---

[144] For an assessment of the rules on cross-examination of police witnesses by the defence so as to bring out past discreditable incidents see D. Wolchover, 'Attacking Confessions with Past Police Embarrassments', *Criminal Law Review*, 1988, p. 573.

[145] That has been the rule – see *Baggott* (1927) 20 Cr App R 92 and *Mondon* (1968) 52 Cr App R 695, but in *Stovell* [2006] EWCA Crim 27, [2006] Crim LR 760 the Court of Appeal said that it would not always necessarily be inappropriate for the prosecution to make a second speech where the defendant was unrepresented.

[146] Consolidated Criminal Practice Direction, section III.28.   [147] Section III.28(a).

[148] See generally I. Edwards, 'The Place of Victims' Preferences in the Sentencing of "Their" Offenders', *Criminal Law Review*, 2002, pp. 689–702. See also generally J. Doak, 'Victims'

Statement by victim's advocate In April 2006 a pilot of a new concept – voluntary victim's advocate – started in five criminal courts.[149] The scheme applied only in murder and manslaughter cases. The purpose was to put before the court, after conviction and before sentence, 'the effect of the murder or manslaughter on the family of the victim'.[150] The family was to be free, 'within the normal requirements of court procedure', to choose how best to express its views – i.e. whether the statement was to be written only, oral testimony by the maker or read to the court by a CPS prosecutor, an independent advocate or a lay friend.

Families should be encouraged to speak through one representative, 'but more than one member may wish to speak'. Any issue between family members as to the making of a statement would be resolved by the judge. The defendant should be made aware of the contents of the statement in advance.

The family would have the assistance of the CPS prosecutor or of an independent advocate to prepare the statement. Where the family decided to present the statement in the form of an oral statement by one of them, the independent advocate should assist as if the family member were a witness with the statement being his or her evidence-in-chief.

The details would be sorted out with the judge at the pre-trial plea and case management hearing (PCMH). The CPS would serve the statement on the court and the defendant prior to the PCMH.

The independent advocate would be paid for out of public funds. If the family wished to pay for their own choice of lawyer, they could do so with the permission of the court.[151]

Time limits on advocacy Historically the courts have allowed counsel to take as long as they need to present their case, but increasingly this relaxed attitude is giving way to a new concern to see that trials do not take more time than is necessary. Thus, the Practice Directions issued in 1995 for proceedings in the Queen's Bench Division and the Chancery Division and for the Family Division stated that the court would increasingly exercise its discretion to limit the length of opening and closing oral submissions, the time allowed for the examination and cross-examination of witnesses, the issues on which it wished to be addressed and reading aloud from documents and authorities.[152] Courts have increasingly used counsel's time estimates as a way of trying to control the length of the case. In *A-G v. Scriven*,[153] a civil case, Lord Justice Simon Brown

Rights in Criminal Trials: Prospects for Participation', 32 (2) *Journal of Law and Society,* 2005, pp. 294–316.

[149] The Central Criminal Court and Crown Courts in Birmingham, Cardiff, Manchester and Winchester.

[150] Protocol on the procedure to be followed in the victims' advocate pilot areas. Issued by the President of the Queen's Bench Division, 3 May 2006 – www.judiciary.gov.uk/docs/victims_advocate_protocol_030506.pdf.

[151] For a discussion of the pros and cons of this initiative see J. Robins, 'Finding a Voice', *Law Society's Gazette,* 29 September 2005, p. 20.   [152] [1995] 1 All ER 385, para. 2.

[153] 4 February 2000, unreported, CA.

said: 'The courts are not required to listen to litigants, whether represented or not, for as long as they like. It is for the court to control its own process, and it is well entitled to bring arguments to a close when it concludes that its process is being abused and that nothing of value will be lost by ending it'. The same applies to criminal cases. In *Butt*[154] the trial judge, having listened to lengthy and repetitive cross-examination and having repeatedly tried to get counsel to close, finally gave her a time limit of ten more minutes to finish. Dismissing the appeal, the Court of Appeal said that judges could impose time limits. Here it was fully justified. Counsel had had ample time.[155]

The decision The final stage is the process of actual decision. In a case with a jury, the judge sums up on the facts and the law (see pp. 521–24 below) and the jury then decides. In a criminal trial with a jury the question of sentence is solely for the judge. Juries, as will be seen, are very rare in civil cases. Usually, therefore, it is simply a matter of the court reaching and announcing its decision.

Reasons for the decision In the High Court, but not always in the county or magistrates' court, the court will normally also give a reasoned judgment. There is growing pressure generated by the Human Rights Act for judicial decisions to be properly reasoned but the requirements in the lowest courts are as yet not very demanding.[156] In the Crown Court, the jury does not give reasons (for discussion of which see pp. 529–30 below). Nor does the judge since it is the jury rather than the judge that gives the decision. The exception is sentencing which is done by the court. The Criminal Justice Act 2003, s. 174 imposes on the court a general statutory duty to give reasons for, and to explain the effect of, the sentence passed.[157]

On the conduct of trials generally see for instance R. du Cann, *The Art of the Advocate* (Penguin, revised edition, 1993).

7. Justice should be conducted in public

It is an old adage that justice must not only be done but must be manifestly seen to be done – a phrase attributed to Lord Chief Justice Hewart in *Sussex Justices, ex p McCarthy*.[158] ('Publicity is the very soul of justice. It is the keenest spur to

---

[154] [2005] EWCA Crim 805, 155 *New Law Journal*, 8 July 2005, p. 1041.

[155] For details of the time limits imposed on cross-examination in the monster case brought unsuccessfully by BCCI against the Bank of England see S. Jeffrey and M. Ayers, 'How Long in the Box?', 156 *New Law Journal*, 1 September 2006, p. 1307. Cross-examination of witness Q was limited by the judge to seven weeks and of witness C to forty days. Both decisions were upheld by the Court of Appeal. After twenty days of cross-examination of witness C, BCCI abandoned its claim.

[156] With regard to the duty to give reasons of magistrates see *R (on the application of McGowan) v. Brent Justices* [2001] EWHC Admin 814, [2002] Crim LR 412 and commentary at 413; and *R v. Civil Service Appeal Board, ex p Cunningham* [1992] ICR 816.

[157] The Explanatory Notes to the Act state that, in doing so, 'it seeks to bring together in a single provision many of the obligations on a court to give reasons when passing sentence which are currently scattered across sentencing legislation' (para. 491).

[158] [1924] 1 KB 256 at 259.

exertion and the surest of all guards against improbity. It keeps the judge himself while trying under trial'.[159]) It is therefore axiomatic that judicial business should be transacted in public. This is a fundamental principle enshrined in Article 6(1) of the European Convention on Human Rights.

There are various distinct issues involved in this phrase. One is physical access to the hearing for the public, including the press. A second concern is access for non-parties to the judgment and other court documents. A third is the special position of the press and the right to publish an accurate account of the proceedings and of the judgment.

Physical access to court proceedings

Although the general principle is clear, there are situations where the basic maxim gives way to other even more important considerations. An obvious example is where a case is heard in camera because of national security considerations[160] and there are other situations where for one reason or another the public and the press have no access to the proceedings. The list is long and seems to be growing.

In *Scott v. Scott*[161] the House of Lords held that although normally a court must sit in public, it can sit in camera if this is necessary to achieve justice. The rule has been applied, for instance, to protect a secret trade process, the affairs of the mentally ill or to prevent tumult or disorder. Convenience, however, is not sufficient reason to sit in camera. In 1982 the Divisional Court ruled that magistrates in Reigate had erred in going into camera for a hearing of charges against a 'supergrass' who had committed his offences *after* he had been given a light sentence for informing. Both defence and prosecution asked for the matter to be dealt with in camera but the Divisional Court said the decision to comply was wrong.[162]

The protection of public decency is normally not a sufficient basis for proceeding in private – see *Scott v. Scott* above, but in *R v. Malvern Justices, ex p Evans*[163] the court held the magistrates in a criminal case had been entitled to sit in camera to spare the defendant from giving embarrassing evidence about her husband that could affect her pending divorce case.[164]

The Civil Procedure Rules state that the general rule is that a hearing is to be in public (CPR 39.2(1)). The court is not, however, required to 'make special arrangements to accommodate members of the public' (CPR 39.2(2)).

According to the CPR 39.2(3) a hearing may be in private if (1) publicity would defeat the object of the hearing; (2) it involves national security; (3) publicity

---

[159] Bentham – cited by Butler-Sloss in *Clibbery v. Allan* [2002] 1 All ER 865 at 872.

[160] For a recent example see *Re A* [2006] EWCA Crim 4, [2006] 2 All ER 1.

[161] [1913] AC 417.

[162] *R v. Reigate Justices, ex p Argus Newspapers* (1983) 5 Cr App Rep (S) 181.

[163] [1988] 1 All ER 371, Div Court.

[164] See also *A-G v. Leveller Magazines* [1979] AC 440, HL and see generally J. Michael, 'Open Justice: Publicity and the Judicial Process', 46 *Current Legal Problems*, 1993, pp. 190–203.

would damage confidential information; (4) a private hearing is necessary to protect the interests of a child or patient; (5) the hearing is one in the absence of the other side ('without notice' – formerly called *ex parte*) and it would be unjust to the absent respondent to have it in public; (6) it concerns uncontentious matters relating to the administration of trusts or of a deceased person's estate; or (7) the court considers it to be in the interests of justice.

The rules for family court proceedings are complicated and vary according to the nature of the case and the level of court.[165] In magistrates' courts the public are not admitted to family court proceedings. Those who can attend are the parties, the legal advisers and witnesses. The media can also attend unless specifically excluded but reporting is not permitted and as a result they rarely do. In the High Court and county courts contested divorces, judicial separation and nullity cases are heard in open court, but these are a small fraction of the cases heard. Most concern financial disputes and disputes over children. In such proceedings the court has a discretion as to whether to allow the public and the media in. Normally they are heard in private.

In November 2005 Baroness Ashton announced that the Government would be consulting about greater openness and accountability in the family court system.[166] A consultation paper issued by the DCA in July 2006 proposed major changes:

- The rules should be the same for all family proceedings in all the courts.
- The media should have a general right to attend unless excluded in the particular case.
- The public should have a right to apply to the court to be allowed to attend.
- The court should have the right to allow the public to attend of its own motion.[167]

Are small claims hearings in public?

Small claims hearings in England used to be held in private, often in the judge's chambers rather than the courtroom. Typically, the parties were seated across the table from each other, with the district judge at its head. The fact that the hearing was in private was said to be one of its most attractive features for people unfamiliar with court procedure. It was therefore surprising that the

---

[165] The DCA Consultation Paper issued in July 2006, n. 167 below, had a 10-page appendix setting out the rules.

[166] 155 *New Law Journal*, 4 November 2005, p. 1655. One of the factors in the Government's decision no doubt was the Report of the House of Commons Constitutional Affairs Committee, *Family Justice: The Operation of the Family Court*, HC 116, Fourth Report Session of 2004–5, February 2005 – see paras. 132–48. The Committee proposed that both the press and the public should be permitted to attend family courts subject to the court's discretion to exclude the public and to impose reporting restrictions (para. 144).

[167] *Confidence and confidentiality: Improving transparency and privacy in family courts*, DCA, July 2006, Cm. 6886. The courts affected and the number of family law applications made to each court in 2004 were the family proceedings magistrates' courts (33,000), the county court (370,000) and the High Court (500).

Practice Direction accompanying the 1999 rules for small claims stated: 'The general rule is that a small claims hearing will be in public' (PD 27, 4.1(1)). It seems clear that this change was prompted by fear that a hearing in private would run foul of Article 6(1) of the European Convention on Human Rights that in the determination of his civil rights and obligations everyone is entitled 'to a fair and public hearing'.[168]

The rules state that although the hearing will generally be held in public, the judge can order a small claims case to be heard in private 'if the parties agree or there is some special reason for holding it in private' (PD 27, 4.1(2)). In practice, the parties commonly agree and things go on much as before.

Moreover, 'in public' does not necessarily mean in the courtroom. It can be 'in public' even if it is in the judge's private room. The small claims Practice Direction (PD 27, 4.2) says: 'a hearing . . . will generally be in the judge's room but it may take place in a courtroom'. A different Practice Direction not restricted to small claims (PD 39, 1.10) says that unless there is a notice on the door stating that the proceedings are private 'members of the public will be admitted where practicable'. If the hearing is in the judge's room, the concept of it being 'in public' is obviously more notional than real.

Special measures directions

The Youth Justice and Criminal Evidence Act 1999 (Part II, Ch. 1) added a further dimension to the closed court issue in the form of a 'special measures direction' under which (see p. 431 below) a court can seek to protect a vulnerable witness, *inter alia*, by clearing the court of the public, including the press, though one member of the press must be allowed to stay to represent the press (s. 25(3)). Vulnerable witnesses for this purpose include anyone under seventeen, anyone suffering from a mental or physical disorder or disability or significant impairment of intelligence and social functioning and complainants in sexual offence cases.

In *Richards*[169] the Court of Appeal dismissed an application for leave to appeal based on Article 6 of the European Convention on Human Rights against the trial judge's decision to clear the court when a witness to a murder refused to give evidence unless this was done. There was no suggestion that the eighteen-year-old witness qualified as 'vulnerable' but the court held that there was a common law power to do what was required in the interests of justice.

Access to court documents and the judgment

So far as concerns access to the judgment, in *Forbes v. Smith*[170] Justice Jacob said: 'the concept of a secret judgment is one which I believe to be inherently abhorrent'. Only in cases where there was cause for secrecy such as in a trade secrets case should the judgment be regarded as a secret document. A judgment given

---

[168] See *Scarth v. United Kingdom* (1999) 27 EHRLR CD 37.   [169] [1999] Crim LR 764.
[170] [1998] 1 All ER 973 at 974.

in chambers was normally to be regarded as a public document unless it was given in camera – as in that particular case.

However, it is increasingly the case that courts make decisions on the basis of material that has not been read out in open court.

Under the old RSC Order 63, r. 4 a member of the public could, for a fee, inspect a copy of any writ or other originating process and any judgment or court order. Strangely, the same did not apply in the county courts. CCR Order 50, r. 10(2) stated that someone who was not a party to the proceedings could only obtain copies of documents from the court records with the leave of the court.

The 1999 rules (as amended)[171] provide for the keeping of a publicly accessible register of claims and of documents issued by the court. (To date the only registers actually available were in the QBD's Central Office and Chancery Chambers in the Royal Courts of Justice). Access to court documents depends on whether one is a party to the proceedings.

Unless the court otherwise orders, a party is entitled to every document on the file. With permission of the court, a party is entitled to any other document filed by a party or communication between the court and a party and another person.

A non-party was entitled without permission, unless the court otherwise ordered, to a copy of the claim form that had been served and of a judgment given in public.[172] In October 2006 this was extended to cover the particulars of claim, the defence, reply and any counterclaim.[173] The new rule was stated to be retrospective. The Law Society applied for permission to judicially review the retrospective effect of the new rule. On 5 October the High Court issued an interim declaration stating that the new rule would only apply to proceedings commenced after 2 October 2 2006 and the Court Service accepted this as permanent.[174]

If a non-party wishes to inspect and copy any document not available to the public, he must seek the leave of the court. (This does not yet apply however in the county courts where the facilities for computer searching are not yet in place.) The court has jurisdiction to grant an application even after the case is over.[175]

PD 39, 1.11 states that when a hearing takes place in public, members of the public may obtain a transcript of any judgment. PD 39, 1.12 states that when a judgment is given or an order is made in private, a member of the public must get the leave of the judge to obtain a transcript.

---

[171] CPR 5.4 and PD 5, para. 4 as amended in 2004. See 154 *New Law Journal*, 17 September 2004, p. 1355; *Law Society's Gazette*, 21 July 2005, p. 37.

[172] CPR 5.4(2). See *Dian AO v Davis Frankel & Mead* [2004] EWHC 2662 (Comm) [2005] 1 All ER 1074 and commentary I. Grainger, 'Public Access to Court Files', 24 *Civil Justice Quarterly*, 2005, pp. 304–08.

[173] See G. Lewson, 'Civil exposure', 156 *New Law Journal*, 13 October 2006, p 1545.

[174] See 156 *New Law Journal*, 8 December 2006, p. 1860 and www.hmcourts-service.gov.uk.

[175] *Re Guardian Newspapers Ltd* [2004] EWHC 3092, Ch.

Witness statements which stand as evidence (i.e. where the written statement is taken as evidence) are open to inspection during the trial (but not thereafter) unless the court otherwise orders (CPR 32.13).

See also *Practice Statement* [1998] 2 All ER 667 on access to judgments for the press and law reporters.

Discovering what happened in chambers Open access to decisions given in chambers was the subject of *Hodgson v. Imperial Tobacco Ltd*,[176] an action by cancer sufferers against tobacco companies. The Court of Appeal held that what happened during proceedings in chambers was private but not confidential or secret. Information about such proceedings and the judgment or order could and should be made available to the public when requested. Moreover, save in the exceptional circumstances identified in the Administration of Justice Act 1960, s. 12(1) or where a court with power to do so ordered otherwise, it was not contempt of court to reveal what occurred in chambers provided any comment made did not substantially prejudice the administration of justice. The judge had therefore been wrong to make a 'gagging order'.

Wardship, guardianship and adoption cases are usually heard in chambers. In undefended divorce cases no evidence is heard in open court. Ancillary proceedings concerning maintenance and custody of children are normally heard in chambers. Domestic proceedings in magistrates' courts are in private. In the Family Division a commentator has observed that, since chambers' hearings are the rule and open court hearings the exception, 'a situation has been created which is causing concern even among some judges'. So little in the way of reported decisions were emerging from this quarter that 'lawyers specialising in divorce related cases are faced with a virtual famine of modern day case law'.[177]

However, in *Clibbery v. Allan*[178] the Court of Appeal held that although family proceedings involving children or ancillary relief were protected from publication without the court's permission, that did not apply to all family proceedings heard in private. Whether they were protected would depend on the nature of the proceedings and whether the administration of justice would be impeded by publication.

Physical access to proceedings in chambers

A chambers hearing can be in the judge's private room or it can be in the normal courtroom with a notice stating that the court is sitting in chambers, but, even when held in chambers, the proceedings are normally to be regarded as being in public. This was recognised by Jacob J in *Forbes v. Smith*.[179] ('A chambers hearing is in private, in the sense that members of the public are not given admission as of right to the courtroom'.) Courts, the judge said, sat in chambers or in open court generally only as a matter of administrative convenience.

---

[176] [1998] 2 All ER 673.
[177] R.P. Pearson, 'Open Justice', *Solicitors' Journal*, 19–26 December 1986, p. 969.
[178] [2002] 1 All ER 865.   [179] [1998] 1 All ER 973.

Thus in the Chancery Division the normal practice was for urgent applications for interlocutory injunctions to be made in open court, whereas in the Queen's Bench Division they were made in chambers. There was no logic or reason for the difference. It was abolished by the Civil Procedure Rules. The Commercial Court sat in chambers but with its doors open. So normally did the Patent Court. If there was an appeal from a chambers hearing to the Court of Appeal it was heard in open court.[180]

Reporting of judicial proceedings

Normally judicial proceedings can be reported. The Contempt of Court Act 1981, s. 4 states: 'subject to this section, a person is not guilty of contempt of court under the strict liability rule in respect of a fair and accurate report of legal proceedings held in public, published contemporaneously and in good faith'.

Section 4 of the 1981 Act gives the courts the power to direct that publication be postponed 'where it appears to be necessary for avoiding a substantial risk of prejudice to the administration of justice'. Such orders must be formulated with precision.[181]

Under s. 11 of the Contempt of Court Act 1981, a court, having power to do so, may direct that a name or other material not be published if it appears to the court to be necessary. Use of this power by the courts has proved very controversial. Until 1988 there was no right of appeal against the exercise of the power by the Crown Court or higher courts, but this was changed by s. 159 of the Criminal Justice Act 1988. There have been a number of decisions, mainly by the Divisional Court, on challenges to s. 11 orders made by magistrates. From these it seems clear that the courts should not, for instance, prevent publication of the name of a witness or party simply to protect them from embarrassment. Thus in 1987 the Divisional Court held that justices in Malvern and Evesham had been wrong to prohibit publication of a former Conservative MP's name and address when he appeared on a motoring charge. He had claimed that publication of the details would expose him to harassment by his wife. Lord Justice Watkins said that s. 11 of the 1981 Act was not enacted 'for the benefit of the comfort and feelings of defendants',[182] but it would be legitimate to ban reporting of a witness's name in a blackmail case.[183]

---

[180] In *Storer v. British Gas Plc* [2000] 1 WLR 1237 the Court of Appeal quashed a decision of an industrial tribunal because the room in which the hearing took place was in an area marked 'Private. No admittance to the public beyond this point', the door to which was fitted with a push-button lock.

[181] See *Practice Direction (Contempt: Reporting Restrictions)* [1982] 1 WLR 1475. On s. 4 orders see especially *R v. Horsham Justices, ex p Farquharson* [1982] QB 762; *R v. Leveller Magazines Ltd* [1979] AC 440, HL.

[182] *R v. Evesham Justices, ex p McDonagh* [1988] 1 All ER 371. See to similar effect *Trustor AB v. Smallbone* [2000] 1 All ER 811. See also *Scarth v. United Kingdom* (1999) 27 EHRLR CD 37.

[183] In September 2006 the media were barred from publishing the names of two immigration judges who were central figures in a sensational case involving video recordings of their sexual

Even chambers hearings to which the public are not admitted are generally capable of being reported. The Administration of Justice Act 1960, s. 12(1)[184] states: 'the publication of information relating to proceedings before any court sitting in private shall not of itself be contempt of court except in the following cases . . .' The stated exceptions are proceedings that relate to the exercise of the inherent jurisdiction of the High Court in relation to minors, or that are brought under the Children Act 1989 or otherwise relate wholly or mainly to the maintenance or upbringing of a minor. Subject to the exceptions, if reporters can find out what happened in chambers, they can publish it. (The exceptions do not apply where the communication is to a spouse or partner, a close family member, a lawyer, a lay adviser or McKenzie friend, a health care professional, mediator etc.[185])

Section 97(2) of the Children Act 1989 with regard to Children's Act proceedings makes it a criminal offence to publish any material which is intended or likely to identify any child involved in any proceedings before the High Court, county court or magistrates' court unless the court is satisfied that the welfare of the child requires it. The section has been held to be compatible with Article 6(1) of the ECHR which guarantees the right to a fair trial including the right to a public hearing.[186] However, contrary to what had previously been assumed, the Court of Appeal ruled in June 2006 that it only applies while the proceedings are actually live.[187] At that point continuing restrictions on publishing information are based on the Administration of Justice Act 1960, s. 12 (above).

The Court of Appeal's decision in *Stanton v. Stanton* in June 2006[188] marked an important shift in the courts' attitude to publication of the details of cases. The court unanimously lifted an injunction preventing a father from talking and writing about his own case including identifying his ten-year-old daughter. The court ruled that judges had to balance in each case whether anonymity should outweigh the right to freedom of expression. Publicity would not be allowed if it would cause distress to a child.

Reporters who attend the youth court in the magistrates' courts (which as seen above is not open to the public) can report the proceedings but must not report anything which would lead to the child being identified unless the court permits it.[189] Photographs are equally prohibited. By contrast, by virtue of s. 39

---

relationship, the alleged use by one of them of cocaine and a charge of blackmail against an attractive illegal immigrant whom they had both employed as a cleaner and with whom one of them had had a sexual relationship. Commenting in *The Guardian* (25 September) Marcel Berlins said that since the names of the judges were probably known to the entire immigration judiciary, to many in the legal world, to the media covering the trial and to their friends and families, the only people left ignorant would be those to whom the names meant nothing.   [184] As amended by the Children Act 1989, s. 108(5) and Sch. 13, para. 14.

[185] Family Proceedings (Amendment No 4) Rules 2005, SI 2005/1976.

[186] *P v. BW* [2003] EWHC 1541 (Fam), [2003] 4 All ER 1074.

[187] *Stanton v. Stanton* [2006] EWCA Civ 878.   [188] *Ibid.*

[189] Children and Young Persons Act 1933, s. 49 (as amended).

of the 1933 Act, in the Crown Court and the magistrates' court the press can identify a juvenile unless the court prohibits such publication. The adult court can order the media not to publish information that would lead to the identification of a child but it cannot give directions as to what material it can or cannot publish to give effect to the order.[190]

See further G. Robertson and A. Nicol, *Media Law* (5th edn, forthcoming 2007).

Televising trials

Cameras are not permitted in court, so television of legal proceedings, now commonplace in the USA,[191] is not permitted. In March 2003 the Lord Chancellor gave permission for an experiment with televising of appellate level cases. The pilot allowed broadcasters to produce news bulletins, features and documentary material but only for demonstration purposes. They could not be broadcast.[192]

In November 2004 the DCA issued a consultation paper inviting views as to whether the rules should be changed.[193] It published the responses to the consultation exercise in June 2005.[194] The Government's conclusion:

> 1. It is clear from the response to consultation that support for widespread broadcasting is limited, and that there is grave concern about the potential impact on participants, especially witnesses and jurors, and on the trial process. On the other hand, many respondents did feel that broadcasting could increase understanding of court processes and make courts more accessible.
>
> 2. In light of the responses, we are exploring whether there are options which might achieve these benefits, without risking harm to participants or any negative impact on the administration of justice.[195]
>
> Any proposals for change would be the subject of a further public consultation on the detail.[196]

Since then there has been no further word on the subject from the DCA.

---

[190] *R (Gazette Media Co Ltd) v. Teesside Crown Court* [2005] EWCA Crim 1983, [2005] Crim LR 157 criticised in A. Gillespie and V. Bettinson, 'Preventing Secondary Victimisation Through Anonymity', 70 *Modern Law Review*, 2007, pp. 114–27.

[191] However, not in the US Supreme Court.

[192] F. Gibb, 'Irvine ready to allow TV cameras in Appeal Court', *The Times*, 10 March 2003; 'Camera in Court', *Counsel*, February 2005, p. 13. See also R. Smith, 'Let the Cameras In', *Counsel*, March 2005, p. 29.

[193] *Broadcasting Courts*, consultation paper 28/2004, 15 November 2004.

[194] CP (R) 28/04, 30 June 2005.   [195] At p. 42.

[196] In July 2005 Sky News transmitted a live, verbatim transcript of the summing-up in the case of a much publicised murder case. The latest technology allowed it to publish the text on a split screen with a reporter outside the court providing commentary. It was said to be the first live transmission of court stenography. A protocol had been agreed with the DCA allowing, at the discretion of the trial judge, live transmission of stenography from the opening and closing speeches, the summing-up and the verdict, as well as delayed transmission of the evidence of witnesses (*Law Society's Gazette*, 7 July 2005, p. 11).

Protecting the witness

The principle that justice should be conducted in public is sometimes qualified where the witness requires special protection.

In exceptional circumstances the identity of witnesses such as members of the security service can be concealed even from the other side. In June 1999 the Divisional Court held that Lord Saville's inquiry into the shootings in Londonderry on 'Bloody Sunday' acted unreasonably in denying a claim for anonymity of seventeen members of the parachute regiment. Knowing their names was not vital for the inquiry to perform its task, while disclosing them put their lives at risk.[197] Ordering that the identity of the witness be concealed is not a breach of the ECHR when it is necessary to protect the witness from the threat of serious violence or death.[198]

Special measures directions for vulnerable witnesses[199]

In recent years efforts have been made to ease the process of giving evidence for vulnerable witnesses and especially for children.

The chief issue has been whether children should be able to give evidence by live video link or even by pre-recorded interview instead of in the actual court-room.[200] The first step taken in that direction was s. 32(1) of the Criminal Justice Act 1988 which allowed children under fourteen in Crown Court cases of violence, sexual assault or cruelty to give evidence by live closed circuit television with the permission of the court. The aim was to protect the child from having to face the allegedly abusing adult.[201]

In 1989 the Pigot Committee reported.[202] The Committee took the view that a child should never be required to give evidence in public as a witness unless the

---

[197] *R v. Lord Saville of Newdigate, ex p A* [1999] NLJR 965. The Court of Appeal upheld the ruling [1999] NLJR 1201. In a trial in Belfast in June 1989 Lord Chief Justice Hutton held that in the particular circumstances of the case such an order could be made, but in that instance the defence raised no objection. The defendants were accused of taking part in the gruesome and notorious murder of two British army corporals who had blundered into an IRA funeral. The prosecution asked the court to rule that some twenty-seven media witnesses could give their evidence without being identified and that they should not be seen by the accused, the public or the press, but only by the court and the lawyers for each side. The judge held that the witnesses could give their evidence behind a large curtain. See G. Marcus, 'Secret Witnesses', *Public Law*, Summer 1990, p. 207.   [198] *Davis* and *Ellis* [2006] EWCA Crim 1155, [2007] Crim LR 70.

[199] See A. Keane, *The Modern Law of Evidence* (6th edn, 2006) pp. 155–66.

[200] For a summary of the developments in the law with extensive citation of the literature see D. Cooper, 'Pigot Unfulfilled: Video Recorded Cross-examination under Section 28 of the Youth Justice and Criminal Evidence Act 1999', *Criminal Law Review*, 2005, pp. 456–66.

[201] For a description of how this procedure operates and of some of its problems see C. Champness, 'Children's Evidence in Criminal Proceedings', *Law Society's Gazette*, 8 March 1989, p. 14.

[202] *Report of the Advisory Group on Video Recorded Evidence*, Home Office, December 1989. There was also a report by the Scottish Law Commission (*The Evidence of Children and Other Potentially Vulnerable Witnesses*, Discussion Paper No. 75, June 1988). For an evaluation of this report in the light of English law and practice see J. McEwan, 'Child Evidence: More Proposals for Reform', *Criminal Law Review*, 1988, p. 813.

child himself expressed a wish to do so.[203] It recommended that both a child's evidence-in-chief and cross-examination should be presented in the form of pre-recorded video interviews. The entirety of a child's evidence should be taken at a pre-trial hearing. If the interview by the police had been videoed, it should be shown at the pre-trial hearing with both sides able to ask further questions. If the original police questioning had not been videoed, the child's examination-in-chief and cross-examination would take place at the pre-trial hearing. In either case, the whole of the pre-trial hearing would be video recorded and shown at the trial. At the time all of this was considered too controversial.[204]

The Criminal Justice Act 1991 represented a compromise approach. Section 54[205] permitted the Crown Court or a youth court at the trial of a case to which s. 32 of the 1988 Act (above) applied to admit as evidence-in-chief a video recording of an interview with a child unless: (1) the child was not available for cross-examination; or (2) there had been a failure to comply with rules about disclosing the circumstances in which the recording was made; or (3) it would not be in the interests of justice to admit the recording. The child had to be called and could be cross-examined in court, though not by the accused himself (s. 55(7)).[206] (This was widely referred to as 'half-Pigot'.)

The legislative culmination of these efforts was the Youth Justice and Criminal Evidence Act 1999[207] which has no fewer than eighteen sections giving courts the power to give a 'special measures direction' to assist witnesses, *other than the defendant*, who might have difficulty giving evidence or who might be reluctant to do so.[208] The reason given for excluding the defendant was that he could choose not to give evidence – an unconvincing justification.

The special measures that can be authorised under the 1999 Act include: screens to ensure that the witness cannot see the accused (s. 23); allowing the witness to give evidence from outside the court by live television link (s. 24); clearing the press and public from the court so that evidence can be given in private (s. 25); removal of the judge's and barristers' wigs and gowns (s. 26); allowing an interview with the witness video recorded before the trial to be shown at the trial as the witness's evidence-in-chief (s. 27); allowing the cross-examination of the witness to be conducted in a pre-recorded video recording (s. 28); and questioning through an intermediary (s. 29).

---

[203] Pigot, para. 2.26.   [204] See references in D. Cooper, n. 202 above at n. 49.

[205] Inserting a new s. 32A into the 1988 Act.

[206] The Home Office and the Department of Health jointly produced a *Memorandum of Good Practice on Video Recorded Interviews with Child Witnesses for Criminal Proceedings* (HMSO, 1992). For a description see B. Ward, 'Children's Evidence', *Solicitors' Journal*, 3 July 1992, p. 644 and by the same author, 'Interviewing Child Witnesses', 142 *New Law Journal*, 6 November 1992, p. 1547.

[207] The Act was preceded by the Home Office White Paper *Speaking Up for Justice*, the Report of the Home Office Interdepartmental Working Group on the Treatment of Vulnerable or Intimidated Witnesses in the Criminal Justice System, 1998.

[208] For a discussion of the implications and complexities of the 1999 Act with regard to child witnesses see L.C.H. Hoyano, 'Variations on a Theme by Pigot: Special Measures Directions for Child Witnesses', *Criminal Law Review*, 2000, pp. 250–73.

Vulnerable witnesses for this purpose are (1) those under the age of seventeen (s. 16(1)); (2) persons who suffer from a mental disorder, mental impairment or significant learning disability, or physical disorder or disability which the court considers likely to affect the quality of their evidence (s. 16(2)); and (3) persons whom the court is satisfied would give less than their best evidence because of fear and distress caused by giving evidence (s. 17).

If on an application or of its motion the court decides that a witness is eligible for assistance in the form of special measures it must determine which special measure would be likely to improve the quality of the witness's evidence.

Witnesses under seventeen are automatically eligible for special measures. There are three groups: (1) children giving evidence in a sexual offence case; (2) children giving evidence in a case involving an offence of violence, abduction or neglect; and (3) those giving evidence in any other case. In all three categories there is a statutory presumption that the witness's evidence-in-chief will be given by a pre-recorded video unless this would not improve the quality of the evidence.

In the case of the first two groups, which are described as being in need of 'special protection', the court does not have to consider whether special measures will improve the quality of their evidence. That requirement is treated as being satisfied (s. 21(5)). Witnesses in need of special protection will have a video recording of their evidence-in-chief admitted and will have their cross-examination conducted via live television link unless exceptionally the court exercises its power under s. 27(2) on the ground that this would not be in the interests of justice. The House of Lords held in 2005 that the mandatory presumption in s. 21(5) did not breach the defendant's right to a fair trial under Article 6 of the European Convention on Human Rights.[209] A critical comment on the Divisional Court's decision in the same case pointed out that the mandatory presumption had 'the bizarre effect of teenagers giving evidence against teenagers through live television, in many cases the witnesses being older than the defendants'.[210] How could it be fair that the older and more mature witness would be protected from face to face cross-examination to which the defendant was exposed? The jury was likely to regard one as the victim and the other as the criminal simply because one was protected and the other was not. 'The whole notion of the presumption of innocence gets turned on its head'.[211]

---

[209] *R v. Camberwell Green Youth Court, ex p D and ex p G* [2005] UKHL 4, [2005] 2 Cr App R 1. For commentary see J. Doak, 'Child Witnesses: Do Special Measures Directions Prejudice the Accused's Right to a Fair Hearing', 9 *International Journal of Evidence and Proof*, 2005, pp. 291–5.

[210] M. Sikand, 'Special Measures: Protecting Young Witnesses or Prejudicing Young Defendants?', 7 *Archbold News*, 2003, p. 6.

[211] *Ibid.* In *R (S) v. Waltham Forest Youth Court* [2004] EWHC Admin 715, [2004] 2 Cr App R 335 the thirteen-year-old defendant, S, a vulnerable child with learning difficulties, was too afraid to speak out against her older co-defendants who had threatened her. The Divisional Court held that the express terms of the statute made it impossible to allow S to give evidence by TV link.

Implementation of these measures has gone in stages. Home Office Circular 39/2005 set out the position with regard to each category of special measure. All Crown Courts and magistrates' courts were able to give special measures directions for screens, live TV links and clearing the court. Pre-recorded evidence-in-chief was permitted in all Crown Courts under s. 16 but only in pilot courts under s. 17 and in magistrates' courts under s. 16 only for child witnesses in need of special protection.

The Home Office announced in 2004 that it was not going ahead with implementation of the most controversial of the special measures – allowing cross-examination by pre-recorded interview under s. 28[212] – described as 'a central feature of "full Pigot" '.[213]

For Home Office guidance see *Achieving best evidence in criminal proceedings: guidance for vulnerable or intimidated witnesses, including children* (available on www.cps.gov.uk and www.homeoffice.gov.uk).[214]

In June 2004 the Home Office published *Are special measures working? Evidence from surveys of vulnerable and intimidated witnesses* (Research Study 283). The vast majority of witnesses who had used special measures found them helpful – especially live link and video recorded evidence-in-chief.

On 1 December 2004 the Home Office announced a wide-ranging inquiry into the future of children's evidence.[215] At the time of writing this had not yet been published.

In October 2005 a study of CPS data involving over 6,000 vulnerable and intimidated witnesses showed that a clear majority of special measures applications were successful. TV links were the most popular with video recorded examination-in-chief a clear second favourite but a long way behind.[216]

NB Lord Justice Auld recommended that in due course consideration should be given to allowing *all* critical witnesses in cases of serious crimes to give evidence-in-chief by pre-recorded video.[217] This proposal was translated into legislative form in s. 137 of the Criminal Justice Act 2003. With the permission of the court, the witness in indictable-only offences and specified either-way offences can be allowed to give evidence-in-chief by a video recording made

---

[212] For a discussion see D. Cooper, n. 202 above. See also D. Birch and R. Powell, *Meeting the Challenge of Pigot: Pre-Trial Cross-Examination under Section 28 of the Youth Justice and Criminal Justice Act 1999* (February 2004).　　[213] Hoyano, n. 208 above at p. 265.

[214] See also D. Heraghty, 'Gearing Up for Greater Use of Video Evidence', 153 *New Law Journal*, 28 March 2003, p. 460; L. Ellison, *The Adversarial Process and the Vulnerable Witness* (OUP, 2001); D. Birch, 'A Better Deal for Vulnerable Witnesses?', *Criminal Law Review*, 2000, pp. 223–49; and L.C.H. Hoyano, 'Striking a Balance between the Rights of Defendants and Vulnerable Witnesses: Will Special Measures Directions Contravene Guarantees of a Fair Trial?', *Criminal Law Review*, 2001, pp. 948–69.

[215] Press release, 'Giving Child Witnesses the Support they Need' – www.cjsonline.gov.uk.

[216] P. Roberts, D. Cooper and S. Judge, 'Coming Soon to a Court Near You! Special Measures for Vulnerable and Intimidated Witnesses', 169 *Justice of the Peace*, 24 September and 1 October 2005, pp. 749–51 and 769–74 at 770. The first two authors conducted the survey – see *Special Measures for Vulnerable and Intimidated Witnesses: An Analysis of CPS Monitoring Data*, 2005 – www.cps.gov.uk.　　[217] Auld, pp. 555–6.

when the matters were fresh in his memory. He would then give oral evidence only as to matters not adequately dealt with in the video recording. The court must be satisfied that the witness's recollection was significantly better when he made the recording and that it is in the interests of justice. This provision has not yet, however, been brought into force. For the time being, as Professor Birch has said, this 'explosive device' remains 'tucked away with the [harmless looking] provisions about memory-refreshing and ticking merrily'.[218]

8. The exclusionary rules of evidence

One of the chief differences between the English and the continental systems is that the English excludes various categories of evidence in spite of the fact that they are relevant. These exclusionary rules of evidence fall into three main categories: (1) evidence excluded because it might be unduly prejudicial; (2) evidence excluded because it is inherently unreliable; and (3) evidence excluded because it is against the public interest that it be admitted.

Evidence excluded because it might be unduly prejudicial

Bad character and prior convictions

The general principle was that evidence of the defendant's previous misconduct and of his disposition or his propensity to act in a particular way were generally excluded until he had been convicted. There were said to be two reasons. First, the fact that the defendant behaved in a particular way before does not in itself provide evidence that he did the act of which he now stands accused. Secondly, insofar as it does provide such evidence, there is a danger that a jury would give it undue weight.

By contrast, in systems based on the continental civil law, the defendant's character and background are fully admissible in evidence. In the United States, his prior convictions are admissible if the defendant gives evidence.

The basic rule was subject to important exceptions:

- Where the defendant himself introduced his own prior record – for instance to show that he was a thief not a rapist.
- Where the defendant asserted that he was a person of good character, the prosecution could introduce evidence to rebut the assertion.
- Where the defence attacked the character of prosecution witnesses, the prosecution could introduce evidence to show what sort of person was 'throwing mud' (the so-called 'tit for tat' rule).
- The 'tit for tat' rule applied also where one defendant blamed another defendant (known as 'a cut-throat defence').

---

[218] D. Birch, 'Criminal Justice Act 2003 (4) Hearsay: Same Old Story, Same Old Song', *Criminal Law Review*, 2004, p. 555 at 52.

- Where there was sufficient similarity between the facts of the present case and the facts in the previous case (the 'similar facts' rule).

The rules had been developed piecemeal over many decades mainly through judicial decisions.[219] The topic was exceedingly complex and controversial. In 1993 the Runciman Royal Commission recommended that the whole question of the admissibility of bad character evidence should be referred to the Law Commission.[220] The Government referred the issue to the Law Commission in 1994. In 1996 the Commission produced a consultation paper[221] but it took until 2001 for it to produce its Final Report and Draft Bill.[222] Broadly, the Draft Bill would have enacted the general prohibition on evidence of the defendant's bad character and restated the existing exceptions in tidier form.

Empirical evidence

In the *Crown Court Study* conducted for the Runciman Royal Commission, the defendant had previous convictions in almost four-fifths (77 per cent) of contested cases.[223]

The Law Commission's 1996 consultation paper referred to empirical evidence of how jurors treat evidence of previous misconduct based on a study conducted for the Commission.[224] The research showed that recent convictions for similar offences increased the perceived probative effect of the offence charged. Knowledge of a previous conviction for an offence of dishonesty did not decrease the defendant's credibility as a *witness* but a previous conviction for indecent assault on a child had a distinct negative impact on the jurors' perception of the defendant's credibility whatever the charge.[225]

Influenced by the empirical evidence as to the potential impact on jurors of the evidence of bad character, the Law Commission proposed four safeguards: first, that leave should normally be required for the admission of such evidence,

---

[219] For a brief overview see C. Tapper, 'The Criminal Justice Act 2003 (3) Evidence of Bad Character', 2004 *Criminal Law Review*, pp. 533–5. Tapper points out that much of the existing law was the result of decisions of the House of Lords in the previous decade i.e. it was not very old at all.   [220] Runciman, p. 126, para. 30.

[221] *Evidence in Criminal Proceedings*, consultation paper no. 141. For commentary and discussion see *Criminal Law Review*, February 1997.

[222] *Evidence of Bad Character in Criminal Proceedings*, Cm. 5257, Law Com No. 273. For commentary and discussion see J. McEwan, 'Previous Misconduct at the Crossroads: Which "Way Ahead"?', *Criminal Law Review*, 2002, pp. 180–91; P.Mirfield, 'Bad Character and the Law Commission', 6 *International Journal of Evidence and Proof*, 2002, pp. 141–62.

[223] M. Zander and P. Henderson, *The Crown Court Study* (Royal Commission on Criminal Justice, Research Study No. 19, 1993) section 4.6.1.

[224] Published as an appendix to the Commission's paper and separately as S. Lloyd-Bostock, 'The Effects on Juries of Hearing about the Defendant's Previous Criminal Record: A Simulation Study',*Criminal Law Review*, 2000, p. 734 and *The Effects on Magistrates of Learning that the Defendant has a Previous Conviction* (2000, LCD Research Series No 3/2000).

[225] For a critical assessment both of the empirical data and of the Law Commission's reliance on it see M. Redmayne, 'The Law Commission's Character Convictions', 6 *International Journal of Evidence and Proof*, 2002, pp. 71–93.

secondly, that such evidence be subject to a heightened test of relevance, thirdly, that the conditions of admissibility be set out in detail and, fourthly, that such evidence should be admitted only by a strongly worded inclusionary discretion. As will be seen, none of these safeguards was adopted in the legislation.

Auld report (2001)

Lord Justice Auld's *Review of the Criminal Courts of England and Wales* was published in the same month as the Law Commission's Final Report. Auld said that the law on the admissibility of bad character evidence was unduly complex and difficult to apply, that it often failed to distinguish between relevant and irrelevant evidence and arguably left too much discretion to judges. In his view there was much to be said 'for a more radical view than has so far found favour with the Law Commission, for placing more trust in the fact finders and for introducing some reality into this complex corner of the law',[226] but, given that the Law Commission was about to produce its Final Report, he did not make any specific recommendations.

The Government's White Paper (2002)

In its White Paper *Justice for All* in July 2002 the Government said that it opposed the routine introduction of all previous convictions as that might prejudice the fact finders unfairly against the accused. ('Juries and judges need to make their decisions on the basis of the evidence of whether or not the defendant committed the crime with which he is charged rather than his previous reputation' (para. 4.55).) However, it continued:

> We favour an approach that entrusts relevant information to those determining the case as far as possible. It should be for the judge to decide whether previous convictions are sufficiently relevant to the case, bearing in mind the prejudicial effect, to be heard by the jury and for the jury to decide what weight should be given to that information in all the circumstances of the case (para. 4.56).

Thus, where a doctor was charged with indecent assault against a patient the judge should be able to rule that the prosecution could introduce evidence that the doctor had previously been acquitted in two previous separate trials on the similar charges involving other patients. Or, where the defendant was charged with assaulting his wife, the judge should be able to rule that previous convictions for assault occasioning bodily harm and evidence by witnesses of past occasions when he was seen striking his wife be admitted in evidence. Unless the court thought the information would have a disproportionately prejudicial effect, the fact finders should be allowed to know about previous convictions and other misconduct relevant to the offence (para. 4.57).

---

[226] Auld, Ch. 11, p. 567, para. 120.

The Government, in short, favoured a much more radical approach than the Law Commission.[227] This was implemented in the Criminal Justice Act 2003. The bad character provisions of the Act were brought into force in December 2004.[228]

The Criminal Justice Act 2003

Definition of bad character Evidence of a person's 'bad character' is defined in the Act as 'evidence of, or of a disposition towards, misconduct on his part' (s. 98). This could include evidence showing that a person was guilty of an offence of which he was acquitted.[229] 'Misconduct' is defined as 'the commission of an offence or other reprehensible behaviour' (s. 99).[230]

Evidence of bad character of a non-defendant Section 100(1) sets out the circumstances in which evidence can be given of the previous misconduct of someone other than the defendant – such as a witness. The first requirement is that the leave of the court has to be obtained. There is no comparable requirement with regard to such evidence concerning the defendant.[231] Secondly, the evidence can only be introduced if either: (1) it is important explanatory evidence; (2) it has substantial probative value in relation to a matter in issue and that issue is one of substantial importance in the case; or (3) the parties agree that the evidence should be given.

For evidence of a non-defendant's bad character to be admissible as 'important explanatory evidence' it must be such that: '(a) without it, the court or jury would find it impossible or difficult properly to understand other evidence in the case and (b) its value for understanding the case as a whole is substantial' (s. 100(2)). The court is required to take into account factors such as the nature and number of previous events and when they occurred. If the evidence is tendered to show that someone else was responsible for the crime, the court has to consider the extent to which it shows or tends to show that to be the case. These rules give witnesses more protection than under the previous law.

Evidence of the defendant's bad character Sections 101–106 set out the circumstances in which evidence of the defendant's bad character would be admissible.

---

[227] For a critical comparison between the Law Commission's proposals and the provisions of the Criminal Justice Act 2003 see Tapper, n. 219 above. He found the differences 'both profound and disturbing' (at p. 537).

[228] For an assessment of the early case law on these provisions see A. Waterman and T. Dempster, 'Bad Character: Feeling Our Way One Year On', *Criminal Law Review*, 2006, pp. 614–28.

[229] Preserving the effect of the House of Lords decision in *Z* [2000] AC 483 that three complaints of rape of which the defendant had been acquitted could be admitted in a subsequent trial for rape.

[230] For an exploration of the meaning of this phrase see R. Munday, 'What Constitutes "Other Reprehensible Behaviour" under the Bad Character Provisions of the Criminal Justice Act 2003?', *Criminal Law Review*, 2005, pp. 24–43. He deplored the word 'reprehensible' as 'evocative of Victorian social moralising'.

[231] By contrast, the Law Commission's Bill did require leave. As Professor Tapper observed, the Commission regarded the requirement of leave 'as the pivot upon which avoiding prejudice turned' (n. 219 above at p. 541).

Instead of the previous exclusionary rule with exceptions – which the Law Commission thought should be continued – the approach is inclusionary subject to limited judicial discretion to exclude such evidence where to admit it would be unfair.

Section 101(1) provides that evidence of a defendant's bad character is admissible where any of seven gateways apply. Sections 102–106 provide further clarification regarding the gateways. The seven gateways are where:

(a) The parties agree to it being given.
(b) The defendant introduces the evidence himself.
(c) It is 'important explanatory evidence'. Section 102 adds that it is important explanatory evidence if (1) without it the court or the jury would find it impossible or difficult properly to understand other evidence in the case; or (2) its value for understanding the case as a whole is substantial.
(d) It is relevant to an important matter in issue[232] between the defendant and the prosecution. Section 103(1) extends the meaning of 'a matter in issue' in providing that it includes whether he has a propensity (a) to commit that kind of offence 'except where his having such a propensity makes it no more likely that he is guilty of the offence'; or (b) to be untruthful 'except where it is not suggested that the defendant's case is untruthful in any respect'.[233]

Section 103(1) (a) and (b) represent a major change in the law. As regards (a), it is no longer necessary, as it was under the former law, to show striking similarity. The test is simple relevance. There is no need to show 'enhanced probative value' or 'enhanced relevance'.[234] Propensity to commit that kind of offence can be established by proof that he has been convicted of an offence of the same description or of the same category[235] – unless the court considers this would be unjust by reason of the length of time since the conviction 'or for any other reason' (s. 103(2) and (3)).

There is no minimum number of events necessary to demonstrate propensity. In cases of unusual behaviour, such as arson or child sexual abuse, a single

---

[232] Section 112 adds, somewhat unnecessarily, that 'important matter' means 'a matter of substantial importance in the context of the case as a whole'.

[233] For a disquisition as to the possible meaning of these provisions see R. Munday, 'Bad Character Rules and Riddles: "Explanatory Notes" and True Meanings of Section 103(1) of the Criminal Justice Act 2003', *Criminal Law Review*, 2005, pp. 337–54.

[234] *Hanson, Gilmore and Pickstone* [2005] EWCA Crim 824, [2005] 1 WLR 3169. In *Hanson* the Court of Appeal upheld a conviction for stealing a carrier bag containing £600 from a bedroom after the defendant had pleaded guilty when the judge said he would allow the prosecution to prove his previous convictions for dishonesty. In *Gilmore* the Court of Appeal upheld a theft conviction where G had been found with a bag of stolen goods in an alleyway, the jury having heard of his three previous convictions for shoplifting.

[235] Two offences are of the same category, *inter alia*, if they belong to the same category prescribed by an order of the Home Secretary. The Criminal Justice Act 2003 (Categories of Offences) Order 2004, SI 2004/3346 created two categories – one for offences of dishonesty, the other of offences against children. In *Hanson*, n. 234 above at [8], the Court of Appeal held that s. 103(2) was not exhaustive of the types of conviction that could be relied on to show propensity.

instance could be enough.[236] Even a single previous conviction for shoplifting could show propensity 'if the *modus operandi* has significant features shared by the offence charged'. This may require the court to inquire into the circumstances of previous convictions.[237]

As regards s. 103(1) (b), in *Hanson*[238] the Court of Appeal said it made admissible evidence of convictions of offences that involved telling lies and also prior convictions in contested cases where the defendant gave evidence and his word was plainly disbelieved:

(e) It has 'substantial probative value in relation to an important matter in issue between the defendant and a co-defendant'. This, therefore, is available only to defendants as between themselves. Section 104(1) adds that evidence which is relevant to the question whether the defendant has a propensity to be untruthful is admissible under (e) 'only if the nature of his defence is such as to undermine the co-defendant's defence'. This appears to be a considerably more restrictive rule than under the previous law.[239]

(f) To 'correct a false impression given by the defendant' by putting his character in evidence. An assertion is treated as made by the defendant if made by a defence witness or in answer by *any* witness in cross-examination in response to a question asked by the defence 'that is intended to elicit it or is likely to do so' (s. 105).

(g) The defendant has attacked the character of another person.[240] Under the previous law, evidence admitted under the 'tit for tat' rule went only to credibility not to guilt. This is no longer so. In *Highton*[241] the Court of Appeal held that once evidence has been admitted under gateway (g), it can properly be applied under another gateway.[242]

---

[236] *Hanson*, n. 234 above at [9].

[237] In *Hanson*, n. 234 above, the Court of Appeal warned that judges should not permit the trial 'unreasonably to be diverted into an investigation of matters not charged in the indictment' ([12]).   [238] Note 234 above at [13].

[239] For an exploration of the serious questions as to the interpretation of gateway (e) and s. 104 see R. Munday, 'Cut-throat Defences and the Propensity to be Untruthful under Section 104 of the Criminal Justice Act 2003', *Criminal Law Review*, 2005, pp. 624–37. His conclusion (at 637) was that the provisions have 'introduced a highly uncertain regime, where one can anticipate considerable variation from one court to another' which was hardly satisfactory 'when what is being removed without fanfare, is a defendant's traditional entitlement to defend himself by all means when a co-defendant has undermined the foundation of his case'. See also J. Hartshorne, 'Defensive Use of a Co-accused's Confession and the Criminal Justice Act 2003', 8 *International Journal of Evidence and Proof*, 2004, pp. 165–78.

[240] As further defined in s. 106. Under the previous law the attack had to be on a prosecution witness or the deceased victim. Also it only applied if he gave evidence. Neither restriction applies to gateway (g).

[241] *Highton, Van Nguyen and Carp* [2005] EWCA Crim 1985, [2005] 1 WLR 3472.

[242] For critical commentary see for instance R. Munday, 'The Purposes of Gateway (g): Yet Another Problematic of the Criminal Justice Act 2003', *Criminal Law Review*, 2006, pp. 300–18.

The Act specifically states that under (d) and (g) (but not the other gateways) the defendant can apply to the court for the evidence not to be admitted on the ground that admitting it would have such an adverse effect on the fairness of the proceedings that the court ought not to permit it (s. 101(3)), but although the court does not have that discretion to exclude the evidence in relation to the other gateways, it would appear still to have the general discretion to exclude evidence that would make the proceedings unfair under s. 78 of PACE (as to which see p. 479 below).[243]

Criticism of the bad character provisions

The bad character proposals in the Bill were strongly criticised by the all-party House of Commons Home Affairs Committee. It did not agree that prior similar convictions should be admitted automatically unless the defendant succeeded in persuading the trial judge to rule against admissibility. ('We believe that these provisions could lead to miscarriages of justice in some cases. In particular we are concerned at the prospect of using a defendant's previous record to prop up what might otherwise be a weak case. We are also concerned that this will increase the temptation for the police to pursue "the usual suspects".'[244]) It agreed with the Criminal Bar Association that 'propensity for misconduct should not justify automatic admission of the defendant's bad character'.[245] It was concerned that the test for admitting the defendant's bad character was lower than that for admitting the bad character of witnesses. ('In our view, there should be a standard test requiring the bad character to have "substantial probative value" in relation to a matter in issue, which is itself of substantial importance in the context of the case as a whole'.[246]) Its overall conclusion was blunt: 'We recommend that [the clauses] which relate to the admissibility of a defendant's bad character, be deleted from the Bill'.[247] The Government rejected the Committee's advice.

The then Lord Chief Justice, Lord Woolf, on behalf of the judiciary was also highly critical of these provisions. He spoke about the Bill in a speech on the Second Reading in the House of Lords on 16 June 2003. In an unusual move he said that he did not have time in his speech to deal with all the matters in issue and that he would place a lengthy document in the library setting out 'what the judiciary, whom I represent, regard as being the problem areas':[248]

> 13. The provisions as a whole are extremely confusing and will prove very difficult to interpret. They will result in lengthy arguments in court, more appeals and more scope for technical errors on the part of the trial judge that

---

[243] In *Highton*, n. 241 above, Lord Woolf said: 'judges may consider that it is a sensible precaution, when making rulings as to the use of evidence of bad character, to apply the provision of section 78 and exclude evidence where it would be appropriate to do so under section 78 . . .' (at [13]).   [244] 2002–3, 2nd Report, December 2002, HC 83, para. 116.

[245] *Ibid*, para. 119.   [246] *Ibid*, para. 122.   [247] *Ibid*, para. 123.

[248] With Lord Woolf's permission, the writer published the gist of the twelve-page document in the *New Law Journal*, 8 August 2003, pp. 1228 and 1242 and 15 August, pp. 1264–6.

could give rise to convictions being overturned. Evidence that would previously have been considered neither admissible nor relevant will apparently be treated as both admissible *and* relevant.

15. An example of the sort of complications that are likely to arise as a consequence of chapter 1 is provided by clause 96 [which became s. 103 (ed.)]. That clause is designed to introduce into a trial an issue as to whether a defendant has a propensity to commit an offence or a propensity to be untruthful and then allow evidence of bad character to be given. This evidence of propensity is particularly dangerous. A trial should relate to whether an accused has committed an offence or is untruthful and not questions as to whether the defendant has a *propensity*. Again the judiciary consider this provision is likely to complicate proceedings and prolong trials without any benefit . . .

16. Another curiosity relates to the provisions as to the defendant's bad character. The judge is allowed to exclude evidence of bad character if it would have 'such an adverse effect on the fairness of the proceedings that the court ought not to admit it', but this discretion does not apply to all the situations where evidence of bad character can be admitted. In addition, the clause addresses when the judge is to exclude the evidence. It would be preferable if this clause and many similar clauses gave the judge a discretion to admit such controversial evidence and not to exclude it (clause 93(3) [which became s. 101(3)]).

Despite the Lord Chief Justice's criticisms of the bad character provisions, the case law after they came into force shows that both trial and appellate judges have accepted that the 2003 Act has completely changed the position. Moreover the Court of Appeal has said that the trial judge's 'feel' for the case is usually the critical ingredient of the decision. The Court of Appeal said that it would apply the same approach to the judge's ruling on admissibility of bad character evidence as it did to the exercise of judicial discretion.[249] In other words, appeals are likely to fail – and most have in fact failed.

Use of prior convictions in civil proceedings

Previous convictions could not be admitted in evidence in civil proceedings arising out of the same facts. A conviction for dangerous driving was therefore not admissible in subsequent proceedings for damages resulting from the same incident. This rule, known as the rule in *Hollington v. F Hewthorn & Co Ltd*,[250] was abolished by the Civil Evidence Act 1968, s. 11. The conviction is now rebuttable evidence of the facts involved in the offence, save in libel proceedings where the conviction is deemed to be irrebuttable evidence of the facts.

Evidence excluded because it is inherently unreliable

Children
The law affecting the evidence of children has always caused problems.

---

[249] *Renda* [2005] EWCA Crim 2826, [2006] 2 All ER 553 at [3].　　　[250] [1943] KB 587.

Children's evidence on oath

The basic rule at common law was that evidence had to be given on oath. In order to take the oath the witness had to understand its significance. Until 1991 there was no statutory rule as to the age at which a child was allowed to take the oath. It was regarded a matter for the judge in the case to determine whether the child had an appreciation of the solemnity of the occasion and of the special responsibility to tell the truth conveyed by the oath. In *Hayes*[251] the court said that the dividing line was probably between eight and ten. In 1972 the Criminal Law Revision Committee recommended that in criminal cases children under fourteen should always give evidence unsworn. This was implemented twenty years later in the Criminal Justice Act 1991.[252]

Children's unsworn evidence

Although the basic rule was that evidence had to be given on oath, in fact the courts would accept unsworn evidence. In criminal cases this was already known in the seventeenth century in cases of 'rape, buggery, witchcraft, and such crimes which are practised upon children'.[253] In 1779 it was held that a child could only give evidence on oath.[254] It took another century until the Criminal Law Amendment Act 1885 before children were allowed to give unsworn evidence. The 1885 Act applied only in cases involving unlawful sexual intercourse with girls under thirteen. It was extended to all criminal cases by the Children and Young Persons Act 1933, s. 38 though the 1933 Act provided that the unsworn evidence of a child required corroboration. Curiously, however, in civil cases unsworn evidence from children was not permitted until the Children Act 1989.

As to the age at which unsworn evidence could be admitted, a court ruled in 1958 that it had been wrong to accept the unsworn evidence of the five-year-old daughter who was the victim of her father's alleged incest,[255] but in two cases in 1990 the Court of Appeal refused to grant leave to appeal against a conviction for incest based on the unsworn evidence of a child of six.[256] This issue with regard to criminal cases has now been clarified by legislation.

Recent reforms

The rules with regard to the evidence of children have recently been altered partly in response to a more positive attitude to the evidence of children[257] and

---

[251] [1977] 1 WLR 234.

[252] Section 52 inserted a new s. 33A into the Criminal Justice Act 1988: 'A child's evidence in criminal proceedings shall be given unsworn'.

[253] Hale, *History of the Pleas of the Crown*, 1736, p. 284.   [254] *Brasier* (1779) East PC 443.

[255] *Wallwork* (1958) 42 Cr App Rep 153. In *Wright* (1987) 90 Cr App Rep 91 this was extended to a six-year-old.   [256] *B* (1990) Times, 1 March; *Z* [1990] 2 QB 355.

[257] For a review of empirical research evidence see J.R. Spencer and R. Flin, 'Child Witnesses – Are They Liars?', *New Law Journal*, 24 November 1989, p. 1603. Their conclusion was that the evidence did not support the traditional view that children are more likely to tell lies than adults, and it contradicted the view that the younger the child, the more likely it is that he or

partly in response to a concern about the difficulty of getting convictions in sex abuse cases involving young children.

Competence

The Youth Justice and Criminal Evidence Act 1999 established that the question of competence to give evidence in criminal cases is not to be treated as a matter of age. Section 53(1) states that a person of any age is competent to give evidence in a criminal case. (In a case in 2006 the Court of Appeal upheld the trial judge's decision to allow a girl of three and a half to give evidence.[258]) A person is not competent, however, if he cannot understand questions put to him or give understandable answers (s. 53(2)).[259] In order to assess whether a child can give intelligible testimony the judge should either watch a video taped interview or should ask the child questions (or both) so as to determine if he or she can understand questions and answer them in a coherent and comprehensible manner.[260] The question is one on which expert evidence can be received (s. 54(5)).[261]

The oath

As has been seen, in 1991 the rule was adopted that children aged fourteen should give evidence on oath while the evidence of children under fourteen would always be unsworn. The Youth Justice and Criminal Evidence Act 1999, s. 55 confirmed this in a provision which states that a witness in a criminal case may not be sworn unless he has reached the age of fourteen 'and he has a sufficient appreciation of the solemnity of the occasion and of the particular responsibility to tell the truth which is involved in taking the oath' (s. 55(2)). The test has however now been significantly watered down. If the witness is able

Footnote 257 (*cont.*)

she will lie. On the empirical evidence see also R. Bull, 'Children as Witnesses', 4 *Policing*, 1988, p. 130; and D. Birch, 'Children's Evidence', *Criminal Law Review*, 1992, p. 262 at 263–4. One piece of research was reported by G. Davies, A. Tarrant and R. Flin, 'Close Encounters of the Witness Kind: Children's Memory / a Simulated Health Inspection', *British Journal of Psychology*, 1989. The study tested 128 boys and girls split into age groups of six to seven and ten to eleven. The test involved direct confrontation between the child and an adult stranger in which the child was touched and an article of clothing (shoes) removed. The two age groups did not differ in their ability to help produce a photofit of the man. The report says: 'even the youngest subjects tested could have provided evidence on a number of points relevant to the main theme of events which would have been accurate in essentials and of interest to the court'. See also J. Plotnikoff and R. Woolfson, *In Their Own Words: The Experience of 50 Young Witnesses in Criminal Proceedings* (NSPCC/Victim Support, 2004).

[258] *Powell* [2006] EWCA Crim 3, [2006] Crim LR 781. The defendant's appeal was allowed on other grounds.

[259] For an application of s. 53 in a case where the videoed interview of an 81-year-old rape victim who had long-term delusional problems and had been diagnosed with early Alzheimer's disease was allowed see *R v. D* [2002] EWCA Crim 990, [2003] QB 90.

[260] Cf *DPP v. M* [1997] 2 All ER 749.

[261] This cancelled the 1997 decision that it was not appropriate to permit expert evidence to be given on the issue on the ground that the question was one well within the competence of a judge or magistrate (*G v. DPP* [1997] 2 All ER 755).

to give intelligible testimony, the Act provides that it is to be presumed that the witness is fit to take the oath unless evidence to the contrary is given. Giving intelligible testimony means understanding questions put to him and giving answers that can be understood (s. 55(8)). Again, expert evidence can be given on the matter (s. 55(6)).

Corroboration

As has been noted, the unsworn evidence of children in criminal cases had to be corroborated (Children and Young Persons Act 1933, s. 38). Moreover, the unsworn evidence of one child could not corroborate the unsworn evidence of another child, however cogent the evidence.[262] The effect of these rules was to make it impossible in some cases to get convictions of offenders in extremely serious sexual abuse cases.

The requirement of corroboration for the unsworn evidence of children was abolished by the Criminal Justice Act 1988, s. 34(1). Section 34(3) also provided that unsworn evidence could corroborate the evidence, whether sworn or unsworn, of anyone.

Prior to 1988 the sworn evidence of a child did not technically require corroboration but the judge had to warn the jury of the danger of relying on such uncorroborated evidence. The requirement of that warning was abolished by s. 34(2) of the 1988 Act – unless such a warning is required in relation to the evidence of an adult witness.

Persons of defective intellect

Where it is alleged that a witness lacks the mental capacity to testify, it is for the judge to decide whether he understands the nature of the oath.

Parties

Until modern times, both in civil and criminal cases, the parties themselves were not permitted to give evidence because it was thought that their evidence would be unreliable. This was changed for civil cases in 1851 by the Evidence Act of that year. In criminal cases defendants were not permitted to give evidence on oath until 1898, though before that date the judges allowed accused persons to make an unsworn statement from the dock. The present rules regarding occasions when parties need not give evidence fall under the different heading of evidence excluded for reasons of public policy – see below.

Spouses of parties

The spouse of a party was incompetent as a witness on the same basis as the party himself on the grounds of the likely unreliability of the evidence. It was not until the Evidence Amendment Act 1853 that a spouse became a competent witness in a civil case and in the Criminal Evidence Act 1898 that a spouse

---

[262] *Hester* [1973] AC 296.

became a competent witness for the defence in a criminal case. (As will be seen (p. 462 below), the spouse is not normally competent for the prosecution.) It seems, however, that a spouse is not a compellable witness for the defence.[263]

Hearsay evidence

Hearsay evidence, very simply defined, is an assertion made by someone who is not present in court as a witness. If A is the witness, what B said to A is first-hand hearsay; what B said to C, who told A, is second-hand hearsay. A document is hearsay evidence unless its author is there to introduce it in evidence.[264]

The rule excluding hearsay evidence as inherently unreliable has been regarded as one of the essential features of the common law principle that a trial, especially in a criminal case, should be based on evidence given by live witnesses in open court subject to cross-examination. At the Nuremberg trial of the Nazi war criminals there was a clash between the continental systems which permit hearsay evidence and the common law systems which basically reject it. In that situation the common law countries agreed to accept hearsay evidence.

A dramatic example of the impact of the exclusion of hearsay evidence is *Sparks v. R*:

> ### *Sparks v. R* [1964] 1 All ER 727, Judicial Committee of the Privy Council
> A girl of three was sexually assaulted. The mother asked what the person who did it looked like. She said, 'it was a coloured boy'. The defendant, a staff sergeant in the US Air Force, was a white man. The trial court ruled that the mother could not give her daughter's statement in evidence. On appeal, *inter alia*, against this ruling, Lord Morris, giving the judgment of the Board, said:
>
> It becomes necessary therefore to examine the contentions which have been advanced in support of the admissibility of the evidence. It was said that 'it was manifestly unjust for the jury to be left throughout the whole trial with the impression that the child could not give any clue to the identity of her assailant'. The cause of justice is, however, best served by adherence to rules which have long been recognised and settled. If the girl had made a remark to her mother (not in the presence of the appellant) to the effect that it was the appellant who had assaulted her and if the girl was not to be a witness at the trial, evidence as to what she had said would be the merest hearsay. In such circumstances it would be the defence who would wish to challenge a contention, if advanced, that it would be 'manifestly unjust' for the jury not to know that the girl had given a clue to the identity of her assailant. If it is said that hearsay evidence should freely be admitted and that there should be concentration in any particular case on deciding as to its value or weight, it is sufficient to say that our law has not been evolved on such lines, but is firmly based on the view that it is wiser

---

[263] See T.M.S. Tosswill, 'The Accused's Spouse as a Defence Witness', *Criminal Law Review*, 1979, p. 702 and M. Cohen, 'Are Wives Really so Incompetent?', *Criminal Law Review*, 1980, p. 222.

[264] The definition of the hearsay rule at common law given in C. Tapper (ed.), *Cross and Tapper on Evidence* is: 'a statement other than one made by a person while giving oral evidence in the proceedings was inadmissible as evidence of any fact stated' (10th edn, 2004) p. 578.

and better that hearsay should be excluded save in certain well-defined and rather exceptional circumstances. [The appeal was allowed on other grounds.]

In *Myers v. DPP*[265] the prosecution foundered because of the hearsay rule. The accused took part in a conspiracy involving the purchase of wrecked cars with their log books, then disguising stolen cars so as to make them conform to the log books of the wrecked cars and selling them as renovated wrecks. In order to prove that the cars were the stolen rather than the wrecked ones, the prosecution called an officer in charge of the records of the manufacturers of the stolen cars to produce microfilms of the cards filled in by workmen showing the numbers of the cylinder blocks which coincided with the cylinder block numbers of the cars sold by the defendants. The majority of the House of Lords held that the admission of the records would be a breach of the rule against hearsay evidence because, as Lord Reid said: 'the entries on the cards were assertions by the unidentifiable men who made them that they had entered numbers which they had seen on the cars'. That problem was dealt with almost immediately by the Criminal Evidence Act 1965, which made business or trade records admissible.

In *R v. Kearley*[266] K was accused of possession of drugs with intent to supply. Drugs had been found in his flat. While the police were there, ten phone calls were received in which the caller asked to speak to him about getting drugs. The prosecution wanted to introduce evidence of these calls through evidence of the police officers who intercepted the calls. After five days of argument the House of Lords ruled (three to two) that the calls were inadmissible as hearsay evidence!

There have always been a considerable number of exceptions to the hearsay rule, some statutory, some common law, and in recent years there were a succession of statutory exceptions and amendments of the rule. As will be seen (p. 451 below) in 1995, on the recommendation of the Law Commission, the hearsay rule was effectively abolished in civil cases. In the same year the Law Commission published a report recommending drastic reform of the rule for criminal cases (see pp. 453–54 below). The Government accepted the recommendations in full but, in the event, they were not implemented. Instead, the Government introduced an even more radical reform in the Criminal Justice Act 2003.

The rule only applies if the statement in question is to be introduced in order to establish the truth of its contents. If it is to be introduced for some other purpose, it does not count as hearsay evidence. This is confusing not only for the student, it causes confusion even for the courts. The distinction drawn is between 'hearsay' and 'direct evidence'. Thus, for instance, the printout from an intoximeter measuring blood alcohol level has been treated not as hearsay but as direct ('real') evidence of the mechanical process.[267] In *Taylor v. Chief Constable of Cheshire*[268] the prosecution case depended in part on what three police officers had seen in a video recording allegedly showing the appellant

[265] [1965] AC 1001.   [266] [1992] 2 AC 228, [1992] 2 All ER 345, HL.
[267] *Castle v. Cross* [1985] 1 All ER 87.   [268] [1987] 1 All ER 225.

committing theft from a shop, but the video had mistakenly been erased before the trial. The evidence of what was on the video was held by the Divisional Court not to be hearsay at all but rather direct evidence of what was seen happening at a particular time and place. Similarly, the courts have held that a sketch made by a police officer from a description given by a witness was not hearsay,[269] that a photofit picture compiled by a police officer was not hearsay[270] and that in some circumstances a computer printout is not hearsay.[271]

However, in *Townsend*[272] the court refused to extend this to a piece of paper on which a victim of a mugging had written the assailant's car number with a defective ball-point pen which only made indentations. The police had been able to blow up the indentations which matched the defendant's car number, but they had lost the original piece of paper.

Another form of evidence which looks confusingly as if it should be treated as hearsay evidence is when it is introduced simply to permit a witness to refresh his memory (for instance in the very common situation where a police officer is permitted to 'refresh' his memory from his notebook) or to show a previous inconsistent statement or a prior consistent statement.

Another example of evidence that is not hearsay is where the statement is introduced not to show the truth of the statement but rather to show a person's mental state. Thus in *Subramaniam v. Public Prosecutor*[273] the court allowed evidence of threats allegedly made by terrorists to the appellant to be admissible not to show that they intended to carry out those threats but to demonstrate his state of mind where his defence to the charge was duress.

A cynical comment on these examples of 'non-hearsay' is to see them all as ways simply of avoiding the rule – a view expressed by Professor Adrian Zuckerman:

> The methodology just described illustrates a fairly common tendency in this area. A certain type of statement is taken to be reliable. To avoid exclusion the court searches for a convenient tag which may be given to this type of evidence so that it may pass for something other than hearsay. To fulfil its function the tag or label must be associated with admissible evidence . . . Once the label is attached to a piece of evidence, the inhibiting effect of the hearsay rule disappears as if by magic.[274]

There are in addition a long list of recognised exceptions to the rule.

---

[269] *Smith, Percy* [1976] Crim LR 511.
[270] *Cook* [1987] Crim LR 402.   [271] *Wood* [1982] Crim LR 667.   [272] [1987] Crim LR 411.
[273] [1956] 1 WLR 965. Cf *Blastland* [1986] AC 41 where the House of Lords ruled that the out-of-court statement could only be introduced to show a state of mind where the state of mind was in issue. The charge was murder and buggery. The defence was that the offences had been committed by someone else. The defence wished to introduce statements made by that person to others revealing knowledge of the murder at a time when it was not generally known. The House of Lords held that the purpose of introducing the statement was not to show the other person's state of mind but to show that he had committed the murder. It was therefore not admissible.   [274] *Principles of Criminal Evidence* (Clarendon Press, 1989) p. 197.

Exceptions to the hearsay rule

At common law, an early exception recognised was that a deposition taken
before a coroner or justice of the peace might be read at a subsequent trial if the
witness was dead or too ill to travel. The exception did not, however, extend to
cases where the witness was simply untraceable, even if it could be shown that
diligent efforts had been made to find him. These exceptions were in the
Criminal Justice Act 1925, s. 13(4)(a) which provided also for the situation
where the witness whose deposition is to be read is proved to be insane or kept
out of the way by means of the procurement of the accused or on his behalf.

Another common law exception was for the *dying declaration*. This allowed
the prosecution in a murder or manslaughter case to introduce in evidence a
statement made by the deceased purporting to identify his assailant, providing
he had a 'settled and hopeless expectation of death'. If he believed he had a
chance of recovery the exception did not apply. For a modern example of the
rule, in *Nembhard v. R*[275] the Judicial Committee of the Privy Council upheld a
conviction for murder where the only evidence against the accused was the
deceased's alleged statement to his wife that he was going to die and that the
defendant had shot him.

From a practical point of view, a more important common law exception in
criminal cases was for *admissions or confessions*. If it were not for this exception,
a police officer would not be able to tell the court about the accused's alleged
self-incriminatory statement. The rationale for the exception was that people
do not make false statements to the police to their own detriment; therefore
there would be an inherent probability that the statement was true, which
would avoid the vice of hearsay statements that they are inherently unreliable
and not subject to cross-examination. The rationale is wholly unconvincing.
First, as is nowadays well known, people do make untrue confessions and
admissions – whether to protect others or out of some form of pressure or psychological weakness. Secondly, the issue with regard to confessions in a contested case is typically not whether the confession was true or false but whether
it was made at all. The real reason for the exception is the need for it if criminals are to be brought to book.

Another common law exception was for a statement made so close to the
event as in effect itself to be part of the event (the *res gestae* rule). It used to be
thought that the statement had to be actually contemporaneous with the
event,[276] but this requirement was abandoned. In *Andrews*[277] Lord Ackner said
that a *res gestae* statement was admissible if it was made in circumstances which

---

[275] [1982] 1 All ER 183.

[276] In *Bedingfield* (1879) 14 Cox CC 341 the court refused to admit under the *res gestae* doctrine a
statement by the victim who came out of her house with her throat slit ('see what Harry's
done') because it was not made at the moment of the murderous attack.

[277] [1987] 1 All ER 513. A was charged with murder by stabbing. The victim was found bleeding
heavily a few minutes after the stabbing. A police officer arrived a few minutes later. The
victim told the police that the defendant had carried out the stabbing. This statement was
admitted as part of the *res gestae* and the ruling was upheld by the House of Lords.

were sufficiently spontaneous and contemporaneous with the event to preclude the possibility of concoction or distortion. It had to be so closely associated with the event that the victim's mind was still dominated by it.[278]

The common law also allowed statements in *public documents* such as a birth or marriage certificate to be admitted without requiring that the author of the document has to come to court to give evidence. At common law, however, the rule required that the document be available for public inspection.[279]

There was another common law exception to the hearsay rule for family law matters especially where they affected children. The attitude of the courts was not, however, consistent. Sometimes the courts ruled that in family law cases the hearsay rule could be relaxed,[280] but in other cases they insisted on strict compliance with the rules.[281] The Children (Admissibility of Hearsay Evidence) Order 1990[282] provided that the hearsay rule did not apply in civil proceedings before the High Court or a county court concerning the upbringing, maintenance or welfare of a child. The Order also provided that the hearsay rule did not apply in relation to such proceedings in juvenile courts. In 1991 this rule was applied to magistrates' courts.

Reform of the hearsay rule in civil cases

In civil cases the main statutes until 1995 were the Civil Evidence Acts of 1938, 1968 and 1972. Under the 1938 Act, statements in original documents could be admitted to establish a fact of which direct oral evidence would be admissible if the maker of the statement had personal knowledge of the matter or it was part of a continuous record in the performance of a duty and the witness could not attend because he was dead, ill or abroad, or if all reasonable efforts to find him had been made without success. It also allowed the statement to be admitted if the witness was present to avoid delay or cost. The maker of the statement had to have personal knowledge of the facts stated and there were specific requirements that he authenticate the document. Also the statement had to be one made in writing.

The Civil Evidence Act 1968 broadened admissible hearsay to oral statements and also to mechanically recorded statements made by someone under a duty to record such information supplied to him by someone with personal

---

[278] In *Turnbull* (1984) 80 Cr App Rep 104 the court admitted a statement made in a pub some 200 yards away from the scene of the attack and some forty-five minutes after it had occurred.

[279] In *Lilley v. Pettit* [1946] KB 401 the court held inadmissible the regimental records of the army unit of the defendant's husband where she had been charged with falsely entering her husband's name as father of her child. The prosecution wanted to prove that the husband had been abroad at all material times. The evidence was not admissible because the records were not public.

[280] See for instance *Official Solicitor v. K* [1965] AC 201; *Hurwitt v. Hurwitt* [1979] 3 FLR 194; *Edwards v. Edwards* [1986] 1 FLR 187; *Thompson v. Thompson* [1986] 1 FLR 212n; *Webb v. Webb* [1986] 1 FLR 541.

[281] See especially *H v. H; K v. K* [1990] Fam 86; *Bradford City Metropolitan Council v. K and K* [1990] Fam 140 ('the *Bradford* case' and 9 *Civil Justice Quarterly*, 1990, p. 228).

[282] SI 1990/1115.

knowledge of the facts. Procedural safeguards required notice to be given in advance to the other side, with full particulars of the hearsay statement in question. If the other party objected, the person whose statement was to be given had to be called in person, unless he was dead, ill or abroad, or could not reasonably be expected to remember the matter. The Civil Evidence Act 1972 made the evidence of expert witnesses admissible in the form of their reports without having to call them.

In January 1991 the Law Commission proposed in a consultation paper that the hearsay rule should be completely abolished for civil proceedings.[283] The Commission suggested that, despite reform of the hearsay rule, it was not only difficult to understand but increasingly difficult to reconcile with recent procedural developments such as pre-trial exchange of witness statements. The hearsay rule in civil proceedings had already been abolished in Scotland by the Civil Evidence (Scotland) Act 1988. There was still a case for keeping the hearsay rule in criminal proceedings, especially in jury trials, but jury trials in civil cases were now exceedingly rare. The chief advantage of abolition of the rule would be to simplify the rules of evidence and the elimination of technical objections to the admissibility of relevant evidence. It should be for the parties to decide what evidence would assist their case. In practice they would resort to hearsay evidence only where it was the best they could find. The Law Commission's views were broadly confirmed in its final report published in 1993.[284]

The Government implemented the recommendation in the Civil Evidence Act 1995. The same rules were extended to civil proceedings in magistrates' courts as from April 1999.[285]

The guiding principle in the 1995 Act is that evidence is not to be excluded on the ground that it is hearsay and that the court will decide what weight to give it. The concept of hearsay evidence remains and it will often be regarded as less persuasive than direct evidence, but it is no longer to be excluded on that ground.

Parties are under a duty to give each other notice of their intention to adduce hearsay evidence.[286] Failure to give notice does not mean that the evidence cannot be introduced but the court can take that failure into account in considering what weight to place on the evidence and when making costs orders (s. 2).[287] A party can call for cross-examination of a person whose statement has been tendered as hearsay evidence and who has not been called to give oral

---

[283] *The Hearsay Rule in Civil Proceedings* (Law Com No. 117, 1991).
[284] *The Hearsay Rule in Civil Proceedings* (Law Com No. 216).
[285] Magistrates' Courts (Hearsay Evidence in Civil Proceedings) Rules 1999, SI 1999/681.
[286] See now CPR, r. 33.
[287] The Law Commission Report (Part III, para. 3.7) said that it appeared that the notice requirement under the previous English legislation had 'fallen into disuse' and that 'the prescribed time limits were not complied with'. Under the Civil Evidence (Scotland) Act 1988 hearsay evidence is admissible without any requirement of advance notice. One commentator suggested that we would have done better to follow the Scotland Act – see J. Peysner, 'Hearsay is Dead! Long Live Hearsay', 2 *International Journal of Evidence and Proof*, 1998, pp. 232–46.

evidence (s. 3). Section 4 guides the court as to what factors to weigh in such evidence, such as whether it would have been reasonable and practicable to have called the maker of the statement and when the statement was made, e.g. was it made contemporaneously, or whether there was any motive to conceal or misrepresent matters.

Reform of the hearsay rule in criminal cases

In criminal cases, too, the hearsay rule was gradually transformed by statute – a process that culminated in the Criminal Justice Act 2003.

1967–2003

- The Criminal Justice Act 1967, s. 9 made admissible written witness statements where they were signed, a copy had been served in advance on the other party and no counter-notice had been served objecting to the statement being tendered in evidence. This was used very frequently. Section 2 of the 1967 Act (later s. 102 of the Magistrates Courts Act 1980) made written statements admissible in committal proceedings on a similar basis, namely, that they were written, signed and tendered in advance. Again, this was much used. The Criminal Procedure and Investigations Act 1996 carried it much further by making *any* written statement and deposition admitted in evidence in committal proceedings admissible at trial providing the statement was signed by a magistrate. The accused could object to the statement or deposition being read as evidence at his trial but the trial court could overrule the objection if it considered it 'to be in the interests of justice'.[288]
- The Criminal Evidence Act 1965 reversed the House of Lords decision in *Myers v. DPP* (p. 447 above) by providing that business and trade records made under a duty to record the information admissible. This legislation was superseded by the much wider provisions of the Police and Criminal Evidence Act 1984, which in turn was superseded by the even wider provisions of the Criminal Justice Act 1988.

  PACE, s. 68 made admissible statements in any document that formed part of a record compiled by a person under a duty or on the basis of information supplied by someone acting under a duty, where the maker of the document was unavailable to give evidence. The supplier of the information had to be dead, ill or physically unable to give evidence, abroad or whose whereabouts were not known, or it had to be a situation where it would not be reasonable to expect him to remember the matters recorded.

  Section 68 of PACE was replaced by Part II and Sch. 2 of the Criminal Justice Act 1988. The purpose of Part II was to establish a new basis for the admissibility of documentary hearsay in criminal proceedings. It classified documents into three categories: first-hand hearsay, business documents and

---

[288] Section 68 and Sch. 2, paras. 1 and 2. For a savage critique of this provision see R. Munday, 'The Drafting Smokescreen', 147 *New Law Journal*, 30 May 1997, p. 792; 6 June 1997, p. 860.

documents which might fall into either category that had been prepared specifically for the purpose of criminal proceedings.

Section 23 made any first-hand hearsay admissible provided the maker was unavailable to give evidence because he was dead or unfit or abroad and it was not reasonably practicable to secure his attendance, or that he could not be found in spite of all reasonable steps taken. These provisions were similar to those in s. 68 of the 1984 Act, but it was no longer possible to tender someone's hearsay statement on the basis that he could not reasonably be expected to remember the matter. Nor could the maker's statement be admitted when he could not be identified after reasonable efforts made.

Section 24 considerably widened the previous exception for business records by no longer requiring that the business document had to have been made by someone acting under a duty. It was only necessary to prove that the information contained in the document had been supplied by someone who had or might reasonably be supposed to have had personal knowledge of the matter.

Where a statement was prepared for the purposes of a criminal investigation or prosecution it could be introduced in evidence on proof regarding the absence of the maker that he was dead, unfit, abroad etc. or that he did not give evidence 'through fear or because he [was] kept out of the way'.[289]

• The Runciman Royal Commission expressed the view that 'in general, the fact that a statement is hearsay should mean that the court places rather less weight on it, but not that it should be inadmissible in the first place'.[290] The probative weight of the evidence should, it thought, 'in principle be decided by the jury for themselves' (ibid). It recommended that 'hearsay evidence should be admitted to a greater extent than at present' (ibid), but because of the complexity of the hearsay rule it thought that the issues needed thorough exploration by the Law Commission.

• The Government referred the question of the hearsay rule to the Law Commission in April 1994 and a year later, in July 1995, the Commission produced a 266 page consultation paper.[291] The consultation paper suggested that it was right to retain the hearsay rule in criminal cases as a protection to the accused. In civil cases the finders of fact were judges; in criminal cases they were jurors and magistrates, but the rules needed reform: 'The rule is excessively complex; this complexity leads to confusion, anomalies and wasted time, both for the court and for the parties. The rule results in the exclusion of cogent evidence even when it is the defence that seeks to adduce it' (para. 9.2).

---

[289] See further D.J. Birch, 'The Criminal Justice Act – The Evidence Provisions', *Criminal Law Review*, 1989, pp. 15–31.   [290] Runciman, p. 125, para. 26.

[291] *Evidence in Criminal Proceedings: Hearsay and Related Topics* (Law Com No. 138, 1995). For commentary on the consultation paper see A.A.S. Zuckerman, 'The Futility of Hearsay', *Criminal Law Review*, 1996, pp. 4–15; D.C. Ormerod, 'The Hearsay Exceptions', *ibid*, pp. 16–28; P. Murphy, 'Hearsay: the Road to Reform', 1 *International Journal of Evidence and Proof*, 1997, pp. 107–27 and 'Practising Safe Hearsay: Surrender may be Inevitable, but Shouldn't We Take Precautions?', *ibid*, 1997, pp. 105–21.

The Law Commission proposed that as a general rule hearsay should remain inadmissible subject to listed statutory exceptions. These would be first-hand oral or documentary hearsay of identified witnesses. The categories of exception would be: (1) where the witness was dead or too ill to attend court; (2) where such steps had been taken as were reasonably practicable to secure his attendance but without success and he was abroad or could not be found; or (3) where the witness refused to give evidence although physically available. They would not extend to evidence of any fact of which the witness's oral evidence would not be admissible.

The Commission proposed that there should be a residual discretion to admit hearsay falling outside the stated categories and other preserved exceptions which would extend to multiple as well as first-hand hearsay. This should be available only if it appeared to the court that (1) the evidence was so positively and obviously trustworthy that the opportunity to test it by cross-examination could safely be dispensed with; and (2) the interests of justice required that it be admitted.

The Commission also recommended that s. 69 of PACE regarding computers should be repealed. In the absence of evidence to the contrary it should be assumed that a computer or other mechanical instrument was functioning properly. This was effected by s. 60 of the Youth Justice and Criminal Evidence Act 1999.

The Law Commission's Final Report reaffirmed the main recommendations in the consultation paper.[292]

In December 1998 the Government announced that it accepted all the recommendations of the Law Commission's Report – lock, stock and barrel.[293] However, the legislation to give effect to this commitment was delayed for years and in the end it was not implemented.

In October 2001 Lord Justice Auld's *Review of the Criminal Courts* said of the hearsay rule:

> It is common ground that the present law is unsatisfactory and needs reform. It is complicated, unprincipled and arbitrary in the application of the many exceptions. It can exclude cogent and let in weak evidence. It wastes court time in requiring it to receive oral evidence when written evidence would do. And it confuses witnesses and prevents them from giving their accounts in their own way.[294]

---

[292] Law Com No. 245, Cm. 3670, 1997. For commentary on the Final Report see J.D. Jackson, 'Hearsay: the Sacred Cow that Won't be Slaughtered?' 2 *International Journal of Evidence and Proof*, 1998, pp. 166–90; C. Tapper, 'Hearsay in Criminal Cases: An Overview of Law Commission Report No 245', *Criminal Law Review*, 1997, p. 771; cf J. Spencer, 'Hearsay Reform: A Bridge not Far Enough?', *Criminal Law Review*, 1996, p. 29. (Professor Spencer was the original consultant to the Law Commission but withdrew because of his dissatisfaction with the 'unduly timid' proposals in the consultation paper. He then became an adviser to Lord Justice Auld on his review.)

[293] House of Lords, *Hansard*, 17 December 1998, vol. 599, WA, col. 184.

[294] Auld, p. 557, para. 96.

The Law Commission's proposals, Auld said, looked at individually, represented useful improvements on the present law. They relaxed some of the rigidity of the present rule through a widening of the exceptions and the introduction of a limited inclusionary discretion, but 'their implementation would not significantly change the present landscape nor, I believe, remove much of the scope for dispute that disfigures and interrupts our present trial process'.[295] He suggested that a further review be undertaken with a view to making hearsay evidence 'generally admissible subject to the principle of the best evidence, rather than generally inadmissible subject to specified exceptions as proposed by the Law Commission' (p. 560). Fact finders should be trusted to assess the weight of the evidence.

The Government's July 2002 White Paper *Justice for All* said:

> We believe the right approach is that, if there is good reason for the original maker not to be able to give the evidence personally (for example, through illness or death) or where records have been properly compiled by businesses, then the evidence should automatically go in, rather than its admissibility being judged. Judges should also have a discretion to decide that other evidence of this sort can be given. This is close to the approach developed in civil proceedings (para. 4.61).

The Government did not adopt Lord Justice Auld's recommendations that the topic should be further studied by another committee nor that the best evidence rule should be adopted. Instead the Criminal Justice Act 2003, Ch. 2 contained a complete restatement – as opposed to a codification – of the law on hearsay in criminal proceedings. Although the restatement retained much of the existing law, it also represented a considerable shift toward admitting more evidence. The hearsay provisions were brought into force in April 2005.

The Criminal Justice Act 2003, ss. 114–136[296] The provisions start in s. 114(1) by establishing that hearsay evidence, whether oral or written, is admissible under four headings: (1) under statute; (2) under any common law rule specifically preserved by the 2003 Act; (3) if all the parties agree; and (4) if 'the court is satisfied that it is in the interests of justice for it to be admissible'.

The last category (4) gives the judge the possibility of admitting hearsay that does not fit into any other category. Depending on how the courts apply it, this 'safety valve' could prove to be of great importance. It could extend to any form of hearsay evidence including multiple hearsay.[297]

---

[295] *Ibid*, p. 559, para. 102.
[296] For a commentary see for instance D. Birch, 'Hearsay: Same Old Story, Same Old Song?', 2004, *Criminal Law Review*, p. 556.
[297] Lord Cooke of Thorndon in the House of Lords debate on the Bill suggested that this safety valve was the most important provision in the hearsay reform package giving the courts a 'flexible weapon to achieve justice in criminal law'. He drew attention to the fact that 'in other common law countries, particularly Canada and New Zealand, the courts have moulded the judge-made law so as to accept broadly a residual discretion to admit hearsay evidence of sufficient apparent reliability'. (House of Lords, *Hansard*, 18 September 2003, cols. 1109 *et seq.*)

Section 114(2)(a)–(i) sets out the factors that the court must take into account when deciding whether the evidence is reliable enough to admit under subsection (1)(d) – the probative value of the evidence and how important it is, what other evidence there is, the circumstances in which it was made, the reliability of the maker of the statement, how reliable it is that the statement had been made, why oral evidence is not available, the difficulty of challenging the statement and the extent to which that difficulty would prejudice the party facing it.

Section 116(2) sets out a series of categories under which first-hand hearsay evidence, oral or documentary,[298] is automatically admissible, provided that the witness is unavailable to testify because he is dead, ill, absent abroad, has disappeared or is in fear (which subsection (3) says must be widely construed and includes fear of the death or injury of another person or of financial loss). The identity of the person must be established to the court's satisfaction. The discretion and leave provisions in ss. 25 and 26 of the 1988 Act have been removed except where the witness is said to be in fear. Leave under subsection (2)(e) can only be given if it is in the interests of justice after weighing the relative effect of admitting or excluding the evidence. The court is specifically required to consider whether a 'special measures' direction under the Youth Justice and Criminal Evidence Act 1999 (giving evidence behind a screen, live link, video recorded evidence etc. – p. 432 above) might work as an alternative to admitting the evidence as hearsay (subsection (4)).[299]

Business and other documents previously permitted under s. 24 of the Criminal Justice Act 1988 are permitted under s. 117. Section 118 preserves eight categories of hearsay evidence permitted at common law, including 'public information' (such as dictionaries, maps, birth certificates or court records), *res gestae* (pp. 449–50 above)[300] and confessions. Dying declarations have not been preserved, but they could be admissible under s. 116.

Under the previous law an assertion made in a previous statement did not become evidence of its truth unless it was adopted by its maker in evidence. Under ss. 119 and 120 reversing the traditional rule, virtually any earlier statement by a witness that comes into evidence can be evidence of its own truth. Section 119 applies to previous inconsistent statements.[301] Section 120 applies to previous consistent statements that become evidence to rebut an allegation of recent fabrication and to previous statements put in evidence through cross-examination. Similarly, under s. 120 a 'recent complaint' by a complainant can be evidence of the truth of the allegation provided the complaint was made as

---

[298] The equivalent previous provision in s. 23 of the 1988 Act was confined to documentary evidence.   [299] For the ECHR implications see *Sellick* [2005] Crim LR 722.

[300] *Res gestae* is wider than s. 116 as it could cover the spontaneous statement of an unidentified person as in *Gibson* (1887) 18 QBD 857.

[301] For an example see *Joyce and Joyce* [2005] EWCA Crim 1785. Two eye witnesses to shootings became hostile witnesses at trial. The Court of Appeal upheld the trial judge's decision to admit their earlier statements identifying the accused.

soon as could reasonably be expected and the maker claims that at the time the matter was fresh in his mind.[302]

Multiple hearsay is permitted if one of the stages of hearsay is admissible under the provisions as a business document, a witness's previous statement or a recent complaint or all the parties agree to its admission or the court is satisfied that the interests of justice require its admission (s. 121).

Under s. 139 a witness is allowed to refresh his memory from statements made at a time when his recollection is likely to have been 'significantly better'.[303]

When it is brought into force, s. 137 will permit the court to give leave for the evidence of a witness to a serious offence[304] to be given in the form of a video recording made when the event was still fresh in his memory. (As noted above, Professor Birch has described this as 'an explosive device'.[305])

The Criminal Justice Act contains several different safeguards in addition to the 'safety valve' in s. 114(1)(d):

- If there is any question as to the capability of a witness whose hearsay is sought to have admitted, the court must exclude it unless the party that wants to adduce the hearsay can show on a balance of probability that the witness was capable (s. 123). It follows that the identity of the witness must first be established.[306] The test of capability is based on understanding questions put and giving answers that can be understood.

- The court is required to admit evidence that undermines the absent witness's credibility or that shows that he made other inconsistent statements. The court may also admit material that could have been put to the witness in cross-examination if he had been there to testify (s. 124).

- If the judge considers that the hearsay evidence is so unconvincing as to make a conviction unsafe he must either direct the jury to acquit or stop the case and order a retrial (s. 125).

- The court is given a discretion to exclude hearsay evidence on the ground that it would result in undue waste of time having regard to its likely value (s. 126).

---

[302] Professor Spencer (n. 292 above) suggested that the rule against using a witness's previous statement, also known as the rule against narrative, was based on two remarkable propositions – that memory improves with time and that the stress of a trial enhances the power of recall. A further argument against the rule, as Auld noted in his report, is that the problem of inability to cross-examine the witness does not apply to the previous statements of someone in the witness box. Professor Birch, referring to these weighty arguments, said she found it astonishing that the Government missed the opportunity of abolishing the rule (n. 296 above at p. 570).

[303] Under the previous law there was a requirement that the earlier statement have been contemporaneous with the event.

[304] An offence triable only on indictment or prescribed either-way offences (s. 137(1)).

[305] Note 296 above at p. 572.

[306] Article 6(3)(d) of the ECHR guarantees that the defendant has the 'right to examine or have examined witnesses against him'. He cannot challenge the witness unless he has been identified.

Rules of court require that in some circumstances notice be given of an intention to rely on hearsay evidence and counter notices setting out objections.[307]

Speaking on the Second Reading of the Bill in the House of Lords, Lord Woolf, Lord Chief Justice, said of the hearsay provisions:[308]

> 22. We question whether the complexity of the provisions is necessary. What has happened is that the complex common law rules are being replaced by complex statutory rules, some of which are a repetition of the common law rules.
>
> 23. What happens now in civil proceedings is that a judge has a general discretion to determine how matters are to be proved. The judge has to exercise the discretion in the interests of justice . . . If it is not first-hand evidence, then it has the disadvantage that it has not been tested by cross-examination. Whether this matters depends on the circumstances. If we have got to the stage where it is considered that it is safe to allow juries to hear hearsay evidence, then we must be accepting that they can be trusted to use that evidence in accordance with the directions of the judge. Instead of the detailed and complex provisions which are contained in Chapter 2, what is needed is a simple rule putting the judge in charge of what evidence is admissible and giving him the responsibility of ensuring that the jury uses the evidence in an appropriate manner.

The Court of Appeal has on several occasions ruled that the statutory hearsay provisions are not *per se* incompatible with Article 6(3)(d) of the ECHR.[309] Compatibility depends on a variety of considerations and ultimately on the exercise by the court of judicial discretion.[310]

US Supreme Court and hearsay In marked contrast to the reform of the hearsay rule in England, see the 2004 decision of the US Supreme Court in *Crawford v. Washington*.[311] The court insisted on the defendant's right guaranteed by the Sixth Amendment to confront prosecution witnesses and to test their evidence by cross-examination. In a murder trial the trial court allowed in evidence of a recorded statement of the defendant's wife made during police interrogation to the effect that the killing was not self-defence. The trial court's

---

[307] An amendment in 2006 to the Criminal Procedure Rules Part 34 limited the notice requirement to cases where it is in the interests of justice for it to be admitted (CJA 2003, s. 114(d)), or the witness is unavailable (s. 116), or the evidence is a business or other such document (s. 117) or it is multiple hearsay (s. 121).

[308] In his 'Background Notes' laid in the library of the House of Lords and published by the writer – see n. 248, p. 441 above.

[309] *Sellick* [2005] EWCA Crim 651; *Al Khwaja* [2005] EWCA Crim 2697; *Xhabri* [2005] EWCA Crim 3135; *Tahery* [2006] EWCA Crim 529. See also the decision of the Judicial Committee of the Privy Council in *Grant v. The State* [2006] UKPC 2, [2006] Crim LR 837.

[310] However see the decision in *E* where the Court of Appeal upheld the trial judge's ruling not to admit the complainant's video evidence in a rape case. The decision in *Sellick* was distinguished. Although satisfied that the complainant was unfit (CJA 2003, s. 116(2)(b)) and in fear (CJA 2003, s. 116(2)(e)) and that the defendant was not responsible, the judge concluded that the hearsay evidence was the sole or decisive evidence in the case and that it would be unfair to admit it since the accused would not be able to test the evidence by cross-examination. [2006] Crim. LR 839.　　[311] (2004) 541 US 36.

ruling was in line with the Supreme Court's 1981 decision in *Ohio v. Roberts*[312] which held that the Sixth Amendment right to be 'confronted with the witnesses against him' did not prevent admission of an unavailable witness's statement if it bore 'adequate indicia of reliability' as falling within one of the recognised exceptions to the hearsay rule or possessing 'particularised guarantees of trustworthiness'. In *Crawford* the Supreme Court overruling its decision in *Ohio v. Roberts* said:

> (d) The Confrontation Clause commands that reliability be assessed in a particular manner: by testing in the crucible of cross-examination. *Roberts* allows a jury to hear evidence, untested by the adversary process, based on a mere judicial determination of reliability, thus replacing the constitutionally prescribed method of assessing reliability with a wholly foreign one (25–27).
>
> (e) *Roberts'* framework is unpredictable. Whether a statement is deemed reliable depends on which factors a judge considers and how much weight he accords each of them. However, the unpardonable vice of the *Roberts* test is its demonstrated capacity to admit core testimonial statements that the Confrontation Clause plainly meant to exclude (27–30).
>
> (f) The instant case is a self-contained demonstration of *Roberts'* unpredictable and inconsistent application. It also reveals *Roberts'* failure to interpret the Constitution in a way that secures its intended constraint on judicial discretion. The Constitution prescribes the procedure for determining the reliability of testimony in criminal trials, and this court, no less than the state courts, lacks authority to replace it with one of its own devising (30–32).[313]

The gist of the Supreme Court's ruling was that if an out-of-court statement is 'testimonial' in nature, its admission in evidence breaches the defendant's right of confrontation even if it appears to be wholly reliable.[314]

Identification evidence

Possibly the most notorious source of miscarriages of justice is identification evidence raising the question whether such evidence ought to be wholly excluded in criminal cases unless corroborated. The question was examined by the Devlin Committee on *Evidence of Identification in Criminal Cases*.[315] The Committee rejected this view but recommended that the judge should be required to warn the jury that it was unsafe to convict on the basis of eyewitness evidence unless the circumstances of the identification were exceptional or there was substantial evidence of some other sort. A judge who gave such

---

[312] (1981) 448 US 56.

[313] The official headnote issued by the Reporter of Decisions – www.bailii.org – World Collections – North America – United States – Supreme Court decisions.

[314] For approving commentary see S. Clark, 'Who Do You Think You Are? The Criminal Trial and Community Character' in A. Duff et al. (eds.), *The Trial on Trial (2)*, (Oxford, 2006) pp. 83–97 at pp. 90–4. ('The act of accusation without a willingness to confront is simply an unacceptable act of ignoble cowardice – an act worthy of outrage, and not to be abetted by the state' (p. 94).) See also W.E. O'Brien, 'The Right of Confrontation: US and European Perspectives', 121 *Law Quarterly Review*, 2005, pp. 481–510.

[315] House of Commons Paper 338, 1976.

warning should indicate the kind of case where exceptionally it might be reasonable to rely on eyewitness evidence. Failure to give the warning would be grounds to quash the conviction. So too would a finding by the Court of Appeal that the case was not such as to justify reliance on eyewitness evidence or that there was insufficient supporting evidence.

The Court of Appeal in *R v. Turnbull*[316] acted on the report only a few weeks after the report was published though it did not give full effect to the Committee's recommendation. Sitting with five judges, the court laid down new guidelines for trial judges in cases involving disputed identification evidence. Lord Widgery for the court said that the trial judge should warn the jury of the special need for caution before relying on identification evidence. He should instruct them as to the reason for such warning and should refer to the possibility that a mistaken witness was a convincing one and that even a number of such witnesses could be mistaken. Secondly, he should direct the jury to examine very closely the circumstances in which the identification came to be made:

> How long did the witness have the accused under observation? At what distance? In what light? Was the observation impeded in any way, as for example by passing traffic or a press of people? Had the witness ever seen the accused before? How often? If only occasionally, had he any reason for remembering the accused? How long elapsed between the original observation and the subsequent identification to the police? Was there any material discrepancy between the description of the accused given to the police by the witness when first seen by them and his actual appearance? (at p. 228).

If there were such discrepancies, the prosecution should inform the defence. The court said that in setting out its guidelines it had tried to follow the recommendations of the Devlin Committee. A failure to follow the guidelines was likely to result in a conviction being quashed,[317] but the courts have resisted the suggestion that *Turnbull* requires them to follow a formula.[318]

The rules for identification procedures are now to be found in the PACE Code of Practice on Identification Evidence (Code D) revised as from 1 January 2006.[319]

---

[316] [1977] QB 224.

[317] For cases in which convictions were subsequently quashed as a result of a failure to follow the guidelines see for instance *R v. Hunjan* (1978) 68 Cr App Rep 99; *Bentley* [1991] Crim LR 620; *Fergus* (1993) 98 Cr App Rep 313.

[318] See for instance *Mills* [1995] Crim LR 884 and *Mussell; Dalton* [1995] Crim LR 887. See also E. Grayson, 'Identifying Turnbull', *Criminal Law Review*, 1977, p. 509; and J.D. Jackson, 'The Insufficiency of Identification Evidence Based on Personal Impression', *Criminal Law Review*, 1986, p. 203.

[319] See M. Zander, *Police and Criminal Evidence Act 1984* (5th edn, Sweet & Maxwell, 2005 and First Supplement, 2006). For cases on the admissibility of evidence obtained in breach of the identification rules see *ibid*, paras. 8–116 and 8–121. For a recent evaluation of the rules see A. Roberts, 'The Problem of Mistaken Identification: Some Observations on Process', 8 *International Journal of Evidence and Proof*, 2004, pp. 100–19.

Judicial warnings regarding uncorroborated evidence

Until very recently the judges were required to give the jury a warning about
the danger of relying on the uncorroborated evidence of children (p. 445
above), accomplices giving evidence for the prosecution and complainants in
a sexual offence. The Law Commission recommended in 1991 that the rules
requiring such warnings should be abolished.[320] This was effected in the
Criminal Justice and Public Order Act 1994, s. 32(1). In *Makanjuola and
Easton*[321] the Court of Appeal held that although there was no longer a rule
requiring a warning about uncorroborated evidence, one could be given on a
discretionary basis where the judge thought it necessary. It gave guidelines as
to how the matter should be approached. The guidelines provoked a good deal
of debate.[322]

Section 33 of the 1994 Act also abolished the requirement of actual corroboration for a number of offences under the Sexual Offences Act 1956.

Judicial warnings regarding cell confessions

Evidence in a criminal case in the form of a confession allegedly made to a cell
mate in prison is open to the danger that it was fabricated by the witness to gain
some advantage for himself. In *Benedetto*[323] the Privy Council seemed to require
that once it was established that a prisoner had a motive for lying a specific and
detailed warning should always be given to the jury about the danger of convicting on cell confession evidence, but in the high profile case of *Stone*[324] the
Court of Appeal said that not every case involving a cell confession required
such a warning. There were no fixed rules. The nature of the warning would
depend on the facts of each case. In the case of a two-line confession, there
would generally be a need to warn the jury that such confessions were easy to
concoct and difficult to prove and that prisoners could have many motives to
lie. If the informant had a significant criminal record or a history of lying, this
should be pointed out, but where, as in that case, an alleged confession would
not be easy to invent, it would be absurd to require the judge to say that cell confessions were easy to concoct. Similarly, where as in that case, the defence had
not cross-examined the informant about the motive of hope of advantage the
judge was not required to warn the jury of that possibility. Warnings about the
possibility that the prisoner informant might give tainted evidence had to arise
from the evidence.

[320] *Corroboration of Evidence in Criminal Trials*, Cm. 1620, 1991.
[321] [1995] 2 Cr App Rep 469, [1995] 3 All ER 730.
[322] See commentary in *Criminal Law Review*, 1996, pp. 44 at 45 and 815 at 816; D.J. Birch,
'Corroboration: Goodbye to All That?', *Criminal Law Review*, 1995, pp. 524–39; P. Mirfield,
'Corroboration after the 1994 Act', *ibid*, pp. 448–60; J. Hartshorne, 'Corroboration and Care
Warnings after *Makanjuola*', 2 *International Journal of Evidence and Proof*, 1998, pp. 1–12. See
also *Warwick Muncaster* [1999] Crim LR 409.   [323] [2003] 1 WLR 1545.
[324] [2005] EWCA Crim 105, [2005] Crim LR 569. Michael Stone was convicted of the horrific
murders of Lin Russell and her daughter Megan and of the attempted murder of Megan's
sister Josie.

Evidence excluded because its admissibility would be against the public interest

There are various categories of excluded evidence that can conveniently be collected under this head.

The evidence of spouses in criminal cases

A spouse was generally not able to give evidence for the prosecution in a criminal case even if willing to give evidence.[325] She was not competent as a witness. There were some exceptions where the wife was permitted to give evidence but was not compellable, mainly involving offences against the wife herself, her property or against their children. In *Hoskyn v. Metropolitan Police Commissioner*[326] the House of Lords held that a woman who married the defendant two days before the trial could not be *compelled* to give evidence against her new husband in a case arising out of a serious assault on her! In *R v. Pitt*[327] the Court of Appeal said that a wife who was competent but not compellable to give evidence for the prosecution against her husband remained free to decide whether to give evidence until the moment that she entered the witness box and was unaffected by whether she had previously given a statement to the police or had given evidence at the committal proceedings, but once she decided to give evidence she became like any other witness and had to answer all questions save those that might incriminate her. Moreover, she could be treated as a hostile witness if that would be legitimate with an ordinary witness. This should be explained to her before she started to give evidence. The general exclusionary rule applied even after judicial separation and possibly after divorce with regard to matters that occurred during the marriage.

In its 1972 11th Report, the Criminal Law Revision Committee (CLRC) recommended that the rule should be modified to make the wife *competent* to give evidence for the prosecution if willing to do so. She should be *compellable* (as opposed to being merely competent) in cases involving violence against her or against children of the household under sixteen.[328] If the parties were divorced, the CLRC thought that they should be treated for all purposes as if they had never been married – even with regard to matters occurring during the marriage.

PACE, s. 80 broadly carried into effect the CLRC's proposals. It provides, first, that a spouse is always competent for the prosecution save where he or she is charged jointly with the same offence. (The exception does not apply, however, where he or she is no longer liable to be convicted for that offence by virtue of having pleaded guilty or otherwise.) The Act, secondly, made the spouse always compellable for the defence – save for the same exception where she is charged jointly with him.[329] The Act extended the CLRC's proposals by making a spouse

---

[325] See *R v. Mount* (1934) 24 Cr App Rep 135.   [326] [1978] 2 All ER 136.

[327] [1982] Crim LR 513.   [328] Paragraphs 149–50.

[329] In *R (on the application of CPS) v. Registrar General of Births, Deaths and Marriages* [2002] EWCA Civ 1661, [2003] 1 All ER 540 the Court of Appeal held that it was not contrary to public policy for the defendant to marry in order to take advantage of s. 80. The prosecution

compellable for the prosecution not only in cases of violence to children of the family under sixteen, but also in cases of violence or a sexual offence against *anyone* under sixteen whether or not they were family members. Thirdly, PACE implemented the CLRC's proposal that a spouse should be competent for a co-accused regardless of whether his or her spouse consented. Fourthly, the Act laid down that after the marriage has been terminated, both spouses become competent and compellable as if they had never been married – even regarding events that occurred during the marriage.

Evidence that might incriminate the witness

Any witness in any case, other than the defendant himself, is entitled to refuse to answer a question that might expose him to a criminal charge. (The equivalent of the American 'taking the Fifth Amendment'.) If the privilege is invoked, it is for the judge to decide whether the questions have to be answered. It seems that the privilege may extend to cover answers that could incriminate a spouse, but it does not go beyond that to protect other family members.

In *Re O (disclosure order)*[330] the Court of Appeal held that convicted persons could be required to make full disclosure of their assets for the purposes of potential confiscation proceedings under the Criminal Justice Act 1988, but because of the principle of not requiring a person to incriminate himself, the order would be subject to a condition that no disclosure made in compliance with the order should be used as evidence in the prosecution of an offence alleged to have been committed by the person required to make the disclosure.

The accused is not a compellable witness

An accused person in a criminal case has a right to remain silent in the dock. That was and remains the case. In fact the great majority of defendants who plead not guilty do give evidence. (In the *Crown Court Study* done for the Royal Commission on Criminal Justice over 70 per cent of defendants gave evidence.[331])

The basic rule was that the prosecution were not permitted to comment on the fact that the defendant chose not to go into the witness box.[332] The judge was allowed, in his discretion, to draw the jury's attention to the fact but he could not suggest that silence constituted evidence against the defendant.[333]

---

was therefore not entitled to ask the prison authorities and/or the Registrar of Births, Deaths and Marriages to refuse to allow the wedding until after the defendant's trial.

[330] [1991] 1 All ER 330.

[331] M. Zander and P. Henderson, *The Crown Court Study* (Royal Commission on Criminal Justice, Research Study No 19, 1993) p. 114.

[332] Criminal Evidence Act 1898, s. 1(b), but see *R v. Brown and Routh* [1983] Crim LR 38 where it was held the rule had not been infringed even though the prosecution counsel did comment on the defendants' failure to give evidence in the sense that he said the prosecution's case was uncontradicted.

[333] *R v. Martinez-Tobon* [1994] 2 All ER 90, CA. Provided the judge told the jury that they should not assume guilt from a refusal to give evidence, comment was permitted. Where the defence

Until 1982, if the defendant chose to give evidence he could either go into the witness box and thereby subject himself to cross-examination or he could make a statement from the dock on which he could not be cross-examined.

The CLRC in its 1972 11th Report recommended drastic reform of the rules along the lines of its recommendations regarding silence in the police station (p. 166 above):[334]

- That if the prosecution had established a *prima facie* case, the accused should formally be asked to go into the witness box and told that, if he failed to do so, adverse inferences could be drawn. Failure to do so could also amount to corroboration where corroboration was required. In the view of the Committee the existing rule was much too favourable to the defence. Normally it should be incumbent on the accused to give evidence, but it would not become contempt of court to refuse.
- The prosecution and judge should be entitled to comment on the accused's failure to give evidence. The prohibition on comment was wrong in principle and entirely illogical.
- The right to make an unsworn statement from the dock should be abolished. It was rarely exercised in trials on indictment save in cases where the accused wanted to attack prosecution witnesses without making himself liable to the revelations of his own prior convictions. It was wrong to give the accused this choice.

These proposals were received with much less criticism than those made by the CLRC with regard to the right of silence in the police station.

The Philips Royal Commission on Criminal Procedure (1981)[335] disagreed with the CLRC on the first two points. It did not favour putting pressure on the accused to give evidence or allowing comment on his refusal to testify, but it did agree that the right of the defendant to make an unsworn statement from the dock should be abolished. It was anomalous that a defendant should be able to give evidence without being subject to the possibility of perjury proceedings. He should be required to submit himself to the oath and cross-examination.

The Government followed the advice of the Philips Commission. The Criminal Justice Act 1982, s. 72 abolished the right of the defendant to make an unsworn statement from the dock but it preserved the right of an unrepresented accused to address the court in the same way that counsel could, by way of submissions or in mitigation of sentence.

The Runciman Royal Commission on Criminal Justice said that the balance was held correctly in the standard direction given to juries:

Footnote 333 (*cont.*)
  case involved facts which were at variance with the prosecution's case and which were within the defendant's knowledge, such comment might be legitimate. The nature and strength of such comment was a matter for the judge.
[334] Criminal Law Revision Committee, *Evidence (General)*, Eleventh Report, 1972, Cmnd. 4991, paras. 102–13. [335] Philips, paras. 4.63–7.

> The defendant does not have to give evidence. He is entitled to sit in the dock and require the prosecution to prove its case. You must not assume that he is guilty because he has not given evidence. The fact that he has not given evidence proves nothing one way or the other. It does nothing to establish his guilt. On the other hand, it means that there is no evidence from the defendant to undermine, contradict, or explain the evidence put before you by the prosecution.

Where the defendant did not give evidence, the prosecution could question, and the judge could comment on, the explanation given by counsel but, the Royal Commission said, 'neither the prosecution nor the judge should invite the jury to draw from the defendant's failure to give evidence the inference that his or her explanation is less deserving of being believed'.[336]

The Government, however, rejected the view of the two Royal Commissions and instead implemented the recommendation of the CLRC made in 1972. The Criminal Justice and Public Order Act 1994, s. 35 states that at the trial of someone [. . .][337] at the conclusion of the prosecution's case, the court must:

> Satisfy itself . . . that the accused is aware that the stage has been reached at which evidence can be given for the defence . . . and that, if he chooses not to give evidence, or having been sworn, without good cause refuses to answer any question, it will be permissible for the court or jury to draw such inferences as appear proper from his failure to give evidence or his refusal without good cause to answer any question (s. 35(2)).

The court or jury may draw such inferences as appear proper from the failure to give evidence or refusal to answer questions (s. 35(3)).

The rule does not apply if it appears to the court that 'the physical or mental condition of the accused makes it undesirable for him to give evidence' (s. 35(1)(b)).

A Practice Direction dealt with the procedure to be followed.[338] If the defendant is legally represented and the court is informed that he does not intend to give evidence, the judge should, in the presence of the jury, inquire of the lawyer: 'have you advised your client that the stage has now been reached at which he may give evidence and if he chooses not to do so, or, having been sworn, without good cause refuses to answer any questions, the jury may draw such inferences as appear proper?' If this assurance is given, the case proceeds. If not, the case should briefly be adjourned for that to be done.

If the accused is not legally represented the judge should say to the defendant:

> You have heard the evidence against you. Now is the time for you to make your defence. You may give evidence on oath, and be cross-examined like any other witness. If you do not give evidence, or having been sworn, without good cause refuse to answer any question, the jury may draw such inferences as appear

---

[336] Runciman, p. 56, para. 27.

[337] '[who has attained the age of fourteen years]'. The words in square brackets were removed by the Crime and Disorder Act 1998, s. 35.

[338] *Practice Direction (Crown Court: Evidence: Advice to Defendant)* [1995] 1 WLR 657.

proper. That means they may hold it against you. You may also call any witness or witnesses whom you have arranged to attend court. Afterwards you may also, if you wish, address the jury by arguing your case from the dock, but you cannot at that stage give evidence. Do you now intend to give evidence?

In *Cowan*[339] Lord Chief Justice Taylor, for the Court of Appeal, said there were certain essential matters on which the judge must direct the jury under s. 35, namely:

- The burden of proof remains on the prosecution at all times.
- The defendant is entitled to remain silent.
- An inference from failure to give evidence cannot on its own prove guilt.
- The jury must be satisfied that the prosecution have established a case to answer before drawing an inference from silence.
- The jury may draw an adverse inference if, despite any evidence relied on by the accused to explain his silence or in the absence of such evidence, the jury concludes the silence can only sensibly be attributed to the accused having no answer or none that would stand up to cross-examination.

There needs to be some evidential basis or some exceptional factors in the case to justify the judge NOT permitting the jury to draw an adverse inference from the failure to give evidence.

For the recommended text of the Judicial Studies Board's latest specimen direction for the judge to give to the jury see the JSB's Website – www.jsboard. co.uk – Publications – Bench Books – Specimen Directions No. 39.

Legal professional privilege

As has been seen (pp. 90–93) communications between a client and his legal adviser generally cannot be given in evidence by the lawyer without the permission of the client if they were made either (1) with reference to proceedings in being or then contemplated; or (2) to enable the client to receive, or the lawyer to give, legal advice.

The privilege is that of the client not the lawyer and can only be waived by the client. (There is no equivalent privilege for communications between doctor and patient, priest and penitent or journalist and his source, though, as has been seen (p. 228 above), these categories do now have some immunity under the Police and Criminal Evidence Act with regard to certain pre-trial police searches.) The privilege is intended to promote candour between a client and his lawyers.

In the Police and Criminal Evidence Act 1984 legal professional privilege is defined to include not only communications but also documents and other articles mentioned in or enclosed with privileged communications if the communication was in connection with the giving of legal advice or in connection with or contemplation of legal proceedings and for the purpose of such proceedings (s. 10). It also includes not only communications for these purposes between

---

[339] [1996] QB 373.

the client and the lawyer, but also with third persons such as accountants or others involved in legal advice or legal proceedings.[340]

For the position regarding legal professional privilege in light of the lawyer's obligations to report his client under the Money Laundering Act 2002 see p. 91 above.

Evidence obtained at a 'trial within a trial'

It is a common feature of Crown Court cases that the admissibility of evidence is considered by the judge, usually in the absence of the jury. This is known technically as a *voir dire* or, less formally, as a 'trial within a trial'.

If the accused makes admissions during the *voir dire*, the prosecution cannot give evidence of them once the trial resumes.[341] If, however, the defendant used the *voir dire* to boast of having committed the offences in question or used the occasion to make a political speech, that would be irrelevant to the issue of admissibility and different considerations would apply.

When the trial is in the magistrates' courts, a challenge to the admissibility of a confession cannot easily be conducted in the same way. There is no jury to withdraw while the court makes up its mind on the question of admissibility. On the other hand, it is not satisfactory for the magistrates to consider admissibility at the same time as considering the question of weight and truth. In *F (an infant) v. Chief Constable of Kent*[342] Lord Chief Justice Lane said: 'where matters are being conducted before magistrates, there is no question of a "trial within a trial" because magistrates are judges of both fact and law and determine questions of guilt and innocence', but this does mean that, where a confession is to be challenged, the chances of a fair trial are inevitably greater in the Crown Court than in the magistrates' court.[343]

---

[340] See T.R.S. Allen, 'Legal Privilege and the Principle of Fairness in the Criminal Trial' (1987) *Criminal Law Review*, p. 449.

[341] *R v. Brophy* [1981] 2 All ER 705, HL. B was accused of forty-nine counts of terrorism offences including twelve murders by explosions. There was no evidence against him other than admissions made during interrogations. During the trial within a trial as to their admissibility he said he had been a member of the IRA for years. The trial judge ruled that the statements made in the interrogations were inadmissible. There was therefore no evidence against B on the first forty-eight counts. The forty-ninth count was being a member of the IRA. This was allowed to be proved by the admissions made during the *voir dire*. On appeal, the House of Lords held that this was not proper, even though it had been a voluntary admission in answer to questions from his own counsel. Anything which emerged only at the *voir dire* and was relevant to the *voir dire* could not be admissible at the trial: 'If such evidence, being relevant, were admissible at the substantive trial, an accused person would not enjoy the complete freedom that he ought to have to contest the admissibility of his previous statements' (at p. 709, per Lord Fraser). He would not feel free if what he said at the *voir dire* could be used against him at the trial. See also *Wong Kam-Ming* [1980] AC 247, PC. For a discussion of whether there are any exceptions to the rule either at common law or as a result of the rules on inferences from silence see P. Mirfield, 'Two Side-effects of Sections 34 to 37 of the Criminal Justice and Public Order Act 1994', *Criminal Law Review*, 1995, pp. 612 at 617–24.

[342] [1982] Crim LR 682.

[343] For a discussion of this issue see W.M.S. Tildesley and W.F. Bullock, 'Challenging Confessions in the Magistrates' Courts', 147 *Justice of the Peace*, 16 April 1983, p. 243.

In *R v. Liverpool Juvenile Court, ex p R*[344] it was argued on behalf of the juvenile accused that the *Chief Constable of Kent* case had in effect been displaced by the provisions of s. 76 of the Police and Criminal Evidence Act 1984 which dealt with the admissibility of confessions (see below). The Divisional Court upheld the contention. It ruled that, where the question of the admissibility of a confession is raised by the accused, the magistrates must hold a trial within a trial at which the defendant would be entitled to give and call evidence relating purely to the question of admissibility.[345]

To protect police informers

The courts have for decades recognised the principle that the identity of police informers should, if possible, be kept secret and that surveillance methods should not necessarily become known to the defence. As long ago as 1890 Lord Esher MR referred to the rule protecting the disclosure of the name of an informant as a rule in public prosecutions.[346] In *Rankine*[347] the appellant argued on appeal that his conviction was unsafe and unsatisfactory because he had not been allowed by the trial judge to cross-examine the police witnesses as to the location of the observation point from which they had allegedly seen him repeatedly selling drugs. The Court of Appeal refused to quash the conviction.[348]

However, this principle of public interest exclusion of evidence may have to give way to the even higher principle that the defendant should not be unfairly impeded from establishing his innocence. Thus, in *Brown*[349] the Court of Appeal quashed convictions because the trial judge had refused to allow police officers to be questioned about the details of their surveillance operation.

Note that no equivalent tenderness is shown toward the defendant when his case on appeal is that the jury considered material that should not have been known to them. The principle in such cases is that the Court of Appeal will not permit such a contention to be put.[350]

See generally J.A. Andrews, 'Public Interest and Criminal Proceedings', 104 *Law Quarterly Review*, 1988, pp. 410–21.

Cross-examination of rape victims

At common law a rape victim giving evidence against her alleged attacker could be cross-examined about her sexual past. The purpose of the Sexual Offences (Amendment) Act 1976, s. 2 was to restrict such questions. No such questions could be asked without the leave of the judge and no such questions could be asked about the sexual experience of the complainant with anyone other than the defendant. Moreover the Act provided that the judge should only give such

---

[344] [1987] 2 All ER 668.

[345] For comment see B. Gibson, 'Justices and Trials Within Trials – Yet Again', 151 *Justice of the Peace*, 2 May 1987, p. 275.   [346] *Marks v. Beyfus* (1890) 25 QBD 494.

[347] [1986] QB 861.   [348] See to the same effect *Johnson* [1988] 1 WLR 1377.

[349] (1987) 87 Cr App Rep 52.   [350] See *Thompson*, p. 532 below.

consent if satisfied that it would be unfair to the defendant to refuse to allow the evidence to be adduced.

It was felt that the 1976 Act did not do the job[351] and the Youth Justice and Criminal Evidence Act 1999 returned to the issue.

Section 41 of the 1999 Act provided that evidence or questioning about a complainant's sexual conduct was not admissible as evidence of whether he or she consented to the offence except where the evidence or questions related to acts at or about the time of the incident that was the subject of the charge. Evidence or questioning about sexual behaviour was admissible, however, in relation to whether sex took place or whether the defendant believed his alleged victim consented, provided it related to specific instances of sexual behaviour at or about the time in question and that its main purpose was not to impugn the witness's character.[352]

In *R v. A (No 2)*[353] the House of Lords held that, despite the wording of s. 41, the complainant could be asked questions about her sexual conduct that, if excluded, would endanger the defendant's right to a fair trial under Article 6 of the ECHR. The defendant had been barred by the trial judge from asking questions about their sexual relationship during the three weeks before the alleged rape. The House of Lords upheld the Court of Appeal's decision thereby overturning the trial judge's ruling and Parliament's intention in passing s. 41.[354]

Phone tap evidence

Telephone-tap intercept evidence, even if lawfully obtained in the UK,[355] is inadmissible in a criminal trial.[356] The topic has been much debated in recent years and it is now widely thought that the Government's policy is mistaken. Opposition to a change is based at least partly on the fear that admitting such evidence would lead to the methods used in covert surveillance becoming known to criminals and terrorists. Professor John Spencer has powerfully argued that this is unconvincing.[357] For one thing, if security considerations made it undesirable to use the evidence in a particular case the prosecutors would not use it. If it had to be revealed as unused material (see p. 290 above), that could be done under the special procedure for public interest immunity for such material (p. 297 above). In the final analysis the prosecution could drop the case.

---

[351] See L. Ellison, 'Cross-Examination in Rape Trials', *Criminal Law Review*, 1998, pp. 605–15.

[352] See N. Kibble, 'The Sexual History Provisions: Charting a Course between Inflexible Legislative Rules and Wholly Untrammelled Judicial Discretion', *Criminal Law Review*, 2000, p. 274.

[353] [2002] AC 45, [2001] 3 All ER 1.

[354] For discussion see J. Temkin, 'Sexual History Evidence: Beware the Backlash', *Criminal Law Review*, 2003, p. 217; and D. Birch, 'Untangling Sexual History Evidence: A Rejoinder to Professor Temkin', *Criminal Law Review*, 2003, p. 370.

[355] If it is obtained legally abroad, it is admissible: *R v. P* [2002] 1 AC 146.

[356] The Regulation of Investigatory Powers Act 2000 (RIPA 2000), s. 17. See generally D. Ormerod and S. McKay, 'Telephone Intercepts and their Admissibility', *Criminal Law Review*, 2004, pp. 15–38.

[357] 'Tapping into the Telephones', 155 *New Law Journal*, 4 March 2005, p. 309.

Spencer suggests that at least part of the real reason is that it might expose the Home Secretary's actions to unwelcome scrutiny in the courts. The authorisation of telephone tapping is done not by a judicial person but by the Home Secretary.[358] If such evidence were admissible, the courts would be able to examine the way that he and his officials use the power.

In August 2006 the Joint Parliamentary Human Rights Committee recommended that the ban on intercept evidence be lifted.[359] It said that the DPP strongly supported this view issue The Joint Committee urged that this be dealt with as a matter of urgency. The protection of sources was handled appropriately in other countries and could be handled here too.

In September 2006 the Attorney General, Lord Goldsmith, and the Director of Public Prosecutions, Ken MacDonald QC, both publicly added their voices to support a change in the rule. Both said that they had been convinced by the experience of the US and of Australia that admissibility of intercept evidence was a vital tool in the fight against organised crime and terrorism and that the problems could be handled.[360]

Evidence obtained by improper means

The common law made a distinction between *confessions* that were improperly obtained and other kinds of evidence obtained in regular ways. Broadly, confessions were liable to be excluded, whilst other evidence was normally admitted in evidence.

Confessions

The common law There was a well-established common law rule going back some two hundred years that a confession could not be admitted in evidence if it was 'involuntary', defined to mean obtained as the result of a threat or promise held out by a person in authority.[361]

The rule was expressed in the Judges' Rules, principle (e) of the preamble of which stated: 'it is a fundamental condition of the admissibility in evidence against any person . . . that it shall have been voluntary in the sense that it has

---

[358] Before 1985 the Home Secretary issued warrants without any clear powers to do so. In 1985 the Interception of Communications Act – in response to the Strasbourg Court's decision in *Malone v. United Kingdom* (1984) 7 EHRR 7 – confirmed the Home Secretary as the person responsible for authorisation. That system was perpetuated in the RIPA 2000.

[359] *Counter-Terrorism Policy and Human Rights: Prosecution and Pre-Charge Detention*, 24th Report of Session 2005–6, 1 August 2006, HL 240, HC 1576.

[360] *The Guardian*, 21 and 22 September 2006. The newspaper reported that the move also had the backing of the Association of Chief Police Officers, the Conservative Party and Liberty.

[361] This was held to include a father – see *R v. Moore* (1972) 56 Cr App Rep 373 and *R v. Cleary* (1963) 48 Cr App Rep 116. In *R v. Thompson* (1978) Times, 18 January it was held to include also a social worker who said: 'Do not admit something you have not done but it is always the best policy to be honest. If you were concerned tell him about it and get the matter cleared up for your own sake'. The judge excluded the accused's confession. On the concept of the person in authority see P. Mirfield, 'Confessions – the "Person in Authority" Requirement', *Criminal Law Review*, 1981, p. 92.

not been obtained from him by fear of prejudice or hope of advantage, exercised or held out by a person in authority or by oppression'. An example of the principle being applied was *R v. Smith*, decided in 1959:

R v. Smith [1959] 2 QB 35, Courts Martial Appeal Court

The appellant, a soldier, was charged with the murder by stabbing of a soldier of another regiment during a barrack-room fight. Immediately after the fight the appellant's regimental sergeant-major put his company on parade and indicated that the men would be kept there until he learnt who had been involved in the fighting. At the trial the judge-advocate admitted in evidence a statement made by the appellant to the sergeant-major at that parade, confessing to the stabbing. Evidence was also given of a subsequent confession made the following day to a sergeant of the Special Investigation Branch after a caution had been administered.

Lord Chief Justice Parker, giving the judgment of the court, stated the facts and continued:

The court is quite clear that while there was nothing improper in the action taken by the regimental sergeant-major, the evidence of what took place was clearly inadmissible at the prisoner's trial. What the sergeant-major did might well have been a very useful course of action in order to enable further inquiries to be made, but the court is satisfied that if the only evidence against the prisoner was a confession obtained in those circumstances, it would be quite inadmissible at his trial. It has always been a fundamental principle of the courts, and something quite apart from the Judges' Rules of Practice, that a prisoner's confession outside the court is only admissible if it is voluntary. In deciding whether an admission is voluntary the court has been at pains to hold that even the most gentle, if I may put it in that way, threats or slight inducements will taint a confession. To say to all those on parade, 'You are staying here and are not going to bed until one of you owns up' is in the view of this court clearly a threat. It might also, I suppose, be looked upon as an inducement in that the converse is true, 'If one of you will come forward and own up, the rest of you can go to bed'; but whichever way one looks at it, the court is of the opinion that while the action was perfectly proper and a useful start no doubt to inquiries, evidence in regard thereto was clearly inadmissible.

The court then considered the second confession made by the accused the next morning. It ruled that this was admissible because the effect of the threat or inducement was then spent.

The *Smith* case did not end in the defendant's conviction being quashed. An even more striking case was that of *R v. Zaveckas*[362] because the court there did quash the conviction when it found that the confession had followed an improper promise. The case was even more remarkable in that the promise came as the result of a request from the accused. He was told by the police that an identification parade had been arranged and if he was not picked out he

---

[362] [1970] 1 All ER 413.

would be allowed to go. He asked whether he would be given bail at once if he made a statement. The officer said 'yes' and he then made a statement admitting guilt. The Court of Appeal Criminal Division ruled that the statement should have been held inadmissible because it was an inducement held out by a person in authority. With regret, the court said, it had to quash the conviction. Similarly, in *Northam*[363] the Court of Appeal quashed a conviction based on a confession after the accused had asked a police officer whether it would be possible for a second offence to be taken into consideration at his forthcoming trial rather than being the basis of a later separate trial. The police officer said the police would have no objection. The Court of Appeal said this amounted to a fatal inducement.

The common law objection to the admissibility of confessions obtained through *oppression* appears to be more recent than for confessions obtained by threats or promises. The preamble to the Judges' Rules mentioned 'oppression' as one reason for a confession being found 'involuntary'.[364]

Confessions obtained as a result of threats, promises or oppression were inadmissible in law. Once they were classified in this way the judge had no discretion. Confessions obtained in breach of the Judges' Rules, by contrast, were only inadmissible in the judge's discretion, though it was not easy to get the judges to exercise this discretion. In *Prager* Lord Justice Edmund Davies dealt with the submission by counsel that a statement was inadmissible because the police had not cautioned the defendant before questioning him, even though they plainly had plenty of evidence justifying reasonable suspicion, and that the questioning was therefore in breach of Rule 2 of the Judges' Rules which required a suspect to be cautioned when the police had sufficient admissible evidence reasonably to suspect him. The defendant was taken from his house in the early hours of the morning and on arrival at the police station was questioned at length about complicity in espionage activities. The Court of Appeal refused to hold that the confession should have been excluded.[365]

Pre-PACE changes in the admissibility rules regarding confessions In its 1972 11th Report, the CLRC recommended by a majority that confessions should only be excluded where it was likely that the threat or inducement would produce an unreliable confession. It would be for the judge to imagine that he was present at the questioning and to consider in the light of all the evidence 'whether at the point when the threat was uttered or the inducement offered, any confession which the accused might make as a result of it would be likely to be unreliable'. The proposed test would apply not to the confession actually made but 'to any confession which he might have made in consequence of the threat or inducement' (para. 65). The Committee did not make it clear whether

---

[363] (1967) 52 Cr App Rep 97.

[364] For judicial statements on the subject see for instance *Prager* [1972] 1 WLR 260; *Westlake* [1979] Crim LR 652; *Hudson* [1981] Crim LR 107; *Gowan* [1982] Crim LR 821.

[365] See to same effect *Conway v. Hotten* [1976] 2 All ER 213; *Greaves v. D* [1980] Crim LR 435; *Lam Chi-ming* [1991] AC 212, [1991] 3 All ER 172, PC.

the test should relate to the reasonable defendant in that situation or to the accused himself i.e. whether it should be objective or subjective.

The CLRC's proposal was at first not implemented by legislation but in the period between the CLRC's Report and enactment of the Police and Criminal Evidence Act 1984, the common law changed to come somewhat into line with the approach adopted by the CLRC. This was mainly achieved by two cases. In the first, *DPP v. Ping Lin*,[366] the defendant confessed after the officer in the case had assured him: 'if you show the judge that you have helped the police to trace bigger drug people, I am sure that he will bear it in mind when he sentences you'. The House of Lords upheld the trial judge's decision to allow the confession to be given in evidence. The question of voluntariness, the Law Lords held, was one of fact and causation.

The second case, *Rennie*,[367] went even further. The officer admitted that the defendant confessed in return for a promise from the officer that he would in that event not bring the suspect's sister and mother into the affair. The Court of Appeal upheld the trial judge's decision to admit the confession. Giving judgment, Lord Chief Justice Lane said it was for the court simply to take a common sense view of whether the confession had been of the defendant's own free will. The fact that his confession was induced wholly or in part because he hoped the police would then not charge his mother or his sister did not make it involuntary.

Plainly, the test of whether a confession was voluntary had undergone a sea-change since decisions like *Smith* in 1959 and *Zaveckas* in 1970.

The Philips Royal Commission   The Philips Royal Commission on Criminal Procedure (1981) criticised the common law rule with regard to confessions (as it then stood) on the ground that it was unrealistic. It assumed, first, that suspects in the police station could be free from fear of prejudice or hope of advantage and, secondly, that it was possible to tell to what extent any particular suspect was affected by such fear or hope. Both assumptions, the Commission said, were false. Research conducted for the Commission by Dr Barrie Irving showed that even a trained psychologist present at the questioning of suspects could not tell what pressures were responsible for suspects making statements, but fear of prejudice and hope of advantage were in the very nature of the situation, regardless of what precisely was said or done by the police.[368]

The Commission thought it would be better to abandon the vain attempt to distinguish between voluntary and involuntary confessions and to concentrate instead on the behaviour of the police officer. If the suspect was subjected to torture, violence, the threat of violence or inhuman or degrading treatment, any subsequent confession should be inadmissible. This would mark society's 'abhorrence of such conduct'.[369] Any lesser breach of the rules of questioning should only

---

[366] [1975] 3 All ER 175.   [367] [1982] 1 All ER 385.
[368] Philips, para. 4.73 based on B. Irving, *Police Interrogation: A Case Study of Current Practice* (Royal Commission Research Study No. 2, 1980).   [369] Philips, para. 4.132.

be liable to the consequence that the trial judge would warn the jury of the danger of relying on the resulting confession if there was no independent evidence.[370]

PACE The proposal that the voluntariness test should be abolished met with considerable opposition and the Conservative Government did not accept it. The Police and Criminal Evidence Act instead based its approach on the inadmissibility of any confession obtained as a result of oppression or which was obtained in consequence of something 'likely in the circumstances to render unreliable any confession which might be made by the accused in consequence thereof':

Police and Criminal Evidence Act 1984, s. 76

(1) In any proceedings a confession made by an accused person may be given in evidence against him in so far as it is relevant to any matter in issue in the proceedings and is not excluded by the court in pursuance of this section.

(2) If, in any proceedings where the prosecution proposes to give in evidence a confession made by an accused person, it is represented to the court that the confession was or may have been obtained –

   (a) by oppression of the person who made it; or

   (b) in consequence of anything said or done which was likely, in the circumstances existing at the time, to render unreliable any confession which might be made by him in consequence thereof,

the court shall not allow the confession to be given in evidence against him except in so far as the prosecution proves to the court beyond reasonable doubt that the confession (notwithstanding that it may be true) was not obtained as aforesaid.

Oppression As defined in s. 76(8), oppression 'includes torture, inhuman or degrading treatment, and the use or threat of violence'.

  Various points arise:

- The burden of proof on questions of the admissibility of confessions lies on the prosecution – s. 76(2).
- When any question of the admissibility of a confession arises, it is for the judge to rule as to whether the evidence is admissible and for the jury to decide on whether it is to be believed.[371]
- There is supposed to be a trial within a trial to determine the admissibility of a confession, even in the magistrates' court.[372] Moreover, the Court of Appeal has said *obiter* that the question of its admissibility cannot be considered by the court after the confession has been given in evidence,[373] but this seems questionable.[374]

---

[370] Philips, para. 4.133.

[371] *McCarthy* (1980) 70 Cr App Rep 270; *Ragho Prasad s/o Ram Autar Rao v. R* [1981] 1 All ER 319.   [372] *R v. Liverpool Juvenile Court, ex p R* [1988] QB 1.

[373] *Sat-Bhambra* (1988) 88 Cr App Rep 55, [1988] Crim LR 453.

[374] See Professor J.C. Smith – a comment on the case after the report in the *Criminal Law Review* at p. 454.

- A judge's direction that the jury may rely on a confession if they regard it as true even if it has or may have been made as a result of oppression is incompatible with Article 6 of the ECHR.[375]
- There have hardly been any cases in which the courts have held that there was oppressive conduct by the police. In *Fulling*[376] the Court of Appeal made it clear that oppression would exist only very rarely. It gave the word its meaning in the *Oxford English Dictionary* as: 'the exercise of authority or power in a burdensome, harsh or wrongful manner; unjust or cruel treatment of subjects, inferiors etc; the imposition of unreasonable or unjust burdens'.[377]

In *Beales*[378] the trial judge found that questioning of the suspect for thirty-five minutes(!) 'stepped into the realm' of oppression because the police officer deliberately misled the suspect as to the existence of evidence of the offence, but the judge said that even if the police conduct was not oppressive under s. 76(2)(a) the confession was certainly unreliable under s. 76(2)(b). On the facts of the case it seems unlikely that the Court of Appeal would have upheld the trial judge's finding that there was evidence of oppression.

In *Davison*[379] where there had been a whole series of breaches of the Act and the Codes of Practice, the judge held that the prosecution had failed to discharge the burden of proof on it to show that the confessions in a series of interviews had not been obtained as a result of oppression. He seemed to regard the unlawful detention of the suspect as of prime significance.

In the case of Timothy West in 1988, the trial judge held that police had been oppressive in constantly interrupting the defendant, shouting at him, using foul language to indicate that he was lying and making it clear that they would continue questioning him until he confessed.

In *Paris, Abdullahi and Miller*[380] (known as the case of the 'Cardiff Three'), the Lord Chief Justice in the Court of Appeal said the court had been horrified by the hectoring and bullying manner of the police questioning of Miller who denied the murder charge over 300 times over some thirteen hours before making admissions. ('Short of physical violence, it is hard to conceive a more hostile and intimidating approach to a suspect. It is impossible to convey on the printed page the pace, force and menace of the officer's delivery'.) The Court of Appeal quashed all three convictions after they had served four years' imprisonment. (Eleven years later, after testing of DNA evidence that had been overlooked at the time of the original investigation, the real murderer was identified and convicted.)

In the George Heron case in November 1993, Mitchell J ruled that confessions and admissions to the murder of a seven-year-old girl were inadmissible because

---

[375] *Mushtaq* [2005] UKHL 25, [2005] 3 All ER 885. For a question as to which institutions would be trusted see [2006] Crim LR 834.   [376] [1987] QB 426.

[377] For an elegant essay in the form of a Socratic dialogue on the meaning of oppression see R. Munday, 'The Court, the Dictionary, and the True Meaning of "Oppression": A Neo-Socratic Dialogue on English Legal Method', 26 *Statute Law Review*, 2005, pp. 103–24.

[378] [1991] Crim LR 118.   [379] [1988] Crim LR 442.   [380] (1992) 97 Cr App Rep 99.

they had been obtained by oppression. The questioning had been conducted without any hectoring or shouting, but the judge held that oppression existed in falsely telling the accused that he had been identified, in pounding him with being a killer and with sexual motives for the killing and in telling him that it was in his interest to tell the truth when it had been made clear that the police regarded the truth to be that he had done the killing. The police had been engaged in breaking the defendant's resolve to make no admissions.

It is worthy of note that in both the Cardiff Three case and the George Heron case the suspect had had his legal adviser present throughout the interviews.

Unreliability The formula adopted in s. 76(2)(b) (p. 474 above) was effectively that recommended by the CLRC in its 1972 Report. The fact that the new test abandoned the previous law as reflected in decisions like *Zaveckas* (p. 471 above) is confirmed by the provision in PACE Code C that if a suspect asks an officer what action will be taken by the police if the person being questioned answers questions, makes a statement or refuses to do either, the officer may inform him what action he proposes to take in that event provided that the action is itself proper and warranted (Code C, para. 11.5). But officers are still admonished not to indicate 'except in answer to a direct question' what action will be taken if the person being interviewed answers questions, makes a statement or refuses to do either (*ibid*).

The issue of reliability of confessions has given rise to a number of different points:

- The words 'in consequence of anything said or done' mean said or done by someone other than the suspect.[381]
- The test of 'likely in the circumstances existing at the time' is objective and hypothetical. It is not what the officer thought was the suspect's mental state but what it actually was.[382] The circumstances existing at the time can include the fact that the suspect had a very low IQ or was very suggestible.[383] Also the truth or otherwise of the confession does not come into the question.
- Although the words of the subsection seem to require a causal link between what was said and done in fact, in some of the cases the courts have found a confession to be unreliable where there was no such link. The courts have treated breaches of the Code as sufficient to establish unreliability even without any evidence that the breaches led directly to the admissions or confession.[384]

---

[381] *Goldenberg* [1988] Crim LR 678.   [382] *Everett* [1988] Crim LR 826.

[383] *Silcott, Braithwaite and Raghip* (1991) Times, 9 December; *McKenzie* (1992) 96 Cr App Rep 98, CA.

[384] See for instance *DPP v. Blake* [1989] 1 WLR 432 and *Doolan* [1988] Crim LR 747. The latter was an especially striking case since some of the breaches considered relevant by the court occurred *after* the confession.

Examples of things said or done which have been held to constitute grounds for holding a confession to be unreliable include: an offer of bail,[385] minimising the significance of a serious (sex) offence and suggesting that psychiatric help might be appropriate,[386] saying to a defendant who has previously denied the offence, 'Do I gather that you are now admitting the offence?',[387] falsely telling the suspect that his voice has been recognised on tape,[388] falsely telling the suspect that he has been identified by a witness[389] and indicating that the suspect will have to stay in the police station until the matter is cleared up.[390]

Examples of things *not* said or done which have been held to be grounds for holding a confession to be unreliable include: failure to obtain a solicitor,[391] breaches in the provisions of Code C[392] or failure to see that the suspect has an appropriate adult,[393] but such grounds will not *necessarily* result in a confession being held to be inadmissible.[394]

Runciman Royal Commission The Runciman Commission, by a majority of eight to three, rejected the suggestion that a confession should only be admissible if corroborated, but it recommended that the judge should be required to give the jury a warning, adapted to the circumstances of the case similar to that in identification cases, about the dangers of relying on an uncorroborated confession.[395]

For further reading on confession evidence see: D.J. Birch, 'The PACE Hots Up: Confessions and Confusions under the 1984 Act', *Criminal Law Review*, 1985, p. 95 and 'The Evidence Provisions', *Northern Ireland Legal Quarterly*, 1989, p. 411; I. Dennis, 'Miscarriages of Justice and the Law of Confessions: Evidentiary Issues and Solutions', *Public Law*, 1993, pp. 291–313; I.H. Dennis, *The Law of Evidence* (3rd revised edn, Sweet and Maxwell, 2006) Ch. 6; M. Zander, *The Police and Criminal Evidence Act 1984* (5th edn, Sweet and Maxwell, 2005 and First Supplement, 2006) pp. 341–60.

Evidence, including confessions, illegally or improperly obtained

Whereas the common law historically took a strict view of the admissibility of confession evidence, its approach to other evidence was different. Until 1979 the rule was that the courts had a discretion as to whether such evidence should be admitted. There were many cases in which this proposition had been stated. The origin of the doctrine was a *dictum* of Lord Chief Justice Goddard, giving the judgment of the Privy Council in *Kuruma, Son of Kaniu v. R*: 'No doubt in a criminal case the judge always has a discretion to disallow evidence if the strict rules of admissibility would operate unfairly against the accused . . . If, for

---

[385] *Barry* (1991) 95 Cr App Rep 384, CA.   [386] *Delaney* (1988) 88 Cr App Rep 338, CA.
[387] *Waters* [1989] Crim LR 62, CA.   [388] *Blake* [1989] 1 WLR 432.
[389] *Heron*, p. 475 above.   [390] *Jasper* (24 April 1994, unreported), CA.
[391] *McGovern* (1990) 92 Cr App Rep 228, CA; *Chung* (1990) 92 Cr App Rep 314, CA.
[392] *Delaney* (1988) 88 Cr App Rep 338, CA; *Doolan* (1991) 12 Cr App Rep (S) 634, CA.
[393] *Everett* [1988] Crim LR 826; *Moss* (1990) 91 Cr App Rep 371, CA.
[394] *Waters* [1989] Crim LR 62; *Maguire* (1989) 90 Cr App Rep 115, CA.
[395] Runciman, p. 68, para. 87.

instance, some admission of some piece of evidence, e.g. a document, had been obtained from a defendant by a trick, no doubt the judge might properly rule it out'.[396] See also *Jeffrey v. Black*[397] in which Lord Chief Justice Widgery said that the discretion, though not often exercised, certainly existed: 'But if the case is exceptional, if the case is such that not only have the police officers entered without authority, but they have been guilty of trickery or they have misled someone, or they have been oppressive or they have been unfair, or in other respects they have behaved in a manner which is morally reprehensible, then it is open to the justices to apply their discretion and decline to allow the particular evidence to be let in as part of the trial'. But there were few cases in which the discretion was exercised.

In 1980 in *Sang*[398] the House of Lords either abolished the discretion or at least drastically curtailed it. The case concerned a defence of entrapment – the defendant claimed that he had been induced to commit the offence by an informer acting on the instructions of the police. All the judges in the House of Lords ruled that there was no such defence as entrapment in English law, but they went on to consider the more general question whether a judge had a discretion to exclude relevant evidence. They ruled, again unanimously, that (save for confessions or evidence tantamount to a confession) no discretion existed to exclude evidence simply on the ground that it had been illegally or improperly obtained! Such illegality might be a factor to be taken into account in sentencing or might be the basis for civil proceedings or disciplinary action against the police. The only basis for excluding relevant evidence was where its effect would be unduly prejudicial – for example, evidence of previous similar acts[399] – or where it would be unfair to admit it, but unfairness could not be shown merely by the fact that the evidence had been illegally obtained. In fact the nature of 'unfairness' that would entitle the judge to exclude evidence in his discretion is obscure. Lord Scarman, for instance, said that each case must depend on its circumstances: 'All I would say is that the principle of fairness, though concerned exclusively with the use of evidence at trial, is not susceptible to categorisation or classification, and is wide enough in some circumstances to embrace the way in which, after the crime, evidence has been obtained from the accused'.[400]

The Philips Royal Commission The Royal Commission on Criminal Procedure recommended that the admissibility of improperly obtained evidence other than confessions be substantially confirmed. It did not accept the view that illegally

---

[396] [1955] AC 197 at 204.   [397] [1978] 1 All ER 555.

[398] [1980] AC 402, [1979] 2 All ER 1222. For comment on *Sang* see J.D. Jackson, 'Unfairness and the Judicial Discretion to Exclude Evidence', *New Law Journal*, 1980, p. 585. See generally J.D. Heydon, 'Illegally Obtained Evidence', *Criminal Law Review*, 1973, p. 690 and A.J. Ashworth, 'Excluding Evidence as Protecting Rights', *Criminal Law Review*, 1977, p. 723.

[399] As in *Noor Mohamed v. R* [1949] AC 182 or *Harris v. DPP* [1952] AC 694.

[400] [1979] 2 All ER 1222 at 1247.

or improperly obtained evidence should basically be excluded, as it is in the United States under the doctrine of 'the fruit of the poisoned tree'.[401]

The Commission said it was not appropriate to use the rules as to the admissibility of evidence to discipline the police or to discourage police malpractice. First, it could only affect the small minority of cases where the defendant pleaded not guilty and would therefore not discourage improper behaviour by the police in the majority of cases. Secondly, the challenge on admissibility would be so distant in time from the moment of the improper conduct as not to be an effective deterrent. Experience in the United States suggested that it was not effective as a deterrent to misconduct by the police. The proper way to deter or to deal with misconduct by the police was through police disciplinary and supervisory procedures, civil actions for damages and the machinery of complaints against the police.[402]

The Commission equally did not favour the 'reverse onus' exclusionary rule recommended by the Australian Law Reform Commission, under which improperly obtained evidence is inadmissible unless the prosecution can satisfy the judge that there was some special reason why the impropriety should be condoned. Such a rule, the Commission said, would be difficult to administer in a uniform way. It would not reduce trials within trials. The fact that the judge had a discretion would weaken the deterrent effect on the police.

PACE The Government adopted a different approach from that proposed by the Royal Commission. At a very late stage of the Bill it introduced an expanded version of the common law discretion. This became s. 78, which has been by far the most frequently used section of the Act:

> 78. (1) In any proceedings the court may refuse to allow evidence on which the prosecution proposes to rely to be given if it appears to the court that, having regard to all the circumstances, including the circumstances in which the evidence was obtained, the admission of the evidence would have such an adverse effect on the fairness of the proceedings that the court ought not to admit it.
>
> (2) Nothing in this section shall prejudice any rule of law requiring a court to exclude evidence.

The impact of s. 78 has been remarkable. Contrary to what most commentators expected, the judges have forged the somewhat ambiguous words of the section

---

[401] The Royal Commission's Report attracted severe criticism from some quarters for its failure to recommend an exclusionary rule– see for instance J. Driscoll, 'Excluding Illegally Obtained Evidence – Can We Learn from the United States?', *Legal Action Group Bulletin*, June 1981, p. 131. See also by same author, 'Excluding Illegally Obtained Evidence in the United States', *Criminal Law Review*, 1987, p. 553. The US rule is in the process of development. In *US v. Patane* 542 US 630 (2004) the Supreme Court held that where the fruit of a voluntary statement is physical evidence (in that case a gun), the fact that the suspect had not been cautioned (in that case because the suspect said he knew his rights) did not mean that the evidence (of the gun) had to be excluded. The privilege against self-incrimination was not engaged, the court said, since the evidence was the gun not his voluntary statement that he had a gun in the house.   [402] Philips, paras. 4.123–8.

into a powerful weapon to hold the police accountable for breaches of the law and of the Codes of Practice.

The most common basis for the Court of Appeal to apply s. 78 has been 'significant and substantial' breaches of the PACE rules. The cases concern (1) breaches of the Act and or the Codes such as failure to tell the suspect (D) his rights, not giving D access to a solicitor, not cautioning D, not providing an appropriate adult, not complying with the formalities regarding interviews and not complying with identification procedures; and (2) obtaining evidence by tricks, undercover police work and the like.[403]

The Court of Appeal has repeatedly said that each case must be decided on its own facts. It has refused to lay down guidelines as to how the discretion under s. 78 should be exercised. The decision to exclude evidence is not taken to penalise the police.[404] In order to succeed under s. 78 the defence has to establish that a significant and substantial breach of the rules or other impropriety has occurred, which affects the fairness of the proceedings and which is sufficiently serious to require that the court excludes the evidence. In *Walsh*[405] the Court of Appeal said: 'The task of the court is not merely to consider whether there would be an adverse effect on the fairness of the proceedings, but such an adverse effect that justice requires the evidence to be excluded'.[406]

There are now a very large number of decisions interpreting and applying s. 78. Reviewing this mass of case law for the 2005 edition of his book on PACE the writer expressed his impression:[407]

> Not that the courts have articulated a consistent and all-embracing theory for the application of s. 78. Various principles explaining the exercise of the discretion to exclude evidence have been suggested by academic commentators. These include the Reliability principle (to promote the reliability of evidence), the Disciplinary principle (to penalise the police for breaches of the rules as a way of promoting adherence to the rules), and the Protective principle (to protect the accused).[408] Many cases could be said to fall within those broad approaches – but there is little or no sign that the judges themselves deal with the problems in that way. The evidence from the cases is to the contrary.[409]

---

[403] For references to the actual cases see for instance the writer's book, *The Police and Criminal Evidence Act 1984* (5th edn, 2005) pp. 368–76.

[404] See for instance *R v. Delaney* (1988) 88 Cr App Rep 338, CA.

[405] (1989) 91 Cr App Rep 161.

[406] For the view that the courts tend to exercise the discretion in s. 78 against professional criminals see M. Doherty, 'Judicial Discretion: Victimising the Villains?', 3 *International Journal of Evidence and Proof*, 1999, pp. 44–56.

[407] M. Zander, *The Police and Criminal Evidence Act 1984* (5th edn, 2003, Sweet & Maxwell) paras. 8–61–2.

[408] See A. Ashworth and M. Redmayne, *The Criminal Process* (3rd edn, Clarendon Press, 2005) pp. 314–32; and P. Roberts and A.A.S. Zuckerman, *The Principles of Criminal Evidence* (3rd edn, Oxford, 2005) pp. 147–75.

[409] See M. Hunter, 'Judicial Discretion: Section 78 in Practice', *Criminal Law Review*, 1994, p. 558 reporting on an empirical study in Leeds Crown Court. The judges she interviewed were unanimous in rejecting the idea that they considered any of these theoretical principles when

The writer believes rather that s. 78 has become established and accepted as a means for the courts to determine what breaches of the rules or improper conduct are unacceptable on a case by case basis without any clearly articulated theory. Usually, even when there has been some breach or impropriety, the court allows the evidence in and even when it finds there to have been impropriety, the Court of Appeal usually ends by dismissing the appeal, but there have also been many cases, including non-confession cases, in which the appeal court has quashed a conviction because of such improprieties. In the great majority of such cases the court's chief concern seems to be that the verdict should be based on reliable evidence, but sometimes, the court is expressing a more fundamental concern directed not so much to the result in the particular case as to a view that the system demands a minimum of procedural correctness and moral integrity.[410]

To some extent the decisions of the courts applying s. 78 can be systematised. Certain basic distinctions have emerged, but there remains (and will always remain) a significant and irreducible degree of discretion left to the court . . . Professor Diane Birch, writing about the entrapment cases, has suggested that 'the more principled the discretion can be said to be, and the more its underlying aims can be articulated, the more consistent will be the decisions made under it'.[411] She cites another academic view of the need to avoid the 'mushiness and unpredictability of a general doctrine of exclusion for "unfairness"'.[412] Consistency in the application of a discretion to exclude evidence on the grounds of unfairness may be desirable but in the end it is unattainable.

Evidence obtained by torture In December 2005, the House of Lords, in a case heard by seven law lords, held unanimously that evidence of any kind obtained by torture is inadmissible in judicial proceedings regardless of whether the torture was conducted by British or by foreign agents.[413] The Special Immigration Appeals Commission had held that the fact that evidence had been, or might have been, procured by torture inflicted by foreign agents, provided it was without the complicity of the British authorities, did not make it legally inadmissible. The Court of Appeal by a majority of two to one, upheld the decision. Each of the law lords wrote an opinion rejecting the Court of Appeal's view.[414] They relied primarily on the common law, though Lord Bingham also based himself on international law as taken into account by the ECHR.[415]

deciding whether to exclude disputed evidence. The writer cannot say that he is surprised at this finding which would probably be equally true of the Court of Appeal.

[410] See further I.H. Dennis, 'Reconstructing the Law of Criminal Evidence', 42 *Current Legal Problems*, 1989, p. 21 and A.A.S. Zuckerman, 'Illegally Obtained Evidence: Discretion as a Guardian of Legitimacy', 40 *Current Legal Problems*, 1987, p. 55.

[411] 'Excluding Evidence from Entrapment: What is a "Fair Cop"?', 73 *Current Legal Problems*, 1994, p. 89.

[412] J.D. Heydon, 'Entrapment and Unfairly Obtained Evidence in the House of Lords', *Criminal Law Review*, 1980, p. 134.

[413] *A v Secretary of State for the Home Department (No 2)* [2005] UKHL 71, [2006] 1 All ER 575.

[414] In the All England Law Reports, the judgments run to 63 pages.   [415] At [52].

However, their lordships were not prepared to extend the common law exclusionary rule to evidence obtained as a result of inhuman or degrading treatment.

Also, they recognised that although the courts could not take evidence procured by torture into account, the executive in the person of the Home Secretary could do so when deciding whether to impose control orders on terrorism suspects.[416]

Irregularly obtained real evidence in Scotland In the leading case of *Lawrie v. Muir* decided in 1950 by a full bench of the High Court of Justiciary, Lord Cooper stated that whether irregularly obtained real evidence should be admitted must be determined according to the balance between the need to preserve civil liberties and the need to ensure that justice is done.[417] Until then, in Scotland, real evidence which had been obtained irregularly was always in practice admitted. Tracing the history of this doctrine since 1950 Professor Peter Duff wrote:[418]

> Unfortunately, for a number of reasons, no clear framework has evolved to guide judges in this task. First, the various, traditional rationales for excluding improperly obtained evidence have all frequently been cited: the 'reliability principle' (i.e. ensuring the reliability of the evidence); the 'disciplinary principle' (i.e. controlling the police and prosecution authorities); the 'vindicatory principle' (i.e protecting or vindicating the rights of the accused). As is the situation elsewhere, it is not clear which of these rationales motivates the decisions of the Scottish courts and this has led to inconsistencies in the application of the law. As we shall see, in one case the court will cite one of these three principles, leading to a particular result, and in another similar case the court will cite another, leading to a different result . . .
>
> Secondly, and to some degree related to the first reason, there is some confusion as to what factors are relevant in determining whether evidence should be admitted and the weight to be attributed to these. Among the issues which have been taken into account by the Scottish courts are: the gravity of the crime; the extent of the irregularity; the urgency of the investigation; the need to preserve evidence; the authority and identity of those who obtained the evidence; the motive of those responsible for the impropriety; the extent of the infringement of the accused's rights; and the issue of fairness to the accused. The judiciary has tended to 'pick and mix' from this list, sometimes being heavily influenced by a particular factor and on other occasions, dismissing the same factor as of no account. This has led to considerable inconsistency and uncertainty in the law.

(One difference between the English and the Scottish position is that whereas s. 78 explicitly gives the judge a discretion, in Scotland the judge technically has

---

[416] For the suggestion that the reasoning in the judgment is not as solid as one might wish see N. Rasiah, 'A v Secretary of State for the Home Department (No 2): Occupying the Moral High Ground', 69 *Modern Law Review*, 2006, pp. 991–5.

[417] 1950 JC 19 at 26.

[418] P. Duff, 'Irregularly Obtained Real Evidence: The Scottish Solution?', 8 *International Journal of Evidence and Proof*, 2004, p. 77 at 78–9.

no discretion. The admissibility question is treated as a matter of law. In England the appeal court is reluctant to interfere with the trial judge's exercise of discretion. In Scotland, Professor Duff says, the appeal court is ready to 'fine-tune' decisions on admissibility reached below.)

Exclusion of improperly obtained evidence in New Zealand[419] In 1992, the New Zealand Court of Appeal created a rule for the exclusion of evidence obtained in breach of New Zealand's Bill of Rights Act 1990.[420] The rule provided that such evidence was presumed to be inadmissible unless the prosecution was able to persuade the court otherwise.[421] In practice, once a breach was established the evidence was normally excluded. However, this *prima facie* exclusionary rule did not last long. In 2002, in *Shaheed*[422] the Court of Appeal, sitting with seven judges, abolished the rule it had created only ten years earlier. Six of the seven judges decided that exclusion should instead be based on a balancing of different factors similar to the discretion to exclude evidence on the basis of unfairness which applied in non-Bill of Rights cases. The balancing of a variety of factors is what operates explicitly in Scotland and implicitly in England under s. 78.

See also I.H. Dennis, *The Law of Evidence* (3rd revised edn, Sweet and Maxwell, 2006) Ch. 8.

The ECHR and the fairness of trials

In *Khan (Sultan) v. United Kingdom*[423] the European Court of Human Rights held that although there had been breaches of Articles 8 and 13 of the Convention, the defendant had not been deprived of his right to a fair trial under Article 6(1) of the Convention. The case concerned reception of evidence from a listening device installed on his home by the police.[424] The Strasbourg Court reached the same decision in *PG and JH v. United Kingdom*[425] which concerned covert listening devices both at the suspects' home and at the police station. The House of Lords adopted the same approach in *Sultan Khan*[426] and *P.*[427] In both it held that the question whether the trial was fair should be judged by application of s. 78.

Further reading A. Ashworth, 'Article 6 and the Fairness of Trials', *Criminal Law Review*, 1999, pp. 261–72; Sir Robert Walker, 'The Impact of European

---

[419] See R. Mahoney, 'Abolition of New Zealand's *Prima Facie* Exclusionary Rule', *Criminal Law Review*, 2003, pp. 607–17.

[420] *Butcher* [1992] 2 NZLR 257; *Kirifi* [1992] 2 NZLR 8.

[421] For the argument that the English system should adopt the same rule for evidence obtained in breach of the ECHR see D. Ormerod, 'ECHR and the Exclusion of Evidence: Trial Remedies for Article 8 Breaches?', *Criminal Law Review*, 2003, p. 61.

[422] [2002] 2 NZLR 377, CA.   [423] (2000) 31 EHRR 1016, [2000] Crim LR 684.

[424] For critical comment see Professor Ashworth's commentary in the *Criminal Law Review*, 2000 at pp. 684–86.   [425] [2002] Crim LR 308.   [426] [1997] AC 558.

[427] [2001] 1 AC 146, HL.

Standards on the Right to a Fair Trial in Civil Proceedings in United Kingdom
Domestic Law', *European Human Rights Law Review*, 1999, pp. 4–14; F.G.
Jacobs, 'The Right to a Fair Trial in European Law', *European Human Rights Law
Review*, 1999, pp. 141–56.

For fuller treatment see especially B. Emmerson and A. Ashworth, *Human
Rights and Criminal Justice* (2nd edn, Sweet and Maxwell, 2006).

Abuse of process

The court can stop a case under the separate common law doctrine known as
'abuse of process' if it regards it contrary to the public interest to permit it to
continue.[428] In *R v. Horseferry Road Magistrates' Court, ex p Bennett*[429] the
House of Lords ruled that a stay was appropriate where B had been forcibly
abducted and brought to this country to face trial for false pretences in disregard of extradition laws. Lord Griffiths said that the judiciary should not 'countenance behaviour that threatens either human rights or the rule of law' and
that if a serious abuse of power has occurred the court 'should express its disapproval by refusing to act upon it'.[430] The same doctrine was applied in 2005
by the Court of Appeal in *Grant*[431] when it stayed a case for conspiracy to
murder[432] because the police had deliberately eavesdropped upon and tape
recorded privileged conversations between the defendant and his solicitor. The
case is the more striking in that the taped conversations did not produce any
material of assistance to the prosecution. The mere fact of the eavesdropping
was so serious an abuse of process as to require the quashing of the murder
conviction.

In *Shahzad*[433] by contrast, the House of Lords refused to apply the doctrine
in a case where S was lured by a customs officer to come to this country to collect
a shipment of heroin S had sent here. ('The conduct of the customs officer was
not so unworthy or shameful that it was an affront to the public conscience to
allow the prosecution to proceed'.[434]) In a speech, with which the other four
Law Lords agreed, Lord Steyn said:

> The speeches in *Bennett* conclusively establish that proceedings may be stayed
> in the exercise of the judge's discretion not only where a fair trial is impossible,
> but also where it would be contrary to the public interest in the integrity of the
> criminal justice system that a trial should take place. An infinite variety of cases
> could arise. General guidance as to how the discretion should be exercised in
> particular circumstances will not be useful, but it is possible to say that in a case
> such as the present the judge must weigh in the balance the public interest in
> ensuring that those who are charged with grave crimes should be tried and the

---

[428] For application of abuse of process in the context of delay see pp. 255, 368–69 above.

[429] [1994] AC 42, [1993] 3 All ER 138.   [430] [1994] AC 42 at 62.

[431] [2005] EWCA 1089, [2005] Crim LR 955.

[432] The prosecution's case was that G had recruited a gunman to kill his wife's lover.

[433] [1996] 1 All ER 353.   [434] Per Lord Steyn at 361.

competing public interest in not conveying the impression that the court will adopt the approach that the end justifies any means.[435]

See further M. Mackarel and C. Gane, 'Admitting Irregularly or Illegally Obtained Evidence from Abroad into Criminal Proceedings – a Common Law Approach', *Criminal Law Review*, 1997, pp. 721–9. The authors criticise the laxity of common law courts in the United States, Canada, Australia and the UK for their failure to apply the standard set by the House of Lords in *Bennett*. Lord Steyn in *Shahzad* said that the court had to undertake a balancing exercise. Mackarel and Gane suggest that 'the balance has been tipping heavily in favour of the requirements of effective crime control, to the extent that the irregular and illegal activities of law enforcement agencies are considered to have little bearing on the fairness or the propriety of any subsequent trial'.[436]

See generally D. Corker and D. Young, *Abuse of Process and Fairness in Criminal Proceedings* (Butterworths, 2002).

[435] *Ibid.*   [436] At p. 728.

Chapter 5

The jury

1. The origins of the jury system

The original concept of the jury was precisely the opposite of what it later became. The members of the jury were chosen as persons who were likely to know what had happened or, if not, they were supposed to find out before the trial. In the thirteenth century it was 'the duty of the jurors, so soon as they have been summoned, to make inquiries about the facts of which they will have to speak when they come before the court. They must collect testimony; they must weigh it and state the net result in a verdict'.[1] Medieval juries came more to speak than to listen.

The transformation of the medieval active jury into the passive courtroom triers of fact is not well understood either in its timing or its causes. Probably in the later fifteenth century, but certainly by the sixteenth, it had become expected that the jury would be ignorant of the facts of the case.

2. Eligibility for jury service

Until 1974 eligibility for jury service was governed largely by wholly out-of-date property qualifications. This was the subject of inquiry by the Morris Committee, which reported in 1965 and whose report was implemented by the Juries Act 1974.

Composition of the jury list

> ***Report of the (Morris) Departmental Committee on Jury Service,* 1965, Cmnd. 2627, paras. 38–42**
> 38. Under the present qualifications eligibility is in practice confined to 'householders'. In general, this is taken to mean the person who is liable to pay the rates in respect of separately rated accommodation. In most families this is the husband (which is why, as will be seen later, only a relatively small proportion of jurors are women).

---

[1] F. Pollock and F.W. Maitland, *The History of English Law* (2nd edn, 1898) pp. 624–5. See also Miriam Peck, 'Origins and History of Trial by Jury' in *Fraud (Trials Without a Jury) Bill 2006–07*, House of Commons, Research Paper 06/57, 23 November 2006, pp. 36–39.

39. Another restriction on the householder's eligibility is that his premises must be rated at not less than £30 in the counties of London and Middlesex and not less than £20 elsewhere. At the time the Juries Act 1825 was passed, there must have been relatively few houses with the necessary rateable value. Successive revaluations have enormously increased the number of houses rated at the qualifying value, and we were informed by the Government Social Survey that 81 per cent of domestic hereditaments in England and Wales are at present rated at £30 or more; no figure is readily available for those rated at £20 or more, but we have been told that for the country as a whole the proportion excluded by the rateable value limitation is now unlikely to exceed 10 per cent . . .

42. It is estimated that there are 7.15 million names marked as eligible for jury service on the 1964 electoral registers for England and Wales, which is 22.5 per cent of the 31.77 million names on the registers.

The Morris Committee recommended that, subject to certain exempted categories, juries ought to be selected from all those on the electoral register. This was eventually implemented in the Juries Act 1974. Under this Act a person is eligible for jury service who is between eighteen and seventy,[2] on the register of electors[3] and has been resident in the UK for at least five years since the age of thirteen.

Those ineligible, disqualified or excused

Certain persons, however, have been 'ineligible', 'disqualified' or 'excused'. Those *ineligible* were mainly persons who it was thought would exercise undue influence in the jury room by virtue of their professional knowledge about the justice business – judges, lawyers, other fee earners in solicitors' offices, court staff, police officers, prison officers, probation officers and the like.[4]

The list of those ineligible also includes clergymen of any religious denomination on the ground that they might exert undue influence in the jury room by virtue of their office. The Runciman Royal Commission on Criminal Justice recommended that this last category of exclusion from jury service be abolished. ('We do not see why clergymen and members of religious orders should not be eligible for jury service'.[5])

[2] Until 1988 the age limit was sixty-five but the Criminal Justice Act 1988, s. 119 provided that a person who is between sixty-five and seventy is eligible though he cannot be required to serve.
[3] Lord Justice Auld's report (Ch. 5, para. 23, p. 144) recommended that this should be broadened to include persons on other specified publicly maintained lists or directories, for instance, by the Driver and Vehicle Licensing Authority, the Department for Work and Pensions, the Inland Revenue and telephone directories. The proposal was intended to address the finding of Home Office research that close to 10 per cent of those eligible to register on the electoral roll are not registered. This proposal was not adopted by the Government.
[4] In *R v. Salt* [1996] Crim LR 517 the Court of Appeal quashed the conviction when the supervising usher in the court, not for the first time, contacted his son when there were insufficient numbers to serve on a jury. The court held that the selection of the son of an usher who regularly attended as a juror fell within the spirit of the disqualification in Sch. 1 of the Juries Act.   [5] Runciman, p. 132, para. 57.

Lord Justice Auld took a much more radical approach. He urged that we follow the example of several American states of abolishing this form of ineligibility. ('In my view, no one should be automatically ineligible or excusable from jury service simply because he or she is a member of a certain profession or holds a particular office or job'.[6])

This recommendation was adopted in the Criminal Justice Act 2003. Schedule 33 of the Act removes the status of 'ineligibility' for jury service except for persons who are 'mentally disordered'[7] or disqualified. Those eligible for jury service therefore now include judges, lawyers and police officers![8] Anyone who previously was ineligible who does not wish to serve must now apply for excusal or deferral (on which see below).

The Bar Council issued advice to barristers as to how they should act as jurors:

> If selected to serve on a jury, it is axiomatic that a member of the Bar does so as part of his/her duty as a private citizen. It is neither necessary or appropriate to conceal his/her profession from other jurors, but it is not necessary to volunteer such information immediately. Members of the Bar should expect to be treated as equal members of the jury, and should insist that they are not accorded any special status.
>
> The most important thing for barristers to note is that they are sitting on the jury as part of the tribunal of fact, and not in their capacity as barristers.
>
> Where a jury is required to leave court during the trial, a member of the Bar on the jury should not offer any explanation as to the reason, and should not give any explanation beyond what the judge has told the jury, even if asked.
>
> A member of the Bar should not express any advice or opinion as to the law, or as to any direction of law given by the judge, any time. A barrister may, like any other jury member, send a note to the judge asking any relevant question of fact or law. However, also like every other member of the jury, he must accept that it is for the judge, not the jury, to decide issues of law. The barrister must, therefore, accept the judge's directions as to any issue of the law, even if he considers it to be incorrect.[9]

Guidance issued to solicitors was in virtually identical terms.[10] Judges received guidance in the form of a letter from the Lord Chief Justice.[11] It warns that judges acting as jurors should 'avoid the temptation to correct guidance [from the trial judge] they perceive to be inaccurate as this is outside the scope of their role as jurors', but nothing in the guidance, it states, 'detracts from the ability of judges sitting as jurors to bring their general knowledge of life to bear on the deliberations of the jury'.

---

[6] Auld, Ch. 5, para. 14, p. 140.

[7] Defined in new Sch. 1, Part 1 of the Juries Act 1974 inserted by Sch. 33, para. 15 of the Act.

[8] In *Abdroikov* [2005] EWCA Crim 1986, [2005] 4 All ER 869 the Court of Appeal held that having a police officer or a CPS employee on the jury did not in itself offend the principles of fairness.   [9] *Counsel*, August 2004, p. iv.

[10] www.lawsociety.org.uk – search – jury service – 29 September 2005.

[11] For the text see the judiciary Website – www.judiciary.gov.uk – search – jury service – 15 June 2004.

Disqualified The Juries Act 1974 (Sch. 1, Part 2) has a list of categories of persons disqualified from jury service by reason of their criminal convictions. Lord Justice Auld did not propose any change in this category of exclusion from jury service but the Criminal Justice Act 2003 brings the list up to date.[12]

The Runciman Royal Commission[13] said that research might show that 'contrary to general belief, the role played by jurors with prior criminal convictions is indistinguishable from the role played by any other category of juror'. It recommended that s. 8 of the Contempt of Court Act be amended to permit research on juries to be done. This has not been implemented. (On the issue of such research, see p. 513 below.)

In *R v. Mason*[14] the Court of Appeal held that it was lawful for the police to scrutinise jury panels. If names showed up with disqualifying criminal convictions the information could be passed to prosecuting counsel who could eliminate such people from a case by using the procedure known as 'stand by for the Crown' – see p. 498 below.[15] In 1987 the Home Secretary announced that the police would in future make random checks of would-be jurors to see whether any were disqualified. An unpublished Home Office study had shown that one in every twenty-four juries had on it a disqualified person. The checks would be made between the time that the jury was summoned and the date of jury service.[16] The system was instituted in 1988. Each Crown Court Centre outside London was supposed to provide the police quarterly with a batch of names for checking.

The Runciman Royal Commission said however that the Association of Chief Police Officers had told it that often courts did not fulfil this requirement and frequently the information given was insufficient to enable a search of the records to be made.[17] No doubt also sometimes the police failed to make the checks. It has been held that it is not correct for the judge to institute inquiries as to whether a particular juror was disqualified.[18] However, either the chief constable or the DPP can require a Criminal Records Office check in any case in which they consider it would be in the interests of justice.[19]

---

[12] It provides that those disqualified include: (1) persons who have ever been sentenced to life imprisonment or to a term of youth custody or detention of more than five years or to be detained during Her Majesty's pleasure; (2) anyone who in the previous ten years has served any part of a prison sentence, youth custody or detention or has been detained in a young offender institution or has had a suspended sentence of imprisonment or has been the subject of a community service order, community punishment order or community order as defined in the Criminal Justice Act 2003; and (3) anyone who in the previous five years has been subject to a probation order or a community rehabilitation order. (Sch. 1, Part 2 of the Juries Act 1974 inserted by Sch. 33, para. 15 of the 2003 Act.)   [13] Runciman, p.132, para. 59.

[14] [1980] 3 All ER 777.

[15] See also the *Annex to the Attorney General Guidelines on Jury Checks: Recommendations of the Association of Chief Police Officers* [1988] 3 All ER 1086 authorising checks in cases where the police thought it particularly important that disqualified persons should not serve on the jury.

[16] *The Times* and *The Guardian*, 26 September 1987.   [17] Report, p. 133, para. 60.

[18] In *Obellin, Williams and Martin* [1997] 1 Cr App Rep 355 the Court of Appeal quashed convictions for robbery because the judge asked the prosecution to carry out a Criminal Records Office check on one juror after they had begun their deliberations.

[19] *Annex to the Attorney General's Guidelines on Jury Checks* – 88 Cr App R 123 at 125.

As will be seen (p. 492 below), jury summoning is now done centrally for the whole country by the Central Summoning Bureau. Lord Justice Auld's report said that one of the first things the Bureau should do was to establish an electronic link with the police criminal records system 'to enable automatic checks on any previous convictions of potential jurors'.[20] That has now been achieved. The handling of the checks for disqualifying criminal convictions is now an automatic electronic process.[21]

Excusals Some persons were formerly excused as of right being persons deemed to have more important business elsewhere, such as MPs, members of the House of Lords, full-time members of the forces, and doctors, dentists and others in the medical profession.

Lord Justice Auld recommended that excusal as of right be abolished.[22] The Government accepted the recommendation[23] and it was implemented in the Criminal Justice Act 2003.[24] As was seen above, the new principle is that no one is excusable from jury service unless they can show good reason, in which case jury service should normally be deferred to another date.

The Solicitor General told the House of Commons that it was estimated that removing the categories of 'ineligible' and 'excused as of right' would add some four million names to the pool from which jurors are drawn.[25]

It has always been possible to request excusal on an individual *ad hoc* basis and this is very common. Something like a quarter of a million persons are summoned for jury service per year. A 1999 Home Office research study, based on a sample of 50,000 people summoned for jury service, found that only about a third (34 per cent) were actually available for service. Those who were ineligible, excused as of right or disqualified accounted for 13 per cent of the sample. Some 8 per cent had moved from their address and another 7 per cent simply failed to attend.[26] No fewer than 38 per cent of the Home Office sample were excused *ad hoc* on an individual basis.[27] Lord Justice Auld's report said of this category that 'it is taken up in the main by those who are self-employed or in full-time employment who can make out a case for economic or other hardship for themselves or others if they have to give up their work for even a short period and also by parents who are unable to make alternative arrangements for the care of their children'.[28]

---

[20] Chapter 5, para. 16, p. 141.
[21] Information provided to the writer by the Central Summoning Bureau, 24 September 2006.
[22] Auld, Ch. 5, para. 37, p. 150.
[23] White Paper, *Justice for All*, Cm. 5563, July 2001, para. 7.27.
[24] Schedule 33, para. 3 repealing the Juries Act 1974, s. 9(1) which gave persons listed in Sch. 1, Part 3 of the Act excusal as of right.
[25] House of Commons, Standing Committee B, 13 February 2003, cols. 1057–8.
[26] One of Auld's recommendations was that there should be 'rigorous and well-publicised enforcement of the obligation to undertake jury service' with fixed penalties, subject to a right of appeal. (Auld, Ch. 5, para. 26, p. 145.)
[27] J. Airs and A. Shaw, *Jury Excusal and Deferral* (Home Office Research and Statistics, Research Findings No. 102, 1999).   [28] Auld, Ch. 5, para. 39, p. 151.

In fact, however, the Home Office research study on which this statement was based showed a different picture. The most common reason for excusal (not mentioned by Auld) was medical – accounting for no less than 40 per cent of the total excused. Care of children and the elderly accounted for another 20 per cent. The juror being an essential worker or financial reasons accounted for another 20 per cent. The great variety of miscellaneous other reasons included not being a resident (9 per cent), being a student (6 per cent) and transport problems (overall only 1 per cent but in some rural areas as much as 30 per cent).

The Home Office study found that of the 34 per cent of the sample who were available for jury service, nearly half had had their jury service deferred, in quite a few cases more than once. Reasons for deferral were similar to those for excusal but prior holiday arrangements accounted for a third (34 per cent).

Applications for excusal which formerly went to the court's summoning officer now have to be made to the national Central Summoning Bureau (see p. 492 below) but there is a right of appeal against refusal to the judge. The latest Practice Direction on excusal recognises that the Criminal Justice Act 2003 has led to an increase 'in the number of jurors with professional and public service commitments'. Applications for excusal should be 'considered with common sense and according to the interests of justice'.[29]

The court has power to discharge a jury summons if it considers that the person will not be able to act effectively as a juror on account of disability[30] or 'insufficient understanding of English'.[31]

There is *no formal literacy test* for jury service. The Runciman Royal Commission said with regard to the question whether there should be such a test, that the *Crown Court Study* carried out for the Commission[32] showed that jurors and jury foremen broadly claimed to understand the issues they were trying. Inevitably, this was a subjective judgment and moreover there were some jurors and even some whole juries who were confused. The matter, it said, should be the subject of research.[33] (On jury research see p. 513 below.)

Lord Justice Auld said that it was becoming increasingly necessary for jurors to have a reasonable command of written English. Even in simple cases there were usually documents that they must be capable of understanding, but there was no obvious solution to the problem. The present system of leaving the judge as the final filter during the process of jury selection was 'probably the best that can be achieved'.[34] The judge should give the panel 'an ample and tactfully expressed warning of what they are in for, and offer them a formula that would enable them to seek excusal without embarrassment'.[35] If all else failed, the prosecution had its right to 'stand by' (p. 498 below).

---

[29] *Consolidated Criminal Practice Direction* [2002] 3 All ER 904, para. IV 42.1 as amended by [2005] 3 All ER 89.   [30] Juries Act 1974, s. 9B.   [31] Juries Act 1974, s. 10.

[32] M. Zander and P. Henderson, *Crown Court Study* (Royal Commission on Criminal Justice, Research Study No. 19, 1993).   [33] Auld, p. 135, para. 72.

[34] Auld, Ch. 5, para. 50, p. 155. The Court Service Guidance on Jury Summoning states that a person who has inadequate English should be excused.   [35] Auld, Ch. 5, para. 50, p. 155.

3. The process of jury selection

The random nature of jury selection has been described as the essence of the jury system: see *R v. Sheffield Crown Court, ex p Brownlow*.[36] The trial judge discharged the first jury selected and ordered a jury to be drawn from a different area because it was thought there was a danger of intimidation. The Court of Appeal quashed the conviction on the ground that the judge had improperly interfered with the jury selection process which was basically an administrative rather than a judicial function. The judge had the power to discharge individual potential jurors on the ground that they might not be able to perform their duties but he could not interfere with the composition of the jury panel or of an individual jury.

The actual process of selecting the names for the panel used to be somewhat haphazard. Each summoning officer had his own method and many were hardly 'random' in any sense recognisable by a statistician. In 1981 a new system, developed by the Lord Chancellor's Department in consultation with the Royal Statistical Society, was introduced nationally. Even then, however, the system as it was actually operated was less than completely random. An article in *The Law Magazine*[37] pointed out that the electoral register was not wholly representative of the population. Nearly 7 per cent were on the register wrongly because they had moved or died, about one-fifth of those from the new Commonwealth were not registered, and nearly one-fifth of those between the ages of twenty-one and twenty-four were not registered because of their mobility.

In 2001 a single Central Summoning Bureau operating a computerised system was established for the whole country. (www.courts-service.gov.uk. See also www.juror.cjsonline.org.)

The summons comes with an explanatory leaflet about jury service, a leaflet on jurors' expenses including a form regarding claims for loss of earnings, and a reply envelope to return a form stating that the person concerned is either qualified to serve or is not qualified, with the reason. Failure to give this information or giving false information is an offence.

The method of determining the composition of the jury for the particular case varies somewhat from court to court. Ballotting is supposed to be done by putting the appropriate number of cards into the ballot box and drawing them in such a way that the jury bailiff cannot see the names on the cards. The cards are then transferred to the courtroom ballot box for the final ballot.

Usually about twenty or so names are drawn and these individuals are brought into the back of the court. (They are often called 'the jury in waiting'.) The clerk of the court is given cards, each of which has the name and address of a juror in waiting. He reads out twelve names and those persons go into the jury box.

---

[36] [1980] QB 530. In *Tarrant* [1998] Crim LR 342.   [37] 30 October 1987, p. 20.

4. Challenging of jurors

At common law, either party can challenge the whole panel on the ground that the person conducting the summoning acted improperly or was biased. This form of challenge ('challenge to the array') is nowadays virtually unheard of, but the parties also have the right to challenge individual jurors ('challenge to the polls').

The position of the parties with regard to selection of the jury was historically somewhat different. The prosecution could only challenge jurors if they had some reason ('challenge for cause', see below), but they could also exercise a right known as 'stand by for the Crown' or simply 'stand by', which means that the prospective juror stands to one side. If a jury can be empanelled without him (as would almost always be the case), he is not required. If not, he must be accepted unless the prosecution can show cause why he should not be a juror in that case.[38] In practice, the prosecution only rarely exercise their right either of stand by or of challenge for cause.

Peremptory challenge

The defence in a criminal case have traditionally had the right to challenge numbers of prospective jurors without giving any reason – the so-called right of 'peremptory challenge'. Originally the number of such challenges permitted was thirty-five. In 1509 this was reduced to twenty; in 1948 it was reduced to seven and in 1977 to three. After all peremptory challenges had been exhausted, the defence had only a right of challenge for cause – with no limit to the numbers that could be challenged in that way, but from the mid-1980s the right of peremptory challenge became highly controversial.

It was suggested that the right was being 'abused' by defence lawyers who would use it, especially in London, to eliminate from the jury persons who were educated or looked intelligent or middle class. There was no hard evidence to support the allegation but it gained some currency.

In January 1986 great impetus was given to the campaign to abolish the right of peremptory challenge in the Report of the Roskill Committee on Fraud Trials. The Committee was divided on the issue but by a majority of seven to one it recommended that the right should be abolished. It thought that the interests of the accused could be adequately safeguarded by the right of challenge for cause.

The majority said that the right conflicted with the principle that the jury should be selected randomly. Since co-accused could each exercise three such challenges, the panel might be reduced by a considerable number. It concluded:

> We have considerable sympathy with the exercise of the right of peremptory challenge in pursuit of an aim of securing a better racial or sexual balance on a

[38] See J.F. McEldowney, 'Stand by the Crown: An Historical Analysis', *Criminal Law Review*, 1979, p. 272.

jury, but we have no sympathy with its exercise where that exercise is, as the evidence suggests is too often the case, largely tactical. The aim of the jury is to secure a verdict which is just to prosecution and defence alike after a proper appraisal of the evidence. That aim ought not to be hampered by the use of the right of peremptory challenge in the hope of replacing a juror whose appearance and address may suggest a capacity to understand the real issues or a bias in favour of the prosecution by one whom it is hoped may be less able to understand or may be more likely to be biased in favour of the defence [para. 7.29] . . . Our evidence shows that the public, the press and many legal practitioners now believe that this ancient right is abused cynically and systematically to manipulate cases toward a desired result. The current situation bids fair to bring the whole system into disrepute. We conclude that in respect of fraud trials such manipulation is wholly unacceptable and must be stopped [para. 7.37].

In a White Paper published in March 1986 the Home Office said that it was contrary to the interests of justice that persons should be removed from the jury because they were thought to have insight or respect for the law which was inimical to the defence. The problem was most acute in cases involving several defendants if they pooled their challenges. The Government had no wish to interfere unnecessarily with a long-standing right that could be used in ways that were consistent with justice, but as far as practicable, and providing it did not seriously prejudice a defendant's right to a fair trial, juries should be composed of a random selection of those who were neither ineligible nor disqualified.[39] The 1986 White Paper was followed by legislation in the Criminal Justice Act 1988, s. 118 of which provided simply: 'The right to challenge without cause in proceedings for the trial of a person on indictment is abolished'.

Empirical evidence published by the Home Office at the time when the Criminal Justice Bill was going through Parliament did not support the view that the use of peremptory challenge affected the outcome of trials,[40] but that did not stop the legislation going forward.

Challenge for cause

In the United States prospective jurors can be asked questions to establish whether they are biased.[41] Sometimes this process can take hours and even days or weeks. Selection of the jury in the celebrated trial of O.J. Simpson in 1994 took forty days.

In England, by contrast, questions may not be put unless a foundation of fact has first been laid.[42] This means that in practice challenges for cause are

---

[39] *Criminal Justice: Plans for Legislation*, March 1986, Cmnd. 9658, para. 35.

[40] See J. Vennard and D. Riley, 'The Use of Peremptory Challenge and Stand By of Jurors and Their Relationship to Final Outcome', *Criminal Law Review*, 1988, p. 731.

[41] For a description see M. George, 'Jury Selection, Texas Style', 138 *New Law Journal*, 24 June 1988, p. 438 and R. May, 'Jury Selection in the United States: Are there Lessons to be Learned?', *Criminal Law Review*, 1998, pp. 270–3.

[42] *Chandler (No 2)* [1964] 1 All ER 761.

extremely rare and the jury selection process typically takes only minutes. Since normally nothing is known about the prospective jurors other than their names and addresses, there is usually no basis on which a challenge for cause can be launched. At one time, the lists available to the parties at least showed the jurors' occupations, but that was ended in 1973.

Those entitled to inspect the list of names on the panel include the defendant, solicitor and counsel for any party, and police officers involved in the case. Instructions to Crown Court staff state that requests from anyone else, or if the official is in any doubt, should be referred to a superior officer. A record of any request to inspect the panel list must be kept. Concern about jury intimidation has increased in recent years,[43] but it has not reached the point where it has been thought that the right to look at the panel should be withheld.

The American approach is based on the attempt to eliminate bias by asking potential jurors questions about their views and experience. The English approach is to take the jury 'warts and all'. The English approach was set out in a Practice Note in 1973 as a result of what happened in the so-called Angry Brigade case. Alleged anarchists were being tried for attempts to bomb the homes of prominent Conservative politicians. The judge acceded to a defence request that he put questions to prospective jurors. He asked them to exclude themselves for a variety of reasons, for instance if they were subscribing members of the Conservative Party, if they had relatives in the police force or serving in the armed forces in Northern Ireland, or if they were constituents of any of several prominent persons whose homes were alleged to have been the subject of actual or projected bombings. As a result, thirty-nine people were challenged on behalf of the eight defendants and another nineteen admitted they fell into one or other of the judge's categories.[44]

Shortly after the case was concluded, however, the Lord Chief Justice issued the Practice Note to stop such questions.[45] The text has been renewed and slightly revised from time to time – most recently in 2005:[46] 'It may be appropriate for a judge to excuse the juror from that particular case where the potential juror is personally concerned with the facts of the particular case or is closely connected with a prospective witness'.

The previous version of the Practice Note went on: 'He or she may also be excused on grounds of personal hardship or conscientious objection to jury service', but this sentence was dropped in 2005. The 2005 version does however recognise difficulties for potential jurors created by very long cases.

---

[43] The Runciman Royal Commission recommended that an acquittal should be cancelled and a retrial be instituted where it was subsequently established that jurors had been bribed or intimidated (p. 177, para. 74). This was implemented in the Criminal Procedure and Investigations Act 1996, s. 54. As will be seen, p. 548 below, the Criminal Justice Act 2003, s. 46 provides that where jury tampering appears to have taken place the judge can decide either to discharge the jury and continue without one or to terminate the trial. The section is not yet in force.   [44] *The Guardian*, 31 May 1972.   [45] [1973] 1 All ER 240.

[46] *Amendment to the Consolidated Criminal Practice Direction (Jury Service)* [2005] 3 All ER 89.

It also refers to unexpected difficulties arising in the course of a case through 'professional or personal circumstances' – mentioning a breakdown in childcare arrangements or urgent parliamentary business for an MP which might lead the judge to adjourn the case or to discharge that juror and continue with a reduced number of jurors.

The judge's discretion

In *R v. Ford*[47] Lord Chief Justice Lane said that the trial judge has a residual discretion to discharge a juror who ought not to be serving even in the absence of any objection by any party. 'The basic position is that a juror may be discharged on grounds that would found a challenge for cause. In addition jurors who are not likely to be willing or able properly to perform their duties may also be discharged'.

The question of conscientious objection to jury service was considered in *R v. Crown Court at Guildford, ex p Siderfin*[48] in which the Divisional Court held that a member of the Plymouth Brethren could be entitled to excusal not because of her beliefs as such but because they prevented her from taking part in the jury's deliberations. Since 'she would not participate at all in the usual discussion between jurors which is an integral part of the jury system', she would be unable to perform her duties as a juror. (The court also held that a judge hearing an appeal from a chief clerk's refusal of such an application to be excused jury service should consider sympathetically any request for the person to be legally represented.)

Questionnaires for jury selection

The trial in 1995 of Kevin and Ian Maxwell, sons of the notorious business magnate Robert Maxwell, was scheduled to last some six months. The trial judge, Mr Justice Phillips (now Lord Chief Justice Phillips), adopted a highly unusual method of selecting the jury. First, two groups of 400 potential jurors were summoned to the Old Bailey. Of these, 650 were immediately excused for reasons of personal non-availability including holiday plans, child-minding responsibilities, work commitments and the like. The remaining 150 were invited to complete a twenty page questionnaire with some forty questions specifically relating to the Maxwell trial. This was designed to test their availability for an unusually long case and was also directed to their knowledge of the case and possible resulting prejudice. The judge and counsel in open court then went through the list of these 150 questionnaires classifying them as A (no reason to exclude), C (should be excluded for any reason, including illiteracy) and B (uncertain). There were fifty-two Cs. The jury was then selected by ballot drawn from the remaining hundred or so jurors. As each name was drawn, if counsel or the judge had any queries on the basis of the questionnaire or the classification, the juror was asked to come into the court room and they were

---

[47] (1989) 89 Cr App Rep 278 at 280.   [48] [1989] 3 All ER 7.

asked questions by the judge to clarify the issue. The individual then left the court room and the judge and counsel together decided whether that person should or should not serve as a juror.

In *R v. Tracey Andrews*[49] the Court of Appeal said that the use of a question-naire to establish whether potential jurors were biased should be avoided save in most exceptional circumstances.

Jury selection and pre-trial publicity

It is not a valid ground of objection that the juror has previous knowledge of the case from the media. In *R v. Maxwell* Phillips J said that because the minds of potential jurors might have become 'clogged with prejudice' by pre-trial pub-licity about the case he would permit questions to be put in the jury question-naire and further questions to be posed when he questioned potential jurors in open court (see above). But in a ruling on jury selection given on 27 April 1995 he said: 'The fact that a juror may have read or heard prejudicial matter about a defendant, *and even formed an adverse opinion of him on the basis of it, does not of itself disqualify the juror on the ground of bias*' (emphasis supplied). He cited a *dictum* of the Ontario Court of Appeal:

> In this era of rapid dissemination of news by the various media, it would be naive to think that in the case of a crime involving considerable notoriety, it would be possible to select twelve jurors who had not heard anything about the case. Prior information about a case and even the holding of a tentative opinion about it, does not make partial a juror sworn to render a true verdict according to the evidence.[50]

Phillips J cited with approval the observation of the High Court of Australia: 'in the past too little weight may have been given to the capacity of jurors to assess critically what they see and hear and their ability to reach their decisions by ref-erence to the evidence before them'.[51]

Procedure for challenge for cause

In 1989 the Judicial Studies Board published a recommended procedure for challenge for cause based on recommendations of the Law Commission. If counsel can state the ground of challenge without prejudicing his client in the eyes of the jury or embarrassing the juror, the matter can be dealt with in open court. If not, the sworn jurors should be sent to the jury room and the rest of the panel, *including the challenged juror*, should leave the court. The judge should then decide whether to exclude the press and the public. Challenges should never be heard in the judge's room.

---

[49] [1999] Crim LR 156 and commentary at 157; 148 *New Law Journal*, 4 December 1998, p. 1812.
[50] *R v. Hubbert* (1975) 29 CCC (2d) 279 at 291.
[51] *R v. Glennon* (1992) 173 CLR 592. The study carried out for the New Zealand Law Commission (p. 376 above) suggests that pre-trial publicity is probably not the threat to the jury's decision-making that has been feared.

Stand by for the Crown

When the defence right of peremptory challenge was abolished in 1988, the Attorney General issued guidelines as to how the prosecution's right to 'stand by for the Crown' was to be used:[52]

Attorney General's guidelines on the exercise by the Crown of its right of stand by

1. Although the law has long recognised the right of the Crown to exclude a member of a jury panel from sitting as a juror by the exercise in open court of the right to request a stand by or, if necessary, by challenge for cause, it has been customary for those instructed to prosecute on behalf of the Crown to assert that right only sparingly and in exceptional circumstances. It is generally accepted that the prosecution should not use its right in order to influence the overall composition of a jury or with a view to tactical advantage . . .

5. The circumstances in which it would be proper for the Crown to exercise its right to stand by a member of a jury panel are: (a) where a jury check authorised in accordance with the Attorney General's Guidelines on Jury Checks reveals information justifying exercise of the right to stand by in accordance with para. 9 of the guidelines and the Attorney General personally authorises the exercise of the right to stand by; or (b) where a person is about to be sworn as a juror who is manifestly unsuitable and the defence agree that, accordingly, the exercise by the prosecution of the right to stand by would be appropriate. An example of the sort of exceptional circumstances which might justify stand by is where it becomes apparent that . . . a juror selected for service to try a complex case is in fact illiterate.

Juries and the problem of race

The question whether the courts have any way of achieving a racial mix in a case where that seems to be desirable was the subject of a number of conflicting court decisions in the 1980s.[53]

In *Ford*[54] the trial judge refused an application for a multi-racial jury in a case where the defendant was accused of reckless driving and driving a vehicle without authority. Lord Lane, the Lord Chief Justice, giving the judgment of the Court of Appeal, said that the judge had a discretion to discharge a particular juror who was unfit to serve, for instance because he was deaf or blind or otherwise incompetent to serve, but this discretion did not extend to discharging a competent juror in order to secure a jury drawn from a particular section of the community nor otherwise to influence the overall composition of the jury. 'For

[52] *Practice Note* [1988] 3 All ER 1086.
[53] *Binns* [1982] Crim LR 522 and 823; *Danvers* [1982] Crim LR 680; *Newton Rose* (1981) Times, 11 November; *Bansall, Bir, Mahio and Singh* [1985] Crim LR 151; *McCalla* [1986] Crim LR 335; *Frazer* [1987] Crim LR 418; *Thomas* (1989) 88 Cr App Rep 370.
[54] [1989] 3 All ER 445.

this latter purpose the law provides that "fairness" is achieved by the principle of random selection'.[55]

The court disapproved suggestions to the contrary in earlier cases such as *Binns, Bansall* and *Thomas* (n. 53 above). Lord Lane said that there was no principle that juries should be racially balanced – for that would depend on an underlying premise that jurors of a particular racial origin were incapable of giving an impartial verdict in accordance with the evidence.

In its evidence to the Runciman Royal Commission on Criminal Justice, the Commission for Racial Equality (CRE) argued that something had to be done to ensure that a jury be racially mixed where this seemed relevant. Restoration of the right of peremptory challenge (above) would help, but on its own it would not be sufficient. One way would be to give the trial judge a statutory right to stand by jurors in order to achieve a racially mixed jury. If the judge refused to exercise this power, the CRE proposed that the defence counsel should have the right to stand by unlimited numbers of jurors until an acceptable racial mix was achieved – the equivalent right to the prosecution's right of 'stand by for the Crown'.

The Runciman Royal Commission was persuaded by the CRE that in a small number of racially sensitive cases something needed to be done to secure that the jury should be racially balanced.[56]

The Commission unanimously proposed that in such a case either side could ask the judge to authorise a special procedure so as to ensure that the jury contains up to three members of ethnic minority communities. If the judge agreed, the jury bailiff would continue drawing names randomly until three such people were drawn. This procedure should not apply, as the CRE had proposed, merely because the defendant thought that he could not get a fair trial from an all-white jury. The judge would have to be persuaded that it was reasonable because of the special and unusual features of the case. Thus, a black defendant charged with burglary would not normally succeed with such an application, but black people accused of violence against a member of an extremist organisation who had been making racial taunts against them and their friends might succeed.[57]

The CRE thought it would be impracticable to provide that the ethnic minority members of the jury should be drawn from the same ethnic minority group as the defendant. The Royal Commission thought that this should be an issue that the judge could be asked to consider.

---

[55] At 449. *Ford* was applied in *Smith (Lance Percival)* [2003] EWCA Crim 283, [2003] Crim LR 633 where the Court of Appeal held that a trial judge had no power to empanel a jury, let alone discretion as to how the jury was composed. The defendant, who was black, appealed on the ground, *inter alia*, that he had been convicted by an all-white jury. The court held that there was nothing in the ECHR jurisprudence that impugned the way that juries were selected.

[56] 'The Court of Appeal in *Ford* held that race should not be taken into account in selecting juries. Although we agree with the court's position with regard to most cases, we believe that there are some exceptional cases where race should be taken into account'. (Runciman, p. 133, para. 62.)   [57] Runciman, p. 133, para. 63.

The Royal Commission's proposal proved controversial. Lord Taylor, the Lord Chief Justice at the time, was against it. Speaking to the Leeds Race Issues Advisory Council he said: 'Though put forward for the best of motives, this proposal seems to me the thin edge of a particularly insidious wedge. The jury is the foundation of our system. It is drawn at random from the law-abiding inhabitants of the locality in which a case is tried. We must on no account introduce measures which allow the state to start nibbling away at the principle of random selection of jurors'. Jurors must not be seen as 'representing the views of the community, or of discrete parts of it, nor indeed of representing either the complainant or the victim'.[58]

Lord Justice Auld in his report made the same recommendation as the Runciman Royal Commission. Juries, he admitted, were clearly at risk of one or more of their number bringing prejudice of one sort or another to their task, but such prejudice was usually invisible and 'we are content to assume that it will be overcome or cancelled by differing views of other members'.[59] Membership of a race is usually visible and, he argued, 'it is this quality of visible difference and the prejudice that it may engender that singles out race for different treatment from other special interest groups in the courtroom'.[60]

The Government rejected the proposal. In its White Paper *Justice for All* it gave six reasons. Implementing the proposal, it said,[61] would potentially:

- Undermine the fundamental principle of random selection and would not achieve a truly representative jury of peers.
- Assume bias on the part of the excluded jurors when no prejudice had been proved.
- Place the selected minority ethnic jurors in a difficult position – as if they were expected to represent the interests of the defendant or the victim.
- Generate tensions and divisions in the jury room.
- Place undue weight on the views of the specially selected jurors.
- Place a new burden on the court to determine which cases should attract an ethnic minority quota and provide a ground for unmeritorious appeals.

As a member of the Runciman Royal Commission, the writer was party to its unanimous recommendation on ethnic minority representation. This is one of the two of its 352 recommendations on which he later changed his mind.[62]

Jury vetting

In 1978, during the so-called 'ABC' trial of a soldier and two journalists under the Official Secrets Act, it was revealed that in some cases the prosecution vet

---

[58] *The Times*, 1 July 1995.   [59] Auld, Ch. 5, para. 59, p. 158.   [60] *Ibid.*

[61] White Paper, *Justice for All*, July 2001, para. 7.29.

[62] See M. Zander's response to the Auld Review, www.criminal-courts-review – Major Reports/Comments, p. 13.

the jury panel. On the first day of the trial, counsel for one of the defendants learned from the clerk of the court that prosecution counsel had had a list of the potential jurors. 'Anyone who is known to be disloyal would obviously be disqualified', said Mr John Leonard QC for the prosecution. (In fact the Crown had not taken objection to anyone on the list.)

During the trial it emerged that the foreman of the jury had been a member of the elite Special Air Service Regiment (the SAS). When this fact was made known on television, the trial judge discharged the jury. As a direct result, in October 1978 the Attorney General, Mr Sam Silkin QC, published guidelines for vetting of jury panels which he had actually established three years earlier but which had not previously been published.[63] These guidelines have subsequently been redrafted several times. They identify two categories of case in which additional checks are required – cases involving national security and terrorist cases:[64]

> 5. The particular aspects of these cases which may make it desirable to seek extra precautions are (a) in security cases a danger that a juror, either voluntarily or under pressure, may make an improper use of evidence which, because of its sensitivity, has been given in camera, (b) in both security and terrorist cases the danger that a juror's political beliefs are so biased as to go beyond normally reflecting the broad spectrum of views and interests in the community to reflect the extreme views of sectarian interest or pressure groups to a degree which might interfere with his fair assessment of the facts of the case or lead him to exert improper pressure on his fellow jurors.
>
> 6. In order to ascertain whether in exceptional circumstances of the above nature either of these factors might seriously influence a potential juror's impartial performance of his duties or his respecting the secrecy of evidence given in camera, it may be necessary to conduct a limited investigation of the panel. In general, such further investigation beyond one of criminal records made for disqualifications may only be made with the records of police Special Branches. However, in security cases, the investigation may, additionally, involve the security services. No checks other than on these sources and no general inquiries are to be made save to the limited extent that they may be needed to confirm the identity of a juror about whom the initial check has raised serious doubts.

Such checks require the personal approval of the Attorney General. If the check shows that any juror should be excluded from the trial it is done by telling prosecution counsel who would ask that juror to 'stand by for the Crown'.

Use made of jury vetting
There is virtually no information about the use of jury vetting. In his original statement in 1978 the Attorney General said that in the three years since he had laid down his guidelines jury vetting had occurred in 25 cases. At that time the

---

[63] See *The Times*, 11 October 1978.
[64] The latest version is (1989) 88 Cr App Rep 123, [1988] 3 All ER 1086.

categories of cases in which jury vetting was permitted included organised crime which was later withdrawn. The authorities know that such cases are likely to provoke a row.[65] The number of such cases is probably even fewer today than in the late 1970s.[66]

5. The size of the jury

As Lord Justice Auld's report said, the fact that the English jury consists of twelve persons is 'a matter of tradition rather than logic'.[67] In Scotland the number is fifteen. Auld made no recommendation for a change in this regard, but he did suggest that in long cases, where they consider it appropriate, judges should have a right to swear alternate or reserve jurors, to meet the contingency of the jury being reduced in number by illness or any other reason of necessity.[68] This recommendation was not adopted by the Government.

6. Who serves on juries?

There has for many years been debate as to whether those who served on juries were drawn disproportionately from certain social groups and whether some elements of society avoided jury duty. In fact a very large national study of jury membership (the *Crown Court Study*) showed that this was not so.[69] The study had returns from some 8,300 jurors in over 800 trials.

Sex Males were slightly over-represented – 53 per cent as against 48 per cent in the whole population, but foremen were much more disproportionately male – 78 per cent.[70]

Social class The social class measures were somewhat crude but it appeared that 19 per cent were skilled manual (compared with 23 per cent in the general population), 7 per cent were unskilled manual (exactly the same as the general population) and 29 per cent were professional/managerial (compared with 31 per cent in the general population).[71]

Work status The great majority of the jurors were working (69 per cent full-time, 13 per cent part-time). Only 2 per cent had been unemployed for over two years. 6 per cent were retired persons.[72]

---

[65] As occurred in 1979 when *The Guardian* (20 September) printed details of information obtained through jury vetting from the police computer in relation to the trial of six anarchists.

[66] This issue has not been raised for debate for many years. For strong criticism of the practice of vetting, see H. Harman and J. Griffith, *Justice Deserted* (National Council for Civil Liberties, 1979); P. Duff and M. Findlay, 'Jury Vetting – the Jury Under Attack', *Legal Studies*, 1983, p. 159. See also R.J. East, 'Jury Packing: A Thing of the Past?', 48 *Modern Law Review*, 1985, p. 518. East took an even more serious view of jury vetting, seeing it as part of a general erosion of civil liberties.   [67] Auld, Ch. 5, para. 17, p. 142.

[68] Auld, Ch. 5, para. 20, p. 143.

[69] M. Zander and P. Henderson, *The Crown Court Study* (Royal Commission on Criminal Justice, Research Study No. 19, 1993).   [70] *Ibid*, section 8.13.1, p. 234.

[71] *Ibid*, Table 8.41, p. 238.   [72] *Ibid*, Table 8.40, p. 237.

However, now that the categories of 'ineligible' for jury service and 'excused as of right' have effectively been eliminated, the whole controversy about the composition of juries has presumably ceased to be of interest or concern.

7. The extent to which juries are used

Civil cases

There is a *right* to have trial by jury only in the following civil cases: libel, slander, malicious prosecution, false imprisonment and allegations of fraud. Since the Supreme Court Act 1981, the right to trial by jury in the categories listed above has been subject to the proviso in s. 69(1) that the court can refuse jury trial if it is of the opinion that 'the trial requires prolonged examination of documents or accounts or any scientific or local investigation which cannot conveniently be made with a jury'.[73] One advantage of trial by judge as against trial by jury is that it results in a reasoned judgment. (Both parties in the 'Holocaust denial' libel action brought by David Irving against Penguin Books and Professor Deborah Lipstadt agreed that the case was too complex for a jury. The trial, which lasted from January to April 2000, ended with a devastating 150 page judgment by Mr Justice Gray demolishing Irving's arguments.[74])

In other cases trial is without a jury unless the court 'in its discretion orders it to be tried with a jury'.[75]

Prior to the 1981 Act the judges had what appeared to be a complete statutory discretion as to whether to order trial by jury. The Administration of Justice Act 1933 provided that 'Any action to be tried in the Queen's Bench Division could, in the discretion of the court or judge, be ordered to be tried either with or without a jury'.

In 1937, the Court of Appeal sitting with five judges, said that the question of trial by jury was really one for the discretion of the court.[76] Lord Wright said the discretion of the judge was 'completely untrammelled'.[77] The *Annual Practice*, the practitioners' bible, in interpreting the decision said 'the discretion of the judge is absolute'. When the Rules of the Supreme Court were revised in 1958, RSC Order 36, r. 1(3) was amended to read: 'the discretion of a court or judge

---

[73] In 1994 the Court of Appeal denied an application from two unemployed environmental campaigners that the libel action brought against them in respect of a leaflet by McDonald's fast food chain should be heard by a jury. The Court of Appeal said that the scientific issues would make it impossible for the case to be tried satisfactorily by a jury. The two campaigners conducted their own case – which went on for over a year and became the longest libel action in recorded history. (See national newspapers 26 March 1994 and a year later D. Mills, '"McLibel 2" bite back against Big Mac', *Legal Action*, April 1995, p. 9.) In *Racz v. Home Office* [1994] 1 All ER 97 the House of Lords upheld the Court of Appeal's denial of jury trial even though the action could have raised the issue of an award of exemplary damages.

[74] For an account of the case see R. Evans, *Telling Lies About Hitler* (Verso, 2002).

[75] Supreme Court Act, 1981, s. 69(3). For a brief review of the cases see 14 *Civil Justice Quarterly*, 1995, p. 152.   [76] *Hope v. Great Western Rly Co* [1937] 2 KB 130.   [77] At p. 138.

in making or varying any order under this rule is an absolute one'. Nothing could be clearer.

In 1966 the issue came again before the Court of Appeal sitting again with five judges in a case where jury trial had been allowed for a claim for damages in a road accident which left the plaintiff a permanent quadriplegic. Lord Denning, giving the judgment of the court, explained why trial by jury was normally not appropriate for personal injury cases:

Ward v. James [1966] 1 QB 273, [1965] 1 All ER 563, Court of Appeal, Civil Division
Lord Denning MR:

Relevant considerations today
Let it not be supposed that this court is in any way opposed to trial by jury. It has been the bulwark for our liberties too long for any of us to seek to alter it. Whenever a man is on trial for serious crime, or when in a civil case a man's honour or integrity is at stake, or when one or other party must be deliberately lying, then trial by jury has no equal, but in personal injury cases trial by jury has given place of late to trial by judge alone, the reason being simply this, that in these cases trial by judge alone is more acceptable to the great majority of people. Rarely does a party ask in these cases for a jury. When a solicitor gives advice, it runs in this way: 'if I were you, I should not ask for a jury. I should have a judge alone. You do know where you stand with a judge, and if he goes wrong, you can always go to the Court of Appeal, but as for a jury, you never know what they will do, and if they do go wrong, there is no putting them right. The Court of Appeal hardly ever interferes with the verdict of a jury'. So the client decides on judge alone. That is why jury trials have declined. It is because they are not asked for . . . This important consequence follows: the judges alone, and not juries, in the great majority of cases, decide whether there is negligence or not. They set the standard of care to be expected of the reasonable man. They also assess the damages. They see, so far as they can, that like sums are given for like injuries. They set the standards for awards. Hence there is a uniformity of decision. This has its impact on decisions as to the mode of trial. If a party asks for a jury in an ordinary personal injury case, the court naturally asks: 'Why do you want a jury when nearly everyone else is content with judge alone?' I am afraid it is often because he has a weak case, or desires to appeal to sympathy. If no good reason is given, then the court orders trial by judge alone. Hence we find that nowadays the discretion in the ordinary run of personal injury cases is in favour of judge alone . . .

Lessons of recent cases
. . . Recent cases show the desirability of three things: first, *assessability*: in cases of grave injury, where the body is wrecked or the brain destroyed, it is very difficult to assess a fair compensation in money, so difficult that the award must basically be a conventional figure, derived from experience or from awards in comparable cases. Secondly, *uniformity*: there should be some measure of

uniformity in awards so that similar decisions are given in similar cases; otherwise there will be great dissatisfaction in the community, and much criticism of the administration of justice. Thirdly, *predictability*: parties should be able to predict with some measure of accuracy the sum which is likely to be awarded in a particular case, for by this means cases can be settled peaceably and not brought to court, a thing very much to the public good. None of these three is achieved when the damages are left at large to the jury. Under the present practice the judge does not give them any help at all to assess the figure. The result is that awards may vary greatly, from being much too high to much too low. There is no uniformity and no predictability . . .

The case caused a great hullabaloo. The Court of Appeal, it was said, had struck down one of the sacred rights of an Englishman – the right to trial by jury. This was in fact not the case as the civil jury had already virtually ceased to exist even before the decision. In 1963, three years before *Ward v. James*, the number of jury trials in London in the Queen's Bench Division was twenty-seven out of a total of 962 (2.8 per cent).[78] Nevertheless, the Court of Appeal was obviously concerned to allay public disquiet and within a month it found a case[79] in which it disclaimed any intention to abolish civil juries:

Hodges v. Harland and Wolff Ltd [1965] 1 All ER 1086, Court of Appeal, Civil Division

[The plaintiff, while employed by the defendant, was operating a diesel driven air compressor. The spindle on that machine was not properly guarded as required by the relevant Regulations, 1960. The spindle caught and tore the plaintiff's trousers and avulsed his penis and scrotal skin. One effect of the injury was that the plaintiff still had the sexual urge without the ability to perform the sexual act. On the summons for directions, trial by jury was ordered by the judge. On appeal:]

Lord Denning MR: . . . Naturally enough, we have been referred to the recent decision of this court in *Ward v. James*. It is a mistake to suppose that this court in that case took away the right to trial by jury. It was not this court but Parliament itself which years ago took away any absolute right to trial by jury and left it to the discretion of the judges. This court in *Ward v. James* affirmed that discretion and said that, as the statute has given a discretion to the judge, this court would not fetter it by rigid rules from which the judge was never at liberty to depart. What *Ward v. James* did was this. It laid down the considerations which should be borne in mind by a judge when exercising his discretion; and it is apparent that, on those considerations, the result will ordinarily be trial by judge alone. It will not result in trial by jury save in exceptional circumstances. That is no great change. It has been the position for many years. As it happened, in *Ward v. James* itself, the result was trial by jury.

In this present case the judge, it seems to me, has borne all the relevant considerations in mind. He said, 'this is a unique case'. So it is. Counsel for the defendants

---

[78] For the history of the decline of the civil jury see Lord Devlin, *Trial by Jury*, Ch. 6.
[79] The two cases were reported in the same volume of the All England Law Reports.

urged that there were one or two cases in the books where a man had retained the sexual urge without the ability to perform the sexual act. That may be so, but they were very different from this. I think that the judge was well entitled to take the view that this was an exceptional case, and in the circumstances to exercise his discretion in favour of trial by jury. Indeed, when a judge exercises his discretion and takes all the relevant considerations into account, it is well settled that the burden is on anyone coming to this court to show that he was wrong. I see nothing wrong in the way that Mr Justice Lyell dealt with this case in ordering trial by jury . . .

I think that this case was properly decided by the judge. The appeal fails and must be dismissed.

Lord Justices Davies and Salmon agreed.

In 1995 the Law Commission in a consultation paper said it thought that juries should *never* be used for personal injury cases:

> Given the difficulty of assessing damages for non-pecuniary loss in personal injury cases and the judicial tariff that has been developed to ensure a measure of consistency and uniformity, we consider it unsatisfactory that juries might ever be called upon to assess compensatory damages for personal injury. Juries do not have the benefit of knowledge of the scale of values that has been developed and the inevitable consequence is unacceptable inconsistency with awards in other cases.[80]

Like the Court of Appeal in *Ward v. James*, the Law Commission rejected the idea that the jury should be provided with a scale of values, or upper and lower sums, leaving it for them to fix the actual amount.

Juries for libel and slander cases – the Faulks Committee

The role of the jury in libel and slander actions was considered by the Faulks Committee. In its report in 1974[81] the Committee concluded that juries should no longer be available as of right in defamation actions but that instead there should be the same discretion to permit a jury as in all other cases. They had several reasons:

- Although juries were perfectly able to determine some questions that arose in defamation actions, there were other matters (such as whether a plea of justification succeeded or technical legal concepts such as fair comment and qualified privilege) where a judge was normally more competent.
- Libel actions often turned on barbed subtleties, specialist jargon or group attitudes of warring factions where the jury was not likely to have any relevant insight or knowledge.
- Contrary to the popular view that judges were remote from the life of the community, they were in fact well in touch with the emotions, conventions, language and way of life of the rest of the community. ('The idea that judges

---

[80] *Damages for Personal Injury: Non-Pecuniary Loss*, consultation paper 140, 1995, para. 4.83 at p. 125.   [81] *The Law of Defamation*, 1974, Cmnd. 5709.

live in an ivory tower is wholly out-dated. They go by train and bus, they look at television and they hear, in matrimonial, criminal, accident and other cases, every kind of expression which the ordinary man uses, and they have learnt how he lives' (para. 484).)

- Judges gave their reasons, whereas juries did not. It was more satisfactory for both sides to know the reasons.
- Juries had difficulties with complex cases.
- Juries were unpredictable.
- Trial by jury was more expensive.
- The existing rule gave the right of decision as to mode of trial to whichever side wanted jury trial. No matter how strong the case against jury trial, the party who wanted it would prevail. This was unjust to the other party and wrong in principle.

The Committee concluded by saying that it believed that 'much of the support for jury trials is emotional and derives from the undoubted value of juries in serious criminal cases where they stand between the prosecuting authority and the citizen'.[82]

It did not recommend that the possibility of jury trial should be removed altogether because there were some cases in which a jury would be better than a judge:

> We recognise it to be undesirable, that a judge sitting alone should be embroiled in a matter of political, religious or moral controversy. The same might be true where any party has been outspokenly critical of the Bench. Broadly, where the issue is whether the words were true or false and the subject is one that raises strong feelings among the general public so that a judge alone might be suspected, however mistakenly, of prejudice conscious or unconscious, we should expect that trial by jury might be awarded – but that in cases which did not involve such controversial questions a judge alone would be more likely to be selected.[83]

However, the Committee did have a recommendation on the subject of whether juries should continue to deal with damages.

Juries and damages in defamation cases

The Committee came to the conclusion that it was not right that juries should continue to award damages. The jury simply lacked the necessary knowledge and experience. There were two possible alternatives. One was that the judge should fix the amount of damages without any help from the jury. The other was that the judge would fix the actual amount having had guidance from the jury as to the appropriate scale. The Committee favoured the second. The jury should determine whether the damages were to be 'substantial/moderate/nominal or contemptuous' and the judge should fix the actual amount.[84] The Committee also said that the Court of Appeal should be empowered to review

[82] Paragraph 496.   [83] Faulks, para. 503.   [84] Faulks, para. 513.

the amount of damages and should have the power to substitute its own figure for that of the jury.[85]

In its 1995 consultation paper on *Damages for Personal Injury: Non-Pecuniary Loss* the Law Commission said that it had reluctantly come to the conclusion that the Faulks Committee's recommendation to split the determination of liability and damages between judge and jury was unworkable in libel actions.

In the late 1980s the question of the jury's competence in the assessment of damages came into issue again as a result of some huge libel awards:

- £450,000 to Martin Packard against a Greek newspaper (with a circulation of fifty copies in England), 1987.
- £300,000 to Koo Stark against the *Daily Mirror* regarding an alleged relationship with Prince Andrew, 1988.
- £500,000 to Jeffrey Archer against the *Daily Star* regarding an allegation that he had visited a prostitute, 1988. (This sum had to be paid back with costs and interest after Archer was imprisoned for perjury in the case!)
- £650,000 against *Private Eye* for Sonia Sutcliffe, wife of the 'Yorkshire Ripper', regarding an allegation that she had cashed in on his notoriety, 1989. (The award was set aside by the Court of Appeal which ordered a retrial. She eventually accepted £60,000 in settlement.)

These cases led to a change in the rules so as to permit the Court of Appeal to substitute its own award for that of the jury – as had been recommended in 1974 by the Faulks Committee, but the problem continued:

- £250,000 against Mirror Group Newspapers for broadcaster Esther Rantzen regarding her reputation and integrity as someone concerned about sexual abuse of children. Reduced on appeal to £110,000.[86] The Court of Appeal said the award was excessive by any objective standard of reasonable compensation. It invoked Article 10 of the European Convention as one of the reasons for its decision. The courts' previous reluctance to intervene should be re-examined. The courts, it said, should subject large awards of damages to more searching scrutiny than had been the case in the past. The question to be asked was whether a reasonable jury could have thought the award was necessary to compensate the plaintiff and re-establish his reputation.

The Law Commission, in its 1995 consultation paper on *Damages for Personal Injury: Non-Pecuniary Loss*, proposed that the judge in directing the jury in defamation or other cases should inform the jury of the range of awards for non-pecuniary loss in personal injury cases. The Law Commission's view had hardly been expressed when it became the law of the land through a ruling by the Court of Appeal in a case brought by rock star Elton John against the *Sunday Mirror*.[87] The court reduced what it called the jury's 'manifestly excessive' award

[85] Faulks, para. 514.   [86] *Rantzen v. Mirror Group Newspapers* [1993] 4 All ER 975.
[87] *John v. Mirror Group Newspapers Ltd* [1996] 2 All ER 35.

of £350,000 to £75,000. In doing so it held that in future lawyers and judges could and should give juries clear guidance with regard to damages. It described juries in libel actions as 'sheep loosed on an unfenced common with no shepherd'. Sir Thomas Bingham MR said:

> It is in our view offensive to public opinion, and rightly so, that a defamation plaintiff should recover damages for injury to reputation greater, perhaps by a significant factor, than if that same plaintiff had been rendered a helpless cripple or an insensate vegetable. The time has in our view come when judges, and counsel, should be free to draw the attention of juries to these comparisons.

Mentioning figures would not, it thought, develop into an auction. Figures mentioned by counsel would tend to be the upper and lower bounds of a realistic bracket. The jury would remain free to choose a figure within or outside the bracket.

The Court of Appeal took the same approach in *Thompson v. Metropolitan Police Commissioner*.[88] The court held that in cases involving actions for unlawful acts by police officers, juries should be told about damages awarded in personal injury cases even if the case did not involve personal injuries. Exemplary damages should be from £5,000 to £25,000 with £50,000 an absolute maximum. (The court reduced damages of £220,000 awarded by the jury to £35,000.)

However, in *Gleaner Co Ltd v. Abrahams*,[89] the Privy Council said that because damages in personal injury cases could be mentioned in defamation cases in one jurisdiction did not mean that it was necessarily right in another jurisdiction. There was an element of deterrence in libel cases which did not exist in personal injury cases. It dismissed the defendant's appeal against an award of 35 million Jamaican dollars (equivalent to £533,000).

Criminal cases

Cases tried at the Crown Court (called 'trial on indictment') where the accused pleads not guilty to one or more charges have hitherto always been heard by juries.

Cases tried on indictment are of two kinds: the very serious offences that can only be tried at the higher level and offences triable either way.[90] The great majority of either-way cases are tried summarily.

The basic concept regarding the disposition of either-way cases has been that if either the magistrates or the defendant think that the case should be heard in the Crown Court that view prevails. The magistrates cannot insist on summary trial if the defendant wants trial by jury; the defendant cannot insist on summary trial if the magistrates think it should be dealt with by the Crown Court. The Criminal Justice Act 2003 retained this fundamental principle.

---

[88] [1997] 2 All ER 762.   [89] (2003) Times, 22 July.
[90] For the allocation of such cases see pp. 315–22 above.

Where a number of defendants are jointly charged with an either-way offence and one elects to be tried on indictment, all must be sent for trial on indictment.[91]

8. Aids to the jury

The question of whether, and if so how, to assist the jury has exercised a succession of official committees. The Morris Committee in 1965 recommended that jurors be sent a leaflet with information about their duties and about local arrangements. It did not think that they should be encouraged to take notes, though if they wished to do so, facilities to do so should be provided. ('The process of note-taking is one that requires a good deal of experience and skill. Because of their training, judges are able to make accurate and reasonably complete notes, and at the same time to observe all that is happening and to keep control over the proceedings. Not all jurors can be expected to have the same skill and training. Experience shows that as a general rule it may well be better for jurors to concentrate on listening, observing and reflecting'.[92])

The *Crown Court Study* found that in the great majority of cases one or more members of the jury did take notes and most jurors said that they found their notes to be useful.[93]

The Morris Committee was doubtful whether jurors should be informed that they could ask questions. ('If positive encouragement were given to jurors to ask questions there would be a risk in a criminal case of some question prejudicial to the accused being asked inadvertently, and there would also be some risk of the proceedings getting out of hand'.[94]) In the *Crown Court Study*, the great majority of jurors (70 per cent) said that they had been told they could ask questions, but of those who had wanted to do so, only 17 per cent had had the courage to do so.[95]

Jurors now receive a good deal of information about jury service – both beforehand in the form of material sent out with the jury summons and at the start of their jury service. This includes the showing of a video. The HM Courts Service Website (www.hmcourtsservice.gov.uk) has a helpful thirty-three page booklet *Your Guide to Jury Service* with sections on: preparing for your first day, your first day at court, selecting/empanelling a jury, who's who in court, the trial process, in the jury deliberation room, complaints, frequently asked questions and a glossary of some commonly used legal terms.

The Roskill Committee gave attention to ways of making the jury's task easier, especially in complex cases. The prosecution, it said, should prepare schedules and summaries of the relevant contents of documentary evidence. Glossaries of

---

[91] *R v. Brentwood Justices, ex p Nicholls* [1990] 3 All ER 516.
[92] *Report of the (Morris) Departmental Committee on Jury Service*, 1965, Cmnd. 2627, para. 282.
[93] M. Zander and P. Henderson, n. 69 above, p. 173, section 6.2.3.
[94] Morris Committee, para. 283.
[95] M. Zander and P. Henderson, n. 69 above, p. 174, section 6.2.4.

technical terms should be made for the jury. Modern techniques of presentation of information should be utilised, including any appropriate forms of visual aid.

This exhortation was taken to heart. Cases run by the Serious Fraud Office rejoice in a full battery of hi-tech methods. Specially designed court rooms in Chichester Rents in Chancery Lane, for instance, have a proliferation of TV monitors and computer systems for presentation of evidence to the jury. The jury itself has TV monitors on which they can see the head and shoulders of the witness, but the TV monitors are constantly in use also to project documents and graphics. In these huge cases with thousands of documents, the IT expert is now a vital member of the lawyers' support team.[96]

The Runciman Royal Commission also made recommendations designed to ease the jury's task. It thought that writing materials should always be provided, that technological aids should be provided where appropriate and that the judge should explain to the jury that they have a right to ask questions and to take notes.[97]

Lord Justice Auld devoted considerable attention to the problem of providing more assistance to the jury. His recommendations included the following:

- Jurors should be provided with a copy of the indictment or charge.
- The judge should give jurors a fuller introduction to their task including the structure and practical features of the trial, a word about their manner of working, for example as regards note-taking and the time and manner of their deliberations.
- He should give them a summary of the case and the questions they were to decide supported with a written aide-memoire (a Cases and Issues Summary) agreed in draft by the lawyers and approved by the judge. The judge's summary should identify the nature of the charges, the evidence agreed, the matters of fact in issue and a list of the likely questions for their decision. If the issues narrowed or widened in the course of the trial, the Case and Issues Summary should be amended and re-issued.[98]

Auld acknowledged that 'many criminal practitioners may not initially welcome the proposal for an agreed Case and Issues Summary'.[99] They might believe 'that it would be impracticable in the hurly burly of their life, preparing cases for trial – often in the cracks of the day while engaged in the trial of other cases'.[100]

There are a considerable number of reasons why Auld's proposal of an agreed Case and Issues Summary poses problems:

- It is common in Crown Court cases for both prosecution and defence barristers to receive the brief for the trial at the last minute – the day before the trial

[96] See also the Criminal Justice Act 1988, s. 31 which permits the court to approve special means for conveying complex information.   [97] Runciman, pp. 134–5.
[98] Auld, Ch. 11, paras. 21–3, pp. 520–1.   [99] *Ibid*, para. 24, p. 522.   [100] *Ibid*.

or the morning of the trial.[101] In that situation how could there be an agreed case statement?

- Counsel at trial is frequently different from counsel who dealt with the matter before trial. Again, this is true for both the prosecution and the defence.[102]
- There is no system that reliably enables counsel to know the name of opposing counsel in advance of the trial. In more substantial cases they might have that knowledge but in ordinary run-of-the-mill cases, usually they would not.[103] How could they agree a document if they do not know each other's identity?
- Even if counsel does know the name of the then opposing counsel, since it is normal for counsel to change during the pre-trial stage, there would be no way of knowing whether that counsel will still be acting when the matter comes to trial.
- If, as would often happen, the appreciation of the facts changes as the case preparation moves along, the Case and Issues Summary would have to be updated – with further resulting problems of getting agreement.
- Presumably the Case and Issues Summary would have to be settled by counsel, but what would be the role of the defence solicitors and the CPS? The Auld report said nothing about this. Many solicitors would find it very unsatisfactory to be excluded from the process, but having them involved would add significantly to the complication and delay involved.
- Would the lawyers in practice get instructions from the defendant? There are, notoriously, serious difficulties in criminal cases in getting instructions from the defendant. If he is on bail, he frequently does not manage to get himself to his solicitors' office; if he is in custody, his solicitors and barristers commonly do not manage to get to the prison.
- Since there would be no advantage to the defendant in agreeing a statement such as Auld had in mind, defendants and their lawyers would drag their feet and would not be co-operative. Why should they be? As has been seen, this is well known to be the case with defence disclosure despite the fact that failure to produce a defence disclosure statement may result in adverse comment by the judge (CPIA 1996, s. 11(3)). Plotnikoff's and Woolfson's research[104] established

---

[101] In the *Crown Court Study* half (51 per cent) of all prosecution barristers and one-third (31 per cent) of defence barristers in contested cases received the brief in the case on the day before the hearing or on the day itself (n. 69 above, section 2.1.3).

[102] The *Crown Court Study* showed that close to half of all briefs were returned. Prosecution barristers in contested cases said their brief had previously been returned in 59 per cent of cases. For defence barristers the proportion was 44 per cent (n. 69 above, section 2.1.6). It could not be assumed that a statement drafted by the (usually more junior) counsel who acted earlier would be thought adequate by the trial advocate.

[103] The Court Service's *Review of the Effectiveness of Plea and Directions Hearings in the Crown Court*, January 1998 asked counsel when they were informed of opposing counsel's identity. 92 per cent of defence counsel and 96 per cent of prosecution counsel answered on the day of the PDH (para. 5.31).

[104] J. Plotnikoff and R. Woolfson, *A Fair Balance? Evaluation of the operation of disclosure law* (Home Office, RDS Occasional Paper No. 76, 2001) – available on www.homeoffice.gov.uk/rds/index.html.

that this was virtually a dead letter. The defence statement was generally either framed in a way that revealed little or it was not entered at all. Yet prosecutors generally did not ask the court to direct that further particulars be given nor did they generally ask the judge to comment adversely on the absence or inadequacy of the defence statement.[105] One reason was that judges seemed to be as unenthusiastic about enforcing the statutory obligation as prosecutors. If that is true of defence statements which are supposed to be helpful to the prosecution, how much more would it be true of Auld's proposed case statements which would mainly be intended to be helpful only to the jury?

9. The quality of jury decision-making

There is as yet no systematic study of the jury based on observation or recording of their deliberations. The Contempt of Court Act 1981 makes such research impossible. Section 8 of the Act states that it is contempt of court 'to obtain, disclose, or solicit any particulars of statements made, opinions expressed, arguments advanced or votes cast by members of a jury in the course of their deliberations in any legal proceedings'.[106] The Runciman Commission recommended that s. 8 of the Contempt of Court Act be amended to permit authorised research in the jury room.[107] Lord Justice Auld disagreed.[108]

In 2005 the Department of Constitutional Affairs published a consultation paper canvassing the question whether such research should be permitted.[109] In light of the consultation the Government announced that it favoured more research and that it was not opposed to amending the 1981 Act, but that that should not be done until there were specific questions to be answered that could not be sufficiently investigated without altering the law.[110]

Studies of jury decision-making have mainly been based on the impressions of judges, lawyers, or police officers, or on simulations with 'shadow' or 'mock' juries.

One early study was the famous Chicago project based on the impressions of judges conducted by Professors Harry Kalven, Jr. and Hans Zeisel of Chicago University and published as *The American Jury*.[111] The work was based on 3,576

---

[105] Plotnikoff and Woolfson research study.

[106] The lengthy questionnaire addressed to jurors in the Crown Court study done for the Runciman Royal Commission was not exempt from the provisions of the 1981 Act. The questions asked were all carefully drafted and officially approved on the basis that they did not infringe the provisions of s. 8.   [107] Runciman, recommendation 1, p. 188.

[108] Auld, Ch. 5, paras. 82–7, pp. 166–8.

[109] *Jury Research and Impropriety*, DCA, consultation paper 04/2005, January 2005. For the text of the consultation papers and the summary of responses see www.dca.gov.uk – Publications – Consultation Papers – January 2005. For the writer's actual response against the idea, contrary to the view of the Runciman Royal Commission to which he signed up in 1993, see www.lse.ac.uk – Law Department – Who's Who – academic staff (emeritus).

[110] For an account of the responses to the consultation paper and an assessment of the Government's decision see P. Ferguson QC, 'Jury Research and Impropriety', 155 *New Law Journal*, 2 December 2005, p. 1840.   [111] (Little Brown & Co, 1966).

actual criminal trials and the replies to a questionnaire from the 555 trial judges involved. (Jurymen could not be approached.) The results showed that judges and juries agreed to acquit in 13 per cent of cases and agreed to convict in 62 per cent of cases, yielding a total agreement rate of 75 per cent. In cases where judge and jury disagreed, it was found that the jury was more lenient than the judge in 19 per cent and less lenient in 3 per cent. Just over half of the disagreements which seemed explicable were caused by different approaches to the evidence. Nearly one-third were due to jury reaction to the law and about one-tenth were due to jury sentiments about the defendant himself. The authors summarised their conclusions:

Harry Kalven, Jr. and Hans Zeisel, 'The American Jury', *New Society*, 25 August 1966, p. 290

It may be useful to put quite general and interrelated questions: why do judge and jury ever disagree, and why do they not disagree more often?

The answer must turn on the intrinsic differences between the two institutions. The judge very often perceives the stimulus that moves the jury, but does not yield to it. Indeed it is interesting how often the judge describes with sensitivity a factor which he then excludes from his own considerations.

The better question is the second. Since the jury does at times recognise and use its *de facto* freedom, why does it not deviate from the judge more often? Why is it not more of a wildcat operation? In many ways our single most basic finding is that the jury, despite its autonomy, spins so close to the legal baseline.

The study does not answer directly, but it does lay the ground for three plausible suggestions. As just noted, the official law has done pretty well in adjusting to the equities, and there is therefore no great gap between the official values and the popular. Again, the group nature of the jury decision will moderate and brake eccentric views. Lastly, the jury is not simply a corner gang picked from the street; it has been invested with a public task, brought under the influence of a judge, and put to work in solemn surroundings. Perhaps one reason why the jury exercises its very real power so sparingly is because it is officially told it has none.

The jury thus represents a uniquely subtle distribution of official power; an unusual arrangement of checks and balances. It represents also an impressive way of building discretion, equity, and flexibility into a legal system. Not the least of the advantages is that the jury, relieved of the burdens of creating precedent, can bend the law without breaking it.

Whether or not one comes to admire the jury system as much as we have, it must rank as a daring effort in human arrangement to work out a solution to the tensions between law and equity and anarchy.[112]

---

[112] For an extended discussion of the book see *Criminal Law Review*, 1967, pp. 555–86, but for doubts about the statistical methodology of the study see A.E. Bottoms and M. Walker, 'The American Jury: A Critique', 67 *Journal of the American Statistical Association*, 1972, p. 773. For the authors' rejoinder, see *ibid*, p. 779. For an assessment in 1991 see V. Hans and N. Vidman, 'The American Jury at Twenty-Five Years', *Law and Social Inquiry*, 1991, p. 323.

The first English study, by the Oxford Penal Research Unit, was based primarily on the views of barristers and the police. Its principal finding was that most acquittals were 'attributable to a single cause – the failure of the prosecution (normally the police) to provide enough information, or to present it in court in a way that would convince both judge and jury of the defendant's guilt'.[113] Very few verdicts were found to be perverse.

The writer's study of acquittals at the Old Bailey and the Inner London Crown Court was based on questionnaire interviews with the barristers for the prosecution and the defence. It was striking that there was no great difference of view between prosecution and defence lawyers as to the likely reasons for the acquittals. Again, there was little evidence of perverse verdicts.[114]

For the report of a series of experiments with 'mock' juries who listened to tape recorded trials, see A.P. Sealy and W.R. Cornish, 'Juries and their Verdicts', 36 *Modern Law Review*, 1973, p. 496; and LSE Jury Project, 'Juries and the Rules of Evidence', *Criminal Law Review*, 1973, p. 208.

A study based on thirty cases heard by 'shadow' juries conducted by the Oxford Penal Research Unit showed the jury approaching its task very soberly. The shadow juries listened to real cases and when the real jury withdrew to consider their verdicts, so did the shadow jury. The authors summarised their results:

Sarah McCabe and Robert Purves, *The Shadow Jury at Work*, 1974, pp. 60–3

Of course the 'shadow' jury discussions and verdicts were not comparable with those of the real jury since the future of the defendant was not at risk, but the fact that many of our volunteers felt like jurors encourages us to make certain comparisons where real and 'shadow' jury verdicts agree . . .

Summary of results

3. The 'shadow' juries showed considerable determination in looking for evidence upon which convictions could be based; when it seemed inadequate, they were not prepared to allow their own 'hunch' that the defendant was involved in some way in the offence that was charged to stand in the way of an acquittal . . .

5. There was little evidence of perversity in the final decisions of these thirty groups. One acquittal only showed that sympathy and impatience with the triviality of the case so influenced the 'shadow' jurors' view of the evidence that they refused to convict. One other unexpected acquittal seemed to be wholly due to dissatisfaction with the evidence.

A less positive view of jury decisions emerged from a later piece of research by Professors John Baldwin and Michael McConville.[115] They selected a random sample in Birmingham Crown Court of 500 defendants who pleaded not guilty. In the event, 116 of these were acquitted by the judge before the case had run its

---

[113] S. McCabe and R. Purves, *The Jury at Work* (Blackwell, 1972) p. 11.
[114] M. Zander, 'Are Too Many Professional Criminals Avoiding Conviction?', 37 *Modern Law Review*, 1974, p. 28.   [115] *Jury Trials* (Clarendon, 1979).

full course and another fourteen changed their plea to guilty during the case. This left 370, of which 114 ended in acquittal. The researchers asked the trial judge, the defence solicitor, the prosecuting solicitor, the police and the defendant himself about these cases – the first three groups by questionnaire and the last two by interview. The response rate was very high (over 95 per cent for the judges, the prosecuting solicitors and the police). The table below shows the opinions of the different groups regarding the 114 acquittal cases.

	Judge per cent	Defence solicitor per cent	Prosecuting solicitor per cent	Police per cent
No strong view expressed that the acquittal was not justified	62	83	65	48
Some doubts about the acquittal	6	7	9	8
Serious doubts about the acquittal	32	10	26	44
Total	100 (114)	100 (114)	100 (114)	100 (114)

(Source: *Jury Trials*, Table 5, p. 46)

The acquittal was seen as doubtful or highly questionable by one respondent in thirty instances (27 per cent of the 114), by two respondents in sixteen (14 per cent) and by three or more respondents in twenty-eight (25 per cent).[116] There were forty-one cases in which both judge and one other respondent found the acquittal doubtful.[117]

Convictions were less often found doubtful or highly questionable, but 8 per cent were so regarded by one or more respondents (2 per cent by one respondent, 3 per cent by two and 3 per cent by three or more respondents).[118]

The researchers concluded that in respect of a few acquittals it might be said 'that the jury's verdict was primarily conditioned by its sympathy for the defendant or antipathy towards the victim' and 'some questionable convictions can possibly be explained on the basis of sympathy with the victim or prejudice against the defendant', but in general 'the performance of the jury did not always appear to accord with the principle underlying the trial system in England that it is better to acquit those who are probably guilty than to convict any who are possibly innocent. On the contrary, the jury appeared on occasion to be over ready to acquit those who were probably guilty and insufficiently prepared to protect the possibly innocent'.[119] There was nothing in the composition of the jury (age, sex or social class) that correlated with the decisions.

[116] *Ibid*, Table 6, p. 47.   [117] *Ibid*, p. 54.   [118] *Ibid*, Table 9, p. 51.   [119] *Ibid*, p. 128.

The study is significantly different from previous studies in suggesting a considerable measure of disagreement between jury verdicts and those of the other key actors.

By contrast the *Crown Court Study* was broadly very positive. As previously noted, the study was based on the responses of jurors, prosecution and defence barristers, judges and police officers concerned in some 800 contested cases in every Crown Court in England and Wales in a two-week period in February 1992.

Did the jury understand the evidence? Jurors were asked: 'How difficult was it for you to understand the evidence in this case?' Over 90 per cent thought it 'not at all difficult' (50 per cent) or 'not very difficult' (41 per cent).[120] The same question was asked in cases where there was scientific evidence. The results were very similar – 56 per cent 'not at all difficult', 34 per cent 'not very difficult'.[121]

Jurors were then asked: 'Do you think the jury as a whole was able to understand the evidence?' The response broadly was Yes. Over 90 per cent thought that all the jury understood the evidence (56 per cent) or that most understood (41 per cent). The response from jury foremen was virtually identical.[122] There were 143 juries (17 per cent of the 821 in the study) in which one or more jurors said 'Only a few understood' or 'None of them understood'. 116 juries had one such member, twenty had two such members, six had three and one had four.[123]

The prosecution and defence barristers were asked whether they thought the jury had trouble understanding the evidence. 94 per cent of prosecution barristers and 90 per cent of defence barristers thought they had no trouble.[124] As a result of an oversight this question was not put to the judges, but they were asked whether the jury could understand the scientific evidence in cases where there had been some. In no fewer than 93 per cent of these cases the judges thought all the scientific evidence was understandable by the jury.[125]

The answers for the question 'Could the jurors remember the evidence?' were much the same.[126]

Was the jury's verdict surprising? Different participants in the trial were asked: 'In your view, was the jury's decision surprising in the light of the evidence?' In the great majority of cases the answer was No. The verdict was surprising in the view of 27 per cent of the CPS, 25 per cent of the police, 18 per cent of the defence solicitors, 15 per cent of the prosecution barristers and 14 per cent of the judges and the defence barristers.[127]

The great majority of respondents in all the categories thought the verdict was understandable in the light of the evidence. Those who thought it was against the weight of the evidence but explicable gave a long list of explanations: sympathy for the defendant, antipathy toward the complainant, case too trivial or stale, misconduct by the police, concern over sentence and quality or lack of

---

[120] M. Zander and P. Henderson, n. 69 above at section 8.2.1.   [121] *Ibid* at section 8.2.2.
[122] *Ibid* at section 8.2.3.   [123] *Ibid.*   [124] *Ibid*, p. 177, Table 6.15.   [125] *Ibid.*
[126] *Ibid*, p. 178, Table 6.16; p. 209, Table 8.9.   [127] *Ibid*, p. 163, Table 6.5.

quality of the respective counsel. Hardly any respondents thought the decision was against the judge's direction on law.

The prosecution and defence lawyers and the judges all agreed that 2–4 per cent of jury decisions were inexplicable. The police thought that 8 per cent were inexplicable.

When the judges, the prosecution barristers and the police thought that the verdict was against the weight of the evidence it was an acquittal in about 90 per cent of instances. When defence barristers and defence solicitors thought the verdict was against the weight of the evidence just under half were acquittals.[128]

On the basis of these figures it appears that 'problematic jury acquittals' constituted 31 per cent of all jury acquittals for prosecution barristers, 29 per cent for the judges and 16 per cent for defence barristers.[129] Jury acquittals are about one-third of all acquittals in the Crown Court (see p. 538 below). On that basis, problematic acquittals would be around one-tenth of all acquittals.

The *Crown Court Study* also showed that there were some (though far fewer) problematic convictions. Judges and prosecution barristers thought that 2 per cent of convictions were problematic, whereas defence barristers thought that 17 per cent were problematic.[130]

Research by Julie Vennard, then of the Home Office Research and Planning Unit, supports the view that juries decide rationally and on the basis of the evidence.[131]

Length of jury deliberations In most cases the jury was out for a very short period – in over half (52 per cent) for under two hours and in three-quarters (77 per cent) for under four hours.[132] There were eight cases (1 per cent) in which the jury stayed together overnight. (At the time of the survey it was a rule that once the jury had begun their deliberations, they were not allowed to separate until they reached their verdict, known as 'sequestration of the jury'. Now, under the Criminal Justice and Public Order Act 1994, s. 43, it is in the judge's discretion whether he permits the jury to go home while they are deliberating.)

Not surprisingly, the length of jury deliberations was closely associated with the length of the case. Thus where the case lasted under half a day, the jurors reported being out for under two hours in 96 per cent of cases. When the case lasted three to four days the jurors were back within two hours in only 15 per cent of cases. When it lasted over two weeks, the jurors took more than four hours in three-quarters of the cases.[133] (The English record is probably still the Maxwell trial in 1996 where the jury were out for seven days of deliberations spread over ten days and eleven nights.)

---

[128] *Ibid*, Table 6.9.   [129] *Ibid*, p. 170.   [130] *Ibid*, pp. 170–1.

[131] J. Vennard, 'The Outcome of Contested Trials' in D. Moxon (ed.), *Managing Criminal Justice* (1985) pp. 126–51; and *Evidence and Outcome: a Comparison of Contested Trials in Magistrates' Courts and the Crown Court* (Home Office Research and Planning Unit, Research Bulletin No. 20, 1986) p. 48.

[132] M. Zander and P. Henderson, n. 69 above, Table 8.23, p. 225.   [133] *Ibid*.

For an unscientific and distinctly jaundiced account of the experience of serving on a jury, see the lecture of the late Professor Ely Devons of the London School of Economics, 'Serving as a Juryman in Britain', 28 *Modern Law Review*, 1965, p. 561. See also articles in 140 *New Law Journal*, 14 September 1990, pp. 1264–76; 'Jury Service: A Personal Observation', *LAG Bulletin*, 1979, p. 278; and Trevor Grove, *The Juryman's Tale* (Bloomsbury Publishing, 2000).

10. Respective roles of judge and jury

During the trial the jury is normally passive, simply listening to the case as it develops. Sometimes the jury will ask a question by passing a note to the judge. The judge will then decide whether, and if so how, the question should be answered. Sometimes he will invite the views of the lawyers for both sides. At each break they are usually warned by the judge not to discuss the case among themselves or with anyone else until they reach their deliberations at the end.

The judge's role in the adversary system, as has been seen, is also largely passive if the comparison is with that of the judge in the continental system, but by comparison with the jury, the judge is quite actively involved. In particular, he will have to rule on points of law as they arise, especially with regard to the admissibility or otherwise of evidence. If this involves lengthy debate, the jury will be asked to withdraw. The judge knows more about the case than the jury in that he has access to the pre-trial papers. At the close of the prosecution's case he may have to deal with a submission that there is no case to answer (see pp. 523–24 below).

For the view that there should be greater interaction between judge and jury with regard to fact finding see J. Jackson and S. Doran, 'Judge and Jury: Towards a New Division of Labour in Criminal Trials', 60 *Modern Law Review*, 1997, pp. 759–78.

The judge is supposed to sum up for the jury on both the law and the facts.[134]

Summing up the law

In *McVey*[135] the Court of Appeal spelled out the minimum content of every summing up: 'it is trite to say that every summing up must contain at least a direction to the jury as to the burden and standard of proof, and as to the ingredients of the offence or offences which the jury are called upon to consider'. The problem of what is meant by this *dictum* was considered in a lecture entitled 'Summing Up the Law' by the late Professor Edward Griew:[136]

---

[134] For a valuable review of the empirical evidence see P. Darbyshire, 'What can we Learn from Published Jury Research? Findings for the Criminal Courts Review 2001', *Criminal Law Review*, 2001, pp. 970–9. See especially W. Young, 'Summing-up to Juries in Criminal Cases – What Jury Research says about Current Rules and Practice', *Criminal Law Review*, 2003, pp. 665–89.   [135] [1988] Crim LR 127.   [136] *Criminal Law Review*, 1989, pp. 768–80.

Directing the jury as to the burden of proof means telling them who has to prove the case; it means telling them that the prosecution must prove the defendant's guilt, not the defendant his innocence. Directing them as to the standard of proof means telling them that the case has to be proved beyond reasonable doubt – commonly expressed by saying that they may convict the defendant only if they are sure of his guilt.[137]

In recent years the Court of Appeal has laid down 'model' or 'specimen' directions or standard forms of words in which directions on particular matters can or ought to be given. A number are now embodied in a document issued to all judges who sit in the Crown Court by the Judicial Studies Board with the approval of the Lord Chief Justice. They are published on the Board's Website.[138] The foreword warns: 'They are an invaluable tool – but must be a servant not a master . . . They must be adapted to the needs of the individual case'.

In his lecture, Professor Griew criticised the tendency of judges to give the jury more law than it needed for the purpose of its decision[139] and to use overly technical and complex language. American research showed that a good many judicial directions on law to juries were 'totally incomprehensible to an alarming percentage of jurors'.[140] No doubt similar research in this country would yield similar results. 'Our juries continue to be addressed in language relatively rich in abstract and latinate words and in sentences that are often very long'.

In the *Crown Court Study*, 61 per cent of jurors said they found the judge's summing up 'not at all difficult' to understand and another 33 per cent found it 'not very difficult' to understand. When asked if other members of the jury found it difficult, a quarter were not sure but 65 per cent thought they did not.[141] But saying that they understood does not mean that they did understand. Even less does it show whether the jury followed the judge's direction on the law.[142]

In 'Summing up – a judge's perspective', Madge J argued for greater use of written directions to juries on the law.[143] In his experience, giving the jury a written copy of his instructions on the law had positive results: fewer requests

---

[137] For an empirical study of what magistrates, ordinary citizens and professionals in the criminal justice system understand by the admonition 'only convict if you are sure of the defendant's guilt' see M. Zander, 'The Criminal Standard of Proof – How Sure is Sure?', 150 *New Law Journal*, 20 October 2000, p. 1517.

[138] www.jsboard.co.uk (Publications – Bench books – Specimen Directions).

[139] Professor Griew suggested (at pp. 770–1) that in *McVey*, above, the Court of Appeal quashed a conviction of a plainly guilty person because the judge's direction on the ingredients of the offence was insufficient even though the missing words were unnecessary to the jury's decision.

[140] Notably R.P. Charrow and V.R. Charrow, 'Making Legal Language Understandable: A Psycholinguistic Study of Jury Instructions', *Columbia Law Review*, 1979, p. 1306; W.W. Schwarzer, 'Communicating with Juries: Problems and Remedies', 69 *California Law Review*, 1981, p. 731.   [141] M. Zander and P. Henderson, n. 69 above, sections 8.6.2–3.

[142] For references to other literature on whether jurors understand judges' directions on the law see *Evidence in Criminal Proceedings: Previous Misconduct of a Defendant* (Law Commission consultation paper 141, 1996) pp. 127–8.   [143] *Criminal Law Review*, 2006, pp. 817–27.

from juries for further instructions, quicker jury decisions, more conviction and fewer hung juries. He also argued for less judicial comment on the facts.

Summing up on the facts

The job of the judge in summing up the facts according to the Court of Appeal is to 'state matters impartially, clearly and logically'.[144] His task therefore is to remind them of the evidence and to marshal it in a convenient way which is fair to both sides.[145]

To what extent can he go beyond this to comment on the evidence and thereby seek to influence the jury's decision? There is no doubt that English judges do this. (It is famously said that Sergeant Sullivan at the end of an Old Bailey trial invited the judge to ask the jury whether they found for the defendant or his Lordship.) In the notorious case of the 'Birmingham Six' whose convictions for involvement in IRA terrorist bombings were ultimately quashed, the trial judge, Bridge J (as he then was), during a three-day summing up gave innumerable indications that in his view the prosecution's evidence was to be preferred to that of the defence. Nor did he see anything wrong with leading the jury to its conclusion. 'I am of the opinion', he told the jury, 'that if a judge has formed a clear view, it is much better to let the jury see that and say so and not pretend to be a kind of Olympian detached observer'.

For an unusually strong summing up on the facts in a civil case see that of Caulfield J in the libel action very unwisely brought in 1987 by Mr Jeffrey Archer against the *Daily Star*, arising out of the allegation that he had visited a prostitute.[146] There was, the judge said, no accounting for the tastes of happily married men and the fact that the jury would not expect Mr Archer, deputy chairman of the Conservative Party, to visit a prostitute, did not mean that it was not possible, but he asked the jury to consider whether it was probable. He invited the jury to remember the evidence of Mrs Mary Archer. 'Your vision of her will probably never disappear. Has she elegance? Has she fragrance? Would she have, apart from the strain of his trial, a radiance?' Mr Archer, the judge said, was a sportsman. 'You may think he's fit looking . . . Is he in need of cold, unloving, rubber-insulated sex in a seedy hotel?'[147]

The danger that the judge will try to influence the jury is the greater in cases where the accused has previous convictions, because the judge knows of their existence from the outset. They are in his file, allegedly so that he can steer counsel away

---

[144] *Berrada* (1989) 91 Cr App Rep 131n. The trial judge had said that the defendant's allegation that police officers had fabricated an interview was 'really monstrous and wicked' and 'utterly monstrous'. The court quashed the conviction.

[145] It seems that in a short case in which the issues are simple it is not necessarily a fatal defect in a summing up that the evidence has not been discussed: see *Attfield* (1961) 45 Cr App Rep 309.

[146] Four years later Lord Archer, as he had become, was imprisoned for perjury and perverting the course of justice in the libel proceedings.   [147] *The Times*, 24 July 1987.

from questions which might otherwise lead to their becoming admissible. (This is less significant now that previous convictions are much more widely admissible.)

In the United States the rule in most states is that the judge in a criminal trial must express no opinion on the weight or credibility of the evidence of witnesses or on the merits of either side.

Even if judges are prevented from commenting, they can of course still convey to the jury their basic view through a mixture of inflexion of the voice, 'body language', timing and other signs which would not register in the official transcript. (The Court of Appeal has, however, indicated that in extreme cases it would allow evidence from those present in court as to 'non-verbal communication' by the trial judge trying to persuade the jury.[148]) The only way to prevent such influence would be to prohibit the judge from summing up at all on the facts – which is the usual rule in the USA. There is little doubt that when the judge sums up for a conviction the impression of impartial justice being done is diminished.[149]

In the *Crown Court Study*, the barristers, the CPS, the defence solicitor and the judge were asked: 'Did the summing up favour either side?' In each category of respondents the majority said No, but of those who said Yes, more in each category thought it favoured the prosecution than the defence.[150] Defendants were asked about the fairness or otherwise of the judge during the trial and in the summing up. The defendant thought the judge had been fair in the summing up in 73 per cent of cases and unfair in 27 per cent.[151]

The Runciman Royal Commission thought it would be wrong to lay down a rule as to how far the judge should sum up on the facts. Cases and circumstances varied. Sometimes there would be no need for a summing up at all. The need to be fair to both sides, the Commission said, required 'that judges should be wholly neutral in any comment that they make on the credibility of the evidence'.[152] It was 'inappropriate for judges to intrude their own views of whether or not a witness is to be believed'.[153] Implementation of that recommendation would presumably require some kind of ruling or Practice Statement by the Lord Chief Justice. This has not happened.[154]

Lord Justice Auld took a radical approach to the judge's summing up: 'The judge should no longer direct the jury on the law or sum up evidence in the detail that he now does'.[155] His basic recommendations were:[156]

- The judge should continue to remind the jury of the issues and, save in the most simple cases, the evidence relevant to them, and should always give the jury an adequate account of the defence, but he should do it in more summary form than is now common.

---

[148] *Hircock* [1969] 1 All ER 47.

[149] See generally D. Wolchover, 'Should Judges Sum Up on the Facts?', *Criminal Law Review*, 1989, p. 781.   [150] M. Zander and P. Henderson, n. 69 above, Table 4.21, p. 130.

[151] *Ibid.*, p. 132.   [152] *Ibid.*, p. 124, para. 23.   [153] *Ibid.*

[154] For support for the Royal Commission's view that it should happen see D. Osborne, 'Breaking New Ground', *Counsel*, February 1998, pp. 16–17.

[155] Auld, Ch. 11, para. 44, p. 533.   [156] Auld, pp. 537–8.

- The judge should devise and put to the jury a series of written factual questions, the answers to which could logically lead only to a verdict of guilty or not guilty; the questions should correspond with those in the updated Case and Issues Summary, supplemented as necessary in a separate written list prepared for the purpose, and each question should be tailored to the law as the judge knows it to be and to the issues and evidence in the case.
- The judge, where he considers it appropriate, should be permitted to require a jury to answer publicly each of his questions and to declare a verdict in accordance with those answers.
- So far as possible, the judge should not direct the jury on the law, save by implication in the questions of fact that he puts to them for decision.

In Auld's view, 'simplification of the way in which judges direct and sum up to juries was essential for the future well-being of our system of trial by judge and jury'.[157] The Court of Appeal bore ultimate responsibility for the elaborate and complex structure now enshrined in the Judicial Studies Board's specimen directions. What was needed, he suggested, was 'a fundamental and practical review of the structure and necessary content of a summing up with a view to shedding rather than incorporating the law and to framing simple factual questions that take it into account'. Perhaps, he thought, 'a body drawn from the judiciary and the Judicial Studies Board could be given a blank sheet of paper and charged with the task'.

The Auld report was published in October 2001. Five years later, there was no sign that such a body would be established or that Auld's radical proposals regarding the judge's summing up would be adopted.

Directing an acquittal

A high proportion of acquittals are directed by the judge. As has been seen, there are two forms of such acquittal: (1) where the prosecution enter no evidence at all (called an 'ordered acquittal') and (2) after a submission by the defence at some stage after the case has begun and usually at the end of the prosecution's case that there is no case to answer (a 'directed acquittal').

The withdrawal of a case from the jury poses a delicate problem. Can the judge decline to put the case to the jury if he thinks that the prosecution's case is merely weak? The Court of Appeal considered this question in 1981 in *R v. Galbraith*.[158] Lord Lane, the Chief Justice, said there were two schools of thought. One was that the judge should stop the case if in his view it would be unsafe or unsatisfactory to convict.[159] The other was that the judge should only stop the case if there was no evidence on which a jury properly directed could

---

[157] *Ibid*, para. 49, p. 535. Auld did not mention the findings of the *Crown Court Study* (sect. 8.6.2) suggesting that the jury may not in fact have as great difficulties with the summing up as some believe.   [158] [1981] 1 WLR 1039.

[159] See for instance *Mansfield* (1977) 65 Cr App Rep 276.

properly convict. Before the Criminal Appeal Act 1966 the second test had been applied, but under the 1966 Act the Court of Appeal was required to quash a conviction where it found that under the circumstances it was unsafe or unsatisfactory (see p. 693 below). Since then a practice had grown up of asking the trial judge to take a view as to whether conviction would be safe by submitting that there was no case. This involved the judge invading the province of the jury. It invited the trial judge to consider the weight and the reliability of the prosecution's evidence – precisely the issues that had to be considered by the jury.

In *Galbraith* Lord Lane answered the question in this way:

> How then should the judge approach a submission of 'no case'? (1) If there is no evidence that the crime alleged has been committed by the defendant, there is no difficulty. The judge will of course stop the case. (2) The difficulty arises where there is some evidence but it is of a tenuous character, for example because of inherent weakness or vagueness or because it is inconsistent with other evidence. (a) Where the judge comes to the conclusion that the prosecution evidence, taken at the highest, is such that a jury properly directed could not properly convict upon it, it is his duty, upon a submission being made, to stop the case. (b) Where however the prosecution evidence is such that its strength or weakness depends on the view to be taken of a witness's reliability, or other matters which are generally speaking within the province of the jury and where on one possible view of the facts there *is* evidence upon which a jury could properly come to the conclusion that the defendant is guilty, then the judge should allow the matter to be tried by the jury. It follows that we think the second of the two schools of thought is to be preferred.[160]

Even where the judge has rejected a submission of no case he may still direct the jury to acquit if in light of the developing defence case he subsequently comes to the conclusion that no reasonable jury properly directed could convict,[161] but such a power must be exercised very sparingly.

The Runciman Royal Commission Report recommended that *Galbraith* should be reversed so that a judge could stop a case if he or she took the view that the prosecution's evidence was demonstrably unsafe or unsatisfactory or too weak to be allowed to go to the jury.[162] This recommendation has not been acted upon.

Sometimes the judge, whilst not going so far as to direct the jury to acquit, makes it very clear in his summing up that he thinks an acquittal is the right result. He sums up strongly for an acquittal. There is nothing to prevent this even if the judge goes beyond the proper limits. The matter is unlikely to become the subject of comment from the Court of Appeal since the prosecution has no right

---

[160] At p. 1042. For comment and discussion see R. Pattenden, 'The Submission of No Case – Some Recent Developments', *Criminal Law Review*, 1982, p. 558; D. Wolchover, 'Stopping the Trial in Suspect Cases', 132 *New Law Journal*, 1982, p. 527. For the effect of this ruling in magistrates' courts see N. Yell, 'Submissions of "No Case to Answer"', *Justice of the Peace*, 1981, p. 406.   [161] *Brown (Davina)* [2001] Crim LR 675, CA.
[162] Runciman, p. 59, para. 41.

of appeal against an acquittal (other than on a point of law taken by the Attorney General, the outcome of which does not affect the defendant – see p. 667 below). (For a classic instance of the judge 'summing up for an acquittal' see the summing up of Mr Justice Cantley in the Jeremy Thorpe case.[163])

Directing a conviction

Views have differed as to whether it is ever legitimate for the judge to direct the jury to convict. Lord Devlin thought it to be unconstitutional.[164] There is no doubt that the judge must leave to the jury any issue that has to be decided by them. In *Leer*[165] the Court of Appeal considered a direction to convict where the accused had been charged with possessing an offensive weapon after being found with a fishing knife. The judge ruled that his answers to police questioning as to why he had the knife did not amount to a reasonable excuse and that he therefore had no defence to put forward and he directed them to convict. The Court of Appeal quashed the conviction because the judge should have left the issue to the jury. It would have been surprising if the jury had decided to acquit but such a decision on the evidence would not have been perverse.[166]

However, what if an acquittal would be perverse? Can the judge direct a conviction then? In *DPP v. Stonehouse*[167] the House of Lords by a majority of three to two held that he could not. Lord Salmon said there was a difference between directing the jury to acquit or to convict. If there was no evidence on which they could reasonably convict, he should direct an acquittal. This rule had been established a long time ago to protect the accused against being wrongly convicted. 'But there is no converse rule . . . If the judge is satisfied that on the evidence, the jury would not be justified in acquitting the accused and indeed that it would be perverse of them to do so, he has no power to pre-empt the jury's verdict by directing them to convict. The jury alone has the right to decide that the accused is guilty'.[168] Lord Salmon did accept that it would be perfectly in order for the judge to sum up to the jury 'in such a way as to make it plain that he considers the accused is guilty and should be convicted'.[169] Lord Edmund-Davies said there was an unfortunate tendency in the courts these days to withdraw issues from the jury which were properly theirs. Whether this sprang from distrust of the jury's capacity 'or from excessive zeal in seeking to simplify their task, it needs careful watching'.[170] The judge could give a strong lead to the jury but he should not direct them to convict.

The view expressed in *Stonehouse* was confirmed by a unanimous House of Lords in *Wang*, allowing an appeal from the Court of Appeal.[171] The decision, given in a single opinion, was a ringing endorsement of the dominant role of the jury:

---

[163] *Daily Telegraph*, 19 and 20 June 1979.   [164] *Trial by Jury*, 1966, p. 84 and Appendix II.
[165] [1982] Crim LR 310.   [166] See also *R v. Clemo* [1973] RTR 176n.
[167] [1978] AC 55.   [168] At 80.   [169] *Ibid.*   [170] At 88.
[171] [2005] UKHL 9, [2005] 1 All ER 782 and see the commentary in [2005] Crim LR 646–8.

In England and Wales it has been possible to assume, in the light of experience and with a large measure of confidence, that jurors will almost invariably approach their important task with a degree of conscientiousness commensurate with what is at stake and a ready willingness to do their best to follow the trial judge's directions. If there were to be a significant problem, no doubt the role of the jury would call for legislative scrutiny. As it is, however, the acquittals of such high profile defendants as *Ponting*,[172] *Randle and Pottle*[173] have been quite as much welcomed as resented by the public, which over many centuries has adhered tenaciously to its historic choice that decisions on the guilt of defendants charged with serious crime should rest with a jury of lay people, randomly selected, and not with professional judges . . . We would accordingly allow the appeal, quash the appellant's conviction and answer the certified question by saying that there are no circumstances in which a judge is entitled to direct a jury to return a verdict of guilt [16, 18].[174]

In June 2006 the Court of Appeal put a gloss on Lord Bingham's *dictum* in *Wang* that there were 'no circumstances in which a judge is entitled to direct a jury to return a verdict of guilty'.[175] Lord Justice Tuckey said this did not mean that in every such case the conviction must be held to be unsafe.[176] It depended on whether the jury was given an opportunity to consider its verdict. In *Kelleher*[177] the judge had directed the jury that 'there can only be one verdict in this case and that is one of guilty'. The jury retired and brought back a guilty verdict. The Court of Appeal dismissed their appeals against conviction. In these two cases the appellants raised no defence in law and in each case the judge had directed the jury to convict which they did *without retiring*. The Court of Appeal quashed the convictions as the question of the defendant's guilt had been completely taken away from the jury. (One has to say that this distinction based on whether the jury actually retires seems unconvincing.)

On the historic role of the jury see T.A. Green's magisterial *Verdict According to Conscience: Perspectives on the English Criminal Trial, 1200–1800* (Chicago

---

[172] [1985] Crim LR 318. Clive Ponting, a senior civil servant, was prosecuted under the Official Secrets Act for leaking to an MP information about the sinking of the Argentinian ship *The General Belgrano* during the Falklands War. The judge thought Mr Ponting had no defence. He therefore intended to direct the jury to convict but was dissuaded from doing so by counsel for the prosecution who drew the judge's attention to what he termed 'recent authorities'. The judge said that although all the elements of the offence had been made out and there was no defence, he told the jury that they were at liberty to bring in whatever verdict they considered right. The jury acquitted – presumably because they felt that Mr Ponting had acted honourably and perhaps correctly (ed.).

[173] [1991] 1 WLR 1087. The defendants were tried at the Old Bailey for helping the spy George Blake to escape from prison twenty-five years earlier. They were prosecuted after they wrote a book about their exploit. The trial judge ruled that they had no defence to the charge. In his closing speech to the jury Pat Pottle said: 'We do not deny the things we are accused of doing. Not only do we not deny it, we say it was the right thing to do'. The jury acquitted both men (*The Times*, 5 July 1991) (ed.).

[174] In *Caley-Knowles* and *Jones* [2006] EWCA Crim 1611, [2007] Crim LR 61, 4 October the Court of Appeal said that Lord Bingham's statement in *Wang* that there were 'no circumstances in which a judge is entitled to direct a jury to return a verdict of guilty' meant in every such case.   [175] At [17].   [176] *Caley-Knowles* and *Jones*, n. 174 above.

[177] [2003] EWCA Crim 3525.

University Press, 1985). Green shows that part of the role of the jury was to mitigate the rigour and harshness of the criminal law and its penalties by acquitting guilty defendants, not just in the occasional case but on a massive scale.

Should the jury be prohibited from returning a perverse verdict?

In one of the most controversial passages in his report, Lord Justice Auld recommended 'that the law should be declared, by statute if need be, that juries have no right to acquit defendants in defiance of the law or in disregard of the evidence, and that judges and advocates should conduct criminal cases accordingly'.[178] In his view, the ability of juries to acquit in defiance of the law and in disregard of their oaths was 'a blatant affront to the legal process and the main purpose of the criminal justice system – the control of crime – of which they are so important a part'.[179] The jury's role was 'to find the facts and, applying the law to those facts, to determine guilt or no'.[180] They were not there 'to substitute their view of the propriety of the law for that of Parliament or its enforcement for that of the appointed Executive, still less on what may be irrational, secret and unchallengeable grounds'.[181]

The writer criticised this proposal in his response to the Auld report:[182]

> I regard this proposal as wholly unacceptable – a serious misreading of the function of the jury. The right to return a perverse verdict in defiance of the law or the evidence is an important safeguard against unjust laws, oppressive prosecutions or harsh sentences. In former centuries juries notoriously defied the law to save defendants from the gallows. In modern times the power is used, sometimes to general acclaim, sometimes to general annoyance, usually one imagines to some of each.

> Auld quotes E.P. Thompson's eloquent passage in describing the function of the jury:

>> The English common law rests upon a bargain between the Law and the People. The jury box is where people come into the court; the judge watches them and the jury watches back. A jury is the place where the bargain is struck. The jury attends in judgment, not only upon the accused, but also upon the justice and humanity of the law . . . [*Writing by Candlelight*, 1980]

> This exactly captures the position, which I would say is part of the unwritten constitution of this country. Auld says that he regards the ability of juries to acquit and to convict in defiance of the law and in disregard of their oaths, as a 'blatant affront to the legal process and the main purpose of the criminal justice system – the control of crime – of which they are so important a part'. I believe that this statement, perhaps the least attractive sentence in the whole report, reflects deep distrust of the jury. It is based I believe on an authoritarian attitude that disregards history and reveals a grievously misjudged sense of the proper balance of the criminal justice system.

---

[178] Auld, Ch. 5, para. 107, p. 176.   [179] *Ibid.*   [180] *Ibid.*   [181] *Ibid.*
[182] Accessible on www.criminal-courts-review.org.uk – Comments received, pp. 18–19.

In the Introduction to his Report[183] Sir Robin quotes, with apparent approval, from the concluding sentence in my Dissent to the Report of the Runciman Royal Commission, 'the integrity of the criminal justice system is a higher objective than the conviction of any individual'. But the concern for justice and for the integrity of the system is too important to be entrusted solely to the judges. The jury have a role in that regard too.

The Runciman Royal Commission dealt with this issue in a short paragraph – which was not mentioned by Auld:

> Although juries are under a solemn duty to return a verdict in accordance with the evidence, they do from time to time perversely return a verdict contrary to the evidence. Until there is research on jury deliberations it is impossible to say confidently why this happens, but it is plausible to suppose that it is because the jury has taken an unfavourable view of the prosecution or of the law under which it is brought or the likely penalty. We do not, however, think that these cases justify the introduction of a right of appeal against acquittal.[184]

I cannot imagine that on a constitutional matter of this importance any Government would prefer the view of an individual judge, however distinguished, to the unanimous contrary view of a recent Royal Commission. I believe that the present system provides the right balance in telling the jury that they must decide the case in light of the law and the evidence but allowing them to ignore either or both if they believe that to be the right course. We have lived with that system for hundreds of years. I believe that there is no acceptable reason to consider changing it.

The Government stated in its White Paper that it did not accept Lord Justice Auld's recommendation. ('Nor do we intend to legislate to prevent juries from returning verdicts regarded as perverse where the verdict flies in the face of the evidence, as has happened very occasionally'.[185])

Asking the jury questions

The jury does not give reasons for its decisions. In a criminal case it simply says 'guilty' or 'not guilty'. In a civil case it finds for the plaintiff or defendant and, if for the plaintiff, it may have to determine the damages. But in a decision in February 1999 the Court of Appeal created an exception to the general rule. It held that where there was more than one possible basis for a verdict of guilty of manslaughter 'it might be convenient and desirable' for the judge to invite the jury to indicate the basis on which they returned that verdict. The purpose of such an inquiry would be to assist the judge with regard to sentence. Lord Justice Rose said that in summing up, the judge might hand to the jury written questions identifying the different possible verdicts as between murder and manslaughter and also as to the reasons for manslaughter. Alternatively, after a manslaughter verdict was returned, a judge might ask the jury what was the basis

---

[183] Page 10, para. 8.   [184] Report, p. 177, para. 75.
[185] White Paper, *Justice for All*, Cm. 5563, July 2001, para. 4.50.

of that verdict – provided that he had warned the jury in his summing up of his intention to ask that question. But there was no obligation on the jury to answer. Nor was there any requirement of unanimity as to the reasons for the verdict.[186]

This proposal seems completely novel and highly problematic. So far as is known, the suggestion has not been taken up.

Is the jury's unreasoned verdict compatible with the European Convention on Human Rights?

Article 6 of the ECHR states that one of the incidents of a fair trial is a public pronouncement of a reasoned decision. If this applies to jury trial, the Strasbourg Court could hold jury trial with its inscrutable verdict to be contrary to the Convention. Addressing this question in his report, Lord Justice Auld said: 'For a number of reasons, I incline to the view of a number of eminent British commentators[187] that the Strasbourg Court, in taking account of the way in which our system of jury trial works as a whole, would not consider our juries' unreasoned verdicts to breach Article 6'.[188]

He instanced the following reasons:

- The Strasbourg case law was not precise about the content of reasons required to satisfy the fair trial test.
- The test was not exacting. As well as allowing for different national traditions, the court had stressed that the general duty to give reasons did not require detailed answers.
- Courts were not required by the Strasbourg case law to indicate the evidence they accept and why.
- The Strasbourg Court had ruled that the publicly unreasoned decision of a Danish jury was not contrary to the Convention.[189]
- In *Condron v. United Kingdom*[190] the court had said: 'The fact that the issue of the applicant's silence was left to a jury cannot of itself be incompatible with the requirement of a fair trial'.[191] This, Auld suggested, showed that the court was prepared to accept the jury's verdict as the final word in a judgment of which the summing up furnished the overt reasoning process.
- In considering the fairness of the trial the Strasbourg Court looked at the trial and the appeal process together. The Court of Appeal did have a limited capacity to quash a conviction if it considers that it was contrary to the evidence.[192]

186   *R v. Jones (Douglas)* (1999) Times, 17 February.
187   He cited Professor John Spencer in his advice to the Auld Review and Harris, O'Boyle and Warbrick, *The Law of the European Convention on Human Rights* (1995) p. 215.
188   Auld, Ch. 5, para. 92, p. 170.
189   *Saric v. Denmark*, application no. 31913/96, decision of 2 February 1999.
190   (2000) 31 EHRR 1.   191   At [57].
192   However, Auld cited the court's statement in *Condron v. United Kingdom* (above at [46]) that jury verdicts in England 'are not accompanied by reasons which are amenable to review on appeal'.

- There was no general continental consensus as to what is meant by the reasoning ('motivation') of a judicial decision. In France, for instance, it could mean no more than an indication of the legal principles applied by the court.

However, Lord Justice Auld did consider that 'the time has come' for the trial judge to give the jury a series of written factual questions leading logically only to a verdict of guilty or not guilty.[193]

11. Majority jury verdicts

In Scotland, since time immemorial, there has been a majority verdict based on a bare majority of eight or more out of the fifteen who sit on a Scottish jury. Historically in England, however, the jury's decision had to be unanimous – though the reality of unanimity must sometimes have been questionable. In some cases dissenters would probably have 'given in' rather than have a hung jury or just to bring the proceedings to a speedy conclusion.[194]

In 1967, the then Home Secretary, Mr Roy Jenkins, introduced proposals in the Criminal Justice Bill to permit a majority verdict of not less than ten out of twelve. The reason he gave was the spate of recent 'jury nobbling' cases – though the evidence for this was thin. The total proportion of jury disagreements resulting in a retrial appeared to be about 4 per cent and few of these, presumably, would have been due to any form of tampering with the jury.

The proposal provoked great controversy at the time, but in the interim it seems to have become accepted.[195] Lord Justice Auld dealt with this topic in nine lines. His Review, he said, had 'produced little support for change either in the levels of the required majorities or for reversion to unanimity in all cases or for any form of intermediate verdict, such as that of "not proven" in use in Scotland'.[196]

The proportion of guilty verdicts by majority is just over a fifth.[197] There are no equivalent official figures for the proportion of acquittals by a majority, since the jury is not permitted to reveal that an acquittal was by a majority, for fear that it would be treated as a second-class acquittal.[198] (In the *Crown Court Study* it was possible to establish from the jury questionnaires that the proportion of acquittals by a majority was exactly the same as convictions by a majority.[199])

The court is not supposed to consider the possibility of a majority verdict until at least two hours and ten minutes have elapsed.[200] In a complex case the judge will wait much longer than that.

---

[193] Auld, Ch. 5, para. 97, p. 172.

[194] For the particular danger of this happening on a Friday afternoon see P. Darbyshire, 'Notes of a Lawyer Juror', 150 *New Law Journal*, 14 September 1990, p. 1264 at 6–7.

[195] See, however, G. Maher, 'Jury Verdicts and the Presumption of Innocence', *Legal Studies*, 1983, p. 146 for a powerful argument that majority verdicts are inconsistent with the requirement that proof of guilt be beyond a reasonable doubt.

[196] Auld, Ch. 5, para. 75, p. 164.

[197] See the annual *Judicial Statistics*, Table 6.11. In 2004 it was 23 per cent; in 2005 it was 21 per cent.

[198] Criminal Justice Act 1967, s. 13(2).   [199] M. Zander and P. Henderson, n. 69 above, p. 162.

[200] *Practice Direction* [2002] 3 All ER 936, para. 46.

In *R v. Reynolds*[201] the Court of Appeal Criminal Division quashed a conviction for theft because the foreman of the jury stated that there was a majority of ten in favour of conviction but he did not also state that there were two members of the jury who disagreed. The court held that the provisions of s. 17(3) of the 1967 Act were mandatory in stating that the court 'shall not accept [a majority verdict] unless the foreman of the jury has stated in open court the number of jurors who respectively agreed to and dissented from the verdict'. In *R v. Pigg*[202] the House of Lords overruled *Reynolds*. The Law Lords held unanimously that, although it was a mandatory requirement that the number who agreed on conviction and the number who dissented must be made known, the precise form of words used was not an essential part of that requirement. It was enough if the words used by the foreman of the jury and the clerk of the court made it clear to an ordinary person how the jury was divided. If the foreman said that ten agreed to convict it could be inferred that two dissented!

However, what if the jury is completely deadlocked? For many years the judge was permitted in that situation to give what was known as a *Walhein* direction, approved in the case of that name.[203] In that case, the jury told the judge that they were having difficulty in reaching a unanimous verdict. (At that date there was no such thing as a majority verdict.) The judge then directed them:

> You are a body of twelve men. Each of you has taken an oath to return a true verdict according to the evidence; but, of course, you have a duty not as individuals, but collectively. No one must be false to that oath; but in order to return a collective verdict, the verdict of you all, there must necessarily be argument and a certain amount of give and take and adjustment of views within the scope of the oath you have taken; and it makes for great public inconvenience and expense if jurors cannot agree owing to the unwillingness of one of their number to listen to the arguments of the rest. Having said that, I can say no more.

This direction seemed to condone pressure on the dissenting minority to fall into line. Since the introduction of majority verdicts in 1967 it has seemed inappropriate. In *Watson*[204] the Court of Appeal approved a new direction to replace that in *Walhein*:

> Each of you has taken an oath to return a true verdict according to the evidence. No one must be false to that oath, but you have a duty not only as individuals but collectively. That is the strength of the jury system. Each of you takes into the jury box with you your individual experience and wisdom. You do that by giving your views and listening to the views of the others. There must necessarily be discussion, argument and give and take within the scope of your oath. That is the way in which agreement is reached. If, unhappily, [ten of] you cannot reach agreement you must say so. It is a matter for the discretion of the Judge as

---

[201] [1981] 3 All ER 849.   [202] [1983] 1 All ER 56.   [203] (1952) 36 Cr App Rep 167.
[204] [1988] QB 690.

to whether he gives that direction at all and if so, at what stage of the trial. There will usually be no need to do so.[205]

12. Retrials on jury disagreement

When the jury disagrees and cannot reach a verdict, the prosecution are entitled to start afresh. It is a matter of discretion over which the court has no control – though occasionally the judge remonstrates with the prosecutor about the desirability of pursuing a particular case. (It has been argued that the prosecution should have to ask leave and that the court should take into account the same factors regarded as relevant when the Court of Appeal considers whether to order a retrial on quashing a conviction.[206])

There are no regular statistics about the extent to which retrials occur as a result of jury disagreements. In 1981, according to a Home Office Research Unit paper, there were some 370 retrials due to this cause – about 1.5 per cent of the 25,000 or so contested cases in the Crown Court that year.[207]

13. Will the courts consider what happened in the jury room?

What happens if it is suggested that one or more jurors has behaved improperly? If the matter is raised on appeal the ancient common law rule is clear.[208] Appeal courts will not receive evidence as to what transpired in the jury room. In *Boston v. Bagshaw & Sons*[209] all twelve members of the jury swore affidavits that they had given the opposite result of what they intended. The Court of Appeal refused to change the decision. Giving the judgment of the court Lord Denning said:

> To my mind it is settled as well as anything can be that it is not open to the court to receive any such evidence as this. Once a jury has given their verdict, it is accepted by the judge, and they have been discharged, they are not at liberty to say they meant something different . . .
>
> The reasons are twofold: first, to secure the finality of decisions arrived at by the jury; secondly, to protect the jury themselves and to prevent them being exposed to pressure or inducement to explain or alter their views.

The rule is the same in criminal cases. In *Thompson*[210] the Court of Criminal Appeal refused to inquire into an allegation that the jury had been moving

---

[205] See further M.J. Reville, 'Directing the Hung Lamp of Freedom', *Law Society's Gazette*, 26 October 1988, p. 19; P. Robertshaw, 'Exhorting Hung Juries', *Criminal Law Review*, 1997, p. 805.   [206] J. Hall, 'Hung Juries and Retrials', *Archbold News*, 27 June 2001, p. 6.

[207] See S. Butler, *Acquittal Rates* (Home Office Research and Planning Unit Paper No. 16, 1983) p. 7. On the juror's duty to reach a decision see *R v. Schot and Barclay* [1997] Crim LR 827. In Robertshaw's article, n. 205 above, it was stated that in 1991 there were ninety hung trials in the whole country – of which no fewer than seventy-nine (88 per cent) occurred in one court, the Inner London Crown Court!

[208] In 1785 in *Vaise v. Delavel* 1 TR 11, 99 ER 944 Lord Mansfield said that the court could not receive an affidavit from a juror as to the nature of the jury's deliberations.

[209] [1966] 1 WLR 1135n.   [210] [1962] 1 All ER 65.

toward an acquittal until one member of the jury had produced a list of the defendant's previous convictions upon which they convicted. Lord Chief Justice Parker gave the judgment of the court:

> . . . There is absolutely no doubt that information as to the prisoner's previous convictions must be kept from a jury, and if what was said to have happened did happen it would have been highly improper. This court is now asked to inquire into the matter, and to adjourn the case in order to see whether the alleged statement by the juryman can be supported by some statement or affidavit made by him. The court has come to the conclusion that it is perfectly idle to adjourn the case for that purpose because the court is quite satisfied that they would have no right at all to inquire what did occur in the jury room. It has for long been a rule of practice, based on public policy, that the court should not inquire, by taking evidence from jurymen, what did occur in either the jury box or the jury room.

The common law rule was endorsed in 2004 by a four to one decision of the House of Lords in *Connor* and *Mirza*.[211] In each case a letter had been written to the trial court by a juror after majority verdicts of guilty. In one the letter alleged that other jurors had been racially prejudiced against the defendant; in the second the juror alleged that other jurors had rushed to finish the case against the two defendants with inappropriate speed. The Court of Appeal applied the common law rule. It also held that the Contempt of Court Act 1981, s. 8 prohibited complaint about or inquiry into such allegations. The House of Lords, Lord Steyn dissenting, held that the principle of the confidentiality of a jury's deliberations underpinned the independence and impartiality of the jury as a whole. The rule prohibiting inquiry applied even if it appeared that egregious impropriety had occurred. This was because of the common law rule not because of the Contempt of Court Act. Section 8 of the 1981 Act had no application to the court that had responsibility for handling contempt.

The Law Lords conceded that there were some exceptions. The distinction is not always easy to draw. In *Ellis v. Deheer*[212] evidence was received that some of the jurors had been unable to hear what the foreman said in giving the jury's verdict and that they were in disagreement with it. In *Ras Behari Lal*[213] the Privy Council upheld an inquiry held as to whether a juror had been able to understand English. In *Spencer*[214] the House of Lords quashed convictions of nurses who had been found guilty of violence against patients at Rampton Hospital when someone who had been removed from the jury because of possible bias against the defendants had given lifts to and from the trial to three of the jurors. In *Young*[215] the Court of Appeal ordered a retrial after it emerged that during an overnight adjournment in a hotel members of the jury had used a ouija board to consult the deceased in a séance! (In *Connor* and *Mirza* the Law Lords said that if the evidence was that the jurors had used a ouija board *in* the jury room

---

[211] [2004] UKHL 2, [2004] 1 All ER 925, [2004] Crim LR 1041. The speeches take fifty-five pages in the law report.   [212] [1922] 2 KB 113.   [213] (1933) 50 TLR 1, PC.
[214] [1986] 2 All ER 928.   [215] [1995] QB 324.

or that they had decided the case by drawing lots or tossing a coin, that evidence could be admitted. There would in effect have been no deliberations.) In K[216] the Court of Appeal quashed a conviction when the day after the case was finished the jury bailiff discovered in the jury room material that had been downloaded from the internet.

The House of Lords in *Connor* and *Mirza* said that if a juror had concerns about the improper conduct of fellow jurors he should bring such concerns to the attention of the trial judge.[217] That, the Law Lords said, could extend to other persons properly concerned, such as the jury bailiff or the clerk of the court. It would also be permissible to send a sealed letter to the defendant's lawyers or even to a Citizens' Advice Bureau if it was to be passed on unopened to the proper authorities. It was not permissible, however, to write as had happened in that case to the defendant's mother.[218]

The judge then has a variety of options. He would normally discuss these with counsel for both sides. He may warn the jury about the matter and exhort them to behave properly. He has the option of discharging the jury. Whether he can and should conduct an inquiry as to what happened in the jury room was considered by the House of Lords in *Smith*.[219] While the jury in that case were considering their verdict the judge had received a letter from one of the jurors alleging that some jurors had been badgering, coercing and even intimidating other jurors into changing their verdict. The judge gave the jury a further direction which included exhortation not to be bullied or cajoled into a verdict with which they did not agree. The Court of Appeal certified for the House of Lords the question what inquiry could properly be made as to what had transpired in the jury room. The five Law Lords agreed that the convictions should be quashed on the ground that the judge's direction to the jury had been inadequate. It had not mentioned the jury's duty to follow the judge's directions on the law, to adhere to the evidence without speculation and to decide on the verdict without bargaining or pressure.

As to whether the trial judge could inquire into what happened in the jury room, Lord Carswell (with whom the four other judges agreed) said that although there might be some matters into which the judge can and should inquire – he gave as an example an allegation that a juror had used a mobile telephone – 'I do not think that it is necessary or desirable to attempt to draw up a

---

[216] [2005] EWCA 346, [2005] Crim LR 574.

[217] *Practice Direction (Criminal Proceedings: Consolidation)* [2002] 1 WLR 2870 was amended so as to make this clear to jurors – [2004] 1 WLR 665 ('Judges should ensure that the jury is alerted to bring any concerns about fellow jurors to the attention of the judge at the time and not wait until the case is concluded' and the judge should instruct the jury that they had 'a duty to bring to the judge's attention promptly, any behaviour among jurors or by others affecting the jurors, that causes concern').

[218] *A-G v. Scotcher* [2005] UKHL 36, [2005] 3 All ER 1 in which sentence of the juror for contempt of court was upheld. It was no defence to the charge that the juror's purpose in writing to the mother had been to prevent a miscarriage of justice.

[219] [2005] UKHL 12, [2005] 2 All ER 29, [2005] Crim LR 476.

precise definition of the situations in which it would be legitimate for the judge to question jurors'.[220] In the case in question questioning jurors would not have been appropriate. It would be unlikely to reveal the truth and could have made the situation worse.

In *Smith* the letter to the judge identified the juror who wrote it. In the earlier case of *Robinson*[221] the judge received an anonymous letter about what was going on in the jury room. In order to discover whether it came from a member of the jury the judge drafted first one and then a second questionnaire. Both were given to the jurors to complete in order to discover whether they had written the anonymous letter. They all denied it and without further inquiry (rightly or wrongly) the judge concluded that it had been written by someone not on the jury. Commenting in *Smith*, Lord Carswell simply said: 'I do not consider that issuing a questionnaire of the type used in *R v. Robinson* would have been appropriate in this case'.[222] The question of what inquiries by the trial judge are permissible remains open.

The Strasbourg Court has given decisions on these matters that pull in slightly different directions. In *Gregory v. United Kingdom* G complained that he had not had a fair trial due to racial discrimination. While the jury were considering their verdict, a note had been passed to the trial judge saying that the jury were showing racial overtones and that one juror should be excused. The judge warned the jury to put aside any prejudice and to decide the case on the evidence. Rejecting the complaint, the court said it was accepted that 'it was not possible under English law for the trial judge to question the jurors about the circumstances that gave rise to the note'. It also acknowledged 'that the rule governing the secrecy of jury deliberations is a crucial and legitimate feature of English trial law which serves to reinforce the jury's role as the ultimate arbiter of fact and to guarantee open and frank deliberations among jurors'.[223]

In *Sander v. United Kingdom*[224] the Strasbourg Court held by four to three that the defendant had not had a fair trial because the trial judge had not taken sufficiently robust action to deal with an allegation by one juror of racial prejudice by two other jurors. He had told the jurors to search their consciences, overnight and to let the court know if they could not decide the case on the evidence. Having received such assurance the next day, he allowed the trial to proceed. The court held that he had failed to provide sufficient guarantees to exclude any objectively justified or legitimate doubts about the jury's impartiality.[225]

In 2005, in its consultation paper regarding research in the jury room (p. 513 above), the Government raised the question whether any further steps should be taken to deal with the problem of impropriety in the jury room. It indicated, however, that it did not itself consider that any changes were needed, other than

---

[220] At [20].   [221] [2002] EWCA Crim 2489.   [222] At [21].
[223] (1988) 25 EHRR 577 at [44].   [224] (2001) 31 EHRR 1003.
[225] For critical comment see M. Zander, 'The Complaining Juror', 150 *New Law Journal*, 19 May 2000, p. 723.

informing jurors about what could constitute impropriety and of how they could draw it to the attention of the trial judge. In November 2005 the Government stated that its decision was to allow the common law to develop on a case by case basis rather than introduce statutory changes.[226]

For discussion of these issues see K. Quinn, 'Jury Bias and the European Convention on Human Rights: a Well-Kept Secret?' *Criminal Law Review*, 2004, pp. 998–1014; P.R. Ferguson, 'The Criminal Jury in England and Scotland: the Confidentiality Principle and the Investigation of Impropriety', 10 *International Journal of Evidence and Proof*, 2006, pp. 180–211.

14. Publication of the secrets of the jury room

Jurors are told that they must not reveal anything that occurs in the jury room either during the trial or after it has finished. But what is the position if the press publish details of jury deliberations? The question came up for decision after the sensational Jeremy Thorpe case[227] when the *New Statesman* in 1979 published an interview with a member of the jury in which he gave details of the jury discussions. Proceedings for contempt were instituted by the Attorney General but, surprisingly, the Attorney General lost.[228] The Divisional Court held that disclosure of the secrets of the jury room could be contempt but it depended on the circumstances. It would be contempt if disclosure tended to imperil the finality of jury verdicts or to affect adversely the attitude of future jurors or the quality of their deliberations. In this case, the court found, there were no special features which made publication a contempt. There had been no payment of money to the juror. The article did not suggest that anything improper had occurred. In fact it showed that the jury had approached their task in a sensible and responsible manner. There was no suggestion that the article could have interfered with the administration of justice.

The media's victory was shortlived. As has been seen, the Contempt of Court Act 1981, s. 8 made it contempt 'to obtain, disclose or solicit any particulars of statements made, opinions expressed, arguments advanced or votes cast by members of a jury in the course of their deliberation in any legal proceedings'. It makes no difference whether the case is identified or whether any payment is made for such disclosure. The clause was introduced against the advice of the Government by Lords Hutchinson and Wigoder and was supported by the Criminal Bar Association, the Senate of the Four Inns of Court and the Lord Chief Justice. The Lord Chancellor, Lord Hailsham, declared it to be 'far too draconian'. However, he was defeated in the House of Lords and the Government did not seek to have the clause overturned when the Bill returned to the House of Commons.

---

[226] See www.dca.gov.uk – Publications – Consultation Papers – January 2005.
[227] The leader of the Liberal Party was charged with conspiracy to murder his alleged homosexual lover. He was acquitted after a trial lasting thirty-one days.
[228] *A-G v. New Statesman and Nation Publishing Co Ltd* [1980] 1 All ER 644.

It is noteworthy that when the issue had been put to the Criminal Law Revision Committee for consideration in 1967 it did not think there was any need for legislation. The Committee said juries were reminded of their duty to maintain secrecy by a notice on the walls of the jury room and that there seemed to be few breaches of this understanding: 'We are of opinion that secrecy has been well maintained and that such breaches or attempts to break it as have become known so far have not established a mischief so extensive or serious that it calls for legislation and punishment'.[229] It accepted that it was not then a criminal offence to disclose what had happened in the jury room though in certain circumstances it might amount to contempt of court. But it did not think the problem was sufficiently serious to warrant legislation. For one thing it did not think it right to make punishable the inevitable minor disclosures as people spoke to their families and friends after the case about the experience of being jurymen. Such disclosures, the Committee said, though they should not be encouraged, few would regard as deserving of punishment. Under the Contempt of Court Act 1981 such disclosures could theoretically be the subject of proceedings for contempt – though in practice this is unthinkable.

See further J. Jaconelli, 'Some Thoughts on Jury Secrecy', *Legal Studies*, March 1990, p. 91.

In *A–G v. Associated Newspapers Ltd*[230] the House of Lords rejected an appeal by the owners of the *Mail on Sunday* which had been fined £60,000 for contempt in publishing views of jurors in the Blue Arrow fraud case. The information had been obtained not from the jurors directly but from transcripts of paid interviews purportedly carried out by a researcher. The House of Lords held that it made no difference whether the publication of what had transpired in the jury room came directly from jurors or indirectly from others.

15. Does the jury acquit too many defendants?

The suggestion that too many guilty defendants are acquitted was powerfully urged in the 1970s by Sir Robert Mark when he was Commissioner of the Metropolitan Police. The best-publicised occasion for the expression of these views was his 1973 Dimbleby Lecture on BBC1:

Sir Robert Mark, 'Minority Verdict', BBC, 1973, pp. 8–14

What we do know about trials in higher courts doesn't justify any complacency. Indeed, there is one fact I can mention which should be enough in itself to demand some kind of enquiry. This is the rate of acquittals. Of all the people in England and Wales who plead not guilty and are tried by jury, about half are acquitted . . .

Every acquittal is a case in which either a guilty man has been allowed to go free or an innocent citizen has been put to the trouble and expense of defending

---

[229] Criminal Law Revision Committee, Tenth Report, *Secrecy of the Jury Room*, 1968.
[230] [1994] 1 All ER 556.

himself. There must be some rate of failure. We can't always expect to convict the guilty or never to prosecute the innocent, but in my opinion a failure rate of one in two is far too high. I doubt whether it would be tolerated in many other kinds of activity, so I think it's something that certainly needs looking into. In the absence of any reliable research no one can say with any certainty why the acquittal rate is so high. A fairly high number of acquittals are undoubtedly by direction of the judges, as soon as they've heard the prosecution case. Since 1967 cases are no longer sifted effectively by a Magistrate, and the higher courts are cluttered up by cases which in my opinion should never have got there at all.

My own view is that the proportion of those acquittals relating to those whom experienced police officers believe to be guilty is too high to be acceptable . . .

I wouldn't deny that sometimes common sense and humanity produce an acquittal which could not be justified in law, but this kind of case is much rarer than you might suppose. Much more frequent are the cases in which the defects and uncertainties in the system are ruthlessly exploited by the knowledgeable criminal and by his advisers.

Sir Robert Mark's strictures on the high 'failure rate' in English trials need some further explication and comment.

The acquittal rate is based on contested cases, whereas the majority of defendants in the Crown Court plead guilty. The proportion pleading guilty in Crown Courts currently is around three-fifths. (In 2004, of defendants tried in the Crown Court, 58 per cent pleaded guilty to all charges. In 2005 the proportion was 60 per cent.[231] The proportion is lower than it was. For many years it was around 70 per cent.)

The proportion of defendants pleading not guilty to all counts who are acquitted is around two-thirds. (In both 2004 and 2005 it was exactly 66 per cent.[232]) This is a high proportion – higher even than the figure of which Sir Robert Mark complained.

However, only a minority of acquittals are actually by a jury. In 2005, 57 per cent of all acquittals of defendants pleading not guilty to all charges were ordered by the judge when the prosecution offered no evidence at the start of the case and another 12 per cent were directed by the judge at the close of the prosecution's case on the ground that there was insufficient evidence to put to the jury.[233] The jury were therefore only responsible for the remaining 31 per cent of the acquittals. This represents 7 per cent of the total number tried in the Crown Court.[234]

The fact that some 7 per cent of those tried in the Crown Court are acquitted by the jury could be mainly attributable to the fact that the burden of proof is a high one. Even assuming that all those acquitted were guilty (a wholly

[231] *Judicial Statistics 2004*, Cmnd 6565, Table 6.8, p 90; *ibid.*, 2005, Cmnd 6799, Table 6.8, p 90.

[232] *Ibid*, Table 6.9.

[233] *Ibid*, Table 6.10. For a study of these cases see J. Baldwin, 'Understanding Judge Ordered and Directed Acquittals in the Crown Court', *Criminal Law Review*, 1997, pp. 536–55.

[234] *Ibid*, calculated from Tables 6.8 and 6.10.

impermissible and unrealistic assumption), a significant number would rightly be acquitted simply because the prosecution failed to prove its case beyond a reasonable doubt. If proof must be beyond a reasonable doubt (and no one has suggested otherwise), it is inevitable that a considerable number of guilty defendants will be acquitted because the evidence of their guilt cannot be produced.

Contrary to what Sir Robert Mark asserted, professional criminals do not appear to do better in the criminal justice system than others. Indeed, if anything the reverse. Taking defendants with a prior record, the evidence is that they have a statistically *lower* chance of an acquittal than defendants with no prior record.[235] Moreover, the worse the record, the worse the chances of an acquittal.[236] In Baldwin and McConville's 1979 study they got from the police details not only of prior convictions but also of prior acquittals and of suspected involvement in criminal activity. From this they built up a profile of each defendant on a scale of criminal professionalism. For this exercise there were close to 5,000 defendants in the sample – 2,406 in Birmingham and 2,292 in London, a total of 4,698. Of these, 2,265 (48 per cent) were defined by the police information as 'low' on the criminal professionalism score, 1,448 (31 per cent) as 'medium', 647 (14 per cent) as 'high' and 227 (5 per cent) as 'very high'. When these scores were compared with acquittals and especially the 'questionable acquittals', it was found that 'only a minuscule proportion of all cases end in the questionable acquittal of any defendant who, on the measures used here, could be regarded as a professional criminal. Indeed, of those scoring highly on the professionalism scale in each city, no more than one in eighty was said to have been questionably acquitted'.[237]

The only evidence that provides *any* support for Sir Robert Mark's thesis was that of John Mack, who contrasted the careers of the top criminals in his area of research (from names supplied by the police) with that of two other categories of lesser criminals. He called his three groups the Main Group, the Lesser Group and the Small Fry. On average the Small Fry were convicted on 85 per cent of charges brought against them, the Lesser Group on 80 per cent and the Main Group on 75 per cent.[238] This does show that the Main Group were somewhat more successful in avoiding charges than the others, but the difference can hardly be said to be great and the police success rate in getting convictions in three-quarters of the charges brought against the top villains seems, if anything, remarkably high. Moreover, as Mack showed, when the serious criminals are convicted they tend to get longer sentences. Mack compared the time not spent in prison from the age of seventeen for his three groups. The Small Fry spent on average 83 per cent of their time not in prison compared with 70 per cent for the Lesser Group and 74 per cent for the Main Group.[239]

---

[235] This is shown by a number of studies including even one conducted by the Metropolitan Police – see M. Zander, 37 *Modern Law Review*, 1974, p. 39, Table 3; McCabe and Purves, *The Jury at Work* (Blackwell, 1972) p. 39, Table 4; Metropolitan Police, *Law Society's Gazette*, 1 March 1973, Table 1.   [236] M. Zander, 37 *Modern Law Review*, 1974, p. 41.
[237] *Jury Trials* (1979) pp. 110–12.   [238] J. Mack, 39 *Modern Law Review*, 1976, p. 255.
[239] *Ibid*, p. 252.

Nor was Sir Robert's attack on crooked lawyers supported by the small amount of evidence on this issue. In Baldwin and McConville's study of 370 contested jury trials in Birmingham they interviewed the police officers in the cases about the reasons for the acquittals. They reported: 'There was not a single serious allegation of any practice which could possibly be described as corrupt'.[240] In another study the same two authors looked at 2,000 cases heard in seven London Crown Courts in the light of the 'solicitors blacklist' maintained by Scotland Yard. (They had been sent a copy anonymously.) The firms on the list appeared on behalf of 223 defendants in the sample. Of these, 50 per cent pleaded guilty – a proportion that was slightly *higher* than for the rest of the sample. Of those who pleaded not guilty, the acquittal rate was 53 per cent, which was not very different from that of 47 per cent of the rest of the sample. Of the defendants identified to the researchers by the police as serious professional criminals, only ten out of seventy-two had employed firms on the blacklist.[241]

Finally, the minority of cases that are contested are likely, by definition, to be the doubtful ones in which one might expect a fairly high acquittal rate. This common sense view is supported by the evidence which shows that many not guilty pleas are based on a defence that the accused lacked the necessary knowledge or intent (*mens rea*) to be guilty of the offence. It is perhaps not surprising that, in such cases particularly, the jury (or magistrates) will interpret conflicting testimony by giving the defendant the benefit of the doubt.

16. Trial on indictment without a jury

Hitherto in England and Wales trial on indictment has meant trial by jury. The Criminal Justice Bill 2002–3 Part 7 provided for trial on indictment by a judge without a jury in three situations: (1) on application by the defendant (clause 41); (2) on the ground of the complexity or length of the case (clause 42) and (3) where there was a danger of jury tampering (clause 43).

The House of Lords Committee stage debate on these provisions took place on 15 July 2003. Twenty peers spoke. Apart from the Minister, Baroness Scotland QC, only two of the twenty supported the Government. There were seventeen speeches denouncing the provisions as an unacceptable incursion on the sanctity of trial by jury. After a debate of three and a half hours, the Lords rejected all three clauses by the overwhelming majority of 210 to 136.[242] (The vote was taken on clause 41 but the debate grouped all the Part 7 provisions together so that defeat for clause 41 meant defeat for them all.)

The Government immediately announced that it would restore the Part 7 provisions when the Bill returned to the Commons. In the event, the defendant's

---

[240] *Jury Trials*, 1979, p. 118.
[241] J. Baldwin and M. McConville, 'Allegations Against Lawyers', *Criminal Law Review*, 1978, pp. 744–5.   [242] House of Lords, *Hansard*, vol. 651, 15 July 2003, cols. 768–814.

right to opt for trial by judge alone was quietly dropped but the other two provisions were retained and were eventually included in the Act as ss. 43 and 44 respectively. (See further p. 546 below.)

The Domestic Violence, Crime and Victims Act 2004, ss. 17–20 has novel provisions for trial without jury for some offences when other similar offences can be tried with a jury. An application would be made by the prosecution. There are three pre-conditions: (1) the case must have so many counts that trial by jury of all of them would be impracticable; (2) trial by jury is possible of counts that can be regarded as sample counts; and (3) it is in the interests of justice (s. 17).

At the time of writing only s. 44 (jury tampering) had been brought into force.

This section on trial on indictment without a jury begins with consideration of the 'Diplock courts' in Northern Ireland.

'Diplock courts' in Northern Ireland

A survey of all cases tried in the first six months of 1973 in Belfast showed an acquittal rate of 16 per cent for Protestant defendants as against 6 per cent for Catholics. A Committee headed by Lord Diplock was sent to inquire into the problem of jury verdicts in terrorism cases. The Committee's Report identified various problems including intimidation of witnesses by terrorists and the danger of perverse acquittals of Loyalist terrorists by predominantly Protestant juries. The Committee recommended the suspension of jury trial for certain offences [243] The recommendation was implemented in the Northern Ireland (Emergency Provisions) Act 1973 in relation to 'scheduled offences', broadly those regularly committed by terrorists – murder, other serious offences against the person, firearms and explosives charges, arson, robbery, aggravated burglary and intimidation.

The system of trial in Diplock courts was basically left intact subject to certain significant innovations: a decision to convict requires a reasoned judgment (and reasoned judgments are normally also given for acquittals), there is an automatic right of appeal against conviction, sentence or both and if the judge rules that a confession is inadmissible, he can withdraw and direct that the trial be conducted by a different judge. There were also changes made in the rules governing the admissibility of confessions.

A major study of the system published in 1995 stated that from 1973 to then, well over 10,000 defendants had passed through Diplock courts. 'The average annual figure decreased from over 1,000 in the early years to a level of over 400 in each year from 1991 to 1993'.[244]

---

[243] *Report of the Commission to Consider Legal Procedures to Deal with Terrorist Activities in Northern Ireland*, 1972, Cmnd. 5185.

[244] J. Jackson and S. Doran, *Judge without Jury: Diplock Trials in the Adversary System* (Clarendon Press, 1995) p. 19. On the Diplock courts see also K. Boyle, T. Hadden and P. Hillyard, *Law*

The study by Jackson and Doran showed that although the acquittal rate in Diplock courts for each of the ten years from 1984 to 1993 ran below that in ordinary jury trials, in seven of those ten years it was over 40 per cent and in four of the ten years it was over 50 per cent.[245] The guilty plea rate in Diplock court cases was not significantly different from the rate in ordinary trials. In both Diplock courts and ordinary Northern Ireland trials the guilty plea rate was considerably higher than in jury cases in England and Wales. In Northern Ireland between 1984 and 1993 it was over 80 per cent in seven out of ten years in Diplock courts and in six out of ten years in ordinary trials.[246]

The authors of the study found that although in Diplock courts the judges had more possibility for involving themselves in the fact-finding process than in jury trials, they generally did not do so. ('There was, however, no clear evidence from our survey that judges necessarily acted in a more inquisitorial manner when sitting in the absence of the jury. The general, though not universal, view expressed by the judges who spoke to us was that it was inappropriate to deviate from the umpireal role required in adversarial proceedings'.[247])

In 1987 the Government decided to abolish the right of trial by jury in civil actions in Northern Ireland where previously jury trials were used in the overwhelming majority of such cases.[248]

In August 2006 it was announced that as part of the process of 'normalisation', it was intended that Diplock courts should be abolished before summer 2007, but judge-only trials would be retained for exceptional cases. The DPP was to have the power to certify judge-only trial on the basis that in his view there was a risk of jury intimidation or interference with the administration of justice.[249]

Defendant allowed to opt for trial by judge alone

The Runciman Royal Commission did not mention 'jury waiver', namely permitting defendants to opt for trial by judge alone. This is widely used in the United States[250] and to some extent in Canada,[251] New Zealand[252] and Australia. Lord Justice Auld proposed that, subject to the consent of the court, the defendant be given the choice in all trials on indictment. The judge should decide after hearing representations from both sides. He did not favour making the

Footnote 244 (*cont.*)
   and State (Martin Robertson, 1975) and by the same authors, *Ten Years on, Northern Ireland* (Cobden Trust, 1980); J. Jackson, 'Diplock and the Presumption against Jury Trial: a Critique', *Criminal Law Review*, 1992, p. 755.   [245] Table 2.2, p. 35.   [246] *Ibid*, Table 2.3, p. 41.
[247] *Ibid*, p. 288.   [248] Jury Amendment (Northern Ireland) Order 1987, SI 1987/1283.
[249] *Replacement Arrangements for the Diplock Court System* (Northern Ireland Office consultation paper, 11 August 2006) – www.nio.gov.uk.
[250] According to the Auld report (Ch. 5, para. 111, p. 178) in 1993 some 14 per cent of all serious federal cases were tried by judge alone.
[251] It has applied to all indictable offences since 1985 – Canadian Criminal Code, RSC C-46, ss. 473 and 476.
[252] Offences carrying a maximum of fourteen years' imprisonment or a mandatory life term are excluded – Crimes Act 1961, ss. 361 A–C and 361B(5).

defendant's option subject to the consent of the prosecution as was the case in most jurisdictions in the United States.

In his view, trial by judge alone had a potential for providing 'a simpler, more efficient, fairer and more open form of procedure than is now available in many jury trials, with the added advantage of a fully reasoned judgment'.[253]

To avoid 'judge shopping', the defendant should be required to opt for trial at an early stage. Where the defendant had co-defendants who did not want trial by judge alone the best solution was that adopted in New Zealand where the judge would order that either all or none be tried by judge alone.[254]

The Government accepted the recommendation that the defendant be permitted to opt for trial by judge alone[255] and included it in the Criminal Justice Bill 2002–3. As has been seen, however, clause 41 was defeated in the Lords and was not re-introduced.

Non-jury courts for fraud and other complex trials

There have for many years been a variety of voices raised to urge that long, complex fraud cases should be tried by some form of special tribunal. The campaign for such reform had been going on since the late 1960s when it was promoted in particular by the then Lord Chief Justice, Lord Parker. In 1983 the idea was put forward separately by the Chairman of the Law Commission, by the Lord Chief Justice, Lord Lane, by a Law Lord, Lord Roskill, and by Lord Hailsham, the Lord Chancellor, in the Hamlyn Lectures. In November of that year the Government set up the Roskill Committee 'to consider in what ways the conduct of criminal proceedings arising from fraud can be improved, and to consider what changes in existing law and procedure would be desirable to secure the just, expeditious and economical disposal of such proceedings'.

The Roskill Committee concluded that long fraud cases were so complex that it was not reasonable to expect jurors to be able to cope. There were often multiple defendants and many charges. 'The background against which frauds are alleged to have been committed – the sophisticated world of high finance and international trading – is probably a mystery to most or all of the jurors, its customs and practices a closed book'.[256] The language of accountancy would be unfamiliar. The evidence often ran into hundreds or even thousands of documents. Research conducted for the Committee by the Medical Research Council's Applied Psychology Unit at Cambridge on understanding by jurors of a one-hour summing up in a fraud case confirmed the 'view of experienced observers and the promptings of common sense, that the most complex of fraud cases will exceed the limits of comprehension of members of a jury'.[257] Many jurors were simply out of their depth in such cases.

---

[253] Auld, Ch. 5, para. 117, p. 180.   [254] *Ibid*, para. 118, pp. 180–1.
[255] White Paper, *Justice for All*, Cm. 5563, July 2001, para. 4.27.   [256] Roskill, para. 8.27.
[257] *Ibid*, para. 8.34.

There was one dissentient, Mr Walter Merricks. In a powerful statement he effectively demolished the Committee's reasoning. First, he pointed to the weight of expert evidence received by the Committee which was 'overwhelmingly in favour of retaining the jury'.[258] The Committee thought there were cases that were not prosecuted because of the difficulty of presenting very complex cases to the jury, but analysis by the DPP of all his fraud cases in 1983 showed that there was only one out of seventy-one not prosecuted in which the decision not to prosecute was caused by the complexity of the evidence.

Mr Merricks suggested that it had become a convention of the unwritten constitution that citizens should not be subjected to more than a short period of imprisonment otherwise than on a jury's verdict. Parliament should not be invited to abrogate this constitutional right without evidence that jury trial had broken down in serious fraud cases *and* that all possible procedural improvements had been considered and found inadequate. There was a danger that if a special expert tribunal were set up, the trial would become simply an exchange between lawyers and the tribunal in impenetrable jargon. The function of a trial as a publicly comprehensible exposition of the case would be threatened. Moreover, the fundamental issue in most fraud trials was one of dishonesty. It would be dangerous to entrust this judgment to experts. The legal standard of dishonesty was the standard of the ordinary man and experts were not ordinary men. It would also be difficult to define the cases in which the special tribunal would be appropriate.

Mr Merricks' dissent attracted much notice and support in comments on the Roskill Committee Report. He had clearly had the better of the argument. The Government gave the report generally a warm welcome but its proposal on this particular issue was too controversial and, after hesitating for a period, the Government announced that it would not be implemented.

In 1993 the Runciman Royal Commission said that in the absence of research into juries it had no basis for making any recommendations for dispensing with juries in long fraud cases.[259]

In February 1998, a year into the life of the Blair Government, the Home Office published a consultation paper (*Juries in Serious Fraud Trials*) which invited views on whether the system should be altered and, if so, how. It referred to the Court of Appeal's decision in the *Blue Arrow* trial quashing the conviction on the ground that the case had become unmanageable and said that there was a significant risk of a miscarriage of justice resulting from the volume and complexity of the issues presented to the jury. The consultation paper canvassed a number of possible options: special juries, a judge sitting on his own, a special tribunal and a judge sitting with a jury.

Views were asked for by June 1998 but in fact nothing further happened with regard to this issue before Lord Justice Auld was appointed in December 1999 to undertake his review of the criminal courts.

---

[258] *Ibid*, p. 192, para. C5.   [259] Runciman, p. 136, para. 76.

Lord Justice Auld's report

Auld recommended that in serious and complex fraud cases the trial judge should be empowered to order trial by himself sitting with lay members (or, where the defendant opted for trial by judge alone, by himself alone). Either party should have a right of appeal against the judge's decision to the Court of Appeal.

Of the various arguments, Auld said that the two that weighed most heavily with him were 'the burdensome length and increasing speciality and complexity of these cases, with which jurors, largely or wholly strangers to the subject matter, are expected to cope'. The average length of cases prosecuted by the Serious Fraud Office was six months. ('The fact is that many fraud and other cases . . . now demand much more of the traditional English jury than it is equipped to provide'.[260])

Auld rejected having special juries made up of persons with special qualifications. It would be too difficult to compose lists of persons with the requisite qualifications and it would be unreasonable to expect them to serve for such long cases. He said that there had been little support for the idea of trial in such cases by a panel of judges. He agreed with those who argued that this would unduly strain valuable and limited judicial resources. He said that he had wavered as to whether trial in such cases should be by judge alone or by judge sitting with lay members. In the end he considered that the defendant should be entitled to express a preference, with the decision left to the judge. If he decided that trial should be with lay members, he should, after hearing representations, determine from which (if any) speciality(ies) they should be drawn. The Lord Chancellor, after consulting professional bodies, could establish and maintain a panel of suitable persons.[261] In the first instance the new system might be restricted to cases prosecuted by the Serious Fraud Office.

The White Paper

In its White Paper *Justice for All*[262] the Government said that that there were a small number of serious and complex fraud trials that placed a huge strain on all concerned and where the time commitment was a burden on jurors' personal and working lives. As a result it was not always possible to find a representative panel of jurors. The Government had concluded there should be a more effective form of trial in such cases. It rejected Auld's view that trial in such cases might be by judge with lay members. It recognised that the expertise of such persons could help the trial proceed. 'However, identifying and recruiting suitable people raises considerable difficulties, not least because this would represent a substantial commitment over a long period'. It therefore proposed that such cases should be tried by judge alone. It did not expect there to be more than fifteen to twenty such trials a year.[263] It asked for views as to whether trial by judge alone should be extended to other long and complex cases.

---

[260] Auld, Ch. 5, para. 183, p. 204.   [261] Auld, Ch. 5, pp. 205–9 and 213.
[262] Cm. 5563, July 2001, para. 4.28.   [263] *Ibid*, para. 4.30.

The Criminal Justice Act 2003

In the event, the Government decided to extend trial by judge alone to a much wider category of cases. Clause 42 of the Criminal Justice Bill 2002–3 provided for the prosecution to apply for a trial on indictment in the Crown Court to be conducted by judge alone on grounds of length or complexity. Such an application would have to satisfy two tests.

The first concerned the likely impact of the trial on the jurors. The length or complexity of the trial had to be such that it was likely to be so burdensome on the jury as to make it necessary in the interests of justice to conduct the trial without a jury (subsection (4)(a)) or that the trial would be likely to place an excessive burden on the life of a typical juror (subsection (4)(b)). The Explanatory Notes accompanying the Bill said that in deciding whether the burden on a typical juror would be excessive, the judge would need to take account of factors such as the impact of the trial on his or her working and private life and the physical and mental demands it would make.[264]

The second condition that had to be satisfied related to the sort of issues and evidence that the jury would have to consider – that the complexity or length (or both) would be attributable to the need to address arrangements, transactions or records of a financial or commercial nature or that related to property (subsection (5)(a)) and to the likely nature or volume of the evidence (subsection (5)(b)).

The Explanatory Notes accompanying the Bill (para. 228) said that in making his decision the judge might be expected to have regard to factors such as the seriousness of the offence charged and the seniority of the defendant's position – though all relevant factors would have to be taken into account.

After the clause was defeated in the Lords (p. 000 above) it was re-introduced by the Government. However, in order to get it through, the Home Secretary, Mr David Blunkett, was forced to give an undertaking that it would not be implemented until there had been further consultation about the best way of dealing with the problem and that confirmation would require an affirmative resolution in both Houses of Parliament.[265] Consultation took the form of a half-day seminar as to the various options convened by the Attorney General, Lord Goldsmith, attended by some fifty persons representing the various interest groups.[266]

In June 2005 the Attorney General announced that the Government would be pressing ahead with implementation of s. 43.[267] It hoped that the provision would be brought into force from 1 January 2006. A debate on an Order to achieve this was scheduled for 29 November in the Lords but in the face of the prospect of defeat the Attorney General withdrew the Order – though he said he was still committed to trial without juries for a small number of very difficult cases.[268] However, in March 2006 he finally conceded that the provision would

---

[264] Paragraph 231.   [265] House of Commons, *Hansard*, 20 November 2003, cols. 1027–8.
[266] The writer was one of those who attended.   [267] *The Guardian*, 22 June 2005.
[268] *The Guardian*, 26 November 2005; *New Law Journal*, 2 December 2005, p. 1835.

not be implemented. On the Report stage of the Fraud Bill Lord Goldsmith stated that the attempt to find an acceptable compromise having failed, the Government had decided not to proceed with s. 43. Instead – when parliamentary time allowed – it would instead bring forward a new Bill dealing with the matter.[269] The Fraud (Trials Without a Jury) Bill was introduced on 16 November 2006. The Bill activates s. 43 of the Criminal Justice Act 2003 subject to one change – that the initial application for a non-jury trial and the trial itself must both be heard by a High Court judge.[270]

Until now whether the jury can understand the evidence in long fraud trials has never been investigated in the context of an actual case, but in 2006 the question was put to the test in the inquiry after the collapse of *R v. Rayment*, known as the Jubilee Line Case. The case began on 25 June 2003. On 22 March 2005, almost two years later, it was terminated after the prosecution announced its decision not to oppose a defence application to discharge the jury. The prosecution accepted that, as a matter of law, no jury could be expected to remember and assess evidence that had been given a year or even eighteen months earlier. Costs of some £25 million had been wasted and in view of the public disquiet, the Attorney General asked the Chief Inspector of the CPS to inquire into the reasons for this expensive fiasco.

The Chief Inspector's report totally exonerated the jury from any blame. ('No responsibility for the inconclusive outcome of the case can properly be attributed to the capabilities or conduct of the jury'.[271])

In his report the Chief Inspector stated that eleven of the twelve members of the jury had been interviewed by the review team. They had been furious when they discovered from the newspapers that the reason for the termination of the case on which they had sat for almost two years was their assumed inability to remember the evidence:

> Taken as a whole they did not appear to have had difficulty understanding the evidence or the essentials of the case presented to them. Most of them insisted they had a good or very good grasp of what the case was about from the prosecution opening onwards; that they understood very well the charges and the different combinations of [the seven] defendants and counts; and that when the case collapsed they had a clear understanding of the evidence.[272]

The fact that they said that they understood the evidence obviously did not prove that they actually did understand it. The Chief Inspector's report makes a highly significant (and probably unique) contribution in considering this question:

> During a group interview in early August 2005 they showed quite impressive familiarity with the charges, issues and evidence, despite the length of time that

---

[269] House of Lords, *Hansard*, 14 March 2006, col. 1130.
[270] For a resumé of the background, the history and the arguments see Miriam Peck, House of Commons Research Paper, n. 1, p. 486 above.
[271] *Review of the Investigation and Criminal Proceedings relating to the Jubilee Line Case* (HM CPS Inspectorate, June 2006) Executive Summary, para. 9.   [272] *Ibid*, p. 106, para. 11.7.

had elapsed, and the fact that they did not have their notes or access to documents nor an opportunity to think back and refresh their memories. They recalled particular parts of the evidence, particular witnesses and the substance of their evidence. They recalled the different counts . . . Occasionally there were individual failures of recollection, but one advantage of the jury system is that not all jurors are likely to have forgotten the same piece of evidence, if it is of any importance.[273]

So much for the argument that jurors cannot be expected to remember and understand the evidence in long complex cases.

Trial by judge alone because of jury tampering

The White Paper *Justice for All* (July 2001) said that where an attempt had been made to intimidate or influence the jury the judge had a common law power to stop the trial but no power to continue the trial without a jury. The Government intended to legislate to give the judge power to continue the trial without the jury. It asked whether this power should also exist where it was anticipated that there was a serious risk that the jury would be subject to bribery or intimidation. In such cases the courts currently ordered police protection for the jury. Quite apart from being extremely costly and burdensome for the police, such protection might have to continue over a period of months, and could be extremely disruptive and an unreasonable intrusion in the lives of jurors.

Under the Criminal Justice Act 2003 s. 44[274] a judge can order that the trial be conducted without a jury if the prosecution satisfy him (1) that 'there is evidence of a real and present danger that jury tampering would take place' and (2) that despite any efforts that might be made to prevent it, 'the likelihood that it would take place would be so substantial as to make it necessary in the interests of justice for the trial to be conducted without a jury'. Under s. 46 the judge (exercising his common law powers) may discharge the jury during the trial because jury tampering appears to have taken place. If he is minded to discharge the jury on such grounds, he must allow the parties to make representations. If he then discharges the jury he must order that the trial continues without a jury unless in the interests of justice he decides that he must terminate it. If he decides instead to stop the trial he may order that a new trial will be conducted without a jury – providing he is satisfied that the two conditions in s. 44 are fulfilled.

Trial by jury of sample counts only

The Domestic Violence, Crimes and Victims Act 2004 introduced a new concept – trial by judge and jury of sample counts followed after conviction by trial by judge alone of other similar counts.

---

[273] *Ibid.*   [274] In force from July 2006 – SI 2006/No. 1835.

The provisions for a two-stage trial process were based on the recommendations of the Law Commission in its report *Effective Prosecution of Multiple Offending*.[275] The Law Commission Report stated that its work on the problem was prompted by the decision of the Court of Appeal in *Kidd*[276] in which the court held that it offended a fundamental principle for the defendant to be sentenced not only for the specimen offences of which he had been convicted but also for other offences for which they were specimens that he had not agreed could be taken into consideration. The ruling meant that in such cases the defendant would escape being sentenced for the true range of his offences. This was the problem addressed by the Law Commission.

Following the Law Commission's recommendation, s. 18 of the 2004 Act provides that the prosecution may apply to a Crown Court judge for a trial on the basis that some but not all counts in the indictment may be tried by a judge without a jury. Three conditions must be satisfied: (1) that the number of counts in the indictment is such 'that a trial by jury involving all those counts would be impracticable'; (2) that each count or group of counts tried with a jury can be regarded as a sample of counts which could be tried without a jury; and (3) that it 'is in the interests of justice' for an order to be made under the section. (At the time of writing the provision was not yet in force.)

Young defendants

Defendants under eighteen charged with an indictable offence other than murder must be tried summarily unless the offence is one of certain grave offences for which they may be sentenced to a long term of imprisonment or where they are charged with an adult and the magistrates consider it to be in the interests of justice that all should be tried together. Lord Justice Auld stated that in 1999 close to 5,000 young defendants were committed for trial in the Crown Court and nearly 1,000 were committed to the Crown Court for sentence.

Auld recommended that all cases involving young defendants committed to the Crown Court for trial or sentence should instead be put before a special sitting of the youth court constituted by a judge sitting with at least two experienced youth panel magistrates and exercising the full powers of the Crown Court.[277] The court should have the power to sit in private. ('Notwithstanding the public notoriety that such cases now attract through intense media coverage, I consider that the court proceedings should normally be entitled to the same privacy as those in the present youth court'.[278]) The only exception should be where the young defendant was tried jointly with an adult. Such cases should continue to be subject to the Practice Direction issued in February 2000[279] as a

---

[275] No. 277, 2002.
[276] [1998] 1 WLR 604. (The decision is also referred to as *Canavan*.)
[277] Auld, Ch. 5, para. 211, p. 216.   [278] Auld, Ch. 5, paras. 185–95 and 206, pp. 205–9 and 213.
[279] [2000] 1 Cr App Rep 483, [2000] 2 All ER 285.

result of the cases of Thompson and Venables, both eleven years old when they were convicted at the Crown Court of the murder of two-year-old James Bulger. The European Court of Human Rights held in December 1999 that they had not had a fair trial.

The Practice Direction stated that the trial of young defendants should, if practicable, be in a courtroom in which all the participants are on the same level, the defendant should be allowed to sit with family members and his legal representatives, the trial should be conducted in language that he can follow and on a timetable that takes account of his concentration span, robes and wigs should not be worn unless the defendant asks or the court orders that they should be and the court should be prepared to order that attendance be restricted to a small number of persons. Facilities for reporting the trial must be provided but they can be restricted in the courtroom itself. If so, they must be relayed to another room to which the media have free access.

The Government's White Paper *Justice for All* (July 2001) said that many welcomed the proposal in Auld to take young defendants out of the Crown Court. Certainly, the younger the defendant, the stronger that case. 'There was however some concern over those in the older age group'. One option would be to give the Crown Court a discretion to retain cases involving sixteen- and seventeen-year-olds. As regards young defendants charged with adults, the Government invited further views.

The Criminal Justice Act 2003 did not include any provisions on this topic.

17. The operation of the jury (and trials) in former times

An American scholar, Professor John Langbein of the University of Chicago, writing in 1978, demonstrated from the Old Bailey Sessions Papers for the period 1670–1730 that at that time the criminal trial proceeded in a way that would now be regarded as most improper. The Old Bailey Sessions Papers were so-called 'chap books'– pamphlets written by non-lawyers for sale to the general public, each pamphlet recounting the details of the latest cases.

They ran from 1674 for nearly two and a half centuries. (Over 100,000 of the trials from 1674 – 834 are now freely accessible at www.oldbaileyonline. org.) During that time they underwent major changes of format and function, from chap books to newspapers to true law reports. The newspaper phase had been reached by the mid-1680s. At that time they were published regularly and they recounted a considerable number of cases. The Old Bailey sat eight times a year and a Sessions Paper was produced for each session. In the early years they ran to four pages and everything was highly compressed. In the 1720s they were eight pages long and in the 1730s they burgeoned to twenty page pamphlets. In the late 1730s the reports of a single session required two twenty page pamphlets. They were seemingly written mainly for laymen and are therefore not an ideal source for understanding of the system of trial, but Langbein says that they 'are probably the best accounts we shall ever have of what transpired in ordinary English criminal courts before the late eighteenth century'.[280]

The features of the trial at that time included the following:

- A single jury was empanelled to hear a large number of cases. Typically, there were only two twelve man juries for the whole sessions – a London jury and a Middlesex jury. A session lasted several days and processed fifty to a hundred felony cases. In December 1678, for instance, there was a two-day session. On the Wednesday morning the London jury tried two cases; the Middlesex jury tried seven. In the afternoon the London jury tried three cases. The next morning the Middlesex jury had eight cases and the London jury six. On Thursday the London jury was discharged whilst the Middlesex jury had six cases. Between them the two juries returned verdicts in thirty-two cases involving thirty-six accused in two days!
- The cases were commonly tried and decided in batches. The jury would hear a number of trials and would then go off to deliberate on all the cases together. In the cases in December 1678, for instance, the Middlesex jury which heard twenty-one cases deliberated only three times. The first batch consisted of seven cases, the second of eight cases and the last of six cases.
- Many of the jurors were veterans of earlier sessions. Jurors it seemed were drawn from a tiny cohort.
- As is obvious from these facts, trials took place at amazing speed. Most cases were not guilty pleas but they were disposed of in short order. Typically a jury heard twelve to twenty cases in a day. Many of the not guilty pleas, it is true, were somewhat half-hearted. The accused made no reply or offered no evidence or brought only character witnesses. One reason for the striking speed of events was that trials tended to take place within a few weeks of the event and the recollection of witnesses was therefore fresh. Most of the trials at the December sessions concerned crimes that had occurred in October or November. Also the cases were normally based on committal papers prepared and even presented by the justice of the peace or his clerk. The committal procedure often resulted in the accused making a statement or confession and the not guilty plea that then followed was more *pro forma* than real. There were no lawyers either for prosecution or defence. The prosecution was at least allowed to have a barrister whereas the defence was not. In important cases, reported as State Trials, the prosecution was always represented, but in ordinary cases normally it was not. In the December 1678 session, for instance, there was no mention of any prosecution counsel in any of the thirty-two cases. In the absence of a lawyer there was no opening and closing speech, no examination or cross-examination of witnesses and no motions on points of evidence. Questioning of witnesses was done by the judge himself or by the accused. The accused could not give sworn evidence but he could question both prosecution witnesses and call and

---

[280] J.H. Langbein, 'The Criminal Trial Before Lawyers', 45 *University of Chicago Law Review*, 1978, pp. 263 and 271.

question defence witnesses. He would be asked by the judge what reply he made to prosecution evidence and it was normal for him to respond rather than to rely on any right of silence or right not to incriminate himself. (Langbein says that in the entire sixty-year period from the 1670s he did not come across a single case in which an accused person refused to speak in reliance on the right of silence.) Also the judge gave few instructions to the jury about each case. Jury deliberations were often perfunctory. Sometimes the jury did not even retire to reach a verdict.

- The judge played a far more directing role than would be permissible today. In *Bushell*'s case in 1670 the principle was established that jurors could not be fined for returning a verdict contrary to the trial judge's instructions, but *Bushell*'s case was untypical. The Old Bailey Sessions Papers show the judge normally exercising so much influence over the jury that Langbein suggests 'it is difficult to characterise the jury functioning autonomously' (at p. 285). The judge often served in effect as examiner-in-chief of both the witnesses and the accused. In this capacity, as well as in summing up to the jury, he exercised what seems to have been a wholly unrestricted power to comment on the merits of the case. Sometimes the judge did not bother to use the power, but when he felt like it he would tell the jury what verdict to find and normally the jury followed the judge's indications.

- Sometimes if the judge did not think the evidence for one side or the other was sufficient, he would stop the trial and tell the party in question to get evidence on the point in question and start again. Today the double-jeopardy rule prevents the prosecution from stopping a case that is going badly and starting afresh, but in the seventeenth and eighteenth centuries this occurred not infrequently. The power seems to have been used mainly in order to assist the prosecution rather than the defence.

- There is evidence in the reports of some instances of exchanges between the judge and the jury as the case was proceeding. The jury would comment as the case was developing, or would ask questions or would ask for certain witnesses to be called. Moreover it often gave reasons for its decisions and sometimes would be questioned about the verdict by the judge.

- In some instances the judge rejected a verdict, probed the jury's reasoning, argued with the jury, gave further instructions and told it to go away to deliberate afresh. If the judge did not agree with a jury's conviction of the defendant, it was common for him to recommend a pardon or commutation of sentence and such recommendations were often influential.

- The Old Bailey Sessions Papers also threw light on the rules of evidence that were then applied. Hearsay evidence seemed to be admitted quite commonly. If the judge ruled that hearsay evidence should be excluded, no warning was normally given to the jury to disregard the excluded evidence. Nor was the jury sent out of the court room while the argument went on as to the admissibility of the evidence. Since there was normally no lawyer for either side, this was not appropriate.

The Sessions Papers also show that evidence of previous convictions was frequently considered by the jury as part of the evidence.

Langbein suggests that the modern concept of fairness to the accused requiring exclusion of evidence that would taint the jury had not developed by that time. At a time when the judge dominated the jury there was little thought of keeping prejudicial evidence away from them. The law of evidence, with its modern exclusionary rules, developed not in order to control the judges but as part of the rise of the lawyer as a participant in the criminal process. The rise of lawyers cost the judges their commanding role and thereby made the jury more dangerous, since the judge could not control it so well.

The rule that the accused could not have a lawyer started to break down in about the 1730s. Until then, according to Langbein, the absence of defence counsel was justified by three main arguments. First, the trial judge was supposed to serve as defence counsel. Secondly, the requirement of a high degree of proof was regarded as a safeguard. If proof of that level could be mustered against the prisoner it would be useless for him to have a lawyer since he would plainly be guilty. Thirdly, the accused knew more about the case than anyone else and could not therefore be properly served by an intermediary. On the other hand, curiously, lawyers *were* allowed for misdemeanour cases though not normally for felonies. Lawyers were also permitted if there was some point of law to argue. If the court did not see the point, however, it was left for the accused himself to raise it and to persuade the judge to allow him to have a lawyer. Defence lawyers began to play a role in examining and cross-examining witnesses in the 1730s, though the accused himself continued to play the same role as before as well. There was no real differentiation of function between counsel and the accused, but gradually the role of the lawyer developed and, as Langbein puts it, the lawyers eventually broke up the ancient working relationship between judge and jury 'and cost the judge his mastery of the proceedings' (at p. 314).

In the period covered by the Sessions Papers studied by Langbein, the accused in effect therefore lacked the safeguards both of the inquisitorial and of the adversarial systems. There was neither proper investigation of claims of non-guilt nor rules of evidence, the assistance of counsel nor appropriate rules for the selection, instruction and control of the jury.

Another American scholar, Professor Malcolm Feeley of the University of California, conducted a study of 3,500 cases at the Old Bailey from 1687 to 1912.[281] He found that in the 1830s, trials accounted for no less than 95 per cent of all adjudications, but trials were completely different from what we now think of when we use that word:

> Typically defendants were not represented by lawyers; they rarely confronted witnesses in any meaningful way; they rarely challenged evidence or offered

---

[281] M.M. Feeley, 'Legal Complexity and the Transformation of the Criminal Process: The Origins of Plea Bargaining', 31 *Israel Law Review*, 1997, pp. 183 and 188.

defences of any kind. And when the accused or someone in his or her behalf did occasionally take the stand, more often than not, they did not offer a spirited defence, but offered perfunctory excuses or defences, pleas for mercy, or in the case of witnesses, offered testimony as to good character or mitigating factors. Indeed the eighteenth and early nineteenth century trial (and earlier) more closely resembled the modern sentence hearing or plea bargaining process than it does a full-fledged modern jury trial.

On the origins of defence lawyers see J. Langbein, 'The Prosecutorial Origins of Defence Counsel in the Eighteenth Century: the Appearance of Solicitors', 58 *Cambridge Law Journal*, 1999, pp. 314–65.

See also an illuminating, long article by S. Landsman, 'The Rise of the Contentious Spirit: Adversary Procedure in Eighteenth Century England', 75 *Cornell Law Review*, 1990, pp. 498–609.

FURTHER READING ON THE JURY SYSTEM

J. Baldwin and M. McConville, *Jury Trials* (Clarendon Press, 1979).

Z. Bankowski and G. Mungham, 'The Jury as Process' in P. Carlen (ed.), *The Sociology of Law* (University of Keele, 1976).

W.R. Cornish, *The Jury* (Penguin, 1971).

P. Darbyshire, 'The Lamp that Shows that Freedom Lives – Is it Worth the Candle?', *Criminal Law Review*, 1991, p. 740.

P. Darbyshire, 'What can we Learn from Published Jury Research? Findings for the Criminal Courts Review 2001', *Criminal Law Review*, 2001, pp. 970–9.[282]

Lord Devlin, *Trial by Jury* (Stevens, 1966) and 'The Conscience of the Jury', 107 *Law Quarterly Review*, 1991, p. 398.

P. Duff and M. Findlay, *The Jury Under Attack* (Butterworths, 1988).

S. Enright and J. Morton, *Taking Liberties: The Criminal Jury in the 1990s* (Weidenfeld and Nicolson, 1990).

M.D.A. Freeman, 'The Jury on Trial', *Current Legal Problems*, 1981, p. 65.

T. Grove, *The Juryman's Tale* (Bloomsbury, 2000).

H. Kalven, Jr. and H. Zeisel, *The American Jury* (Little Brown, 1966) and the review of their book by E. Griew, 'The Behaviour of the Jury – A Review of the American Evidence', *Criminal Law Review*, 1967, p. 569.

P. Thornton, '50th Anniversary Article: Trial by Jury: 50 Years of Change', *Criminal Law Review*, 2004, p. 683.

For an overview of the jury in continental countries see R. Munday, 'Jury Trial, Continental Style', *Legal Studies*, July 1993, pp. 204–24. For developments in Spain and Russia see articles by the American scholar Professor S. Thaman, 'Spain Returns to Trial by Jury', 21 *Hastings International and Comparative Law Review*, 1998, pp. 291–537; and 'The Resurrection of Trial by Jury in Russia', 31 *Stanford Journal of International Law*, 1995, pp. 61–274.

---

[282] The full study is on the DCA Website together with the Auld Review – www.criminal-courts-review.org.uk. It is available in hard copy as Occasional Paper Series 49 from Kingston Law School, Kingston University.

For information and assessment of juries in England, Scotland, Ireland, Canada, America, New Zealand, Spain and Russia see N.J. Vidmar (ed.), 'Juries of the World', a special issue of *Law and Contemporary Problems*, vol. 62, 1999.

For an even broader survey of countries around the world under the title 'The Lay Participation in the Criminal Trial in the XXIst Century' see *Revue Internationale de Droit Penal*, 2001 (1) and (2) – some 600 pages (almost all in English).

Chapter 6

Costs and the funding of legal proceedings

The cost of legal proceedings is widely regarded as the single greatest concern confronting the justice system.[1] For civil justice the costs concern a variety of funders – individuals, companies, trade unions, insurers and the public purse. For criminal justice the costs fall mainly on the taxpayer.

The problem of costs bedevils all legal systems – who should pay them, how to keep them under control and what assistance is available for those unable to afford them. These are some of the topics addressed in this chapter.[2]

1. The new rules

In civil cases the court's power to award costs in contentious[3] matters flows from the Supreme Court Act 1981, s. 51 which provides that, subject to statute and rules of court, 'the costs of and incidental to all proceedings . . . shall be in the discretion of the court'. The rules are now to be found in the Civil Procedure Rules Parts 43–48.[4] CPR 44.3(1) says that the court has a discretion as to whether costs are payable by one party to another, the amount of those costs and when they are to be paid.

---

[1] For a startling illustration see *King v. Telegraph Group Ltd* [2004] EWCA Civ 613, [2005] 1 WLR 2282. There were no pre-action costs other than preparing a letter before action but by exchange of statements of case the claimants had incurred costs of £32,000 – including fifty-four hours of a partner's time at £370 per hour and forty-eight hours of a trainee solicitor's time at £146 per hour. Their estimate of the cost of preparing for and handling a five-day court hearing in a libel case was £238,000.

[2] For treatment of costs in civil matters generally the practitioner's bible is *Cook on Costs* published annually. For an instructive short history of the costs rules see Peter Hurst, 'Going Round in Circles', 25 *Civil Justice Quarterly*, 2006, pp. 546-56. For a valuable review see Micheal Cook, 'That was the Costs Year that was', 26 *Civil Justice Quarterly*, 2007, pp. 134–51.

[3] The rules distinguish between costs for 'contentious' and 'non-contentious' matters. Cases which result in legal proceedings being initiated are contentious, even if they settle before any court hearing. In contentious matters, there were formerly different rules for the High Court and the county court. In April 1999, the difference between costs in the High Court and the county court was abolished.

[4] They replaced Rules of the Supreme Court (RSC) Order 62 and County Court Rules (CCR) Order 38.

Who pays?

Under the old rules the position regarding contentious matters was clear and almost mechanical. Although according to the rules the court had a complete discretion, in fact, save in exceptional circumstances, the loser paid. At the end of the case, counsel for the winner asked for the 'usual order as to costs' which was made more or less automatically. The application was dealt with in seconds. Where a case settled, the settlement was normally on the basis that the loser paid the winner's costs. (For exceptions to the 'costs follow the event' rule see pp. 577–85 below. For discussion of the rule see pp. 571–73.)

CPR 44.3(2) states that the general rule still is 'that the unsuccessful party will be ordered to pay the costs of the successful party', but the 'Woolf reform' rules made several major changes from the previous system. The most important was that the court has a much wider duty to exercise its discretion as to who pays costs at the end of a case. CPR 44.3(4) states that in deciding what order to make, the court must take into account all the circumstances including the conduct of all the parties and whether a party has succeeded on part of his case even though he has not succeeded overall. So a party that has lost may still get his costs in respect of matters on which he won. For the contrast between the old 'winner takes all' approach and the new more nuanced approach see *Re Elgindata Ltd (No 2)*[5] compared with, say, *Jones v. University of Warwick*.[6] As an example of the new approach there have been cases (p. 145 above) where a successful party has been deprived of his costs because he unreasonably refused to take part in alternative dispute resolution.

Issues versus percentage basis Assessing who has won on particular issues can be a time-consuming exercise. In *Verrechia v. Metropolitan Police Commissioner*[7] the Court of Appeal said that an order allowing or disallowing costs by reference to success on particular issues should only be made if there was no other order that could appropriately reflect the justice of the case. The costs of making the determination might be disproportionate to the benefit gained. A 'percentage' order would often produce a fairer result than an 'issues based' order. Wherever practicable, the judge should endeavour to form a view as to the percentage of costs to which the winning party should be entitled or, alternatively, whether justice would be done by awarding costs from or until a particular date.

---

[5] [1993] 1 All ER 232.
[6] [2001] EWCA Civ 535, [2001] All ER (D) 135 (Apr) – defendants got no costs even though they won the issue at the hearing as to the admissibility of a video of the claimant filmed secretly in her home because of the way in which the film had been obtained. For examples of the application of the new approach see J. Ross, 'Apportionment of Costs – Winner does not Take All', 152 *New Law Journal*, 15 March 2002, p. 401; M. Goodwin, 'Costs losers', 146 *Solicitors' Journal*, 15 November 2002, p. 104; M. Ditchburn, 'Winner Takes All?', 147 *Solicitors' Journal*, 28 February 2003, p. 216; P. Jones, 'Bad Conduct can Escalate "Reasonable" Costs', 154 *New Law Journal*, 23 July 2004, p. 1149; and 155 *New Law Journal*, 17 June 2005, p. 939.   [7] [2002] EWCA Civ 605, [2002] 3 All ER 385.

Factors to be taken into account in assessing the amount of costs

CPR 44.5 states that when determining the amount of costs, the court must take into account not only matters that had previously to be taken into account (the amount involved, the importance and complexity of the matter, the skill required and the time spent) but also '(a) the conduct of all the parties including in particular (i) conduct before, as well as during, the proceedings; and (ii) the efforts made, if any, before and during the proceedings in order to try to resolve the dispute'. Thus the court can take into account whether it was reasonable to raise or to pursue particular allegations, whether a party exaggerated his claim and the way in which the case was pursued or defended.

The overall effect of the new costs rules was summarised in *Cook on Costs*:

> The new Rules are not a mere codification of what was already there. They introduced a new philosophy and approach to costs. In the past the court had been concerned only to decide whether or not to award costs to one party or the other at the end of a hearing, with any costs awarded being quantified at the end of the proceedings if the parties could not agree them. Now costs permeate every aspect of civil litigation: the courts are charged with the responsibility of managing cases to ensure that the work undertaken by the parties (and therefore the costs they incur) are proportionate to the issues, while costs orders may be made as sanctions to ensure that the conduct of the parties (both before and during the proceedings) is in compliance with the new procedural code. As well as seeking to achieve proportionality and using costs orders as sanctions, the new regime also aims to make the amount of costs more predictable by requiring the parties to provide estimates of their costs at various stages of the litigation, and for costs on the fast track to be fixed, initially for the trial only, but eventually for the whole action . . . The concepts of proportionality and of the winner of litigation no longer virtually automatically receiving all, or indeed any, of his costs, have also brought about fundamental changes in the conduct of litigation (p. 78).

Assessment (formerly 'taxation')

If the loser is ordered to pay the winner's costs it does not mean *all* those costs but only such costs as are assessed to be due, which will depend on the basis on which the court has ordered them to be paid. The assessment is carried out by court officials and judges. This assessment was previously known as 'taxation' and those who conducted the process were Taxing Masters. From April 1999 taxation was renamed 'detailed assessment' and 'summary assessment'. Taxing Masters became 'Costs Judges', Taxing Officers became 'Authorised Court Officers' and the Supreme Court Taxing Office became the 'Supreme Court Costs Office'. Any party aggrieved at a decision in a detailed assessment hearing can appeal to a judge of the next tier. The appeal from the Authorised Court Officer is as of right. In most other cases the aggrieved person will need permission (formerly 'leave') to appeal.

Summary assessment is where the court that has heard the case assesses the costs right away so that the actual amount to be paid by the loser can be determined there and then (CPR 43.3). The Practice Direction states that 'the general rule is that the court will make a summary assessment of the costs in a fast track case and at the end of any other hearing lasting less than a day' (CPR, PD 44.7). That means that in county court cases summary assessment is the norm. It also generally applies in interlocutory (pre-trial) hearings where the court decides that one party should pay the costs 'in any event' regardless of the ultimate outcome of the case, but summary assessment does not apply where there is substantial dispute about the costs. Failure to produce a summary statement can be treated as a waiver of a claim for costs.

Judge Michael Cook (author of *Cook on Costs*) has written: 'It is a truth universally acknowledged that the costs provisions are the least successful part of the Civil Procedure Rules and that the least successful part of the costs provisions is summary assessment'.[8] The reason, he said, was that the judges were performing a function that was not within their competence:

> At the end of an exhausting fast track hearing, there is often the pantomime of two barristers addressing a former barrister (the trial judge) who has had a one-hour Judicial Studies Board crash course on costs, on matters of which none of them has any practical experience. There is a one-page statement of costs prepared by someone who is not present in court, which contains references to a file of papers which is also conspicuous by its absence. The judge has to choose between two sets of figures apparently plucked from the air, or arrive at his own by the same route.

Detailed assessment is when the bill is assessed at some point, weeks or months after the case is finished.[9] It is common for the bills to be prepared by specialist costs draftsmen – itself a costly business.[10] Recently there have been indications that judges, restless about the huge level of costs, are prepared to make radical reductions in costs.[11]

---

[8] 'Costs Rules are a Plodder's Charter', 17 *Litigation Funding*, February 2002, p. 8.

[9] See M. Bacon, *Solicitors' Journal*, 1999, pp. 680 and 740.

[10] In a case in 2006 it was estimated that the costs hearing would itself take some 30–40 days with claimants' costs in excess of £350,000. This followed a trial at which the claimants had been awarded damages of over £10 million plus costs to be assessed if not agreed. The claimants' costs of the trial were first estimated at £3.9 million and subsequently came to £4.7 million. The defendants were given leave to appeal on condition that they paid £2 million on account for costs plus £150,000 as security for the costs of the appeal. When the defendants failed to pay anything the court ordered that they be debarred from taking part in the detailed assessment. (*Days Healthcare UK Ltd v. Pihsiang Machinery Manufacturing Co Ltd* [2006] EWHC 1444, QB, [2006] 4 All ER 233.) For details of the Association of Law Costs Draftsmen see J. Robins, 'Fellows Who Draft a Response to the Battle on Costs', *Law Society's Gazette*, 14 July 2005, p. 22.

[11] In *King v. Telegraph Group Ltd* [2005] EWHC 90015 (Costs) the Senior Costs Judge reduced the claimant's bill by nearly 40 per cent. In *Henry v. BBC* [2005] EWHC 1034, QB the judge and the Senior Costs Judge reduced the figure claimed from £957,000 to £506,500 – a reduction of 47 per cent.

Costs-only proceedings The 1999 reforms introduced the new concept of proceedings solely for assessment of costs when there is complete agreement on all other matters (CPR 44.12A). The application is made under CPR Part 8. As will be seen, this innovation has been used in an enormous number of cases.

Orders for payment of costs must now be paid within fourteen days Pre-CPR, an assessment of interim costs was not made until the end of the case. The significance of CPR 44.8 requiring payment within fourteen days is that it powerfully concentrates the minds of those considering whether to make interim applications. They have to be ready to back their judgment that an interim application is worthwhile with real money. It has had the intended effect of significantly reducing the number of such applications.

Proportionality CPR 1.1(2) states that 'proportionate' refers to the amount of money involved, the importance of the case, the complexity of the issues and *the financial position of each party*. The Practice Direction supplementing CPR 44.5 expressly states that 'proportionate' does not necessarily mean a fixed percentage as there will be costs that have to be incurred even in small cases and that solicitors 'are not required to conduct litigation at rates which are uneconomic' (para. 11.2).

In *Lownds v. Home Office*[12] the Court of Appeal addressed the question of the relationship between 'reasonable' and 'proportionate'. Pre-CPR the test had been reasonableness. The trouble with that test, Lord Denning said, was that 'it institutionalised, as reasonable, the level of costs which were generally charged by the profession at the time when the professional services were rendered' (at [2]). If a rate of charge was commonly adopted it was taken to be reasonable. Now the court also had to consider whether the costs were proportionate. CPR 44.3 in fact does not use the word 'proportionate' but, Lord Denning said, 'the considerations which should be taken into account when making an order for costs are redolent of proportionality' (at [3]). But where there is a clash between proportionality and reasonableness, which takes precedence? The claimed costs in that case were £17,000 plus VAT in a medical negligence case that settled for £3,000. The District judge allowed costs of just under £15,000 plus VAT. Most of the costs had been incurred before the CPR came into force and on that ground the Court of Appeal said it would not interfere with the decision. But it considered what its approach would be in respect of costs post-CPR. The crucial point to emerge from the decision was that costs that are *necessarily* incurred should be allowed even if the result is disproportionate. There should be a two-stage process. First, look to see if the costs as a whole are disproportionate. If they are not, check to make sure that each item was reasonably incurred and that the cost for each item was reasonable. If the global costs are disproportionately high, check to see whether any costs have been incurred unnecessarily. Costs that have been incurred unnecessarily may be recoverable from one's own client but they are not recoverable from the losing party.

---

[12] [2002] EWCA Civ 365, [2002] 1 WLR 2450.

In *Giambrone v. JMC Holidays Ltd*[13] action was brought by 652 claimants against a company that ran holidays. After a costs hearing lasting two and a half days the Costs Judge held that the claimed costs were disproportionate. The claimants appealed unsuccessfully. Morland J who heard the appeal said that a Costs Judge should be able to deal with overall proportionality in a matter of an hour or less. He also said that appeals against a preliminary decision on proportionality were to be discouraged.[14]

Costs estimates In fast track and multi-track cases the parties must file cost estimates at various stages – with the allocation questionnaire, with the pre-trial checklist, and at other stages as ordered by the court. (Litigants in person are exempt.) The estimates should show costs under ten different headings and should differentiate between costs already incurred and those to be incurred.[15] Copies must be served not only on the court and the other side but also on the lay client. The estimates must be updated. The purpose of estimates is to keep the parties informed, to assist the court in deciding what case management decisions to make and what, if any, costs orders to make. The court can take the estimate(s) into account when assessing the reasonableness of any costs claimed. In *Leigh v. Michelin Tyre Plc*[16] the Court of Appeal identified three circumstances in which the court may do so: (1) where there is a significant difference between the estimated costs and the costs claimed, the difference calls for an explanation. In the absence of a satisfactory explanation, the court may conclude that the costs claimed are unreasonable; (2) the estimated costs can be taken into account if the other party shows that he relied on them – for instance in not making a settlement offer because the estimate was low; and (3) if the court considers that different case management decisions would have been made had the estimate been more accurate – for instance by reducing the number of expert witnesses. In *Leigh* the Court of Appeal did not penalise an estimate that turned out to be far out because there was an explanation and the paying party failed to show either reliance on the estimate or that different case management decisions would probably have been made. The court rejected the claim that an inaccurate estimate should, by definition, be penalised. An estimate was not a costs capping order.

In June 2005, flowing from the decision in *Leigh*, the rules were amended to provide that if claimed costs exceed the costs estimate by more than 20 per cent the excess will not be recoverable unless there is a 'satisfactory explanation'.[17]

The different bases of costs

The level of costs depends on the basis of the assessment ordered by the court. Before 1986 there were five different costs orders that could be made at the end

---

[13] [2002] EWHC 2932, QB, [2003] 1 All ER 982.   [14] At [56].
[15] Costs PD 43, paras. 6.1–6.6.   [16] [2003] EWCA Civ 1766.
[17] PD 43, para. 6.5A. See 'Judges Cracking Down on Costs', *Law Society's Gazette*, 13 April 2006, p. 3 warning that the senior judiciary were clamping down on inaccurate costs estimates.

of the case as to the basis of 'taxation'. They were: 'party and party costs', 'common fund costs', 'trustee basis', 'solicitor and own client basis' and 'indemnity basis'.[18] In 1986 the system was changed. 'Party and party costs' was replaced by the 'standard basis' of taxation which became the norm for both privately funded and legal aid cases. On the standard basis all costs were allowed that were reasonably incurred, with any doubts being resolved in favour of the paying party. The other bases of costs (trustee, common fund and solicitor and own client) were abolished and replaced by the 'indemnity' basis under which all costs were allowed except insofar as they are of an unreasonable amount or have been unreasonably incurred, with doubts being resolved in favour of the party being paid.

These definitions were slightly modified in the April 1999 rules. Thus standard fees still do not allow costs that have been unreasonably incurred or that are unreasonable in amount, but they must also be 'proportionate to the matters in issue' – a new concept. As before, any doubts are resolved in favour of the paying party (CPR 44.4). Costs assessed on the indemnity basis are presumed to have been reasonably incurred and to be of a reasonable amount if they were incurred with the express or implied approval of the client. They are presumed to have been unreasonably incurred if they are of an unusual nature or amount and the solicitor did not warn the client that as a result he might not recover all of them from the other party (CPR 48.8).

It was held in *McPhilemy v. Times Newspapers Ltd (No 2)*[19] that an order for indemnity costs is not penal and carries no stigma or implied disapproval of the defendant's conduct and that the claimant can get interest on indemnity costs.

Non-contentious costs

If there are no proceedings or they are in a tribunal,[20] costs are non-contentious. Non-contentious matters are governed by the Solicitors' (Non-Contentious Business) Remuneration Order 1994, Article 3 which prescribes that a solicitor's remuneration shall be such sum as may be fair and reasonable having regard to all the circumstances and in particular to the complexity of the matter or the difficulty or novelty of the issues raised, the skill and responsibility involved, the time it takes,[21] the number of documents, where the work is done, the amount of money involved and the importance of the matter to the client.

2. Controls on costs

There are a variety of methods for seeking to protect the payer of costs from excessive charges.

---

[18] These five categories of costs were described by Sir Robert Megarry, Vice Chancellor, in *EMI Records Ltd v. Wallace Ltd* [1982] 2 All ER 980.

[19] [2001] EWCA Civ 933, [2001] 4 All ER 861, [2002] 1 WLR 934.

[20] Other than the Lands Tribunal.

[21] For an exploration of this issue see M. Cook, 'Solicitors' Hourly Rates', 24 *Civil Justice Quarterly*, pp. 142–50.

'Between party' and 'solicitor and own client' assessment of costs

As has been seen, assessment of contentious costs (previously called taxa-tion) is assessment by the court. By far the most common is where the loser asks for the winner's bill to be assessed – now called 'between party' (for-merly 'party and party') assessment, but such assessment does not reduce the total bill. It only determines what each party is to pay – the distribution of the burden of costs as between winner and loser. The procedure to reduce the bill absolutely is for the client to challenge his own lawyer's bill by what is called a 'solicitor and own client' taxation, or assessment, under the Solicitors' Act 1974, Part III. The client does not have to pay the amount by which the bill is reduced. Such assessments are extremely rare – partly because clients feel embarrassment at challenging their solicitors' bills, partly through ignorance of the availability of the facility and partly because, unless the client succeeds in getting the bill reduced by more than one-fifth, he has to bear the costs of the taxation. The solicitor is only required to inform the client of this right at the stage of issuing legal proceedings to sue for unpaid fees and now before entering a conditional fee contract. Many clients prob-ably pay the bill without ever realising that they have a statutory right to chal-lenge it. The right of challenge exists even if there is a written agreement between lawyer and client as to the level of fees and even if the bill has already been paid.

Fixed costs

Fixed costs have become a major new factor. There are various types:

Minor items In the past fixed costs were confined to minor standard items in civil litigation such as photocopies, attendance to issue or serve summonses, attendance to deliver documents, issuing proceedings, entering a judgment, enforcing a judgment etc. They apply where the claim is for a specified sum of money and summary judgment is obtained or the claim is one where the court gives a fixed date for the hearing when it issues the claim and judgment is given for delivery of goods.

Small claims Fixed costs have always been a feature of small claims cases where the only costs normally recoverable are fixed costs attributable to issuing the claim, court fees, experts' fees not exceeding £200 each and loss of earnings by a party or witness up to £50 a day. If the case involves seeking an injunction, the cost of obtaining legal advice up to £260 can be recovered. Costs on a summary assessment in relation to an appeal may also be allowed.[22] A party who acts unreasonably can be ordered to pay such costs as are assessed.

---

[22] For a horror story illustrating this exception see *Gregory v. Turner* [2003] EWCA Civ 183, [2003] 2 All ER 1114.

Fixed costs for fast track cases Lord Woolf in his two *Access to Justice* reports expressed the hope that *all* fast track costs would be fixed, but in the event, the only part of the case for which fixed costs could be agreed by April 1999 when the CPR were implemented was in respect of the day in court. The fixed amounts, which include the fee for preparation for advocacy, are the same regardless of the length of the trial.[23] (Fast track cases are supposed to be finished within one day but that does not guarantee that one day will always suffice.) The court has a discretion to increase or decrease the amounts because of the conduct of the parties or of the lawyers (CPR 46.3).

Fixed fees in fast track cases however became much more important through an initiative of the Civil Justice Council through its Predictable Costs Sub-Committee and negotiations in what came to be called 'the Big Tent' between the different interest groups. These bore their first fruit in December 2002 when there was agreement on fixed costs for road accident cases above the small claims limit and under £10,000 that settled without recourse to legal proceedings. This new scheme became effective as from October 2003. Save for exceptional cases, the costs are on a sliding scale of £800 plus 20 per cent of the agreed damages up to £6,000 and 15 per cent from £6,000 to £10,000.[24] Where in such cases there is a Conditional Fee Agreement (pp. 632–33 below), the success fee payable to the successful solicitor is restricted to 12.5 per cent.[25]

As of June 2004, the limiting of Conditional Fee Agreement success fees in road traffic cases was extended to cover all road traffic cases other than those within the small claims limit.[26] As from October 2004 success fees for both solicitors and barristers in bodily injury employment claims up to any figure also became subject to fixed percentages.[27] In 2005 agreement, again brokered by the Civil Justice Council, was reached for the application of the same approach to success fees for industrial disease claims.[28]

---

[23] The hearing fees are on a scale depending on the value of the claim. Where the award does not exceed £3,000 the fixed fee is £350; where it is between £3,000 and £10,000 it is £500; where it is over £10,000 the fixed fee is £750. Where a solicitor attends with counsel, a fixed sum of £250 is added (CPR 46.2).

[24] For the details see 153 *New Law Journal*, 10 October 2003, p. 1497. For further details see the Civil Justice Council's Website www.civiljusticecouncil.gov.uk; and two articles by Professor Peysner, the chairman of the Civil Justice Council's sub-committee – 'Searching for Predictable Costs', *Journal of Personal Injury Litigation*, 2002, p. 162; and 'Finding Predictable Costs', 22 *Civil Justice Quarterly*, 2003, pp. 349–70. See also his 'Predictability and Budgeting', 23 *Civil Justice Quarterly*, 2004, pp. 15–37. For a practitioner's view see K. Underwood, 'Current Issues – Fixed Costs and Conditional Fees', 24 *Civil Justice Quarterly*, 2005, pp. 388–95.   [25] 154 *New Law Journal*, 23 January 2004, p. 92.

[26] For solicitors, the limit for pre-trial settlement is again 12.5 per cent – or 100 per cent if there is a trial. For barristers, it is the same except that in fast track cases it is 50 per cent if there is a settlement within fourteen days of the trial date and in multi-track cases it is 75 per cent if there is a settlement within twenty-one days of the trial date: SI 1306/2004; *Law Society's Gazette*, 10 June 2004, p. 36.

[27] 25 per cent, rising to 100 per cent if a trial takes place. An additional 2.5 per cent is allowed where the claim is funded by a membership organisation such as a trade union. *Law Society's Gazette*, 7 October 2004, p. 5.   [28] *Law Society's Gazette*, 18 August 2005, p. 22.

Lord Woolf intended that his proposed fixed-costs regime for fast track cases under which between parties costs would be subject to a ceiling would also affect the level of costs charged by solicitors to their own clients,[29] but so far at least there is no such rule. CPR 48.8 provides that a solicitor can charge his own client more than the amount he can recover from the other side providing there is a written agreement with the client expressly permitting it. The fixed costs scheme devised by the Civil Justice Council for road accident cases only applies to between parties costs, so CPR 48.8 applies there too.

Legal aid work As will be seen fixed fees are already of major importance in legal aid work and will become even more so (see pp. 620–22 below).

In civil work, the Legal Services Commission (LSC) has already to an extent moved from payment by the hour to fixed fees. By 2006 when Lord Carter reported, firms were getting a fixed sum per case, regardless of the complexity of the case, the time spent or the amount of disbursements incurred.[30] If the case was exceptional[31] it fell outside the scheme. From September 2004 the scheme was voluntary. In April 2005 it became compulsory.[32]

During the initial stage the fees paid were 'tailored' to firms – the amount was based on the firms' average case costs in the year 2003–4, initially plus an increase of 2.5 per cent. It was intended that from April 2006 fixed fees would be based instead on national or regional figures but in October 2005 the LSC announced that the transition from the 'tailored' fees would be postponed to April 2007. Announcing the change, it claimed that it was responding to suppliers' requests for a period of stability before further changes are introduced.[33] As will be seen (p. 622 below) in its consultation paper of July 2006, the LSC proposed that 'tailored fixed fees' would be replaced by fixed and graduated fees.

An advantage of fixed fees for firms was an end to the hated LSC cost compliance auditing (see p. 600 below). There was also the guarantee that payment would be made without deduction. A majority of legal aid firms of solicitors joined the voluntary scheme. Bindman & Partners, one of the country's leading legal aid firms, refused to do so. A partner in the firm explained why:[34]

> We do not consider it right for civil legal aid work to be paid on a flat rate. Payment should depend on the work undertaken, and be underpinned by assessment of the quality and reasonableness of the work done. Severing this link exposes clients to arbitrary factors which will influence whether they get advice and assistance, and the nature and extent of the help they receive. This must be contrary to the interests of justice. It places publicly funded clients in a

---

[29] Such a system operated in Germany. (Woolf's *Interim Report*, Annex V, p. 263.) For fuller treatment see D. Leipold, 'Limiting Costs for Better Access to Justice' in Zuckerman and Cranston (eds.), *Reform of Civil Procedure – Essays on 'Access to Justice'* (Clarendon Press, 1995) pp. 265 and 266–75.

[30] The LSC eventually agreed to pay any increase in overall average disbursement costs.

[31] Initially defined as one that cost at least three times the fixed fee or £2,500, whichever was the lower.   [32] Lawyers doing mental health work could choose whether to take part.

[33] LSC, *Focus*, No. 49, December 2005, p. 2.

[34] S. Chahal, 'Putting solicitors in a fix', *Law Society's Gazette*, 28 October 2004, p. 15.

wholly different and less advantageous position in comparison with privately paying clients.

We also see serious adverse practical consequences for our clients. Suppliers will take on cases which are 'easy', short term and predictable, at the expense of other clients. Clients who need interpreters, or home visits, or are in hospital or prison, will be discriminated against in favour of those who can get to the office and speak English. Particular kinds of cases where legal expertise is most required – such as those before the social security commissioner – will become wholly impracticable to take on, while the temptation to take on cases that require little legal input and can be cheaply concluded will be irresistible . . .

The ulterior purpose of the scheme, Ms Chahal said, was to meet the demand by the DCA to deliver more acts of publicly funded legal advice and assistance for the same money.

Fixed fees were a central part of the proposals put forward by Lord Carter in his 2006 Review of funding for legal aid (p. 620 below). But the prospects for implementation of these proposals, at least as scheduled for 2007, were uncertain. [35]

On fixed fees see K. Underwood, *Fixed Costs* (2nd edn, Lexis Nexis Butterworths, 2006). See also P. Owston and S. McCall, 'New Thinking for a New World', *Legal Aid Review*, March 2005, p. 12.

Scale fees

In cases in the county court, other than small claims cases, the level of fees was formerly controlled by scales depending on the amount in issue. Until 1991 there were four scales; from 1991 there were three.[36] Scale fees in the county court went out with the implementation of the Woolf reforms in April 1999.

In the High Court, the old approach of scales for different items of work had been replaced in 1986 by discretion which meant the solicitor had to justify each item in his detailed bill of costs.

Conveyancing, which was formerly the single largest source of solicitors' work,[37] used to be subject to scale fees that were treated as both *maxima* and *minima* – the fee was set by reference to the value involved and the Law Society allowed no competition between solicitors through undercutting. In 1973 this system was replaced by a requirement that the charge be 'fair and reasonable' and from 1984 solicitors were permitted to advertise their fees. These reforms

---

[35] On 19 October 2006 the *Law Society's Gazette*, in a front page story headed 'Falconer climbs down over fixed-fee rates', reported that the Lord Chancellor had 'conceded that the Government realised that there are significant problems with fixed fees' and that implementation might have to be delayed.

[36] Lower Scale – under £100, Scale 1 – £100–3,000, Scale 2 – over £3,000.

[37] Conveyancing of residential property, which in the mid 1960s represented half of solicitors' gross income, had reduced by the end of the 1990s to some 10 per cent – see J. Jenkins, *The Changing Legal Market Place in England and Wales* (Law Society, 1999) para. 7.1.

introduced competition and caused fees to come down,[38] but the Law Society has continued to the present day to issue 'guidance' on how to calculate the value element in non-contentious work, based on a percentage of the value of the property. There are fee scales in the form of 'guidance' covering domestic conveyancing, probate and charges when acting for a mortgage lender.

The Office of Fair Trading (OFT) in its 2002 report *Competition in professions* (www.oft.gov.uk) said that although charges had dropped over the previous decade, the fact that conveyancing and probate charges varied widely suggested that the market was not highly competitive. ('A greater degree of price convergence would be expected in the presence of strong competition or price transparency'.[39]) It also noted that bank charges for probate work were even higher than those of solicitors. The OFT said that especially in the field of probate work the fee guidance might inhibit or distort competition.

Pre-emptive cost capping orders

The courts post-Woolf have introduced a new order capping costs prospectively. There was no specific power in the CPR to do so but the judges deduced the power from the courts' general powers of case management in CPR, r. 3. In *AB v. Leeds Teaching Hospitals NHS Trust*[40] Gage J set a cap on costs in a case for damages for unlawful retention by hospitals of organs of deceased patients. Over 2,000 claims had been notified. The potential damages were estimated at £10–15 million. The lawyers' estimate was that they would need 3,410 hours in preparing the case. Despite the fact that the lead solicitors had agreed cost plans with the Legal Services Commission, the judge reduced this to 1,750 hours and put a cap on the claimants' costs in respect of the generic issues of £506,500.[41] The cap based on the estimate limited what the claimants could recover if they succeeded, unless the court ordered otherwise.

The concept was approved by the Court of Appeal in *King v. Telegraph Group*.[42] The Court of Appeal, referring to early decisions in which cost capping orders had been made,[43] said that they could be made equally in defamation

---

[38] The Law Society Working Party stated in 1994 that solicitors' conveyancing charges fell in real terms between 1986 and 1993 by no less than 45 per cent: 'Adapting for the Future', *Report of the Law Society's Special Working Party on Conveyancing Services*, 1994, p. 9.   [39] OFT, para. 217, pp. 64–5 and similarly para. 219.

[40] [2003] EWHC 1034, QB.

[41] 153 *New Law Journal*, 23 May 2003, p. 792; 12 *Independent Lawyer*, July/August 2003, p. 11.

[42] [2004] EWCA Civ 613, [2005] 1 WLR 2282. The claimant had a conditional fee agreement (CFA – see p. 630 below) but no insurance to cover the risk of losing. The result was that if the claimant won, the defendants would have to pay the claimant's costs (estimated at some £400,000) plus the success fee under the CFA (probably 100 per cent) whereas if the defendant publisher won, it would be unlikely to recover any costs at all in respect of its costs of some £400,000.

[43] *Solutia UK Ltd v. Griffiths* [2001] EWCA Civ 61, [2001] 2 Costs LR 247; *AB v. Leeds Teaching Hospitals NHS Trust*, n. 40 above; *Various Ledward Claimants Meadway HA* [2003] EWHC 2551, QB.

cases. The court said that the power to make a pre-emptive costs order applied both prospectively and retrospectively. Making such an order retrospectively would however be wholly exceptional.[44] The order must be applied for in good time. If it came too close to the trial it would be refused. The court cannot intervene of its own motion. It has to wait for an application.[45]

The reason for granting the order is that there is a real and substantial risk that otherwise costs would be disproportionately or unreasonably incurred and that that risk cannot be managed by ordinary case management and a detailed assessment of costs after the trial.[46]

Remuneration certificates in non-contentious matters

The Law Society has traditionally provided a free service in reviewing bills in non-contentious matters. The client asks for a remuneration certificate. If the certificate suggests a lower fee, that is then the fee that the solicitor may charge. Remuneration certificates cannot result in the bill being increased. This procedure is very little used. As from 1994 the system was modified so that it applies only if the bill is for an amount under £50,000 and only if the client has paid at least half the solicitors' costs plus disbursements and VAT. The solicitor must pay back to the client any amount paid him which the remuneration certificate states is excessive. In exceptional circumstances the requirement to pay half the bill can be waived by the Law Society.

Legal aid work

Legal aid work is subject to fee rates and systems laid down by statutory rules and regulations. Payments for legal aid work are subject to a variety of controls. Much legal aid work was paid under hourly rates set by the DCA. (The basic hourly rate for civil legal aid court work in non-family law matters in 2003 was a paltry £74. This rate was the same for the whole country irrespective of the level of fee earner. This basic rate had not been increased for almost ten years since 1994!) Payments for prescribed family law work were paid on somewhat higher rates.

The prescribed rate could be increased if the work was done with exceptional competence, skill or expertise, with exceptional dispatch or if it involved

---

[44] *Petursson v. Hutchinson 3G UK Ltd* [2004] EWHC 2609, TCC. In that case a retrospective order was refused. In *AB v. Leeds Training Hospital NHS Trust*, n. 40 above, the order applied both prospectively and retrospectively.

[45] For an example see *Henry v. BBC* [2005] EWHC 2503, QB, [2006] 1 All ER 154. In that case, if the BBC lost, the costs it would have to pay, including the claimant's success fee, were estimated at £1.6 million. If it won, because of a limit of £100,000 on the claimant's insurance, it was unlikely to recover more than a fifth of its costs of some £500,000. The judge said that it was a prime candidate for a costs capping order but the application had come too late.

[46] For a review of the case law by District Judge Lethem see 'Capping the Costs Gusher', *Litigation Funding*, June 2006, pp. 6–9.

exceptional circumstances or complexity. In the county court the remuneration allowed could be doubled; in the High Court it could be trebled.

Standard and graduated fees From the mid-1980s the Government increasingly paid legal aid fees by way of either standard or graduated fees. The standard fee was either wholly, or more or less, fixed for the category of case. So in the Crown Court, standard fees were introduced for solicitors in respect of contested cases lasting under two days, guilty pleas, committals for sentence and appeals. The solicitor claimed either 'the lower standard fee' or 'the principal standard fee' or he delivered a bill in the traditional way. The determining officer decided the appropriate fee. In the case of barristers, the standard fee laid down one fee.[47] However, it was found that in a high proportion of cases the lawyers used the 'escape clause' to charge by the hours worked.

Graduated fees are more flexible because they take more variables into account. Graduated fees were introduced in 1997. They initially applied to all Crown Court cases other than those lasting more than ten days or where there were more than eighty witnesses or over 1,000 pages of material. The system provided a base fee determined by the most serious offence charged. The base fee could then be increased by five factors: the size of the brief, the length of the trial, the number of defendants represented, other hearings pre-and post-trial and certain other work by counsel.[48]

Graduated fees were progressively extended to capture more cases. Since October 2005 they have applied to all Crown Court cases except very high cost cases (now defined as trials lasting forty-one days or over).

In May 2001 graduated fees were introduced for payment of barristers in family work in magistrates' courts, county courts and the High Court.[49]

Very high cost cases are managed by individual contracts with the Legal Services Commission. Work is agreed in advance and there are fixed rates for preparation and court attendance.

Wasted costs orders

The Courts and Legal Services Act 1990, s. 4 provided for 'wasted costs orders' against legal representatives. Under the section (and under ss. 111 and 112) the court may disallow or, as the case may be, order the legal representative concerned to meet the whole or any part of the wasted costs (s. 4(6)). Wasted costs are defined as costs incurred by any party (1) as a result of any 'improper,

---

[47] See 'Standard fees in the Crown Court', *Law Society's Gazette*, 23 September 1987, p. 2672; A. Edwards, 'Standard Fees: a Survival Guide', *New Law Journal*, 7 October 1988, p. 722.

[48] For a description of the history and the system see *Counsel*, May/June 1996, pp. 12–15. For an exploration of the mysteries of the system see P. W. Tague, 'Barristers' Selfish Incentives in Counselling Defendants over the Choice of Plea', *Criminal Law Review*, 2007, p. 3 at 11–17.

[49] See the Community Legal Service (Funding) (Counsel in Family Proceedings) Order 2001, SI 2001/1071.

unreasonable or negligent act or omission on the part of any representative or any employee of a representative' or (2) which, in the light of any such act or omission, the court considers it is unreasonable to expect that party to pay.

The wasted costs order jurisdiction has been fraught with difficulties. A series of test cases on 'wasted costs orders' were decided in *Ridehalgh v. Horsefield*.[50] All six appeals were successful. The orders should not have been made.[51] The Lord Chief Justice's 1995 Practice Direction (p. 124 above) had emphasised the importance of wasted costs orders: 'the paramount importance of reducing the cost and delay of civil litigation makes it necessary for judges sitting at first instance to assert greater control over the preparation for and the conduct of hearings than has hitherto been customary. Failure by practitioners to conduct cases economically will be visited by appropriate orders for costs, including wasted costs orders',[52] but the Court of Appeal's decision in *Ridehalgh v. Horsefield* suggested that an appeal by the lawyers from a wasted costs order would often, if not usually, succeed. In *Persaud v. Persaud*[53] the Court of Appeal, citing *Ridehalgh* and *Medcalf v. Weatherill*,[54] said that there had to be something akin to abuse of process for a wasted costs order to be made. Mere negligence was not sufficient:[55]

> Wasted costs are dealt with in CPR 48.7 and the accompanying Practice Direction. The Practice Direction states that the court will generally take the question in two stages. First, it should be satisfied that there is evidence which 'if unanswered would be likely to lead to a wasted costs order being made' and that the wasted costs order proceedings are justified 'notwithstanding the likely costs involved'. The second stage is for the court, having heard the lawyer, to consider whether it is appropriate to make a wasted costs order (PD 48, 2.6).

Lord Justice Auld in his report was distinctly unenthusiastic about wasted costs orders:

> The third possible financial sanction is to make a wasted costs order against the legal representatives on one side or another, but again there are often practical limitations on the court of identifying who is at fault on the prosecution side, counsel, those instructing him or the police – and on the defence side, counsel,

---

[50] [1994] Ch 205, [1994] 3 All ER 848.

[51] The conduct complained of in the appeals, variously, was: both parties' solicitors misconstrued a complex statute, solicitors (like their own expert and counsel) failed to realise that the client had fundamentally (and fatally for the claim) misdescribed the location of a piece of machinery; solicitors failed to serve the other side with notice of legal aid; solicitors pursued a misconceived application in reliance on specialist counsel and failed to progress negotiations even though counsel advised that the parties were too far apart to achieve a sensible compromise; honest solicitors relied on the client's untruthful instructions; and counsel instructed at the eleventh hour was inadequately prepared at the hearing.

[52] [1995] 1 All ER 385, para. 1.

[53] (6 March 2003, unreported) Case No. AC9500972, CA; 147 *Solicitors' Journal*, 14 March 2003, p. 301.   [54] [2002] UKHL 27, [2003] 1 AC 120.

[55] For a case in which a wasted costs order was made where the judge delivered severe criticism of the barristers, including QCs, see *Re G (care proceedings)*.

his solicitor or the defendant. And wide use of such cumbrous satellite proceedings would be both an impractical and expensive way of achieving efficient preparation for trial.[56]

A study of the case law and insurance statistics confirmed Auld's concerns. The wasted costs jurisdiction was flawed for six reasons:

> . . . First, it is very costly proportionate to the amount recovered. Secondly, judges can initiate a wasted costs enquiry, which is unfair and even more disproportionately costly. Thirdly, it is procedurally complex. Fourthly, it is unpredictable whether the client would waive privilege, and what the consequences will be . . . Fifthly, it is not possible for solicitors and barristers to make contribution claims against each other. Sixthly, it is mostly used against lawyers representing legally aided litigants from whom costs cannot be recovered.[57]

NB *Advocates' former immunity from suit is ended* Until the twenty-first century both barristers and solicitors had immunity from actions for negligence with regard to the work they did in court and in preparation of court work.[58] In *Arthur JS Hall & Co v. Simons*[59] the House of Lords, sitting with seven judges, changed that rule. They held that advocates no longer had immunity from suit, unanimously in respect of their conduct of civil proceedings and by a majority of four to three in respect of criminal proceedings. (The judgments take some eighty pages in the law reports.[60])

It seems that fears that the change in the immunity would lead to a flood of claims against barristers have proved unfounded.[61]

3. Should costs follow the event?

Civil cases

As already noted, under the CPR the rule that the loser pays the allowable costs of the winner is no longer so hard-edged and clear-cut as before but CPR 44.3(2) states that to be the general rule.

In the United States the rule is the opposite – namely each side generally pays his or its own costs. There is a great deal of debate in the United States as to the merits and demerits of the 'cost shifting rule', as it is known there. By

---

[56] Auld, p. 491, para. 230.
[57] H. Evans, 'Wasted Costs', 64 *Modern Law Review*, 2001, p. 51. For earlier articles see P. Jones and N. Armstrong, 'Living in Fear of Wasted Costs', 13 *Civil Justice Quarterly*, 1994, pp. 208–32; A. Murdie, 'Costs against Non-Parties and Wasted Cost Orders against Representatives', *Legal Action*, January 1998, p. 20.
[58] *Rondel v. Worsley* [1969] 1 AC 191, HL and *Saif Ali v. Mitchell & Co* [1980] AC 198, HL. See also *Kelley v. Corston* [1997] 4 All ER 466.   [59] [2002] 1 AC 615, [2000] 3 All ER 673.
[60] See M. Seneviratne, 'The Rise and Fall of Advocate's Immunity', 21 *Legal Studies*, 2001, pp. 644–62.
[61] J. Bennett, 'Blasts from the Past', *The Lawyer*, 13 September 2004 – www.thelawyer.com. The article, which details several of the cases, states that according to the Bar's insurers, the level of claims was stable.

contrast, in England there is very little discussion of the pros and cons of the costs rule.

The alleged advantages of the rule that costs normally follow the event include the following:

- It 'makes the winner whole' – restores him financially somewhat to the position that he was in before the wrong done to him.
- It recognises that the winner has won. By contrast, if he had to pay his own costs, the fruits of the litigation would be diminished by his costs, which to that extent would diminish his victory. In smaller cases the costs would eat up a huge proportion or even all of the damages.
- If the client is advised that he has good prospects of success, the costs-follow-the-event rule encourages meritorious litigation. (The overwhelming majority of plaintiffs win – whether on a settlement or after a trial.)
- The rule also helps to discourage unmeritorious or nuisance actions. A person with no reasonable prospects of success will think twice before bringing an action if he is told that he will have to pay his opponent's as well as his own costs.

The alleged disadvantages of the rule include the following:

- The rule operates harshly where both sides have been responsibly and competently advised that they have good prospects of success. If both sides have acted reasonably why should the loser pay most of the winner's costs? (That remains the case under the post-Woolf reforms.)
- The rule operates harshly where the outcome of the litigation turns on uncertainties and complexities of the law. It is unfair that the losing litigant should bear such a heavy burden of costs because the law is obscure. (Again, that unfairness is not reduced by the post-Woolf rules.)
- The rule operates harshly where one party loses on most of the issues raised at the trial but wins overall on a point that absorbs very little of the time in the case. Why should the opponent pay such a heavy price when he succeeded with regard to a high proportion of time taken by the trial? (The post-Woolf rules impact on that problem to the extent that the court can allocate the burden of costs in accordance with the costs of the issues won and lost.)
- The rule may deter meritorious as well as unmeritorious litigation. Some would-be litigants will not be willing to take the risk of losing even if they are advised that they have good chances of success.
- The pressure to abandon sound causes of action for fear of the cost of losing will bear most heavily on the economically weaker party.
- The rule has an inflationary effect on the cost of litigation as each side tends to spend more and more in order to ensure success and thereby avoid the risk of paying costs. Often the litigation is actually more about who pays the costs than about the apparent subject of the litigation. (That still operates powerfully despite the attempt in the Woolf reforms to keep costs in proportion to the amount at stake.)

- Moreover, the rule certainly does not prevent nuisance actions – they are a well-known phenomenon.
- The rule increases the unpredictability of the costs factor in litigation. It is bad enough that one cannot know what one's own lawyers are going to charge, it is worse that one may also have to pay an unknown amount in respect of one's opponent's costs. (That obviously does not apply to fixed costs.)

In his Report, Lord Woolf said that, on balance, the indemnity rule should be retained subject to a requirement that the court takes account of the conduct of the parties in its allocation of costs.[62]

The costs-follows-the-event rule and group actions

Special problems arise when there are many plaintiffs suing collectively as a group. The question became a matter of acute public concern in 1987, in the course of the litigation brought by over a thousand plaintiffs for the effects suffered as a result of use of the anti-arthritis drug Opren. In *Davies v. Eli Lilly & Co*[63] the court held that if the action were to go ahead, all the plaintiffs, other than those on legal aid, had to be regarded as being liable for their share of the ultimate costs of the action if they failed.[64]

One of the plaintiffs in the case then challenged the power of the court to make an order regarding costs before the end of the case. RSC Order 62, r. 3 said that costs should follow the event except when the court saw fit to make some other order. To follow the event, the plaintiff argued, must mean that the case was finished. The Court of Appeal rejected the argument. Normally the order would be made at the end of the case but it could be made earlier if the interests of justice required it. In any event, the judge's order in this case had not been for payment but for apportionment between plaintiffs.

In *Aiden Shipping Co Ltd v. Interbulk Ltd, The Vimeira*[65] the House of Lords held that the court had the widest possible discretion to order anyone to pay costs – even if they were not parties to the proceedings. The only proviso was that the order had to be fair in the circumstances. Such an order was highly appropriate where some 'lead actions' were selected raising common issues which could be litigated in order to settle those issues. In *Ward v. Guinness Mahon & Co*[66] it was held that each of the ninety-nine claimants should only be liable for one-ninety-ninth's part of the overall costs, in other words several, rather than several and joint liability.

---

[62] *Interim Report*, June 1995, p. 204, paras. 23–4.

[63] [1987] 3 All ER 94, [1987] 3 All ER 94.

[64] Most of the plaintiffs were elderly pensioners. Obviously they could not afford this risk and it seemed as if the cases brought by non-legally aided plaintiffs would have to be withdrawn. At the last moment, however, a 'fairy godparent' in the form of a wealthy philanthropist, Godfrey Bradman, came forward and guaranteed the costs of the non-legally aided plaintiffs, which it was thought would be well in excess of £1 million. (See *The Times* and *The Guardian*, 23 July 1987.)   [65] [1986] 2 All ER 409.   [66] [1996] 4 All ER 112.

Group actions, as has been seen (p. 66 above), are now governed by CPR Part 19 which provides for the making of a Group Litigation Order (GLO). In July 2000, CPR 48.6A codified the guidance in the case law on costs issues in such cases. It provides that unless the court orders otherwise, any order for common costs[67] against group litigants imposes on each such litigant several liability for an equal share of those costs. However, in respect of liability toward his own solicitors, a group litigant is responsible for his own solicitor and client costs as well as an equal share of the common costs.

The court may make provision for the costs contribution of a party who joins the group late or leaves it early. In December 2001 the Court of Appeal gave a single decision in three GLO actions respectively concerning the MMR vaccine, oral contraceptives and exposure to asbestos in each of which there was an almost identical cost-sharing order made by the trial judge.[68] The chief question was whether the share of generic costs of discontinuers and those who settled were to be determined when they discontinued or settled or rather at the end of the case. If the former, funders of the litigation, notably the Legal Services Commission, would not be able to recover their costs even if they had funded a successful claim. The Court of Appeal held that the proper time for that decision was at the end of the case. So defendants cannot get pre-emptive orders exempting them from paying the common costs of discontinuers even though they might end up losing in respect of those common issues. Writing about the case the co-ordinating solicitors for the solicitors said: 'The judgment means practitioners involved in representing claimants in group claims can breathe a sigh of relief and the Legal Services Commission is able to look positively again on funding these claims . . . The only people unhappy with the judgment will be the defendants'.[69]

For an account of the development of this area of litigation and discussion of the issues raised see C.J.S. Hodges, *Multi-Party Actions* (Oxford University Press, 2000) and M. Mildred, 'Group Actions' in G.G. Howells (ed.), *The Law of Product Liability* (Butterworths, 2000). For a highly critical review of the dismal story of unsuccessful English group actions funded at public expense and suggestions for improving the system see D. Collins, 'Multi-party Actions', 31

---

[67] 'Common costs' are defined as costs incurred in relation to the GLO issues, individual costs incurred while it is a test case or costs incurred by the lead solicitor in administering the group litigation – see CPR 48.6A(2)(b).

[68] *Afrika v. Cape plc; X v. Schering Health Care Ltd; Sayers v. Merck, SmithKline Beecham plc* [2001] EWCA Civ 2017, [2002] 1 WLR 2274.

[69] M. Day and G. Matthews, 'Fairer Multi-party Actions', 146 *Solicitors' Journal*, 15 February 2002, p. 142. They began their article: 'It is no exaggeration to say that the future of multi-party actions hung by a thread while the judgment of the Court of Appeal was awaited'. See also on this important decision M. Mildred, 'Cost-sharing in Group Litigation: Preserving Access to Justice', 65 *Modern Law Review*, 2002, pp. 597–602; and M. Goldberg, 'Counting the Cost of Group Actions', 152 *New Law Journal*, 22 March 2002, p. 437; but for a much gloomier assessment two years later see F. Bawden, 'Group Dynamic', 18 *Independent Lawyer*, 2004, pp. 10–13.

Manitoba Law Journal, 2006, pp. 211–34. ('Recent English group actions have demonstrated a waste of public resources on unmeritorious claims . . .')

By direction of the Lord Chancellor there is now only £3 million annually available for multi-party actions. The dire implications of this cap on funding were explored by Jon Robins in 'A Bitter Pill to Swallow', *Independent Lawyer*, November 2006, pp. 14–17.

The costs liability of non-parties

In what circumstances can someone who helps to finance another person's litigation be made liable for the other side's costs? In *Arkin v. Borchard Lines Ltd*[70] the Court of Appeal distinguished three categories of funders.

'Pure funders' were those with no personal interest in the litigation, who did not stand to benefit, were not funding it as a matter of business and did not involve themselves in controlling or influencing its course. Generally the court would not make an order for costs in such a case. The court gave priority to the public interest in the funded party getting access to justice over that of the successful unfunded party recovering his costs. An example was *Hamilton v. Al-Fayed (No 2)*[71] where several hundred individuals had contributed to a fighting fund to enable Neil Hamilton MP to bring a libel action against Mohammed Al-Fayed, the owner of Harrods. The court refused to make a costs order against nine of the major contributors to the fund.

In the second category, the non party not only funded the litigation but substantially controlled or benefited from it, so as to make himself the 'real' party. Here justice ordinarily required that a costs order be made. An example was where a costs order was made against insurers who funded and conducted the proceedings in their own interests[72] or a costs order against a shareholder of a company who was not a party to the litigation against the company but who had controlled the conduct of the litigation in his own interest.[73]

The third category was where the funder supported the litigation for commercial or financial reasons. In such a case, where the funder was in effect purchasing a stake in the litigation for profit it was unfair that he should be protected from all liability for the costs of the opposing party. In a case where the professional funder provided some of the funding it could be made liable for the other side's costs to the extent of the funding provided. The court said it saw no reason in principle why the same approach should not apply where the funder provided the greater part or the whole of the costs. In *Arkin* the funding body had provided the money for expert evidence on a contingency basis of a share in the proceeds if the case was won. It expected that it would have to provide some £600,000 but in fact provided £1.3 million. The costs order was limited to a contribution of £1.3 million toward the successful defendant's costs

---

[70] [2005] EWCA Civ 655, [2005] 3 All ER 613.   [71] [2002] EWCA Civ 932.

[72] *TGA Chapman Ltd v. Christopher* [1998] 1 WLR 12.

[73] *CIBC Mellon Trust Co v. Wolfgang Otto Stolzenberg (No 3)* [2005] EWCA Civ 628.

(which were over £6 million). The court said this would have the beneficial effect that professional funders would cap their liability or otherwise ensure that the costs remained proportionate.[74]

A comment on the decision in *Arkin* posed the question whether professional funders in this context might include the lawyers on a Conditional Fee Agreement where the lawyers are in effect funding the case on the basis that if they win they can claim a success fee of up to 100 per cent of their costs.[75]

In *Total Spares & Supplies Ltd v. Antares SRL*[76] the judge made a costs order against an Italian company to which the defendant company had transferred a substantial part of its business just two weeks before litigation against it commenced. The Italian company was run substantially by officers of the defendant company. The judge found that the transfer had been made in order to frustrate any costs order.[77]

This argument was raised in *Hodgson v. Imperial Tobacco Ltd*[78] a case brought by cancer sufferers against three tobacco companies. The court held that with regard to liability for costs, the position of the lawyers under Conditional Fee Agreements was the same as that of lawyers normally.[79]

Criminal cases

The principle that costs follow the event in criminal cases affects both the defence costs and those of the prosecution. Where the defendant is convicted, in addition to any contribution he may have had to make in respect of his own defence, he can be ordered to pay something toward the costs of the prosecution. The courts vary in their policy as to whether to order such payments. The power to order costs arises under s. 18 of the Prosecution of Offences Act 1985,[80] which says that where the defendant is convicted at the Crown Court or a magistrates' court he can be ordered to pay the whole or any part of the prosecution

---

[74] In *Campbells Cash and Carry Property Ltd v. Fostiff Property Ltd* [2006] HCA 41 the High Court of Australia held by five to two that third party litigation funding was not an abuse of process or contrary to public policy. The third party litigation funder had underwritten the costs in exchange for one-third of any amounts recovered plus the benefit of any costs order. For a discussion of third party litigation funding developments in Australia see *Litigation Funding*, August 2006, p. 8.

[75] K. Ashby and C. Glasser, 'Extending Liability for Financing', 155 *New Law Journal*, 17 June 2005, p. 928. For comment rejecting the proposition see J. Peysner, 'Arkin . . . Again', 155 *New Law Journal*, 9 September 2005, p. 1326.　　[76] [2006] EWHC 1537, Ch.

[77] For comment see P. Gearon, 'Third Parties Beware', 156 *New Law Journal*, 1 September 2006, p. 1312.　　[78] [1998] 2 All ER 673.

[79] The action collapsed a year later when forty-seven of the fifty-three claimants abandoned their action after a pre-trial ruling by the judge suggested they were unlikely to succeed. The plaintiffs' solicitors, Leigh Day & Co and Irwin Mitchell, who had been funding the litigation under the CFA, were said to have lost £2.5 million (*The Times*, 27 February 1999). In 2004 Martyn Day, one of the leading lawyers handling multi-party actions, said of these cases: 'Successful cases are good business. Unsuccessful cases are a disaster [for a firm]. A total disaster' (18 *Independent Lawyer*, 2004, p. 10).

[80] Supplemented by the Costs in Criminal Cases (General) Regulations 1986, SI 1986/1335.

costs.[81] The court may make any order it considers just and reasonable. For a helpful statement of the principles to be applied see *R v. Northallerton Magistrates' Court, ex p Dove.*[82] The sum ordered to be paid should be within the defendant's means, should not be grossly disproportionate to the fine and should not be greater than the costs actually incurred. The purpose of the order is to compensate the prosecution not to punish the defendant.

The Attorney General told the House of Commons in November 1987 that it was the policy of the Crown Prosecution Service always to make an application for costs against all convicted defendants unless in the particular circumstances it was apparent that such an application would 'lack merit or that an order for costs would be impractical'.[83]

A defendant who is acquitted and who has paid some or all of his defence costs may be entitled to ask for the whole or part of his costs to be paid out of public funds.

Under s. 16 of the Prosecution of Offences Act 1985, when a defendant is acquitted the court may make an order ('a defendant's costs order') of such amount as the court 'considers reasonably sufficient to compensate him for any expenses properly incurred by him in the proceedings' (subsection(6)):

> Where the defendant is acquitted, he ought normally to be awarded his costs. This is the rule, laid down repeatedly by a series of Practice Notes. The latest, issued in 2004, provides that such an order should normally be made 'unless there are positive reasons for not doing so' – for example 'where the defendant's own conduct has brought suspicion on himself and has misled the prosecution into thinking that the case against him was stronger than it was'.[84]

However, in fact costs are only rarely given to the acquitted defendant by magistrates, probably because they tend to feel that such an order reflects badly on the prosecution. A refusal of an order is supposed to be exceptional, but in fact it is the order itself that is exceptional. The Practice Direction states that when refusing to make a costs order the court should give its reasons and should explain in open court that this does not involve any suggestion that the defendant is guilty.

4. Exceptions to the rule that costs follow the event

There are a variety of situations where the costs-follow-the-event rule does not apply.

No costs in small claims in county courts

As was seen, in cases allocated to the small claims track, unless he has behaved unreasonably, the loser pays only 'restricted costs' (CPR 27.14): the fixed costs

---

[81] For further details see *Practice Note* [1991] 2 All ER 924, [1991] 1 WLR 491.
[82] [1999] Crim LR 760.   [83] House of Commons, *Hansard,* 6 November 1987, col. 819.
[84] *Practice Direction* [2004] 2 All ER 1070 at paras. 2.1 and 2.2.

payable on issue of the proceedings, the fee payable on allocation (which is not payable if the claim is for under £1,000), the travelling expenses of a witness, up to £50 a day loss of earnings for each party or witness, a sum not exceeding £200 for an expert's fees plus travelling expenses and costs of enforcement. But restricted costs only apply after the case has been allocated to the small claims system by the District judge. There is therefore a possibility of having to pay costs in respect of things done before the case was allocated.

The costs rule in small claims litigation is designed to facilitate and encourage use of the courts by ordinary citizens. The theory is that if they conduct the case themselves and then lose, they have little in the way of costs to pay and they will therefore not be frightened to bring the case. The trouble with the theory is that the inability to recover costs may penalise rather than benefit the litigant by in practice denying him the use of a lawyer. He either has to be prepared to pay for it or do without. It is for that reason that, so far at least, personal injury and housing cases involving sums of between £1,000 and £5,000 have been excluded from the small claims system. The exception officially recognises that the services of a lawyer in such cases may often be crucial and the winning claimant should be able to recover the cost from the other side.

Legal aid cases

Under the former legal aid scheme, an assisted litigant was protected against the normal operation of the costs-follows-the-event rule by a special rule which limited what he could be asked to pay in respect of his opponent's costs to the same amount, if any, as he had been required to contribute toward his own costs. (Something between 80 per cent and 90 per cent of those who got civil legal aid were not subject to a contribution with regard to their own costs and were therefore not at risk of having to pay anything if they lost.) This rule applies equally under the arrangements which came into force in April 2000 when the legal aid scheme became the Community Legal Service and the Legal Aid Board was replaced by the Legal Service Commission.[85]

Where a non-assisted person succeeds in an action against a legally aided person the effect of the rule meant that usually such a person got little, if anything, by way of costs from his defeated opponent. The Legal Aid Act 1988, s. 18 provided that a person in that situation could make a claim on the Legal Aid Fund in respect of first instance proceedings by showing that he would otherwise suffer 'severe financial hardship'[86] and in all cases that it was 'just and

---

[85] Access to Justice Act 1999, s. 11 and the Community Legal Service (Costs) Regulations 2000, SI 2000/441.

[86] Lord Mackay, in a 1996 White Paper, said that the test would be eased to permit recovery by the unassisted successful litigant if he could show that he would otherwise suffer financial hardship. The requirement that it be 'severe' would be dropped (p. 34, para. 4.30). Lord Irvine's 1998 White Paper *Modernising Justice* confirmed that Labour would make the same change (p. 36, para. 3.29).

equitable in all the circumstances' for such an order. This system too was continued under the Access to Justice Act 1999, s. 11[87] – except that as from 2001 only individuals can apply and they need only show financial hardship. The requirement that the hardship be severe was dropped.[88]

With regard to proceedings at the appellate level it has been held to be 'just and equitable' to make an order in favour, *inter alia*, of building societies, insurance companies, a police authority and local authorities. In *R v. Secretary of State for the Home Department, ex p Gunn*[89] the Court of Appeal held that an order could be made in favour even of a Government department despite the fact that under the new rules the court had to have regard to the resources of the non-funded party in deciding what was just and equitable.[90]

Some costs of litigant in person

The traditional rule was that a successful litigant in person, unless he was a practising solicitor, could not recover anything in respect of his own time and labour in preparing his own case.[91] The reason for the rule (at least that given in 1884) was 'private expenditure of labour and trouble by a layman cannot be measured. It depends on the zeal, the assiduity, or the nervousness of the individual'.[92] Such considerations did not apply where the litigant was a solicitor. A practising solicitor could recover costs in respect not only of his own skill and labour, but also that of his clerk or that of his firm,[93] but the principle that a litigant in person who was a solicitor could recover costs as if he had employed a solicitor did not extend to members of other professions.[94]

In 1973 the House of Lords held that a successful litigant in person was entitled to claim for payments made to a solicitor who assisted him with the preparation of his case. Lord Reid said he should have 'such sums as were reasonably necessary for him to spend in order to prepare his written case and equip himself to appear and argue his case in person'.[95]

The Litigants in Person (Costs and Expenses) Act 1975 took the matter further. It provided that litigants in person are entitled to recover costs, including compensation for their own time and effort, but the level of remuneration for their own time was – and remains – pitifully low. It was originally set at a nominal £9.25 per hour and that figure has not been increased. In *Mainwaring v. Goldtech Investments Ltd*[96] a litigant in person put in a bill for £87,250 charging her time at

[87] See the Community Legal Service (Cost Protection) Regulations 2000, SI 2000/824, reg. 5. See also 30 *Focus*, pp. 32–3.

[88] Community Legal Service(Costs Protection) (Amendment No 2) Regulations 2001, SI 2001/3812.   [89] [2001] EWCA Civ 891, [2001] 3 All ER 481.

[90] See generally J. Simons, 'Recovering Costs from the Legal Services Commission', 154 *New Law Journal*, 15 October 2004, p. 1528.   [91] *Buckland v. Watts* [1970] 1 QB 27, CA.

[92] *London Scottish Benefit Society v. Chorley* (1884) 13 QBD 872 at 877.

[93] *Malkinson v. Trim* [2002] EWCA Civ 1273, [2003] 2 All ER 356.

[94] *Sisu Capital Fund Ltd v. Tucker* [2005] EWHC 2321, Ch, [2006] 1 All ER 167.

[95] *Malloch v. Aberdeen Corpn (No 2)* [1973] 1 All ER 304.   [96] [1997] 1 All ER 467.

a basic rate of £75 per hour, uplifted to £125 in respect of research and £200 an hour in respect of preparation and advocacy. The court held that she was only entitled to charge at the going rate for litigants in person who suffered no pecuniary loss, namely £9.25 per hour! However, in *R (on the application of Wulfsohn) v. Legal Services Commission*[97] the Court of Appeal awarded the litigant in person, who had spent over 1,200 hours on the case, total costs of £10,460. (The trial judge had awarded him £120.) In *Hart v. Aga Khan Foundation (UK)*[98] the Court of Appeal held that an actress who spent some 250 hours in studying technical matters in connection with her action could only recover for forty hours' worth because that is what it would have taken a solicitor.

The 1975 Act provided that if the litigant in person in a civil case has suffered actual financial loss by reason of the work done on the case, such loss can be recovered – subject to a maximum of two-thirds of the rate that would have been allowed if a solicitor had done the work.[99]

An amendment to the rules in October 2002 stated that where the litigant can prove financial loss, recoverable costs include 'the amount that he can prove he has lost for time reasonably spent on doing the work',[100] but if he cannot prove financial loss, he can only claim £9.25 per hour for 'the time reasonably spent on doing the work'.[101] (The Civil Justice Council in 2005 urged that the right to try to establish financial loss should be removed as it absorbed undue judicial time and in 85 per cent of cases was unsuccessful.[102])

The two-thirds restriction laid down by the 1975 Act also applies if the litigant in person is himself a practising solicitor, though not if he employs another firm.[103] A barrister who conducts his own defence in a criminal case can recover remuneration in respect of his professional time and skill.[104]

One useful change made in the CPR in 1999 is the rule that the litigant in person can recover 'payments reasonably made by him for legal services relating to the conduct of the proceedings'.[105] This would seem to permit 'unbundled' legal services where the litigant in person does much of the work on his case but uses professional lawyers as and when needed and, if he wins, can then recover their proper costs. A further amendment to the rules in October 2002 added to recoverable costs 'the costs of obtaining expert assistance in assessing the costs claim'.[106]

However, where a lay litigant employs someone other than a solicitor to assist him, his costs may not be recoverable. Andre Agassi, the tennis star, in an appeal

---

[97] [2002] EWCA Civ 250, [2002] All ER (D) 120 (Feb).   [98] [1984] 1 WLR 994.

[99] Previously, RSC Order 62, r. 18(2), now CPR 48.6(2).   [100] CPR 48.6(4)(a).

[101] CPR 48.6(4)(b). Under the Employment Appeal Tribunal Rules 2004 the figure is £25 per hour increasing by £1 each year from 2006.

[102] *Improved Access to Justice – Funding Options and Proportionate Costs*, August 2005, pp. 62–3.

[103] This is the effect of CPR 48.6(6) which now includes a practising solicitor in the definition of a litigant in person. Pre-1999 the rule (RSC Order 62, r. 18(6)) specifically excluded from the definition of litigant in person anyone who was a practising solicitor.

[104] *Khan v. Lord Chancellor* [2003] EWHC 12, QB, [2003] 2 All ER 367.   [105] CPR 48.6(3)(b).

[106] CPR 48.6(3)(c). E Fennell, 'Is the Route into Law now too Tailor-made?', *The Times*, 17 October 2006, p. 3 (www.timesonline.co.uk/aw).

to the courts from the decision of the tax commissioners, employed tax experts who instructed a barrister. The tax experts were allowed under the Bar's rules (see pp. 799–800 below) to instruct a barrister and the case in the court was presented by the barrister. Despite this, the Court of Appeal held that Mr Agassi was a litigant in person because the tax experts were not solicitors entitled to conduct litigation.[107] Having won his court case, he therefore could not recover from the Revenue the costs charged by the tax experts as legal advisers – though the court held that he could recover as disbursements their costs as tax experts. (To add insult to injury, Agassi subsequently lost the tax appeal in the House of Lords.)

The litigant in person costs rules do not apply to cases brought in the small claims system, the limit for which since 1999 has been £5,000. In small claims cases, the litigant normally cannot recover costs whether he employs lawyers or acts in person.

Where the winner is not liable to pay – the indemnity principle

The costs-follow-the-event rule provided, as has been seen, that when the winner is indemnified against his costs, the indemnity covers his actual costs and no more. It follows that if he won the case and had no costs because his solicitor had agreed to work for nothing, nothing could be recovered from the other side. This was the principle – and the problem – of the indemnity principle. Why, however, should the lawyer not be permitted to promise his own client that he will charge him nothing and still recover his proper costs from the other side if the case succeeds? If the arrangement qualifies as a Conditional Fee Agreement (CFA), the matter is now regulated by statute (see below), but if not, the indemnity rule applied – until it was modified as from June 2003.[108]

The May 1999 consultation paper *Controlling Costs* said that the Lord Chancellor was considering abolishing the indemnity rule but was concerned that its removal should not lead to an increase in legal costs being awarded by the courts. The indemnity principle provided a cap on the costs which could be recovered from the loser. Without it solicitors would technically be free to claim costs without bounds, subject only to assessment by the court.

The Access to Justice Act 1999, s. 31 paved the way for abolition of the indemnity principle. It provided that Rules of Court might make provision, *inter alia*, for securing that the amount awarded to a party in respect of costs to be paid by him to his representatives 'is not limited to what would have been payable by

---

[107] *Agassi v. Robinson* [2005] EWCA 1507. See D. Capper, 'Costs Recovery under Bar Licensed Access Scheme', 26 *Civil Justice Quarterly*, 2007, pp. 23–27.

[108] *Gundry v. Sainsbury* [1910] 1 KB 645; *General of Berne Insurance Co v. Jardine Reinsurance Management Ltd* [1998] 2 All ER 301; Solicitors Act 1974, s. 60(3). The authorities were described and the issues discussed in the writer's 'Will the Revolution in the Funding of Civil Litigation in England Eventually Lead to Contingency Fees?', 52 *DePaul Law Review*, 2002, p. 259 at 271–8.

him to them if he had not been awarded costs'. The Explanatory Notes to the Act stated that the purpose was 'to limit or abolish the common law principle known as the indemnity principle'. However, it was not until 2 June 2003 that this actually happened.[109] As from the same date a new rule has provided that recoverable costs in CPR Parts 44–48 include costs incurred by the provision of advocacy or litigation services under a CFA where the client is only liable to pay his lawyer's fees and expenses to the extent that they are recovered 'whether by way of costs or otherwise'.[110] 'By way of costs' means from the loser; 'or otherwise' would recover from the damages.[111] The Explanatory Note to the statutory instrument says:

> This in effect abrogates in relation to this type of conditional fee agreement the so-called indemnity principle – the principle that the amount which can be awarded to a party in respect of costs to be paid by him to his legal representatives is limited to what would have been payable by him to them if he had not been awarded costs. Solicitors will to this extent be able to agree lawfully with their clients not to seek to recover by way of costs anything in excess of what the court awards or what it is agreed will be paid . . .

NB Clause 185 of the Legal Services Bill introduced in November 2006 gives a court the discretion to make a costs order in favour of a party whose legal representation has been provided pro bono. The money would be paid to a designated charity established to distribute money to organisations that conduct pro bono work.

Contemptuous damages

If the claimant wins only contemptuous damages he will normally be ordered to pay the costs despite having technically won the action. The order that he pay the 'loser's' costs reflects the true meaning of the result. Contemptuous damages are traditionally expressed in the form of the smallest coin then in circulation. In *Dering v. Uris*[112] Dering, a Polish prisoner doctor at Auschwitz, sued for libel over a passage in Leon Uris's well-known novel *Exodus* in which he was said to have participated in more than a hundred atrocious experimental operations at the concentration camp. The author, defending, brought witnesses who had survived the operations whose evidence showed Dering's conduct at Auschwitz in extremely poor light. The libel action in effect turned into a war crimes trial of Dering. In the event, the jury awarded him a half-penny damages and the judge ordered that he pay the costs. (He died shortly after the court's decision.)

---

[109] Access to Justice Act 1999 (Commencement No 10) Order 2003, SI 2003/1241.
[110] Civil Procedure (Amendment No 2) Rules 2003, SI 2003/1242.
[111] See D. Marshall, 'The New CFA Regulations', 153 *New Law Journal*, 30 May 2003, p. 833. For the background see J. Peysner, 'A Revolution by Degrees: From Costs to Financing and the End of the Indemnity Principle' – www.webjcli.ncl.ac.uk.   [112] [1964] 2 QB 669.

Family law ancillary relief applications

As from April 2006, ancillary relief applications in family law matters are subject to a new rule that normally there will be no order as to costs unless the court considers that an order should be made on the ground of conduct at any stage.[113] The motive was to make the question of costs part of the overall financial settlement between the parties rather than a separate matter tacked on after the substantive issues had been decided. Costs have to be paid out of the matrimonial 'pot' and the court divides up what is left between the parties.[114]

Public interest cases

The court sometimes exercises its discretion by making no order as to costs where it takes the view that the losing party does not deserve to be penalised in costs. A familiar example is the long established practice of granting the Revenue leave to appeal to the House of Lords on terms that it will pay the taxpayer's costs in any event. If the Revenue want a point of tax law cleared up, it should be done at the expense of the general body of taxpayers.

In *New Zealand Maori Council v. A-G of New Zealand*[115] Lord Woolf, giving judgment for the Privy Council, expressed this policy in a case concerning threats to the survival of the Maori language (taonga):

> Although the appeal is to be dismissed, the applicants were not bringing the proceedings out of any motive of personal gain. They were pursuing proceedings in the interests of taonga which is an important part of the heritage of New Zealand. Because of the different views expressed by the members of the Court of Appeal on the issues raised on this appeal, an undesirable lack of clarity inevitably existed in an important area of the law which it was important that their Lordships examine and in the circumstances their Lordships regard it as just there should be no order as to the costs on this appeal.

In *R v. Lord Chancellor, ex p Child Poverty Action Group* Dyson J refused to grant the pre-emptive costs order requested. The rule that costs follow the event should normally apply even in public law cases, but he accepted that there was a category of very exceptional case where the court would make no order as to costs and an even more exceptional category where it would make an early pre-emptive order in public interest challenge cases providing that the public body should in effect subsidise proceedings brought against it. The pre-conditions for such an order were that the issues raised were truly ones of general public importance and that the court could assess the merits at an early stage so as to

---

[113] Family Proceedings (Amendment) Rules 2006, SI 2006/352 and Practice Direction. There was a consultation paper in October 2004, CP(L)29/04 (*Costs in Ancillary Relief Proceedings and Appeals in Family Proceedings*).

[114] For an explanation of the change and its implications see Judge Michael Cook, 'Costs out of the Matrimonial Pot', 25 *Civil Justice Quarterly*, 2006, pp. 261–72; S. Gold, 156 *New Law Journal*, 17 March 2006, p. 448.   [115] [1994] 1 AC 466 at 484.

make a pre-emptive decision. The applicant should not have a private interest in the matter. The court would have to consider the respective financial means of the parties and the probable level of costs. It would be more likely to make an order 'where the respondent clearly has a superior capacity to bear the costs of the proceedings than the applicant, and where it is satisfied that, unless the order is made, the applicant will probably discontinue the proceedings, and will be acting reasonably in so doing'.[116]

The first such order – known as a Protective Costs Order (PCO) – was made in December 2002 in *R (on the application of the Campaign for Nuclear Disarmament) v. Prime Minister*.[117] The relevant rule is now CPR 44.3. The order in that case – which concerned an attempt to have the then impending war in Iraq declared illegal – was the more remarkable in that it was made before permission had been given to make the judicial review application.[118]

The issue was considered further by the Court of Appeal in *R (Corner House Research) v. Secretary of State for Trade and Industry*.[119] The court allowed an appeal against the refusal of a PCO in judicial review proceedings brought by a small non-governmental organisation regarding the failure to consult over a new anti-corruption policy issued by the Export Credits Guarantee Department. In a lengthy judgment delivered by Lord Phillips MR, the court approved of the conditions for the grant of a PCO laid down by Dyson J (as he then was) in *R v. Lord Chancellor, ex p CPAG* (above) but it added some further details:

- A PCO would be more likely to be granted if those acting for the applicant were doing so pro bono.
- If not, the claimant would normally have a conditional fee agreement and there should normally be a cost capping order for the applicant's costs – including the success fee on CFAs.
- Such an order should be restricted to solicitors' fees and a modest fee for a single advocate of junior counsel status.
- If the application for a PCO failed, the applicant would pay the court fee and the defendant's costs on the application.
- The judge would consider whether to grant a PCO on the papers. If he was minded to refuse the request, the applicant could ask for a hearing – limited to one hour.

The Public Law Project was allowed to intervene in the case as an interested third party. Commenting on the Court of Appeal's decision, its solicitor criticised the court's indication that the PCO would restrict the applicant to modest fees of a

---

[116] [1998] 2 All ER 755 at 766.   [117] [2002] EWCA 2712, Admin, Case No. AC9500930.
[118] In *Weir v. Secretary of State for Transport* (21 April 2005, unreported) QBD a PCO limiting costs to £1.35 million was refused to a claimant who was a member of the Railtrack Private Shareholders Action Group because they were claiming compensation which indicated they had a private interest in the outcome.
[119] [2005] EWCA Civ 192, [2005] 4 All ER 1.

single junior counsel. ('The two propositions – exceptional cases and limited costs recovery – may well prove irreconcilable in many cases'.[120]) Also, she asked, why should the court be more willing to grant a PCO if the lawyers for the applicant were acting pro bono? That had no bearing on the merits of an application. Cost caps to include the success fee on CFAs, she said, would restrict access to justice for claimants. Many small organisations would not be able to risk applying for a PCO if losing meant having to pay the costs of the application.[121]

For a proposed variant on PCOs in public law cases see J. Beagent and J. Hickman, 'Costs protection certificates – bridging the funding gap', 155 *New Law Journal*, 16 December 2005, p. 1914. Their suggestion was that in public law cases persons whose means took them outside the legal aid scheme should be able to ask the Legal Services Commission for a 'costs protection certificate' which would limit or totally extinguish the claimant's liability for the other side's costs. Respondent public authorities would remain liable to pay costs if they lost but would not be able to recover costs if they won. Part of the cost of the scheme could be defrayed by charging a fee for making the application.

See further the 38-page *Report of the Working Group on Facilitating Public Interest Litigation* published in July 2006.[122] The Working Group, convened by Liberty, funded by the Nuffield Foundation and chaired by Kay L.J, brought together government lawyers, lawyers acting for claimants and representatives of other interested bodies. It focused on when it was appropriate for the courts to make PCOs. It recommended, inter alia, that having a private interest in the outcome of the case should not be an absolute bar to getting a PCO. Also the court should place little emphasis on whether the lawyers were acting pro bono.

It identified three types of possible PCO: 1) The party with the PCO not liable for the opponent's costs if they lost, but could recover costs if they won; 2) Neither side liable for the other's costs; 3) The party's liability for the opponent's costs under a PCO capped in advance.

For an overall assessment see R. Clayton QC, 'Public Interest Litigation, Costs and the Role of Legal Aid', *Public Law*, 2006, pp. 429–42.

NB As seen above, cl. 185 of the Legal Services Bill 2006–07 allows a court to make a costs order in favour of a party whose legal representation has been provided pro bono.

5. The legal aid system

Introduction

It is recognised in most civilised countries that there is a significant denial of justice if the state does not assist poor persons to meet the costs of lawyers. In

---

[120] L. Whitfield, *Legal Action*, May 2005, p. 31 at 32.

[121] These would include the defendant's costs of acknowledging service – *R (Mount Cook Land Ltd and Mount Eden Land Ltd) v. Westminster City Council* [2003] EWCA Civ 1346.

[122] www.liberty-human-rights.org.uk/publications/6-reports/litigating-the-public-interest.pdf.

England this recognition goes back many decades. The first major legislation establishing the legal aid system on a modern footing was the Legal Aid Act 1949 passed by the Attlee Government in the post-Second World era.

The scheme has had three main stages. The first was from 1949 to 1989 when the scheme, though funded by the state, was run by the Law Society under the authority of the Legal Aid Act 1949. The second, from 1989 to 1999, was when it was run by the statutory Legal Aid Board established by the Legal Aid Act 1988. The third era beginning in April 2000 is the current system run by the Legal Services Commission under the authority of the Access to Justice Act 1999. The second stage could be seen as a seamless progression from the first. The third marked a radical break. It is widely accepted that the system is now in serious difficulties.

The scheme as it developed from 1949 had certain main characteristics:

- It covered both civil and criminal proceedings in all the courts.
- It covered legal advice and assistance short of legal proceedings.
- Any firm of solicitors could undertake legal aid work.
- Though funded by the Treasury, the service was at first wholly and later mainly provided by private practitioners.
- To get legal aid for representation in court there was a means test and a merits test.
- Depending on his means, the legally aided person could be asked to pay a contribution toward the cost.
- There was no ceiling on total expenditure. The system was demand-led.

These characteristics were in the second as much as in the first stage. The most important difference between the third stage as from April 2000 and the preceding fifty years is that there is now an overall ceiling on expenditure. But because of the obligations imposed by the European Convention on Human Rights the cap on expenditure does not apply to criminal legal aid. The result is that the funds available for the civil scheme are always at the mercy of the costs of the criminal scheme which have been rising exponentially.

The other major difference between the third stage beginning in 2000 and the previous fifty years is that whereas previously any firm of solicitors could undertake legal aid work, now only firms that have a contract with the Legal Services Commission can do so.

The change from a demand-led service to one that is restricted by a ceiling on expenditure was introduced by Tony Blair's Labour Government but Labour was implementing plans developed by the previous Conservative Government.[123] When it was proposed by Lord Mackay, the Conservative Lord Chancellor, Lord Irvine, wrote: 'Capping is crude'. It would, he said, 'lead at worst to substantial exclusion from justice and at best to long waiting lists'. The availability of legal

---

[123] See the 1995 Green Paper, *Legal Aid – Targetting Need*, Cm. 2854 and the 1996 White Paper, *Striking the Balance*, Cm. 3305.

aid should not depend on where the individual lives or when application is made. It should depend on means and merits.[124] But it was Lord Irvine as Labour Lord Chancellor who brought in the Access to Justice Act 1999 which established the present scheme.

The 1999 Act was foreshadowed in a White Paper, *Modernising Justice*, published in December 1998:[125]

- There would be a new body, the Legal Services Commission (LSC), responsible for running the Community Legal Service (CLS).
- Its functions would be to 'develop, in co-operation with local funders and other interested bodies, local, regional and national plans to match the provision of legal services to identified needs and priorities'.[126]
- The CLS would replace legal aid in civil and family cases.
- Criminal legal aid would be the responsibility of the new Criminal Defence Service (CDS).
- Resources would be directed where most needed.
- The CLS would operate under a controlled (i.e. capped) budget.
- All providers of funded legal services would require a contract from the LSC.
- Contracts would specify and limit the work that could be undertaken.
- The way forward included fixed prices and competitive tendering.
- A Funding Code would set out criteria for funding decisions.
- The funding assessment would consider three questions: (1) would another type of service be better; (2) could the matter be funded some other way; and (3) did the merits of the case justify public funding?
- As under the legal aid scheme, the general test would be whether a reasonable person able to fund the case with his or her own money would be prepared to pursue it, but the criteria applied would not as before only be the strength of the case and the prospects of success. They would also include 'the importance and potential benefit to the assisted person and the likely cost', 'the wider public interest' and 'the availability of resources and the likely demands on those resources'.[127]

(1) The civil legal aid scheme

The proposals outlined in the White Paper were incorporated in the Access to Justice Act 1999. The Act established the LSC.

---

[124] Lord Irvine, 'The Legal System and Law Reform under Labour' in D. Bean (ed.), *Law Reform for All* (Blackstone, 1996).

[125] Cm. 4155. For analysis see M. Zander, 'The Government's Plans on Legal Aid and Conditional Fees', 61 *Modern Law Review*, 1998, pp. 538–50.

[126] White Paper, p. 15, para. 2.11. On assessing the need for legal services by the LSC see P. Pleasence et al, 'Needs Assessment and the Community Legal Service in England and Wales', 11 *International Journal of the Legal Profession*, 2004, pp. 213–32.

[127] White Paper, para. 3.26.

The LSC, like the Legal Aid Board, has a mixed board of lawyers and non-lawyers.[128] (Of the first three chairmen, two were non-lawyers.) The LSC is responsible for publicly funded civil legal services through the CLS and criminal legal services through the CDS. It publishes an annual report.[129] The annual report and other publications issued by the LSC can be accessed on its Website – www.legalservices.gov.uk.[130]

A great deal of valuable information about the legal aid scheme is also to be found in Lord Carter's Review of Legal Aid Procurement, *Legal Aid – a market-based approach to reform* (the Carter Report) published in July 2006.

The new scheme changed the names of the different parts of the scheme and to some extent the nature of the categories and added a number of new features.[131]

The nature of provision

The Funding Code became operative as from 1 April 2000.[132]

The LSC funds civil legal services under the headings of Controlled and Licensed Work.

'Controlled Work' covers all Legal Help and Help at Court and Legal Representation before Mental Health Review Tribunals, the Immigration Appeal Tribunal and Immigration Adjudicators. These services are provided under the terms of the provider's General Civil Contract where the decision as to whether to provide services is made by the provider under a contract that limits the number of cases that may be taken (known as 'matter starts'). The firm gets a global sum calculated by the LSC on the basis of the number and kind of its 'matter starts'. The contract specifies the number of matter starts

---

[128] Details of the members and their business, financial and other interests appear in the annual report.

[129] Less detailed as to information and especially statistics than given by its predecessor, the Legal Aid Board, but there are plenty of colour photos. As from 2005–6 much of the statistical information was hived off to – www.legalservices.org.uk – About Us – Corporate information – Our publications – Statistical information.

[130] Note especially *Focus* published several times a year by the LSC with the latest information on both the civil and criminal schemes and *Focus on CDS* which concentrates just on the CDS. Both are accessible on the Website.

[131] 'Legal aid for civil proceedings' became 'Legal representation', sub-divided into 'Investigative Help' limited to making inquiries to permit assessment in cases likely to be expensive and 'Full representation'. 'Legal aid for criminal proceedings' became 'funded services' provided by the CDS. 'Legal advice and assistance' for matters that had not reached court proceedings (widely known as the Green Form scheme) became 'Legal Help'. 'Assistance by way of representation' (ABWOR) permitting representation in certain cases without a full legal aid certificate became 'Help at Court'. 'Support funding' (new) is a funding mix of the state plus a conditional fee agreement (CFA) divided into 'Investigative Support' (new) and 'Litigation Support' (new). 'Approved Family Help' (new) is help in family cases short of Full Representation. 'General Family Help' (new) covers negotiations in a family dispute where no mediation is in progress. 'Family Mediation' (new) is for disputes relating to children, money or property. For a fuller glossary of new terms see LSC, 30 *Focus*, April 2000, pp. 42–3.

[132] For the text of the Funding Code see www.legalservices.gov.uk. For an overview see 30 *Focus*, April 2000, pp. 19–30. For the relevant regulations see 29 *Focus*, March 2000, pp. 28–57. For a helpful explanation of the Funding Code see *Legal Action*, December 2003, pp. 17–18.

under different headings – family, actions against the police, clinical negligence, debt, education, public law, welfare benefits etc. By far the largest number of contracts are issued with regard to family matters.[133] The number of matter starts can be adjusted on application.

With regard to Controlled Work there are limits to the amount that may be spent on the case without further authority from the LSC. (The current limit for Legal Help is £500 for most cases. In cases where Controlled Legal Representation is provided before a tribunal the limit is £1,500. In immigration and asylum cases the limit is five hours' work.)

A firm with a contract for Controlled Work also has the right to apply to the LSC for a certificate to provide representation in civil proceedings. Certificates are issued on a case-by-case basis. (Emergency work can be conducted without prior authority.)

'Licensed Work' covers other Legal Representation (not including very expensive cases which are managed under individual contracts). Licensed Work contracts do not limit the number of cases that can be started. Instead, an application for funding has to be made to the LSC in each case and a decision is made on the basis of financial eligibility of the client and the merits of the case. Licensed Work is typically for firms that handle specialised litigation.

The funding priorities

A direction given by the Lord Chancellor under the Access to Justice Act 1999 (AJA), s. 6(1) together with guidance issued under s. 23 set the funding priorities as envisaged in the 1988 White Paper.[134] In drawing up its plans the LSC was required to give top priority to certain Children Act proceedings (as defined in the Funding Code)[135] and to civil proceedings where the client is at real and immediate risk of loss of life or liberty. Any such case should be funded provided it meets the merits test criteria. After that the LSC 'should generally give the following categories higher priority than others', namely:

- Help with social welfare issues that will enable people to avoid or climb out of social exclusion, including help with housing proceedings and advice relating to debt, employment rights and entitlement to social security benefits.
- Domestic violence proceedings.
- Proceedings concerning the welfare of children (including those under Parts IV or V of the Children Act, adoption proceedings and proceedings concerning residence).

---

[133] In 2005–6 family law accounted for 43 per cent of all contract categories and 36 per cent of all matter starts. The next largest categories of matter starts were housing (14 per cent), debt (13 per cent), welfare benefits (13 per cent) and immigration (12 per cent). (LSC Statistical Information, 2005–6, Tables CLS1 and CLS2.) These statistical tables are now to be found at www.legalservices.gov.uk – About Us – Corporate Information – Our Publications – Statistical Information.   [134] See 29 *Focus*, March 2000, pp. 17–18.

[135] Public law child protection cases for which legal aid was previously available without a means or merits test.

- Proceedings against public authorities alleging serious wrong-doing, abuse of position or power or significant breach of human rights.

Exclusions from the scheme

Under legal aid there was a short list of types of matters that were excluded: defamation, relator actions, election petitions and judgment summonses: the AJA has a longer list of excluded categories. The AJA excluded, in particular, services relating to allegations of negligently caused injury, death or damage to property, other than allegations of clinical negligence.[136] These matters were excluded on the ground that they were suitable for funding under CFAs (see below). Personal injury due to something other than negligence was not excluded. Other areas of work excluded were conveyancing, boundary disputes, the making of wills, matters of trust law, defamation[137] and malicious falsehood, company or partnership law and other matters arising out of business.[138] It is thought that such matters do not have sufficient priority to justify public funding.

Exceptions to the exclusions

The Lord Chancellor may give directions under the AJA, s. 6(8)(a) permitting the LSC in specified circumstances to fund services that are generally excluded. The categories include cases that have a significant wider public interest and cases against public authorities alleging serious wrong-doing, abuse of position or power or a significant breach of human rights. Another category is personal injury cases with very high investigative costs before it can be determined whether the case could be funded under a CFA. The Lord Chancellor may authorise funding in individual cases following a request from the Commission (s. 6(8)(b)).

The Lord Chancellor's Guidance states that funding of a case in an otherwise excluded category may be considered where '(i) there is significant wider public interest; or (ii) the case is of overwhelming importance to the client; or (iii) there is convincing evidence that there are other exceptional circumstances such that without public funding for representation it would be practically impossible for the client to bring or defend the proceedings, or the lack of funding would lead to obvious unfairness in the proceedings'.[139]

---

[136] AJA 1999, Sch. 22, para. 1(a).
[137] In February 2005 in the famous 'McLibel' case of *Steel and Morris v. United Kingdom* (2005) Times, 16 February the Strasbourg Court ordered the Government to pay the two defendants £57,000 compensation for failing to give them legal aid to defend the action brought against them by McDonalds. See Hudson, 'Free Speech and Equality of Arms – the Decision in *Steel & Morris v. United Kingdom*', *European Human Rights Law Review*, 2005, pp. 301–9.
[138] AJA 1999, Sch. 2, para. 1(a).
[139] The third category was added in light of *R (on the application of Jarrett) v. Legal Services Commission* [2001] EWHC Admin 389, [2001] All ER (D) 111 (Jun) which concerned the exclusion of director disqualification cases. This might be sufficient to meet the need for legal aid in exceptional cases identified by the Strasbourg Court in the 'McLibel' case (n. 137

The Commission has a Public Interest Advisory Panel. A summary of its reports on individual cases is published in its publication *Focus* and also on the Website – www.legalservices.gov.uk – Guidance – Public Interest Reports.[140]

In addition to establishing that the matter in question is within the scope of the scheme, the applicant has to satisfy a merits test and a means test.

The merits test

Under the previous scheme an applicant could not get civil legal aid unless he satisfied the Legal Aid Board that he had reasonable grounds for taking, defending or being a party to the proceedings.[141] He could be refused legal aid if in the circumstances it appeared to the Board 'unreasonable that he should be granted representation'.[142]

The first part of the test was whether there were sufficient prospects of the client being successful. The second part, the 'reasonableness test', was more elastic. The usual interpretation was whether a reasonable solicitor would advise a reasonable client, who had the means, to spend his own money on the case. This excluded most small claims, as solicitors would not normally advise their clients to proceed, but although financial benefit as compared with the cost was the normal criterion, it did not always apply. There were cases affecting the applicant's status, reputation or dignity where legal aid could be appropriate even though the financial benefit was small.

The Funding Code radically transformed the merits test. As foreshadowed in the 1998 White Paper, it now requires consideration of wider criteria and different measures of likely success depending on the type of case.[143] The essence of the matter is not merely prospects of success but cost benefit. The tests are set out in the General Funding Code (section 5).[144] They are different for the different categories. For Legal Help, they are whether there is sufficient benefit to the client having regard to the circumstances, including his personal circumstances, to justify the work and whether it is reasonable for the work to be funded by the CLS having regard to any other potential sources of funding. For Help at Court, they are those tests plus: Is advocacy appropriate, will it be of real benefit to the client and would Legal Representation be more appropriate? For Emergency Representation, the test is merely whether it is in the interests of justice.

Funding for Full Representation will be refused if the prospects of success are unclear or poor or are borderline and the case does not appear to have a

---

above). The Government indicated after the judgment that it did not intend to extend legal aid generally to defamation cases. (Lord Falconer, House of Lords, *Hansard*, 22 February 2005.)

[140] See also K. Ashton, 'Public Interest Litigation – Realising the Potential', *Legal Action*, July 2001.

[141] Legal Aid Act 1988, s. 15(2).   [142] *Ibid.*, s. 15(3).

[143] For research by the Legal Aid Board into the capacity of solicitors to judge prospects of success see P. Pleasence, 'Can Solicitors Pick Winners?', *New Law Journal*, 29 January 1999, p. 138.   [144] For a description see *Legal Action*, December 2003, pp. 17–18.

significant wider public interest or to be of overwhelming importance to the client.

If the claim is for damages and it does not have a significant wider public interest, Full Representation will be refused unless:

- Where prospects of success are 'very good' (80 per cent or better), likely damages will exceed likely costs. Where prospects of success are 'good' (60–80 per cent), likely damages exceed likely costs by two to one. Where prospects of success are moderate (50–60 per cent), likely damages exceed likely costs by four to one.
- If the claim is not primarily for damages (including one which has over-whelming importance to the client) but does not have a wider public significance, Full Representation will be refused unless the likely benefits justify the likely costs, such that a reasonable private paying client would be prepared to litigate. If the claim does have a significant wider public interest, it may be refused unless the likely benefit to the applicant and others justify the likely costs, having regard to the prospects of success and all other circumstances.

Funding for very high cost cases[145] will be refused unless it appears reasonable for funding to be granted in the light of the resources available and likely future demands on those resources.[146] These cases are handled by the Special Cases Unit. Each case has an individual contract based on an agreed case plan with prices costed for each stage.

The means test and contributions

Under the legal aid scheme there were three categories of applicant: (1) those who qualified for free legal aid; (2) those who qualified for legal aid subject to a contribution; and (3) those who did not qualify for legal aid because of excessive income or capital or both. The great majority (around 85 per cent) of those who got civil legal aid paid no contribution.

The CLS has the same basic structure of eligibility tests regarding income and capital and for calculating eligibility.[147] The rates for the year are announced annually to come into force in April.[148]

For some kinds of work there is no contribution.[149] The contribution in respect of income in 2006 was payable for those whose monthly disposable

---

[145] In respect of Investigative Help or Full Representation cases where costs are likely to exceed £25,000 and in respect of Litigation Support cases where a conditional fee agreement is in place and funding is sought for costs above £15,000 or disbursements above £5,000.

[146] This affordability criterion does not apply to Special Children Act Proceedings and judicial review proceedings in which funding is to continue or other proceedings in which the life or liberty of the client is at risk. (See 32 *Focus*, pp. 12–13.)

[147] The details were set out in 36 *Focus*, November 2001, pp. 16–23.

[148] For the year from April 2006 the gross income limit was £2,350 per month (more with four or more dependent children), the limit for 'disposable income' was £649 per month and the capital limit was £8,000 (£3,000 for immigration cases).

[149] Legal Help, Help at Court, Family Mediation, Help with Mediation and Legal Representation before the Asylum and Immigration Tribunal.

income was above £279 and below £649. It was assessed in three income bands.[150] The contribution from disposable capital between £3,000 and £8,000 is either the excess capital over £3,000 or the likely costs whichever is the lesser. If capital is under £3,000 there is no contribution in respect of capital.

To arrive at the figure for disposable income or disposable capital a considerable number of deductions are allowed from the gross figures. Thus for income, allowable deductions include national insurance, tax, child care expenses incurred because of employment, rent or mortgage payments up to £545 per month and a fixed amount for each dependent relative. In calculating capital one may exclude the value of one's home up to £100,000 after allowing for any mortgage again up to £100,000.[151]

The statutory charge

When a legally aided person won his case, the legal aid fund recouped itself for his costs first from costs paid by the loser, secondly, from his contribution and, thirdly, from any damages awarded to him or from property recovered or preserved by the litigation. This so-called 'statutory charge' on the damages could in some cases have the effect of wiping out the net benefit of the litigation. The Legal Aid Board had the power to delay activating the statutory charge.[152] This power to delay was commonly used to avoid a sale of the matrimonial home by the wife when it had been awarded to her in the matrimonial proceedings for her and the children to live in, but the claim remained effective and was met when the wife later sold. Under the CLS, the statutory charge is in most respects essentially the same. (It does not apply to sums expended by the LSC in funding Legal Help, Help at Court, Family Mediation or Help with Mediation.[153])

Pre-CLS, the statutory charge was the cost of the funded services or the value of the house whichever was the lesser. Now when the operation of the charge is postponed the charge applies to the whole cost of the funded services so that if the value of the property increases in value above the amount due, the LSC can take its full pound of flesh.[154]

Legal Help

Legal Help (formerly 'legal advice and assistance' otherwise known as the Green Form) permits the solicitor to give advice and assistance short of representation

---

[150] For a monthly disposable income between £280 and £411, a quarter of income in excess of £275. For a disposable income between £412 to £545, £34 plus a third of income in excess of £411. For a disposable income between £546 to £649, £78.70 plus a half of income in excess of £545.

[151] The LSC provoked considerable criticism in 2004 when it canvassed abolition of the disregard of the first £100,000 of equity but in the event this was not pursued.

[152] *Hanlon v. Law Society* [1980] 2 All ER 199.

[153] Unless in the case of Legal Help, Help at Court or Help with Mediation the work was in connection with family, clinical negligence or personal injury proceedings or a dispute which might give rise to such proceedings.   [154] See further 29 *Focus*, March 2000, pp. 11–13.

at a hearing. Within the limits of his contract with the LSC, it is within the discretion of the solicitor what work he undertakes by way of Legal Help.

There is no merits test. There was a fairly stringent means test administered by the solicitor himself. Until 1993 a contribution was payable by those just above the free limit but as from April 1993 Green Form help was only available to those eligible to obtain it free. That remains the position under the present scheme.

In 2005–6, Legal Help accounted for 708,500 acts of assistance (not including immigration matters) provided by solicitors (450,000), not-for-profit organisations (163,100), CLS Direct telephone advice (73,600), pilots and other (21,900).[155]

The Legal Help scheme allows up to two hours' work (or three hours in divorce work). If the matter requires more work, the lawyer must apply to the LSC for an extension.

Help at Court

Help at Court (formerly Assistance by Way of Representation, known as ABWOR) is a scheme to enable representation in certain matters to be handled without the full requirement of a legal aid certificate. It applied to domestic proceedings in magistrates' courts, proceedings before mental health review tribunals, representation in police applications under PACE for a warrant of further detention and representation in certain child care proceedings.

It is for the solicitor to determine whether the client is financially eligible and whether the case is within the scope of the Act.[156] Again, there is no contribution from the client.

Immigration and asylum work

The LSC's annual report for 2002–3 reported a significant increase in services provided in immigration and especially asylum work. In the two years from 2000–1 the cost had more than doubled from £81 million to £174 million. The rise was due to various factors including increases in the numbers of asylum seekers and faster processing by the Home Office resulting in more appeals (19,395 in 2000, 64,125 in 2002). There was concern about the poor quality of some of the advice given in this field. There were particular concerns about the use of devolved powers by providers to self-grant certificates for judicial review in immigration cases, the success rate for which was only 13 per cent. 'Radical measures' would be required in 2003–4. The first such measure was that devolved power to grant certificates was removed as from April 2003. Applications for funding had to be made to the LSC.[157]

In June 2003 the Government published a consultation paper proposing further radical measures:[158]

---

[155] LSC *Annual Report 2005–06*, Table 3, p. 18.   [156] 29 *Focus*, March 2000, p. 14.
[157] 41 *Focus*, March 2003, p. 2.
[158] *Public Consultation on Proposed Changes to Publicly Funded Immigration and Asylum Work*, consultation paper 07/03.

- Time limits for number of hours of advice paid for different types of matter (five hours for initial advice in an asylum case;[159] three hours for non-asylum immigration cases) and maximum amounts allowed for disbursements. The *maxima* to attach to the client and to apply therefore if the client changed advisers.
- Maximum fees for preparing appeals or for applying for leave to appeal (but not for substantive hearings).
- Payments would only be made to accredited advisers and case workers.
- The accreditation scheme would also be applied to interpreters.[160]
- To exclude useless attendances – for instance at interviews with the Home Office.

These proposals provoked severe criticism from the advice sector, especially as to the proposed five-hour time limit for asylum work. The House of Commons Constitutional Affairs Committee in a report in October 2003[161] commended the idea of accreditation of advisers to reduce the amount of poor quality work but criticised the five-hour time limit as unrealistic and likely to be counterproductive.

In light of these criticisms, the proposals were slightly modified so that instead of an absolute time limit there was a cost or time threshold beyond which providers require the consent of the LSC to continue working on the matter. Funding for attendance and making representations at the Home Office was withdrawn altogether. These changes became effective as from April 2004.

The accreditation scheme became effective as from April 2005. By then all practitioners undertaking publicly funded work in the field had to achieve accreditation by passing two written examinations and a videotaped skills assessment.

Another important change made as from April 2005 was that legal aid would only be paid retrospectively, if at all, to appellants challenging appeal decisions made by the new Asylum and Immigration Tribunal. Lawyers are only paid if the judge considers the case had a significant prospect of being overturned at the outset. (The House of Commons Constitutional Affairs Committee described the retrospective payment system as 'unprecedented' and expressed concern as to the negative effect this would have on suppliers.[162])

In April 2005 the campaigning organisation Asylum Aid and Bail for Immigration Detainees published *Justice Denied: asylum and immigration legal aid – a system in crisis*.[163] One of the main points made in their document was

---

[159] The five hour cap on initial advice was in contrast to the fourteen to twenty hours allowed in the LSC's April 2003 Manual.

[160] Over £10 million annually is spent on interpreter services by the police.

[161] Fourth Report, Session 2003–4, HC 1171.

[162] *Legal Aid: Asylum Appeals* (House of Commons Constitutional Affairs Committee, Fifth Report, Session 2004–5, 15 March 2005, HC 276) para. 22.

[163] Available at www.biduk.org/pdf/Justice per cent20Denied/JusticeDeniedFullReport.pdf and www.asylumaid.org.uk/Publications/Justicedenied.pdf. For a summary and commentary see 'asylum legal aid crisis: evidence from the frontline'.

the poor quality of the sections of the LSC that dealt with immigration and asylum funding requests and applications: 'The issue of poor quality Home Office decisions is now mirrored by the LSC'. The funding cuts had driven many high quality, experienced legal practitioners from the field because the cuts made it impossible for them to carry out the work properly. The precipitous decline in the number of solicitors' firms doing this work is very marked. The Law Society said that just in the six months from September 2005 to February 2006 the number had dropped from 302 to 264.[164] (In 2003 there were 617 contracted suppliers.)

In May 2006 a further blow for those working in the field came with the announcement that the LSC proposed to axe the contracts of firms that failed to achieve a 40 per cent success rate in immigration asylum appeals. The President of the Law Society was quoted as saying: 'As with retrospective funding for appeals, the Commission appears to be singling out immigration solicitors for particularly onerous contract requirements'.

The system in operation

Numbers of providers At the time of the establishment of the LSC some 11,000 firms of solicitors were providing legal aid services. The Law Society predicted that under the new system there would be some 6,000 contracting firms. In fact the number of solicitors' firms with contracts from the CLS is already well below that figure and as a result of the implementation of the Carter Review (see below) it is likely to decrease further. The Carter Review in July 2006 stated that there were just under 4,100 firms providing funded services. Over 2,500 firms (62 per cent) did more than one form of legal aid work (crime, family and other civil). The rest did just one category – 597 did only crime, 776 did only civil work and 236 did only family work.[165] Research carried out for the Law Society by consultants LECG in light of the Carter proposals predicted that if implemented as many as 800 firms (double what Lord Carter had predicted) doing criminal legal aid work would be forced out of business.[166]

By contrast, contracts with not-for-profit agencies has been slowly rising. In March 2006 it was 970.

Numbers of persons being assisted The LSC's Annual Report for 2005–6 stated that during the year the LSC delivered 2.6 million 'acts of assistance':[167] Licensed Work 194,000, Controlled Work 801,400, criminal other than Crown Court 1,489,000 and Crown Court 121,500.[168]

Matter starts In 2005–6 there were 283,300 'matter starts' in family law and 498,700 in other work (solicitors 235,000, not-for-profit agencies 190,000 and

[164] 20 *Independent Lawyer*, May 2006, p. 8.   [165] Carter Review, p. 38.

[166] *Law Society's Gazette*, 28 September 2006, p. 1.

[167] *Annual Report, 2005–06*, p. 6. An editorial in *Legal Action* acidly drew attention to the fact that acts of assistance were actually provided by solicitors and not-for-profit agencies rather than by the LSC. The editorial also queried the figures which it suggested included some double counting. (Issue of September 2006, p. 3.)   [168] *Annual Report, 2005–06*, Table 1, p. 7.

LSC Direct 73,600). The total of 781,900 was 13 per cent up on the figure for 2004–5.[169]

Overall expenditure The LSC's Annual Report for 2005–6 reported total net cash expenditure of £2.1 billion: Licensed Work £547 million, Controlled Work £284 million, CDS £502 million, Crown Court £695 million and administration costs £97 million.[170]

Research into need The introduction of a limited budget requires attention to the targetting of legal aid funds on the basis of 'need'. This means having knowledge of populations vulnerable to the experience of legal problems, the impact of problems, the strategies used to deal with problems and the effectiveness of different strategies. The LSC conducts important research into the need for legal services through the Legal Services Research Centre.[171]

CLS Quality Mark The Quality Mark or Specialist Quality Mark is a quality assurance standard for legal information, advice and specialist services launched together with the CLS in April 2000. Providers of services apply for the Quality Mark at the appropriate level depending on the services they offer. The CLS publishes annually a Directory split into regional volumes of organisations that have applied for or obtained a Quality Mark. There are over 10,000 organisations quality marked at one or more of the five levels: Self Help Information, Assisted Information, General Help, General Help with Casework and Specialist.

As will be seen, Lord Carter's review of procurement of legal aid (July 2006) proposed the transfer of quality assurance for solicitors from the LSC to the Law Society. But it seemed likely that at least some aspects of the SQM would survive as LSC contract requirements.[172]

A *CLS Quality Mark* for barristers' chambers (QMB) was launched in autumn 2002. When the QMB was introduced, the LSC said that ultimately it would be compulsory for chambers doing publicly funded work but this threat was withdrawn after complaints by the Bar Council that such restriction of client choice would breach the Human Rights Act.

CLS Directory Line Callers are provided with details of providers in their area – if possible at least one solicitor and one not-for-profit provider.

CLS Direct In July 2004 the CLS launched CLS Direct (tel. 0845 345 4 345).[173] Callers can get free advice (charged at local call rates) on a variety of topics: debt, education, housing, employment, consumer problems and welfare benefits. The phones are manned 9am to 5pm by qualified advisers from firms or

---

[169] LSC, *Statistical Information 2005–06*, Table CLS2, p. 4. (See n. 133 above.)

[170] *Annual Report, 2005–06*, Table 1, p. 7.

[171] For an account of the methods used by the LSC to assess 'need' and for the main findings of the first periodic survey of justiciable problems see P. Pleasence et al, 'Needs Assessment and the Community Legal Service in England and Wales', 11 *International Journal of the Legal Profession*, 2004, pp. 213–55.

[172] See V. Ling, 'Grasping the Nettle of Quality Assurance', *Independent Lawyer*, October 2006, p. 29.

[173] For details see LSC, 45 *Focus*, August 2004, p. 6.

agencies that have contracts with the LSC.[174] In 2005–6 the helpline received over half a million calls. Some 164,000 callers received free advice from a specialist adviser. Another 207,000 were given information as to how to find local advice providers. A means test is applied. Some 70 per cent of callers are found to be eligible for legal aid.[175]

The service also provides information leaflets available free of charge through a dedicated Leafletline (tel. 0845 300 0343). The leaflets can be downloaded from www.clsdirect.org.uk or the *Just Ask* Website (www.justask.org.uk). In 2005–6 over 2.1 million leaflets were distributed directly to the public and another 371,000 were downloaded from the Website.[176]

Community Legal Service Partnerships (CLSPs) The purpose of CLSPs was to bring together organisations offering legal and advice services – solicitors, law centres, Citizens' Advice Bureaux, local authority advice services and the like. They were launched in 2000 as a key plank of the CLS. By March 2003 over 99 per cent of the population of England and Wales was covered by a CLSP, but research three years on by the Advice Service Alliance showed they were not a success. Many partnerships 'were dormant or dying on their feet'.[177] They had been deserted by private practice solicitors and crucial community groups.[178] What was the point of better co-ordination and analysis of what were the problems when there was less and less money to spend? In 2004 the LSC informed CLSPs in London that because of a lack of resources it was 'no longer able to provide the same levels of leadership and administration' as before.[179]

Community Legal Advice Centres (CLACS) and Networks (CLANS) In March 2006 the CLS published a five year plan.[180] It stated that with local authorities it planned to establish 'community legal advice centres and networks' to provide services that would range from basic advice to legal representation in the full range of social welfare problems.[181] (A CLAC would be a single entity providing

---

[174] For discussion see A. Griffith, 'Telephone Advice: Complement or Alternative', *Legal Action*, July 2004, p. 6.

[175] In July 2004 the LSC published an evaluation of CLS Direct which was then a pilot project. It showed that clients liked the fact that the service was delivered by telephone when they could speak from their own home, telephone interviews tended to be more focused so that cases were resolved more quickly and outcomes were as good or better than traditional casework. 85 per cent of clients said they would recommend the service to someone else (*Improving access to advice in the Community Legal Service*).   [176] *Annual Report, 2005–06*, p. 16.

[177] 'Partnerships and the Community Legal Service' accessible at www.asauk.org.uk and A. Griffith, 'Time to Rethink CLS Partnerships?', *Legal Action*, February 2003, p. 9. See also R. Moorhead, 'Third Way Regulation? Community Legal Service Partnerships', 64 *Modern Law Review*, 2001, pp. 543–62.

[178] 'CLSPs: Good Idea or Good for Nothing?' *Independent Lawyer*, May 2004, p. 7.

[179] *Law Society's Gazette*, 5 August 2004, p. 1.

[180] *Making Legal Rights a Reality*, March 2006 – www.legalservices.gov.uk/civil/innovations/strategy_for_cls.asp.

[181] For the research background see a report by the Legal Services Research Centre (LSRC), P. Pleasence et al, *Causes of Action, Civil Law and Social Justice* (2nd edn, TSO, 2006). A summary of the finding is available at www.legalservices,gov.uk/docs/news/Summary-Main - Findings-revised-Mar05.pdf. The 2006 survey compares its results with those in 2001 and

the whole bundle of core social welfare law services; a CLAN would be a group of CLS organisations working together to provide the same legal services as a CLAC.[182]) Contracts would be awarded after a tendering process.[183] The LSC planned to open twelve centres over the first year. This was to be the LSC's third venture into directly salaried services.[184]

The consequences for solicitors' firms, law centres and not-for-profit agencies providing such CLS funded services in the area could be serious. The LSC warned that where there was a CLAC or a CLAN 'we may reduce or not renew some of our other social welfare contracts from April 2007'.[185] In the longer term, the LSC added: 'Our direction of travel is clearly one where all legally aided social welfare advice and representation is provided by a combination of Centres, Networks and CLS Direct subject to continuing evaluation to ensure quality, access and value'.[186]

For a sharply critical and pessimistic reaction see O. Hansen, 'CLACs and CLANs – a New Reality?, *Legal Action*, August 2006, pp. 8–9. In his view, if the CLS meant what it was now saying, the future for current providers of social welfare legal services was bleak.

See also S. Williams, 'Access to Justice or Tesco Law?', 157 *New Law Journal*, 13 October 2006, p. 1537.

For the view that neither local authorities nor private practitioners were likely to be interested in bidding for CLACs see P. Rohan, 'Jump or be Pushed', *Independent Lawyer*, November 2006, pp. 26–27.[187]

In November 2006 a network of Inner London solicitors' firms and not-for-profit agencies established their own experimental CLAN covering civil, family and criminal defence work. A client who came into any of the networked offices would have any other legal aid problem dealt with by the appropriate firm without having to shop around. All the members of the network would be Specialist Quality Mark (SQM) qualified. The hope was that, if it worked, practitioners in other parts of the country would set up their own networks.[188]

Quality control

Quality control has been one of the central issues for publicly funded legal services. From 1994 this was done through franchising of firms. From 2000 the

---

2004. For an article by two of those involved see 'Research Details Impact of Civil Justice Problems', *Legal Action*, May 2006, p. 8. See also S. Hynes, 'Legal Failings Create Social Exclusion', *Independent Lawyer*, May 2006, p. 28.

[182] *Making Legal Rights a Reality*, pp. 8 and 9.

[183] LSC, 50 *Focus*, April 2006, p. 4.

[184] 156 *New Law Journal*, 31 March 2006, p. 528. As will be seen, the Public Defender Service has eight offices wholly funded by the LSC. The LSC has also established a salaried immigration and asylum legal service in Birmingham – see LSC, 45 *Focus*, August 2004, p. 17.

[185] *Making Legal Rights a Reality*, p. 9.   [186] *Ibid*, p. 10.

[187] The same issue of *Independent Lawyer* at p. 28 carried an article by V. Ling, 'Why the sums don't add up on CLACs', as to why the tenders for the Leicester and Gateshead pilot CLACs failed to attract any interest from private practice.

[188] Lucy Scott-Moncrieff, 'A Starter CLAN', *Legal Action*, October 2006, pp. 6–7.

LSC introduced contracting for particular areas of work in which firms say they had competence. The LSC gave a Quality Mark and a Specialist Quality Mark as quality assurance standards. All contractors had to have at least the Quality Mark. Over many years practitioners complained bitterly of the way in which these issues were handled.[189] The House of Commons Constitutional Affairs Committee in a report in 2004 on civil legal aid was scathing about the way in which LSC audits were carried out:

> The current system of auditing solicitors' costs is arbitrary, inaccurate and bureaucratic. Furthermore, it is not linked to quality of advice given. It is clearly punishing competent and honest solicitors and is operated in a way which completely fails to attract the support of the profession. This is the most serious criticism of the current system for managing legal aid work that we have found.[190]

With a view to improving its relations with suppliers in 2004 the LSC introduced the Preferred Supplier initiative. Preferred Suppliers were service providers who performed to the highest standards both in terms of quality and value who, once identified, would enjoy a variety of advantages in the form principally of reduced bureaucracy and greater autonomy.

After a pilot with twenty-five firms,[191] the LSC in March 2006 issued a consultation paper[192] proposing that over the next three years the Preferred Supplier Scheme would not merely be rolled out nationally. It would be applied to *all* contracted firms, so that by 2009 only suppliers that satisfied the higher tests for Preferred Supplier status would get contracts from the LSC. (Presumably this foreshadows a yet further reduction in the number of suppliers.)

The consultation paper recognised that the relationship between the LSC and providers was not working well and that it needed to be changed:

> 2.7 The current relationship between the Commission and legal service providers is not functioning as effectively as it could. This is hampering both the good quality, value for money legal service providers with whom the future of legal aid rests, and the Commission. Our objective is to move away from a system that has relatively low upfront entry criteria but then relies heavily on intrusive checking and audit. We recognise that this has also become a system where we have traditionally set up management systems to address the problems caused by those legal service providers who do not provide good quality and value for money services, do not comply with legal aid rules and do not provide good ser-

---

[189] 'We have seen them come and go, the franchise management audit, the transaction criteria audit, contract compliance audits, liaison audits, desktop audits and peer reviews . . . Lever arch files containing consultation papers, research papers and correspondence with the LSC over the past ten years would fill a couple of decent sized rooms'. (S. Hewitt, 'The Preferred Supplier Pilot', *Legal Aid Review*, March 2005, p. 18.)

[190] *Civil Legal Aid – Adequacy of Provision*, July 2004, Fourth Report of the Session 2003–4, para. 87.

[191] For a positive assessment of the scheme from one of the pilot firms see S. Hewitt, n. 189 above.

[192] *Quality Relationships Delivering Quality Outcomes*, March 2006 – www.legalservices.gov.uk. See also LSC, *Focus*, April 2006, pp. 2–3.

vices for clients. It then applies these rules to all of our providers. However, this has not wholly addressed the issue of the poorest performers whilst alienating and getting in the way of a constructive and effective relationship with the best.

To be a Preferred Supplier providers would have to achieve a rating of one or two at Peer Review and File Assessment in all major categories in which they undertake work, have a good history of compliance with legal aid requirements, give value for money and have a soundly financed and sustainable business.

Preferred Suppliers would have a greater and potentially increasing range of devolved decision-making powers. Billing and claiming processes would be simplified. Inspection and auditing would be significantly reduced. A Relationship Manager for each Supplier would be appointed by the LSC to help develop a partnership between the firm and the LSC. The basic concept was to set the bar higher for firms at the point of entry into publicly funded work and thereafter greatly to reduce the scope of auditing and inspection.

Peer review

In November 2005 the LSC published a report on peer review.[193] An earlier consultation paper indicated that peer review, where firms are judged by experienced practitioners, would be used nationally as the best measure of quality of advice and legal work and would be the LSC's key quality measure. The previous ways of evaluating standards used by the LSC notoriously had not addressed the quality of advice directly. Peer review would be able to do that. The reviewers would examine a sample of fifteen case files drawn randomly using a standard criteria[194] and ratings system[195] developed by Professor Avrom Sherr and a team at the Institute of Advanced Legal Studies (IALS).[196] The IALS would own and manage the system. It would have charge of issues such as consistency and training of reviewers. The LSC's role would only be to administer the scheme; it would have no involvement in the actual process of any review. The report stated that the LSC was 'committed to accepting the judgments of the reviewer'. Representations from the firm in question about the review[197] would be considered by the reviewer and another senior member of the reviewers' panel. The IALS would seek to achieve a unanimous report,

---

[193] *Independent Peer Review? The Process*, November 2005 – www.legalservices.gov.uk/peerreview. The report was the result of a consultation paper *Independent Peer Review of Legal Advice and Legal Work*, April 2005. The LSC drew rare praise for having listened to the profession's response to the consultation paper – 'Groups Line Up to Praise LSC over Peer Review Scheme', *Independent Lawyer*, December 2005, p. 4.

[194] Assessing the information obtained from the client, the advice given and the steps taken after the advice.

[195] With a scale of 1–5: (1) Excellence, (2) Competence Plus, (3) Threshold Competence, (4) Below Competence, (5) Failure in Performance.

[196] See R. Moorhead, A. Sherr et al, *Quality and Cost – Final report on the contracting of civil, non-family advice and assistance pilot'*, 2001. The research covered a huge sample – 140,000 cases including 87,000 closed cases.   [197] From firms with a rating of 4 or 5 – and possibly 3.

if necessary by bringing in another person with relevant expertise. Any doubt would be resolved in favour of the body being reviewed. A review resulting in a rating of 4 or 5 would be followed by a second review by a different reviewer – immediately in the case of a rating of 5; after six months in the case of a rating of 4.[198]

Specialist Support reprieved

In 2000 the CLS piloted Specialist Support – the funding of specialist advice services that could be drawn on by holders of CLS contracts. By 2004 there were nineteen providers of Specialist Support.[199] In April 2005, *Focus* stated: 'the Legal Services Commission is pleased to report that the Specialist Support services have proven invaluable and continue to offer solicitors and advisors the support needed to improve access to justice and services to the client'.[200] The services provided free advice, support, mentoring and low cost training. The support for the expert services offered had been 'excellent with many organisations stressing how invaluable the services have been'.[201] The funding at that time was some £2.3 million.

In June 2005 the nineteen providers concluded a lengthy renegotiation of their three year contracts with the LSC. However, in July, without prior warning, they were informed that the new contracts would not be signed pending a general review of LSC expenditure.

Given the warmth of its endorsement of the value of this service it was a considerable shock when in January 2006 the LSC informed the providers of Specialist Support that all their contracts were being terminated. The director of the CLS explained to providers at a meeting in February that the service no longer fitted into the CLS' priorities as the money was better spent on providing services directly to the public.[202]

The decision was received with widespread criticism. On 7 March, one of the nineteen providers, the Public Law Project, started proceedings for judicial review against the LSC which three days later resulted in an interim injunction extending the Specialist Support Service until October 2006. The Constitutional Affairs Committee of the House of Commons held an emergency meeting and on 14 March issued a report that was highly critical of the LSC's decision.[203] On 22 March the LSC informed the Committee that it had decided to rethink the matter. In the meanwhile, the notices of termination would be withdrawn.[204]

---

[198] For a practitioner's positive account of peer review see Legal Aid Practitioner's Group, *Legal Aid Review*, December 2005, pp. 18–19.

[199] Most providers were organisations – Liberty, MIND, Citizens' Advice Specialist Support Unit, Child Poverty Action Group, Shelter, Joint Council for the Welfare of Immigrants, Disability Law Services, Terence Higgins Trust and the Public Law Project. A few were barristers' chambers or solicitors' firms.   [200] 47 *Focus*, p. 22.   [201] *Ibid.*

[202] *Legal Action*, March 2006, p. 4.

[203] Fourth Report of the Session 2005–6, HC 919, 14 March 2006. See *Law Society's Gazette*, 16 March 2006, p. 3.   [204] See *Legal Action*, May 2006, p. 5.

(2) Criminal legal aid[205]

The 1998 White Paper *Modernising Justice* also set out the Government's plans for criminal legal aid. The Government would set up a new Criminal Defence Service (CDS) to replace the current criminal legal aid system.[206]

The CDS would be separate from the CLS running the civil scheme. The two schemes would have separate budgets but the Lord Chancellor caused consternation when he said in the debates on the Access to Justice Bill: 'What is available for civil legal aid is what is left over from the budget after the prior claims of criminal legal aid have been met'.[207] The Lord Chancellor's words proved all too prophetic.

The White Paper said that most publicly funded criminal defence services would be provided by lawyers in private practice, under contracts, working wherever possible on prices fixed in advance. Fixed prices created an incentive to keep delay to a minimum, they rewarded efficiency and allowed quick and certain payment. So far as possible, contracts would cover the full range of criminal defence services from advice in the police station to Crown Court representation. If a case required the services of a specialist advocate this would be provided under a separate contract. Very expensive cases – defined then as those expected to last more than twenty-five days – would be handled by individually negotiated contracts. If the CDS and the firm chosen by the defendant could not agree on terms, the client might be required to choose a different firm from the panel. This would enable the CDS to keep a tight rein on expenditure instead of handing over a blank cheque as the then existing system effectively did.

All contracts would include quality requirements. Firms would have to give assurances that both solicitors and their unqualified representatives had the appropriate knowledge and skills. The Law Society's accreditation scheme first introduced for police station advice (p. 181 above) could be developed for this purpose or, if that did not happen, the CDS would be expected to start its own.

Clients would still have choice of firm provided it had a contract. Change of firm would require the consent of the CDS and would not normally be possible. (The Government later stated that if a client asked for the duty solicitor in the police station he would normally be required to stay with the duty solicitor's firm for the rest of the case. If, however, he asked for his own solicitor in the police station but ended up with the duty solicitor he would have the right to change to the solicitor of his choice.) Most firms that undertook a significant amount of criminal work would remain part of the scheme, but they should

---

[205] For an account of the story of criminal legal aid from its start to the present see E. Cape, 'The Rise (and Fall?) of a Criminal Defence Profession', *Criminal Law Review*, 2004, pp. 401–16.

[206] On the previous scheme see an excellent collection of essays in R. Young and D. Wall (eds.), *Access to Criminal Justice: Legal Aid Lawyers and the Defence of Liberty* (Blackstone, 1996).

[207] House of Lords, *Hansard*, 21 January 1999, col. 738.

have to compete for work. One way to meet both these objectives would be to make firms bid for a larger or smaller share of the work available. Firms would be awarded more or fewer duty solicitor 'slots' on the basis of the prices they offered both for that work and for subsequent representation.

The CDS became operational as from April 2001. From that date funding of private practice solicitors to provide advice and assistance on criminal matters, including in the police station and representation in the magistrates' court, had to be through the General Criminal Contract.

Under the system, applications for funding for legal representation, as before, were made to and decided by the court.

The merits test

The merits test previously was simply whether it was 'in the interests of justice'. Prior to the Legal Aid Act 1988 the statutory formula of 'the interests of justice' was not further defined. Instead there was a non-statutory list of criteria that were supposed to be applied to the interpretation of the test for cases to be heard in the magistrates' courts. These non-statutory, so-called 'Widgery criteria',[208] were replaced with a statutory gloss on the 'interests of justice' in s. 22 of the Legal Aid Act 1988.[209] The criteria for the grant of what is now called a 'right to representation' are whether the defendant is likely to face a sentence depriving him of his liberty or loss of livelihood or serious damage to reputation; whether the case involves a substantial question of law or the defendant may be unable to understand the proceedings or to state his own case; whether the defence involves the tracing and interviewing of witnesses or expert cross-examination; or that it is in the interests of someone else that the defendant is represented.

Where the case was being tried in the Crown Courts, it has been regarded as normally in the interests of justice for legal aid to be granted – as can be seen from the remarkable fact that year on year some 95 per cent of those tried in the Crown Court, regardless of whether they plead guilty or not guilty, are represented out of public funds. (In 2005, it was 94 per cent of those tried and 80 per cent of those who appeared for sentence only.[210]) Unlike the position in other countries, members of the Criminal Bar, including its most eminent members, spend most of their working lives representing publicly funded defendants.

However, whether a particular applicant for legal aid in the magistrates' court got it has depended as much as anything on the accident of which court he applied to. Courts varied considerably in their policy as regards the granting of

---

[208] So called because they were formulated by the (Widgery) Report of the Departmental Committee on *Legal Aid in Criminal Proceedings*, 1966, Cmnd. 2934, para. 180.

[209] This is now to be found in virtually identical language in Sch. 3 of the Access to Justice Act 1999, para. 5(2) ('criteria for grant of right').

[210] The figures are given each year in the annual *Judicial Statistics*, Tables 10.2 and 10.4.

legal aid.[211] Research found considerable differences in interpretation of the criteria. It also found that many (perhaps most) grants of legal aid were made in situations where the criteria did not apply, or where, if they did apply, they were given little weight by court clerks. Instead, the system that seemed to operate in most courts was that for some offences legal aid was automatically granted, for others almost automatically refused, while in the middle was a grey area where the arguments presented by or, more likely, on behalf of the applicant could make a difference. Some court clerks were too generous, some were too severe.[212] The problem has not been the subject of recent inquiry but no doubt that continued to be the case.

The Legal Aid Act 1988, s. 21(7) provided that where a doubt arose as to whether legal aid should be granted to a person, 'the doubt shall be resolved in that person's favour'. There was no equivalent in the Access to Justice Act 1999.

The Criminal Defence Service Act 2006 transferred responsibility for the grant of legal aid to the LSC. In order to promote consistency in decision-making (and to have better control) the LSC delegated the actual decision not to the courts but to the court staff. The interests of justice test is therefore now an administrative act. But a person refused legal aid has the right to appeal to the magistrates, guided by instructions from the Commission.[213]. The LSC announced that 'legal advisers will initially work with administrative staff to carry out the interests of justice test in order to embed the new procedure'.[214]

The means test and contributions

The basis of the means test used to be imprecise. Courts were supposed to follow broadly the same financial tests as applied to civil cases. The general test was whether it appeared to the court that the applicant's means were such that he required assistance in meeting the costs. Unlike the civil scheme, however, the criminal scheme had no upper limit – so even a relatively affluent person could qualify if the case was likely to be a long and costly one. The test was what a person could reasonably be expected to afford without altering their life style.

Contributions From the start the criminal legal aid scheme had a contribution aspect but again this was on a very different basis from that in the civil scheme. Until 1982, the court had a complete discretion as to whether to ask for a down-payment or to demand a contribution after the completion of the case. Both the contribution order and its amount were entirely in the discretion of the court and, inevitably, courts varied considerably in their approach.

---

[211] R. Young, 'The Merits of Legal Aid in the Magistrates' Courts', *Criminal Law Review*, 1993, pp. 336–44 and R. Young and A. Wilcox, 'The Merits of Legal Aid in the Magistrates' Courts Revisited', *Criminal Law Review*, 2007, pp. 109–28. The latter article revisits the findings of the research carried out in 1992 and considers how discretion is likely to be operated under the Criminal Defence Act 2006.

[212] *Criminal Law Review*, 1993, pp. 336 and 343.

[213] For details of the instructions see A. Keogh, 'In the Interests of Justice?', *Independent Lawyer* October 2006, pp. 26–27.   [214] LSC, 20 *Focus on CDS*, September 2006, p. 8.

This was changed by the Legal Aid Act 1982, the chief purpose of which was to raise more revenue from contributions. The Act proceeded on the basis that defendants should have to pay for their legal defence whatever they could afford according to rigid criteria as in civil cases. This policy was continued by the Legal Aid Act 1988.

The fruits of this legislation were however meagre. Only a tiny proportion of defendants were ordered to pay contributions and the aggregate amount of money recovered was small. In May 1999, Mr Geoff Hoon, Minister of State, told the House of Commons: 'the total value of contributions collected is barely enough to pay for the direct costs of running the system'.[215] (In 2000 the total amount recovered in the form of contributions was £5.9 million – under 1 per cent of expenditure on criminal legal aid.[216]) The system was not merely unproductive, it was also erratic and inefficient. The system of vetting legal aid applications was repeatedly censured by the National Audit Office and in the annual reports of the Comptroller and Auditor General.

The Government's solution, Mr Hoon told the Standing Committee on the Access to Justice Bill in May 1999, was to scrap means testing for applicants and instead all courts other than magistrates' courts should have a duty to consider at the end of a case, whether a defendant should pay his defence costs. That would be done by a Recovery of Defence Costs Order.[217]

The new system abolishing up-front contributions became effective as from October 2000.[218] From that date anyone who successfully applied for a Right to Representation Order got legal representation initially without charge. Those tried in the magistrates' courts, or who were sent to the Crown Court for sentence only, or who appealed to the Crown Court could not be asked to make a contribution. Save in exceptional circumstances, the same was true for someone who was acquitted in the Crown Court.

However, anyone committed for trial in the Crown Court who is convicted or who pleads guilty can be liable for defence costs. Such a person has to fill in a Form B setting out his financial situation. If no Form B was filled in, save in exceptional circumstances, the judge *has* to order the defendant to pay the full amount of the defence costs to the Legal Services Commission.[219] If Form B is filled in and discloses sufficient income or other assets, the court can make a Recovery of Defence Costs Order. The regulations exempt the first £3,000 of the defendant's capital, the first £100,000 of the equity in his principal home and income of up to £24,000 per annum. The judge has a duty to consider making an order at the end of the case. He has to decide whether the information before him is sufficient. His powers include the power to investigate the defendant's

[215] House of Commons, Standing Committee E, 29 April 1999, col. 83.
[216] *Judicial Statistics*, 2000, p. 102, Table 10.7.
[217] House of Commons Standing Committee E, 11 May 1999, col. 239.
[218] Legal Aid Act 1988 (Modification) Regulations 2000.
[219] Criminal Defence Service (Recovery of Defence Costs Orders) Regulations 2001, SI 2001/856, reg. 13.

partner and any other third party where it appears that the defendant has deliberately removed assets.

If in doubt, the judge can refer the matter to the LSC for a report.[220] The LSC then sends a report to the judge who can 'make any necessary further inquiry'.[221]

The abolition of means testing for cases dealt with by magistrates coincided with, and was assumed to have been the cause of, a significant rise in the number of grants of criminal legal aid. Panicked by this increase, the DCA in May 2004 published a draft Bill, accompanied by a consultation paper[222] aimed at making two major changes. One was to transfer authority to grant criminal legal aid from the courts to the LSC. The second was to reintroduce a means test.[223] The motivation behind the Bill was clear. The consultation paper stated: 'Expenditure on criminal legal aid in 2002/03 exceeded original provision by more than £140 million. The numbers of individuals applying for and getting public funding had risen by about 40 per cent'.[224] The courts were being too generous in making grants of legal aid. ('There is some evidence that courts have been too favourable to defendants . . .'[225]) Also, many who previously would have been privately represented or who would have represented themselves were applying for, and getting, legal aid. The re-introduction of the means test would 'focus the resources on those that need help most'.[226]

The proposals in the Draft Bill were the subject of an unusually critical report by the House of Commons Constitutional Affairs Select Committee.[227] The Committee approved of the objective of controlling the rising cost of criminal legal aid and the policy that those who can afford to pay for their own defence should do so, but it considered that the proposals were unworkable, ill-considered and likely to prove ineffective – and in breach of the ECHR.

When the Bill was introduced into Parliament it had been altered by the Government to give the task of means testing, as before, to court clerks.[228] It had also been changed to give the applicant a right of appeal against a refusal of legal

---

[220] *Ibid*, reg. 7.   [221] *Ibid*, reg. 12(b).

[222] *Draft Criminal Defence Service Bill*, consultation paper and Explanatory Notes, 2004, Cm. 6194.

[223] The DCA's consultation paper offered three possible models: (1) a simpler version of the old means test with no upper limit for income and a contribution of a flat rate 10 per cent of anticipated costs; (2) an 'all or nothing' model where the defendant would be eligible if his gross household income was below £25,000 and his gross capital was under £5,000; and (3) a 'sliding scale' model where contributions would be paid only on income on a sliding scale.

[224] DCA consultation paper, Annex C, para. 11. The number of cases in which defendants got legal aid orders for trials in the magistrates' courts in the years 1993–8 fluctuated between 432,000 and 494,000. In 1998–9 it rose to 503,000. In the following two years it was down to 475,000 and 467,000, but in 2001–2 it rose extraordinarily to 598,000. In 2002–3 the figure was 576,000.   [225] DCA consultation paper, para. 40.   [226] *Ibid*, para. 49.

[227] Fifth Report of Session 2003–4, HC 746–1. For an account of the criticisms see 18 *Independent Lawyer*, September 2004, pp. 4–5.

[228] Under the Draft Bill the LSC would have delegated means testing to solicitors. The Select Committee and many others pointed out that this would create a serious conflict of interest issue.

aid on the grounds of the interests of justice[229] (though not on means).[230] The appeal would be in writing – initially to the justices' clerk and if refused, to the magistrates.[231]

The Criminal Defence Service Act 2006 took effect on 2 October 2006.[232] It applies only to cases in the magistrates' courts but there were plans to extend it to Crown Court cases in 2007.

The DCA promised that the new means test would be light on bureaucracy and that it would not cause delays in the criminal process but there was little hope that this would prove to be the reality. The applicant had to submit an Application for Legal Aid in criminal proceedings form (CDS14) plus a fully completed Financial Statement form (CDS15). The forms are long and complicated.[233] Many applicants will need help to fill them in. It was predictable that court staff would be spending time helping applicants do so.

If the defendant was helped with the forms by a solicitor who represented him at the first hearing before the legal aid issue had been decided, the lawyers theoretically could claim a modest fee of £75 under 'Early Cover' even if legal aid was ultimately refused. However, the £75 fee was subject to what criminal lawyers were calling 'nonsensical' provisions seemingly designed to ensure that they could not make an Early Cover claim.[234] In the first week of the operation of the means test hundreds of criminal defence solicitors across the country signed protocols pledging that they would refuse to represent clients until they knew they would receive legal aid, in protest at the 'shambolic' means-testing system.[235]

---

[229] The Joint Committee on Human Rights expressed concern that the Government might be intending to move toward a discretion as to whether the interests of justice required representation rather than a right as required by the ECHR. (*Scrutiny: Second Progress Report, 2004–05*, February 2005, HL 41, HC 305, para. 2.10.)

[230] There would only be an appeal on means to the LSC and then only for a change of circumstances or miscalculation of the figures by court staff. The Joint Committee on Human Rights suggested that the lack of an appeal to an independent tribunal on eligibility with regard to means would be open to challenge under the ECHR, n. 229 above, p. 16.

[231] Both the Joint Human Rights Committee and the Constitutional Affairs Committee criticised the Draft Bill for failure to provide such a right of appeal which they said would be a breach of Article 6 of the ECHR. See the decision of the Strasbourg Court in *Granger v. United Kingdom* (1990) 12 EHRR 469.

[232] See the Criminal Defence Service (Financial Eligibility) Regulations 2006, SI 2006/2492. Detailed information in relation to the means test can be found at www.legalservices.gov.uk/ criminal/getting-legal_aid/index.asp. A full account of the legislation and of its likely costs and benefits is to be found in the Regulatory Impact Statement issued by the DCA – www.dca. gov.uk/risk/crime-defence-act-ria.pdf.

[233] For the forms go to the LSC Website – www.legalservices.gov.uk/criminal/forms//cds.asp.

[234] Early Cover was originally only payable if (1) the defendant had submitted his application within two days of being charged; (2) no decision on legal aid had been reached by 9am on the day of the hearing; and (3) the first hearing advanced the case and an adjournment was justified. Where legal aid is refused on the interests of justice test, the lawyer could claim for one hour's work under what was called Pre-Order Cover. (See *Law Society's Gazette*, 21 September 2006, p. 3.)

[235] *Law Society's Gazette*, 5 October 2006, p. 1. For a weary comment on the shambles and a suggestion that LSC incompetence might show that it was not fit for purpose see A. Keogh,

The furore over the implementation of the new system was so great that the Government was forced to amend the scheme. In a letter addressed to practitioners on 23 November 2006 the LSC's Director of the CDS announced that:

- where a defendant qualified for legal aid, the solicitor would be guaranteed payment from the date when the court received the original application even if the application was rejected because of some technical defect;
- application forms would no longer require the counter-signature of the applicant's partner if evidence was provided that the partner was unable to sign;
- payment under the Early Cover scheme would be made if the application form was submitted within five (as compared with two) working days from first instructions, providing this was not after the first hearing;
- all the forms were being reviewed with a view to making them simpler and shorter.[236]

A client who is in custody and who therefore cannot provide the necessary documentation can sign a Statement of Truth (CDS17), but this depends on his being able to state both his income and his outgoings from memory. (What mentally disordered defendants were supposed to do was not clear.)

Under the new means test, defendants whose 'adjusted' income[237] is below £11,900 get legal aid automatically.[238] Those whose adjusted income is above £20,740 do not qualify. Those earning between £11,900 and £20,740 have their finances examined to see whether their 'disposable' income after deductions for various forms of expenditure[239] brings it below £3,156. (If the individual has a partner, the partner's resources must be added-in unless he/she has a contrary interest in the case.) Eligible defendants pay no contribution. No account is taken of capital.

The LSC set targets for its staff of 90 per cent of applications being processed by 5pm on the day after the application, 99 per cent by 5pm on the third day and 100 per cent by 5pm on the sixth working day. This was ambitious.

Where someone needs legal aid but his application is refused there are two fail-safe provisions. If a court considers that it would be in the interests of justice for an unrepresented defendant to have representation, then provided that the person is eligible under the means test, a representation order must be

---

'Means Testing – a Sign of Things to Come?', 156 New Law Journal, 6 October 2006, p. 1489. For a news item 'Means testing branded bureaucratic nightmare' see ibid, p. 1491. See further, Ed Cape, 'Criminal Legal Aid Means-Testing: Fair Justice? Fair Price?', Legal Action, January 2007, pp. 6–7.

[236] On 17 January 2007 the Government announced that, starting in May, it would be carrying out a review of the first six months of the operation of the new means testing system (Law Society's Gazette, 25 January 2007, p. 4).

[237] Gross annual income divided by weighting = adjusted income. 'Weighting' for a single adult is 1.00 plus the total weighting for children. The weighting for a couple is 1.64 plus weighting for children. Weighting for children varies according to age from 0.15 for those under one year to 0.59 to those between sixteen and eighteen.

[238] So do those on Income Support, income-based Jobseeker's Allowance or a State Pension, anyone under sixteen or under eighteen if in full-time education.

[239] Tax, National Insurance, rent or mortgage payments, an allowance for cost of living expenses etc.

granted.[240] Also, the LSC has the power to make a representation order in favour of someone whose means take him outside the limits of the scheme where he 'does not have sufficient means to pay for the cost of legal assistance'.[241]

The Government estimated that under the new means test, of the 650,000 currently getting representation orders, some 110,000 would no longer be eligible, with potential savings of some £35 million.

Very High Cost cases

Special rules apply in very high cost criminal cases – now defined as any case predicted to last for forty-one days or more at trial.[242] Such cases absorb a grotesquely large proportion of the total criminal defence budget – 1 per cent of Crown Court cases accounting for about half of *all* Crown Court legal aid expenditure. Regulations provide that such cases require an individual case contract. They are managed by the Complex Crime Unit at the LSC. There is a three-monthly case plan. The work to be done is agreed in advance. Fees are based on the seniority of the practitioner and the level of seriousness and complexity of the case.[243] The LSC's annual report for 2005–6 said it entered into 414 such contracts in the year.[244]

Duty solicitor schemes in magistrates' courts

A national scheme for the establishment of duty solicitor schemes in magistrates' courts was provided for by the Legal Aid Act 1982. The basic idea was that the defendant who comes to court without having seen a lawyer should have someone to provide preliminary advice – as to his plea, whether to ask for an adjournment and whether to apply for legal aid or bail – and representation. Originally the scheme was run by the Law Society through regional committees. The running of the schemes became part of the responsibility of the Legal Aid Board when it took over the management of the scheme in 1988.

The scheme continued broadly unaffected by the transfer of responsibility to the LSC.

In 2005–6, the numbers assisted under the scheme were 86,000 at a total cost of £19.8 million.[245]

---

[240] Criminal Defence Service (Representation Order and Consequential Amendments) Regulations 2006, para. 10.

[241] Criminal Defence Service (Financial Eligibility) Regulations 2006, SI 2006/2492, para. 14(1)(b).

[242] Changed from twenty-five days in 2004. LSC, 14 *Focus on CDS*, March 2004, p. 5; and 16, December 2004, p. 3. Originally, shorter cases where defence costs were likely to be above £150,000 were also within the definition, but this measure was dropped in August 2004.

[243] In 2004, proposals for changes in the payment of barristers in these cases led to an unprecedented strike. The strike was settled with agreement for an extra £17 million. (*Law Society's Gazette*, 1 July 2004, pp. 1 and 16–17.)

[244] Table 6, p. 22. This does not necessarily equate to the number of cases as there may be more than one contract per case.   [245] LSC, *Annual Report 2005–06*, Table 6, p. 22.

Duty solicitor schemes in police stations

As was seen above (p. 178), duty solicitor schemes were set up under PACE to assist detainees in the police station. Like the schemes for courts, they were originally run by the Law Society, then by the Legal Aid Board and now by the LSC.

They operate on either a rota or a panel basis[246] with local practitioners. Such schemes cover all the 1,645 police stations in the country.[247] There are elaborate rules as to the qualifications required and the selection process involved for those participating in these schemes. The Law Society and the LSC have in recent years made serious attempts to improve the quality of the advice given under the scheme, both by solicitors and others (known as 'representatives').[248]

In around two-thirds of cases the solicitor called out is the suspect's own solicitor. There is a fixed fee for telephone calls (regardless of whether they are routine or for advice)[249] and a higher fee for attendance at the police station.

From the outset there has been no means test and no contribution in respect of work done under either of the duty solicitor schemes.

In 2004, cutbacks in the scheme were implemented as a way of saving money.[250] The basic policy was that less serious matters and matters where the lawyer cannot in practice achieve anything of significance for the client should either be removed from the scheme or restricted to telephone advice only. Payment is now made only for telephone advice if the client is detained for a non-imprisonable offence, for various driving offences (driving with excess alcohol or failing to produce a specimen), for breach of bail conditions or failing to appear. Payment for attendance at the police station is paid for however if one of the exceptions applies and the Sufficient Benefit Test is satisfied.

The exceptions are: If an interview or identification procedure is going to take place; the client, being a juvenile or mentally vulnerable, is entitled to assistance from an appropriate adult; the client requires an interpreter or is otherwise unable to communicate over the telephone; the client complains of serious mal-treatment by the police or the lawyer is already at the police station. But even if

---

[246] In rota schemes the solicitors are nominated in advance for a set period during which they must make themselves fully available – night or day. In panel schemes the phone service running the scheme calls one solicitor after another until it finds one available. Rota schemes tend to be used in urban areas, panel schemes in less busy rural areas.

[247] The number of firms serving a particular police station varies greatly. The Carter Review (p. 24, para. 17) contrasted Bristol with thirty-one firms per police station against London with 85.

[248] In November 2005 these requirements were extended to solicitors acting for their own clients – see *Focus on CDS*, October 2005, p. 5. At the same time the Law Society was engaged in a consultation exercise as to whether those already accredited under the Criminal Litigation Accreditation Scheme should have to re-qualify every five years (*ibid*, p. 4). For an exchange as to the merits of this proposal see *Independent Lawyer*, December 2005, p. 24.

[249] Until 2004 a higher fee was paid for calls involving advice.

[250] The changes were heralded by consultation papers published in 2003 by the DCA and the LSC both with the same title *Delivering Value for Money in the Criminal Defence Service?*

an exception applies the lawyer will only be paid for attendance at the police station if it would be of sufficient benefit to the client.[251]

In October 2005, as noted above, the LSC began an experiment (called CDS Direct) with a telephone advice service staffed by qualified employees[252] for matters restricted to telephone advice only – unless one of the exceptions applies. In two areas, Liverpool and Boston, the pilot covered all police station work other than indictable-only cases and cases where the time of the interview is known when the request for the duty solicitor is made. In those two areas, the CDS Direct lawyer gives initial advice and decides whether attendance in the police station is necessary, in which case the matter is passed on to a solicitor's firm.[253]

In 2005–6, 766,000 suspects in the police station were advised under the scheme.[254] Roughly 80 per cent of the cost is for advice given in the police station and 20 per cent for advice given over the telephone. The total cost in 2005–6 was £171 million.[255]

For the recommendations of the Carter Review regarding police station duty solicitor services see pp. 620–21 below.

Public defenders

The most controversial proposal in the 1998 White Paper *Modernising Justice* was that, in addition to contracting with lawyers in private practice, the CDS would also be able to use publicly funded salaried lawyers. Evidence from other countries, it said, suggested that properly funded salaried defenders could even be more cost-effective and could provide a better service than lawyers in private practice.[256] But before taking the first steps in this direction, the CDS would take account of the pilot scheme involving public defence solicitors which was currently running in Scotland.[257]

The Public Defender Services (PDS) was set up in May 2001 as a four year pilot project. In its first year it had opened three Public Defender Offices. By

---

[251] For details see *Legal Action*, October 2004, p. 14.
[252] Solicitors holding the Law Society's Police Station Qualification or accredited police station representatives.
[253] LSC, 15 *Focus on CDS*, August 2004, p. 8; 16, December 2004, p. 3; and 18, October 2005, p. 3.
[254] Lord Carter's Review of Legal Aid Procurement – *Legal Aid: A market-based approach to reform*, July 2006 (Carter Review), p. 24. In 2001–2, the figure was 616,400. The rise in the four years to 2005–6 was 24 per cent.
[255] Carter Review, p. 24. In 2001–2, the figure was £126.9 million. The rise in the four years to 2005–6 was 35 per cent.
[256] The White Paper cited T. Goriely, *Legal Aid Delivery Systems: which offer the best value for money in mass casework?* (LCD Research Series No 10, December 1997).
[257] See A. Watson, 'The Public Defence Solicitors' Office: The Background to its Introduction in Scotland', *Scottish Law Gazette*, September 1998, p. 117. In June 2000 the LCD published a consultation paper, *Criminal Defence Service: Establishing a Salaried Defence Service and Draft Code of Conduct for Salaried Defenders Employed by the Legal Services Commission.* See also T. Goriely, 'Evaluating the Scottish Public Defence Solicitors' Office', 30 *Journal of Law and Society*, 2003, pp. 84–101.

2004 there were eight.[258] The PDS's final report on the pilot was published in 2006.[259] This claimed that the pilot had been a success. All eight offices had achieved the category one (highest) rating, all but one had 'competent plus' rating in peer review and there was high client satisfaction. In 2005–6 the service dealt with 5,900 cases.[260]

Private practitioners understandably felt aggrieved about the level of funding provided by the PDS for staff, premises and other facilities but Anthony Edwards[261] told the Criminal Law Solicitors' Association annual conference in 2001 that although the PDS plainly was unfair competition this was to miss the point. Setting up a pilot PDS was a part of the Labour Party's manifesto at the last election. 'Like it or not, fair or not, an elected Government is entitled to carry out its manifesto commitments.'

In February 2003 the Law Society canvassed the idea that a salaried public defender (and civil legal) service might be a solution to the crisis in legal aid funding.[262] The legal aid practitioner's journal *The Independent Lawyer* described this as a 'spectacular volte face' by the Society which had previously been, at best, deeply sceptical about salaried provision for legal services.[263] Ironically though, the Law Society was warming to the PDS just as the Government seemed to be losing enthusiasm for the project. Baroness Patricia Scotland QC, the Government minister, in a letter to the Legal Aid Practitioner's Group, had confirmed that expansion of the pilot project from its existing eight offices had been halted. ('No new PDS offices will be opened in 2003 . . . unless external factors, such as the collapse of coverage in a particular area, necessitates the [Legal Services Commission] starting a new office'.) The minister's statement followed confirmation by the LSC[264] that the PDS was more expensive than private practice – 'which would seem to rule out a nationwide service being a solution to the funding crisis'.[265]

See generally D. O'Brien and J.A. Epp, 'Salaried Defenders and the Access to Justice Act 1999', 63 *Modern Law Review*, 2000, pp. 394–412. Their conclusion was that the primary reason for the reforms was the desire to control legal aid costs, but if lessons were learnt from other jurisdictions, a well managed state salaried service could provide a service that would match the quality of the service provided by private practitioners. Equally, if managed poorly, it would be an inferior service. In other words, no delivery model was inherently inferior

---

[258] In Birmingham, Cheltenham, Chester, Darlington, Liverpool, Middlesbrough, Pontypridd and Swansea.

[259] *Public Defender Service Annual Report 2004–05* –www.legalservices.gov.uk/docs/pds/ PDSannual_report_final.pdf.   [260] LSC, *Annual Report 2005–06*, p. 23.

[261] An experienced defence solicitor and member of the LSC who had been appointed Professional Head of Service for the PDS.

[262] Law Society consultation paper, *The Future of Publicly Funded Legal Services*, February 2003.   [263] Issue 8, March 2003, p. 3.

[264] See 5 *Independent Lawyer*, October 2002, p. 10.

[265] 8 *Independent Lawyer*, March 2003, p. 3.

or superior, but the PDS should offer a complementary service not one that simply competed with private practice.[266]

In its 2001 report *Public Defenders: Learning from the US experience* JUSTICE said that 'what was clear without exception was that, within each US jurisdiction, the public defender system was acknowledged to be superior, in terms of quality, support and resources, to the publicly funded private bar operating alongside it' (p. 7). Criticisms of US public defender systems, it said, were 'not based on arguments about the inadequacy of salaried as against private providers, but rather on the inadequate resourcing and running of the indigent defence system as a whole in many states, but where nevertheless the salaried defender is likely to produce the best service on offer' (p. 7).

An evaluation of the Scottish Public Defender System (PDSO) found that the quality of the PDSO's advocacy was similar to that of private practice though there were differences in the ways they processed cases. PDSO cases were somewhat more likely to end with a conviction (88 per cent compared with 83 per cent of private practice clients). The difference appeared to be a tendency on the part of the PDSO clients to plead guilty earlier, whereas if the case was dragged out there was a possibility the prosecution would drop the case. Client satisfaction with salaried defenders was lower than that of private practice clients. PDSO clients were also less likely to say they would use the office again.[267]

For an independent evaluation of the English PDS pilot see L. Bridges, E. Cape, P. Fenn, A. Mitchell, R. Moorhead and A. Sherr, *Evaluation of the Public Defender Service in England and Wales* (2007, www.legalservices.gov.uk/criminal/pds/ evaluation.asp – Related Documents). This report showed that the PDS model could provide services of the same quality as private practice but at a higher price, largely due to the requirement that they compete on a 'level playing field' – the costs of the service being spread amongst small numbers of clients. Whether the PDS concept has any future in the context of Lord Carter's market-based reform project for criminal legal aid (see pp. 620–22 below) is uncertain.

Law centres

Most legal aid expenditure has always been for services provided by lawyers in private practice (known in the US as 'judicare'). A minuscule proportion of the resources disposed of by the Legal Aid Board went to law centres – salaried lawyers, mainly in poverty areas, who are not in private practice. The first law centre was set up in 1970.[268] Since then some fifty or so have been established. Their funding came variously from ordinary legal aid, grants from local

---

[266] For a useful short summary of the pros and cons see N. Rose, 'Defending the Cause', *Law Society's Gazette*, 11 November 2004, pp. 20–2.

[267] C. Tata et al, 'Does Mode of Delivery Make a Difference to Criminal Case Outcomes and Clients' Satisfaction? The Public Defence Solicitor Experiment', *Criminal Law Review*, 2004, pp.120–35.

[268] For the history see M. Zander, *Legal Services for the Community*, 1978, Ch. 2.

authorities, from foundations and charities and in a few cases direct grants from the Legal Aid Board. The LSC took over these grants, but by 2003 it had decided that it would only support law centres through contracts like other providers. In 2005 just over half (55 per cent) of the funding of law centres came from the LSC. Payments made by the LSC to law centres, which were just over £5 million in 2000–1, rose to nearly £11 million in 2005–6.[269]

In 2006 the LSC announced that it would not be continuing the annual grant to the Law Centres Federation, the law centres' central organising body (www.law-centres.org.uk). The grant of £165,000 supported the directorate and policy work as well as administration and running costs. Happily the threat was subsequently withdrawn – though future long-term funding from the LSC was to be reviewed.[270]

Also, as already noted, in 2006 the LSC announced its plan (p. 598 above) to establish 'Community Legal Advice Centres (CLACS) and Networks (CLANS) that provide access to a service which ranges from basic advice to legal representation in the full range of social welfare problems as well as children and family legal problems'.[271] They sounded remarkably like law centres. One wondered why the LSC did not merely announce that it had decided to build on and develop the existing exemplars. (Leicester and Gateshead, the first two areas with invitations to tender for CLACS, both had existing law centres.)

Legal aid for tribunals?

With a few exceptions tribunals have been outside the legal aid scheme. (The exceptions currently are the Employment Appeal Tribunal, the Mental Health Review Tribunal, the Immigration Adjudicators, the Immigration Appeals Tribunal, the Protection of Children Act Tribunal, the Proscribed Organisations Appeal Tribunal and certain proceedings before the Special and General Commissioners of Income Tax.)

Not that legal representation in tribunals is regarded as irrelevant. It is widely recognised that legal representation does make a difference in tribunal cases as much as in court cases. The explanation simply has always been insufficiency of funds.

The not-for-profit sector in legal services

There is state funding, mainly from other sources, for advice given by non-lawyer agencies (known as 'the advice sector' or the 'not-for-profit sector'). By far the biggest are Citizens' Advice Bureaux. The annual report for 2005–6 stated that there were 475 bureaux regularly offering advice at some 3,400 outlets. Most were Citizens' Advice Bureaux but they included prisons, courts, schools and colleges, libraries and shopping centres. Some 2.75 million people had used the service during the year. Some 5.25 million new problems had been

---

[269] Information provided to the writer by the LSC, 10 October 2006.
[270] See *Independent Lawyer*, April 2006, pp. 6, 22 and 26.   [271] LSC, 50 *Focus*, p. 4.

handled. Many have a legal component. The advice given by bureaux is free of charge and non-means tested. The advisers are some 20,000 trained lay volunteers plus some full-time staff. The budget was £103 million. The funding for local bureaux comes mainly from local authorities and the Legal Services Commission. The central organisation, the National Association of Citizens' Advice Bureaux, is mainly funded by a grant from the Department of Trade and Industry. The service provided now includes an online advice service – www.adviceguide.org.uk. For the annual report see www.nacab.org.uk.

The declining proportion of the population eligible for civil legal aid

The proportion of the population eligible for legal aid depends on the relationship between the means test and the resources of the members of the population.

In 1991, a Government consultation paper *Eligibility for Civil Legal Aid* commented critically on the view that a particular proportion of the population 'should' be eligible for legal aid. This view, it said, presupposed that the distribution and level of means in the population remained constant relative to the cost of litigation. Also it did not relate means to costs.

The figures showed a decline in eligibility – whether one looked at proportion of households (from 77 per cent eligible in 1979 to 61 per cent in 1990) or population (from 74 per cent eligible in 1979 to 66 per cent in 1990).[272]

At the end of the 1980s it was thought that around half of the population were eligible for legal aid.[273]

A report by the LSC's Legal Services Research Centre found that in 2001–2 28 per cent of what were called 'benefit units'[274] were fully eligible for Legal Representation and another 18.5 per cent were eligible for Legal Representation on a contribution basis.[275]

Why has the cost of criminal legal aid risen so much?

A study for the LSC published in 2005 considered the causes of rising expenditure on criminal legal aid well above increases in inflation and general levels of public spending.[276]

[272] Table 3, p. 85.
[273] See C. Glasser, *Law Society's Gazette*, 9 March 1988, p. 11; 20 April 1988, p. 11; 5 April 1989, p. 9; and M. Murphy, *Legal Action*, October 1989, p. 7.
[274] 'Benefit unit' refers to a single adult or couple living as married and any dependent children. Benefit unit is a standard Government term.
[275] L. Buck and G. Stark, *Means Assessment: Options for Change* (Legal Services Research Centre, Research Paper No. 8, February 2001) p. 9 – accessible at www.lsrc.org.uk/publications.htm. See also the same authors, 'Simplicity versus Fairness in Means Testing: The Case of Civil Legal Aid', 24(4)*Fiscal Studies*, 2003, pp. 427–49.
[276] E. Cape and R. Moorhead, *Demand Induced Supply? Identifying Cost Drivers in Criminal Defence Work*, July 2005 – accessible at www.lsrc.org.uk/publications.htm.

The largest increases occurred in Crown Court cases due to substantial increases in volume of work and in the average cost per case. The second most significant element of increasing cost was police station work. One reason was higher volume of work – more people arrested, more held in custody and more asking for a solicitor. The rise in the average cost per case appeared to reflect concentration on more serious cases and outcomes that were more detrimental to suspects (more cautions, charges and remands in custody) and more investigation techniques (DNA and drug testing).

Magistrates' court costs were the most stable part of the criminal defence budget but there had been a substantial increase in volume of work at the turn of the new century. The abolition of the means test was not the only reason. There had been an increase (of some 150,000) in the numbers charged. Increases in the likelihood of receiving a prison sentence and procedural innovations (such as plea before venue) made more grants of legal aid legitimate.

The most important conclusion of the study was that the level of increase – the cause of constant adverse comment by politicians and the media – was due to a significant extent to decisions beyond the remit and the direct influence of either the LSC or lawyers. The report criticised the Government for only rarely taking the legal aid expenditure implications of policy into account. A stark example was the abolition of the means test implemented by the Access to Justice Act 1999. In 2004, when proposing re-introduction of the means test, the DCA said that it was likely that between 75,000 and 150,000 grants of representation orders 'arose as a result of the abolition of the means test'.[277] Yet the only reference to the possible financial implications made in the White Paper that preceded the 1999 Act had been that the cost of collecting contributions was not much less than the total of contributions collected. The Home Office 2001 White Paper *Criminal Justice: The Way Ahead* promised the biggest injection of new resources for the criminal justice system in twenty years to pay, *inter alia*, for 9,000 more police, 700 new CPS staff and an extra 2,600 prison places. There was no sign that the impact on criminal legal aid had been considered. The Home Office's 'Narrowing the Justice Gap' project launched in 2002 reflected the manifesto commitment 'to bring 100,000 more crimes to justice', but the framework document made no reference to the legal aid expenditure consequences of the new targets.[278]

Cape and Moorhead said there were two principal implications:

---

[277] DCA consultation paper, *Criminal Defence Service Bill*, 2004, Cm. 6194, para. 75.

[278] Other examples given in the report were the White Paper *Justice for All*, July 2002, Cm. 5563 which promised a significant increase in police numbers and police powers; the Government's strategic plan for criminal justice *Cutting Crime, Delivering Justice*, July 2004, Cm. 6288 promising 150,000 more offences brought to justice and an improvement in police detection rates from 19 per cent to at least 25 per cent; and the Home Office consultation paper *Policing: Modernising Police Powers to Meeting Community Needs*, August 2004 proposing major increased police powers. In each case there was no sign that the legal aid implications had even been considered, let alone costed. By contrast the White Paper *Safety and Justice*, 2003, Cm. 5847 on domestic violence did try to cost the likely increase in legal aid expenditure implicit in its recommendations.

1. Existing management of supply by way of fixed fees and in the future, competitive tendering, has no mechanism for understanding and reflecting upward pressures on the amount of work which needs to be done for clients.

2. The setting of a capped civil legal aid budget alongside an uncapped criminal budget is problematic where the total of the two budgets is *de facto* capped. There are strong arguments for separating the two budgets and for ensuring that mechanisms for predicting and managing the criminal budget take proper account of criminal justice reform.[279]

They finished their report:

> It is easy to understand the desire of Government to reform criminal justice policy, without properly funding the defence side of the equation. Supplier-induced demand provides a convenient political justification for so doing, but our analysis shows that the system itself creates significant demand: it has increased the number and seriousness of cases being processed through the police stations and the courts and it has probably increased the volume of work that needs to be done on those cases. At the moment those demands are being met out of the civil legal aid fund, reductions in profitability for private practitioners or, perhaps most worryingly, reductions in the quality of service being provided to defendants.[280]

Clearly influenced by the report, in September 2005 the DCA announced that Government departments had to take account of the implications for the legal aid budget when putting forward proposals for reform.[281] Civil servants were required first to contact the DCA's legal aid strategy team to determine whether legal aid was in issue. If so, the second stage required actual costing.

Whilst welcoming this announcement, Cape and Moorhead said it was not enough. It was limited to proposals for new criminal sanctions or civil penalties, which was far too narrow. (For instance it would not apply to the proposal that an extra 150,000 offenders should be brought to justice.) Also, there was no indication that the Government department in question might be required to reconsider its proposals nor that it could be made to contribute to the legal aid cost. They also challenged the statement in the DCA document that preparing a legal aid impact statement was 'not a difficult process'. If that was so, they observed, 'why have decades gone by with no adequate legal aid costing being conducted?'[282]

Where now with the funding of legal aid?

The most serious problem of legal aid is that there is not enough money to fund it – even though the level of expenditure per head of the population is the highest

---

[279] At p. 70.   [280] *Ibid.*   [281] See www.dca.gov.uk/laid/impact-test.htm.
[282] E. Cape and R. Moorhead, 'Legal aid impact tests: good start but not enough', 155 *New Law Journal*, 23 September 2005, p. 1373. The new approach got off to 'a shaky start' when, launching the pilot for allowing victims' families in murder and manslaughter cases to address the court, the minister, Harriet Harman, admitted that the Government had no idea what it might cost. (18 *Independent Lawyer*, October/November 2005, p. 5.)

in the world. The cost rose so much that retrenchment became politically inevitable. Since the mid-1990s the system has been in crisis and there has been a bewildering series of proposals and initiatives to try to deal with the issue.

Competitive tendering[283]

In January 2005 the LSC published a consultation paper proposing a new system of competitive tendering in London (*Improving Value for Money for Publicly Funded Criminal Defence Services in London*). London was chosen for the pilot because of oversupply of firms doing the work. Initially the tendering would be for police station and magistrates' court work (worth some £110 million). London would be divided into ten to fifteen 'bid zones'. The LSC hoped to make savings not only through fixed prices but on travel and waiting time which would be part of the bid price rather than being charged separately. It would save also from abolition of its hated cost compliance audits.

The legal profession was mainly strongly opposed to the proposals. Even those who were reconciled to the idea of price-competitive tendering (PCT) criticised the LSC's paper. The LSC claimed that PCT would improve quality as well as saving money but critics argued that there was nothing that would improve standards. The LSC said that all but around 5 per cent of existing suppliers would go straight on to the bid panel at which point the only criterion would be price.[284] ('Bids will be assessed and contracts awarded on the basis of price. No other factors will be considered at this stage as all suppliers will have passed the quality threshold'.) Fisher Meredith was peer reviewed and placed among the top three firms in the country. Its managing partner, Stephen Hewitt, said this would count for nothing in the bid round where the firm might be undercut 'by a bloke with a mobile phone working out of the front room'.[285]

Far from raising standards, there would be a levelling down. Bidding should be on the 'best value' basis widely used by public sector bodies[286] that took into account a variety of factors – IT, supervision, training, equal opportunities etc. (The LSC had used a best value approach when awarding civil contracts in 2004 and agreed that it was 'a tried and tested method'.)

The pilot was scheduled to begin in August 2005, but after the setting up of Lord Carter's Review (see below) it was postponed. His first report in February 2006 made PCT part of his plan to be introduced over a three year period.

---

[283] For the economists' assessment leading to the adoption by the LSC of the idea of price-competitive tendering see 18 *Independent Lawyer*, March 2005, p. 15.

[284] The 5 per cent not passported straight into the bid round would be subject to peer review to see whether it should be permitted to join the bid round.

[285] *Independent Lawyer*, March 2005, p. 12.

[286] See *Legal Aid Review*, March 2005, pp. 8–9.

The Carter Review

In July 2005 the Lord Chancellor published a forty-six page paper *A Fairer Deal for Legal Aid*.[287] At the same time he announced that he had appointed Lord Carter of Coles to undertake a wide-ranging review of the funding of legal aid with special reference to criminal legal aid.[288] Lord Carter's report came in two parts – the first on 9 February 2006[289] and the second on 13 July 2006.[290]

On the same day as his final report the DCA and the LSC published a ninety-six page joint consultation paper *Legal Aid: A Sustainable Future* setting out proposals for the implementation of the Carter reforms and a raft of proposals concerning Civil, Family and Immigration legal aid.

Carter's proposals amount to a fundamental restructuring of legal aid procurement using a market-based approach. The stated aims are to ensure sustainable, high quality legal aid services at an affordable cost using fixed prices, block contracts, consolidation of suppliers and eventually price-competitive tendering.

Carter's sixty-two proposals included:

- The concentration of criminal legal aid work in fewer and larger firms.
- Competitive tendering for legal aid contracts based on best value measured by price, quality and capacity.
- The LSC to continue to set the quality standards but the actual vetting of standards of barristers and solicitors' firms to be taken over by the Bar Council and the Law Society using peer review.
- Revised graduated fees for Crown Court advocates and a new graduated fee scheme for solicitors in the Crown Court and in the magistrates' courts to reward earlier preparation and resolution of cases.
- The whole fee to be paid to the first barrister instructed on a case regardless of whether he ends up doing the trial. That barrister would be responsible for the payments to any substitute advocate.[291]
- Working practices of barristers' clerks and chambers to be revised to make it possible to identify the trial advocate at an early stage.

---

[287] Cm. 6591.

[288] For the terms of reference and other information about the Review including its publications see www.legalaidprocurementreview.gov.uk.

[289] *Procurement of Criminal Defence Services: Market Based Reform.* For comment and discussion in the legal journals see *Law Society's Gazette*, 16 February 2006, pp. 1, 8 and 15; 23 February 2006, p. 5; 21 April 2006, p. 1; 4 May 2006, p. 1; *Counsel*, March 2006, pp. 4 and 6; May 2006, p. 15; *Independent Lawyer*, March 2006, pp. 12–15; *Legal Action*, March 2006, p. 3; *Legal Aid Review*, April 2006, pp. 4–7.

[290] *Legal Aid – A market based approach to reform.* For comment and discussion in the legal journals see *Law Society's Gazette*, 20 July 2006, pp. 1 and 15; *Counsel*, August 2006, pp. 5 and 8–9; *Legal Action*, August 2006, pp. 3 and 6–7; *Legal Aid Review*, July 2006, pp. 2 and 10–11; LSC, 51 *Focus*, August 2006, pp. 2–5; *Law Society's Gazette*, 26 October 2006, p. 3; *Legal Action*, November 2006, pp. 6–9; *Law Society's Gazette,* 26 October 2006, p. 3; *Legal Action,* November 2006, pp. 6–9.

[291] As to how this would work see J. Chase, 'Composite Fees', *Counsel*, November 2006, pp. 23–4. See also the Bar Council's Response to the Joint DCA/LSC Consultation Paper, *Legal Aid: A Sustainable Future*, October 2006, paras. 68–70.

- Fixed fees (to include travel and waiting time)[292] for work carried out in police stations.[293]
- Fees should be the same for duty and own client work and for work done in and out of office hours.
- All police station clients should have to be routed through a call centre even if they wished to have a particular solicitor.
- Solicitors should be restricted with regard to cases they could take from outside their own area to something like 20 per cent of their cases.
- The firm that began the work on a case should be expected to carry the case through to its conclusion.
- Tighter control of very high cost cases (VHCC).
- Standard fees for civil and family Legal Help and new graduated fees for solicitors in private Family and Child Care proceedings.
- A single contract for criminal and civil work and for solicitors' firms and not-for-profit agencies (NFPs).[294]
- The Government should set aside £4 million to help firms prepare for the new regime and £6 million for IT modernisation.

Implementation should be phased over the three years 2007–10. The resulting savings could be of the order of £100 million against the 2005–6 spend. This would allow a significant redistribution of moneys from criminal to civil legal aid. Fees paid to barristers in VHCC cases would reduce. Junior barristers would get a 16 per cent increase to make up for ten years of stagnation of fees.

On the day of publication the Lord Chancellor, Lord Falconer, said: 'Because of the inclusive way Lord Carter has carried out his review . . . we can move quickly towards implementing it. That's why I'm starting immediately a full consultation on what he is proposing. The Carter Review provides the blueprint. Now we have to get on with the job'.[295]

In his first immediate reaction, the Chairman of the Bar, Stephen Hockman QC, said: 'This is as good an outcome as is available, and the proposals are worthy of very serious consideration'. The President of the Law Society,

---

[292] Commenting, the Legal Aid Practitioner's Group said this would penalise firms for the inefficiency of the courts, prosecutors, police and others who caused the delay (13 *Legal Aid Review*, July 2006, pp. 11–12). Around a quarter of all attendance at police station costs are attributable to travel (20 per cent) and waiting time (6 per cent) – Carter Review, p. 24, para. 14.

[293] Jane Hickman, a partner in a leading defence solicitors' firm, warned that it would mean that obstructive police could choose to keep the solicitor waiting for hours knowing his fee was slipping away. (*Law Society's Gazette*, 20 July 2006, p. 3.)

[294] *LAG* (August 2006, p. 3) commented that this would be bad news for NFPs. ('It will change the way they work, forcing them to spend less time on their most vulnerable and needy clients in order to improve "efficiency"'.)

[295] *Law Society's Gazette*, 20 July 2006, p. 3. However, at the Law Society's annual conference in October the Lord Chancellor admitted that the Government had gone 'back to the drawing board' on fixed fees for legally aided family and civil work, that the introduction of fixed fees might be put back a year and competitive tendering for contracts brought forward a year, so that both would begin in 2008. (*Law Society's Gazette*, 19 October 2006, p. 1.)

Mr Kevin Martin, was less welcoming: 'Lord Carter is proposing a system with fewer, larger legal aid firms. We are not convinced that this will provide access to justice'.[296]

The DCA/LSC's consultation paper

The consultation period was three months to 12 October 2006. Consultation was on the basis of a 102 page paper issued jointly by the DCA and the LSC (*Legal Aid: A sustainable future*) published on the same day as the Carter Review.[297] This began with twenty-one questions arising from Carter, but most of the consultation paper (pp. 21–88) dealt with Civil, Family and Immigration legal aid and posed a further fifty-eight questions regarding those topics.[298]

The proposals in the consultation paper included:

- Providers who do not have a minimum income (£25,000 or perhaps £50,000) would probably not get a contract. (The LSC 'believe that it is uneconomic for both the LSC and the provider to deliver this small amount of legal aid work, and this is consistent with our proposals for preferred supplier of moving towards fewer and larger contracts'.[299])
- A move from paying for services that providers choose to deliver to paying for services the LSC wishes to purchase. Licensed work (p. 589 above) to cease.
- Instead of the LSC and providers having contracts for different categories of work, there would be one unified contract for all categories.
- Different contracts and different payments for solicitors and NFPs to cease. All providers to have the same contract.
- By April 2009 all contracting bodies to meet a high peer review quality rating (level 1 or 2) – to be managed by the Institute of Advanced Legal Studies at London University.
- All the new remuneration schemes to come into operation in April 2007.
- Hourly rates and tailored fixed fees (p. 565 above) in Civil, Family and Immigration and Asylum work to be replaced by fixed and graduated fee schemes.[300]
- The statutory charge (p. 593 above) will longer apply to Legal Help work.
- The proposals to be cost neutral though fixed fees would reduce the inflationary pressure on the legal aid budget caused by the rise in the average case costs.

---

[296] *Ibid.*

[297] Consultation paper 13/06, July 2006 – www.dca.gov.uk and www.legalservices.gov.uk. The Director of the Legal Aid Practitioner's Group (LAPG) complained: 'The LSC's consultation paper came like a bolt from the blue. We had no prior warning that it even existed, let alone of what it would contain'. LAPG had fundamental objections to both the content and the timetable 'and to the way in which this consultation was sprung on the profession without prior discussion and without warning'. It was counterproductive and 'seriously damages the attempt to find a more co-operative way of working between the Commission and the profession'. (14 *Legal Aid Review,* October 2006, p. 4.)

[298] The consultation paper included a summary of the Carter recommendations (Appendix A, pp. 89–99).   [299] Consultation paper, para. 2.24.

[300] On graduated fee schemes see p. 569 above.

On 25 July 2006 the House of Commons Constitutional Affairs Committee announced that it was setting up an inquiry into the implementation of Carter. The announcement[301] stated that concerns had been expressed that the proposed reforms might have an adverse effect on the provision of legal services since smaller firms were unlikely to be awarded contracts. This was expected to have a disproportionate effect on rural firms and firms owned by ethnic minority practitioners. It was also possible that the quality of provision could suffer 'since lawyers would be encouraged to spend less time on cases if they were only receiving fixed fees'.

The Committee called for evidence (not more than 3,000 words long) to be submitted by 2 October.[302] It proposed to take oral evidence in the new year with a report envisaged at the earliest in the spring. It was clear that its report would not be completed in time to influence Government decisions following the consultation started in July 2006.

The Bar's reaction

The Bar was on the whole quite pleased with the Carter Review. It welcomed in particular the proposed aggregate increase of 16 per cent in the graduated fee schemes which would restore the effect of inflation over the years when there had been no increase. Also, cash cuts to the old scheme made in July 2005 would be reversed through the new graduated fee scheme. It accepted as fair the proposed redistribution of funds from the small number of vastly expensive long cases to the large number of one-to-ten day cases. There was to be no change to the rate or to the way that barristers were paid for civil legal aid or under the barristers' family graduated fees scheme. The Bar's main regret was that the increases in fees to junior barristers were to be delayed until April 2007.

On 12 October 2006, the closing date, the Bar Council submitted a 140 page response to the joint DCA/LSC consultation paper.[303]

The Law Society's reaction

The Law Society, understandably, was much more critical of the Carter Review since the proposed savings of some £100 million on criminal legal

---

[301] Press Notice No. 35 of session 2005–6.   [302] It received over 250 submissions.

[303] www.barcouncil.org.uk (thirty-four pages plus over a hundred pages of appendices). The response dealt with: (1) the diversity implications of Carter; (2) the quality assurance proposals for advocates; (3) payment of the fee to the first advocate instructed; (4) the revised advocacy graduated fee scheme; (5) the new scheme for very high cost cases; (6) the proposal that barrister and solicitor advocates might be paid under the same scheme; (7) price-competitive tendering for Crown Court advocates; (8) payment of assigned advocates in the magistrates' courts; (9) the proposals for family legal aid; (10) the proposals for civil legal aid; and (11) the proposals for a Review Panel. The twelve appendices mainly set out Bar Council proposals. The response urged, *inter alia*, that the proposed harmonisation of barristers' and solicitors' graduated fees and competitive tendering should both await full appraisal of the new scheme.

aid would mainly affect solicitors.[304] On 2 October the Law Society submitted a memorandum to the Constitutional Affairs Committee inquiry into the implementation of the Carter Review. On 12 October, again the closing date, it submitted its 125-page response to the DCA/LSC consultation paper.[305]

The Law Society said it did not object in principle to market principles being applied but warned that it would not guarantee access to justice in some categories of law and in some geographical areas. Nor did it oppose graduated fees, but current fees and those proposed threatened the viability of law firms 'thereby posing a serious risk to the legal aid system'.[306]

Carter recommended that legal aid work should be concentrated in fewer and larger firms and reckoned that as a result some 400 firms would have to close or merge. The independent economic analysis conducted for the Law Society by LECG[307] put the number of criminal legal aid firms that would have to close or merge at double that number.[308] LECG also warned that, apart from the impact on solicitor firms, 'a real risk is that supply might be disrupted . . . making it unclear at this point whether there will be enough capacity to provide services in all areas'.[309] Flexibility in contract caseloads, scheduling of the implementation plan and fee levels might be needed to ensure continued coverage.[310]

Lord Carter envisaged that the saving of £100 million on the criminal legal aid budget would be achieved by way of efficiencies 'without compromising quality and access to services for clients'.[311] In the Law Society's view, legal aid suppliers working on tight margins[312] were already operating on a highly efficient basis. 'It is difficult to envisage how further efficiencies can be made without quality being compromised'.[313] It was unreasonable to expect them to absorb the cost of inefficiences in the police station and court systems, the effect of which would be greatly exacerbated by fixed fees.[314] The LECG report warned that 'a major risk for the reforms is that following a long history of limited firm profits and related problems, the transition to a new structure may be disruptive . . . Many experienced practitioners and firms may leave legal aid

---

[304] Carter Review, p. 3, para. 8. This would include a £10 million cut in both police station and magistrates' court fees.   [305] www.lawsociety.org.uk.

[306] Law Society's submission to the Constitutional Affairs Committee, 2 October 2006, para. 5.

[307] LECG Ltd, *Legal Aid Reforms Proposed by the Carter Review – Analysis and Commentary*, September 2006 – accessible on www.lawsociety.org.uk.

[308] There were some 2,200 firms performing lower criminal defence (CDS) work. 58 per cent of the firms were doing under the 200 case target proposed by Carter. That represented 1,300 firms performing 17 per cent of total CDS work. 'To meet the 200 case target a minimum of about 800 of these small firms would need to merge into larger firms' (n. 307 above, Executive Summary, para. 1.5a).   [309] *Ibid.*   [310] *Ibid.*   [311] Carter Review, p. 3, para. 8.

[312] LECG estimated that the profit margins of criminal legal aid practices ranged from minus 6 per cent to 2 per cent depending on firm size. These, it said, 'compare unfavourably with typical market-determined profit rates in broadly equivalent service industries' (n. 307 above, para. 1.5e).   [313] Note 307 above, para. 10.   [314] See to the same effect n. 307 above.

work and prospects for long term performance may not be attractive enough to attract new recruits. This could do lasting damage to sustainability and leave the system in little better condition than at present'.[315] There would be a need for sensitive implementation and adequate financial returns in the longer term.[316]

Fixed fees worked on the 'swings and roundabouts' principle. On simple matters the fixed fee would be higher than a fee calculated on the basis of hourly rates, but for more complex matters the fee would be lower. Clients with more complex cases would find it more difficult to get representation. Suppliers who specialised in more complex areas of work would be at a particular disadvantage. The proposals had an escape clause for matters where costs exceed the fixed fee by a factor of four but this multiplier was set too high. Specialists would be compelled to take on more standard cases to remain viable. For the more general suppliers there would be no incentive to take on more specialist cases. The Law Society warned that this would cause a 'lowest common denominator' approach.[317]

The new fee structures would favour volume suppliers. Firms in rural areas or small towns would be likely not to have the volume of legal aid work to qualify for the new contracts. ('They may abandon legal aid work altogether in favour of private paying clients or simply close down, hastening the steady exodus from legal aid work'.[318])

Carter's final report rejected the suggestion that his proposals would impact adversely and disproportionately on black and minority ethnic (BME) communities and suppliers. Citing the report by MDA commissioned by the LSC,[319] the Law Society disagreed. Most BME firms were small and were therefore at risk under the Carter reforms. ('The Carter proposals pose similar risks to those identified by the MDA research as they envisage a significant contraction in the supplier base through the setting of minimum contract sizes and price-competitive tendering. The proposals represent the greatest challenge to small firms in respect of which BME suppliers are disproportionately represented'.[320]) Since BME clients appeared to be more likely to instruct a solicitor from a BME managed firm, the disappearance of such firms would have an adverse impact on BME communities.[321]

---

[315] Note 307 above, para. 1.5e.

[316] *Ibid.* 'After years of restricted rates and low profits much of the supplier base is fragile and susceptible to lasting harm if the transition is not carefully implemented and evaluated' (*ibid*, para. 1.5i).   [317] Note 306 above, para. 15.

[318] *Ibid*, para. 20. In 2001 there were 3,500 solicitors' offices providing criminal legal aid; in September 2005 the number had reduced to 2,651 (*ibid*, para. 8).

[319] MDA, *Research on Ethnic Diversity amongst Suppliers of Legal Aid Services,* April 2006. See *Law Society's Gazette,* 21 April 2006, p. 1.   [320] Note 306 above, para. 17.

[321] *Ibid*, para. 18. The MDA study (p. 5) made such a finding with regard to civil legal aid and the Law Society considered the same was probably the case for criminal work: 'This is because BME clients' choice of solicitor is often influenced by the need for a representative with a shared racial, religious or cultural identity, or linguistic ability' (n. 306 above, para. 18).

A considerable head of steam was building up in opposition to the Carter proposals.[322] This included threats of strike action by solicitors.[323] A letter addressed to the Lord Chancellor from 28 leading City firms, including Clifford Chance, Herbert Smith and Eversheds, said:

> The current proposals mean that it simply will not make commercial sense for solicitors to take on legal aid. Committed as our legal aid colleagues are to public service, they will be forced to leave the public sector. We urge you to reconsider your plans and safeguard the future of this vital public service.[324]

In all, the DCA received no fewer than 2,372 responses to its consultation over Carter and the joint DCA/LSC consultation paper. On 28 November they published a summary of the responses.[325] This reported that points raised regarding criminal legal aid included:

- a general agreement that there was a need for modernisation in the procurement of legal aid;
- a concern that fixed fees could favour larger firms and be more difficult for smaller firms, including BME firms;
- that the inclusion of travel and waiting within a fixed fee could adversely affect rural firms;
- the potential impact on both firms and clients of any limits to own client work;
- the tension between ensuring quality whilst achieving a sustainable level of profit under fixed fees;
- the need for sufficient flexibility to reflect the complexities of preparing defence cases in the revised litigators fees;
- agreement in principle with the tendering of VHCC work but balanced with the need to ensure panel areas are large enough to secure national coverage; and
- the benefits of increased remuneration for the junior Bar and the anticipated positive effect this could have on wider diversity objectives.

Points raised in respect of the proposals for Civil, Family and Immigration Legal Aid, it said, included:

- a widespread concern that the proposed fee schemes were set at levels that are too low;

---

[322] For the views of the Legal Aid Practitioners Group see 13 *Legal Aid Review*, July 2006, pp. 11–12; and 14 *Legal Aid Review*, October 2006, pp. 8–13. For the views of the Legal Action Group see *LAG*, March 2006, p. 3; and November 2006, pp. 3 and 6–9.

[323] *Law Society's Gazette*, 16 November 2006, p 3. In January 2007, at a Special Law Society meeting, more than 400 criminal law practitioners voted overwhelmingly to reject Carter's competitive tendering proposals (*Law Society's Gazette*, 25 January 2007, pp. 1, 16).

[324] 156 *New Law Journal*, 24 November, 2006, p. 1779; *The Lawyer*, 27 November 2006, p. 3.

[325] DCA/LSC, *Legal Aid: a sustainable future – analysis of responses*, November 2006 – www.dca.gov.uk or www.legalservices.gov.uk, 71pp.

- a widespread concern about the concept of fixed fees that are based on an average with some cases costing more and some less;
- a widespread concern that the proposals will drive firms out of legal aid and this will affect access to justice for vulnerable clients;
- respondents in all categories consider that the proposed exceptional rate is set too high at four times the fee; and
- there was little consensus as to whether regional or national rates would be the preferred option across any categories.

The Government's decision

The Lord Chancellor announced his decisions on 28 November 2006.[326] In essence, the Government was standing firm on the Carter proposals but it was making some conciliatory minor adjustments:

Criminal legal aid
Police station work
- The move to fixed fees was confirmed but the date of implementation would be put back six months from April to October 2007.[327]
- The inclusion of travel and waiting in police station fees was confirmed but the fees would be reconfigured according to new boundary areas to take account of local sensitivities. [328]
- Best value competitive tendering for police station work was not only confirmed but would be brought in a year earlier by October 2008 instead of 2009–10.

Magistrates' courts
- Revised standard fees including travel and waiting time would be introduced from April 2007 in urban but not in rural areas.
- The feasibility of introducing graduated fees in April 2008 would be 'carefully considered' given the introduction of price competitive tendering that October.[329]
- Best value competitive tendering to be introduced in October 2008 instead of 2009–10.

Crown Court
- Revised graduated fees for advocates would be introduced as promised in April 2007.

---

[326] For his Ministerial statement see House of Lords, *Hansard*, 28 November 2006, WS col.? The DCA/LSC put out a joint document *Legal Aid Reform: the Way Ahead*, November 2006, Cm 6993, 66pp.

[327] Fixed fees for police station work and graduated fees for solicitors in the Crown Court would be introduced in October rather than April 2007.

[328] The Consultation document had proposed that the fees would be set by the Criminal Justice System areas.

[329] The Consultation document had said that graduated fees would be introduced in April 2008.

- The litigators graduated fees scheme would be introduced in October rather than in April 2007.
- A single graduated fees scheme for advocates and litigators subject to best value competitive tendering to be introduced by October 2008.[330]

Minimum contract size for criminal work
- To be decided early in 2007.

Very high cost cases in the Crown Court
- A panel of suppliers for these cases would be introduced in October 2007. Detailed proposals on qualification and selection for the panel to be the subject of further consultation.[331]

Civil Legal Aid
Unified contract
- Standard terms to be introduced in April 2007 – minimum income level to be fixed later.[332]

Tailored fixed fee replacement scheme
- New fixed fees to be implemented for solicitors and the not-for-profit sector in October rather than April 2007.
- Travel and waiting time to be included but disbursements to be paid in addition to the fixed fees.
- Payment on an hourly basis – the escape threshold – where the fee is three (rather than four) times the fixed fee.
- Not-for-profit sector to be paid the same fees as solicitors from October 2007.

It was obvious that the Government's announcement would provoke a strong reaction from the legal profession – especially from solicitors.[333]

Amending the duty solicitor arrangements
On the same day as the Government unveiled its decisions on the Carter proposals, the LSC issued yet another new consultation paper[334] – this time on the way that duty solicitor slots are allocated and on the rules as to what work can be undertaken by different categories of fee earners.

---

[330] The Consultation document had merely said it should be considered.
[331] The Consultation document had said a best value tendering panel of suppliers for VHCCCs would be established by October 2007.
[332] The Consultation document proposed a minimum income level of £25,000 or £50,000.
[333] Senior judges weighed in too. See the strong criticisms of the Master of the Rolls and the President of the Family Division to the Commons Constitutional Affairs Committee inquiry into the Carter proposals on 23 January 2007 – www.parliament.uk – Committees – Constitutional Affairs Commitee (HC 223-iii).
[334] LSC, *Market Stability Measures*, November 2006, 59pp.

International comparisons

Given the depth and breadth of criticism of the English system, it is striking that the UK has by far the highest per capita expenditure on legal aid of any country in the world. The subject was explored by Professor John Flood and Ms Avis Whyte of Westminster University.[335] As to comparative expenditure they cited a report by the European Commission for the Efficiency of Justice.[336] This showed criminal and civil legal aid expenditure in England and Wales at £1.9 billion. The next highest total was Germany with £319 million.[337] A table showing the expenditure of ten jurisdictions[338] showed that England and Wales was seventeen times that of the United States and four times that of the Netherlands.[339] No other jurisdiction came close:

> In the global picture, the United Kingdom is an odd, outlying case radically different from every other country: it spends far more on legal aid in total and greater amounts per capita. It also appears to generate huge numbers of cases . . . From one perspective it may appear that the United Kingdom celebrates the virtues of access to justice for all above most others; from another it may seem that the United Kingdom is acutely profligate in its spending on legal aid, not necessarily achieving value or satisfaction for money.[340]

Other recent publications on legal aid

R Moorhead and P. Pleasence, *After Universalism – Re-engineering Access to Justice* (Oxford University Press, 2003).

Legal and Advice Services: A Pathway to Regeneration, DCA and Law Centres Federation, February 2004 – www.dca.gov.uk.

Independent Review of the Community Legal Services by Matrix Research and Consultancy Ltd with Sheffield University, April 2004[341] – www.dca.gov.uk/pubs/reports/clsreview.pdf.

Geography of Advice, National Association of Citizens' Advice Bureaux, 2004.[342]

House of Commons, Constitutional Affairs Committee, Fourth Report of the 2003–4 session, *Civil Legal Aid – Adequacy of Provision*, HC 391, July 2004.

---

[335] J. Flood and A. White, 'What's Wrong with Legal Aid? Lessons from Outside the UK', 25 *Civil Justice Quarterly*, 2006, pp. 80–98.   [336] *Ibid* at p. 83.

[337] R. Esthuis, *European Judicial Systems 2002: Report on the CEPJ Evaluation Scheme* (CEPE, 2004) p. 15 at 83.

[338] In order from the lowest to the highest: United States, Germany, France, New South Wales, Quebec, Ontario, British Columbia, Netherlands, New Zealand, England and Wales.

[339] Flood and White, n. 335 above at p. 84.   [340] *Ibid* at p. 97.

[341] For a summary and comments see *Legal Aid Review*, July 2004, pp. 8–14.

[342] For a summary and comments from the chief executive of the Citizens' Advice Bureaux see D. Harker, 'The Geography of Advice', *Legal Aid Review*, July 2004, pp. 17–18.

Making Legal Rights a Reality – the Legal Services Commission's Strategy for the Community Legal Service, Vol. 1: A Consultation Paper, Vol. 2: An Overview, LSC, July 2005 – www.legalservices.gov.uk – search.[343]

A Fairer Deal for Legal Aid, DCA, July 2005 – www.dca.gov.uk/laid/laidfull paper.pdf.[344]

For a major research report on civil justice related problems see P. Pleasence, A. Buck, N. Balmer, A. O'Grady, H. Genn and M. Smith, *Causes of Action: Civil Law and Social Justice* (Legal Services Research Centre, 2004).[345]

6. Conditional fees and contingency fees

The English system traditionally rejected contingent fees as a method of financing litigation.[346] Under the contingency fee system, a client typically pays nothing if he loses, whereas if he wins, the lawyer takes his fee out of the damages. The fee charged by the lawyer in the event of a win is normally assessed on a percentage basis. In the United States contingency fees are the normal method of financing personal injury litigation. What is less well known is that they are also now permitted in every Canadian province.[347]

From the client's point of view the great attraction of a contingency fee is that he normally pays nothing unless and until the case is won – and that the amount paid to the lawyers is then directly related to the amount obtained by way of damages. In the USA the usual percentage, save in very high recoveries, is one third. The cost of losing is wholly, or at worst, mainly, borne by the lawyer. Normally the client is not even required to put up any money to cover disbursements.

The original objection to contingency fees in England was that they are maintenance (the financial support of someone else's litigation) and champerty (the taking of a financial interest in the outcome of someone else's litigation).[348]

---

[343] For a summary by the CLS' director see *Legal Action*, August 2005, p. 6. For a discussion of responses see J. Robins, ' Where Next for Civil Legal Aid?', 18 *Independent Lawyer*, December 2005, pp. 6–7. For critical comment see 'Substance or Spin?', *Legal Action*, May 2006, p. 3.

[344] For comments see *Legal Aid Review*, October 2005, pp. 4–6.

[345] For a brief account of the research findings by its lead author see P. Pleasence, 'Furthering Social Justice', *Legal Aid Review*, July 2004, p. 19. A summary is available at www.legalservices. gov.uk/docs/news/Summary-Main-Findings-revised-Mar05.pdf.

[346] The prohibition of contingency fees applies only to contentious work as defined by the Solicitors Act 1974. Contingency fees *are* permitted in non-contentious work. This includes Employment Tribunal cases.

[347] See M. Zander, 'Contingency Fees – the Canadian Experience', *Litigation Funding*, June 2002, p. 12; and 'Green Light for Contingency Fees', December 2002, p. 16. The leading Ontario case is *McIntyre Estate v. Ontario* [2002] 61 OR (3d) 257, CA holding that a contingency fee was not champertous or maintenance and was recoverable. The decision led to amendment of the Solicitors Act to permit Ontario lawyers to enter into contingency fee agreements. In 2006 the court held that this ruling only extended, however, to qualified lawyers and did not apply to others such as paralegals – *Tri Level Claims Consultants Ltd v. Kolionitis* (2006) 15 CPC (6th) 1241.

[348] For a recent review of the history and rationale of maintenance and champerty see *Giles v. Thompson* [1993] 3 All ER 321 at 328 per Lord Justice Steyn.

Maintenance and champerty were illegal until the Criminal Law Act 1967, but in abolishing the criminal offences of maintenance and champerty the 1967 Act expressly preserved the rules making such arrangements improper for solicitors.[349] The concern was that a lawyer who has a financial stake in the outcome of the litigation may be tempted into unethical conduct.[350] Given this opposition, it may be thought to have been illogical that, as will be seen, the system does now allow 'conditional fees' which are another form of payment by results. In fact the opposition to contingency fees is weakening and there are even signs that they may be allowed, at least in some circumstances.

CFAs – the history (1989–1995)

Conditional fee agreements (CFAs) came out of the 1989 Green Papers on reform of the legal profession (p. 778 below). One of the three Green Papers[351] asked whether contingent fees should be permitted. It suggested that possible reform might take three different forms. One option was to allow unrestricted contingency fees. (The Green Paper said: 'It is considered that this would not be in the public interest'.[352]) A second option was to have contingency fees but to control the percentage of the damages that could be taken by the lawyers ('restricted contingency fees'). A third option was to adopt the Scottish system of 'speculative fees' under which the solicitor agreed that he would only be paid if he won the case.[353] A possible variant would be to agree that if the case was won, the lawyer would get an agreed success fee based on a percentage of his costs.

The White Paper issued in July 1989 stated that there had been a clear consensus in favour of the third option.[354] The Courts and Legal Services Act 1990, s. 58 gave effect to this by legitimising 'conditional fee agreements' (an improvement on the racy sounding 'speculative' fees). The permissible level of success fee (then called 'uplift') was to be set by statutory instrument.

The Lord Chancellor's Department's subsequent consultation paper suggested that, at least in the first instance, the maximum uplift might be set at 10 per cent and that this would not be part of any costs order payable by the opponent. It also suggested that conditional fees be restricted for the time being to personal injury cases.

Responding to the consultation paper both the Law Society and the Consumers' Association argued that an uplift of 10 per cent was too low to lure

---

[349] *Wallersteiner v. Moir (No 2)* [1975] 1 All ER 849, Denning MR dissenting.

[350] For the unenforceability of a champertous agreement see *Aratra Potato Co Ltd v. Taylor Joynson Garrett* [1995] 4 All ER 695, Div Court.   [351] *Contingency Fees*, Cm. 571, 1989.

[352] Paragraph 4.9.

[353] The Scottish system was later regulated in the case of barristers by the Act of Sederunt (Fees of Advocates in Speculative Actions) 1992, SI 1992/1897 and in the case of solicitors by the equivalent SI 1992/1879.

[354] *Legal Services: A Framework for the Future*, 1989, Cm. 740, p. 41.

lawyers into taking on potentially difficult and complex cases. The Law Society said it hoped the maximum would be raised to 20 per cent, though there could be an argument for 100 per cent – on the basis that this would enable the lawyer to break even if half the cases taken on a conditional fee basis were successful.[355]

In the event, the Lord Chancellor agreed on a maximum uplift of 100 per cent.[356] So, what had been previously discussed as a modest charge to the client of 10–15 per cent of the fees was at the last moment changed to the very different proposition that, in the event of winning the case, the lawyer might receive double his fee. Moreover whereas the basic fee is made up of overheads and profit, the success fee would be pure profit – though profit that would have to fund the cost of cases that were lost where no fee was earned.

CFAs – the start

It took another five years before CFAs became operational. The first rules for the new system were the Conditional Fees Agreements Regulations 1995 which came into force in July 1995.[357] The rules were very strict. There had to be a legally binding contract between the client and the solicitor setting out the details of the arrangement. There were extensive technical requirements – which later proved to be a serious matter. The Law Society's model agreement to be entered into between the solicitor and the client recommended that solic-itors' success fees should never take more than 25 per cent of the client's damages.[358]

The Law Society's model agreement provided that if the case was won, the client was liable to pay disbursements, basic costs and a 'success fee', plus VAT, though it also explained that normally disbursements and basic costs would be recovered from the other side.[359] If the case was lost, the client was liable to pay the solicitor's disbursements (which might or might not include barristers' fees – see below) and the other side's costs and disbursements.

The model agreement recited that the solicitor had explained to the client whether he was eligible for legal aid, the situation as regards liability for costs and disbursements and the right to have the solicitor's bill vetted by a solicitor and own client taxation (p. 563 above).

Where the barrister in the case has a conditional fee agreement with the solic-itors, his fee is a disbursement recoverable from the other side, but if he wins, the client has to pay the barrister's success fee in addition to the solicitors' success fee. If he loses, the client pays nothing in respect of the barrister's fee.

---

[355] *Law Society's Gazette*, 1 May 1991, p. 10.

[356] In Scotland, the Lord President of the Court of Session had agreed in 1992 that the permissible uplift in 'speculative actions' could be 100 per cent – see the speech of Lord Hope of Craighead in *Campbell v. MGN (No 2)* [2005] UKHL 61, [2005] 4 All ER 793 at [41].

[357] SI 1995/1674.

[358] For a guide to the topic see M. Napier and G. Wignall (eds.), *A Guide to Funding Litigation* (Law Society, 2006).　　[359] *Law Society's Gazette*, 28 June 1995, p. 30.

The client who lost was still at risk of having to pay the other side's costs. This risk could be covered by insurance and a great variety of insurance products have developed. As will be seen, legal expenses insurance (LEI) was already quite well established (p. 648 below), but that is insurance taken out before the event (BTE). The product now developed was insurance taken out after the event (ATE).

Recoverability of success fees and insurance premiums

In October 1997, Lord Irvine, then the new Lord Chancellor, provoked uproar when he announced that conditional fee agreements would replace legal aid for all damages and money claims. The threat was subsequently somewhat modified, but essentially the Lord Chancellor stuck to his basic policy. In March 1998 he published a consultation paper.[360] This stated that the Government wished to extend CFAs to any proceedings other than family and criminal cases. More significantly, the consultation paper also asked for views as to whether the losing defendant should pay the ATE insurance premium payable by the plaintiff to cover against the risk of losing and/or the success fee payable by the plaintiff. The Government said that it was minded to make these changes but was 'keen to learn whether they would be welcomed in making conditional fees more useful and attractive'.

As was to be expected, there were a variety of reactions. The Legal Aid Board[361] said it could see no objection to the general availability of CFAs for money claims. Making insurance premiums recoverable had the disadvantage that defendants with the strongest case would end up paying the highest amount as the success fee would be highest in such cases. If the success fee were recoverable, solicitors would have an incentive to charge an excessive uplift even on claims with a low risk. 'There would be a danger of lawyer-driven litigation as lawyers would have an incentive to pursue claims regardless of whether the damages claimed were small or trivial'. It might be so attractive to lawyers that litigation might be encouraged even between wealthy or corporate litigants who might otherwise settle without going to court.

Both the Bar Council and the Law Society said that they agreed with the Government that the success fee and the premium should be recoverable. The Legal Action Group agreed that the success fee and the insurance premium should be recoverable but the proposed 25 per cent cap on damages should be made statutory to prevent solicitors and their clients agreeing an unreasonably high success fees.

The Government moved swiftly. The first step was to extend the scope of conditional fees. Under s. 58 of the Courts and Legal Services Act 1990 CFAs had originally been limited to three categories of litigation – personal injury,

---

[360] *Access to Justice with Conditional Fees.*
[361] *The Legal Aid Board's response to the Lord Chancellor's consultation paper*, May 1998.

insolvency and cases brought in Strasbourg under the European Convention on Human Rights. In July 1998, under the Conditional Fee Agreements Order 1998, they were extended to cover all civil cases other than family work.[362]

This policy of expanding the role of CFAs was further elaborated in the provisions of the Access to Justice Act 1999. There were several developments. One was to extend CFAs to family ancillary work solely relating to financial matters and property.[363] (All cases involving the welfare of children as well as criminal proceedings remain outside the scope of conditional fees.) A second development was to extend CFAs to proceedings other than court proceedings, such as arbitrations.[364] The third development was to make a premium payable for an ATE insurance policy against the risk of having to pay costs recoverable from the losing defendant. The insurance policy need not be one associated with a CFA.[365] The fourth, and perhaps the most important, development was that a success fee payable by the client was also recoverable from the losing defendant.[366]

It was suggested that the recoverable success fee element in CFAs was in breach of the ECHR Article 6 right to a fair trial or the Article 10 right to freedom of expression in that it imposed on defendants a liability in costs that was not reasonable and proportionate.[367] In *King v. Telegraph Group Ltd* the Court of Appeal rejected the argument.[368] The defendants sought cost-capping orders against an impecunious CFA claimant with no insurance cover. Lord Justice Brooke conceded that the fact that publishers were at risk of having to pay up to twice the reasonable costs of the claimant was bound to have a chilling effect on the publisher's freedom of expression rights under ECHR Article 10. But it was not for the courts to thwart the intention of Parliament that a claimant be able to bring a defamation action with a CFA and without insurance. The following year the House of Lords took the same view. Whether one thought the policy was wise or not, it was proportionate and therefore permissible for Parliament to impose on unsuccessful defendants in defamation actions the burden of paying costs that reflected not only the costs of that case but also of other cases where the claimant lost.[369]

---

[362] See now the Conditional Fee Agreements Order 2000, SI 2000/823.

[363] Access to Justice Act 1999, s. 27 inserting a new s. 58A into the 1990 Act: see subsection(1).

[364] Section 58 of the CLSA 1990 did not cover arbitrations. It was held in *Bevan Ashford v. Geoff Yeandle (Contractors) Ltd* [1998] 3 All ER 238 that CFAs in arbitration cases were nevertheless lawful because of the policy implicit in s. 58. As has been seen, this decision was confirmed by s. 27 of the Access to Justice Act 1999 inserting a new s. 58A into the Courts and Legal Services Act 1990. Section 58A(4) applies CFAs to 'any sort of proceedings for resolving disputes (and not just proceedings in a court)'.   [365] Access to Justice Act 1999, s. 29.

[366] New s. 58A(6) in the CLSA 1990 inserted by s. 31 of the Access to Justice Act 1999 states that a costs order against someone who has a CFA can include any 'success fees' payable under the CFA. The same is not the case in Scotland. The success fee there must be paid by the successful claimant out of his damages.

[367] K. Ashby and C. Glasser, 'The Legality of Conditional Fee Uplifts', 24 *Civil Justice Quarterly*, 2005, pp. 130–5.   [368] [2004] EWCA Civ 613, [2005] 1 WLR 2282.

[369] *Campbell v. MGN (No 2)* [2005] UKHL 61, [2005] 4 All ER 793. The well-known model, Naomi Campbell, won modest damages of £3,500 for publication of an article about her drug

The recoverability of the ATE insurance premium and of the success fee had dramatic and far-reaching effects. It obviously made CFAs much more attractive to claimants. Now a client with a 'no win, no fee' CFA and an ATE policy could litigate effectively free from financial risk. He was in an even better position than a legally aided litigant on a nil contribution since there was no 'statutory charge' to deprive him of part of his damages. Claimants' lawyers were also well satisfied. Instead of looking to their own clients for payment of the success fee out of the damages, they could now collect it from the losers (or rather their insurers). The Law Society's recommendation that the success fee should not result in taking more than 25 per cent of the damages was no longer necessary and was dropped. Claimants' insurers had a booming business.

Claims management companies

There was a new phenomenon of 'claims management companies' offering various forms of 'no win, no fee' deals through mass marketing on television and in the press. For a time these firms prospered extraordinarily. In 2000, Claims Direct, the market leader, which spent up to £1.5 million per month on advertising, announced a pre-tax profit of £10.1 million on a turnover of £39.6 million. The Accident Group (TAG) with some 700 solicitor firms on its panel had a turnover in 2002 of £243 million. But both went bust, respectively in 2002 and 2003. Partly this was the result of press criticism based on the experience of disgruntled clients. Also, the courts held that the premiums charged to clients and the fees charged to panel solicitors were wholly or in part irrecoverable.[370] The resulting litigation, which threatens the very existence of many of the firms of solicitors that were taking referrals from the claims management companies, has been going on ever since.[371] (The Compensation Act 2006 was passed

addiction. The appeal to the House of Lords was on a CFA. The profit costs claimed by the lawyers on the CFA came to £288,468. The amount claimed in respect of the success fee was £279,981.35! (*ibid at* [5]). (The bill of costs served by Ms Campbell's solicitors in respect of the trial and of the proceedings in the Court of Appeal, which were not on a CFA, were for £377,070 and £114,755 respectively (*ibid* at [2]).) For the suggestion that a CFA with 100 per cent uplift could contravene the EC doctrine of effective enforcement of Art 81 and/or Art 82 by discouraging a defendant from asserting his rights for fear of having to pay exorbitant costs see G. Cumming, 'Conditional Fees and Enforcement of EC Competition Law: England and Scotland; Ordinary Civil Courts and the Competition Tribunal', 25 *Civil Justice Quarterly*, 2006, pp. 529–45.

[370] Notably *Sharrat v. London Central Bus Co (No 2)* [2004] EWCA Civ 575, [2004] 3 All ER 325 – known as the TAG case. For reflections by the lawyer for the successful defendant insurers see A. Parker, 'Where there's blame . . .', 154 *New Law Journal*, 18 June 2004, pp. 914–15. See further n. 371 below.

[371] The Law Society advised solicitors to reimburse their clients. (*Law Society's Gazette*, 2 September 2004, p. 39.) Worse for the solicitors was that the ATE insurer who paid an average of £1,700 per lost case sued some 700 firms for negligently taking on 'bogus or unwinnable' claims. It was said that these claims involved aggregate sums of £100 million. (See *Law Society's Gazette*, 13 January 2005, p. 1; 13 April 2006, p. 1; 11 May 2006, p. 14.) For an overview of the battle for this market between solicitors and claims management companies see N. Hanson, 'Staking claims', *Law Society's Gazette*, 24 June 2004, pp. 22–5.

mainly in order to introduce a regulatory system for claims management companies.[372] The system went into operation as from November 2006. The head of claims management regulation predicted that regulation would reduce the number of claims management companies from about 200 to half that number. Many of the existing firms would cease business rather than apply for the necessary authorisation to act as claims managers.[373])

'Costs wars'

From the point of view of the defence insurance industry these developments were most unwelcome. Instead of having to pay just the winner's damages and costs, it now also had to finance the ATE premium and the success fee. Moreover, the television and press advertising by the claims management companies was resulting in significant growth in the number of claims.

This led to two developments. One was 'costs negotiators', employed by insurance companies to negotiate settlements with claimants' lawyers, paid on a commission basis by reference to their success in reducing the bill.[374] The second was a wave of satellite litigation with insurers taking every conceivable point (and some inconceivable ones) to try to avoid, or at least delay, having to shoulder these new and unexpected liabilities for which they had not budgeted. As each point was litigated there were thousands or tens of thousands of other cases awaiting the outcome. Commonly there was no dispute between the parties as to liability or damages. The dispute was purely as to the costs – fought out under the new procedure introduced in 1999 by the Civil Procedure Rules for Part 8, costs-only proceedings. (Some felt that the introduction of costs-only proceedings had proved to be one of the less helpful features of the Woolf reforms of civil procedure.[375])

Insurers said, for instance, that they would not reimburse the success fee and ATE insurance premium where the case settled without legal proceedings being issued – on the ground that until proceedings were issued there was no insurable risk. The point was rejected by the Court of Appeal in *Callery v. Gray*.[376]

---

[372] On the problems of regulating the claims management companies see J. Robins, 'Too Hot to Handle', *Law Society's Gazette*, 4 May 2006, pp. 18–20.

[373] *Law Society's Gazette*, 21 September 2006, p. 5.

[374] In *Ahmed v. Powell* [2003] EWHC 9011 (Costs) Chief Costs Judge Master Hurst held that employees of costs negotiators did not have rights of audience in detailed assessments and that the fees they charged insurers were irrecoverable as champertous. See M. Bacon, 'No Right of Audience', 147 *Solicitors' Journal*, 28 February 2003, p. 215. (In the judgment it was stated that in a period of two years one such firm, acting on behalf of an insurer in some 27,700 claims, had achieved reductions in costs of £20.8 million. For a defence of costs negotiators see G. Cooke, 'The Case for Defence', *Litigation Funding*, August 2005, p. 7. Surprisingly, costs negotiators have their uses even in fixed costs regimes. Cooke stated that his firm had clocked up savings over £1 million in a year in supposedly fixed costs cases.)

[375] For an account of progress in the costs war see J. Robins, 'Figuring out a Truce', *Law Society's Gazette*, 14 July 2005, pp. 20–2.

[376] [2001] EWCA Civ 117, [2001] 3 All ER 833, [2001] 1 WLR 2112.

The chief reason was the practical consideration that that was the result required if CFAs were to survive as a viable marketable proposition. ('There is overwhelming evidence from those engaged in the provision of ATE insurance that unless the policy is taken out before it is known whether a defendant is going to contest liability, the premium is going to rise substantially. Indeed the evidence suggests that cover may not be available in such circumstances'.[377]) The court held that the claimant could recover a reasonable success fee and a reasonable ATE insurance premium for cover against the risk of losing arranged when the solicitor was first instructed. In *Callery v. Gray (No 2)*[378] the Court of Appeal held that the premium of £350 that had been charged was reasonable and therefore recoverable in full. It also held that in modest and straightforward claims for compensation arising from road traffic accidents it was reasonable for a success fee of a maximum of 20 per cent to be agreed at the outset.

It posited, *obiter*, that it might be appropriate for there to be a two-stage success fee – initially of 100 per cent, but reducing to as little as 5 per cent if the claim settled before the end of the protocol period. That would encourage defendants and their insurers to settle early. (The suggestion of a two-stage success fee proved to be of great significance.)

On appeal, the House of Lords unanimously dismissed the appeal on the recoverability of the success fee and by four to one dismissed the appeal on the recoverability of the ATE insurance premium. (The Law Lords were told there were 150,000 cases awaiting the outcome of the case.) It in effect washed its hands of the whole business saying that regulation of CFAs was a matter for the Court of Appeal. (None of the live judgments mentioned the two-stage success fee.[379])

In September 2002 the Court of Appeal in *Halloran v. Delaney*[380] dropped a bombshell by holding that in simple cases that are settled without the need to start proceedings the recoverable success fee should normally be 5 per cent, unless the court was persuaded that a higher uplift was appropriate. (It added for good measure that the 5 per cent normal success fee should apply retrospectively to any case decided since August 2001 when both *Callery* decisions were available.[381])

In *KU v. Liverpool City Council*[382] the Court of Appeal said the success fee must be considered on the basis of the facts that were known, or that should

---

[377] *Ibid* at [99].   [378] [2001] EWCA Civ 1246, [2001] 4 All ER 1, [2001] 1 WLR 2142.

[379] [2002] UKHL 28, [2002] 3 All ER 417, [2002] 1 WLR 2000. For a critical review of these judicial decisions see M. Zander, 'Where are we now on Conditional Fees? – Or Why This Emperor is Wearing Few, if Any, Clothes', 65 *Modern Law Review*, 2002, pp. 919–30. This Case Note said that Lord Hoffman's speech had ripped to pieces the theoretical basis of the Court of Appeal's approach to the issue.

[380] [2002] EWCA Civ 1258, [2003] 1 All ER 775, [2003] 1 WLR 28.

[381] For critical comment see M. Zander, 'Where are we Heading with the Funding of Civil Litigation?', 22 *Civil Justice Quarterly*, 2003, pp. 23 and 29–32. For the history of success fees see 155 *New Law Journal*, 11 February 2005, pp. 214–15.

[382] [2005] EWCA Civ 475. For a discussion see 'Restricting the Scope of Split Success Fees', 155 *New Law Journal*, 20 May 2005, p. 765.

have been known, to the solicitor at the time the CFA was entered. Where according to that test the success fee was reasonable, the court could not decide on a different, much lower, success fee because at a later stage the risks became lower. If the solicitor wished to claim a high success fee for a risk that might come about in the future, the CFA should provide for a two-stage success fee.

However, the court does have power to change the success fee if it considers it was unreasonably high and increasingly the Court of Appeal is exerting pressure to reduce success fees. In *KU v. Liverpool City Council* it reduced the single-stage success fee of 100 per cent to 50 per cent. (The Court of Appeal in that case said that Costs Judges should be more willing to approve high success fees in cases that have gone a long way towards trial if the claimant solicitor has agreed a much lower success fee for early settlement.) In *Begum v. Klarit*[383] in a case which it described as a 'stone-cold certainty' it reduced a success fee of 100 per cent for counsel and 70 per cent for the solicitors to 15 per cent.[384]

The costs war between insurers and claimants involved many cases that raised only pure technicalities. The CFA regulations which had been drafted to protect clients proved to be a minefield to be exploited by lawyers for the insurers whose objective was to discover some failure by the claimant's lawyers to comply with the regulations which would make the CFA unenforceable so that they could avoid having to pay up.[385]

In May 2003 the Court of Appeal gave a judgment that was clearly intended to put an end to the extraordinary wave of satellite litigation in which insurers challenged CFAs on minor technicalities. Six consolidated appeals were heard together in *Hollins v. Russell*.[386] Lord Justice Brooke giving the judgment of the court, said that a CFA would only be unenforceable if in the circumstances of the particular case the conditions applicable to it by virtue of s. 58 of the Courts

---

[383] [2005] EWCA Civ 210.

[384] Lord Justice Brooke said: 'We find it hard to understand how responsible counsel could have agreed with responsible solicitors a success fee of 100 per cent in respect of this appeal, or how responsible solicitors could have agreed with their clients a success fee of 70 per cent. Success fees negotiated, if that is the right word, at that level discredit and devalue the whole of the arrangements for conditional fee agreements'.

[385] For articles examining a slew of such cases see G. Wignall, 152 *New Law Journal*, 16 August 2002, p. 1268; 6 December 2002, p. 1836; 2 May 2003, p. 676; G. Exall, 'Civil Litigation Brief', 146 *Solicitors' Journal*, 28 June 2002, p. 582 and 20 December 2002, p. 1160; S.J. Brown, 'CFAs – Privilege, Disclosure and Non-compliance', 152 *New Law Journal*, p. 1812; A. Dennison, 'Muddy Waters', 153 *New Law Journal*, 17 January 2003, p. 49. The last of these concerned the 'TAG Test Case, Tranche 1' which was said to affect almost 250,000 cases and 700 firms of solicitors. The Senior Costs Judge held that it was not a breach of the CFA Regulations for the firms to delegate the function of explaining and agreeing the funding arrangements to non-solicitor agents. It was a victory for the claimants, but in May 2003 the same Costs Judge, deciding the second Tranche of the TAG Test Case, held that a large part of the moneys (close to £1,000 per case) paid in respect of the funding arrangements were not genuine ATE insurance premiums and were therefore not recoverable under the 1999 Act. The Court of Appeal upheld the decision: *Sharratt v. London Central Bus Co Ltd* [2003] EWCA Civ 7128, [2003] 1 WLR 2487, [2003] 4 All ER 590. The financial consequences for the 700 solicitors' firms concerned were extremely serious.   [386] [2003] EWCA Civ 718, [2003] 4 All ER 590.

and Legal Services Act 1990 had not been complied with in light of their statutory purposes. Costs Judges should consider whether the particular departure from a regulation or statutory requirement, either on its own or together with any other such departure, had had a materially adverse effect on the protection afforded to the client or upon the proper administration of justice. If the answer was no, then the departure was immaterial and the statutory conditions were satisfied. The parliamentary purpose was to enhance access to justice, not to impede it, and to create better ways of delivering litigation services, not worse ones. These purposes would be thwarted if those who rendered good service to their clients under CFAs were at risk of going unremunerated at the culmination of the bitter trench warfare which had been such an unhappy feature of the recent litigation scene. Satellite litigation about costs had become a growth industry that was a blot on the civil justice system. CFAs should only be declared unenforceable if the breach mattered and if the client could have relied on it successfully against his own solicitor.

In 2006 the Court of Appeal's decision in *Rogers v. Merthyr Tydfil County Borough Council* regarding challenges by insurers to ATE premiums was clearly aimed, like that in *Hollins v. Russell*, at reducing satellite litigation.[387]

New rules introduced as from 2 June 2003 created what has been called a 'CFA Lite' or 'CFA Simple' under which many of the troublesome consumer protection rules introduced to safeguard the CFA client were swept away.[388] Also in June 2003 the DCA issued a consultation paper entitled *Simplifying Conditional Fee Agreements* and a year later in June 2004 it published a further consultation paper *Making Simple CFAs a Reality* in response to the earlier consultation exercise. The 2004 paper proposed further simplifying the regulations for CFAs. In its response to that consultation published in August 2005, the Government said it had concluded that there was no need for any regulations. The responsibility for policing the whole area should fall on the Law Society.[389] In pursuit of this, the Law Society produced a shorter, model CFA.[390]

The new regime was implemented as from 1 November 2005. Under new professional conduct requirements, solicitors came under a duty to make clear to clients the terms of the agreement, in what circumstances, if any, the client

---

[387] [2006] EWCA Civ 1134. The court upheld a claim for recovery of a premium of £4,860 on the ATE policy in respect of an action with agreed damages of £3,105. For a discussion of the implications see 156 *New Law Journal*, 29 September 2006, pp. 1471–2; and 27 October 2006, p. 1639.

[388] See the Conditional Fee Agreements (Miscellaneous Amendments) Regulations 2003, SI 2003/1240 and D. Marshall, 'The New CFA Regulations', 153 *New Law Journal*, 30 May 2003, pp. 833 and 837.

[389] The DCA's paper *New Regulation for Conditional Fee Agreements* (August 2005, CP (R) 22/04) stated: 'We will rely on the primary legislation to provide the minimum Government legislative framework for the use of CFAs by legal representatives and professional regulation to provide the practical governance of the use of CFAs. This would very clearly focus primary responsibility for all client care, contractual and guidance matters on solicitors and the Law Society's professional rules of conduct, supporting costs guidance and proposed new model CFA.   [390] For web references see *Law Society's Gazette*, 18 August 2005, p. 3.

would be required to pay anything and his right to have any bill from his solicitor assessed. The solicitor must also explain any interest he has in recommending an insurance policy or other funding.[391]

The critical question now was how breaches of the conduct code would be regarded. What breaches would make a CFA unenforceable?[392]

Hopes that *Hollins v. Russell* and the new regulations had dealt with the problem of satellite litigation arising from technical defects in CFAs were dashed by the Court of Appeal's 2006 decision of *Garrett v. Halton Borough Council and Myatt v. National Coal Board*.[393] The court held that if there had been a material breach of the rules it was not necessary for the defendants who challenged the CFA to show that the client had suffered any loss. The fact that the claimant did not object did not prevent the defendant's insurers from objecting. Secondly, the question should be determined by reference to the circumstances existing at the time the CFA was entered into. Both parts of the decision gave unexpected support to the insurers. It was predicted that the costs war would spark back into life.[394]

This will not happen however in cases under the new predictable (or fixed) costs regime established for road traffic cases (p. 564 above). It has been held that for such costs and the fixed success fee to be recoverable there is no need to establish that the underlying CFA was valid.[395]

CFAs – the balance sheet

The House of Commons Constitutional Affairs Committee considered CFAs in its 2006 report *Compensation Culture*.[396] A paper prepared by the Advice Service Alliance (March 2005)[397] said that people who took out ATE insurance were sometimes forced by the insurers to accept low settlements. Another issue was that many people wrongly believed that 'no win, no fee' meant they would have nothing to pay, whereas if they lost, even with ATE insurance, they might have to pay the premium on the policy. There had been mis-selling of ATE policies to people who already had BTE policies.

In its report *No Win, No Fee, No Chance* (December 2004) Citizens Advice Bureaux too had highlighted concerns about CFAs: inappropriate high pressure selling on behalf of claims management companies (e.g. salesmen approaching injured persons in hospitals), loan financed insurance premiums and other costs eroding the value of claimants' compensation, perverse incentives for

[391] For details see 155 *New Law Journal*, 16 September 2005, pp. 1347–8.
[392] For consideration of this in the light of the case law see D. Chalk, 'CFAs after 1 November – a Brave New World?', 155 *New Law Journal*, 18 November 2005, p. 1744. See also Judge Michael Cook, 'That was the Costs Year that was', 26 *Civil Justice Quarterly*, 2007, p. 134 at 138–42.
[393] [2006] EWCA Civ 1017 discussed by J. Morgan QC in *Law Society's Gazette*, 27 July 2006, pp. 28–9.   [394] N. Rose, 'Back into the Trenches', *Litigation Funding*, August 2006, p. 4.
[395] *Nizami v. Butt* [2006] EWHC 159, QB.
[396] Third Report of Session 2005–6, HC 754-I, 1 March 2006, paras.12–18.
[397] *Claiming Compensation* – www.advicenow.org.uk/compensation.

lawyers, for instance, in cherry-picking high value cases and declining to take up small though valid claims. There had been and remained inadequate consumer protection though the Compensation Act 2006 would belatedly regulate claims management companies.

The Constitutional Affairs Committee said it agreed with the conclusion drawn by the Citizens' Advice Bureaux that the introduction of CFAs, with a class of unregulated intermediaries acting as claims managers, had adversely affected the reputation of legal service providers generally. The statistics showed that the number of claims had not increased since the introduction of CFAs, but the increased awareness of the public that it was possible to sue without personal financial risk, combined with media attention to apparently unmeritorious claims, had contributed to a widely held opinion that we did indeed have a compensation culture.

The courts and contingency arrangements

Despite the development of CFAs, the courts have so far refused to recognise any other form of contingency arrangements. In *Awwad v. Geraghty & Co*[398] the defendant solicitors agreed to act for the claimant in libel proceedings on the basis of normal full rate fees if he won but at a lower rate if he lost. The agreement was made in 1993 – after the Courts and Legal Services had authorised CFAs but before 1995 when they first became operational. The case settled and the solicitor sent a bill to the client at the lower rate. The client refused to pay and initiated the procedure whereby the court vets the lawyer's bill.

The judge at first instance held that the agreement was unlawful and unenforceable so that the firm was not entitled to recover any costs. On appeal the firm argued that the common law did not make the fees irrecoverable or, if it did, they were entitled to recover reasonable remuneration on a *quantum meruit* basis. The Court of Appeal held that it was against public policy for a solicitor to act under a contingency arrangement – even one specifying a normal fee – save if the agreement was sanctioned by statute. The courts would not enforce such an agreement and where public policy refused enforcement, there could be no *quantum meruit*.[399] The court conceded that there were many considerations that favoured such arrangements. Such an agreement was of advantage to the client. It did not increase the costs liability of the losing party. It did not involve any division of the spoils as a contingency fee agreement did. There was therefore no extra incentive for the lawyer to stir up litigation. The temptation for the lawyer to act improperly

---

[398] [2000] 1 All ER 608.

[399] The Ontario Court of Appeal took a contrary view in *Tri Level Claims Consultants Ltd v. Kolionitis* (2006) 15 CPC (6th) 1241 in which, as noted above, it held that recovery of contingency fees was permitted for lawyers but not for paralegals. The paralegals' firm had spent thirteen hours pursuing the claim. The court said the contract for payment was neither unconscionable nor unfair and that the firm should be paid on a *quantum meruit* basis at the rate of $100 an hour.

was less than where there was a CFA or one where the lawyer got a success fee on winning. There was nothing improper in a lawyer agreeing to act for his normal fees but having in mind – for reasons of friendship or in order to foster future work – not to exact the fee if the client lost. But Parliament had recently addressed itself to the problem, first in the 1990 Act and more recently in the Access to Justice Act 1999. Lord Justice Schieman said: 'I see no reason to suppose that Parliament foresaw significant parallel judicial developments of the law'.[400]

The position at the time of writing was therefore fraught. The costs issues arising from the introduction of conditional fees had so bedevilled the litigation system as to cause massive and unprecedented disruption. Solicitors' firms that went in for CFAs on a large scale were going unpaid while one test case after another wound its way its way through the courts. Some were facing bankruptcy. It was uncertain whether *Hollins v. Russell* would bring the costs war to an end.

Conditional fees, introduced in 1995 by the Lord Chancellor as his solution to the financing of civil litigation, had produced a mass of unexpected problems and recoverability of success fees and ATE insurance premiums, introduced in 1999, had thrown the system into chaos. The question increasingly being asked was whether contingency fees might be a better option.[401]

For research on CFAs see:

S. Yarrow, *The Price of Success – Lawyers, Clients and Conditional Fees* (1997). Based on a sample of 200 CFA personal injury cases undertaken by 121 firms all of which were personal injury specialists. It was undertaken before many of the cases had been completed.

S. Yarrow, *Just Rewards?* (University of Westminster, 2000). Based on a sample of 197 cases supplied by a representative sample of fifty-eight solicitors' firms specialising in personal injury work. The research consisted of interviews with lawyers in sixteen of the fifty-eight firms and details of just over half of the 197 cases (56 per cent) that were completed. Fieldwork ended in March 2000. (The study found, *inter alia*, that the success fees written into the CFA 'were higher than would have reflected the actual, very low, risk of losing'.[402])

P. Fenn, A. Gray and N. Rickman, *The Impact of Conditional Fees on the Selection, Handling and Outcomes of Personal Injury Cases* (DCA Research Study No. 6/2002). Based on cases closed mostly in 2000 and 2001. (The cases therefore were not subject to the recoverability of success fees and ATE insurance premiums which only applied to cases that started after April 2000.)

P. Fenn, A. Gray, N. Rickman and Y. Mansur, *The Funding of Personal Injury Litigation: Comparisons over Time and Across Jurisdictions* (DCA Research Study No. 2/2006 – www.dca.gov.uk – Publications – Research).

---

[400] At 628. See, however, *R (on the application of Factortame Ltd) v. Secretary of State for Transport, Local Government and the Regions (No 8)* [2002] EWCA Civ 932, [2003] QB 381, [2002] 4 All ER 97 where the Court of Appeal upheld a contingency fee for a firm of accountants who assisted the lawyers in litigation to be paid out of the damages.

[401] For an upbeat assessment see G. Langdon-Dawn, 'The Burning Question', *Litigation Funding*, June 2006, p. 4.　　　[402] At p. 7.

According to the last of these studies, 'regardless of referral route, conditional fee agreements are now the predominant means of finance for personal injury claims'. For cases started after 2002, CFAs accounted for 93 per cent of accident management company[403] cases, 99 per cent of trade union cases, 91 per cent of BTE insurance cases and 86 per cent of the 'other' cases in the study.

Should contingency fees be permitted?

The principal reason given for banning contingency fees has always been a concern over ethical standards – the fear that the claimant's lawyer might stoop to dirty tricks in order to make sure of winning and earning his fee. No win, no fee. On the other hand, the greater the damages, the fatter the fee. The lawyer's direct financial interest in the outcome of the litigation might act not simply as a spur to greater activity but a temptation from the path of righteous conduct.

This pass was sold however with the introduction of conditional fees. In a CFA, the lawyer has a direct financial interest in the outcome. If the case is won, the lawyer can charge a substantial success fee up to 100 per cent of his costs which in many ordinary cases can be as much or more than the damages.[404] (It is also worth noting in this context that the new fixed fee for road traffic offences that settle without proceedings for under £10,000 (p. 564 above) has a sliding scale for the fee, dependent on the level of damages.)

In a report to the Lord Chancellor in 1997 Sir Peter Middleton said:

> There is no essential difference in principle between conditional and contingency fees. Indeed, in some ways the latter may be preferable. Contingency fees create an incentive to achieve the best possible result for the client, not just a simple win. And they reward a cost-effective approach in a way that conditional fees, where the lawyers' remuneration is still based on an hourly bill, do not. Opponents of contingency fees usually cite the experience of them in the United States of America. However, considering the differences between the two jurisdictions – notably the cost-shifting rule and the fact that juries here do not generally set damages – we should re-assess whether those concerns may be misplaced.[405]

Contingency fees create a problem of potential conflict of interest between the lawyer and the client as the lawyer's financial interests may or may not be the same as those of the client. But the same is true of CFAs.

While CFA success fees remain recoverable from the losing litigant, claimants are unlikely to prefer a contingency fee arrangement under which the lawyer would take his fee out of the damages. Under the existing arrangements, the claimant with a CFA can both have his cake and eat it. He gets his full damages and his lawyer receives his costs and his success fee from the other side.

---

[403] Such companies refer claimants to solicitors.
[404] Lord Woolf's *Interim Report* showed that in a sample of cases in the Supreme Court Taxing Office the average costs allowed in cases worth £12,500 or less were £12,044.
[405] *Report to the Lord Chancellor, Review of Civil Justice and Legal Aid*, 1997, para. 5.49.

However, it is by no means obvious that this is the ideal solution. The recoverability of success fees not only spawned a monstrous wave of satellite litigation. It has also thrown a considerable burden of extra costs on defendants' insurance companies – costs that naturally are passed on to the general body of premium payers. If success fees are a proper inducement to get lawyers to engage in cases where there is a risk of getting no fee if one loses, it may be fairer that the cost should be borne by the client as a deduction from his damages than by the general public.

It would now be a considerable step to put the genie of 'recoverability' back into the bottle. That step would be the more difficult politically if it was associated with permission for lawyers to enter into contingency fee arrangements, but the question whether contingency fees should be permitted is now on the legal-political agenda.[406]

The advantages of contingency fees over conditional fees include the following:

- They are much simpler to explain to the client.
- Since contingency fees are calculated as a percentage of the recovery they are, by definition, proportionate to the damages. (Concern that the lawyer's contingency fees may in big cases nevertheless be unreasonably high can to some extent be controlled by regulation requiring a sliding scale of percentages.)
- The client may benefit from the incentive for the lawyers to maximise the damages.
- Unlike CFAs, contingency fees do not have a built-in incentive for lawyers to pad their costs in order to earn higher success fees.
- Contingency fees would probably not generate the incredible volume of satellite litigation that has been stirred up by conditional fees.

Contingency fees are compatible with the English 'fee-shifting' rule as is clear from Canada where the loser pays the winner's costs, as in England, and contingency fees are permitted, as in the USA. Ontario was the last Canadian province to accept contingency fees which it did in the recent case of *McIntyre Estate v. Ontario*.[407] The Ontario Court of Appeal in that case had to decide whether the Ontario Champerty Act 1897 meant what it said: 'All champertous agreements are forbidden'. The court held that it did not. The reason that contingency fees had been thought to be against public policy was that they were thought to be open to abuse but, the court said, there was no evidence that lawyers who acted on a contingency basis performed to a lower ethical standard than those who were paid regardless of outcome. From a public policy point of view, the attitude towards permitting the use of contingency fees had undergone enormous

---

[406] In May 2004 the Better Regulation Task Force attached to the Cabinet Office said that contingency fees need not lead to an explosion in the 'compensation' culture if there were safeguards such as costs shifting (i.e. a rule that the loser pays the costs of the winner) and a maximum percentage that could be charged. (*Better Routes to Redress*, 2004, p. 30.)

[407] [2002] OJ No. 3417, 10 September 2002 (Docket No. C36074).

change over the previous century. All the other Canadian provinces had enacted legislation to permit such arrangements and 'overwhelmingly, those studying these issues have recommended that for reasons of promoting access to justice, contingency fee agreements should be permitted' (para. 62). Whether a particular contingency fee was unlawful, the court said, turned on whether the lawyer had an improper motive, which in turn depended, *inter alia*, on whether the agreed fee structure was fair and reasonable. (In the particular case the court said that could not be decided until the end of the case.)

In *Raphael Partners v. Lam*[408] the Ontario Court of Appeal upheld as reasonable and enforceable a contingency fee of 15 per cent of the first $1 million recovered and 10 per cent of each additional $1 million *plus* any costs recovered. (The total fee was $2.5 million plus the costs of $461,000.)

In Ontario therefore the move to legitimate contingency fees was initiated by the courts re-interpreting public policy on maintenance and champerty.

If contingency fees were to be legitimated in England either by the courts or by the legislature, the question would be whether the claimant's lawyers should have the contingency fee from damages *and* costs from the other side, as in *Raphael v. Lam*, or simply the contingency fee from the damages, as in the United States, or whether there should be some combination of contingency fee and ordinary costs. If the successful litigant's lawyers were entitled to recover both full costs in the ordinary way and the full contingency fee, the contingency fee would be somewhat like the CFA success fee but paid by the client out of the damages rather than by the losing litigant. It would build up the lawyers' 'war chest' to meet the costs in cases that are litigated and lost or where after investigation the case does not go forward – and it would increase profits, making this form of practice the more economically attractive to lawyers. But to allow the lawyers to take both costs from the loser and the contingency fee out of the damages could result in them getting remuneration that was unreasonably high.

These issues came under active consideration in Ontario in the aftermath of the decision in September 2002 in *McIntyre Estate* (above). In October 2002, only weeks after that decision, the Law Society of Upper Canada acted by amending the Rules of Professional Conduct to allow contingency fee agreements, save in family and criminal matters (Revised Rule 2.08(3)). The commentary to the rule stated that in determining the appropriate percentage or other basis of a contingent fee, 'the lawyer and the client should consider a number of factors, including the likelihood of success, the nature and complexity of the claim, the expense and risk of pursuing it, the amount of the expected recovery and who is to receive an award of costs'. It continued: 'If the lawyer and client agree that the costs award is to be paid to the lawyer, a smaller percentage of the award than would otherwise be agreed upon for the contingent fee after considering all relevant factors, will generally be appropriate'. It concluded: 'The test is whether the fee in all of the circumstances is fair and reasonable'.

---

[408] *Ibid.*

A few weeks later, the Ontario legislature passed the Justice Statute Law Amendment Act 2002. This amended the Solicitors Act by making it clear that contingency fee arrangements, providing they are in writing, are permissible, save in a criminal or family law matter (s. 28.1). The new provisions state that a court should not reduce an order of costs solely because there is a contingency fee agreement in existence (s. 20.1). This was to deal with cases where the fee payable under the contingency arrangement would not adequately compensate the lawyer for the work he had done, but the approval of the court is required for payment of both the contingency fee and the whole or part of ordinary costs and under the legislation such approval can only be given if there are exceptional circumstances (s. 28.8). The minister is able to prescribe a maximum percentage for contingency fees but the court may allow a fee above that limit where it is fair to do so. For the regulations see Ontario Regulation 195/04. They provide, *inter alia*, that the contingency fee payable by the claimant cannot exceed the amount of his damages.

Dissatisfaction in England, notably among the higher judiciary, with the results of the recoverability regime introduced by Lord Irvine's Access to Justice Act 1999 make it conceivable that the Ontario legislation could become a model for changes in the English system.

In 2005 a report issued by the Civil Justice Council came down against American style contingency fees but recommended that 'consideration should be given to the introduction of contingency fees on a regulated basis along similar lines to those permitted in Ontario by the Solicitors Act 2002 particularly to assist access to justice in group actions and other complex cases where no other method of funding is available'.[409] More and more significant voices are being heard as to the advantages of contingency fees.[410]

Contingency Legal Aid Fund (CLAF)

The idea of a Contingency Legal Aid Fund (CLAF) has been mooted for many years as an adjunct to legal aid. The basic idea is simple. Create a fund from contributions by successful litigants who agree to pay a stated percentage of their damages into the Fund which is then used to pay the costs of unsuccessful claimants. The concept avoids the main alleged danger of contingency fees of lawyers being tempted into unethical conduct because of the financial importance of winning.

---

[409] M. Napier, Costs Judge P. Hurst, R. Musgrove and J. Peysner, *Improved Access to Justice – Funding Options and Proportionate Costs* (Civil Justice Council, August 2005) p. 39.

[410] See J. Robins, 'Support is Growing for a Controversial "Contingent Legal Aid Fund"', 34 *Independent Lawyer*, January/February 2006, p. 18. Having referred to the CJC's 2005 report (above), Robins cited Lord Chief Justice Phillips who told the Commons Constitutional Affairs Committee 'that the costs imposed by conditional fees represented a greater burden on society than the £37 million their introduction saved from the legal aid budget'. Two years earlier, Lord Phillips said it was time to consider contingency fees 'particularly for group actions that may involve issues of public interest but where litigants cannot get funding'. (*Law Society's Gazette*, 24 June 2004, p. 18.)

The CLAF concept has been promoted in particular by JUSTICE,[411] the Law Society[412] and the Bar,[413] but it has not been implemented in the UK. One reason (known as the problem of 'adverse selection') is the difficulty of getting sufficient numbers of clients with promising actions to agree to give up a percentage of their damages to make the system economically viable by creating the fund. The problem of adverse selection existed before CFAs. It is the greater now that with a CFA backed by BTE or ATE insurance a claimant can sue knowing that if he wins he will get his full damages and if he loses he is not liable to pay anything. The only situation in which the CLAF would be attractive to the claimant would be in the less promising case which no solicitor would take on a CFA and/or no insurer would back with ATE cover. How could such cases generate sufficient moneys in the Fund?

In the parliamentary debates leading to the Access to Justice Act 1999 the CLAF concept was discussed.[414] Though unpersuaded of the merits of a CLAF alongside CFAs, the Lord Chancellor was eventually persuaded to introduce a Government amendment to permit the establishment of a CLAF.[415]

In August 2005 the Civil Justice Council in its paper *Improved Access to Justice – Funding Options and Proportionate Costs* recommended that the Legal Services Commission 'should give further consideration' to the idea. It referred especially to the scheme that had operated successfully in Hong Kong since 1984.[416] It did not explain, or even discuss, how the problem of 'adverse selection' could be addressed.

Lord Carter in his Review in July 2006 also referred to the idea with a new twist, namely that the fund could be supported by CFA style success fees. He recognised that because of adverse selection a contingent legal aid fund could not be self-financing in direct competition with CFAs. It might have scope where CFAs were not available. Alternatively, a success fee or profit-making element might be added to the legal aid scheme – perhaps through a levy on damages or a levy from costs.[417]

FURTHER READING

For discussion of ethical problems in England raised by conditional fees and/or contingency fees see D. Luban, 'Speculating on Justice: The Ethics and Jurisprudence of Contingency Fees' in S. Parker and C. Stamford (eds.), *Legal Ethics and Legal Practice*

[411] *CLAF Proposals for a Contingency Legal Aid Fund*, 1978.
[412] Most recently in the Law Society's consultation paper *The Future of Publicly Funded Legal Services*, February 2003, paras. 71–7.   [413] *An Idea Whose Time Has Come*, August 1997.
[414] See especially House of Lords, *Hansard*, 21 January 1999, vol. 596, cols. 782–90.
[415] House of Commons, Standing Committee E, 13 May 1999, cols. 376–80. See the Access to Justice Act 1999, s. 28.
[416] The Hong Kong scheme is described at pp. 92–6 of the CJC's report – see www.costsdebate.civiljusticecouncil.gov.uk.
[417] Lord Carter's Review of Legal Aid Procurement, *Legal Aid: A market-based approach to reform*, July 2006, Annex 3.1. pp. 142–3. For a discussion see J. Robins, 'Carter Breathes Life into CLAF', *Litigation Funding*, August 2006, pp. 10–11.

(1995); S. Simkins, 'An Ethical Choice? A Practical Reaction to the Death of Legal Aid in Personal Injury and Medical Negligence Claims', *Journal of Personal Injury Litigation*, 1998, p. 128; C. Graffy, 'Conditional Fees: Key to the Courthouse or the Casino', 1(1) *Legal Ethics*, 1998, p. 70; S. Yarrow and P. Abrams, 'Conditional Fees: The Challenge to Ethics', 2(2) *Legal Ethics*, 1999, p. 192; R. O'Dair, 'Legal Ethics and Legal Aid: The Great Divorce?', 52 *Current Legal Problems*, 1999, p. 419; *The Ethics of Conditional Fee Arrangements* (Society for Advanced Legal Studies, 2001).

For writing about contingency fees in England see especially R.C.A. White, 'Contingent Fees: A Supplement to Legal Aid?', 41 *Modern Law Review*, 1978, p. 286; T. Swanson, 'The Importance of Contingency Fee Agreements', 11 *Oxford Journal of Legal Studies*, 1991, p. 193; N. Rickman, 'The Economics of Contingency Fees in Personal Injury Litigation', 10(1) *Oxford Review of Economic Policy*, 1994, p. 34; J. Peysner, 'What's Wrong with Contingency Fees?', 10(1) *Nottingham Law Journal*, 2001, p. 22; M. Zander, 'If Conditional Fees, Why Not Contingency Fees?', 152 *New Law Journal*, 24 May 2002, p. 797.

For consideration of contingency fees in the USA see for instance H.M. Kritzer, 'Seven Dogged Myths Concerning Contingency Fees', 80 *Washington University Law Quarterly*, 2002, pp. 730–94. (Professor Kritzer has published a series of articles on the subject accessible on his Website: www.polisci.wisc.edu/~kritzer/research/research.htm.) See also the Symposium on Contingency Fee Financing of Litigation in America, 47 *DePaul Law Review*, 1998, pp. 227–477.

7. Legal expenses insurance (LEI)

Before the event (BTE) insurance against legal costs has been familiar for years, notably in the context of house insurance and motoring, but in the past twenty or so years the insurance industry has started to market policies covering a wider range of legal problems. Most policies issued in the UK are 'add-ons' to existing policies, usually of motor or home insurance policies. It has been estimated that about seventeen million people have cover under such policies – though they are often unaware of the fact. The 'add-on' policies cost the customer around a mere £15–20. Some of them also provide free, telephone legal advice. (Abbey Legal Protection, for instance, announced in 1998 that they were employing eight solicitors and four barristers to provide advice to their legal expenses insurance clients seven days a week and twenty-four hours a day.[418])

Typically such LEI policies cover lawyers' fees, court costs, costs of witnesses and experts – and costs of the opponent if the insured is ordered to pay them. Normally there is a maximum liability per claim which may be £25,000 or £50,000. Many of the policies cover all the members of the family.

The policy normally provides that only cases that have a reasonable prospect of success will be supported, but the insured has a right to choose his own lawyer.[419] Many insurers, however, reserve the right to reject the client's

---

[418] *Law Society's Gazette*, 5 March 1998, p. 4.

[419] This is required by the Insurance Companies (Legal Expenses Insurance) Regulations 1990, SI 1990/1159 implementing EC Directive 87/34 which came into force on 1 July 1990.

nomination. It is not clear whether this is lawful under the EC Directive. Most insurers also retain the right to withdraw cover if a reasonable settlement is unlikely to be obtained or if the insured refuses a reasonable offer. (In these respects insurance is much like having legal aid.)

Most policies exclude matrimonial disputes. Many also exclude building disputes, defamation, tax matters and defence of criminal prosecutions involving violence.

It was said in 1991 that the Association of British Insurers estimated that total premiums were then worth about £40–50 million pa, which represented a significant increase of some 100 per cent on the previous two or three years. This divided between 50 per cent motor related, 20 per cent general family policies and 30 per cent commercial.

A survey carried out in 1991 for the Law Society and the Consumers' Association suggested that 7 per cent of the population had some form of legal expenses insurance proper.[420]

The significance of BTE policies was boosted by the Court of Appeal's decision in *Sarwar v. Alam*.[421] S had been injured while a passenger in A's car. S sued A. His solicitor took the case on a CFA. The case was settled save for the costs. In CPR Part 8 costs-only proceedings the trial judge held that S's solicitors were not entitled to recover the ATE premium on the CFA because he was covered by A's BTE policy which covered both damages and costs. The fact that S was not aware that he was covered was irrelevant. On appeal, the Court of Appeal noted that two-fifths of all motor policies carried such cover and that normally it extended to passengers. Allowing the appeal, the court said there were in this case reasons that justified the solicitors advising that a separate ATE policy be taken out so that the ATE premium was recoverable. But it said, *obiter*, that in motor accident cases it was desirable that solicitors should ask clients to bring to their first interview any relevant motor insurance, household insurance or other stand-alone BTE insurance policy whether belonging to the client or a spouse or partner living in the same house as the client. If BTE cover was available, the claim was modest and there were no features of the cover that made it inappropriate. The solicitors should refer the case to the BTE insurer without further ado.

In *Samonini v. London General Transport Services*[422] the Court of Appeal went a step further by holding that a CFA would be unenforceable if the solicitor

---

[420] See *Legal Expenses Insurance in the UK* (Law Society, January 1991) summarised in *Law Society's Gazette*, 6 February 1991, p. 3 and *Solicitors' Journal*, 7 June 1991, p. 608. See also the *Which?* survey, April 1991, pp. 223–9. For a broad assessment including international comparisons see two papers in A. Zuckerman and R. Cranston (eds.), *Reforming Civil Procedure – Essays on Access to Justice* (Clarendon Press, 1995): N. Rickman and A. Gray, 'The Role of Legal Expenses Insurance in Securing Access to the Market for Legal Services', pp. 305–25 and V. Prais, 'Legal Expenses Insurance', pp. 431–6.

[421] [2001] EWCA Civ 1401, [2001] 4 All ER 541.

[422] [2005] EWHC 90001 (Costs) (19 January 2005); *New Law Journal*, 11 March 2005, p. 377; 1 July 2005, p. 1017.

failed to investigate the existence of a BTE policy – even when none actually existed!

Commenting on *Sarwar*, Professor John Peysner suggested that it could have profound effects. Over the previous two or three years, as a matter of deliberate policy, liability insurers and legal expenses insurers had created joint ventures to bolt on legal expenses cover at modest or no extra charge to house and motor insurance policies. The hope was that they could be used to defeat the recoverability of costly ATE insurance premiums and success fees in CFAs. Solicitors on the panels of legal expenses insurers charged modest rates without success fees. By replacing the client's own lawyer with the insurer's panel lawyer, cheap lawyers would replace expensive ones:

> The implication is that the market for this type of work will alter its profile from provision by a range of independent solicitors buying after-the-event premiums on the open market . . . to a relatively small number of panel solicitors (possibly no more than 200 firms in the whole country) who will corner the market for modest claims. Their work will be controlled by legal expenses insurers who are closely linked to the insurers for the defendant . . . A scheme where access to legal help is concentrated in a few hands, in the absence of an effective regulator, is a matter of serious concern.[423]

In Germany LEI already plays a major role as may be seen from the following:[424]

- An estimated 44 per cent of all households are covered by LEI.
- LEI companies fund some 3.6 million cases per year.
- LEI companies pay lawyers more than 1.5 billion euros per year – which represents on average a quarter of fees earned by lawyers.

The Lord Chancellor's March 1998 consultation paper (*Access to Justice with Conditional Fees*) said that the Government was keen to encourage the use of legal expenses insurance more generally, both BTE and ATE insurance. It wanted to do what it reasonably could to assist the legal expenses insurance industry and would welcome views on how it could facilitate the development of such insurance whether through changes in the law or otherwise (para. 4 13, p. 30). But it is easier to pose the question than to find an answer.

In August 2005 the Civil Justice Council in its paper *Improved Access to Justice – Funding Options and Proportionate Costs* also backed LEI as one of the ways of improving access to justice. It rehearsed the various advantages of LEI. It avoided the uncertainties of CFAs and finding lawyers to act. As an add-on policy it was extremely inexpensive and there was no means test limit. Its range

---

[423] J. Peysner, 'Turning into Trouble', 10(2) *Nottingham Law Journal*, 2001, pp. 64 and 66–7. See to similar effect D. Lock. 'Funding Faces Tough Future', 16 *Litigation Funding*, 2001, p. 6.

[424] M. Killian and F. Regan, 'Legal Expenses Insurance and Legal Aid – Two Sides of the Same Coin? The Experience from Germany and Sweden', 11 *International Journal of the legal profession*, 2004, p. 233 at 238. See also M. Killian, 'Alternatives to Public Provision: the Role of Legal Expenses Insurance in Broadening Access to Justice: the German Experience', *Journal of Law and Society*, 2003, p. 31.

included areas where costs recovery was not available such as employment matters and small claims. It thought that 'encouragement should be given to the further expansion and public awareness of BTE'. But it did not have any practical suggestions as to how this might be done.

One aspect of the system that is not widely known is that solicitors routinely pay insurance companies referral fees of several hundreds of pounds in order to be able to handle these cases.[425]

8. Pro bono work done by the profession

It has always been the case that lawyers have done work pro bono – i.e. free of charge, but in recent years both sides of the profession have made efforts to institutionalise the concept of pro bono work.

At the Bar the way was led by young members of the profession, who in 1972 set up the Free Representation Unit (FRU) to represent clients free of charge in tribunal cases. FRU has some 270 volunteer representatives. It does not deal with the public directly but takes cases that are referred by referral agencies such as Citizens' Advice Bureaux. In 2005–06, it represented a total of 864 clients mainly in employment, social security and immigration cases.

In August 1996, on the initiative of Mr (as he then was) Peter Goldsmith QC, former chairman of the Bar, the Bar Pro Bono Unit was launched as a charity to provide free legal advice and representation in deserving cases where legal aid is not available and the applicant cannot afford legal assistance. Advice and representation is provided by barristers who have volunteered their services. Each volunteer agrees to donate a minimum of three days a year. In its first eight years over 1,800 barristers (including 240 QCs) volunteered their services and some 2,500 individuals were assisted.[426]

In 2000 the Bar launched 'Bar in the Community' which provides barristers willing to serve on the Management Committee of voluntary sector organisations. Over 500 barristers have volunteered. (See www.barprobono.org.uk.)

Equivalent institutional pro bono activity by the solicitors' branch started in 1992[427] with the decision by twenty-four City firms together with some barristers' chambers to provide assistance to Citizens' Advice Bureaux with free advice on debt, housing and employment matters. In August 1993 ten major City firms said they would do pro bono work for Liberty.[428] In March 1995 it was

---

[425] For critical comment see J. Robins, 'School for Scandal', *Litigation Funding*, June 2006, pp. 2–3.

[426] Lord Goldsmith, 'A Decade of Achievement', *Counsel*, September 2006, pp. 20–1.

[427] The suggestion that the English profession should follow the example of the American in undertaking pro bono work was first made by the writer several decades ago: M. Zander, 'Pro Bono Publico', *Law Society's Gazette*, 27 September 1972. For discussion of the somewhat belated adoption of this suggestion see A. Boon and R. Alley, 'Moral Agendas? Pro Bono Publico in Large Law Firms in the United Kingdom', 60 *Modern Law Review*, 1997, pp. 630–54 and A. Boon and A. Whyte, 'Charity and Beating Begins at Home: the Aetiology of the New Culture of *Pro Bono Publico*', 2 *Legal Ethics*, 1999, p. 167.

[428] *Solicitors' Journal*, 27 August 1993.

announced that over forty law firms in different parts of the country had pledged to provide at least £5,000 worth of free advice annually to community projects aimed at job creation, inner city regeneration and environmental improvements.[429]

The Law Society's Pro Bono Working Party which reported in May 1994 was not prepared to recommend that solicitors be obliged to take part in pro bono work.[430] But in November 1996 a meeting organised by solicitor Andrew Phillips (later Lord Phillips of Sudbury) with the backing of the Law Society and the charity Business in the Community established the Solicitors' Pro Bono Group to boost the amount of such work done by the solicitors' branch.[431]

The Group started work in September 1997.[432] In March 1998 it launched a national membership drive with the backing, *inter alia*, of the Lord Chief Justice. Take-up at that time was not remarkable. There were some 160 members ranging from substantial firms to trainee solicitors. Five years later, in Spring 2003, the number of members had only crept up to 220, of which 189 were firms.

However, by 2006 pro bono work by solicitors was on a much more substantial footing. Several of the larger firms have full-time pro bono administrators. *The Lawyer*, published fortnightly, has a column in each issue highlighting some new pro bono development. From this it appears that a more generous and more systematic approach to pro bono work had finally begun to emerge among some leading solicitors' firms. (In 2005, for instance, Allen & Overy spearheaded a scheme for large law firms to donate interest earned on client accounts to the charity Legal Support Trust. It was anticipated that over three years some £200,000 would be donated.)

In January 2006 the Solicitors' Pro Bono Group renamed itself Law Works – see www.lawworks.org.uk. Law Works had some fifty clinics nationally operating each week providing an estimated 28,000 pieces of advice annually.

In 2002 Lord Goldsmith (then as Attorney General) established a new pro bono committee comprising the Government's law officers, the main pro bono organisations, the Bar Council and the Law Society (www.probonouk.net).[433]

Each year since 2002 there has been an annual pro bono week to promote the concept. See the Website for details of the range of events. (In 2002 there were eleven events. In June 2006 there were over fifty.[434])

In the United States, law students have been engaged in real-life pro bono work on a major scale for decades.[435] In the UK this is a recent development and,

---

[429]   *The Lawyer*, 15 March 1995, p. 1.

[430]   See E. Gilvarry, 'The Pro Bono Push', *Law Society's Gazette*, 25 May 1994, p. 4.

[431]   Start up funding for the Solicitors' Pro Bono Group was provided by Allen & Overy, Clifford Chance, Clyde & Co, Dibb Lupton Alsop, Freshfields, Hammond Suddards, Herbert Smith, Linklaters, Lovell White Durrant, Norton Rose and Slaughter & May.

[432]   See *Law Society's Gazette*, 17 September 1997, p. 12.

[433]   J. Robins, 'Social conscience', *The Lawyer*, 9 June 2003, p. 18.

[434]   For an overview of the pro bono scene see *Law Society's Gazette*, 1 June 2006, pp. 16–17.

[435]   Described over 30 years ago by the writer: 'Clinical Legal Education', 123 *New Law Journal*, 22 February 1973, pp. 181–83. In 2006 the Harvard Law School reported that the staff for clinical

as yet, on a modest scale. A survey of 95 law schools published in October 2006 showed that over half (53 per cent) were involved in some form of pro bono activity and others said they intended to become involved. Some ran clinics, some offered only advice, some offered representation, some worked on innocence projects investigating alleged miscarriage of justice cases, some involved placements with other organisations such as Citizens' Advice Bureaux or the Free Representation Unit. Financial support from the respective institutions for pro bono activities averaged £22,000.[436]

programmes consisted of 6 faculty members, 25 instructors, 11 lecturers on law and 8 clinical fellows. Student enrolment had risen from 300 students in 2001-02 to 576 students. The number of students doing clinical work in the Human Rights field was over 100. In the academic year 2006-07, new clinics were offered in Child Advocacy, Death Penalty, Environmental Law, Intellectual Property, Internet, Mediation and Negotiation. (*Harvard Law Today*), September 2006.   [436] For details of the survey see www.lawworks.org.uk.

Chapter 7

Appeals

An appeal system is necessary to perform a variety of functions. One is to provide an opportunity for the disappointed litigant to test the validity of the decision at first instance. A second is to allow the court 'to correct an error, unfairness or wrong exercise of discretion which has led to an unjust result'.[1] A third purpose of the appeal system is to preserve some measure of uniformity in the decision-making of lower courts. The doctrine of precedent is an important aide in this process. Lower courts are encouraged and in some circumstances are required to follow the indications of the higher courts on matters of law and practice, the assessment of damages and even fact-finding.[2] A fourth function of the appeal court is to keep the law abreast of changing circumstances. A fifth reason is to promote public confidence in the administration of justice.[3]

In the earliest days of the system the appeal process was exceedingly limited. In civil cases, procedure was by writ of error and the basis of the appeal was that there was some error appearing on the face of the record. Since only certain things appeared on the record there were many issues on which no appeal was possible. Later the courts allowed each party to move a Bill of Exceptions, in which the trial judge was asked to note that a particular point had been rejected by the judge and this was then treated as part of the record for the purpose of an appeal. This helped somewhat, but it was still limited in scope and required the point to be seen and taken at the trial itself. Moreover, a further problem was that if the appeal was successful the court had no power to substitute its own decision for that of the court below. It could only order a fresh trial.

Appeals on questions of fact were even more difficult. Originally, when cases were heard by juries and the jury was supposed to decide cases of its own knowledge a wrong verdict was practically a matter for the disciplining of the

---

[1] Bowman, *Review of the Court of Appeal (Civil Division)*, September 1997, p. 25. The Bowman Review – see below – said that the mere fact that there was an error does not mean that there should be a successful appeal. The important point is to establish 'whether what has happened means that a judgment or order should not be allowed to stand' (*ibid*).

[2] The operation of the precedent system is considered in the writer's *The Law-Making Process* (6th edn, Cambridge University Press, 2004).

[3] For an exploration of the nature, functions and limitations of appeals in the context of recent reforms see R. Nobles and D. Schiff, 'The Right to Appeal and Workable Systems of Justice', 65 *Modern Law Review*, 2002, pp. 676–701.

jury. A writ of attaint could be brought to try the truth of the jury's verdict and, if the attaint jury thought the first jury was mistaken, the first jury was liable to punishment. It was only in the seventeenth century that juries were no longer liable to be punished for their verdicts and that the common law courts were prepared to order a new trial on the ground that a jury's decision had been against the weight of the evidence.

Juries in civil cases are now virtually unknown so the question normally is whether the appeal court is prepared to interfere with a decision rendered by the trial judge. As will be seen, the appeal court has the power to take a different view of the facts from that of the court below – though it is generally reluctant to do so – but in other respects, the appellate court has extensive powers not only to order a retrial but to substitute its own decision.

In criminal cases the situation was even more remarkable. There was no appeal from conviction at all until well into the nineteenth century. At some point the judges started informally to refer a question of law to other judges before they summed up to the jury or before sentence was executed. In 1848 this informal arrangement was regularised with the establishment of the Court for Crown Cases Reserved, but it was still available only on reference from the judge – though the procedure was extended also to quarter sessions. In the last seventy years of the nineteenth century Parliament considered the question of an appeal in criminal cases no fewer than twenty-eight times, but it was only after an especially serious miscarriage of justice, the Adolf Beck case, that the Court of Criminal Appeal was finally established in 1907. Its powers include quashing a conviction, ordering a retrial and reducing the sentence.

1. The structure of appeal courts

Civil cases

In the nineteenth century the appeal courts in civil cases were in a considerable muddle. Appeals from the old Court of Common Pleas went to the Court of King's Bench. Appeals from the old Court of Exchequer went to the Court of Exchequer Chamber. When the Court of King's Bench began hearing cases at first instance in the sixteenth century, a second Court of Exchequer Chamber was set up to hear appeals from that body. In 1830 the two courts of Exchequer Chamber were replaced by a third. This court was established to hear appeals from all three common law courts – Queen's Bench, Common Pleas and Exchequer. The members of the court were drawn from the two from which the appeal did not come. In addition there was the Court of Appeal in Chancery which heard appeals from the Court of Chancery, not in the traditional way by writ of error but by a rehearing. Appeals from the Court of Admiralty went to the Privy Council and from 1833 to the Judicial Committee of the Privy Council. Appeals from the Divorce Court established in 1857 went at first from the single judge to the full court and from 1868 to the House of Lords.

The Judicature Commissioners reported in 1869 and recommended a new structure. They proposed that there should be one Supreme Court, comprising a High Court and a Court of Appeal. The Court of Appeal should take appeals from all the divisions of the High Court. This reform was achieved in the Judicature Acts 1873–1875. Its constitution and the statutory framework are now to be found in the Supreme Court Act 1981. In 1966 the Court of Criminal Appeal became the Court of Appeal Criminal Division, so that from that date there was a Civil Division and a Criminal Division of that court.

The Civil Division is presided over by the Master of the Rolls and sits in several divisions – almost always, though not invariably, in London. Lord Justices of Appeal sit as the judges. The Court of Appeal normally sits with three judges. However, the Supreme Court Act 1981 provided for two-judge courts to hear appeals on interlocutory matters or any other matter prescribed by order made by the Lord Chancellor and the Access to Justice Act 1999 stated that the Court of Appeal is validly constituted if it consists of one or more judges.[4] A two-judge court is not uncommon even in cases significant enough to be reported.[5] For very important cases the Court of Appeal occasionally sits with five judges.

The Court of Appeal Civil Division sometimes sits with two Lord Justices and one High Court judge and occasionally sits with one Lord Justice and two High Court (puisne) judges. Retired Lord Justices also often sit. A two-judge court may be composed of two Lord Justices or one Lord Justice and one puisne.[6]

Until very recently the Court of Appeal Civil Division heard appeals from both the High Court and the county court, but, as will be seen below, under the post-Woolf reforms of the appellate system, since May 2000 most appeals from the county court now go to the High Court. The basic concept introduced by these reforms is that an appeal should go to the next level in the hierarchy and that second appeals be severely restricted.[7]

Appeals from the civil jurisdiction of the magistrates' courts go to the Divisional Court of the Family Division, which consists of two or three judges usually of the High Court. Appeals from the Divisional Court in a civil case lie to the Court of Appeal.

Appeals from the Court of Appeal have hitherto gone to the House of Lords. In modern times the House of Lords in its appellate judicial role has consisted of judges specifically appointed for the purpose as Lords of Appeal in Ordinary

---

[4] Access to Justice Act 1999, s. 59 substituting a new s. 54(2) into the Supreme Court Act 1981.
[5] In the 2001 law reports 10 per cent of decisions of the Court of Appeal Civil Division were given by a two-judge court. (R. Munday, 'Judicial Configurations', 61 *Cambridge Law Journal*, 2002, p. 612 at 655, n. 156.)
[6] Munday's article, n. 5 above, shows that in 2001 28 per cent of the court's reported decisions included at least one puisne judge.
[7] For the Website of the Court of Appeal Civil Division see www.civilappeals.gov.uk. The Website, *inter alia*, gives a guide as to the different routes of appeal, contains links to the most recent judgments of the court and to relevant Civil Procedure Rules and practice directions.

(generally referred to as Law Lords), plus the Lord Chancellor[8] and any former Lord Chancellors.

The House of Lords usually sits with five judges but on occasion seven are empanelled. The hearings are conducted in one of the committee rooms of the Palace of Westminster, but judgment is given in the legislative chamber itself. Nowadays the judgments (called 'speeches') are not read. The procedure consists simply of the presiding judge putting the issue to the vote as if it were an ordinary legislative matter. ('My Lords, I beg to move that the Report of the Appellate Committee be now considered'.) When this has been approved ('the Contents have it'), each Law Lord stands up in order of seniority and says merely that he would allow or dismiss the appeal 'for the reasons given in my printed speech'.

In 2005 the House of Lords dealt with sixty-eight civil appeals (of which nineteen concerned human rights issues) and twelve criminal appeals.[9]

The judicial functions of the House of Lords are as old as Parliament itself. By 1600 it enjoyed an undisputed role as a court of appeal. It heard cases by way of writ of error from the Courts of Exchequer Chamber. Until 1844 lay peers were able to participate in the judicial work and occasionally they did so. The appellate jurisdiction of the House of Lords was threatened and almost abolished in the court reforms of the 1873–5 era but in the end it was preserved in the Appellate Jurisdiction Act 1876, which provided for salaried Law Lords. Though nominally the final appeal remained in the hands of the hereditary chamber, in reality it was transferred to a court of law under the control of a professional judiciary.

In 2000 the Report of the Royal Commission on reform of the House of Lords concluded: 'There is no reason why the second chamber should not continue to exercise the judicial functions of the present House of Lords'.[10] It recommended that the Law Lords should continue to be *ex officio* members of the reformed second chamber.

Creation of a Supreme Court On 14 July 2003 a Government consultation paper set out proposals for establishing a new Supreme Court.[11] This was a highly controversial proposal but it was eventually passed into law.[12] The

---

[8] On 12 June 2003 the Prime Minister, Tony Blair, announced the abolition of the office of Lord Chancellor. In the event the office of Lord Chancellor survived but shorn of the previous right to sit judicially in the House of Lords, whilst that jurisdiction continues (see below.)

[9] *Judicial Statistics, 2005*, Table 1.4, p. 14.

[10] *A House for the Future*, Cm. 4534, 2000, pp. 92–3.

[11] DCA, *Constitutional Reform: A Supreme Court for the United Kingdom*, consultation paper 11/03. For discussion see I.R. Scott, 22 *Civil Justice Quarterly*, 2003, pp. 318–23.

[12] See for instance Lord Bingham of Cornhill, 'A new Supreme Court for the United Kingdom', Constitution Unit UCL annual lecture, 2002 and 'The Old Order Changeth', 122 *Law Quarterly Review*, 2006, pp. 211–23; Lord Steyn, 'The Case for a Supreme Court', 118 *Law Quarterly Review*, 2002, p. 382; Lord Hope, 'A Phoenix from the Ashes? Accommodating a New Supreme Court', 121 *Law Quarterly Review*, 2005, pp. 253–72; Lord Cooke, 'The Law Lords: An Endangered Heritage', 119 *Law Quarterly Review*, 2003, pp. 49–67. See also Lord Windlesham's two-part article on the story of the Constitutional Reform Act 2005,

Constitutional Reform Act 2005 replaces the appellate jurisdiction of the House of Lords by a Supreme Court. The first justices of the Supreme Court will be the then sitting Lords of Appeal in Ordinary.[13] The Act provided, however, that the establishment of the Supreme Court would not take place 'unless the Lord Chancellor is satisfied that the Supreme Court will at that time be provided with accommodation in accordance with written plans that he has approved' (s. 148(4)). The Lord Chancellor may approve such plans only if, having consulted the current Lords of Appeal in Ordinary, he is satisfied that the accommodation 'will be appropriate for the purposes of the court' (s. 148(5)).

The Supreme Court is to be in the Middlesex Sessions building on Westminster Square opposite the Houses of Parliament, which is being converted (at an estimated cost of £30 million).[14] The latest official forecast as to when the building will be ready is October 2009.[15]

Radical reform of civil appeals following Bowman

The civil appeal system has recently undergone drastic reform – described by Lord Brooke as 'the most significant changes in the arrangements for appeals in civil proceedings in this country for 125 years'.[16] Previously, litigants had extensive rights of appeal. In the case of a final judgment there was generally the right to appeal to the Court of Appeal; in the case of an interlocutory decision by the Master or District judge there was generally the possibility of two appeals – first to the judge and then on to the Court of Appeal. Appeals from a District judge or Master to a judge were full re-hearings. Appeals to the Court of Appeal were more restricted in their nature.

In his Final Report *Access to Justice* (1996) Lord Woolf recommended that leave to appeal should be required for all interlocutory appeals, that some appeals should lie to lower courts than the Court of Appeal, that all appeals should be of the 'limited Court of Appeal rehearing type' and that there should be greater uniformity in the procedure for appeal.

Instead of moving ahead with these recommendations, the Lord Chancellor announced in March 1996 that there would be a full separate review of the Civil

Footnote 12 (*cont.*)

> *Public Law*, 2005, pp. 806–23 and 2006, p. 35; and I.R. Scott, 22 *Civil Justice Quarterly*, 2003, pp. 318–23. For consideration of the functions of the House of Lords and the Judicial Committee of the Privy Council see A. Le Sueur and R. Cornes, *What do the Top Courts do?*, Constitution Unit, June 2000.

[13] Including any female Lord of Appeal in Ordinary. In 2006 Baroness Hale was both the first and so far the only woman to have been appointed.

[14] Planning permission for the refurbishment was given on 7 September 2006. The actual work was scheduled to begin in April 2007.

[15] The work itself was costed at £30 million. The cost of moving the old courts into new premises would be another £20 million. (There is every reason to suppose that these would prove to be considerable underestimates.) The costs of running the new Supreme Court would be of the order of £8–10 million a year compared with £3–4 million in the House of Lords. For a drawing of what the new Supreme Court would look like see *Law Society's Gazette*, 14 September 2006, p. 4.

[16] *Tanfern Ltd v. Cameron MacDonald (Practice Note)* [2000] 1 WLR 131 [50].

Division of the Court of Appeal under the chairmanship of Sir Jeffrey Bowman, former senior partner of Price Waterhouse. The terms of reference were to inquire into the court's rules, procedures and working methods, its jurisdiction and the legal and administrative support system. The five other members of the review team included Lord Woolf, who at the time was still Master of the Rolls. (He became Lord Chief Justice in 2000.)

The Bowman report was published in September 1997.[17] (Due to the complex nature of routes of appeal in family matters, Bowman recommended that a specialist committee should examine this area. The Family Appeal Review Group, chaired by Lord Justice Thorpe, published its recommendations in July 1998.)

The Bowman report said that the Court of Appeal was being asked to consider appeals that were not of sufficient weight or complexity to require two or three of the country's most senior judges and which had already been through one or more levels of appeal.[18] The same considerations of justice, expedition and moderation of costs should apply to appeals as to first instance proceedings. An appeal should no longer be seen as an automatic further stage in a case. A dissatisfied litigant's right should be not to appeal but to have his request to appeal considered. The requirement of permission to appeal should be the norm. Also appeals should be dealt with in ways proportionate to the grounds of complaint and the subject matter of the dispute. More than one level of appeal could normally only be justified if there was an important point of principle or practice at stake.

The report made 146 recommendations. Many were implemented by the Access to Justice Act 1999 (AJA 1999) and CPR Part 52 which came into force from 2 May 2000. (The new scheme was described in detail in the judgment of the Court of Appeal delivered by Lord Justice Brooke in *Tanfern* (n. 16 above).) The same system was applied to small claims cases as from October 2000.

AJA 1999 provides that where an appeal is taken to a county court or the High Court, no further appeal can be taken to the Court of Appeal unless the Court of Appeal considers that '(a) the appeal would raise an important point of principle or practice, or (b) there is some other compelling reason for the Court of Appeal to hear it' (s. 55(1)).

---

[17] Note 1 above. For a lengthy review see J. Jacob, 'The Bowman Review of the Court of Appeal', 61 *Modern Law Review*, 1998, pp. 390–400. For an assessment of the impact of the Bowman reforms see two studies by J. Plotnikoff and R. Woolfson, *Evaluation of the Impact of the Reforms in the Court of Appeal (Civil Division)* (DCA Research Study No. 5, 2003) and *Evaluation of Appellate Work in the High Court and the County Courts* (DCA Research Study No. 7, 2005). The first found that there had been improvement in the processing of the court's caseload. Waiting times and pending caseloads had reduced substantially and the length of hearings had not increased. The extension of the requirement for permission to appeal had proved effective at filtering out many unmeritorious appeals without the need for a full appeal hearing, but costs had not reduced. The second report canvassed a great range of issues.

[18] Thus a decision by a District judge in a non-family case in the county court could be appealed to a Circuit judge and then to the Court of Appeal. In High Court cases an appeal lay against an interlocutory decision by a Master or District judge to a High Court judge and then to the Court of Appeal.

AJA 1999, s. 56 gives the Lord Chancellor the power by statutory instrument to prescribe alternative routes for the destination of appeals. This was done by the Access to Justice Act 1999 (Destination of Appeals) Order 2000, SI 2000/1071 (Destination Order). (For details again see the Court of Appeal's decision in *Tanfern* (above).)

The Destination Order provides that appeals which previously would have gone to the Court of Appeal will now go to a lower court. The general principle is that appeal lies to the next level of judge in the judicial hierarchy. Thus appeals from Masters or District judges of the High Court lie to a High Court judge (Article 2). Appeals from a District judge of the county court lie to a Circuit judge (Article 3). Appeals from any other county court judge (i.e. a Circuit judge or recorder) lie to a High Court judge (Article 3).

However, Article 4 of the Destination Order sets out two exceptions. Article 4(a) provides that the normal route of appeal does not apply where a 'final decision'[19] is given in a multi-track case.[20] An appeal lies instead direct to the Court of Appeal.

Article 4(b) provides that where a final decision is made by a specialist jurisdiction, regardless of the level of the judge, appeal lies direct to the Court of Appeal.

Article 5 provides that second appeals go to the Court of Appeal itself.

AJA 1999, s. 57 gives the Master of the Rolls the power to 'call in' any appeal going to a lower court so that it can be heard instead by the Court of Appeal. This power will enable the Court of Appeal to give a ruling on issues that are causing serious difficulties.

Running the office The Supreme Court Act 1981 created the position of Registrar of Civil Appeals who took office in 1982. The Registrar was a judicial officer with limited judicial powers such as granting extensions of time in which to appeal, leave to amend, ordering security for costs and resolving listing disputes. He also had administrative responsibilities, including deciding 'constitutions' (which judges sit in the up to eleven courts that may be sitting at any time). Constitutions generally stay together for three or so weeks. He did not, however, have line management responsibility for the Civil Appeal Office which was also set up in 1982. The Civil Appeal Office processes all appeals and applications for leave to the Court of Appeal.

Bowman recommended that the Head of the Civil Appeals Office should have line management responsibility for the staff and for the running of the office. His judicial functions should normally be performed by two designated senior legal officers, though anyone dissatisfied with their decision should have the right to refer it to a Lord Justice. Accepting this recommendation, AJA 1999, s. 70 abolished the office of Registrar of Civil Appeals. His administrative

---

[19] As to the meaning of 'final decision' see *Scribes West Ltd v. Relsa Anstalt* [2004] EWCA Civ 965.

[20] The exception does not apply to cases not on the multi-track – *Clark (Inspector of Taxes) v. Perks* [2001] 1 WLR 17 at [7] and [54].

functions were taken over by the Head of Civil Appeals. There is now an informative Website – www.civilappeals.gov.uk – which, amongst many other items, includes an interactive guide to the appeal system.

Bowman said that the office should undertake much more management of a case from beginning to end. ('Lord Woolf laid great emphasis in his [Access to Justice Report] on case management and the role of the judges in this process. We believe that the principle of case management can be applied in the Court of Appeal and that the Lords Justices have a very important role to play'.[21]) However, much of the management should be done by staff in the office rather than the judges.

The full-time staff increased from nineteen to seventy, including ten lawyers. The main duties of the lawyers are to write brief legal abstracts of each case onto the computer for the benefit of the judges. They also prepare summaries of cases of litigants in person. A recent development has been the introduction of some (currently ten) part-time 'judicial assistants' – young, high-calibre pupil barristers or trainee solicitors, who typically spend one term working there.[22]

In April 1999 a fifty-four page Practice Note was published consolidating with some amendments all the principal Practice Directions relating to proceedings in the Court of Appeal.[23] See now the Practice Direction attached to Part 52.[24]

Criminal cases

Appeals from the old quarter sessions and assize courts went to the Court of Criminal Appeal. When the Court of Appeal Criminal Division was established in 1966, they went to that court instead. Then in 1972 when the Crown Courts replaced the quarter sessions and assize courts, appeals accordingly went from the Crown Court to the Court of Appeal Criminal Division.

The Court of Appeal Criminal Division sits normally with three judges. The presiding judge is either the Lord Chief Justice or a Lord Justice of Appeal. The other judges can be Lord Justices, High Court judges or senior Circuit judges. In fact it seems that nowadays it is quite rare for the court to consist of three Lord Justices.[25]

---

[21] Note 1 above at p. 75.

[22] For a description of the work done by the judicial assistants in the Court of Appeal see *Counsel*, June 1998, p. 22; June 2002, p. 18 and the Website.   [23] [1999] 2 All ER 490.

[24] On practice directions generally see J.A. Jolowicz, 'Practice Directions and Civil Procedure Rules', 59 *Cambridge Law Journal*, 2000, p. 53.

[25] Munday's article, n. 5 above at p. 656, showed that none of the forty-three cases reported in the two volumes of the 2001 *Criminal Appeal Reports* had three Lord Justices. Indeed, in only one of the forty-three cases were two Lord Justices sitting. In thirty-six of the cases the court consisted of one Lord Justice and two puisne judges. In five cases it consisted of one Lord Justice, one puisne judge and one Circuit judge and one case was heard by two judges, a serving Lord Justice and a recently retired Lord Justice.

Appeals from the Court of Appeal Criminal Division go, with leave, to the House of Lords.

Appeals from decisions of the magistrates' courts in criminal cases may go in two alternative directions. There can be an appeal to the Crown Court, which sits for this purpose with a judge and two or more magistrates but without a jury. Alternatively appeals lie by way of case stated (see p. 677 below) from the magistrates' court to the Divisional Court of the Queen's Bench Division sitting with two or three High Court judges, though the Lord Chief Justice often presides in the Divisional Court.

Appeals from the appellate jurisdiction of the Crown Court go to the Divisional Court of the Queen's Bench Division on a point of law by way of case stated. Appeals in criminal cases go direct from the Divisional Court to the House of Lords.

Lord Justice Auld in his Review of the Criminal Courts recommended that both appeals as of right to the Crown Court by way of rehearing and appeals to the Divisional Court by way of case stated or for judicial review should be abolished. Appeals from the magistrates' court, he proposed, should be to a single judge in the Crown Court and such an appeal should require leave. There would be a possibility of a further appeal to the Court of Appeal which would exercise the supervisory jurisdiction now exercised by the Divisional Court.[26] However, these recommendations were not accepted by the Government.[27]

The Judicial Committee of the Privy Council

The Judicial Committee of the Privy Council is primarily a Commonwealth court. It is the final court of appeal for various countries of which the Queen is Head of State and UK overseas territories. (For the complete list see the Judicial Committee's Website – www.privy-council.org.uk – Jurisdiction.)

The right of appeal from Australia was abolished in 1986, Singapore abolished the appeal to the Judicial Committee in 1994 and New Zealand abolished it as from 2004.[28] The twelve independent countries in the Caribbean all had the Judicial Committee as the final court of appeal. In February 2001 the Agreement Establishing the Caribbean Court of Justice (CCJ) was ratified. The objective was that the CCJ would replace the Judicial Committee as the final court of appeal. This has not happened yet. Four of the twelve countries (Antigua, the Bahamas, St Kitts and St Vincent) refused to ratify the court's appellate jurisdiction.[29] Then in 2005 the Judicial Committee held that the legislation passed

---

[26] Auld, Ch. 12, pp. 620–2.

[27] Its response to the report attached to the 2002 White Paper *Justice for All* said: 'We consider that the existing arrangements work satisfactorily' (p. 43).

[28] For an account of the debates in the New Zealand Parliament see R. Cornes, 'Appealing to History: the New Zealand Supreme Court Debate', 24 *Legal Studies*, 2004, pp. 210–27.

[29] See D. O'Brien, 'The Caribbean Court of Justice and Reading Down the Independence Constitutions of the Commonwealth Caribbean: The Empire Strikes Back', *European Human Rights Law Review*, 2005, pp. 607–27.

in Jamaica to make the switch was procedurally flawed and therefore void. At the time of writing only Barbados and Guyana had validly enacted the relevant legislation.

The Judicial Committee was given a new (albeit, as it turned out, temporary) role under the devolution Acts passed by the Blair Government in 1998. The devolution legislation for Scotland, Wales and Northern Ireland made the Judicial Committee of the Privy Council the final court of appeal on devolution matters because it was felt inappropriate that the House of Lords, being a part of the Westminster Parliament, should be the arbiter of devolution matters, including decisions as to the competence of the devolved assemblies. Normally the decisions of the Judicial Committee, though treated with great respect, are not binding on the UK courts, but decisions on devolution matters are binding on all courts in the United Kingdom – though not on the Judicial Committee itself.[30]

Under the three devolution Acts the Judicial Committee may take references on devolution issues arising in the course of litigation; it may hear appeals against determination of a devolution issue from the High Court, the Court of Appeal, the Inner House of the Court of Session in Scotland or the Court of Appeal in Northern Ireland.[31] The House of Lords may refer devolution issues to the Judicial Committee – though each of the three Acts state that it may also decide the matter itself if it 'considers it more appropriate'.[32]

However, the Constitutional Reform Act 2005, s. 41 provides that devolution appeals will go to the new Supreme Court when that court starts sitting. The Government's consultation paper on the setting up of the court[33] stated that on balance the Government believed that it would be right to transfer the jurisdiction on devolution cases from the Judicial Committee to the new Supreme Court with arrangements which enabled additional Scottish and Northern Ireland judges to sit in such cases where that was appropriate: 'The establishment of the new court gives us the opportunity to restore a single apex to the UK's judicial system where all the constitutional issues can be considered' (para. 20).

The Judicial Committee includes the present and retired Law Lords, past Lord Chancellors and past and retired Lord Justices of Appeal. The composition of the Judicial Committee is by convention a matter for the Senior Law Lord. The devolution Acts, however, contained provisions specifically excluding Commonwealth judges from hearing devolution cases.[34]

---

[30] See the Scotland Act 1998, s. 103; Government of Wales Act 1998, Sch. 8, para. 32; and the Northern Ireland Act 1998, s. 82.

[31] Scotland Act, ss. 32, 33, 98 and Sch. 6; Government of Wales Act 1998, s. 109 and Sch. 8; Northern Ireland Act 1998, ss. 11, 79 and 82 and Sch. 10.

[32] Scotland Act 1998, Sch. 6, para. 32; Government of Wales Act 1998, Sch. 8, para. 29; Northern Ireland Act 1998, Sch. 10, para. 32. For a Practice Note on devolution in Wales see [1999] 3 All ER 466.

[33] *Constitutional reform: a Supreme Court for the United Kingdom*, 2003, consultation paper 11.

[34] Scotland Act 1998, s. 103(2); Government of Wales Act 1998, Sch. 8, para. 33; Northern Ireland Act 1998, s. 82(2).

2. The appeal process

A right to appeal?

Civil cases

The position as regards right to appeal has been transformed by the reforms flowing from the Woolf and Bowman reports.

AJA 1999, s. 54 provides for rights of appeal to be exercised only with permission as prescribed by rules of court. The Explanatory Notes to the Act stated that, with few exceptions, rules would require permission to appeal to be obtained in all appeals to the county courts, High Court or Civil Division of the Court of Appeal. The exceptions were appeals against committal to prison, against a refusal of *habeas corpus* and against secure accommodation orders under the Children Act 1989.[35] The rules are in CPR 52.3.

CPR 52.3(6) provides that permission to appeal will only be given where '(a) the court considers that the appeal would have a real prospect of success; or (b) there is some other compelling reason why the appeal should be heard'.

A refusal of permission must be reasoned to comply with Article 6 of the ECHR.[36] There is no appeal against a refusal.[37] However, if the refusal of permission to appeal is made on the papers, the would-be appellant is entitled to have the matter reconsidered by the same court at an oral hearing.

CPR 52.13(2) provides that where the county court or High Court has decided an appeal, the Court of Appeal will not give permission for a second appeal unless it considers that the case raises an important point of principle or practice or there is 'some other compelling reason'. In *Uphill v. BRB (Residuary) Ltd*[38] the Court of Appeal considered the meaning of the phrase 'some other compelling reason'. The first requirement was that normally the prospects of success be very high, but more was normally required. The criteria for a second appeal were not the same as for a first appeal. Leave for a second appeal could, for instance, be given where the judge on the first appeal made a decision that was perverse or was plainly wrong. It could be given if it was inconsistent with a decision of a higher court. Leave might also be given if the applicant had only a real (as opposed to a very good) chance of an appeal where the first decision was tainted with some procedural irregularity which rendered the first decision unfair.

A commentator described the decision in *Uphill* as harsh: 'No one expects a right to appeal every decision. However, justice should not be simply about

---

[35] CPR 52.3 sets out some of the exceptions. Other exceptions were dealt with by Lord Justice Brooke in his judgment in *Tanfern* (n. 16 above) at [24]–[26].

[36] *Yams v. Plender* [2001] 1 WLR 32 at [17].

[37] Access to Justice Act 1999, s. 54(4). For a disturbing illustration of the effect of this provision see *Gregory v. Turner* [2003] EWCA Civ 183, [2003] 2 All ER 1114. The Court of Appeal commiserated with the claimant that it did not have the power to allow an appeal in a case where something had plainly gone wrong below.

[38] [2005] EWCA Civ 60, [2005] 3 All ER 264.

saving the public purse and having empty lists in the Court of Appeal. A system that prevents a party from appealing a decision that the court acknowledges to be wrong is not one that can be said to be dealing with cases justly'.[39]

Less than six months after the decision in *Uphill*, a differently constituted Court of Appeal held that a more flexible approach was required in certain cases.[40] A distinction should be drawn between cases which had already received judicial consideration twice before and those where that was not the case. But, apart from that, the Court of Appeal said that the Court should be able to hear an appeal where an important point of practice arose. In that case it arose because two county court judges had made the same error in applying the law. A second appeal was justified to correct 'a worrying tendency in judges at that level'.[41]

Another commentator pointed out that the court's screening process is not cost-free. A great deal of judicial time was taken in dealing with permission applications. A better system might be that of the Employment Appeal Tribunal where weak cases were listed for a preliminary hearing in the absence of the other side. This was especially well adapted for eliminating weak litigant in person appeals.[42]

In 2005 almost three-fifths (58 per cent) of applications for permission to appeal were refused by the Court of Appeal. Of the appeals heard, 38 per cent were allowed, 46 per cent were dismissed, 14 per cent were disposed of by consent and 2 per cent were disposed of in some other way.[43]

Appeals to the House of Lords require leave either of the Court of Appeal or of the House of Lords itself. Such appeals are supposed always to be on points of law of general public importance.[44] No reasons were given for a refusal by the House of Lords to give leave but this was changed in April 2003. The change was prompted by a belief that it was required by European Community law, but, it was stated, 'so as not to discriminate between petitions which raise a question of Community law and those which do not, the Appellate Committee will briefly indicate their reasons for refusing any petition for leave to appeal'.[45]

In 2005 there were 255 petitions to the House of Lords requesting permission to appeal that were disposed of, of which seventy-nine (31 per cent) were successful.[46] The Law Lords heard 102 appeals. There were eighty-nine judgments during the year, of which 57 per cent were allowed and 43 per cent were dismissed.[47]

---

[39] R. Preston-Jones, 'An Uphill Struggle', 155 *New Law Journal*, 8 April 2005, pp. 532–3.

[40] *James Cramp v. Hastings Borough Council; Rainbow Phillips v. London Borough of Camden* [2005] EWCA Civ 1005, [2005] 4 All ER 1014.

[41] At [68]. For commentary see T. Jenns, 'Is it all Downhill for Second Appeals?', 25 *Civil Justice Quarterly*, 2006, pp. 439–50.

[42] A. Jack, 'Permission to appeal, revisited', *New Law Journal*, 10 June 2005, p. 910.

[43] *Judicial Statistics, 2005*, Table 1.4.

[44] For an exploration of this issue see L. Blom-Cooper and G. Drewry, *Final Appeal* (Clarendon Press, 1972) pp. 117–51.   [45] 38th Report from the Appeal Committee, 3 April 2003.

[46] *Judicial Statistics, 2005*, Table 1.3.   [47] *Ibid*, Table 1.4.

Criminal cases

In criminal cases no leave is required for an appeal from the magistrates' court – whether by way of rehearing to the Crown Court or by way of case stated on a point of law to the Divisional Court of the Queen's Bench Division. Leave is, however, required for an appeal from the Crown Court to the Court of Appeal Criminal Division. The exception was for an appeal on a point of law only where no leave was required until 1995 when the exception was abolished by the Criminal Appeal Act 1995, s. 1.

Leave is also required for an appeal to the House of Lords, obtainable either from the Court of Appeal (or the Divisional Court) or from the House of Lords itself. In addition, in a criminal case, the Court of Appeal (or the Divisional Court) must certify that the case raises a point of law of general public importance. To this extent it is harder to appeal in a criminal than in a civil case, since there is no equivalent requirement in civil cases. The Runciman Royal Commission recommended that the requirement of this certificate be abolished,[48] but this has not been implemented.

The House of Lords has no jurisdiction in criminal appeals from Scotland.[49] The new Supreme Court likewise will have no jurisdiction in such cases.[50]

Each year the House of Lords hears many more civil than criminal appeals. In 2005 it heard seventy-five appeals from the Court of Appeal Civil Division as against twelve from the Criminal Division.[51]

Appeals by the prosecution

The prosecution basically has had no right of appeal against an acquittal, but there were two exceptions. One was in an appeal on a point of law by way of case stated from the magistrates' court to the Divisional Court. If the appeal succeeds, the case can be sent back to the magistrates with a direction to convict or to reconsider the matter in the light of the Divisional Court's ruling on the point of law. But where the prosecution applies instead for an order of judicial review to quash an acquittal for some breach of natural justice or lack of jurisdiction, there is no power to do this unless the original trial can be held to have been a total nullity.[52]

Until 1972 there was no right for the prosecution to appeal from acquittals in the Crown Court. The Criminal Justice Act of that year gave the prosecution a

---

[48] Runciman, p. 178, para. 79.

[49] See C. Himsworth and A. Paterson, 'A Supreme Court for the United Kingdom: Views from the Northern Kingdom', 24 *Legal Studies*, 2004, pp. 99–118.

[50] Constitutional Reform Act 2005, s. 40(3) provides that an appeal from Scotland lies to the Supreme Court 'if an appeal lay from that court to the House of Lords at or immediately before the commencement of this section'.   [51] *Judicial Statistics, 2005*, Table 1.4.

[52] *R v. Dorking Justices, ex p Harrington* [1983] 3 All ER 29, applying *R v. Middlesex Quarter Sessions Chairman, ex p DPP* [1952] 2 QB 758, in which the court held that nothing could be done when the trial judge quite wrongly told the jury that it 'was a complete waste of their time to listen to the prosecution evidence' and invited them to acquit, which they did.

limited right of appeal. Section 36 provided for an appeal on a point of law by the Attorney General in a case tried on indictment where the defendant has been acquitted. However, the acquitted defendant is not affected by the outcome of the appeal. If the Attorney General is successful it simply clarifies the law.[53] In *A-G's Reference (No 1 of 1975)*[54] the court said that the procedure should be used exclusively 'for short but important points which require a quick ruling of this court before a potentially false decision of law has too wide a circulation in the courts'.[55]

The next development was the Criminal Justice Act 1988, s. 36 of which gave the Attorney General, with leave of the Court of Appeal, the right to refer cases to the court on the grounds that the sentence is 'unduly lenient'. This does have an effect on the disposition of the actual case.

In the years 2001–5 Lord Goldsmith, as Attorney General, referred 698 cases, an average of 140 cases per year. The Court of Appeal agreed to reconsider 521 of these (75 per cent). In 414 of the 521 (79 per cent) the sentence was increased.[56]

The Runciman Royal Commission recommended that where a person is convicted of conspiracy to pervert the course of justice by 'jury nobbling' in a case which led to an acquittal, the prosecution should be entitled to restart the case against the acquitted defendant.[57] Section 54 of the Criminal Procedure and Investigations Act 1996 gave the High Court the power to quash the conviction if satisfied that the acquittal would not have occurred had it not been for the interference with or intimidation of the jury.

The Royal Commission rejected the suggestion that the prosecution should have a right to appeal against a perverse verdict or where a defendant was acquitted (or convicted on a less serious charge) as a result of an error by a prosecution witness. ('We have every sympathy for the victims and families of victims in such cases, especially where they have suffered bereavement or injury. We believe, however, that the right answer is for the investigating and prosecuting authorities to prepare their cases thoroughly'.[58])

As was seen above, Lord Justice Auld proposed that there should be legislation to provide that juries may not give perverse acquittals – which was not accepted by the Government. He did not however go so far as to propose that the prosecution should have a right to appeal against a perverse verdict.

Appeals against terminating rulings The Criminal Justice Act 2003, Part 9 gives the prosecution the right to appeal against a ruling by a Crown Court judge that there is no case to answer or any other ruling that terminates the trial made at

---

[53] For a comment on the section see D.J. Stephens, 'In Jeopardy', *Criminal Law Review*, 1972, p. 361 and J. Jaconelli, 'Attorney General's References – a Problematic Device', *Criminal Law Review*, 1981, p. 543.   [54] [1975] 3 WLR 11 at 13.

[55] See W.T. West, 'Wrongful Acquittals', 147 *Justice of the Peace*, 8 October 1983, p. 647.

[56] *The Guardian*, 14 June 2006. The Solicitor General told the House of Commons in 2003 that in the previous fourteen years, 845 cases had been referred to the Court of Appeal and 606 (72 per cent) had resulted in the sentence being increased. On average the Attorney General referred just under half the cases that were sent to him. (House of Commons, *Hansard*, vol. 402, 24 March 2003, col. 23 WA.)   [57] Runciman, p. 177, para. 74.   [58] *Ibid*, para. 76.

a pre-trial hearing or during the trial at any stage before the start of the judge's summing up.[59] This includes not only rulings that are terminating in themselves but also those that are so serious a blow to the prosecution that, in the absence of a right of appeal, it would offer no, or no further, evidence.

The provisions were based on, but went considerably beyond, recommendations first proposed by the Law Commission.[60] They had the support of Lord Justice Auld.[61]

Leave to appeal must be obtained either from the judge or the Court of Appeal. A ruling effectively acquitting the defendant will not take effect while the prosecution decides whether to appeal and, if an appeal is pursued, until it is concluded, but the prosecution has to give an undertaking that if the appeal is unsuccessful, the defendant must be found not guilty. Defence costs are payable by the prosecution.

Both the prosecution and the defence have the right to appeal to the House of Lords on a point of law of general public importance.

The Criminal Justice Act 2003, Part 9 also gives the prosecution the right in cases involving qualifying offences as defined in Sch. 4, Part 1 to appeal against a ruling on evidence which significantly weakens the prosecution's case. This has however not yet been brought into force.

Abolition of the double jeopardy rule

It has for centuries been a generally accepted principle that a person should not be put in peril of conviction twice for the same offence. The principle is expressed in the ancient common law doctrine of *autrefois acquit*, better known as the rule against double jeopardy.

Largely stimulated by the Stephen Lawrence case, the question was raised whether the rule against double jeopardy should be curtailed. In 1999 the Macpherson Report on the Stephen Lawrence case recommended that the Court of Appeal be given the power to permit prosecution appeals after acquittal where 'fresh and viable' evidence is presented.[62] In June 2000 the Home Affairs Committee of the House of Commons recommended that the double jeopardy rule should be relaxed where there was new evidence that made an acquittal unsafe, where the offence carried a life sentence and the Attorney General

---

[59] The Law Commission said that appeals during the course of the trial 'would be wholly impracticable, would throw the system into chaos and would be contrary to long established principle'. (*Double Jeopardy and Prosecution Appeals*, Law Com Report No. 267, 2001, para. 7.38.) For concern about the likely resulting delays see H. Blaxland QC, 'Prosecution Appeals', 18 *Independent Lawyer*, July–August 2004, p. 15.

[60] *Prosecution Appeals Against Judges' Rulings*, Law Com consultation paper 158, 2000; and final report *Double Jeopardy and Prosecution Appeals*, Law Com Report No. 267, 2001. For critical comment on the consultation paper see R. Pattenden, 'Prosecution Appeals Against Judges' Rulings', *Criminal Law Review*, 2000, pp. 971–86. For a broadly approving assessment of the provisions in the Act see I. Dennis, 'Prosecution Appeals and Retrial for Serious Offences', *Criminal Law Review*, 2004, pp. 619–25.   [61] Auld, Ch. 12, pp. 634–5.

[62] *Report of an Inquiry into the Stephen Lawrence case* by Lord Macpherson of Cluny, Cm. 4262, 1999, recommendation 38.

considered it to be in the public interest for the conviction to be quashed.[63] In March 2001 the Law Commission in its report *Double Jeopardy and Prosecution Appeals* recommended that in murder cases[64] the Court of Appeal should be given power to set aside an acquittal where there was apparently reliable and compelling new evidence of guilt and it was in the interests of justice to do so.

Lord Justice Auld in his report in October 2001 agreed with the Law Commission's recommendation but proposed that it should be extended to 'other grave offences punishable with life and/or long terms of imprisonment as Parliament might specify'. ('Why should an alleged violent rapist or robber, who leaves his victim near dead . . . not be answerable to the law in the same way as an alleged murderer?'[65])

The Law Commission proposed that the personal consent of the DPP should be required for an application to quash an acquittal. Auld agreed and urged that the DPP's consent should also be required for the reopening of an investigation after an acquittal.

The White Paper *Justice for All* (July 2002) signalled that the Government intended to implement these recommendations[66] and they were included in the Criminal Justice Bill 2002–3, Part 10. The provisions were extremely controversial[67] but they were passed and brought into force in April 2005.

The Criminal Justice Act 2003, ss. 75–97

- The provisions affect a person who has been acquitted anywhere in the world, except Scotland, of a qualifying offence, as defined in Sch. 5, Part 1.[68] The Schedule lists twenty nine offences all carrying a maximum sentence of life imprisonment and which according to the Explanatory Notes accompanying the Act 'have a particularly serious impact either on the victim or on society more generally'.
- The provisions are retrospective and therefore apply to acquittals that occurred before the Act.[69]
- The prosecutor may apply to the Court of Appeal for an order quashing an acquittal and permitting a retrial for a qualifying offence.[70]

---

[63] *The Double Jeopardy Rule*, 3rd Report of the 1999–2000 session, HC 190, paras. 21–4 and 39–41.

[64] In its earlier consultation paper, at para. 5.29, it had proposed that the power should apply to all cases in which the sentence would be likely to be at least three years' imprisonment.

[65] Auld, Ch. 12, para. 60, p. 633.   [66] Paragraphs 4–63–66.

[67] For two articles written before the Bill was published see I. Dennis, 'Rethinking Double Jeopardy: Justice and Finality in the Criminal Process', *Criminal Law Review*, 2000, pp. 933–51 and P. Roberts, 'Justice for All? Two Bad Arguments [and Several Good Suggestions] for Resisting Double Jeopardy Reform', 6 *International Journal of Evidence and Proof*, 2002, pp. 197–217. For an assessment after the Act was passed see I. Dennis, 'Prosecution Appeals and Retrial for Serious Offences', *Criminal Law Review*, 2004, pp. 625–38. For the parliamentary debates see especially House of Lords, *Hansard*, 17 July 2003.

[68] Section 75(1), (4) and (5). Scotland is excluded because the Scottish devolved executive decided not to adopt this modification of the double jeopardy rule.   [69] Section 75(6).

[70] Section 76.

- It requires the personal written consent of the DPP.[71]
- An application can only be made once.[72]
- The DPP must be satisfied that there is 'new and compelling evidence' that the acquitted person is guilty of a qualifying offence and that it is in the public interest for the application to proceed.[73]
- The test whether the evidence is 'new' is merely that it was not adduced in the trial leading to the acquittal.[74]
- Evidence is 'compelling' if it is reliable, substantial and if, 'in the context of the outstanding issues, it appears highly probative of the case against the acquitted person'.[75]
- It is irrelevant whether the new evidence would have been admissible or inadmissible.[76]
- To make the order for a new trial the Court of Appeal must be satisfied that there is 'new and compelling evidence' (s. 78) and that such a trial is in the interests of justice (s. 79).[77]
- The interests of justice test must be determined having regard in particular to (1) whether existing circumstances make a fair trial unlikely; (2) the length of time since the offence was committed; (3) whether it is likely that the new evidence would have been available at the time of the original proceedings but for a failure by an officer or prosecutor to act with due diligence; and (4) whether an officer or prosecutor has failed to act with due expedition since the new evidence became available.[78]
- The person concerned is entitled to be present at the hearing of the application.[79]
- The Court of Appeal can make an order restricting reporting of the case in order to ensure that there can be a fair trial.[80]
- The retrial of an acquitted person must take place on an indictment preferred by the direction of the Court of Appeal. The arraignment must be within two months of the order for a retrial unless the court allows a longer period.[81]
- Re-opening an investigation after an acquittal requires the written consent of the DPP. A reinvestigation for these purposes means arrest or questioning the acquitted person, searching him or premises owned or occupied by him, searching a vehicle owned by him, seizing anything in his possession or taking his fingerprints or a bodily sample from him. The DPP can only give his consent if he is satisfied that there is sufficient new evidence already or that such new evidence is likely to come to light if the investigation goes ahead.[82]
- If urgent action is needed to prevent an investigation being substantially and irrevocably prejudiced or to prevent death or serious injury, it is permitted provided it is authorised by an officer of the rank of superintendent or above.[83]

---

[71] Section 76(3).   [72] Section 76(5).   [73] Sections 76(4) and 78.   [74] Section 78(2).
[75] Section 78(3).   [76] Section 78(5).   [77] Section 77.   [78] Section 79.
[79] Section 80(5).   [80] Section 82.   [81] Section 84.   [82] Section 85.   [83] Section 86.

The first person to be convicted under the provisions was Billy Dunlop for the murder in 1989 of twenty-two year old Julie Higgs. Her mother campaigned over seventeen years for a change in the double jeopardy rule. Dunlop was tried for the murder but twice the jury failed to agree and in 1991 he was formally acquitted. Later, while in prison for assaulting a former girlfriend, he confessed to a prison officer that he had killed Julie Higgs. He was tried for perjury and given a six year sentence. When the double jeopardy rule was changed, Cleveland Police reopened the case. On 11 September 2006 at the Old Bailey Dunlop pleaded guilty to the murder and on 6 October he was sentenced to life imprisonment. (*Dunlop* [2006] EWCA Crim 1354, [2007] 1 All ER 593.)

Practice and procedure of appeals

An appeal was formerly said to be by way of rehearing, but with one exception this did not mean what it appeared to mean. The exception was an appeal from the magistrates' court to the Crown Court where the case started (and still starts) afresh with all the witnesses as if it had never been heard before. (Lord Justice Auld recommended that this form of appeal should be abolished,[84] but the recommendation was not adopted by the Government.)

In all other cases the appeal court heard the appeal on the basis of the decision below. In other words, the appellant argued that something went wrong in the court below and for that purpose he would normally have to show what did happen – by producing the judgment which he claimed was wrong in law or by having a transcript of the whole or part of the proceedings below to show that, for instance, the decision was against the weight of the evidence or that some impropriety had occurred. Occasionally, but very rarely indeed, the Court of Appeal was prepared to listen to witnesses, but only if they were new and then only in exceptional circumstances. Otherwise, testimony was presented to the appeal court via the written word through the transcript of the trial or a note of the proceedings taken by the judge, the lawyers or the court clerk.

Under the former Rules of the Supreme Court, the Court of Appeal had 'all the authority and jurisdiction of the court or tribunal from which the appeal was brought' and the power 'to give any order which ought to have been given or made, and to make such further order as the case may require'.[85] Its powers meant that the Court of Appeal was indeed a court of appeal – as opposed to what in continental systems is called a court of cassation where the court basically has to reach its decision on the basis of the findings of fact of the court below and may not even have the power to substitute its own decision so that it can only quash the decision and send the case back for a new start.[86]

---

[84] Auld, Ch. 12, p. 622.

[85] Supreme Court Act 1981, s. 15(3); RSC Order 59, rr. 10(1) and (3).

[86] That traditionally was the position in France though in modern times the Cour de Cassation does have the power to substitute its own decision thus blurring the distinction between appeal and cassation.

Under the new rules for civil appeals that came into force in May 2000 (Part 52 of the CPR), there is still reference to re-hearing[87] but this form of appeal is now relegated to a secondary position by the new rule that, subject to two exceptions, 'every appeal will be limited to a review of the decision of the lower court'.[88] The exceptions are where a Practice Direction makes different provisions[89] and, secondly, where 'the court considers that in the circumstances of an individual appeal it would be in the interests of justice to hold a re-hearing'.

The intention apparently was that 'review' is to be different from, and probably something more limited than, 'rehearing'. The question is what is that difference and, in particular, does an appeal court, and especially the Court of Appeal, retain the previous power to reach its own decision with regard to all, or any aspect of, the case? An appeal court still has all the powers of the lower court[90] including the power to 'affirm, set aside or vary any judgment or order made or given by the lower court',[91] to receive oral evidence or evidence which was not before the lower court if it so orders[92] and to draw any inference of fact which it considers justified on the evidence.[93]

In what way therefore does the new power of revision differ from the previous power to rehear? It has been argued that 'rehearing' should now be confined to the rare case of a real rehearing of the entire case, whereas 'revision' should be used in relation to all the other powers of the court.[94] If this is correct, not much will have changed. It seems more likely that the intention was to effect a significant change but mainly with regard to interlocutory appeals. In *Tanfern Ltd* (above) Lord Justice Brooke, having set out the CPR provisions that as a general rule every appeal will be limited to a review of the decision below (CPR 52.11(1)), went on:

> This marks a significant change in practice, in relation to what used to be called 'interlocutory' appeals from District judges or Masters. Under the old practice, the appeal to a judge was a rehearing in the fullest sense of the word, and the judge exercised his/her discretion afresh, while giving appropriate weight to the way the lower court had exercised its discretion in the matter. Under the new practice, the decision of the lower court will attract much greater significance, The appeal court's duty is now limited to a review of that decision, and it may only interfere in the quite limited circumstances set out in r. 52.11(3).[95]

---

[87] As opposed to 'rehearing' in the former rules – presumably a spelling change that was not intended to have significance.   [88] CPR 52.11(1).

[89] The most relevant provision of the Practice Direction is para. 9.1 which requires a hearing if the appeal is from a minister, person or body who (1) did not hold a hearing to come to that decision or (2) held a hearing but the procedure did not provide for consideration of evidence.   [90] CPR 52 10(1).   [91] CPR 52.10(2)(a).

[92] CPR 52.11(2). The rule now says that the court will *not* receive oral evidence or fresh evidence unless it so orders; the previous rule (RSC Order 59, r. 10(2)) said it should not do so except on special grounds.   [93] CPR 52.11(4).

[94] J. A. Jolowicz, 'The New Appeal: Re-hearing or Revision or What?', 20 *Civil Justice Quarterly*, 2001, pp. 7–12.

[95] Note 16 above at [31]. On the difference between 'review' and 're-hearing' see also *Assicurazioni Generali Spa v. Arab Insurance Group (BSC)* [2002] EWCA Civ 1642, [2003] 1 WLR 577 per Lord Justices Clarke at [6] and Ward at [193].

There are several features of the appeal system which should be noted.

The procedure for civil appeals
Applying for leave

Where an application for leave to appeal reaches the Court of Appeal Civil Division the way it was handled depended on whether it was prepared by a lawyer or a litigant in person. If the application was prepared by a lawyer, it was normally sent to a single Lord Justice who considered it on the papers, without a hearing. If he refused leave, the applicant had the right to renew the application to the full court where it was argued *ex parte* (in the absence of the other side) before two other Lord Justices. If the application was presented by a litigant in person, it could be dealt with in the same way or, alternatively, since litigants in person are more likely to renew their applications, it could be heard immediately in open court by two Lord Justices as a way of cutting out one stage.

The Bowman Committee proposed some changes. All applications for leave should be considered initially by a single Lord Justice. He could then do one of three things: (1) allow the application on the papers; (2) decide to hear the application in open court either alone or with another Lord Justice; or (3) if minded to refuse leave, to write to the applicant giving reasons but offering to hold an oral hearing. If the offer was not accepted within the time limit, the application would be dismissed on the papers with no right of renewal. These proposals were adopted.

In the year 2004–5 there were 917 cases in which the decision was made on the papers alone. (In 35 per cent permission was refused.) There were 749 cases in which the application was heard in open court. These are mostly applications by unrepresented defendants. (In 79 per cent permission was refused.) There were 391 cases in which there was a renewed application – oral hearing after a paper refusal. (In 68 per cent permission was refused.[96])

The procedure for criminal appeals
Applying for leave

All appeals require leave, which is usually sought from the Court of Appeal. Applications for leave are made to a single judge (normally a High Court judge) who deals with the matter by considering the papers only. There is no hearing. If he refuses leave, the applicant has the right to renew the application by asking for leave from the full court of three judges. This is at an actual hearing in open court, though usually neither the prosecution nor the applicant is present. It is very rare for leave to be given by the full court. If leave is given, quite frequently the hearing of the application is combined with the hearing of the appeal, counsel having been warned in advance to prepare themselves for the argument on the merits.

---

[96] *Master of the Rolls Review of the Legal Year 2004–5*, Graph 6, p. 30 (www.civilappeals. gov.uk).

One unsatisfactory feature of the system is that if the defendant is legally aided (most are)[97] his lawyers' duties cease after they have advised as to whether there are grounds of appeal and, if so, have drafted them. The legal aid certificate does not cover advice as to whether to renew an application once it has been turned down by the single judge. Application for legal aid for the renewal hearing can however be made to the Registrar.

The Runciman Royal Commission said this was a gap in the system which should be closed by providing that the original legal aid cover also the question of renewing the application after it has been turned down by the single judge.[98] This recommendation was not implemented.

If leave to appeal is granted, the Registrar of Criminal Appeals prepares a summary of the appellant's case[99] and assigns counsel, usually the same barrister who appeared at the trial. The Registrar therefore has a dual function, as administrative officer of the court and in something like the role of instructing solicitor.

The success rate on a renewal to the full court, not surprisingly, is statistically much affected by whether the appellant is represented.[100]

Time loss rules

The court can order that some of the time spent appealing does not count toward the sentence, as a penalty for making a frivolous application. This threat acts powerfully on the minds of prisoners. In 1966 the grounds for quashing a conviction were altered and became more favourable to the appellant (see p. 693 below). News of this resulted in a flood of new applications for leave to appeal, which were running at the rate of about 12,000 a year compared with about 2,000 in 1963. This caused an announcement to be made in 1970 by the Lord Chief Justice, Lord Parker, that in future the power to order that time does not count if the application was thought to be frivolous would be used more often.[101] The announcement had an immediate and dramatic effect. The numbers of applications for leave went down by about half and remained at that lower figure of some 6,000 a year for several years.

Would-be appellants were reminded of the existence of the power in a further Practice Note in 1980.[102] The warning was in fierce and forbidding terms: 'It

---

[97] Currently around 95 per cent of defendants in the Crown Court have legal aid and an unknown additional proportion are represented privately.   [98] Runciman, p. 167, para. 25.

[99] The summary, which can run to many pages, is prepared by lawyers employed by the Registrar or by barristers employed *ad hoc*. They do not make recommendations. Formerly these summaries were not seen by the appellant's lawyers, but this was changed by Lord Taylor after he became Lord Chief Justice.

[100] In a sample of cases between October and December 1990, only 22 per cent of defendants who renewed their application from the single judge to the full court had counsel, but their success rate was 48 per cent compared with 15 per cent of the much larger number without counsel. (Evidence of Lord Chancellor's Department to Runciman Royal Commission, Ch. 4, Table 2.) See also K. Malleson, *Review of the Appeal Process* (Royal Commission Research Study No. 17, 1993) p. 32.   [101] *Practice Note* [1970] 1 WLR 663.

[102] [1980] 1 All ER 555. See now *Practice Direction (Criminal Proceedings: Consolidation)* [2002] 1 WLR 2870.

may be expected that such a direction [ordering loss of time for a hopeless appeal] will normally be made unless the grounds are not only settled and signed by counsel, but also supported by the written opinion of counsel'.

What is often not realised by prisoners is how rarely the power to order that time spent appealing should not count is exercised or that the power is limited to adding on ninety days to the sentence. An action against the UK Government under the European Convention on Human Rights challenging the legality of the power was rejected by the Strasbourg Court in March 1987. The European Court of Human Rights was told that, although there were no statistics, loss of time was ordered in some sixty or so cases per year by the single judge or the full court. The normal order was for twenty-eight days to be added on, though such orders ranged from seven days to sixty-four days.[103] (In later years the number of such orders is much lower still. In 1998 there were four, in 1999 two, in 2000 none and in 2001 two. In April 2005 the Court of Appeal said it was a power that had been too little used.[104])

Research conducted for the Runciman Royal Commission on Criminal Justice showed that there was a great deal of misinformation in the prisons about the time loss rules. Many prisoners were under the erroneous impression that *all* the time spent appealing could be added on by the Court of Appeal. (This error was less surprising when seen against the fact that many solicitors appeared to share the same misapprehension and that over half of all solicitors responding to the survey thought that the Court of Appeal still had the power to increase sentences which had been abolished twenty-five years earlier!) A third of the sample of prisoners who did not appeal said the threat of time being added on had been the reason.[105]

The Runciman Commission recommended that prisoners – and lawyers – be made aware of the true position. ('We think it wrong that appellants who spend several months awaiting appeal should be left with the impression that if they fail, those months will be added to their sentences. Nor should they have reason to fear that the Court of Appeal will increase their sentence'.[106]) It recommended that the Court of Appeal issue a new Practice Direction dealing with the issue and that the official guides issued by the Criminal Appeal Office, the Bar Council and the Law Society make matters clear, even though the result would be likely to be an increase in the number of applications for leave to appeal. ('We would regard it as an unavoidable result of correcting an important piece of misinformation common among prisoners' (*ibid*).) This recommendation, however, was not acted upon.

The great majority of appeals are against sentence. In the ten years 1995–2005 the number of applications for leave to appeal against conviction fluctuated

[103] *Monnell and Morris v. United Kingdom* (1987) 10 EHRR 205.
[104] *Kuimba* (2005) Times, 17 May. See also *Hart, George, Clarke, Brown* (2007) Times, 16 February.
[105] J. Plotnikoff and R. Woolfson, *Information and Advice for Prisoners about Grounds for Appeal and the Appeals Process* (Royal Commission Research Study No. 18, 1993) pp. 79–82.
[106] Runciman, pp. 165–6, para. 19.

from a high of 2,393 (in 1995) to a low of 1,661 (in 2005). The number of applications for leave to appeal against sentence fluctuated in the same period between a high of 7,160 (in 1997) and a low of 5,178 (in 2005).[107]

In 2005, of the applications for leave to appeal considered by a single judge, 24 per cent were granted against conviction and 33 per cent against sentence.[108]

Of those applications which were refused by the single judge, 50 per cent were renewed to the full court against conviction and 27 per cent against sentence.[109] A quarter (25 per cent) of the renewed applications against conviction and two-fifths (40 per cent) of those against sentence were successful.[110]

Of the appeals heard by the full court during 2005, 37 per cent (twenty-two) against conviction were allowed and 71 per cent (1,534) against sentence were allowed.[111]

Legal advice for appellants in criminal cases

The Access to Justice Act 1999, s. 26 states that 'representation' includes advice and assistance as to any appeal. The official Guide to practitioners on criminal appeals states in para 1.1 that no one convicted or sentenced in the Crown Court should be without advice or assistance on appeal.[112] The solicitor's brief to a barrister must include instructions to the barrister to give advice and assistance as to the prospects of an appeal in the event of a conviction or sentence. The advice must be whether there are grounds of appeal. If so, the grounds must be drafted. The procedure requires that counsel fill out a form right away at court telling the client whether it is thought that there are grounds of appeal or whether counsel needs time to consider the matter. He is required then to deliver written advice to the solicitor within fourteen days, including, where appropriate, signed grounds of appeal. The solicitors should send it on to the client so that he receives it within twenty-one days measured from his conviction or sentence.

Research done for the Runciman Royal Commission showed that in various respects this system was not at that time functioning as it should. Thus 9 per cent of prisoners said they had not been visited in the cells at the end of the case and 23 per cent said they had been visited but an appeal had not been discussed. The Royal Commission said it regarded these as serious matters and called on both branches of the profession to 'take all necessary steps to ensure that practitioners not only perform their duty to see the client at the end of the case, as most do, but also give preliminary advice both orally and in writing'.[113] No later research has inquired into whether this exhortation has been heeded.

---

[107] *Judicial Statistics, 2005*, Table 1.7.   [108] *Ibid.*   [109] *Ibid.*   [110] *Ibid.*

[111] *Ibid*, Table 1.8.

[112] *A Guide to Proceedings in the Court of Appeal, Criminal Division* [1997] 2 Cr App Rep 459 and the current edition of *Archbold Criminal Pleading Evidence & Practice.* The Guide is also accessible at www.courtservice.gov.uk – Publications – Guidance.

[113] J. Plotnikoff and R. Woolfson, *Information and Advice for Prisoners about Grounds for Appeal and the Appeals Process* (Royal Commission Research Study No. 18, 1993) pp. 164–5, para. 14.

Where it appears that the defendant has submitted his own grounds, the Criminal Appeal Office writes to the solicitors who acted at the trial to ask if advice was given. If the reply is affirmative, no doubt the Criminal Appeal Office assumes that the solicitors were discouraging about the prospects of an appeal.

Appeals by way of case stated

An appeal may be brought against a decision of the magistrates' court on the ground that it is wrong in law or in excess of jurisdiction by asking the magistrates to state a case to the Divisional Court (Magistrates' Courts Act 1980, s. 111(1)). This must be done within twenty-one days. There is no power to give an extension of time. In a criminal case the prosecution may ask for a case to be stated, as can the defence. The magistrates draw up a statement of the facts found, the cases cited, the decision and the issue for the consideration of the Divisional Court. If the appeal is based on the argument that there was no evidence on which the magistrates could have reached their decision, the case stated also includes a resumé of the evidence. The court supplies the parties with a draft of the case to be stated and invites their comments. In the event that a party is dissatisfied with the way in which the case has been put, he can apply to the Divisional Court asking for the case to be remitted to the magistrates for restatement of the facts. The magistrates can refuse to state a case on the grounds that it is a frivolous request. However, an unreasonable refusal to state a case can be the subject of an application for judicial review.[114]

As noted above (p. 662) Lord Justice Auld recommended that the right to appeal from the magistrates' court to the High Court by way of case stated should be abolished,[115] but this recommendation was not acted upon.

Leapfrog appeals

In 1969 a new procedure was devised to enable appeals to go direct from the High Court to the House of Lords in certain limited circumstances.

To the House of Lords

Administration of Justice Act 1969

Section 12(3) – that a point of law of general public importance is involved in that decision and that that point of law either:

(a) related wholly or mainly to the construction of an enactment or of a statutory instrument, and has been fully argued in the proceedings and fully considered in the judgment of the judge in the proceedings, or

(b) is one in respect of which the judge is bound by a decision of the Court of Appeal or of the House of Lords in previous proceedings, and was fully

---

[114] *Sunworld Ltd v. Hammersmith and Fulham London Borough Council* [2000] 2 All ER 837, Div Court. See generally A. Murdie, 'Appeals by Case Stated from the Magistrates' Court', *Solicitors' Journal*, 6 October 1995, p. 984; J. A. Backhouse, 'Right of Appeal by way of Case Stated – Should it be Simplified?', 156 *Justice of the Peace*, 16 May 1992, p. 310.

[115] Auld, p. 623.

considered in the judgments given by the Court of Appeal or the House of Lords (as the case may be) in those previous proceedings . . .

The power has been used very little.

To the Court of Appeal Civil Division

Where an appeal would otherwise be heard on appeal by the county court or the High Court it can be transferred direct to the Court of Appeal if the Master of the Rolls or the court from which the appeal is taken or the court to which the appeal is going considers that it raises an important point of principle or practice or 'there is some other compelling reason for the Court of Appeal to hear the case'.[116]

To the Court of Appeal Criminal Division

Lord Justice Auld recommended in his report that the leapfrog appeal be extended to criminal cases for use where there are conflicting decisions of the Court of Appeal that can only be resolved by the House of Lords.[117] This has not been implemented.

General

In the early 1960s a team of eminent English and American judges and lawyers spent a period in each other's countries studying the appeal system. The object was for each to assess the strengths and weaknesses of both systems. A member of the American team reported on the meeting.[118] What follows distils the main points of comparison at that time and (in editorial square brackets or footnotes) what has happened to the English system in the intervening forty or more years. As will appear, although the English system has moved somewhat in the direction of the American system, many of the differences identified then are still valid.

The decision

In the United States, almost all decisions are reserved and rendered in written form. Rarely is one pronounced from the bench. Furthermore, an attempt is always made to have the judges agree upon an opinion for the court as a whole, or, if that cannot be done, to secure as broad a base of agreement as possible.

While concurring opinions are not unusual and even multiple separate dissents not unknown, it is not expected that each judge will express his own views. The ideal is a unanimous opinion for the court, or, failing that, one majority opinion and one dissent.

[The English system is moving strongly in that direction. In his 2001–2 annual report as Master of the Rolls Lord Phillips said: 'it is now more common for a

---

[116] Access to Justice Act 1999, s. 57 and CPR 52.14.   [117] Auld, Ch. 12, para. 117, p. 657.
[118] D. Karlen, 'Appeal in England and the United States', 78 *Law Quarterly Review*, 1962, p. 371.

constitution of the court to deliver a single judgment to which all members of the court have contributed. This is a trend which has my support. Profusion of precedent is the bain of judges and practitioners alike. A single judgment reduces the material that has to be read, avoids the opportunity for differences of interpretation and provides greater clarity' (ed.).[119]]

> In England, few decisions are either reserved or written. In the Court of Appeal, the practice is for each judge to express his individual views orally and extemporaneously immediately upon the close of argument. In the Court of Criminal Appeal a single opinion for the court is customarily expressed, but almost always orally and extemporaneously. Only in the House of Lords and the Privy Council are decisions customarily reserved and written.

[This was the position in the Civil Division and remains the position in the Criminal Division, but the proportion of cases in which the decision is reserved in the Civil Division is now very considerable. The Bowman report in 1997 said that the Court of Appeal reserved judgment in a quarter to a third of cases. The Master of the Rolls' annual reports show that the proportion has now risen to over half.[120] As the simpler appeals were dealt with by lower courts, the proportion of complex cases heard by the Court of Appeal in which it was necessary to reserve judgment was inevitably rising (ed.).]

> The American approach entails different internal operating procedures than are usual in England. Conferences, both formal and informal, are a prominent feature of American practice. So are exchanges of memoranda and draft opinions. On the other hand, since reading and writing are by their nature solitary operations, American judges, who are compelled to do much of both, spend many, if not most, of their working hours alone. They are frequently required to shift their attention from one case to another and then back again, because, with cases being heard in batches, several are awaiting decision at any given time.
>
> To the limited extent that the English practice conforms to the American pattern, the same internal procedures doubtless apply. In the great majority of English appeals, however, the judges follow a vastly different routine. Most of their working time is spent together sitting on the bench, listening and talking rather than reading and writing. The discussions they hold are brief and seemingly casual, although highly economical, by reason of the fact that cases are heard and decided one at a time. The judges' minds are already focused on the problems at hand and not distracted by other cases which have been heard and are awaiting decision. They whisper between themselves on the bench; they converse as they walk to and from the courtroom; and they indirectly make comments to each other as they carry on Socratic dialogues with counsel, but they

---

[119] For a critical discussion of the trend toward single judgments in the Court of Appeal see R. Munday, '"All for One and One for All" – The Rise to Prominence of the Composite Judgment within the Civil Division of the Court of Appeal', 61 *Cambridge Law Journal*, 2002, pp. 321–50.

[120] In the five years from 2001–2 to 2004–5 it was respectively 52 per cent, 54 per cent, 55 per cent, 61 per cent and 55 per cent – Graph 4.

do not ordinarily exchange memoranda or draft opinions or engage in full scale conferences.[121]

In short, the appellate judge in England spends most of his working time in open court, relatively little in chambers, whereas his counterpart in America spends most of his working time in chambers, and relatively little in open court. This is neatly illustrated by the times of sitting for comparable courts in the two nations. In the United States Court of Appeals for the Second Circuit, each judge hears arguments one week out of four, and uses the other three for studying written briefs and records on appeal, conferring with his brother judges, and writing opinions. By way of contrast, each judge on the English Court of Appeal hears arguments, day after day, five days a week, throughout each term.

[Following Bowman, the judges in the Court of Appeal Civil Division nowadays have a significant proportion of working time for writing but the difference between the two systems remains (ed.).]

Supporting personnel

In the United States, most appellate judges have law clerks, sometimes more than one. These typically are young men, recently graduated from law school with fine academic records, who serve for a period of a year or two. They are chosen by and answerable to the judges, although paid out of public funds. The services they perform vary greatly from one judge to another, but in general they carry on research, prepare memoranda, discuss the cases to be decided with the judges for whom they work, and sometimes even draft opinions or parts of opinions to be rendered. They participate in the decisional process to the extent that their judges wish them to participate . . .

In England there are no law clerks.[122]

[Professor Karlen made the point that since in the English system written briefs are not used and most opinions are given extemporaneously at the close of oral argument, it was difficult to see what use law clerks would be in most English appellate courts. As will be seen, skeleton arguments – mini versions of the fully argued American written brief – are now an established part of the English system, but about half the decisions of the Court of Appeal Civil Division and the overwhelming majority of the decisions of the Court of Appeal Criminal Division are still rendered extemporaneously at the end of the case. The young judicial assistants now employed by the Court of Appeal Civil Division are, so far at least, a pale reflection of the US style law clerk. Their work consists

---

[121] See to like effect K. Malleson, 'Decision-making in the Court of Appeal: the Burden of Proof in an Inquisitorial Process', 1 *International Journal of Evidence and Proof*, 1997, pp. 175–86 (ed.).

[122] As has been seen, the Court of Appeal Civil Division does now employ young judicial assistants. For a fascinating, and perhaps disturbing, insider's description (and critique) of the way the justices of the US Supreme Court and their clerks operate as seen by a former clerk see E. Lazarus, *Closed Chambers* (1999, Penguin). See also G. R. Smith, 'A Primer of Opinion Writing for Law Clerks', 26 *Vanderbilt Law Review*, 1973, p. 1203 (ed.).

typically in preparing summaries and analysis of the issues in a case. They are not involved in the writing of a judge's written judgments (ed.).]

Finality

In the United States, appellate decisions possess less finality. New trials can be granted in all types of cases, criminal as well as civil. Rehearings are frequently asked for and occasionally allowed. Existing side by side with appeals are a variety of methods of collateral attack, including *habeas corpus*, sometimes entailing successive re-examination of a single case by courts of co-ordinate jurisdiction.

Finally, the American doctrine of precedent is such that a decision is never beyond the reach of challenge in a new lawsuit. If conditions or thinking have changed, sometimes if only the personnel of the court has changed, there is always the possibility that the unwanted decision may be overruled.

[The difference between the two civil systems in this respect is even greater today than it was then, since the Court of Appeal has taken such strong action post-Bowman to reduce second appeals. As will be seen, retrials in criminal cases are not quite so rare today as they were then but they are still very rare (ed.).]

Oral argument

In the United States, oral arguments are secondary in importance to the briefs, and are rigidly limited in duration. In the United States Supreme Court, one hour is allowed to each side, but in many appellate courts, less time than that is permitted, frequently no more than fifteen minutes or a half-hour for each side. Reading by counsel is frowned upon. The judges do not wish to hear what they can read for themselves. They expect to get all the information they need about the judgment below, the evidence, and the authorities relied upon from studying the briefs and record on appeal. They do not even encourage counsel to discuss in detail the precedents claimed to govern the decision, preferring to do that job by themselves in the relative privacy of their chambers, with or without the assistance of law clerks.

In England, where there are no written briefs,[123] oral arguments are all-important. They are never arbitrarily limited in duration. While some last for only a few minutes, others go on for many days, even weeks. The only controls ordinarily exercised over the time of oral arguments are informal, *ad hoc* suggestions from the judges. Thus when counsel wishes to cite a case as authority, the presiding judge may ask him: for what proposition? If the judges indicate that they accept the proposition as stated, there is no need to read the case. Similarly if counsel has persuaded the judges on a certain point, they may indicate that it is unnecessary for him to pursue it further. If counsel for the appellant, by the time he finishes his argument, has failed to persuade the court that the decision below should be reversed or modified, the court informs counsel for the respondent that it does not wish to hear from him at all, and proceeds forthwith to deliver judgment. Despite such controls as these, the time spent in England in oral arguments tends to be very much greater than that spent in the United States.

---

[123] As already noted, written 'skeleton arguments' are, however, now required – see below (ed.).

[As will be seen below, the English system does now make some attempts to restrict oral argument but so far at least they have not gone far. The basic difference between the system is still very great indeed (ed.).]

Various steps have been taken to improve the efficiency of the Court of Appeal. One is to pay vastly more attention to getting the parties to prepare the bundle of documents for the court in proper form.[124] Another is to have the judges pre-read so that when the oral argument commences the judges will be able to focus on the important issues.

Skeleton arguments

The beginnings of the skeleton argument were in a Practice Note issued in 1983 by Lord Donaldson, the then Master of the Rolls.[125] The Practice Note said that the points which counsel intended to argue should be set out in not more than one or two sentences together with full references to be used in support of each point. The skeleton should also contain anything that would otherwise have to be dictated to the bench such as propositions of law, chronologies of events, lists of *dramatis personae* or, where necessary, glossaries of terms. No one would be held to the contents of such a document. The document should, however, be sent to the court (and the other side) well before the hearing or, at the latest, when counsel rose.[126]

A somewhat similar development had already taken place in the House of Lords. In 1982 in *MV Yorke Motors v. Edwards*[127] Lord Diplock set out what the House of Lords would in future require by way of written documents in a case. Previously the case presented by the parties would contain a summary of the facts, the proceedings in the courts below, the judgments and the arguments on appeal. Now, Lord Diplock said, the case should start 'with a statement of what the party conceives to be the issues that arise on the appeal'.[128] Counsel should bear in mind that the members of the appellate committee would have read the judgments below. Each issue should be mentioned in a sentence or two. If there were points that it was not intended to pursue, this should be stated; conversely, if it was intended to take a point that was not argued below, the case should mention the fact. If there was an intention to ask the House of Lords not to follow one of its own previous decisions, this should be made clear. Heads of argument should be prepared setting out the chief authorities to be relied on. Lord Diplock said that it was not intended to move towards the American written brief. Counsel for one side had put in a document of thirty-nine pages, which was far too long. Counsel for the other side had put in one a sixth of that length, which was perfectly adequate.

What started as an experiment with a voluntary system became mandatory in 1989. The rule is now stated in the Practice Direction accompanying CPR,

---

[124] See Practice Direction 39 PD 3, para. 3.2.   [125] [1983] 2 All ER 34.
[126] For a powerful critique of the innovation of skeleton arguments see F. A. Mann, 'Reflections on English Civil Justice and the Rule of Law', 2 *Civil Justice Quarterly*, 1983, p. 320.
[127] [1982] 1 All ER 1024.   [128] At 1025.

r. 52.4. The post-CPR *White Book* states that paras. 5.10 and 5.11 of the Practice Direction 'replace voluminous earlier practice directions concerning skeleton arguments'. They should be succinct: 'The practice of drafting diffuse skeleton arguments (which some advocates favoured under the former regime) is not appropriate'.[129]

Since 1999 the rule has been that the skeleton argument must be presented with the application for permission to appeal, failing which within fourteen days thereafter. Lists of authorities (with the relevant passages marked up) are supposed to be handed in not less than seven days before the hearing.[130]

The new approach was criticised by David Pannick QC. He argued that it would be wasteful for counsel to prepare a skeleton argument many months before the hearing of the appeal. A skeleton prepared so long in advance would lack quality and focus. Also, the lawyers would have to prepare the case twice – once to draft the skeleton argument and again for the actual appeal hearing.[131] Lord Woolf, replying, said early presentation of the skeleton was vital if the court was to be able to take the necessary case management decisions.[132]

Restrictions on oral argument?

One of the features of American appellate practice, as has been seen, is drastic restriction of oral argument. This has not yet come to the English system. Despite the new emphasis on case management by the courts, counsel are still permitted to argue their case at length – indeed generally at the length that *they* think appropriate.

In 1991 an American scholar, Professor Robert Martineau, spent three months in the Court of Appeal Civil Division to study the English oral tradition. He started with the hypothesis that the American system could probably learn much from the English. He ended with the opposite conclusion. Moreover, surprisingly, he was not overly impressed with the quality of the oral advocacy he observed. ('Most English barristers are not effective appellate advocates'.) The situation in England seemed to him to be pretty much the same as in the USA. In both countries, he thought, 15 per cent of appellate advocates were highly competent, 30–40 per cent were competent and 50–60 per cent were incompetent.[133]

---

[129] *Civil Procedure*, 2003, 52.4.3.

[130] Note *Haggis v. DPP* [2003] EWHC 2481 (Admin), [2004] 2 All ER 382. Lord Justice Brooke set out the rules and added: 'It is now high time that practice in this respect is tightened up so that unnecessary time is not wasted either by the parties waiting for the other side to file skeleton arguments in accordance with the rules, or by the court in being bombarded at a very late stage, sometimes after it has already done its pre-reading, with the late arrival of skeleton arguments and important authorities' ([34]).

[131] *The Times*, 26 January 1999.   [132] *The Times*, 2 February 1999.

[133] W. Hein, *Appellate Justice in England and the United States*, 1991; and see an article based on the book by the present writer – 'A Brief Encounter', 141 *New Law Journal*, 12 April 1991, p. 491.

The chief step taken so far towards limited oral argument in the Court of Appeal has been a rule that counsel is required to give an estimate of time for the case. There are no penalties as yet for overrunning. Martineau, whose research was pre-Woolf reform, found that even judges who pre-read the papers generally left counsel to develop his oral argument in his own way and at his own length, out of belief in the virtues of the oral tradition. This was confirmed in a paper by Lord Justice Leggatt written for the Anglo-American judicial exchange in 1994.[134] He acknowledged that skeleton arguments help by telling the judges what appeals are about before they start but 'it sometimes effects little perceptible saving of time because counsel are suffered to repeat orally what they have already rendered in writing'. That some presiding judges allowed that to happen was 'another example of the oral tradition dying hard'. He suggested that the court was in that respect falling between two stools because skeleton arguments (which were sometimes of inordinate length) were required, yet oral argument essentially was open-ended. The Practice Direction required counsel to open his appeal by going directly to the ground of appeal in the forefront of the appellant's case but this enjoinder was not always obeyed.

Lord Justice Leggatt said that 'immoderate periods of time are spent in informing the courts about the facts and the law, as distinct from presenting the reasons why they support the cause of the one side or the other'. In 1954 there had been eight Lord Justices, in 1974 sixteen and in 1994 there were twenty-nine. (In 2006 there were thirty-seven.) Yet the delays increased. The average time taken from setting down to judgment had risen to an average of 8.4 months from an average between 1985 and 1994 of 7.3 months. It was clear, he suggested, that the only alternative to increasing the number of judges was to reduce the time taken to resolve appeals. 'That can only be done by reversing the traditional practice of allowing counsel to state how long they want and substituting a system whereby the court stipulates the length of time for which counsel shall be permitted to address the court'.

In 1986 the Commercial Court introduced a table of the periods for which particular kinds of oral application would be allowed to last, unless counsel had previously obtained permission to take more time.[135] This, Lord Justice Leggatt said, worked well and more time was only rarely sought. It was the experience of commercial judges that 'competent counsel can on demand tailor their submissions to take no longer than a stipulated period of time, however short':

> Not only can counsel adapt to the time available, but unless the curtailment is too drastic, the quality of the argument will almost always be improved. Increase in the intensity of oral argument may reasonably be expected to increase its quality. The best counsel are invariably concise; lesser counsel would usually be

---

[134] 'The Future of the Oral Tradition in the Court of Appeal', 14 *Civil Justice Quarterly* ,1995, p. 11.

[135] *Admiralty and Commercial Courts Guide*, F10. *Civil Procedure*, 2006, vol. 2, 2A-93.

better if they were so. That they are not concise is mainly due to lack of the discipline that limitations of time impose.[136]

Lord Justice Leggatt said that, although he had no statistics on the matter, it was comparatively uncommon for members of the court to change their minds about whether to allow or dismiss an appeal once they had read the skeleton arguments. There was no reason to suppose that the judges would change their minds less often if speeches were shorter.

In ordinary cases the appellant's solicitors must lodge an estimate of time needed for the hearing, signed by counsel. A copy must be sent to the respondent who then has the opportunity of disagreeing the time estimate. Failure to do so is taken as acceptance of the proposed time limit. Any revised time estimate must be lodged with the court, signed by the advocate concerned.

Since 1991 the House of Lords too has required that counsel should notify the Judicial Office how many hours were needed for argument and broadly expects them to keep within that estimate.[137]

The Bowman Committee said in its 1997 report that although it did not favour the drastic American approach to time limits for oral argument, it did think that 'there is a greater need to impose appropriate time limits for individual appeals'.[138] But it did not wish 'to see counsel being prevented from making relevant submissions because they are abruptly cut off in mid-sentence'.[139]

3. Appeal decisions

The grounds of appeal

An appeal can be brought on a variety of grounds. In a civil case it can be on fact or law, on the amount of damages, on the wrong exercise by the trial court of a discretion or an allegation that the court exceeded its jurisdiction.

In a criminal case the appeal can be against conviction or sentence. If the appeal is against conviction, it can be either on the facts (that the court or the jury reached the wrong result), on a point of law, on a question of mixed fact and law or on any other ground which appears sufficient (Criminal Appeal Act 1968, s. 1(2)(b)).

Mistakes of counsel Incompetent representation by counsel at the trial is not in itself a ground of appeal[140] though if the advocate was flagrantly incompe-

---

[136] Note 134 above at p. 15.
[137] *Procedure Direction* [1991] 3 All ER 608. See also the Patent Court *Practice Direction* [1998] 3 All ER 372 which required the parties to give estimates of time needed for the trial and for the judge to read the papers before the hearing. Parties were reminded of 'the court's power to impose guillotines on the duration of submissions and cross-examination'. This power, the Practice Direction warned, 'will be exercised in any case where it is of the view that a case is not being conducted with reasonable expedition' (para. 21).   [138] Bowman, p. 88.
[139] *Ibid*, p. 99.   [140] *Gautam* [1988] Crim LR 109; *Day* [2003] EWCA Crim 1060.

tent it used to be said that that might be a ground of appeal.[141] However, in 1993 in *Clinton*[142] the Court of Appeal took a different approach. It held that the test was whether the conviction was safe. If counsel's conduct rendered the verdict unsafe (or unsatisfactory)[143] the court would not seek to assess the qualitative value of counsel's alleged incompetence but would seek to assess its effect on the trial and the verdict.[144]

The Runciman Royal Commission (1993) recommended that the Court of Appeal's attitude to errors by counsel be based (as suggested in *Clinton*) by its effect rather than on the degree of incompetence. ('It cannot possibly be right that there should be defendants serving prison sentences for no other reason than that their lawyers made a decision which later turns out to have been mistaken. What matters is not the degree to which the lawyers were at fault but whether the particular decision, whether reasonable or unreasonable, caused a miscarriage of justice'.[145])

This now represents the Court of Appeal's basic approach,[146] though mention of 'flagrant incompetence' still occur.[147]

The approach adopted by the Strasbourg Court is based on the question – was the defendant deprived of his right to a fair trial?[148] In *Thakrar*[149] the Court of Appeal said: 'The test is whether in all the circumstances, the conviction is safe. Nonetheless, if such failures have prevented an appellant from having a fair trial, within the meaning of Article 6 of the European Convention on Human Rights, that will normally mean that the conviction is unsafe and should be quashed'.

Only one appeal

In *Pinfold*[150] it was held that an appellant only has a right to appeal once. The court had no jurisdiction to hear a second appeal, even on the grounds of fresh evidence. The only recourse for the defendant then was to ask the Home Secretary to refer the case back to the Court of Appeal under his powers under s. 17 of the Criminal Appeal Act and is now to try to get the Criminal Cases Review Commission (CCRC) (see pp. 725–29 below) to do so.

---

[141] *Ensor* [1989] 1 WLR 497; *Crabtree, Foley, McCann* [1992] Crim LR 65.

[142] [1993] 2 All ER 998.

[143] As will be seen below, the statutory formula 'unsafe or unsatisfactory' was changed to 'unsafe'.

[144] Followed in *Boal* [1992] 3 All ER 177; *Irwin* [1987] 2 All ER 1085; *Ahluwalia* [1992] 4 All ER 889.   [145] Runciman, p. 174, para. 59.

[146] See for instance *Thakrar* [2001] EWCA Crim 1096; *Harrison* [2002] EWCA Crim 2309; *Day* [2003] EWCA Crim 1060.

[147] *Boodram* [2001] UKPC 20, [2002] 1 Cr App Rep 103. The Judicial Committee quashed a conviction on account of counsel's 'multiple failures' – 'the worst case of the failure of counsel to carry out his duties in a criminal case that their Lordships have come across' (at [39]). The barrister who appeared at the retrial had for instance not been aware that it was a retrial and when he became aware he did not inquire as to what had happened at the first trial. There was no need to embark on an inquiry as to the impact of the failures. The defendant had not had a fair trial.   [148] See the commentary on *Nangle* [2002] Crim LR 506 at 507.

[149] [2001] EWCA Crim 1096, para. 35.   [150] [1988] 2 All ER 217.

It has been held that when the CCRC refers a case back to the Court of Appeal, the court is not bound by the decision in *Pinfold* and in exceptional circumstances it can therefore reconsider an issue that it has previously determined.[151]

Powers of the Court of Appeal

Court of Appeal Civil Division

The Court of Appeal can make any order which could have been made in the court below and substitute its own decision as to liability, *quantum* of damages or costs. It is not limited to points raised in the notice of appeal. It can, though it rarely does, take further points itself, for instance, as to the illegality of a contract.

The court can order a retrial. However, where the court was considering an award of damages by a jury, it had no power to substitute its own award for that of the jury unless the parties consented (which generally they did). Absent such consent, it had to order a retrial. The Courts and Legal Services Act 1990, s. 8 gave a power for rules to be made to permit the court to change the amount of damages.[152] Usually, the Court of Appeal intervenes to reduce damages but it can increase them.[153]

Court of Appeal Criminal Division

The Court of Appeal Criminal Division can quash a conviction or reduce a sentence. Since 1966 it has not had the power to increase sentences, though, curiously, this power is still exercisable by the Crown Court when it hears appeals from the magistrates' courts. The Court of Appeal also has a right to order a retrial.

The grounds for allowing appeals

Civil cases

Pre-CPR

Under the former system there was no rule in either statute or the rules of court as to the grounds for allowing an appeal. The Rules of the Supreme Court simply said that the Court of Appeal 'shall have power to draw inferences of fact and to give any judgment and make any order which ought to have been given or made, and to make such further or other order as the case may require'.[154] Case law and commentaries, such as the *White Book* for the High Court and the equivalent *Green Book* for the county court, established the principles on which the courts acted.

---

[151] *Thomas* [2002] EWCA Crim 941, [2002] Crim LR 912; *Wallace Duncan Smith (No 3)* [2002] EWCA Crim 2907, [2003] 1 Cr App Rep 648; *Mills (No 2), Poole (No 2)* (2003) Times, 26 June.

[152] See RSC (Amendment No 3) 1990, SI 1990/2599, reg. 13, amending CPR Sch. 1, RSC Order 59, r. 11.

[153] For a rare example see *Clark v. Chief Constable of Cleveland Constabulary* (1999) 21 *LS Gaz* 38 when the court increased an award of damages for malicious prosecution from £500 to £2,000.   [154] RSC Order 59, r. 10(3).

The rules on the hearing of appeals now provide that the appeal court will allow an appeal 'where the decision of the lower court was (a) wrong; or (b) unjust because of a serious procedural or other irregularity in the proceedings in the lower court' (CPR 52.11(3)). These rules apply not just to the Court of Appeal; they apply to all civil courts exercising appellate functions.

The editors of the *White Book* suggest that 'wrong' presumably means that the court below erred in law, erred in fact or erred in the exercise of its discretion.

As regards errors of fact, the Court of Appeal has always been chary of taking a different view of the facts from that taken by the trial court, especially where the findings of fact were based on testimony given by witnesses. When the decision was that of a jury the reluctance was even greater. The position was described by the House of Lords in a case in 1927.

SS Hontestroom (Owners) v. SS Sagaporack (Owners) [1927] AC 37, HL

[In actions arising out of a collision between two ships the trial judge found that the *Sagaporack* was wholly to blame. His decision was reversed by the Court of Appeal which found the other ship was wholly to blame.

On appeal to the House of Lords, Lord Sumner, giving the judgment for the majority, said:]

The learned President, after seeing both pilots, accepted the story of the *Hontestroom.* Though he does not expressly say so, it is evident that he regarded the *Hontestroom*'s pilot as an honest and a credible witness and, conversely, that he did not accept the story of the pilot of the *Sagaporack,* not thinking that his memory could be trusted . . .

What then is the real effect on the hearing in a Court of Appeal of the fact that the trial judge saw and heard the witnesses? I think it has been somewhat lost sight of. Of course, there is jurisdiction to retry the case on the shorthand note, including in such retrial the appreciation of the relative values of the witnesses, for the appeal is made a rehearing by rules which have the force of statute: Order 68, r. 1. It is not, however, a mere matter of discretion to remember and take account of this fact; it is a matter of justice and of judicial obligation. None the less, not to have seen the witnesses puts appellate judges in a permanent position of disadvantage as against the trial judge, and, unless it can be shown that he has failed to use or has palpably misused his advantage, the higher court ought not to take the responsibility of reversing conclusions so arrived at, merely on the result of their own comparisons and criticisms of the witnesses and of their own view of the probabilities of the case. The course of the trial and the whole substance of the judgment must be looked at, and the matter does not depend on the question whether a witness has been cross-examined to credit or has been pronounced by the judge in terms to be unworthy of it. If his estimate of the man forms any substantial part of his reasons for his judgment the trial judge's conclusion of fact should, as I understand the decisions, be let alone. In *The Julia* (1860) 14 Moo PC 210 at 235 Lord Kingsdown says: 'they, who require this Board, under such circumstances, to reverse a decision of the court below upon a point of this description, undertake a task of great and almost insuperable difficulty . . . We must, in order to reverse, not merely entertain doubts whether the decision below is right, but be convinced that it is wrong'. . ..

My Lords, for these reasons I do not propose to retry this case, nor do I think that the Court of Appeal should have done so.

For rarely expressed scepticism about the value to trial courts of observing the demeanour of the witnesses, see, however, a lecture given by Sir Thomas Bingham (as he then was) given at an early stage of his illustrious judicial career – 'The Judge as Juror', *Current Legal Problems*, 1985, p. 1 at 6–13.

Sometimes, the court would reverse a judge's finding of fact on the ground that it was plainly wrong[155] and, very exceptionally, the Court of Appeal was prepared to reverse even a jury's decision if it found it to be perverse. An example was *Grobbelaar v. News Group Newspapers Ltd.*[156] The Court of Appeal set aside a jury's award of £85,000 libel damages awarded to Bruce Grobbelaar, the famous goalkeeper. He sued the *Sun* newspaper which, in a series of sensational articles published over seven days, had accused him of taking bribes to fix games. The Court of Appeal said it had a duty to intervene where the verdict was so plainly wrong that no jury acting reasonably could have reached such a decision on a balance of probabilities. Having regard to the evidence, Grobbelaar's story was simply incredible and he should not be permitted to retain an unmerited award of damages.[157] On appeal, the House of Lords reversed the Court of Appeal's decision on the ground that although the Court of Appeal could and should quash a perverse jury decision, it did not agree that the jury's decision was perverse. (Any satisfaction Mr Grobbelaar might have taken in the Law Lords' decision will have been considerably diminished by their decision to reduce his award of damages to a nominal £1 and to order that he pay two-thirds of the *Sun* newspaper's costs.[158])

The position was somewhat different when the appeal court was asked to review the drawing of inferences from facts by the trial judge. In such cases the appeal court regarded itself as permitted to draw different inferences even though it had not seen the witnesses (*Benmax v. Austin Motor Co Ltd*[159]), but in *Biogen Inc v. Medeva Plc*[160] Lord Hoffmann warned against treating *Benmax* as authorising an appellate court to undertake a fresh evaluation of the evidence where there was no question of the credibility of witnesses. The need for judicial caution in reversing the judge's evaluation of the fact was based on much more than professional courtesy:

---

[155] See for instance *The Ikarian Reefer* [1995] Lloyd's Rep 455 reversing the finding that insured shipowners had not intentionally scuttled their vessel.

[156] [2001] EWCA Civ 33, [2001] 2 All ER 437.

[157] For critical commentary on the decision see P. Robertshaw, 'The Review Roles of the Court of Appeal: *Grobbelaar v. News International*', 64 *Modern Law Review*, 2001, pp. 923–32.

[158] [2002] UKHL 40, [2002] 4 All ER 732. The Law Lords said that although the jury must have accepted that G had corruptly accepted bribes, it must also have found that he did not in fact 'throw' matches. To that extent, on the evidence, the jury's decision was not perverse, but the Law Lords held that it would be an affront to justice if a court of law were to award substantial damages to a man shown to have acted in such flagrant breach of his legal and moral obligations. [159] [1955] AC 370 or *Whitehouse v. Jordan* [1981] 1 All ER 267.

[160] [1997] RPC 1 at 45.

It is because specific findings of fact, even by the most meticulous judge, are inherently an incomplete statement of the impression which was made upon him by the primary evidence. The expressed findings are always surrounded by a penumbra of imprecision as to emphasis, relative weight, minor qualification and nuance . . . of which time and language do not permit exact expression but which play an important part in the judge's overall evaluation.

An appellate court, Lord Hoffmann said, should be very cautious in differing from the judge's evaluation.

The Court of Appeal's attitude to altering awards of damages was similar. It was more reluctant to interfere with an award by a jury than a judge though it would alter an award even of a jury if it thought it to be wholly wrong,[161] but the court would uphold an award of damages even if it thought it was considerably more than it would itself have awarded.[162]

With regard to review of discretionary decisions, the classic rule was that the appeal court would not interfere, even if it disagreed with the decision, unless it could be shown that the judge below had erred in law or had acted on wrong principles – such as taking into account irrelevant matters, acting under a misapprehension of fact or failing to exercise the discretion.[163]

Post-CPR

The position since the introduction of the CPR is much the same. In *Designers Guild Ltd v. Russell Williams (Textiles) Ltd*[164] the House of Lords held that the Court of Appeal had been wrong to substitute its own assessment of the evidence for that made by the trial judge. The question at issue was whether there had been infringement of copyright. Lord Bingham said that the Court of Appeal had approached this issue 'more in the manner of a first instance court making original findings of fact than as an appellate court reviewing findings already made . . . It was not for the Court of Appeal to embark on the issue of substantiality afresh, unless the judge had misdirected himself, which in my opinion he had not'.[165] Lord Hoffmann said that although the issue had not involved assessment of the credibility of witnesses, nevertheless the trial court had had the benefit of expert testimony. The court's decision involved the application of a not altogether precise legal standard to a combination of features of varying importance. The case fell into a class of case in which an

---

[161] For examples see *Lewis v. Daily Telegraph Ltd* [1964] AC 234 (damages manifestly too high) or *English and Scottish Co-op Properties Mortgage and Investment Society Ltd v. Odhams Press Ltd* [1940] 1 KB 440 (damages manifestly too low).

[162] In *Blackshaw v. Lord* [1983] 2 All ER 311 the court refused to interfere with libel damages of £45,000 awarded by a jury even though all three judges thought it was far too high.

[163] See for instance *Culver v. Beard* [1937] 1 All ER 301 (court refused to change allocation of case from county court to High Court); *Stevens v. Walker* [1936] 2 KB 215 (court interfered because the judge had not considered matters he should have taken into account); *Eagil Trust Co Ltd v. Pigott-Brown* [1985] 3 All ER 119 (dismissal for want of prosecution – court's role is to review the exercise of discretion, not to substitute its own decision).

[164] [2001] 1 All ER 700.   [165] At 702.

appellate court should not reverse a judge's decision unless he has erred in principle.

In *Assicurazioni Generali SpA v. Arab Insurance Group (BSC)*[166] Lord Justice Ward said that two factors led appellate judges to be cautious about interfering:

> First, the appellate court recognises that judging the witness is a more complex task than merely judging the transcript. Each may have its intellectual component but the former can also crucially rely on intuition. That gives the trial judge the advantage over us in assessing the witness's demeanour, so often a vital factor in deciding where the truth lies. Secondly, judging is an art not a science. So the more complex the question, the more likely it is that different judges will come to different conclusions and the harder it is to determine right from wrong. Borrowing language from other jurisprudence, the trial judge is entitled to 'a margin of appreciation' (at [196]).

This is familiar language which could equally have come from the pre-CPR era.

As to what constitutes sufficient error in the exercise of discretion to justify interference by the appeal court, in *Tanfern Ltd* (n. 16 above) Lord Justice Brooke referred to Lord Fraser's speech in *G v. G (Minors: Custody Appeals)*:[167]

> The appellate court should only interfere when they consider that the judge of first instance has not merely preferred an imperfect solution which is different from an alternative imperfect solution which the Court of Appeal might or would have adopted, but has exceeded the generous ambit within which a reasonable disagreement is possible.[168]

Again, that represents business as usual.

Criminal cases

The conditions for the court to allow an appeal were first laid down in s. 4 of the Criminal Appeal Act 1907. (As will be seen, this was replaced by s. 2 of the Criminal Appeal Act 1966, which became s. 2 of the Criminal Appeal Act 1968, which in its turn was replaced by s. 2 of the Criminal Appeal Act 1995.)

Criminal Appeal Act 1907

4.–(1) The Court of Criminal Appeal on any such appeal against conviction shall allow the appeal if they think that the verdict of the jury should be set aside on the ground that it is unreasonable or cannot be supported having regard to the evidence, or that the judgment of the court before whom the appellant was convicted should be set aside on the ground of a wrong decision of any question of law or that on any ground there was a miscarriage of justice, and in any other case shall dismiss the appeal:

Provided that the court may, notwithstanding that they are of opinion that the point raised in the appeal might be decided in favour of the appellant, dismiss the appeal if they consider that no substantial miscarriage of justice has actually occurred.

---

[166] [2002] EWCA Civ 1642.   [167] [1985] 1 WLR 647.   [168] At 652.

The Court of Appeal's attitude to jury verdicts in criminal cases was, if anything, even more deferential than that it adopted in civil cases. The case that follows was typical:

R v. Hopkins-Husson (1949) 34 Cr App Rep 47, CA

[Lord Chief Justice Goddard, giving the judgment of the court, said:]

With regard to the other six cases, the jury found a verdict of not guilty in five of them, and in the case of one boy, a boy called Allan Simpson, they found the appellant guilty. It is fair and right to say that the learned judge said in terms that he was surprised at the verdict, and he himself would obviously have preferred a verdict of acquittal; but it is also right to say that from a very early period in the history of this court it has been laid down, and has been laid down frequently since, that the fact that the trial judge was dissatisfied with the verdict, although it is a matter to be taken into account in this court, must not be taken as a ground by itself for quashing the conviction. If it were, it would mean that we should be substituting the opinion of the judge for the opinion of the jury, and that is one of the things which this court will never do.

In just the same way it has been held from an equally early period in the history of this court that the fact that some members or all the members of the court think that they themselves would have returned a different verdict is again no ground for refusing to accept the verdict of the jury, which is the constitutional method of trial in this country. If there is evidence to go to the jury, and there has been no misdirection, and it cannot be said that the verdict is one which a reasonable jury could not arrive at, this court will not set aside the verdict of guilty which has been found by the jury.

A commentator in 1966, describing the attitude of the court to its powers, wrote:

The broad picture that emerged was a court concerned in appeals against conviction, with the judge's direction, evidence and procedure and the occasional point of substantive law rather than the 'merits' of the case. An appellant who could point to a clear misdirection, the wrongful admission or exclusion of evidence or some procedural irregularity, had better prospects of success than the appellant who simply claimed that he was innocent and that the jury had come to the wrong decision.[169]

A JUSTICE Committee in 1964 thought 'it seems absurd and unjust that verdicts which experienced judges would have thought surprising and not supported by really adequate evidence, should be allowed to stand for no other reason than that they were arrived at by a jury'.[170] In 1965 the Donovan Committee took a similar view:

Under the terms of s. 4(1), if it is strictly construed, there is, in the case of an innocent person who has been wrongly identified and in consequence wrongly

---

[169] M. Dean, 'Criminal Appeal Act 1966', *Criminal Law Review*, 1966, pp. 535 and 539.
[170] JUSTICE, *Criminal Appeals*, 1964, para. 59.

convicted, virtually no protection conferred by his right to appeal . . . provided that the evidence of identification was, on the face of it, credible. We think that this defect should be remedied.[171]

It recommended the adoption of a broader formula (one originally proposed in 1907 by F.E. Smith, the later Lord Birkenhead, Lord Chancellor, during the debates on the Criminal Appeal Bill), that the court should quash a conviction where the verdict in the opinion of the court was 'under all the circumstances of the case unsafe or unsatisfactory'. This was duly achieved in the Criminal Appeal Act 1966, which was then incorporated into the 1968 Act and became s. 2(1)(a) of that Act.

Criminal Appeal Act 1968

2.–(1) Except as provided by this Act, the Court of Appeal shall allow an appeal against conviction if they think:

(a) that the verdict of the jury should be set aside on the ground that under all the circumstances of the case it is unsafe or unsatisfactory; or
(b) that the judgment of the court of trial should be set aside on the ground of a wrong decision of any question of law; or
(c) that there was a material irregularity in the course of the trial, and in any other case shall dismiss the appeal:

Provided that the court may, notwithstanding that they are of opinion that the point raised in the appeal might be decided in favour of the appellant, dismiss the appeal if they consider that no miscarriage of justice has actually occurred.

In the case of an appeal against conviction the court shall, if they allow the appeal, quash the conviction.

In the final appeal of the Birmingham Six the prosecution argued that the two words 'unsafe' and 'unsatisfactory' in s. 2(1)(a) had separate meanings and that therefore convictions could be unsatisfactory but not unsafe. The Court of Appeal rejected this view. The two words, it said, were indistinguishable. (As will be seen, this re-emerged as a question in interpretation of the 1995 Act – see pp. 701–04 below.)

Cooper and the 'lurking doubt' test

In 1969 the Court of Appeal Criminal Division decided the *Cooper* case, in which it pronounced a philosophy with regard to the way in which the court should approach jury verdicts that was very different from the approach shown in the *Hopkins-Husson* decision.

R v. Cooper [1969] 1 QB 267, CA

[The defendant was convicted of assault occasioning actual bodily harm after an incident in which a twenty-two year old girl was attacked by one of a group of

---

[171] *Report of the Interdepartmental Committee on the Court of Criminal Appeal*, 1965, Cmnd. 2755, p. 33, para. 145.

three drunken youths. At an identification parade six weeks after the offence she picked out the defendant. In his own words: 'She never looked at anyone else' and according to the court she clearly had no doubt at all. The question for the court was whether the conviction was unsafe by reason of the evidence at the trial that B had told D that he rather than the defendant had committed the attack. There was close physical similarity between the defendant and B. Nevertheless the jury convicted.

Lord Justice Widgery, giving the judgment of the court, said:]

It has been said over and over again throughout the years that this court must recognise the advantage which a jury has in seeing and hearing the witness, and if all the material was before the jury and the summing-up was impeccable, this court should not lightly interfere. Indeed, until the passing of the Criminal Appeal Act 1966, provisions which are now to be found in s. 2 of the Criminal Appeal Act 1968, it was almost unheard of for this court to interfere in such a case.

However, now our powers are somewhat different, and we are indeed charged to allow an appeal against conviction if we think that the verdict of the jury should be set aside on the ground that under all the circumstances of the case it is unsafe or unsatisfactory. That means that in cases of this kind the court must in the end ask itself a subjective question, whether we are content to let the matter stand as it is, or whether there is not some lurking doubt in our minds which makes us wonder whether an injustice has been done. This is a reaction which may not be based strictly on the evidence as such; it is a reaction which can be produced by the general feel of the case as the court experiences it.

The court said that after due consideration it had decided that the conviction should be quashed as unsafe.

If the very broad 'lurking doubt' test as formulated in *Cooper* reflected the Court of Appeal's normal attitude, a high proportion of appellants against conviction might stand a reasonable chance of getting their convictions overturned. In fact, however, the Court of Appeal was not easily persuaded to adopt the 'lurking doubt' test. One expert stated in 1983: 'the "lurking doubt" test, enunciated by Lord Widgery when he was first appointed, has been quietly buried'.[172] Research carried out for JUSTICE almost twenty years after the decision stated that only six reported cases had been found where the court had quashed a conviction on the grounds that there was a lurking doubt about the conviction and there was nothing new to throw doubt on it.

An important insight into the Court of Appeal's marked reluctance to use the 'lurking doubt' test was supplied by former Lord Justice Lawton, a vastly experienced criminal appeal judge, in his evidence to the Runciman Royal Commission:

Until the decision of the Court of Appeal in *R v. Cooper* it had been assumed that

[172] T. Sargant, *More Law Reform Now* (Barry Rose, 1983) p. 91. Sargant was the Director of JUSTICE.

a conviction should not be quashed unless there was some reason in law for doing so. In that case however it was adjudged that the court could apply a subjective test had it a lurking doubt or reasoned unease which made it wonder whether an injustice had been done. In simpler terms this means that the court can quash a conviction if it has a hunch that there has been an injustice. This cannot be a sound way of administering criminal justice; and since 1969 the judges seem to have appreciated that it was not because only six appeals have been allowed on this ground.

In other words, the judges did not apply the 'lurking doubt' test because they did not like it. They believed that to apply it would be to usurp the function of the jury.

Report of the Runciman Royal Commission

The Runciman Royal Commission said it had received conflicting evidence about the 'lurking doubt' test. On the one hand, there were those who pointed out that the Court of Appeal had only very rarely acknowledged that it was applying this test. On the other hand, it had been suggested to the Royal Commission that the Court of Appeal had not infrequently allowed appeals on what had in truth been the 'lurking doubt' principle, even though there had been no reference to the phrase. These were cases where there was no error at the trial nor any error in law, 'but nevertheless the combined experience of the three members of the court leads them to conclude that there may have been an injustice in the trial and in the jury's verdict'. They consequently allowed the appeal on the ground that, at the least, the jury's verdict was unsatisfactory. 'There is no real difference between this approach and an application of the "lurking doubt" principle'.[173]

The Royal Commission's conclusion on the matter was to encourage the court to use this power when it felt it right to do so:

> We fully appreciate the reluctance felt by judges sitting in the Court of Appeal about quashing a jury's verdict. The jury has seen the witnesses and heard their evidence; the Court of Appeal has not. Where, however, on reading the transcript and hearing argument the Court of Appeal has a serious doubt about the verdict, it should exercise its power to quash. We do not think that quashing the jury's verdict where the court believes it to be unsafe undermines the system of jury trial. We therefore recommend that, as part of the redrafting of s. 2, it be made clear that the Court of Appeal should quash a conviction notwithstanding that the jury reached their verdict having heard all the relevant evidence and without any error of law or material irregularity having occurred if after reviewing the case, the court concludes that the verdict is or may be unsafe.[174]

For an example of the Court of Appeal adopting this approach see *R v. Haughton*.[175] The case was referred back to the Court of Appeal by the Home

---

[173] Runciman, p. 171, para. 45.   [174] Runciman, pp. 171–2, para. 46.
[175] Unreported, Case No. 589/SI/91, 21 May 1992.

Secretary on the ground that the ESDA test appeared to show that police officers had fabricated the appellant's confession. The Court of Appeal rejected that argument, but it said that its duty was 'to review the case generally'. Having done that, it found that the verdict was unsafe and unsatisfactory even though there was nothing new that had not been before the jury.

As will be seen below, the Government accepted the Royal Commission's proposal that s. 2 be redrafted but it did not adopt the proposal in the form suggested by the Commission. The status of the 'lurking doubt' test was uncertain.

Do appeal judges have the time it takes?

A practical point made in a powerful lecture on the problem of miscarriages of justice by the distinguished Australian judge, Justice Michael Kirby, is that appeal judges do not have the time to consider the trial evidence properly. Nor, typically, do they have the time, all of them, to read the entirety of the transcript of what may have been a trial lasting many days or even weeks. 'They visit the evidence, on the invitation of counsel, skipping from one passage to another. Rarely do they capture the subtle atmosphere of the trial, for such things do not readily emerge from cold pages. These are the reasons why so much deference is paid to the advantages of the trial judge or jury, who see the evidence unfold in sequence and observe the witnesses giving their testimony.'[176]

Lord Justice Auld's report painted a picture of a court that was under enormous pressure:

> It is no secret that the judge allotted the task of giving the judgment of the court in each case will often need to prepare in advance some provisional notes of the relevant facts, issues and law as a reference for his judgment. The volume and speed of the work is such that the judges could not cope if they did not do that . . . Working at such speed gives the judges of the court little time to focus on anything but the application of the law to the particular facts before them . . . It is thus difficult for them to apply and develop the law in a principled and consistent manner . . . This is a serious shortcoming in the main judicial institution in this country responsible for declaring and developing the criminal law as well as for applying it.[177]

Quashing the jury's verdict on account of error at trial

Research by Professor Kate Malleson shows that by far the most frequent reason for the Court of Appeal to quash a conviction is because of some error at trial, usually error by the trial judge in the form of misdirection of the jury on the law

---

[176] 'Miscarriages of Justice', The Child and Co Lecture, London, 1991, p. 26. The evidence of the Lord Chancellor's Department to the Runciman Royal Commission stated that in a typical week in September 1991, the one Division of the Court of Appeal Criminal Division that was then sitting was provided with 4,800 pages of documentation. About half the Court of Appeal's time was spent on sentence appeals. Such appeals were declining while the proportion of appeals against conviction was increasing. In a normal sitting day, each Division of the court could deal with up to ten sentence cases and one or two conviction cases.   [177] Auld, Ch. 12, pp. 643–4, para. 000.

or some other defect in the summing up, or a wrong decision to allow or to exclude evidence.[178]

Under the Criminal Appeal Act 1968, errors at trial could be dealt with in three ways. One was to treat the error as inconsequential by applying 'the proviso' (see pp. 699–700 below). The second was to quash the conviction and order a retrial (see pp. 714–15 below). The third and, according to Malleson's research, by far the most common was to quash the conviction.

A majority of the Runciman Royal Commission proposed a different approach:

> (1) If the court believes that the conviction is safe despite the error, the appeal should be dismissed.
>
> (2) If the court believes the error has rendered the verdict unsafe, the appeal should be allowed and the conviction quashed.
>
> (3) If it believes the conviction may be unsafe as a result of the error, it should quash the conviction and order a retrial.[179]

Three of the Commission's members wished to add a further category for cases where there is an error at trial sufficiently serious to affect the trial materially but not sufficiently serious to make the conviction unsafe. In such a case they thought the court should order a retrial. The majority disagreed: 'The majority of us do not believe that a person who is clearly guilty should be accorded a retrial merely because there has been some error at the trial'.[180]

As will be seen, the minority's approach eventually prevailed in the judicial interpretation of the new statutory formula but in 2006 the Government signalled that it wanted the majority's view to be adopted.

Quashing the jury's verdict on account of pre-trial malpractice or procedural irregularity

Where an appeal is based on some pre-trial matter (which might be anything from fabrication of evidence to some serious irregularity in the implementation of PACE) a majority of nine out of eleven members of the Runciman Royal Commission thought the Court of Appeal should only act if it thought the matter was such as to make, or maybe make, the conviction unsafe. If there was plenty of other, untainted evidence showing the defendant to be guilty, his conviction should not be quashed even if there were some gross impropriety in the pre-trial handling of the case. The minority of two (which included the writer) thought that there could be occasions when the court should quash a conviction even though there was clear evidence of guilt.

The majority view

49. In the view of the majority, even if they believed that quashing the convictions of criminals was an appropriate way of punishing police malpractice, it would be

---

[178] In the 1990 and 1992 samples in her research for the Runciman Royal Commission, trial errors were involved in 83 per cent and 82 per cent of successful appeals. (K. Malleson, *Review of the Appeal Process*, Royal Commission on Criminal Justice, Research Report No. 17, 1993, p. 22, Table 1.2.)   [179] Auld, p. 170, para. 38.   [180] *Ibid.*

naive to suppose that this would have any practical effect on police behaviour. In any case it cannot in their view be morally right that a person who has been convicted on abundant other evidence and may be a danger to the public should walk free because of what may be a criminal offence by someone else. Such an offence should be separately prosecuted within the system. It is also essential, if confidence in the criminal justice system is to be maintained, that police officers involved in malpractice should be disciplined, and in this connection we attach great importance to the recommendations in chapter three, which should lead to more effective police disciplinary procedures. The Court of Appeal must report any cases of malpractice by police officers which come to their attention to chief officers of police. We also envisage that the more serious the malpractice the less likely it is that the court would conclude that the verdict could be safe.

50. In the view of the majority, the minority view is illogical. It would only be effective if the judge at first instance had allowed the tainted evidence to be heard by the jury. If the judge had properly excluded the evidence then the verdict would be unassailable. The minority view must logically involve the trial judge in stopping a case on the basis of tainted evidence which he or she nevertheless proposed to exclude. The majority believe this to be unacceptable precluding as it must the jury from returning a verdict on the basis of evidence which was safe, admissible, and probative. It is only the tainted evidence which is excluded by s. 78 of PACE. That section does not allow the court to stop the case if there remains admissible probative evidence to support it [p. 23].

The minority view
[The minority view was expressed in the writer's dissent:]

68. The moral foundation of the criminal justice system requires that if the prosecution has employed foul means, the defendant must go free even though he is plainly guilty. Where the integrity of the process is fatally flawed, the conviction should be quashed as an expression of the system's repugnance at the methods used by those acting for the prosecution.

69. The majority's position would I believe encourage serious wrongdoing from some police officers who might be tempted to exert force or fabricate or suppress evidence in the hope of establishing the guilt of the suspect, especially in a serious case when they believe him to be guilty. There have unfortunately been some gross examples of such conduct.

70. The position adopted by the majority also seems to me to risk undermining the principle at the heart of s. 78 of PACE which explicitly gives the court the power to exclude evidence on the ground that it renders the proceedings 'unfair'. The word 'unfair' expresses the underlying moral principle and the Court of Appeal has repeatedly used this new statutory power very broadly to express its refusal to uphold convictions based on unacceptable police practices even when it could not be said that the misconduct had any impact on the jury's verdict.

71. Section 78 would of course remain – but the majority would in effect be encouraging the Court of Appeal to undercut a part of its moral force by saying that the issue of 'unfairness' can be ignored where there is sufficient evidence to show that the defendant is actually guilty. Any judge concerned to discourage

prosecution malpractice would I believe be dismayed by the majority's position. In terms of the message sent to the police service and other prosecution agencies it could undo much of the good effect being achieved by the attitude of the judges to s. 78 of PACE.

72. But the matter goes beyond discouraging prosecution malpractice. At the heart of the criminal justice system there is a fundamental principle that the process must itself have integrity. The majority suggest that the answer to prosecution wrongdoing in the investigation of crime is to deal with the wrongdoers through prosecution or disciplinary proceedings. Even were this to happen (and often in practice it would not), the approach is not merely insufficient, it is irrelevant to the point of principle. The more serious the case, the greater the need that the system upholds the values in the name of which it claims to act. If the behaviour of the prosecution agencies has deprived a guilty verdict of its moral legitimacy the Court of Appeal must have a residual power to quash the verdict no matter how strong the evidence of guilt. The integrity of the criminal justice system is a higher objective than the conviction of any individual.[181]

Applying 'the proviso'

No one suggests that a conviction should be quashed, or even a retrial ordered, where the matter complained of by the appellant is trivial. (In the United States this is known as 'harmless error'.) Here the matter was previously dealt with by what was called 'the proviso'.

The proviso referred to here is that at the end of the Criminal Appeal Act 1968, s. 2 – p. 693 above – 'Provided that the court may, notwithstanding that they are of opinion that the point raised in the appeal might be decided in favour of the appellant, dismiss the appeal if they consider that no miscarriage of justice has actually occurred'.

The application of the proviso was explored by Michael Knight in his book on criminal appeals. In this he showed that, contrary to what was often maintained, the great majority of cases where the power of the proviso had been exercised were cases of serious error in the trial. Before substantiating this controversial assertion, he set out the test which the court had developed for the application of the proviso.

Michael Knight, *Criminal Appeals*, 1970, pp. 9–53

The test which the appellate court goes by is not the degree of error but whether there is, despite the fault, sufficient evidence and a sufficient direction for a reasonable jury inevitably to convict for, if so, there is no substantial miscarriage of justice.[182] However, if it is correct to say that the error can have had any crucial influence on a reasonable jury the conviction must be quashed, for to uphold it then would be a miscarriage of justice. The court metaphorically blots out the fault – the error in the direction, the piece of inadmissible evidence, the impact of the wrongly drafted indictment – and asks if, without it, there is a strong

---

[181] Runciman, dissent, pp. 234–5.
[182] The test was laid down in *Stirland v. DPP* [1944] AC 315 (ed.).

enough case for an inevitable conviction. And if they can answer 'yes' to this question, they show the Nelson Touch by turning a blind eye to the fault (p. 16).

Knight gave numerous examples of cases where the proviso was applied in spite of serious errors in the trial, e.g.:

- *Haddy*[183] – jury wrongly invited to infer guilt from the accused's silence.
- *Farid*[184] – jury not warned by the judge that corroboration is desirable for the evidence of accomplices.
- *Whybrow*[185] – misdirection as to intent in attempted murder.
- *Slinger*[186] – judge did not tell the jury that the onus of proof lay on the prosecution.

Knight also produced sixteen examples of cases where the proviso was applied although the jury had wrongly been informed of the defendant's previous convictions (pp. 19–21). He continued:

> Certainly in recent years the appellate court in their judgments go extremely carefully through the evidence other than the inadmissible evidence wrongly let in plus the direction, or the direction minus the offending portion plus the evidence, to show that it is fair to say that a reasonable jury would inevitably have convicted. This definite and very often scrupulous care betrays a sense of uneasiness and dislike which can be taken as further recognition of the regularity of use – in serious fault cases [of the proviso] (p. 21).
>
> The line between some of the cases where the proviso has been exercised and some where it has not is sometimes so narrow as to be almost non-existent, and the answer to this conundrum lies in the amount of evidence and the standard of the direction outside of the fault.
>
> Occasionally, use of the proviso is declined because a particular fault is of its nature so serious that, even though the appellate court would like to uphold the conviction, and, even though there probably would be sufficient evidence and direction apart from the fault to justify in their opinion an inevitable finding of guilty by a reasonable jury, their desire to have a deserved conviction must be sacrificed to the general principle of fairness in our criminal trial. This is the principle stated in *Maxwell v. DPP*.[187] It is often better that one guilty man should escape than that the general rules evolved by the dictates of justice for the conduct of criminal prosecutions should be disregarded or discredited . . .

The redrafting of s. 2

The Runciman Royal Commission The Royal Commission unanimously agreed that the Criminal Appeal Act 1968, s. 2 needed to be redrafted,[188] but the Commission was not agreed as to how it should be redrafted. The majority of eight recommended that the different grounds of appeal set out in s. 2(1)(a),

---

183 (1944) 29 Cr App Rep 182.   184 (1945) 30 Cr App Rep 168.
185 (1951) 35 Cr App Rep 141.   186 (1961) 46 Cr App Rep 244.   187 [1935] AC 309.
188 For an article detailing the drafting defects of the section see R. Buxton, 'Miscarriages of Justice and the Court of Appeal', 109 *Law Quarterly Review*, 1993, p. 66.

(b) and (c) (p. 693 above) should be replaced by a single new ground – that the conviction 'is or may be unsafe'. If the court is satisfied that the conviction *is* unsafe it should quash the conviction; if the court is satisfied that the conviction *may be* unsafe it should quash the conviction and order a retrial unless there are reasons which make a retrial impracticable or undesirable.[189] Under that scheme the proviso would be redundant.

The minority of three argued that it would be confusing to wrap up all possible grounds of appeal in the one word 'unsafe'. That word implied that there was something wrong with the jury's verdict whereas the defect might be 'some irregularities or errors of law or procedure which did not necessarily affect the jury's verdict but were so serious that the conviction should not stand'.[190] Furthermore, in the view of the minority, an umbrella formula would not give the Court of Appeal sufficient guidance. In the view of the minority the grounds of appeal should distinguish between appeals claiming that the jury reached the wrong result and those alleging material irregularities or errors of law or procedure in or before the trial.[191]

The Criminal Appeal Act 1995 The Government did not accept the Royal Commission's recommendation that the formula should distinguish between 'is unsafe' and 'may be unsafe'. The formula in the new Act is simply whether the conviction is unsafe. The Criminal Appeal Act 1995, s. 2 replaced the Criminal Appeal Act 1968, s. 2 (including the proviso) with the following new provision: 'subject to the provisions of this Act, the Court of Appeal (a) shall allow an appeal against conviction if they think that the conviction is unsafe; and (b) shall dismiss such an appeal in any other case'.

The Government therefore rejected the view of the minority but it also rejected the majority's view that the formula should include the words 'or may be unsafe'. The Home Office minister speaking in the Committee stage of the Bill said: 'The difficulty with the phrase "may be unsafe" is that it is inherently uncertain. Almost any conviction may be unsafe. The test might well result in the Court of Appeal having to allow a considerably greater number of appeals than at present, simply because it did not know for certain that the conviction was safe'.[192] Also, 'may be unsafe' had about it a suggestion of subjectivity on the part of someone other than the Court of Appeal. 'That would go far broader than current practice and far broader than the Committee would wish . . . We do not intend it to result in fewer convictions being overturned than at present. We want to consolidate the existing practice of the Court of Appeal' (*ibid*).

The late Professor Sir John Smith, addressing this issue, basically agreed with the Government's view that the words 'may be unsafe' added nothing:

> A conviction is unsafe if the court has nothing more than a lurking doubt whether the appellant is guilty – that is the court thinks that he may have been

---

[189] Runciman, p. 170, para. 38.   [190] *Ibid*, p. 169, para. 3.   [191] *Ibid*.
[192] House of Commons, Standing Committee B, 21 March 1995, col. 27.

wrongly convicted. What then is the difference between 'we think that the appellant may have been wrongly convicted?' and 'we think that it may be that he may have been wrongly convicted?' Surely there is no difference. Either the court has a lurking (or greater) doubt, or it does not. It is submitted that the Government was right to insist on the exclusion of the words, 'or may be', which could have led only to confusion, and possibly, to the court feeling obliged to give a narrow meaning to 'unsafe'.[193]

The Court of Appeal had previously quite often quashed a conviction on the ground that there was an error of law or a material irregularity even though it probably had no doubt that the defendant was guilty. If the court were to hold that a conviction was only 'unsafe' if the court had a lurking (or greater) doubt about the defendant's conviction, that would be a drastic restriction of the court's power, but the parliamentary debates make it clear that this was not the Government's intention. In moving the Second Reading of the Bill, the Home Secretary said of this section: 'in substance, it restates the existing practice of the Court of Appeal . . .'[194]

The Home Office minister rejected an amendment to retain the words 'or unsatisfactory'. The Government, he said, agreed with the majority of the Royal Commission that there was no real difference between 'unsafe' and 'unsatisfactory'. It had been argued by some that 'unsafe' referred to evidential flaws whilst 'unsatisfactory' connoted procedural flaws, but in the Government's view 'the word "unsafe" is sufficient to deal with convictions which are unacceptable because of flaws in the manner in which a case is prosecuted or tried, and because of evidence which undermines the prosecution case. If a procedural flaw is sufficiently serious to cast doubt on the safety of a conviction, the court will allow the appeal'.[195]

Speaking in the Second Reading debate in the House of Lords, the Lord Chief Justice, Lord Taylor, said the new formula – whether the conviction is unsafe – 'will in my view be concise, just and comprehensible to the ordinary citizen without narrowing the present grounds of appeal'.[196]

On the redrafting of s. 2 see D. Schiff and R. Nobles, 'Criminal Appeal Act 1995: the Semantics of Jurisdiction', 58 *Modern Law Review*, 1996, pp. 299–320. See also A. Clarke, 'Safety or Supervision', *Criminal Law Review*, 1999, p. 108; V. Tunkel, 'When Safe Convictions are Unsafely Quashed', 149 *New Law Journal*, 1999, p. 1089; L.H. Leigh, 'Lurking Doubt and the Safety of Convictions', *Criminal Law Review*, 2006, pp. 809–16.

At first it seemed that, despite what had been said in Parliament, changing 'unsafe or unsatisfactory' to the simple 'unsafe' had resulted in a significant narrowing of the Court of Appeal's power to quash a conviction where something has gone wrong either at the trial or pre-trial but there is enough evidence to

---

[193] *Criminal Law Review*, 1995, p. 922.
[194] House of Commons, *Hansard*, 6 March 1995, col. 24.   [195] *Ibid*, col. 27.
[196] House of Lords, *Hansard*, 15 May 1995, col. 311.

show that the defendant was correctly found guilty. In *R v. Chalkley and R v. Jeffries*[197] the police arrested C in connection with credit card frauds as a pretext in order to be able to place a listening device in his home in connection with conspiracies to commit robberies. The defendants changed their plea to guilty after the judge ruled that the evidence of the tape recorded conversations was admissible. The Court of Appeal held that the court had no power to allow an appeal 'if it does not think the conviction unsafe but is dissatisfied in some way with what went on at the trial'.[198] (The decision in *Chalkley* was applied by the Court of Appeal in several later cases – *Kennedy*,[199] *Hewitson and Bramwich*,[200] *Rajcoomar*[201] and *Thomas*.[202])

However, in *Mullen*[203] the Court of Appeal took a completely different approach. The appellant had been brought unlawfully to this country by collusion between the British and the Zimbabwean authorities. He was deported without regard to normal extradition procedures. He was convicted here of terrorist offences and was sentenced to thirty years' imprisonment. Some years later he was given leave to appeal out of time on the ground that the whole trial was vitiated by the illegality of his deportation. The Court of Appeal held that, despite the gravity of the charges, the conduct of the British authorities was so shameful that it was an affront to the public conscience to allow the conviction to stand. There had been a blatant and extremely serious failure to adhere to the rule of law. All the relevant circumstances had to be weighed. Here they came down decisively against the prosecution. In light of conflicting views expressed in the cases, the meaning of the word 'unsafe' in the Criminal Appeal Act as amended in 1995 was sufficiently ambiguous to permit recourse to *Hansard* from which it was apparent that the new form of s. 2 was intended to restate the previous practice of the Court of Appeal which had allowed abuse of process as a ground for quashing a conviction. Furthermore, for a conviction to be safe, it had to be lawful. If it resulted from a trial that should never have taken place, it could hardly be regarded as safe. In his commentary in the *Criminal Law Review*, Professor Sir John Smith wrote: 'We seem now to be close to achieving the result intended by Parliament – i.e. no change'.[204]

Cases following *Mullen* in which convictions were quashed despite there being little doubt as to the factual guilt of the accused include *Togher*,[205] *Davis, Johnson and Rowe*[206] and *Sargent*.[207] By 2003 it seemed that the Court of Appeal had rejected the approach in *Chalkley*.

---

[197] [1998] 2 Cr App Rep 79, [1998] 2 All ER 155.   [198] At 172.

[199] [1999] 1 Cr App Rep 54.   [200] [1999] Crim LR 307.   [201] [1999] Crim LR 728.

[202] [2000] 1 Cr App Rep 447.   [203] [2000] QB 520, [1999] Crim LR 561.

[204] Note 203 above at pp. 562–3.

[205] [2001] Cr App Rep 457, [2001] 3 All ER 463. For commentary see especially R. Nobles and D. Schiff, 'Due Process and Dirty Harry Dilemmas: Criminal Appeals and the Human Rights Act', 64 *Modern Law Review*, 2001, pp. 911–22.

[206] [2000] Crim LR 1012. For commentary see Professor Andrew Ashworth at 1017.

[207] [2001] UKHL 54, [2003] Crim LR 276.

In his report in October 2001 Lord Justice Auld (who gave the court's judgment in *Chalkley*) called for legislative clarification of whether the approach in *Chalkley* or that in *Mullen* was to be preferred. ('In my view, consideration should be given to amendment of the present statutory test to make clear whether and to what extent it is to apply to convictions that would be regarded as safe in the ordinary sense of that word but follow want of due process before or during trial'.[208]) He did not, however, indicate his own preference. Pending any such statutory amendment, it seems that the Court of Appeal has decided that it is *Mullen* rather than *Chalkley* that should prevail.

However, on 19 April 2006 in a ministerial statement on compensation for miscarriages of justice Mr Charles Clarke, the then Home Secretary, announced that 'an urgent review' would be undertaken with the Lord Chancellor and the Attorney General 'of the statutory test the Court of Appeal must use in deciding whether to quash a conviction'. The Home Secretary proposed 'to examine whether and if so to what extent an error in the trial process necessarily means a miscarriage of justice'.

On 18 September 2006 a consultation paper (*Quashing Convictions*)[209] issued jointly by the Home Secretary, the Lord Chancellor and the Attorney General announced that the Government had *decided* to change the position by legislation. ('The Government believes that the law should not allow people to go free where they were convicted and the court are [sic] satisfied they committed the offence' (para. 31).)

The consultation paper identified three options: (1) to reinstate the proviso (pp. 691, 699 above) so that a conviction would not be quashed if the court considered that no miscarriage of justice has occurred;[210] (2) to replace the proviso with a different formula to achieve the same result[211] or (3) to recast the test to require the Court of Appeal to re-examine the evidence ('akin to the task of the jury').[212] In view of its reservations about each option it asked for other suggestions as to how the objective could be achieved.[213]

It would be surprising if the Government achieves its objective. It will be difficult, and maybe impossible, to prevent the Court of Appeal from doing what it thinks is right to uphold the integrity of the legal process.

Has the Human Rights Act changed the position? What is the relationship between the statutory test of 'unsafe' under the 1995 Act and the question whether the defendant has had a fair trial within the meaning of the European

---

[208] Report, p. 614, para. 10.   [209] www.homeoffice.gov.uk and www.cjsonline.gov.uk.

[210] The Government said it did not rule out option 1 but it suffered from disadvantages – for instance that 'miscarriage of justice' required interpretation. Also, commentators had thought that the proviso added little to the test (para. 34).

[211] This would be implementing Lord Justice Auld's approach expressed in *Chalkley* (para. 35).

[212] The Government said it did not favour reconstituting the Court of Appeal as a trial court 'hearing all the witnesses and supplanting the jury as a tribunal of fact' (para. 38).

[213] For critical response to the Government's position see the editorial in the November 2006 issue of the *Criminal Law Review* at p. 955 and Peter Ferguson QC, 'Retrials and Tribulations', 156 *New Law Journal*, 20 October 2006, pp. 1582–83

Convention on Human Rights? If there have been breaches of the defendant's right to a fair trial under Article 6 of the Convention does that mean that the conviction is automatically unsafe? In July 2000 the Court of Appeal dealing with the matter in *Davis, Johnson and Rowe* said the two questions must be kept separate. It was not helpful to think in terms of there being a presumption that a finding of a breach by the European Court meant that the conviction was unsafe. The effect of a breach of the Convention on the safety of the conviction would vary according to the nature and degree of the breach.[214]

A few months later in *Togher*, Lord Woolf, giving the judgment of the court, said that 'the circumstances in which there will be room for a different result before this court and before the European Court because of unfairness based on the respective tests we employ will be rare indeed' and 'if a defendant has been denied a fair trial it will be almost inevitable that the conviction will be regarded as unsafe'.[215]

However, in *Cranwell*[216] the Court of Appeal said: 'Although in very many cases a trial which is unfair will result in a conviction which is unsafe, this is not necessarily the case. There may be cases, for example, in which, though there has been unfairness, the evidence of the guilt of the defendant is so strong that there can be no doubt that the verdict is safe'.

It seems unlikely that the Strasbourg Court will rule that a breach of the Convention automatically makes a conviction unsafe.[217] In *Condron v. United Kingdom* the Strasbourg Court said: 'In the court's opinion, the question whether or not the rights of the defence guaranteed to an accused under Article 6 of the Convention were secured in any given case cannot be assimilated to a finding that his conviction was safe in the absence of any enquiry into the issue of fairness'. It seems equally unlikely that legislative amendment to the 1995 Act will lay down such a rule.[218] In all probability therefore the matter will remain fuzzy. In most cases 'unfair' will equate to 'unsafe' but in some cases it will not.[219] There will be no rule. The real question for the future is whether the number of exceptions is great or small.

For a powerful statement that the courts should give particular emphasis to the right to a fair trial see A. Jennings, A. Ashworth and B. Emmerson, 'Silence and Safety: The Impact of Human Rights Law', *Criminal Law Review*, 2000, pp. 879 and 893–4 which concluded: 'One effect of bringing Convention rights into English law must be to ensure, at every level of the criminal process, that justice is not only done but is seen to be done'. D. Ormerod has argued that breaches of the Convention should at least create a presumption that the evidence be excluded – 'ECHR and the Exclusion of Evidence: Trial Remedies for Article 8 Breaches?', *Criminal Law Review*, 2003, p. 61.

---

[214] [2000] Crim LR 1012 at 1015. See to the same effect the court's decision in *Francom* [2000] Crim LR 1018 per Lord Woolf.   [215] [2001] 1 Cr App Rep 457, [2001] 3 All ER 463 at [33].

[216] [2001] EWCA Crim 1216.   [217] (2000) 8 BHRC 290 at para. 65.

[218] K. Malleson and S. Roberts proposed such an amendment in 'Streamlining and Clarifying the Appellate Process', *Criminal Law Review*, 2002, pp. 272 and 277.

[219] See for example *Lyons* [2002] UKHL 44, [2002] 4 All ER 1028 dealt with below (p. 707).

See also Professor Andrew Ashworth's Hamlyn Lectures, *Human Rights, Serious Crime and Criminal Procedure* (Sweet & Maxwell, 2002).

For scepticism as to the likelihood of the Court of Appeal changing its traditional approach in light of the Human Rights Act see R. Nobles and D. Schiff, 'Due Process and Dirty Harry Dilemmas' which concluded:

> The grounds for appeal have undergone a number of changes since the Court of Criminal Appeal was founded in 1907. In each case, the formal grounds for quashing convictions, represented by the statutory wording of the court's jurisdiction, has mattered less than the court's sense of what constitutes an appropriate basis for appeal, based on its own professional experience. Those standards have always included a strong deference towards a jury's verdict, and a willingness to regard less serious breaches of due process as insufficient reasons to quash convictions. Changing the Court of Appeal's legal authority by statutory amendment has, in the past, done little to alter its treatment of appeal cases. The Human Rights Act can be viewed as simply another alteration to the formal grounds for appeal, but unless it alters the court's view of what constitutes a serious irregularity it will make little difference to the outcome of appeals. While the language of rights may be a new addition to Court of Appeal judgments it will not, by itself, alter the court's view of which irregularities justify freeing those thought to be guilty . . . of serious offences'.[220]

Is the test of unsafeness that of then or of now? Since the Court of Appeal normally hears an appeal within a relatively short time after the trial, it is not often that the relevant law or procedure will have changed significantly in the interim, but where the Court of Appeal deals with a case that has been referred to it by the Criminal Cases Review Commission, the trial may have occurred years earlier. (In the case of Derek Bentley it occurred forty-five years earlier; in the James Hanratty case it took place forty years earlier.) When considering whether the original conviction is unsafe should the Court of Appeal apply the standards applicable at the time of the trial or those applicable at the time of the review?

In *Bentley*[221] in a judgment given by Lord Bingham, the Court of Appeal held that the statutory law of homicide had to be taken as it was at the time of the trial but that the common law was that current at the time of the review and the conduct of the trial and the judge's direction of the jury should likewise be judged by the standards that would now apply. This has remarkable implications. Commenting on the decision, Professor Sir John Smith wrote: 'How many convictions of, say, more than twenty years ago could be regarded as "safe" in the light of the changed, but relevant, conditions of today?' It was depressing, he said, to think that so many, perhaps a majority of the convictions in our courts, were 'unsafe' – i.e. wrong in law. 'Is there any satisfactory way of preventing this rewriting of legal history? No one really believes that the present common law was the common law in 1189'.[222]

---

[220] Note 205 above at p. 922.   [221] [2001] 1 Cr App Rep 307, [1999] Crim LR 330.
[222] [1999] Crim LR 330 at 332. See to the same effect a critique of Lord Bingham's judgment by F. Bennion, 'Rewriting history in the Court of Appeal', 148 *New Law Journal*, 14 August 1998,

In a commentary on a further case raising the same issue,[223] D.C. Ormerod suggested a differentiation between three types of case: (1) cases where new evidence has come to light which throws doubt on the conviction; (2) cases where there is no new material but there is a new understanding of material in existence at the time of the trial – for instance, new scientific knowledge and (3) cases where there has been a change in the law's attitude prompted solely by legal developments, such as more liberal procedures or changes, perhaps driven by the ECHR, with regard to such matters as the admissibility of evidence, providing access to legal advice or with regard to disclosure of unused evidence. It was the third category that gave rise to problems. 'If the Court of Appeal is prepared to quash convictions as "unsafe" because the law has changed its perception of what is "fair" to defendants, irrespective of whether that also undermines the reliability of the conviction, this really opens the floodgates'. Even if the third category were restricted to cases of potential unreliability, it would leave an enormous number of cases open to challenge, for example, 'all convictions based on old disclosure rules'.

In *Hanratty (decd)*[224] the Court of Appeal seems to have taken the point. The court said:

> In order to achieve justice, non-compliance with rules which were not current at the time of the trial may have to be treated differently from rules which were in force at the time of the trial. If certain of the current requirements of, for example, a summing up are not complied with at a trial which takes place today this can almost automatically result in a conviction being set aside but this approach should not be adopted in relation to trials which took place before the rule was established. The fact that what has happened did not comply with a rule which was in force at the time of the trial makes the non-compliance more serious than it would be if there was no rule in force. Proper standards will not be maintained unless this court can be expected when appropriate, to enforce the rules by taking a serious view of a breach of the rules at the time they are in force. It is not appropriate to apply this approach to a forty year old case.[225]

The court upheld the conviction even though it found that much material that today would be required to be disclosed by the prosecution had not been disclosed.

See also *Lyons*[226] where the House of Lords refused to apply the current standard of fairness because at the time of the convictions the admissibility of the incriminating statements taken under compulsory powers of questioning had been authorised by statute.[227] This was despite the fact that the Strasbourg

---

p. 1228. ('The past is a foreign country; they do things differently there. Or to put it even more succinctly: You can't change history, and you shouldn't even try' (at 1243).) However, the principle enunciated in *Bentley* was applied in *O'Brien, Hall, Sherwood* [2000] Crim LR 676, CA.   [223] *King* [2000] Crim LR 835 at 838–41.

[224] [2002] EWCA Crim 1141, [2002] 3 All ER 534, [2002] Crim LR 650.   [225] At [98].

[226] [2002] UKHL 44, [2002] 4 All ER 1028.

[227] A statement taken under compulsory power of questioning was admissible in evidence at a subsequent prosecution by virtue of the Companies Act 1985, s. 434(5).

Court had ruled the convictions to be unfair[228] and Parliament had as a result changed the law.[229]

The power to receive fresh evidence

The Court of Appeal, both civil and criminal, had and still has full power to receive fresh evidence. The issue has rather been how the court chooses to exercise that power.

In civil cases, pre-CPR, the Rules of the Supreme Court (Order 59, r. 10) provided that although the court had the power to receive fresh evidence, 'no such evidence . . . shall be admitted except on special grounds'. The *White Book*'s gloss pre-CPR stated: 'After there has been a trial or hearing on the merits, fresh evidence will not be admitted in the Court of Appeal unless the conditions in *Ladd v. Marshall* are satisfied. A strict approach is adopted'.

The CPR puts the matter even more narrowly: 'Unless it orders otherwise, the appeal court will not receive (a) oral evidence; or (b) evidence which was not before the lower court' (CPR 52.11(2)). But despite the fact that there is no longer reference to 'special grounds', the principles laid down by the Court of Appeal in *Ladd v. Marshall* still govern the situation.[230] Lord Phillips has said that the principles of *Ladd v. Marshall* are consistent with those of the overriding objective in the CPR.[231]

In *Ladd v. Marshall*[232] the plaintiff called the defendant's wife as his witness. She was a reluctant witness and said she did not remember a particular incident. Judgment was given for the defendant. Subsequently, after she had obtained a divorce, she informed the plaintiff's solicitors that she now did remember the incident and that she wished to change her evidence. The plaintiff asked the court either to order a new trial or itself to hear the evidence. The Court of Appeal dismissed the appeal. Lord Denning gave the court's judgment:

> To justify the reception of fresh evidence or a new trial, three conditions must be fulfilled: first, it must be shown that the evidence could not have been obtained with reasonable diligence for use at the trial; secondly, the evidence must be such that, if given, it would probably have an important influence on the result of the case, though it need not be decisive; thirdly, the evidence must be such as is presumably to be believed, or in other words, it must be apparently credible, though it need not be incontrovertible.
>
> We have to apply those principles to the case where a witness comes and says: 'I told a lie but nevertheless I now want to tell the truth'. It seems to me that the fresh evidence of such a witness will not as a rule satisfy the third condition. A confessed liar cannot usually be accepted as being credible.

---

[228] *Saunders v. United Kingdom* (1997) 2 BHRC 358 and *IJL v. United Kingdom* (2000) 9 BHRC 222.

[229] Under the Youth Justice and Criminal Evidence Act 1999, s. 59 and Sch. 3 statements made under compulsory powers of questioning are inadmissible.

[230] See *Hertfordshire Investments Ltd v. Bubb* [2000] 1 WLR 2318 at 2325 per Lord Justice Hale.

[231] See *Hamilton v. Al Fayed* (2001) Times, 16 January, CA.   [232] [1954] 1 WLR 1489, CA.

With regard to criminal cases, the Criminal Appeal Act 1968, s. 23(2) permitted the court to receive fresh evidence if 'it appears to them that the evidence is likely to be credible and would have been admissible' and 'there is a reasonable explanation for the failure to adduce it' in the earlier proceedings. On the recommendation of the Runciman Royal Commission, the definition of admissible fresh evidence was broadened by the Criminal Appeal Act 1995 to evidence 'which appears to the court to be capable of belief'.[233]

The decision of the Court of Criminal Appeal in *R v. Flower*[234] showed that the court's policy regarding the admission of fresh evidence was similar to that expressed for civil cases in *Ladd v. Marshall*. Widgery J, giving the judgment of the court, said:

> When this court gives leave to call fresh evidence which appears at the time of the application for leave to be credible, it is still the duty of the court to consider and assess the reliability of that evidence when the witness appears and is cross-examined, and this is particularly true when evidence is called in rebuttal before this court. Having heard the fresh evidence and considered the reliability of the witness, this court may take one of three views with regard to it. If satisfied that the fresh evidence is true and that it is conclusive of the appeal the court can, and no doubt ordinarily would, quash the conviction. Alternatively, if not satisfied that the evidence is conclusive, the court may order a new trial so that a jury can consider the fresh evidence alongside that given at the original trial. The second possibility is that the court is not satisfied that the fresh evidence is true but nevertheless thinks that it might be acceptable to, and believed by, a jury, in which case as a general proposition the court would no doubt be inclined to order a new trial in order that the evidence could be considered by the jury, assuming the weight of the fresh evidence would justify that course. Then there is a third possibility, namely that this court, having heard the evidence, positively disbelieves it and is satisfied that the witness is not speaking the truth. In that event, and speaking generally again, no new trial is called for because the fresh evidence is treated as worthless and the court will then proceed to deal with the appeal as though the fresh evidence had not been tendered.

A dramatic example of the narrowness of the approach of the Court of Appeal to fresh evidence was the case of Luke Dougherty. Dougherty was charged with shoplifting, having been identified by two witnesses. The offence occurred at a time when Dougherty was in fact on a bus outing with some twenty others, many of whom knew him. In the event only two were produced as witnesses at the trial. One was his girlfriend and the other was someone with previous convictions. The jury disbelieved the alibi and convicted. He received a sentence of six months' imprisonment and the judge also activated a nine months' suspended sentence, making fifteen months in all.

The case was taken up by JUSTICE. On the application for leave to appeal, the single judge ruled that there was no ground to appoint a solicitor and that

---

[233] Criminal Appeal Act 1968, s. 23(2)(a) inserted by the Criminal Appeal Act 1995, s. 4(1) – replacing 'likely to be credible'.   [234] (1965) 50 Cr App Rep 22.

the fresh evidence could not be called. In conversation between counsel for Dougherty and the Registrar of the Court, the Registrar said that 'this kind of case is unlikely to get off the ground' and that there were various unreported decisions in which the court had refused to allow the calling of fresh evidence where counsel at the trial had not called witnesses in spite of the client's request that they be called. When the case was argued before the full court, the fresh evidence point was not even argued. Counsel proceeded instead on a different issue (that of the dock identification). Nevertheless the court in dismissing the appeal said that if the point had been argued, 'the conditions necessary before such evidence could be received before this court could not be fulfilled'.

JUSTICE pursued its concern over the case and eventually in November 1972, through the good offices of the former Lord Chancellor, Lord Gardiner, it was referred back to the Court of Appeal by the Home Secretary. Dougherty's release was ordered immediately by the court. An examination of the alibi witnesses was then ordered and on the hearing the prosecution did not contest the contention on behalf of Dougherty that the conviction was unsafe and unsatisfactory.

The whole sorry story was told in the Report of the Devlin Committee on Identification Evidence, which was set up partly as a result of this case.[235] The report said that our administration of justice was based on the adversary system and the trial retained many characteristics of a battle. ('In a battle it is the responsibility of each side to get all its troops on the field on time. Napoleon could not appeal against the verdict of Waterloo on the ground that Marshall Grouchy and his army were still on their way when Blucher and the Prussians arrived in the nick of time'.[236]) Under the adversary system, relief was granted if the lack of evidence at the time of trial was due to misfortune, but not if it was due to lack of diligence or to a deliberate decision to do without the evidence. The rule was the same for civil as for criminal cases. However, it was no longer acceptable that an innocent person should continue to spend time in prison 'on the principle of "woe to the conquered"'. But the remedy lay chiefly with the executive in exercising the Royal Prerogative of Mercy by pardon (as to which see p. 720 below).

A more relaxed attitude to the problem of fresh evidence was shown by the Court of Appeal Civil Division in *Dixon v. Dixon*.[237] A husband was ordered to pay maintenance for a child that he claimed was not his. After the magistrates' court hearing, the husband had blood tests done which showed conclusively that the child was not his. He applied to the Divisional Court for leave to appeal out of time against the order for periodic payments and for leave to admit the fresh evidence of the blood test. The Divisional Court refused leave to admit the fresh evidence on the ground that the evidence was available or could have been available if the husband had used reasonable diligence at the time of the hearing before the magistrates.

---

[235] *Report of the Departmental Committee on Evidence of Identification in Criminal Cases*, 1976, House of Commons Paper 338, Ch. 2.   [236] Paragraph 6.3.   [237] (1983) 133 NLJ 305.

On appeal, the Court of Appeal remitted the matter to the magistrates to hold a re-hearing with the fresh evidence. The court said it was a very serious matter to exclude evidence which was wholly conclusive in favour of an applicant on the ground that it could have been available with reasonable diligence at the time of the hearing. It would be most undesirable that an order of the court should be allowed to stand which was based on crucial facts that everyone knew were incorrectly stated.

A few months later the House of Lords took a less generous view. In *Linton v. Ministry of Defence*[238] it upheld a decision from Northern Ireland denying a fresh trial and permission to introduce fresh evidence to a plaintiff who had been shot by a soldier. He claimed that he was an innocent passer-by caught in a hail of bullets exchanged between soldiers and IRA terrorists. The army claimed that he had been one of the terrorists himself. He sued for damages for his injuries. A crucial piece of evidence concerned an employment card which he said he had had in his jeans' back-pocket, which proved that he was on his way to a job interview at the time of the incident. He was unable, however, to explain on cross-examination why it was neither bloodstained nor crumpled. The barrister for the army suggested to the jury that he had not in fact had it on him and the jury rejected his claim.

On appeal he sought to introduce fresh evidence of two kinds. First, he said he now remembered that he had actually been carrying the card in his jacket, which would explain why it was not bloodstained or crumpled. Secondly, he wanted to produce the entry in the hospital record where he was taken unconscious after being shot, which showed that his effects included an employment card which Lord Scarman said was almost certainly the card which he had been talking about at the trial.

Giving judgment for a unanimous House of Lords, Lord Scarman said that the appellant had satisfied the second and third of the tests laid down in *Ladd v. Marshall*. The evidence was important and it was apparently credible, but he could not satisfy the first test. He (or his lawyers) had lacked reasonable diligence in not producing the new evidence at the trial. 'Ours is an adversarial system and it is the duty of a plaintiff to come to court with the evidence to prove his case'. He cited with approval the *dictum* of the Lord Chief Justice of Northern Ireland in the court below: 'A new trial cannot be granted or fresh evidence admitted just because the result of the first trial was or may have been occasioned or made more likely by the unsuccessful party's inattention or faulty memory or by an innocent mistake'.

Sometimes, however, the Court of Appeal receives fresh evidence even though there is no reasonable explanation as to why it was not adduced at the trial – simply on the basis that it is expedient to do so in the interests of justice.[239] The trouble is that the attitude of the court is unpredictable. In *Dosoruth v. Mauritius*[240] the Judicial Committee of the Privy Council said that

---

[238] (1983) 133 NLJ 1103.   [239] As in *Cairns* [2000] Crim LR 473.
[240] [2004] UKPC 51, [2005] Crim LR 474.

before ordering a retrial on the basis of evidence that could have been adduced at the trial it had to be persuaded that it was in the interests of justice, having regard to the constitutional right of the accused to a fair trial.

Appeals which attempt to raise for the first time the diminished responsibility of the appellant will normally not succeed – on the ground that the evidence should have been produced at the trial, but again, sometimes the court makes an exception.[241]

The Runciman Royal Commission suggested that possibly the court had construed its powers too narrowly. It was understandable that the court should view fresh evidence with suspicion. There was the fear that the allegedly fresh evidence might be manufactured. It agreed that defendants and their lawyers should not be encouraged to think of trials 'as nothing more than a practice run which in the event of a conviction will leave them free to put an alternative defence to the Court of Appeal in whatever manner they please'.[242]

On the other hand, the court should 'be alive to the possibility that the fresh evidence, if true, may exonerate the appellant or at least throw serious doubts on the conviction'.[243] The court had to consider whether the fresh evidence was available at the trial and, if so, whether there was a reasonable explanation for the failure to adduce it. It had been suggested to the Commission that the attitude of the court had on occasion been excessively restrictive. It said: 'We would urge that in general the court should take a broad, rather than a narrow, approach to them'.[244] Thus, where the witness wished to change his evidence, the Court of Appeal was right to look at it very carefully, but if there were some reasonable explanation why the witness gave the previous evidence from which he wants to depart, the court should receive it.[245]

Despite the frequently narrow and negative attitude of the Court of Appeal to its powers to receive fresh evidence, there is no doubt that the court has the power to receive any admissible evidence if it so chooses and it can call and hear such evidence on its own initiative. It seems that it can even receive evidence that is inadmissible under the rules of evidence.[246] (The Runciman Royal Commission said that if there were convincing but inadmissible evidence showing that a miscarriage of justice had occurred it should be dealt with through the Royal Prerogative of Mercy rather than by the Court of Appeal. 'If the fresh evidence sought to be admitted is inadmissible under the rules of evidence, in our view the court should not receive it'.[247])

Fresh evidence can be introduced by the prosecution just as much by the defence. That is what happened in the appeal hearing in 2002 in the case of James Hanratty who was hanged for murder in 1962. The case, which had always been the subject of controversy, had been referred back to the Court of

---

[241] For an example see *Neaven* [2006] EWCA Crim 955, [2006] Crim LR 909. For a review of the cases see the commentary at 910–11.   [242] Runciman, p. 173, para. 55.   [243] *Ibid.*

[244] *Ibid*, para. 56.   [245] *Ibid*, p. 174, para. 57.   [246] *D and J* [1996] 1 All ER 881 at 886, CA.

[247] Report, p. 176, para. 67.

Appeal by the Criminal Cases Review Commission. The prosecution wished to introduce DNA evidence obtained in 2000 after the body was exhumed at the request of the defence, which, it argued, proved conclusively that Hanratty was not innocent but guilty. Allowing the application, the Court of Appeal held that the overriding consideration was whether the evidence would assist the court to achieve justice.[248]

The situation is obviously different when the fresh evidence concerns matters that occurred after the trial, but here too the appeal courts have traditionally taken a rather narrow approach on the basis that there should be an end to litigation and that cases should not be re-opened unless there are very good grounds. Thus in *Mulholland v. Mitchell*[249] the plaintiff had suffered very serious injuries and damages had been assessed by the judge on the basis that he could be looked after either at home or in an ordinary nursing home. The appeal was on the basis that after the trial his condition had deteriorated dramatically. The Court of Appeal allowed fresh evidence to be given to establish the facts. On appeal to the House of Lords, the Law Lords held that the Court of Appeal had exercised its discretion reasonably but, generally, fresh evidence should not be admitted relating to a matter of uncertainty taken into account by the judge unless the basis on which he had given his decision had been clearly falsified by subsequent events.

When a case is referred back to the Court of Appeal (formerly by the Home Secretary and now by the Criminal Cases Review Commission, pp. 725–29 below) the power to receive fresh evidence is less restrictive than on an ordinary appeal.[250]

New points taken on appeal

The Court of Appeal's attitude to new points taken on appeal is similar to its attitude to fresh evidence. If they could have been taken at the trial, the Court of Appeal will generally not allow them to be advanced for the first time at the appellate stage. So in *Re Tarling*[251] Gibson J in a *habeas corpus* case said: 'It is clear to the court that an applicant for *habeas corpus* is required to put forward on his initial application the whole of the case which is then fairly available to him – it becomes an abuse of process to raise in subsequent proceedings matters which could, and therefore should, have been litigated in earlier proceedings'.[252] In the same year in *Maynard*[253] Lord Justice Roskill said: 'We have often said in this court that where a question, and in particular a question of the admissibility of evidence, is deliberately not raised at the trial it is only in very rare cases that we allow the matter to be raised in this court for the first time. To hold otherwise would be to encourage counsel to keep points of this kind up their sleeve and then reserve them for the Court of Appeal and thus have a second bite at

---

[248] *R v. Hanratty* [2002] EWCA Crim 1141, [2002] 3 All ER 534.   [249] [1971] AC 666.
[250] *McGrath* [1949] 2 All ER 495; *Sparkes* [1956] 1 WLR 505; *Swabey* [1972] 2 All ER 1094; *Graves* [1978] Crim LR 216.   [251] [1979] 1 All ER 981.   [252] At 987.
[253] (1979) 69 Cr App Rep 309.

the forensic cherry'. (It was noted earlier that it is now required by the Bar's Code of Conduct that points be drawn to the trial court's attention rather than withheld for use on an appeal and that this is now also required by the courts as part of their drive to improve the efficiency of the process (p. 390 above.)

In *Stirland v. DPP*[254] the House of Lords rejected any firm rule that the courts could not allow an appeal on admissibility of evidence where counsel had failed to take objection at the trial, but, it said, 'the failure of counsel to object may have some bearing on the question whether the accused was really prejudiced'. It was not 'a proper use of counsel's discretion to raise no objection at the time in order to preserve a ground of objection for a possible appeal'.[255]

The power to order retrials

Until 1988 the power to order a retrial in a criminal case existed only in one situation – where the court allowed an appeal on the ground of fresh evidence. The basic statutory provision regulating the right to order retrials was s. 7 of the Criminal Appeal Act 1968:

> 7–(1) Where the Court of Appeal allow an appeal against conviction [and do so only by reason of evidence received or available to be received by them under s. 23 of this Act][256] and it appears to the court that the interests of justice so require, they may order the appellant to be retried.

The question whether there ought to be a general right to order a retrial was considered in 1954 by the Tucker Committee[257] and in 1964 by a committee of JUSTICE. The Tucker Committee was divided on whether there should be a general power to order a retrial (five to three against). The JUSTICE committee was divided nine to four in favour. Both committees were unanimous that there should be a power to order a retrial when there was fresh evidence.

A general power to order retrials became law through s. 43 of the Criminal Justice Act 1988. It applies whenever the court thinks it to be in the interests of justice. However, there was not at first any great increase in the tiny number of retrials ordered. In the nineteen month period from August 1989 to March 1991 only four retrials were ordered by the Court of Appeal Criminal Division.[258] But this has changed significantly. In the years 1995–2004 the number of retrials ordered was respectively 52, 53, 33, 73, 70, 72, 58, 50, 45 and 66.[259]

The Runciman Royal Commission strongly supported the Court of Appeal ordering more retrials:

> We welcome and wish to encourage the increasing exercise of this power. Although . . . retrials will not be practicable or desirable in a significant

---

[254] [1944] AC 315.   [255] At 328. See also *R v. Cox (Andrew Mark)* [1995] Crim LR 741.

[256] The words in brackets were removed by the Criminal Justice Act 1988, s. 43 (ed.).

[257] *Report of the Departmental Committee on New Trials in Criminal Cases*, 1954, Cmnd. 9150.

[258] House of Commons, *Hansard*, 11 March 1991, vol. 187, cols. 361–2.

[259] *Judicial Statistics 2005 (Revised)*, Table 1.8. No figure was given for 2005.

number of cases, they offer the Court of Appeal an attractive solution for its understandable reservations about speculative prediction of a hypothetical jury's decision. Where the court is not in doubt, there is no difficulty in allowing or dismissing the appeal as appropriate. Where, on the other hand, the court is in doubt and would like to see the evidence or arguments more fully tested, then, other things being equal, retrials seem to all of us the better way to proceed, even if some of us would not like them to be as frequently ordered as would others.[260]

The Royal Commission was split down the middle as to what should happen if for one or another reason a retrial, though desirable, was felt to be impracticable and fresh evidence was not involved. Six members of the Commission thought that in that situation the Court of Appeal should quash the conviction on the basis that, by definition, to want a retrial it must already have decided that the conviction, at the least, might be unsafe. Five members of the Commission thought that in that situation the Court of Appeal should still decide the matter for itself.[261]

In *Reid v. R*[262] Lord Diplock, giving the judgment of the Judicial Committee of the Privy Council, said that the factors the court should consider when deciding whether to order a retrial included the seriousness and prevalence of the offence, the probable duration and cost of a new trial, the ordeal to be faced by the defendant in being tried a second time, the lapse of time since the commission of the offence and its effect on the quality of the evidence and the strength of the prosecution case. A retrial should not be permitted where the prosecution failed for lack of evidence. ('It is not in the interests of justice as administered under the common law system of criminal procedure that the prosecution should be given another chance to cure evidential deficiencies in its case against the defendant'.[263])

The rule regulating retrials does not prevent the court from ordering a new trial where none has taken place initially – for example because the jury failed to agree on a verdict. Sometimes the court holds that an irregularity vitiates the trial and orders a fresh start (*venire de novo*). In order for *venire de novo* to lie, the court must be in a position to rule that the trial was void from the outset – a nullity.[264] In *Rose* the House of Lords quashed a conviction for murder when the judge was shown to have brought pressure on the jury to hasten its decision. But it held that *venire de novo* could not be ordered as the trial had been validly commenced and could not be said to have been void from the outset.[265]

---

[260] Runciman, p. 175, para. 65.   [261] *Ibid*, para. 66.   [262] [1980] AC 343, PC.   [263] At 350.

[264] For examples see *Crane v. DPP* [1921] 2 AC 299 and *Cronin* [1940] 1 All ER 618. For examples of cases where the court did not feel able to order a retrial on this ground see *Neal* [1949] 2 KB 590; *McKenna* [1960] 1 QB 411 and the House of Lords decision in *Rose* [1982] 2 All ER 731.

[265] The most authoritative study of the issue is by Sir Robin, later Lord, Cooke in 71 *Law Quarterly Review*, 1955, p. 100.

In fresh evidence cases should the Court of Appeal order retrials or decide for itself?

In his book, *The Judge*, Lord Devlin argued powerfully that the Court of Appeal had started to usurp the function of the jury in deciding doubtful cases by either quashing the conviction or by applying the proviso.[266] He took as his text *Stafford v. DPP*[267] and the 'Luton Murder Case', in which the Court of Appeal repeatedly refused to order a new trial even though crucial new evidence came to light.[268]

In *Stafford* the House of Lords held unanimously that the task of the Court of Appeal in fresh evidence cases was to decide whether *it* thinks the verdict unsafe or unsatisfactory. It should consider the weight of the evidence and not concern itself so much with the question as to what effect it might have had on a jury. Lord Devlin had strongly criticised this approach on the ground that it usurped the function of the jury.[269] Under the rule adopted in *Stafford*, Stafford was not, in his view, convicted by a jury but rather by a mixed trial by judges and jury. It was in effect now the judges who had to evaluate the impact of fresh evidence. ('If the court has no reasonable doubt about the verdict, it follows that the court does not think that the jury could have one; and conversely, if the court says that a jury might in the light of new evidence have a reasonable doubt, that means that the court has a reasonable doubt'.[270]) The danger of that approach in Lord Devlin's view was that it could lead to an end to the jury. ('If judge and jury are bound to give the same answer why bother with a jury?'[271])

The issue came up again in *Pendleton*.[272] P was convicted in 1985 of a murder committed in 1971. In 1999 the case was referred back to the Court of Appeal by the Criminal Cases Review Commission in light of fresh evidence. The Court of Appeal received the fresh evidence but held that it did not affect the safety of the conviction. P appealed to the House of Lords and, surprisingly, persuaded their Lordships to overturn the Court of Appeal's decision. (Lord Hobhouse in a concurring opinion expressed his disquiet that the House of Lords should become involved in a question that was properly the province of the Court of Appeal.) On the question of principle the Law Lords unanimously affirmed *Stafford*. Lord Bingham, with the approval of all the judges, said that the test to be applied was the effect of the fresh evidence on their minds, not the effect it would have had on the mind of the jury.[273] But in approving *Stafford*, Lord Bingham put a slightly new spin on the issue. Mr Michael Mansfield, counsel

---

[266] (OUP, 1979) pp. 148–76.   [267] [1974] AC 878.

[268] For the story of this case see Ludovic Kennedy, *Wicked Beyond Belief*.

[269] *The Judge*, pp. 148–76.   [270] Citing *Stafford v. DPP* per Lord Dilhorne at 893.

[271] For an illustration of the principle being applied see *R v. Trevor* [1998] Crim LR 652. See further P. O'Connor, 'The Court of Appeal: Retrials and Tribulations', *Criminal Law Review*, 1990, pp. 620–5 and generally K. Malleson, 'Miscarriages of Justice and the Accessibility of the Court of Appeal', *Criminal Law Review*, 1991, p. 323.

[272] [2001] UKHL 66, [2002] 1 All ER 524, [2002] Crim LR 398.   [273] At [19].

for the appellant, had argued for the view urged by Lord Devlin. This, Lord
Bingham said, had the merit of reminding the Court of Appeal that it was not
and should never become the primary decision-maker. Secondly, it reminded
the Court of Appeal that it had an imperfect and incomplete understanding of
the full processes which led the jury to convict:

> For these reasons it will usually be wise for the Court of Appeal, in a case of any
> difficulty, to test their own provisional view by asking whether the evidence, if
> given at the trial, might reasonably have affected the decision of the trial jury to
> convict. If it might, the conviction must be thought to be unsafe [19].

The question for consideration, Lord Bingham said, was 'whether the conviction is safe and not whether the accused is guilty'. That question had to be separated from the quite different question whether there could or should be a
retrial. ('A conviction cannot be thought unsafe if a retrial can be ordered but
safe if it cannot'.)

In his concurring speech Lord Hobhouse took a more robust approach. He
pointed out that if the jury's decision should be paramount, it was Mr
Mansfield's argument that was unprincipled 'since it is he who is seeking to
escape from the verdict of a jury merely upon the possibility (which will exist
in almost every case) that the jury might have returned a different verdict'.

Commenting on the decision, Professor Sir John Smith suggested that if Lord
Devlin were alive he would not have been satisfied by it but that did not mean
that the decision was wrong: 'Giving effect to Lord Devlin's opinion would have
meant that in all cases where fresh evidence was admissible there would have to
be either a new trial or, if that was impracticable, a final acquittal'.[274]

In *Mills (No 2), Poole (No 2)*[275] the Court of Appeal, quashing two 1990
murder convictions, held that what it called the *Pendleton* impact test as a range
of permissible intrusion into the jury's thought processes was equally applicable where the new matter was one of argument either of law or interpretation
of or inference from the evidence at the trial.

The Runciman Royal Commission considered Lord Devlin's criticism that
the Court of Appeal usurped the function of the jury if it decided the effect of
fresh evidence on the result. It agreed with Lord Devlin save if the fresh evidence
was so clear cut as to satisfy the Court of Appeal that it rendered the conviction
unsafe – in which case it should quash the conviction. Otherwise, having admitted fresh evidence on the basis that it was relevant and capable of belief which
could have affected the outcome of the case, it should order a retrial unless that
was not practicable or desirable. ('The Court of Appeal, which has not seen the
other witnesses in the case nor heard their evidence, is not in our view the
appropriate tribunal to assess the ultimate credibility and effect on a jury of
fresh evidence'.[276])

---

[274] [2002] Crim LR 400.   [275] [2003] EWCA Crim 1753, (2003) Times, 26 June.
[276] Runciman, p. 175, para. 62.

Where a retrial was not practicable or was otherwise undesirable in an appeal based on fresh evidence the Royal Commission unanimously said that there was no alternative other than the Court of Appeal deciding the matter for itself.[277]

It is to be noted that there is in fact no way of taking away from the Court of Appeal the duty of deciding what *it* thinks about fresh evidence since, unavoidably, it always has to decide the initial questions – is the evidence capable of belief and significant? This is not usurping the role of the jury but it does involve consideration of the credibility and importance of the evidence – *pace* Lord Devlin.

The matter was put plainly by the Judicial Committee of the Privy Council:

> While . . . the Court of Appeal and this House may find it a convenient approach to consider what a jury might have done if they had heard the fresh evidence, the ultimate responsibility rests with them and them alone for deciding the question [whether or not the verdict is unsafe].[278]

Does the criminal appeal system make sense?

Under this provocative title Professor John Spencer of Cambridge University has suggested a number of issues that deserve reconsideration:[279]

- The system allows an appeal from magistrates' courts as of right by way of rehearing, whereas an appeal from the Crown Court is not a rehearing and requires leave.
- The prosecutor can appeal from the magistrates' court against an acquittal but cannot appeal against an inadequate sentence. In Crown Court cases it is basically the other way round.
- On appeal from the magistrates' court to the Crown Court, the sentence can be increased, whereas on appeal from the Crown Court to the Court of Appeal there is no power to increase sentence.
- A person who is convicted and sentenced to imprisonment goes to prison whilst he is appealing. ('This is a feature of our system which, in my experience, our colleagues from continental Europe find both shocking and astonishing'.[280])
- The prosecution has no right to appeal against a perverse jury acquittal. (Professor Spencer shares Lord Justice Auld's view that this is wrong – as to which see p. 527 above.)
- The prosecution in a Crown Court case cannot directly challenge an acquittal that results from a failure of due process or a misapplication of the criminal law. An Attorney General's Reference can set the law straight but has no effect on the acquittal.
- Under the Criminal Justice Act 2003 the prosecution has the right to interlocutory appeals. There is no equivalent right for the defence – for instance

---

[277] *Ibid*, para. 63.
[278] *Dial v. State of Trinidad and Tobago* [2005] 1 WLR 1660 per Lord Brown at [31]. See also *Harris* [2005] EWCA Crim 1980 at [101].   [279] *Criminal Law Review*, 2006, pp. 677–94.
[280] At p. 685.

against a ruling that there is a case to answer or that contested prosecution evidence is admissible. The right to appeal later after conviction is not the equivalent.

- The Court of Appeal Criminal Division is seriously overworked. (According to Sir Robin Auld, 'five or six hours' preparation a day in addition to normal sitting hours, sometimes longer, and much of the weekend is not unusual'.[281]) This affects both the quality of work and the capacity of the court to hear appeals on disputed facts involving hearing witnesses. A solution, he suggested, would be to have regional Courts of Appeal staffed by senior Circuit judges to handle most appeals against sentence and simple appeals against conviction. The court in London would handle only the more important and difficult cases.[282]

4. Dealing with alleged miscarriage of justice cases

The problem of the machinery for dealing with miscarriages of justice has been a contentious issue for years. It came sharply into focus especially in the context of three famous IRA cases – the Guildford Four, the Maguire Seven and the Birmingham Six.[283] In all three cases all the defendants had their convictions quashed by the Court of Appeal. In all three the defendants had served long terms of imprisonment. In all three it took years of campaigning to get them set free and in each case it was eventually proved that they had been the victims of a miscarriage of justice. The Government announced the establishment of the Royal Commission on Criminal Justice on 14 March 1991, the day that the Birmingham Six had their convictions quashed. One of the topics specifically referred to in the Commission's terms of reference was 'the arrangements for considering and investigating allegations of miscarriages of justice when appeal rights have been exhausted'. As will be seen below, the Royal Commission recommended that a new system be established for dealing with this problem and the recommendation was implemented in the Criminal Appeal Act 1995.

A distinguished role in this long battle to set things right was played by JUSTICE, the British Section of the International Commission of Jurists. Its

---

[281] Runciman, Ch. 12, p. 642, para. 79.

[282] Lord Justice Auld, for the same reason, proposed that for straightforward appeals the court should sit with two instead of three judges – two High Court judges or a High Court judge with a Circuit judge. (Auld, Ch. 12, p. 646, para. 92.)

[283] Mountains of newsprint, major television programmes and books all played an important part in the saga of these three cases. On the Guildford Four and Maguire cases see in particular G. McKee and R. Franey, *Time Bomb* (Bloomsbury, 1988), R. Kee, *Trial and Error* (Hamish Hamilton, 1986) and Sir John May, *Interim Report on the Maguire Case*, July 1990, HMSO, HC 556 and *Second Report on the Maguire Case*, 1992, HC 296. On the case of the Birmingham Six see especially C. Mullin's *Error of Judgment* (Poolbeg, 1990). Apart from the reports and articles referred to in the following pages see also the special issue of the *New Law Journal* on miscarriages of justice, 17 May 1991.

report in 1968, *Home Office Review of Criminal Convictions*, was effectively the first to examine the issue critically. Between the JUSTICE report of 1968 and the report of the Runciman Royal Commission in 1993 the topic was inquired into by the Devlin Committee (1970),[284] the House of Commons Home Affairs Committee (1982)[285] and by JUSTICE again (1989).[286] The main recommendations of these reports, which were covered in earlier editions of this work, are not included here as they are now of purely historical interest.

Powers of the Home Secretary

When someone has exhausted his right of appeal to the courts his last recourse is to appeal to the executive. The minister responsible for such matters is the Home Secretary. The Home Secretary has various powers that may be deployed.

Free pardon

The minister can recommend that the person be given a free pardon. This wipes out the effects of conviction and sentence though, curiously, not the conviction itself.[287] In *R v. Secretary for the Home Department, ex p Bentley*[288] the Divisional Court held that the courts could review the refusal by the Home Secretary to recommend the grant of a pardon. The court accepted that to get a free pardon it was necessary to establish both moral and technical innocence. See to the same effect the evidence of the Home Office to the Home Affairs Committee of the House of Commons in 1982: 'it is a long-established policy that the free pardon, as an exceptional act of grace, should be confined as far as possible to those who are morally as well as technically innocent. This "Clean Hands" doctrine means that the Home Secretary must be satisfied before recommending a free pardon that in the incident in question the defendant had no intention of committing an offence and did not in fact commit one'.[289]

Most free pardons occur in road traffic and other minor offences, usually for technical reasons. Frequently, for instance, the reason is that a whole batch of speeding convictions has to be cancelled when it turns out that the stretch of road in question was not properly marked in accordance with the regulations. The Home Office's evidence in 1982 to the House of Commons Home Affairs Committee gave statistics about the use of the free pardon. In the eight-year period from 1972–1980 there had been 2,180 instances in which free pardons had been granted with regard to the original conviction. In nine-tenths of the

---

[284] *Evidence in Identification in Criminal Cases*, 1976, House of Commons Paper 338.
[285] *Miscarriages of Justice*, Sixth Report from the Home Affairs Committee, 1982, Cm. 421. See also *The Government Reply to the Sixth Report from the Home Affairs Committee*, 1983.
[286] *Miscarriages of Justice*.   [287] See *Foster* [1984] Crim LR 423.
[288] [1993] 4 All ER 442.
[289] Quoted in JUSTICE, *Miscarriages of Justice*, 1982, p. 3, para. 12.

cases the conviction had been for minor motoring offences. There had also been a total of 1,519 cases in which action had been taken on other grounds, such as compassionate remission of imprisonment or early release resulting from assistance given to the prison authorities.[290]

For a suggestion that failure to exercise the power of mercy might in some circumstances be open to judicial review see B.V. Harris, 'Judicial Review and the Prerogative of Mercy?' in *Public Law*, 1991, p. 386.

Conditional pardon

The conditional pardon substitutes one form of punishment for another, again leaving the original conviction standing.[291]

Remission

Remission, also under prerogative, consists of a reduction in a sentence without a change in the nature of the sentence.

Reference to the Court of Appeal Criminal Division under the Criminal Appeal Act 1907, s. 17

The Home Secretary could refer a case to the Court of Appeal. In the eight years 1981–9 the Home Secretary referred a total of thirty-nine cases involving fifty-four defendants. In eighteen of these cases the appeals were allowed.[292] The Report of the Runciman Royal Commission stated that in the three years 1989–92 there were a total of twenty-eight cases referred involving fifty-nine defendants. Thirty-five had their convictions quashed. Two were ordered to be retried and in both cases the defendant was acquitted. One appeal was dismissed. The rest were then still pending.[293]

Other powers

In particular cases, the Home Secretary releases a prisoner on licence by virtue of his sentence of life imprisonment. Although these powers are normally exercised on considerations not affecting the original conviction, there is some evidence that they are occasionally used in this way.

Principles upon which the Home Secretary exercised his powers

The 1968 JUSTICE report (above) reported on the criteria for acting adopted by the Home Office:

---

[290] *Miscarriages of Justice*, Sixth Report of the Home Affairs Committee, 1982, Cm. 421, Appendix A, p. 7.

[291] As to pardons see A.T.H. Smith, 'The Prerogative of Mercy, the Power of Pardon and Criminal Justice', *Public Law*, 1983, p. 398; A. Wolfgarten, 'Free Pardon', *Solicitors' Journal*, 28 February 1986, p. 157.

[292] Home Office evidence to the May Inquiry into the Guildford and Woolwich pub bombings.

[293] Report, p. 181, n. 5.

The overriding factor governing the exercise of the powers available to the Home Secretary is a proper concern to avoid even the appearance of interfering with the independence of the judiciary. Home Secretaries have accordingly taken a very restricted view of the proper scope for executive intervention – a matter which has been dealt with before a competent court is not normally considered to be reviewable. As a consequence, a Home Secretary will only intervene in cases where evidence is presented by the petitioner which was not available to the courts which dealt with the case. At the level of executive review, the onus of proof is effectively reversed. In cases where the petitioner fails to convince the Home Secretary of his innocence, but establishes that a serious doubt exists as to his guilt, he may be granted some remission of his sentence, or released on licence if the sentence is appropriate. Remission is more commonly granted however in respect of matters arising during the currency of the sentence, such as ill health, or as reward for assistance to the police or prison authorities.

Prisoners, inevitably, had great difficulty in putting their points effectively. They usually had no legal or other professional help. Unless there was a public campaign by the media or some individual journalist or an organisation like JUSTICE, the Home Office usually paid little attention to prisoners' petitions. Perhaps understandably, neither the Home Office nor the police showed much enthusiasm for re-examining cases.

The case for an independent body

The case for a new independent system to investigate miscarriages of justice was made by the Home Affairs Committee in 1982 and by JUSTICE in 1989. In October 1989 the Home Secretary and the Attorney General appointed Lord Justice May to inquire into the circumstances leading to the conviction of the Guildford Four and the Maguire family in respect of the pub bombings in Guildford and Woolwich in 1974.[294] The inquiry was partly about the circumstances of the particular cases but it was also about the general problem of miscarriages of justice. Many of those who gave evidence to the May Inquiry supported the call for some form of independent body to assist the Home Secretary to identify cases. In addition to JUSTICE they included the Criminal Bar Association, the Law Society, the National Association of Probation Officers, the Society of Labour Lawyers and the Legal Action Group.

The most significant evidence to the May Inquiry on this matter was the oral statement of Mr Douglas Hurd, then the Foreign Secretary, who had been the Home Secretary between 1985 and 1989 and in that capacity had been concerned with the Maguire case. In his evidence on 2 October 1991 Mr Hurd said

---

[294] Sir John May was a member of the Runciman Royal Commission. The *general* question of the machinery for handling miscarriage of justice cases was transferred by his Inquiry to the Royal Commission.

that he was now persuaded that the power to refer possible miscarriages of justice should be removed from the Home Secretary and given to an independent standing body with investigative facilities.

In 1987 he had told the House of Commons that cases should be referred to the Court of Appeal only when new evidence or new considerations of substance cast doubt on a conviction. It was important that Home Secretaries not bow to other pressures. He told the May Inquiry that Home Secretaries came under 'fairly continuous pressure in case after case to use the power to reopen arguments already before the courts'. In the face of that, successive Home Secretaries had 'tried to establish rules and criteria which would enable them to exercise the power without getting into a position where they are in effect substituting themselves for the court'. He explained to the May Inquiry that he had refrained from referring the cases back to the Court of Appeal for fear of undermining public confidence. It would be better if these pressures could be handled by some new machinery. Possibly it might consist of some form of 'court of last resort' or an independent investigatory bureau, but it should have the power itself to refer cases to the Court of Appeal.

The Runciman Royal Commission

The Runciman Commission's recommendations on the machinery for dealing with miscarriage of justice cases were unanimous. The main recommendation was that the responsibility for dealing with these cases should be taken from the Home Office and given instead to a new body independent of Government. Most of the witnesses who gave evidence to the Runciman Commission, including the Home Office, the Home Secretary and two former Home Secretaries, had urged this upon the Commission.

The Royal Commission said:

> Our recommendation is based on the proposition, adequately established in our view by Sir John May's Inquiry, that the role assigned to the Home Secretary and his Department under the existing legislation is incompatible with the constitutional separation of powers as between the courts and the executive. The scrupulous observance of constitutional principles has meant a reluctance on the part of the Home Office to enquire deeply enough into the cases put to it and, given the constitutional background, we do not think that this is likely to change significantly in the future.[295]

It recommended that a new body be set up 'to consider alleged miscarriages of justice, to supervise their investigation if further inquiries are needed, and to refer appropriate cases to the Court of Appeal'.[296] It suggested that the new body might be called the Criminal Cases Review Authority. (In the event, the Government decided instead that it should be called the Criminal Cases Review Commission (CCRC). For convenience the new body will be referred to here as

---

[295] Runciman, p. 182, para. 9.   [296] *Ibid*, para. 11.

the CCRC, whether reference is being made to the recommendations of the Royal Commission or to the provisions of the Criminal Appeal Act 1995.)

The Royal Commission proposed that the applicant could apply to the new body only after his appeal against conviction had been turned down or he had been refused leave to appeal. The CCRC would investigate the case if it thought an investigation was called for. Where it instructed the police to conduct investigations, it would be responsible for supervising the investigation and would have the power to require the police to follow up lines of inquiry it thought necessary. If the investigation suggested that a miscarriage of justice might have occurred, the CCRC would refer the case to the Court of Appeal which would consider it as if it were an appeal referred by the Home Secretary under s. 17. The CCRC would provide the court with a statement of reasons and such (admissible) supporting material as it thought desirable.[297] If it considered there were no grounds for a reference it would explain this decision, with its reasons, to the applicant.[298]

The CCRC would be independent of Government but there would have to be a minister answerable for it in Parliament. That should be the Home Secretary. The CCRC would report annually to the minister who would lay the report before Parliament. The chairman should be appointed by the Queen on the advice of the Prime Minister. The other members could be appointed by the Lord Chancellor.[299]

The Court of Appeal should have power to refer cases to the CCRC for investigation and the CCRC would report to the Court of Appeal about the outcome of any such investigation, but the CCRC would be wholly separate from the Court of Appeal and would not form a part of the court structure.[300]

When the Court of Appeal received a reference from the CCRC it would ensure that the defence and the prosecution had a copy of the statement of reasons and the supporting material together with any additional material that it thought fit, so far as that was not prohibited by public interest immunity.[301] The appellant would present his case as he saw fit and he would be able, as before, to raise any matter of fact or law regardless of whether it was included in the papers sent to the CCRC.[302]

The Home Secretary could continue, very exceptionally, to exercise the Royal Prerogative of Mercy especially for cases that the Court of Appeal could not consider under the existing rules, for instance because of the rules of evidence.[303]

The CCRC should not be subject to judicial review in respect of its decisions.[304]

The CCRC should consist of several members, some lawyers and some lay persons. Not all would need to be full-time. The chairman should not be a

---

[297] *Ibid*, pp. 182–3, paras. 12 and 16.   [298] *Ibid*.   [299] *Ibid*, p. 183, paras. 13–14.
[300] *Ibid*, para. 15.   [301] *Ibid*, para. 13 and pp. 186–7, para. 31.   [302] *Ibid*, p. 183, para. 16.
[303] *Ibid*, p. 184, paras. 17–18.   [304] *Ibid*, para. 19.

serving member of the judiciary.[305] The body should be supported by a staff of lawyers and administrators and it should have access to specialist advisers such as forensic scientists, as necessary. It might be desirable for it to have on its staff one or two people expert in investigations especially to assist it in supervising police investigations.[306]

In its annual report the CCRC should be able to draw attention to general features of the criminal justice system which it found unsatisfactory and to make any recommendations for change it thought fit.[307]

The Royal Commission did not attempt to define the test the new body should use in deciding whether to investigate a case. ('In practice, it will need no further justification for investigating a case than a conclusion on the part of its members that there is, or may be on investigation, something to justify referring it to the Court of Appeal'.[308]) The CCRC would need to devise its own rules and procedures for selecting cases for investigation.

The CCRC should be resourced sufficiently to enable it when appropriate to discuss cases direct with applicants. ('It is not always possible for people who have suffered a miscarriage of justice and then been sentenced to a long term of imprisonment to set out their case clearly and cogently in writing and an interview may sometimes be the best way of convincing the [Commission] that the case is one worth investigation'.[309])

The Royal Commission considered but rejected the idea that investigations should be carried out by persons other than the police. ('Given the size and scope of the inquiries that sometimes have to be made in these cases, and the resources required, there is in our view no practicable alternative to the police carrying out the investigation'.[310])

There would need to be adequate arrangements for granting legal aid to convicted persons after they had lost their appeals to enable them to make representations to the Commission.[311]

The Criminal Cases Review Commission (CCRC)

The recommendations of the Royal Commission were implemented in the Criminal Appeal Act 1995. The Act established the CCRC, consisting of not fewer than eleven persons, all of whom have to be appointed by the Queen on the recommendation of the Prime Minister. At least one-third must be legally qualified. At least two-thirds must be persons with knowledge or experience of the criminal justice system. There is no prohibition on a serving judge being on, or chairman of, the Commission.[312] The Commission began work in 1997.

---

[305] *Ibid*, para. 20.   [306] *Ibid*, p. 185, para. 21.   [307] *Ibid*, para. 22.   [308] *Ibid*, para. 24.
[309] *Ibid*, para. 25.   [310] *Ibid*, p. 186, para. 28.   [311] *Ibid*, p. 187, para. 32.
[312] The first chairman, Sir Frederick Crawford, was a lay person, a distinguished scientist. The second chairman, Professor Graham Zellick, was an academic lawyer and university administrator.

In Scotland, following the recommendations of the Sutherland Committee,[313] an equivalent Scottish Criminal Cases Review Commission was set up in 1999.[314]

The CCRC's power to refer a case to the Court of Appeal applies not only to Crown Court conviction issues but also to Crown Court sentencing issues and to conviction and sentence cases dealt with by magistrates.[315] It also includes Northern Ireland cases.

A reference to the Court of Appeal cannot be made unless the Commission 'considers that there is a *real possibility* that the conviction, verdict, finding or sentence would not be upheld were the reference to be made . . . because of an argument, or evidence, not raised in the proceedings which led to it or on any appeal or application for leave to appeal against it' (s. 13(1)(a), (b) emphasis supplied). In the case of a sentence, it must be a new point of law or information (s. 13(1)(c)).

A pre-condition is that an appeal has been determined or leave to appeal has been refused. However, the CCRC retains a discretion to make a reference even if these conditions are not fulfilled 'if it appears to the Commission that there are exceptional circumstances which justify making it' (s. 13(2)).[316]

The minister told the House of Commons during the Committee Stage of the Bill that these criteria were wide enough 'to enable a conviction, verdict or finding to be referred if there was new evidence, or new argument in relation to evidence which has already been raised, which is of sufficient weight in the context of the whole case to give rise to a real possibility of the conviction, verdict or finding not being upheld on appeal'.[317]

In *R v. Criminal Cases Review Commission, ex p Pearson*[318] the Divisional Court said the Commission's task was to predict what view the Court of Appeal would take as to whether a conviction was unsafe. That phrase included cases in which the court, though not persuaded of the appellant's innocence, was 'subject to some lurking doubt or uneasiness whether an injustice has been done'.[319] That was a judgment entrusted to the CCRC and to no one else. If a decision not to refer a case was challenged, the courts would not consider whether the CCRC's judgment had been objectively right or wrong, only whether it was reasonable and lawful. The CCRC can refer a case even where the Court of Appeal would not have granted leave to appeal out of time because of its policy not to do so where the appeal is based on a change in the law (*Director of Revenue and Customs Prosecutions (R) v. Criminal Cases Review Commission* [2006] EWHC 3064 (Admin)).

---

[313] *Criminal Appeals and Alleged Miscarriages of Justice*, 1996, Cmnd. 3425, Ch. 5.

[314] The Crime and Punishment (Scotland) Act 1997, s. 24 inserted a new Part (XA) into the Criminal Procedure (Scotland) Act 1995.

[315] For consideration of the CCRC's power in cases dealt with by the magistrates' courts see K. Kerrigan, 'Miscarriage of Justice in the Magistrates' Court: the Forgotten Power of the Criminal Cases Review Commission', *Criminal Law Review*, 2006, pp. 124–39.

[316] On consideration of s. 13(1) and (2) see *Poole* [2003] EWCA Crim 1753, [2003] Crim LR 60.

[317] House of Commons, Standing Committee B, 30 March 1995, col. 126.

[318] [1999] 3 All ER 498.   [319] At 503, citing *Cooper*, p. 693 above.

The Scottish Commission has broader statutory powers. It may refer a case if it believes '(a) that a miscarriage of justice may have occurred; and (b) that it is in the interests of justice that a reference should be made'.[320] So, at least according to the statutes, unlike the English Commission, the Scottish is not required to 'second guess' the Court of Appeal's approach to the referral.[321]

In a decision of major importance, the House of Lords in *Kansal (No 2)*[322] held that an appellant who had been convicted before the implementation of the Human Rights Act 1998 could not rely on Convention rights in an appeal heard after the implementation of the Act.[323] This has obvious implications for the work of the CCRC since it will have to adopt the same approach.

During the Lords Committee stage of the Criminal Appeal Bill, the minister rejected a Labour attempt to amend the Bill so as to permit a reference where a point was new because it had not been adequately considered at the trial or the appeal. That amendment, Baroness Blatch said, 'would enable the Commission to refer a case on no grounds other than that, in its opinion, the courts had given insufficient consideration to some matter or matters that had come before it'.[324] That would not be right 'as it would put the Commission in the invidious position of asserting its opinion or judgment on a matter above that of the courts' (*ibid*). The CCRC was not 'a court of last resort, second guessing, sitting over and above the appellate courts' (*ibid*).

However, 'where an argument was so poorly presented that the courts may have been misled, or where the appellant's case was not put to the court, then the Commission could reasonably regard such matters as new and could refer' (*ibid*).

When making a reference the CCRC gives the court and all the parties a statement of its reasons (s. 14(4)). Equally, if the CCRC decides not to refer a case, it must give a statement of its reasons to the applicant (s. 14(6)).

Originally, regardless of the CCRC's reasons for the reference to the Court of Appeal, the convicted person was at liberty to raise any points he wished. However, this was changed by the Criminal Justice Act 2003, s. 315[325] which prohibits an appeal on grounds other than those referred to the court by the CCRC unless the court gives leave for any other grounds to be raised.

---

[320] Criminal Procedure (Scotland) Act 1995, s. 194C as amended.

[321] See, however, the decision of the High Court of Justiciary in *Crombie v. Clark* 2001 SLT 635 which suggests that the Scottish Commission must have some regard to the likely attitude of the High Court. The difference in the statutory provision was based on the Sutherland Committee's apparent view that the English criteria were too stringent – see its report at para. 5.62. For consideration of the implications of the difference between the English and the Scottish statutes in this regard see P. Duff, 'Criminal Cases Review Commissions and "Defence" to the Courts: The Evaluation of Evidence and Evidentiary Rules', *Criminal Law Review*, 2001, pp. 341–62 and the follow-up correspondence at pp. 761–3.

[322] [2001] UKHL 62, [2002] 2 AC 69, [2002] 1 All ER 257.

[323] Applied in *Rezvi* [2002] UKHL 1, [2003] 1 AC 1099, [2002] 1 All ER 801; *Benjafield* [2002] UKHL 2, [2003] 1 AC 1099, [2002] 1 All ER 815; and *Lyons* [2002] UKHL 44, [2002] 4 All ER 1028.   [324] House of Lords, *Hansard*, 8 June 1995, col. 1515.

[325] Inserting new subsections (4A) and (4B) into s. 14 of the Criminal Appeal Act 1995.

In *R v. Secretary of State for the Home Department, ex p Hickey (No 2)*[326] the Divisional Court held that before the Home Secretary made a decision whether to refer a case under s. 17 of the 1968 Act the convicted prisoner was entitled to disclosure of fresh information revealed by inquiries about his case. Lord Justice Simon Brown, giving judgment, said that advance disclosure was required in the interests of both fairness and informed decision-making and the guiding principle as to the level of disclosure should be such as to enable the petitioner to present his best case effectively. He could only do that if he adequately appreciated the nature and extent of the evidence that had been produced by the Home Secretary's inquiries. The CCRC is subject to the same duty of disclosure.

The CCRC has the power to obtain documents (ss. 17 and 18). This includes access 'to all relevant information held by the Secretary of State, whether it is representations by, or on behalf of, any person claiming wrongful conviction, or police reports, forensic science reports, opinions from lawyers, doctors, and other independent experts, transcripts of legal proceedings, correspondence and records of telephone conversations'.[327] It does not, however, receive advice to ministers about cases from their civil servants. That would put the CCRC in an invidious position. It would be vulnerable to the charge of having been unduly influenced by the views taken during the earlier consideration of the case by a different authority.

The powers of the Scottish Commission are greater since, on application to a court, it may seek documents held by anyone (not only by public bodies) and it can apply for a warrant to compel anyone to give a statement on oath (known as a precognition).

The Court of Appeal has the power to direct the CCRC to investigate and report to the court.[328] Originally this power only existed with regard to appeals against conviction. It was hardly ever used. The Criminal Justice Act 2003 extended the power to include also applications for leave to appeal.[329]

As proposed by the Royal Commission, when investigations are conducted on behalf of the CCRC they are generally conducted by the police. In supervising or directing the police, the CCRC play a role similar to that played by the Independent Police Complaints Commission. The CCRC can require a chief officer of police to appoint a person from his own force or another force to carry out an investigation (s. 19). It also has a power of veto over the selection of the officer by the chief constable (*ibid*). It can direct the actual investigations made and can sack the investigating officer (s. 20). In practice, however, the CCRC generally carries out its own investigations.

At the outset the CCRC took over the existing Home Office caseload (279 files). Understandably, there was a considerable initial surge of fresh applications – some of which related to cases previously rejected by the Home Office.

---

[326] [1995] 1 All ER 490.   [327] House of Lords, *Hansard*, 8 June 1995, col. 1529.
[328] Section 23A of the Criminal Appeal Act 1968 inserted by s. 5 of the Criminal Appeal Act 1995.
[329] Criminal Justice Act 2003, s. 313. This came into force in September 2004 and applied to cases lodged after that date.

The case intake in 2004–5 was 955, the highest figure to date. In 2005–6 it was 938 and it was expected to continue at that level. It has not yet been below 800. The backlog of cases, though reducing, is still great and the delay in getting a case reviewed is considerable. The number of cases where the review process had not yet begun peaked at 1,208 in May 1999, but had been reduced to 338 by March 2002. In March 2006 it was down to 200.[330]

The CCRC has a residual power under s. 16 of the 1995 Act to refer cases to the Home Secretary for consideration of the Royal Prerogative of Mercy where a reference to the Court of Appeal is not possible. This might occur where the CCRC is convinced that the applicant is innocent but the Court of Appeal would appear not to be able to quash the conviction. By March 2006 no such reference had been made.

All the posts on the board of the CCRC including that of chairman are advertised publicly. In March 2006 the CCRC had total staff of around a hundred including forty-six case review managers. (By comparison, in 1995, C3 in the Home Office had a staff of twenty-one.) Expenditure in 2005–6 was £7.75 million.

The Commission started handling cases as from 31 March 1997. By July 2006, it had received a total of 8,856 cases and had completed 8,163. There had been a total of 318 referrals to the Court of Appeal – an average of some thirty-five per year compared with an average of under ten per year by the Home Secretary pre-CCRC.

Of the 318 referrals, 287 had been determined. Over two-thirds (69 per cent) had resulted in the conviction being quashed; just under one-third (31 per cent) in it being upheld. There were only thirty sentence references of which 83 per cent were varied and 17 per cent were upheld.[331]

A great deal of information about its work, including the annual report, is available on the CCRC's Website: www.ccrc.gov.uk.

FURTHER READING

On the pre-CCRC era see for instance K. Malleson, 'The Criminal Cases Review Commission', *Criminal Law Review*, 1995, pp. 929–37. See also R. Nobles, D. Schiff et al, 'The Inevitability of Crisis in Criminal Appeals', *International Journal of the Sociology of Law*, 1993, p. 21; D.S. Greer, 'Miscarriages of Criminal Justice Reconsidered', 57 *Modern Law Review*, 1994, pp. 58–74; R. Nobles and D. Schiff, 'Miscarriages of Justice: A Systems Approach', 58 *Modern Law Review*, 1995, pp. 299–320.

For an assessment of the work of the CCRC see A. James, N. Taylor and C. Walker, 'The Criminal Cases Review Commission: Economy, Effectiveness and Justice', *Criminal Law Review*, 2000, pp. 140–53; R. Nobles and D. Schiff, 'The Criminal Cases Review

---

[330] CCRC, *Annual Report*, 2005–6, Figure 3.

[331] *Annual Report*, 2005–6, updated from the CCRC's Website, 15 August 2006 – www.ccrc.gov.uk – Case Statistics.

Commission: Reporting Success?', 64 *Modern Law Review*, 2001, pp. 280–99; the House of Commons Select Committee on Home Affairs, *The Work of the Criminal Cases Review Commission*, HC 106 (1999); HC 429 (2000).

For discussion of the relationship between the CCRC and the Court of Appeal see R. Nobles and D. Schiff, 'The Criminal Cases Review Commission: Establishing a Workable Relationship with the Court of Appeal', *Criminal Law Review*, 2005, pp. 173–89; the response from the CCRC's Chairman, Professor Graham Zellick, *ibid*, pp. 937–50 and the reply from R. Nobles and D. Schiff, *ibid*, pp. 951–4. See also P. Duff, 'Criminal Cases Review Commission and "Deference" to the Courts: the Evaluation of Evidence and Evidentiary Rules', *Criminal Law Review*, 2001, pp. 341–62.

See also generally C. Walker and K. Starmer (eds.), *Miscarriages of Justice: A Review of Justice in Error* (Blackstone Press, 1999); R. Nobles and D. Schiff, *Understanding Miscarriages of Justice: Law, the Media and the Inevitability of Crisis* (OUP, 2000).

Compensation for wrongful conviction

Until 1988 compensation for wrongful conviction was paid by the Home Office on an *ex gratia* basis. Such payments, it was explained in a parliamentary statement in 1976, were made 'not as recognition of liability but in recognition of hardship suffered'.[332] Normally it was on the basis that there had been some 'misconduct or negligence on the part of the police or some public authority'.[333] Such payments could be made to persons who had received a free pardon or whose convictions had been quashed after a reference to the Court of Appeal by the Home Secretary.

In 1985 the Home Secretary announced that in future he would pay such compensation where this was required by international obligations:

> The International Covenant on Civil and Political Rights (Article 14.6) provides that, 'when a person has by a final decision been convicted of a criminal offence, or he has been pardoned, on the ground that a new or newly discovered fact shows conclusively that there has been a miscarriage of justice, the person who has suffered punishment as a result of such conviction shall be compensated according to law, unless it is proved that the non-disclosure of the unknown fact in time is wholly or partly attributable to him'.
>
> I remain prepared to pay compensation to people who do not fall within the terms of the preceding paragraph but who have spent a period in custody following a wrongful conviction or charge, where I am satisfied that it has resulted from serious default on the part of a member of a police force or some other public authority.
>
> There may be exceptional circumstances that justify compensation in cases outside these categories. In particular, facts may emerge at trial or on appeal within time, that completely exonerate the accused person. I am prepared, in

---

[332] House of Commons, *Hansard*, 29 July 1976, vol. 916, cols. 328–30.
[333] Statement of the Home Office Minister, House of Commons, *Hansard*, 1977, vol. 929, cols. 835–6.

principle, to pay compensation to people who have spent a period in custody or have been imprisoned in cases such as this. I will not, however, be prepared to pay compensation simply because at the trial or an appeal the prosecution was unable to sustain the burden of proof beyond a reasonable doubt in relation to the specific charge that was brought.[334]

The courts held that the matter was entirely one for ministerial discretion[335] and that there was no duty to give reasons.[336]

In November 1987 the Home Office unexpectedly announced during the debate on the Criminal Justice Bill that it intended to move an amendment to give a statutory right of compensation where a court's final decision resulted in a conviction which was later reversed on the ground that new facts showed conclusively that the defendant was the victim of a miscarriage of justice – unless it was shown that the non-disclosure of the facts was due to the defendant's own fault.[337]

Section 133(1) of the Criminal Justice Act 1988 states: 'When a person has been convicted of a criminal offence and when subsequently his conviction has been reversed or he has been pardoned on the ground that[338] a new or newly discovered fact[339] shows beyond reasonable doubt that there has been a miscarriage of justice, the Secretary of State shall pay compensation for the miscarriage of justice . . . unless the non-disclosure of the unknown fact was wholly or partly attributable to the person convicted'. It is for the Home Secretary to make the decision whether compensation is payable (s. 133(3)). If payable, the amount is determined by an assessor appointed by the Home Secretary (s. 133(4)).

Persons who did not fall within s. 133 of the 1988 Act could still be compensated under the *ex gratia* discretionary scheme if they showed that they had spent a period in custody following a wrongful conviction or charge and the Home Secretary was satisfied that it had resulted from serious default on the part of a police force or of some other public authority, or where there were other exceptional circumstances, in particular the emergence of facts which completely exonerated the accused person.[340] (As will be seen, this discretionary scheme was suddenly abolished in 2006.)

In 2002 in *Mullen* the Divisional Court ruled that the Criminal Justice Act 1988, s. 133 only provided compensation for those ultimately proved

---

[334] House of Commons, *Hansard*, 29 November 1985, vol. 87, WA col. 689.

[335] *R v. Secretary of State for the Home Office, ex p Chubb* [1986] Crim LR 809, Div Court.

[336] *R v. Secretary of State for the Home Department, ex p Harrison* [1988] 3 All ER 86.

[337] House of Lords, *Hansard*, 19 November 1987, cols. 398–9. This became s. 133 and Sch. 12 of the Criminal Justice Act 1988.

[338] The new facts must be the principal ground not just supporting grounds – *R (on the application of Murphy) v. Secretary of State for the Home Department* [2005] EWHC 140 (Admin), [2005] 2 All ER 763.

[339] This does not include facts that come to the notice of the defence after conviction but before an appeal. They must be facts that come to light after the appeal process is complete. (*Murphy case*, n. 338 above.)

[340] Statement of the then Home Secretary, Mr Douglas Hurd, 29 November 1985. The full text is set out in Lord Steyn's speech in *Mullen* (n. 341 below) at [28]. For a case in which the

innocent.[341] As was seen above (p. 703) the claimant had served ten years of a thirty-year sentence for IRA terrorism offences when his conviction was quashed by the Court of Appeal on the ground that his deportation to the UK after being arrested in Zimbabwe had been unlawful as an abuse of process. The Divisional Court held that 'miscarriage of justice' in the International Covenant on Civil and Political Rights (above) had a narrow meaning and that the Criminal Justice Act 1988, s. 133(1) was intended to have the same narrow meaning. This decision was reversed by the Court of Appeal.[342] The court said that the *travaux préparatoires* to the International Covenant showed that the phrase 'miscarriage of justice' was used in its wider rather than its narrower sense. There was no indication that the parties had intended that the claimant had to establish his innocence. Even if that were wrong, the phrase 'miscarriage of justice' was wide enough to embrace such circumstances as had occurred in this case. The presumption of innocence required that Acts of Parliament be interpreted on the basis that it had not been intended that the state should proceed on the footing that a wrongly convicted man was guilty. If Parliament had intended that the claimant had to be proved innocent it could have said so.

The House of Lords allowed an appeal by the Home Secretary and restored the Divisional Court's decision.[343] Lord Steyn held that only someone who was clearly innocent was entitled to compensation. Lord Bingham, with whom the other Law Lords agreed, said he would hesitate to accept the argument that innocence should be a prerequisite for a successful claim. He thought that the statutory scheme also covered cases where there had been 'failures of the trial process', but this was not a case where there had been a failure in the trial process. It was right that the abuse of process should have led to M's conviction being quashed but the wrongful acts did not affect the fairness of the trial nor did they throw doubt on the jury's verdict. Moreover there was no reason to doubt M's guilt.[344]

The Criminal Appeal Act 1995 added a new subsection 4A to s. 133 that in assessing the amount of compensation with regard to loss of reputation, the assessor should have regard in particular to (1) the seriousness of the offence

---

Footnote 340 (*cont.*)
    discretionary scheme was considered – though not applied – see *R (on the application of A Daghir) v. Secretary of State for the Home Department* [2004] EWHC 243.

[341] *R (Mullen) v. Secretary of State for the Home Department* [2002] EWHC 230 (Admin), [2002] 1 WLR 1857.

[342] [2002] EWCA Civ 1882, [2003] QB 993, [2003] 1 All ER 613. For a discussion see S. Roberts, '"Unsafe" Convictions: Defining and Compensating Miscarriages of Justice', 66 *Modern Law Review*, 2003, pp. 441–51.

[343] [2004] UKHL 18, [2004] 3 All ER 65, [2004] Crim LR 837.

[344] For discussion of the issues raised by this case with particular reference to the presumption of innocence see R. Nobles and D. Schiff, 'Guilt and Innocence in the Criminal Justice System: A Comment on *R (Mullen) v. Secretary of State for the Home Department*', 69 *Modern Law Review*, 2006, pp. 80–91. See also P. Ferguson QC, 'Compensating Miscarriages of Justice', 154 *New Law Journal*, 4 June 2004, pp. 842–3.

and the severity of the punishment; (2) the conduct of the investigation and prosecution and (3) any other convictions of the person and any punishment in respect of those previous convictions. No doubt subsection (c) of this amendment was intended to lower the level of damages paid in such cases.

In June 1997 the Home Secretary issued a document to guide applicants: 'Compensation for Miscarriages of Justice: Note for Successful Applicants'. The note stated: 'In reaching his assessment, the assessor will apply principles analogous to those governing the assessment of damages for civil wrongs' (para. 5).[345]

A rare glimpse of the workings of the system came in judicial review proceedings brought by cousins Vincent and Michael Hickey, who spent nearly twenty years in prison wrongly convicted of murdering paperboy Carl Bridgewater, and Michael O'Brien who had spent eleven years in prison after being wrongly convicted of the murder of newsagent Philip Saunders. The independent assessor, Lord Brennan QC, former chairman of the Bar, had awarded Vincent Hickey £506,000, Michael Hickey £990,000 and O'Brien £650,000. The awards to Michael Hickey and Vincent Hickey were reduced by 20 per cent and 25 per cent respectively because of their previous criminal record. In each case the amount attributable to loss of earnings was reduced by £60,000 representing the living expenses they had saved by virtue of being in prison! In his judgment Justice Kay held that the deduction for saved living expenses was wrong, but he upheld the assessor's rejection of a claim for the costs of financial advice and counselling costs for one of the mothers.[346]

The Home Secretary's statement of April 2006

On 19 April 2006 the then Home Secretary, Mr Charles Clarke, in a Written Ministerial Statement, announced major changes to the compensation system designed, he said, 'to modernise and simplify the system, and to bring about a better balance with the treatment of victims of crime'.[347] ('Compensation payments for miscarriages of justice have increased sharply over the last few years and are now running at an average of well over £250,000 – with more than 10 per cent of that amount also paid in legal fees. In contrast no legal costs are payable under the scheme for victims of crime and the average amount received by each victim is less than one-fiftieth of what is paid to those eligible under the miscarriage of justice scheme'.[348])

He announced that with immediate effect:

---

[345] For consideration of the assessor's approach to damages see R. Kapila, 'Compensation for Miscarriages of Justice', 153 *New Law Journal*, 16 May 2003, p. 742.

[346] *R (on the application of O'Brien) v. Independent Assessor* [2003] EWHC 855 (Admin), [2003] NLJR 668.   [347] House of Commons, *Hansard*, 19 April 2006, 15 WS.

[348] For reaction to the Home Secretary's announcement see 156 *New Law Journal*, 28 April 2006, p. 695 (news report); G. Langdon-Down, 'State of Denial', *Law Society's Gazette*, 11 May 2006, p. 20; P. Ferguson QC, 'Cut-price Justice', 156 *New Law Journal*, 12 May 2006, pp. 778–9.

- The discretionary scheme of compensation would be abolished for new applications.[349]
- When determining compensation the assessor would take greater account of criminal convictions of applicants. (He already took some account, but typically deductions were modest, ranging from 5–20 per cent. By contrast, reductions in payments to victims of crime were much higher ranging up to 100 per cent in serious cases.)
- The assessor would take greater account of conduct by the applicant which contributed to the circumstances leading to the miscarriage of justice.
- Legal costs with regard to applications for compensation would be paid by reference to the fees paid under the Legal Help scheme (p. 588 above. Currently £46 per hour).[350]
- Claims and supporting material should be submitted within six months. The assessor would give his final decision within twelve months. (Currently claims were taking an average of more than three years to settle.)

Changes requiring legislation:

- Deductions from compensation payments under s. 133 in respect of prior convictions could only be made in respect of non-pecuniary loss. Legislation would extend this to pecuniary loss. It would provide that in exceptional circumstances the amount of compensation could be reduced to nil because of criminal convictions and/or contributory conduct by the applicant.
- The maximum amount of compensation payable under the statutory scheme would be £500,000 and the maximum payable in respect of loss of earnings would be one and a half times the gross average industrial earnings.

The Home Secretary's Ministerial Statement announced, as noted above, that 'an urgent review' would be undertaken with the Lord Chancellor and the Attorney General 'of the statutory test the Court of Appeal must use in deciding whether to quash a conviction'. The Home Secretary proposed 'to examine whether and if so to what extent an error in the trial process necessarily means a miscarriage of justice'. (On this issue see pp. 703–04 above.)

---

[349] In 2005 the statutory scheme cost some £6 million; the discretionary scheme cost some £2 million a year.
[350] With regard to current cases, the change would apply to legal costs incurred after 19 April 2006. The Home Secretary said that dealing with miscarriages of justice had become 'a massive industry for the legal profession'. His changes would mean the end of an industry that had been getting large amounts of money for individuals who did not deserve it. (*The Times*, 20 April 2006, p. 4.)

Chapter 8

The legal profession

1. The component parts of the profession

The Bar

Origin

The Bar dates back to the end of the thirteenth century. Originally and for a very long time, barristers could and did receive instructions direct from the lay client. It was not until the nineteenth century that it was finally settled that a barrister had to have instructions from a solicitor to appear in court.

Inns of Court

A barrister must be a member of one of the four Inns of Court. The profession's connection with what are now the Inns of Court dates back to the early fourteenth century when, on the dissolution of the crusading order of the Knights Templar, the buildings were occupied by the lawyers who had previously lived in the area around the courts. By the end of the fourteenth century there were four societies in existence – the Inner and Middle Temples, Lincoln's Inn and Gray's Inn. In the seventeenth century the right to practice in the Royal Courts became restricted to members of the Inns of Court and since that time they have enjoyed a monopoly over the right of admission to the Bar.

There are three categories of members of the Inns – benchers, barristers and students. Control of the Inns is vested in the benchers who are appointed by the existing body of benchers, normally from the ranks of judges and senior practitioners.

The Inns today have five main functions. They own and administer accommodation which is rented to barristers for professional chambers and to other persons for professional, commercial or residential purposes. They provide law libraries and common rooms for barristers and students. They provide lunches and dinners for their members. They award scholarships and bursaries for students and young barristers. They also play some part in the training of students and young barristers.

Most of the income of the Inns (some 90 per cent) comes from rents. In 1974 the Inland Revenue agreed to treat the Inns as charities except to the extent that their income was applied to non-charitable purposes.

In June 2000 a Working Party on the Future of the Inns of Court chaired by Sir Murray Stuart-Smith recommended that membership of the Inns should be offered to solicitors entitled to appear in the higher courts – on payment of an entrance fee of £1,000.[1] The recommendation, however, proved highly controversial and it was not adopted.[2]

Entry and training

Qualification for the Bar involves three stages: the academic stage, institutional vocational training and professional vocational training (pupillage).

Joining an Inn and 'keeping term' A would-be barrister must become a member of one of the four Inns of Court[3] and must then 'keep term'. Traditionally keeping term meant simply eating the required number of dinners in one's Inn. Today it means attending educational events organised by the Inn.[4]

The academic stage The academic stage is normally fulfilled by taking a law degree but a person with a degree in some other subject is permitted to pass the academic stage by taking a one-year conversion course known as the Common Professional Examination (CPE) or Diploma in Law which for this purpose is deemed to be the equivalent of a law degree. About one quarter of all barristers enter the Bar via this route.

The vocational stage before Call – the BVC Thereafter, one must take the one-year full-time Bar Vocational Course (BVC)[5] which is designed to train young beginners in the practical skills they will actually need in practice.[6] The course

---

[1] R. Seabrook, 'Read Beyond the Headlines', *Counsel*, August 2000, p. 14. See also M. Bowley, 'A Missed Opportunity', 150 *New Law Journal*, 16 June 2000, p. 907.

[2] On 27 November 2000 the four Inns of Court in a press statement regarding the report said: 'This proposal was canvassed extensively throughout the membership of the four Inns, three of them holding open meetings to encourage the widest possible debate. It became clear that there was insufficient support for the proposal to be accepted at the present time. The fundamental problem lies in the structural and practical distinction between the two professions, which the members of the Inns do not believe should be compromised'. The statement said that 'the Council of the Inns of Court will however keep these developments under review'.

[3] Until recently one had to join an Inn before registering for the vocational training course but this rule was abolished in 1997.

[4] The requirement used to be to eat thirty-six dinners spread over twelve terms, of which there were four per year. The process therefore took at least three years, two of which had to be before Call to the Bar. That rule was changed so that students could 'keep term' by eating only twelve dinners spread over two years, one year of which could be after Call. More recently the dining requirement has been linked (as it was in the sixteenth and seventeenth centuries) to educational activities. From May 1998, 'keeping term' has meant attending twelve 'qualifying sessions' spread over two years. A 'qualifying session' is defined as 'an event of an educational and collegiate nature arranged by or on behalf of an Inn'. (C. Graffy, 'Coming to Terms with Keeping Terms', *Counsel*, March/April 1997, p. 14.)

[5] Alternatively, the course can be taken part-time over two years.

[6] See M. Taylor, 'Pioneering Legal Skills Training', *Legal Action*, April 1995, p. 6; J. Shapland, 'Training for the Bar', *Counsel*, January/February 1995, p. 19. For more recent appraisals of

is given by the Inns of Court School of Law and a number of other providers. (For further information see www.bvconline.co.uk.)

Until 1997 the only way to become a practising barrister was to take the course provided by the Inns of Court School of Law (ICSL) in London. In a report in March 1991, the Taylor Working Party recommended that entry to vocational training for the Bar should be led by the requirement of numbers of practising barristers and that there should be a limit of 700 to 800 on the numbers admitted to the ICSL, the maximum the institution could accommodate. Instead, in June 1994, the Bar Council decided to permit institutions other than the ICSL to teach the BVC. The recommendation that there should be a limit on numbers admitted to the course was abandoned. Currently, including the Inns of Court School of Law, there are a total of eight: BPP Law School, the College of Law (London), Nottingham Trent University, the University of Northumbria, the University of the West of England (Bristol), the Cardiff Law School and Manchester Metropolitan University.[7]

Between them, the institutions offering the BVC have some 1,750 places. (There are between 2,500 and 3,000 applications for these places.)

Call to the Bar Students who have successfully completed the BVC have until now been entitled to be Called to the Bar and therefore to call themselves 'Barrister at law' – though they had no right of audience and therefore could not practise until they completed pupillage (see below). In 1995 the Bar Council concluded that Call to the Bar should be deferred until the completion of pupillage, but it was more than a decade before this policy was implemented. In 2004 the Bar Council resolved that for anyone commencing the BVC after September 2008, 'provisional' Call would be available after completion of the first six months of pupillage.[8] This would entitle them to appear in court during the second six months of pupillage. On satisfactory completion of the second six months the student could be Called to the Bar.[9]

'Graduates of an Inn' Since persons who have completed the BVC would no longer be entitled to the title 'Barrister at law', consideration was given to whether some alternative status might be created for the benefit of home students who were unsuccessful in getting a pupillage or for the benefit of overseas students who do the BVC before returning to their own countries. A Working Party chaired by Ian Glick QC considered whether they could be given the title 'Graduate' of their Inn. A majority of the Working Party was against the proposal but a significant minority favoured the suggestion. The draft Training Regulations issued by the Bar for consultation in April 2006 included regulations for the status of Graduate of an Inn. Steps toward implementation were

the BVC see A. Keane, 'The Check Up', *Counsel*, June 2004, p. 24 and P. Newman, 'Time to Shape Up', *Counsel*, April 2006, p. 18.

[7] For further information see www.legaleducation.org.

[8] See N. Bastin, 'Modern Times', *Counsel*, November 2004, p. 14.

[9] In April 2006 the Bar Council issued a consultation paper and Draft Training Regulations regarding the details of this plan – see www.legaleducation.org.uk.

however halted following the establishment in January 2006 of a new regulatory system for the Bar – as to which see p. 835 below. The Bar Standards Board which took over responsibility for regulating the Bar as from that date decided that, rather than adopting the Bar Council's decision, it would itself decide the matter afresh. It appointed Sir Michael Buckley, a former Parliamentary Ombudsman, as adviser; commissioned MORI to undertake market research; published a consultation paper;[10] held a number of workshops; and aimed to publish a policy paper for debate early in 2007.[11]

Pupillage After the BVC, would-be barristers who want to practise in this country have to find a set of chambers willing to take them on to do pupillage. The BVC provides only simulations.[12] Pupillage puts flesh on the skeleton by providing real-life experience under tutelage of a pupil master/mistress.[13] There is no formal examination at the end of pupillage. (The rules were recently amended to permit the first six months of pupillage to be spent in employment rather than with a barrister in private practice and to allow the second six months to be spent training with a solicitor or a lawyer in an EU country.)

Pre-1996, applicants had to apply for pupillages directly to chambers. As a result, chambers were inundated with applications; would-be pupils had to send dozens, or even hundreds, of applications. Inevitably the system favoured those with contacts. In order to bring order into the system and to create a more level playing field, the Bar established the Pupillage Applications Clearing House (PACH) to operate in a similar way to the UCAS system for entry to university. As from April 1996, students were permitted to make only a limited number of applications. PACH collected the application forms, transmitted them to the participating chambers and communicated chambers' decisions to applicants. About 80 per cent of chambers participated in this system.[14]

In October 2000 the Bar Council decided to move to a new online system of application – the On Line Pupillage Application System (OLPAS).[15] The new system went live in October 2002. As from 1 January 2003, save for recognised exceptions, all pupillage vacancies must be advertised on the OLPAS Website (www.pupillageonline.co.uk).[16] One is only permitted applications to twenty-four sets of chambers. The system has a summer and an autumn season.

---

[10] www.barcouncil.org.uk – Bar Standards Board.

[11] G. Leggatt QC, 'A Vexed Quest?ion', *Counsel*, November 2006, p. 10.

[12] For the proposal that the course should include a period in chambers see N. Bastin, 'Survival of the Fittest', *Counsel*, October 1999, p. 28.

[13] For discussion of the issues see N. Bastin, 'New Pupils for a New Century', *Counsel*, April 1998, p. 30; J. Shapland et al, *Pupillage and the Vocational Course* (1995); J. Shapland and A. Sorsby, *Starting Practice: Work and Training at the Junior Bar* (1995); J. Shapland and A. Sorsby, *Good Practice in Pupillage* (Bar Council, 1998).

[14] For discussion of the failings of PACH see N. Shaw, 'The Class of 2000', *Counsel*, February 2001, p. 18.   [15] 'The Way we are to Recruit', *Counsel*, December 2000, p. 16.

[16] The exceptions are for pupillages sponsored with recognised training organisations, overseas pupils who intend to return to their own countries, solicitors or other qualified lawyers and academic lawyers.

Chambers are prohibited from making offers in respect of summer applicants before 31 July and in respect of autumn applicants before 31 October.[17]

The number of pupillages has been declining – probably a sign of more difficult times. In 2001 the number of pupillages was 808. In 2004 it was 572. A year later it had fallen to 527. Competition for pupillages is fierce. A survey in Spring 2006 showed that only 18 per cent of students on the Bar Vocational Course received a pupillage offer. Over half did not even receive an offer of an interview and half of those interviewed were not offered a pupillage.[18]

The funding of the BVC The cost of the BVC in 2006–7 ranged between £7,000 and £12,000, plus maintenance, estimated at that date at £6,500–7,500.

As recently as 1990–1, over 60 per cent of students on the BVC received some kind of local education authority grant and nearly 50 per cent received a grant covering their fees in full. This situation has changed dramatically. Six years later, in 1996–7, only 6 per cent of students on the BVC had a grant and less than 3 per cent received an award covering full fees.[19] (Students on the BVC raised the money needed for the vocational course mainly from a combination of loans (26 per cent), Inn scholarships (28 per cent) and parental support (25 per cent) with the balance made up of a variety of sources.[20]) By 2003, local authority funding for the BVC had effectively ceased. The 2006 survey of BVC students reported that nearly half were supported by family or a partner and a third had debts in excess of £20,000.[21]

The 2002 Report of the (Mountfield) Committee to Review Financial Support for Entrants to the Bar[22] said (paras. 5–6) that the effect of the withdrawal of local authority support for the BVC year had been compounded by the imposition of fees of £1,100 for the undergraduate period and the complete replacement of university maintenance grants by student loans. The result was that the average student left university with a debt of £10,000 and, on some estimates, more. If the student had to pay for the BVC and for subsistence he would approach pupillage with a debt of £25,000. For the student who had previously taken the one-year CPE to transfer from a non-law degree, the debt could be of the order of £36,000.

Referring to the broader social effects of such high debts, the 2002 Mountfield Report said:

> There is a wide consensus that the Bar needs to reflect, and be seen to reflect, the society it serves. Unless it does so, the Bar will increasingly be viewed with hostility and envy by the world at large, as an apparently privileged group drawn from a restricted segment of British society. The social background, gender and ethnic balance had been improving, driven by changes in higher education and by enlightened attitudes by the Bar. There is now a grave and immediate danger

---

[17] For a discussion of the fairness of the system see M. Bowley QC, 'Loaded Dice?', *Counsel*, May 2006, p. 20.   [18] *Law Society's Gazette*, 19 October 2006, p. 4.
[19] *Report of the (Goldsmith) Working Party on Financing Entry to the Bar*, 1998, p. 22.
[20] Goldsmith Report, p. 21.   [21] M. Bowley QC, 'Loaded Dice?', *Counsel*, May 2006, p. 22.
[22] Accessible on www.barcouncil.org.uk.

that these trends will be reversed because of the changes in public support for students in higher education and the debt burden of students contemplating a career at the Bar. The social bias in the university system and even further back in the chain, in the school system, has the result that academically high achievers, as conventionally measured, tend to be concentrated in the white middle classes. Fewer than one in five young people from the lower socio-economic groups participate in higher education, well below the 45 percent who participate from the higher ones [p. 3, paras. 8–9].

The Inns of Court provide significant sums in scholarships. In 1998 the Goldsmith Report said that the Inns of Court provided about £1.75 million scholarship and other moneys for students during the BVC year. The Mountfield Report said that by 2002 this had risen to some £2.3 million. A general review of funding entry to the profession said that around a quarter of Bar students at that time received financial help from the Inns, with over half obtaining between £3,000 and £6,000.[23]

The 1998 Goldsmith Report recommended that the Bar should provide or procure direct financial assistance to the number of BVC students who were likely to get tenancies, which it took to be around 500. In respect of those 500 the Bar should increase its contribution to supporting the cost of the BVC year by £2 million per annum. One way to achieve this would be if more chambers provided funding for the BVC year, which it, however, did not think was likely to be achievable. The best way, it thought, would be to raise money through an annual subscription for membership of the Inns of Court or by loans.

Four years later, the Mountfield Report said that chambers provided some £0.33 million in respect of the BVC year.[24] In the Committee's view this was insufficient. It recommended that there should be a levy on the senior members of the profession to make it possible to fund some 400 BVC scholarships of about £8,000. Such funding, it said, was necessary to enable the Bar to compete for the ablest entrants with the support provided, for instance, by City solicitors' firms. According to the Report, the cost would be some £3.5 million, which it said was about 0.25 per cent of the Bar's gross income. The levy, it recommended, should be based on barristers' gross income which should be imposed either wholly or mainly on those earning over £100,000. The money could be raised by requiring a charge of 0.25 per cent of gross income for those earning between £100,000 and £250,000 and 0.5 per cent for those earning above £250,000. (That would translate to £250 for the former and £625 for the latter – though the actual cost would be only half after tax and national insurance.) The practising Bar, led by the Commercial Bar, rejected the Mountfield proposal.[25]

The funding of pupillage So far as concerns the funding of pupillage, in 1989, a working party under William Blackburne QC recommended that the Bar should finance a scheme by a levy on the profession whereby pupils would

[23] R. Epstein, 'Learning the Law – Finding the Funds', 152 *New Law Journal*, 25 January 2002, pp. 91–2.   [24] Annex D.   [25] *Counsel*, October 2002, p. 6; December 2002, p. 5.

receive a minimum income of £6,000 pa during their pupillage year. The report led to the establishment of a second working party under Sir Nicholas (now Lord) Phillips which took the view that it was neither practical nor lawful to impose on the Bar a scheme such as that proposed by the Blackburne Working Party. Instead it proposed that each set of chambers should be expected to offer a quota of funded pupillage places. The target would be 450 such funded places. This recommendation was adopted by the Bar Council in January 1990 and began in that year. By 1997, chambers were putting £5.3 million into the scheme and five years later in 2002 that figure had risen to £6 million.[26] The Goldsmith Report in 1998 proposed that the minimum of £6,000 pa should be increased to £10,000.[27] This proposal was implemented as from 31 December 2002,[28] but many chambers pay well above the guaranteed minimum. Between £18,000 and £35,000 seems to have been the range in 2005 but in October of that year it was reported that chambers at 3 Verulam Buildings were the first to offer over £40,000 and that other leading sets would follow suit.[29]

Some chambers were in addition offering guaranteed earnings in the first years in practice. Four New Square was said to be the most generous, offering a total of £150,000 for the first three years of tenancy. The earnings were split so that a new tenant would received £60,000 in the first year, reducing to £40,000 in the third year. Fountain Court gave new tenants £37,000, the same amount paid to pupils. Maitland Chambers offered £70,000 over the first two years.[30] A year later it was reported that by autumn 2007 a third of the Bar's biggest civil sets would be paying pupils over £40,000.[31]

Continuing education From October 1997, new practitioners have been required to undertake a total of forty-two hours of continuing education over a three-year period which must include further advocacy training and courses in ethics. In addition, attendance at an approved accountancy course is required.

The concept was gradually extended and as from January 2005 an obligation to engage in continuing education applied to all practising barristers however senior.[32] The requirement after the initial three years is to complete twelve CPD hours per calendar year, of which four hours must be satisfied through

---

[26] The Mountfield Report, 2002, Annex D.

[27] In the second six months of the pupillage, £5,000 could be earned by way of guaranteed receipts.

[28] *Counsel*, April 2002, p. 5. See also E. Bowles, 'To Fund or not to Fund?', *Counsel*, February 2001, p. 10. There was obviously a possibility that the mandatory payment of £10,000 would result in fewer pupilages – see 152 *New Law Journal*, 22 November 2002, p. 1744, reporting that the latest annual survey of the Bar by BDO Stoy Hayward suggested that the number of pupilages could drop by as many as 139.   [29] *The Lawyer*, 31 October 2005, p. 2.

[30] *Ibid.*   [31] *The Lawyer*, 23 October 2006, p. 4.

[32] *Counsel*, June 2002, p. 26. See www.legaleducation.org.uk. On the importance of continuing legal education for barristers whether employed or in independent practice see Report of the Collyear Committee, *Education and Training for the Bar, Blueprint for the Future*, June 1999.

'accredited courses'.[33] (Details of accredited courses are available on the on-line database at www.legaleducation.org.uk.)[34]

Numbers at the Bar and recruitment

There has been a remarkable growth in the size of the Bar over the past thirty or so years. During the 1950s the number of barristers fluctuated at or some-what below the figure of 2,000, but in the fifty or so years since then the number has increased six fold. In 2006 it was 11,818.

A considerable minority of those Called to the Bar each year are from over-seas. It is still the case that many qualify who never intend to practise.

As seen above, the Bar estimated in 1991 that in the next decade it would need some 400 to 500 new 'starts in practice' to maintain an adequate flow into the private profession,[35] plus another 150 to 200 or so coming to the Employed Bar to provide manpower for the Government Legal Service, the Crown Prosecution Service, commerce, finance and industry, local government, the armed forces, parliamentary counsel, etc.[36]

It is estimated that in addition to barristers in private practice, there are something under 3,000 or more 'employed' barristers working as lawyers in commerce, industry and other fields.[37] (On the position of 'employed' barris-ters see p. 760 below.) There are also 'non-practising barristers' defined as bar-risters who are neither in chambers nor employed who may or may not be practising law. (The category includes lecturers, MPs, barristers working in law centres and some who offer specialised services from home or a private office.[38] Their organisation, called the Employed and Non-Practising Barristers' Association (ENPBA), has a Website – www.enpba.org.)

Chambers

A barrister does not have an office; he works in 'chambers'. In the past every practising barrister had to be a member of professional chambers. (As will be seen below a barrister who has been in practice for at least three years can now practice from home – but, though growing, this is still highly exceptional.)

Numbers of sets The number of sets of chambers hovers around 350 – a slight decline recently resulting from mergers.[39] (In 1992–3 there were a total of 373 sets; five years later in 1997 there were 417 sets. In 2005 there were 360.[40])

---

[33] *The Lawyer*, 5 November 2001, p. 33 and 1 August 2005, p. 21.
[34] See generally the CPD and Training Supplement in 156 *New Law Journal*, 17 November 2006, pp. 1747–59.
[35] The Bar Council's statistics stated that in 2004 there were (only) 315 persons who obtained tenancies in chambers – www.barcouncil.org.uk/documents/TenanciesObtained_2004.doc. As at July 2005 there were 527 engaged in pupillage.
[36] *Report of the (Taylor) Bar Entry and Training Working Party*, 1991.
[37] The Bar Council's statistics put the number in December 2005 at 2,800.
[38] See G. Parasie, 'Time, Gentlemen Please', *Counsel*, December 1999, p. 26.
[39] See D. Platt, 'The Urge to Merge', *Counsel*, April 2000, p. 21.
[40] Source: the Bar's Annual Report.

Practising outside the Inns of Court Until 1987 there was an unwritten rule that London barristers had to practise in the physical precincts of the Inns of Court. The rule was supported by the long-standing policy that barristers should be charged rents by the Inns that were distinctly lower than the going level of commercial rents. This rule, combined with the explosion of numbers at the Bar, resulted in a serious accommodation crisis. (A survey in 1986 showed that 10 per cent of London barristers were sharing a desk. Inner Temple had 2.14 barristers per room!)

In summer 1987 the Bar Council issued a statement that the Bar and the Inns had reached agreement on a new policy to ensure the availability of sufficient accommodation for the practising profession, especially in London. The two crucial elements were that the accommodation would, if necessary, be outside the Inns and that the rent would be at a commercial level. The capital for the development would come from moneys raised by mortgage on the properties of the Inns, which were then thought to be worth over £200 million.[41]

At first, the change in policy did not seem to have much effect, but gradually more and more chambers began to move out of the hallowed precincts of the Inns to more spacious and modern office accommodation in the neighbourhood.

An article in the Bar's journal *Counsel* in July 1991 said that 'only a few years ago, any suggestion that chambers should move out of the confines of the Inns would have been greeted with horror as a culture-shocking break with the past'. But now it was no longer so. ('What has promoted the departure of about a dozen sets from the Temple in the last twelve months has been overcrowding'. In some cases the Inns had assisted the process of moving out by becoming intermediate landlords.[42])

Practising from home The Benson Royal Commission on Legal Services in 1979 recommended that a barrister should be permitted to practise from home without a clerk but it took a decade, until 1989, before this was allowed. A barrister who has been in chambers for not less than three years is permitted to practise on his own. The first year in which the Bar Council statistics reported the number of sole practitioners was 1993 when there were sixty-eight out of a total of 7,735 barristers in private practice (0.8 per cent). In 2005 it was 281 out of 11,818 (2.3 per cent).[43]

Chambers outside London Traditionally the Bar has been heavily a London-based profession but the proportion of barristers practising in the provinces has increased significantly. In the 1960s it was about one quarter. In the late 1990s it was one third. In 2005 it was two-fifths.

[41] *New Law Journal*, 26 June 1987, p. 580.
[42] *The Lawyer* reported on 7 June 2004, p. 5 that a set was moving out of the Inns to have more space. It had barristers working four to a room. Another article described how legal aid lawyers were moving out to reduce chambers' expenses – S. Hindmarsh, 'Legal Aid Barristers leading the Exodus of Chambers from the Inns of Court', 33 *Independent Lawyer*, December 2005, p. 16.
[43] For one barrister's account of practising on her own see M. Macpherson, 'Home Alone', *Counsel*, April 2005, p. 27. The Bar Sole Practitioners Group holds an annual conference.

The number of towns and cities outside London where there is a local Bar recently more than doubled. (In 1978 there were twenty-eight cities outside London where barristers practised; twenty years later in 1997/8 there were fifty-eight.[44]) The trend is to establish more local Bars.

The report *Strategies for the Future*, issued in October 1990 by the Bar Council, said that reflecting the Government's policy there was likely to be a long-term trend towards administering justice from a small number of major regional centres. As part of this policy more legal services activity was likely to take place outside London. The county courts were taking on an increasing number of the larger cases. The Bar should 'support and encourage the broad policy of the further development of legal centres outside London'.[45]

Size of chambers Barristers' chambers have been getting larger and larger. The same 1990 report said: 'The ability of barristers to organise themselves into economic units that offer the best combination of efficiency and accessibility is critical to the future of the Bar'.[46] The size of chambers had doubled in the previous twenty years to an average size of about fifteen, but the upward trend continued. The report recommended that the optimum size of chambers was at least twenty-five and that it could in some instances be as high as fifty or even more. ('Only highly specialised sets in high fee-earning areas of the law will be able to practise successfully in smaller units'.[47]) One reason for increasing the size of chambers was increased profitability. Barristers in larger chambers had higher gross and net earnings.

A study published in 1999 showed that some 15 per cent of barristers were practising in chambers of over fifty members, 14 per cent were practising in chambers of between forty-one and fifty members, 30 per cent were in chambers with thirty-one to forty members and 24 per cent in chambers with twenty-one to thirty members. Only about 17 per cent were in chambers with under twenty members.[48] By 2006 the average size of chambers had risen to thirty-three. Analysis in 2006 of the top thirty sets of chambers showed two with over a hundred members (162 and 137), three with between seventy-five and a hundred members (eighty-eight, eighty-six and seventy-seven) and only one with fewer than forty members. Most had been between forty and sixty members.[49] *The Times* reported in October 2006 that the largest set in the country, with 180 barristers, had its centre in Birmingham with Bristol and London annexes. The second largest with 170 tenants was also in Birmingham.[50]

---

[44] The figure for 2006 was not available.

[45] Paragraph 3.16. For the exploration of these trends by a geographer and a barrister see further M. Blacksell and C. Fussell, 'Barristers and the Growth of Local Justice in England and Wales', 19 *Transactions British Institute of Geography NS*, 1994, pp. 482–93. Their conclusion was that 'a more loosely-knit and regionally diverse legal culture was beginning to emerge' at the Bar.

[46] Paragraph 3.24.   [47] Paragraph 3.28.

[48] BDO Stoy Hayward, *Report on the 1999 Survey of Barristers' Chambers*, p. 8.

[49] The Lawyer, *UK 100 Annual Report 2006 The New Order*, pp. 60–4.

[50] *The Times*, 31 October 2006, Law, p. 5.

Efficiency The 1990 Bar Council report also dismissed as out-of-date the notion that chambers were still Dickensian in aspect. 'Most sets are now computerised either substantially or to some extent, with applications ranging from word processing, document transmission (fax) and routine accounting such as fee recording and billing, to more complex applications such as legal databases or the production of management information'.[51] (A study had shown that non-computerised sets of chambers had between £0.5 million and £1 million more fees outstanding than computerised sets, resulting in a loss of interest on capital of up to £130,000 pa. This obviously far exceeded the annual cost of leasing basic level computerisation.)

Turnover Barristers' chambers nowadays are multi-million pound enterprises. A survey of the top thirty sets in 2006 showed turnover ranging from £11.5 million to £34 million. All the top eight sets had turnover of more than £25 million.[52]

Chambers' contribution Barristers contribute to chambers' expenses pro rata according to income. Reports from the top thirty sets showed considerable differences with a few paying as much as 20 per cent or even more, most in the 12–15 per cent range and some around 10 per cent. The lowest was a set that had a range from 6–11 per cent. One set had a sliding scale – 15 per cent up to the first £200,000, 10 per cent for the next £100,000 and 2 per cent above that.[53]

The barrister's clerk

The rule has been that each set of chambers must have a clerk.[54] Most sets have more than one clerk – the senior clerk and a number of junior clerks. The junior clerks perform functions that are normally understood by the term 'clerical', but senior clerks have functions that go well beyond this. The Benson Royal Commission on Legal Services[55] described the role as having three main components:

- *Office administrator and accountant* He maintains the accounts for the chambers as a whole and ensures that each member of chambers has adequate secretarial and other similar services.
- *Business manager* He works for each member of chambers individually in maintaining his professional diary, checking court lists for cases in which he is retained, negotiating fees, sending out fee notes and reminders and keeping the individual accounts.
- *Agent* Advising barristers on the development of their practices, ensuring that beginners receive work according to their abilities and experience, advising solicitors as to which barristers to instruct and advising on the allocation of work as between members of chambers.

---

[51] *Strategies for the Future*, 1990, para. 3.25.
[52] The Lawyer, *UK 100 Annual Report 2006 The New Order*, pp. 60–4.   [53] *Ibid.*
[54] As was seen above, this rule was changed in 1990 but few barristers choose to practise without a clerk. For a description of such a rare case see P. Norman, 'Practice without a Clerk', 147 *New Law Journal*, 11 July 1997, p. 1039.   [55] 1979, para. 34.3.

This dry recital does not, however, convey the extent to which the clerk is the lynch-pin of the whole system. A high proportion of work coming into any set of chambers is actually allocated by the clerk. Sometimes the solicitor asks on behalf of the lay client for Mr A. The clerk informs him that Mr A is not available to take the case on that date but that he has an excellent Mr B who is available. The solicitor client will commonly agree to the suggestion that Mr B does the case – especially if he has previously been to those chambers and been broadly satisfied with the quality of the barristers he has instructed. Or the solicitor may be told that Mr A is available, but a day or so before the hearing he is told by the clerk that unfortunately Mr A has not completed his previous case (he is 'part heard' elsewhere) and the clerk suggests Mr B or Miss C, both of whom are from the same chambers. The solicitor usually has little choice but to accept the recommendation, especially at the last moment. Another common situation is when the solicitor says from the outset that he has a particular kind of routine case and asks the clerk to find someone of the appropriate level of experience from his chambers to handle it.

The clerk also plays a crucial role in negotiating private sector fees. (Fees paid from public funds are not fixed by the clerk.) Traditionally the clerk's remuneration was on a commission basis – typically in the order of 5–7 per cent of gross chambers' income without any contribution to chambers' expenses or 8–10 per cent of gross income with the clerk making some contribution towards expenses like a barrister member. The senior clerk therefore has a direct financial stake in the level of fees earned by his principals. His interest is to set the fees as high as possible consistent with the aim of not losing the work. A solicitor who wishes to discuss the fee with the barrister is permitted to do so, but it is very rarely done. The earning capacity of the clerks is therefore extraordinary. A senior clerk on full commission could be drawing anything from 5 per cent to 10 per cent of the professional earnings of fifty or more barristers. He will be earning considerably more than most members of the chambers. However, the modern trend is for the senior clerks to be paid on a salary rather than a commission basis or on a combination of salary and commission.[56] *The Lawyer* reported in 2000 that senior clerks were 'facing concerted pressure to reduce their earnings as chambers cut overheads'. Senior clerks at the five leading commercial sets were 'earning between £100,000 and £350,000 a year'.[57]

The system is gradually changing with the growth in the size, complexity and modernisation of chambers and the increasing concern at the Bar for a more acceptable image. A woman clerk, for instance, is no longer a rarity. Clerks are increasingly likely to have considerable educational and other qualifications. Traditionally clerks came straight from school with few, if any, qualifications.

---

[56] The 2001 BDO Stoy Hayward *Survey of Barristers Chambers* showed (p. 25) that 35 per cent of chief clerks were on salary only (compared with 23 per cent in 1999), while 29 per cent were on commission only (compared with 35 per cent in 1999 and 43 per cent in 1997).

[57] 16 October 2000, p. 1.

Today they need considerable skills to mastermind a multi-million pound business. Sets of chambers looking for a new chief clerk are these days increasingly likely to advertise for an 'Administrator', 'Practice Manager' or 'Chief Executive'. (By 2001 some 22 per cent of chambers had a Practice Manager or Chief Executive.[58])

The Bar's 1990 report, 'Strategies for the Future', said (para. 3.46) that the clerking arrangements suffered from a number of weaknesses including:

- The wide range of functions and skills required of clerks.
- Inadequate specialist skills in marketing, performance management, information technology and accountancy.
- High costs associated with the commission-based remuneration of the clerk ('with some clerks earning significantly more than experienced barristers within their employing chambers').
- The potential for patronage or influence over the careers of barristers and undue lack of accountability to members of the set.
- Unclear contractual relationships.

The report recommended that chambers should aim to have a staff (on normal pensionable employment contracts) consisting of two main figures. One would be the Practice Manager, dealing with such matters as marketing and promotion, pricing, fee negotiation, practice development and accommodation strategy. The second would be the Administrator, dealing with accounting, billing, secretarial services, information technology, library facilities, etc. They should be remunerated by a basic salary plus an annual performance-related bonus awarded by a management committee. 'There should be no commission or percentage element'.[59] (The Practice Manager, it suggested, might in 1990 earn a maximum of, say, £48,000; the Administrator, say, £29,000.[60])

Such new arrangements would need to be phased in. To convert the clerking system into an effective management capability would 'require determined action from the profession'.[61]

In 2001 a new concept was born with the founding of Clerksroom, a company providing clerking services to barristers as well as arbitrators and mediators. In August 2006, their Website (www.clerksroom.com) stated that it was working for fifty-eight barristers, 184 arbitrators and 479 mediators. Most of the barristers are sole practitioners working from home. Members pay a 'chambers contribution' of 10 per cent of their earnings – less than they would pay in normal chambers because there is no room rental.[62]

The only extended treatment of the arcane subject of the clerking system is John Flood's book *Barristers' Clerks* (Manchester University Press, 1983). For a short and racy piece see R. S. Chahal, 'Clerks No More on Borrowed Time', *The*

---

[58] BDO Stoy Hayward, *Survey of Barristers Chambers*, 2001, p. 20.   [59] Paragraph 3.53.
[60] Paragraph 3.55. These figures seem ludicrously low given the actual earnings (even in 1990) of senior clerks.
[61] Paragraph 3.49.   [62] *The Lawyer*, 6 February 2006, p. 4.

Lawyer, 29 October 1996 and by the same author, 'A Tough Niche to Carve', *The Lawyer*, 4 February 1997.

Queen's (or King's) Counsel

Originally the division in the profession was between 'sergeants-at-law' and barristers. The first King's Counsel were appointed in the seventeenth century but at that time the title did not signify seniority in the profession but rather the function of assisting the law officers of the Crown in cases in which the Crown had an interest. In the course of the eighteenth and nineteenth centuries, appointments to the rank of King's Counsel came to be regarded as a mark of pre-eminence in the profession. By the end of the nineteenth century, no more appointments of sergeants-at-law were made and the senior rank amongst barristers was limited to King's (or Queen's) Counsel – otherwise known as KC or QC or 'leaders' or 'silks'.

QCs were appointed by the Queen on the advice of the Lord Chancellor. Toward the end of each year a notice was published in the legal journals informing practitioners who wished to be considered to submit their names to the Lord Chancellor. Only those who applied were considered. The process of selection has been described by the Lord Chancellor.[63] Applicants put in their *curriculum vitae* and the Lord Chancellor had inquiries made about each applicant by senior members of his staff. The list of applicants was sent to the Law Lords, the judges in the Court of Appeal and to all High Court judges as well as to certain senior Circuit judges. The list also went to the Chairman of the Bar and to the leaders of the circuits and specialist Bars. Those consulted were encouraged to express their views about those on the list – after having taken discreet soundings among other leading silks. The Lord Chancellor's staff met the Bar Leaders and the Presiding Judges from each circuit. The staff had some thirty-five meetings on the subject. A provisional list of appointments was discussed with the Heads of Divisions (Lord Chief Justice, Master of the Rolls, President of the Family Division and Vice Chancellor, head of the Chancery Division).

A Bar Council Working Party (the Kalisher Committee) set up 'to investigate the methods, procedures and criteria for the appointment of Queen's Counsel', which reported in 1994, recommended that the pool of those consulted should be wider still – for instance by including Masters and Resident Circuit judges in main court centres.[64]

The Lord Chancellor took into account not only the personal qualities of the applicant but also the total number of silks generally and the total number in the field in which the applicant practices. (The form filled out by those consulted had a space 'Ready for silk now, but not recommended for appointment this year because other, named, candidates are preferred in this field'.)

---

[63] Lord Mackay, 'The Myths and Facts about Silk', *Counsel*, October 1993, p. 11.
[64] See C. Frazer, 'The Silk Round', *Counsel*, July/August 1994, p. 22.

A person who was not appointed one year could apply again and it was common to apply several times before being appointed.

The proportion of QCs to junior barristers was kept at about 10 per cent. The percentage of successful applicants in the eight years up to 2002 was 12–17 per cent, except for 2002 when it jumped to 26 per cent and 2003 when it was 31 per cent.[65] The number of appointments in 2002 was dramatically higher than in any previous year. Between 1994 and 2001 the annual number was around seventy with a high of seventy-eight. For whatever reason,[66] it jumped in one year from 77 in 2001 to 113 in 2002 and to 121 in 2003.[67] The total number of QCs in December 2002 (the last year of the old system) was 1,145 – 10.6 per cent of the practising Bar.

A person applies to become a QC for a number of reasons. One is the desire for advancement in the profession. QCs generally enjoy higher incomes and have a higher status. (They even have a separate bench to sit on in court.) The second reason is to lighten the load of work. The work of barristers is divided between advocacy, opinion and 'paper work', meaning in the main drafting of pleadings and similar documents. By tradition, paper work is reserved for junior barristers. It is not very well remunerated and is burdensome. Practitioners are usually happy to escape this work and to concentrate their efforts on advocacy in heavy cases and opinion work.

Applying for silk, however, is a gamble, mainly because of the old 'Two Counsel' rule. This was the rule that, normally, a Queen's Counsel should appear in court only with a junior as well. (There used to be a further rule that the junior was paid a fee equivalent to two-thirds of that paid to the QC. This was abolished by the Bar in 1971, but the junior is still commonly paid the equivalent of either two-thirds or half the leader's fee.)

In 1976 the Monopolies and Mergers Commission in a special report (*Two Counsel Rule*) stated that this restrictive rule was contrary to the public interest, though it accepted that paper work (e.g. drafting) should normally be done by juniors. This report was accepted by the Bar, which abolished the Two Counsel rule at the next AGM in 1977. Since then a QC has had the right to appear in court without a junior. But he is entitled to expect that a junior will be instructed unless the contrary is stated, and he may decline to accept instructions to appear without a junior if he thinks this would prejudice his ability to conduct the case or any other case or to fulfil his other professional obligations. In general, QCs tend to be employed in heavy matters where two counsel are appropriate.

It follows that when applying for silk the applicant must consider that clients are willing to pay not only the higher fees normally paid to leaders but also the fee of the junior who would normally appear with him. Some of those

---

[65] *Counsel*, June 2002, Table 1, p. 42; June 2000, Table 1, p. 47.
[66] There was speculation that it was a defensive response to the threatening sounds about the institution emanating from the Office of Fair Trading – on which see pp. 778–80 below.
[67] *Counsel*, June 2001, p. 42; June 2003, p. 47.

appointed as QCs do not become successful as leaders even though they had been highly successful as juniors.

The question whether the institution of silk should be abolished came up periodically. In 1999 an early day motion proposing the abolition of QCs tabled by Mr Andrew Dismore, a backbench Labour MP, won the support of over a hundred MPs. He also put down a series of parliamentary questions which elicited, *inter alia*, that the LCD's selection process cost the taxpayer a fair amount of money. Mr Geoff Hoon, at that time Minister of State in the LCD, told the House of Commons during the Committee stage of the Access to Justice Bill that the total cost was of the order of £130,000, of which £120,000 was attributable to the elaborate consultation process.[68] The Bar Council accepted that this cost should instead be borne by applicants and the Government introduced an amendment to the Access to Justice Bill to permit this.[69] In 1999 the fee was fixed at £335. By 2002 it had been raised to £720. (As will be seen (p. 806 below) under the new system it is far higher still.)

Mr Dismore's efforts to persuade the Government to abolish QCs initially met with less success. His proposed amendment was very simple: 'The office of Queen's Counsel is abolished'. Of the various arguments he deployed the most weighty was the inflationary effect on fees. ('It simply enables QCs to charge more money for doing exactly the same work.'[70]) Speaking to the amendment, the minister, Mr Hoon, said that the rank of Queen's Counsel had existed since the end of the sixteenth century when it was first bestowed on Francis Bacon. Not that the Government would regard that as conclusive. ('We are a reforming Government and we would not be afraid to abolish an institution whose only value is as a relic of the past.'[71]) However, he said, Lord Irvine (who until he became Lord Chancellor in May 1997 was himself a practising QC) took 'a positive view' of the value of Queen's Counsel. 'By identifying the best advocates through a tough system of peer and judicial assessment, the award of silk is a kite mark of quality.' It enabled lawyers and clients to identify the leading members of the profession and to make more informed choices. It also provided an incentive to attain the highest standards of advocacy and integrity. It was right that the system should be conducted under the Government's auspices. The process of selection was open and was explained in a guide that was available on the LCD's Website.[72]

In July 1999, however, the Lord Chancellor announced that he had asked Sir Leonard Peach, former Commissioner for Public Appointments, to examine the selection procedures for appointing both QCs and judges. The Peach Report was published in December 1999.[73] It found that:

---

[68] House of Commons, Standing Committee E, 11 May 1999, col. 358.
[69] *Ibid*, col. 357. See the Access to Justice Act 1999, s. 45.   [70] *Ibid*, col. 363.
[71] *Ibid*, cols. 372–3.   [72] *Ibid*, cols. 373–4.
[73] *An Independent Scrutiny of the Appointment Processes of Judges and Queen's Counsel in England and Wales*, December 1999.

- The judges and the Bar's representatives seen were 'largely content' with the system.
- The officers of the Law Society were opposed to the concept of silk and were 'firmly opposed to the consultation system'.[74]
- Some specialist groups of barristers and solicitors, notably employed lawyers, felt they were unfairly excluded from consideration.
- Equal opportunity and ethnic minority representatives agreed that the system needed revision to give them a better chance of appointment.[75]

Sir Leonard made proposals for minor changes:

- The assessment form should be slightly restructured.
- The number of consultees nominated by the applicant should be restricted to three to six – 'an unlimited number simply aids the well known candidate'.
- All applicants should be required to give reasons for their own suitability for silk in relation to the criteria.
- A table should be published showing the fee earnings of candidates in quartiles. (This was implemented.[76])
- There should be power in exceptional circumstances to interview someone regarded as a good candidate about whom there is insufficient information.

By recommending only minor changes in the system, the Peach Report in effect validated it. But in March 2001 the Office of Fair Trading (OFT) in its wide-ranging report on restrictions on competition in professions (*Competition in professions*)[77] raised the fundamental question whether the award of the title Queen's Counsel was on balance of value to consumers. The OFT has real powers and this report represented a serious threat to the continued existence of the rank of Queen's Counsel. (On the OFT's report see pp. 778–79 below.)

Speaking at the Bar's annual conference in 2002, Lady Justice Hale questioned whether the Bar was sensible to rely on a Government minister to bestow this mark of superior quality. She asked: 'What is a profession, a large part of whose function is to stand up for the citizen against the state, doing when it looks to Government for preferment?'[78]

In March 2003, the Bar Council's Working Party on Judicial Appointments and Silk, chaired by Sir Iain Glidewell, a former Court of Appeal judge, recommended that silks should no longer be appointed by the Lord Chancellor.

---

[74] The Law Society had earlier announced that it would no longer take part in the consultation processes of appointing judges and QCs. ('Law Society turns its back on "secret soundings"', *Solicitors' Journal*, 1 October 1999, p. 895.)

[75] For research on this see K. Malleson and F. Banda, *Factors Affecting the Decision to Apply for Silk and Judicial Office* (LCD Research Series, June 2000) – www.lcd.gov.uk/research/2000/res00fr.htm.

[76] See *Counsel*, June 2002, p. 42. The table showed that the average earnings of all applicants was £206,000 (£269,000 for successful and £184,000 for unsuccessful candidates).

[77] OFT 328.   [78] *Counsel*, December 2002, p. 32.

Instead, appointment should be on the recommendation of a panel chaired by a retired senior judge and a broad membership.[79]

A month later, on 2 April 2003, Lord Irvine, the Lord Chancellor, giving evidence to the new House of Commons Select Committee on his Department, stated that he would shortly be issuing a consultation paper which would invite views both on the method of appointing silks and on 'whether the status of Queen's Counsel should continue to exist or not'.[80] The consultation paper was published in July 2003, but before then, on 29 April, at the annual ceremony in the House of Lords when the new QCs are sworn in, Lord Irvine, with no prior warning, announced that the competition for appointment as Queen's Counsel for 2004 was being suspended. 'The question I must resolve', he told the no doubt astonished and probably dismayed silks and their families, 'is whether the award of a quality mark is of such central importance to the effective operation of our legal system that it should continue to be made by the state. If the view prevails that a quality mark should still be awarded, but independently of Government, then the state should stand aside and the grant of a quality mark would become an issue for the professions alone: the rank of Queen's Counsel would therefore go'.[81] It was clear that the 2003 batch of new QCs, if not the last to be appointed, was likely to be the last selected under the traditional system.[82]

For consideration of the pros and cons of the rank of Queen's Counsel and for the establishment of a new system for the selection of QCs see pp. 801–06 below.

Partnerships among barristers

It is a rule of Bar conduct and etiquette that barristers may not form partnerships. The members of chambers share the services of the clerk and share office expenses such as secretarial facilities, library and other costs, but they may not agree to share fees. The traditional basis of the rule is that the barrister is an individual and should take responsibility for his work as an individual. Nowadays when so much of the work is either not earmarked for any individual or gets reallocated because of the eventual non-availability of the selected individual, the reasons for the rule have somewhat altered.

The issue has from time to time been considered by the Bar. In 1961 a committee recommended that the rule be adhered to and this view was taken again by a different committee in 1969 and again by the Senate of the Four Inns of Courts and the Bar when it came to give evidence to the Benson Royal Commission on Legal Services.

The Benson Commission in its report in 1979 did not go into the issue very deeply, but it unanimously adopted the then prevailing view that partnerships should not be allowed. Partnerships, it thought, would erode the right of the

---

[79] See *Counsel*, April 2003, p. 8.   [80] Oral evidence of 2 April 2003, Q 73.
[81] See S. Hawthorne, 'Last of the Line?', *Counsel*, June 2003, p. 46.
[82] Lord Irvine told those present: 'If silk goes, that would make you the last in an illustrious line of leading counsel recognised by the state as leaders of the profession'.

client to select a particular individual by reason of his capabilities. ('Both by law and in practice, a partnership involves the sharing of work and responsibility and a common interest in earning profits so that if one member of a partnership cannot, or does not wish to, deal with a particular matter another partner, who may not either be known, or acceptable, to the client does so.'[83]) The Commission said it was particularly influenced by the fact that partnerships would restrict the client's choice – especially in some of the small specialised Bars and in provincial centres, some of which only had one set of chambers.

Another problem with partnerships, which the Commission did not mention, is that many members of the Bar perform part-time judicial functions. It would presumably be impossible for one member of a partnership to appear as an advocate in a case in which a partner was the judge. This would mean that if the barrister came to court and found that his partner was to be the judge he would have to withdraw at the last moment. Even if the problem were appreciated earlier, it would still create administrative difficulties, which would add yet a further dimension to the already complex matter of listing cases.

The Royal Commission concluded: 'Partnerships would often we think be convenient or advantageous to barristers but the point of overriding importance is the public interest. We therefore consider that partnerships between barristers should not be permitted.'[84]

A later inquiry into the issue resulted in a statement by the Bar in May 1987 that it adhered to the rule that barristers could not form partnerships, but that it would for the first time permit 'purse sharing' arrangements in the form of the pooling of fees and their distribution according to some agreed formula. Solicitors would have to be informed that such arrangements operated in the chambers and barristers in such chambers would not be allowed to appear against each other or in a case in which a member of the chambers was acting as judge.[85] This system for distribution of fees, if it exists at all, is exceedingly rare.

One of the many proposals canvassed in the famous (or infamous) Green Papers issued in January 1989 by the then Lord Chancellor, Lord Mackay (p. 778 below), was that barristers should be able to form partnerships with one another. The Bar's response on this (as on virtually all the proposals in the Green Papers) was strongly critical.

The matter was considered again by the 1990 Bar Council's report entitled 'Strategies for the Future'. This said that the supposed advantages of partnership were greatly exaggerated. In particular, a partnership no longer had any distinct tax benefits. In its view most of the main advantages of a partnership in terms of a cohesive group structure could be achieved without a formal partnership. A set of chambers, it suggested, needed a clear and efficient decision-making structure to permit it to assess options and determine courses of action on the basis of full discussion – but without the need for unanimous decisions.

---

[83] Paragraph 33.65.   [84] Paragraph 33.66.   [85] *Law Society's Gazette*, 27 May 1987, p. 1566.

The present informal consensus process needed to be replaced by machinery that allowed for rapid and effective decisions to be taken for all. The larger the set, the greater the need for such machinery.

The question of partnerships at the Bar was raised in 2001 by the Office of Fair Trading in its report *Competition in professions*. (For the details and further developments see pp. 778–81 below.)

Women at the Bar

In 1955 women made up only 3.2 per cent of the practising Bar. The proportion has steadily risen: by 1965, 4.6 per cent; 1975, 7.1 per cent; 1985, 13 per cent and 1995, 22 per cent. In 2005, it was 29 per cent.[86] In 2005, 49 per cent of those Called to the Bar were women.

In 2001 it was reported that of barristers of up to five years' Call, women were 38 per cent of the cohort.[87] Of the cohort of over ten, fifteen and twenty years' Call the proportions were 21 per cent, 17 per cent and 14 per cent.[88] Because women have only quite recently begun to come into the profession in large numbers there are very few in the ranks of senior practitioners, let alone on the bench as judges. Women QCs are under 10 per cent of all QCs. (As at October 2006 there were 1,284 QCs practising at the English Bar, of whom 118 (9.2%) were women.[89])

One aspect of the problem is that so few women put themselves forward for consideration. Women barristers are currently around 30 per cent of the practising Bar. In both 2002 and 2003, only 10 per cent of applicants for silk were women. In 2005, the first year of the new system, the proportion of female applicants rose to 15 per cent.[90]

Of the sixty-six women who applied for silk in 2005, exactly half succeeded. (This compared with only 23 per cent in 2003.) The proportion of successful women was higher than for successful male applicants (38 per cent) or of ethnic minority applicants (42 per cent).[91] The thirty-three women made silk were 19 per cent of the 175 who were awarded the title. Women therefore fared relatively well in the first year of the new system.

For details of a survey of women barristers regarding their experience of sex discrimination see B. Hewson, 'Sex and the Bar', *Counsel*, February 1993, p. 12. See also C. Barton and C. Farrelly, 'Women in the Legal Profession', 148 *New Law Journal*, 24 April 1998, p. 599; K. Malleson and F. Banda, *Factors Affecting the Decision to Apply for Silk and Judicial Office*, LCD Research Series, June 2000 – www.dca.gov.uk/research/2000/res00fr.htm; D. Nicolson, 'Demography, Discrimination and Diversity: a New Dawn for the British Legal Profession?', 12 *International Journal of the Legal Profession*, 2005, pp. 2001–8.

---

[86] Bar Council's Annual Report.
[87] BDO Stoy Hayward report, *Survey of Barristers Chambers*, 2001, para. 3.2.
[88] DCA, *Judicial Appointments, 5th Annual Report, 2002–2003*, p. 19.
[89] Information supplied by the Bar Council.
[90] *Law Society's Gazette*, 17 November 2005, p. 1.   [91] *The Lawyer*, 31 July 2006, p. 15.

Ethnic minorities at the Bar

In 2006, ethnic minority barristers made up 10 per cent of the practising Bar and 17 per cent of pupils were from the ethnic minorities.[92] (Ethnic minorities constitute some 7 per cent of the whole population.)

This appears somewhat encouraging but there has been concern for many years about the problems of members of ethnic minorities in getting entry to the Bar and even more about the fact that most practise in chambers consisting largely of members of the minority in question. Research in 1989 showed that more than half of chambers had no ethnic minority tenants and slightly more than half of the practising black barristers were concentrated in sixteen sets.

In October 1991, the Bar Council adopted a race-equality policy which included a recommendation to all chambers that they should aim to have 5 per cent of their members drawn from ethnic minorities. This recommendation does not seem to have had much, if any, impact. The policy also envisaged a Code of Practice on the non-discriminatory selection and treatment of pupils and tenants and for the distribution of work in chambers. The Bar's Equality and Diversity Code was promulgated in 2004. It requires chambers to appoint an equality officer and to have an equality policy. The Chairman of the Bar warned that the Bar Standards Board established to regulate the Bar as from 1 January 2006 (see p. 835 below) planned to develop its own equality and diversity strategy and would be 'looking closely at compliance with the Equality and Diversity Code'.[93]

In 2002, the number of ethnic minority barristers applying for silk was nineteen out of 429 (4 per cent). Seven were appointed – 6 per cent of the 113 appointments made and 37 per cent of those from ethnic minorities applying. In 2003, the number applying was twenty-three out of 394 (6 per cent). The same number, seven, were appointed – again 6 per cent of the total appointed and 30 per cent of those applying from ethnic minorities. In 2004, the system was in abeyance. In 2005, ethnic minority applicants were twenty-one out of 443 (5 per cent).[94] Ten were appointed – 6 per cent of those appointed and 42 per cent of those applying from ethnic minorities.

See further the report of the DCA's Legal Services Consultative Panel, *The Legal Profession: Entry, Retention and Competition*, May 2005 and the DCA's response *Diversity in the Legal Profession: A Report on Government Proposals*, December 2005. See also D. Nicolson, 'Demography, Discrimination and Diversity: a New Dawn for the British Legal Profession?', 12 *International Journal of the Legal Profession*, 2005, pp. 2001–8.

Circuits

The country is divided into six circuits, each with its own rules and customs, officers and controlling committee. A barrister can only be a member of one

---

[92] Bar Council's Annual Report, 2005.

[93] S. Hockman QC, 'Equality and Diversity', *Counsel*, May 2006, p. 3.

[94] Press Release, 11 November 2005 – www.qcapplications.org.uk/press.

circuit but he can appear in a court on another circuit. The circuit is concerned with the administration of criminal justice in its area together with the Circuit Administrator who is a senior official of the Lord Chancellor's Department. The circuits are also concerned with the establishment of new chambers in their area. The circuit leader will take an interest in the conduct of members of the circuit and will give advice and guidance to any barrister who seems to require it. The circuits have no formal function in respect of disciplinary proceedings.

Advertising by barristers

In 1989 the Bar Council changed its rules to permit a barrister to engage in any advertising or promotion in connection with his practice which conforms to the British Code of Advertising Practice, including the use of photographs, statements of rates and methods of charging, statements about the nature and extent of his services and, with the client's written consent, the name of any professional or lay client. Such advertising must not be inaccurate or likely to mislead, or be likely to diminish public confidence in the legal profession. It must not make comparisons with other barristers ('knocking copy' or fee comparisons) or include statements about the quality of the barrister's work, the size or success of his practice or his success rate.[95] Initially most chambers confined their advertising to chambers' brochures, but it is now common for chambers and even individual barristers to have their own Websites.

The OFT's report, *Competition in Professions*, March 2001, said that the restriction on direct comparison with other barristers and on referring to success rates 'may restrict competition, perhaps especially for individuals and smaller clients, and they may limit the ability of prospective clients to compare relative value for money' (p. 15).

In its response, the Bar Council said that the Bar's attitude to advertising had undergone a sea-change – moving from one in which all advertising was prohibited with a few exceptions, to one in which all advertising was permitted with a few exceptions.

With regard to advertising success rates it argued that such advertising would be inherently misleading, partly because often there is no clear definition of success or failure and also for the fundamental reason that the outcome of a case depends on many factors other than the skill of the advocate. The more skilful a barrister the more likely that he will be instructed in the most difficult cases. No member of the profession would regard success rates as an indication of quality of the barrister but there was a danger that uninformed persons might do so. Also if success rates could be advertised barristers might tend to avoid the more difficult cases in order not to compromise their position in some league table. Those consulted unanimously took the view that the prohibition on such advertising should remain. These arguments were apparently persuasive as the

---

[95] *Bar Code of Conduct* (2004, 8th edn) para. 710 – the Code can be accessed on the Bar Council's Website – www.barcouncil.org.uk.

OFT said in its *Progress Statement* of April 2002: 'We do not at present intend to pursue this issue further' (para. 3.24, p. 14).

Different considerations, the Bar's response stated, applied to comparative advertising. No one favoured comparisons in terms of quality, or criticisms of individuals or other sets of chambers. Such comparisons were calculated only to disparage while being unverifiable. But comparing fees would not be open to that objection providing it was accurate and not likely to mislead. The Bar Council changed the rule to make that possible on 23 March 2002 with effect from that date. (One consequence is that the world now knows what top QCs earn.[96])

Management of the Bar

For over a century the affairs of practitioners have been run by the Bar Council. Its origins were the Bar Committee, created in 1883 which in 1895 became the General Council of the Bar. But the Bar Council was expressly barred from interfering with 'the property, jurisdiction, powers or privileges of the Inns'. Over decades relations between the Bar Council and the Inns of Court were strained. The Inns owned all the properties. They controlled admission to the Bar and disciplinary matters but the rulings of the Bar Council on matters of etiquette became recognised as binding on barristers as a whole.

In the second half of the twentieth century the strained relationship led to repeated attempts to find the right formula for a working system. In 1966 the Senate of the Four Inns of Court was established to provide one body that could act collectively in matters of common interest. It had seven representatives from each Inn and six representatives of the Bar Council, but it could take no decisions that involved expense to the Inns without getting their agreement. This proved unsatisfactory.

---

[96] On 28 April 2003, under the heading 'Fees Squeezed at Commercial Bar', *The Lawyer* reported that although three QCs (Lord Grabiner, Jonathan Sumption and Gordon Pollock) now charged £1,000 per hour, the 'headline rate' across the rest of the Commercial Bar had been 'hit hard'. Due to competitive pressures and the relatively slow rate of incoming work, a range as 'low' (sic) as £500–600 per hour was prevalent among the forty top commercial silks. Lord Grabiner had previously made headlines as the first barrister to earn over £1 million per year. The record brief fee is said to have been one of £3 million paid to Gordon Pollock in the abortive case brought by the liquidators of BCCI against the Bank of England – *The Lawyer*, 12 January 2004, p. 1.

In August 2006 it was reported that there were 18 commercial and tax silks who had earned over £2m in the previous year and that two 'were even understood to have gatecrashed the elite £3m-a-year club'. There were around 30 barristers earning more than £1m a year. Hourly rates had remained static during the past year. 'Most silks are charged at around the same rate as a partner in a law firm, with an average fee being £500 an hour. Junior barrister rates could be as low as £35 an hour rising to £350 per hour for a senior junior. (*The Lawyer*, 21 August 2006, p. 4)

The same issue of *The Lawyer* (p. 1) reported that Linklaters had no fewer than 124 partners earning £1m or more during the previous year.; that Slaughter and May had 90, and Allen & Overy had 85, a quarter of its equity partners. In all there were 392 London-based private practice partners who took home more than £1m in 2005–6.

In 1972 a committee chaired by Lord Pearce pointed to the fact that there were no fewer than six autonomous bodies to run a profession, at that time, of fewer than 3,000 practitioners – the four Inns, the Senate and the Bar Council. There was a multiplicity of overlapping committees – in 1971 some sixty-one standing bodies. The whole system was wasteful of manpower, accommodation, money and time. Junior members were virtually excluded from all decision-making. There was a critical shortage of accommodation for practitioners in London. The Inns had no common rent policy, no common policy on libraries and lacked control over pupils. The Pearce Committee concluded that there should be one effective central governing body with sufficient financial resources to carry out its policies.

In 1974 a new body, the Senate of the Four Inns of Court and the Bar, was set up with a slight majority of practitioners.[97] Its remit was to lay down general policy for the profession and to decide on the contents of the Consolidated Regulations of the Inns. The Inns agreed to abide by the general policy laid down by the Senate subject to the understanding that they would not be expected to bear an unfair burden of cost. The Bar Council was a sub-committee of the Senate.

In 1979 the report of the Benson Royal Commission on Legal Services said that these arrangements were 'neither sufficiently co-ordinated nor adequately representative of the profession as a whole' (para. 32.67). The Senate should have the power to take decisions binding on the Inns. Some sixty members of the Senate should be elected by the Bar in such a way as to ensure adequate representation for different levels of seniority, specialists, barristers practising in different parts of the country and those employed in commerce and industry. There was no need to have barristers appointed by the Inns or the Senate. It would be right to continue to have some representation of the judges in the Senate. A method should be found to have between ten and twenty whether by appointment, election by the judges or co-option. The Inns should have representatives in the form of the Treasurer and Chairman of its Finance Committee.

In 1986 a new committee under the chairmanship of Lord Rawlinson recommended that the management of the Bar should be in the hands solely of practitioners. The government of a profession, particularly one like the Bar which engaged in a great deal of publicly funded work, should not be in the hands even partially of judges. There should be a new General Council of the Bar and of the Inns of Court consisting of barristers alone. Decisions which might affect the Inns should be taken by a Treasurers' Council of the Inns

---

[97] It had six representatives of each Inn appointed by the benchers, three barrister representatives of each Inn elected by the members of the Inns other than the benchers and thirty-nine barristers elected by the Bar, of whom eighteen had to be practising juniors and under seven years since Call. There were ten *ex-officio* members, such as the Law Officers and the leaders of the six circuits, and up to sixteen additional members appointed by the Senate.

consisting of the Treasurers, certain other benchers, the chairman of the Council of Legal Education and the officers of the new Bar Council. The Treasurers' Council would have power to refer back to the Bar Council any policies, but if the Bar Council affirmed the policy, the Treasurers' Council would have the duty to secure its implementation. (The relationship would be like that between the House of Commons and the House of Lords, with the Commons having the ultimate power to insist on a policy.) The Bar Council would include a system of constituencies.[98] These proposals were adopted by the Bar and came into effect on 1 January 1987.[99]

In 1991, Lord Benson, the former Chairman of the Royal Commission on Legal Services, urged that the time had come to place management of all the Inns' properties under the authority of the Bar Council.[100] Very large sums of money would be needed to modernise the properties held by the Inns to bear the cost of improving recruitment, the vocational training of students, remuneration in pupillage and continuing professional education. The Bar, though tiny, still had six governing bodies – the Bar Council, the four Inns of Court and the Treasurer's Council. The division of responsibility was wasteful in time and money. The Inns owned extremely valuable properties in London and were therefore one of the best-endowed professions in the country. Each of the Inns managed its properties in its own way. For years they had charged low rents and had therefore failed to build up reserves. Now they would have to borrow large sums at high interest. The Inns were reluctant to allow the Bar Council to decide how to administer their valuable assets. Under the 1987 agreement the Bar could in theory impose its will on the Inns but the procedure was complex.

In 1999, the Bar Council moved to make subscription to the Bar Council compulsory. It persuaded the Government to introduce an amendment to the Access to Justice Bill which gave the Bar Council the right to make subscriptions mandatory.[101]

The problem of the management of the Bar continued to be an issue. In 1996, Martin Bowley QC said: 'The central issue . . . is that we just cannot afford the waste of resources, both human and financial, involved in our current system of government which involves a Bar Council, four Inns of Court, six Circuits and something like twenty specialist associations, all with differing agendas and differing priorities'.[102]

For the most recent developments following the report of Sir David Clementi see pp. 823–36 below.

---

[98] It should consist of two representatives of each circuit (of whom one would be a junior barrister), one from each Bar Association, three representatives of each Inn and fifty-one elected members, of whom nine would be Queen's Counsel and twelve would be under seven years' Call.

[99] See *Law Society's Gazette*, 28 May 1986, p. 1628; 23 July 1986, p. 2321 and also *Counsel*, September/October 1994, pp. 10–14.   [100] *Counsel*, July 1991, pp. 14–15.

[101] Access to Justice Act 1999, s. 46.   [102] *Counsel*, May/June 1996, p. 16.

Employed and 'non-practising' barristers

As has been seen, there are many barristers who, having been Called to the Bar, do not become self-employed barristers in chambers but who do provide legal services. They used to be called 'non-practising barristers', despite the fact that they worked as lawyers, but in the 1980s those who offered legal services to their own employer came to be called 'employed barristers'. Until the end of the 1980s, employed barristers had no right to appear as advocates in the courts. But in 1989 the Bar Council agreed that employed barristers should be treated in the same way as solicitors. Providing they had completed pupillage or had been in employment for five years they were given the same rights of audience as solicitors in the lower courts. They were also permitted to instruct barristers in private practice, but they were not allowed to conduct litigation. In 1997, as will be seen below, employed solicitors were granted full rights of audience and the Bar Council moved to grant similar rights to employed barristers, but these moves were overtaken by the Access to Justice Act 1999 which required the Bar Council to grant full rights of audience to employed barristers who satisfied equivalent training requirements to those for self-employed barristers. In order to obtain rights of audience in the higher courts a barrister must not only have completed pupillage but must for three years following pupillage work from the office of a 'qualified person'. The majority of employed barristers and most solicitors do not at present meet the criteria for being 'qualified persons'.[103] This creates a barrier for newly qualified barristers.

There are now three categories of employed barristers. There are employed barristers who offer legal services only to their own employer. This is the position of barristers who are employed in the Government legal service or local government and in-house lawyers in commerce, finance and industry.[104]

Secondly, there are barristers who offer legal services to the general public through their employers. They can only hold themselves out as practising barristers if they have higher rights of audience and work for an organisation approved under the Code of Conduct. The organisations that are approved include solicitors' firms and law centres.

Thirdly, there are employed barristers who may not hold themselves out as barristers – for instance because although they work for an approved organisation such as a firm of solicitors, they have not done pupillage. (A large number of City firms employ barristers. Allen & Overy, for instance, employs as many as 150 barristers most of whom are not practising.) Another group are those

---

[103] Defined as someone who for six years has practised as a barrister or a member of an authorised body and for the previous two years has made such practice his primary occupation and who has been entitled to exercise a right of audience in all the courts (Code of Conduct rule 203.3).

[104] Those who were Called before January 2002 need only to have completed their Bar Vocational Course (or the previous Bar Finals) to be eligible for this status. Those Called after January 2002 need also to have completed a pupillage.

who may have higher rights of audience but who offer legal services to the public at large working for non-authorised organisations such as accountants' firms or as claims advisers for insurance companies.

For the view that employed barristers feel cast as 'second class citizens' by the Bar Council see L. Trevelyan, 'Bar to Progress', *Law Society's Gazette*, 10 February 2005, p. 20.

For the implications of the Clementi report and its aftermath see pp. 823–36 below.

The solicitors' branch

Origin and history

The solicitors' branch grew out of the variety of different practitioners who operated in different capacities in the legal system other than the barrister and the sergeant-at-law. By the late thirteenth century, attorneys existed to handle the technicalities of law suits. Solicitors seem first to have emerged in the sixteenth century. By the end of the seventeenth century the different categories included sergeants, Queen's Counsel and junior barristers, solicitors, attorneys, conveyancers or scriveners, pleaders and proctors. Pleaders were absorbed by the Bar, scriveners' work was taken over by solicitors and attorneys, and the differences between attorney and solicitors were gradually eliminated. Attorneys were advisers to the parties, solicitors were especially associated with matters concerned with land and proctors were concerned with ecclesiastical law and matrimonial affairs.

The Judicature Act 1873 merged the functions of solicitors, attorneys and proctors and the title 'solicitor' was adopted as a generic title for them all. Statute now reserves that title to those qualified as solicitors. (There is no equivalent statute in relation to barristers.)

For information about the profession at present, including much statistical information covering recent years, see www.research.lawsociety.org.uk. Note especially very helpful fact sheets. See also the annual publication *Trends in the Solicitors' Profession Annual Statistical Report* accessible on the Law Society's Website – www.lawsociety.org.uk.

On the history of the profession see for instance M. Birks, *Gentlemen of the Law* (Stevens, 1960).

Entry and training

The process of qualifying to be a solicitor, as for the barrister, consists of an academic stage, a stage of institutional vocational training and a period of 'on the job' training formerly known as articles and today called traineeship.

The academic stage A person wishing to be a solicitor can pass the academic requirement by taking a law degree but, as with barristers, a non-law degree plus the one-year law conversion course (the CPE) is deemed to be the equivalent. In 2004–5 there were 7,356 persons admitted as solicitors. Of these 69 per cent came by way of direct entry and 22 per cent were by transfer, mainly from over-seas.[105] Of those who came by direct entry, just over three-quarters had law degrees and 23 per cent had non-law degrees. Of the transfers, 13 per cent were former barristers, 10 per cent were legal executives and 2 per cent were justices' clerks whilst 75 per cent were foreign lawyers – (in order) from Australia, New Zealand, North America, Singapore/Malaysia, Hong Kong, Scotland, EU coun-tries and the Indian sub-continent.[106]

Vocational training for solicitors – the Legal Practice Course The Law Society's vocational Legal Practice Course (LPC) was drastically reformed as from 1993. The aim was to make the course more genuinely vocational, based as much as possible on skills training. The course is taught at the five branches of the College of Law and at over twenty universities. Whereas previously the course was virtually identical wherever it was taught, there is now a measure of freedom for teaching institutions subject to accreditation by the Law Society's Legal Practice Course Board. The content has a practical basis with an empha-sis on the use of 'black letter law' and practical know-how.[107] The course can be either full-time over one year or part-time over two academic years.[108] The course was further revised in 1997 to place greater emphasis on law in general and business law in particular to give more opportunity for options.[109]

In 2001 eight leading City firms started a more specialised bespoke 'LPC+' course. City LPC was delivered originally by Nottingham Law School, the Oxford Institute of Legal Practice and the BPP Law School. (Subsequently three of the firms[110] broke away from the consortium to set up a course with the College of Law in London. The other five[111] decided to work with the BPP only.) Bespoke courses specifically tailored to the needs of particular firms seem likely to grow.[112]

In January 2005 the Law Society put forward a package of reform proposals prepared by its Training Framework Review Group. The central feature of the

---

[105] Law Society, *Trends in the Solicitors' Profession, Annual Statistical Report 2005 (Annual Statistics 2005)*, Table 9.5. In respect of 8 per cent no information was available as to the route of entry.   [106] *Annual Statistics 2005*, Table 9.6.

[107] The course consists of both compulsory subjects (conveyancing, wills, probate, administration, business law and practice, and litigation and advocacy) and optional subjects. Matters of professional conduct and the influence of European law, revenue law and financial services law are supposed to be taught throughout the course. Skills training is supposed to focus on interviewing and advising, legal research, writing and drafting, negotiating and advocacy.

[108] See further *Law Society's Gazette*, 23 May 1990, p. 4; 20 June 1990, p. 2; 6 February 1991, p. 6; 2 October 1991, p. 4. For critical assessment and a reply see *Legal Action*, July 1994, p. 8 and September 1994, p. 9. See also the study by the Policy Studies Institute – M. Shiner and T. Newburn, *Entry into the Legal Professions: The Law Student Cohort Study Year 3* (Law Society, 1995).

[109] For a description see N. Savage, 'Reshaping the Legal Practice Course', 147 *New Law Journal*, 19 September 1997, p. 1358.   [110] Clifford Chance, Linklaters and Allen & Overy.

[111] Freshfields Bruckhaus Deringer, Herbert Smith, Lovells, Norton Rose and Slaughter & May.

[112] In September 2006 Berwin Leighton Paisner signed up on a new LPC+ course aimed at smaller firms. (*Law Society's Gazette*, 21 September 2006, p. 22.)

proposal was that the Legal Practice Course should no longer be compulsory.[113] There would be other ways of qualifying. Instead of skills being taught in the classroom and being tested in hypothetical exams, they could be acquired and assessed in real-life situations. This would make it possible to earn whilst learning, so reducing the cost of qualifying. There would be no minimum period of study and preparation prior to qualification.

The proposal that the LPC become optional attracted intense critical response[114] and in view of the widespread negative reaction it was eventually abandoned.[115] The LPC therefore remains compulsory, but the new LPC (dubbed LPC2), due to come into effect in 2008, will have various different features. One major difference is that instead of all providers having to run the same course they will have considerable freedom to devise their own course.

In January 2006, responsibility for the training system was taken over by the Law Society's new Regulation Board. The Training Framework Review Group which had previously done the work was abolished.[116] In May 2006 the Regulation Board published draft proposals. The framework document stated: 'The key regulatory role for the Law Society Regulation Board is to achieve consistency of the learning outcomes and demonstration by candidates of the minimum standards, rather than to ensure that all LPC students have a consistent or equivalent experience'.

Centrally set assessments detached from any prescribed course would be introduced, initially for the financial, business skills and professional ethics modules. There would be more skills assessments.[117] There would be a variety of elective subjects. Students would be able to apply for exemptions from parts of the course they had already covered in the form of equivalent experience. There would also be 'robust' assessment of trainees' work-based learning through the completion of a 6,000 word portfolio during the training contract.[118]

The number of places for full-time students on the LPC in the three years from 2003–5 was 7,859, 8,345 and 8,843. (That is the number of places not the number of students.) The number of part-time places in those years was 1,700, 2,256 and 2,498.[119]

Funding the LPC For those who obtain traineeship contracts with large firms, the costs of the LPC course are normally paid by the firm. (According to the

---

[113] *Law Society's Gazette*, 20 January 2005, p. 3; 27 January 2005, p. 18.

[114] N. Johnson, 'The Training Framework Review – What's All the Fuss About?' 155 *New Law Journal*, 2005, p. 357.   [115] *Law Society's Gazette*, 27 October 2005, p. 1.

[116] *The Lawyer*, 23 January 2006, p. 3. For discussion of this development see *The Lawyer*, 13 February 2006, pp. 24–9.

[117] The Association of LPC Providers argued that this could increase the cost of the course by up to £1,000 per pupil. (*The Lawyer*, 24 July 2006, p. 8.)

[118] *Law Society's Gazette*, 27 October 2005; 16 December 2005; 25 May 2006, p. 4. *The Lawyer*, 7 August 2006, p. 22. For an overall description of the proposals by the chairman of the Regulation Board see P. Williamson, 'Solicitors of the Future', 156 *New Law Journal*, 17 November 2006, pp. 1756–7.   [119] *Annual Statistics 2005*, Table 8.3, p. 40.

2002 Mountfield Report,[120] the typical financial package offered by the large firms covered: costs of the course, CPE as well as LPC, plus maintenance of £5,000 pa, a salary of £28,000 for the first year of the traineeship, £32,000 for the second year and £50,000 on qualification.) Obviously, few small firms can offer such inducements.

In 2002, the Legal Services Commission, to encourage young lawyers into publicly funded work, started to pay LPC fees for a hundred students a year. The grants continue after the LPC to cover a part of the trainee's salary for the traineeship stage. Grants were being targetted at firms in smaller urban and rural areas. Firms must derive over 50 per cent of their income from legal aid. The grants are premised on an expectation that the solicitor will stay with the firm for at least two years after qualification.[121]

Traineeship Hitherto the basic post-LPC training-on-the-job has been two years in a solicitors' office under a formal training contract. In August 2006 the new Law Society Regulation Board (LSRB) published a consultation paper entitled *A New Framework for Work Based Learning* (www.lawsociety.org.uk). This invited views on radical proposals designed to create a more flexible system aimed at reducing the cost of training and the bottleneck for would-be solicitors who had passed the LPC but could not get a training contract.[122]

The main features of the proposed new system would be:

- A move away from the two-year training contract to a period of assessed learning involving an initial planning session and four review sessions at not less than four-month intervals. (So qualification would be possible after sixteen months.)
- A route to qualification for individuals not working in an accredited organisation or under a formal training arrangement through the guidance of LSRB trained 'portfolio supervisors'.
- A standard portfolio template as an assessment tool for the period of work-based learning.
- The development of an improved validation and monitoring process for organisations seeking accreditation as training organisations and a lighter touch, in-house assessment regime for individuals employed in those organisations.

A distinction would be drawn between trainees working in accredited organisations and others. The LSRB would no longer prescribe the detailed structure and content of training in accredited organisations. Anyone wishing to qualify as a solicitor would be able to present themselves for assessment regardless of

---

[120] *Report of the Committee on Financial Support for Entrants to the Bar,* July 2002, Annex B.
[121] See the Legal Services Commission's consultation paper *Developing Legal Aid Solicitors*; Press Release of 12 June 2002 ('Over £1.5 million to help fund the next generation of legal aid solicitors') – www.legalservices.gov.uk.
[122] The page one story in the *Law Society's Gazette,* 17 August 2006 was headed 'Board sets training revolution in motion'.

where or how they had gained their experience and whether it had been obtained under a structured training environment or by working in some other legal environment at an appropriate level. (The costs of the reviews for those not employed in accredited organisations would fall on the trainee.) The intention would be for the standard of competence for all entrants to match that achieved by newly qualified solicitors under the existing system.[123] A two-year pilot project would start in September 2007. The pilot would be evaluated before full implementation of the new system.

Trainee registrations are at record levels – having exceeded 5,000 per annum for six consecutive years. (In 2004–5 there were 5,732 new traineeships registered compared with 4,170 ten years earlier, an increase of over a third.[124]) Well over half (61 per cent) were women (compared with 54 per cent in 1990–1).[125] Of those with known ethnicity, ethnic minority trainees were 18 per cent.[126]

Since 1987, the Law Society has recommended national minimum starting salaries for trainee solicitors. From 1993–9 the rates were frozen at the 1992 levels. From 2003 there was also a recommended salary (as opposed to minimum salary). (From August 2006 the recommended salary was £17,527 in Central London and £15,605 in the rest of the country, with the recommended minimum as £17,110 and £15,332.) It was reported in 2006 however that the Law Society's new Regulatory Board was contemplating ditching minimum pay 'in an effort to grow the number of training contract places available to students'.[127] Despite growth over the previous five years in the number of students taking the LPC the number of training contracts had remained almost static.

Most trainees are paid over the minimum rate. The average starting salary in 2004–5 was £20,794 – though in Central London it was £27,094.[128] Male trainees were offered starting salaries that on average were 7 per cent above that for females.[129]

The small number of large firms took a completely disproportionate number of the trainees. Almost a third (31 per cent) of all traineeships registered in 2004–5 were with the 0.3 per cent of firms with eighty-one or more partners and a further 15 per cent with firms with twenty-six to eighty partners. (These firms accounted for 1.4 per cent of all firms.) Fifteen per cent of trainees were with the 3 per cent of firms with eleven to twenty-five partners, 15 per cent were with the 9 per cent of firms with five to ten partners and 24 per cent were with the 86 per cent of one to four partner firms.[130]

Continuing education The Law Society introduced compulsory continuing education for new entrants as from 1984. In 1990 it was extended to all members of the profession qualifying after 1987. They have to undertake sixteen hours per

---

[123] For further details and differing views see *Law Society Gazette*, 21 September 2006, pp. 20–1.
[124] *Annual Statistics 2005*, chart 6, p. 41.　　[125] *Ibid*, Table 8.7, p. 42.
[126] *Ibid*, Table 8.8, p. 42. With regard to 7 per cent of trainees there was no information as to ethnicity.　　[127] *The Lawyer*, 4 September 2006, p. 11.
[128] *Annual Statistics 2005*, para. 8.13, p. 46.　　[129] *Ibid*, para. 8.14, p. 46.
[130] *Ibid*, Table 8.11, p. 45.

annum at continuing education courses or activities of one sort or another for the rest of their careers. As from November 1998 the same obligation to undertake continuing education was extended to all solicitors of whatever seniority. The obligation can be met by engaging in a variety of educational activities.[131]

Number of solicitors

A person who acts as a solicitor within the meaning of the Solicitors Act 1974 must hold an annual practising certificate. In 2005, there were 126,142 solicitors on the Roll of whom 100,938 (80 per cent) held practising certificates.[132] Of these, 78,092 (77 per cent) were in private practice.[133]

There has been a dramatic increase in the number of solicitors with practising certificates. For the first half of the twentieth century, it was under 20,000. In 1950, it was 17,000. In 1975, the number was just under 30,000; in 1985, 44,500; in 1995, 66,100. In the decade to 2005, it grew by 34,000 to just over 100,000.[134]

The large growth in the size of the Bar in the 1960s and 1970s was fuelled to a considerable extent by the exponential increase in grants of representation under legal aid. This was not the case for the solicitors' branch since legal aid forms only a small proportion of their income.[135] The growth was attributable rather to the spread of home ownership in the population. As will be seen below, until 1986 solicitors had a monopoly of the handling of conveyancing which accounted for a very large part of their income. (In 1901, only about 10 per cent of dwellings were owner-occupied; the figure in 1971 was 50 per cent and in 1990 was 67 per cent.[136])

The structure of the solicitors' profession

Solicitors practise in firms. A firm may have more than one office. The annual statistics published by the Law Society show the number of firms broken down by numbers of partners. In 2004–5, there were 9,728 firms with a total of 12,650 offices.[137]

As has been seen, the great majority of firms are small, but it is the largest firms of which one hears most often. According to the 2004 profile of the 'Top 100' firms by *The Lawyer*,[138] there were several firms with over 1,000 fee earners.[139]

---

[131] See generally the CPD and Training Supplement in 156 *New Law Journal*, 17 November 2006, pp. 1747–59. The penultimate article in the supplement by the chairman of the Regulation Board (pp. 1756–70) indicated that the Board would in future be looking at ways of placing emphasis on outcomes rather than on CPD hours spent.

[132] *Ibid*, para. 1.3, p. 13. Those without a practising certificate include retired solicitors and others not pursuing a career in the legal profession.   [133] *Ibid*, Table 2.2.

[134] *Ibid*, p. 13.

[135] In 1999–2000 it was 13 per cent of gross fees. The figure was not available after 2001 but it is unlikely that the percentage increased.

[136] For an overall assessment of the changing profile of the profession see N. Rose, 'Strength in Numbers', *Law Society's Gazette*, 8 July 2004, pp. 24–5.

[137] *Annual Statistics 2005*, Table 3.1, p. 23.   [138] 5 May 2004, p. 16

[139] Clifford Chance (2,684 lawyers including 406 equity partners), Freshfields (2,225 lawyers, 516 equity partners), Linklaters (2,000 lawyers, 390 equity partners), Allen & Overy (1,879

Their importance, however, is enormous. In 2005, firms with eighty-one or more partners, around 0.3 per cent of the total number of firms, employed just over one-fifth (22 per cent) of all solicitors. Firms with twenty-six or more partners, 1.5 per cent of the total, employed well over a third (38 per cent) of all solicitors. (At the other end of the spectrum, sole practices, 46 per cent of all firms employed 8 per cent of all solicitors.[140])

The firms with twenty-six or more partners in 1999–2000 generated no less than 50 per cent of the profession's gross fees. (This figure was not available after 2001.) As has been seen, they also train half of all the entrants to the profession.

'Assistant solicitors' are qualified solicitors who are not partners. In recent years a new category has emerged of 'associate solicitors' whose status is between that of assistant solicitor and partner. In 2005, solicitors in firms were partners (34 per cent), assistant solicitors (36 per cent), associate solicitors (13 per cent), consultants (4 per cent), sole practitioners (5 per cent) and other (7 per cent).[141]

A solicitor normally cannot establish his own practice within three years of admission to the Roll. He needs the permission of the Law Society to do so.

The fee earners in solicitors' firms also include 'legal executives'.

Legal executives

It has been a familiar feature of solicitors' offices for well over a hundred years that they employ unadmitted staff on professional work. Formerly they were known as 'managing clerks', but since the founding of the Institute of Legal Executives in 1963 they have generally been known as legal executives, regardless of whether they were actually members of the Institute. In 2005, there were some 22,500 members of the Institute (including students). There are reckoned to be approximately another 10,000 unadmitted staff in solicitors' offices who are not members of the Institute.

The Institute has three grades of membership – students, Associates (who have passed four papers in law and have served in solicitors' office for at least three consecutive years) and Fellows (who must be twenty-five or over, have served eight years in a solicitors' office and who must have passed an examination comprising three papers out of a choice of thirteen).

For further information see the Institute's Website www.ilex.org. See also A.M. Francis, 'Legal Executives and the Phantom of Legal Professionalism: the Rise and Rise of the Third Branch of the Legal Profession', 9 *International Journal of the Legal Profession*, 2002, pp. 5–25. For a comparison between qualifying as a solicitor via a university degree and via being a legal executive see J. Beavan, 'Qualification: an Alternative Option', 155 *New Law Journal*, 2005, pp. 1535–6.

As will be seen, legal executives now have significant rights of audience.

---

lawyers, 312 equity partners), Lovells (1,153 lawyers, 235 equity partners), Eversheds (1,712 lawyers, 172 equity partners) and DLA (1,212 lawyers, 113 equity partners).

[140] *Annual Statistics 2005*, Table 4.1, p. 27.   [141] *Ibid*, Table 4.1, p. 27.

The distribution of solicitors' offices in the community

The first systematic national study of the location of solicitors' offices was carried out by Ken Foster on the basis of the Law List in 1971.[142] Wide differences emerged in the distribution of solicitors' offices. Various socio-economic factors were then tested to attempt to explain this unequal distribution of solicitors. The strongest correlation was between the distribution of solicitors and the amount per head of retail sales. These high correlations, Foster suggested, indicated that 'the location of solicitors and their offices is governed principally by economic considerations very similar to those that govern the location of retail distribution outlets'.[143]

A second study of the distribution of solicitors was carried out on the data for 1985 by Kim Economides and Mark Blacksell.[144] Like Foster, they plotted the distribution of solicitors in the Solicitors and Barristers Directory. The results showed a very uneven distribution. 'At a regional level, the southeast dominated, with almost half the total and the lowest regional value for the number of persons per solicitor. There was a broad band of relatively well-provided counties stretching from the southwest to East Anglia, while poorly-provided counties covered the north and east Midlands.'[145] However, more detailed scrutiny of the data, at district rather than county level, revealed a more complex and more interesting pattern which ran somewhat counter to the general distribution picture. Solicitors were disproportionately well represented in rural areas and poorly represented in rapidly expanding suburban populations on the fringes of the major centres of population.

Women in the solicitors' profession

The remarkable rise in the number of women in the profession is similar to that at the Bar. As recently as 1960 there were virtually no women solicitors. In 1970, they were a mere 3 per cent of those with practising certificates. In 1980, the proportion was 10 per cent, in 1990 25 per cent and in 2005 42 per cent. Since 1994 more than half of those admitted as solicitors have been women. In 2004–5, the proportion was 60 per cent.[146]

It seems, however, that women still do not enjoy parity in promotion prospects. The distribution of solicitors in private practice in 2005 is given in the Table below. It shows that 44 per cent of men compared with 20 per cent of women were partners. In part this might be because women have only relatively recently begun to enter the profession in significant numbers. But the *Statistical Report* goes on to show that with equivalent levels of experience a higher proportion of men achieve partnership.[147] Thus, of solicitors with ten to nineteen years' experience, 68 per cent of men were partners (or sole practitioners) compared with 45 per

[142] 'The Location of Solicitors', *Modern Law Review*, 1973, p. 153.   [143] *Ibid* at pp. 161–2.
[144] 'Access to Justice in Rural Britain: Final Report', 16 *Anglo–American Law Review*, 1985, pp. 353–75.   [145] *Ibid* at pp. 357–8.   [146] *Annual Statistics 2005*, Table 9.3, p. 48.
[147] *Ibid*, para. 2.10, p. 18.

	All solicitors per cent	Women per cent	Men per cent
Partners	34	20	44
Sole practitioners	5	3	7
Associate solicitors	13	16	11
Assistant solicitors	36	53	25
Consultant	4	2	6
Other	7	6	8
Total	100	100	100

(Source: *Annual Statistical Report*, 2005, Table 2.9, p. 17)

cent of women. This could be partly because, compared with men, women take a greater number of career breaks and accumulate fewer years of post-qualifying experience. No doubt it is also due to some extent to gender discrimination.[148]

Ethnic minorities in the solicitors' profession

The proportion of solicitors from the ethnic minorities has risen considerably in recent years. In 1995 they were 3.8 per cent of solicitors with practising certificates. By 2005, this had risen to an estimated 8.7 per cent.[149] Of the students enrolling with the Law Society in 2004–5, no fewer than 25 per cent were from ethnic minority groups[150] – compared with 14 per cent in 1991–2.[151]

In 2005, 18 per cent of trainee solicitors and 13 per cent of new admissions to the Roll were from ethnic groups.[152]

By far the largest single category of ethnic minority admissions was Asian (56 per cent). Others were African (12 per cent), Chinese (7 per cent) and Afro-Carribbean (5 per cent).[153] The figures for ethnic origin of those admitted as solicitors is not complete since the information about ethnic origin was only available in 2004–5 for 76 per cent of those admitted.

A further breakdown of the ethnic minority admissions showed that 63 per cent were women – an even higher proportion than for admissions generally. Within the ethnic minorities, the proportion of female admissions was highest amongst Afro-Carribbeans (82 per cent).[154]

[148] See further C.M.S. McGlynn, 'The Business of Equality in the Solicitors' Profession', 63 *Modern Law Review*, 2000, pp. 442–56; H. Sommerlad, 'Women Solicitors in a Fractured Profession: Intersections of Gender and Professionalism in England and Wales', 9 *International Journal of the Legal Profession*, 2002, pp. 213–34; D. Nicolson, 'Demography, Discrimination and Diversity: a New Dawn for the British Legal Profession?', 12 *International Journal of the Legal Profession*, 2005, pp. 201–28; Law Society, *Women Solicitors*, Fact Sheet, 2005 – www.research.lawsociety.org.uk.
[149] *Annual Statistics 2005*, para. 2.12, p. 19. The ethnicity information was available for 87.9 per cent of practising solicitor holders.   [150] *Ibid*, Table 8.5, p. 38.
[151] *Annual Statistics 2001*, para. 8.5, p. 56.
[152] *Annual Statistics 2005*, Table 8.8, p. 42 and Table 9.9, p. 54.   [153] *Ibid*, Table 9.11, p. 55.
[154] *Ibid*, para. 9.11, p. 55.

Whereas 36 per cent of White Europeans in private practice are at partnership level, the corresponding proportion from minority ethnic groups is significantly lower at 22 per cent.[155] In March 2006, Trevor Phillips, chair of the Commission for Racial Equality, warned the profession that without visible improvement the profession was 'inviting Government to consider tougher legislation' which would force it to do better.[156]

In May 2005 the Lord Chancellor's Legal Services Consultative Panel called for law firms and barristers' chambers to undertake diversity monitoring including keeping records for QCs and partners and to publish the results on their Website.[157] In July 2006, however, a Government minister said she was 'appalled' at the lack of response by law firms with regard to publishing their diversity statistics.[158]

Management of the solicitors' branch

The profession is run by the Law Society which was established by Royal Charter in 1831 and by 121 autonomous local law societies. The Law Society is both the professional association concerned with the advancement of the interests of solicitors and the governing body concerned with dealing with complaints against solicitors and disciplinary matters. It is therefore both the trade union and the regulator. (As will be seen, in 2006 these two roles were separated and under the Legal Services Bill complaints against solicitors are to be entirely removed.)

The Law Society issues practising certificates to those in private practice. It administers the Compensation Fund against which clients defrauded by solicitors can complain and recoup their losses.[159] It also manages the system of training for those wishing to qualify as solicitors through its College of Law. Practice Rules regulating the practice, conduct and discipline of solicitors were until now promulgated by the Law Society with the approval of the Master of the Rolls under the authority of the Solicitors Act 1933, s. 31.

The 121 local law societies perform less important functions. They deal with complaints from the public, help solicitors in difficulties and assist would-be entrants to secure positions in firms. They may arrange lectures and social events. They also play a role in shaping Law Society policy by reacting to proposals emanating from Chancery Lane.

---

[155] *Ibid*, para. 2.15, p. 22.

[156] 156 *New Law Journal*, 31 March 2006, p. 526. He was speaking at the launch of a survey by the Black Solicitors Network showing that many of the top solicitors' firms in the UK had no black or ethnic minority partners.

[157] *The Legal Profession: Entry, Retention and Competition*, May 2005, www.dca.gov.uk/atoj/lscp/lscofr.2.htm.

[158] *The Lawyer*, 31 July 2006, p. 4. Bridget Prentice MP, Parliamentary Under Secretary of State at the DCA, said that only thirty-four of *The Lawyer UK 100* had replied to the DCA's request despite repeated reminders.

[159] In 2005, payments from the Fund amounted to £13.3 million. (Law Society's *Annual Report*, 2005, p. 27.)

The Law Society is run by its Council, which until 2000 consisted of seventy-five members elected by solicitors throughout the country. The country was divided into constituencies, each of which had a proportionate number of Council members depending on the number of solicitors who practised in that area.

As is normal for a professional body, the Law Society has always been the butt of criticism from its members, but in the past few years the level of criticism has reached new heights (or depths). Dissatisfaction seems to centre partly on the way the Society deals with substantive issues – such as the catastrophe of the shortfall of several hundred million pounds on the Solicitors' Indemnity Fund (SIF) and the resulting gigantic increases in insurance premiums, partly on what is felt to be general inefficiency and partly on lack of rapport with the concerns of the ordinary practitioner. Criticism from outside the profession is also endemic – notably over the Law Society's handling of complaints by clients.

The crisis over the SIF, after a long and agonising saga, eventually led in June 1999 to a decision by a reluctant Council of the Law Society to allow solicitors to opt between the previously compulsory mutual Fund and making equivalent alternative insurance arrangements in the open market.[160]

The perceived problem of inefficiency and general malaise led to the Council asking for advice from Pearson Group chairman, Sir Dennis (now Lord) Stevenson, a businessman experienced in helping ailing companies. His verdict: 'The Law Society does not work. Its very structure prevents effective decision-making, and when decisions are made, there is no means of ensuring that they are implemented'. He recommended that the Society's 141 committees and working parties should be reduced to a core, that greater use be made of *ad hoc* task forces, that an executive committee should oversee implementation of the Council's policy decisions and that elections should be restricted to the Deputy Vice President level to avoid damaging contests.[161] The Council took his advice. In January 1999 some fifty committees were abolished. A new organisational system was established that came into existence as from January 2000. In the meanwhile a small Interim Executive Committee and twelve working parties on major policy areas were established.[162]

In 1999–2000 the Law Society engaged in a further bout of major reform. In December 1999 the Interim Executive Committee approved the appointment of consultants Corporate Edge to advise on a redefinition of the Society's activities. In April 2000 the Council received reports from three working

---

[160] *Law Society's Gazette*, 30 June 1999, p. 3. The story can be traced over months through the columns of the *Gazette*. For a potted history of professional indemnity insurance for solicitors see *Law Society's Gazette*, 17 February 1999, p. 22. For a full account see M. Davies, 'Wither Mutuality? A Recent History of Solicitors' Professional Indemnity Insurance', 5 *International Journal of the Legal Profession*, 1998, pp. 29–61. For the new scheme see *Law Society's Gazette*, 11 August 1999, p. 46; 20 April 2001, p. 24; *New Law Journal*, 15 June 2001, p. 881; *The Lawyer*, 25 June 2001, p. 33.   [161] *The Lawyer*, 22 September 1998, p. 1.

[162] For the developing story see *Law Society's Gazette*, 20 September 1998, p. 4; 18 November 1998, p. 22; 25 November 1998, p. 22; 2 December 1998, p. 15; 20 January 1999, p. 16; 26 May 1999, p. 18.

parties on the Future of Regulation, Regulation Review, and Sections and Specialisation. It agreed that reform should be taken forward by a specially convened Reform Co-ordination Group. This eventually resulted in a consultation paper which was sent to the profession in October 2000. The consultation paper made a number of central proposals:

- *An enlarged and more representative Council* – size to be increased from seventy-five to a hundred – representation not only for geographical constituencies but also for sectional and specialist interests possibly to be elected by national ballot or nominated by the interest groups – primary role of Council to approve strategic priorities, determine policy and set budget – it would elect and delegate authority to a Main Board – the Council would only meet four to six times a year.
- *Redesignation of the Society's functions* – proposed they be Standards, Adjudication and Compliance, Law reform, Representation, Services, and Finance and Administration.[163]
- *A Board per function, chaired by a Council member* – each Board to consist of a mixture of Council, non-Council and lay members – the first two named Boards to have 50 per cent lay membership.
- *The Main Board to operate as 'cabinet' government* – consisting of three office holders, Council member chairs of the individual boards, the Chief Executive and the staff director of each function – its role overseeing the strategic plan and budget.

The reform package met opposition,[164] but it was approved by the profession – first in responses to the consultation exercise and then at a Special General Meeting in May 2001. The postal ballot, in which over 17,000 voted, approved a series of resolutions by more than the required two-thirds majority.[165]

The Society's annual report for the year ending December 2001 gave details of the initial phase under the new system. The new Council had sixty-one seats for geographical constituencies plus up to thirty-nine specialist seats and five lay members. So far, thirty-six of the thirty-nine seats had been designated. The first lay members had been appointed by the Master of the Rolls in July 2001. The Standards Board had eight Council members and three lay members. Half the members of the Compliance Board which dealt with enforcement of rules, regulations and standards were lay persons.

It is not required that qualified solicitors be members of the Law Society, but over 80 per cent are.

---

[163] See further p. 835 below.

[164] See for instance D. Keating, 'Reform at the Law Society', 150 *New Law Journal*, 29 September 2000, p. 1396; M. Mears, 'Keep the status quo', *Law Society's Gazette*, 16 November 2000, p. 26.

[165] See M. Napier, 'End of the Beginning', *Law Society's Gazette*, 3 May 2001, p. 20; and for the resolutions passed see 'The Law Society's Special General Meeting', *Law Society's Gazette*, 11 May 2001, p. 14.

For the recommendations regarding regulation in the report by Sir David Clementi, the profession's response and the Legal Services Bill see pp. 824–27, 834–35 below.

For the view that the Law Society had lost its way in coming to terms with contemporary conditions see A.M. Francis, 'Out of Touch and Out of Time: Lawyers, their Leaders and Collective Mobility within the Legal Profession', 24 *Legal Studies*, 2004, pp. 322–48.

2. The divided profession

Many assume that the division of the legal profession goes back into the mists of antiquity, but this is not so. As Australian scholar John Forbes pointed out, division presupposes two or more parts of a whole, but it was not until the seventeenth or even eighteenth century that solicitors could be said to have emerged as a distinct or identifiable professional group. The Bar had by then had centuries of development. The distinction in those days was therefore not between two parts of the same profession, but between lawyers and sub-lawyers. In 1765 Blackstone set out the hierarchy of the legal profession without even mentioning solicitors. Even a hundred years later Dicey lectured on legal education without referring to solicitors. Until the late eighteenth and into the early nineteenth century, solicitors could be described as 'an unorganised, ill-disciplined, ill-educated category of sub-professional agents, living wholly or partly on the sub-professional trivia of litigation and conveyancing and sharing even this subject matter with court clerks, law students and laymen'.[166]

However, in the nineteenth century the solicitors' branch gradually established itself and carved out areas of work in which it specialised. The Bar was persuaded first to give up seeing clients direct and then to cease to do conveyancing. In return the Bar had a monopoly over the right to appear as an advocate (the 'right of audience') in the higher courts and a virtual monopoly over appointments to the bench.

In 1979, the Benson Royal Commission on Legal Services concluded unanimously that the divided profession was in the public interest mainly on the ground that it promoted specialisation (*Cmnd* 7648, 1979, para. 17.45).

Today the division is still maintained. One cannot practise both as a barrister and a solicitor at the same time. Barristers and solicitors are not (yet at least) permitted to form partnerships. The Bar is still the senior branch. The solicitor attends on the barrister in his chambers rather than the reverse. The barrister is in charge of the running of the case and will tell the solicitor how he intends to conduct it. The barrister team and the solicitor team in a case still tend to work separately in doing their respective parts of the work. Barristers no longer have their former monopoly with regard to rights of audience in the higher courts, but they still do by far the bulk of that work. (The Law Society has

---

[166] M. Birks, *Gentlemen of the Law* (Stevens, 1960) p. 105.

conceded that in some cases it is not necessary for a solicitor to attend counsel at court.[167])

Similarly, although barristers no longer have their former monopoly over all higher judicial appointments[168] the great majority of such appointments have been and still are from the ranks of barristers. (Thus in 2004–5 of eleven High Court judges appointed, none was a solicitor; of 145 recorders appointed, only four were solicitors.[169])

There are more and more signs of overlap in the work done by barristers and solicitors and of direct competition between the two branches. The Bar's Response to the 2001 OFT report said: 'All the services that barristers provide can now be and are increasingly provided by solicitors'.[170] In 2003 it even became possible for lay clients to seek advice from a barrister without the intervention of a solicitor (see pp. 799–800 below). This was the most radical step yet in the changing relationship between the two branches of the profession.

For the Bar's statement of the value of having an independent referral profession see Appendix 9 and 10 to the Bar Council's Response to the DCA/LSC Consultation Paper, *Legal Aid: A Sustainable Future*, October 2006 – www.barcouncil.org.uk.

For the effect of the Government's Legal Services Bill introduced in November 2006 see pp. 823–36 below.

Transfer between the two branches

It has become very much easier than it previously was to transfer from one branch to the other. Under the Qualified Lawyer Transfer Regulations 1990 a barrister wishing to practise as a solicitor must pass a test in Professional Conduct and Accounts (a combined paper). In addition, they must either have completed twelve months' pupillage and twelve months' legal practice after pupillage or complete two years' legal practice. Providing they have had recent advocacy experience, they do not have to re-qualify for rights of audience in the higher courts.[171] Barristers who switch to practice as solicitors do not, as formerly, have to disbar themselves. They remain subject to the Bar Council Code as 'non-practising barristers'. Solicitors who switch to become barristers do not have to come off the Roll but they cannot have a practising certificate. Unless they have higher rights of audience, solicitors transferring to the Bar must undertake pupillage.

---

[167] See *Guide to the Professional Conduct of Solicitors*, 20.04 (www.lawsociety.org.uk) which replaced the version of 20.04 in the printed Guide. It applies in magistrates' courts, small claims, fast track and in some Crown Court cases – where the solicitor considers it reasonable in that neither the client's interests nor the interests of justice will be prejudiced.

[168] Solicitors gained the right to be appointed recorders and Circuit judges by the Courts Act 1971. (See also the Administration of Justice Act 1977, s. 12.) They won the right to be appointed judges in the High Court and above by the Courts and Legal Services Act 1990, s. 71.   [169] www.dca.gov.uk/judicial/ja-arep2005/parttwo.htm#f.   [170] Paragraph 2.19.

[171] Courts Qualifications Regulations 2000 made under the Access to Justice Act 1999.

About seventy solicitors apply each year to become barristers; some 150–200 barristers apply each year to become solicitors.

3. Law centres

Law centres as noted above (p. 614), are offices providing legal services in poverty areas staffed by lawyers whose salaries are paid out of public funds. The funding is a mixture of central and local Government money and ordinary payments out of the legal aid fund. For the clients the services are entirely free of charge.

Law centres were first proposed in 1968 in the Society of Labour Lawyers' pamphlet *Justice for All*. At the time the concept was opposed by the Law Society, which saw law centres as a threat to the private practitioner. The first centre was set up in 1970 in North Kensington. By the end of that decade there were some thirty. During most of the 1980s there were some fifty law centres and that remains the approximate number.

The original opposition of the Law Society melted away as it began to be appreciated that law centres could refer paying work to the local profession whilst handling unremunerative work that the profession was not keen to undertake. Law centres are generally regarded as an important resource filling gaps in the legal aid system, often specialising in areas of work that private practitioners do not handle.

Law centre lawyers have developed skills and specialisms which have been copied by private practitioners. They have pioneered means of delivering legal services such as twenty-four hour services (a precursor of the police station Duty Solicitor scheme), multi-plaintiff work in areas other than personal injuries, peripatetic advice sessions, advice over the telephone for those who find it difficult to get to the office or pro-active lawyering, for instance through advice and training to groups. Law centres have also played a major role in providing representation in tribunals and thereby opening up an area of need not covered by the traditional legal aid system.

Law centres also play an important role as specialists. The DTI for instance awarded the Law Centres Federation (LCF) £150,000 to fund a one-year project to train lawyers and caseworkers in new legislation on equality legislation. The London Discrimination Unit, in the Lambeth Law Centre, funded by the Commission for Racial Equality, the Big Lottery Fund and the Association of London Government, takes discrimination cases from across London. The Law Centres Federation received a grant of £1.4 million from the Disability Rights Commission to fund caseworkers in law centres.[172]

---

[172] Examples were given by Steve Hynes, Director of the Law Centres Federation, in an article on specialist funding for law centres in 34 *Independent Lawyer*, January/February 2006, p. 21.

4. The use of solicitors, and clients' perceptions

There have been various surveys about use of lawyers.[173] The main findings of these surveys are:

- Use of lawyers is common. Nearly three-fifths of people over eighteen had seen a solicitor with regard to a personal problem at some point. 14 per cent had done so in the previous twelve months.[174] 34 per cent had used a solicitor in the past five years for a personal problem.[175]
- The age group that uses lawyers most are those between twenty-five and thirty-four.[176] Given that buying a home is the most common reason for using a solicitor, this is not surprising.
- The main services are buying and selling a home, making a will, divorce and matrimonial problems, dealing with someone's estate and compensation for injury.[177]
- Use of lawyers varies by socio-economic group. A solicitor in 1977 was used by 25 per cent of the professional class, 21 per cent of employers and managers, 19 per cent of intermediate and junior non-manual workers, 13 per cent of skilled manual workers and workers who worked on their own account, 11 per cent of semi-skilled workers and 10 per cent of unskilled manual workers.[178]
- Those in non-manual households (one-third of the population) accounted for over a half of all use of lawyers for the buying and selling of property, dealing with the estates of deceased persons and making or altering wills.[179] In divorce, motoring offences and personal injury claims arising out of road traffic accidents those who used lawyers were roughly in proportion to their size in the general population.[180] Manual households used lawyers considerably more (proportionately) than non-manual in claims for industrial injury compensation and marginally more in offences other than motoring,[181] but in matters which were not connected with property, 'the profile of users of lawyers' services by socio-economic group is not greatly different from that of the adult population in general.[182]

    These results demonstrate that use of lawyers is problem-connected even more than it is type-of-person connected. In other words, socio-economic

---

[173] The largest study was that conducted in the late 1970s for the Benson Royal Commission on Legal Services based on interviews with a random sample of 7,941 households (Cmnd. 7648, 1979, vol. 2, pp. 173–298 (Royal Commission)). A study by the Law Society's Research and Planning Unit was based on interviews with a representative sample of 1,630 people aged over eighteen (J. Jenkins and V. Lewis, *Client Perceptions*, Research Study No. 17, 1995 ('Jenkins and Lewis, 1995')). See also J. Jenkins, E. Skordaki and C. Willis, *Public Use and Perception of Solicitors' Services* (Law Society Research Study No. 1, 1989) and R. Craig, M. Rigg, R. Briscoe and P. Smith, *Client Views* (Law Society Research Study No. 40, 2001).

[174] Royal Commission, Table 8.3, p. 185.   [175] Jenkins and Lewis, 1995, n. 173 above, p. 5.
[176] Royal Commission, para. 8.27, p. 184; Law Society, 1995, pp. 5–6.   [177] All three surveys.
[178] Royal Commission, Table 8.8, p. 190.   [179] *Ibid*, para. 8.110.   [180] *Ibid*, para. 8.111.
[181] *Ibid*, para. 8.112.   [182] *Ibid*, para. 8.115.

background is not the best explanation of the fact that different categories in the socio-economic scale use lawyers to a different extent. In fields where property is involved (conveyancing, probate, wills, etc.), naturally those with property see lawyers much more than those without. Since this is the largest single source of work for the solicitors' profession it explains why lawyer use seems to reflect the differences between classes, but the impression is misleading. If one looks at non-property types of work, the use of lawyers is relatively even as between members of different socio-economic backgrounds.

- The image of solicitors is generally good. Of the professions evaluated (the others were bank managers, estate agents, dentists, NHS doctors and social workers), solicitors came in the middle range, with doctors rated most highly on all criteria.[183] The vast majority of clients were extremely satisfied with their own solicitor.[184]
- People distinguished between their own solicitor and the profession as a whole. Thus 31 per cent thought solicitors were approachable and easy to talk to. When asked about their own solicitor, the percentage was 74 per cent.[185]

The ratings for all the professions were generally down from the previous survey in 1989. ('The evidence supports the opinion that the public are now more questioning and demand higher level of service from all professions'.[186])

For a study by the Consumers' Association conducted since the establishment of the Community Legal Service see *The Community Legal Service: Access for All?*, 2000, summarised in *Legal Action*, July 2000, pp. 8–9.

For a major empirical study of what people do when they have a legal problem see H. Genn, *Paths to Justice* (Hart, 1999). For the follow-up study in Scotland see H. Genn and A. Paterson, *Paths to Justice: Scotland* (Hart, 2001).

5. Reform of the profession – current issues

Reform of the legal profession has been a live topic for most of the period since the 1960s. For over forty years the profession has been the subject of a series of reports, Green Papers, White Papers and a succession of statutes, culminating in the Legal Services Bill 2006–07 to implement the recommendations of the report in 2003 by Sir David Clementi.

In the 1960s the affairs of the profession were examined in three reports from the now defunct National Board for Prices and Incomes (1968, 1969 and 1971). In the 1970s the Monopolies Commission produced three reports affecting the legal profession on restrictive practices generally (1970), the Two Counsel Rule (1976) and restrictions on advertising (1976). The Benson Royal Commission on Legal Services published its report in 1979.[187] In 1988, the Marre Committee set up jointly by the Bar Council and the Law Society to deal with rights of audience,

---

[183] Jenkins and Lewis, 1995, n. 173 above, Ch. 3.   [184] *Ibid*, para. 3.9.
[185] *Ibid*, para. 3.10.   [186] *Ibid*, para. 3.12.
[187] Cmnd. 7648.

published its report *A Time for Change.* (For reasons of space, these reports are dealt with here only to the extent necessary to understand current issues.)

The aggregate effect of all these inquiries was not great. In January 1989, the then Lord Chancellor, Lord Mackay, launched three Green Papers making a whole raft of radical proposals for reform of the profession. The Green Papers provoked uproar.[188] The legal profession and the judges reacted fiercely forcing Mrs Thatcher's Government to retreat.[189] The White Paper published in July 1989 was significantly less radical than the Green Papers of January.[190] The White Paper was broadly implemented in the Courts and Legal Services Act 1990 (CLSA).[191] That Act created a new structure for dealing in particular with the endless battles over rights of audience.

Seven years later, in December 1997, Lord Irvine, the incoming Labour Lord Chancellor, indicated that he was dissatisfied with the system for dealing with rights of audience created by the CLSA and that fresh legislation would be introduced to reform it. A consultation paper (*Rights of Audience and Rights to Conduct Litigation: The Way Ahead*) was issued in June 1998 followed in December 1998 by a wide-ranging White Paper (*Modernising Justice*) dealing with legal services, civil legal aid, the civil courts, criminal justice and criminal defence. At the same time Lord Irvine published his Access to Justice Bill which became the Access to Justice Act 1999.

The Report of the Office of Fair Trading The next major development was the publication in March 2001 of the Office of Fair Trading's report *Competition in Professions.*[192] The OFT's report was commissioned under s. 2 of the Fair Trading Act 1973. The terms of reference were to identify restrictions which

---

[188] There were three Green Papers: *The Work and Organisation of the Legal Profession* (Cm. 570, 1989), *Conveyancing by Authorised Practitioners* (Cm. 572, 1989) and *Contingency Fees* (Cm. 571, 1989). For an extended review of the proposals in the Green Papers see 'The Green Paper on Contingency Fees', 8 *Civil Justice Quarterly*, April 1989, pp. 97–103; and 'The Realignment of the English Legal Profession', 8 *Civil Justice Quarterly*, July 1989, pp. 202–14.

[189] For a detailed account of the battle over the Green Papers see M. Zander, 'The Thatcher Government's Onslaught on the Lawyers: Who Won?', 24 *International Lawyer*, 1990, pp. 753–85. For a more recent account of the story see Ch. 2 of R. Abel's book *English Lawyers between Market and State* (OUP, 2003) and the writer's assessment of Abel's account in 11 *International Journal of the Legal Profession*, 2004, pp. 123–30.

[190] *White Paper on Legal Services* (Cm. 740, July 1989). For a review of the White Paper see 'The White Paper on Legal Services', 9 *Civil Justice Quarterly*, January 1990, pp. 6–12.

[191] For an account of the CLSA 1990 see 'Courts and Legal Services Act 1990', 10 *Civil Justice Quarterly*, April 1991, p. 97.

[192] OFT 328 – accessible on www.oft.gov.uk. For a summary see 151 *New Law Journal*, 23 February 2001, p. 370. The report was on restrictions on competition in three professions – lawyers, accountants and architects – but the lawyers were the main focus. The recommendations in the report were wide-ranging and potentially extremely serious for both branches of the profession: the professions to lose their partial exemption from competition law; banks, insurance companies and building societies to be allowed to compete for conveyancing and probate work; solicitors and barristers employed by non-lawyers to be permitted to offer legal services to the public; scrapping of the rank of QC; abolition of the restrictions on lay clients having direct access to barristers; on barristers forming partnerships

have the effect of 'preventing, restricting or distorting competition in professional services to a significant extent'. Although any consumer benefits claimed
for the restrictions were also to be identified, the terms of reference expressly
stated that the question whether such benefits justified the restrictions was to
be left 'for further consideration'.

Section 9 of the Competition Act 1998 sets out the criteria that must be met
if a restrictive agreement is to be given an exemption. The test is a narrow economic one – namely, whether (1) the restriction on competition in question is
justified on the ground that it improves production, distribution or economic
progress, while allowing consumers a fair share of the resulting benefit and (2)
does not impose restrictions that are not indispensable to the attainment of
those objectives or give the profession concerned the possibility of eliminating
competition in respect of a substantial part of the work in question.

The OFT's document consisted of two parts – the 137 page report of its consultants, Law and Economics Consulting Group Ltd (LECG), and its own nineteen page conclusions based on that report. LECG's report was prepared under
severe time constraints and was based on skimpy field research. (For instance,
it did not include a visit to a single set of chambers!) They also drew up their
extensive reform agenda despite admitting that their inquiries 'did not uncover
significant concerns among users of professional services, whether about
quality, price or innovation' (para. 20). (The report said that there were two
possible explanations. 'One is that the professions are providing a high standard
of service at a reasonable price. The other is that they may not be, but that clients
have difficulty in judging whether they have received good service and what
would constitute a reasonable price' (para. 20).)

Despite these manifest shortcomings, the OFT adopted LECG's report. It
called for consideration of legislative action by Government. It urged the professions to take prompt action to remove those restrictions that did not have a
proper justification and warned that, failing readiness to take such action within
twelve months, it would 'use its available powers with a view to removal of those
restrictions' (para. 49).

The then Secretary of State at the Department of Trade and Industry, Mr
Stephen Byers, said in the Commons on 8 March 2001 that the Government
accepted and would implement the recommendation to make the professions
fully subject to competition law (which happened),[193] but that for the rest it
seemed appropriate to consider comments on the report and that the Government would be issuing a formal consultation paper.

The Bar's Response The Bar published a forty-one page Response to the OFT
in February 2002.[194] It started with why the divided profession was in the public

---

and on barristers and solicitors forming multi-disciplinary partnerships etc. This was, in
effect, a reprise of Lord Mackay's 1989 Green Papers.

[193] The Enterprise Act 2002 repealed Sch. 4 of the Competition Act 1998.

[194] Accessible on www.barcouncil.org. The Response was prepared by a committee chaired by Sir
Sydney Kentridge QC, the doyen of the Bar.

interest. (LECG's report had not addressed this question.[195]) The divided profession not only had the advantages of enabling barristers to hone specialist skills as advocates and of providing objective advice to solicitors and their clients, it also enabled them to do their work 'more efficiently and cheaply than solicitors'.[196] This was because barristers' overheads were so much lower – typically 28 per cent of gross income compared with 70 per cent for solicitors.[197] The market for their services, the Bar said, would work less efficiently if the client did not have the solicitor to match the barrister to the client's needs and to monitor the quality of the barrister's work. The divided profession also promoted competition between solicitors by giving even small firms access to the full range of expertise at the Bar which enabled them better to compete with larger firms. Eighty per cent of solicitors' firms had five or fewer partners. The availability of the Bar enabled them 'to provide a much higher quality and range of services than would otherwise be possible'.[198] The divided profession also permitted barristers to operate the cab-rank rule which prohibited picking and choosing clients. (The rule requires a barrister to accept instructions with regard to work within his competence on being offered a proper fee.[199]) Because, as a result, barristers were not identified with their clients, even the most unpopular could secure proper representation. The cab-rank rule did not apply to solicitors. The Bar ended the general introductory section of its Response by quoting this writer, commenting on the OFT report, that it was an over-simplification to believe:

> . . . that equating the work done by professional people to business will necessarily improve the position of the consumer when the reality is that sometimes it may rather worsen it. Certainly one wants competition to ensure that professional fees are no higher than they need to be and that professional rules do not unnecessarily inhibit efficiency, but what one looks for from the professions even more is standards, integrity and concern for the client of a higher order than that offered in the business world.[200]

[195] Except that it stated that it had no objection to the title 'barrister' and 'solicitor' continuing provided that restrictions on direct access of clients to barristers and on conducting litigation were removed (para. 252, p. 74). The OFT report itself had said: 'The dual structure of the legal profession, with its separate roles for solicitors and barristers, may add unnecessarily to costs'. In the Director General's view, rather than pressing now for restructuring to end the dual structure of the legal profession, 'the best approach is to address its remaining adverse effects through further liberalisation of professional rules' (para. 49).

[196] Paragraph 2.10.

[197] It quoted the current average hourly rates for barristers: up to five years' Call, £78; five to ten years' call, £113; over ten years' Call, £166; QCs, £293 – by comparison with the rates for solicitors: up to five years' post-qualification, £181; over five years' post-qualification £245; equity partner £323. BDO Stoy Hayward, *Survey of Barristers' Chambers*, 2001, para. 6.5.

[198] Paragraph 2.17.

[199] See A. Watson, 'Advocacy for the Unpopular: The Barrister's Cab-rank Rule in England and Wales – Past, Present and Future?', 162 *Justice of the Peace*, 20 June 1998, pp. 476, 499 and 576.

[200] M. Zander, 'Should the Legal Profession be Shaking in its Boots?', 151 *New Law Journal*, 23 February 2001, p. 369.

The Response then addressed the specific restrictive rules at issue: partnerships, including multi-disciplinary partnerships, direct access to barristers by lay clients, advertising, the right to conduct litigation, Queen's Counsel and legal professional privilege. The arguments are noted in the relevant sections below.

The Law Society's Response The Law Society's Response to the OFT's report in December 2000 (www.lawsociety.org.uk) was quite brief. It stated that the Law Society had a Working Party on Multi-disciplinary Partnerships and a Regulation Review Working Party reviewing all the current restrictions on competition. It explained the rules regarding entry to the profession, fee sharing with non-solicitors and advertising and argued that they were in the public interest.

In April 2002, the OFT issued a twenty-one page progress statement.[201] The accompanying press release was headed 'Competition in professions – improvement but more action needed'.

In July 2002, the LCD issued a consultation paper (*In the Public Interest?*)[202] regarding the topics in the OFT's report which fell to the Department.[203] It stated: 'On all the issues raised in this consultation, the Government's position is that the market should be opened up to competition unless there are strong reasons why that should not be the case, such as evidence that real consumer detriment might result from such a change' (p. 5). The Government had decided to review the whole regulatory framework for legal services, the first step of which would be to settle the scope of such an exercise and how to complete it. It posed a series of questions.

In November 2002, both the Bar and the Law Society published their responses to the LCD's consultation paper *In the Public Interest?*[204]

Also in November 2002, the OFT issued a brief response to the LCD's consultation paper *In the Public Interest?* (press release, 21 November 2002.)

On 24 July 2003, Lord Falconer, Lord Chancellor and Secretary of State for Constitutional Affairs, announced that there was to be a wide-ranging review of the regulation of the legal services market aimed at promoting competition and innovation and improving services for the customer. It would be led by Sir David Clementi, an accountant, chairman of Prudential Plc and former Deputy Governor of the Bank of England. He was asked to complete his review by the end of 2004.[205]

[201] OFT 385, www.oft.gov.uk. [202] DCA consultation paper 07/02 – www.dca.gov.uk.
[203] Four topics were addressed: legislation on conveyancing and probate, multi-disciplinary partnerships for solicitors, legal professional privilege and the QC system.
[204] For the Bar's response see www.barcouncil.org.uk; for the Law Society's response (*Quality, Choice and the Consumer Interest*) see www.lawsociety.org.uk.
[205] The Clementi Review was announced in the DCA's twenty-page report of July 2003 *Competition and Regulation in the Legal Services Market* (CP(R2) 07/02) giving the Government's response on the matters raised in the consultation paper *In the Public Interest?* of July 2002. The 2003 report included a five page Annex A on opening up the market for probate services. It also had annexed to it a 133-page Scoping Study prepared by three academics, Robert Baldwin, Kate Malleson and Martin Cave, and Sheila Spicer of the LCD. (Sheila Spicer was then seconded to Sir David Clementi's inquiry.)

The DCA's 2003 report also announced that:

- The probate market would be opened up to banks, building societies and insurance companies, subject to the controls in ss. 54 and 55 of the Courts and Legal Services Act 1990 which would be brought into effect, as recommended by the OFT. The Government's calculation was that, over a decade, solicitors were unlikely to lose more than 7–8 per cent of their market share in this area, which represented only one per cent of solicitors' overall gross income. (See p. 819 below.)
- The Government favoured allowing new types of businesses such as multidisciplinary partnerships (MDPs) giving 'one-stop' services and corporations wider access to the market but would leave it to the Clementi Review to recommend how best to regulate them to safeguard the independence of the professions and consumers' interests. ('Appropriate regulation, adequate and stringent enough to protect both the interests of the public and the core values of the professions, is the key to the successful development of these new style businesses'.[206])
- Legal professional privilege would not be extended to clients of non-lawyers. (There was no evidence that the existing privilege was significantly distorting the market in favour of lawyers and it was contrary to the public interest to increase the right of non-disclosure, both from the courts and from the Revenue and Customs and Excise.) But the Government later changed its mind. Clause 182 of the Legal Services Bill introduced in November 2006, would confer privilege on any non-lawyer providing advocacy services, litigation services, conveyancing or probate services as what the Bill calls 'authorised persons' (see further p. 000 below).
- Pending the Clementi Review, the conveyancing market would not be opened up to banks or building societies. (The set-up costs for Government in respect of regulation would be high. In the early 1990s, take-up by such competitors was low. The conveyancing market was no longer a monopoly and was already competitive.)

The Clementi Review The Review published a seventy-nine page consultation paper in March 2004 and its Final Report (*Review of the Regulatory Framework for Legal Services in England and Wales*) in December 2004. The Final Report (considered further below, pp. 823–41) made far-reaching recommendations regarding three topics:

- *Regulation of legal services* There should be a single regulator for the entire market – the Legal Services Board (LSB) – with a majority of non-lawyers. The LSB would authorise Front Line Regulators (FLRs) such as the Bar Council and the Law Society to carry out day-to-day regulation.

---

[206] For a sharp critical reaction from a sole practitioner to the prospect of what has been dubbed 'Tesco law' see C. Sutton, 'A "Special Offer" the Public must Refuse', *New Law Journal*, 1 August 2003, p. 1185.

- *Complaints* There should be a new single body – the Office of Legal Complaints – to handle all legal services complaints.
- *New ways of providing legal services* There should a new form of provider of legal services – Legal Disciplinary Partnerships (LDPs) – with non-lawyer partners, providing lawyers were in the majority. Non-lawyer ownership of LDPs should be permitted subject to a test of 'fit to own'.

In October 2005, the Government responded to the Clementi Report in a 158 page White Paper (*The Future of Legal Services: Putting Consumers First*).[207] The White Paper indicated that the Government accepted the recommendations of the Report except that with regard to LDPs it would go further than Clementi by allowing Alternative Business Structures (ABS), with a majority of non-lawyers (and even non-lawyer owners) to provide legal services.

On 24 May 2006 the Government published the Draft Legal Services Bill.[208] The Draft Bill was sent for consideration to a Joint Committee of both Houses which was required to complete its work and to report by 25 July. The Committee published its response on time.[209] In September 2006 the Government published its response to the Joint Committee's Report. On 23 November 2006 the Legal Services Bill was introduced by the Lord Chancellor in the House of Lords.

What follows is a treatment of a variety of current topics including in particular issues raised by the OFT and by the Clementi Report. A topic that is not treated is that of fusion or unification of the two branches of the legal profession. At one time this issue excited a great deal of interest. The writer wrote extensively on the subject.[210] In the first five editions of this work a considerable amount of space was given to the subject, but in the sixth edition (1992) this material was dropped – not because the topic lacked interest, but because it no longer seemed to be of practical importance. The Benson Royal Commission on the Legal Services in its 1979 Report had concluded unanimously that the divided

---

[207] Cm. 6679 – www.dca.gov.uk.

[208] The Draft Bill (172 pp.), Explanatory Notes (66 pp.) and the Full Regularity Impact Statement (82 pp.) are all accessible on www.dca.gov.uk/legist/legalservices.htm. For a three-part series by S. Young analysing the Draft Bill see 'Tomorrow's World', 156 *New Law Journal*, 1 September 2006, p. 1304; 8 September, p. 1351; 15 September, p. 1391.

[209] The Joint Committee's Report (HC 1154, HL 232) was published on 25 July 2006. Accessible at www.parliament.gov.uk – Business-Committees – Committees in Full – Former Committees – Draft Legal Services Bill.

[210] The argument for unification of the legal profession was perhaps most fully developed in M. Zander, *Lawyers and the Public Interest* (Weidenfeld and Nicolson, 1968, now out of print) pp. 270–332. See also P. Reeves, *Are Two Legal Professions Necessary?* (Waterlows, 1986). For a direct response to the arguments in *Lawyers and the Public Interest* see G. Gardiner, 'Two Lawyers or One?', 23 *Current Legal Problems*, 1970, p. 1. See also R.E. Megarry, *Lawyer and Litigant in England* (Stevens, 1962); C.P. Harvey, *The Advocate's Devil* (Stevens, 1958); E.J. Cohn, 'The German Attorney – Experiences with a United Profession', 9 *International and Comparative Law Quarterly*, 1960, pp. 580–99 and 10 *International and Comparative Law Quarterly*, 1961, pp. 103–22; and F.A. Mann, 'Fusion of the Legal Profession', *Law Quarterly Review*, July 1977, p. 367. For the history see J. Forbes, 'Division of the Profession: Ancient or Scientific', *Law Society's Gazette*, 26 January 1977, p. 67.

profession was in the public interest.[211] It seemed improbable that this verdict would be overturned. The relevant Green Paper in 1989 proposed that barristers and solicitors should be permitted to form partnerships with each other and the Courts and Legal Services Act 1990, s. 66 permitted both barristers and solicitors to enter into partnerships with, respectively, non-barristers and non-solicitors. But it also specifically permitted the Law Society and the Bar Council to make rules prohibiting their members from entering into such partnerships and both branches had such rules. The 1990 legislation left it to the profession to regulate the matter and with both branches of the profession strongly opposed to 'fusion', the issue did not seem to be a live one. The fact that the OFT did not deal with the question in its 2001 report on restrictions on competition in the professions confirmed this view. Implementation of the Clementi Report by the Legal Services Act 2007 is unlikely to change the position. Even if the Legal Services Board were one day to require the two branches to abolish their rules forbidding private practice partnerships between barristers and solicitors, one cannot imagine many taking advantage of the possibility. The overwhelming majority of barristers and solicitors clearly favour the divided profession and it seems safe to predict that it will continue into the indefinite future.

Rights of audience for lawyers

The battle between barristers and solicitors over rights of audience in the higher courts has over the years been the issue between the two branches of the legal profession that has provoked sharper differences than any other. The right of audience is a technical term meaning the right to appear for a client as an advocate in a court or tribunal. Traditionally the question of who can appear as an advocate in an English court was decided by the judges.[212] From the nineteenth century, Parliament also became involved through legislation. (Thus, for instance, since their establishment in 1846, legislation provided that both barristers and solicitors have the right to appear as advocates in the county courts.) In recent years the battle expanded beyond the respective interests of barristers and solicitors in private practice to the question whether rights of audience in the higher courts should be given to employed lawyers and especially those employed by the Crown Prosecution Service.

In 1979, the Benson Royal Commission, by a bare majority of eight to seven, recommended that the Bar should retain its ancient monopoly over the right of audience in the higher courts. Ten years later in 1989 the Green Paper proposed instead that the right to appear as an advocate should be based not on status as a barrister or a solicitor but on individual qualification for the particular court. The test should be whether the relevant professional body had been authorised

---

[211] Benson Report, 1979, Cmnd. 7648, Ch. 17, pp. 187–202.
[212] For a helpful modern review of the history and the cases see *Abse v. Smith* [1986] QB 536, [1986] 1 All ER 350.

to certify advocates and whether the individual had the prescribed qualifications. Lay advocates could also be given rights of audience.

However, after furious debate, the 1989 White Paper more or less abandoned the 1989 Green Paper approach. The White Paper proposed that the members of both professional bodies would be deemed to enjoy their existing rights of audience. Thus, on qualification, barristers in private practice would have full rights of audience in all the courts, solicitors in private practice would have their existing rights of audience in the lower courts and such other rights of audience in the higher courts as they already enjoyed and lawyers employed other than in private practice would only have rights of audience in the lower courts.

However, additional rights of audience could be sought by the Law Society and by bodies representing employed lawyers, or even by bodies representing non-lawyers. The White Paper laid out a complex process by which such claims would be handled.[213]

This scheme was translated into law in the Courts and Legal Services Act 1990 (CLSA) subject to the requirement that decisions fulfil the 'statutory objective'[214] and the 'general principle'.[215]

As soon as the CLSA received Royal Assent, the Law Society put in its application for additional rights of audience and, shortly after, a second application was put in by the Head of the Government Legal Service and the Director of Public Prosecutions on behalf of Government lawyers and the CPS respectively.

There then ensued a tortuous process lasting several years. (The story was told by the writer in some six pages in the 8th edition of this work and at much greater length elsewhere.[216]) In brief, in 1993 solicitors won the right to qualify as advocates in the higher courts.[217] The Lord Chancellor and the Lord Chief

---

[213] The claim had to be put to the Lord Chancellor who referred it to his Advisory Committee on Legal Education and Conduct (ACLEC). If ACLEC approved, it then had to be approved by the Lord Chancellor with the concurrence of four senior judges (the Lord Chief Justice, the Master of the Rolls, the President of the Family Division and the Vice-Chancellor of the Chancery Division). The Lord Chancellor and the four judges had to consider the matter 'having regard' to the views of the Advisory Committee. Each judge had to agree; each therefore had a veto. Failure to agree had to be explained in written reasons (which were subject to judicial review for unreasonableness). In addition, the question had to be referred to the Director General of the Office of Fair Trading for his assessment from the point of view of competition policy.

[214] Section 17(1) stated: 'The general objective of this Part is the development of legal services . . . by making provision for new or better ways of providing such services and a wider choice of persons providing them, while maintaining the proper and efficient administration of justice'.

[215] Section 17(3) stated: 'As a general principle' the question whether a person should be granted a right of audience or be granted a right to conduct litigation had to be determined by reference 'only' (emphasis supplied) to four considerations: qualifications, being a member of a professional body capable of enforcing rules of conduct, whether it had an equivalent to the Bar's cab-rank rule and whether the rules of conduct were 'appropriate in the interests of the proper and efficient administration of justice'.

[216] M. Zander, 'Rights of Audience in the Higher Courts in England and Wales since the 1990 Act: What Happened?', 4 *International Journal of the Legal Profession*, 1997, pp. 167–196.

Justice greatly irritated the solicitors' branch when they decided in 1994 that solicitor advocates in the higher courts could not wear wigs – a decision that stands to the present day and that still rankles.[218]

After much further argument, in February 1997, the Conservative Lord Chancellor announced acceptance of the Law Society's request for extended rights of audience for employed solicitors subject to certain conditions. The Bar requested the same extension for employed barristers but, whilst this was under consideration, Lord Irvine, the new Labour Lord Chancellor, announced that he would be introducing major changes in the system for granting rights of audience. He was clearly frustrated both by the cumbersome nature of the vetting system under the CLSA 1990, at the low take-up of their new rights of audience by solicitors[219] and at the barriers put in the way of employed lawyers. The qualification rules for solicitors would be eased. Employed lawyers would basically be given the same rights of audience as lawyers in private practice. The Lord Chancellor's Advisory Committee (ACLEC) would be abolished. The proposal to give employed lawyers (i.e. CPS employees) the right to have full rights of audience provoked huge controversy and focused especially on whether CPS advocates could be sufficiently independent.[220]

The Lord Chancellor's promise (or threat) was implemented by the Access to Justice Act 1999. Section 36 provided that every barrister and every solicitor has rights of audience in all the courts 'exercisable in accordance with the qualification regulations and rules of conduct' of the Bar Council and the Law Society. These regulations were promulgated in March 2000 (see below).

AJA 1999, s. 37 added that qualification regulations were invalid insofar as they imposed special restrictions on employed lawyers as to the courts or the cases in which the right of audience could be exercised. The Lord Chancellor attempted to meet concerns about the independence of employed lawyers by s. 42 which stated that everyone exercising rights of audience 'has (a) a duty to the court to act in the interests of justice; and (b) a duty to comply with rules of conduct of the body relating to the right and approved for the purposes of this

---

[217] For the original regulations laying down the mode of qualification for extended rights of audience for solicitors in private practice see *Law Society's Gazette*, 17 December 1993, pp. 29–30.

[218] See Practice Direction (Court Dress) – *The Times*, 20 July 1994. On the history of the wigs see J.F. McLaren, 'A Brief History of Wigs in the Legal Profession', 6 *International Journal of the Legal Profession*, 1999, pp. 241–50. (In 2003, the LCD initiated a consultation exercise on court attire including wigs – see *Counsel*, June 2003, p. 5. For the results of the Bar's own survey, in which 3,751 barristers took part, see *Counsel*, July 2003, pp. 21–2.)

[219] He was quoted as saying of the low take-up: 'There must therefore be a question whether solicitors have a significant appetite to become advocates'. (*Law Society's Gazette*, 17 February 2000, p. 4.)

[220] Unsurprisingly, the Bar and the great majority of judges strongly opposed the change. For a sceptical view see also M. Zander, 'Will the Reforms Serve the Public Interest?, 148 *New Law Journal*, 3 July 1998, p. 969. For the contrary view see for instance A. Darlington, 'The CPS and Rights of Audience', *New Law Journal*, 1997, p. 1395. Both Lord Bingham, then Lord Chief Justice, and Lord Woolf, then Master of the Rolls, supported the change – see House of Lords, *Hansard*, vol. 595, 14 December 1998, cols. 1125–6 and 1153.

section; and those duties shall override any obligation which the person may have (otherwise than under the criminal law) if it is inconsistent with them'.(The Explanatory Notes said this meant that an advocate must refuse to do anything that is not in the interests of justice.)

Where under the 1990 Act the four designated senior judges had a veto over any changes to rights of audience or rules of conduct, under the 1999 Act they merely have to be consulted.[221] Sir Sydney Kentridge QC, one of the most distinguished members of the South African as well as of the English Bars, wrote that implementation of the proposals to transfer the power over rights of audience from the judges to a Cabinet Minister 'would constitute a quiet constitutional revolution'. The Lord Chancellor would be able to change the rules without the consent either of the Bar or of the judges – 'a decision which could seriously undermine the independence of the Bar, and in the hands of another Lord Chancellor less committed to the independence of the Bar, destroy it'. During apartheid in South Africa there were frequent threats from the Government to place the Bar under the control of a central council with Government nominated members. 'This proposal was consistently and successfully resisted by the whole of the Bar . . . It was well understood that to remove the control of the profession from the provincial Bar Councils and General Council of the Bar would have meant the end of the independence of the profession'.[222]

The effect of the changes Take-up by solicitors of the new right to seek rights of audience in the higher courts was slow. The first solicitor to appear in the higher courts did so in February 1994. By 2000, when the regulations under the AJA 1999 were being worked out, the number of solicitors who had qualified for rights of audience in the higher civil or higher criminal courts or both was only some 1,000. (Over two-thirds (69 per cent) had qualified for criminal proceedings, 15 per cent had qualified for civil proceedings and 16 per cent had qualified for both civil and criminal cases.)

Research conducted for ACLEC before the AJA 1999 suggested that this somewhat sluggish start to the new era of rights of audience in the higher courts for solicitors was unlikely to alter swiftly. There were many reasons. One was the cost of qualification which had risen from £2,000 in 1994 to some £4,000. Another was the difficulty of the exam. (In September 1995 only 29 per cent of the fifty-three candidates passed the evidence and procedure test.[223]) For City firms, one reason was the problem of enabling their members to get the required 'flying hours' of advocacy in the lower courts when such firms rarely had cases in those courts. City firms argued that they should be allowed to train

---

[221] AJA 1999, Sch. 5, paras. 5 and 6.

[222] S. Kentridge, 'A Quiet Revolution?', *Counsel*, December 1998, p. 24. See also R. de Wilde, 'A Constitutional Issue – the Judges and the Bar', 148 *New Law Journal*, 2 October 1998, p. 1424 and Lord Ackner powerfully supporting the same view, 'More Power to the Executive?', 148 *New Law Journal*, 16 October 1998, p. 1512. See also to the same general effect M. Zander, 'More Louis XIV than Cardinal Wolsey', 148 *New Law Journal*, 24 July 1998, p. 1084.

[223] *Law Society's Gazette*, 14 February 1996, p. 1.

their members themselves.[224] But the main reasons were that solicitors did not yet see higher court advocacy fitting in with their way of practising and that they preferred to continue to use the Bar.[225]

Implementation of the rights of audience provisions in the AJA 1999 did result in a simpler, cheaper system of qualification for solicitors. The Higher Rights Qualification Regulations 2000 provided for three routes to qualification:

* *Exemption* – For solicitors who have practised as barrister or solicitor for at least three years and who can demonstrate some experience of advocacy in the higher courts as well as extensive experience in the lower courts.
* *Accreditation* – For solicitors who have practised for three or more years as a barrister or solicitor who by reason of their experience of litigation in the higher courts have a sound understanding of the applicable procedure, evidence and ethics can apply for a Certificate of Eligibility to attempt an Advocacy Assessment. And
* *Development* – Training and assessment in higher court procedure, evidence, ethics and advocacy skills plus one year's litigation and advocacy experience working with a mentor. Six months of the year can be during the solicitor's training contract period.[226]

From January 2007 only the third of these routes will be available.[227] For further details see the Law Society's Website.[228]

By 2006, about a fifth of the 2,700 CPS solicitors had qualified for rights of audience in the higher courts.[229] (Of these, a little over half had criminal certificates, just over 20 per cent had civil certificates and a quarter had both.)

However, no hard information is available regarding the crucial question as to how often such rights of audience are actually being used by solicitors.[230] There were signs that some firms were developing advocacy training on a

---

[224] *The Lawyer*, 6 February 1996. In 1998 the Law Society eased the problem by agreeing a third training route to qualification by use of a discretion with regard to advocacy experience in the lower courts. See *The Lawyer*, 28 April 1998, p. 3.

[225] See 'Solicitor Advocates no Threat to Bar', *Solicitors' Journal*, 15 November 1996, p. 1092; G. Davis et al, 'Solicitor Advocacy and Higher Court Rights', 147 *New Law Journal*, 14 February 1997, p. 212; M. Zander, 'The Long Shadow of the Bar', 148 *New Law Journal*, 2 October 1998, p. 1422; L. Hickman, 'A Higher Calling', *Law Society's Gazette*, 5 May 2001, p. 38. See also R. Kerridge and G. Davis, 'Reform of the Legal Profession: An Alternative Way Ahead', 62 *Modern Law Review*, 1999, pp. 807–23.

[226] See L. Flannery, 'Expanding your Portfolio: Training as a Solicitor Advocate', 155 *New Law Journal*, 11 March 2005, p. 367.

[227] Originally the cut-off date was 31 October 2005 but an extra year was added for the exemption route at the request of the CPS – see *Law Society's Gazette*, 29 September 2005, p. 5; 155 *New Law Journal*, 4 November 2005, p. 1654.

[228] www.lawsociety.org.uk – Contents – Law Society Members – Our services (Specialist Panels) – Rights of Audience in the Higher Courts.

[229] The 2004–5 annual report gave the figure as 544 of 2,723 prosecutors.

[230] For the Scottish experience with similar reforms see G. Hanlon and J.D. Jackson, 'Last Orders at the Bar? Competition, Choice and Justice for All – the Impact of Solicitor Advocacy', 19 *Oxford Journal of Legal Studies*, 1999, pp. 555–82.

significant scale.[231] In 2005, Herbert Smith hired two QCs to head-up the firm's specialist advocacy unit.[232] The unit had forty-three solicitor advocates and another forty who were in the process of obtaining the higher rights qualification. The firm hoped to be the first to be accredited to provide its own higher rights training.[233] In September 2006 it was reported that Evershed had followed Herbert Smith's lead to become the second major UK firm to launch a dedicated in-house advocacy service with the hire of the most senior junior barrister from Fountain Court Chambers.[234] But so far at least, use of these higher rights of audience has been on a modest scale. A solicitor-advocate, lamenting the 'disturbing lack of progress in the trial arena and at the higher end of the advocacy spectrum', said it was due to 'a failure to overcome the traditional and ingrained briefing habits, and an unnecessary degree of deference to the Bar'.[235] In the writer's view, this is likely to continue.

The position with regard to the CPS is somewhat different as it is a national organisation which can operate a national policy to use its own employees as advocates instead of the independent Bar. There are indications that this is happening. In a speech in May 2006 the DPP, Ken Macdonald QC, said:

> The public prosecuting authority, so that we can have more ownership of our cases, and so that I can hold my prosecutors more accountable for their decisions, are going to do much more Higher Court advocacy than we have traditionally done, and already we see the difference that's having, in terms of the desire that people outside have to join us. For the first time ever we now have waiting lists around the country, of lawyers in private practice, who want to join the CPS, and when we recently announced twenty five places on a legal trainee scheme nationally, to graduates of law schools, we received, within three and a half weeks, two and a half thousand applications.[236]

This development is obviously threatening for the Criminal Bar. In March 2006 the DPP and the Chairman of the Bar set up the CPS/Bar Advocacy Liaison Group to provide a forum in which the CPS and the Bar can raise related advocacy and service-delivery issues. In November 2006, the Group published the *CPS/Bar Framework of Principles for Prosecution Advocates.*[237] The Framework states:

> The Bar understands that the CPS wishes to increase the number of in-house prosecutors with higher rights of audience and also to deploy in-house

---

[231] 'Top City Firms take Advocacy In-house', *Law Society's Gazette*, 30 March 2000, p. 1; 'City Firm joins Advocacy Trend', *Law Society's Gazette*, 6 April 2000, p. 1; 'Advocacy Training Courses attract the Interest of Mid-sized Commercial Firms', *Law Society's Gazette*, 22 June 2000, p. 9; 'Linklaters to Introduce its own Advocacy Qualification', *Law Society's Gazette*, 17 August 2000, p. 8; 'The Best of Both Worlds', *The Lawyer*, 11 March 2002, p. 27; and more generally N. Armstrong and D. Urpeth, 'Solicitor Advocacy', *New Law Journal*, 2 June 2000, p. 835.

[232] The QCs had to take the Qualified Lawyers Training Test to be admitted to the Roll of Solicitors.   [233] *Law Society's Gazette*, 28 April 2005, p. 5; 27 October 2005, p. 25.

[234] *The Lawyer*, 25 September 2006, p. 1.

[235] M. Hardie, 'Giving up Old Habits', *Law Society's Gazette*, 27 October 2005, p. 14.

[236] Speech at King's College London, 23 May 2006.   [237] Accessible via Google.

prosecutors more often on the full range of case types in the Crown Court. This will provide career opportunities for employed barristers but will inevitably affect the amount of work available to the self-employed Bar.

The CPS recognises that the self employed Bar provides a valuable service to the CPS by offering high quality self employed barristers to undertake prosecution work. Self employed barristers bring wide experience and understanding to their prosecution work and the CPS is determined to ensure that there remains a flourishing self employed Bar with barristers of skill and ability at all levels who are willing and able to play their part in prosecuting a full range of work for the CPS.

The Framework sets out the intended working arrangements between the CPS and the independent Bar. Thus, for example, if the case is likely to be contested, a barrister instructed to conduct the trial should also conduct the Plea and Case Management Hearing (PCMH). Where this is not possible, the Framework states that that the CPS must be informed at the earliest opportunity to permit alternative arrangements to be made. This might involve instructing a CPS advocate as replacement. On the vexed issue of returned briefs, the Framework states: 'It is the intention of the CPS and the Bar that only rarely should PCMH briefs be returned and only in very exceptional circumstances should a trial brief be returned.'[238]

A CPS pilot scheme for extending advocacy in the Crown Court in Hampshire and Hertfordshire led to complaints in 2005 from the Criminal Bar Association that the CPS were 'cherry-picking work'.[239] Commenting, the *Law Society's Gazette* pointed out editorially: 'The Bar is right to say that the CPS, as a public body, must show that handling cases in-house offers better value for money. If this then allows CPS lawyers to cherry-pick their cases (which it denies in any case), well – why not?'[240]

As to whether CPS advocates are competent, the HM Chief Inspector's Annual Report on the CPS for 2001–2 stated that inspectors saw 187 advocates perform. The general level of performance was good. About half were rated 'competent in all respects', about 25 per cent were rated 'above average in some respects' and about 10 per cent were 'very good'. Under 10 per cent were 'less than competent' or 'very poor'.

Rights of audience for non-lawyers

The 1989 Green Paper had suggested that bodies other than lawyers could be authorised to licence advocates in the courts. This was confirmed in the 1989 White Paper and was reflected in the machinery of the CLSA 1990 described above. A body representing, say, accountants, surveyors or patent agents could

---

[238] It would be remarkable if this was achieved. In the *Crown Court Study,* 59 per cent of prosecution barristers said their brief had been returned by another barrister and the CPS said that the brief had been returned in 66% of cases. (1993, Sect. 2.1.6, p. 32.)

[239] *Law Society's Gazette*, 17 February 2005, p. 1.   [240] *Ibid*, p. 13.

apply to be approved by the Advisory Committee, the designated judges and the Lord Chancellor in precisely the same way as the Bar Council and the Law Society which were approved as authorised bodies by the Act.

In 1993 the Institute of Legal Executives (ILEX) applied to become an authorised body to grant rights of audience for certain civil proceedings in county courts, magistrates' courts and coroners courts. (In open court in the county court for matters within the jurisdiction of District judges and in magistrates' courts in specified matrimonial proceedings.) ACLEC approved the application in December 1995. ILEX applied to the Lord Chancellor in March 1996 and the application was approved in November 1997. The new rights of audience became effective as from April 1998. They apply to Fellows of ILEX with at least five years' post-qualification experience.

In May 2006, the Department for Constitutional Affairs announced that Fellows of ILEX would be given the right of audience in criminal proceedings in the magistrates' courts and youth courts and in bail applications in the Crown Court. The Legal Services Consultative Panel (which, as will be seen, replaced ACLEC in 1999) had recommended this development in March 2006. ILEX Fellows would have to take a six-day advocacy course to qualify. A statutory instrument would be made to give effect to the announcement.[241]

The second application for rights of audience for non-lawyers to be approved was made in 1991 by the Chartered Institute of Patent Agents. It applied for its members to conduct litigation and to have rights of audience in patent and related intellectual property proceedings in the High Court. At first the application foundered on various objections raised by ACLEC, but it was reactivated and eventually a fresh application was made. This was formally approved by ACLEC in November 1998 and by the designated judges and the Lord Chancellor in May 1999.

Rights of audience and other extended powers for non-lawyers in the CPS The Narey Report on Delay in the Criminal Justice System (February 1997) proposed that non-lawyers in the CPS should be able to review files and to present uncontested cases in the magistrates' courts. 'One of the things which most struck me on visiting CPS offices was the amount of entirely straightforward work being handled in the office and at court by lawyers. Much of this work must be dispiriting. I am convinced that administrative staff, managed by lawyers and dealing exclusively with uncontested cases, could successfully and efficiently present cases at court, freeing lawyers to concentrate on contested cases' (p. 15).

The Labour Government acted on the Narey recommendation in the Crime and Disorder Act 1998 but took it further than Narey proposed. Section 53 gave the DPP the power to designate non-lawyers in the CPS to conduct bail applications and all proceedings in the magistrates' courts other than (1) contested cases (from the opening until conviction); (2) cases which can only be tried on

---

[241] *Law Society's Gazette*, 25 May 2006, p. 5; *Legal Executive Journal*, June 2006, p. 2.

indictment or where the defendant has opted for Crown Court trial; or (3) cases in which a notice of transfer to the Crown Court (p. 345 above) has been served.

Concern had been expressed in 1997 by Lord Bingham, the Lord Chief Justice, who said that the proposal for lay CPS staff to review files and to prosecute undefended cases 'appears to reflect a belief that such matters are relatively straightforward and call for little technical understanding. In many cases this is no doubt true. In other cases it is not'.[242] *Justice of the Peace* commenting editorially said:

> We see this as yet another disappointing development in the still young life of the CPS. Low morale, overstretched resources and the recent loss of many experienced lawyers have all hit the service very hard indeed. Despite the Government's denials we are in no doubt that the true reason behind this initiative is to cut costs . . . Administrative staff in the CPS do fine work day in day out, but they are not lawyers and appropriate qualifications and experience are necessary to carry out proper case reviews and to prosecute even simple guilty pleas. Assurances about 'appropriate training' for the new 'lay reviewers and presenters' do not allay our concerns, and they will not allay the concerns of others.[243]

The journal said it was especially noteworthy that the Government replaced the Narey recommendation that lay prosecutors should be subject at all times to direction by legally qualified staff with the very different requirement of 'subject to such instructions as are given to him by the Director'. ('The danger we foresee is that lay prosecutors, after passing their initial and as yet unspecified training, will be issued with numerous circulars on how to do this or that and then be left to get on with it with little, if any, *de facto* supervision by lawyers (*ibid*).)

The Glidewell Report which was published after the provisions dealing with this issue had already been adopted in the Crime and Disorder Bill, said that many CPS lawyers were opposed to the Narey proposals for an expanded role for non-lawyers in the CPS seeing them as 'an attack on their proper area of work'.[244] The point was also made that even in the simplest of cases there can be difficulties with which a non-lawyer could not be expected to deal competently. Non-lawyers expressed the fear that they might be obliged to do work for which they had neither aptitude nor training. Glidewell rejected these worries, but it drew a distinction between lay review and lay representation. With regard to lay representation, if the list included only guilty plea cases within the Narey criteria it saw no disadvantage and considerable advantage in the prosecution being presented by an experienced but not legally qualified caseworker, but if the list included a mixture of cases it would be 'positively wasteful' to have both the lawyer and a non-lawyer to present the cases. Also non-lawyer caseworkers would have to be trained to do the work and only those who wanted to do such work should be used. There should be no element of compulsion.

[242] J. Malpas, 'Lay Prosecutors: Revolution by the Back Door', *The Lawyer*, 12 August 1997, p. 2.
[243] 162 *Justice of the Peace*, 14 March 1998, p. 194.
[244] *Review of the Crown Prosecution Service*, Cm. 3960, June 1998 (Glidewell), p. 130, para. 16.

As to review of case files by non-lawyers, Glidewell said it had 'more reserva-tions'.[245] The Narey recommendation related to a substantial proportion of cases prosecuted by the CPS:

> If it means no more than ensuring that the statement of evidence apparently jus-tifies the charge, that the charge is within the agreed criteria and that the defen-dant, usually after having legal advice (which will often be from a duty lawyer) intends to plead guilty, then we think that an experienced caseworker could properly so decide . . . but if more than that is to be involved in the process of reviewing expedited cases, the skills necessary for such review will be those of a lawyer. If a lawyer is to acquire them, he will require both instruction in the law and practice and some experience. Whether the overall benefit in those circum-stances will be worthwhile, we doubt.

It is to be noted that both Narey and Glidewell's stated pre-condition for non-lawyers to undertake either the review or the presentation function was that they be properly trained for the task. A CPS survey of lay presenters later found that 43 per cent of respondents stated that they had done work beyond the strict criteria laid down by the CPS.[246]

The issue came up again in October 2005. The 2004–5 CPS annual report referred to what it called 'the extended remit' of Designated Case Workers (DCWs).[247] CPS lawyers objected strongly to this development. Kris Venkatasami, a CPS lawyer and national convenor for the prosecutors' union, the First Division Association, said: 'In our opinion, this is all about cutting corners and trying to get justice on the cheap. The Law Society's council member for the CPS com-plained that case workers were "civil servants who have no external ethical pro-fessional body to exercise any sanction"'.[248]

Lay representation in small claims cases The 1989 Green Paper supported the recommendation of the Civil Justice Review that litigants should have the right to select a lay representative in small claims cases and debt and housing cases in the county court. This was implemented in s. 11 of the Courts and Legal Services Act 1990, which gave the Lord Chancellor the power to make such pro-vision by order. In 1992 the Lord Chancellor issued a Practice Direction giving effect to s. 11[249] in respect only of small claims cases. The order entitled anyone to speak at a small claims hearing on behalf of a party. The party being repre-sented must be present. The court retained the power to bar a lay representative who behaves in an unruly fashion.

The 1999 CPR preserved that position in small claims cases: 'A party may present his own case at a hearing or a lawyer or lay representative may present

---

[245] Glidewell, p. 130, para. 19.   [246] *Law Society's Gazette*, 27 October 2005, p. 20.
[247] DCWs would undertake work in early administrative hearings; presentations in court in cases where a youth was charged with an adult and a guilty plea was expected; all cases, including youth court cases, after a guilty plea where the court orders a pre-sentence report; 'totting up' motoring cases where the defendant seeks to avoid disqualification on grounds of exceptional hardship and applications for the removal of a driving disqualification (Appendix D, p. 53).
[248] *Law Society's Gazette*, 27 October 2005, p. 21.   [249] SI 1992/1966.

it for him'. But, unless the court agrees, the lay representative can only present the case if the lay client is present (CPR PD 27.3). See also p. 408 above for the position of the 'McKenzie man'.

Conducting litigation

Prior to the CLSA 1990 it was an offence under the Solicitors Act 1974, s. 20 for anyone other than a solicitor to start or to conduct litigation in any civil or criminal court, except as a litigant in person. The 1989 Green Paper proposed that this monopoly should be ended and that anyone should be capable of becoming a litigator. The 1989 White Paper confirmed this proposal. It stated that the right to conduct litigation, like the right to appear as an advocate, should be granted to practitioners by the professional bodies or institutions to which they belonged if the bodies could demonstrate that they could set and maintain appropriate standards of competence and conduct. All litigators would also be subject to the existing powers of the High Court over solicitors as officers of the court. The Law Society would become an authorised body under the Act. Other bodies could become authorised bodies by an Order in Council made, following advice from ACLEC, on the recommendation of the Lord Chancellor and subject to the concurrence of the four designated judges.

This scheme was implemented by ss. 28–29 of the CLSA 1990. By 1999 no new body had been granted the right to initiate or to conduct litigation. The application by a newly formed Institute of Commercial Litigators was rejected by ACLEC in February 1996. The Institute was informed by the Committee that the application fell 'far short of what is required by the statutory objective and the general principle'.

However, in the LCD's June 1998 consultation paper *Rights of Audience and Rights to Conduct Litigation* the question was posed whether legislation should authorise bodies other than the Law Society to conduct litigation. The two bodies which would be obvious candidates, it suggested, were the Bar Council and the Institute of Legal Executives both of which were authorised bodies with regard to rights of audience. There would be no compulsion to take up rights to conduct litigation and most barristers would probably prefer not to do so. But some, such as those employed as lawyers in commerce and industry, might find it useful to be able to become authorised litigators (para. 5.5). Most legal executives worked in solicitors' offices but some might benefit from being able to set up their own independent practices.

This suggestion was implemented in the Access to Justice Act, s. 40 which made both the Bar Council and the Institute of Legal Executives authorised bodies for this purpose. The Bar has exercised this power – but only in respect of employed lawyers providing such services for their own employers.[250]

---

[250] See the Employed Barristers (Conduct of Litigation) Rules – www.barcouncil.org.uk – (Rules and Guidance). Exceptionally, an employed barrister may offer the service to the public – i.e. when employed in a solicitor's office or a law centre.

The 2001 OFT report *Competition in Professions* (see p. 778 above) said the restriction on private practitioners conducting litigation 'prevents potential efficiencies and limits the numbers of lawyers who are able to conduct litigation on behalf of clients'.[251] In its Response the Bar argued that adding a few barristers to the number of lawyers eligible to conduct litigation would produce negligible benefits for consumers. They already had 85,000 lawyers in some 8,000 firms available for the purpose. On the other hand, to permit barristers to perform the function would undermine the distinction between barristers and solicitors. By absorbing time in collecting evidence, correspondence and handling disclosure, it would dilute the barristers' specialist skills and would thereby seriously diminish the quality of their advocacy and advice. Also barristers' overheads would increase if they had to maintain the systems and staff necessary to conduct litigation. If barristers were to handle client moneys they would need to be regulated as solicitors are regulated. Such a regulatory system could cost as much as £1 million per year to run.

In a statement issued on 25 April 2002 regarding progress the OFT said it remained concerned that the Bar did not intend to lift the blanket prohibition on the conduct of litigation by barristers in independent practice and that it would be investigating the matter further. It did not object to the divided profession but to a rule that imposed specialisation and which restricted what barristers were free to do. Permitting barristers who wished to conduct litigation to do so would not prevent other barristers from continuing to be specialists who did not offer that service. The OFT said it was not persuaded by the argument about the cost of regulating the holding of client moneys. One solution would be to prohibit it. Another would be to find cost effective ways of solving the problem.

Neither the LCD's consultation paper *In the Public Interest?* (July 2002) nor the OFT's Response to the consultation paper (November 2002) referred to the topic.

If barristers were permitted to conduct litigation it seems unlikely that any significant number would avail themselves of the possibility.

Claims assessors

The Lord Chancellor announced in June 1999 that he was setting up a committee to examine the activities of claims assessors who assisted claimants with their claims in return for a commission on damages recovered. The *Solicitors' Journal* reported that lawyers groups had long been warning 'that consumers [were] being ripped off by unscrupulous and incompetent assessors'. They were wholly unregulated. Anyone could set himself up to bring compensation claims for a share of the damages. Because they were not permitted to issue legal proceedings they were tempted to settle for too low a figure rather than hand the case to a solicitor. Also their fees were unregulated. A Law Society spokesman

---

[251] OFT, 2001 at p. 15. Based on the view expressed in the LECG Report at paras. 258–61.

was quoted as saying: 'At worst, these unqualified legal advisers are just cowboys or crooks. At best, they can only provide a second-rate service'.[252] The Committee reported in April 2000 that it did not think that there was a present need for legislation.[253]

Legal Services Consultative Panel

The 1989 Green Paper proposed that the Lord Chancellor should have an advisory committee with a lay majority. The functions of the advisory committee, it suggested, should include advice on the arrangements for legal education and training, on the need for recognising areas of specialisation and how specialists should be trained and on codes of conduct.

The 1989 White Paper confirmed that there would be an advisory committee with a lay majority. The committee was established by the CLSA 1990, s. 20. Its duty was to assist 'in the maintenance and development of standards in the education, training and conduct of those offering legal services' (s. 21(1)). Its functions, set out in Sch. 2 of the Act, included advising the Lord Chancellor on all stages of education and training of lawyers, qualification regulations and rules of conduct (whether related to advocacy or the conduct of litigation or not) and specialisation schemes.

The Advisory Committee on Legal Education and Conduct (known as ACLEC) was clearly intended to be the lead policy-making body under the CLSA 1990 – with the designated judges playing a subsidiary monitoring role.

Replacement of ACLEC In its June 1998 consultation paper (above) the Lord Chancellor's Department said that the Government intended to abolish ACLEC. The committee, it said, had attracted distinguished membership, but it had not succeeded in 'significantly furthering the statutory objective of developing new or better ways of providing legal services and a wider choice of persons providing them' (para. 4.6). Partly this might have been due to the carefully balanced membership representative of various legal interest groups. (ACLEC, in its response to the consultation paper, stoutly defended its record.[254])

The consultation paper proposed that there should be a new body to be called the Legal Services Consultative Panel appointed for their individual expertise rather than as representatives of interest groups (para. 4.16). The Panel would be asked to consider all applications from new bodies for authorisation under the CLSA 1990, any applications for the approval of rule changes on which the Lord Chancellor required advice 'and any other matters concerning the provision of legal services on which the Lord Chancellor required advice' (para. 4.17).

---

[252] *Solicitors' Journal*, 18 June 1999, p. 575.
[253] *Report on the Activities of Non-legally Qualified Claims Assessors and Employment Advisers –* accessible on www.dca.gov.uk – Major Reports/Reviews.
[254] See also 'Farewell to ACLEC' by Lord Justice Potter, its last chairman, in *Counsel*, April 1999, p. 26.

The Panel was established as of 1 January 2000.[255] (For details of its membership, its work and the advice it has given to the Lord Chancellor see www.dca.gov.uk/atoj/lscp/lscpfr2.htm.)

Right of direct access to the Bar for professional and lay clients

In earlier times there was no rule preventing barristers from dealing directly with clients, but by the mid-nineteenth century it had become an understanding. In 1888 the Attorney General gave an opinion that in contentious matters a barrister should not act or advise without the intervention of a solicitor – chiefly because the barrister was not in a position to ascertain the facts of the case.[256] It remained permissible, though uncommon, for barristers to accept instructions directly from clients in non-contentious matters, but in 1955 the then Attorney General declared the practice to be wrong and this opinion was adopted by the Bar Council at its 1956 Annual General Meeting.

The 1989 Green Paper recommended that lay clients should have a right of direct access to barristers. Many commentators, including the writer, argued that this could lead to the destruction of the Bar as a second-tier consultancy service and the Government conceded the point. The 1989 White Paper (para. 11.7) said that this matter would be left to the Bar to determine.

That year, in the context of the furious debate over the Green Papers, the Bar altered its rules to permit Direct Professional Access (DPA) to some professional clients to instruct barristers direct, without having to go via a solicitor. A decade later there were nearly forty professional bodies with this right. They included: architects, accountants, loss adjusters, ombudsmen, actuaries, valuers and auctioneers, Royal Town Planning Institute, Royal Institution of Chartered Surveyors, Association of Average Adjusters, Chartered Association of Certified Accountants, Institution of Mechanical Engineers, Institution of Chemical Engineers, Institute of Taxation, Institute of Chartered Secretaries and Administrators.

In May 1996 the Bar Council agreed in principle that bureau workers in designated Citizens' Advice Bureaux should be able to refer work direct to a barrister.[257] After completion of a pilot, this scheme became effective for advice agencies with franchises from the Legal Aid Board as from January 1999.[258]

A Bar Council Policy Unit appointed in 1994 'to think the unthinkable' produced a consultation paper in February 1994 which, amongst other things, proposed that direct access for *lay clients* to a barrister should be permitted in non-contentious work – i.e. for legal advice. For contentious matters (litigation) the lay client should also be allowed direct access to a barrister but the barrister should then be under a duty to refer the client to an appropriate

---

[255] Access to Justice Act 1999, s. 35(3) and Sch. 5.   [256] (1888) 85 LT Jo 176.
[257] See H. Heilbron, 'Moving with the Times – an Opportunity for the Bar', *Counsel*, July/August 1996, p. 18.   [258] See D. Payne, 'Welcome Advice', *Counsel*, April 1999, p. 24.

professional intermediary who would usually be a solicitor. This proposal was considered but rejected at the Bar's Annual Meeting in July 1994.

Spokesmen for the Labour Party (notably Mr Paul Boateng MP) said before the 1997 General Election that a Labour Government would abolish the rule prohibiting direct access for lay clients to a barrister but, in the event, after Labour was returned to power in the General Election this threat was quietly dropped.

Neither the LCD's 1998 consultation paper nor the Access to Justice Act 1999 contained any provision on the subject.

However, in October 1998 the Bar Council issued a short but potentially important consultation paper addressing the issue of direct access. 'Contracts and Access to the Bar' prepared by a sub-committee, known as the Contracts Working Party, under the Chairmanship of James Munby QC (who had also chaired the Bar Council Policy Unit which produced the 1994 consultation paper). The Munby Committee said that barristers were restricted not only by rules about the source of their work (i.e. from whom they were permitted to receive instructions), but also regarding the nature of the work they could do. They were not permitted to do certain categories of work done by solicitors – defined in the Bar's Code of Conduct, para. 901. (This 'excepted work' includes the management, administration or general conduct of a lay client's affairs, the management, administration or general conduct of litigation and the receipt and handling of clients' money.)

The Munby Committee suggested that the Bar had various options. One was to maintain the status quo. The second was to expand the categories eligible to refer DPA work. The third was to permit direct access by lay clients. The fourth was both to permit direct access to lay clients and to scrap the restrictions on the work that barristers could do. The fifth was also to permit barristers to conduct litigation. The last two would lead to an assimilation of the functions and roles of barristers and solicitors.

Direct licensed access (DLA) Expansion of the categories of those able to refer clients to the barrister could include people not members of a professional body provided they were recognised by the Bar Council as (1) competent in some identifiable area of expertise or experience; (2) having the necessary skills to organise papers and information; and (perhaps) (3) subject to some suitable disciplinary or regulatory tribunal or at least some rules. There were many potential candidates including banks, building societies, insurance companies, trade unions, trade associations, employers' associations, consumer bodies, housing associations and charities.

If the Bar Council had the responsibility for deciding who had the right to refer to barristers, this would free 'individual barristers and chambers from the administrative and other burdens of dealing with any and every layman who simply walks in off the street'. Also unrestricted direct access by lay clients would raise overheads and would have significant client care implications (para. 5.5).

The Munby Committee said it saw no reason to distinguish between contentious and non-contentious work for the purpose of the direct access rules. It did not think that holding to the status quo was right. It was strongly opposed to permitting unrestricted direct access. If the Bar was going to survive it would do so 'only because there is a real and perceived difference between what barristers do and what solicitors (and others) do . . . Barristers should do barristers' work; they should not do solicitors' work' (para. 5.9(4)).

So the choice effectively lay between an extension of DPA, the introduction of DLA or the extension of direct access to all lay clients. There was little scope for extension of DPA. There were few professional bodies not already on the list that would satisfy the criteria. The Munby Committee favoured DLA over direct access to all lay clients.

This view prevailed. In 1999 the Bar Council approved a scheme for DLA called BarDIRECT.[259] The scheme was extended to include police forces, probation services, trading standards offices, clinical negligence and other insurers, trading companies, banks, insolvency practitioners and trades unions. By 2003 over a hundred licences had been approved.[260]

The future success of licensed access/BarDIRECT was dealt a potentially serious blow, however, by the Court of Appeal's December 2005 decision in the case of Andre Agassi and the taxman. Agassi employed non-lawyer tax experts who instructed a barrister. As already noted, the Court of Appeal ruled that the tax experts' fees (other than disbursements) were not recoverable against the Revenue because they were not lawyers. Unless this rule is changed by legislation, licensed access/BarDIRECT will not be attractive to litigants.

In March 2001 the OFT's report *Competition in Professions* said that while there was no objection to a barrister choosing not to deal with clients without the intermediary of a solicitor, there was objection to the professional rule denying freedom of choice. In response to the criticism, the Bar Council, acting on the recommendation of a committee chaired by Sir Sydney Kentridge, unanimously approved changes to its professional rules to broaden the scope for lay clients to have direct access to barristers.

The Kentridge Committee's recommendation was that the new regime should be implemented cautiously, with restricted direct access in criminal and family cases, notably for advice and in a very few court matters where it is clear that the additional role of the solicitor is not necessary. A consultation paper on the response to the OFT's report was issued by the Bar in April 2002. This proved to be the most controversial issue in the consultation paper. A working group then put forward detailed rules. The final version was approved by the Bar Council on 29 March 2003 and by the Lord Chancellor in June 2004. The scheme became effective in July 2004.

---

[259] See J. Munby, 'Extending a Helping Hand', *Counsel*, October 1999, p. 26.
[260] The list was published in *Counsel*, March 2003, p. vi.

In June 2004 BarDIRECT and DPA were renamed 'licensed access' and 'direct access' was renamed 'public access'.

Under the rules, public access is permitted in civil work, excluding family and immigration matters, providing it can be done without a solicitor. It can be undertaken in limited categories of family and criminal work such as advice (but not advice in police stations) and appeals but not for trials. Special Bar Council approved training is a requirement.[261] Barristers with under three years' experience cannot undertake public access work. The barrister is required to send a client care letter setting out what he or she is and is not able to do, the likely fees to be charged and any other information the client needs.[262] The barrister cannot start work on the matter until he has a copy of the letter countersigned signed by the client. It specifies that all work must be paid for in advance! The barrister may not write to the client on headed notepaper, he may not hold client moneys (and therefore cannot issue proceedings or applications) and he cannot take on work on the instructions of a lay client which involves the investigation of facts or the taking of statements from witnesses. Also, if acting in litigation, the only costs recoverable from the other side are £9.25 per hour for a litigant in person.[263]

However, in operating public access, the 'cab-rank rule' does not apply.[264]

By September 2005, nearly 600 barristers had attended the one-day training course and some 380 had made their details available to the public.[265]

Non-practising employed barristers

In 1990 the Bar authorised a new type of practice – that of 'non-practising employed barristers' working, say, for a firm of accountants or foreign lawyers. Such a barrister was allowed to advise his firm's clients but not to hold himself out to be a practising barrister nor to appear as counsel in court, but the rules only allow a non-practising barrister to call himself such if he has completed a pupillage.

The consultants LECG in their report attached to the OFT's report *Competition in Professions* said that only about a hundred individuals had registered with the Bar Council to continue using the title.[266] It doubted whether

[261] The training consists of a one-day course.
[262] See *Counsel*, February 2003, p. iv. For views as to the prospects see L. Heathfield, 'Handle with Care', *Counsel*, May 2003, p. 15; P. Bennett, 'Moving the Goalposts', *Counsel*, May 2003, pp. 18–19; L. Trevelyan, 'Access All Areas', *Law Society's Gazette*, 5 August 2004, p. 18; A. Speaight QC, 'Giant Leap?', *Counsel*, October 2004, p. 20.   [263] Practice Direction 52.4.
[264] For one barrister's view of the seriously negative effect of the restrictions see L. Sinclair, 'Public Access: Hold the Gates?', 155 *New Law Journal*, 24 June 2005, p. 984. ('In the author's personal experience, each of these restrictions has been instrumental in ensuring that there is minimal, if any, benefit to working with a barrister directly'.) For a very up-beat assessment see A. Heppinstall, 'Public Access to the Bar is Good for All', 155 *New Law Journal*, 16 September 2005, p. 1360.
[265] 155 *New Law Journal*, 9 September 2005, p. 1304. For the current list see www.barcouncil.org.uk. For the experience of three barristers with Direct Public Access see 'Reaching Out', *Counsel*, November 2006, pp. 12–13.   [266] Paragraph 269, p. 77.

the requirement of a pupillage as the basis for using the title was necessary. It called this a backward step to inhibit a source of competition for non-advocacy services.

Queen's Counsel

Eligibility of solicitors The 1989 Green Paper did not question the value of the status of QC but it proposed that all those who held full advocacy certificates should be eligible to become QCs. The 1989 White Paper amended this by stating that the Lord Chancellor would in future regard as eligible those who held rights of audience *either* in the High Court *or* the Crown Court. This did not need legislation and was therefore not included in the CLSA 1990.

From July 1995 solicitor advocates became eligible to apply to become QCs. However, by 2003 only eight had been appointed.[267] In the eight years 1996–2003 there were a total of 3,837 applications for silk, an average of 480 per year. Of these, only seventy-three (1.9 per cent) were made by solicitors. (In 2005, the first year of the new reformed system, there were 443 applications of which twelve (2.7 per cent) were from solicitors. In 2002–3, the last year of the old system, the number of solicitor applicants had been ten out of 394 (2.5 per cent).[268])

Should QCs continue to exist?

The Bar's Response to the OFT report argued that the QC system had real value both for the purchasers of advocacy services and to the administration of justice. Appointment as QC was public recognition of outstanding ability. It was of value to purchasers of advocacy services such as solicitors and especially to those who did not regularly instruct counsel in the particular field of work. Internationally it helped to make English advocates competitive in litigation and arbitrations outside the UK. It also helped to maintain standards since QCs were selected not only for their legal skills. Integrity and independence were also assessed. The question whether it should be the Lord Chancellor who made the selection was, it suggested, a constitutional rather than a competition question. At least no one suggested that political considerations played any part in the process.

The OFT suggested that there was inadequate peer review. The Bar said, on the contrary, the selection process involved an intense and wide-ranging process of peer review. The OFT pointed out that there were no professional examinations that had to be taken to become a QC. The Bar's reply was that what was being

---

[267] One, Laurence Collins, formerly a partner in City firm Herbert Smith, in 2000 became the first solicitor to be appointed a High Court judge and in 2007 was appointed a Lord Justice of Appeal.

[268] *Law Society's Gazette*, 17 November 2005, p. 1.

assessed – experience, advocacy skills and professional qualities demonstrated in practice – were not measurable by formal examinations. The OFT argued that there was no continuous quality appraisal of QCs. The Bar said it was not aware that this caused any problem. Market forces were the main safeguard, but there might be a case for a procedure whereby the rank of QC could be removed if the Lord Chancellor was satisfied that there had been a serious or sustained failure to meet the standards reasonably to be expected of a QC.[269]

In its report on progress in April 2002, the OFT (para. 3.39) said a quality mark was only of value to consumers if it was awarded according to clear criteria and in a transparent way. Whether the QC system met this condition was open to debate. Another condition was that the mark should be capable of being lost as well as won. The QC system did not qualify in that regard. Also, it said, 'we remain concerned that the QC system may operate to distort competition'. One sign of this was 'the step-change in fees that QCs are said to command upon taking silk'; another was that 'custom and practice had given rise to some *de facto* demarcations as to what work is and is not suitable for QCs'. It had also been suggested that the system displayed elements of a quota system and that some quantitative as distinct from purely qualitative criteria might apply. (It added, pointedly: 'We note with interest that the number of QCs appointed in 2002 is markedly higher than in any other recent year'.[270])

The LCD's consultation paper *In the Public Interest?*, issued in July 2002, devoted eleven pages to the issue. It seemed to lean toward affirmation of the utility of the status of QCs 'in so far as users of a service are insufficiently informed about the full range of quality on offer, an effective and accurate mark of quality which differentiates the leading players will improve the amount of information available to users of the service' (para. 127). Not all users of the service would have the information to identify the top specialists. Since barristers were self-employed, many of the usual mechanisms to signal information on quality – such as becoming a partner – were not available to barristers. In the absence of reliable information on the quality of providers, users would tend to stick with the barristers they had tried previously. A mark of quality 'therefore facilitates competition by enabling the user to "switch" to new providers, i.e. to instruct with confidence a barrister of whom they have little or no experience' (para. 131). The QC system also provided a career structure within the legal system 'marking the achievement of a level of status, excellence and seniority which is broadly analogous to that found within other professions (senior

---

[269] Paragraphs 7.1–15.

[270] As noted above, in previous years the number appointed was sixty to seventy and the success rate of applications was as low as an average of 14 per cent. In 2002 the number was 113 from 429 applications, a success rate of 26 per cent. In 2003 it was even higher – 121 from 394 applications, a success rate of 31 per cent. This apparent 'watering of the brandy' led to criticism – see B. Malkin, 'Irvine under Fire for Silk Appointment Hike', *The Lawyer*, 21 April 2003, p. 2.

partners in solicitors' firms, hospital consultants, professors in the academic world, etc.)' (para. 134).

On the question of increased fees the paper said that there was considerable overlap between what could be earned by a successful junior and a QC. The junior could be earning more than the QC even in the same area of practice.

The Law Society in its response to the consultation paper criticised the system. It referred to the evidence it gave in 1999 to the enquiry by Sir Leonard Peach on the operation of the judicial and QC appointments procedures (p. 750 above) when it said: 'The designation is a mark of patronage that is inappropriate in the modern age' (para. 5.3). The Council of the Law Society had confirmed that opinion in September 2000 in deciding to continue to remain outside the automatic consultation process for judicial appointments and silk.

The Law Society in its Response to the July 2002 consultation paper (para. 5.5) said it had three main concerns. One was about the consultation process which at least gave excessive weight to the views of the judges and not enough to key consumers such as solicitors. Secondly, it was undesirable for leaders of an independent profession to be selected by a Government minister – though there was no evidence that the appointment function had been abused in the recent past. Thirdly, there was concern that, 'at least until very recently', a quota system had operated. The QC system was helpful in identifying specialists for non-specialists.

However, it said that solicitors reported 'a substantial increase in fees when barristers are appointed QC – indeed, solicitors thought that this was the whole point, from the applicants' perspective' (Q 57, p. 60). It agreed with the OFT that 'reports from solicitors suggest a step-change [in higher fees] that is not always justified by the superior skills claimed' (Q 59, p. 60). Sometimes a QC was instructed solely because the client was anxious to have apparent equality of arms with the opponent. Another point of criticism was that the courts too often placed greater weight on an argument put by a QC than on the same argument put by a junior.

If the system continued, the Law Society thought it should be replaced by an accreditation system for experienced members of the Bar. ('Ideally, accreditation would be achieved by candidates being able to demonstrate by objective methods that they had achieved the required level of work experience and specialised knowledge' (para. 5.8).) Such a scheme would also require members to seek re-accreditation, say, every five years. No indication was given as to what 'objective methods' could be used for such accreditation.

Given the markedly approving tenor of the LCD's presentation of the issues in July 2002, it was surprising that, as has been seen, on 2 April 2003 the Lord Chancellor told the new House of Commons Select Committee on his Department that he would be issuing a consultation paper to canvass, *inter alia*, the question whether the QC system should continue to exist and even more surprising that on 29 April 2003 he announced that he was suspending the entire process of selection.

The Government's further consultation paper[271] was issued on 14 July 2003. Its substantive part was thirty-one pages long. In the Foreword the new Lord Chancellor, Lord Falconer, said: 'I have no predetermined answers to the questions raised in this paper', but the paper gave rather more emphasis to the negative aspects of the system than had its July 2002 paper.

It first addressed whether it was appropriate for the appointment to be made by the Queen on the advice of ministers. There was need for a strong case to justify it. ('The indications from customers certainly suggest that the rank of QC in the legal services market does not provide a useful kitemark in practice, and that the market might work more effectively if the QC mark were to be removed' (para. 22).) The Government's provisional view was that retention of the rank in its present form could only be justified if:

- It serves a helpful purpose for users of legal services.
- Any benefits clearly outweigh any problems and in particular the extent to which it may distort competition in the market for legal services and its possible effect on fees.
- Its possible benefits cannot be provided in other ways free of such disadvantages (p. 22).

The responses to *In the Public Interest?* had not produced many concrete examples of the QC rank being used as an effective guide when selecting an advocate:

> A number of respondents said that it had a general usefulness, but more detailed responses tended to argue that what was relevant to an instructing solicitor was the individual advocate's experience and skills. They had frequently found the right junior counsel to be of better value than a QC. It was also said that the rank of QC drove up legal costs unjustifiably. There was a perception that QCs were now instructed in circumstances where their particular skills were not really needed: for example because it might be thought that judges would pay more attention to a QC's argument, or because a simple equality of arms was needed – just because the other side had already instructed a QC. Such perceptions could have the effect of tilting the market in favour of QCs and against experienced juniors (para. 49).

Abolition of the rank could therefore have two beneficial effects. First, it could lead to a more effective reliance on information about individual advocates and their skills 'so that consumers would pay only the price reflecting the real value of the service they are buying rather than paying for a badge or QC "brand"' (para. 50). Providing information flowed freely, the market would determine which barristers could command higher prices on the basis of the quality of their work (para. 50). Secondly, if QCs lowered their fees to be competitive with experienced juniors, costs would come down. (On the other hand, if

---

[271] *Constitutional Reform: the Future of Queen's Counsel*, consultation paper 08/03 (accessible on www.dca.gov.uk – Publications – consultation papers – 2003).

individuals were already paid according to their skills, there would be little or no change. A different possibility was that experienced juniors might put their fees up.)

Lord Falconer's consultation paper considered the implications for existing QCs if the rank were removed and the ways in which it might be done. The final section discussed what sort of award system might replace the present system. Annexes dealt with the current criteria for the award, the current selection procedures, the position in other jurisdictions and quality marks in other UK professions and trades.[272]

On 26 May 2004 Lord Falconer in a Written Statement in the House of Lords announced his decision. The Lord Chancellor would no longer be involved in the selection of QCs, but respondents to the consultation paper had been clear about the value of maintaining a kitemark for advocacy services – 'both to recognise excellence and to provide useful information for consumers'. The Government had therefore asked the Bar Council and the Law Society (and their counterparts in Northern Ireland) to develop a scheme for accrediting leading advocates to replace the existing arrangements. The professions would be responsible for selecting the candidates. The Lord Chancellor would recommend to the Queen that those on the list were appointed, subject to the possibility that in exceptional circumstances he would depart from the recommended names.[273] The Lord Chancellor said that the decision was an interim measure pending a market study of what areas of law demonstrated a need for better consumer information.

In December 2004 it was reported that the Bar Council and the Law Society had agreed on extending QC accreditation beyond advocacy to other work. There would be a 'competency framework'[274] having taken 'structured references' from judges, practitioners and clients. The scheme would indicate the broad field of law – civil, criminal or family – in which the successful applicants had demonstrated excellence. If QCs ceased to perform to a satisfactory standard, the award could be revoked.

The nine person Selection Panel when first constituted was chaired by a layman.[275] It had a senior judge (female), two QCs (one male, one female),[276] a solicitor in private practice (female), a senior prosecutor solicitor (male)[277] and three other laymen (one male, two female). Five of the nine therefore were

---

[272] A summary of the responses to the consultation paper was published by the DCA in January 2004. The individual reponses were published in February 2004. Both documents are accessible on www.dca.gov.uk – Publications – consultation papers – 2003.

[273] House of Lords, *Hansard*, 26 May 2004, col. WS 54.

[274] The criteria were: integrity, understanding and using the law, analysing case material and preparing arguments, persuading and responding to the unfolding case, working with the client and working in the team. The competencies were: oral and written advocacy, case management and dispute resolution.

[275] Sir Duncan Nichol, formerly Chief Executive of NHS Management Executive, and also chairman of the Parole Board.   [276] Nominated by the Bar Council.

[277] The solicitors are nominated by the Law Society.

female and four were lay. One of the lay persons was from an ethnic minority. The Secretariat was headed by a senior and experienced civil servant seconded by the DCA.

The process includes a 'self-assessment' completed by the applicant. With regard to referees, the applicant must list judges before they have appeared in cases of substance, complexity or particular difficulty in the previous two years. (Where there are fewer than twelve referees, the two years is extended to three years.) The candidate must also identify a number of practitioners by whom he has been led or against whom he has appeared.

The Selection Panel decides which named referees to ask for references (in the cases of judges, four). There is also an interview with a member of the Selection Panel and an external expert.[278]

Successful candidates receive their Letters Patent at a ceremony presided over by the Lord Chancellor or the Lord Chief Justice.

The new system is required to be self-financing. The fee for applying in 2007 was £2,500 plus VAT. Successful candidates were required to pay a further £3,000 plus VAT (to cover the cost of the appointment ceremony and of the Letters Patent).[279]

Unsuccessful candidates receive feedback. There is a complaints procedure involving a senior serving judge.[280]

As noted above, of the 443 applicants on the first round under the new system, 15 per cent were women (up from 10 per cent in the last round under the old system), but, as also noted, hopes, and indeed expectations, that there would also be an increase in the number of solicitor applicants were not realised.

There were 175 appointments – 141 men and thirty-three women.[281] Ten were from ethnic minority backgrounds; four were solicitors.[282]

This new system is on trial. One of its architects suggested that the initial procedures had proved too onerous and complicated. The 443 applications on the first round had generated nearly 4,500 references. Sir Duncan Nichol, who chaired the Selection Panel, was quoted as saying that he would be seeking ways to reduce the burdens on judicial, practitioner and client referees.[283]

BarMark and Quality Mark

In 1999 the Bar Council introduced the BarMark scheme whereby chambers can be accredited as efficient. To qualify, the chambers has to be able to show that its systems and documentation are consistent with the required quality standards. The tests, which are conducted by the British Standards Institution

---

[278] For a description of the Selection Panel's working methods by one of the lay members see K. Singh, 'High Octane', *Counsel*, September 2006, pp. 37–8.   [279] www.qcapplicationss.org.uk.
[280] W. Blair QC and R. Knowles QC, 'Racing Silks', *Counsel*, April 2005, p. 16 and 'The Silk Route Re-opens', *Counsel*, August 2005, pp. 10–12; J. Robins, 'Making the Grade', *Law Society's Gazette*, 12 May 2005, p. 22.   [281] One did not disclose his/her gender.
[282] For full statistics and comparison with the previous ten years see *Counsel*, August 2006, pp. 32–3.
[283] '"Laborious" QC Competition under Review', 156 *New Law Journal*, 11 August 2006, p. 1268.

(BSI), are quite demanding. There is a one-off initial charge of £350 plus VAT and thereafter BSI has a daily charge of £645 per auditor. In 2006 the number of sets with the qualification was forty-one.[284]

Alternatively, chambers can qualify for the Legal Services Commission's Quality Mark for the Bar launched in 2002. Over a hundred sets have the Quality Mark.[285] The LSC does not charge for providing this service.

For discussion of, and proposals on the problem of assessing quality of advocates, see Appendix 1 of the Bar Council's Response to the joint DCA and LSC Consultation Paper, *Legal Aid: A Sustainable Future,* 12 October 2006 – www.barcouncil.org.uk.

Partnerships between lawyers and between lawyers and non-lawyers

As has been seen, under the Bar's own rules barristers are not permitted to form partnerships. (The sole exception to the rule is that, curiously, a barrister has for many years been allowed to form a partnership with an overseas lawyer.) In 1979 the Report of the Benson Royal Commission on Legal Services supported the rule forbidding partnerships. Ten years later, the February 1989 Green Paper proposed (1) that barristers and solicitors should be able to form partnerships with each other; (2) that each should be able to join in partnerships with members of other professions ('multi-disciplinary partnerships' or 'MDPs'); (3) that each should be able to join in partnership with foreign lawyers ('multi-national partnerships' or 'MNPs') and (4) that barristers should be able to form partnerships with other barristers.

However, the July 1989 White Paper (Ch. 12) played a very different tune. ('The Government . . . believes that the regulation of how the members of professional bodies organise themselves to meet their clients' needs is best left to the professions themselves, subject to a proper scrutiny to avoid unnecessary or undesirable anti-competitive effects' (para. 12.2).)

The Courts and Legal Services Act 1990, s. 66 abolished the statutory prohibition on solicitors forming partnerships with non-solicitors and stated that there is no common law rule that prevents barristers from forming such relationships, but s. 66 also specifically permits the Bar to make rules preventing barristers from entering such partnerships. The Bar has so far maintained its prohibition on partnerships.

Partnerships between barristers

The publication in February 2001 of the report of the OFT *Competition in Professions* (p. 778 above) suddenly made the issue – at least of partnerships between barristers – a live one. The OFT's report said:

---

[284] See J. Chase, 'Nine Easy Steps to BarMark Status', *Counsel,* June 2000, p. 28; J. Woolf, 'Getting into Shape', *Counsel,* May 2005, p. 26; and the Bar Council's Website – www.barcouncil.org.uk – Services to Barristers. Curiously, the number in 2006 was lower than in 2003 when it was sixty. (*Counsel,* February 2003, p. vi.)   [285] In July 2006 the number was 129.

The requirement that only sole practitioners can supply barristers' services is anomalous in the context of professional services and beyond. A similar requirement for, say, booksellers would have clear disadvantages in terms of, *inter alia*, costs, price, efficiency, innovation and choice. While bookselling and the supply of legal services by barristers have rather different economic characteristics, the same general economic principles should apply. Moreover, the sole practitioner requirement might also have the effect of deterring some people from a career as a barrister who would be at least as able professionally as those who become barristers, but who do not have the financial resources to fall back on if their flow of business were to fall off, or who are quite reasonably averse to such financial risk. Lifting of the restriction could therefore help to broaden access to and diversity in the profession.[286]

The Bar's Response to the OFT's report devoted six pages to the topic. It argued that the rule ensured the widest availability of barristers' services to the public in three ways:

- Competition was promoted by maximising the number of competing undertakings – barristers in the same chambers often appeared against each other which would be impossible if they were partners – this was especially important in specialised fields with small numbers of practitioners.
- Minimising costs – individuals working for themselves had lower overheads.
- The 'cab-rank principle' (p. 780 above) would be undermined with partnerships – conflict of interest problems would be greatly increased as the barrister would have to consider not only the interests of his own clients but those of all the clients of the partnerships. Even if there were no technical conflict of interest, partners would sometimes pressurise each other not to take a client – representation would be subject to the will of the majority. The accompanying report by consultants LEGG suggested that the freedom to form partnerships was more important than the cab-rank rule. This showed 'little understanding of the importance of the rule to British justice'. To reduce this valuable public benefit in the name of personal financial advantage and greater security for barristers was contrary to the public interest.

Features that made the OFT's comparison with bookselling inappropriate included:

- The adversarial nature of litigation with the potential for conflicts of interest.
- The small number of barristers with relevant specialist skills.
- The public interest in ensuring that such expertise was as widely available as possible.
- The public duties to which barristers were subject.

---

[286] At p. 15 and see also the accompanying report of the consultants LECG, pp. 80–2.

There was no evidence that the rule deterred would-be entrants. There was a heavy demand for pupillages and tenancies. Most entrants did not have private means and were dependent on funding provided by chambers.

In its April 2002 progress statement regarding *Competition in professions* the OFT responded to the Bar's three main arguments. It questioned whether it was true that abolishing the rule would diminish competition. Not all specialist areas were small and moreover competition rules existed to prevent concentration of work in few hands. As to the relative overhead costs of barristers and solicitors it was premature to draw the conclusion that this was due to a difference in their respective business structures. As to the cab-rank rule, it would still apply to barristers not in partnerships and might apply also to those in partnerships. The OFT said that it intended to give further detailed consideration to the issue.

Partnerships between barristers and members of other professions

The OFT report did not address additional words to the prohibition on barristers forming multi-disciplinary partnerships (MDPs). The consultants LECG's report said the arguments were similar to those that applied to partnerships between barristers. It concluded that the current restrictions on barristers forming MDPs were 'inhibiting competition, potential cost efficiencies and customer choice and convenience'.[287]

The Bar's Response said that all the reasons for prohibiting barristers from forming partnerships with one another applied equally to MDPs. In addition, MDPs would give rise to difficulties of differing professional standards, differing approaches to conflicts of interest and differing rules concerning client confidentiality and the operation of legal professional privilege.[288] The consultants LECG's report recognised these difficulties but did not propose any solution to them. There had been no support in the consultation conducted by the Kentridge Committee for barristers to enter MDPs. In conclusion on this topic, it quoted a recent speech by Lord Woolf, Lord Chief Justice, in which, referring to the OFT report he had said: 'I want to say that I believe that partnership is inconsistent with the independence of the Bar and with the public interest'.

MNPs and MDPs for solicitors

Section 66(1) of the Courts and Legal Services Act 1990 provided: 'Section 39 of the Solicitors Act 1974 (which, in effect, prevents solicitors entering into partnership with persons who are not solicitors) shall cease to have effect'. However, subsection (2) went on to permit the Law Society to continue to prohibit or restrict such partnerships.

One of the few policies proposed in the 1989 Green Papers that was implemented was the recommendation that solicitors should be permitted to form

---

[287] Paragraph 291, p. 82.   [288] Page 19, para. 3.27.

partnerships with foreign lawyers (MNPs). Under the Multinational Practice Rules 1991 an MNP operating in England and Wales has to comply with all the rules that apply to solicitors. All the partners must be either solicitors or Registered Foreign Lawyers (RFLs). (One becomes an RFL by going through a process of registration with the Law Society, set out in s. 89 and Sch. 14 of the CLSA.[289]) In 2003 there were over 200 MNPs registered with the Law Society.

However, partnerships between solicitors and members of other professions (MDPs) are still prohibited by reason of the Solicitors' Practice Rules 4 and 7. Rule 4 prohibits solicitors employed by non-solicitors acting for third parties; Rule 7 prohibits solicitors sharing fees with non-solicitors. Whether MDPs should be permitted has been the subject of deep divisions in the profession since the 1980s.

In 1987, in response to a consultation document issued by the Law Society, 54 per cent of respondents favoured a relaxation of the ban on mixed partnerships. In January 1993 the Law Society issued a fresh consultation document (*Multi-Disciplinary Practice*) inviting the profession's views. The response rate to the survey conducted by the Law Society was very low, but of those who replied, 49 per cent of solicitors and 56 per cent of Local Law Societies were opposed to MDPs, 33 per cent were in favour. The Council of the Law Society decided in March 1994 to take no further action on the matter for the time being.

In June 1996, the Law Society issued another consultation paper on the question (*MDPs: Why? . . . Why Not?*) It stated that solicitors could currently work with non-lawyers in four different ways short of partnership: (1) A firm of solicitors could have a close association with a firm of non-lawyers with a referral arrangement. Most of the major accountancy firms had such arrangements with firms of solicitors. They were permitted – provided the firm had only lawyer owners and fees were not shared with non-lawyers. (2) A solicitor could have a business that was not a solicitors' business with a non-lawyer. Such a firm could provide business adviser services but not legal services. (3) A solicitor employed by non-lawyers could do legal work for customers but not as a practising solicitor. (4) A solicitor who is not practising could own a non-lawyer business jointly with a non-lawyer. Such a business was not a practice.

The consultation paper set out the pros and cons of MDPs in general and proposed six alternative models. This time a large majority of those who responded favoured relaxation of the rules and in October 1999 the Council resolved that solicitors who wished to do so should be allowed to provide any legal service through any medium to anyone whilst still providing safeguards to protect the public interest. It was accepted that this would require legislation.[290] It autho-

---

[289] For a review of the various forms of alliances being formed with European lawyers see 'Rocky Road to Union', *Law Society's Gazette*, 26 June 2001, p. 26.

rised its working party to develop two interim models of MDPs: Model A, a solicitors' firm with a minority of non-solicitor partners, and Model B, 'linked' partnerships of lawyers and non-lawyers to share fees.

The main interim model proposed by the working party was Model A – 'Legal Practice Plus' – which would allow solicitors to take non-solicitors into partnership (NSPs) provided the practice remained in the control of the solicitor partners and the services provided were of the kind normally provided by a solicitor's practice. The proposal was that the NSPs would be regulated by the Society under a contractual scheme established under its Charter (as opposed to its statutory) powers. In return for being entered on a register, NSPs would agree to be subject to Law Society regulation.

Under Model B solicitors could fee-share but not enter into partnerships with a non-solicitor business. Examples might include franchising and licensing arrangements.

A third model being canvassed, dubbed 'TescoLaw', would allow any organisation, including supermarkets, to deliver legal services provided it was properly regulated.[291] Regulation might be achieved by 'ring fencing' the solicitors' practice part of the operation as an incorporated practice. This would require legislation to allow non-solicitors to participate in the ownership and control of an incorporated practice. The Law Society would also need new powers to disqualify individuals from owning a practice so as to protect the public.

The Law Society said that consideration was also being given to relaxation of the restrictions on employed solicitors acting for third parties. Solicitors employed by non-solicitors could act as solicitors only for their employers, though there was an exception, for instance, for trade unions and for lawyers employed by law centres. If this rule were removed, the regulation of solicitors employed by non-solicitors could be achieved by a system where individual practitioners rather than business structures were regulated.

The consultants LECG for the OFT report *Competition in Professions* said that there was some demand for MDPs among solicitors – notably in the fields of property (solicitors with surveyors and estate agents), financial services (solicitors with accountants and financial advisers) and family law (solicitors and mediators). In its view, the current restrictions on the formation of MDPs were 'inhibiting competition, potential cost efficiencies, and customer choice and convenience'.[292] However, it admitted that 'there could be a risk that a small number of accountancy firms could come to dominate the market for legal services', though this, it said, should be addressed by competition law against abuse of a dominant position.

[290] See 'Multi-disciplinary Partnerships on Horizon after "Seismic" Vote', *Law Society's Gazette*, 20 October 1999, p. 3.
[291] See J. Robins, 'Basket Cases', *The Lawyer*, 18 February 2002, p. 22; M. Patterson, 'Deregulation Cannot be Avoided', *Solicitors' Journal*, 5 April 2002, p. 300.
[292] Paragraph 204, p. 62.

In its April 2002 statement on progress, the OFT said the Law Society had been active in addressing the issues raised in its 2001 report. The Law Society Council had adopted a recommendation from its Regulatory Review Working Party to amend Practice Rule 4, subject to the implementation of measures necessary for consumer protection. This amendment would allow solicitors employed by non-solicitors to provide services to members of the public. The Council was to be asked by the Working Party to reconsider a proposal, which it had previously rejected, to remove the ban in Practice Rule 7 on sharing fees with non-solicitor professionals. Legislation might be needed to enable the Law Society to regulate non-solicitor partners of MDPs. These were concerns for the Lord Chancellor's Department to address.

The LCD, in its consultation paper *In the Interests of Justice?* issued in July 2002, devoted sixteen pages to MDPs and the provision of legal services by lawyers employed by non-lawyers. It said that the Government's position was that unjustified restrictions on competition should be removed subject to the need for adequate protection of the consumers. It asked for answers to thirty relevant questions.

In its Response, the Law Society devoted fifteen pages to the topic.[293] It anticipated that liberalisation of the rules would bring potential benefits both to consumers and to the public. Capital injections whether through MDPs or commercial organisations offering legal services direct to the public could increase competition. Significant capital investment could help solicitors to market a range of methods of delivery of services to consumers. Increasingly organisations would want to meet the diverse expectations of clients which might lead to changes in traditional office hours, remote access, access to services through the internet and the like.[294] Many firms were concerned that they could not compete effectively with well resourced non-qualified providers of legal services. Liberalisation of rules allowing input of venture capital would help firms to compete on a more level playing field. Some firms already employed other professionals such as accountants. With MDPs they could offer such persons partnerships – 'giving them a real stake in the future prosperity of their business'.[295] If solicitors employed in commerce and industry could offer legal services to the public, new career options would open for members of the profession which might for instance be attractive to those wishing to work part-time or to take career breaks.

Addressing 'perceived risks', the Law Society said MDPs could result in a reduction of choice for consumers if monster accountant firms swallowed solicitors' firms. It was even more concerned that the result could be a shrinking of consumer access to legal services. Larger organisations would be likely to be attracted to the profitable areas of work such as probate, personal injury and professional negligence and to neglect less profitable ones affecting people

---

[293] *Quality, Choice and the Public Interest*, pp. 37–52 – www.lawsociety.org.uk.
[294] *Ibid*, para. 3.20, p. 42.   [295] *Ibid*, para. 3.21, p. 42.

facing social exclusion, the poor, the homeless and those with mental health problems. Solicitors practising in the field of social welfare law might become increasingly thin on the ground. To minimise that risk the Government should provide proper level of funding for those services.

A related issue was that larger commercial organisations were likely to take tough commercial decisions as to the closing of satellite offices in smaller communities. In the same way that banks, building societies and supermarkets had moved away from small market towns towards more central locations, so too might large organisations offering legal services. Technology would help to bridge the gap through video conferencing and internet access, but a significant proportion of clients were not ready for such developments, preferring face-to-face contact with an adviser. Research suggested that under half the population was willing to consider video conferencing or the internet to obtain legal advice.[296]

The risks to the profession mirrored the risks to the public. 'The liberalisation of practice, opening up competition, could lead to the gradual disintegration of the current high street network of firms . . . this could have a significant impact for consumers on choice of and access to legal advice'. A major concern was whether MDPs and incorporated practices would provide the necessary commitment to train young solicitors.

The Law Society's conclusion was that, while it was likely to be possible to provide a satisfactory *regulatory* framework for solicitors employed by commercial organisations to provide services to the public by adopting the incorporated practice regime, there was a 'strong possibility that such a development could seriously damage access to justice, especially in rural areas'.[297] It urged the Government to undertake further research and to carry out detailed economic analysis before taking firm decisions.

In 2002 the European Court of Justice ruled that the Netherlands (and therefore the other member states) had the right to prevent lawyers from entering into MDPs with accountants, though it accepted that this might restrict competition in legal services.[298] The Netherlands Bar had refused to allow two Dutch lawyers to enter into partnership respectively with Arthur Andersen and Price Waterhouse-Coopers on the ground that it threatened the lawyer's duty to act for clients in complete independence, to avoid all risk of a conflict of interest and to observe strict professional secrecy. The judges found there was incompatibility between the advisory activities of the lawyers and the supervisory activities of accountants who are not subject to the same duty of secrecy as legal practitioners.[299]

---

[296] *Ibid*, para. 3.30, p. 44.   [297] *Ibid*, para. 3.32, p. 45.

[298] Case C-309/99 *Wouters* [2002] ECR I-1577 (judgment of 19 February 2002).

[299] For a helpful and succinct general overview of these issues see A. Bogan, 'Multi-disciplinary Partnerships – Is it a Brave New World or a Glimpse into Chaos', 151 *New Law* Journal, 9 March 2001, p. 354; S. Young, 'Multi-disciplinary Partnerships', 152 *New Law Journal*, 29 November 2002, p. 1810. See also 8 *International Journal of the Legal Profession*, 2001, a special issue with

Incorporation and limited liability partnerships (LLPs)

Solicitors were permitted to incorporate by the Solicitors Incorporated Practice Rules 1988. The chief advantage of incorporation is the protection it gives to the personal assets of partners not involved in the actionable advice. Unlike accountants or surveyors, solicitors are not (yet at least) allowed to issue shares, to seek outside investment or to offer directorships to non-solicitors.

Another important consideration is financial disclosure. Annual accounts must be filed at Companies House.[300]

The issue of limited liability has been under consideration for some years especially as a result of the fear of massive claims against lawyers' and accountants' firms.[301] Under the ordinary rules for partnerships, joint and several legal liability of the partners is unlimited unless it is expressly limited. If an attempt is made to provide for express exclusion, the cap may only be for amounts over the minimum compulsory level of professional indemnity cover (£2 million for partnerships and £3 million for limited liability partnerships).[302]

LLPs are new and are becoming extremely popular. The Limited Liability Partnerships Act 2000 became effective as from April 2001. An LLP is a form of body corporate with members instead of partners. The members act as agents of the LLP not of each other. In the event of a claim, only members who assume a personal duty of care to a client are liable for the losses arising from the LLP's work. Innocent members are no longer liable. Moreover the members' liability is limited to the capital they have in the firm. Private wealth is therefore not at risk. An LLP does not have share capital so the potential tension between directors and shareholders does not arise. The LLP can sue and be sued. In some ways it is like a partnership. It is taxed like a partnership in the hands of its members. The main disadvantage is the requirement of financial transparency. An LLP must file 'true and fair' accounts audited to generally accepted accounting standards – including a requirement, if the total divisible profit exceeds £200,000, to show the income of the highest paid member.[303] (The requirements as to financial disclosure in the United States are less demanding. Clifford Chance became an LLP under New York law, it is

Footnote 299 (*cont.*)
   four articles on MDPs: J. Fish, 'Ethics, MDPs and the European Dimension', pp. 103–8; E. Deards, 'MDPs: a Cause for Concern or Celebration?', pp. 125–50; L.S. Terry, 'MDPs: Reflections from the US Perspective', pp. 151–60; and A.A. Paterson, 'Multi-disciplinary Partnerships – a Critique', pp. 161–8.
[300] See C. Davis, 'Coming Aboard', *Law Society's Gazette*, 15 May 1996, p. 26.
[301] In December 1995, for instance, the 150 partners of accountants Binder Hamlyn were ordered to pay damages of £34 million for failing in their duty of auditing. (*The Times*, 1 December 1995 and 8 December 1995.)
[302] On capping of liability see M. Ellis, 'Cap Happy', *The Lawyer*, 27 June 2005, p. 28.
[303] See D. Furst and S. Gale, 'Nowhere to Hide', *The Lawyer*, 24 January 2005, p. 23. For an article reporting on the accounts presented by Allen & Overy, the first of the 'magic circle' firms to release its LLP accounts, see *The Lawyer*, 11 July 2005, p. 2.

said, in order to gain the benefits without the disadvantage of financial disclosure.[304])

By July 2006, no fewer than thirty-eight of the UK's top hundred law firms had converted to LLP status and a significant number of other firms were going through the conversion process.[305]

LLPs are not subject to corporation tax. Limited companies are. Shareholders of the company are taxed on the profits they extract whether as bonuses or dividends. The effective rate of tax paid by members of an LLP is lower – one of the reasons why they are regarded by many as more attractive. Members of an LLP are also entitled to claim tax relief against the interest on loans taken out for contributions of capital. However, in the post-Clementi world when outside investment in law firms becomes possible (see p. 832 below), investors may prefer to take an equity stake in a limited company.[306]

Conveyancing

Until the 1970s, conveyancing of residential property accounted for half the solicitors' profession's income. (For small firms, which are the great majority, it is still a major factor today.[307]) Solicitors enjoyed a statutory monopoly. The continuation of the monopoly was therefore felt to be of critical importance to solicitors. In 1979, the Benson Royal Commission on Legal Services recommended by ten to five that, on balance, it was in the public interest that the monopoly continue – mainly so as to give the consumer the protection of work done by a person with the necessary skills. The Government at first accepted this recommendation but subsequently it changed its mind. The Administration of Justice Act 1985 permitted competition for solicitors from licensed conveyancers. The solicitors' profession was deeply apprehensive about competition from licensed conveyancers but this proved an unreal fear. The competition turned out to be insignificant. (In 1999 the Law Society stated that solicitors

---

[304] There has been a good deal of writing on the pros and cons of LLPs. See R. Foster, 'Limited Liability Partnerships – Could they Save your Home?', 152 *New Law Journal*, 14 June 2002, p. 919; C. Roberts, 'Reaching the Limit', *The Lawyer*, 17 May 2004, p. 29; B. Gripton, 'Follow the Leader', *The Lawyer*, 17 May 2004, p. 35; P. Garry and P. Ashford, 'Members Only', *The Lawyer*, 8 November 2004, p. 25; Q. Wastie, 'Under Pressure', *The Lawyer*, 8 November 2004, p. 29; P.J. McDonnell QC, 'Know your Limit', *The Lawyer*, 27 June 2005, p. 36; C. Ives, 'Structural Shift', *The Lawyer*, 27 June 2005, p. 40; M. Shierson, 'The Ghost of Business Past', *The Lawyer*, 17 October 2005, p. 20; I. Cooper, 'LLP – Limitless Preparation?', 155 *New Law Journal*, 28 October 2005, p. 1637.

[305] *The Lawyer*, 2 October 2006, p. 35.

[306] N. Carter-Pegg and B. Potter, 'Limited Appeal', *The Lawyer*, 2 October 2006, p. 35.

[307] Figures for 2003 showed that for sole practitioner firms it accounted for 40 per cent of fee income and for two to five and six to twelve solicitor firms it was the largest single source of fee income at 19 per cent and 20 per cent respectively. By contrast, for firms with 41–170 solicitors it was only 5 per cent of fee income. Overall for the profession it was 9 per cent. (Law Society's Strategic Research Unit, *Solicitors Firms 2003 Research Findings*, Table 1 – www.research.lawsociety.org.uk.)

accounted for 95 per cent of the market share in the provision of conveyancing services. Licensed conveyancers accounted for 4 per cent. The remaining 1 per cent was attributable to DIY.[308])

In 2006 there were 967 licensed conveyancers, of whom 315 had full licences allowing them to practise on their own or in a partnership or a recognised body. The rest were employed mainly by small firms of solicitors or other licensed conveyancers.[309] (There were an estimated 15,000 solicitors working in the field of conveyancing.)

In 1989 a much more potent threat emerged in the proposal in the Government's Green Paper that banks, building societies and other financial institutions should be permitted to compete for conveyancing work with solicitors in private practice – though the financial institutions would be required to use either solicitors or licensed conveyancers.[310] The proposal caused consternation among solicitors.

The proposal survived in the 1989 White Paper – subject to several qualifications, all designed to promote a 'level playing field': (1) There would have to be an identified solicitor or licensed conveyancer responsible for the conveyancing part of the transaction. (2) The client would have to be offered at least one personal interview with the solicitor or licensed conveyancer to review any possible conflict of interest between the client and the provider of the service. (3) In order to restrict conflicts of interest, a code of practice would prevent financial institutions ('authorised practitioners') from providing services both to buyer and seller. They would also be prohibited from offering conveyancing services if they (or a subsidiary or associated company) were also providing estate agency services to another party. These restrictions could not be overridden even by written consent. (4) The code of practice would prohibit 'tying in' by a rule that conveyancing services should not be made conditional on other services being undertaken or other services be made conditional on conveyancing services being undertaken.

The signals were that the financial institutions would not want to compete by using *in-house* solicitors or licensed conveyancers. They appeared likely to compete instead by using existing local practitioners on non-exclusive panels. The threat to the profession was that profit margins would be cut even further and that solicitors' firms that were not on the panels would lose much of their conveyancing work.

The Courts and Legal Services Act 1999, ss. 34–52 enacted provisions which permitted non-lawyers to become 'authorised practitioners' to undertake conveyancing work in competition with solicitors in private practice. The process would be supervised by an independent regulatory authority (the Authorised Conveyancing Practitioners Board) and be subject to regulations. The Board

---

[308] Law Society, *The Changing Legal Market Place*, September 1999, p. 31, para. 7.4.
[309] Website of the Council for Licensed Conveyancers – www.conveyancer.org.uk.
[310] *Conveyancing by Authorised Practitioners*, 1989, Cm. 572.

was set up in 1991 and draft regulations were circulated for comment. But in March 1992 the Lord Chancellor unexpectedly announced that he had decided to postpone the implementation of the scheme because of a lack of demand from potential providers.[311] The reason appeared to be a lack of serious interest in undertaking the work by the financial institutions for whom it was designed.

A little over ten years later the topic was reactivated when the OFT in its report *Competition in Professions* (2001) recommended that 'fresh consideration should be given to implementing the parts of CLSA 1990, ss. 34–52 not so far implemented, with a view to increase competition in the provision of conveyancing services' (p. 17). Solicitors, it said, faced little competition. (The report of its consultants LECG said that the wide variation in solicitors' charges for conveyancing work indicated a lack of competition.) Implementation of the rest of ss. 34–52 'would allow, for example, banks and building societies to provide conveyancing services' (p. 17).

In its consultation paper, *In the Interests of Justice* in July 2002, the LCD said: 'The Government favours opening up the conveyancing market further and in principle is willing to incur the cost of establishing an independent regulator, if that represents good use of public funds'.[312] The conveyancing market was in the process of considerable developments. The Land Registry already delivered many of its services on-line and was moving toward a system of electronic conveyancing. This 'could ignite the interest of potential new providers of conveyancing services' (para. 8, p. 13).

On the other hand, the consultation paper suggested, the introduction of new non-solicitor providers threatened the existence of small firms. For firms with fewer than five partners, residential conveyancing represented nearly a quarter (23 per cent) of gross fee income. Loss of that income could lead to firms closing or amalgamating which would be of especial concern in rural areas where there were fewest firms. The Government had made 'rural proofing' a part of its formal policy-making process.

The Law Society, in its response *Quality, Choice and the Public Interest* in November 2002, drew attention to the range of protections enjoyed by solicitors' clients including in particular compulsory indemnity insurance and full reimbursement from the Compensation Fund where there had been fraud by a solicitor. If banks and building societies could offer conveyancing, there was the prospect of buyers and borrowers being required to use the in-house service with the consequential loss of independent advice. The 1991 draft regulations had dealt with this by requiring that the client must have a personal interview with a solicitor. The financial institutions disliked this as it would have reduced their profits.

The Law Society agreed with the LCD that the effect of competition with banks and building societies might be the disappearance of large parts of the

---

[311] House of Lords, *Hansard*, 11 March 1992, WA col. 71.
[312] Paragraph 6, p. 12. The cost of running the Board it thought would be some £1.3 million, some of which would be recovered through a levy on fees charged by the Board to authorised practitioners – para. 15, p. 16.

network of solicitors' firms. It recommended that the only satisfactory vehicle in regulatory terms to enable new providers to enter this market would be through enabling employed solicitors to provide services to the employers' customers through ring-fenced incorporated solicitors' practices – provided that a proper scheme of regulation for such bodies could be developed.

On 24 July 2003, in the course of announcing the setting up of the Clementi Review, the DCA announced that pending the review, the conveyancing market would not for the time being be opened up to banks and building societies.[313]

Probate

Prior to the CLSA 1990, it was an offence for anyone other than a solicitor, barrister or notary to draft for a fee the papers on which a grant of probate or letters of administration depend. (Probate is granted where the deceased left a will to enable his affairs to be dealt with; if there is no will, the equivalent authorisation is called letters of administration.) The 1989 Green Paper proposed that this monopoly should be abolished. It offered two possible ways of achieving more competition. One was to widen the class of persons who could apply for probate for reward, the second was to abolish the restriction altogether.

The response to the Green Paper strongly supported the former rather than the latter alternative and this was stated to be the Government's decision. The CLSA 1990, s. 54 stated that banks, building societies and insurance companies could also do such work provided that they were parties to a scheme for complaints and complied with any regulations made by the Lord Chancellor for such a scheme.[314] Section 55 would enable the Lord Chancellor – subject to the approval procedure set out in Sch.9 of the Act which requires him to consult the Legal Services Consultative Panel and the President of the Family Division – to add to the list of approved bodies whose members could provide probate services, but this scheme was not implemented.

The OFT's report *Competition in Professions* (2001) recommended that fresh consideration should be given to activating ss. 54 and 55 so as to promote competition in this field. The LCD's consultation paper *In the Public Interest?* said again, as it had for conveyancing, that the Government favoured the opening up of the market and was in principle willing to incur the cost providing that represented a good use of public money. It invited views whether the method of regulation proposed in s. 54 and the approval procedure in s. 55 were sufficient protection for consumers.

---

[313] *Competition and Regulation in the Legal Services Market*, p. 9. One of the reasons given was that the conveyancing market was no longer a monopoly and was already competitive. ('Providers are now ready to give fixed quotes to consumers who may shop around'.)

[314] The Financial Services and Markets Act 2000 (FSMA) altered the reference to banks, building societies and insurance companies in s. 54 to persons with permission under Part IV of the FSMA to accept deposits or effect contracts of insurance. This would bring in credit unions.

The Law Society in its response (*Quality, Choice and the Public Interest*, November 2002) urged that implementing ss. 54 and 55 would provide significantly weaker protections for the users of new providers than was available for solicitors' clients. It would confuse members of the public about regulators. The Law Society was considering whether solicitors employed by bodies such as banks and lending organisations should be allowed to offer probate service to their customers through an incorporated solicitors' practice, but basically the existing arrangements worked well. The main problem, it suggested, was the absence of safeguards against excessive fees charged by banks and trust corporations.

In the course of announcing the setting up of the Clementi Review the Government stated that ss. 54 and 55 would be activated. Contrary to the view of practitioners, the Government considered that there was no sufficient risk of detriment to access to justice or to consumers to justify excluding new providers having access to the market. Practitioners would lose some work but it was unlikely that it would be more than 7–8 per cent of market share which represented less than 1 per cent of solicitors' overall gross income.[315]

The Government's decision was implemented by statutory instrument which took effect in December 2004.[316] The effect is to allow approved bodies to exempt non-lawyers from the monopoly previously enjoyed by solicitors by virtue of the Solicitors Act 1974, s. 23. However, the Lord Chancellor's post-Clementi White Paper *The Future of Legal Services: Putting Consumers First* stated that to date there had been no applications from any bodies for 'approved status'.[317]

Cost information and client care

The Solicitors' Costs Information and Client Care Code requires that clients 'are given the information they need to understand what is happening generally and in particular on (1) the cost of legal service both at the outset and as the matter progresses and (2) responsibility for client matters. Clients should be given the best information possible about the likely costs, including a breakdown between fees, disbursements and VAT. The Code states that giving the best information includes agreeing a fixed fee or giving a realistic estimate or giving a forecast within a range of possible costs or explaining why none of those is possible. The solicitor is supposed to explain on what basis charges are calculated. If charging is on an hourly basis, that should be made clear.

---

[315] *Competition and Regulation in the Legal Services Market*, July 2003, p. 11 and Annex A.
[316] Courts and Legal Services Act 1990 (Commencement No 11) Order 2004, SI 2004/2959. For a discussion of the issue see N. Cobb, 'Plans for the Probate Market', 154 *New Law Journal*, 2004, p. 1561.
[317] Cm. 6679, October 2005, p. 84. For an assessment of the likely impact of the Clementi reforms for wills and probate practitioners see N. Bird, 'Putting Consumers First?', 156 *New Law Journal*, 24 March 2006, p. 492.

All solicitors' firms are under an obligation to have a written complaints procedure. Clients must be told the name and status of the person who is handling the matter and who to contact in case they have a complaint. Failing to comply with these rules has serious consequences. In *Pilbrow v. Pearless De Rougemont & Co*[318] the client paid £800 on account of the bill but then refused to pay the balance of £1,800 on the ground that he had asked to see a solicitor but the matter had been handled by someone who was not a solicitor nor a qualified legal executive. Despite the fact that the work had been done competently, the court upheld the client's refusal to pay the solicitors' bill.

For the full text of the eighteen page Solicitors' Costs Information and Client Care Code, as amended in March 1999, see *Law Society's Gazette*, 21 April 1999. The full text of the Code can be found at www.lawsociety.org.uk.

Complaints

The handling of complaints against lawyers has been a contentious issue for decades.[319] Each branch of the legal profession had its own system[320] and for the past thirty and more years legislation has added an external monitoring dimension.

The first form of the external dimension was the statutory Lay Observer appointed under the Solicitors Act 1974 to review the way complaints against solicitors had been handled. The Lay Observer existed from 1974 to 1990. In 1990 under ss. 21–26 of the Courts and Legal Services Act the concept was expanded into the office of the Legal Services Ombudsman (LSO) whose remit includes supervision of complaints against not only solicitors but barristers, legal executives, licensed conveyancers and patent agents.[321] Since the solicitors' profession is by far the largest of these professions, it is not surprising that the bulk of the LSO's work concerns solicitors. In 2005–6, 89 per cent of the matters dealt with by the LSO concerned solicitors, 10 per cent concerned barristers.

In her 2005–6 Annual Report the LSO said: 'It is common knowledge that the Law Society has for many years been struggling to provide an effective complaints-handling service. Ombudsman's reports going back over a decade have been critical of their performance'. Despite serious efforts by the Law Society to find the right answer to the problem of establishing an efficient

[318] [1999] 3 All ER 355, CA.
[319] For a more detailed account of the story see the 9th edition of this work, pp. 782–6.
[320] For a comparative study see M. Ross and Y. Enoch, 'Complaints against Solicitors: A Comparative Study of the Solicitors' Complaints Procedures in Scotland, England and Wales, and Northern Ireland', *Scottish Law and Practice Quarterly*, 1996, pp. 145–58, 216–23 and 331–9.
[321] For an evaluation of the role of the ombudsman five years on see R. James and M. Seneviratne, 'The Legal Services Ombudsman: Form Versus Function?', 58 Modern Law Review, 1995, pp. 187–209. See also M. Seneviratne, 'Consumer Complaints and the Legal Profession: Making Self-regulation Work', 7 *International Journal of the Legal Profession*, 2000, pp. 39–58.

system, the criticisms, if anything, have become even sharper.[322] ('Once again this year, the Ombudsman's recommendations highlight repeated instances of basic errors, poor administration, poor decision-making and poor service on the Law Society's part'.) By contrast, the Bar's handling of complaints was the subject of relatively little criticism.[323]

The Access to Justice Act 1999, s. 51 gave the Lord Chancellor the power to appoint a Legal Services Complaints Commissioner with powers to set standards and targets for complaints handling and the power to fine professional bodies if they were not met.[324] These provisions did not come into force immediately. The Act provided that they would only be activated if it appeared to the Lord Chancellor 'that complaints about members of any professional body are not being handled effectively and efficiently'. In the event, the power was activated in October 2004 when the Legal Services Ombudsman, Ms Zahida Manzoor, was given the additional role of Complaints Commissioner. The Commissioner works with an Advisory Board set up in 2004. In 2006 she added a Consumer Board.[325]

However, all of this was quickly overtaken by the latest developments stemming from the recommendation of the Clementi Review that the handling of complaints should be taken entirely away from the profession and given instead to a new independent Office of Legal Complaints. The Government accepted the recommendation and the relevant provisions were included in the Draft Legal Services Bill (May 2006) and the Legal Services Bill (November 2006). (See further p. 838 below.) The Office of the Legal Services Ombudsman and the Office of the Legal Services Complaints Commissioner would both be abolished.

EU lawyers – reciprocal rights[326]

Foreign lawyers can practise law in England providing they do not falsely hold themselves out to have qualifications which they do not have or undertake work reserved to nationally qualified barristers or solicitors.

---

[322] See the LSO's annual reports accessible at www.olso.org. For a brief bullet-point account of the main events from 1990 to 2000 see the LSO's annual report for 2000–1, pp. 9–12.

[323] On the Bar's system see M. Ross and Y. Enoch, 'Procedures for Complaint against Counsel in the United Kingdom: Internal Purification versus External Vindication?', 19 *Civil Justice Quarterly*, 2000, pp. 405–31.

[324] In 2006, the Commissioner levied a fine of £250,000 on the Law Society for unsatisfactory performance. The fine was 'for the inadequacy' of its plan to improve complaints handling. (See the Commissioner's annual report 2005–6, p. 15.) The Law Society's President and the Chairman of its Consumer Complaints Board said that the Commissioner's targets were 'unachievable and unrealistic'. (*Law Society's Gazette,* 26 May 2006, p. 1.)

[325] *Law Society's Gazette,* 9 February 2006, p. 3. For the membership of both bodies see the Commissioner's annual report – www.olscc.gov.uk.

[326] Based on the information on the Law Society's Website – www.lawsociety.org.uk – Overseas lawyers in England and Wales. See also I. Katsirea and A. Ruff, 'Free Movement of Law Students and Lawyers in the EU: a Comparison of English, German and Greek Legislation', 12 *International Journal of the Legal Profession*, 2005, pp. 367–406.

There are three EU Directives that apply to European lawyers working in Great Britain. The first is the 1977 Services Directive.[327] This allows lawyers to cross borders within the European Union and provide temporary services, including advocacy services in local courts, but the host country can impose conditions with regard to reserved litigation and advocacy work and can prohibit the foreign lawyer from undertaking reserved conveyancing and probate work. The UK permits a European lawyer to do reserved litigation and advocacy work if instructed with a UK lawyer who is able to do that work. The foreign lawyer operating under the Services Directive is barred from doing conveyancing or probate work.

The second is the 1989 Mutual Recognition of Diplomas Directive[328] under which each state requires lawyers applying for recognition to undergo certain tests. In the case of the Law Society these are prescribed by the Qualified Lawyers Transfer Regulations 1990.

The third is the Establishment of Lawyers Directive which came into force in March 2000 after being in gestation for more than twenty years.[329] This Directive has three main consequences:

- European Union lawyers have the right to practise law – including the law of another EU member state in which they are established – under their own professional title (Article 3). So a German lawyer working in London can hold himself out to advise clients on English law. Equally, English lawyers can practise under their title of barrister or solicitor in other EU countries. The lawyer wishing to avail himself of this must be registered with a competent authority in the host state. The relevant competent authority in England would be the Law Society or the Bar Council. If the work in question is a reserved activity (litigation and advocacy) the lawyer must be instructed together with a UK lawyer able to do that work.
- Once registered, EU lawyers have the right to representation in the professional association and have a full right to vote in elections.
- After three years of 'practice of host state law', under Article 10 of the Directive, EU lawyers have the right to be admitted to the local profession without examination. They have to make clear the nature of their qualifications on their notepaper so that the public are not misled but the Law Society may require some evidence that the lawyer has indeed been practising English law during the previous three years. The foreign lawyer can choose whether he wants to become a barrister or solicitor.[330]

---

[327] 77/249/EEC implemented in the UK by the European Communities (Services of Lawyers) Order 1978, SI 1978/1910.

[328] 89/48/EEC implemented in the UK by the European Communities (Recognition of Professional Qualifications) Regulations 1991, SI 1991/824 substituted by SI 2000/1960.

[329] 98/5/EC implemented by the European Communities (Lawyer's Practice) Regulations 2000, SI 2000/1119.   [330] *The Lawyer*, 31 May 1999, p. 7.

The Establishment Directive makes registration mandatory for EU nationals working as lawyers in England on a permanent basis. By July 2006 only some 250 EU lawyers had registered with the Law Society under the Directive, a considerably lower number than were thought to be working in this country. Whether the relatively small number who have registered is because they did not know about the requirement, or because of the cost (£825 in 2006) or for other reasons was not known.

From the Clementi Review to the Legal Services Bill

Announcing the establishment of the Clementi Review, Lord Falconer said, 'The legal services regulatory system is complex and fragmented. There is a wide range of regulators with overlapping powers and responsibilities.[331] . . . We need to establish whether the system meets the demands of a modern, changing legal services market.'[332]

The terms of reference of the Review were: 'To consider what regulatory framework would best promote competition, innovation and the public and consumer interest in an efficient, effective and independent legal sector and to recommend a framework which will be independent in representing the public and consumer interest, comprehensive, accountable, consistent, flexible, transparent, and no more restrictive or burdensome than is clearly justified.'

The Review had a small staff but the report was clearly the work of Sir David Clementi himself. There can be little doubt that his work will have a very significant impact on the future of the legal profession and the delivery of legal services here and very probably in other countries as well. The Legal Services Bill is a major piece of legislation.[333] If the old system it replaces was complex, the new system can hardly be described as simple.[334]

The three main topics addressed in turn by the Clementi Review,[335] the Draft Legal Services Bill,[336] the 82-page long Regulatory Impact Statement accompanying the Draft Bill,[337] the report of the Joint Parliamentary Committee examining the Draft Bill,[338] the Government's Response to the report of the Joint

---

[331] According to the 133-page Scoping Study attached as Appendix B to the report (n. 205 above) there were no fewer than 22 regulators involved in legal services.

[332] DCA Press Release No. 310/03, 24 July 2003.

[333] When first published in May 2006 the Draft Bill ran to no fewer than 172 pages with 159 clauses and 15 Schedules. The Bill published in November 2006 had swollen to 204 clauses and 24 Schedules and was a staggering 304 pages long. No doubt by the time it reaches the statute book, it will be longer still. For a critical appraisal see Kerry Underwood, 'The Legal Services Bill – Death by Regulation?', 26 *Civil Justice Quarterly*, 2007, pp. 124–33.

[334] See for instance the 40 pages of Schedules 11 to 14 of the Bill dealing with the licensing rules for Alternative Business Structures.   [335] www.legal-services-review.org.uk

[336] www.dca.gov.uk/legist/legalservices.htm.

[337] The Regulatory Impact Statement is on the same Website as the Draft Bill – see n. 336 above. It included a valuable six-page summary of expected 'benefits and costs' – i.e. pros and cons – in relation to each of the main topics in the legislation.

[338] www.parliament.gov.uk – Business – Committees – Committees in Full – Former Committees – Draft Legal Services Bill.

Committee[339] and the Bill itself were: the regulatory system, the complaints system and business structures for the provision of legal services. They are dealt with here in that order.

The regulatory system

Clementi said that the current regulatory system was 'outdated, inflexible, over-complex and insufficiently accountable or transparent'.[340] The Law Society was overseen in many of its functions by the Master of the Rolls, much of the Bar Council's work and that of the Council for Licensed Conveyancers and the Institute of Legal Executives by the DCA, the Chartered Institute of Patent Agents by the Department of Trade and Industry and the Faculty Office over-seeing notaries by the Archbishop of Canterbury. There were no clear princi-ples or objectives underlying the system and it had insufficient regard to the interests of consumers. Reforms had been piecemeal, often adding to the list of inconsistencies (p. 2).

In his consultation paper Clementi set out two main regulatory models. The first, referred to as Model A, involved stripping out all regulatory functions from the front-line practitioner bodies – i.e. the Law Society and the Bar Council. All their functions would be vested in a Legal Services Authority. They would undertake all the regulatory functions: entry standards and training, rule-making, monitoring and enforcement, complaints and disci-pline.

Model B gave responsibility for the regulatory functions to front-line practi-tioner bodies subject to supervision by a Legal Services Board (LSB). Model B+, a variant of model B, would require the front-line bodies to separate their reg-ulatory functions from their representative functions.

Clementi's conclusion was that regulatory functions, other than complaints and discipline, would best be served by Model B+.[341] The conclusion was accepted by the Government and was given effect in Part 2 of the Legal Services Bill.

The Bill establishes the LSB.[342] The Board must 'so far as is reasonably prac-ticable, act in a way – (a) which is compatible with the regulatory objectives, and (b) which the Board considers most appropriate for the purpose of meeting those objectives'.[343]

The 'regulatory objectives', all of which save one were proposed in Clementi, are set out in cl. 1 of the Bill: '(a) supporting the constitutional principle of the rule of law; (b) improving access to justice; (c) protecting and promoting the interests of consumers; (d) promoting competition in the provision of legal services within

---

[339] www.dca.gov.uk – Legislation – Legal Services Bill – Further background on the Legal Services Bill – Latest News.

[340] The view of the Scoping Study, n. 205 above, cited by Clementi in his consultation paper issued in March 2004, para. 2, p. 7.   [341] Clementi, p. 49, para. 70.

[342] Clause 2 and Sch. 1.   [343] Clause 3(2).

subsection (2);[344] (e) encouraging an independent,[345] strong, diverse and effective legal profession; (f) increasing public understanding of the citizen's legal rights and duties; (g) promoting and maintaining adherence to the professional principles'.[346] The Joint Parliamentary Committee on the Draft Bill recommended (para. 5) that in the Explanatory Notes it be made clear that the objectives were not ranked in any particular order lest it be thought that they were ranked in order of importance. This was adopted. (See Explanatory Notes, para. 26.)

The Board must have regard to the principles under which the regulatory activities should be 'transparent, accountable, proportionate, consistent and targetted only at cases in which action is needed' and any other principle it thinks represents the best regulatory practice and the public interest.[347] (Approved regulators are placed under the same obligation by clause 27(3).)

The first chairman and a majority of the members of the Board must be lay persons. The Secretary of State[348] would appoint all the members of the Board.[349] The Board must establish a Consumer Panel to represent the interests of consumers (cl. 8). (The Joint Parliamentary Committee (para. 17) recommended that there should be a parallel Practitioner Panel including academics. This was not adopted.)

The Bill provides that named existing bodies are approved front-line regulators.[350] Other bodies may, however, apply to the Board to become approved regulators. If, having taken advice,[351] the Board accepts the application, it would recommend the Secretary of State to designate that body as an approved regulator in relation to the stated activities.[352] The Secretary of State is not obliged to accept the recommendation.[353]

---

[344] Subsection (2) defines these as 'services such as are provided by authorised persons (including services which do not involve the carrying on of activities which are reserved legal activities)'. Section 12 describes as 'reserved activities': exercising rights of audience, the conduct of litigation, reserved instrument activities, probate and notarial activities and the administration of oaths.(Sch. 2 defines the reserved activities, Sch. 3 defines the exemptions.) Under s. 17 a person is an 'authorised person' if he is authorised to carry on the relevant activity. The Joint Parliamentary Committee (para. 216) recommended that will writing for a fee should be an additional reserved activity. This was not adopted.

[345] The Joint Parliamentary Committee (para. 4) urged that 'independent' should be inserted before 'strong'.   [346] The last in the list of objectives was added by the Government.

[347] Clause 3(3).

[348] The term 'Secretary of State', rather than 'Lord Chancellor', is used throughout the Bill.

[349] Schedule 1, paras. 1 and 2. The appointments would be made according to 'Nolan principles', namely, in accordance with the Commissioner for Public Appointment's Code of Practice (Explanatory Notes, para. 38). The Joint Parliamentary Committee (para. 9) urged that the Secretary of State should be required to consult the Lord Chief Justice. The Government did not adopt this recommendation.

[350] They are listed in Sch. 4 which also sets out the reserved activities in question in each case. Both the Law Society and the Bar Council are listed as approved regulators with regard to rights of audience, the conduct of litigation, reserved instrument activities, probate activities and the administration of oaths.

[351] Advice must be sought from the Office of Fair Trading, the Consumer Panel, the Lord Chief Justice and such other persons it considers it reasonable to consult.

Any alteration by an approved regulator of its regulatory arrangements takes effect only when approved.[354] The Secretary of State can by order extend the reserved legal activities but he can only do so on the recommendation of the Board.[355]

The Bill gives the Board extensive powers to regulate approved regulators. These include the power to:

- Require information.[356]
- Issue guidance.[357]
- Set regulatory targets and monitor compliance.[358]
- Direct a regulator to take specific action.[359]
- Direct a regulator to change its regulatory arrangements.[360]
- Publicly censure an approved regulator.[361]
- Impose a financial penalty on an approved regulator.[362]
- Intervene directly (through an 'intervention direction') in an approved regulator's regulatory functions.[363]

The Joint Parliamentary Committee urged that objective thresholds should be established for the exercise of the Board's powers and that it should only be able to intervene to take over the functions of an approved regulator 'if there is clear evidence that serious damage might otherwise be caused to the regulatory objectives' (para. 178). The recommendation was not adopted.

The Secretary of State also has a variety of powers under the Bill. The Joint Parliamentary Committee's Report highlighted the matter of the minister's powers, which it set out in Appendix 9 of its report. Sir David Clementi told the Joint Committee that one of his concerns about the Draft Bill was 'How often the Secretary of State seems to appear in this Bill as somebody who is making decisions. I had envisaged that he would set up the framework, make sure the objectives were there and then as far as possible stand back from it'. He thought that 'important points of public policy' should fall to the Secretary of State, whilst 'more technical regulatory matters should fall to the LSB'. The Joint Committee said it agreed that the Secretary of State had too much involvement (para. 150). It recommended that each of the minister's powers in the Draft Bill be reconsidered and only retained if necessary (para. 155).

With one exception,[364] the Bill does not provide for any right of appeal against regulatory decisions by the LSB. The Joint Parliamentary Committee on the Draft Bill recommended (para. 18) that there be a right to ask a judge for

---

[352] Schedule 4, para. 16(2).   [353] Schedule 4, para. 17(1)(a).

[354] Schedule 4, para. 19(1) provides for various possible forms of approval – e.g. by the Board or where the Board has decided that the alteration is exempt from the requirement of approval or where it is an alteration made in compliance with a performance target direction given by the Board under clause 31.

[355] Clause 17 and Sch. 6. This applies equally to an order stating that an activity would no longer be reserved (cl. 25).   [356] Clause 54.   [357] Clause 158.   [358] Clause 30.

[359] Clause 31 and Sch. 7.   [360] Clause 31(3)(b).   [361] Clause 34.   [362] Clause 36.

[363] Clause 40 and Sch 8.

leave to appeal to the High Court. The Government did not accept the recommendation.

If the OFT is of the opinion that the regulatory arrangements of an approved regulator 'prevent, restrict or distort competition within the market for reserved legal services to any significant extent, or are likely to do so', it may issue a report to that effect.[365] The Board must consider the report and must notify the OFT what, if any, action it proposes to take.[366] If the OFT considers that the Board has not given proper consideration to its report, it may give a copy to the Secretary of State.[367] He must then seek the advice of the Competition Commission.[368]

The Secretary of State may direct the Board to take such action as he considers appropriate in connection with any matter raised in a report by the OFT.[369] This is a potentially far-reaching power.

The Board has the power to make rules for a levy from approved regulators to cover the costs of the Board and the Office for Legal Complaints.[370]

Clementi considered that the costs of the LSB might be shared between the Government and the profession.[371] The Government rejected this approach. The White Paper stated: 'The Government starts from the position that the legal profession should pay the cost of its regulation. The LSB will therefore make a charge on all FLRs[372] to pay for the costs of its regulation'.[373] The professions were understandably indignant that their members should have to pay for what had previously been funded by the taxpayer. (And no doubt the cost will prove to be even higher than Clementi estimated.[374])

The Joint Committee said it was not convinced by the Government's costings of the new regulatory framework and urged it to revisit this question.[375] It also hoped that the Government would give further consideration to funding the start-up costs of the new system. The profession, it said, should not be expected to fund the public policy considerations currently funded by the Government.[376]

But the Government declined to budge. Its Response said bleakly, 'The Government has made it clear that it proposes that the legal professions should pay the full cost of these reforms. The basic principle is that those being regulated should bear the cost of regulation'.[377]

---

[364] There is an appeal against the imposition of a financial penalty (cll. 38, 94).

[365] Clause 56. [366] Clause 57. [367] Clause 58. [368] Clause 58(4). [369] Clause 60(1).

[370] Clause 166. [371] Review, p. 89, paras. 35 and 36. [372] Front-line regulators.

[373] White Paper, para. 9.1. Clementi estimated annual costs of the new system would be £79.5 million. (Appendix to the Clementi Review.)

[374] The Explanatory Notes published with the Legal Services Bill in November 2006 (paras. 505–9) stated that an analysis by PricewaterhouseCoopers('PwC') of the cost of regulating the legal services sector in 2005–06 estimated it to be around £97.4m. About £12m had been spent by Government and £85.4m by the professional bodies. PwC calculated annual running costs under the new regulatory framework at £87.9m, £9.6m less than at present.

[375] Joint Report, Recommendation 55. [376] Joint Report, para. 467, Recommendation 57.

Complaints

The concern about the complaints system identified by the Clementi Review arose at different levels. At the operational level there was an issue about efficiency especially with regard to the Law Society's system,[378] at the oversight level there was concern over the overlapping powers of the oversight bodies and at the level of principle there was the question whether lawyers should run the system of handling complaints against lawyers.

Clementi recommended that a new Office for Legal Complaints (OLC) take over the handling of consumer complaints against all providers of legal services regulated by the LSB.[379] The OLC should first try to mediate. If this failed, the OLC should investigate further and come to a decision. Its powers should include requiring an apology, ordering a reduction in fees, requiring that work be re-done and faults be remedied and ordering compensation.[380] Complaints raising issues of professional misconduct should be referred to the FLR[381] but this should not delay the granting of redress in respect of the consumer complaint.[382]

The Government stated in the White Paper that Clementi's recommendation was accepted. The maximum level of compensation that the OLC could award would be £20,000.[383]

The relevant provisions giving effect to the Clementi proposals on complaints are in Part 6 of the Legal Services Bill (cll. 109–157). The OLC will be accountable to the Board and will be funded through a combination of a general levy on legal services providers and a 'polluter pays' mechanism.[384] The Board

---

[377] Response, p. 35.
[378] In relation to the Law Society, 'In the main, concerns have centred around the issues of substantial delay in dealing with complaints, and questionable quality in terms of the outcome. This was initially attributed to poor management of the complaints handling process, and inadequate resourcing' (Clementi, p. 57, para. 17).
[379] Clementi, p. 66, para. 46. The Law Society's reaction was positive. The Bar Council's was strongly negative on the ground that its procedures had not been criticised. In September 2006, however, the Bar Standard's Board new independent commissioner said he intended to overhaul the Bar's disciplinary and complaints system to increase transparency and efficiency. Robert Behrens, who was appointed in June 2006, said there were three key weaknesses in the existing scheme – the views of complainants were not taken into account enough, there was not enough feedback to people the subject of complaint and the system was not transparent enough (*The Lawyer*, 18 September 2006, p. 6). [380] Clementi, pp. 67–8, paras. 49 and 50.
[381] The Joint Parliamentary Committee urged that the Bill be amended to allow the OLC to refer to the professional bodies complaints that raised both consumer and conduct issues (para. 44). [382] Clementi, pp. 68–9, paras. 52 and 53.
[383] White Paper, 2005, para. 8.11; Legal Services Bill cl. 135. Under the old scheme, the maximum until 2005 was £5,000. It was raised to £15,000 in January 2006. The average IPS award was around £400.
[384] The Joint Parliamentary Committee recommended that this should only apply to those found guilty (para. 52). The recommendation was not adopted. The Explanatory Notes to the Bill (para. 318) state: 'It is envisaged that the ombudsman scheme rules . . . will apply a combination of periodic (annual) fees for approved regulators and a "polluter pays" mechanism to fund legal complaints handling. The "polluter pays" mechanism will mean that the respondent of a complaint, whether the complaint is upheld or not so long as it is not first excluded from the scheme, is charged for the handling of the complaint.' This is the same as

will appoint the members of the OLC in consultation with the Secretary of State.[385]

Legal service providers will still be required to maintain in-house complaints handling arrangements. These will continue to be the first port of call for consumers. Save in exceptional circumstances, the OLC will not consider complaints that have not been considered in-house.[386] If the complaint is not resolved in-house, consumers will be able to refer the matter to the OLC. Complaints will be handled by caseworkers, who will attempt to mediate.

The OLC will only handle complaints about inadequate professional service. Allegations of professional misconduct involving potential disciplinary matters will remain the province of the FLRs.

The methodology for handling complaints will follow the Financial Ombudsman Service model.[387] Its essence is that the complaint is first passed by an ombudsman to a caseworker who investigates and attempts to find a mutually acceptable solution – sometimes involving informal guidance from an ombudsman. The caseworker cannot make a binding determination. The Explanatory Notes state that an ombudsman would become directly involved 'if the parties do not accept the caseworker's solution' in which case 'the caseworker would submit the complaint to an ombudsman for binding determination' (para. 361).

Alternative Business Structures

In its July 2003 consultation paper (*Competition and Regulation in the Legal Services Market*)[388] the Government expressed its support for the principle of enabling legal services to be provided by alternative business structures. ('Such new structures would provide an opportunity for increased investment and therefore enhanced development and innovation; for improved efficiency and lower costs'.[389])

The rules that restrict the way that legal services can be provided were identified for the Clementi Review by the OFT:[390]

- Rules prohibiting partnerships between barristers and between barristers and other professionals (lawyers and non-lawyers).
- Rules prohibiting barristers employed in solicitors' firms from becoming partners.

---

the Financial Ombudsman Service scheme.

[385] Sch. 15, para. 1.   [386] Clause 123.

[387] For the procedures of the Financial Services Ombudsman see the annual reports –. www.financial-ombudsman.org.uk. The system was established under the Financial Services and Markets Act 2000. It replaced the Banking Ombudsman, the Building Societies Ombudsman, the Insurance Ombudsman, the Investment Ombudsman, the Securities and Future Complaints Bureau and the Personal Investment Authority Ombudsman Bureau. Commending the scheme he operates, Mr Walter Merricks, Chief Financial Ombudsman, said they had reduced the unit cost of complaints to £433 in 2005 compared with the costs of the Law Society's system which were over £1,500 per case. (*Law Society's Gazette*, 3 August 2006,

- Rules prohibiting solicitors from entering into partnership with other professions (lawyers and non-lawyers).
- Rules that (with a small number of exceptions)[391] prevent solicitors in the employment of businesses or organisations not owned by solicitors (e.g. banks and insurance companies) from providing legal services to third parties.

Clementi drew a distinction between Legal Disciplinary Partnerships (LDPs) and Multi-Disciplinary Practices (MDPs). LDPs are law practices that permit lawyers from different professional bodies, for instance, barristers and solicitors, to work together on an equal footing. MDPs are practices which bring together lawyers and other professionals (e.g. accountants or chartered surveyors) to provide legal and other services to third parties.

Clementi recommended that LDPs be permitted but that any decision as to whether MDPs be approved should be postponed until there had been experience with LDPs. LDPs should be a distinct 'ring-fenced legal entity'. They would be required to identify a lawyer in the firm as Head of Legal Practice responsible to the regulator for the firm's compliance in its conduct of legal business with the regulatory rules. The manager of an LDP, however, could be a non-lawyer. He too would have to be identified to the regulator. He would have to sign a Code of Practice. Lawyers would have to be a majority in the management structure of an LDP. Non-lawyer ownership of LDPs should be permitted subject to a 'fit to own' test. New capital should increase capacity and exert a downward pressure on prices. New investors might bring new ideas about how legal services might be provided.[392] Outside investors would be prohibited from interfering in individual cases and from having access to client files.

However, the Government went considerably further than Clementi in deciding not to restrict Alternative Business Structures to LDPs.[393] The White Paper stated that different types of lawyers (barristers and solicitors) and lawyers and non-lawyers would be permitted to work together on an equal footing in Alternative Business Structures (ABS firms). ABS firms would have to be licensed by an authorised ABS regulator (or in the absence of any such regulator by the LSB itself). ABS firms would be able to tap into outside investment.[394]

The potential benefits for consumers, the White Paper suggested, would be more choice, reduced prices, better access to justice, improved consumer service, greater convenience and increased consumer confidence. The potential advantages for providers included increased access to finance, better spread of

---

p. 12.)   [388] CP (R2) 07/02, DCA.   [389] Paragraph 54.   [390] Clementi, p. 105, para. 2.

[391] Notably law centres where lawyers and non-lawyers can work together on an equal footing.

[392] Clementi, p. 115, para. 35.

[393] This was unexpected. *The Law Society's Gazette* of 20 October 2005 headed its page one story

risk, increased flexibility, better prospects for high-quality non-lawyers and more choice for new legal professionals.[395]

The White Paper said that the Government expected that the Board would want to be satisfied that an FLR that wanted to regulate ABS firms would have rules that did not restrict different kinds of lawyers or lawyers and non-lawyers from working together on an equal footing.[396]

The Joint Committee urged the Government to re-think its approach to Legal Disciplinary Partnerships (LDPs) and amend the draft Bill to make provision for LDPs without outside ownership.[397]

The Government's Response accepted the recommendation and indicated that the Bill would be amended to enable professional bodies to regulate entities that fell short of the full ABS model. ('This would allow the Law Society, for example, to remove the current restriction that requires a solicitors' firm to be fully owned and managed by solicitors. It could instead provide for the regulation of entities which are managed or owned by different types of lawyers (e.g. a solicitor and a barrister) without the need for the issue of a full ABS licence. This should reduce a potential burden on firms and reduce costs to the consumer, while enabling greater liberalisation in the delivery of services'.[398])

The Joint Committee found itself most troubled by the Government's decision to go well beyond what Clementi had recommended with regard to alternative business structures. ('We have been told about the potential for conflicts of interest in ABS firms, both between lawyers and shareholders and between lawyers and non-lawyers. We are worried both about the speed of approach and the level of uncertainty about the impact of the reforms, particularly on access to justice in rural areas and legal aid provision. Our over-riding concern is that nothing in the reforms should have a detrimental impact on the quality of legal services provided by a legal professional to a client . . . Given the level of uncertainty about the impact of ABS provisions we urge the Government to use "less haste and more care" and follow the Clementi Report in their approach'.) The Joint Committee urged a step-by-step approach 'starting with the least controversial model – partnerships of different types of lawyers without outside ownership or management – before going into the deeper waters surrounding more complex forms of ABSs where real issues of conflicts of interest and uncertainty of impact may arise'.[399]

'Falconer Stuns with Green Light to MDPs'.   [394] White Paper, p. 39, para. 6.1.

[395] White Paper, pp. 40–1. By contrast, influential solicitor Andrew Phillips recommended that the ABS provisions in the Legal Services Bill should be 'thrown into the deepest hole in hell'. Formerly Lord Phillips of Sudbury, he said that external ownership of law firms would drive high street firms out of business and increase the size of legal aid deserts. His campaign against ABSs was being supported by the Legal Aid Practitioners Group, the Sole Practitioners Group and the Legal Action Group. (*Law Society's Gazette*, 18 January 2007, p 4.)

[396] White Paper, p. 43.   [397] Joint Report, Recommendation 32.   [398] Response, p. 22.

The Government's Response said it did not believe that a prescribed timetable was necessary or appropriate. ('It should be for the LSB to make a judgment whether a regulator has the appropriate arrangements in place to regulate and address the risks of various kinds of ABSs . . . There is no reason artificially to delay implementation and the benefits to clients'.[400])

But the Government had a change of heart. Speaking on the Second Reading debate in the Lords on 6 December 2006, Lord Falconer said that the Bill would permit the setting up of LDPs, with no non-lawyer managers or owners. They would not be ABSs and so they would not have to wait for the setting up of the Legal Services Board and the ABS licensing system. They could be established as soon as the Act was enacted.[401] ('...the fact that we are allowing [LDPs] to emerge in advance of alternative business structures answers a key recommendation from the Joint Committee'.[402] It also, he said, reflected Sir David Clementi's evidence to the Joint Committee when he said, 'I think LDPs are walking and we should learn to walk before we get into the running and sprinting involved in MDPs'.[403]

The Joint Parliamentary Committee said it was also concerned about the possible adverse international impact of the ABS structure. Evidence it had received from the German Federal Bar suggested that ABS firms with non-lawyer shareholders and management by a majority of non-lawyers would be illegal there.[404] ('If this is the case, this would necessitate a fundamental re-think of this policy. We are also concerned lest the provisions in the draft Bill would move England and Wales out of step with other European countries'.[405]) The Government's Response said it did not agree: 'It should be left to individual firms, who know their international markets and clients better than Government, to make their own judgments'.[406]

ABS firms were the subject of Part 5 of the Bill (cll. 70–108) and Schs. 10–14. The Explanatory Notes[407] stated that where non-lawyers act as partners, directors or owners of an ABS firm, it would need to operate as a licensed body. An ABS firm is any structure that could potentially deliver a reserved legal service,[408] other than those currently permitted to do so. Examples, some of which are currently permitted, include MDPs, partnerships, limited liability partnerships, unlimited liability incorporated practices, private limited companies, public limited companies and mutual societies.[409] Prospective ABS firms (called 'licensed bodies') would have to be licensed by a 'licensing authority'. Licensed authorities could be approved regulators (see above) that have also been approved as licensing authorities. The Board itself could also be a licensing authority.

---

[399] Joint Report, para. 291 and Table 5, Recommendation 37.
[400] Response, p. 25.
[401] By virtue of the provisions in Schedule 16 (The Law Society, Solicitors, Recognised Bodies and Foreign Lawyers), para 74 (Legal services bodies).   [402] Col. 1166.   [403] *Ibid.*
[404] See to the same effect 'German Regulator Stokes Fears over Bill', *Law Society's Gazette*, 6 July 2006, p. 1.   [405] Joint Report, para. 329, Recommendation 41.   [406] Response, p. 27.

Licensing authorities would have the power to adopt different rules for not for profit organisations and trades unions or to waive or modify the rules for such organisations.[410]

The licensing rules for ABSs are set out in Schs. 11–14 – a total of no less than 40 pages! They require, inter alia, that there be a designated Head of Legal Practice[411]and a designated Head of Finance and Administration[412] and that both must be approved by the licensing authority. The licensed body must have 'suitable arrangements in place' to ensure that it, its managers and employees comply with the duties imposed on them and that they maintain the professional principles set out in s. 1(3).

Schedule 13 sets out immensely detailed rules about ownership of an ABS. Non-authorised persons may only hold what is called a 'restricted interest' in an ABS with the approval of the relevant licensing authority.

An interest in a licensed body arises when a person owns shares in it, has the right to share in its capital, is a partner in it, or is in some other way entitled to share in its profits or obliged to contribute to its losses.

A 'restricted interest' is either 'a material interest' or 'a controlled interest'. A 'material interest' in a company with shares arises when a person owns 10 per cent or more of the shares in it or its parent company; or can exercise or control the exercise of 10 per cent of the voting power in it or in its parent company; or can exercise significant influence over the management of the company or its parent company by virtue of his shareholding or voting power.[413] (The licensing authority is permitted to specify a lower proportion than 10 per cent.[414])

A 'controlled interest' in a company with shares is any proportion of shares specified in the rules that is greater than the material interest level. [415]

The licensing authority must be satisfied that the person is a fit and proper person to hold the interest and that his interest does not compromise adherence by the licensed body to the professional principles.[416]In reaching that decision the licensing authority must have regard to the person's 'probity and financial position', the person's associates and 'any other matter which may be specified in licensing rules'.[417]

Schedule 14 deals with the licensing authority's extensive power of intervention when it suspends or revokes a licence.

NB The Legal Services Bill and resources for research

A provision in the Bill that could prove to be of importance was cl. 11 headed 'Advice and research functions of the Consumer Panel'. This provided that the Legal Services Board may request its Consumer Panel to carry out research for the Board. Whether this proves to be significant will depend on the use made of the possibility by the Board and the resources available for the purpose.

---

[407] Explanatory Notes, para. 174.   [408] See n. 343 above.   [409] Explanatory Notes, para. 175.
[410] *Ibid*, para. 180.   [411] Sch. 11, para. 11.   [412] Sch. 11, para. 13.   [413] Sch. 13, para. 3.(1).

Research is capable of assisting in improving standards of work as much, or even more than, complaints or disciplinary systems. Complaints and disciplinary systems deal with the individual case. Research can discover how the area of work in question is being handled generally from which lessons can be learnt that apply to all practitioners in the field. The issues handled by complaints and disciplinary system tend to be viewed by the rest of the profession as not applying to them. Research can identify systemic problems which can then be addressed on a broad front.

If this is understood by the Legal Services Board, the addition of a research dimension through the Consumer Panel could be of great value.

Clementi – what has happened?

The Bar Council and the Law Society separate regulatory from representational functions

Clementi was clear that the representational and the regulatory functions of the FLRs had to be separated:

> My terms of reference include a requirement to propose a framework that promotes the public and consumer interest, promotes competition, promotes innovation and is transparent. The framework needs to meet these criteria and be seen clearly to do so. I do not believe that the current combination of regulatory and representative powers, in particular within the Law Society and the Bar Council, permit a framework that gets close to meeting this requirement . . . A key recommendation of this Review is that the regulatory and representative functions of front-line regulators should be clearly split.[418]

Both the Law Society and the Bar Council fell well short of good governance practice for a regulatory body:

> Regulatory bodies should have lay involvement in their decision making functions. The Law Society has some lay involvement in certain sub-committees and its main Council of 105 includes five lay members. The Bar Council has some lay involvement in sub-committees, but the Council itself, with around 120 members, has no lay content. The size and make-up of both the Law Society Council and the Bar Council are representative in nature. They are inappropriate for a decision making regulatory body.[419]

Another problem was that the President of the Law Society and the Chairman of the Bar Council held office for only one year. 'Such a short term of office might be appropriate for a representative role but not for a senior regulatory position'.[420]

The choice was between creating two separate bodies (as with the General Medical Council and the British Medical Association) or ring-fencing the regulatory function from the representational function within a single body.

---

[414] Sch. 13, para. 3(2).   [415] Sch. 13, para. 4.   [416] Sch. 13, para. 6.   [417] *Ibid.*

The Law Society's response to the Clementi consultation paper accepted the basic principle of separation of functions. In 2003 it had set up a Governance Review Group chaired by Baroness Prashar, First Civil Service Commissioner. In its Interim Report (May 2004) the Review Group had proposed a Regulatory Board of some fifteen to twenty members, half of whom should be lay. All members should be appointed through an independent procedure based on merit.[421] Clementi thought these were the right criteria for the LSB to apply.[422]

Clementi reported in December 2004. Within a month, in January 2005, the Law Society's Council voted to create two new bodies: one dealing solely with consumer complaints and the other dealing with all other regulatory matters. The representative functions would remain with a much smaller Council. The Regulation Board would have sixteen members with a solicitor chairman and a majority of solicitor members. The complaints board would have twelve members with a lay chairman and a majority of lay members. A proposal that council members could be members of either board was defeated. So too was a proposal for some element of election of solicitor members.

Before the debate, the Lord Chancellor, Lord Falconer, told Council members that reaching this decision 'should allow you to retain the ability to regulate your own profession'.[423]

When the issue was put to the profession in a postal referendum, solicitors narrowly endorsed the decision by 52.4 per cent against 47.6 per cent.[424]

The new system went live as from 1 January 2006.[425] (On 29 January 2007 the Solicitors Regulation Board was renamed the Solicitors Regulatory Authority.)

The Bar moved in the same way. In April 2005 the Bar Council published for consultation proposals to establish a new parent committee, the Bar Standards Board (BSB) with significant lay membership and the barrister members of which would not be members of the Bar Council. It would initiate proposals, provide an independent supervision of all regulatory matters relating to barristers including rule-making, discipline, casework, standards and quality. Its duty would be to give preference to the public interest.[426] The proposals were adopted.[427] The new structure became operational as from 1 January 2006. The first chair of the BSB was Ruth Evans, chief executive of the National Consumer Council, who also chairs the standards committee of the General Medical Council.

Prospects for Alternative Business Structures

At the time of writing, the new era of ABSs was only a talking point. However the signs were that there was interest amongst potential clients. In September

---

[418] Clementi, pp. 31–2, paras. 24–5.   [419] *Ibid*, p. 37, para. 33.   [420] *Ibid*, para. 34.

[421] See N. Rose, 'Split Personality', *Law Society's Gazette*, 15 July 2004, p. 20.

[422] Clementi, p. 39, paras. 38 and 39.   [423] *Law Society's Gazette*, 27 January 2005, p. 3.

[424] 155 *New Law Journal*, 16 September 2005, p. 1339. Only 15,000 of the 123,500 solicitors balloted voted.

[425] See N. Rose, 'The enforcers', *Law Society's Gazette*, 27 July 2006, pp. 22–5.

[426] *Counsel*, April 2005, p. ii.

[427] The advertisements for the posts of Chairman and membership of the BSB and its four

2006 the *Law Society's Gazette* published a report of research by Capita Legal Services showing that 47 per cent of respondents to a survey would be happy to use new providers of legal services for divorce, residential property, conveyancing and will-writing. The on-line survey was of 1,385 consumers and 240 small-business owners. A question asked which non-lawyer bodies or institutions would be trusted to provide legal services. The Citizens' Advice Bureau was first of the top ten choices. Seven of the ten were financial institutions such as banks, building societies and insurance companies. The other two places were taken by Tesco and the AA.[428] Commenting on the results, an editorial warned it showed that 'unless traditional small and medium sized practices begin to market their assets and to modernise, they could easily be swept aside'.[429]

In October 2006, the Halifax became the first major bank to enter the legal services market with the launch of Halifax Legal Solutions offering 'everyday legal products' at fees that it claimed would be considerably lower than those offered by high street solicitors. The services would include discounted conveyancing, will preparation and a 24-hour legal helpline for which there would be an annual charge of £89. Conveyancing would be provided by HammondsDirect, a member of the Halifax's fixed-fee conveyancing law firm panel launched in 2005 which had already been used by some 50,000 customers. But the Halifax said that it had no plan to buy a law firm when the Legal Services Bill came into force.[430]

Legal expenses insurance firm DAS announced that it too would be setting up its own law firm once the Legal Services Bill was enacted. Initially at least it would concentrate on personal injury (PI) work. It handled around 15,000 PI cases a year. As a starting point it would aim to deal with a quarter of those in the law firm. It would require a staff of about 40.[431]

The Northern Ireland 'Clementi' takes a different view

By a coincidence, on the same day that the Legal Services Bill was introduced in the House of Lords, the Northern Ireland equivalent of the Clementi report was published in Belfast.

The Report (*Legal Services in Northern Ireland: Complaints, Regulation, Competition*[432]) was the work of the Legal Services Review Group established by Government in December 2005 to recommend to the Minister of Finance and Personnel how the legal professions in Northern Ireland should be regulated.

---

committees went out in July 2005. (*Counsel*, August 2005, p. iv.)

[428] *Law Society's Gazette*, 21 September 2006, p. 3. Other providers mentioned included newspapers, utility and telephone companies and football clubs! The AA stated in November 2005 that it was set to offer legal services to the general public when the market was opened in 2007. It planned to offer wills, conveyancing and personal injury work direct to the public. (*Law Society's Gazette*, 17 November 2005, p. 5.)   [429] *Ibid*, p. 16.

[430] *Law Society's Gazette*, 2 November 2006, p. 1.

[431] *Law Society's Gazette*, 4 January 2007, pp.1–2.

The chairman of the Review Group was Professor Sir George Bain, former Vice Chancellor of Queen's University, Belfast.[433]

The terms of reference invited the Review Group to consider the Northern Ireland system in light of the Clementi Report and the Government's October 2005 White Paper.[434] In his foreword Sir George Bain said:

> 4. . . . we fully accept Clementi's principles and objectives for the regulation of legal services. But we have not accepted some of his recommendations for England and Wales because we believe they are inappropriate for Northern Ireland. Northern Ireland is different – different in size, different in the nature and structure of its legal professions, and different in its history of regulation. Hence different recommendations are needed – recommendations that capture the principles of good regulation but also recognise these other differences.

There are some 500 solicitors' firms spread around the Province and some 560 barristers who all practise from the Bar Library in Belfast.

Regulation

Bain found the Northern Ireland regulatory situation was broadly satisfactory:

> 8. We found that the legal professions have discharged their regulatory functions in a reasonable manner. The regulatory failure in England and Wales has not occurred in Northern Ireland. Nor is there the regulatory maze in Northern Ireland that Clementi encountered in England and Wales. Hence simply to apply Clementi's proposals to Northern Ireland would not be appropriate . . .
>
> 9. We believe that the professions themselves should continue to discharge regulatory responsibilities, but subject to enhanced oversight arrangements, and, where it adds value, increased lay participation. Oversight should be applied to both solicitors and barristers by a Legal Services Oversight Commissioner helped by advice from the Lord Chief Justice for Northern Ireland.

The Oversight Commissioner should have an audit function in relation to professional rules. The regulatory and representative functions of the professional bodies did not need to be separated for general aspects of regulation though they should be separated for complaints handling.

Complaints

In regard to complaints, Bain said:

> Although we found that the professional bodies have generally discharged their responsibilities in this area fairly, we identified a number of areas where the system requires to be strengthened in the public and consumer interest. Given the relatively few complaints made about lawyers in Northern Ireland, we

---

[432] 23 November 2006. Accessible on www.dfpni.gov.uk.

[433] The seven other members were: a QC, a former President of the Law Society, a legal academic, the Director of the Law Centre, an academic economist, an accountant and the policy head of the Federation of Small Businesses.

believe that they should continue to administer complaints handling, but subject to several important changes.

11. We consider that lay participation should be increased so that all complaints are heard by a majority of non-lawyers, including a lay chair. We believe this change will provide the necessary openness and transparency required to give consumers the confidence to make a complaint when they have received poor service.

12. Increased lay participation should be coupled with strengthened oversight,[435] with the Legal Services Oversight Commissioner having wide-ranging powers, including an auditing function and the ability to set and monitor targets. The proposed system should be more accessible and more accountable than before and complaints committees should be functionally separate from their professional bodies.[436] The eligibility to make a complaint should also be considerably widened.[437]

13. Compensation awards should give consumers effective and adequate redress, including a simplified process for pursuing a claim for professional negligence for smaller value cases. We set our limits lower than those proposed elsewhere in these islands; at £3,500 for misconduct and poor service, and £3,500 for professional negligence.

The Oversight Commissioner should have a small staff and sufficient resources 'to ensure that consumers in Northern Ireland are afforded an effective level of oversight to protect them'.[438] Funding should be by the professions.[439] The Commissioner should have the power to:

- audit individual complaint files;
- monitor and set targets for the complaint handling duties of both professional bodies;
- select lay persons from the available pool to handle specific cases;
- advise the professional bodies on their other regulatory functions, including rule-making.

He should make an annual report to Parliament.

Alternative business structures

The Bain Review Group rejected the whole package of Clementi reforms aimed at broadening the way in which legal services could be delivered.

---

[434] *The Future of Legal Services: Putting the Consumer First.*

[435] Lay people should be in a majority on all committees and they should be chaired by a lay person (Recommendation 7).

[436] Responsibility for complaints-handling should be transferred from the Bar Council to the Benchers 'to achieve functional separation between regulation and representation' (Recommendation 8). Complaints committees of the Law Society should be functionally separate from the Law Society's Council (Recommendation 10). The Solicitors' Disciplinary Tribunal should continue to have a lawyer chair but the majority of members should be lay persons (Recommendation 11).

[437] Eligibility to make a complaint should be open to anyone and be subject to oversight by the Oversight Commissioner (Recommendation 16).   [438] Recommendation 30.

[439] There should be a general levy on all practitioners and a specific levy on those found guilty of

17. We believe that competition is in the best interests of the consumer and hence to be welcomed. We found that it exists in Northern Ireland, with a general practice model of solicitors' practices providing advice to consumers throughout Northern Ireland, supported by an independent Bar Library from which about 560 barristers compete with each other to provide advocacy services to clients.

18. We were impressed by the existing model that gives anyone in any part of Northern Ireland the chance to obtain advice on any matter from the top barristers in Belfast. While we considered the alternative models being proposed in England and Wales – Legal Disciplinary Practices and Multi-Disciplinary Practices – we believe that allowing such models in Northern Ireland would not have the desired effect of increasing competition. Indeed, we consider that they could actually reduce it. We accordingly leave the existing restrictions on such parties as they are. We also concluded that allowing external ownership of legal firms could carry with it unwanted problems, and we recommend no change to this restriction for Northern Ireland.

Conclusion

The Executive Summary of the Bain Report concluded:

22. Our recommendations were unanimously agreed by representatives not just from the legal professions on the Review Group, but also from those who represent the voices of the voluntary sector, the business sector and the consumer. We believe that these proposals should be effective and proportionate for Northern Ireland, and should place the consumer in at least as good a position as those in other parts of these islands, but without the high costs and complex structures that have been recommended in these areas.

Competition: other aspects

The Bain Report equally rejected the proposal that the statutory bar on competition from licensed conveyancers should be lifted.

But it did recommend changes in the rules on direct access to a barrister for advice. It recommended that the Bar Council should consider widening the existing Direct Professional Access Scheme to allow members of the general public to access barristers directly for advice.[440]

It also recommended the Government to consider amending the Judicature (NI) Act 1978 to allow solicitor advocates to appear, subject to conditions, in the higher courts.[441] The Bar Council should consider its rules on the rights of audience of employed barristers.[442]

The Irish Competition Authority follows Clementi

Two weeks after the publication of the Legal Services Bill and the Northern Ireland report, the Irish Competition Authority published a 220-page report on competition in legal services.[443]

---

poor service or misconduct (Recommendation 31).
[440] Recommendation 40.   [441] Recommendation 41.   [442] Recommendation 42.

The Report called for the dismantling of a raft of restrictive practices affecting the legal profession and the establishment of an independent body – to be known as the Legal Services Commission – with overall responsibility for regulating the profession and the market for legal services.

Many of the recommendations concerned matters that had already been reformed in the English system.[444] Others were similar to those that emerged from the Clementi report. They included:

- the establishment of the Legal Services Commission (LSC) much in the same form as the Legal Services Board under the English Legal Services Bill;
- separation of the regulatory and the representative functions of the Law Society and the Bar;
- abolition of the Law Society's monopoly over the training of solicitors and the Inns of Court's monopoly over the training of barristers. A provider of education and training for solicitors and for barristers should require the permission of the LSC which would be responsible for the standards of education and training;
- barristers should be permitted to join in partnership;
- the state, as the largest buyer of legal services, should consider the introduction of competitive tendering for legal services;
- the Legal Services Commission should consider alternative business structures.

Reform of the regulation of legal services in Scotland

In March 2004 Scottish ministers commissioned research into the Scottish legal services market in response to the report by the European Commission entitled *Competition in Professional Services* that invited member states and professional bodies to review professional rules and regulations and eliminate those that could be seen as restrictive of competition, disproportionate and not objectively justified.

In May 2006 the Research Working Group published A Report on the Legal Services Market in Scotland.[445] Compared with the market in England and Wales (valued at some £19bn) that in Scotland was small (some £1bn). The regulatory framework in Scotland was not complex. It was not comparable to the 'regulatory maze' described in the Clementi Report.

---

[443] *Competition in Professional Services Solicitors & Barristers*, December 2006, www.tca.ie.

[444] Introduction of licensed conveyancers. Much greater freedom for both barristers and solicitors to advertise. Employed lawyers to be permitted to represent their employers in court. Easier transfer from one branch of the profession to the other. Taxing Masters not to allow junior barrister a fee equivalent to two-thirds of that paid to a leader – they should be paid only for the work they actually do. Solicitors to be required to issue meaningful fee or fee estimate letters. Abolition of scale fees based on a percentage of the value of the assets. Establish objective criteria for awarding the title of Senior Counsel, together with a procedure for monitoring and removing the title. Solicitors to be eligible to become Senior Counsel.

[445] www.scotland.gov.uk/Publications/2006/04/12093822/0.

The Legal Profession and Legal Aid (Scotland) Bill introduced in the Scottish Parliament in March 2006 proposed the establishment of a Scottish Legal Complaints Commission independent of the legal profession. The Commission will receive complaints that it has not been possible to resolve at source. It will also have jurisdiction to deal with low value negligence complaints where the award is expected to be under £20,000 which would provide consumers with an alternative to pursuing a claim through the court system.

A note supplied to the writer in December 2006 from the Access to Justice Division of the Scottish Executive Justice Department stated:

> A possible next step would be a consultation exercise, based on issues identified in the report of the Research Working Group on the legal services market in Scotland and the Scottish implications of the recommendations made by Sir David Clementi ('MacClementi'). At this stage in the second session of the Scottish Parliament, it is too late to embark on a consultative process which could not result in legislation before the elections in May 2007 for the next session of the Scottish Parliament. It will therefore be for the incoming Administration in May 2007 to consider the case for taking forward a 'MacClementi' reform agenda in Scotland.

Index

Abrams, P., 54, 126, 135, 146n, 648
Abuse of process, 484
Access to a lawyer in police station,
    delay, 177
    duty solicitor, 176
    research data, 180
    terrorism cases, 176
Access to court documents, 425–26
Access to Justice Act 1999,
    appeals, 659–60
    CLAF, 646
    conducting litigation, 794
    indemnity principle, 581
    leave to appeal, 664
    Legal Services Commission, 387–88
    Legal Services Complaints Commissioner,
        821
    'recoverability' of CFA insurance premiums
        and success fees, 634
    rights of audience, 786
Access to proceedings in chambers, 427
Acknowledgment of service, 76
Acquittals,
    Diplock courts, 542
    directing, 523
    juries, 537–40
    research, 515
Adler, Professor Michael, 46
Administrative Justice and Tribunals Council,
    46
Admiralty Court, 3, 4
Advance disclosure, See DISCLOSURE, CIVIL
    and INFORMATION SUPPLIED TO THE
    OTHER SIDE
Adversary system, 379–401
    exceptions, 384–92
    expert witness, 390–91
    inquisitorial system compared, 395–98
    judicial role in, 380–84

small claims, a special system, 384–89
tribunals and the adversary system, 398–99
Woolf Report, 393
Advisory Committee on Legal Education and
    Conduct (ACLEC), See LORD
    CHANCELLOR'S ADVISORY COMMITTEE
Alibi defence, 302
Allocation of cases – civil, 11–12, 50–51, 67,
    78
Allocation of cases – criminal, 315–22
Alternative Business Structures (ABSs),
    829–33, 835–36, 838–39
Alternative dispute resolution (ADR), 141–50
Andrews, N., 92n, 117n, 141, 382n, 394
Anonymity for victims and defendants in sex
    offences cases, 376
Anti-terrorism, Crime and Security Act 2001,
    213
'Anton Piller order', 102
Appeals,
    abolition of House of Lords, 2, 657–58
    Anglo-American comparisons, 678–82
    applying for leave, 673–74
    Bowman reforms, 658–61
    Bowman Report (1997), 659
    case stated, 677
    Criminal Appeal Act 1995, 701–08
    Crown Court, heard by, 662
    double jeopardy rule, 668–71
    errors at trial, 696–97
    findings of fact, 688–90, 692–96
    fresh evidence, 708–13
    grounds for allowing appeals,
        civil, 687–91
        criminal, 691–96
    grounds for appealing, 685–86
    history, 655–66
    Judicial Committee of the Privy Council,
        662–63

Appeals (*cont.*)
   leapfrog, 677–78
   leave to appeal, 673–74
   legal advice for appellants, 676–77
   loss of time, 674–75
   'lurking doubt' test, 693–96
   mistakes of counsel, 685–86
   new points on appeal, 713–14
   only one appeal, 686
   oral argument, 683–85
   perverse verdicts, 527–28
   powers of Court of Appeal, 687
   prosecution, 666–71
   proviso, the, 699–700
   retrials, 714–18
   review or re-hearing, 671–72
   right of, 664–68, 673–74
   single judge procedure, 673–74
   skeleton argument, 682–83
   structure of appeal courts, 655–63
   terminating rulings, 667–68
   time-limits on argument, 683–85
   unduly lenient sentence, 667
   'unsafe' verdicts, 701–08
Appropriate adult, 190–91
Arrest,
   citizen's, 202
   common law, 200–01
   detention by a civilian for 30 minutes,
      203
   detention for questioning, 207–08
   giving the reason for arrest, 204–05
   informing someone of whereabouts, 188
   necessity test, 201
   non-arrestable offences, abolished, 201
   PACE amended by SOCPA, 201
   procedure, 203–05
   reasonable grounds required, 201
   remedies for unlawful, 206–07
   search of arrested person, 220
   search of premises after an arrest, 220–22
   serious arrestable offences, abolished, 182
   under warrant, 200
   when does it occur, 203–04
   without warrant, 200–01
Ashworth, Professor Andrew, 156, 252n, 273,
      326, 327n, 478n, 480n, 483, 703, 705,
      706
Assizes,
   abolition, 16–17
Attorney General,
   Guidelines on disclosure, 288–89

   prosecutions, 266
   unduly lenient sentence appeals, 667
Auld, Lord Justice, *Review of the Criminal
      Courts* (2001)
   aids for the jury, 511
   appeal judges pressure of time, 696
   bad character, 437
   bail appeals, 279, 284
   Case and Issues Summary, 511–12
   case management, 345
   case stated, 662
   charging, 248
   committals for sentence only, 18
   committal proceedings, 345
   Court Service, 1
   CPS, 248
   criminal procedure code, 153
   defendant's right to jury trial, 321
   disclosure, 293–94, 307–08
   double jeopardy, 669
   established, 1, 152, 347
   evidence by pre-recorded video, 434
   fraud trials, 545
   Government's Response, 152
   hearsay evidence, 454–55
   IT, 40
   joint inspection unit, 37
   judge's summing up on fact and law, 522
   jurisdiction of magistrates' courts, 30
   jury aids, 511
   jury not giving reasons, 529
   jury selection, 487–88, 490
   lay and professional magistrates, 30
   laying an information, 206
   making magistracy more representative, 23,
      26
   managing the criminal justice system, 1,
      34–36
   middle tier of jurisdiction, 39
   not proven verdict, 530
   perverse verdicts, 527–28
   'pre-trial assessment', 354–55
   pre-trial hearings, 352–54
   private prosecution, 270
   prosecution appeals, 668
   questions to the jury, 530
   racial mix of jurors, 500
   sanctions, 356
   sentence canvass, 331
   sentence discount,
   terms of reference, 155–56
   ticketing of judges, 19

time-limits, 366, 368
training of magistrates, 27
wasted costs orders, 360, 570
young defendants, 548–50
Automatic striking out, 123

Bad character evidence, 435–42, 438–42
Bail, 273–87
    appeals against grant, 284
    appeals against refusal, 283
    Bail Act 1976, 277
    bail hostels, 276, 287
    conditions, 276, 279
    concerns regarding, 285
    courts, 276–84
    information schemes, 286
    Law Commission on bail and the ECHR,
        278
    length of remand period, 283
    Nottingham Justices case, 282
    police station, 275–76
    street bail, 275
    surety, 280–81
Baldwin, Professor John, 8n, 9, 25n, 58, 156n,
        157, 158, 175n, 181, 184n, 249n, 322n,
        323, 324, 325n, 384, 385, 386, 387, 388,
        389, 324, 325n, 384, 385, 387, 388
Bar/barristers
    advertising, 756–57
    BarDIRECT, 799–800
    BarMark, 806–07
    cab-rank rule, 780
    chambers, 742–45
    circuits, 755
    clerks, 744–48
    complaints against, 820
    complaints against, 820
    direct access to, 799–800
    employed, 760
    entry and training, 736–42
    ethnic minorities, 755
    funding entry, 739–41
    management, 757–59
    numbers, 742
    partnerships, 752–54
    training and entry, 736–42
    Queen's Counsel, 748–52, 801–06
    women, 754
BCCI v Bank of England, 49, 82, 417n, 422n,
        757n
Beeching Royal Commission on Assizes and
    Quarter Sessions (1969), 16

Benson Royal Commission on Legal Services,
    See ROYAL COMMISSION ON LEGAL
    SERVICES
Better Regulation Task Force, 55, 56n, 644n
'Big Tent', 564
Bingham, Lord, 415, 509, 657n, 689, 785n, 792
Bowen LJ, 131
Bowman Report on Civil Appeals (1997),
        654n, 658, 660, 661, 664, 673, 679, 680,
        681, 685
Bridges, Professor Lee , 152n, 179, 181, 182n,
        322, 324, 337, 338, 362, 614
Brooke, LJ., 41–42, 43
Bugging, 234–38
Burns, Suzanne, 63, 132, 140n, 141

'Cab-rank' rule, 780, 808, 809
Calderbank letter, 83
Cantley Working Party on Personal Injury
    Litigation Procedure (1979), 47, 57n,
    114
    delay, 120–21
Cape, Professor Ed, 173n, 182, 210, 238n, 310,
        603, 614, 616n , 617–18
Carter, Lord, Review of Legal Aid
    Procurement (2005 06), 388, 596, 611,
    612n, 620 28
Case Disposal Manual, 253
Case management, 114–28, 347–61
    American research, 126
    Australian experience, 128
    courts' duty of, 50
    Practice Statement (1995), 124
Case Preparation Project, 357–62
Case stated, appeal, 677
Cases and Issues Summary for jurors, 511
Caution,
    new,
    old,
Cautioning, as an alternative to prosecution,
    255–58
CDS Direct, 612
Cell confessions, 461
Central Summoning Bureau, 492
Challenges, jury selection,
    for cause, 494–96
    peremptory, 493–94
Chancery Division, 5
Charging standards, 254–55
Charging the suspect, 248–50
    Code for Crown Prosecutors, 250–53
    Full Code Test, 250–51

Charging the suspect (*cont.*)
  Guide to case disposal, 253–54
  Threshold Test, 252
Children,
  appropriate adult, 190–91
  evidence of, 442–45
  interviewing, 190–91
  See also VULNERABLE WITNESSES
Citizen's arrest, 202
Civil courts,
  allocation of cases, 11–12, 50–51, 67, 78
  three tracks, 50
  unification, 13–16
Civil Justice Council,
  'Big Tent', 564
  contingency fees, 646
  court fees, 72
  legal expenses insurance, 650
  predictable costs, 564, 565, 580
  small claims jurisdiction level, 8
Civil legal aid, *See* LEGAL AID
Civil Procedure Rules (CPR), 51–52
CLAF, 646
Claim form, 68
Claims assessors, 795–96
Claims Direct, 635
Claims management companies, 635–36
Class actions, 63–66
Class bias in prosecutions, 243–44
Clementi Review of Regulation of Legal
      Services Market (2004)
  Alternative Business Structures(ABSs),
      829–33, 835–36, 838–39
  appointed, 781
  complaints against lawyers, 828–29
  consultation paper, 782
  developments, 834
  final report, 782
  Government response, 783
  regulation of the legal profession, 824–27,
      834
  terms of reference, 823
Clerks to the justices, 33
Closed court, 423–24
Coaching the witness, 418
Code for Crown Prosecutors, 250–53
Codes of Practice (PACE), 151
Committals for sentence only, 18
Committal proceedings, 340–44
Community Legal Services *see* LEGAL AID
COMPASS IT system, 41–42

Compellability,
  accused person, 463–66
  spouses, 445–46, 462
Compensation Act 2006, 56, 635
Compensation culture, 55–56
Compensation for miscarriages of justice,
      730–34
Competence of children to give evidence,
      444
Competitive tendering for legal aid work, 587,
      617, 619, 620, 621n, 623n, 625, 627,
      628
Complaints against lawyers, 821, 828, 837–38
Computerisation for the courts, 40–42
Computerised Summons Production Centre,
      74
Concordat, the, 3
Conditional cautions, 258
Conditional fees (CFAs), 630–640
  claims management companies, 635–36
  'costs wars', 636–40
  history, 631–32
  recoverability of success fees and insurance
      premiums, 633–35
  start, 632–33
  success fees, 631–32
Confessions,
  admissibility, 470–77
  cell, 461
  false, 159
  oppression, 474
  unreliability, 476–77
  voluntary, 470–73
Contempt through publicity, 370–76
Contingency fees, 641–46
Contingency Legal Aid Fund (CLAF), 646
Controls on costs,
  assessment of costs (formerly taxation),
      558–59
  fixed costs, 563–66, 577–78, 587, 603, 617,
      619–27
  legal aid work, 568–69
  predictable costs, 564
  remuneration certificates, 568
  scale fees, 566
  taxation of costs, 558–59
  wasted costs orders, 569
  See also COSTS
Control orders, 214–17
Conveyancing, 566, 567, 570, 766, 773, 778,
      782, 815–18, 837

Convictions, admissibility, *See* PRIOR
   CONVICTIONS
Cost capping orders, 567–68
Costs
  acquittal on, 577
  assessment, detailed and summary, 558–59
  'between party', 563
  capping, 567–68
  Civil Justice Council's 'Big Tent', 564
  compliance auditing, 565
  controls, 562–71
  costs estimates, 561
  costs only proceedings, 560
  detailed assessment, 559
  factors to be taken into account, 558
  fast track, 564–65
  fixed, 563–66
  follow-the-event *See* Costs Follow the Event
  graduated fees, 569
  group actions, 573
  Group Litigation Orders, 574
  indemnity basis, 562
  indemnity rule, 581–82 *See also* COSTS-
    FOLLOW THE-EVENT
  legal aid work, 565, 568–69, 578–79
  new rules, 556
  non-contentious, 562
  non-parties, 575
  party and party, 562
  predictable, 564
  pro bono representation, 582
  proportionality, 560
  remuneration certificates, 568
  road traffic cases, 564
  scale, 566
  small claims, 563
  solicitor and own client assessment, 563
  standard basis, 562
  standard fees, 569
  starting cases, 72
  summary assessment, 559
  Very High Cost cases, 569
  wasted, 569–71
  who pays, 557
  See also CONDITIONAL FEES, CONTINGENCY
    FEES, CONTROLS ON FEES, COSTS-
    FOLLOW-THE-EVENT
Costs-follow-the-event,
  civil cases, 557
  CPR 44.3(1), 556
  criminal cases, 576–77

pros and cons, 571–73
exceptions,
  contemptuous damages, 582
  criminal cases, 576–77
  group actions, 573–75
  indemnity principle, 581–82
  legal aid cases, 578–79
  litigants in person, 579–81
  non-party funders, 575–76
  public interest cases, 583–84
  small claims, 577–78
'Costs wars', 636
Council on Tribunals, 46
County courts
  jurisdiction, 7
  small claims, *See* SMALL CLAIMS
  work of, 7
Court fees, 71–73
Court of Common Pleas, 3
Court of Exchequer, 3
Court of Protection, 6
Courts Act 2003, 1, 11, 22n, 37–39
Courts and Legal Services Act 1990 (CLSA)
  Advisory Committee to Lord Chancellor,
    785, 786
  conditional fees, 631
  'general principle', 785
  rights of audience, 785
  'statutory objective', 785
Court Service, 1, 38 355
Covert surveillance, 234–38
Crime and Disorder Act 1998
  abolition of committal proceedings for
    indictable-only offences, 344
  jurisdiction of court clerks, 33
Criminal Appeal Act 1995,
  Criminal Cases Review Commission, 725
  unsafe convictions, 701
Criminal Cases Management Framework, 361
Criminal Cases Review Commission (CCRC),
  725–30
Criminal courts,
  allocation of cases between higher and
    lower, 315–22
  management, 34–37
Criminal Defence Service(CDS), 587, 603,
  605, 607n, 608, 612n, 617n
Criminal Justice Act 2003
  bad character, 438
  bail from the court, 278, 279, 284
  bail on condition extended, 276

Criminal Justice Act 2003 (*cont.*)
　charging by CPS, 245
　committal for sentence only, 18
　committal proceedings abolished, 289, 340
　conditional cautions, 258
　defence disclosure, 308–10
　detention for question, time limit, 209, 212
　double jeopardy, 669–701
　evidence by video recording, 434
　fraud trials, 546
　hearsay evidence, 455–58
　jury eligibility, 488, 489, 490
　jury tampering, 548
　laying an information abolished, 206
　magistrates' sentencing powers, 30, 321
　non-intimate sample, 223–24
　prior convictions, 438
　prosecution appeals, 667–68
　prosecution disclosure, 294
　reasoned decisions on sentencing, 422
　reference to Commission by Court of
　　Appeal, 728
　reference to CCRC, 727
　sentence indication, 331
　Sentencing Guidelines Council, 331
　street bail, 275
　terrorism detainees, time limit, 212
　time limit, 367
　trial on indictment by judge alone, 540, 546,
　　548
Criminal Justice and Public Order Act 1994
　　(CJPOA)
　abolition of committal proceedings, 343
　bail, 276
　right of silence, 170
Criminal Law Revision Committee (CLRC)
　　11th Report (1972)
　adverse inferences from silence, 166
　confessions, admissibility, 472
　defendant's failure to give evidence, 464
　right to silence, 166
Criminal legal aid, 603–12
Criminal Procedure Rules, 153–54
Cross-examination, 108, 382, 388, 396,
　　419–20, 422n, 432, 459, 464
　special measures in rape cases, 468–69
Crown Court,
　division of work with magistrates' court,
　　315–22
　establishment, 16
　judicial manpower, 18–19
　work of, 17–18

Crown Court Study (1993), 152 n 9
　barrister's brief delivered when, 364
　CPS pressure on prosecution barrister, 271
　defendants testifying, proportion, 463
　experts, 306
　judge aware of uncalled relevant witness,
　　383
　judge influencing the jury, 522
　innocent who plead guilty, 324
　jurors taking notes, 510
　jurors' understanding, 491, 517, 520
　jury composition, 502
　jury decisions, 517, 518
　length of jury deliberations, 518
　listing information supplied, frequency, 355
　majority acquittals, 530
　officer in charge of the case a constable,
　　313
　pre-trial conference with defence barrister,
　　frequency, 353
　pre-trial review, value, 119n
　previous convictions of defendants, 436
　returned briefs, 512, 790
　telling the defendant his sentence prospects,
　　329
　Turner on sentence discount, 329
　unwelcome pressure on prosecution
　　barristers by CPS,
　weakness of prosecution cases, 259, 325
Crown Prosecution Service (CPS)
　cautioning as an alternative to prosecution,
　　255–58
　charging, 248–50
　Code for Prosecutors, 250–53
　conditional cautions, 258
　decision to prosecute, 250–58
　Designated Case Workers, 793
　discretion to prosecute, 241–44
　discontinuance by, 258
　establishment, 246
　failure to prosecute, 262–63
　Full Code Test, 250–51
　Glidewell Report, 247
　Guide to case disposal, 253
　independence from police, 263–64
　prosecuting barristers and, 271–73
　reasons for not prosecuting, 252
　reasons for prosecuting, 251
　rights of audience for lawyers and non-
　　lawyers, 786–90, 791–93
　three stages, 264–66
　Threshold Test, 252

Custody officer, 187
Custody record, 188
Custody time limits, 208

Damages,
    General, 69
    Special, 68
Darbyshire, Dr Penny, 20–24, 31, 32, 34, 327,
        519, 530
Davies, Mark, 28
Deaf suspects, questioning, 191
Default judgment, 81–82
Defence,
    access to forensic facilities, 299
    disclosure, 302–09
    preparation of cases, 362–65
Defence case preparation, research, 362–65
Defence disclosure, criminal, 302–09
Defendant, not a compellable witness, 463–66
Delay,
    Cantley Committee (1979), 120
    civil cases, 119–26
    Civil Justice Review (1985–88), 121
    criminal cases, 365–70
    Evershed Committee (1953), 120
    Goriely et al, 126
    Heilbron-Hodge (1992), 121
    KPMG Peat Marwick (1994), 124
    Practice Direction (1995), 124
    Winn Committee (1969), 120
    Woolf reforms (1995. 1996), 125–26
Detention for questioning, 207–17
    legality, 207
    terrorism, 212–17
    time-limits, 208–11
    See also POLICE STATION, POLICE
        QUESTIONING
Devlin, Lord, 399, 459, 505n, 525, 554, 710,
        716–17, 720
    Committee on Identification, 710
    retrials, 716–17
Diamond, SS., 29n
Dignan, J., 25, 26
Dingwall, R., 59, 139
'Diplock courts', 541–42
Direct access to barristers, 797–98
Directed acquittal, 259, 523–25
Directing the jury to acquit/convict, 523–27
Disclosure, civil, 86–99
    CPR, 88–90
    legal professional privilege, 87, 90–94
    medical records, 96

non-parties, 97–98
pre-Woolf, 86–87
public interest immunity (PII), 94–95
subsequent use of disclosed document,
    98–99
third-party, 97–98
use of disclosed document, 98–99
witness (mere witness rule), 98
Woolf's proposals, 87–88
Disclosure, criminal See INFORMATION
    SUPPLIED TO THE OTHER SIDE
Disclosure Protocol (2006), 310–11
Discovery (civil), See DISCLOSURE
Discretion in prosecutions, 241–44
    judicial control of, 260
    police, 241–43
Dismissal for want of prosecution, 123
Dismore, A., MP, 750
District judges, 6, 7, 20
Divided legal profession, 773–75, 779–80
Divisional Court of the Queen's Bench
        Division, 4
DNA, 223, 224, 225, 475, 713
Dock, defendant's unsworn statement, 445,
    469
Donovan Committee (1965), 692
Double jeopardy rule, abolition, 668–71
Dougherty, Luke, 709
Draft Legal Services Bill 2006, 783, 824, 832
Drafting of documents, 69–71
Drug testing, 224
Duty solicitor schemes, 610–12

Early Administrative Hearings (EAHs), 351
Effective Trial Management Programme,
        350n, 357, 361
'Either way offences', 316–17
Entry on premises,
    bugging, 234–38
    with consent, 232
    with warrant, 226, 231
    without warrant, 226
    See also SEARCH AND SEIZURE
Ethnic minority,
    barristers, 755
    magistrates, 24
    solicitors, 769
EU Directives, 821
European lawyers, right of establishment,
        821–22
European small claims proposal, 9n, 68
Evaluating criminal justice systems, 155–56

Evershed Committee on *Supreme Court*
    Practice and Procedure (1953)
  delay, 120
  robust summons for directions, 114
Evidence,
  accused person not compellable, 463–66
  bad character, 435–42, 438–42
  children, 442–45
  confessions, 470–77
  contrary to public interest, 462–83
  discretion to exclude evidence, 477–82
  exclusionary rules, 435–83
  experts, *See* EXPERT WITNESSES
  hearsay, 446–59
  identification, 459–60
  improperly obtained evidence, 470–83
  informers, 468
  legal professional privilege, 466–67
  New Zealand, 483
  parties, 445
  prior convictions, 435–42
  propensity, 439–40, 442
  rape victims, 468–69
  Scotland, 482
  self-incrimination, 463
  similar fact evidence, 436, 438–40
  spouses, 445, 462
  'tit for tat' rule, 435, 440
  unduly prejudicial, 435–42
  United States, 458
  unreliable, 442–62
  voir dire, 467
  vulnerable witnesses, 431
  See also CHILDREN'S EVIDENCE
Examination-in-chief, 417
Exchange of witness statements, 104–08
Excluded material, 228–29
Exclusionary rules of evidence, 435–77
Expert witnesses,
  Academy, 112
  calling, 394
  disclosure of, 309
  duties, 299, 390
  'hired guns', 109
  legal professional privilege, 93
  no property in, 100
  Protocol, 112
  single, 78, 113

False confessions, 159
Family court work, 10–11, 13–14, 15
Family Division, 5

Farquharson Guidelines, 270, 271, 273
Fast and Fair scheme, 63
Fast track,
  allocation, 12, 51, 78
  case management conferences, 116, 117
  characteristics, 51
  costs, 137, 559, 561, 564, 565
  directions hearings, 115, 116
  disclosure/ discovery, 88
  expert evidence, 110–11, 113, 416
  fixed costs, 564, 65
  jurisdiction, 12
Faulks Committee on Defamation (1971),
    506–08
Fenn, P., 135, 136, 614, 642
Financial Services Ombudsman, 44, 143,
    829n
Fingerprints, 217–18
Fiss, O., 59
Fixed costs, 563–66, 577–78, 587, 603, 617,
    619–27
Footwear impressions, 218
Forensic material, access for defence,
    299–300
Fraud Review (2006), 258, 295, 314, 315, 327,
    335, 336n
Fraud trials without jury, 543–48
Free pardon, 720
'Freezing order' (Mareva injunctions),
  civil, 102–03
  criminal, 240
French criminal justice reforms, 1993, 2000,
    401n
Fresh evidence, 708–13
Funding Code, *See* LEGAL AID

Galanter, Professor Marc, 59, 134
'General damages', 69
General warrants forbidden, 233
Genn, Professor Hazel, 54n, 57, 59, 146, 147,
    149, 404, 405, 407, 630, 777
Gladwell, D., 133n
Glidewell Report
  CPS, 247–48, 255, 264, 265
  Queen's Counsel, 751–52
Goldsmith, Lord, 217n, 264–65, 266, 470, 546,
    547, 651, 652, 667, 739, 740, 741
Goriely, Tamara, 54, 58, 62n, 113, 126, 135,
    139, 612n, 613n
Graduated fees, 314, 565, 569, 620, 621, 623,
    624, 627, 628
Graduates of an Inn, 737

Green Papers (1989), 778n
Green, T.A., 526
Group actions, 63–66
Group Litigation Order (GLO), 66
Grove, Trevor, 519
Gudjonsson, G, 159, 170n
Guilty pleas, 322–40
    Criminal Justice Act 2003, 331
    innocent who plead guilty, 322–24
    judge's involvement, 327–34
    plea bargaining, 322–36
    plea before venue, 337–40
    role of the lawyers, 324–25
    sentence canvass, 329–34
    sentence discount, 326–27, 329–36
    supergrasses, 335

Hansen, Ole, 324, 325, 599
Harris, Don, 56n
Hawkins, K., 59, 83, 268, 413n
Hearsay evidence,
    civil cases, 446–52
    criminal cases, 452–59
Hedderman, C., 22n, 318n, 319n, 343n
Heilbron-Hodge Report on Civil Justice
    (1992), 121
Helping the police with their inquiries,
    199–200
Henham, R., 327n
Herbert, A., 337n
High Cost legal aid cases, see Very High Cost
    cases
High Court, 3–6
Hodgson, J., 181, 182n, 191, 362, 400, 401n
'Holding charges', 211
Home Secretary,
    pardon, 720
    reference to Court of Appeal, 721
Hoogstraten, van, N., 77n
House of Lords, abolition of judicial function,
    2, 657–58
Human Rights Act 1999
    civil procedure rules, and, 53
Hung jury, 530
Hurd, Lord, (Douglas), 168

Identification evidence, 459
Immunity of advocates, 571
Immunity from prosecution, 335–36
Incorporation of solicitors' practices, 814
Indemnity principle of costs, 581–82
Informers, protection, 468

Information supplied to the other side,
    disclosure, criminal,
    Auld, 293–94, 307–08
    Criminal Justice Act 2003, 294–97, 308–10
    Criminal Procedure and Investigations Act
        1996 (CPIA), 305–06
    defence disclosure, 302
    Disclosure Protocol (2006), 310–12
    evidence the prosecution do not intend to
        use (unused material), 290–97
    evidence the prosecution intend to use,
        288–90
    prosecution disclosure, 288–302
    public interest immunity, 297–99
    scientific evidence, 299–301
    unused material, 290–97
Innocent who plead guilty, 322–24
Inns of Court, 735
Inquisitorial system, 395–98
Inspecting witness statements, 425–27
Inspectorate for the courts, 37–38
Institute of Legal Executives, 767
Insurance, legal costs,
    before-the-event (BTE, LEI), 648–51
    after-the-event (ATE), 633–5
Interim remedies, 101–04
Interlocutory work, 6
Interpreters, 191
Interviews in police stations *See* POLICE
    DETENTION, QUESTIONING IN POLICE
    STATION
Intimate samples, 223
    destruction, 224–25
Intimate searches, 222–23
Intrusive surveillance, 234–38
Ipp, DA, 392
Irish Competition Authority Report (2006),
    839–40
Issue of civil proceedings, 74–76
Issue of criminal summons, 205–06
IT, 40–42

Jacob, Sir Jack, 114, 140, 141, 393, 399
Jacob, Joseph, 52, 53, 112n, 141, 659n
James Committee (1975), 316–17
Jolowicz, Professor JA., 661, n.24
Journalistic material, 229
Jubilee Line Case, 547
Judge alone trial, 540–50
Judges,
    adversary system, 380–87
    calling witnesses, 382–83

Judges (*cont.*)
 Crown Court in, 18–19
 directing an acquittal, 523
 directing a conviction, 525
 fact finders, as, 688–89
 Focusing judicial resources appropriately
   (2005), 15–16
 interventionist, 386–87
 plea bargaining, and, 327–34
 summing up on fact, 521
 summing up on law, 519
 'ticketing', 19
Judges' Rules, 159–60
Judgment in default, 80–81
Judicial assistants, 661, 680
Judicial Committee of the Privy Council,
   662–63
Jury,
 acquittal rate, 537–40
 age, 486–87
 aids, 510–13
 asking of questions by the jury, 510
 asking questions of the jury, 528
 Central Summoning Bureau, 492
 challenge for cause, 494–96, 497
 challenging, 493–97
 civil cases, 503–09
 contempt of court, 536
 Court of Appeal and jury room, 532–36
 criminal cases, 509–10
 damages' decisions, 504–09
 disqualified, 489
 eligibility for jury service, 486–88
 ethnic mix, 498–500
 excused, 490–91
 Faulks Committee, 506–08
 former times, 550–54
 fraud cases, 543–48
 gender, 502
 history, 486, 55–54
 hung jury, 532
 ineligible, 487–88
 libel proceedings, 507–08
 literacy test, 491
 majority verdicts, 530–32
 Maxwell case, 496, 497
 Morris Committee, 486–87
 origins, 486
 peremptory challenge, 493–94
 perverse verdicts, 527–28
 pre-trial publicity affecting selection, 497

 publication of jury room secrets, 536–37
 quality of decision-making, 513–19
 questionnaires for jury selection, 496–97
 racial mix, 498–500
 roles of judge and jury, 519–27
 secrecy, 536–37
 size, 502
 social class, 502
 stand by for the Crown, 498
 summoning, 492
 tampering, 548
 unreasoned decision, ECHR compatibility,
   529–60
 used in civil cases, 503–07
 used in criminal cases, 509–10
 vetting, 500–02
 work status, 502
Justices' clerks, role, 31
Justices of the peace, *See* MAGISTRATES
Juveniles,
 appropriate adult, 190–91
 questioning, 190–91
 trials for indictable offences, 550

Kalven, H., 513, 554
Karlen, Delmar, 678
Kelcey, I., 365
Kentridge, Sir Sydney QC, 779n, 787, 799,
   809
Kirby, Hon Michael, 663–64
KPMG Peat Marwick report on delay (1994),
   124

Langbein, Professor John, 399, 400, 550
Law centres, 614–15, 775
Law Commission,
 Attorney General's consent to prosecution,
   266
 bail, 278, 279
 challenge of jurors for causes, 497
 court of protection, 6
 double jeopardy, 669
 hearsay evidence, civil, 447, 451
 hearsay evidence, criminal, 453, 454, 455
 juries in personal injury cases, 506, 508
 prior convictions, admissibility, 436, 227n,
   439
 prosecution appeals, 668
 trial for specimen offences, 549
 uncorroborated evidence, 461
Law Officers as prosecutors, 266

Law Society, 770
  reorganisation, 770–72
  selection of QCs, 751
Lawrence, Stephen, 199, 262, 269, 668
Legal aid,
  Access to Justice Act 1999, 587
  Advice and Assistance, 588n
  Approved Family Help, 588n
  Carter Review, 620–29
  CDS Direct, 612
  civil, 587–602
  Community Legal Service(CLS), 596–99
  CLS Direct, 597
  Community Legal Advice Centres (CLACS),
    598–99
  Community Legal Advice Networks
    (CLANS), 598–99
  competitive tendering, 619
  contributions,
    civil, 592–93
    criminal, 605–10
  Controlled Work, 588, 589
  cost, 597
  criminal, 603–14
  Criminal Defence Service (CDS), 603–04
  duty solicitor schemes, 610–12
  Early Cover, 608n
  eligibility, 616
  Emergency Representation, 591
  exclusions, 590
  Focus, 588n
  Full Representation, 591
  Funding Code, 588
  funding priorities, 589
  future, 618
  General Civil Contract, 588
  glossary of terms, 588n
  group litigation, 573–74
  Help at Court, 588, 594
  history, 586
  immigration and asylum work, 594
  international comparisons, 629
  Investigative Help, 588n
  Legal Aid: A Sustainable Future (2006),
    622
  Legal Help, 588, 593–94
  Legal Representation, 588
  Legal Services Commission, 587, 588
  Licensed Work, 589
  Litigation Support, 588n
  matter starts, 596
  means test,
    civil, 592–93
    criminal, 605–10
  merits test,
    civil, 591
    criminal, 604–05
  Modernising Justice (1998), 587, 603
  not-for-profit sector, 596, 615–16
  numbers of providers, 596
  partnerships, 598
  peer review, 601
  Preferred Supplier initiative, 600–01
  proportion of population eligible, 616
  public defenders, 612–14
  quality control, 599
  Quality Mark, 597
  reasons for rising cost, 616–18
  Recovery of Defence Costs Order, 606
  research, 597
  Scottish Public Defence Solicitors' Office,
    614
  Specialist Support, 602
  statutory charge, 593
  Support Funding, 588n
  tribunals, 615
  Very High Cost Cases, 610
  Widgery criteria, 604
Legal Disciplinary Partnerships (LDPs), 783,
  830, 833
Legal executives,
  number, 767
  rights of audience, 791
Legal expenses insurance (LEI), 648–50
Legal profession, ch 8
  division, 773
  transfer between branches, 774
  See also BAR, BARRISTERS, INNS OF COURT,
    OFFICE OF FAIR TRADING, QUEEN'S
    COUNSEL, SOLICITORS, ROYAL
    COMMISSION ON LEGAL SERVICES
Legal professional privilege,
  civil, 782, 90–93
  criminal, 228n, 229, 231, 239, 240, 309,
    466–67
Legal Services Board (LSB), 782, 824–40
Legal Services Commission (LSC), 587–88
  See also Legal aid
Legal Services Consultative Panel, 796
Legal Services Ombudsman, 820
Legatt report (*Tribunals for Users – One
  System, One Service*), 2001, 43, 44, 46

Leigh, Professor Leonard, 397, 702

Levi, M., 118n

Libra IT system, 41n

Licensed conveyancers, 815, 816, 840, 841

Lidstone, K., 162, 227n, 230n, 231, 268

Lightman, J., 50, 117, 130, 131, 394

Limited liability partnerships, 814, 815n, 831

Listing, 116, 117, 121, 130

Litigants in person, 101, 406–07, 408–11, 579,
    580

Lord Chancellor, proposed abolition of, 1n

Lord Chancellor's Advisory Committee on
    Legal Education and Conduct
    (ACLEC), 796

Lord Chancellor's Department (LCD),
    abolition of, 1n

'Lurking doubt' test, 693–95

Macdonald, Sir Kenneth, DPP, 217n, 250n,
    266, 360, 470, 789

Magistrates,
  age, 24
  appointment, 22
  District Judges (Magistrates' Courts), 20
  ethnic minority representation, 24
  gender, 24
  number, 20
  political balance, 25–26
  recruitment, 23
  selection process, 22–23
  sentencing powers, 30
  social class, 24–25
  stipendiaries, 20
  training, 27–28

Magistrates' Courts, 9, 19–34
  clerks, 31–34, 38
  division of work with Crown Court,
    315–22
  either way offences in, 316–21
  inspectorate, 37
  jurisdiction, 9, 20–21
  lay and professional magistrates, 29–30
  managing, 36
  number, 20

Majority verdicts, 530–32

Malleson, Profesor Kate, 382, 674n, 680n, 696,
    697, 705n, 716n, 729, 751n, 781

Managing the courts, 34–39

'Mareva' injunction, 53, 102

Mark, Sir Robert, 537–40

Martineau, Professor Robert, 683, 684

McCabe, Sarah, 515, 539n

McConville, Professor M., 152n, 156n, 175n,
    181, 210n, 244, 322n, 323–25, 327n,
    362, 515, 539, 540

'McKenzie man', 408–10, 429

Mediation, 142–49

Medical records, disclosure, 96

Medical treatment for suspects, 190

Mentally disordered suspects, 191

'Mere witness' rule, 98

Merricks, Walter, 544, 829n

Middleton, Sir Peter, 643

Miscarriages of justice, 719–34
  compensation, 730–34

Mode of Trial Bill No.1, 320

Mode of Trial Bill No 2, 320

Money laundering, 91, 92

Moorhead, Richard, 54n, 62n, 126, 135, 406n,
    408n, 409, 411, 598n, 601n, 614, 616n,
    617, 618, 629

Morgan, Professor Rod, 22–25, 29, 205n,
    210n, 279n, 287

Morris Committee on Jury Service (1965),
    486

Motions (now called 'applications'), 79

Moxon, D., 22n, 260n, 318n, 319n, 343n, 518n

Multi-disciplinary partnerships (MDPs), See
    PARTNERSHIPS

Multi-national partnerships (MNPs), See
    PARTNERSHIPS

Multi-party actions, 63–66, 573–75

Multi-track,
  ADR, 143
  allocation, 51, 78
  case management conferences, 109
  characteristics, 87–88
  delay, 126
  directions hearings, 116
  disclosure/discovery, 87
  time limits, 130
  See also Woolf Report

Narey Report, Review of Delay in the Criminal
    Justice System (1997), 33 n 150, 320

New Jersey study of case management, 352

New Zealand, improperly obtained evidence,
    483

New Zealand jury study, 118

NHS Redress Bill 2005, 57

Nobles, Professor Richard, 143n, 654n, 702,
    703n, 706, 729, 730, 732n

No property in a witness, 99–100
Non-intimate samples, 223–24
    destruction, 224–25
Non-jury trials on indictment,
    defendant opting for trial by judge alone,
        542–43
    'Diplock courts', 541–42
    jury tampering, 548
    long fraud cases, 543–48
    trial of sample counts only, 548–49
    young defendants, 549
Non-practising employed barristers,
Northern Ireland,
    Bain Report on legal services (2006),
        836–39)
    Diplock courts, 541–42
    right to silence, 168
    supergrasses, 335–36

Oath taking, children, 443
O'Brien, D., 81–82
Office of Fair Trading (OFT) Report,
        Competition in professions (2001),
        778–79
    advertising, 756, 757
    Bar's Response to OFT, 779–80
    conveyancing monopoly, 567
    Law Society's Response to OFT, 781
    partnerships at the Bar, 754
    Queen's Counsel, 751
Official Referee, 5
'One shotters', 59
Open court, 422–31
Opening speech, 417
Oppression, 160, 192, 471, 472, 474–6
Opren case, 573
Orality, 415–17
Otton Working Party on Litigants in Person
        (1995), 410–11
'Overriding objective',
    Civil, 48–50, 52, 61, 75, 82, 88, 90, 130, 131,
        132, 139, 144
    Criminal, 153–55, 347, 390, 392, 708
Oxford Penal Research Unit, 515
Oxford Socio-Legal Centre, 56

PACE, *See* POLICE AND CRIMINAL EVIDENCE
        ACT 1984
Pardon, 720
Part 36 offers, 82–86
Particulars of claim, 69

Partnerships, between
    barristers, 752–54, 807–09, 829–30
    barristers and non-barristers, 809
    lawyers and foreign lawyers (MNPs),
        809–10
    lawyers of different kinds (LDPs), 830
    lawyers and non-lawyers (MDPs/ABSs),
        810–13, 830–33, 835–36, 838–39
Paterson, Professor Alan, 58, 382, 666n, 777,
    814n
Payment into court (Part 36 offers), 82–86
Peach Report, *An Independent Scrutiny of the
    Appointment Processes of Judges and
    Queen's Counsel* (1999), 750–51
Peremptory challenge, 493–94
'Personal records', 228
Perverse jury verdicts, 515, 525, 527–28, 667
Peysner, Professor John, 51n, 54, 62, 80, 113,
    117n, 133, 134, 135, 136, 137, 139, 147,
    451n, 564n, 576n, 582n, 646n, 648, 650
Phillips, J. (later Lord Chief Justice), 372, 496,
    646n, 741
Philips Royal Commission *See* ROYAL
    COMMISSION ON CRIMINAL
    PROCEDURE
Phone tapping, *See* TELEPHONE TAPPING
Photographs, 218
Pigot Committee on Video Recorded
    Evidence, 431–32
Plea bargaining, *See* GUILTY PLEAS
'Plea before venue', 319–20
Plea and Case Management Hearings
    (PCMH), 349–50
Plea and directions hearings (PDHs), 349
Pleadings, 69–71
Pleasence, Pascoe, 57n, 59, 587n, 591n, 597n,
    598n, 629, 630
Plotnikoff, Joyce, 117n, 128, 292n, 293, 294n,
    295, 307, 353n, 444n, 512, 513, 659n
    675n, 676n
Police and Criminal Evidence Act 1994
    (PACE)
    access to solicitor in police station (s. 58),
        176–77
    admissibility of evidence (ss.76, 78), 474,
        479
    arrest (s.24), 201–02
    confessions, admissibility (s.76), 474
    custody officer (s.36), 187–88
    discretion to exclude evidence (s. 78),
        479–83

Police and Criminal Evidence Act 1994
    (PACE) (*cont.*)
  excluded material (s.11), 228–29
  informing someone of arrest (s.56), 183
  intimate samples (s.62), 223
  intimate search (s.55), 222
  non-intimate samples (s.63), 224
  search after an arrest (ss.18, 32), 220–22
  search, no arrest, 228–31
  seizure of evidence (s.19), 239–40
  special procedure material (Sch.1), 230
  stop and search (Code A), 196–99
  time-limits on detention for questioning
    (ss.41–44), 209–11
  unfair proceedings (s. 78), 479–83
Police detention *See* ACCESS TO A LAWYER,
    ARREST, POLICE STATION,
    QUESTIONING OF SUSPECTS
Police discretion to prosecute, 241–44
Police questioning of suspects, *See*
    QUESTIONING OF SUSPECTS
Police station,
  bail from, 275–76
  conditions of detention, 189–91
  conduct of interviews, 190
  custody officer, 187–88
  duty solicitors, 610–12
  record of interview, 188
  regime in, 187–91
  tape-recording of interviews, 183–85
  video-recording of interview, 186
Practice Directions, significance of, 52n
Practice Direction on Case Management 1995,
    124–25
Pre-action protocols, 60–65
'Precognosing' of witnesses, Scotland, 290
Predictable costs, 564
Pre-emptive cost capping orders, 567–68
Preparatory hearings, 350
Press reporting of judicial proceedings,
    428–30
Pre-trial assessment, 354–55
Pre-trial case management,
  civil cases, 114–40
  criminal cases, 347–62
Pre-trial conference with barrister, frequency,
353
Pre-trial depositions, 101
Pre-trial hearings, utility of, 118, 351–53
Pre-trial preparation,
  pre-trial assessment, 354–55
  pre-trial hearings, 349 –54

Pre-trial publicity affecting,
  fair trial, 370–76
  jury verdicts, 376
Pre-trial reviews, 351
Pre-trial rulings, 350–51
Pre-trial settlement conference, 118
Prior convictions, admissibility, 435–42
Private prosecutions, 268–70
Privilege to promote settlement, 60
    See also LEGAL PROFESSIONAL PRIVILEGE
Privy Council, 662–63
Probate, 3, 4, 5, 7, 567, 777, 778n, 781n, 782,
    812, 818–19, 822, 825
Probate, Divorce and Admiralty Division, 5
Pro bono work, 651–53
'Propensity', 435, 439–42
Prosecution system, 241–73
  appeal by prosecution, 666–68
  Auld, 248
  Case Disposal Manual, 253–54
  cautioning, as an alternative, 255–58
  charging standards, 254–55
  Code for Prosecutors, 250–53
  CPS charging, 248–50
  Customs and Excise, 267
  decision to prosecute, 250–55
  discontinuance, 258
  discretion to prosecute, 240–44
  duties of prosecuting lawyers, 270–71
  failure to prosecute, remedies, 262–63
  Farquharson Guidelines, 270–71
  Glidewell Report, 247
  independence from the police, 263–64
  judicial control of, 260–62
  law officers, 266
  Philips Royal Commission, 245
  private, 268–70
  prosecution counsel and the CPS, 271–73
  prosecution counsel and the judge, 273
  Serious Fraud Office, 267
Protective Costs Order, 584
Proviso, 'the', 699–700
Public Defender, *See* CRIMINAL DEFENCE
    SERVICE and LEGAL AID
Public interest immunity, 297–99
Publicity and contempt of court, 370–78
Public justice, 422–430
Pupillage, 738–41
Purves, Robert, 515, 539n

Quarter Sessions, abolition, 16
Queen's Bench Division (QBD), 4

Queen's Counsel, 748–52, 801–06
  Andrew Dismore's campaign, 750
  appointment system, 748,
  Bar's arguments in favour, 801–02
  cost of application, 806
  ethnic minority, 755, 806
  Glidewell Working Party (2003), 751–52
  history, 748
  Kalisher Committee report (1994), 748
  Monopolies and Mergers Commission's
    report (1976), 749
  Law Society's withdrawal, 803
  Lord Chancellor's Department's
    consultation papers (2002, 2003), 802,
    804
  new system, 805–06
  number, 749, 806
  Office of Fair Trading Reports (2001, 2002),
    751, 802
  Peach Committee report(1993), 750–01
  reasons for applying 749
  solicitors eligible, 801
  suspended April 2003, 752
  women, 754, 806
Questioning of suspects
  access to lawyer, 175–82
  after charge, 168
  caution, 167–68
  danger of false confession, 159
  detention for, 207–08
  duty to answer, 162–64
  importance, 156–57
  improper pressure, 191–92
  investigative interviewing, 158
  juveniles, 190–91
  mentally disordered, 191
  quality, 157–58
  right to silence, 161–75
  tape recording, 183–85
  voluntary statements, 192, 470–72

Rand Corporation,
  case management, 126–28
  delay, 139
Rape victims, protection from cross-
  examination, 468–69
Recorders, 6, 16, 17, 19
Recording of stops, 199
Recording of stops and searches, 198–99
Reference to Court of Appeal Criminal
  Division, 727–28
Remuneration certificate, 568

'Repeat players', 59
Reporting of legal proceedings, 428–30
Representation,
  advantages, 402–05
  handicaps for the unrepresented, 405–11
  litigants in person, 408–11
  magistrates' courts, 405–07
  small claims cases, 402–04
  tribunal cases, 407–08
Representative actions, 63–66
Reprimands and warnings, 256
Retrials, 714–18
Returned briefs, 790
Revenue and Customs Prosecutions Office
  (RCPO), 267
Review of the Criminal Courts, See AULD
Review of Regulation of Legal Services Market
  (Clementi, 2003–04), *See Clementi*
Rickman, N., 135, 136, 642, 648, 649n
Right of silence, 165–82, 463–66
  accused person is not a compellable witness,
    463–66
  in police questioning, 165–82
  research, 173–75
  self-incrimination rule, 463
Right to trial by jury, *See* TRIAL BY JURY
Rights of audience,
  employed lawyers, 789–90
  legal executives, 791
  'McKenzie man', 408–10
  non-lawyers, 799–93
  small claims, 793–94
  solicitors, 784–89
Roberts, Professor Simon, 59, 142, 150
Rosenberg, M., 352
Roskill Committee on Fraud Trials,
  defence disclosure, 303
  jury trial, 543–44
Royal Commission on Assizes and Quarter
  Sessions (Beeching, 1969), 16
Royal Commission on Criminal Justice
  (Runciman, 1993)
  adversary system, 395
  committal proceedings, 343
  confession evidence, 477
  Criminal Cases Review Commission
    (CCRC), 723
  defence disclosure, 304
  disclosure of scientific evidence, 299
  expert evidence, 306
  fresh evidence, 709, 712, 717
  Galbraith, 524

Royal Commission on Criminal Justice (*cont.*)
grounds for allowing appeals, 697, 700
hearsay evidence, 453
inquisitorial system, 397
judge summing up facts, 522
jury aids, 511
jury composition, 502
jury research, 513
jury trial for either way offences, 318
'lurking doubt' test, 695
miscarriages of justice, machinery, 723
opening speech, 417
pre-trial process, 349n
prosecution disclosure of unused material,
   292
racial mix of jury, 499
retrials, 714
retrial after jury tampering ends with
   acquittal, 667
right of silence, 169, 465
right to trial by jury, 318
sentence canvass, 330
tems of reference, 155
Zander dissent
   on defence disclosure, 304–05
   on pre-trial malpractice, 528
   on pre-trial process, 349n
Royal Commission on Criminal Procedure
   (Philips, 1981)
access to a lawyer in police station, 176
committal proceedings, 342
confessions, admissibility, 473
defence disclosure, 302
improperly obtained evidence, 478–79
independent prosecution system, 245
right to silence, 167, 464
search of premises, 227–28, 231
seizure of evidence, 239
stop and search, 195–96
time-limits on detention for questioning,
   209
terms of reference, 155
Royal Commission on Legal Services (Benson,
   1979)
access to lawyers in police stations, 176
divided legal profession, 773
multi-disciplinary partnerships, 807
partnerships for barristers, 752–53
right of audience, 784
solicitors' conveyancing monopoly, 815
Rule Committees, 39, 52

Runciman Royal Commission *See* ROYAL
   COMMISSION ON CRIMINAL JUSTICE
Russell, Neil, 22, 23, 24, 25, 29, 418n

Sanctions,
   civil cases, 128–32
   criminal cases, 355–57
Sanders, Professor Andrew, 22n, 156n, 179,
   180, 210, 243, 271n, 325n, 605n
Scale fees, 566
Scientific facilities for defence, 300
Schiff, Professor David, 654n, 702, 703n, 706,
   729, 730, 732
Scotland,
   detaining witnesses, 164
   improperly obtained evidence, 482
   majority jury verdicts, 530
   no opening speech, 417
   Report on the Legal Services Market (2006),
      840
   requirement to give name and address, 164
   time-limits for trials, 366
Scott, Professor Ian R., 14, 64, 120n, 657n
Scott, Sir Richard/Lord, 72
Scottish Public Defence Solicitors' Office,
   613–14
Search and seizure,
   arrested person, 220–22
   'bug and burgle' provisions, 234–38
   premises, after an arrest, 220–22
   premises, no arrest, 225–31
   See also ENTRY ON PREMISES
Search by consent, 232
'Search order' (formerly Anton Piller), 102
Search warrants, 231
Sefton, M., 406, 411, 617–18
'Seize and sift', 240
Seizure of evidence, 239–40
Self-incrimination, 463
Seneviratne, Professor Mary, 51n, 54, 80, 90,
   113, 117n, 133, 134, 135, 136, 137, 139,
   147, 571n
Senior Court of England and Wales, 2
Sentence canvass, 329–34
Sentence discount, 326–27, 329–36
Sentencing, scale levels, 316
'Serious arrestable offence', abolished, 182
Serious Organised Crime Agency, 267
Serious Organised Crime and Police Act 2005
   (SOCPA),
   all premises warrants, 231

arrest, 201
arrestable offences to indictable offences, 221
civilian custody officers, 187
'disclosure notice', 164
footwear impressions, 218
immunity from prosecution, 335
photographs, 218
Service of proceedings, 74–75
Settlement of civil litigation, 55–60
Sexual history, cross-examination on, 468–69
Shapland, Professor Joanna, 54n, 101, 370n,
    736n, 738n,
Silence, *See* RIGHT OF SILENCE
Silkwood, Karen, 101
Similar fact evidence, 436
Single civil court, 13–16
Single joint experts, 78, 113
Skeleton arguments, 682–83
Slapper, G., 244, 268n
Small claims system,
    analysis of special characteristics, 384
    costs, 577–78
    created, 7
    European Small Claims Procedure, 9n, 68
    judge's role, 386–87
    jurisdiction, 7–8
    numbers, 9
    pre-trial review, 118
    procedure, 384
    satisfaction with, 385, 388–89
    standard directions, 115
Solicitors,
    access to in police stations, 175–82
    client care, 819
    complaints against, 820
    continuing education, 765–66
    conveyancing, 815–18
    distribution of, 768
    entry and training, 761–66
    ethnic minorities, 769
    history, 761
    incorporation, 814–15
    legal executives, 767
    limited liability, 814–15
    management, 770–73
    multi-disciplinary partnerships, 809–13
    multi-national partnerships, 810
    numbers, 766
    personnel, 767
    probate, 818–19
    rights of audience, 784–90

size of firms, 767
structure of the profession, 766–67
use of, 776
vocational training, 762–66
women, 768
Special Advocate, 214, 217, 298
'Special damages', 68
Special Immigration Appeal Tribunal, 214
Special measures directions for vulnerable
    witnesses, 431
Special procedure material (PACE Sch.1), 230
Spencer, Professor John, 279n, 400, 443n,
    454n, 457n, 469, 470, 529, 718
Spouse, evidence of, 445–46, 462
'Stand by for the Crown', 498
Standard disclosure, 88
Standard fees, 562, 569
Statement of truth, 69
Statutory charge, 593
'Statutory objective', 785
Stay of prosecution, 368–69
Stevenson, Sir Dennis (now Lord), 771
Stipendiary magistrates (now District Judges),
    20
Stop and question, 192–94, 199
Stop and search, 192–99
    random, 197
    records, 198–99
    voluntary, 198
Street bail, 275
Summary judgment, 81
Summing up on fact and law, 519–23
Summons for directions, 114
Summons or arrest, 205
Summons Production Centre, 74
Supergrasses, 335
Supreme Court (House of Lords), 657–58
Surety, 280

Tague, Professor Peter, 325
'Taken into consideration' (TICs), 336
Tape-recording interviews, 183–85
Tata, C., 325n, 290n, 614n
Taxation of costs, 558–59
Technology and Construction Court, 5
Telephone hearings, 71, 79–80
Telephone tapping, 234–38, 469
Televising trials, 430
Terrorism cases,
    access to lawyer in police station, 171, 176,
        177, 178

Terrorism cases (*cont.*)
control orders, 214
cordoning off an area, 195
duty to answer questions, 162–63
excluded material not exempt, 228n
indefinite detention without charges,
213–14
Joint Parliamentary Human Rights
Committee Report (2006), 217
production order, 230
right of silence, 174n
Special Independent Counsel, 298
stop and question, 194
stop and search randomly, 197–98
tape-recording of interviews, 185
time-limits for detention for questioning,
212–13
video recording, 185
'Tesco law', 782n, 811, 837
Thaman, S., 554
Thompson, EP., 527–28
Threshold Test, 250
'Ticketing' of judges, 19
'TICs', 336
Time limits,
advocacy, 421–22
criminal cases, 366–68
police detention, 208–10
Torture evidence, inadmissibility, 481–82
Transfer to crown court, 345
Trial by judge alone, 540–50
Trial by jury,
the right to have, civil cases, 503–07
the right to have, criminal cases, 315–22,
509–10
See also Jury
Trial on indictment without a jury, 540–50
Tribunals, Courts and Enforcement Bill, 2006,
44
Tribunal Service, 43–45
Tribunal system, 42–46

Ultra sound scans, 222
'Unsafe' verdicts, 693–708
Unduly lenient sentence, appeals, 667
'Unused material, disclosure, 290–97

Venue of civil cases, 73
Very High Cost cases, 610
Victim's advocate, 421
Victim's personal statement, 421
Video-link, 283, 353, 354, 431

Video identification, 219
Video-taping of police station interviews, 186
Vidmar, NJ., 555
Voir dire, 467
Voluntary Bill of Indictment, 346
'Voluntary' searches,
persons, banned, 198
premises, 232
Vulnerable witnesses, 431–35

Wasted costs order, 117, 124, 129, 356, 357,
373, 569–71
'Widgery criteria', 604
Wigs, 786
Winn Committee on Personal Injuries (1968),
automatic directions, 114
compulsory exchange of witness statements,
104, 105
delay, 120
exchange of witness statements, 95
pleadings, 70
'Without prejudice' negotiations, 60
Witness,
accused not compellable, 463
adversary system, calling, 382–84
children, 442–45
discovering identity of opponent's, 104–06
examination of, 417–20
exchange, 104–06
expert, 108–14
judge calling, 382
no property in, 99
protection of vulnerable, 431–35
witness statements, 106–08
See also CHILDREN'S EVIDENCE
Wolchover, D., 172, 186, 273, 367n, 412, 420n,
522n, 524n
Women,
barristers, 754
solicitors, 768
Woolf, Lord, career, 12n
Woolf, Lord, criticisms of the Criminal Justice
Act 2003, 441, 458
Woolf reforms, assessment, 54–55, 59, 112–13,
125–26, 132–40
Woolf Reports on Access to Justice (1995,
1996)
adversary system, 381, 393–94
ADR, 143–44
allocation of civil cases, 78
case management conferences, 117–18
Civil Procedure Rules, 12n, 51–52

costs, 135, 138, 557, 564
costs-only hearings, 636
court control, 125
cross-examination, restricting, 108
defences, drafting, 77
delay, 125–26
directions hearings, 115–17
disclosure/discovery, 87–90
divisions of High Court, 14–15
established, 12
expert witnesses, 109–11
fast track cases, 12, 51, 116, 125
High Court and county court, 13–14
indemnity rule of costs, 573
judicial training to promote consistency, 387
leave to appeal requirement, 658
multi-party actions, 65–66
multi track cases, 12, 51, 116
'overriding objective', 48
payment into court, 83
pleadings, 70
pre-action protocols, 60–63
pre-trial case management, 114–18
pro-active judges, 116
research, 54
right of reply, 77
sanctions, 128–30
single method of starting claims, 67
small claims, 7n, 51, 115–16, 387
summary judgment, 81–82
unification of high court and county court, 13
user-friendly language, 53
venue, 73
witness statements, 107–08
Woolfson, Richard, 117n, 292n, 293, 294n, 295, 307, 353n, 444n, 512, 513, 659n, 675n, 676n
Wynne, A., 25, 26

X-rays of suspects, 222

Youth Justice and Criminal Evidence Act 1999,
caution for those who have not had legal advice, 171
competence of child witnesses, 444
compulsorily obtained evidence not admissible, 164
computer evidence, 454
oath taking by children, 444
prohibition on reporting identifying witness affected by 'fear or distress', 378
rape cases, cross-examination of victim by accused, 468–69
right of silence and legal advice, 171
sexual offences, cross-examination by defendant of victim banned, 419
special measures directions for vulnerable witnesses, 425, 432–35

Zander, Professor Michael,
abolition of ACLEC, 785n
Auld Report on perverse jury verdict, response, 527–28
Case Preparation Project, 360
disclosure, 307
PACE, s 78, 480–81
Runciman Royal Commission, Dissent, defence disclosure, 304–05
pre-trial malpractice, 698–99
pre-trial process, 354n
sanctions, 356
Woolf reforms, 12n and 132–40
Zedner, Professor Lucia, 397
Zeisel, H., 513, 554
Zuckerman, Professor Adrian, 12, 49, 85, 94, 122n, 128, 132, 139n, 141, 394, 448, 453n, 480n, 565n, 649n